THE McGRAW-HILL INTRODUCTION TO LITERATURE

Second Edition

Gilbert H. Muller
The City University of New York
LaGuardia

John A. Williams
Rutgers University

McGraw-Hill, Inc.
New York   St. Louis   San Francisco   Auckland   Bogotá   Caracas
Lisbon   London   Madrid   Mexico City   Milan   Montreal   New Delhi
San Juan   Singapore   Sydney   Tokyo   Toronto

This book was developed by STEVEN PENSINGER, Inc.

This book was set in Baskerville by ComCom, Inc.
The editors were Steve Pensinger and Jean Akers;
the designer was Karen K. Quigley;
the production supervisor was Denise L. Puryear.
R. R. Donnelley & Sons Company was printer and binder.

Cover photo: Romare Bearden, *The Piano Lesson,* 1983
Collage and water color, 29 × 22".
Courtesy, Estate of Romare Bearden.

THE McGRAW-HILL INTRODUCTION TO LITERATURE

Permissions Acknowledgments appear on pages 1117–1128 and on this
page by reference.

This book is printed on acid-free paper.

1 2 3 4 5 6 7 8 9 0 DOC DOC 9 0 9 8 7 6 5 4

ISBN 0-07-044246-0

Library of Congress Cataloging-in-Publication Data

The McGraw-Hill introduction to literature / [selection and
    introductions by] Gilbert H. Muller, John A. Williams.—2nd ed.
        p.   cm.
    Includes index.
    ISBN 0-07-044246-0
    1. Literature—Collections.   I. Muller, Gilbert H., (date).
II. Williams, John Alfred, (date).
PN6014.M1376   1995
    808—dc20   94-17019

About the Authors

Gilbert H. Muller, who received a Ph.D. in English and American literature from Stanford University, is currently professor of English and special assistant to the president at the LaGuardia campus of the City University of New York. He has also taught at Stanford, Vassar, and several universities overseas. Dr. Muller is the author of the award-winning *Nightmares and Visions: Flannery O'Connor and the Catholic Grotesque, Chester Himes,* and other critical studies. His essays and reviews have appeared in *The New York Times, The New Republic, The Nation, The Sewanee Review, The Georgia Review,* and elsewhere. He is also a noted author and editor of textbooks in English and composition, including *The Short Prose Reader* with Harvey Wiener, and, with John A. Williams, *Bridges: Literature across Cultures* and *Ways In: Approaches to Reading and Writing about Literature.* Among Dr. Muller's awards are the National Endowment for the Humanities Fellowships, a Fulbright Fellowship, and a Mellon Fellowship.

John A. Williams, the Paul Robeson Professor of English at Rutgers University, is the author of twelve novels, among them *The Man Who Cried I Am* (1967), *!Click Song* (1982), *Jacob's Ladder* (1987), and *Trio: Clifford's Blues* (1994); and ten nonfiction works that include studies on Richard Wright and Martin Luther King, Jr. (1970), Richard Pryor (1991), and Malcolm X (1993). In addition, he has edited or co-edited ten books, among them *Amistad I and II.* A former journalist, Williams is also a poet and playwright and a recipient of the Rutgers University Lindback Foundation Award for Distinguished Teaching.

To
Laleh, Parisa, and Darius
And to
Lori, Greg, Dennis, and Adam
And as well to
Margo, John Gregory, Nancy, and David

Contents

F i c t i o n

Understanding Fiction 3

P o e t r y

Understanding Poetry   263

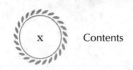

16. Meter, Rhythm, and Sound 335

17. Structure and Form 346

18. An Anthology of Poetry 357

D r a m a

Preface

The McGraw-Hill Introduction to Literature, now in its second edition, is a dynamic and diversified anthology for college students enrolled in literature and composition courses. It contains fiction, poetry, and drama of American and international appeal. Designed with an eye to both the uniqueness and the universality of outstanding literature, this text offers a unified, multicultural approach to meaning, form, technique, and values in fiction, poetry, and drama. If literature, as Paul Valéry declared, is "the art of playing on the minds of others," then what we have attempted to create in this anthology is an appreciation of the strategies and themes by which first-rate authors capture and engage the imagination, intellect, and emotions of a broad range of readers.

The organization of *The McGraw-Hill Introduction to Literature* reflects organically the prime ways in which the teaching of literature actually is done—by genre, subject, theme, and technique. However, instead of fragmenting these approaches, we combine them in order to show how readers experience the thrill and meaning of a text through the author's handling of the key elements of his or her craft. The anthology contains three traditional main sections, each with a prefatory essay: Fiction, Poetry, and Drama. While these three genres are not the only forms of literature, what we call literature is most often expressed through them. Within each of these three major sections there are self-contained chapters—excellent modules for instruction—arranged around literary selections that reveal the application of specific technique. These chapters on strategy and technique contain concise introductory essays and exercises for discussion and writing. Each distinct chapter, by isolating within the genre a specific technique in relationship to theme, asserts the primacy of method in the author's discovery, exploration, and evaluation of a subject. The extensive anthologies arranged alphabetically at the end of the fiction, poetry, and drama sections enhance the teacher's flexibility in

fitting *The McGraw-Hill Introduction to Literature* to personal, pedagogical, and classroom expectations. Through these basic organizational strategies, we offer teachers holistic yet flexible materials for instruction and direct students toward the shared methods and themes—and thus the universality—of all fine literature.

Teachers will immediately recognize the literary excellence of many of the classical and contemporary authors and selections in this anthology and will be intrigued perhaps by their unique positioning within and across chapters. Included are Shakespeare and Dickinson, Hemingway and Welty, Sophocles and Ibsen, Hughes and Plath, Beckett and Borges—scores of major writers and those chestnuts that we look forward to teaching in a variety of literature and composition courses. Yet in *The McGraw-Hill Introduction to Literature* there are also writers and works that are lesser known but still of high rank and of considerable interest. We think that teachers will be delighted to discover or rediscover Katherine Philips and Chínua Achebe, Bharati Mukherjee and Hernando Téllez, Sterling A. Brown and Leslie Marmon Silko. In fact, this anthology offers a broader range of women, ethnic, and international authors than most comparable texts, and thus advocates, we believe, both a truly American and a pluralistic literature.

In keeping with our attempt to offer a pluralistic anthology and to address the needs and expectations of a varied group of students, we offer detailed apparatus for many of the selections in *The McGraw-Hill Introduction to Literature*. Questions for discussion and writing appear after many selections. The questions range from the simple to the complex. All questions encourage students not only to understand and appreciate literature, but also to use the skills essential for critical thought—to develop and refine abilities to analyze, compare, classify, and define concepts and to defend critical positions. The recommended writing projects for many selections also are geared to short paragraphs, essays, and longer comparative papers. Consequently this anthology will be very useful in composition courses where writing through literature is stressed, as well as in introductory and more specialized literature courses. An extensive glossary provides students with basic definitions helpful in discussing and writing about literature. Moreover, a section entitled "Biographical Profiles" helps students to understand authors in this anthology. This apparatus is supported by an inclusive instructor's guide offering assistance in the exploration of all materials in the anthology and also by a companion text, *Ways In: Approaches to Reading and Writing about Literature.*

In preparing *The McGraw-Hill Introduction to Literature,* we have sought the eloquence, formal brilliance, and plain human interest of writers from the United States and abroad, from the fifth century B.C. to the 1990s, who can tell us and our students something about our common estate. "I am quite at a loss," wrote Henry James, "to imagine anything that people might like or dislike." We trust that students will enjoy enough of this anthology to make literature meaningful for them. Through male and female authors representing diverse ethnic, racial, and cultural backgrounds, we express the faith that good literature best reflects the human condition, for better or worse, to a far greater extent than films or television. Even these media, so easy to absorb if not delight, could not exist without the written word.

We would like to express our thanks for the many useful comments and suggestions provided by colleagues who reviewed this text during the course of its development,

especially to Herman L. Asarnow, University of Portland; James L. Battersby, Ohio State University; Warren B. Benson, West Valley College; Dennis R. Gabriel, Cuyahoga Community College, Western Campus; John Hanes, Duquesne University; Rosalie Hewitt, Northern Illinois University; Perry Lentz, Kenyon College; Dan McLeod, San Diego State University; Gratia Murphy, Youngstown State University; Frank Ross, Eastern Michigan University; J. Chesley Taylor, Washington State University; and Suzanne Wolkenfeld. Special appreciation is extended to Alan Gerstle for his superlative work on the instructor's manual.

Gilbert H. Muller
John A. Williams

F iction

Gabriele Münter. *Boating*. 1910. Oil on canvas. 49 1/4" X 28 7/8".
Milwaukee Art Museum, Gift of Mrs. Harry Lynde Bradley.

UNDERSTANDING FICTION

A lice Walker, whose short story "Roselily" appears in this anthology, recounts in an essay the process whereby she absorbed tales from her mother, who in turn had received these stories from earlier ancestors and "anonymous" black women. These stories "came from my mothers lips as naturally as breathing." Their creative spark reflects the vitality of a long oral tradition.

Fiction began as storytelling, perhaps at night around warming campfires or anywhere else that people gathered. In those times the stories were sung or told in verse. Fiction comes directly from ancient oral traditions found in numerous cultures of the world.

Sometimes there were storytelling or story-singing contests, as in the classical age of Greek letters, when poet-playwrights read their works, more in verse than not, to audiences gathered for the festivals of Dionysus, which ran from autumn through spring each year. These early stories usually were about figures or events familiar to particular groups, and such stories often became well known. Eventually, embellishments on the standard tales (as they were then called) were applauded and encouraged. New characters with new characteristics appeared; new conflicts requiring other than the usual solutions were portrayed.

However much adorned, the stories that have lived the longest may symbolize basic human concerns that have remained unchanged. The story of Prometheus is a good example. We know the Prometheus story well as it has come down from the Greeks. Prometheus, pitying human beings, steals fire from the gods and brings it to earth, thus enriching human life with warmth and light. The same basic story is told in many variations all over the world. However, the heroes who steal from the gods or from other powerful beings range from ordinary mortals like King Arthur of England (securing Excalibur) to Rama of India (pulling his bow) to crafty animals (lizards, birds, or insects). At their core, though, such stories are essentially Promethean. However, it is only in the story of Prometheus that the hero is punished by the more powerful beings. In the other stories these beings exact no retribution.

Clearly, a story can have as many variations as it has storytellers, and we all tend to be storytellers, given enough encouragement. Saying "Can you top this?" or telling a fish story is as old as humanity itself. Stories may be viewed as conduits through which are passed history, cultural values, knowledge, and entertainment. Fiction provides us, as Richard Wright acknowledged of his own experience, with "vague glimpses of life's possibilities."

The short story and the novel (which may be considered a longer, more complicated story) are the major forms of fiction used today. The novella, or short novel, is a transitional form between the short story and the novel. The three forms evolved from the earlier tale, fable, legend, and myth.

Fiction, whether short or long, suffers from (or just possibly is enriched by) a preponderance of definitions, many of which are imposed upon the works by persons other than the creators of them. There are times when it is important to let the writers themselves say what fiction is or is not and what it should do or should not do. Nevertheless, if reading a work of fiction makes us believe in its content and its characters, then the work should be considered successful; for fiction is intended first to find believers, and belief must precede any other reaction to the work. A work of fiction usually possesses character, plot, setting, point of view, theme, and, sometimes, symbols. The way language is used to establish each of these elements helps to create within us a reaction to the work.

The choice of language is only one of several ways to tell us what fiction is. Thomas Berger in his novel *Killing Time* (1972) states, "A work of fiction is a construction of language and otherwise a lie." Constructions of language shape civilization. (Lies are told for no other reason than to be believed.) Next, we confront E. L. Doctorow's assertion, "There is no fiction or nonfiction as we commonly understand the distinction." A third perspective comes from Nobel laureate Isaac Bashevis Singer: "At best, art can be nothing more than a means of forgetting the human disaster for a while." Singer's lies, then, are "white," and his "constructions of language" are illusions.

Explanations of "fiction" abound. Flannery O'Connor holds that the written word has more meaning than the spoken, a fact that gives fiction more importance, perhaps more moral force, than speech. For Herman Melville, fiction offers more reality "than life itself can show." And for Amy Tan, fiction is predicated on "the power of language—the way it can evoke an emotion, a visual image, a complex idea, or a simple truth." In any event, it is clear that fiction is a statement by a writer about a real or imaginary world, past, present, or future; it is a response to the enormous pulsations of the universe by a writer who is part of it. How do we or should we respond to such a statement? Do we feel pleasure? Should fiction make us pause to reflect?

The question of what fiction does or should do, if anything, draws relatively clear opinions from fiction writers. "It has," says Singer, "the magical power of merging causality with purpose, doubt with faith, the passions of the flesh with the yearnings of the soul. . . . The zeal for messages has made many writers forget that storytelling is the raison d'être of artistic prose."

We think this means that good fiction, without having a discernible "message," can fulfill a deep moral need for the reader, just as a writer may feel a moral compulsion to create fiction. Flannery O'Connor seems to support this stance: "It is the nature of fiction not to be good for much else unless it is good in itself." This statement seems to imply that it is possible for fiction not to have any value other than that of being good fiction—possessing an intrinsic worth, with all other factors being extraneous.

Time and again writers stress the need, first of all, to tell a story, a good story. William Faulkner, also a Nobel laureate, said that "the primary job of any writer is to tell you a story, a story out of human experience—I mean by that, universal, mutual experience, the anguishes and troubles and griefs of the human heart, which is universal, without regard to race or time or condition. He wants to tell you something which has seemed to him so true, so moving, either comic or tragic, that it's worth repeating."

Fiction can be a shared experience—a sharing of statements, observations, and moods. The writer invites you into his or her created, ordered world so you can view your life from a new perspective. As Nobel laureate Toni Morrison observes, fiction can alert readers to "unaccountable beauty . . . the intricateness or simple elegance of the writer's imagination . . . the world that the imagination evokes."

Former *Esquire* and *Saturday Evening Post* fiction editor Rust Hills believes that contemporary fiction "has much to tell us about how we live, presents a kind of complex truth about ourselves and our society that can be found neither in the analyses and statistics of the psychologists and sociologists nor in the recently popular 'new reportage' . . . when we try to understand any past civilization we turn first to Art." Fiction may provide us with knowledge where before there was ignorance.

Telling a good story is considered by many to be a primary function of fiction, but telling a truthful story seems to be equally important. According to Joseph Conrad, all art "may be defined as a single-minded attempt to render the highest kind of justice to the visible universe, by bringing light to the truth, manifold and one, underlying its every aspect. . . ." Conrad's opinion raises a problem. Is the writer's truth more truthful than anyone else's? Or might his truth merge with that of the reader? Truth is joined, made "manifold and one," and that characteristic, along with others, makes for good fiction. Perhaps this is what Grace Paley means when she states that fiction writing bears with it certain moral responsibilities, saying, "Everyone, real or invented, deserves the open destiny of life." We are once again faced with the fact that good fiction may awake in readers a sense of moral thought and action and that the action considered often is that of creating a story. Yet we must be careful about the "truth" of a writer's vision. For example, the African writer Chinua Achebe, whose story "Civil Peace" appears in this anthology, has taken issue with the "truth" of Conrad's "classic" *Heart of Darkness*, finding in it the "depersonalization of a portion of the human race."

Most people feel that there is a story or novel within them waiting for an opportunity to get out, and perhaps that is as it should be. Flannery O'Connor, a fine guide to the materials of fiction, declares, "The fact is that the materials of the fiction writer are the humblest. Fiction is about everything human and we are made of dust. . . ." No one has ever been able to say for sure where even the "humblest" materials come from, how they are gathered and fashioned into the shape of a story or novel. We simply do not know. Yet we do recognize, in one way or another, the ability of a good writer of fiction to take the most ordinary materials and render them into extraordinary works.

Edgar Allan Poe writes, "Either history affords [the writer] a thesis—or one is suggested by an incident of the day—or at best, the author sets himself to work in the combination of striking events to form merely the basis of his narrative—designing, generally, to fill in with description, dialogue or authorial command, whatever crevices of fact or action may, from page to page, render themselves apparent." Somewhere in the creative process, Poe is saying, is an experience the writer has had which he or she desires to share with others. This view is shared by Leo Tolstoy: "Art is a human activity consisting in this, that one man consciously by means of certain external signs, hands on to others feelings he has lived through, and that others are infected by these feelings and also experience them. . . ."

James Baldwin articulates a similar perspective: "One writes out of one thing only—

one's own experience. Everything depends on how relentlessly one forces from this experience the last drop, sweet or bitter, it can possibly give."

Often the writer tries to share *un*common experience in order to extend our knowledge. Certainly Ernest Hemingway was such a writer. Hemingway, indeed, implies that Dostoevsky's greatness was a result of extreme hardship: "Dostoevsky was made by being sent to Siberia." It was also Hemingway's opinion, shared by a number of writers, including James Joyce and Richard Wright, that writers "are forged in injustice as a sword is forged."

The idea that fiction is based on personal experience, which then seeks universal acceptance, refers, of course, to only one method by which fiction is created. The most widely held opinion is that fiction is created from a mixture of fact and fancy. We sense this admixture of fact and fancy in a writer like Jorge Luis Borges, who is so intrigued by the labryinth in his fiction that he terms this structure "a symbol of bewilderment, a symbol of being lost in life."

Although fiction comes in several forms, our basic concern in this text is with the short story, which was created and defined in the United States early in the nineteenth century. While the short prose narrative—the tale—goes back to the eighth century B.C., Edgar Allan Poe is said to have first recognized the genre of the short story in Nathaniel Hawthorne's *Twice-Told Tales* in 1842. The term "story," as opposed to "tale," is believed to have originated in the Henry James collection *Daisy Miller: A Study; and Other Stories,* which was published in 1883.

Of Hawthorne's short stories Poe wrote that the form belonged "to the loftiest region of art." As to the mechanics of creating the story, Poe added that "having conceived with deliberate care a certain unique or single *effect* to be wrought out, he [the writer] then invents such incidents—he combines such events as may best aid him in establishing his preconceived effects." Furthermore, "if his very initial sentence tend not to the outbringing of this effect, then he has failed in his first step. In the whole composition there should be no word written, of which the tendency, direct or indirect, is not to the pre-established design."

Poe's rules influenced the rise both of the short story and of poetic forms in the United States and abroad. How do these rules stand up after 150 years? Isaac Bashevis Singer states: "Unlike the novel, which can absorb and even forgive lengthy discussions, flashbacks, and loose construction, the short story must aim directly at its climax. It must possess uninterrupted tension and suspense. Also, brevity is its very essence. The short story must have a definite plan. . . ." Both Poe and Singer eschew didactic elements in the short story, but it often happens that such elements find their way into a work even in the conceptual stage. Given many writers' concern for truth and justice, didactic sections may perhaps be excused. One definition of "didactic," it is worth noting, is "morally instructive."

Short story writers now are legion, and they have, like the form, contributed much to literature from the early stages of the industrial revolution to today's age of supertechnology. It is often said, and it is probably true, that most people in most modern societies find themselves with diminishing time to read. Novels are longer and demand more time and thought from us; short stories may demand more consideration for shorter periods of time and perhaps have not quite so much labyrinthian plot. The short story may be perfect for our age—and even perfect for certain writers. As Alice Munro admits, she started writing short stories because she didn't have time to write anything else!

As an integral part of literature, the short story, like the novel, must first of all tell us a story. The various interpretations of the story, the question of which philosophy it might propound, and whether the author succeeded—all such considerations come long after the facts of creation and publication. It may happen that as literature becomes more and more just another product of the entertainment factory, the labels attached to literature may come to bear more weight than the works themselves. We, of course, hope this will not happen.

By whatever means a story is created and however it is structured, whether it imitates life, expresses it, affects it, or projects it, language ultimately makes the story work. Language is the final mold of all the other elements of fiction—language shows what it is and what it does, reveals how it was created, and gives it the ultimate form it demands. A contemporary novelist and poet, Judith Ortiz Cofer, who grew up in the United States initially speaking Spanish, describes her acquisition of a second lan-guage—English—as an emergence from the bottom of a swimming pool: "I managed to surface and breathe the air of the real world . . . for I needed to communicate almost as much as I needed to breathe." Language creates character, action, mood, tone, symbols, and so on. Concepts do not. Everything in the world, as a highly fluent chimpanzee in Bernard Malamud's novel *God's Grace* (1982) declares, might very well be the genesis of a story, but it takes language for the telling. In good fiction, in all great literature, it is language that we see, feel, and hear. Language is both the wrapper on the package and one of the gifts inside it.

In the sections that follow, we explore how authors use language to create theme, plot, character, point of view, setting, tone, and symbolism. A brief essay introduces each of these elements of storytelling, which is illustrated by three reading selections with questions to help clarify each topic or technique.

1 . T h e m e

"Cut a good story anywhere," wrote Anton Chekhov, "and it will bleed." Chekhov's observation reflects brilliantly the organic connection between subject (or content) and form in short fiction and, indeed, in all literature. A good story is like the finely molded and tuned body of a champion sprinter: flesh shaped to frame and given swift purpose; form and content that should not be altered. In each short story the writer shapes content and organizes and refines material in order to produce through a fusion of content and form an interpretation of life. It is this wedding of content (notably characters and events) and form (technique, style) that gives a story its main meaning, or theme.

A theme is a distillation of everything that happens in a story's human drama. Whereas the subject is simply the topic of the tale (that is, what the story is overtly about), our understanding of the theme grows from our perception and evaluation of the story—it is our understanding of what the work says about the subject. For instance, we might say that the subject of Anton Chekhov's "The Lady with the Pet Dog" is love. (Other topics could be advanced as the main subject of this superlative tale.) However, stating the theme of this story would take more than one word; normally at least a sentence and, in a very real sense, often an entire essay might be required. A sentence like the following might qualify as a statement of the theme: "The desire for true love can obsess and consume a person's life." Sadly, when we thus extract subject and theme from a story, without considering the questions of *how* and *why* they emerge, we reduce the quality of the tale, and we lose sight of that special genius that writers can sometimes bring to their subjects. "I would be unable to write about anything that did not seem to me both unique and universal," declares Joyce Carol Oates. To justify the abstraction of subject and theme from a story, we must also seek out the formal patterns and stylistic devices used by the author to communicate the subject and the theme.

The nature of a writer's subject influences the stylistic and other technical decisions that he or she will make in order to give a story both form and meaning. Robert Louis Stevenson (author of *Treasure Island* and of several superb short stories) stated that "with each new subject . . . the true artist will vary his method and change the point of attack." In other words, each new subject—love, war, youth, marriage, revenge, or a combination of topics—dictates the correct strategies and approaches. Each aspect of style and technique—imagery, plot, characterization, point of view, symbolism, mood, tone, and so forth—is a way of getting at the subject of the tale and of shaping its meaning. Ultimately, of course, all the elements of a story are involved in the creation of meaning. "The whole story is the meaning," stated Flannery O'Connor, who used decidedly unusual points of attack to convey her subjects and themes to an audience that she described wryly as blind, hard of hearing, and in need of technical shocks. In considering theme, we should examine the whole story or, for purposes of special analysis, certain aspects of the tale.

We like to search for themes in literature because they make works meaningful and relevant. It helps us to know, for example, that a writer like Luisa Valenzuela has stated that the overriding theme in her fiction offers a "damning version of recent Argentine history." However, we want to explore theme in a balanced and intelligent way, remembering that all the elements in a story contribute to the illumination of meaning. Writers themselves are usually interested in meaning; they search for the "truth" about how we think, feel, act, and perceive. At the same time, they generally do not want to preach, moralize, or convey a message. "For messages," stated the American writer of detective fiction James M. Cain, "I use Western Union." Theme in most good fiction is conveyed not through stating a moral or a didactic point, but rather in a key imaginative insight or a *series* of such insights into the human condition.

Just as there is typically a series of insights in a short story, there may be more than one subject and, as a consequence, more than one theme. Complex stories—for instance Shirley Jackson's "The Lottery"—may have multiple subjects and meanings that have been engineered consciously by an author who wants to mystify. Jackson delights in obscuring her subject, forcing readers to ponder the perplexing nature of the modern condition. What, you will have to ask yourself when you read "The Lottery," is the subject of the tale? Is the subject violence, religion, or historical or social processes? And what theme or themes are generated by these topics? Indeed, *is* there a theme? For we have to admit that theme does not always function as a unifying element in short fiction. A story can simply be a slice of life; a striving for special effects, as in Poe and much supernatural fiction; a premium on suspense and intrigue, as in detective and espionage fiction; or a willful attempt to destroy traditional concepts of content and form, as in much contemporary "antifiction."

Some stories handle theme intensively, while others blur theme, create multiple themes, or ignore theme entirely. Stories, after all, come in many shapes and sizes. The short story writer Hortense Calisher might be correct when she says that the short story "is an apocalypse served in a very small cup." Yet we never know for sure what the outcome of all this fire and brimstone will be. Fortunately, there is more often than not an explosion of meaning in the tightly compressed world of short fiction. In the spirit of Henry James, a writer will, according to the "subject," "method," and "point of attack," produce fiction that deals either with the attitudes and conventions of society and the age; with moments of intellectual or moral crisis; with individual feelings and emotions; or with the realms of the mind and the poetic imagination. Even in the

current era of experimentation and acute artistic self-consciousness, a fiction writer's natural impulse is to give shape and meaning to his or her art.

In shaping the materials of their art, writers of fiction understand both the tradition behind their craft and the need to "make it new." Kate Chopin, who appears in this chapter, was an admirer of Maupassant, translating many of his stories from the French. She especially liked Maupassant's "escape from tradition and authority," as she wrote in an article for *The Atlantic Monthly* in 1896. But in "imitating" the French writer's simplicity and directness, she turned her fictive materials toward decidedly feminist situations and themes.

Writers, however, do not reduce their stories to single, prescriptive themes. Nor do they necessarily provide messages, morals, or answers. As Chekhov declared, the artist "must set the question, not solve it." Authors ask not one question, but a series of questions: Why is life the way that it is? What human (and inhuman) impulses and motivations govern our lives? What are the critical events in the human drama? What details offer clues to an understanding of human nature? These are some of the essential questions that fiction writers traditionally ask, and they are the questions that we seek to answer in any consideration of subject and theme.

Anton Chekhov

THE LADY WITH THE PET DOG

I

A new person, it was said, had appeared on the esplanade: a lady with a pet dog. Dmitry Dmitrich Gurov, who had spent a fortnight at Yalta and had got used to the place, had also begun to take an interest in new arrivals. As he sat in Vernet's confectionery shop, he saw, walking on the esplanade, a fair-haired young woman of medium height, wearing a beret; a white Pomeranian was trotting behind her.

And afterwards he met her in the public garden and in the square several times a day. She walked alone, always wearing the same beret and always with the white dog; no one knew who she was and everyone called her simply "the lady with the pet dog."

"If she is here alone without husband or friends," Gurov reflected, "it wouldn't be a bad thing to make her acquaintance."

He was under forty, but he already had a daughter twelve years old, and two sons at school. They had found a wife for him when he was very young, a student in his second year, and by now she seemed half as old again as he. She was a tall, erect woman with dark eyebrows, stately and dignified and, as she said of herself, intellectual. She read a great deal, used simplified spelling in her letters, called her husband, not Dmitry, but Dimitry, while he privately considered her of limited intelligence, narrow-minded, dowdy, was afraid of her, and did not like to be at home. He had begun being unfaithful to her long ago—had been unfaithful to her often and, probably for that reason, almost always spoke ill of women, and when they were talked of in his presence used to call them "the inferior race."

It seemed to him that he had been sufficiently tutored by bitter experience to call them what he pleased, and yet he could not have lived without "the inferior race" for two days together. In the company of men he was bored and ill at ease, he was chilly and uncommunicative with them; but when he was among women he felt free, and knew what to speak to them about and how to comport himself; and even to be silent with them was no strain on him. In his appearance, in his character, in his whole makeup there was something attractive and elusive that disposed women in his favor and allured them. He knew that, and some force seemed to draw him to them, too.

Oft-repeated and really bitter experience had taught him long ago that with decent people—particularly Moscow people—who are irresolute and slow to move, every affair which at first seems a light and charming adventure inevitably grows into a whole problem of extreme complexity, and in the end a painful situation is created. But at every new meeting with an interesting woman this lesson of experience seemed to slip from his memory, and he was eager for life, and everything seemed so simple and diverting.

One evening while he was dining in the public garden the lady in the beret walked up without haste to take the next table. Her expression, her gait, her dress, and the way she did her hair told him that she belonged to the upper class, that she was married, that she was in Yalta for the first time and alone, and that she was bored there. The stories told of the immorality in Yalta are to a great extent untrue; he despised them, and knew that such stories were made up for the most part by persons who would have been glad to sin themselves if they had had the chance; but when the lady sat down at the next table three paces from him, he recalled these stories of easy conquests, of trips to the mountains, and the tempting thought of a swift, fleeting liaison, a romance with an unknown woman of whose very name he was ignorant suddenly took hold of him.

He beckoned invitingly to the Pomeranian, and when the dog approached him, shook his finger at it. The Pomeranian growled; Gurov threatened it again.

The lady glanced at him and at once dropped her eyes.

"He doesn't bite," she said and blushed.

"May I give him a bone?" he asked; and when she nodded he inquired affably, "Have you been in Yalta long?"

"About five days."

"And I am dragging out the second week here."

There was a short silence.

"Time passes quickly, and yet it is so dull here!" she said, not looking at him.

"It's only the fashion to say it's dull here. A provincial will live in Belyov or Zhizdra and not be bored, but when he comes here it's 'Oh, the dullness! Oh, the dust!' One would think he came from Granada."

She laughed. Then both continued eating in silence, like strangers, but after dinner they walked together and there sprang up between them the light banter of people who are free and contented, to whom it does not matter where they go or what they talk about. They walked and talked of the strange light on the sea: the water was a soft, warm, lilac color, and there was a golden band of moonlight upon it. They talked of how sultry it was after a hot day. Gurov told her that he was a native of Moscow, that he had studied languages and literature at the university, but had a post in a bank; that at one time he had trained to become an opera singer but had given it up, that he owned two houses in Moscow. And he learned from her that she had grown up in Petersburg, but had lived in S—— since her marriage two years previously, that she was going to stay in Yalta for about another month, and that her husband, who needed a rest, too, might perhaps come to fetch her. She was not certain whether her husband was a member of a Government Board or served on a Zemstvo Council,[1] and this amused her. And Gurov learned too that her name was Anna Sergeyevna.

Afterwards in his room at the hotel he thought about her—and was certain that he would meet her the next day. It was bound to happen. Getting into bed he recalled that she had been a schoolgirl only recently, doing lessons like his own daughter; he thought how much timidity and angularity there was still in her laugh and her manner of talking with a stranger. It must have been the first time in her life that she was alone in a setting in which she was followed, looked at, and spoken to for one secret purpose alone, which she could hardly fail to guess. He thought of her slim, delicate throat, her lovely gray eyes.

"There's something pathetic about her, though," he thought, and dropped off.

II

A week had passed since they had struck up an acquaintance. It was a holiday. It was close indoors, while in the street the wind whirled the dust about and blew people's hats off. One was thirsty all day, and Gurov often went into the restaurant and offered Anna Sergeyevna a soft drink or ice cream. One did not know what to do with oneself.

In the evening when the wind had abated they went out on the pier to watch the steamer come in. There were a great many people walking about the dock; they had come to welcome someone and they were carrying bunches of flowers. And two peculiarities of a festive Yalta crowd stood out: the elderly ladies were dressed like young ones and there were many generals.

Owing to the choppy sea, the steamer arrived late, after sunset, and it was a long time tacking about before it put in at the pier. Anna Sergeyevna peered at the steamer and the passengers through her lorgnette as though looking for acquaintances, and whenever she turned to Gurov her eyes were shining. She talked a great deal and asked questions jerkily, forgetting the next moment what she had asked; then she lost her lorgnette in the crush.

The festive crowd began to disperse; it was now too dark to see people's faces; there was no wind any more, but Gurov and Anna Sergeyevna still stood as though waiting to see someone else come off the steamer. Anna Sergeyevna was silent now, and sniffed her flowers without looking at Gurov.

[1] *Zemstvo Council*—county council.

"The weather has improved this evening," he said. "Where shall we go now? Shall we drive somewhere?"

She did not reply.

Then he looked at her intently, and suddenly embraced her and kissed her on the lips, and the moist fragrance of her flowers enveloped him; and at once he looked round him anxiously, wondering if anyone had seen them.

"Let us go to your place," he said softly. And they walked off together rapidly.

The air in her room was close and there was the smell of the perfume she had bought at the Japanese shop. Looking at her, Gurov thought: "What encounters life offers!" From the past he preserved the memory of carefree, good-natured women whom love made gay and who were grateful to him for the happiness he gave them, however brief it might be; and of women like his wife who loved without sincerity, with too many words, affectedly, hysterically, with an expression that it was not love or passion that engaged them but something more significant; and of two or three others, very beautiful, frigid women, across whose faces would suddenly flit a rapacious expression—an obstinate desire to take from life more than it could give, and these were women no longer young, capricious, unreflecting, domineering, unintelligent, and when Gurov grew cold to them their beauty aroused his hatred, and the lace on their lingerie seemed to him to resemble scales.

But here there was the timidity, the angularity of inexperienced youth, a feeling of awkwardness; and there was a sense of embarrassment, as though someone had suddenly knocked at the door. Anna Sergeyevna, "the lady with the pet dog," treated what had happened in a peculiar way, very seriously, as though it were her fall—so it seemed, and this was odd and inappropriate. Her features drooped and faded, and her long hair hung down sadly on either side of her face; she grew pensive and her dejected pose was that of a Magdalene in a picture by an old master.

"It's not right," she said. "You don't respect me now, you first of all."

There was a watermelon on the table. Gurov cut himself a slice and began eating it without haste. They were silent for at least half an hour.

There was something touching about Anna Sergeyevna; she had the purity of a well-bred, naive woman who has seen little of life. The single candle burning on the table barely illumined her face, yet it was clear that she was unhappy.

"Why should I stop respecting you, darling?" asked Gurov. "You don't know what you're saying."

"God forgive me," she said, and her eyes filled with tears. "It's terrible."

"It's as though you were trying to exonerate yourself."

"How can I exonerate myself? No. I am a bad, low woman; I despise myself and I have no thought of exonerating myself. It's not my husband but myself I have deceived. And not only just now; I have been deceiving myself for a long time. My husband may be a good, honest man, but he is a flunkey! I don't know what he does, what his work is, but I know he is a flunkey! I was twenty when I married him. I was tormented by curiosity; I wanted something better. 'There must be a different sort of life,' I said to myself. I wanted to live! To live, to live! Curiosity kept eating at me—you don't understand it, but I swear to God I could no longer control myself; something was going on in me; I could not be held back. I told my husband I was ill, and came here. And

here I have been walking about as though in a daze, as though I were mad; and now I have become a vulgar, vile woman whom anyone may despise."

Gurov was already bored with her; he was irritated by her naive tone, by her repentance, so unexpected and so out of place, but for the tears in her eyes he might have thought she was joking or play-acting.

"I don't understand, my dear," he said softly. "What do you want?"

She hid her face on his breast and pressed close to him.

"Believe me, believe me, I beg you," she said, "I love honesty and purity, and sin is loathsome to me; I don't know what I'm doing. Simple people say, 'The Evil One has led me astray.' And I may say of myself now that the Evil One has led me astray."

"Quiet, quiet," he murmured.

He looked into her fixed, frightened eyes, kissed her, spoke to her softly and affectionately, and by degrees she calmed down, and her gaiety returned; both began laughing.

Afterwards when they went out there was not a soul on the esplanade. The town with its cypresses looked quite dead, but the sea was still sounding as it broke upon the beach; a single launch was rocking on the waves and on it a lantern was blinking sleepily.

They found a cab and drove to Oreanda.

"I found out your surname in the hall just now: it was written on the board—von Dideritz," said Gurov. "Is your husband German?"

"No; I believe his grandfather was German, but he is Greek Orthodox himself."

At Oreanda they sat on a bench not far from the church, looked down at the sea, and were silent. Yalta was barely visible through the morning mist; white clouds rested motionlessly on the mountaintops. The leaves did not stir on the trees, cicadas twanged, and the monotonous muffled sound of the sea that rose from below spoke of the peace, the eternal sleep awaiting us. So it rumbled below when there was no Yalta, no Oreanda here; so it rumbles now, and it will rumble as indifferently and as hollowly when we are no more. And in this constancy, in this complete indifference to the life and death of each of us, there lies, perhaps, a pledge of our eternal salvation, of the unceasing advance of life upon earth, of unceasing movement towards perfection. Sitting beside a young woman who in the dawn seemed so lovely, Gurov, soothed and spellbound by these magical surroundings—the sea, the mountains, the clouds, the wide sky—thought how everything is really beautiful in this world when one reflects: everything except what we think or do ourselves when we forget the higher aims of life and our own human dignity.

A man strolled up to them—probably a guard—looked at them and walked away. And this detail, too, seemed so mysterious and beautiful. They saw a steamer arrive from Feodosia, its lights extinguished in the glow of dawn.

"There is dew on the grass," said Anna Sergeyevna, after a silence.

"Yes, it's time to go home."

They returned to the city.

Then they met every day at twelve o'clock on the esplanade, lunched and dined together, took walks, admired the sea. She complained that she slept badly, that she had palpitations, asked the same questions, troubled now by jealousy and now by the fear that he did not respect her sufficiently. And often in the square or the public garden, when there was no one near them, he suddenly drew her to him and kissed her passionately. Complete idleness, these kisses in broad daylight exchanged furtively in dread of someone's seeing them, the heat, the smell of the sea, and the continual flitting before his eyes of idle, well-dressed, well-fed people, worked a complete change in him; he kept telling Anna Sergeyevna how beautiful she was, how seductive, was urgently passionate; he would not move a step away from her, while she was often pensive and continually pressed him to confess that he did not respect her, did not love her in the least, and saw in her nothing but a common woman. Almost every evening rather late they drove somewhere out of town, to Oreanda or to the waterfall; and the excursion was always a success, the scenery invariably impressed them as beautiful and magnificent.

They were expecting her husband, but a letter came from him saying that he had eye-trouble, and begging his wife to return home as soon as possible. Anna Sergeyevna made haste to go.

"It's a good thing I am leaving," she said to Gurov. "It's the hand of Fate!"

She took a carriage to the railway station, and he went with her. They were driving the whole day. When she had taken her place in the express, and when the second bell had rung, she said, "Let me look at you once more—let me look at you again. Like this."

She was not crying but was so sad that she seemed ill and her face was quivering.

"I shall be thinking of you—remembering you," she said. "God bless you; be happy. Don't remember evil against me. We are parting forever—it has to be, for we ought never to have met. Well, God bless you."

The train moved off rapidly, its lights soon vanished, and a minute later there was no sound of it, as though everything had conspired to end as quickly as possible that sweet trance, that madness. Left alone on the platform, and gazing into the dark distance, Gurov listened to the twang of the grasshoppers and the hum of the telegraph wires, feeling as though he had just waked up. And he reflected, musing, that there had now been another episode or adventure in his life, and it, too, was at an end, and nothing was left of it but a memory. He was moved, sad, and slightly remorseful: this young woman whom he would never meet again had not been happy with him; he had been warm and affectionate with her, but yet in his manner, his tone, and his caresses there had been a shade of light irony, the slightly coarse arrogance of a happy male who was, besides, almost twice her age. She had constantly called him kind, exceptional, high-minded; obviously he had seemed to her different from what he really was, so he had involuntarily deceived her.

Here at the station there was already a scent of autumn in the air; it was a chilly evening.

"It is time for me to go north, too," thought Gurov as he left the platform. "High time!"

III

At home in Moscow the winter routine was already established; the stoves were heated, and in the morning it was still dark when the children were having breakfast and getting

ready for school, and the nurse would light the lamp for a short time. There were frosts already. When the first snow falls, on the first day the sleighs are out, it is pleasant to see the white earth, the white roofs; one draws easy, delicious breaths, and the season brings back the days of one's youth. The old limes and birches, white with hoar-frost, have a good-natured look; they are closer to one's heart than cypresses and palms, and near them one no longer wants to think of mountains and the sea.

Gurov, a native of Moscow, arrived there on a fine frosty day, and when he put on his fur coat and warm gloves and took a walk along Petrovka, and when on Saturday night he heard the bells ringing, his recent trip and the places he had visited lost all charm for him. Little by little he became immersed in Moscow life, greedily read three newspapers a day, and declared that he did not read the Moscow papers on principle. He already felt a longing for restaurants, clubs, formal dinners, anniversary celebrations, and it flattered him to entertain distinguished lawyers and actors, and to play cards with a professor at the physicians' club. He could eat a whole portion of meat stewed with pickled cabbage and served in a pan, Moscow style.

A month or so would pass and the image of Anna Sergeyevna, it seemed to him, would become misty in his memory, and only from time to time he would dream of her with her touching smile as he dreamed of others. But more than a month went by, winter came into its own, and everything was still clear in his memory as though he had parted from Anna Sergeyevna only yesterday. And his memories glowed more and more vividly. When in the evening stillness the voices of his children preparing their lessons reached his study, or when he listened to a song or to an organ playing in a restaurant, or when the storm howled in the chimney, suddenly everything would rise up in his memory; what had happened on the pier and the early morning with the mist on the mountains, and the steamer coming from Feodosia, and the kisses. He would pace about his room a long time, remembering and smiling; then his memories passed into reveries, and in his imagination the past would mingle with what was to come. He did not dream of Anna Sergeyevna, but she followed him about everywhere and watched him. When he shut his eyes he saw her before him as though she were there in the flesh, and she seemed to him lovelier, younger, tenderer than she had been, and he imagined himself a finer man than he had been in Yalta. Of evenings she peered out at him from the bookcase, from the fireplace, from the corner—he heard her breathing, the caressing rustle of her clothes. In the street he followed the women with his eyes, looking for someone who resembled her.

Already he was tormented by a strong desire to share his memories with someone. But in his home it was impossible to talk of his love, and he had no one to talk to outside; certainly he could not confide in his tenants or anyone at the bank. And what was there to talk about? He hadn't loved her then, had he? Had there been anything beautiful, poetical, edifying, or simply interesting in his relations with Anna Sergeyevna? And he was forced to talk vaguely of love, of women, and no one guessed what he meant; only his wife would twitch her black eyebrows and say, "The part of a philanderer does not suit you at all, Dimitry."

One evening, coming out of the physicians' club with an official with whom he had been playing cards, he could not resist saying:

"If you only knew what a fascinating woman I became acquainted with at Yalta!"

The official got into his sledge and was driving away, but turned suddenly and shouted:

"Dmitry Dmitrich!"

"What is it?"

"You were right this evening; the sturgeon was a bit high."

These words, so commonplace, for some reason moved Gurov to indignation, and struck him as degrading and unclean. What savage manners, what mugs! What stupid nights, what dull, humdrum days! Frenzied gambling, gluttony, drunkenness, continual talk always about the same thing! Futile pursuits and conversations always about the same topics take up the better part of one's time, the better part of one's strength, and in the end there is left a life clipped and wingless, an absurd mess, and there is no escaping or getting away from it—just as though one were in a madhouse or a prison.

Gurov, boiling with indignation, did not sleep all night. And he had a headache all the next day. And the following nights too he slept badly; he sat up in bed, thinking, or paced up and down his room. He was fed up with his children, fed up with the bank; he had no desire to go anywhere or to talk of anything.

In December during the holidays he prepared to take a trip and told his wife he was going to Petersburg to do what he could for a young friend—and he set off for S——. What for? He did not know, himself. He wanted to see Anna Sergeyevna and talk with her, to arrange a rendezvous if possible.

He arrived at S—— in the morning, and at the hotel took the best room, in which the floor was covered with gray army cloth, and on the table there was an inkstand, gray with dust and topped by a figure on horseback, its hat in its raised hand and its head broken off. The porter gave him the necessary information: von Dideritz lived in a house of his own on Staro-Goncharnaya Street, not far from the hotel: he was rich and lived well and kept his own horses; everyone in the town knew him. The porter pronounced the name: "Dridiritz."

Without haste Gurov made his way to Staro-Goncharnaya Street and found the house. Directly opposite the house stretched a long gray fence studded with nails.

"A fence like that would make one run away," thought Gurov, looking now at the fence, now at the windows of the house.

He reflected: this was a holiday, and the husband was apt to be at home. And in any case, it would be tactless to go into the house and disturb her. If he were to send her a note, it might fall into her husband's hands, and that might spoil everything. The best thing was to rely on chance. And he kept walking up and down the street and along the fence, waiting for the chance. He saw a beggar go in at the gate and heard the dogs attack him; then an hour later he heard a piano, and the sound came to him faintly and indistinctly. Probably it was Anna Sergeyevna playing. The front door opened suddenly, and an old woman came out, followed by the familiar white Pomeranian. Gurov was on the point of calling to the dog, but his heart began beating violently, and in his excitement he could not remember the Pomeranian's name.

He kept walking up and down, and hated the gray fence more and more, and by now the thought irritably that Anna Sergeyevna had forgotten him, and was perhaps already diverting herself with another man, and that that was very natural in a young woman who from morning till night had to look at that damn fence. He went back to his hotel

room and sat on the couch for a long while, not knowing what to do, then he had dinner and a long nap.

"How stupid and annoying all this is!" he thought when he woke and looked at the dark windows: it was already evening. "Here I've had a good sleep for some reason. What am I going to do at night?"

He sat on the bed, which was covered with a cheap gray blanket of the kind seen in hospitals, and he twitted himself in his vexation:

"So there's your lady with the pet dog. There's your adventure. A nice place to cool your heels in."

That morning at the station a playbill in large letters had caught his eye. *The Geisha* was to be given for the first time. He thought of this and drove to the theater.

"It's quite possible that she goes to first nights," he thought.

The theater was full. As in all provincial theaters, there was a haze above the chandelier, the gallery was noisy and restless; in the front row, before the beginning of the performance the local dandies were standing with their hands clasped behind their backs; in the Governor's box the Governor's daughter, wearing a boa, occupied the front seat, while the Governor himself hid modestly behind the portiere and only his hands were visible; the curtain swayed; the orchestra was a long time tuning up. While the audience was coming in and taking their seats, Gurov scanned the faces eagerly.

Anna Sergeyevna, too, came in. She sat down in the third row, and when Gurov looked at her his heart contracted, and he understood clearly that in the whole world there was no human being so near, so precious, and so important to him; she, this little, undistinguished woman, lost in a provincial crowd, with a vulgar lorgnette in her hand, filled his whole life now, was his sorrow and his joy, the only happiness that he now desired for himself, and to the sounds of the bad orchestra, of the miserable local violins, he thought how lovely she was. He thought and dreamed.

A young man with small side-whiskers, very tall and stooped, came in with Anna Sergeyevna and sat down beside her; he nodded his head at every step and seemed to be bowing continually. Probably this was the husband whom at Yalta, in an access of bitter feeling, she had called a flunkey. And there really was in his lanky figure, his side-whiskers, his small bald patch, something of a flunkey's retiring manner; his smile was mawkish, and in his buttonhole there was an academic badge like a waiter's number.

During the first intermission the husband went out to have a smoke; she remained in her seat. Gurov, who was also sitting in the orchestra, went up to her and said in a shaky voice, with a forced smile:

"Good evening!"

She glanced at him and turned pale, then looked at him again in horror, unable to believe her eyes, and gripped the fan and the lorgnette tightly together in her hands, evidently trying to keep herself from fainting. Both were silent. She was sitting, he was standing, frightened by her distress and not daring to take a seat beside her. The violins and the flute that were being tuned up sang out. He suddenly felt frightened: it seemed as if all the people in the boxes were looking at them. She got up and went hurriedly to the exit; he followed her, and both of them walked blindly along the corridors and up and down stairs, and figures in the uniforms prescribed for magistrates, teachers, and officials of the Department of Crown Lands, all wearing badges, flitted before their eyes, as did also ladies, and fur coats on hangers; they were conscious of drafts and the smell of stale tobacco. And Gurov, whose heart was beating violently, thought:

"Oh, Lord! Why are these people here and this orchestra!"

And at that instant he suddenly recalled how when he had seen Anna Sergeyevna off at the station he had said to himself that all was over between them and that they would never meet again. But how distant the end still was!

On the narrow, gloomy staircase over which it said "To the Amphitheatre," she stopped.

"How you frightened me!" she said, breathing hard, still pale and stunned. "Oh, how you frightened me! I am barely alive. Why did you come? Why?"

"But do understand, Anna, do understand——" he said hurriedly, under his breath. "I implore you, do understand——"

She looked at him with fear, with entreaty, with love; she looked at him intently, to keep his features more distinctly in her memory.

"I suffer so," she went on, not listening to him. "All this time I have been thinking of nothing but you; I live only by the thought of you. And I wanted to forget, to forget; but why, oh, why have you come?"

On the landing above them two high school boys were looking down and smoking, but it was all the same to Gurov; he drew Anna Sergeyevna to him and began kissing her face and hands.

"What are you doing, what are you doing!" she was saying in horror, pushing him away. "We have lost our senses. Go away today; go away at once——I conjure you by all that is sacred, I implore you——People are coming this way!"

Someone was walking up the stairs.

"You must leave," Anna Sergeyevna went on in a whisper. "Do you hear, Dmitry Dmitrich? I will come and see you in Moscow. I have never been happy; I am unhappy now, and I never, never shall be happy, never! So don't make me suffer still more! I swear I'll come to Moscow. But now let us part. My dear, good, precious one, let us part!"

She pressed his hand and walked rapidly downstairs, turning to look round at him, and from her eyes he could see that she really was unhappy. Gurov stood for a while, listening, then when all grew quiet, he found his coat and left the theater.

IV

And Anna Sergeyevna began coming to see him in Moscow. Once every two or three months she left S—— telling her husband that she was going to consult a doctor about a woman's ailment from which she was suffering—and her husband did and did not believe her. When she arrived in Moscow she would stop at the Slavyansky Bazar Hotel, and at once send a man in a red cap to Gurov. Gurov came to see her, and no one in Moscow knew of it.

Once he was going to see her in this way on a winter morning (the messenger had come the evening before and not found him in). With him walked his daughter, whom he wanted to take to school; it was on the way. Snow was coming down in big wet flakes.

"It's three degrees above zero,[2] and yet it's snowing," Gurov was saying to his daughter. "But this temperature prevails only on the surface of the earth; in the upper layers of the atmosphere there is quite a different temperature."

"And why doesn't it thunder in winter, papa?"

He explained that, too. He talked, thinking all the while that he was on his way to a rendezvous, and no living soul knew of it, and probably no one would ever know. He had two lives, an open one, seen and known by all who needed to know it, full of conventional truth and conventional falsehood, exactly like the lives of his friends and acquaintances; and another life that went on in secret. And through some strange, perhaps accidental, combination of circumstances, everything that was of interest and importance to him, everything that was essential to him, everything about which he felt sincerely and did not deceive himself, everything that constituted the core of his life, was going on concealed from others; while all that was false, the shell in which he hid to cover the truth—his work at the bank, for instance, his discussions at the club, his references to the "inferior race," his appearances at anniversary celebrations with his wife—all that went on in the open. Judging others by himself, he did not believe what he saw, and always fancied that every man led his real, most interesting life under cover of secrecy as under cover of night. The personal life of every individual is based on secrecy, and perhaps it is partly for that reason that civilized man is so nervously anxious that personal privacy should be respected.

Having taken his daughter to school, Gurov went on to the Slavyansky Bazar Hotel. He took off his fur coat in the lobby, went upstairs, and knocked gently at the door. Anna Sergeyevna, wearing his favorite gray dress, exhausted by the journey and by waiting, had been expecting him since the previous evening. She was pale, and looked at him without a smile, and he had hardly entered when she flung herself on his breast. That kiss was a long, lingering one, as though they had not seen one another for two years.

"Well, darling, how are you getting on there?" he asked. "What news?"

"Wait; I'll tell you in a moment—I can't speak."

She could not speak; she was crying. She turned away from him, and pressed her handkerchief to her eyes.

"Let her have her cry; meanwhile I'll sit down," he thought, and he seated himself in an armchair.

Then he rang and ordered tea, and while he was having his tea she remained standing at the window with her back to him. She was crying out of sheer agitation, in the sorrowful consciousness that their life was so sad; that they could only see each other in secret and had to hide from people like thieves! Was it not a broken life?

"Come, stop now, dear!" he said.

It was plain to him that this love of theirs would not be over soon, that the end of it was not in sight. Anna Sergeyevna was growing more and more attached to him. She adored him, and it was unthinkable to tell her that their love was bound to come to an end some day; besides, she would not have believed it!

He went up to her and took her by the shoulders, to fondle her and say something diverting, and at that moment he caught sight of himself in the mirror.

---

[2]*three degrees above zero*—Celsius—about thirty-seven degrees Fahrenheit

His hair was already beginning to turn gray. And it seemed odd to him that he had grown so much older in the last few years, and lost his looks. The shoulders on which his hands rested were warm and heaving. He felt compassion for this life, still so warm and lovely, but probably already about to begin to fade and wither like his own. Why did she love him so much? He always seemed to women different from what he was, and they loved in him not himself, but the man whom their imagination created and whom they had been eagerly seeking all their lives; and afterwards, when they saw their mistake, they loved him nevertheless. And not one of them had been happy with him. In the past he had met women, come together with them, parted from them, but he had never once loved; it was anything you please, but not love. And only now when his head was gray he had fallen in love, really, truly—for the first time in his life.

Anna Sergeyevna and he loved each other as people do who are very close and intimate, like man and wife, like tender friends; it seemed to them that Fate itself had meant them for one another, and they could not understand why he had a wife and she a husband; and it was as though they were a pair of migratory birds, male and female, caught and forced to live in different cages. They forgave each other what they were ashamed of in their past, they forgave everything in the present, and felt that this love of theirs had altered them both.

Formerly in moments of sadness he had soothed himself with whatever logical arguments came into his head, but now he no longer cared for logic; he felt profound compassion, he wanted to be sincere and tender.

"Give it up now, my darling," he said. "You've had your cry; that's enough. Let us have a talk now, we'll think up something."

Then they spent a long time taking counsel together, they talked of how to avoid the necessity for secrecy, for deception, for living in different cities, and not seeing one another for long stretches of time. How could they free themselves from these intolerable fetters?

"How? How?" he asked, clutching his head. "How?"

And it seemed as though in a little while the solution would be found, and then a new and glorious life would begin; and it was clear to both of them that the end was still far off, and that what was to be most complicated and difficult for them was only just beginning.

Translated by Avrahm Yarmolinsky

QUESTIONS

1. In what ways are Gurov and Anna Sergeyevna unfulfilled when they first meet?
2. What attracts Gurov to Anna Sergeyevna?
3. Does the story end on an optimistic note, a pessimistic one, or a combination of the two?
4. What is Gurov's general attitude toward women? Does it change or remain the same during the course of the story?

5. It is often said that Chekhov's work foreshadowed the emotional complexity of much twentieth-century writing. Do his characters have the conflicts we find in today's men and women? Explain.
6. State the theme of this story as you perceive it.

Kate Chopin

A RESPECTABLE WOMAN

Mrs. Baroda was a little provoked to learn that her husband expected his friend, Gouvernail, up to spend a week or two on the plantation.

They had entertained a good deal during the winter; much of the time had also been passed in New Orleans in various forms of mild dissipation. She was looking forward to a period of unbroken rest, now, and undisturbed tête-a-tête with her husband, when he informed her that Gouvernail was coming up to stay a week or two.

This was a man she had heard much of but never seen. He had been her husband's college friend; was now a journalist, and in no sense a society man or "a man about town," which were, perhaps, some of the reasons she had never met him. But she had unconsciously formed an image of him in her mind. She pictured him tall, slim, cynical; with eye-glasses, and his hands in his pockets; and she did not like him. Gouvernail was slim enough, but he wasn't very tall nor very cynical; neither did he wear eye-glasses nor carry his hands in his pockets. And she rather liked him when he first presented himself.

But why she liked him she could not explain satisfactorily to herself when she partly attempted to do so. She could discover in him none of those brilliant and promising traits which Gaston, her husband, had often assured her that he possessed. On the contrary, he sat rather mute and receptive before her chatty eagerness to make him feel at home and in face of Gaston's frank and wordy hospitality. His manner was as courteous toward her as the most exacting woman could require; but he made no direct appeal to her approval or even esteem.

Once settled at the plantation he seemed to like to sit upon the wide portico in the shade of one of the big Corinthian pillars, smoking his cigar lazily and listening attentively to Gaston's experience as a sugar planter.

"This is what I call living," he would utter with deep satisfaction, as the air that swept across the sugar field caressed him with its warm and scented velvety touch. It pleased him also to get on familiar terms with the big dogs that came about him, rubbing themselves sociably against his legs. He did not care to fish, and displayed no eagerness to go out and kill grosbecs when Gaston proposed doing so.

Gouvernail's personality puzzled Mrs. Baroda, but she liked him. Indeed, he was a lovable, inoffensive fellow. After a few days, when she could understand him no better than at first, she gave over being puzzled and remained piqued. In this mood she left her husband and her guest, for the most part, alone together. Then finding that Gouvernail took no manner of exception to her action, she imposed her society upon him, accompanying him in his idle strolls to the mill and walks along the batture. She persistently sought to penetrate the reserve in which he had unconsciously enveloped himself.

"When is he going—your friend?" she one day asked her husband. "For my part, he tires me frightfully."

"Not for a week yet, dear. I can't understand; he gives you no trouble."

"No. I should like him better if he did; if he were more like others, and I had to plan somewhat for his comfort and enjoyment."

Gaston took his wife's pretty face between his hands and looked tenderly and laughingly into her troubled eyes. They were making a bit of toilet sociably together in Mrs. Baroda's dressing-room.

"You are full of surprises, ma belle," he said to her. "Even I can never count upon how you are going to act under given conditions." He kissed her and turned to fasten his cravat before the mirror.

"Here you are," he went on, "taking poor Gouvernail seriously and making a commotion over him, the last thing he would desire or expect."

"Commotion!" she hotly resented. "Nonsense! How can you say such a thing? Commotion, indeed! But, you know, you said he was clever."

"So he is. But the poor fellow is run down by overwork now. That's why I asked him here to take a rest."

"You used to say he was a man of ideas," she retorted, unconciliated. "I expected him to be interesting, at least. I'm going to the city in the morning to have my spring gowns fitted. Let me know when Mr. Gouvernail is gone; I shall be at my Aunt Octavie's."

That night she went and sat alone upon a bench that stood beneath a live oak tree at the edge of the gravel walk.

She had never known her thoughts or her intentions to be so confused. She could gather nothing from them but the feeling of a distinct necessity to quit her home in the morning.

Mrs. Baroda heard footsteps crunching the gravel; but could discern in the darkness only the approaching red point of a lighted cigar. She knew it was Gouvernail, for her husband did not smoke. She hoped to remain unnoticed, but her white gown revealed her to him. He threw away his cigar and seated himself upon the bench beside her; without a suspicion that she might object to his presence.

"Your husband told me to bring this to you, Mrs. Baroda," he said, handing her a filmy, white scarf with which she sometimes enveloped her head and shoulders. She accepted the scarf from him with a murmur of thanks, and let it lie in her lap.

He made some commonplace observation upon the baneful effect of the night air at that season. Then as his gaze reached out into the darkness, he murmured, half to himself:

" 'Night of south winds—night of the large few stars!
Still nodding night——' "

She made no reply to this apostrophe to the night, which indeed, was not addressed to her.

Gouvernail was in no sense a diffident man, for he was not a self-conscious one. His periods of reserve were not constitutional, but the result of moods. Sitting there beside Mrs. Baroda, his silence melted for the time.

He talked freely and intimately in a low, hesitating drawl that was not unpleasant to hear. He talked of the old college days when he and Gaston had been a good deal to each other; of the days of keen and blind ambitions and large intentions. Now there was left with him, at least, a philosophic acquiescence to the existing order—only a desire to be permitted to exist, with now and then a little whiff of genuine life, such as he was breathing now.

Her mind only vaguely grasped what he was saying. Her physical being was for the moment predominant. She was not thinking of his words, only drinking in the tones of his voice. She wanted to reach out her hand in the darkness and touch him with the sensitive tips of her fingers upon the face or the lips. She wanted to draw close to him and whisper against his cheek—she did not care what—as she might have done if she had not been a respectable woman.

The stronger the impulse grew to bring herself near him, the further, in fact, did she draw away from him. As soon as she could do so without an appearance of too great rudeness, she rose and left him there alone.

Before she reached the house, Gouvernail had lighted a fresh cigar and ended his apostrophe to the night.

Mrs. Baroda was greatly tempted that night to tell her husband—who was also her friend—of this folly that had seized her. But she did not yield to the temptation. Beside being a respectable woman she was a very sensible one; and she knew there are some battles in life which a human being must fight alone.

When Gaston arose in the morning, his wife had already departed. She had taken an early morning train to the city. She did not return till Gouvernail was gone from under her roof.

There was some talk of having him back during the summer that followed. That is, Gaston greatly desired it; but this desire yielded to his wife's strenuous opposition.

However, before the year ended, she proposed, wholly from herself, to have Gouvernail visit them again. Her husband was surprised and delighted with the suggestion coming from her.

"I am glad, chère amie, to know that you have finally overcome your dislike for him; truly he did not deserve it."

"Oh," she told him, laughingly, after pressing a long, tender kiss upon his lips, "I have overcome everything! you will see. This time I shall be very nice to him."

QUESTIONS

1. Of Mrs. Baroda's feelings toward Gouvernail, the author states, "But why she liked him she could not explain satisfactorily to herself when she partly attempted to do so." At what point do Mrs. Baroda's feelings toward Gouvernail change? What causes this change?

2. The mood of the story is sedate, understated, and enigmatic. How does the physical description of the setting complement this mood?
3. How does the title of the story prove to be an ironic one?
4. Compare and contrast the attraction of Anna Sergeyevna to Gurov in "The Lady with the Pet Dog" with that of Mrs. Baroda to Gouvernail.
5. Kate Chopin is often viewed as an early feminist writer. From what you know of feminism, explain what themes in the story support this characterization.

Shirley Jackson

THE LOTTERY

The morning of June 27th was clear and sunny, with the fresh warmth of a full-summer day; the flowers were blossoming profusely and the grass was richly green. The people of the village began to gather in the square, between the post office and the bank, around ten o'clock; in some towns there were so many people that the lottery took two days and had to be started on June 26th, but in this village, where there were only about three hundred people, the whole lottery took less than two hours, so it could begin at ten o'clock in the morning and still be through in time to allow the villagers to get home for noon dinner.

The children assembled first, of course. School was recently over for the summer, and the feeling of liberty sat uneasily on most of them; they tended to gather together quietly for a while before they broke into boisterous play, and their talk was still of the classroom and the teacher, of books and reprimands. Bobby Martin had already stuffed his pockets full of stones, and the other boys soon followed his example, selecting the smoothest and roundest stones; Bobby and Harry Jones and Dickie Delacroix—the villagers pronounced this name "Dellacroy"—eventually made a great pile of stones in one corner of the square and guarded it against the raids of the other boys. The girls stood aside, talking among themselves, looking over their shoulders at the boys, and the very small children rolled in the dust or clung to the hands of their older brothers or sisters.

Soon the men began to gather, surveying their own children, speaking of planting and rain, tractors and taxes. They stood together, away from the pile of stones in the corner, and their jokes were quiet and they smiled rather than laughed. The women, wearing faded house dresses and sweaters, came shortly after their menfolk. They greeted one another and exchanged bits of gossip as they went to join their husbands. Soon the women, standing by their husbands, began to call to their children, and the children came reluctantly, having to be called four or five times. Bobby Martin ducked under his mother's grasping hand and ran, laughing, back to the pile of stones. His father spoke up sharply, and Bobby came quickly and took his place between his father and his oldest brother.

The lottery was conducted—as were the square dances, the teenage club, the Halloween program—by Mr. Summers, who had time and energy to devote to civic activities. He was a round-faced, jovial man and he ran the coal business, and people were sorry for him, because he had no children and his wife was a scold. When he arrived in the square, carrying the black wooden box, there was a murmur of conversation among the villagers, and he waved and called, "Little late today, folks." The postmaster, Mr. Graves, followed him, carrying a three-legged stool, and the stool was put in the center of the square and Mr. Summers set the black box down on it. The villagers kept their distance, leaving a space between themselves and the stool, and when Mr. Summers said, "Some of you fellows want to give me a hand?" there was a hesitation before two men, Mr. Martin and his oldest son, Baxter, came forward to hold the box steady on the stool while Mr. Summers stirred up the papers inside it.

The original paraphernalia for the lottery had been lost long ago, and the black box now resting on the stool had been put into use even before Old Man Warner, the oldest man in town, was born. Mr. Summers spoke frequently to the villagers about making a new box, but no one liked to upset even as much tradition as was represented by the black box. There was a story that the present box had been made with some pieces of the box that had preceded it, the one that had been constructed when the first people settled down to make a village here. Every year, after the lottery, Mr, Summers began talking again about a new box, but every year the subject was allowed to fade off without anything's being done. The black box grew shabbier each year; by now it was no longer completely black but splintered badly along one side to show the original wood color, and in some places faded or stained.

Mr. Martin and his oldest son, Baxter, held the black box securely on the stool until Mr. Summers had stirred the papers thoroughly with his hand. Because so much of the ritual had been forgotten or discarded, Mr. Summers had been successful in having slips of paper substituted for the chips of wood that had been used for generations. Chips of wood, Mr. Summers had argued, had been all very well when the village was tiny, but now that the population was more than three hundred and likely to keep on growing, it was necessary to use something that would fit more easily into the black box. The night before the lottery, Mr. Summers and Mr. Graves made up the slips of paper and put them in the box, and it was then taken to the safe of Mr. Summers' coal company and locked up until Mr. Summers was ready to take it to the square next morning. The rest of the year, the box was put away, sometimes one place, sometimes another; it had spent one year in Mr. Graves's barn and another year underfoot in the post office, and sometimes it was set on a shelf in the Martin grocery and left there.

There was a great deal of fussing to be done before Mr. Summers declared the lottery open. There were the lists to make up—of heads of families, heads of households in each family, members of each household in each family. There was the proper swearing-in of Mr. Summers by the postmaster, as the official of the lottery; at one time, some people remembered, there had been a recital of some sort, performed by the official of the lottery, a perfunctory, tuneless chant that had been rattled off duly each year; some people believed that the official of the lottery used to stand just so when he said or sang it, others believed that he was supposed to walk among the people, but years and years ago this part of the ritual had been allowed to lapse. There had been, also, a ritual salute, which the official of the lottery had had to use in addressing each person who came up to draw from the box, but this also had changed with time, until now it was felt necessary only for the official to speak to each person approaching. Mr. Summers was very good at all this; in his clean white shirt and blue jeans, with one hand resting carelessly on the black box, he seemed very proper and important as he talked interminably to Mr. Graves and the Martins.

Just as Mr. Summers finally left off talking and turned to the assembled villagers, Mrs. Hutchinson came hurriedly along the path to the square, her sweater thrown over her shoulders, and slid into place in the back of the crowd. "Clean forgot what day it was," she said to Mrs. Delacroix, who stood next to her, and they both laughed softly. "Thought my old man was out back stacking wood," Mrs. Hutchinson went on, "and then I looked out the window and the kids was gone, and then I remembered it was the twenty-seventh and came a-running." She dried her hands on her apron, and Mrs. Delacroix said, "You're in time, though. They're still talking away up there."

Mrs. Hutchinson craned her neck to see through the crowd and found her husband and children standing near the front. She tapped Mrs. Delacroix on the arm as a farewell and began to make her way through the crowd. The people separated good-humoredly to let her through; two or three people said, in voices just loud enough to be heard across the crowd, "Here comes your Missus, Hutchinson," and "Bill, she made it after all." Mrs. Hutchinson reached her husband, and Mr. Summers, who had been waiting, said cheerfully, "Thought we were going to have to get on without you, Tessie." Mrs. Hutchinson said, grinning, "Wouldn't have me leave m'dishes in the sink, now, would you, Joe?," and soft laughter ran through the crowd as the people stirred back into position after Mrs. Hutchinson's arrival.

"Well, now," Mr. Summers said soberly, "guess we better get started, get this over with, so's we can go back to work. Anybody ain't here?"

"Dunbar," several people said. "Dunbar, Dunbar."

Mr. Summers consulted his list. "Clyde Dunbar," he said. "That's right. He's broke his leg, hasn't he? Who's drawing for him?"

"Me, I guess," a woman said, and Mr. Summers turned to look at her. "Wife draws for her husband," Mr. Summers said. "Don't you have a grown boy to do it for you, Janey?" Although Mr. Summers and everyone else in the village knew the answer perfectly well, it was the business of the official of the lottery to ask such questions formally. Mr. Summers waited with an expression of polite interest while Mrs. Dunbar answered.

"Horace's not but sixteen yet," Mrs. Dunbar said regretfully. "Guess I gotta fill in for the old man this year."

"Right," Mr. Summers said. He made a note on the list he was holding. Then he asked, "Watson boy drawing this year?"

A tall boy in the crowd raised his hand. "Here," he said. "I'm drawing for m'mother and me." He blinked his eyes nervously and ducked his head as several voices in the crowd said things like "Good fellow, Jack," and "Glad to see your mother's got a man to do it."

"Well," Mr. Summers said, "guess that's everyone. Old Man Warner make it?"

"Here," a voice said, and Mr. Summers nodded.

A sudden hush fell on the crowd as Mr. Summers cleared his throat and looked at the list. "All ready?" he called. "Now, I'll read the names—heads of families first—and the men come up and take a paper out of the box. Keep the paper folded in your hand without looking at it until everyone has had a turn. Everything clear?"

The people had done it so many times that they only half listened to the directions; most of them were quiet, wetting their lips, not looking around. Then Mr. Summers raised one hand high and said, "Adams." A man disengaged himself from the crowd and came forward. "Hi, Steve," Mr. Summers said, and Mr. Adams said, "Hi, Joe." They grinned at one another humorlessly and nervously. Then Mr. Adams reached into the black box and took out a folded paper. He held it firmly by one corner as he turned and went hastily back to his place in the crowd, where he stood a little apart from his family, not looking down at his hand.

"Allen," Mr. Summers said. "Anderson. . . . Bentham."

"Seems like there's no time at all between lotteries any more," Mrs. Delacroix said to Mrs. Graves in the back row. "Seems like we got through with the last one only last week."

"Time sure goes fast," Mrs. Graves said.

"Clark. . . . Delacroix."

"There goes my old man," Mrs. Delacroix said. She held her breath while her husband went forward.

"Dunbar," Mr. Summers said, and Mrs. Dunbar went steadily to the box while one of the women said, "Go on, Janey," and another said, "There she goes."

"We're next," Mrs. Graves said. She watched while Mr. Graves came around from the side of the box, greeted Mr. Summers gravely, and selected a slip of paper from the box. By now, all through the crowd there were men holding the small folded papers in their large hands, turning them over and over nervously. Mrs. Dunbar and her two sons stood together, Mrs. Dunbar holding the slip of paper.

"Harburt. . . . Hutchinson."

"Get up there, Bill," Mrs. Hutchinson said, and the people near her laughed.

"Jones."

"They do say," Mr. Adams said to Old Man Warner, who stood next to him, "that over in the north village they're talking of giving up the lottery."

Old Man Warner snorted. "Pack of crazy fools," he said. "Listening to the young folks, nothing's good enough for *them*. Next thing you know, they'll be wanting to go back to living in caves, nobody work any more, live *that* way for a while. Used to be a saying about 'Lottery in June, corn be heavy soon.' First thing you know, we'd all be eating stewed chickweed and acorns. There's *always* been a lottery," he added petulantly. "Bad enough to see young Joe Summers up there joking with everybody."

"Some places have already quit lotteries," Mrs. Adams said.

"Nothing but trouble in *that*," Old Man Warner said stoutly. "Pack of young fools."

"Martin." And Bobby Martin watched his father go forward. "Overdyke. . . . Percy."

"I wish they'd hurry," Mrs. Dunbar said to her older son. "I wish they'd hurry."

"They're almost through," her son said.

"You get ready to run tell Dad," Mrs. Dunbar said.

Mr. Summers called his own name and then stepped forward precisely and selected a slip from the box. Then he called, "Warner."

"Seventy-seventh year I been in the lottery," Old Man Warner said as he went through the crowd. "Seventy-seventh time."

"Watson." The tall boy came awkwardly through the crowd. Someone said, "Don't be nervous, Jack," and Mr. Summers said, "Take your time, son."

"Zanini."

After that, there was a long pause, a breathless pause, until Mr. Summers, holding his slip of paper in the air, said, "All right, fellows." For a minute, no one moved, and then all the slips of paper were opened. Suddenly, all the women began to speak at once, saying, "Who is it?," "Who's got it?," "Is it the Dunbars?," "Is it the Watsons?" Then the voices began to say, "It's Hutchinson. It's Bill," "Bill Hutchinson's got it."

"Go tell your father," Mrs. Dunbar said to her older son.

People began to look around to see the Hutchinsons. Bill Hutchinson was standing quiet staring down at the paper in his hand. Suddenly, Tessie Hutchinson shouted to Mr. Summers, "You didn't give him time enough to take any paper he wanted. I saw you. It wasn't fair."

"Be a good sport, Tessie," Mrs. Delacroix called, and Mrs. Graves said, "All of us took the same chance."

"Shut up, Tessie," Bill Hutchinson said.

"Well, everyone," Mr. Summers said, "that was done pretty fast, and now we've got to be hurrying a little more to get done in time." He consulted his next list. "Bill," he said, "You draw for the Hutchinson family. You got any other households in the Hutchinsons?"

"There's Don and Eva," Mrs. Hutchinson yelled. "Make *them* take their chance!"

"Daughters draw with their husbands' families, Tessie," Mr. Summers said gently. "You know that as well as anyone else."

"It wasn't *fair*," Tessie said.

"I guess not, Joe," Bill Hutchinson said regretfully. "My daughter draws with her husband's family, that's only fair. And I've got no other family except the kids."

"Then, as far as drawing for families is concerned, it's you," Mr. Summers said in explanation, "and as far as drawing for households is concerned, that's you, too. Right?"

"Right," Bill Hutchinson said.

"How many kids, Bill?" Mr. Summers asked formally.

"Three," Bill Hutchinson said. "There's Bill, Jr., and Nancy, and little Dave, and Tessie and me."

"All right, then," Mr. Summers said. "Harry, you got their tickets back?"

Mr. Graves nodded and held up the slips of paper. "Put them in the box, then," Mr. Summers directed. "Take Bill's and put it in."

"I think we ought to start over," Mrs. Hutchinson said, as quietly as she could. "I tell you it wasn't *fair*. You didn't give him time enough to choose. *Every*body saw that."

Mr. Graves had selected the five slips and put them in the box, and dropped all the papers but those onto the ground, where the breeze caught them and lifted them off.

"Listen, everybody," Mrs. Hutchinson was saying to the people around her.

"Ready, Bill?" Mr. Summers asked, and Bill Hutchinson, with one quick glance around at his wife and children, nodded.

"Remember," Mr. Summers said, "take the slips and keep them folded until each person has taken one. Harry, you help little Dave." Mr. Graves took the hand of the little boy, who came willingly with him up to the box. "Take a paper out of the box, Davy," Mr. Summers said. Davy put his hand into the box and laughed. "Take just *one* paper," Mr. Summers said. "Harry, you hold it for him." Mr. Graves took the child's hand and removed the folded paper from the tight fist and held it while little Dave stood next to him and looked up at him wonderingly.

"Nancy next," Mr. Summers said. Nancy was twelve, and her school friends breathed heavily as she went forward, switching her skirt, and took a slip daintily from the box. "Bill, Jr.," Mr. Summers said, and Billy, his face red and his feet over-large, nearly knocked the box over as he got a paper out. "Tessie," Mr. Summers said. She hesitated for a minute, looking around defiantly, and then set her lips and went up to the box. She snatched a paper out and held it behind her.

"Bill," Mr. Summers said, and Bill Hutchinson reached into the box and felt around, bringing his hand out at last with the slip of paper in it.

The crowd was quiet. A girl whispered, "I hope it's not Nancy," and the sound of the whisper reached the edges of the crowd.

"It's not the way it used to be," Old Man Warner said clearly. "People ain't the way they used to be."

"All right," Mr. Summers said. "Open the papers. Harry, you open little Dave's."

Mr. Graves opened the slip of paper and there was a general sigh through the crowd as he held it up and everyone could see that it was blank. Nancy and Bill, Jr., opened theirs at the same time, and both beamed and laughed, turning around to the crowd and holding their slips of paper above their heads.

"Tessie," Mr. Summers said. There was a pause, and then Mr. Summers looked at Bill Hutchinson, and Bill unfolded his paper and showed it. It was blank.

"It's Tessie," Mr. Summers said, and his voice was hushed. "Show us her paper, Bill."

Bill Hutchinson went over to his wife and forced the slip of paper out of her hand. It had a black spot on it, the black spot Mr. Summers had made the night before with the heavy pencil in the coal-company office. Bill Hutchinson held it up, and there was a stir in the crowd.

"All right, folks," Mr. Summers said. "Let's finish quickly."

Although the villagers had forgotten the ritual and lost the original black box, they still remembered to use stones. The pile of stones the boys had made earlier was ready; there were stones on the ground with the blowing scraps of paper that had come out of the box. Mrs. Delacroix selected a stone so large she had to pick it up with both hands and turned to Mrs. Dunbar. "Come on," she said. "Hurry up."

Mrs. Dunbar had small stones in both hands, and she said, gasping for breath, "I can't run at all. You'll have to go ahead and I'll catch up with you."

The children had stones already, and someone gave little Davy Hutchinson a few pebbles.

Tessie Hutchinson was in the center of a cleared space by now, and she held her hands out desperately as the villagers moved in on her. "It isn't fair," she said. A stone hit her on the side of the head.

Old Man Warner was saying, "Come on, come on, everyone." Steve Adams was in the front of the crowd of villagers, with Mrs. Graves beside him.

"It isn't fair, it isn't right," Mrs. Hutchinson screamed, and then they were upon her.

QUESTIONS

1. We never learn where the town is located nor its name. Why has Jackson left out these seemingly significant details?
2. What signs are there that the town is preparing for a stoning? What do the characters say that indicates they are preparing for it?
3. Explain the role of mass psychology in the decision of the townspeople to participate in the stoning. Explain the role of tradition in the same decision.
4. What is the theme of the story? What true event or events can you think of that mirror the central action of the story?

2. Plot

Plot is the planned arrangement of actions and events in a narrative; actions and events are causally related, and they progress through a variety of conflicts and opposing forces to a climax and resolution. Because the events in a story are planned, they differ from the myriad random and casual events of real life. Henry James once declared that life is splendid waste, "all inconclusion and confusion." By contrast, life embedded in narrative art is splendid economy—what James termed "all discrimination and selection," a fine focusing of life. Similarly, Edith Wharton, speaking of Russian and French short story writers, found in their handling of plot "a shaft driven straight into the heart of human experience." What happens in a narrative as lives and events unfold is not wasteful, but rather selected, arranged, and patterned according to an author's purpose in creating plot.

Plot might be an artificial arrangement of life, but it is plot that gives a narrative its power, uniqueness, and excellence. It is the basis of narrative art: the shaping of human experience so that we can understand it; the reflection of the author's perceptions and powers of invention; the vehicle through which the artist offers his or her vision of life and the world. And it is plot that gives a story its charm and beauty, as E. M. Forster stressed in his discussion of plot in *Aspects of the Novel:*

> The plot-maker expects us to remember: we expect him to leave no loose ends. Every action or word ought to count; it ought to be economical and spare; even when complicated it should be organic and free from dead matter. And over it, as it unfolds, will hover the memory of the reader (that dull glow of the mind of which intelligence is the bright advancing edge) and will constantly rearrange and reconsider, seeing new clues, new chains of cause and effect, and the final sense (if the plot has been a fine one) will not be of clues or chains, but of something which might have been shown by the novelist right away, only, if he had shown it straight away it would never have become beautiful.

Forster's assessment, which applies to both the novel and short fiction, suggests the subtle ordering and interplay of elements and the meticulous artistry involved in the writer's shaping of plot.

The arrangement and interplay of elements to form plot may assume numerous patterns in fiction, but modern critics have focused on a five-part sequence of events or actions to illustrate a conventional plot. This sequence includes (1) the *beginning* or *exposition,* which among other things introduces an unstable element that sets the plot in motion; (2) *rising action,* a series of events—each event causing the one that follows—which heighten the conflict; (3) the *climax,* the critical or most intense moment in the narrative; (4) *falling action,* a typically brief period in which there is less intensity of effect and an unraveling (what the French term *denouement*) of the conflict; and (5) the ending, or *resolution,* of the conflict.

We can visualize this conventional plot pattern in terms of the accompanying pyramid—a diagram first proposed by the nineteenth-century German critic Gustav Freytag.

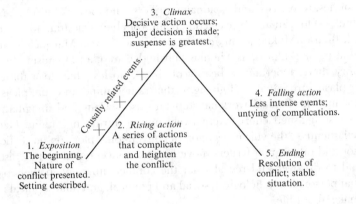

Freytag used this diagram to analyze five-part dramatic tragedy, but the scheme has had widespread utility in the analysis of plot in fiction. In fact, a great part of the pleasure that we experience in the reading of fiction derives from our perception of the rhythm of the narrative as it moves from stage to stage in the plot. We delight in discovering how conflicts arise and develop; how one event causes another in a heightening series of conflicts; how characters caught in these conflicts engage in choices that make the climax and resolution seem almost inevitable. Finally, if the ending is a successful one, we gain satisfaction from the stable situation that emerges—whether it is happy, tragic, mysterious, or whatever—at the conclusion of the tale.

Central to this overview of plot is *conflict,* the opposition of forces. The contemporary American poet, novelist, and critic Robert Penn Warren has put the matter bluntly: "No conflict, no story." Elizabeth Bowen, a modern English short story writer and novelist, is more figurative than Warren, terming conflict a type of combustion. "There must be combustion. Plot depends for its movement on internal combustion." Conflict is at the root of the unstable situation at the start of the plot. Plot itself will pattern this conflict, but it is conflict that translates character and ideas into action. Without conflict, plot cannot exist.

We normally view conflict as the struggle of forces in relation to characters, for conflict at least in part is embodied in characters. When the main character (the protagonist) is fighting or struggling against someone (the antagonist) or something (a nonhuman force can also be the antagonist) outside himself or herself, we term this variety of conflict *external*. When the struggle, or opposition of forces, takes place inside the minds of characters, this type of conflict is *internal*. Thus characters may be involved in a variety of struggles: against other people; against society; against nature; against opposing forces within themselves; against fate or destiny. Seldom do we find a single type of conflict in a good short story. Conflict in short fiction is often subtle and complex, composed of various forces in opposition. To appreciate a complex tale, we have to locate the dramatic center of conflict, from which all other internal and external conflicts—indeed the very contours of plot—seem to radiate. By focusing on a central conflict, we can detect interrelationships among other struggles and elements in the story.

From the viewpoint of the author, plot can be artificial and formulaic or aesthetically valuable, one of fiction's "finer growths," as Forster termed it. Writers of detective stories, mysteries, romances, and espionage thrillers tend to work off standard varieties of plot formulas. Plot can also be exceedingly improbable, melodramatic, or coincidental—as with Bharati Mukherjee in *Jasmine*, or Gabriel García Márquez in much of his fiction. Yet at its best, plot is, as Thomas Hardy declared, an organism: "to a masterpiece in story there appertains a beauty of shape, no less than to a masterpiece in pictorial or plastic art, capable of giving to the trained mind an equal pleasure." Plot involves not just mechanical workmanship but also serious and imaginative artistic response, a distinguished effort to creatively impose form on content. George Eliot might have lamented "the vulgar coercion of conventional plot" on her fiction. Nevertheless, Eliot and other great writers move beyond conventional plot to discover new varieties and to discover and reveal what the conflicts inherent in their plots might mean—what personal, psychological, social and political, and philosophical revelations they can make about life.

Let us imagine—as Yasunari Kawabata, William Faulkner, and Alice Munro must have in the fiction appearing in this section—that the author wants to write a story about boys and girls, men and women. Part of the process of writing such a story would involve the discovery of conflicts and determination of their interrelationship. How to begin these conflicts and end them are always twin agonies, as George Eliot admitted: "Beginnings are always troublesome. Conclusions are the weak points of most authors, but some of the fault lies in the very nature of conclusion, which is at best a negation." And between the beginning and conclusion there is the very large business of organizing and resolving main and minor conflicts, placing protagonists and antagonists in correct relationships, selecting episodes and scenes to dramatize the conflicts, and much more. In developing plot, the author must also select from well-established plotting techniques and occasionally invent new ones: the use of foreshadowing (suggesting or hinting at the resolution beforehand); flashback (creating earlier episodes within the overall progression of action in the plot); and subplots, double plots, and multiple plots. The process whereby authors invent, select, and design all these elements is rarely known to us. What we can perceive is the shape of the narrative—the synthesized product of creativity and craft—the final story itself. And embedded in the story is a plot, the structure of the tale, which permits us to evaluate the quality of the writer's work, the unity of effect, and the way he or she illuminates an idea or theme.

In the stories in this section, we discover meaning through an identification and understanding of the conflicts raised by the narrative. These writers do not categorically state the meaning of these conflicts, but instead reveal it through plot. They develop their subject in unique ways, creating plots that offer brilliantly structured impressions of characters in conflict, but struggling always toward that perfect resolution that is more attainable in fiction, perhaps, than in real life.

Yasunari Kawabata

UP IN THE TREE

Keisuke's house was on the shore where the great river began to enter the sea. Although the river ran alongside the garden, because of the somewhat elevated embankment it could not be seen from the house. The old shore, lined with pines and slightly lower than the embankment, seemed part of the garden, its pines the garden pines. This side of the pines, there was a hedge of Chinese black pine.

Michiko, forcing her way through the hedge, came to play with Keisuke. No, she came just to be with him. Both Michiko and Keisuke were fourth graders. This ducking through the hedge, instead of coming in by the front gate or by the garden gate in back, was a secret between them. For a girl, it wasn't easy. Shielding her head and face with both arms, bent over from the waist, she would plunge into the hedge. Tumbling out into the garden, she would often be caught up in Keisuke's arms.

Shy about letting the people in the house know that Michiko came every day, Keisuke had taught her this way through the hedge.

"I like it. My heart pounds and pounds like anything," Michiko said.

One day, Keisuke climbed up into a pine tree. While he was up there, along came Michiko. Looking neither right nor left, she hurried along by the shore. Stopping at the hedge where she always went through, she looked all around her. Bringing her long, triple-braided pigtails in front of her face, she put them into her mouth halfway along their length. Bracing herself, she threw herself at the hedge. Up in the tree, Keisuke held his breath. When she'd popped out of the hedge into the garden, Michiko did not see Keisuke, whom she had thought would be there. Frightened, she shrank back into the shadow of the hedge, where Keisuke could not see her.

"Mitchan, Mitchan," Keisuke called. Michiko, coming away from the hedge, looked around the garden.

"Mitchan, I'm in the pine tree. I'm up in the pine tree." Looking up toward Keisuke's voice, Michiko did not say a word. Keisuke said, "Come out. Come out of the garden."

When Michiko had come back out through the hedge, she looked up at Keisuke.

"You come down."

"Mitchan, climb up here. It's nice up here in the tree."

"I can't climb it. You're making fun of me, just like a boy. Come down."

"Come up here. The branches are big like this, so even a girl can do it."

Michiko studied the branches. Then she said, "If I fall, it's your fault. If I die, I won't know anything about it."

First dangling from a lower branch, she began to climb.

By the time she'd gotten up to Keisuke's branch, Michiko was gasping for breath. "I climbed it, I climbed it." Her eyes sparkled. "It's scary. Hold me."

"Hmm." Keisuke firmly drew Michiko to him.

Michiko, her arms around Keisuke's neck, said, "You can see the ocean."

"You can see everything. Across the river, and even up the river . . . It's good you climbed up here."

"It *is* good. Keichan, let's climb up here tomorrow."

"Hmm." Keisuke was silent a while. "Mitchan, it's a secret. Climbing up the tree and being up here in the tree—it's a secret. I read books and do homework up here. It's no good if you tell anyone."

"I won't tell." Michiko bowed her head in assent. "Why have you become like a bird?"

"Since it's you, Mitchan, I'll tell you. My father and mother had an awful quarrel. My mother said she was going to take me and go back to her parents' house. I didn't want to look at them, so I climbed a tree in the garden and hid at the top. Saying, 'Where's Keisuke gone to?' they looked all over for me. But they couldn't find me. From the tree, I saw my father go all the way to the ocean to look. This was last spring."

"What were they quarreling about?"

"Don't you know? My father has a woman."

Michiko said nothing.

"Since then, I've been up in this tree a lot. My father and mother still don't know. It's a secret," Keisuke said again, just to make sure. "Mitchan, starting tomorrow, bring your schoolbooks. We'll do our homework up here. We'll get good grades. The trees in the garden are all those big camellia trees with lots of leaves, so nobody can see us from the ground or anywhere."

The "secret" of their being up in the tree had continued for almost two years now. Where the thick trunk branched out near the top, the two could sit comfortably. Michiko, straddling one branch, leaned back against another. There were days when little birds came and days when the wind sang through the pine needles. Although they weren't that high off the ground, these two little lovers felt as if they were in a completely different world, far away from the earth.

                                                    Translated by Lane Dunlop

QUESTIONS

1. Kawabata, a Nobel Prize-winning writer, offers a clear description of setting. What is distinctive about the landscape? How do Michiko and Keisuke relate to it? Why do they hide in the pine tree?

2. What words best describe the mood or atmosphere of this story? Point out passages that convey this mood. How do these passages contribute to the plot?
3. How does the author plot this story? How does the action intensify certain conflicts?

William Faulkner

A ROSE FOR EMILY

I

When Miss Emily Grierson died, our whole town went to her funeral: the men through a sort of respectful affection for a fallen monument, the women mostly out of curiosity to see the inside of her house, which no one save an old manservant—a combined gardener and cook—had seen in at least ten years.

It was a big, squarish frame house that had once been white, decorated with cupolas and spires and scrolled balconies in the heavily lightsome style of the seventies, set on what had once been our most select street. But garages and cotton gins had encroached and obliterated even the august names of that neighborhood; only Miss Emily's house was left, lifting its stubborn and coquettish decay above the cotton wagons and the gasoline pumps—an eyesore among eyesores. And now Miss Emily had gone to join the representatives of those august names where they lay in the cedar-bemused cemetery among the ranked and anonymous graves of Union and Confederate soldiers who fell at the battle of Jefferson.

Alive, Miss Emily had been a tradition, a duty, and a care; a sort of hereditary obligation upon the town, dating from that day in 1894 when Colonel Sartoris, the mayor—he who fathered the edict that no Negro woman should appear on the streets without an apron—remitted her taxes, the dispensation dating from the death of her father on into perpetuity. Not that Miss Emily would have accepted charity. Colonel Sartoris invented an involved tale to the effect that Miss Emily's father had loaned money to the town, which the town, as a matter of business, preferred this way of repaying. Only a man of Colonel Sartoris' generation and thought could have invented it, and only a woman could have believed it.

When the next generation, with its more modern ideas, became mayors and aldermen, this arrangement created some little dissatisfaction. On the first of the year they mailed her a tax notice. February came, and there was no reply. They wrote her a formal letter, asking her to call at the sheriff's office at her convenience. A week later the mayor wrote her himself, offering to call or to send his car for her, and received in reply a note on paper of an archaic shape, in a thin, flowing calligraphy in faded ink, to the effect that she no longer went out at all. The tax notice was also enclosed, without comment.

They called a special meeting of the Board of Aldermen. A deputation waited upon her, knocked at the door through which no visitor had passed since she ceased giving china-painting lessons eight or ten years earlier. They were admitted by the old Negro into a dim hall from which a stairway mounted into still more shadow. It smelled of dust and disuse—a close, dank smell. The Negro led them into the parlor. It was furnished in heavy, leather-covered furniture. When the Negro opened the blinds of one window, they could see that the leather was cracked; and when they sat down, a faint dust rose sluggishly about their thighs, spinning with slow motes in the single sunray. On a tarnished gilt easel before the fireplace stood a crayon portrait of Miss Emily's father.

They rose when she entered—a small, fat woman in black, with a thin gold chain descending to her waist and vanishing into her belt, leaning on an ebony cane with a tarnished gold head. Her skeleton was small and spare; perhaps that was why what would have been merely plumpness in another was obesity in her. She looked bloated, like a body long submerged in motionless water, and of that pallid hue. Her eyes, lost in the fatty ridges of her face, looked like two small pieces of coal pressed into a lump of dough as they moved from one face to another while the visitors stated their errand.

She did not ask them to sit. She just stood in the door and listened quietly until the spokesman came to a stumbling halt. Then they could hear the invisible watch ticking at the end of the gold chain.

Her voice was dry and cold. "I have no taxes in Jefferson. Colonel Sartoris explained it to me. Perhaps one of you can gain access to the city records and satisfy yourselves."

"But we have. We are the city authorities, Miss Emily. Didn't you get a notice from the sheriff, signed by him?"

"I received a paper, yes," Miss Emily said. "Perhaps he considers himself the sheriff . . . I have no taxes in Jefferson."

"But there is nothing on the books to show that, you see. We must go by the——"

"See Colonel Sartoris. I have no taxes in Jefferson."

"But, Miss Emily——"

"See Colonel Sartoris." (Colonel Sartoris had been dead almost ten years.) "I have no taxes in Jefferson. Tobe!" The Negro appeared. "Show these gentlemen out."

II

So she vanquished them, horse and foot, just as she had vanquished their fathers thirty years before about the smell. That was two years after her father's death and a short time after her sweetheart—the one we believed would marry her—had deserted her. After her father's death she went out very little; after her sweetheart went away, people hardly saw her at all. A few of the ladies had the temerity to call, but were not received, and the only sign of life about the place was the Negro man—a young man then—going in and out with a market basket.

"Just as if a man—any man—could keep a kitchen properly," the ladies said; so they were not surprised when the smell developed. It was another link between the gross, teeming world and the high and mighty Griersons.

A neighbor, a woman, complained to the mayor, Judge Stevens, eighty years old.

"But what will you have me do about it, madam?" he said.

"Why, send her word to stop it," the woman said. "Isn't there a law?"

"I'm sure that won't be necessary," Judge Stevens said. "It's probably just a snake or a rat that nigger of hers killed in the yard. I'll speak to him about it."

The next day he received two more complaints, one from a man who came in diffident deprecation. "We really must do something about it, Judge. I'd be the last one in the world to bother Miss Emily, but we've got to do something." That night the Board of Aldermen met—three graybeards and one younger man, a member of the rising generation.

"It's simple enough," he said. "Send her word to have her place cleaned up. Give her a certain time to do it in, and if she don't . . . ."

"Dammit, sir," Judge Stevens said, "will you accuse a lady to her face of smelling bad?"

So the next night, after midnight, four men crossed Miss Emily's lawn and slunk about the house like burglars, sniffing along the base of the brickwork and at the cellar openings while one of them performed a regular sowing motion with his hand out of a sack slung from his shoulder. They broke open the cellar door and sprinkled lime there, and in all the outbuildings. As they recrossed the lawn, a window that had been dark was lighted and Miss Emily sat in it, the light behind her, and her upright torso motionless as that of an idol. They crept quietly across the lawn and into the shadow of the locusts that lined the street. After a week or two the smell went away.

That was when people had begun to feel really sorry for her. People in our town, remembering how old lady Wyatt, her great-aunt, had gone completely crazy at last, believed that the Griersons held themselves a little too high for what they really were. None of the young men were quite good enough for Miss Emily and such. We had long thought of them as a tableau, Miss Emily a slender figure in white in the background, her father a spraddled silhouette in the foreground, his back to her and clutching a horsewhip, the two of them framed by the back-flung front door. So when she got to be thirty and was still single, we were not pleased exactly, but vindicated; even with insanity in the family she wouldn't have turned down all of her chances if they had really materialized.

When her father died, it got about that the house was all that was left to her; and in a way, people were glad. At last they could pity Miss Emily. Being left alone, and a pauper, she had become humanized. Now she too would know the old thrill and the old despair of a penny more or less.

The day after his death all the ladies prepared to call at the house and offer condolence and aid, as is our custom. Miss Emily met them at the door, dressed as usual and with no trace of grief on her face. She told them that her father was not dead. She did that for three days, with the ministers calling on her, and the doctors, trying to persuade her to let them dispose of the body. Just as they were about to resort to law and force, she broke down, and they buried her father quickly.

We did not say she was crazy then. We believed she had to do that. We remembered all the young men her father had driven away, and we knew that with nothing left, she would have to cling to that which had robbed her, as people will.

III

She was sick for a long time. When we saw her again, her hair was cut short, making her look like a girl, with a vague resemblance to those angels in colored church windows—sort of tragic and serene.

The town had just let the contracts for paving the sidewalks, and in the summer after her father's death they began the work. The construction company came with niggers and mules and machinery, and a foreman named Homer Barron, a Yankee—a big, dark, ready man, with a big voice and eyes lighter than his face. The little boys would follow in groups to hear him cuss the niggers, and the niggers singing in time to the rise and fall of picks. Pretty soon he knew everybody in town. Whenever you heard a lot of laughing anywhere about the square, Homer Barron would be in the center of the group. Presently we began to see him and Miss Emily on Sunday afternoons driving in the yellow-wheeled buggy and the matched team of bays from the livery stable.

At first we were glad that Miss Emily would have an interest, because the ladies all said, "Of course a Grierson would not think seriously of a Northerner, a day laborer." But there were still others, older people, who said that even grief could not cause a real lady to forget *noblesse oblige*—without calling it *noblesse oblige*. They just said, "Poor Emily. Her kinsfolk should come to her." She had some kin in Alabama; but years ago her father had fallen out with them over the estate of old lady Wyatt, the crazy woman, and there was no communication between the two families. They had not even been represented at the funeral.

And as soon as the old people said, "Poor Emily," the whispering began. "Do you suppose it's really so?" they said to one another. "Of course it is. What else could . . ." This behind their hands; rustling of craned silk and satin behind jalousies closed upon the sun of Sunday afternoon as the thin, swift clop-clop-clop of the matched team passed: "Poor Emily."

She carried her head high enough—even when we believed that she was fallen. It was as if she demanded more than ever the recognition of her dignity as the last Grierson; as if it had wanted that touch of earthiness to reaffirm her imperviousness. Like when she bought the rat poison, the arsenic. That was over a year after they had begun to say "Poor Emily," and while the two female cousins were visiting her.

"I want some poison," she said to the druggist. She was over thirty then, still a slight woman, though thinner than usual, with cold, haughty black eyes in a face the flesh of which was strained across the temples and about the eyesockets as you imagine a lighthouse-keeper's face ought to look. "I want some poison," she said.

"Yes, Miss Emily. What kind? For rats and such? I'd recom—"

"I want the best you have. I don't care what kind."

The druggist named several. "They'll kill anything up to an elephant. But what you want is—"

"Arsenic," Miss Emily said. "Is that a good one?"

"Is . . . arsenic? Yes, ma'am. But what you want—"

"I want arsenic."

The druggist looked down at her. She looked back at him, erect, her face like a strained flag. "Why, of course," the druggist said. "If that's what you want. But the law requires you to tell what you are going to use it for."

Miss Emily just stared at him, her head tilted back in order to look him eye for eye, until he looked away and went and got the arsenic and wrapped it up. The Negro delivery boy brought her the package; the druggist didn't come back. When she opened the package at home there was written on the box, under the skull and bones: "For rats."

IV

So the next day we all said, "She will kill herself"; and we said it would be the best thing. When she had first begun to be seen with Homer Barron, we had said, "She will marry him." Then we said, "She will persuade him yet," because Homer himself had re-marked—he liked men, and it was known that he drank with the younger men in the Elks' Club—that he was not a marrying man. Later we said, "Poor Emily" behind the jalousies as they passed on Sunday afternoon in the glittering buggy, Miss Emily with her head high and Homer Barron with his hat cocked and a cigar in his teeth, reins and whip in a yellow glove.

Then some of the ladies began to say that it was a disgrace to the town and a bad example to the young people. The men did not want to interfere, but at last the ladies forced the Baptist minister—Miss Emily's people were Episcopal—to call upon her. He would never divulge what happened during that interview, but he refused to go back again. The next Sunday they again drove about the streets, and the following day the minister's wife wrote to Miss Emily's relations in Alabama.

So she had blood-kin under her roof again and we sat back to watch developments. At first nothing happened. Then we were sure that they were to be married. We learned that Miss Emily had been to the jeweler's and ordered a man's toilet set in silver, with the letters H. B. on each piece. Two days later we learned that she had bought a complete outfit of men's clothing, including a nightshirt, and we said, "They are married." We were really glad. We were glad because the two female cousins were even more Grierson than Miss Emily had ever been.

So we were not surprised when Homer Barron—the streets had been finished some time since—was gone. We were a little disappointed that there was not a public blowing-off, but we believed that he had gone on to prepare for Miss Emily's coming, or to give her a chance to get rid of the cousins. (By that time it was a cabal, and we were all Miss Emily's allies to help circumvent the cousins.) Sure enough, after another week they departed. And, as we had expected all along, within three days Homer Barron was back in town. A neighbor saw the Negro man admit him at the kitchen door at dusk one evening.

And that was the last we saw of Homer Barron. And of Miss Emily for some time. The Negro man went in and out with the market basket, but the front door remained closed. Now and then we would see her at a window for a moment, as the men did that night when they sprinkled the lime, but for almost six months she did not appear on the streets. Then we knew that this was to be expected too; as if that quality of her father which had thwarted her woman's life so many times had been too virulent and too furious to die.

When we next saw Miss Emily, she had grown fat and her hair was turning gray. During the next few years it grew grayer and grayer until it attained an even pepper-

and-salt iron-gray, when it ceased turning. Up to the day of her death at seventy-four it was still that vigorous iron-gray, like the hair of an active man.

From that time on her front door remained closed, save for a period of six or seven years, when she was about forty, during which she gave lessons in china-painting. She fitted up a studio in one of the downstairs rooms, where the daughters and granddaughters of Colonel Sartoris' contemporaries were sent to her with the same regularity and in the same spirit that they were sent to church on Sundays with a twenty-five-cent piece for the collection plate. Meanwhile her taxes had been remitted.

Then the newer generation became the backbone and the spirit of the town, and the painting pupils grew up and fell away and did not send their children to her with boxes of color and tedious brushes and pictures cut from the ladies' magazines. The front door closed upon the last one and remained closed for good. When the town got free postal delivery, Miss Emily alone refused to let them fasten the metal numbers above her door and attach a mailbox to it. She would not listen to them.

Daily, monthly, yearly we watched the Negro grow grayer and more stooped, going in and out with the market basket. Each December we sent her a tax notice, which would be returned by the post office a week later, unclaimed. Now and then we would see her in one of the downstairs windows—she had evidently shut up the top floor of the house—like the carven torso of an idol in a niche, looking or not looking at us, we could never tell which. Thus she passed from generation to generation—dear, inescapable, impervious, tranquil, and perverse.

And so she died. Fell ill in the house filled with dust and shadows, with only a doddering Negro man to wait on her. We did not even know she was sick; we had long since given up trying to get any information from the Negro. He talked to no one, probably not even to her, for his voice had grown harsh and rusty, as if from disuse.

She died in one of the downstairs rooms, in a heavy walnut bed with a curtain, her gray head propped on a pillow yellow and moldy with age and lack of sunlight.

V

The Negro met the first of the ladies at the front door and let them in, with their hushed, sibilant voices and their quick, curious glances, and then he disappeared. He walked right through the house and out the back and was not seen again.

The two female cousins came at once. They held the funeral on the second day, with the town coming to look at Miss Emily beneath a mass of bought flowers, with the crayon face of her father musing profoundly above the bier and the ladies sibilant and macabre; and the very old men—some in their brushed Confederate uniforms—on the porch and the lawn, talking of Miss Emily as if she had been a contemporary of theirs, believing that they had danced with her and courted her perhaps, confusing time with its mathematical progression, as the old do, to whom all the past is not a diminishing road but, instead, a huge meadow which no winter ever quite touches, divided from them now by the narrow bottle-neck of the most recent decade of years.

Already we knew that there was one room in that region above stairs which no one had seen in forty years, and which would have to be forced. They waited until Miss Emily was decently in the ground before they opened it.

The violence of breaking down the door seemed to fill this room with pervading dust. A thin, acrid pall as of the tomb seemed to lie everywhere upon this room decked and furnished as for a bridal: upon the valance curtains of faded rose color, upon the rose-shaded lights, upon the dressing table, upon the delicate array of crystal and the man's toilet things backed with tarnished silver, silver so tarnished that the monogram was obscured. Among them lay a collar and tie, as if they had just been removed, which, lifted, left upon the surface a pale crescent in the dust. Upon a chair hung the suit, carefully folded; beneath it the two mute shoes and the discarded socks.

The man himself lay in the bed.

For a long while we just stood there, looking down at the profound and fleshless grin. The body had apparently once lain in the attitude of an embrace, but now the long sleep that outlasts love, that conquers even the grimace of love, had cuckolded him. What was left of him, rotted beneath what was left of the nightshirt, had become inextricable from the bed in which he lay; and upon him and upon the pillow beside him lay that even coating of the patient and biding dust.

Then we noticed that in the second pillow was the indentation of a head. One of us lifted something from it, and leaning forward, that faint and invisible dust dry and acrid in the nostrils, we saw a long strand of iron-gray hair.

QUESTIONS

1. In the first line of the story, Emily is referred to as a "fallen monument." In what sense is she a monument? What, if anything, in Faulkner's description suggests this image?
2. Miss Emily's father has a prominent place in her home as well as in the story. What is his significance both when he is alive and after he has died?
3. Who is found dead at the end of the story? Why was he murdered? What suggestions of or references to death occur before the end of the story?
4. How do the people in the town look upon Emily? What is the cause of their attitude toward her?
5. There are five sections in this story, with events shifting between past and present. In an effort to understand the complex plot that Faulkner invents, trace the sequence of events from section to section.

Alice Munro

THE FOUND BOAT

At the end of Bell Street, McKay Street, Mayo Street, there was the Flood. It was the Wawanash River, which every spring overflowed its banks. Some springs, say one in every five, it covered the roads on that side of town and washed over the fields, creating a shallow choppy lake. Light reflected off the water made everything bright and cold, as it is in a lakeside town, and woke or revived in people certain vague hopes of disaster. Mostly during the late afternoon and early evening, there were people straggling out to look at it, and discuss whether it was still rising, and whether this time it might invade the town. In general, those under fifteen and over sixty-five were most certain that it would.

Eva and Carol rode out on their bicycles. They left the road—it was the end of Mayo Street, past any houses—and rode right into a field, over a wire fence entirely flattened by the weight of the winter's snow. They coasted a little way before the long grass stopped them, then left their bicycles lying down and went to the water.

"We have to find a log and ride on it," Eva said.

"Jesus, we'll freeze our legs off."

"Jesus, we'll freeze our legs off!" said one of the boys who were there too at the water's edge. He spoke in a sour whine, the way boys imitated girls although it was nothing like the way girls talked. These boys—there were three of them—were all in the same class as Eva and Carol at school and were known to them by name (their names being Frank, Bud and Clayton), but Eva and Carol, who had seen and recognized them from the road, had not spoken to them or looked at them or, even yet, given any sign of knowing they were there. The boys seemed to be trying to make a raft, from lumber they had salvaged from the water.

Eva and Carol took off their shoes and socks and waded in. The water was so cold it sent pain up their legs, like blue electric sparks shooting through their veins, but they went on, pulling their skirts high, tight behind and bunched so they could hold them in front.

"Look at the fat-assed ducks in wading."

"Fat-assed fucks."

Eva and Carol, of course, gave no sign of hearing this. They laid hold of a log and climbed on, taking a couple of boards floating in the water for paddles. There were always things floating around in the Flood—branches, fence-rails, logs, road signs, old lumber; sometimes boilers, washtubs, pots and pans, or even a car seat or stuffed chair, as if somewhere the Flood had got into a dump.

They paddled away from shore, heading out into the cold lake. The water was perfectly clear, they could see the brown grass swimming along the bottom. Suppose it was the sea, thought Eva. She thought of drowned cities and countries. Atlantis. Suppose they were riding in a Viking boat—Viking boats on the Atlantic were more frail and narrow than this log on the Flood—and they had miles of clear sea beneath them, then a spired city, intact as a jewel irretrievable on the ocean floor.

"This is a Viking boat," she said. "I am the carving on the front." She stuck her chest out and stretched her neck, trying to make a curve, and she made a face, putting out her tongue. Then she turned and for the first time took notice of the boys.

"Hey, you sucks!" she yelled at them. "You'd be scared to come out here, this water is ten feet deep!"

"Liar," they answered without interest, and she was.

They steered the log around a row of trees, avoiding floating barbed wire, and got into a little bay created by a natural hollow of the land. Where the bay was now, there would be a pond full of frogs later in the spring, and by the middle of summer there would be no water visible at all, just a low tangle of reeds and bushes, green, to show that mud was still wet around their roots. Larger bushes, willows, grew around the steep bank of this pond and were still partly out of the water. Eva and Carol let the log ride in. They saw a place where something was caught.

It was a boat, or part of one. An old rowboat with most of one side ripped out, the board that had been the seat just dangling. It was pushed up among the branches, lying on what would have been its side, if it had a side, the prow caught high.

Their idea came to them without consultation, at the same time:

"You guys! Hey, you guys!"

"We found you a boat!"

"Stop building your stupid raft and come and look at the boat!"

What surprised them in the first place was that the boys really did come, scrambling overland, half running, half sliding down the bank, wanting to see.

"Hey, where?"

"Where is it, I don't see no boat."

What surprised them in the second place was that when the boys did actually see what boat was meant, this old flood-smashed wreck held up in the branches, they did not understand that they had been fooled, that a joke had been played on them. They did not show a moment's disappointment, but seemed as pleased at the discovery as if the boat had been whole and new. They were already barefoot, because they had been wading in the water to get lumber, and they waded in here without a stop, surrounding the boat and appraising it and paying no attention even of an insulting kind to Eva and Carol who bobbed up and down on their log. Eva and Carol had to call to them.

"How do you think you're going to get it off?"

"It won't float anyway."

"What makes you think it will float?"

"It'll sink. Glub-blub-blub, you'll all be drownded."

The boys did not answer, because they were too busy walking around the boat, pulling at it in a testing way to see how it could be got off with the least possible damage. Frank, who was the most literate, talkative and inept of the three, began referring to the boat as *she*, an affectation which Eva and Carol acknowledged with fish-mouths of contempt.

"She's caught two places. You got to be careful not to tear a hole in her bottom. She's heavier than you'd think."

It was Clayton who climbed up and freed the boat, and Bud, a tall fat boy, who got the weight of it on his back to turn it into the water so that they could half float, half carry it to shore. All this took some time. Eva and Carol abandoned their log and waded out of the water. They walked overland to get their shoes and socks and bicycles. They did not need to come back this way but they came. They stood at the top of the hill, leaning on their bicycles. They did not go on home, but they did not sit down and frankly watch, either. They stood more or less facing each other, but glancing down at the water and at the boys struggling with the boat, as if they had just halted for a moment out of curiosity, and staying longer than they intended, to see what came of this unpromising project.

About nine o'clock, or when it was nearly dark—dark to people inside the houses, but not quite dark outside—they all returned to town, going along Mayo Street in a sort of procession. Frank and Bud and Clayton came carrying the boat, upside-down, and Eva and Carol walked behind, wheeling their bicycles. The boys' heads were almost hidden in the darkness of the overturned boat, with its smell of soaked wood, cold swampy water. The girls could look ahead and see the street lights in their tin reflectors, a necklace of lights climbing Mayo Street, reaching all the way up to the standpipe. They turned onto Burns Street heading for Clayton's house, the nearest house belonging to any of them. This was not the way home for Eva or for Carol either, but they followed along. The boys were perhaps too busy carrying the boat to tell them to go away. Some younger children were still out playing, playing hopscotch on the sidewalk though they could hardly see. At this time of year the bare sidewalk was still such a novelty and delight. These children cleared out of the way and watched the boat go by with unwilling respect; they shouted questions after it, wanting to know where it came from and what was going to be done with it. No one answered them. Eva and Carol as well as the boys refused to answer or even look at them.

The five of them entered Clayton's yard. The boys shifted weight, as if they were going to put the boat down.

"You better take it round to the back where nobody can see it," Carol said. That was the first thing any of them had said since they came into town.

The boys said nothing but went on, following a mud path between Clayton's house and a leaning board fence. They let the boat down in the back yard.

"It's a stolen boat, you know," said Eva, mainly for the effect. "It must've belonged to somebody. You stole it."

"You was the ones who stole it then," Bud said, short of breath. "It was you seen it first."

"It was you took it."

"It was all of us then. If one of us gets in trouble then all of us does."

"Are you going to tell anybody on them?" said Carol as she and Eva rode home, along the streets which were dark between the lights now and potholed from winter.

"It's up to you. I won't if you won't."

"I won't if you won't."

They rode in silence, relinquishing something, but not discontented.

The board fence in Clayton's back yard had every so often a post which supported it, or tried to, and it was on these posts that Eva and Carol spent several evenings sitting, jauntily but not very comfortably. Or else they just leaned against the fence while the boys worked on the boat. During the first couple of evenings neighborhood children attracted by the sound of hammering tried to get into the yard to see what was going on, but Eva and Carol blocked their way.

"Who said you could come in here?"

"Just us can come in this yard."

These evenings were getting longer, the air milder. Skipping was starting on the sidewalks. Further along the street there was a row of hard maples that had been tapped. Children drank the sap as fast as it could drip into the buckets. The old man and woman who owned the trees, and who hoped to make syrup, came running out of the house making noises as if they were trying to scare away crows. Finally, every spring, the old man would come out on his porch and fire his shotgun into the air, and then the thieving would stop.

None of those working on the boat bothered about stealing sap, though all had done so last year.

The lumber to repair the boat was picked up here and there, along back lanes. At this time of year things were lying around—old boards and branches, sodden mitts, spoons flung out with the dishwater, lids of pudding pots that had been set in the snow to cool, all the debris that can sift through and survive winter. The tools came from Clayton's cellar—left over, presumably, from the time when his father was alive—and though they had nobody to advise them the boys seemed to figure out more or less the manner in which boats are built, or rebuilt. Frank was the one who showed up with diagrams from books and *Popular Mechanics* magazines. Clayton looked at these diagrams and listened to Frank read the instructions and then went ahead and decided in his own way what was to be done. Bud was best at sawing. Eva and Carol watched everything from the fence and offered criticism and thought up names. The names for the boat that they thought of were: Water Lily, Sea Horse, Flood Queen, and Caro-Eve, after them because they had found it. The boys did not say which, if any, of these names they found satisfactory.

The boat had to be tarred. Clayton heated up a pot of tar on the kitchen stove and brought it out and painted slowly, his thorough way, sitting astride the overturned boat. The other boys were sawing a board to make a new seat. As Clayton worked, the tar cooled and thickened so that finally he could not move the brush any more. He turned to Eva and held out the pot and said, "You can go in and heat this on the stove."

Eva took the pot and went up the back steps. The kitchen seemed black after outside, but it must be light enough to see in, because there was Clayton's mother standing at the ironing board, ironing. She did that for a living, took in wash and ironing.

"Please may I put the tar pot on the stove?" said Eva, who had been brought up to talk politely to parents, even wash-and-iron ladies, and who for some reason especially wanted to make a good impression on Clayton's mother.

"You'll have to poke up the fire then," said Clayton's mother, as if she doubted whether Eva would know how to do that. But Eva could see now, and she picked up the lid with the stove-lifter, and took the poker and poked up a flame. She stirred the tar as it softened. She felt privileged. Then and later. Before she went to sleep a picture of Clayton came to her mind; she saw him sitting astride the boat, tarpainting, with such concentration, delicacy, absorption. She thought of him speaking to her, out of his isolation, in such an ordinary peaceful taking-for-granted voice.

On the twenty-fourth of May, a school holiday in the middle of the week, the boat was carried out of town, a long way now, off the road over fields and fences that had been repaired, to where the river flowed between its normal banks. Eva and Carol, as well as the boys, took turns carrying it. It was launched in the water from a cow-trampled spot between willow bushes that were fresh out in leaf. The boys went first. They yelled with triumph when the boat did float, when it rode amazingly down the river current. The boat was painted black, and green inside, with yellow seats, and a strip of yellow all the way around the outside. There was no name on it, after all. The boys could not imagine that it needed any name to keep it separate from the other boats in the world.

Eva and Carol ran along the bank, carrying bags full of peanut butter-and-jam sandwiches, pickles, bananas, chocolate cake, potato chips, graham crackers stuck together with corn syrup and five bottles of pop to be cooled in the river water. The bottles bumped against their legs. They yelled for a turn.

"If they don't let us they're bastards," Carol said, and they yelled together, "We found it! We found it!"

The boys did not answer, but after a while they brought the boat in, and Carol and Eva came crashing, panting down the bank.

"Does it leak?"

"It don't leak yet."

"We forgot a bailing can," wailed Carol, but nevertheless she got in, with Eva, and Frank pushed them off, crying, "Here's to a Watery Grave!"

And the thing about being in a boat was that it was not solidly bobbing, like a log, but was cupped in the water, so that riding in it was not like being on something in the water, but like being in the water itself. Soon they were all going out in the boat in mixed-up turns, two boys and a girl, two girls and a boy, a girl and a boy, until things were so confused it was impossible to tell whose turn came next, and nobody cared anyway. They went down the river—those who weren't riding, running along the bank to keep up. They passed under two bridges, one iron, one cement. Once they saw a big carp just resting, it seemed to smile at them, in the bridge-shaded water. They did not know how far they had gone on the river, but things had changed—the water had got shallower, and the land flatter. Across an open field they saw a building that looked like a house, abandoned. They dragged the boat up on the bank and tied it and set out across the field.

"That's the old station," Frank said. "That's Pedder Station." The others had heard this name but he was the one who knew, because his father was the station agent in town. He said that this was a station on a branch line that had been torn up, and that there had been a sawmill here, but a long time ago.

Inside the station it was dark, cool. All the windows were broken. Glass lay in shards and in fairly big pieces on the floor. They walked around finding the larger pieces of glass and tramping on them, smashing them, it was like cracking ice on puddles. Some partitions were still in place, you could see where the ticket window had been. There was a bench lying on its side. People had been here, it looked as if people came here all the time, though it was so far from anywhere. Beer bottles and pop bottles were lying around, also cigarette packages, gum and candy wrappers, the paper from a loaf of bread. The walls were covered with dim and fresh pencil and chalk writings and carved with knives.

I LOVE RONNIE COLES
I WANT TO FUCK
KILROY WAS HERE
RONNIE COLES IS AN ASS-HOLE
WHAT ARE YOU DOING HERE?
WAITING FOR A TRAIN
DAWNA   MARY-LOU   BARBARA   JOANNE

It was exciting to be inside this large, dark, empty place, with the loud noise of breaking glass and their voices ringing back from the underside of the roof. They tipped the old beer bottles against their mouths. That reminded them that they were hungry and thirsty and they cleared a place in the middle of the floor and sat down and ate the lunch. They drank the pop just as it was, lukewarm. They ate everything there was and licked the smears of peanut butter and jam off the bread-paper in which the sandwiches had been wrapped.

They played Truth or Dare.

"I dare you to write on the wall, I am a Stupid Ass, and sign your name."

"Tell the truth—what is the worst lie you ever told?"

"Did you ever wet the bed?"

"Did you ever dream you were walking down the street without any clothes on?"

"I dare you to go outside and pee on the railway sign."

It was Frank who had to do that. They could not see him, even his back, but they knew he did it, they heard the hissing sound of his pee. They all sat still, amazed, unable to think of what the next dare would be.

"I dare everybody," said Frank from the doorway, "I dare—Everybody."

"What?"

"Take off all our clothes."

Eva and Carol screamed.

"Anybody who won't do it has to walk—has to *crawl*—around this floor on their hands and knees."

They were all quiet, till Eva said, almost complacently, "What first?"

"Shoes and socks."

"Then we have to go outside, there's too much glass here."

They pulled off their shoes and socks in the doorway, in the sudden blinding sun. The field before them was bright as water. They ran across where the tracks used to go.

"That's enough, that's enough," said Carol. "Watch out for thistles!"

"Tops! Everybody take off their tops!"

"I won't! We won't, will we, Eva?"

But Eva was whirling round and round in the sun where the track used to be. "I don't care, I don't care! Truth or Dare! Truth or Dare!"

She unbuttoned her blouse as she whirled, as if she didn't know what her hand was doing, she flung it off.

Carol took off hers. "I wouldn't have done it, if you hadn't!"

"Bottoms!"

Nobody said a word this time, they all bent and stripped themselves. Eva, naked first, started running across the field, and then all the others ran, all five of them running bare through the knee-high hot grass, running towards the river. Not caring now about being caught but in fact leaping and yelling to call attention to themselves, if there was anybody to hear or see. They felt as if they were going to jump off a cliff and fly. They felt that something was happening to them different from anything that had happened before, and it had to do with the boat, the water, the sunlight, the dark ruined station, and each other. They thought of each other now hardly as names or people, but as echoing shrieks, reflections, all bold and white and loud and scandalous, and as fast as arrows. They went running without a break into the cold water and when it came almost to the tops of their legs they fell on it and swam. It stopped their noise. Silence, amazement, came over them in a rush. They dipped and floated and separated, sleek as mink.

Eva stood up in the water her hair dripping, water running down her face. She was waist deep. She stood on smooth stones, her feet fairly wide apart, water flowing between her legs. About a yard away from her Clayton also stood up, and they were blinking the water out of their eyes, looking at each other. Eva did not turn or try to hide; she was quivering from the cold of the water, but also with pride, shame, boldness, and exhilaration.

Clayton shook his head violently, as if he wanted to bang something out of it, then bent over and took a mouthful of river water. He stood up with his cheeks full and made a tight hole of his mouth and shot the water at her as if it was coming out of a hose, hitting her exactly, first one breast and then the other. Water from his mouth ran down her body. He hooted to see it, a loud self-conscious sound that nobody would have expected, from him. The others looked up from wherever they were in the water and closed in to see.

Eva crouched down and slid into the water, letting her head go right under. She swam, and when she let her head out downstream, Carol was coming after her and the boys were already on the bank, already running into the grass, showing their skinny backs, their white, flat buttocks. They were laughing and saying things to each other but she couldn't hear, for the water in her ears.

"What did he do?" said Carol.

"Nothing."

They crept in to shore. "Let's stay in the bushes till they go," said Eva. "I hate them anyway. I really do. Don't you hate them?"

"Sure," said Carol, and they waited, not very long, until they heard the boys still noisy and excited coming down to the place a bit upriver where they had left the boat. They heard them jump in and start rowing.

"They've got all the hard part, going back," said Eva, hugging herself and shivering violently. "Who cares? Anyway. It never was our boat."

"What if they tell?" said Carol.

"We'll say it's all a lie."

Eva hadn't thought of this solution until she said it, but as soon as she did she felt almost light-hearted again. The ease and scornfulness of it did make them both giggle, and slapping themselves and splashing out of the water they set about developing one of those fits of laughter in which, as soon as one showed signs of exhaustion, the other would snort and start up again, and they would make helpless—soon genuinely helpless—faces at each other and bend over and grab themselves as if they had the worst pain.

QUESTIONS

1. What impact does the found boat have upon the lives of the boys? Of the girls? What impact does it have on the relationship between them?
2. What activities do the boys perform that are traditionally masculine? What activities do the girls perform that are traditionally feminine?
3. Compare and contrast the mood and tone the author uses in describing the town, and the mood and tone she uses in describing the actions of the girls and boys. What is the relationship between them?
4. Examine the way the author escalates the action in the story. What incidents, in particular, lead up to the final scene?

3 . Character

Characters are the people in narratives. We generally know their sex, physical features, age, jobs, education, status in society, and family background. In other words, we know their outward form and behavior. Their physical appearance and social background are part of the way that authors handle characterization—the creation, presentation, and development of character in fiction.

Yet character is also a way of being; it determines how a person acts. As such, the writer must go beyond outward appearances that tell us who characters are. The author must reveal the inner qualities that motivate people and that make finely realized characters so memorable for readers. Many of the greatest novels include in their titles the names of such memorable characters: *Don Quixote, Tom Jones, Madame Bovary, Jane Eyre, Huckleberry Finn, Anna Karenina, Ethan Frome, The Great Gatsby, Lolita, Jasmine.* These narratives explore and illuminate the inner development of character, the mental and emotional states of character, the ethical and moral traits of character, the essence of character. In short, the great writer has a rare ability, as Samuel Johnson observed of Samuel Richardson, to "dive into the recesses of the human heart."

In real life, we rarely get as close to the recesses of the human heart as novelists and short story writers do. People in life tend to hide their essential beings, to be unpredictable at times, to defy our best interpretations of them. These facts underscore an essential difference between actual people and invented characters, for the purpose of the author is not to conceal but to reveal character and to fix it for us so that we can understand it. Eudora Welty observes: "Characters in the plot connect us with the vastness of our secret life, which is endlessly explorable." Nevertheless, there are similarities in the ways we attempt to understand real and fictional characters. We do talk about people on an everyday basis, analyzing, criticizing, and comparing them. We try to discover what lies beneath their looks, dress, speech, mannerisms, social gestures, actions, and viewpoints. Sociology and psychology, among other things, have taught us much about the exploration of human nature. In a sense, then, we know how to "create" people, and in doing so we come close to perhaps the greatest mystery in the art of fiction—the ability of the author to breathe life into characters who are, after all, mere constructs of words.

How do we gain insight into the mystery of fictional characterization? Through characterization, great short story writers can convince us, as E. M. Forster wrote, that there is "life within the pages of a book." They have a genius for focusing—in a manner typical of compressed short story art—on key characters who sustain the *felt* existence of a larger world or society. Characters in the hands of a major writer are brought to life by the author's ability to see them vividly, to describe them, to place them in the right relationship to a problem or conflict, and to set them in action.

It is hard to separate character from action in any discussion of fiction. Henry James stressed the interrelationship of these elements when he asked, "What is character but the determination of incident? What is incident but the illustration of character." In a similar vein, F. Scott Fitzgerald posted on the wall of the room in which he wrote, "Character is action." Of course, James admitted that the *starting point* of fiction is probably character. We become interested in action and plot only to the extent that we are absorbed by character—by those figures drawn nominally from "reality" who speak to us about the conflicts, problems, pleasures, possibilities, and mysteries of existence.

Authors, too, are absorbed by their characters. Anthony Trollope in his *Autobiography* declared that the writer of fiction "desires to make his readers so intimately acquainted with his characters that the creations of his brain should be to them speaking, moving, living, human creatures. This he can never do unless he knows those fictitious person-ages himself, and he can never know them well unless he can live with them in the full reality of established intimacy." Similarly, Joseph Conrad wrote of being haunted by his characters, considering them the companions of his imagination. From a slightly differ-ent but nevertheless "intimate" perspective, Turgenev spoke of watching his characters develop. "If I watch them long enough I see them come together, I see them *placed*, I see them engaged in this or that act and in this or that difficulty. How they look and move and speak and behave, always in the setting I have found for them, is my account of them." There is, then, an elusive genius behind character creation—a genius based on imaginative identification and powers of perception. At the same time, we can detect in this set of observations by three great writers certain clues to the ways we "see" and learn about fictional characters.

Basically we learn about people in fiction through *direct* or *indirect* characterization. With direct characterization, the author literally tells us what a character is like—the outer and inner qualities of his or her being. Direct characterization is a procedure far more common in eighteenth- and nineteenth-century fiction than in modern fiction, although the method still is apparent today. More typically, however, modern fiction writers explore characters through indirect methods: what characters do, what they say, how they dress, what they look like, what they think, and what they say and think about one another. When presented with indirect characterization, readers must catch and interpret clues about personality, identify traits, and discover characters' inner motiva-tions.

Regardless of the method of characterization, the author's invented people will be static or dynamic, flat or fully rounded. As a general rule, we can say that a static character—one who doesn't change in the course of the narrative—is relatively flat, or one-dimensional, while a dynamic character who does change is round, or fully dimensional. The terms "flat" and "round" were proposed by E. M. Forster, who in *Aspects of the Novel* (1927) distinguished between flat character types (easily recognized and easily remembered because they are unchanging and unalterable) and round characters. "The test of round character," wrote Forster, "is whether it is capable of surprising in a convincing way. If it never surprises, it is flat. If it does not convince, it is flat pretending to be round. It has the incalculability of life about it."

In practice, and notably in the practice of short fiction, there is often a fusion of static and dynamic, flat and round, properties of characterization. The short story character tends toward giving symbolic and even archetypal impressions that are essentially flat in effect. In fact, the main characters, or protagonists, in the stories in this section start almost as caricatures—people with a dominant trait that excludes all others. Yet gradually we also sense subtly the shifts in being and attitudes forced on these characters either by antagonists ("villains" in the strict sense, or countervailing characters), altered situations, or reduced circumstances. We sense the mystery and irrationality of human nature, the extremes of psychological processes, even the loss of identity—a peculiarly modern feature of short fiction. From formed and predictable characterization, we move across a field or spectrum of possibility in human behavior and response. Characters grow in complexity as we await the consequences of their choices.

The central characters in the stories that follow confront numerous issues and conflicts. They are types (as even the most fully rounded short story characters tend to be) whose motivations, preoccupations, and obsessions become clear to us as we follow the evolving conflicts in the stories. They are rare and beautifully realized figures, conveying sometimes in the barest outlines the primal mystery of personality that every great short story writer attempts to probe. With characterization, the short story writer tries to capture and convey an entire life—sometimes an entire world—in a highly compressed form.

Arna Bontemps

A SUMMER TRAGEDY

Old Jeff Patton, the black share farmer, fumbled with his bow tie. His fingers trembled and the high stiff collar pinched his throat. A fellow loses his hand for such vanities after thirty or forty years of simple life. Once a year, or maybe twice if there's a wedding among his kinfolks, he may spruce up; but generally fancy clothes do nothing but adorn the wall of the big room and feed the moths. That had been Jeff Patton's experience. He had not worn his stiff-bosomed shirt more than a dozen times in all his married life. His swallow-tailed coat lay on the bed beside him, freshly brushed and pressed, but it was as full of holes as the overalls in which he worked on weekdays. The moths had used it badly. Jeff twisted his mouth into a hideous tooth-less grimace as he contended with the obstinate bow. He stamped his good foot and decided to give up the struggle.

"Jennie," he called.

"What's that, Jeff?" His wife's shrunken voice came out of the adjoining room like an echo. It was hardly bigger than a whisper.

"I reckon you'll have to he'p me wid this heah bow tie, baby," he said meekly. "Dog if I can hitch it up."

Her answer was not strong enough to reach him, but presently the old woman came to the door, feeling her way with a stick. She had a wasted, dead-leaf appearance. Her body, as scrawny and gnarled as a string bean, seemed less than nothing in the ocean of frayed and faded petticoats that surrounded her. These hung an inch or two above the tops of her heavy unlaced shoes and showed little grotesque piles where the stockings had fallen down from her negligible legs.

"You oughta could do a heap mo' wid a thing like that'n me—beingst as you got yo' good sight."

"Looks like I oughta could," he admitted. "But ma fingers is gone democrat on me. I get all mixed up in the looking glass an' can't tell wicha way to twist the devilish thing."

Jennie sat on the side of the bed and old Jeff Patton got down on one knee while she tied the bow knot. It was a slow and painful ordeal for each of them in this position. Jeff's bones cracked, his knee ached, and it was only after a half dozen attempts that Jennie worked a semblance of a bow into the tie.

"I got to dress maself now," the old woman whispered. "These is ma old shoes an' stockings, and I ain't so much as unwrapped ma dress."

"Well, don't worry 'bout me no mo', baby," Jeff said. "That 'bout finishes me. All I gotta do now is slip on that old coat 'n ves' an' I'll be fixed to leave."

Jennie disappeared again through the dim passage into the shed room. Being blind was no handicap to her in that black hole. Jeff heard the cane placed against the wall beside the door and knew that his wife was on easy ground. He put on his coat, took a battered top hat from the bedpost and hobbled to the front door. He was ready to travel. As soon as Jennie could get on her Sunday shoes and her old black silk dress, they would start.

Outside the tiny log house, the day was warm and mellow with sunshine. A host of wasps were humming with busy excitement in the trunk of a dead sycamore. Gray squirrels were searching through the grass for hickory nuts and blue jays were in the trees, hopping from branch to branch. Pine woods stretched away to the left like a black sea. Among them were scattered scores of log houses like Jeff's, houses of black share farmers. Cows and pigs wandered freely among the trees. There was no danger of loss. Each farmer knew his own stock and knew his neighbor's as well as he knew his neighbor's children.

Down the slope to the right were the cultivated acres on which the colored folks worked. They extended to the river, more than two miles away, and they were today green with the unmade cotton crop. A tiny thread of a road, which passed directly in front of Jeff's place, ran through these green fields like a pencil mark.

Jeff, standing outside the door, with his absurd hat in his left hand, surveyed the wide scene tenderly. He had been forty-five years on these acres. He loved them with the unexplained affection that others have for the countries to which they belong.

The sun was hot on his head, his collar still pinched his throat, and the Sunday clothes were intolerably hot. Jeff transferred the hat to his right hand and began fanning with it. Suddenly the whisper that was Jennie's voice came out of the shed room.

"You can bring the car round front whilst you's waitin'," it said feebly. There was a tired pause; then it added, "I'll soon be fixed to go."

"A'right, baby," Jeff answered. "I'll get it in a minute."

But he didn't move. A thought struck him that made his mouth fall open. The mention of the car brought to his mind, with new intensity, the trip he and Jennie were about to take. Fear came into his eyes; excitement took his breath. Lord, Jesus!

"Jeff . . . O Jeff," the old woman's whisper called.

He awakened with a jolt. "Hunh, baby?"

"What you doin'?"

"Nuthin. Jes studyin'. I jes been turnin' things round'n round in ma mind."

"You could be gettin' the car," she said.

"Oh yes, right away, baby."

He started round to the shed, limping heavily on his bad leg. There were three frizzly chickens in the yard. All his other chickens had been killed or stolen recently. But the frizzly chickens had been saved somehow. That was fortunate indeed, for these curious creatures had a way of devouring "Poison" from the yard and in that way protecting against conjure and black luck and spells. But even the frizzly chickens seemed now to be in a stupor. Jeff thought they had some ailment; he expected all three of them to die shortly.

The shed in which the old T-model Ford stood was only a grass roof held up by four corner poles. It had been built by tremulous hands at a time when the little rattletrap car had been regarded as a peculiar treasure. And, miraculously, despite wind and downpour it still stood.

Jeff adjusted the crank and put his weight upon it. The engine came to life with a sputter and bang that rattled the old car from radiator to taillight. Jeff hopped into the seat and put his foot on the accelerator. The sputtering and banging increased. The rattling became more violent. That was good. It was good banging, good sputtering and rattling, and it meant that the aged car was still in running condition. She could be depended on for this trip.

Again Jeff's thought halted as if paralyzed. The suggestion of the trip fell into the machinery of his mind like a wrench. He felt dazed and weak. He swung the car out into the yard, made a half turn and drove around to the front door. When he took his hands off the wheel, he noticed that he was trembling violently. He cut off the motor and climbed to the ground to wait for Jennie.

A few minutes later she was at the window, her voice rattling against the pane like a broken shutter.

"I'm ready, Jeff."

He did not answer, but limped into the house and took her by the arm. He led her slowly through the big room, down the step and across the yard.

"You reckon I'd oughta lock the do'?" he asked softly.

They stopped and Jennie weighed the question. Finally she shook her head.

"Ne' mind the do'," she said. "I don't see no cause to lock up things."

"You right," Jeff agreed. "No cause to lock up."

Jeff opened the door and helped his wife into the car. A quick shudder passed over him. Jesus! Again he trembled.

"How come you shaking so?" Jennie whispered.

"I don't know," he said.

"You mus' be scairt, Jeff."

"No, baby, I ain't scairt."

He slammed the door after her and went around to crank up again. The motor started easily. Jeff wished that it had not been so responsive. He would have liked a few more minutes in which to turn things around in his head. As it was, with Jennie chiding him about being afraid, he had to keep going. He swung the car into the little pencil-mark road and started off toward the river, driving very slowly, very cautiously.

Chugging across the green countryside, the small battered Ford seemed tiny indeed. Jeff felt a familiar excitement, a thrill, as they came down the first slope to the immense levels on which the cotton was growing. He could not help reflecting that the crops were good. He knew what that meant, too; he had made forty-five of them with his own hands. It was true that he had worn out nearly a dozen mules, but that was the fault of old man Stevenson, the owner of the land. Major Stevenson had the odd notion that one mule was all a share farmer needed to work a thirty-acre plot. It was an expensive notion, the way it killed mules from overwork, but the old man held to it. Jeff thought it killed a good many share farmers as well as mules, but he had no sympathy for them. He had always been strong, and he had been taught to have no patience with weakness in men. Women or children might be tolerated if they were puny, but a weak man was a curse. Of course, his own children—

Jeff's thought halted there. He and Jennie never mentioned their dead children any more. And naturally he did not wish to dwell upon them in his mind. Before he knew it, some remark would slip out of his mouth and that would make Jennie feel blue. Perhaps she would cry. A woman like Jennie could not easily throw off the grief that comes from losing five grown children within two years. Even Jeff was still staggered by the blow. His memory had not been much good recently. He frequently talked to himself. And, although he had kept it a secret, he knew that his courage had left him. He was terrified by the least unfamiliar sound at night. He was reluctant to venture far from home in the daytime. And that habit of trembling when he felt fearful was now far beyond his control. Sometimes he became afraid and trembled without knowing what had frightened him. The feeling would just come over him like a chill.

The car rattled slowly over the dusty road. Jennie sat erect and silent, with a little absurd hat pinned to her hair. Her useless eyes seemed very large, very white in their deep sockets. Suddenly Jeff heard her voice, and he inclined his head to catch the words.

"Is we passed Delia Moore's house yet?" she asked.

"Not yet," he said.

"You must be drivin' mighty slow, Jeff."

"We might just as well take our time, baby."

There was a pause. A little puff of steam was coming out of the radiator of the car.

Heat wavered above the hood. Delia Moore's house was nearly half a mile away. After a moment Jennie spoke again.

"You ain't really scairt, is you, Jeff?"

"Nah, baby, I ain't scairt."

"You know how we agreed—we gotta keep on goin'."

Jewels of perspiration appeared on Jeff's forehead. His eyes rounded, blinked, becamed fixed on the road.

"I don't know," he said with a shiver. "I reckon it's the only thing to do."

"Hm."

A flock of guinea fowls, pecking in the road, were scattered by the passing car. Some of them took to their wings; others hid under bushes. A blue jay, swaying on a leafy twig, was annoying a roadside squirrel. Jeff held an even speed till he came near Delia's place. Then he slowed down noticeably.

Delia's house was really no house at all, but an abandoned store building converted into a dwelling. It sat near a crossroads, beneath a single black cedar tree. There Delia, a cattish old creature of Jennie's age, lived alone. She had been there more years than anybody could remember, and long ago had won the disfavor of such women as Jennie. For in her young days Delia had been gayer, yellower and saucier than seemed proper in those parts. Her ways with menfolks had been dark and suspicious. And the fact that she had had as many husbands as children did not help her reputation.

"Yonder's old Delia," Jeff said as they passed.

"What she doin'?"

"Jes sittin' in the do'," he said.

"She see us?"

"Hm," Jeff said. "Musta did."

That relieved Jennie. It strengthened her to know that her old enemy had seen her pass in her best clothes. That would give the old she-devil something to chew her gums and fret about, Jennie thought. Wouldn't she have a fit if she didn't find out? Old evil Delia! This would be just the thing for her. It would pay her back for being so evil. It would also pay her, Jennie thought, for the way she used to grin at Jeff—long ago when her teeth were good.

The road became smooth and red, and Jeff could tell by the smell of the air that they were nearing the river. He could see the rise where the road turned and ran along parallel to the stream. The car chugged on monotonously. After a long silent spell, Jennie leaned against Jeff and spoke.

"How many bale o' cotton you think we got standin'?" she said.

Jeff wrinkled his forehead as he calculated.

"'Bout twenty-five, I reckon."

"How many you make las' year?"

"Twenty-eight," he said. "How come you ask that?"

"I's jes thinkin'," Jennie said quietly.

"It don't make a speck o' difference though," Jeff reflected. "If we get much or if we get little, we still gonna be in debt to old man Stevenson when he gets through counting up agin us. It's took us a long time to learn that."

Jennie was not listening to these words. She had fallen into a trance-like meditation.

Her lips twitched. She chewed her gums and rubbed her gnarled hands nervously. Suddenly she leaned forward, buried her face in the nervous hands and burst into tears. She cried aloud in a dry cracked voice that suggested the rattle of fodder on dead stalks. She cried aloud like a child, for she had never learned to suppress a genuine sob. Her slight old frame shook heavily and seemed hardly able to sustain such violent grief.

"What's the matter, baby?" Jeff asked awkwardly. "Why you cryin' like all that?"

"I's jes thinkin'," she said.

"So you the one what's scairt now, hunh?"

"I ain't scairt, Jeff. I's jes thinkin' 'bout leavin' eve'thing like this—eve'thing we been used to. It's right sad-like."

Jeff did not answer, and presently Jennie buried her face again and cried.

The sun was almost overhead. It beat down furiously on the dusty wagon-path road, on the parched roadside grass and the tiny battered car. Jeff's hands, gripping the wheel, became wet with perspiration; his forehead sparkled. Jeff's lips parted. His mouth shaped a hideous grimace. His face suggested the face of a man being burned. But the torture passed and his expression softened again.

"You mustn't cry, baby," he said to his wife. "We gotta be strong. We can't break down."

Jennie waited a few seconds, then said, "You reckon we oughta do it, Jeff? You reckon we oughta go 'head an' do it, really?"

Jeff's voice choked; his eyes blurred. He was terrified to hear Jennie say the thing that had been in his mind all morning. She had egged him on when he had wanted more than anything in the world to wait, to reconsider, to think things over a little longer. Now she was getting cold feet. Actually there was no need of thinking the question through again. It would only end in making the same painful decision once more. Jeff knew that. There was no need of fooling around longer.

"We jes as well to do like we planned," he said. "They ain't nothin' else for us now—it's the bes' thing."

Jeff thought of the handicaps, the near impossibility, of making another crop with his leg bothering him more and more each week. Then there was always the chance that he would have another stroke, like the one that had made him lame. Another one might kill him. The least it could do would be to leave him helpless. Jeff gasped—Lord, Jesus! He could not bear to think of being helpless, like a baby, on Jennie's hands. Frail, blind Jennie.

The little pounding motor of the car worked harder and harder. The puff of steam from the cracked radiator became larger. Jeff realized that they were climbing a little rise. A moment later the road turned abruptly and he looked down upon the face of the river.

"Jeff."

"Hunh?"

"Is that the water I hear?"

"Hm. Tha's it."

"Well, which way you goin' now?"

"Down this-a way," he said. "The road runs 'long 'side o' the water a lil piece."

She waited a while calmly. Then she said, "Drive faster."

"A'right, baby," Jeff said.

The water roared in the bed of the river. It was fifty or sixty feet below the level of the road. Between the road and the water there was a long smooth slope, sharply inclined. The slope was dry, the clay hardened by prolonged summer heat. The water below, roaring in a narrow channel, was noisy and wild.

"Jeff."

"Hunh?"

"How far you goin'?"

"Jes a lil piece down the road."

"You ain't scairt, is you, Jeff?"

"Nah, baby," he said trembling. "I ain't scairt."

"Remember how we planned it, Jeff. We gotta do it like we said. Brave-like."

"Hm."

Jeff's brain darkened. Things suddenly seemed unreal, like figures in a dream. Thoughts swam in his mind foolishly, hysterically, like little blind fish in a pool within a dense cave. They rushed, crossed one another, jostled, collided, retreated and rushed again. Jeff soon became dizzy. He shuddered violently and turned to his wife.

"Jennie, I can't do it. I can't." His voice broke pitifully.

She did not appear to be listening. All the grief had gone from her face. She sat erect, her unseeing eyes wide open, strained and frightful. Her glossy black skin had become dull. She seemed as thin, as sharp and bony, as a starved bird. Now, having suffered and endured the sadness of tearing herself away from beloved things, she showed no anguish. She was absorbed with her own thoughts, and she didn't even hear Jeff's voice shouting in her ear.

Jeff said nothing more. For an instant there was light in his cavernous brain. The great chamber was, for less than a second, peopled by characters he knew and loved. They were simple, healthy creatures, and they behaved in a manner that he could understand. They had quality. But since he had already taken leave of them long ago, the remembrance did not break his heart again. Young Jeff Patton was among them, the Jeff Patton of fifty years ago who went down to New Orleans with a crowd of country boys to the Mardi Gras doings. The gay young crowd, boys with candy-striped shirts and rouged-brown girls in noisy silks, was like a picture in his head. Yet it did not make him sad. On that very trip Slim Burns had killed Joe Beasley—the crowd had been broken up. Since then Jeff Patton's world had been the Greenbriar Plantation. If there had been other Mardi Gras carnivals, he had not heard of them. Since then there had been no time; the years had fallen on him like waves. Now he was old, worn out. Another paralytic stroke (like the one he had already suffered) would put him on his back for keeps. In that condition, with a frail blind woman to look after him, he would be worse off than if he were dead.

Suddenly Jeff's hands became steady. He actually felt brave. He slowed down the motor of the car and carefully pulled off the road. Below, the water of the stream boomed, a soft thunder in the deep channel. Jeff ran the car onto the clay slope, pointed it directly toward the stream and put his foot heavily on the accelerator. The little car leaped furiously down the steep incline toward the water. The movement was nearly as swift and direct as a fall. The two old black folks, sitting quietly side by side, showed no excitement. In another instant the car hit the water and dropped immediately out of sight.

A little later it lodged in the mud of a shallow place. One wheel of the crushed and upturned little Ford became visible above the rushing water.

QUESTIONS

1. Images of paralysis, decay, and deterioration abound in the story. Locate them. How do they help set the tone and mood of the story?
2. The author says that Jeff had "no patience with weakness in men." Why is this an ironic statement? What other ironies exist in the story? How do they help build the story's tension?
3. Where in the story is the suicide foreshadowed? How does Bontemps hint at the purpose of the trip?
4. How would you characterize Jeff Patton's personality? How would you characterize Jennie's?

Isaac Bashevis Singer

GIMPEL THE FOOL

I

I am Gimpel the fool. I don't think myself a fool. On the contrary. But that's what folks call me. They gave me the name while I was still in school. I had seven names in all: imbecile, donkey, flax-head, dope, glump, ninny, and fool. The last name stuck. What did my foolishness consist of? I was easy to take in. They said, "Gimpel, you know the rabbi's wife has been brought to childbed?" So I skipped school. Well, it turned out to be a lie. How was I supposed to know? She hadn't had a big belly. But I never looked at her belly. Was that really so foolish? The gang laughed and hee-hawed, stomped and danced and chanted a good-night prayer. And instead of the raisins they give when a woman's lying in, they stuffed my hand full of goat turds. I was no weakling. If I slapped someone he'd see all the way to Cracow. But I'm really not a slugger by nature. I think to myself, Let it pass. So they take advantage of me.

I was coming home from school and heard a dog barking. I'm not afraid of dogs, but of course I never want to start up with them. One of them may be mad, and if he bites there's not a Tartar in the world who can help you. So I made tracks. Then I looked around and saw the whole market place wild with laughter. It was no dog at all but Wolf-Leib the thief. How was I supposed to know it was he? It sounded like a howling bitch.

When the pranksters and leg-pullers found that I was easy to fool, every one of them tried his luck with me. "Gimpel, the Czar is coming to Frampol; Gimpel, the moon fell down in Turbeen; Gimpel, little Hodel Furpiece found a treasure behind the bath-house." And I like a *golem* believed everyone. In the first place, everything is possible, as it is written in the Wisdom of the Fathers, I've forgotten just how. Second, I had to believe when the whole town came down on me! If I ever dared to say, "Ah, you're kidding!" there was trouble. People got angry. "What do you mean! You want to call everyone a liar?" What was I to do? I believed them, and I hope at least that did them some good.

I was an orphan. My grandfather who brought me up was already bent toward the grave. So they turned me over to a baker, and what a time they gave me there! Every woman or girl who came to bake a pan of cookies or dry a batch of noodles had to fool me at least once. "Gimpel, there's a fair in heaven; Gimpel, the rabbi gave birth to a calf in the seventh month; Gimpel, a cow flew over the roof and laid brass eggs." A student from the *yeshiva* came once to buy a roll, and he said, "You, Gimpel, while you stand here scraping with your baker's shovel the Messiah has come. The dead have arisen." "What do you mean?" I said. "I heard no one blowing the ram's horn!" He said, "Are you deaf?" And all began to cry, "We heard it, we heard!" Then in came Reitze the candle-dipper and called out in her hoarse voice, "Gimpel, your father and mother have stood up from the grave. They're looking for you."

To tell the truth, I knew very well that nothing of the sort had happened, but all the same, as folks were talking, I threw on my wool vest and went out. Maybe something had happened. What did I stand to lose by looking? Well, what a cat music went up! And then I took a vow to believe nothing more. But that was no go either. They confused me so that I didn't know the big end from the small.

I went to the rabbi to get some advice. He said, "It is written, better to be a fool all your days than for one hour to be evil. You are not a fool. They are the fools. For he who causes his neighbor to feel shame loses Paradise himself." Nevertheless the rabbi's daughter took me in. As I left the rabbinical court she said, "Have you kissed the wall yet?" I said, "No; what for?" She answered, "It's a law; you've got to do it after every visit." Well, there didn't seem to be any harm in it. And she burst out laughing. It was a fine trick. She put one over on me, all right.

I wanted to go off to another town, but then everyone got busy matchmaking, and they were after me so they nearly tore my coat tails off. They talked at me and talked until I got water on the ear. She was no chaste maiden, but they told me she was virgin pure. She had a limp, and they said it was deliberate, from coyness. She had a bastard, and they told me the child was her little brother. I cried, "You're wasting your time. I'll never marry that whore." But they said indignantly, "What a way to talk! Aren't you ashamed of yourself? We can take you to the rabbi and have you fined for giving her a bad name." I saw then that I wouldn't escape them so easily and I thought, They're set on making me their butt. But when you're married the husband's the master, and if that's all right with her it's agreeable to me too. Besides, you can't pass through life unscathed, nor expect to.

I went to her clay house, which was built on the sand, and the whole gang, hollering and chorusing, came after me. They acted like bearbaiters. When we came to the well they stopped all the same. They were afraid to start anything with Elka. Her mouth would open as if it were on a hinge, and she had a fierce tongue. I entered the house. Lines were strung from wall to wall and clothes were drying. Barefoot she stood by the tub, doing the wash. She was dressed in a worn hand-me-down gown of plush. She had her hair put up in braids and pinned across her head. It took my breath away, almost the reek of it all.

Evidently she knew who I was. She took a look at me and said, "Look who's here! He's come, the drip. Grab a seat."

I told her all; I denied nothing. "Tell me the truth," I said, "are you really a virgin, and is that mischievous Yechiel actually your little brother? Don't be deceitful with me, for I'm an orphan."

"I'm an orphan myself," she answered, "and whoever tries to twist you up, may the end of his nose take a twist. But don't let them think they can take advantage of me. I want a dowry of fifty guilders, and let them take up a collection besides. Otherwise they can kiss my you-know-what." She was very plain-spoken. I said, "Don't bargain with me. Either a flat 'yes' or a flat 'no'—go back where you came from."

I thought, No bread will ever be baked from *this* dough. But ours is not a poor town. They consented to everything and proceeded with the wedding. It so happened that there was a dysentery epidemic at the time. The ceremony was held at the cemetery gates, near the little corpse-washing hut. The fellows got drunk. While the marriage contract was being drawn up I heard the most pious high rabbi ask, "Is the bride a widow or a divorced woman?" And the sexton's wife answered for her, "Both a widow and divorced." It was a black moment for me. But what was I to do, run away from under the marriage canopy?

There was singing and dancing. An old granny danced opposite me, hugging a braided white *chalah*. The master of revels made a "God 'a mercy" in memory of the bride's parents. The schoolboys threw burrs, as on *Tishe b' Av* fast day. There were a lot of gifts after the sermon: a noodle board, a kneading trough, a bucket, brooms, ladles, household articles galore. Then I took a look and saw two strapping young men carrying a crib. "What do we need this for?" I asked. So they said, "Don't rack your brains about it. It's all right, it'll come in handy." I realized I was going to be rooked. Take it another way though, what did I stand to lose? I reflected, I'll see what comes of it. A whole town can't go altogether crazy.

II

At night I came where my wife lay, but she wouldn't let me in. "Say, look here, is this what they married us for?" I said. And she said, "My monthly has come." "But yesterday they took you to the ritual bath, and that's afterward, isn't it supposed to be?" "Today isn't yesterday," said she, "and yesterday's not today. You can beat it if you don't like it." In short, I waited.

Not four months later she was in childbed. The townsfolk hid their laughter with their knuckles. But what could I do? She suffered intolerable pains and clawed at the walls. "Gimpel," she cried, "I'm going. Forgive me!" The house filled with women. They were boiling pans of water. The screams rose to the welkin.

The thing to do was to go to the House of Prayer to repeat Psalms, and that was what I did.

The townsfolk liked that, all right. I stood in a corner saying Psalms and prayers, and they shook their heads at me. "Pray, pray!" they told me. "Prayer never made any woman pregnant." One of the congregation put a straw to my mouth and said, "Hay for the cows." There was something to that too, by God!

She gave birth to a boy. Friday at the synagogue the sexton stood up before the Ark, pounded on the reading table, and announced, "The wealthy Reb Gimpel invites the congregation to a feast in honor of the birth of a son." The whole House of Prayer rang with laughter. My face was flaming. But there was nothing I could do. After all, I *was* the one responsible for the circumcision honors and rituals.

Half the town came running. You couldn't wedge another soul in. Women brought peppered chick-peas, and there was a keg of beer from the tavern. I ate and drank as much as anyone, and they all congratulated me. Then there was a circumcision, and I named the boy after my father, may he rest in peace. When all were gone and I was left with my wife alone, she thrust her head through the bed-curtain and called me to her.

"Gimpel," said she, "why are you silent? Has your ship gone and sunk?"

"What shall I say?" I answered. "A fine thing you've done to me! If my mother had known of it she'd have died a second time."

She said, "Are you crazy, or what?"

"How can you make such a fool," I said, "of one who should be the lord and master?"

"What's the matter with you?" she said. "What have you taken it into your head to imagine?"

I saw that I must speak bluntly and openly. "Do you think this is the way to use an orphan?" I said. "You have borne a bastard."

She answered, "Drive this foolishness out of your head. The child is yours."

"How can he be mine?" I argued. "He was born seventeen weeks after the wedding."

She told me then that he was premature. I said, "Isn't he a little too premature?" She said she had had a grandmother who carried just as short a time and she resembled this grandmother of hers as one drop of water does another. She swore to it with such oaths that you would have believed a peasant at the fair if he had used them. To tell the plain truth, I didn't believe her; but when I talked it over the next day with the schoolmaster he told me that the very same thing had happened to Adam and Eve. Two they went up to bed, and four they descended.

"There isn't a woman in the world who is not the granddaughter of Eve," he said.

That was how it was—they argued me dumb. But then, who really knows how such things happen?

I began to forget my sorrow. I loved the child madly, and he loved me too. As soon as he saw me he'd wave his little hands and want me to pick him up, and when he was colicky I was the only one who could pacify him. I bought him a little bone teething ring and a little gilded cap. He was forever catching the evil eye from someone, and then I had to run to get one of those abracadabras for him that would get him out of it. I worked like an ox. You know how expenses go up when there's an infant in the house.

I don't want to lie about it; I didn't dislike Elka either, for that matter. She swore at me and cursed, and I couldn't get enough of her. What strength she had! One of her looks could rob you of the power of speech. And her orations! Pitch and sulphur, that's what they were full of, and yet somehow also full of charm. I adored her every word. She gave me bloody wounds though.

In the evening I brought her a white loaf as well as a dark one, and also poppyseed rolls I baked myself. I thieved because of her and swiped everything I could lay hands on, macaroons, raisins, almonds, cakes. I hope I may be forgiven for stealing from the Saturday pots the women left to warm in the baker's oven. I would take out scraps of meat, a chunk of pudding, a chicken leg or head, a piece of tripe, whatever I could nip quickly. She ate and became fat and handsome.

I had to sleep away from home all during the week, at the bakery. On Friday nights when I got home she always made an excuse of some sort. Either she had heartburn, or a stitch in the side, or hiccups, or headaches. You know what women's excuses are. I had a bitter time of it. It was rough. To add to it, this little brother of hers, the bastard, was growing bigger. He'd put lumps on me, and when I wanted to hit back she'd open her mouth and curse so powerfully I saw a green haze floating before my eyes. Ten times a day she threatened to divorce me. Another man in my place would have taken French leave and disappeared. But I'm the type that bears it and says nothing. What's one to do? Shoulders are from God, and burdens too.

One night there was a calamity in the bakery; the oven burst, and we almost had a fire. There was nothing to do but go home, so I went home. Let me, I thought, also taste the joy of sleeping in bed in midweek. I didn't want to wake the sleeping mite and tiptoed into the house. Coming in, it seemed to me that I heard not the snoring of one but, as it were, a double snore, one a thin enough snore and the other like the snoring of a slaughtered ox. Oh, I didn't like that! I didn't like it at all. I went up to the bed, and things suddenly turned black. Next to Elka lay a man's form. Another in my place would have made an uproar, and enough noise to rouse the whole town, but the thought occurred to me that I might wake the child. A little thing like that—why frighten a little swallow like that, I thought. All right then, I went back to the bakery and stretched out on a sack of flour, and till morning I never shut an eye. I shivered as if I had had malaria. "Enough of being a donkey," I said to myself. "Gimpel isn't going to be a sucker all his life. There's a limit even to the foolishness of a fool like Gimpel."

In the morning I went to the rabbi to get advice, and it made a great commotion in the town. They sent the beadle for Elka right away. She came, carrying the child. And what do you think she did? She denied it, denied everything, bone and stone! "He's out of his head," she said. "I know nothing of dreams or divinations." They yelled at her, warned her, hammered on the table, but she stuck to her guns: it was a false accusation, she said.

The butchers and the horse-traders took her part. One of the lads from the slaughter-house came by and said to me, "We've got our eye on you, you're a marked man." Meanwhile the child started to bear down and soiled itself. In the rabbinical court there was an Ark of the Covenant, and they couldn't allow that, so they sent Elka away.

I said to the rabbi, "What shall I do?"

"You must divorce her at once," said he.

"And what if she refuses?" I asked.

He said, "You must serve the divorce, that's all you'll have to do."

I said, "Well, all right, Rabbi. Let me think about it."

"There's nothing to think about," said he. "You mustn't remain under the same roof with her."

"And if I want to see the child?" I asked.

"Let her go, the harlot," said he, "and her brood of bastards with her."

The verdict he gave was that I mustn't even cross her threshold—never again, as long as I should live.

During the day it didn't bother me so much. I thought, It was bound to happen, the abscess had to burst. But at night when I stretched out upon the sacks I felt it all very bitterly. A longing took me, for her and for the child. I wanted to be angry, but that's my misfortune exactly, I don't have it in me to be really angry. In the first place—this was how my thoughts went—there's bound to be a slip sometimes. You can't live without errors. Probably that lad who was with her led her on and gave her presents and what not, and women are often long on hair and short on sense, and so he got around her. And then since she denies it so, maybe I was only seeing things? Hallucinations do happen. You see a figure or a mannikin or something, but when you come up closer it's nothing, there's not a thing there. And if that's so, I'm doing her an injustice. And when I got so far in my thoughts I started to weep. I sobbed so that I wet the flour where I lay. In the morning I went to the rabbi and told him that I had made a mistake. The rabbi wrote on with his quill, and he said that if that were so he would have to reconsider the whole case. Until he had finished I wasn't to go near my wife, but I might send her bread and money by messenger.

III

Nine months passed before all the rabbis could come to an agreement. Letters went back and forth. I hadn't realized that there could be so much erudition about a matter like this.

Meantime Elka gave birth to still another child, a girl this time. On the Sabbath I went to the synagogue and invoked a blessing on her. They called me up to the Torah, and I named the child for my mother-in-law, may she rest in peace. The louts and loudmouths of the town who came into the bakery gave me a going over. All Frampol refreshed its spirits because of my trouble and grief. However, I resolved that I would always believe what I was told. What's the good of *not* believing? Today it's your wife you don't believe; tomorrow it's God Himself you won't take stock in.

By an apprentice who was her neighbor I sent her daily a corn or a wheat loaf, or a piece of pastry, rolls or bagels, or, when I got the chance, a slab of pudding, a slice of honeycake, or wedding strudel—whatever came my way. The apprentice was a goodhearted lad, and more than once he added something on his own. He had formerly annoyed me a lot, plucking my nose and digging me in the ribs, but when he started to be a visitor to my house he became kind and friendly. "Hey, you, Gimpel," he said to me, "you have a very decent little wife and two fine kids. You don't deserve them."

"But the things people say about her," I said.

"Well, they have long tongues," he said, "and nothing to do with them but babble. Ignore it as you ignore the cold of last winter."

One day the rabbi sent for me and said, "Are you certain, Gimpel, that you were wrong about your wife?"

I said, "I'm certain."

"Why, but look here! You yourself saw it."

"It must have been a shadow," I said.

"The shadow of what?"

"Just of one of the beams, I think."

"You can go home then. You owe thanks to the Yanover rabbi. He found an obscure reference in Maimonides that favored you."

I seized the rabbi's hand and kissed it.

I wanted to run home immediately. It's no small thing to be separated for so long a time from wife and child. Then I reflected, I'd better go back to work now, and go home in the evening. I said nothing to anyone, although as far as my heart was concerned it was like one of the Holy Days. The women teased and twitted me as they did every day, but my thought was, Go on, with your loose talk. The truth is out, like the oil upon the water. Maimonides says it's right, and therefore it is right!

At night, when I had covered the dough to let it rise, I took my share of bread and a little sack of flour and started homeward. The moon was full and the stars were glistening, something to terrify the soul. I hurried onward, and before me darted a long shadow. It was winter, and a fresh snow had fallen. I had a mind to sing, but it was growing late and I didn't want to wake the householders. Then I felt like whistling, but remembered that you don't whistle at night because it brings the demons out. So I was silent and walked fast as I could.

Dogs in the Christian yards barked at me when I passed, but I thought, Bark your teeth out! What are you but mere dogs? Whereas I am a man, the husband of a fine wife, the father of promising children.

As I approached the house my heart started to pound as though it were the heart of a criminal. I felt no fear, but my heart went thump! thump! Well, no drawing back. I quietly lifted the latch and went in. Elka was asleep. I looked at the infant's cradle. The shutter was closed, but the moon forced its way through the cracks. I saw the newborn child's face and loved it as soon as I saw it—immediately—each tiny bone.

Then I came nearer to the bed. And what did I see but the apprentice lying there beside Elka. The moon went out all at once. It was utterly black, and I trembled. My teeth chattered. The bread fell from my hands and my wife waked and said, "Who is that, ah?"

I muttered, "It's me."

"Gimpel?" she asked. "How come you're here? I thought it was forbidden."

"The rabbi said," I answered and shook as with a fever.

"Listen to me, Gimpel," she said, "go out to the shed and see if the goat's all right. It seems she's been sick." I have forgotten to say that we had a goat. When I heard she was unwell I went into the yard. The nannygoat was a good little creature. I had a nearly human feeling for her.

With hesitant steps I went up to the shed and opened the door. The goat stood there

on her four feet. I felt her everywhere, drew her by the arms, examined her udders, and found nothing wrong. She had probably eaten too much bark. "Good night, little goat," I said. "Keep well." And the little beast answered with a "Maa" as though to thank me for the good will.

I went back. The apprentice had vanished.

"Where," I asked, "is the lad?"

"What lad?" my wife answered.

"What do you mean?" I said. "The apprentice. You were sleeping with him."

"The things I have dreamed this night and the night before," she said, "may they come true and lay you low, body and soul! An evil spirit has taken root in you and dazzles your sight." She screamed out, "You hateful creature! You moon calf! You spook! You uncouth man! Get out, or I'll scream all Frampol out of bed!"

Before I could move, her brother sprang out from behind the oven and struck me a blow on the back of the head. I thought he had broken my neck. I felt that something about me was deeply wrong, and I said, "Don't make a scandal. All that's needed now is that people should accuse me of raising spooks and *dybbuks.*" For that was what she had meant. "No one will touch bread of my baking."

In short, I somehow calmed her.

"Well," she said, "that's enough. Lie down, and be shattered by wheels."

Next morning I called the apprentice aside. "Listen here, brother!" I said. And so on and so forth. "What do you say?" He stared at me as though I had dropped from the roof or something.

"I swear," he said, "you'd better go to an herb doctor or some healer. I'm afraid you have a screw loose, but I'll hush it up for you." And that's how the thing stood.

To make a long story short, I lived twenty years with my wife. She bore me six children, four daughters and two sons. All kinds of things happened, but I neither saw nor heard. I believed, and that's all. The rabbi recently said to me, "Belief in itself is beneficial. It is written that a good man lives by his faith."

Suddenly my wife took sick. It began with a trifle, a little growth upon the breast. But she evidently was not destined to live long; she had no years. I spent a fortune on her. I have forgotten to say that by this time I had a bakery of my own and in Frampol was considered to be something of a rich man. Daily the healer came, and every witch doctor in the neighborhood was brought. They decided to use leeches, and after that to try cupping. They even called a doctor from Lublin, but it was too late. Before she died she called me to her bed and said, "Forgive me, Gimpel."

I said, "What is there to forgive? You have been a good and faithful wife."

"Woe, Gimpel!" she said. "It was ugly how I deceived you all these years. I want to go clean to my Maker, and so I have to tell you that the children are not yours."

If I had been clouted on the head with a piece of wood it couldn't have bewildered me more.

"Whose are they?" I asked.

"I don't know," she said, "there were a lot. . . . But they're not yours." And as she spoke she tossed her head to the side, her eyes turned glassy, and it was all up with Elka. On her whitened lips there remained a smile.

I imagined that, dead as she was, she was saying, "I deceived Gimpel. That was the meaning of my brief life."

IV

One night, when the period of mourning was done, as I lay dreaming on the flour sacks, there came the Spirit of Evil himself and said to me, "Gimpel, why do you sleep?"

I said, "What should I be doing? Eating *kreplach?*"

"The whole world deceives you," he said, "and you ought to deceive the world in your turn."

"How can I deceive all the world?" I asked him.

He answered, "You might accumulate a bucket of urine every day and at night pour it into the dough. Let the sages of Frampol eat filth."

"What about judgment in the world to come?" I said.

"There is no world to come," he said. "They've sold you a bill of goods and talked you into believing you carried a cat in your belly. What nonsense!"

"Well then," I said, "and is there a God?"

He answered, "There is no God either."

"What," I said, "*is* there, then?"

"A thick mire."

He stood before my eyes with a goatish beard and horns, longtoothed, and with a tail. Hearing such words, I wanted to snatch him by the tail, but I tumbled from the flour sacks and nearly broke a rib. Then it happened that I had to answer the call of nature, and, passing, I saw the risen bread, which seemed to say to me, "Do it!" In brief, I let myself be persuaded.

At dawn the apprentice came. We kneaded the dough, scattered caraway seeds on it, and set it to bake. Then the apprentice went away, and I was left sitting in the little trench by the oven, on a pile of rags. Well, Gimpel, I thought, you've revenged yourself on them for all the shame they've put on you. Outside the frost glittered, but it was warm beside the oven. The flames heated my face. I bent my head and fell into a doze.

I saw in a dream, at once, Elka in her shroud. She called to me, "What have you done, Gimpel?"

I said to her, "It's all your fault," and started to cry.

"You fool!" she said. "You fool! Because I was false is everything false too? I never deceived anyone but myself. I'm paying for it all, Gimpel. They spare you nothing here."

I looked at her face. It was black. I was startled and waked, and remained sitting dumb. I sensed that everything hung in the balance. A false step now and I'd lose Eternal Life. But God gave me His help. I seized the long shovel and took out the loaves, carried them into the yard, and started to dig a hole in the frozen earth.

My apprentice came back as I was doing it. "What are you doing, boss?" he said, and grew pale as a corpse.

"I know what I'm doing," I said, and I buried it all before his very eyes.

Then I went home, took my hoard from its hiding place, and divided it among the children. "I saw your mother tonight," I said. "She's turning black, poor thing."

They were so astounded they couldn't speak a word.

"Be well," I said, "and forget that such a one as Gimpel ever existed." I put on my short coat, a pair of boots, took the bag that held my prayer shawl in one hand, my stick

in the other, and kissed the *mezzuzah*. When people saw me in the street they were greatly surprised.

"Where are you going?" they said.

I answered, "Into the world." And so I departed from Frampol.

I wandered over the land, and good people did not neglect me. After many years I became old and white; I heard a great deal, many lies and falsehoods, but the longer I lived the more I understood that there were really no lies. Whatever doesn't really happen is dreamed at night. It happens to one if it doesn't happen to another, tomorrow if not today, or a century hence if not next year. What difference can it make? Often I heard tales of which I said, "Now this is a thing that cannot happen." But before a year had elapsed I heard that it actually had come to pass somewhere.

Going from place to place, eating at strange tables, it often happens that I spin yarns—improbable things that could never have happened—about devils, magicians, windmills, and the like. The children run after me, calling, "Grandfather, tell us a story." Sometimes they ask for particular stories, and I try to please them. A fat young boy once said to me, "Grandfather, it's the same story you told us before." The little rogue, he was right.

So it is with dreams too. It is many years since I left Frampol, but as soon as I shut my eyes I am there again. And whom do you think I see? Elka. She is standing by the washtub, as at our first encounter, but her face is shining and her eyes as radiant as the eyes of a saint, and she speaks outlandish words to me, strange things. When I wake I have forgotten it all. But while the dream lasts I am comforted. She answers all my queries, and what comes out is that all is right. I weep and implore, "Let me be with you." And she consoles me and tells me to be patient. The time is nearer than it is far. Sometimes she strokes and kisses me and weeps upon my face. When I awaken I feel her lips and taste the salt of her tears.

No doubt the world is entirely an imaginary world, but it is only once removed from the true world. At the door of the hovel where I lie, there stands the plank on which the dead are taken away. The gravedigger Jew has his spade ready. The grave waits and the worms are hungry; the shrouds are prepared—I carry them in my beggar's sack. Another *shnorrer* is waiting to inherit my bed of straw. When the time comes I will go joyfully. Whatever may be there, it will be real, without complication, without ridicule, without deception. God be praised: there even Gimpel cannot be deceived.

Translated by Saul Bellow

QUESTIONS

1. Gimpel is portrayed in three separate stages of his life. In what way does he remain a "fool" throughout? How does the nature of his foolishness transform during these stages?
2. How is Gimpel's character tested when the Spirit of Evil tries to persuade him to urinate into the dough? What lesson does he learn from this incident?
3. The author's style is sometimes referred to as magical realism. What aspects of this story seem to corroborate this? How does the technique reveal itself in Singer's handling of characterization?

Flannery O'Connor

A GOOD MAN IS HARD TO FIND

The grandmother didn't want to go to Florida. She wanted to visit some of her connections in east Tennessee and she was seizing every chance to change Bailey's mind. Bailey was the son she lived with, her only boy. He was sitting on the edge of his chair at the table, bent over the orange sports section of the *Journal*. "Now look here, Bailey," she said, "see here, read this," and she stood with one hand on her thin hip and the other rattling the newspaper at his bald head. "Here this fellow that calls himself The Misfit is aloose from the Federal Pen and headed toward Florida and you read here what it says he did to these people. Just you read it. I wouldn't take my children in any direction with a criminal like that aloose in it. I couldn't answer to my conscience if I did."

Bailey didn't look up from his reading so she wheeled around then and faced the children's mother; a young mother in slacks, whose face was as broad and innocent as a cabbage and was tied around with a green headkerchief that had two points on the top like rabbit's ears. She was sitting on the sofa, feeding the baby his apricots out of a jar. "The children have been to Florida before," the old lady said. "You all ought to take them somewhere else for a change so they would see different parts of the world and be broad. They never have been to east Tennessee."

The children's mother didn't seem to hear her, but the eight-year-old boy, John Wesley, a stocky child with glasses, said, "If you don't want to go to Florida, why dontcha stay at home?" He and the little girl, June Star, were reading the funny papers on the floor.

"She wouldn't stay at home to be queen for a day," June Star said without raising her yellow head.

"Yes, and what would you do if this fellow, The Misfit, caught you?" the grandmother asked.

"I'd smack his face," John Wesley said.

"She wouldn't stay at home for a million bucks," June Star said. "Afraid she'd miss something. She has to go everywhere we go."

"All right, Miss," the grandmother said. "Just remember that the next time you want me to curl your hair."

June Star said her hair was naturally curly.

The next morning the grandmother was the first one in the car, ready to go. She had her big black valise that looked like the head of a hippopotamus in one corner, and underneath it she was hiding a basket with Pitty Sing, the cat, in it. She didn't intend for the cat to be left alone in the house for three days because he would miss her too much and she was afraid he might brush against one of the gas burners and accidentally asphyxiate himself. Her son, Bailey, didn't like to arrive at a motel with a cat.

She sat in the middle of the back seat with John Wesley and June Star on either side of her. Bailey and the children's mother and the baby sat in the front and they left Atlanta at eight forty-five with the mileage on the car at 55890. The grandmother wrote

this down because she thought it would be interesting to say how many miles they had been when they got back. It took them twenty minutes to reach the outskirts of the city.

The old lady settled herself comfortably, removing her white cotton gloves and putting them up with her purse on the shelf in front of the back window. The children's mother still had on slacks and still had her head tied up in a green kerchief, but the grandmother had on a navy blue straw sailor hat with a bunch of white violets on the brim and a navy blue dress with a small white dot in the print. Her collar and cuffs were white organdy trimmed with lace and at her neckline she had pinned a purple spray of cloth violets containing a sachet. In case of an accident, anyone seeing her dead on the highway would know at once that she was a lady.

She said she thought it was going to be a good day for driving, neither too hot nor too cold, and she cautioned Bailey that the speed limit was fifty-five miles an hour and that the patrolmen hid themselves behind bill-boards and small clumps of trees and sped out after you before you had a chance to slow down. She pointed out interesting details of the scenery: Stone Mountain, the blue granite that in some places came up to both sides of the highway; the brilliant red clay banks slightly streaked with purple; and the various crops that made rows of green lack-work on the ground. The trees were full of silver-white sunlights and the meanest of them sparkled. The children were reading comic magazines and their mother had gone back to sleep.

"Let's go through Georgia fast so we won't have to look at it much," John Wesley said.

"If I were a little boy," said the grandmother, "I wouldn't talk about my native state that way. Tennessee has the mountains and Georgia has the hills."

"Tennessee is just a hillbilly dumping ground," John Wesley said, "and Georgia is a lousy state too."

"You said it," June Star said.

"In my time," said the grandmother, folding her thin veined fingers, "children were more respectful of their native states and their parents and everything else. People did right then. Oh look at the cute little pickaninny!" she said and pointed to a Negro child standing in the door of a shack. "Wouldn't that make a picture, now?" she asked and they all turned and looked at the little Negro out of the back window. He waved.

"He didn't have any britches on," June Star said.

"He probably didn't have any," the grandmother explained. "Little niggers in the country don't have things like we do. If I could paint, I'd paint that picture," she said.

The children exchanged comic books.

The grandmother offered to hold the baby and the children's mother passed him over the front seat to her. She set him on her knee and bounced him and told him about the things they were passing. She rolled her eyes and screwed up her mouth and stuck her leathery thin face into his smooth bland one. Occasionally he gave her a faraway smile. They passed a large cotton field with five or six graves fenced in the middle of it, like a small island. "Look at the graveyard!" the grandmother said, pointing it out. "That was the old family burying ground. That belonged to the plantation."

"Where's the plantation?" John Wesley asked.

"Gone With the Wind," said the grandmother. "Ha. Ha."

When the children finished all the comic books they had brought, they opened the lunch and ate it. The grandmother ate a peanut butter sandwich and an olive and would not let the children throw the box and the paper napkins out the window. When there was nothing else to do they played a game by choosing a cloud and making the other two guess what shape it suggested. John Wesley took one the shape of a cow and June Star guessed a cow and John Wesley said, no, an automobile, and June Star said he didn't play fair, and they began to slap each other over the grandmother.

The grandmother said she would tell them a story if they would keep quiet. When she told a story, she rolled her eyes and waved her head and was very dramatic. She said once when she was a maiden lady she had been courted by a Mr. Edgar Atkins Teagarden from Jasper, Georgia. She said he was a very good-looking man and a gentleman and that he brought her a watermelon every Saturday afternoon with his initials cut in it, E. A. T. Well, one Saturday, she said, Mr. Teagarden brought the watermelon and there was nobody at home and he left it on the front porch and returned in his buggy to Jasper, but she never got the watermelon, she said, because a nigger boy ate it when he saw the initials, E. A. T.! This story tickled John Wesley's funny bone and he giggled and giggled but June Star didn't think it was any good. She said she wouldn't marry a man that just brought her a watermelon on Saturday. The grandmother said she would have done well to marry Mr. Teagarden because he was a gentleman and had bought Coca-Cola stock when it first came out and that he had died only a few years ago, a very wealthy man.

They stopped at The Tower for barbecued sandwiches. The Tower was a part-stucco and part-wood filling station and dance hall set in a clearing outside of Timothy. A fat man named Red Sammy Butts ran it and there were signs stuck here and there on the building and for miles up and down the highway saying, TRY RED SAMMY'S FAMOUS BARBECUE. NONE LIKE FAMOUS RED SAMMY'S! RED SAM! THE FAT BOY WITH THE HAPPY LAUGH. A VETERAN! RED SAMMY'S YOUR MAN!

Red Sammy was lying on the bare ground outside The Tower with his head under a truck while a gray monkey about a foot high, chained to a small chinaberry tree, chattered nearby. The monkey sprang back into the tree and got on the highest limb as soon as he saw the children jump out of the car and run toward him.

Inside, The Tower was a long dark room with a counter at one end and tables at the other and dancing space in the middle. They all sat down at a broad table next to the nickelodeon and Red Sam's wife, a tall burnt-brown woman with hair and eyes lighter than her skin, came and took their order. The children's mother put a dime in the machine and played "The Tennessee Waltz," and the grandmother said that tune always made her want to dance. She asked Bailey if he would like to dance but he only glared at her. He didn't have a naturally sunny disposition like she did and trips made him nervous. The grandmother's brown eyes were very bright. She swayed her head from side to side and pretended she was dancing in her chair. June Star said play something she could tap to so the children's mother put in another dime and played a fast number and June Star stepped out onto the dance floor and did her tap routine.

"Ain't she cute?" Red Sam's wife said, leaning over the counter. "Would you like to come be my little girl?"

"No, I certainly wouldn't," June Star said. "I wouldn't live in a broken-down place like this for a million bucks!" and she ran back to the table.

"Ain't she cute?" the woman repeated, stretching her mouth politely.

"Aren't you ashamed?" hissed the grandmother.

Red Sam came in and told his wife to quit lounging on the counter and hurry up with these people's order. His khaki trousers reached just to his hip bones and his stomach hung over them like a sack of meal swaying under his shirt. He came over and sat down at a table nearby and let out a combination sigh and yodel. "You can't win," he said. "You can't win," and he wiped his sweating red face off with a gray handkerchief. "These days you don't know who to trust," he said. "Ain't that the truth?"

"People are certainly not nice like they used to be," said the grandmother.

"Two fellers come in here last week," Red Sammy said, "driving a Chrysler. It was an old beat-up car but it was a good one and these boys looked all right to me. Said they worked at the mill and you know I let them fellers charge the gas they bought? Now why did I do that?"

"Because you're a good man!" the grandmother said at once.

"Yes'm, I suppose so," Red Sam said as if he were struck with this answer.

His wife brought the orders, carrying the five plates all at once without a tray, two in each hand and one balanced on her arm. "It isn't a soul in this green world of God's that you can trust," she said. "And I don't count nobody out of that, not nobody," she repeated, looking at Red Sammy.

"Did you read about that criminal, The Misfit, that's escaped?" asked the grandmother.

"I wouldn't be a bit surprised if he didn't attack this place right here," said the woman. "If he hears about it being here, I wouldn't be none surprised to see him. If he hears it's two cent in the cash register, I wouldn't be a tall surprised if he. . . ."

"That'll do," Red Sam said. "Go bring these people their Co'-Colas," and the woman went off to get the rest of the order.

"A good man is hard to find," Red Sammy said. "Everything is getting terrible. I remember the day you could go off and leave your screen door unlatched. Not no more."

He and the grandmother discussed better times. The old lady said that in her opinion Europe was entirely to blame for the way things were now. She said the way Europe acted you would think we were made of money and Red Sam said it was no use talking about it, she was exactly right. The children ran outside into the white sunlight and looked at the monkey in the lacy chinaberry tree. He was busy catching fleas on himself and biting each one carefully between his teeth as if it were a delicacy.

They drove off again into the hot afternoon. The grandmother took cat naps and woke up every few minutes with her own snoring. Outside of Toombsboro she woke up and recalled an old plantation that she had visited in this neighborhood once when she was a young lady. She said the house had six white columns across the front and that there was an avenue of oaks leading up to it and two little wooden trellis arbors on either side in front where you sat down with your suitor after a stroll in the garden. She recalled exactly which road to turn off to get to it. She knew that Bailey would not be willing to lose any time looking at an old house, but the more she talked about it, the more she wanted to see it once again and find out if the little twin arbors were still standing. "There was a secret panel in this house," she said craftily, not telling the truth but wishing that she were, "and the story went that all the family silver was hidden in it when Sherman came through but it was never found. . . ."

"Hey!" John Wesley said. "Let's go see it! We'll find it! We'll poke all the wood work and find it! Who lives there? Where do you turn off at? Hey Pop, can't we turn off there?"

"We never have seen a house with a secret panel!" June Star shrieked. "Let's go to the house with the secret panel! Hey, Pop, can't we go see the house with the secret panel!"

"It's not far from here, I know," the grandmother said. "It wouldn't take over twenty minutes."

Bailey was looking straight ahead. His jaw was as rigid as a horseshoe. "No," he said.

The children began to yell and scream that they wanted to see the house with the secret panel. John Wesley kicked the back of the front seat and June Star hung over her mother's shoulder and whined desperately into her ear that they never had any fun even on their vacation, that they could never do what THEY wanted to do. The baby began to scream and John Wesley kicked the back of the seat so hard that his father could feel the blows in his kidney.

"All right!" he shouted and drew the car to a stop at the side of the road. "Will you all shut up? Will you all just shut up for one second? If you don't shut up, we won't go anywhere."

"It would be very educational for them," the grandmother murmured.

"All right," Bailey said, "but get this. This is the only time we're going to stop for anything like this. This is the one and only time."

"The dirt road that you have to turn down is about a mile back," the grandmother directed. "I marked it when we passed."

"A dirt road," Bailey groaned.

After they had turned around and were headed toward the dirt road, the grandmother recalled other points about the house, the beautiful glass over the front doorway and the candle lamp in the hall. John Wesley said that the secret panel was probably in the fireplace.

"You can't go inside this house," Bailey said. "You don't know who lives there."

"While you all talk to the people in front, I'll run around behind and get in a window," John Wesley suggested.

"We'll all stay in the car," his mother said.

They turned onto the dirt road and the car raced roughly along in a swirl of pink dust. The grandmother recalled the times when there were no paved roads and thirty miles was a day's journey. The dirt road was hilly and there were sudden washes in it and sharp curves on dangerous embankments. All at once they would be on a hill, looking down over the blue tops of trees for miles around, then the next minute, they would be in a red depression with the dust-coated trees looking down on them.

"This place had better turn up in a minute," Bailey said, "or I'm going to turn around."

The road looked as if no one had traveled on it in months.

"It's not much farther," the grandmother said and just as she said it, a horrible thought came to her. The thought was so embarrassing that she turned red in the face and her eyes dilated and her feet jumped up, upsetting her valise in the corner. The instant the valise moved, the newspaper top she had over the basket under it rose with a snarl and Pitty Sing, the cat, sprang onto Bailey's shoulder.

The children were thrown to the floor and their mother, clutching the baby, was thrown out the door onto the ground; the old lady was thrown into the front seat. The car turned over once and landed right-side-up in a gulch on the side of the road. Bailey remained in the driver's seat with the cat—gray-striped with a broad white face and an orange nose—clinging to his neck like a caterpillar.

As soon as the children saw they could move their arms and legs, they scrambled out of the car, shouting, "We've had an ACCIDENT!" The grandmother was curled up under the dashboard, hoping she was injured so that Bailey's wrath would not come down on her all at once. The horrible thought she had had before the accident was that the house she had remembered so vividly was not in Georgia but in Tennessee.

Bailey removed the cat from his neck with both hands and flung it out the window against the side of a pine tree. Then he got out of the car and started looking for the children's mother. She was sitting against the side of the red gutted ditch, holding the screaming baby, but she only had a cut down her face and a broken shoulder. "We've had an ACCIDENT" the children screamed in a frenzy of delight.

"But nobody's killed," June Star said with disappointment as the grandmother limped out of the car, her hat still pinned to her head but the broken front brim standing up at a jaunty angle and the violet spray hanging off the side. They all sat down in the ditch, except the children, to recover from the shock. They were all shaking.

"Maybe a car will come along," said the children's mother hoarsely.

"I believe I have injured an organ," said the grandmother, pressing her side, but no one answered her. Bailey's teeth were clattering. He had on a yellow sport shirt with bright blue parrots designed in it and his face was as yellow as the shirt. The grandmother decided that she would not mention that the house was in Tennessee.

The road was about ten feet above and they could see only the tops of the trees on the other side of it. Behind the ditch they were sitting in there were more woods, tall and dark and deep. In a few minutes they saw a car some distance away on top of a hill, coming slowly as if the occupants were watching them. The grandmother stood up and waved both arms dramatically to attract their attention. The car continued to come on slowly, disappeared around a bend and appeared again, moving even slower, on top of the hill they had gone over. It was a big black battered hearselike automobile. There were three men in it.

It came to a stop just over them and for some minutes, the driver looked down with a steady expressionless gaze to where they were sitting, and didn't speak. Then he turned his head and muttered something to the other two and they got out. One was a fat boy in black trousers and a red sweat shirt with a silver stallion embossed on the front of it. He moved around on the right side of them and stood staring, his mouth partly open in a kind of loose grin. The other had on khaki pants and a blue striped coat and a gray hat pulled down very low, hiding most of his face. He came around slowly on the left side. Neither spoke.

The driver got out of the car and stood by the side of it, looking down at them. He was an older man than the other two. His hair was just beginning to gray and he wore silver-rimmed spectacles that gave him a scholarly look. He had a long creased face and didn't have on any shirt or undershirt. He had on blue jeans that were too tight for him and was holding a black hat and a gun. The two boys also had guns.

"We've had an ACCIDENT!" the children screamed.

The grandmother had the peculiar feeling that the bespectacled man was someone she knew. His face was as familiar to her as if she had known him all her life but she could not recall who he was. He moved away from the car and began to come down the embankment, placing his feet carefully so that he wouldn't slip. He had on tan and white shoes and no socks, and his ankles were red and thin. "Good afternoon," he said. "I see you all had you a little spill."

"We turned over twice!" said the grandmother.

"Oncet," he corrected. "We see it happen. Try their car and see will it run, Hiram," he said quietly to the boy with the gray hat.

"What you got that gun for?" John Wesley asked. "Whatcha gonna do with that gun?"

"Lady," the man said to the children's mother, "would you mind calling them children to sit down by you? Children make me nervous. I want all you all to sit down right together there where you're at."

"What are you telling us what to do for?" June Star asked.

Behind them the line of woods gaped like a dark open mouth. "Come here," said their mother.

"Look here now," Bailey began suddenly, "we're in a predicament! We're in. . . ."

The grandmother shrieked. She scrambled to her feet and stood staring.

"You're The Misfit!" she said. "I recognized you at once!"

"Yes'm," the man said, smiling slightly as if he were pleased in spite of himself to be known, "but it would have been better for all of you, lady, if you hadn't of reckernized me."

Bailey turned his head sharply and said something to his mother that shocked even the children. The old lady began to cry and The Misfit reddened.

"Lady," he said, "don't you get upset. Sometimes a man says things he don't mean. I don't reckon he meant to talk to you thataway."

"You wouldn't shoot a lady, would you?" the grandmother said and removed a clean handkerchief from her cuff and began to slap at her eyes with it.

The Misfit pointed the toe of his shoe into the ground and made a little hole and then covered it up again. "I would hate to have to," he said.

"Listen," the grandmother almost screamed, "I know you're a good man. You don't look a bit like you have common blood. I know you must come from nice people!"

"Yes mam," he said, "finest people in the world." When he smiled he showed a row of strong white teeth. "God never made a finer woman than my mother and my daddy's heart was pure gold," he said. The boy with the red sweat shirt had come around behind them and was standing with his gun at his hip. The Misfit squatted down on the ground. "Watch them children, Bobby Lee," he said. "You know they make me nervous." He looked at the six of them huddled together in front of him and he seemed to be

embarrassed as if he couldn't think of anything to say. "Ain't a cloud in the sky," he remarked, looking up at it. "Don't see no sun but don't see no cloud neither."

"Yes, it's a beautiful day," said the grandmother. "Listen," she said, "you shouldn't call yourself The Misfit because I know you're a good man at heart. I can just look at you and tell."

"Hush!" Bailey yelled. "Hush! Everybody shut up and let me handle this!" He was squatting in the position of a runner about to sprint forward but he didn't move.

"I pre-chate that, lady," The Misfit said and drew a little circle in the ground with the butt of his gun.

"It'll take a half a hour to fix this here car," Hiram called, looking over the raised hood of it.

"Well, first you and Bobby Lee get him and that little boy to step over yonder with you," The Misfit said, pointing to Bailey and John Wesley. "The boys want to ask you something," he said to Bailey. "Would you mind stepping back in them woods there with them?"

"Listen," Bailey began, "we're in a terrible predicament! Nobody realizes what this is," and his voice cracked. His eyes were as blue and intense as the parrots in his shirt and he remained perfectly still.

The grandmother reached up to adjust her hat brim as if she were going to the woods with him but it came off in her hand. She stood staring at it and after a second she let it fall on the ground. Hiram pulled Bailey up by the arm as if he were assisting an old man. John Wesley caught hold of his father's hand and Bobby Lee followed. They went off toward the woods and just as they reached the dark edge, Bailey turned and supporting himself against a gray naked pine trunk, he shouted, "I'll be back in a minute, Mamma, wait on me!"

"Come back this instant!" his mother shrilled but they all disappeared into the woods.

"Bailey Boy!" the grandmother called in a tragic voice but she found she was looking at The Misfit squatting on the ground in front of her. "I just know you're a good man," she said desperately. "You're not a bit common!"

"Nome, I ain't a good man," The Misfit said after a second as if he had considered her statement carefully, "but I ain't the worst in the world neither. My daddy said I was a different breed of dog from my brothers and sisters. 'You know,' Daddy said, 'it's some that can live their whole life out without asking about it and it's others has to know why it is, and this boy is one of the latters. He's going to be into everything!'" He put on his black hat and looked up suddenly and then away deep into the woods as if he were embarrassed again. "I'm sorry, I don't have on a shirt before you ladies," he said, hunching his shoulders slightly. "We buried our clothes that we had on when we escaped and we're just making do until we can get better. We borrowed these from some folks we met," he explained.

"That's perfectly all right," the grandmother said. "Maybe Bailey has an extra shirt in his suitcase."

"I'll look and see terrectly," The Misfit said.

"Where are they taking him?" the children's mother screamed.

"Daddy was a card himself," The Misfit said. "You couldn't put anything over on him. He never got in trouble with the Authorities though. Just had the knack of handling them."

"You could be honest too if you'd only try," said the grandmother. "Think how wonderful it would be to settle down and live a comfortable life and not have to think about somebody chasing you all the time."

The Misfit kept scratching in the ground with the butt of his gun as if he were thinking about it. "Yes'm, somebody is always after you," he murmured.

The grandmother noticed how thin his shoulder blades were just behind his hat because she was standing up looking down on him. "Do you ever pray?" she asked.

He shook his head. All she saw was the black hat wiggle between his shoulder blades. "Nome," he said.

There was a pistol shot from the woods, followed closely by another. Then silence. The old lady's head jerked around. She could hear the wind move through the tree tops like a long satisfied insuck of breath. "Bailey Boy!" she called.

"I was a gospel singer for a while," The Misfit said. "I been most everything. Been in the arm service, both land and sea, at home and abroad, been twict married, been an undertaker, been with the railroads, plowed Mother Earth, been in a tornado, seen a man burnt alive oncet," and he looked up at the children's mother and the little girl who were sitting close together, their faces white and their eyes glass; "I even seen a woman flogged," he said.

"Pray, pray," the grandmother began, "pray, pray. . . ."

"I never was a bad boy that I remember of," The Misfit said in an almost dreamy voice, "but somewheres along the line I done something wrong and got sent to the penitentiary. I was buried alive," and he looked up and held her attention to him by a steady stare.

"That's when you should have started to pray," she said. "What did you do to get sent to the penitentiary that first time?"

"Turn to the right, it was a wall," The Misfit said, looking up again at the cloudless sky. "Turn to the left, it was a wall. Look up it was a ceiling, look down it was a floor. I forget what I done, lady. I set there and set there, trying to remember what it was I done and I ain't recalled it to this day. Oncet in a while, I would think it was coming to me, but it never come."

"Maybe they put you in by mistake," the old lady said vaguely.

"Nome," he said. "It wasn't no mistake. They had the papers on me."

"You must have stolen something," she said.

The Misfit sneered slightly. "Nobody had nothing I wanted," he said. "It was a head-doctor at the penitentiary said what I had done was kill my daddy but I known that for a lie. My daddy died in nineteen ought nineteen of the epidemic flu and I never had a thing to do with it. He was buried in the Mount Hopewell Baptist churchyard and you can go there and see for yourself."

"If you would pray," the old lady said, "Jesus would help you."

"That's right," The Misfit said.

"Well then, why don't you pray?" she asked trembling with delight suddenly.

"I don't want no hep," he said. "I'm doing all right by myself."

Bobby Lee and Hiram came ambling back from the woods. Bobby Lee was dragging a yellow shirt with bright blue parrots in it.

"Throw me that shirt, Bobby Lee," The Misfit said. The shirt came flying at him and landed on his shoulder and he put it on. The grandmother couldn't name what the shirt reminded her of. "No, lady," The Misfit said while he was buttoning it up, "I found out the crime don't matter. You can do one thing or you can do another, kill a man or take a tire off his car, because sooner or later you're going to forget what it was you done and just be punished for it."

The children's mother had begun to make heaving noises as if she couldn't get her breath. "Lady," he asked, "would you and that little girl like to step off yonder with Bobby Lee and Hiram and join your husband?"

"Yes, thank you," the mother said faintly. Her left arm dangled helplessly and she was holding the baby, who had gone to sleep, in the other. "Hep that lady up, Hiram," The Misfit said as she struggled to climb out of the ditch, "and Bobby Lee, you hold onto that little girl's hand."

"I don't want to hold hands with him," June Star said. "He reminds me of a pig."

The fat boy blushed and laughed and caught her by the arm and pulled her off into the woods after Hiram and her mother.

Alone with The Misfit, the grandmother found that she had lost her voice. There was not a cloud in the sky nor any sun. There was nothing around her but woods. She wanted to tell him that he must pray. She opened and closed her mouth several times before anything came out. Finally she found herself saying, "Jesus, Jesus," meaning, Jesus will help you, but the way she was saying it, it sounded as if she might be cursing.

"Yes'm," The Misfit said as if he agreed. "Jesus thrown everything off balance. It was the same case with Him as with me except He hadn't committed any crime and they could prove I had committed one because they had the papers on me. Of course," he said, "they never shown me my papers. That's why I sign myself now. I said long ago, you get you a signature and sign everything you do and keep a copy of it. Then you'll know what you done and you can hold up the crime to the punishment and see do they match and in the end you'll have something to prove you ain't been treated right. I call myself The Misfit," he said, "because I can't make what all I done wrong fit what all I gone through in punishment."

There was a piercing scream from the woods, followed closely by a pistol report. "Does it seem right to you, lady, that one is punished a heap and another ain't punished at all?"

"Jesus!" the old lady cried. "You've got good blood! I know you wouldn't shoot a lady! I know you come from nice people! Pray! Jesus, you ought not to shoot a lady. I'll give you all the money I've got!"

"Lady," The Misfit said, looking beyond her far into the woods, "there never was a body that give the undertaker a tip."

There were two more pistol reports and the grandmother raised her head like a parched old turkey hen crying for water and called, "Bailey Boy, Baily Boy!" as if her heart would break.

"Jesus was the only One that ever raised the dead," The Misfit continued, "and He shouldn't have done it. He thrown everything off balance. If He did what He said, then it's nothing for you to do but throw away everything and follow Him, and if He didn't then it's nothing for you to do but enjoy the few minutes you got left the best way you can—by killing somebody or burning down his house or doing some other meanness to him. No pleasure but meanness," he said and his voice had become almost a snarl.

"Maybe He didn't raise the dead," the old lady mumbled, not knowing what she was saying and feeling so dizzy that she sank down in the ditch with her legs twisted under her.

"I wasn't there so I can't say He didn't," The Misfit said. "I wisht I had of been there," he said, hitting the ground with his fist. "It ain't right I wasn't there because if I had of been there I would of known. Listen lady," he said in a high voice, "if I had of been there I would of known and I wouldn't be like I am now." His voice seemed about to crack and the grandmother's head cleared for an instant. She saw the man's face twisted close to her own as if he were going to cry and she murmured. "Why, you're one of my babies. You're one of my own children!" She reached out and touched him on the shoulder. The Misfit sprang back as if a snake had bitten him and shot her three times through the chest. Then he put his gun down on the ground and took off his glasses and began to clean them.

Hiram and Bobby Lee returned from the woods and stood over the ditch, looking down at the grandmother who half sat and half lay in a puddle of blood with her legs crossed under her like a child's and her face smiling up at the cloudless sky.

Without his glasses, The Misfit's eyes were red-rimmed and pale and defenseless-looking. "Take her off and throw her where you thrown the others," he said, picking up the cat that was rubbing itself against his leg.

"She was a talker, wasn't she?" Bobby Lee said, sliding down the ditch with a yodel.

"She would of been a good woman," The Misfit said, "if it had been somebody there to shoot her every minute of her life."

"Some fun!" Bobby Lee said.

"Shut up, Bobby Lee," The Misfit said. "It's no real pleasure in life."

QUESTIONS

1. How would you characterize the grandmother? What can you discern about her personality when she expresses her concern about her personal appearance should she die along the highway?
2. Explain The Misfit's personality. Why does The Misfit have such a negative view of life? Based on his experience growing up, is his view justified?
3. Explain O'Connor's use of caricature in her treatment of the characters in this story.
4. How does O'Connor employ dialogue to capture character?

4 . Point of View

Point of view is the position or vantage point from which the author presents the action of the story. It is the point from which the writer decides to tell the tale. "The whole intricate question of method," writes Percy Lubbock in *The Craft of Fiction* (1921), "I take to be governed by the question of point of view—the question of the relation in which the author stands to the story." Through point of view, we are permitted to see from a special narrative perspective the actions, events, and characters that an author creates. Thus point of view is one of the most important technical considerations for fiction writers, because it directly influences all other elements in a tale.

Although the history of fiction reveals numerous ways of disclosing information through different narrative perspectives, criticism traditionally has focused on three major types of point of view: (1) *omniscient*, where the author sees and knows everything, moving across space and time, commenting on character and action, an all-knowing, godlike creator; (2) *first person*, in which the author allows one character to tell the story, thereby limiting himself or herself to what can be seen, heard, felt, thought, or known by that single character; and (3) *third person*, in which actions, thoughts, and perceptions are filtered in the third person (signaled by the pronouns "he," "she," "it," and "they") through the mind of one character or the minds of several characters. By selecting one point of view or by combining points of view, the author attempts to persuade the reader, who hears a special "voice" operating in the story, to accept the world that is being created in fiction and to view the life forces inherent in the tale from a special perspective.

Writers of fiction—from Homer to Wharton to Borges—have always been alert to the need to create a special angle of vision in order to produce an authentic, or believable, world and to illuminate that world. In the early history of both the novel and short fiction, authors would often call attention to the fact that they were telling the tale, and indeed this form of omniscience is one of the oldest points of view, stemming perhaps from the oral tradition. Many of the greatest eighteenth- and nineteenth-century novels—Fielding's *Tom Jones*, Sterne's *Tristram Shandy*, Hawthorne's *The Scarlet Letter*, George Eliot's *The Mill on the Floss*, Kate Chopin's *The Awakening*, Tolstoy's *Anna Karenina*—use this omniscient method. For example, Tolstoy writes in one of the most famous opening paragraphs in fiction: "Happy families are all alike; every unhappy family is unhappy in its own way." In *Anna Karenina*, we hear Tolstoy, the demigod, telling us *his* story, giving us *his* views from the outset of the narrative.

We also sense omniscience or authorial intrusion in some modern fiction. However, as fiction moved toward the twentieth century, it became increasingly unfashionable for authors to adopt a baldly omniscient point of view. James in his prefaces criticized some of his literary contemporaries for authorial intrusion—for inserting themselves into the action and commenting on it. In modern fiction, we do not see and hear the author as directly as we once did. The author, in the words of James Joyce, vanishes: "The artist, like the God of creation, remains within or behind or beyond his handiwork, invisible, refined out of existence, indifferent, paring his fingernails." Of course, there is *always* an implied author in the tale (a point that Wayne Booth posits brilliantly in *The Rhetoric of Fiction*), but typically the voice of the author, his or her second self, assumes a muted presence in modern fiction.

The common aim of many modern fiction writers is to achieve invisibility by utilizing a variety of points of view that we might think of as corresponding to different lenses for a camera. Each change of lens alters the relationship between the form and the subject. Typically, the storyteller will hide behind one of several first-person or third-person lenses, or points of view. With the first-person point of view, the narrator speaks from the "I" frame of reference. Actually the first-person point of view is not a peculiarly modern type; it derives from fictional memoirs, such as Goldsmith's *Vicar of Wakefield*, and from epistolary fiction, such as Richardson's *Clarissa*, and it prevails in such first-person masterpieces as *Jane Eyre*, *Huckleberry Finn*, and *Great Expectations*. Speaking from the "I" vantage point, the imaginary author can project himself or herself as a participant in the action, an observer of the action, or both an observer and a participant. The speaker can be a major or minor character in the story. The advantage of this first-person point of view, which is evident in one story in this section, Hernando Téllez's "Just Lather, That's All," is that a special immediacy and intimacy—a confessional quality—can be achieved. However, there are also significant limitations to the first-person point of view. James, for one, spoke of the "terrible fluidity of self-revelation" with the first-person narrator. Moreover, the narrator cannot see into the minds of others; special angles or perspectives on events cannot be created easily; events that the narrator has not witnessed cannot be recounted reliably. In fact, the very reliability of the first-person narrator can be called into question. Authors, of course, strive to solve these problems. For instance, they often employ the device of a story within a story in order to achieve a more balanced perspective, a framing technique favored by James in *The Turn of the Screw* and by Conrad in *Heart of Darkness*.

Authors can avoid some of the problems posed by first-person point of view (but at the same time raise new issues for themselves) by selecting a third-person point of view. This third-person point of view can be limited or unlimited. With a limited third-person point of view, the action is filtered through the mind or consciousness of only one

character. This strategy appears in a story in this section, David Leavitt's "Gravity." As readers, we know only what the central consciousness thinks and does; we cannot enter into the mind of any other character. This is a popular strategy for modern short story authors and novelists, for they can present "reality" from a consistent perspective. If we perceive reality from a single perspective, we are inclined as readers to detect a resemblance between what we see in fiction and the way we view the world. In addition, with the limited third-person point of view, the inner experiences of one individual tend to unify the world of the tale. Therefore, from this narrative perspective the illusion is created that we are sharing the thoughts, feelings, and perceptions of a character who is confronting the world from a clear angle of vision.

If authors desire a greater perspective on action and events, they can resort to a multiple or unlimited third-person point of view. Here they enter the minds of two or more characters. The scope of the lens is broad; in fact, it can amount for all practical purposes to a form of omniscience. The method can lead to an erosion of the illusion of reality, and thus the short story writer must possess considerable skill in order to move successfully from one consciousness to another without destroying either the unity of the tale or the impression that what is happening is real rather than contrived.

A final variety of third-person point of view arises when authors refuse to enter the mind of any character, achieving what we term an *objective*, or *dramatic*, third-person point of view. In this situation, a writer views characters as we would view other people in normal life. These figures are like characters on the street or figures in a play. We can interpret them only through their actions and words, their behavior and dress, and what others say the street or figures in a play are. The effect created by an objective point of view is very special.

Each type of point of view has its special functions, powers, and limitations. Great writers can either stay within the limits of these modes, mining them successfully, or combine modes. Melville in *Moby Dick*, Dickens in *Bleak House*, and Faulkner in *The Sound and the Fury* work marvelously with mixed modes, "bouncing" us, as Forster said, from one type of point of view to another. Writers also invent new techniques to enrich point of view, as when Joyce, Faulkner, and Virginia Woolf employ "stream of consciousness" methods that put us next to the highly associative thought processes of their characters, or when Jamaica Kincaid employs an experimental second-person or "you" point of view in her very short story, "Girl."

As you read the stories in this section and other stories in the anthology, ask yourself why the author has selected a certain point of view. Who tells the story? Is he or she reliable or unreliable, and why? What are the advantages and disadvantages of point of view in a specific tale? Are there any special features to the point of view? What effects does point of view have on character, language, and setting? Finally, how does point of view contribute to the development of the story's theme?

Characters live for us through point of view and other techniques. They live with or without authorial intrusion, apart from the author's real self. "We must," declared Flaubert, "by an effort of mind, go over to our characters, as it were, not make them come over to us." Point of view accomplishes this transformation. With a successful short story, the lens selected by the author always conveys the best and most illuminating perspective on character and action, subject and theme.

Hernando Téllez

JUST LATHER, THAT'S ALL

He said nothing when he entered. I was passing the best of my razors back and forth on a strop. When I recognized him I started to tremble. But he didn't notice. Hoping to conceal my emotion, I continued sharpening the razor. I tested it on the meat of my thumb, and then held it up to the light. At that moment he took off the bullet-studded belt that his gun holster dangled from. He hung it up on a wall hook and placed his military cap over it. Then he turned to me, loosening the knot of his tie, and said, "It's hot as hell. Give me a shave." He sat in the chair.

I estimated he had a four-day beard. The four days taken up by the latest expedition in search of our troops. His face seemed reddened, burned by the sun. Carefully, I began to prepare the soap. I cut off a few slices, dropped them into the cup, mixed in a bit of warm water, and began to stir with the brush. Immediately the foam began to rise. "The other boys in the group should have this much beard, too." I continued stirring the lather.

"But we did all right, you know. We got the main ones. We brought back some dead, and we've got some others still alive. But pretty soon they'll all be dead."

"How many did you catch?" I asked.

"Fourteen. We had to go pretty deep into the woods to find them. But we'll get even. Not one of them comes out of this alive, not one."

He leaned back on the chair when he saw me with the lather-covered brush in my hand. I still had to put the sheet on him. No doubt about it, I was upset. I took a sheet out of a drawer and knotted it around my customer's neck. He wouldn't stop talking. He probably thought I was in sympathy with his party.

"The town must have learned a lesson from what we did the other day," he said.

"Yes," I replied, securing the knot at the base of his dark, sweaty neck.

"That was a fine show, eh?"

"Very good," I answered, turning back for the brush. The man closed his eyes with a gesture of fatigue and sat waiting for the cool caress of the soap. I had never had him so close to me. The day he ordered the whole town to file into the patio of the school to see the four rebels hanging there, I came face to face with him for an instant. But the sight of the mutilated bodies kept me from noticing the face of the man who had directed it all, the face I was now about to take into my hands. It was not an unpleasant face, certainly. And the beard, which made him seem a bit older than he was, didn't suit him badly at all. His name was Torres. Captain Torres. A man of imagination, because who else would have thought of hanging the naked rebels and then holding target practice on certain parts of their bodies? I began to apply the first layer of soap. With his eyes closed, he continued. "Without any effort I could go straight to sleep," he said, "but there's plenty to do this afternoon." I stopped the lathering and asked with a feigned lack of interest: "A firing squad?" "Something like that, but a little slower." I got on with the job of lathering his beard. My hands started trembling again. The man could not possibly realize it, and this was in my favor. But I would have preferred that

he hadn't come. It was likely that many of our faction had seen him enter. And an enemy under one's roof imposes certain conditions. I would be obliged to shave that beard like any other one, carefully, gently, like that of any customer, taking pains to see that no single pore emitted a drop of blood. Being careful to see that the little tufts of hair did not lead the blade astray. Seeing that his skin ended up clean, soft, and healthy, so that passing the back of my hand over it I couldn't feel a hair. Yes, I was secretly a rebel, but I was also a conscientious barber, and proud of the preciseness of my profession. And this four-days' growth of beard was a fitting challenge.

I took the razor, opened up the two protective arms, exposed the blade and began the job, from one of the sideburns downward. The razor responded beautifully. His beard was inflexible and hard, not too long, but thick. Bit by bit the skin emerged. The razor rasped along, making its customary sound as fluffs of lather mixed with bits of hair gathered along the blade. I paused a moment to clean it, then took up the strop again to sharpen the razor, because I'm a barber who does things properly. The man, who had kept his eyes closed, opened them now, removed one of his hands from under the sheet, felt the spot on his face where the soap had been cleared off, and said, "Come to the school today at six o'clock." "The same thing as the other day?" I asked horrified. "It could be better," he replied. "What do you plan to do?" "I don't know yet. But we'll amuse ourselves." Once more he leaned back and closed his eyes. I approached him with the razor poised. "Do you plan to punish them all?" I ventured timidly. "All." The soap was drying on his face. I had to hurry. In the mirror I looked toward the street. It was the same as ever: the grocery store with two or three customers in it. Then I glanced at the clock: two-twenty in the afternoon. The razor continued on its downward stroke. Now from the other sideburn down. A thick, blue beard. He should have let it grow like some poets or priests do. It would suit him well. A lot of people wouldn't recognize him. Much to his benefit, I thought, as I attempted to cover the neck area smoothly. There, for sure, the razor had to be handled masterfully, since the hair, although softer, grew into little swirls. A curly beard. One of the tiny pores could be opened up and issue forth its pearl of blood. A good barber such as I prides himself on never allowing this to happen to a client. And this was a first-class client. How many of us had he ordered shot? How many of us had he ordered mutilated? It was better not to think about it. Torres did not know that I was his enemy. He did not know it nor did the rest. It was a secret shared by very few, precisely so that I could inform the revolutionaries of what Torres was doing in the town and of what he was planning each time he undertook a rebel-hunting excursion. So it was going to be very difficult to explain that I had him right in my hands and let him go peacefully—alive and shaved.

The beard was now almost completely gone. He seemed younger, less burdened by years than when he had arrived. I suppose this always happens with men who visit barber shops. Under the stroke of my razor Torres was being rejuvenated—rejuvenated because I am a good barber, the best in the town, if I may say so. A little more lather here, under his chin, on his Adam's apple, on this big vein. How hot it is getting! Torres must be sweating as much as I. But he is not afraid. He is a calm man, who is not even thinking about what he is going to do with the prisoners this afternoon. On the other hand I, with this razor in my hands, stroking and re-stroking this skin, trying to keep blood from oozing from these pores, can't even think clearly.

Damn him for coming, because I'm a revolutionary and not a murderer. And how easy it would be to kill him. And he deserves it. Does he? No! What the devil! No one deserves to have someone else make the sacrifice of becoming a murderer. What do you gain by it? Nothing. Others come along and still others, and the first ones kill the second ones and they the next ones and it goes on like this until everything is a sea of blood. I could cut this throat just so, zip! zip! I wouldn't give him time to complain and since he has his eyes closed he wouldn't see the glistening knife blade or my glistening eyes. But I'm trembling like a real murderer. Out of his neck a gush of blood would spout onto the sheet, on the chair, on my hands, on the floor. I would have to close the door. And the blood would keep inching along the floor, warm, ineradicable, uncontainable, until it reached the street, like a little scarlet stream. I'm sure that one solid stroke, one deep incision, would prevent any pain. He wouldn't suffer. But what would I do with the body? Where would I hide it? I would have to flee, leaving all I have behind, and take refuge far away, far, far away. But they would follow until they found me. "Captain Torres' murderer. He slit his throat while he was shaving him—a coward." And then on the other side. "The avenger of us all. A name to remember. (And here they would mention my name.) He was the town barber. No one knew he was defending our cause."

And what of all this? Murderer or hero? My destiny depends on the edge of this blade. I can turn my hand a bit more, press a little harder on the razor, and sink it in. The skin would give way like silk, like rubber, like the strop. There is nothing more tender than human skin and blood is always there, ready to pour forth. A blade like this doesn't fail. It is my best. But I don't want to be a murderer, no sir. You came to me for a shave. And I perform my work honorably. . . . I don't want blood on my hands. Just lather, that's all. You are an executioner and I am only a barber. Each person has his own place in the scheme of things. That's right. His own place.

Now his chin had been stroked clean and smooth. The man sat up and looked into the mirror. He rubbed his hands over his skin and felt it fresh, like new.

"Thanks," he said. He went to the hanger for his belt, pistol and cap. I must have been very pale; my shirt felt soaked. Torres finished adjusting the buckle, straightened his pistol in the holster and after automatically smoothing down his hair, he put on the cap. From his pants pocket he took out several coins to pay me for my services. And he began to head toward the door. In the doorway he paused for a moment, and turning to me he said:

"They told me that you'd kill me. I came to find out. But killing isn't easy. You can take my word for it." And he headed on down the street.

Translated by Donald Yates

QUESTIONS

1. Why does the narrator repeatedly reassure himself that he is a good barber? Do we find him to be reliable? What significance does this have to Torres's explaining at the end that "killing isn't easy"?
2. Does the author portray Torres sympathetically or unsympathetically? Explain your view, considering the importance of point of view.

3. The narrator describes in detail the process of shaving. Why do you suppose so much space is devoted to the specifics of this process?
4. We learn in the last line that Torres knew all along the barber was sympathetic to the rebel cause. Why did he risk his life merely for a shave?
5. What does the author gain by establishing a first-person point of view in this story?

David Leavitt

GRAVITY

Theo had a choice between a drug that would save his sight and a drug that would keep him alive, so he chose not to go blind. He stopped the pills and started the injections—these required the implantation of an unpleasant and painful catheter just above his heart—and within a few days the clouds in his eyes started to clear up; he could see again. He remembered going into New York City to a show with his mother, when he was twelve and didn't want to admit he needed glasses. "Can you read that?" she'd shouted, pointing to a Broadway marquee, and when he'd squinted, making out only one or two letters, she'd taken off her own glasses—harlequins with tiny rhinestones in the corners—and shoved them onto his face. The world came into focus, and he gasped, astonished at the precision around the edges of things, the legibility, the hard, sharp, colorful landscape. Sylvia had to squint through *Fiddler on the Roof* that day, but for Theo, his face masked by his mother's huge glasses, everything was as bright and vivid as a comic book. Even though people stared at him, and muttered things, Sylvia didn't care; he could *see*.

Because he was dying again, Theo moved back to his mother's house in New Jersey. The DHPG injections she took in stride—she'd seen her own mother through *her* dying, after all. Four times a day, with the equanimity of a nurse, she cleaned out the plastic tube implanted in his chest, inserted a sterilized hypodermic and slowly dripped the bag of sight-giving liquid into his veins. They endured this procedure silently, Sylvia sitting on the side of the hospital bed she'd rented for the duration of Theo's stay—his life, he sometimes thought—watching reruns of *I Love Lucy* or the news, while he tried not to think about the hard piece of pipe stuck into him, even though it was a constant reminder of how wide and unswimmable the gulf was becoming between him and the ever-receding shoreline of the well. And Sylvia was intricately cheerful. Each day she urged him to go out with her somewhere—to the library, or the little museum with the dinosaur replicas he'd been fond of as a child—and when his thinness and the cane drew stares, she'd maneuver him around the people who were staring, determined to shield him from whatever they might say or do. It had been the same that afternoon so many years ago, when she'd pushed him through a lobbyful of curious and laughing faces, determined that nothing should interfere with the spectacle of his seeing. What a pair they must have made, a boy in ugly glasses and a mother daring the world to say a word about it!

This warm, breezy afternoon in May they were shopping for revenge. "Your cousin Howard's engagement party is next month," Sylvia explained in the car. "A very nice girl from Livingston. I met her a few weeks ago, and really, she's a superior person."

"I'm glad," Theo said. "Congratulate Howie for me."

"Do you think you'll be up to going to the party?"

"I'm not sure. Would it be okay for me just to give him a gift?"

"You already have. A lovely silver tray, if I say so myself. The thank-you note's in the living room."

"Mom," Theo said, "why do you always have to—"

Sylvia honked her horn at a truck making an illegal left turn. "Better they should get something than no present at all, is what I say," she said. "But now, the problem is, *I* have to give Howie something, to be from me, and it better be good. It better be very, very good."

"Why?"

"Don't you remember that cheap little nothing Bibi gave you for your graduation? It was disgusting."

"I can't remember what she gave me."

"Of course you can't. It was a tacky pen-and-pencil set. Not even a real leather box. So naturally, it stands to reason that I have to get something truly spectacular for Howard's engagement. Something that will make Bibi blanch. Anyway, I think I've found just the thing, but I need your advice."

"Advice? Well, when my old roommate Nick got married, I gave him a garlic press. It cost five dollars and reflected exactly how much I felt, at that moment, our friendship was worth."

Sylvia laughed. "Clever. But my idea is much more brilliant, because it makes it possible for me to get back at Bibi *and* give Howard the nice gift he and his girl deserve." She smiled, clearly pleased with herself. "Ah, you live and learn."

"You live," Theo said.

Sylvia blinked. "Well, look, here we are." She pulled the car into a handicapped-parking place on Morris Avenue and got out to help Theo, but he was already hoisting himself up out of his seat, using the door handle for leverage. "I can manage myself," he said with some irritation. Sylvia stepped back.

"Clearly one advantage to all this for you," Theo said, balancing on his cane, "is that it's suddenly so much easier to get a parking place."

"Oh Theo, please," Sylvia said. "Look, here's where we're going."

She leaned him into a gift shop filled with porcelain statuettes of Snow White and all seven of the dwarves, music boxes which, when you opened them, played "The Shadow of Your Smile," complicated-smelling potpourris in purple wallpapered boxes, and stuffed snakes you were supposed to push up against drafty windows and doors.

"Mrs. Greenman," said an expansive, gray-haired man in a cream-colored cardigan sweater. "Look who's here, Archie, it's Mrs. Greenman."

Another man, this one thinner and balding, but dressed in an identical cardigan, peered out from the back of the shop. "Hello there!" he said, smiling. He looked at Theo, and his expression changed.

"Mr. Sherman, Mr. Baker. This is my son, Theo."

"Hello," Mr. Sherman and Mr. Baker said. They didn't offer to shake hands.

"Are you here for that item we discussed last week?" Mr. Sherman asked.

"Yes," Sylvia said. "I want advice from my son here." She walked over to a large ridged crystal bowl, a very fifties sort of bowl, stalwart and square-jawed. "What do you think? Beautiful, isn't it?"

"Mom, to tell the truth, I think it's kind of ugly."

"Four hundred and twenty-five dollars," Sylvia said admiringly. "You have to feel it."

Then she picked up the big bowl and tossed it to Theo, like a football.

The gentlemen in the cardigan sweaters gasped and did not exhale. When Theo caught it, it sank his hands. His cane rattled as it hit the floor.

"That's heavy," Sylvia said, observing with satisfaction how the bowl had weighted Theo's arms down. "And where crystal is concerned, heavy is impressive."

She took the bowl back from him and carried it to the counter. Mr. Sherman was mopping his brow. Theo looked at the floor, still surprised not to see shards of glass around his feet.

Since no one else seemed to be volunteering, he bent over and picked up the cane.

"Four hundred and fifty-nine, with tax," Mr. Sherman said, his voice still a bit shaky, and a look of relish came over Sylvia's face as she pulled out her checkbook to pay. Behind the counter, Theo could see Mr. Baker put his hand on his forehead and cast his eyes to the ceiling.

It seemed Sylvia had been looking a long time for something like this, something heavy enough to leave an impression, yet so fragile it could make you sorry.

They headed back out to the car.

"Where can we go now?" Sylvia asked, as she got in. "There must be someplace else to go."

"Home," Theo said. "It's almost time for my medicine."

"Really? Oh. All right." She pulled on her seat belt, inserted the car key in the ignition and sat there.

For just a moment, but perceptibly, her face broke. She squeezed her eyes shut so tight the blue shadow on the lids cracked.

Almost as quickly she was back to normal again, and they were driving. "It's getting hotter," Sylvia said. "Shall I put on the air?"

"Sure," Theo said. He was thinking about the bowl, or more specifically, about how surprising its weight had been, pulling his hands down. For a while now he'd been worried about his mother, worried about what damage his illness might secretly be doing to her that of course she would never admit. On the surface things seemed all right. She still broiled herself a skinned chicken breast for dinner every night, still swam a mile and a half a day, still kept used teabags wrapped in foil in the refrigerator. Yet she had also, at about three o'clock one morning, woken him up to tell him she was going to the twenty-four-hour supermarket, and was there anything he wanted. Then there was the gift shop: She had literally pitched that bowl toward him, pitched it like a ball, and as that great gleam of flight and potential regret came sailing his direction, it had occurred to him that she was trusting his two feeble hands, out of the whole world, to keep it from shattering. What was she trying to test? Was it his newly regained vision? Was it the assurance that he was there, alive, that he hadn't yet slipped past all her caring, a little lost boy in rhinestone-studded glasses? There are certain things you've already done before you even think how to do them—a child pulled from in front of a car, for instance, or the bowl, which Theo was holding before he could even begin to calculate its brief trajectory. It had pulled his arms down, and from that apish posture he'd looked at his mother, who smiled broadly, as if, in the war between heaviness and shattering, he'd just helped her win some small but sustaining victory.

QUESTIONS

1. Leavitt has been termed a "poet of the affections." Apply this insight to the complex relationship between Theo and his mother. How does point of view reveal this relationship?
2. Why is Sylvia "shopping for revenge"? Explain the significance of the bowl that she tosses to Theo. In terms of point of view, how do we get inside her mind?
3. Why does the author call his story "Gravity"?
4. How does point of view affect our understanding of the characters in this story?

Jamaica Kincaid

GIRL

Wash the white clothes on Monday and put them on the stone heap; wash the color clothes on Tuesday and put them on the clothes-line to dry; don't walk barehead in the hot sun; cook pumpkin fritters in very hot sweet oil; soak your little cloths right after you take them off; when buying cotton to make yourself a nice blouse, be sure that it doesn't have gum on it, because that way it won't hold up well after a wash; soak salt fish overnight before you cook it; is it true that you sing benna in Sunday school?; always eat your food in such a way that it won't turn someone else's stomach; on Sundays try to walk like a lady and not like the slut you are so bent on becoming; don't sing benna in Sunday school; you mustn't speak to wharf-rat boys, not even to give directions; don't eat fruits on the street—flies will follow you; *but I don't sing benna on Sundays at all and never in Sunday school;* this is how to sew on a button; this is how to make a buttonhole for the button you have just sewed on; this is how to hem a dress when you see the hem coming down and so to prevent yourself from looking like the slut I know you are so bent on becoming; this is how you iron your father's khaki shirt so that it doesn't have a crease; this is how you iron your father's khaki pants so that they don't have a crease; this is how you grow okra—far from the house, because okra tree harbors red ants; when you are growing dasheen, make sure it gets plenty of water or else it makes your throat itch when you are eating it; this is how you sweep a corner; this is how you sweep a whole house; this is how you sweep a yard; this is how you smile to someone you don't like too much; this is how you smile to someone you don't like at all; this is how you smile to someone you like completely; this is how you set a table for tea; this is how you set a table for dinner; this is how you set a table for dinner with an important guest; this is how you set a table for lunch; this is how you set a table for breakfast; this is how to behave in the presence of men who don't know you very well, and this way they won't recognize immediately the slut I have warned you against becoming; be sure to wash every day, even if it is with your own spit; don't squat down to play marbles—you are not a boy, you know; don't pick people's flowers—you might catch something; don't throw stones at blackbirds, because it might not be a blackbird at all; this is how to make a bread pudding; this is how to make doukona; this is how to make pepper pot; this is how to make a good medicine for a cold; this is how to make a good medicine to throw away a child before it even becomes a child; this is how to catch a fish; this is how to throw back a fish you don't like, and that way something bad won't fall on you; this is how to bully a man; this is how a man bullies you; this is how to love a man, and if this doesn't work there are other ways, and if they don't work don't feel too bad about giving up; this is how to spit up in the air if you feel like it, and this is how to move quick so that it doesn't fall on you; this is how to make ends meet; always squeeze bread to make sure it's fresh; *but what if the baker won't let me feel the bread?;* you mean to say that after all you are really going to be the kind of woman who the baker won't let near the bread?

QUESTIONS

1. Who is speaking in this sketch, and to whom? Is the speaker a trustworthy or reliable guide?
2. The author was born in Saint Johns, the capital of the West Indian island nation of Antigua. What do we learn in the story about the culture of this Caribbean island?
3. This is a very short story. Does a theme emerge? Why or why not?

5. Setting

Setting is the place and time of a story—where and when the narrative takes place. Real or imaginary, concrete or symbolic, a "slice of life" or a cultural panorama, a moment or an eternity, setting is the dramatic backdrop for a story. It is the wellspring of a story's mood or atmosphere, the shaper of characters' actions and emotional responses, the prompter of events.

As the place of fiction, setting is generally a physical locale that shapes a story's mood, its emotional aura or quality. Although characterization, plot, and style are also components of mood, it is setting—place, time, landscape, weather—that situates us emotionally in the universe of fiction. Mood is often equated with atmosphere, and with respect to setting this is a useful correspondence, for atmosphere grows from a physical area—a palace room, perhaps, or a Bowery flophouse. It grows also from time in a given place: from the historical moment of Hawthorne's Puritan New England or Chekhov's Russia, the seasonal rhythms of some of Faulkner's greatest stories, the realistic terrain of Hemingway tales, the timeless and magical settings of García Márquez. Atmosphere and mood, at times used interchangeably, are conceived to condition our responses to fiction.

Setting can be dark or light, melancholy or gay, but it cannot exist without description. In her 1920 novel *The Age of Innocence*, which was awarded the Pulitzer Prize for Literature, Edith Wharton re-created the spirit of New York City in the 1870s and the social history of that gas-lit era through elegant sequences of description like the one that follows.

Old-fashioned New York dined at seven, and the habit of after-dinner calls, though derided in Archer's set, still generally prevailed. As the young man strolled up Fifth Avenue from Waverley Place, the long thoroughfare was deserted but for a group of carriages standing before the Reggie Chiverses' (where there was a dinner for the Duke), and the occasional figure of an elderly gentleman in heavy overcoat and muffler ascending a brownstone doorstep and disappearing into a gas-lit hall. Thus, as Archer crossed Washington Square, he remarked

that old Mr. du Lac was calling on his cousins the Dagonets, and turning down the corner of West Tenth Street he saw Mr. Skipworth, of his own firm, obviously bound on a visit to the Miss Lannings. A little farther up Fifth Avenue, Beaufort appeared on his doorstep, darkly projected against a blaze of light, descended to his private brougham, and rolled away to a mysterious and probably unmentionable destination. It was not an Opera night, and no one was giving a party, so that Beaufort's outing was undoubtedly of a clandestine nature. Archer connected it in his mind with a little house beyond Lexington Avenue in which beribboned window curtains and flower-boxes had recently appeared, and before whose newly painted door the canary-coloured brougham of Miss Fanny Ring was frequently seen to wait.

Here the author has set time, place, mood, and a sense of culture, molding character with marvelously compressed and precise description.

Consider also the setting created by one of Wharton's contemporaries, Ernest Hemingway, in this sketch from *In Our Time* (1925):

They shot the six cabinet ministers at half-past six in the morning against the wall of a hospital. There were pools of water in the courtyard. There were wet leaves on the paving of the courtyard. It rained hard. All the shutters of the hospital were nailed shut. One of the ministers was sick with typhoid. Two soldiers carried him downstairs and out into the rain. They tried to hold him up against the wall but he sat down in a puddle of water. The other five stood very quietly against the wall. Finally the officer told the soldiers it was no good trying to make him stand up. When they fired the first volley he was sitting down in the water with his head on his knees.

Here, setting crucially involves time, place, character, action, and style. We are introduced to an execution at sunrise, a harrowing moment that seems to stretch for us interminably, almost as if we are tracking it with a slow-motion camera. The atmosphere or mood is one of unmitigated gloom: the time is autumn, the ground is wet, the dead leaves point us toward the inevitable execution of the cabinet ministers. It doesn't matter that we know little about the identities of the protagonists and antagonists—who the good guys and the bad guys are. Rather, Hemingway gives us a realistic setting, charges it with imagery, symbolism, and irony, and then forces us to extract meaning or a "theme" from this brief, violent vignette of modern life.

Hemingway encountered the poet, dramatist, fiction writer, and journalist Langston Hughes on a battlefield while both were covering the Spanish Civil War. Hughes' story "On The Road," set in the early 1930s in the United States, a time of great hardship for most Americans, reveals the importance of setting as a backdrop for this symbolic, richly ironic tale. The opening paragraphs of the story establish the mood immediately, one of cold, wet, lonely discomfort:

He was not interested in the snow. When he got off the freight, one early evening during the depression, Sargent never even noticed the snow. But he must have felt it seeping down his neck, cold, wet, sopping in in his shoes. But if you had asked him, he wouldn't have noticed it was snowing. Sargent didn't see the snow, not even under the bright light of the main street, falling white and flaky against the night. He was too hungry, too sleepy, too tired.

The Reverend Mr. Dorset, however, saw the snow when he switched on his porch light, opened the front door of his parsonage, and found standing there before him a big black man with snow on his face, a human piece of night with snow on his face—obviously unemployed.

Sargent has landed in a part of the country where black people are not ordinarily seen. He is obviously a "hobo," one of the millions of wandering homeless at that time. He is big and he is black—"a human piece of the night." Hughes has established not only mood, but the possibility of conflict, even on the parsonage porch. How does Christianity play out in this meeting? The irony extends from the parsonage to the jail to a meeting with Christ, which is, of course, Hughes' commentary on Christianity or lack of it in the society of the 1930s.

William Faulkner is yet another writer who, like Wharton, Hughes, and Hemingway, wrote major fiction in the 1920s and 1930s. In his famous story, "A Rose for Emily," which appears in Chapter 2, Faulkner reveals the way in which a setting can be so charged with meaning that it conveys not just atmosphere but also an understanding of the emotional makeup of the central character and a critique of culture. This is how Faulkner describes Emily Grierson's family house.

> It was a big, squarish frame house that had once been white, decorated with cupolas and spires and scrolled balconies in the heavily lightsome style of the seventies, set on what had once been our most select street. But garages and cotton gins had encroached and obliterated even the august names of that neighborhood; only Miss Emily's house was left, lifting its stubborn and coquettish decay above the cotton wagons and the gasoline pumps—an eyesore among eyesores.

In this paragraph, Faulkner reveals the organic function of setting for our experience of fiction. We can *see* this house, a dim and mildly Gothic incarnation of an earlier period in the history of the American South. As we read this story, we apprehend the way the house is a psychological extension of Emily's own personality. Terrors hidden inside this Gothic structure await those readers who enter the interior world of its setting.

If "A Rose for Emily" had been set outside the South, its impact might not have been quite as powerful, nor its mood so awesome. Faulkner's South, like that of Richard Wright, Arna Bontemps, Flannery O'Connor, and Eudora Welty, is a complex and potentially macabre cultural setting, humming with the unceasing potential for conflict. As Eudora Welty once observed, the "sense of place," or sense of setting, in fiction is the center of all our values and concerns. Through setting, we receive a tangible impression of the writer's world.

Nathaniel Hawthorne

YOUNG
GOODMAN BROWN

Young Goodman Brown came forth at sunset into the street at Salem village; but put his head back, after crossing the threshold, to exchange a parting kiss with his young wife. And Faith, as the wife was aptly named, thrust her own pretty head into the street, letting the wind play with the pink ribbons of her cap while she called to Goodman Brown.

"Dearest heart," whispered she, softly and rather sadly, when her lips were close to his ear, "prithee put off your journey until sunrise and sleep in your own bed to-night. A lone woman is troubled with such dreams and such thoughts that she's afeared of herself sometimes. Pray tarry with me this night, dear husband, of all nights in the year."

"My love and my Faith," replied young Goodman Brown, "of all nights in the year, this one night must I tarry away from thee. My journey, as thou callest it, forth and back again, must needs be done 'twixt now and sunrise. What, my sweet, pretty wife, dost thou doubt me already, and we but three months married?"

"Then God bless you!" said Faith, with the pink ribbons; "and may you find all well when you come back."

"Amen!" cried Goodman Brown. "Say thy prayers, dear Faith, and go to bed at dusk, and no harm will come to thee."

So they parted; and the young man pursued his way until, being about to turn the corner by the meeting-house, he looked back and saw the head of Faith still peeping after him with a melancholy air, in spite of her pink ribbons.

"Poor little Faith!" thought he, for his heart smote him. "What a wretch am I to leave her on such an errand! She talks of dreams, too. Methought as she spoke there was trouble in her face, as if a dream had warned her what work is to be done to-night. But no, no; 't would kill her to think it. Well, she's a blessed angel on earth; and after this one night I'll cling to her skirts and follow her to heaven."

With this excellent resolve for the future, Goodman Brown felt himself justified in making more haste on his present evil purpose. He had taken a dreary road, darkened by all the gloomiest trees of the forest, which barely stood aside to let the narrow path creep through, and closed immediately behind. It was all as lonely as could be; and there is this peculiarity in such a solitude, that the traveller knows not who may be concealed by the innumerable trunks and the thick boughs overhead; so that with lonely footsteps he may yet be passing through an unseen multitude.

"There may be a devilish Indian behind every tree," said Goodman Brown to himself; and he glanced fearfully behind him as he added, "What if the devil himself should be at my very elbow!"

His head being turned back, he passed a crook of the road, and, looking forward again, beheld the figure of a man, in grave and decent attire, seated at the foot of an old tree. He arose at Goodman Brown's approach and walked onward side by side with him.

"You are late, Goodman Brown," said he. "The clock of the Old South was striking as I came through Boston, and that is full fifteen minutes agone."

"Faith kept me back a while," replied the young man, with a tremor in his voice, caused by the sudden appearance of his companion, though not wholly unexpected.

It was now deep dusk in the forest, and deepest in that part of it where these two were journeying. As nearly as could be discerned, the second traveller was about fifty years old, apparently in the same rank of life as Goodman Brown, and bearing a considerable resemblance to him, though perhaps more in expression than features. Still they might have been taken for father and son. And yet, though the elder person was as simply clad as the younger, and as simple in manner too, he had an indescribable air of one who knew the world, and who would not have felt abashed at the governor's dinner table or in King William's court, were it possible that his affairs should call him thither. But the only thing about him that could be fixed upon as remarkable was his staff, which bore the likeness of a great black snake, so curiously wrought that it might almost be seen to twist and wriggle itself like a living serpent. This, of course, must have been an ocular deception, assisted by the uncertain light.

"Come, Goodman Brown," cried his fellow-traveler, "this is a dull pace for the beginning of a journey. Take my staff, if you are so soon weary."

"Friend," said the other, exchanging his slow pace for a full stop, "having kept covenant by meeting thee here, it is my purpose now to return whence I came. I have scruples touching the matter thou wot'st of."

"Sayest thou so?" replied he of the serpent, smiling apart. "Let us walk on, nevertheless, reasoning as we go; and if I convince thee not thou shalt turn back. We are but a little way in the forest yet."

"Too far! too far!" exclaimed the goodman, unconsciously resuming his walk. "My father never went into the woods on such an errand, nor his father before him. We have been a race of honest men and good Christians since the days of the martyrs; and shall I be the first of the name of Brown that ever took this path and kept"—

"Such company, thou wouldst say," observed the elder person, interpreting his pause. "Well said, Goodman Brown! I have been as well acquainted with your family as with ever a one among the Puritans; and that's no trifle to say. I helped your grandfather, the constable, when he lashed the Quaker woman so smartly through the streets of Salem; and it was I that brought your father a pitchpine knot, kindled at my own hearth, to set fire to an Indian village, in King Philip's war. They were my good friends, both; and many a pleasant walk have we had along this path, and returned merrily after midnight. I would fain be friends with you for their sake."

"If it be as thou sayest," replied Goodman Brown, "I marvel they never spoke of these matters; or, verily, I marvel not, seeing that the least rumor of the sort would have driven them from New England. We are a people of prayer, and good works to boot, and abide no such wickedness."

"Wickedness or not," said the traveller with the twisted staff, "I have a very general acquaintance here in New England. The deacons of many a church have drunk the communion wine with me; the selectmen of divers towns make me their chairman; and a majority of the Great and General Court are firm supporters of my interest. The governor and I, too—But these are state secrets."

"Can this be so?" cried Goodman Brown, with a stare of amazement at his undisturbed companion. "Howbeit, I have nothing to do with the governor and council; they have their own ways, and are no rule for a simple husbandman like me. But, were I to go on with thee, how should I meet the eye of that good old man, our minister, at Salem village? Oh, his voice would make me tremble both Sabbath day and lecture day."

Thus far the elder traveller had listened with due gravity; but now burst into a fit of irrepressible mirth, shaking himself so violently that his snake-like staff actually seemed to wriggle in sympathy.

"Ha! ha! ha!" shouted he again and again; then composing himself, "Well, go on, Goodman Brown, go on; but, prithee, don't kill me with laughing."

"Well, then, to end the matter at once," said Goodman Brown, considerably nettled, "there is my wife, Faith. It would break her dear little heart; and I'd rather break my own."

"Nay, if that be the case," answered the other, "e'en go thy ways, Goodman Brown. I would not for twenty old women like the one hobbling before us that Faith should come to any harm."

As he spoke he pointed his staff at a female figure on the path, in whom Goodman Brown recognized a very pious and exemplary dame, who had taught him his catechism in youth, and was still his moral and spiritual adviser, jointly with the minister and Deacon Gookin.

"A marvel, truly, that Goody Cloyse should be so far in the wilderness at nightfall," said he. "But with your leave, friend, I shall take a cut through the woods until we have left this Christian woman behind. Being a stranger to you, she might ask whom I was consorting with and whither I was going."

"Be it so," said his fellow-traveller. "Betake you the woods, and let me keep the path."

Accordingly the young man turned aside; but took care to watch his companion, who advanced softly along the road until he had come within a staff's length of the old dame. She, meanwhile, was making the best of her way, with singular speed for so aged a woman, and mumbling some indistinct words—a prayer, doubtless—as she went. The traveller put forth his staff and touched her withered neck with what seemed the serpent's tail.

"The devil!" screamed the pious old lady.

"Then Goody Cloyse knows her old friend?" observed the traveller, confronting her and leaning on his writhing stick.

"Ah, forsooth, and is it your worship indeed?" cried the good dame. "Yea, truly is it, and in the very image of my old gossip, Goodman Brown, the grandfather of the silly fellow that now is. But—would your worship believe it?—my broomstick hath strangely disappeared, stolen, as I suspect, by that unhanged witch, Goody Cory, and that, too, when I was all anointed with the juice of smallage, and cinquefoil, and wolf's bane"—

"Mingled with fine wheat and the fat of a new-born babe," said the shape of old Goodman Brown.

"Ah, your worship knows the recipe," cried the old lady, cackling aloud. "So, as I was saying, being all ready for the meeting, and no horse to ride on, I made up my mind to foot it; for they tell me there is a nice young man to be taken into communion to-night. But now your good worship will lend me your arm, and we shall be there in a twinkling."

"That can hardly be," answered her friend. "I may not spare you my arm, Goody Cloyse; but here is my staff, if you will."

So saying, he threw it down at her feet, where, perhaps, it assumed life, being one of the rods which its owner had formerly lent to the Egyptian magi. Of this fact, however, Goodman Brown could not take cognizance. He had cast up his eyes in astonishment, and, looking down again, beheld neither Goody Cloyse nor the serpentine staff, but this fellow-traveller alone, who waited for him as calmly as if nothing had happened.

"That old woman taught me my catechism," said the young man; and there was a world of meaning in this simple comment.

They continued to walk onward, while the elder traveller exhorted his companion to make good speed and persevere in the path, discoursing so aptly that his arguments seemed rather to spring up in the bosom of his auditor than to be suggested by himself. As they went, he plucked a branch of maple to serve for a walking stick, and began to strip it of the twigs and little boughs, which were wet with evening dew. The moment his fingers touched them they became strangely withered and dried up as with a week's sunshine. Thus the pair proceeded, at a good free pace, until suddenly, in a gloomy hollow of the road, Goodman Brown sat himself down on the stump of a tree and refused to go any farther.

"Friend," said he, stubbornly, "my mind is made up. Not another step will I budge on this errand. What if a wretched old woman do choose to go to the devil when I thought she was going to heaven: is that any reason why I should quit my dear Faith and go after her?"

"You will think better of this by and by," said his acquaintance, composedly. "Sit here and rest yourself a while; and when you feel like moving again, there is my staff to help you along."

Without more words, he threw his companion the maple stick, and was as speedily out of sight as if he had vanished into the deepening gloom. The young man sat a few moments by the roadside, applauding himself greatly, and thinking with how clear a conscience he should meet the minister in his morning walk, nor shrink from the eye of good old Deacon Gookin. And what calm sleep would be his that very night, which was to have been spent so wickedly, but so purely and sweetly now, in the arms of Faith! Amidst these pleasant and praiseworthy meditations, Goodman Brown heard the tramp of horses along the road, and deemed it advisable to conceal himself within the verge of the forest, conscious of the guilty purpose that had brought him thither, though now so happily turned from it.

On came the hoof tramps and the voices of the riders, two grave old voices, conversing soberly as they drew near. These mingled sounds appeared to pass along the road, within a few yards of the young man's hiding-place; but, owing doubtless to the depth of the gloom at that particular spot, neither the travellers nor their steeds were visible. Though their figures brushed the small boughs by the wayside, it could not be seen that they intercepted, even for a moment, the faint gleam from the strip of bright sky athwart which they must have passed. Goodman Brown alternately crouched and

stood on tiptoe, pulling aside the branches and thrusting forth his head as far as he durst without discerning so much as a shadow. It vexed him the more, because he could have sworn, were such a thing possible, that he recognized the voices of the minister and Deacon Gookin, jogging along quietly, as they were wont to do, when bound to some ordination of ecclesiastical council. While yet within hearing, one of the riders stopped to pluck a switch.

"Of the two, reverend sir," said the voice like the deacon's, "I had rather miss an ordination dinner than to-night's meeting. They tell me that some of our community are to be here from Falmouth and beyond, and others from Connecticut and Rhode Island, besides several of the Indian powwows, who, after their fashion, know almost as much deviltry as the best of us. Moreover, there is a goodly young woman to be taken into communion."

"Mighty well, Deacon Gookin!" replied the solemn old tones of the minister. "Spur up, or we shall be late. Nothing can be done, you know, until I get on the ground."

The hoofs clattered again; and the voices, talking so strangely in the empty air, passed on through the forest, where no church had ever been gathered or solitary Christian prayed. Whither, then, could these holy men be journeying so deep into the heathen wilderness? Young Goodman Brown caught hold of a tree for support, being ready to sink down on the ground, faint and overburdened with the heavy sickness of his heart. He looked up to the sky, doubting whether there really was a heaven above him. Yet there was the blue arch, and the stars brightening it.

"With heaven above and Faith below, I will yet stand firm against the devil!" cried Goodman Brown.

While he still gazed upward into the deep arch of the firmament and had lifted his hands to pray, a cloud, though no wind was stirring, hurried across the zenith and hid the brightening stars. The blue sky was still visible, except directly overhead, where this black mass of cloud was sweeping swiftly northward. Aloft in the air, as if from the depths of the cloud, came a confused and doubtful sound of voices. Once the listener fancied that he could distinguish the accents of towns-people of his own, men and women, both pious and ungodly, many of whom he had met at the communion table, and had seen others rioting at the tavern. The next moment, so indistinct were the sounds, he doubted whether he had heard aught but the murmur of the old forest, whispering without a wind. Then came a stronger swell of those familiar tones, heard daily in the sunshine at Salem village, but never until now from a cloud of night. There was one voice, of a young woman, uttering lamentations, yet with an uncertain sorrow, and entreating for some favor, which, perhaps, it would grieve her to obtain; and all the unseen multitude, both saints and sinners, seemed to encourage her onward.

"Faith!" shouted Goodman Brown, in a voice of agony and desperation; and the echoes of the forest mocked him, crying, "Faith! Faith!" as if bewildered wretches were seeking her all through the wilderness.

The cry of grief, rage, and terror was yet piercing the night, when the unhappy husband held his breath for a response. There was a scream, drowned immediately in a louder murmur of voices, fading into far-off laughter, as the dark cloud swept away, leaving the clear and silent sky above Goodman Brown. But something fluttered lightly down through the air and caught on the branch of a tree. The young man seized it, and beheld a pink ribbon.

"My Faith is gone!" cried he, after one stupefied moment. "There is no good on earth; and sin is but a name. Come, devil; for to thee is this world given."

And, maddened with despair, so that he laughed loud and long, did Goodman Brown grasp his staff and set forth again, at such a rate that he seemed to fly along the forest path rather than to walk or run. The road grew wilder and drearier and more faintly traced, and vanished at length, leaving him in the heart of the dark wilderness, still rushing onward with the instinct that guides mortal man to evil. The whole forest was peopled with frightful sounds—the creaking of the trees, the howling of wild beasts, and the yell of Indians; while sometimes the wind tolled like a distant church bell, and sometimes gave a broad roar around the traveller, as if all Nature were laughing him to scorn. But he was himself the chief horror of the scene, and shrank not from its other horrors.

"Ha! ha! ha!" roared Goodman Brown when the wind laughed at him. "Let us hear which will laugh loudest. Think not to frighten me with your deviltry. Come witch, come wizard, come Indian powwow, come devil himself, and here comes Goodman Brown. You may as well fear him as he fear you."

In truth, all through the haunted forest there could be nothing more frightful than the figure of Goodman Brown. On he flew among the black pines, brandishing his staff with frenzied gestures, now giving vent to an inspiration of horrid blasphemy, and now shouting forth such laughter as set all the echoes of the forest laughing like demons around him. The fiend in his own shape is less hideous than when he rages in the breast of man. Thus sped the demoniac on his course, until, quivering among the trees, he saw a red light before him, as when the felled trunks and branches of a clearing have been set on fire, and throw up their lurid blaze against the sky, at the hour of midnight. He paused, in a lull of the tempest that had driven him onward, and heard the swell of what seemed a hymn, rolling solemnly from a distance with the weight of many voices. He knew the tune; it was a familiar one in the choir of the village meeting-house. The verse died heavily away, and was lengthened by a chorus, not of human voices, but of all the sounds of the benighted wilderness pealing in awful harmony together. Goodman Brown cried out, and his cry was lost to his own ear by its unison with the cry of the desert.

In the interval of silence he stole forward until the light glared full upon his eyes. At one extremity of an open space, hemmed in by the dark wall of the forest, arose a rock, bearing some rude, natural resemblance either to an altar or a pulpit, and surrounded by four blazing pines, their tops aflame, their stems untouched, like candles at an evening meeting. The mass of foliage that had overgrown the summit of the rock was all on fire, blazing high into the night and fitfully illuminating the whole field. Each pendent twig and leafy festoon was in a blaze. As the red light arose and fell, a numerous congregation alternately shone forth, then disappeared in shadow, and again grew, as it were, out of the darkness, peopling the heart of the solitary woods at once.

"A grave and dark-clad company," quoth Goodman Brown.

In truth they were such. Among them, quivering to and fro between gloom and splendor, appeared faces that would be seen next day at the council board of the

province, and others which, Sabbath after Sabbath, looked devoutly heavenward, and benignantly over the crowded pews, from the holiest pulpits in the land. Some affirm that the lady of the governor was there. At least there were high dames well known to her, and wives of honored husbands, and widows, a great multitude, and ancient maidens, all of excellent repute, and fair young girls, who trembled lest their mothers should espy them. Either the sudden gleams of light flashing over the obscure field bedazzled Goodman Brown, or he recognized a score of the church members of Salem village famous for their especial sanctity. Good old Deacon Gookin had arrived, and waited at the skirts of that venerable saint, his revered pastor. But irreverently consorting with these grave, reputable, and pious people, these elders of the church, these chaste dames and dewy virgins, there were men of dissolute lives and women of spotted fame, wretches given over to all mean and filthy vice, and suspected even of horrid crimes. It was strange to see that the good shrank not from the wicked, nor were the sinners abashed by the saints. Scattered also among their pale-faced enemies were the Indian priests, or powwows, who had often scared their native forest with more hideous incantations than any known to English witchcraft.

"But where is Faith?" thought Goodman Brown; and, as hope came into his heart, he trembled.

Another verse of the hymn arose, a slow and mournful strain, such as the pious love, but joined to words which expressed all that our nature can conceive of sin, and darkly hinted at far more. Unfathomable to mere mortals is the lore of fiends. Verse after verse was sung; and still the chorus of the desert swelled between like the deepest tone of a mighty organ; and with the final peal of that dreadful anthem there came a sound, as if the roaring wind, the rushing streams, the howling beasts, and every other voice of the unconcerted wilderness were mingling and according with the voice of guilty man in homage to the prince of all. The four blazing pines threw up a loftier flame, and obscurely discovered shapes and visages of horror on the smoke wreaths above the impious assembly. At the same moment the fire on the rock shot redly forth and formed a glowing arch above its base, where now appeared a figure. With reverence be it spoken, the figure bore no slight similitude, both in garb and manner, to some grave divine of the New England churches.

"Bring forth the converts!" cried a voice that echoed through the field and rolled into the forest.

At the word, Goodman Brown stepped forth from the shadow of the trees and approached the congregation, with whom he felt a loathful brotherhood by the sympathy of all that was wicked in his heart. He could have well-nigh sworn that the shape of his own dead father beckoned him to advance, looking downward from a smoke wreath, while a woman, with dim features of despair, threw out her hand to warn him back. Was it his mother? But he had no power to retreat one step, nor to resist, even in thought, when the minister and good old Deacon Gookin seized his arms and led him to the blazing rock. Thither came also the slender form of a veiled female, led between Goody Cloyse, that pious teacher of the catechism, and Martha Carrier, who had received the devil's promise to be queen of hell. A rampant hag was she. And there stood the proselytes beneath the canopy of fire.

"Welcome, my children," said the dark figure, "to the communion of your race.

Ye have found thus young your nature and your destiny. My children, look behind you!"

They turned; and flashing forth, as it were, in a sheet of flame, the fiend worshippers were seen; the smile of welcome gleamed darkly on every visage.

"There," resumed the sable form, "are all whom ye have reverenced from youth. Ye deemed them holier than yourselves, and shrank from your own sin, contrasting it with their lives of righteousness and prayerful aspirations heavenward. Yet here are they all in my worshipping assembly. This night it shall be granted you to know their secret deeds: how hoary-bearded elders of the church have whispered wanton words to the young maids of their households; how many a woman, eager for widows' weeds, has given her husband a drink at bedtime and let him sleep his last sleep in her bosom; how beardless youths have made haste to inherit their fathers' wealth; and how fair damsels—blush not, sweet ones—have dug little graves in the garden, and bidden me, the sole guest, to an infant's funeral. By the sympathy of your human hearts for sin ye shall scent out all the places—whether in church, bed-chamber, street, field, or forest—where crime has been committed, and shall exult to behold the whole earth one stain of guilt, one mighty blood spot. Far more than this. I shall be yours to penetrate, in every bosom, the deep mystery of sin, the fountain of all wicked arts, and which inexhaustibly supplies more evil impulses than human power—than my power at its utmost—can make manifest in deeds. And now, my children, look upon each other."

They did so; and, by the blaze of the hell-kindled torches, the wretched man beheld his Faith, and the wife her husband, trembling before that unhallowed altar.

"Lo, there ye stand, my children," said the figure, in a deep and solemn tone, almost sad with its despairing awfulness, as if his once angelic nature could yet mourn for our miserable race. "Depending upon one another's hearts, ye had still hoped that virtue were not at all a dream. Now are ye undeceived. Evil is the nature of mankind. Evil must be your only happiness. Welcome again, my children, to the communion of your race."

"Welcome," repeated the fiend worshippers, in one cry of despair and triumph.

And there they stood, the only pair, as it seemed, who were yet hesitating on the verge of wickedness in this dark world. A basin was hollowed, naturally, in the rock. Did it contain water, reddened by the lurid light? or was it blood? or, perchance, a liquid flame? Herein did the shape of evil dip his hand and prepare to lay the mark of baptism upon their foreheads, that they might be partakers of the mystery of sin, more conscious of the secret guilt of others, both in deed and thought, than they could now be of their own. The husband cast one look at his pale wife, and Faith at him. What polluted wretches would the next glance show them to each other, shuddering alike at what they disclosed and what they saw!

"Faith! Faith!" cried the husband, "look up to heaven, and resist the wicked one."

Whether Faith obeyed he knew not. Hardly had he spoken when he found himself amid calm night and solitude, listening to a roar of the wind which died heavily away through the forest. He staggered against the rock, and felt it chill and damp; while a hanging twig, that had been all on fire, besprinkled his cheek with the coldest dew.

The next morning young Goodman Brown came slowly into the street of Salem village, staring around him like a bewildered man. The good old minister was taking a walk along the graveyard to get an appetite for breakfast and meditate his sermon, and bestowed a blessing, as he passed, on Goodman Brown. He shrank from the venerable saint as if to avoid an anathema. Old Deacon Gookin was at domestic worship, and the holy words of his prayer were heard through the open window. "What God doth the wizard pray to?" quoth Goodman Brown. Goody Cloyse, that excellent old Christian, stood in the early sunshine at her own lattice, catechizing a little girl who had brought her a pint of morning's milk. Goodman Brown snatched away the child as from the grasp of the fiend himself. Turning the corner by the meeting-house, he spied the head of Faith, with the pink ribbons, gazing anxiously forth, and bursting into such joy at sight of him that she skipped along the street and almost kissed her husband before the whole village. But Goodman Brown looked sternly and sadly into her face, and passed on without a greeting.

Had Goodman Brown fallen asleep in the forest and only dreamed a wild dream of a witch-meeting?

Be it so if you will; but, alas! it was a dream of evil omen for young Goodman Brown. A stern, a sad, a darkly meditative, a distrustful, if not a desperate man did he become from the night of that fearful dream. On the Sabbath day, when the congregation were singing a holy psalm, he could not listen because an anthem of sin rushed loudly upon his ear and drowned all the blessed strain. When the minister spoke from the pulpit, with power and fervid eloquence, and with his hand on the open Bible, of the sacred truths of our religion, and of saint-like lives and triumphant deaths, and of future bliss or misery unutterable, then did Goodman Brown turn pale, dreading lest the roof should thunder down upon the gray blasphemer and his hearers. Often, awaking suddenly at midnight, he shrank from the bosom of Faith, and at morning or eventide, when the family knelt down at prayer, he scowled, and muttered to himself, and gazed sternly at his wife, and turned away. And when he had lived long, and was borne to his grave, a hoary corpse, followed by Faith, an aged woman, and children and grandchildren, a goodly procession, besides neighbors not a few, they carved no hopeful verse upon his tombstone; for his dying hour was gloom.

QUESTIONS

1. How would you characterize the story's setting? What particular passages establish the setting?
2. Goodman Brown tells the man with the staff that he does not want to journey with him through the forest, yet he does so anyway. Explain this seeming paradox.
3. Is the witches' meeting a dream or reality? Why is this setting so memorable? Does it matter to the theme of the story? Explain.
4. Why does Goodman Brown have a negative response to his wife when he sees her in the village? Why has Goodman Brown's life become gloomy and dismal at the end of the story? Describe the setting at the end of this tale.

James Joyce

ARABY

North Richmond Street, being blind, was a quiet street except at the hour when the Christian Brothers School set the boys free. An uninhabited house of two stories stood at the blind end, detached from its neighbors in a square ground. The other houses of the street, conscious of decent lives within them, gazed at one another with brown imperturbable faces.

The former tenant of our house, a priest, had died in the back drawing-room. Air, musty from having been long enclosed, hung in all the rooms, and the waste room behind the kitchen was littered with old useless papers. Among these, I found a few paper-covered books, the pages of which were curled and damp: *The Abbott*, by Walter Scott, *The Devout Communicant* and *The Memoirs of Vidocq*. I liked the last best because its leaves were yellow. The wild garden behind the house contained a central apple-tree and a few straggling bushes under one of which I found the late tenant's rusty bicycle-pump. He had been a very charitable priest; in his will he had left all his money to institutions and the furniture of his house to his sister.

When the short days of winter came dusk fell before we had well eaten our dinners. When we met in the street the houses had grown somber. The space of sky above us was the color of ever-changing violet and towards it the lamps of the street lifted their feeble lanterns. The cold air stung us and we played till our bodies glowed. Our shouts echoed in the silent street. The career of our play brought us through the dark muddy lanes behind the houses where we ran the gauntlet of the rough tribes from the cottages, to the back doors of the dark dripping gardens where odors arose from the ashpits, to the dark odorous stables where a coachman smoothed and combed the horse or shook music from the buckled harness. When we returned to the street light from the kitchen windows had filled the areas. If my uncle was seen turning the corner we hid in the shadow until we had seen him safely housed. Or if Mangan's sister came out on the doorstep to call her brother in to his tea we watched her from our shadow peer up and down the street. We waited to see whether she would remain or go in and, if she remained, we left our shadow and walked up to Mangan's steps resignedly. She was waiting for us, her figure defined by the light from the half-opened door. Her brother always teased her before he obeyed and I stood by the railings looking at her. Her dress swung as she moved her body and the soft rope of her hair tossed from side to side.

Every morning I lay on the floor in the front parlor watching her door. The blind was pulled down to within an inch of the sash so that I could not be seen. When she came out on the doorstep my heart leaped. I ran to the hall, seized my books and followed her. I kept her brown figure always in my eye and, when we came near the point at which our ways diverged, I quickened my pace and passed her. This happened morning after morning. I had never spoken to her, except for a few casual words, and yet her name was like a summons to all my foolish blood.

Her image accompanied me even in places the most hostile to romance. On Saturday evenings when my aunt went marketing I had to go to carry some of the parcels.

We walked through the flaring streets, jostled by drunken men and bargaining women, amid the curses of laborers, the shrill litanies of shopboys who stood on guard by the barrels of pigs' cheeks, the nasal chanting of street-singers, who sang a *come-all-you* about O'Donovan Rossa, or a ballad about the troubles in our native land. These noises converged in a single sensation of life for me: I imagined that I bore my chalice safely through a throng of foes. Her name sprang to my lips at moments in strange prayers and praises which I myself did not understand. My eyes were often full of tears (I could not tell why) and at times a flood from my heart seemed to pour itself out into my bosom. I thought little of the future. I did not know whether I would ever speak to her or not or, if I spoke to her, how I could tell her of my confused adoration. But my body was like a harp and her words and gestures were like fingers running upon the wires.

One evening I went into the back drawing-room in which the priest had died. It was a dark rainy evening and there was no sound in the house. Through one of the broken panes I heard the rain impinge upon the earth, the fine incessant needles of water playing in the sodden beds. Some distant lamp or lighted window gleamed below me. I was thankful that I could see so little. All my senses seemed to desire to veil themselves and, feeling that I was about to slip from them, I pressed the palms of my hands together until they trembled, murmuring: *"Oh love! O love!"* many times.

At last she spoke to me. When she addressed the first words to me I was so confused that I did not know what to answer. She asked me was I going to *Araby*. I forgot whether I answered yes or no. It would be a splendid bazaar, she said she would love to go.

"And why can't you?" I asked.

While she spoke she turned a silver bracelet round and round her wrist. She could not go, she said, because there would be a retreat that week in her convent. Her brother and two other boys were fighting for their caps and I was alone at the railings. She held one of the spikes, bowing her head towards me. The light from the lamp opposite our door caught the white curve of her neck, lit up her hair that rested there and, falling, lit up the hand upon the railing. It fell over one side of her dress and caught the white border of a petticoat, just visible as she stood at ease.

"It's well for you," she said.

"If I go," I said, "I will bring you something."

What innumerable follies laid waste my waking and sleeping thoughts after that evening! I wished to annihilate the tedious intervening days. I chafed against the work of school. At night in my bedroom and by day in the classroom her image came between me and the page I strove to read. The syllables of the word *Araby* were called to me through the silence in which my soul luxuriated and cast an Eastern enchantment over me. I asked for leave to go to the bazaar on Saturday night. My aunt was surprised and hoped it was not some Freemason affair. I answered few questions in class. I watched my master's face pass from amiability to sternness; he hoped I was not beginning to idle. I could not call my wandering thoughts together. I had hardly any patience with the serious work of life which, now that it stood between me and my desire, seemed to me child's play, ugly monotonous child's play.

On Saturday morning I reminded my uncle that I wished to go to the bazaar in the evening. He was fussing at the hallstand, looking for the hat-brush, and answered me curtly:

"Yes, boy, I know."

As he was in the hall I could not go into the front parlor and lie at the window. I left the house in bad humor and walked slowly towards the school. The air was pitilessly raw and already my heart misgave me.

When I came home to dinner my uncle had not yet been home. Still it was early. I sat staring at the clock for some time and, when its ticking began to irritate me, I left the room. I mounted the staircase and gained the upper part of the house. The high cold empty gloomy rooms liberated me and I went from room to room singing. From the front window I saw my companions playing below in the street. Their cries reached me weakened and indistinct and, leaning my forehead against the cool glass, I looked over at the dark house where she lived. I may have stood there for an hour, seeing nothing but the brown-clad figure cast by my imagination, touched discreetly by the lamplight at the curved neck, at the hand upon the railings and at the border below the dress.

When I came downstairs again I found Mrs. Mercer sitting at the fire. She was an old garrulous woman, a pawnbroker's widow, who collected used stamps for some pious purpose. I had to endure the gossip of the tea-table. The meal was prolonged beyond an hour and still my uncle did not come. Mrs. Mercer stood up to go: she was sorry she couldn't wait any longer, but it was after eight o'clock and she did not like to be out late, as the night air was bad for her. When she had gone I began to walk up and down the room, clenching my fists. My aunt said:

"I'm afraid you may put off your bazaar for this night of Our Lord."

At nine o'clock I heard my uncle's latchkey in the halldoor. I heard him talking to himself and heard the hallstand rocking when it had received the weight of his overcoat. I could interpret these signs. When he was midway through his dinner I asked him to give me the money to go to the bazaar. He had forgotten.

"The people are in bed and after their first sleep now," he said.

I did not smile. My aunt said to him energetically:

"Can't you give him the money and let him go? You've kept him late enough as it is."

My uncle said he was very sorry he had forgotten. He said he believed in the old saying: "All work and no play makes Jack a dull boy." He asked me where I was going and, when I had told him a second time he asked me did I know *The Arab's Farewell to his Steed*. When I left the kitchen he was about to recite the opening lines of the piece to my aunt.

I held a florin tightly in my hand as I strode down Buckingham Street towards the station. The sight of the streets thronged with buyers and glaring with gas recalled to me the purpose of my journey. I took my seat in a third-class carriage of a deserted train. After an intolerable delay the train moved out of the station slowly. It crept onward among ruinous houses and over the twinkling river. At Westland Row Station a crowd of people pressed to the carriage doors; but the porters moved them back, saying that it was a special train for the bazaar. I remained alone in the bare carriage. In a few minutes the train drew up beside an improvised wooden platform. I passed out on to the road and saw by the lighted dial of a clock that it was ten minutes to ten. In front of me was a large building which displayed the magical name.

I could not find any sixpenny entrance and, fearing that the bazaar would be closed, I passed in quickly through a turnstile, handing a shilling to a weary-looking man. I found myself in a big hall girdled at half its height by a gallery. Nearly all the stalls were closed and the greater part of the hall was in darkness. I recognized a silence like that which pervades a church after a service. I walked into the center of the bazaar timidly. A few people were gathered about the stalls which were still open. Before a curtain, over which the words *Café Chantant* were written in colored lamps, two men were counting money on a salver. I listened to the fall of the coins.

Remembering with difficulty why I had come I went over to one of the stalls and examined porcelain vases and flowered tea-sets. At the door of the stall a young lady was talking and laughing with two young gentlemen. I remarked their English accents and listened vaguely to their conversation.

"O, I never said such a thing!"

"O, but you did!"

"O, but I didn't!"

"Didn't she say that?"

"Yes. I heard her."

"O, there's a . . . fib!"

Observing me the young lady came over and asked me did I wish to buy something. The tone of her voice was not encouraging; she seemed to have spoken to me out of a sense of duty. I looked humbly at the great jars that stood like eastern guards at either side of the dark entrance to the stall and murmured:

"No, thank you."

The young lady changed the position of one of the vases and went back to the two young men. They began to talk of the same subject. Once or twice the young lady glanced at me over her shoulder.

I lingered before her stall, though I knew my stay was useless, to make my interest in her wares seem the more real. Then I turned away slowly and walked down the middle of the bazaar. I allowed the two pennies to fall against the sixpence in my pocket. I heard a voice call from one end of the gallery that the light was out. The upper part of the hall was now completely dark.

Gazing up into the darkness I saw myself as a creature driven and derided by vanity; and my eyes burned with anguish and anger.

QUESTIONS

1. Does the first-person narrator seem like a child, an adult, or both? Why?
2. Examine Joyce's description of Dublin, especially in the first five paragraphs. What details stand out? What dominant impression emerges? What nationalist statement might Joyce be making?
3. What is the importance of Mangan's sister? How does she contrast with the boy's uncle? How does she contrast with the women whom the boy encounters at the bazaar? Why is the bazaar an important setting in the story?

4. The Irish fiction writer and critic Sean O'Faolain states that a story "must lead toward its point of illumination." (Joyce termed this moment of illumination an *epiphany*.) What is the point of illumination in "Araby"? How does it derive from setting and dictate the theme?

Eudora Welty

A WORN PATH

It was December—a bright frozen day in the early morning. Far out in the country there was an old Negro woman with her head tied in a red rag, coming along a path through the pinewoods. Her name was Phoenix Jackson. She was very old and small and she walked slowly in the dark pine shadows, moving a little from side to side in her steps, with the balanced heaviness and lightness of a pendulum in a grandfather clock. She carried a thin, small cane made from an umbrella, and with this she kept tapping the frozen earth in front of her. This made a grave and persistent noise in the still air, that seemed meditative like the chirping of a solitary little bird.

She wore a dark striped dress reaching down to her shoe tops, and an equally long apron of bleached sugar sacks, with a full pocket: all neat and tidy, but every time she took a step she might have fallen over her shoe-laces, which dragged from her unlaced shoes. She looked straight ahead. Her eyes were blue with age. Her skin had a pattern all its own of numberless branching wrinkles and as though a whole little tree stood in the middle of her forehead, but a golden color ran underneath, and the two knobs of her cheeks were illuminated by a yellow burning under the dark. Under the red rag her hair came down on her neck in the frailest of ringlets, still black, and with an odor like copper.

Now and then there was a quivering in the thicket. Old Phoenix said, "Out of my way, all you foxes, owls, beetles, jack rabbits, coons, and wild animals! . . . Keep out from under these feet, little bob-whites. . . . Keep the big wild hogs out of my path. Don't let none of those come running my direction. I got a long way." Under her small black-freckled hand her cane, limber as a buggy whip, would switch at the brush as if to rouse up any hiding things.

On she went. The woods were deep and still. The sun made the pine needles almost too bright to look at, up where the wind rocked. The cones dropped as light as feathers. Down in the hollow was the mourning dove—it was not too late for him.

The path ran up a hill. "Seem like there is chains about my feet, time I get this far," she said, in the voice of argument old people keep to use with themselves. "Something always takes a hold of me on this hill—pleads I should stay."

After she got to the top she turned and gave a full, severe look behind her where she had come. "Up through pines," she said at length. "Now down through oaks."

Her eyes opened their widest, and she started down gently. But before she got to the bottom of the hill a bush caught her dress.

Her fingers were busy and intent, but her skirts were full and long, so that before she could pull them free in one place they were caught in another. It was not possible to allow the dress to tear. "I in the thorny bush," she said. "Thorns, you doing your appointed work. Never want to let folks pass—no sir. Old eyes thought you was a pretty little *green* bush."

Finally, trembling all over, she stood free, and after a moment dared to stoop for her cane.

"Sun so high!" she cried, leaning back and looking, while the thick tears went over her eyes. "The time getting all gone here."

At the foot of this hill was a place where a log was laid across the creek.

"Now comes the trial," said Phoenix.

Putting her right foot out, she mounted the log and shut her eyes. Lifting her skirt, levelling her cane fiercely before her, like a festival figure in some parade, she began to march across. Then she opened her eyes and she was safe on the other side.

"I wasn't as old as I thought," she said.

But she sat down to rest. She spread her skirts on the bank around her and folded her hands over her knees. Up above her was a tree in a pearly cloud of mistletoe. She did not dare to close her eyes, and when a little boy brought her a little plate with a slice of marble-cake on it she spoke to him. "That would be acceptable," she said. But when she went to take it there was just her own hand in the air.

So she left that tree, and had to go through a barbed-wire fence. There she had to creep and crawl, spreading her knees and stretching her fingers like a baby trying to climb the steps. But she talked loudly to herself: she could not let her dress be torn now, so late in the day, and she could not pay for having her arm or her leg sawed off if she got caught fast where she was.

At last she was safe through the fence and risen up out in the clearing. Big dead trees, like black men with one arm, were standing in the purple stalks of the withered cotton field. There sat a buzzard.

"Who you watching?"

In the furrow she made her way along.

"Glad this not the season for bulls," she said, looking sideways, "and the good Lord made his snakes to curl up and sleep in the winter. A pleasure I don't see no two-headed snake coming around that tree, where it come once. It took a while to get by him, back in the summer."

She passed through the old cotton and went into a field of dead corn. It whispered and shook and was taller than her head. "Through the maze now," she said, for there was no path.

Then there was something tall, black, and skinny there, moving before her.

At first she took it for a man. It could have been a man dancing in the field. But she stood still and listened, and it did not make a sound. It was as silent as a ghost.

"Ghost," she said sharply, "who be you the ghost of? For I have heard of nary death close by."

But there was no answer—only the ragged dancing in the wind.

She shut her eyes, reached out her hand, and touched a sleeve. She found a coat and inside that an emptiness, cold as ice.

"You scarecrow," she said. Her face lighted. "I ought to be shut up for good," she said with laughter. "My senses is gone. I too old. I the oldest people I ever know. Dance, old scarecrow," she said, "while I dancing with you."

She kicked her foot over the furrow, and with mouth drawn down, shook her head once or twice in a little strutting way. Some husks blew down and whirled in streamers about her skirts.

Then she went on, parting her way from side to side with the cane, through the whispering field. At last she came to the end, to a wagon track where the silver grass blew between the red ruts. The quail were walking around like pullets, seeming all dainty and unseen.

"Walk pretty," she said. "This the easy place. This the easy going."

She followed the track, swaying through the quiet bare fields, through the little strings of tree silver in their dead leaves, past cabins silver from weather, with the doors and windows boarded shut, all like old women under a spell sitting there. "I walking in their sleep," she said, nodding her head vigorously.

In a ravine she went where a spring was silently flowing through a hollow log. Old Phoenix bent and drank. "Sweet-gum makes the water sweet," she said, and drank more. "Nobody know who made this well, for it was here when I was born."

The track crossed a swampy part where the moss hung as white as lace from every limb. "Sleep on, alligators, and blow your bubbles." Then the track went into the road.

Deep, deep the road went down between the high green-colored banks. Overhead the live-oaks met, and it was as dark as a cave.

A black dog with a lolling tongue came up out of the weeds by the ditch. She was meditating, and not ready, and when he came at her she only hit him a little with her cane. Over she went in the ditch, like a little puff of milk-weed.

Down there, her senses drifted away. A dream visited her, and she reached her hand up, but nothing reached down and gave her a pull. So she lay there and presently went to talking. "Old woman," she said to herself, "that black dog come up out of the weeds to stall you off, and now there he sitting on his fine tail, smiling at you."

A white man finally came along and found her—a hunter, a young man, with his dog on a chain.

"Well, Granny!" he laughed. "What are you doing there?"

"Lying on my back like a June-bug waiting to be turned over, mister," she said, reaching up her hand.

He lifted her up, gave her a swing in the air, and set her down, "Anything broken, Granny?"

"No sir, them old dead weeds is springy enough," said Phoenix, when she had got her breath. "I thank you for your trouble."

"Where do you live, Granny?" he asked, while the two dogs were growling at each other.

"Away back yonder, sir, behind the ridge. You can't even see it from here."

"On your way home?"

"No, sir, I going to town."

"Why, that's too far! That's as far as I walk when I come out myself, and I get something for my trouble." He patted the stuffed bag he carried, and there hung down a little closed claw. It was one of the bob-whites, with its beak hooked bitterly to show it was dead. "Now you go on home, Granny!"

"I bound to go to town, mister," said Phoenix. "The time come around."

He gave another laugh, filling the whole landscape. "I know you old colored people! Wouldn't miss going to town to see Santa Claus!"

But something held Old Phoenix very still. The deep lines in her face went into a fierce and different radiation. Without warning, she had seen with her own eyes a flashing nickel fall out of the man's pocket onto the ground.

"How old are you, Granny?" he was saying.

"There is no telling, mister," she said, "no telling."

Then she gave a little cry and clapped her hands and said, "Git on away from here, dog! Look! Look at that dog!" She laughed as if in admiration. "He ain't scared of nobody. He a big black dog." She whispered, "Sic him!"

"Watch me get rid of that cur," said the man. "Sic him, Pete! Sic him!"

Phoenix heard the dogs fighting, and heard the man running and throwing sticks. She even heard a gunshot. But she was slowly bending forward by that time, further and further forward, the lids stretched down over her eyes, as if she were doing this in her sleep. Her chin was lowered almost to her knees. The yellow palm of her hand came out from the fold of her apron. Her fingers slid down and along the ground under the piece of money with the grace and care they would have in lifting an egg from under a sitting hen. The she slowly straightened up, she stood erect, and the nickel was in her apron pocket. A bird flew by. Her lips moved. "God watching me the whole time. I come to stealing."

The man came back, and his own dog panted about them. "Well, I scared him off that time," he said, and then he laughed and lifted his gun and pointed it at Phoenix.

She stood straight and faced him.

"Doesn't the gun scare you?" he said, still pointing it.

"No, sir, I seen plenty go off closer by, in my day, and for less than what I done," she said, holding utterly still.

He smiled, and shouldered the gun. "Well, Granny," he said, "you must be a hundred years old, and scared of nothing. I'd give you a dime if I had any money with me. But you take my advice and stay home, and nothing will happen to you."

"I bound to go on my way, mister," said Phoenix. She inclined her head in the red rag. Then they went in different directions, but she could hear the gun shooting again and again over the hill.

She walked on. The shadows hung from the oak trees to the road like curtains. Then she smelled wood-smoke, and smelled the river, and she saw a steeple and the cabins on their steep steps. Dozens of little black children whirled around her. There ahead was Natchez shining. Bells were ringing. She walked on.

In the paved city it was Christmas time. There were red and green electric lights strung and crisscrossed everywhere, and all turned on in the daytime. Old Phoenix would have been lost if she had not distrusted her eyesight and depended on her feet to know where to take her.

She paused quietly on the sidewalk where people were passing by. A lady came along in the crowd, carrying an armful of red-, green-, and silver-wrapped presents; she gave off perfume like the red roses in hot summer, and Phoenix stopped her.

"Please, missy, will you lace up my shoe?" She held up her foot.

"What do you want, Grandma?"

"See my shoe," said Phoenix. "Do all right for out in the country, but wouldn't look right to go in a big building."

"Stand still then, Grandma," said the lady. She put her packages down on the sidewalk beside her and laced and tied both shoes tightly.

"Can't lace 'em with a cane," said Phoenix. "Thank you, missy. I doesn't mind asking a nice lady to tie up my shoe, when I gets out on the street."

Moving slowly and from side to side, she went into the big building and into a tower of steps, where she walked up and around and around until her feet knew to stop.

She entered a door, and there she saw nailed up on the wall the document that had been stamped with the gold seal and framed in the gold frame, which matched the dream that was hung up in her head.

"Here I be," she said. There was a fixed and ceremonial stiffness over her body.

"A charity case, I suppose," said an attendant who sat at the desk before her.

But Phoenix only looked above her head. There was sweat on her face, the wrinkles in her skin shone like a bright net.

"Speak up, Grandma," the woman said. "What's your name? We must have your history, you know. Have you been here before? What seems to be the trouble with you?"

Old Phoenix only gave a twitch to her face as if a fly were bothering her.

"Are you deaf?" cried the attendant.

But then the nurse came in.

"Oh, that's just old Aunt Phoenix," she said. "She doesn't come for herself—she has a little grandson. She makes these trips just as regular as clockwork. She lives away back off the Old Natchez Trace." She bent down. "Well, Aunt Phoenix, why don't you just take a seat? We won't keep you standing after your long trip." She pointed.

The old woman sat down, bolt upright in the chair.

"Now, how is the boy?" asked the nurse.

Old Phoenix did not speak.

"I said, how is the boy?"

But Phoenix only waited and stared straight ahead, her face very solemn and withdrawn into rigidity.

"Is his throat any better?" asked the nurse. "Aunt Phoenix, don't you hear me? Is your grandson's throat any better since the last time you came for the medicine?"

With her hands on her knees, the old woman waited, silent, erect and motionless, just as if she were in armour.

"You mustn't take up our time this way, Aunt Phoenix," the nurse said. "Tell us quickly about your grandson, and get it over with. He isn't dead, is he?"

At last there came a flicker and then a flame of comprehension across her face, and she spoke.

"My grandson. It was my memory had left me. There I sat and forgot why I made my long trip."

"Forgot?" The nurse frowned. "After you came so far?"

Then Phoenix was like an old woman begging a dignified forgiveness for waking up

frightened in the night. "I never did go to school, I was too old at the Surrender," she said in a soft voice. "I'm an old woman without an education. It was my memory fail me. My little grandson, he is just the same, and I forgot it in the coming."

"Throat never heals, does it?" said the nurse, speaking in a loud, sure voice to Old Phoenix. By now she had a card with something written on it, a little list. "Yes. Swallowed lye. When was it—January—two-three years ago—"

Phoenix spoke unasked now. "No, missy, he not dead, he just the same. Every little while his throat begin to close up again, and he not able to swallow. He not get his breath. He not able to help himself. So the time come around, and I go on another trip for the soothingmedicine."

"All right. The doctor said as long as you came to get it, you could have it," said the nurse. "But it's an obstinate case."

"My little grandson, he sit up there in the house all wrapped up, waiting by himself," Phoenix went on. "We is the only two left in the world. He suffer and it don't seem to put him back at all. He got a sweet look. He going to last. He wear a little patch quilt and peep out holding his mouth open like a little bird. I remembers so plain now. I not going to forget him again, no, the whole enduring time. I could tell him from all the others in creation."

"All right." The nurse was trying to hush her now. She brought her a bottle of medicine. "Charity," she said, making a check mark in a book.

Old Phoenix held the bottle close to her eyes and then carefully put it into her pocket.

"I thank you," she said.

"It's Christmas time, Grandma," said the attendant. "Could I give you a few pennies out of my purse?"

"Five pennies is a nickel," said Phoenix stiffly.

"Here's a nickel," said the attendant.

Phoenix rose carefully and held out her hand. She received the nickel and then fished the other nickel out of her pocket and laid it beside the new one. She stared at her palm closely, with her head on one side.

Then she gave a tap with her cane on the floor.

"This is what come to me to do," she said. "I going to the store and buy my child a little windmill they sells, made out of paper. He going to find it hard to believe there such a thing in the world. I'll march myself back where he waiting, holding it straight up in this hand."

She lifted her free hand, gave a little nod, turned round, and walked out of the doctor's office. Then her slow step began on the stairs, going down.

QUESTIONS

1. What can you infer about Phoenix Jackson from her speech? From her dress? From her behavior toward others? How does her relationship to the shifting setting of the story reveal her character?

2. What patterns of imagery can you detect in Welty's handling of setting?

3. What is the mood of the story? What is Phoenix Jackson's mood as she journeys to the clinic? What significance is there in her fantasy life and her forgetfulness? What do they demonstrate about her resolve?

4. Phoenix Jackson must overcome many obstacles on her journey. Do these obstacles have anything in common? Is there anything similar in the way Phoenix Jackson overcomes these obstacles?

6 . T o n e

Tone is the writer's "voice" that we listen for in a work of fiction—his or her attitude toward the subject. Through tone we enter the author's state of mind, sensing the anger, sadness, sympathy, joy, irony—a broad range of attitudes—inherent in the writer's working of materials. Tone not only illuminates theme, but also reinforces mood and creates its own levels of tension and conflict among characters in a tale.

The author's choice and placement of words—that composite of language that we term *style*—often serve as the basis of tone. Recall, for instance, the flat, simple, almost declarative sentences that Hemingway uses to describe the execution in his sketch from *In Our Time,* which appears in the introduction to Chapter 5: "They shot the six cabinet ministers at half-past six in the morning against the wall of a hospital." We might say that Hemingway's journalistic style, his ostensibly detached mode of observation, creates an objective tone in this sketch. However, the tone is actually more subtle and complex. The details are factual, but the stylistic arrangement—the harsh brutality of the simple sentences and the sequence of death imagery—creates a feeling of pity in us, as if Hemingway is shaping our attitude toward the event so that it coincides with his own.

By contrast, if we examine the very short story "Girl" by Jamaica Kincaid, appearing in Chapter 4, we see that the author achieves a sense of tone through entirely different stylistic conventions. Instead of a series of simple sentences, Kincaid creates one extraordinarily long sentence of Faulknerian complexity, trying to capture the totality of Caribbean culture and of women's lives within it. Told from a second-person point of view (instead of Hemingway's third-person perspective), the tone seems harsh, as the mother lectures a daughter on the strategies of survival within a patriarchal culture. The tone of Kincaid herself, as distinguished from the voice of the speaker, might include an element of harshness, but you could argue that Kincaid's tone is also supportive, critical, and even admiring. In other words, the feelings of a character in a story may convey the feelings and ideas—the tone—of the author, or may vary and even be diametrically opposed. Issues of tone can be very simple—as when we assert that the tone of Arna Bontemps's "A Summer Tragedy" is precisely what the title implies—or exceedingly challenging for careful readers of fiction.

One notable aspect of tone is the creation of irony and satire. Irony is used to convey meanings and ideas that differ from or are opposite to the apparent sense of certain words and images. It is the incongruity between appearance and reality. In a similar vein, satire is a comic attack on or criticism of the foibles, weaknesses, and sheer stupidity of humankind. Both irony and satire invite us to pierce the veil of appearance and understand the truth of the human condition.

There are different kinds of irony that are used in both fiction and drama; irony has also been a useful tool for poets (Chaucer), essayists (Swift), and many others. Perhaps the best example of *dramatic irony*, or *tragic irony*, is to be found in Sophocles's *Oedipus Rex*, wherein the protagonist unknowingly creates the structure for his own undoing. This might also be called *irony of fate*, which is to say that the protagonist gets what he deserves or what the gods or fate believes he deserves.

In *verbal irony* the words, by design or not, conceal the real meaning and produce incongruity. This kind of irony can be found in all writing, but it is most prominent in drama. The handkerchief scene in *Othello* (Act III, Scene 4) is an example.

OTHELLO: Give me your hand. This hand is moist, my lady.
DESDEMONA: It yet hath felt no age nor known no sorrow.
OTHELLO: This argues fruitfulness and liberal heart.
    Hot, hot, and moist. This hand of yours requires
    A sequester from liberty, fasting and prayer,
    Much castigation, exercise devout;
    For here's a young and sweating devil here
    That commonly rebels. 'Tis a good hand,
    A frank one.
DESDEMONA: You may, indeed, say so;
    For 'twas that hand that gave away my heart.
OTHELLO: A liberal hand: the hearts of old gave hands;
    But our new heraldry is hands, not hearts.

The above exchange is close to being mockery, another form of irony. Both are forms of wordplay, which is used to move action and blur the perception between what is real and what isn't. Polite banter *(Asteism)* and innuendo are also related to wordplay.

Irony may also encompass *self-effacement;* there are examples of this in Téllez's "Just Lather, That's All," appearing in Chapter 4. *Understatement* is also used in ironic expression; and *low-rating*, or *ranking*, is a contemporary relative of irony often used by comics whose night-club dissertations on individuals and society offer so much barbed amusement.

Paradox, an apparent contradiction that may, however, be a truthful statement, is also related to irony, but it is *satire* that assumes, even in its relationship to irony, a position of importance all its own, as we see in Pirandello's "War." The "censure of humanity has been the dominant quality of satire," according to Shipley. Satire, an expression of

criticism of human frailty and folly, was used by Cervantes, Rabelais, Swift, Voltaire, Lewis, and others. Such censure is designed to improve human institutions.

Fiction lends itself easily to the use of irony in all its forms. In the first of the stories in this section, Pirandello's "War," we see a group of people on a train talking about their sons fighting on the front during World War I. Noble thoughts and sentiments about patriotism, honor, and dying for one's country slowly become juxtaposed ironically against the reality of one couple's loss. Irony finds for us another reality, one we can live with, but it also serves the purpose of pointing up the reality from which we so often flee.

Careful readers will always be alert to what they perceive as the writer's implied attitude toward characters and subject. Through tone, we can sense the fundamental attitude and perspective of the author. Tone can take us to the center of a story's meaning.

Luigi Pirandello

WAR

The passengers who had left Rome by the night express had had to stop until dawn at the small station of Fabriano in order to continue their journey by the small old-fashioned "local" joining the main line with Sulmona.

At dawn, in a stuffy and smoky second-class carriage in which five people had already spent the night, a bulky woman in deep mourning, was hoisted in—almost like a shapeless bundle. Behind her—puffing and moaning, followed her husband—a tiny man, thin and weakly, his face death-white, his eyes small and bright and looking shy and uneasy.

Having at last taken a seat he politely thanked the passengers who had helped his wife and who had made room for her; then he turned round to the woman trying to pull down the collar of her coat and politely inquired:

"Are you all right, dear?"

The wife, instead of answering, pulled up her collar again to her eyes, so as to hide her face.

"Nasty world," muttered the husband with a sad smile.

And he felt it his duty to explain to his traveling companions that the poor woman was to be pitied for the war was taking away from her her only son, a boy of twenty to whom both had devoted their entire life, even breaking up their home at Sulmona to follow him to Rome where he had to go as a student, then, allowing him to volunteer for war with an assurance, however, that at least for six months he would not be sent to the front and now, all of a sudden, receiving a wire saying that he was due to leave in three days' time and asking them to go and see him off.

The woman under the big coat was twisting and wriggling, at times growling like a wild animal, feeling certain that all those explanations would not have aroused even a shadow of sympathy from those people who—most likely—were in the same plight as herself. One of them, who had been listening with particular attention, said:

"You should thank God that your son is only leaving now for the front. Mine has been sent there the first day of the war. He has already come back twice wounded and been sent back again to the front."

"What about me? I have two sons and three nephews at the front," said another passenger.

"Maybe, but in our case it is our *only* son," ventured the husband.

"What difference can it make? You may spoil your only son with excessive attentions, but you cannot love him more than you would all your other children if you had any. Paternal love is not like bread that can be broken into pieces and split amongst the children in equal shares. A father gives *all* his love to each one of his children without discrimination, whether it be one or ten, and if I am suffering now for my two sons, I am not suffering half for each of them but double. . . ."

"True . . . true . . ." sighed the embarrassed husband, "but suppose (of course we all hope it will never be your case) a father has two sons at the front and he loses one of them, there is still one left to console him . . . while . . ."

"Yes," answered the other, getting cross, "a son left to console him but also a son left for whom he must survive, while in the case of the father of an only son if the son dies the father can die too and put an end to his distress. Which of the two positions is the worse? Don't you see how my case would be worse than yours?"

"Nonsense," interrupted another traveler, a fat, red-faced man with bloodshot eyes of the palest gray.

He was panting. From his bulging eyes seemed to spurt inner violence of an uncontrolled vitality which his weakened body could hardly contain.

"Nonsense," he repeated, trying to cover his mouth with his hand so as to hide the two missing front teeth. "Nonsense. Do we give life to our children for our own benefit?"

The other travelers stared at him in distress. The one who had had his son at the front since the first day of the war sighed: "You are right. Our children do not belong to us, they belong to the Country. . . ."

"Bosh," retorted the fat traveler. "Do we think of the Country when we give life to our children? Our sons are born because . . . well, because they must be born and when they come to life they take our own life with them. This is the truth. We belong to them but they never belong to us. And when they reach twenty they are exactly what we were at their age. We too had a father and mother, but there were so many other things as well . . . girls, cigarettes, illusions, new ties . . . and the Country, of course, whose call we would have answered—when we were twenty—even if father and mother had said no. Now, at our age, the love of our Country is still great, of course, but stronger than it is the love for our children. Is there any one of us here who wouldn't gladly take his son's place at the front if he could?"

There was a silence all round, everybody nodding as to approve.

"Why then," continued the fat man, "shouldn't we consider the feelings of our children when they are twenty? Isn't it natural that at their age they should consider the love for their Country (I am speaking of decent boys, of course) even greater than the love for us? Isn't it natural that it should be so, as after all they must look upon us as upon old boys who cannot move any more and must stay at home? If Country exists, if Country is a natural necessity like bread, of which each of us must eat in order not to die of hunger, somebody must go to defend it. And our sons go, when they are twenty, and they don't want tears, because if they die, they died inflamed and happy (I am speaking, of course, of decent boys). Now, if one dies young and happy, without having the ugly sides of life, the boredom of it, the petti-ness, the bitterness of disillusion . . . what more can we ask for him? Everyone should stop crying: everyone should laugh, as I do . . . or at least thank God—as I do—because my son, before dying, sent me a message saying that he was dying satisfied at having ended his life in the best way he could have wished. That is why, as you see, I do not even wear mourning. . . ."

He shook his light fawn coat as to show it; his livid lip over his missing teeth was trembling, his eyes were watery and motionless and soon after he ended with a shrill laugh which might well have been a sob.

"Quite so . . . Quite so . . ." agreed the others.

The woman who, bundled in a corner under her coat, had been sitting and listening had—for the last three months—tried to find in the words of her husband and her friends something to console her in her deep sorrow, something that might show her how a mother should resign herself to send her son not even to death but to a probable danger of life. Yet not a word had she found amongst the many which had been said . . . and her grief had been greater in seeing that nobody—as she thought—could share her feelings.

But now the words of the traveler amazed and almost stunned her. She suddenly realized that it wasn't the others who were wrong and could not understand her but herself who could not rise up to the same height of those fathers and mothers willing to resign themselves, without crying, not only to the departure of their sons but even to their death.

She lifted her head, she bent over from her corner trying to listen with great attention to the details which the fat man was giving to his companions about the way his son had fallen as a hero, for his King and his Country, happy and without regrets. It seemed to her that she had stumbled into a world she had never dreamt of, a world so far unknown to her and she was so pleased to hear everyone joining in congratulating that brave father who could so stoically speak of his child's death.

Then suddenly, just as if she had heard nothing of what had been said and almost as if waking up from a dream, she turned to the old man, asking him:

"Then . . . is your son really dead?"

Everybody stared at her. The old man, too, turned to look at her, fixing his great, bulging, horribly watery light gray eyes, deep in her face. For some little time he tried to answer, but words failed him. He looked and looked at her, almost as if only then—at that silly, incongruous question—he had suddenly realized at last that his son was really dead . . . gone forever . . . forever. His face contracted, became horribly distorted, then he snatched in haste a handkerchief from his pocket and, to the amazement of everyone, broke into harrowing, heart-rending, uncontrollable sobs.

QUESTIONS

1. What point does the author make by having the traveling companions argue over whose plight is the most tragic?
2. Why does the fat man emphasize the term "decent boys" when he makes reference to soldiering and duty? What emotion is hidden behind his reasoning?
3. Why does the fat man break down and cry at the end?
4. What is Pirandello's attitude toward war in this story? How do you know?

Alice Walker

ROSELILY

Dearly Beloved,

She dreams; dragging herself across the world. A small girl in her mother's white robe and veil, knee raised waist high through a bowl of quicksand soup. The man who stands beside her is against this standing on the front porch of her house, being married to the sound of cars whizzing by on highway 61.

we are gathered here

Like cotton to be weighed. Her fingers at the last minute busily removing dry leaves and twigs. Aware it is a superficial sweep. She knows he blames Mississippi for the respectful way the men turn their heads up in the yard, the women stand waiting and knowledge-able, their children held from mischief by teachings from the wrong God. He glares beyond them to the occupants of the cars, white faces glued to promises beyond a country wedding, noses thrust forward like dogs on a track. For him they usurp the wedding.

in the sight of God

Yes, open house. That is what country black folks like. She dreams she does not already have three children. A squeeze around the flowers in her hands chokes off three and four and five years of breath. Instantly she is ashamed and frightened in her superstition. She looks for the first time at the preacher, forces humility into her eyes, as if she believes he is, in fact, a man of God. She can imagine God, a small black boy, timidly pulling the preacher's coattail.

to join this man and this woman

She thinks of ropes, chains, handcuffs, his religion. His place of worship. Where she will be required to sit apart with covered head. In Chicago, a word she hears when thinking of smoke, from his description of what a cinder was, which they never had in Panther Burn. She sees hovering over the heads of the clean neighbors in her front yard black specks falling, clinging, from the sky. But in Chicago. Respect, a chance to build. Her children at last from underneath the detrimental wheel. A chance to be on top. What a relief, she thinks. What a vision, a view, from up so high.

in holy matrimony.

Her fourth child she gave away to the child's father who had some money. Certainly a good job. Had gone to Harvard. Was a good man but weak because good language meant so much to him he could not live with Roselily. Could not abide TV in the living room, five beds in three rooms, no Bach except from four to six on Sunday afternoons. No chess at all. She does not forget to worry her son among his father's people. She wonders if the New England climate will agree with him. If he will ever come down to Mississippi, as his father did, to try to right the country's wrongs. She wonders if he will be stronger than his father. His father cried off and on throughout her pregnancy. Went to skin and bones. Suffered nightmares, retching and falling out of bed. Tried to kill himself. Later told his wife he found the right baby through friends. Vouched for the sterling qualities that would make up his character.

It is not her nature to blame. Still, she is not entirely thankful. She supposes New England, the North, to be quite different from what she knows. It seems right somehow to her that people who move there to live return home completely changed. She thinks of the air, the smoke, the cinders. Imagines cinders big as hailstones; heavy, weighing on the people. Wonders how this pressure finds its way into the veins, roping the springs of laughter.

if there's anybody here that knows a reason why

But of course they know no reason why beyond what they daily have come to know. She thinks of the man who will be her husband, feels shut away from him because of the stiff severity of his plain black suit. His religion. A lifetime of black and white. Of veils. Covered head. It is as if her children are already gone from her. Not dead, but exalted on a pedestal, a stalk that has no roots. She wonders how to make new roots. It is beyond her. She wonders what one does with memories in a brand-new life. This had seemed easy, until she thought of it. "The reasons why . . . the people who" . . . she thinks, and does not wonder where the thought is from.

these two should not be joined

She thinks of her mother, who is dead. Dead, but still her mother. Joined. This is confusing. Of her father. A gray old man who sold wild mink, rabbit, fox skins to Sears,

Roebuck. He stands in the yard, like a man waiting for a train. Her young sisters stand behind her in smooth green dresses, with flowers in their hands and hair. They giggle, she feels, at the absurdity of the wedding. They are ready for something new. She thinks the man beside her should marry one of them. She feels old. Yoked. An arm seems to reach out from behind her and snatch her backward. She thinks of cemeteries and the long sleep of grandparents mingling in the dirt. She believes that she believes in ghosts. In the soil giving back what it takes.

together,

In the city. He sees her in a new way. This she knows, and is grateful. But is it new enough? She cannot always be a bride and virgin, wearing robes and veil. Even now her body itches to be free of satin and voile, organdy and lily of the valley. Memories crash against her. Memories of being bare to the sun. She wonders what it will be like. Not to have to go to a job. Not to work in a sewing plant. Not to worry about learning to sew straight seams in workingmen's overalls, jeans, and dress pants. Her place will be in the home, he has said, repeatedly, promising her rest she had prayed for. But now she wonders. When she is rested, what will she do? They will make babies—she thinks practically about her fine brown body, his strong black one. They will be inevitable. Her hands will be full. Full of what? Babies. She is not comforted.

let him speak

She wishes she had asked him to explain more of what he meant. But she was impatient. Impatient to be done with sewing. With doing everything for three children, alone. Impatient to leave the girls she had known since childhood, their children growing up, their husbands hanging around her, already old, seedy. Nothing about them that she wanted, or needed. The fathers of her children driving by, waving, not waving; reminders of times she would just as soon forget. Impatient to see the South Side, where they would live and build and be respectable and respected and free. Her husband would free her. A romantic hush. Proposal. Promises. A new life! Respectable, reclaimed, renewed. Free! In robe and veil.

or forever hold

She does not even know if she loves him. She loves his sobriety. His refusal to sing just because he knows the tune. She loves his pride. His blackness and his gray car. She loves his understanding of her *condition*. She thinks she loves the effort he will make to redo her into what he truly wants. His love of her makes her completely conscious of how unloved she was before. This is something; though it makes her unbearably sad. Melancholy. She blinks her eyes. Remembers she is finally being married, like other girls. Like other girls, women? Something strains upward behind her eyes. She thinks of the something as a rat trapped, cornered, scurrying to and fro in her head, peering through the windows of her eyes. She wants to live for once. But doesn't know quite what that means. Wonders if she has ever done it. If she ever will. The preacher is odious to her. She wants to strike him out of the way, out of her

light, with the back of her hand. It seems to her he has always been standing in front of her, barring her way.

his peace.

The rest she does not hear. She feels a kiss, passionate, rousing, within the general pandemonium. Cars drive up blowing their horns. Firecrackers go off. Dogs come from under the house and begin to yelp and bark. Her husband's hand is like the clasp of an iron gate. People congratulate. Her children press against her. They look with awe and distaste mixed with hope at their new father. He stands curiously apart, in spite of the people crowding about to grasp his free hand. He smiles at them all but his eyes are as if turned inward. He knows they cannot understand that he is not a Christian. He will not explain himself. He feels different, he looks it. The old women thought he was like one of their sons except that he had somehow got away from them. Still a son, not a son. Changed.

She thinks how it will be later in the night in the silvery gray car. How they will spin through the darkness of Mississippi and in the morning be in Chicago, Illinois. She thinks of Lincoln, the president. That is all she knows about the place. She feels ignorant, *wrong*, backward. She presses her worried fingers into his palm. He is standing in front of her. In the crush of well-wishing people, he does not look back.

QUESTIONS

1. What is the effect of dividing the story between the italicized words of the minister and the "inner thoughts" of Roselily? How does each complement the other?
2. What attitudes and emotions does Roselily seem to display toward her husband-to-be? What seems to be her main motivation in marrying him?
3. Compare and contrast Roselily and her future husband in terms of their values, temperament, attitude, and demeanor.
4. How would you characterize the story's diction? What does it reveal about Roselily's social class and family background?
5. Alice Walker is noted for her particular sensitivity to the struggles of black women in America. How does the tone of this story bear this out?

Amy Tan

TWO KINDS

My mother believed you could be anything you wanted to be in America. You could open a restaurant. You could work for the government and get good retirement. You could buy a house with almost no money down. You could become rich. You could become instantly famous.

"Of course you can be prodigy, too," my mother told me when I was nine. "You can be best anything. What does Auntie Lindo know? Her daughter, she is only best tricky."

America was where all my mother's hopes lay. She had come here in 1949 after losing everything in China: her mother and father, her family home, her first husband, and two daughters, twin baby girls. But she never looked back with regret. There were so many ways for things to get better.

We didn't immediately pick the right kind of prodigy. At first my mother thought I could be a Chinese Shirley Temple. We'd watch Shirley's old movies on TV as though they were training films. My mother would poke my arm and say, *"Ni kan"*—You watch. And I would see Shirley tapping her feet, or singing a sailor song, or pursing her lips into a very round O while saying, "Oh my goodness."

"Ni kan," said my mother as Shirley's eyes flooded with tears. "You already know how. Don't need talent for crying!"

Soon after my mother got this idea about Shirley Temple, she took me to a beauty training school in the Mission district and put me in the hands of a student who could barely hold the scissors without shaking. Instead of getting big fat curls, I emerged with an uneven mass of crinkly black fuzz. My mother dragged me off to the bathroom and tried to wet down my hair.

"You look like Negro Chinese," she lamented, as if I had done this on purpose.

The instructor of the beauty training school had to lop off these soggy clumps to make my hair even again. "Peter Pan is very popular these days," the instructor assured my mother. I now had hair the length of a boy's, with straight-across bangs that hung at a slant two inches above my eyebrows. I liked the haircut and it made me actually look forward to my future fame.

In fact, in the beginning, I was just as excited as my mother, maybe even more so. I pictured this prodigy part of me as many different images, trying each one on for size. I was a dainty ballerina girl standing by the curtains, waiting to hear the right music that would send me floating on my tiptoes. I was like the Christ child lifted out of the straw manger, crying with holy indignity. I was Cinderella stepping from her pumpkin carriage with sparkly cartoon music filling the air.

In all of my imaginings, I was filled with a sense that I would soon become *perfect*. My mother and father would adore me. I would be beyond reproach. I would never feel the need to sulk for anything.

But sometimes the prodigy in me became impatient. "If you don't hurry up and get

me out of here, I'm disappearing for good," it warned. "And then you'll always be nothing."

Every night after dinner, my mother and I would sit at the Formica kitchen table. She would present new tests, taking her examples from stories of amazing children she had read in *Ripley's Believe It or Not*, or *Good Housekeeping, Reader's Digest*, and a dozen other magazines she kept in a pile in our bathroom. My mother got these magazines from people whose houses she cleaned. And since she cleaned many houses each week, we had a great assortment. She would look through them all, searching for stories about remarkable children.

The first night she brought out a story about a three-year-old boy who knew the capitals of all the states and even most of the European countries. A teacher was quoted as saying the little boy could also pronounce the names of the foreign cities correctly.

"What's the capital of Finland?" my mother asked me, looking at the magazine story.

All I knew was the capital of California, because Sacramento was the name of the street we lived on in Chinatown. "Nairobi!" I guessed, saying the most foreign word I could think of. She checked to see if that was possibly one way to pronounce "Helsinki" before showing me the answer.

The tests got harder—multiplying numbers in my head, finding the queen of hearts in a deck of cards, trying to stand on my head without using my hands, predicting the daily temperatures in Los Angeles, New York, and London.

One night I had to look at a page from the Bible for three minutes and then report everything I could remember. "Now Jehoshaphat had riches and honor in abundance and . . . that's all I remember, Ma," I said.

And after seeing my mother's disappointed face once again, something inside of me began to die. I hated the tests, the raised hopes and failed expectations. Before going to bed that night, I looked in the mirror above the bathroom sink and when I saw only my face staring back—and that it would always be this ordinary face—I began to cry. Such a sad, ugly girl! I made high-pitched noises like a crazed animal, trying to scratch out the face in the mirror.

And then I saw what seemed to be the prodigy side of me—because I had never seen that face before. I looked at my reflection, blinking so I could see more clearly. The girl staring back at me was angry, powerful. This girl and I were the same. I had new thoughts, willful thoughts, or rather thoughts filled with lots of won'ts. I won't let her change me, I promised myself. I won't be what I'm not.

So now on nights when my mother presented her tests, I performed listlessly, my head propped on one arm. I pretended to be bored. And I was. I got so bored I started counting the bellows of the foghorns out on the bay while my mother drilled me in other areas. The sound was comforting and reminded me of the cow jumping over the moon. And the next day, I played a game with myself, seeing if my mother would give up on me before eight bellows. After a while I usually counted only one, maybe two bellows at most. At last she was beginning to give up hope.

Two or three months had gone by without any mention of my being a prodigy again. And then one day my mother was watching *The Ed Sullivan Show* on TV. The TV was old and the sound kept shorting out. Every time my mother got halfway up from the sofa to adjust the set, the sound would go back on and Ed would be talking. As soon as she sat down, Ed would go silent again. She got up, the TV broke into loud piano music. She sat down. Silence. Up and down, back and forth, quiet and loud. It was like a stiff embraceless dance between her and the TV set. Finally she stood by the set with her hand on the sound dial.

She seemed entranced by the music, a little frenzied piano piece with this mesmerizing quality, sort of quick passages and then teasing lilting ones before it returned to the quick playful parts.

"*Ni kan,*" my mother said, calling me over with hurried hand gestures, "Look here."

I could see why my mother was fascinated by the music. It was being pounded out by a little Chinese girl, about nine years old, with a Peter Pan haircut. The girl had the sauciness of a Shirley Temple. She was proudly modest like a proper Chinese child. And she also did this fancy sweep of a curtsy, so that the fluffy skirt of her white dress cascaded slowly to the floor like the petals of a large carnation.

In spite of these warning signs, I wasn't worried. Our family had no piano and we couldn't afford to buy one, let alone reams of sheet music and piano lessons. So I could be generous in my comments when my mother bad-mouthed the little girl on TV.

"Play note right, but doesn't sound good! No singing sound," complained my mother.

"What are you picking on her for?" I said carelessly. "She's pretty good. Maybe she's not the best, but she's trying hard." I knew almost immediately I would be sorry I said that.

"Just like you," she said. "Not the best. Because you not trying." She gave a little huff as she let go of the sound dial and sat down on the sofa.

The little Chinese girl sat down also to play an encore of "Anitra's Dance" by Grieg. I remember the song, because later on I had to learn how to play it.

Three days after watching *The Ed Sullivan Show,* my mother told me what my schedule would be for piano lessons and piano practice. She had talked to Mr. Chong, who lived on the first floor of our apartment building. Mr. Chong was a retired piano teacher and my mother had traded housecleaning services for weekly lessons and a piano for me to practice on every day, two hours a day, from four until six.

When my mother told me this, I felt as though I had been sent to hell. I whined and then kicked my foot a little when I couldn't stand it anymore.

"Why don't you like me the way I am? I'm *not* a genius! I can't play the piano. And even if I could, I wouldn't go on TV if you paid me a million dollars!" I cried.

My mother slapped me. "Who ask you be genius?" she shouted. "Only ask you be your best. For you sake. You think I want you be genius? Hnnh! What for! Who ask you!"

"So ungrateful," I heard her mutter in Chinese. "If she had as much talent as she has temper, she would be famous now."

Mr. Chong, whom I secretly nicknamed Old Chong, was very strange, always tapping his fingers to the silent music of an invisible orchestra. He looked ancient in my eyes. He had lost most of the hair on top of his head and he wore thick glasses and had

eyes that always looked tired and sleepy. But he must have been younger than I thought, since he lived with his mother and was not yet married.

I met Old Lady Chong once and that was enough. She had this peculiar smell like a baby that had done something in its pants. And her fingers felt like a dead person's, like an old peach I once found in the back of the refrigerator; the skin just slid off the meat when I picked it up.

I soon found out why Old Chong had retired from teaching piano. He was deaf. "Like Beethoven!" he shouted to me. "We're both listening only in our head!" And he would start to conduct his frantic silent sonatas.

Our lessons went like this. He would open the book and point to different things, explaining their purpose: "Key! Treble! Bass! No sharps or flats! So this is C major! Listen now and play after me!"

And then he would play the C scale a few times, a simple chord, and then, as if inspired by an old, unreachable itch, he gradually added more notes and running trills and a pounding bass until the music was really something quite grand.

I would play after him, the simple scale, the simple chord, and then I just played some nonsense that sounded like a cat running up and down on top of garbage cans. Old Chong smiled and applauded and then said, "Very good! But now you must learn to keep time!"

So that's how I discovered that Old Chong's eyes were too slow to keep up with the wrong notes I was playing. He went through the motions in half-time. To help me keep rhythm, he stood behind me, pushing down on my right shoulder for every beat. He balanced pennies on top of my wrists so I would keep them still as I slowly played scales and arpeggios. He had me curve my hand around an apple and keep that shape when playing chords. He marched stiffly to show me how to make each finger dance up and down, staccato like an obedient little soldier.

He taught me all these things, and that was how I also learned I could be lazy and get away with mistakes, lots of mistakes. If I hit the wrong notes because I hadn't practiced enough, I never corrected myself. I just kept playing in rhythm. And Old Chong kept conducting his own private reverie.

So maybe I never really gave myself a fair chance. I did pick up the basics pretty quickly, and I might have become a good pianist at that young age. But I was so determined not to try, not to be anybody different that I learned to play only the most ear-splitting preludes, the most discordant hymns.

Over the next year, I practiced like this, dutifully in my own way. And then one day I heard my mother and her friend Lindo Jong both talking in a loud bragging tone of voice so others could hear. It was after church, and I was leaning against the brick wall wearing a dress with stiff white petticoats. Auntie Lindo's daughter, Waverly, who was about my age, was standing farther down the wall about five feet away. We had grown up together and shared all the closeness of two sisters squabbling over crayons and dolls. In other words, for the most part, we hated each other. I thought she was snotty. Waverly Jong had gained a certain amount of fame as "Chinatown's Littlest Chinese Chess Champion."

"She bring home too many trophy," lamented Auntie Lindo that Sunday. "All day she play chess. All day I have no time do nothing but dust off her winnings." She threw a scolding look at Waverly, who pretended not to see her.

"You lucky you don't have this problem," said Auntie Lindo with a sigh to my mother.

And my mother squared her shoulders and bragged: "Our problem worser than yours. If we ask Jing-mei wash dish, she hear nothing but music. It's like you can't stop this natural talent."

And right then, I was determined to put a stop to her foolish pride.

A few weeks later, Old Chong and my mother conspired to have me play in a talent show which would be held in the church hall. By then, my parents had saved up enough to buy me a secondhand piano, a black Wurlitzer spinet with a scarred bench. It was the showpiece of our living room.

For the talent show, I was to play a piece called "Pleading Child" from Schumann's *Scenes from Childhood*. It was a simple, moody piece that sounded more difficult than it was. I was supposed to memorize the whole thing, playing the repeat parts twice to make the piece sound longer. But I dawdled over it, playing a few bars and then cheating, looking up to see what notes followed. I never really listened to what I was playing. I daydreamed about being somewhere else, about being someone else.

The part I liked to practice best was the fancy curtsy: right foot out, touch the rose on the carpet with a pointed foot, sweep to the side, left leg bends, look up and smile.

My parents invited all the couples from the Joy Luck Club to witness my debut. Auntie Lindo and Uncle Tin were there. Waverly and her two older brothers had also come. The first two rows were filled with children both younger and older than I was. The littlest ones got to go first. They recited simple nursery rhymes, squawked out tunes on miniature violins, twirled Hula Hoops, pranced in pink ballet tutus, and when they bowed or curtsied, the audience would sigh in unison, "Awww," and then clap enthusiastically.

When my turn came, I was very confident. I remember my childish excitement. It was as if I knew, without a doubt, that the prodigy side of me really did exist. I had no fear whatsoever, no nervousness. I remember thinking to myself, This is it! This is it! I looked out over the audience, at my mother's blank face, my father's yawn, Auntie Lindo's stiff-lipped smile, Waverly's sulky expression. I had on a white dress layered with sheets of lace, and a pink bow in my Peter Pan haircut. As I sat down I envisioned people jumping to their feet and Ed Sullivan rushing up to introduce me to everyone on TV.

And I started to play. It was so beautiful. I was so caught up in how lovely I looked that at first I didn't worry how I would sound. So it was a surprise to me when I hit the first wrong note and I realized something didn't sound quite right. And then I hit another and another followed that. A chill started at the top of my head and began to trickle down. Yet I couldn't stop playing, as though my hands were bewitched. I kept thinking my fingers would adjust themselves back, like a train switching to the right track. I played this strange jumble through two repeats, the sour notes staying with me all the way to the end.

When I stood up, I discovered my legs were shaking. Maybe I had just been nervous and the audience, like Old Chong, had seen me go through the right motions and had not heard anything wrong at all. I swept my right foot out, went down on my knee, looked up and smiled. The room was quiet, except for Old Chong, who was beaming and shouting, "Bravo! Bravo! Well done!" But then I saw my mother's face, her stricken

face. The audience clapped weakly, and as I walked back to my chair, with my whole face quivering as I tried not to cry, I heard a little boy whisper loudly to his mother, "That was awful," and the mother whispered back, "Well, she certainly tried."

And now I realized how many people were in the audience, the whole world it seemed. I was aware of eyes burning into my back. I felt the shame of my mother and father as they sat stiffly throughout the rest of the show.

We could have escaped during intermission. Pride and some strange sense of honor must have anchored my parents to their chairs. And so we watched it all: the eighteen-year-old boy with a fake mustache who did a magic show and juggled flaming hoops while riding a unicycle. The breasted girl with white makeup who sang from *Madama Butterfly* and got honorable mention. And the eleven-year-old boy who won first prize playing a tricky violin song that sounded like a busy bee.

After the show, the Hsus, the Jongs, and the St. Clairs from the Joy Luck Club came up to my mother and father.

"Lots of talented kids," Auntie Lindo said vaguely, smiling broadly.

"That was something' else," said my father, and I wondered if he was referring to me in a humorous way, or whether he even remembered what I had done.

Waverly looked at me and shrugged her shoulders. "You aren't a genius like me," she said matter-of-factly. And if I hadn't felt so bad, I would have pulled her braids and punched her stomach.

But my mother's expression was what devastated me: a quiet, blank look that said she had lost everything. I felt the same way, and it seemed as if everybody were now coming up, like gawkers at the scene of an accident, to see what parts were actually missing. When we got on the bus to go home, my father was humming the busy-bee tune and my mother was silent. I kept thinking she wanted to wait until we got home before shouting at me. But when my father unlocked the door to our apartment, my mother walked in and then went to the back, into the bedroom. No accusations. No blame. And in a way, I felt disappointed. I had been waiting for her to start shouting, so I could shout back and cry and blame her for all my misery.

I assumed my talent-show fiasco meant I never had to play the piano again. But two days later, after school, my mother came out of the kitchen and saw me watching TV.

"Four clock," she reminded me as if it were any other day. I was stunned, as though she were asking me to go through the talent-show torture again. I wedged myself more tightly in front of the TV.

"Turn off TV," she called from the kitchen five minutes later.

I didn't budge. And then I decided. I didn't have to do what my mother said anymore. I wasn't her slave. This wasn't China. I had listened to her before and look what happened. She was the stupid one.

She came out from the kitchen and stood in the arched entryway of the living room. "Four clock," she said once again, louder.

"I'm not going to play anymore," I said nonchalantly. "Why should I? I'm not a genius."

She walked over and stood in front of the TV. I saw her chest was heaving up and down in an angry way.

"No!" I said, and I now felt stronger, as if my true self had finally emerged. So this was what had been inside me all along.

"No! I won't!" I screamed.

She yanked me by the arm, pulled me off the floor, snapped off the TV. She was frighteningly strong, half pulling, half carrying me toward the piano as I kicked the throw rugs under my feet. She lifted me up and onto the hard bench. I was sobbing by now, looking at her bitterly. Her chest was heaving even more and her mouth was open, smiling crazily as if she were pleased I was crying.

"You want me to be someone that I'm not!" I sobbed. "I'll never be the kind of daughter you want me to be!"

"Only two kinds of daughters," she shouted in Chinese. "Those who are obedient and those who follow their own mind! Only one kind of daughter can live in this house. Obedient daughter!"

"Then I wish I wasn't your daughter. I wish you weren't my mother," I shouted. As I said these things I got scared. It felt like worms and toads and slimy things crawling out of my chest, but it also felt good, as if this awful side of me had surfaced, at last.

"Too late change this," said my mother shrilly.

And I could sense her anger rising to its breaking point. I wanted to see it spill over. And that's when I remembered the babies she had lost in China, the ones we never talked about. "Then I wish I'd never been born!" I shouted. "I wish I were dead! Like them."

It was as if I had said the magic words. Alakazam!—and her face went blank, her mouth closed, her arms went slack, and she backed out of the room, stunned, as if she were blowing away like a small brown leaf, thin, brittle, lifeless.

It was not the only disappointment my mother felt in me. In the years that followed, I failed her so many times, each time asserting my own will, my right to fall short of expectations. I didn't get straight As. I didn't become class president. I didn't get into Stanford. I dropped out of college.

For unlike my mother, I did not believe I could be anything I wanted to be. I could only be me.

And for all those years, we never talked about the disaster at the recital or my terrible accusations afterward at the piano bench. All that remained unchecked, like a betrayal that was now unspeakable. So I never found a way to ask her why she had hoped for something so large that failure was inevitable.

And even worse, I never asked her what frightened me the most: Why had she given up hope?

For after our struggle at the piano, she never mentioned my playing again. The lessons stopped. The lid to the piano was closed, shutting out the dust, my misery, and her dreams.

So she surprised me. A few years ago, she offered to give me the piano, for my thirtieth birthday. I had not played in all those years. I saw the offer as a sign of forgiveness, a tremendous burden removed.

"Are you sure?" I asked shyly. "I mean, won't you and Dad miss it?"

"No, this your piano," she said firmly. "Always your piano. You only one can play."

"Well, I probably can't play anymore," I said. "It's been years."

"You pick up fast," said my mother, as if she knew this was certain. "You have natural talent. You could been genius if you want to."

"No I couldn't."

"You just not trying," said my mother. And she was neither angry nor sad. She said it as if to announce a fact that could never be disproved. "Take it," she said.

But I didn't at first. It was enough that she had offered it to me. And after that, every time I saw it in my parents' living room, standing in front of the bay windows, it made me feel proud, as if it were a shiny trophy I had won back.

Last week I sent a tuner over to my parents' apartment and had the piano reconditioned, for purely sentimental reasons. My mother had died a few months before and I had been getting things in order for my father, a little bit at a time. I put the jewelry in special silk pouches. The sweaters she had knitted in yellow, pink, bright orange—all the colors I hated—I put those in moth-proof boxes. I found some old Chinese silk dresses, the kind with little slits up the sides. I rubbed the old silk against my skin, then wrapped them in tissue and decided to take them home with me.

After I had the piano tuned, I opened the lid and touched the keys. It sounded even richer than I remembered. Really, it was a very good piano. Inside the bench were the same exercise notes with handwritten scales, the same secondhand music books with their covers held together with yellow tape.

I opened up the Schumann book to the dark little piece I had played at the recital. It was on the left-hand side of the page, "Pleading Child." It looked more difficult than I remembered. I played a few bars, surprised at how easily the notes came back to me.

And for the first time, or so it seemed, I noticed the piece on the right-hand side. It was called "Perfectly Contented." I tried to play this one as well. It had a lighter melody but the same flowing rhythm and turned out to be quite easy. "Pleading Child" was shorter but slower; "Perfectly Contented" was longer, but faster. And after I played them both a few times, I realized they were two halves of the same song.

QUESTIONS

1. The writer Alice Walker (whose story "Roselily" appears in this chapter) states that Amy Tan's fiction illuminates "the mystery of the mother-daughter bond in ways that we have not experienced before." Apply this assessment to "Two Kinds," with specific reference to the cross-cultural conflicts in the story.

2. Do you find the tone of this story witty and humorous? Why or why not?

3. How do you interpret the conclusion of the story?

7 . Symbolism

A symbol is something that represents something else by convention, habit, resemblance, or association. Symbols in literature have specific referents.

The word "symbol" is derived from the Greek *symbolaeon* and was originally political and not literary. *Symbolaeon* described a group of words that made up a treaty or a contract. The problem was that each of the contractees attached different ideas to the words they agreed to approve. Inasmuch as the symbols a writer uses may mean different things to different people, the problem of understanding symbols still exists. But they are, as D. H. Lawrence defines them, "organic units of consciousness with a life of their own, and you can never explain them away, because their value is dynamic, emotional, belonging to the sense-consciousness of the body and soul, and not simply mental. An allegorical image has meaning."

Perhaps we can simplify the definition to correspond with the one in the first paragraph of this section: symbolism can be defined as the representation of a reality on one level of reference by a corresponding reality on another. "It is easier," Plato wrote, "to say what a thing is like than what it is," so we think of someone "running like the wind," which is only to say, very fast.

There are times when the major symbol of a story may be found in the title, which may also supply the theme. We recognize symbols by the position of importance they hold in a story, and by their frequent recurrence, either in the narrative or in dialogue. The author *intends* for the reader to understand the symbols he or she uses, for they may be the clue to understanding the story itself.

We all understand certain common symbols—rainbows, daybreak, a cross, a flag, and others—but symbols are drawn from nearly every field of human endeavor and have come into literary use from many sources and at different times. The lotus flower, for example, may symbolize perfect form or perfect state of being to Asian readers, but not necessarily to British readers. Steel may symbolize automobiles to a reader in Detroit, but may symbolize an ax to a reader in central Africa.

In addition to the widely understood symbols, there are cultural, national, religious,

and psychological symbols. Whatever the origin of a symbol, if it finds its way into the English language, it enriches literature and, naturally, extends the number and kinds of symbols that can be used.

Jean Toomer's *Cane* (1923) explored symbolism through the dream of a character, Esther:

> Another dream comes. There is no fire department. There are no heroic men. The fire starts. The loafers on the corner form a circle, chew their tobacco faster, and squirt juice just as fast as they can chew. Gallons on top of gallons they squirt upon the flames. The air reeks with the stench of scorched tobacco juice. Women, fat, chunky Negro women, lean scrawny white women, pull their skirts up above their heads and display the most ludicrous underclothes. The women scoot in all directions from the danger zone. She alone is left to take the baby in her arms. But what a baby! Black, singed, woolly, tobacco-juice baby—ugly as sin. Once held to her breast, miraculous thing: its breath is sweet and its lips can nibble. She loves it frantically.

The symbols here have to do with sex, race, and desire; they also relate to Esther's madness. We have only to think of the language Toomer has used: fire (and there is no fire department to quench the flames); the men forming a circle, chewing tobacco so they can squirt juice, (brown) tobacco juice, scorched tobacco juice, tobacco-juice baby; the women raising their dresses, but only Esther is left to take (bear) the baby, which is transformed because she alone is capable of creating that transformation.

The conscious infusion of psychological symbols was taking place at the time Toomer was writing, but it is important to remember that symbolism is not meant to intimidate the reader; rather it is used to add depth to the story and theme.

Allegory, related to symbolism, while often used in a religious context, is a representation of things or ideas that themselves hold deeper meaning. The story of Prometheus is an example of allegory. Metaphor, another relative of symbolism, is a figure of speech in which one thing is substituted for another. Hamlet, in considering whether or not "To take up arms against a sea of troubles," utters a Shakespearean metaphor.

The stories in this section (as in many others) provide symbols in their titles. In each, the dominant symbol is used effectively to convey several meanings, all of which relate to the theme. Although symbolism is the literary tool most under discussion here, note also the presence of irony, tone, and mood, the uses of plot, point of view, character, subject, and theme. When symbols do exist (and Flannery O'Connor was one of many writers who warned against our tendency to "strain the soup too thin" by hunting for symbols everywhere), they add yet another dimension to the technically complex world of short fiction.

Ernest Hemingway

A CLEAN,
WELL-LIGHTED PLACE

It was late and everyone had left the café except an old man who sat in the shadow the leaves of the tree made against the electric light. In the day time the street was dusty, but at night the dew settled the dust and the old man liked to sit late because he was deaf and now at night it was quiet and he felt the difference. The two waiters inside the café knew that the old man was a little drunk, and while he was a good client they knew that if he became too drunk he would leave without paying, so they kept watch on him.

"Last week he tried to commit suicide," one waiter said.

"Why?"

"He was in despair."

"What about?"

"Nothing."

"How do you know it was nothing?"

"He has plenty of money."

They sat together at a table that was close against the wall near the door of the café and looked at the terrace where the tables were all empty except where the old man sat in the shadow of the leaves of the tree that moved slightly in the wind. A girl and a soldier went by in the street. The street light shone on the brass number on his collar. The girl wore no head covering and hurried beside him.

"The guard will pick him up," one waiter said.

"What does it matter if he gets what he's after?"

"He had better get off the street now. The guard will get him. They went by five minutes ago."

The old man sitting in the shadow rapped on his saucer with his glass. The younger waiter went over to him.

"What do you want?"

The old man looked at him. "Another brandy," he said.

"You'll be drunk," the waiter said. The old man looked at him. The waiter went away.

"He'll stay all night," he said to his colleague. "I'm sleepy now. I never get into bed before three o'clock. He should have killed himself last week."

The waiter took the brandy bottle and another saucer from the counter inside the café and marched out to the old man's table. He put down the saucer and poured the glass full of brandy.

"You should have killed yourself last week," he said to the deaf man. The old man motioned with his finger. "A little more," he said. The waiter poured on into the glass so that the brandy slopped over and ran down the stem into the top saucer of the pile. "Thank you," the old man said. The waiter took the bottle back inside the café. He sat down at the table with his colleague again.

"He's drunk now," he said.

"He's drunk every night."

"What did he want to kill himself for?"

"How should I know."

"How did he do it?"

"He hung himself with a rope."

"Who cut him down?"

"His niece."

"Why did they do it?"

"Fear for his soul."

"How much money has he got?"

"He's got plenty."

"He must be eighty years old."

"Anyway I should say he was eighty."

"I wish he would go home. I never get to bed before three o'clock. What kind of hour is that to go to bed?"

"He stays up because he likes it."

"He's lonely. I'm not lonely. I have a wife waiting in bed for me."

"He had a wife once too."

"A wife would be no good to him now."

"You can't tell. He might be better with a wife."

"His niece looks after him. You said she cut him down."

"I know."

"I wouldn't want to be that old. An old man is a nasty thing."

"Not always. This old man is clean. He drinks without spilling. Even now, drunk. Look at him."

"I don't want to look at him. I wish he would go home. He has no regard for those who must work."

The old man looked from his glass across the square, then over at the waiters.

"Another brandy," he said, pointing to his glass. The waiter who was in hurry came over.

"Finished," he said, speaking with that omission of syntax stupid people employ when talking to drunken people or foreigners. "No more tonight. Close now."

"Another," said the old man.

"No. Finished." The waiter wiped the edge of the table with a towel and shook his head.

The old man stood up, slowly counted the saucers, took a leather coin purse from his pocket and paid for the drinks, leaving half a peseta tip.

The waiter watched him go down the street, a very old man walking unsteadily but with dignity.

"Why didn't you let him stay and drink?" the unhurried waiter asked. They were putting up the shutters. "It is not half-past two."

"I want to go home to bed."

"What is an hour?"

"More to me than to him."

"An hour is the same."

"You talk like an old man yourself. He can buy a bottle and drink at home."

"It's not the same."

"No, it is not," agreed the waiter with a wife. He did not wish to be unjust. He was only in a hurry.

"And you? You have no fear of going home before your usual hour?"

"Are you trying to insult me?"

"No, hombre, only to make a joke."

"No," the waiter who was in a hurry said, rising from pulling down the metal shutters. "I have confidence. I am all confidence."

"You have youth, confidence, and a job," the older waiter said. "You have everything."

"And what do you lack?"

"Everything but work."

"You have everything I have."

"No. I have never had confidence and I am not young."

"Come on. Stop talking nonsense and lock up."

"I am of those who like to stay late at the café," the older waiter said. "With all those who do not want to go to bed. With all those who need a light for the night."

"I want to go home and into bed."

"We are of two different kinds," the older waiter said. He was now dressed to go home. "It is not only a question of youth and confidence although those things are very beautiful. Each night I am reluctant to close up because there may be some one who needs the café."

"Hombre, there are bodegas open all night long."

"You do not understand. This is a clean and pleasant café. It is well lighted. The light is very good and also, now, there are shadows of the leaves."

"Good night," said the younger waiter.

"Good night," the other said. Turning off the electric light he continued the conversation with himself. It is the light of course but it is necessary that the place be clean and pleasant. You do not want music. Certainly you do not want music. Nor can you stand before a bar with dignity although that is all that is provided for these hours. What did he fear? It was not fear or dread. It was a nothing that he knew too well. It was all a nothing and a man was nothing too. It was only that and light was all it needed and a certain cleanness and order. Some lived in it and never felt it but he knew it all was nada y pues nada y nada y pues nada. Our nada who art in nada, nada be thy name thy kingdom nada thy will be nada in nada as it is in nada. Give us this nada our daily nada and nada us our nada as we nada our nadas and nada us not into nada but deliver us from nada; pues nada. Hail nothing full of nothing, nothing is with thee. He smiled and stood before a bar with a shining steam pressure coffee machine.

"What's yours?" asked the barman.

"Nada."

"Otro loco mas," said the barman and turned away.

"A little cup," said the waiter.

The barman poured it for him.

"The light is very bright and pleasant but the bar is unpolished," the waiter said.

The barman looked at him but did not answer. It was too late at night for conversation.

"You want another copita?" the barman asked.

"No, thank you," said the waiter and went out. He disliked bars and bodegas. A clean, well-lighted café was a very different thing. Now, without thinking further, he would go home to his room. He would lie in the bed and finally, with daylight, he would go to sleep. After all, he said to himself, it is probably only insomnia. Many must have it.

QUESTIONS

1. How do the older and younger waiter differ? What is each one's attitude toward the old man?
2. Light imagery abounds in this story. At one point, the older waiter says to himself, "It is the light of course but it is necessary that the place be clean and pleasant." Why does he focus so intently on the "atmosphere" of the café? What does the light symbolize?
3. What is the significance of the waiter's prayer? Why is the prayer full of negativity?
4. It seems that the deaf old man and the older waiter have a similar negative attitude toward life. What do they have in common that may have caused this attitude? What might be the key to their both finding happiness?
5. Hemingway is known for his sparse, laconic style and his ability to say much with few words. Does this story bear out this observation? Explain.

Langston Hughes

ON THE ROAD

He was not interested in the snow. When he got off the freight, one early evening during the depression, Sargeant never even noticed the snow. But he must have felt it seeping down his neck, cold, wet, sopping in his shoes. But if you had asked him, he wouldn't have known it was snowing. Sargeant didn't see the snow, not even under the bright lights of the main street, falling white and flaky against the night. He was too hungry, too sleepy, too tired.

The Reverend Mr. Dorset, however, saw the snow when he switched on his porch light, opened the front door of his parsonage, and found standing there before him a big black man with snow on his face, a human piece of night with snow on his face—obviously unemployed.

Said the Reverend Mr. Dorset before Sargeant even realized he'd opened his mouth: "I'm sorry. No! Go right on down this street four blocks and turn to your left, walk up seven and you'll see the Relief Shelter. I'm sorry. No!" He shut the door.

Sargeant wanted to tell the holy man that he had already been to the Relief Shelter, been to hundreds of relief shelters during the depression years, the beds were always gone and supper was over, the place was full, and they drew the color line anyhow. But the minister said, "No," and shut the door. Evidently he didn't want to hear about it. And he *had* a door to shut.

The big black man turned away. And even yet he didn't see the snow, walking right into it. Maybe he sensed it, cold, wet, sticking to his jaws, wet on his black hands, sopping in his shoes. He stopped and stood on the sidewalk hunched over—hungry, sleepy, cold—looking up and down. Then he looked right where he was—in front of a church. Of course! A church! Sure, right next to a parsonage, certainly a church.

It had *two* doors.

Broad white steps in the night all snowy white. Two high arched doors with slender stone pillars on either side. And way up, a round lacy window with a stone crucifix in the middle and Christ on the crucifix in stone. All this was pale in the street lights, solid and stony pale in the snow.

Sargeant blinked. When he looked up, the snow fell into his eyes. For the first time that night he *saw* the snow. He shook his head. He shook the snow from his coat sleeves, felt hungry, felt lost, felt not lost, felt cold. He walked up the steps of the church. He knocked at the door. No answer. He tried the handle. Locked. He put his shoulder against the door and his long black body slanted like a ramrod. He pushed. With loud rhythmic grunts, like the grunts in a chain-gang song, he pushed against the door.

"I'm tired . . . Huh! . . . Hongry . . . Uh! . . . I'm sleepy . . . Huh! I'm cold . . . I got to sleep somewheres," Sargeant said. "This here is a church, ain't it? Well, uh!"

He pushed against the door.

Suddenly, with an undue cracking and screaking, the door began to give way to the tall black Negro who pushed ferociously against it.

By now two or three white people had stopped in the street, and Sargeant was vaguely aware of some of them yelling at him concerning the door. Three or four more came running, yelling at him.

"Hey!" they said. "Hey!"

"Uh-huh," answered the big tall Negro, "I know it's a white folks' church, but I got to sleep somewhere." He gave another lunge at the door. "Huh!"

And the door broke open.

But just when the door gave way, two white cops arrived in a car, ran up the steps with their clubs, and grabbed Sargeant. But Sargeant for once had no intention of being pulled or pushed away from the door.

Sargeant grabbed, but not for anything so weak as a broken door. He grabbed for one of the tall stone pillars beside the door, grabbed at it and caught it. And held it. The cops pulled and Sargeant pulled. Most of the people in the street got behind the cops and helped them pull.

"A big black unemployed Negro holding onto our church!" thought the people. "The idea!"

The cops began to beat Sargeant over the head, and nobody protested. But he held on.

And then the church fell down.

Gradually, the big stone front of the church fell down, the walls and the rafters, the

crucifix and the Christ. Then the whole thing fell down, covering the cops and the people with bricks and stones and debris. The whole church fell down in the snow.

Sargeant got out from under the church and went walking on up the street with the stone pillar on his shoulder. He was under the impression that he had buried the parsonage and the Reverend Mr. Dorset who said, "No!" So he laughed, and threw the pillar six blocks up the street and went on.

Sargeant thought he was alone, but listening to the *crunch, crunch, crunch* on the snow of his own footsteps, he heard other footsteps, too, doubling his own. He looked around, and there was Christ walking along beside him, the same Christ that had been on the cross on the church—still stone with a rough stone surface, walking along beside him just like he was broken off the cross when the church fell down.

"Well, I'll be dogged," said Sargeant. "This here's the first time I ever seed you off the cross."

"Yes," said Christ, crunching his feet in the snow. "You had to pull the church down to get me off the cross."

"You glad?" said Sargeant.

"I sure am," said Christ.

They both laughed.

"I'm a hell of a fellow, ain't I?" said Sargeant. "Done pulled the church down!"

"You did a good job," said Christ. "They have kept me nailed on a cross for nearly two thousand years."

"Whee-ee-e!" said Sargeant. "I know you are glad to get off."

"I sure am," said Christ.

They walked on in the snow. Sargeant looked at the man of stone.

"And you have been up there two thousand years?"

"I sure have," Christ said.

"Well, if I had a little cash," said Sargeant, "I'd show you around a bit."

"I been around," said Christ.

"Yeah, but that was a long time ago."

"All the same," said Christ, "I've been around."

They walked on in the snow until they came to the railroad yards. Sargeant was tired, sweating and tired.

"Where you goin'?" Sargeant said, stopping by the tracks. He looked at Christ. Sargeant said, "I'm just a bum on the road. How about you? Where you goin'?"

"God knows," Christ said, "but I'm leavin' here."

They saw the red and green lights of the railroad yard half veiled by the snow that fell out of the night. Away down the track they saw a fire in a hobo jungle.

"I can go there and sleep," Sargeant said.

"You can?"

"Sure," said Sargeant. "That place ain't got no doors."

Outside the town, along the tracks, there were barren trees and bushes below the embankment, snow-gray in the dark. And down among the trees and bushes there were makeshift houses made out of boxes and tin and old pieces of wood and canvas. You couldn't see them in the dark, but you knew they were there if you'd ever been on the road, if you had ever lived with the homeless and hungry in a depression.

"I'm side-tracking," Sargeant said. "I'm tired."

"I'm gonna make it on to Kansas City," said Christ.

"O.K.," Sargeant said. "So long!"

He went down into the hobo jungle and found himself a place to sleep. He never did see Christ no more. About 6:00 A.M. a freight came by. Sargeant scrambled out of the jungle with a dozen or so more hobos and ran along the track, grabbing at the freight. It was dawn, early dawn, cold and gray.

"Wonder where Christ is by now?" Sargeant thought. "He musta gone on way on down the road. He didn't sleep in this jungle."

Sargeant grabbed the train and started to pull himself up into a moving coal car, over the edge of a wheeling coal car. But strangely enough, the car was full of cops. The nearest cop rapped Sargeant soundly across the knuckles with his night stick. Wham! Rapped his big black hands for clinging to the top of the car. Wham! But Sargeant did not turn loose. He clung on and tried to pull himself into the car. He hollered at the top of his voice, "Damn it, lemme in this car!"

"Shut up," barked the cop. "You crazy coon!" He rapped Sargeant across the knuckles and punched him in the stomach. "You ain't out in no jungle now. This ain't no train. You in jail."

Wham! across his bare black fingers clinging to the bars of his cell. Wham! between the steel bars low down against his shins.

Suddenly Sargeant realized that he really was in jail. He wasn't on no train. The blood of the night before had dried on his face, his head hurt terribly, and a cop outside in the corridor was hitting him across the knuckles for holding onto the door, yelling and shaking the cell door.

"They musta took me to jail for breaking down the door last night," Sargeant thought, "that church door."

Sargeant went over and sat on a wooden bench against the cold stone wall. He was emptier than ever. His clothes were wet, clammy cold wet, and shoes sloppy with snow water. It was just about dawn. There he was, locked up behind a cell door, nursing his bruised fingers.

The bruised fingers were his, but not the *door*.

Not the *club*, but the fingers.

"You wait," mumbled Sargeant, black against the jail wall. "I'm gonna break down this door, too."

"Shut up—or I'll paste you one," said the cop.

"I'm gonna break down this door," yelled Sargeant as he stood up in his cell.

Then he must have been talking to himself because he said, "I wonder where Christ's gone? I wonder if he's gone to Kansas City?"

QUESTIONS

1. The narrator refers to the Reverend as a "holy man." What is the irony behind this title?

2. Christ says to Sargeant, "You had to pull the church down to get me off the cross." What comment is the author making about organized religion?
3. What similarities exist between the life of Christ and that of Sargeant?
4. At what point in the story is it first apparent that the author is not writing a realistic story? Would you term the story symbolic or allegorical? Explain.

Kay Boyle

ASTRONOMER'S WIFE

There is an evil moment on awakening when all things seem to pause. But for women, they only falter and may be set in action by a single move: a lifted hand and the pendulum will swing, or the voice raised and through every room the pulse takes up its beating. The astronomer's wife felt the interval gaping and at once filled it to the brim. She fetched up her gentle voice and sent it warily down the stairs for coffee, swung her feet out upon the oval mat, and hailed the morning with her bare arms' quivering flesh drawn taut in rhythmic exercise: left, left, left my wife and fourteen children, right, right, right in the middle of the dusty road.

The day would proceed from this, beat by beat, without reflection, like every other day. The astronomer was still asleep, or feigning it, and she, once out of bed, had come into her own possession. Although scarcely ever out of sight of the impenetrable silence of his brow, she would be absent from him all the day in being clean, busy, kind. He was a man of other things, a dreamer. At times he lay still for hours, at others he sat upon the roof behind his telescope, or wandered down the pathway to the road and out across the mountains. This day, like any other, would go on from the removal of the spot left there from dinner on the astronomer's vest to the severe thrashing of the mayonnaise for lunch. That man might be each time the new arching wave, and woman the undertow that sucked him back, were things she had been told by his silence were so.

In spite of the earliness of the hour, the girl had heard her mistress's voice and was coming up the stairs. At the threshold of the bedroom she paused, and said: "Madame, the plumber is here."

The astronomer's wife put on her white and scarlet smock very quickly and buttoned it at the neck. Then she stepped carefully around the motionless spread of water in the hall.

"Tell him to come right up," she said. She laid her hands on the bannisters and stood looking down the wooden stairway. "Ah, I am Mrs. Ames," she said softly as she saw him mounting. "I am Mrs. Ames," she said softly, softly down the flight of stairs. "I am Mrs. Ames," spoken soft as a willow weeping. "The professor is still sleeping. Just step this way."

The plumber himself looked up and saw Mrs. Ames with her voice hushed, speaking to him. She was a youngish woman, but this she had forgotten. The mystery and silence of her husband's mind lay like a chiding finger on her lips. Her eyes were gray, for the light had been extinguished in them. The strange dim halo of her yellow hair was still uncombed and sideways on her head.

For all of his heavy boots, the plumber quieted the sound of his feet, and together they went down the hall, picking their way around the still lake of water that spread as far as the landing and lay docile there. The plumber was a tough, hardy man; but he took off his hat when he spoke to her and looked her fully, almost insolently in the eye.

"Does it come from the wash-basin," he said, "or from the other . . . ?"

"Oh, from the other," said Mrs. Ames without hesitation.

In this place the villas were scattered out few and primitive, and although beauty lay without there was no reflection of her face within. Here all was awkward and unfit; a sense of wrestling with uncouth forces gave everything an austere countenance. Even the plumber, dealing as does a woman with matters under hand, was grave and stately. The mountains round about seemed to have cast them into the shadow of great dignity.

Mrs. Ames began speaking of their arrival that summer in the little villa, mourning each event as it followed on the other.

"Then, just before going to bed last night," she said, "I noticed something was unusual."

The plumber cast down a folded square of sack-cloth on the brimming floor and laid his leather apron on it. Then he stepped boldly onto the heart of the island it shaped and looked long into the overflowing bowl.

"The water should be stopped from the meter in the garden," he said at last.

"Oh, I did that," said Mrs. Ames, "the very first thing last night. I turned it off at once, in my nightgown, as soon as I saw what was happening. But all this had already run in."

The plumber looked for a moment at her red kid slippers. She was standing just at the edge of the clear, pure-seeming tide.

"It's no doubt the soil lines," he said severely. "It may be that something has stopped them, but my opinion is that the water seals aren't working. That's the trouble often enough in such cases. If you had a valve you wouldn't be caught like this."

Mrs. Ames did not know how to meet this rebuke. She stood, swaying a little, looking into the plumber's blue relentless eye.

"I'm sorry—I'm sorry that my husband," she said, "is still—resting and cannot go into this with you. I'm sure it must be very interesting. . . ."

"You'll probably have to have the traps sealed," said the plumber grimly, and at the sound of this Mrs. Ames' hand flew in dismay to the side of her face. The plumber made no move, but the set of his mouth as he looked at her seemed to soften. "Anyway, I'll have a look from the garden end," he said.

"Oh, do," said the astronomer's wife in relief. Here was a man who spoke of action and object as simply as women did! But however hushed her voice had been, it carried clearly to Professor Ames who lay, dreaming and solitary, upon his bed. He heard their footsteps come down the hall, pause, and skip across the pool of overflow.

"Katherine!" said the astronomer in a ringing tone. "There's a problem worthy of your mettle!"

Mrs. Ames did not turn her head, but led the plumber swiftly down the stairs. When the sun in the garden struck her face, he saw there was a wave of color in it, but this may have been anything but shame.

"You see how it is," said the plumber, as if leading her mind away. "The drains run from these houses right down the hill, big enough for a man to stand upright in them, and clean as a whistle too." There they stood in the garden with the vegetation flowering in disorder all about. The plumber looked at the astronomer's wife. "They come out at the torrent on the other side of the forest beyond there," he said.

But the words the astronomer had spoken still sounded in her in despair. The mind of man, she knew, made steep and sprightly flights, pursued illusion, took foothold in the nameless things that cannot pass between the thumb and finger. But whenever the astronomer gave voice to the thoughts that soared within him, she returned in gratitude to the long expanses of his silence. Desert-like they stretched behind and before the articulation of his scorn.

Life, life is an open sea, she sought to explain it in sorrow, and to survive women cling to the floating débris on the tide. But the plumber had suddenly fallen upon his knees in the grass and had crooked his fingers through the ring of the drains' trap-door. When she looked down she saw that he was looking up into her face, and she saw too that his hair was as light as gold.

"Perhaps Mr. Ames," he said rather bitterly, "would like to come down with me and have a look around?"

"Down?" said Mrs. Ames in wonder.

"Into the drains," said the plumber brutally. "They're a study for a man who likes to know what's what."

"Oh, Mr. Ames," said Mrs. Ames in confusion. "He's still—still in bed, you see."

The plumber lifted his strong, weathered face and looked curiously at her. Surely it seemed to him strange for a man to linger in bed, with the sun pouring yellow as wine all over the place. The astronomer's wife saw his lean cheeks, his high, rugged bones, and the deep seams in his brow. His flesh was as firm and clean as wood, stained richly tan with the climate's rigor. His fingers were blunt, but comprehensible to her, gripped in the ring and holding the iron door wide. The backs of his hands were bound round and round with ripe blue veins of blood.

"At any rate," said the astronomer's wife, and the thought of it moved her lips to smile a little, "Mr. Ames would never go down there alive. He likes going up," she said. And she, in her turn, pointed, but impudently, towards the heavens. "On the roof. Or on the mountains. He's been up on the tops of them many times."

"It's a matter of habit," said the plumber, and suddenly he went down the trap, Mrs. Ames saw a bright little piece of his hair still shining, like a star, long after the rest of him had gone. Out of the depths, his voice, hollow and dark with foreboding, returned to her. "I think something has stopped the elbow," was what he said.

This was speech that touched her flesh and bone and made her wonder. When her husband spoke of height, having no sense of it, she could not picture it nor hear. Depth or magic passed her by unless a name was given. But madness in a daily shape, as elbow stopped, she saw clearly and well. She sat down on the grasses, bewildered that it should be a man who had spoken to her so.

She saw the weeds springing up, and she did not move to tear them up from life. She sat powerless, her senses veiled, with no action taking shape beneath her hands. In this way some men sat for hours on end, she knew, tracking a single thought back to its origin. The mind of man could balance and divide, weed out, destroy. She sat on the full, burdened grasses, seeking to think, and dimly waiting for the plumber to return.

Whereas her husband had always gone up, as the dead go, she knew now that there were others who went down, like the corporeal being of the dead. That men were then divided into two bodies now seemed clear to Mrs. Ames. This knowledge stunned her with its simplicity and took the uneasy motion from her limbs. She could not stir, but sat facing the mountains' rocky flanks, and harking in silence to lucidity. Her husband was the mind, this other man the meat, of all mankind.

After a little, the plumber emerged from the earth: first the light top of his head, then the burnt brow, and then the blue eyes fringed with whitest lash. He braced his thick hands flat on the pavings of the garden-path and swung himself completely from the pit.

"It's the soil lines," he said pleasantly. "The gases," he said as he looked down upon her lifted face, "are backing up the drains."

"What in the world are we going to do?" said the astronomer's wife softly. There was a young and strange delight in putting questions to which true answers would be given. Everything the astronomer had ever said to her was a continuous query to which there could be no response.

"Ah, come, now," said the plumber, looking down and smiling. "There's a remedy for every ill, you know. Sometimes it may be that," he said as if speaking to a child, "or sometimes the other thing. But there's always a help for everything a-miss."

Things come out of herbs and make you young again, he might have been saying to her; or the first good rain will quench any drought; or time of itself will put a broken bone together.

"I'm going to follow the ground pipe out right to the torrent," the plumber was saying. "The trouble's between here and there and I'll find it on the way. There's nothing at all that can't be done over for the caring," he was saying, and his eyes were fastened on her face in insolence, or gentleness, or love.

The astronomer's wife stood up, fixed a pin in her hair, and turned around towards the kitchen. Even while she was calling the servant's name, the plumber began speaking again.

"I once had a cow that lost her cud," the plumber was saying. The girl came out on the kitchen-step and Mrs. Ames stood smiling at her in the sun.

"The trouble is very serious, very serious," she said across the garden. "When Mr. Ames gets up, please tell him I've gone down."

She pointed briefly to the open door in the pathway, and the plumber hoisted his kit on his arm and put out his hand to help her down.

"But I made her another in no time," he was saying, "out of flowers and things and what-not."

"Oh," said the astronomer's wife in wonder as she stepped into the heart of the earth. She took his arm, knowing that what he said was true.

QUESTIONS

1. When do we get the first inkling of Mrs. Ames's feelings toward her husband? What are they?
2. What significance does water have as a symbol in the story? Does this symbol go through various transformations, and if so, what are they?
3. Is the astronomer portrayed sympathetically or unsympathetically? Explain.
4. What types of observations does Mrs. Ames make about the plumber? How are they similar to what the plumber notices about Mrs. Ames?
5. How are images of height and depth used in the story? How do they contribute to the story's theme?

8. An Anthology of Short Fiction

Chinua Achebe

CIVIL PEACE

Jonathan Iwegbu counted himself extra-ordinarily lucky. "Happy survival!" meant so much more to him than just a current fashion of greeting old friends in the first hazy days of peace. It went deep to his heart. He had come out of the war with five inestimable blessings—his head, his wife Maria's head and the heads of three out of their four children. As a bonus he also had his old bicycle—a miracle too but naturally not to be compared to the safety of five human heads.

The bicycle had a little history of its own. One day at the height of the war it was commandeered "for urgent military action." Hard as its loss would have been to him he would still have let it go without a thought had he not had some doubts about the genuineness of the officer. It wasn't his disreputable rags, nor the toes peeping out of one blue and one brown canvas shoes, nor yet the two stars of his rank done obviously in a hurry in biro, that troubled Jonathan; many good and heroic soldiers looked the same or worse. It was rather a certain lack of grip and firmness in his manner. So Jonathan, suspecting he might be amenable to influence, rummaged in his raffia bag and produced the two pounds with which he had been going to buy firewood which his wife, Maria, retailed to camp officials for extra stock-fish and corn meal, and got his bicycle back. That night he buried it in the little clearing in the bush where the dead of the camp, including his own youngest son, were buried. When he dug it up again a year later after the surrender all it needed was a little palm-oil greasing. "Nothing puzzles God," he said in wonder.

He put it to immediate use as a taxi and accumulated a small pile of Biafran money ferrying camp officials and their families across the four-mile stretch to the nearest tarred road. His standard charge per trip was six pounds and those who had the money were only glad to be rid of some of it in this way. At the end of a fortnight he had made a small fortune of one hundred and fifteen pounds.

Then he made the journey to Enugu and found another miracle waiting for him. It was unbelievable. He rubbed his eyes and looked again and it was still standing there before him. But, needless to say, even that monumental blessing must be accounted also totally inferior to the five heads in the family. This newest miracle was his little house in Ogui Overside. Indeed nothing puzzles God! Only two houses away a huge concrete edifice some wealthy contractor had put up just before the war was a mountain of rubble. And here was Jonathan's little zinc house of no regrets built with mud blocks quite intact! Of course the doors and windows were missing and five sheets off the roof. But what was that? And anyhow he had returned to Enugu early enough to pick up bits of old zinc and wood and soggy sheets of cardboard lying around the neighbourhood before thousands more came out of their forest holes looking for the same things. He got a destitute carpenter with one old hammer, a blunt plane and a few bent and rusty nails in his tool bag to turn this assortment of wood, paper and metal into door and window shutters for five Nigerian shillings or fifty Biafran pounds. He paid the pounds, and moved in with his overjoyed family carrying five heads on their shoulders.

His children picked mangoes near the military cemetery and sold them to soldiers' wives for a few pennies—real pennies this time—and his wife started making breakfast akara balls for neighbours in a hurry to start life again. With his family earnings he took his bicycle to the villages around and bought fresh palm-wine which he mixed generously in his rooms with the water which had recently started running again in the public tap down the road, and opened up a bar for soldiers and other lucky people with good money.

At first he went daily, then every other day and finally once a week, to the offices of the Coal Corporation where he used to be a miner, to find out what was what. The only thing he did find out in the end was that that little house of his was even a greater blessing than he had thought. Some of his fellow ex-miners who had nowhere to return at the end of the day's waiting just slept outside the doors of the offices and cooked what meal they could scrounge together in Bournvita tins. As the weeks lengthened and still nobody could say what was what Jonathan discontinued his weekly visits altogether and faced his palm-wine bar.

But nothing puzzles God. Came the day of the windfall when after five days of endless scuffles in queues and counter-queues in the sun outside the Treasury he had twenty pounds counted into his palms as ex-gratia award for the rebel money he had turned in. It was like Christmas for him and for many others like him when the payments began. They called it (since few could manage its proper official name) *egg-rasher*.

As soon as the pound notes were placed in his palm Jonathan simply closed it tight over them and buried fist and money inside his trouser pocket. He had to be extra careful because he had seen a man a couple of days earlier collapse into near-madness in an instant before that oceanic crowd because no sooner had he got his twenty pounds than some heartless ruffian picked it off him. Though it was not right that a man in such an extremity of agony should be blamed yet many in the queues that day were able to remark quietly on the victim's carelessness, especially after he pulled out the innards of his pocket and revealed a hole in it big enough to pass a thief's head. But of course he had insisted that the money had been in the other pocket, pulling it out too to show its comparative wholeness. So one had to be careful.

Jonathan soon transferred the money to his left hand and pocket so as to leave his right free for shaking hands should the need arise, though by fixing his gaze at such an elevation as to miss all approaching human faces he made sure that the need did not arise, until he got home.

He was normally a heavy sleeper but that night he heard all the neighbourhood noises die down one after another. Even the night watchman who knocked the hour on some metal somewhere in the distance had fallen silent after knocking one o'clock. That must have been the last thought in Jonathan's mind before he was finally carried away himself. He couldn't have been gone for long, though, when he was violently awakened again.

"Who is knocking?" whispered his wife lying beside him on the floor.

"I don't know," he whispered back breathlessly.

The second time the knocking came it was so loud and imperious that the rickety old door could have fallen down.

"Who is knocking?" he asked them, his voice parched and trembling.

"Na tief-man and him people," came the cool reply. "Make you hopen de door."
This was followed by the heaviest knocking of all.

Maria was the first to raise the alarm, then he followed and all their children.

"Police-o! Thieves-o! Neighbours-o! Police-o! We are lost! We are dead! Neighbours, are you asleep? Wake up! Police-o!"

This went on for a long time and then stopped suddenly. Perhaps they had scared the thief away. There was total silence. But only for a short while.

"You done finish?" asked the voice outside. "Make we help you small. Oya, everybody!"

"Police-o! Tief-man-o! Neighbours-o! we done loss-o! Police-o! . . ."

There were at least five other voices besides the leader's.

Jonathan and his family were now completely paralysed by terror. Maria and the children sobbed inaudibly like lost souls. Jonathan groaned continuously.

The silence that followed the thieves' alarm vibrated horribly. Jonathan all but begged their leader to speak again and be done with it.

"My frien," said he at long last, "we don try our best for call dem but I tink say dem all done sleep-o . . . So wetin we go do now? Sometaim you wan call soja? Or you wan make we call dem for you? Soja better pass police. No be so?"

"Na so!" replied his men. Jonathan thought he heard even more voices now than before and groaned heavily. His legs were sagging under him and his throat felt like sand-paper.

"My frien, why you no de talk again. I de ask you say you wan make we call soja?"

"No."

"Awrighto. Now make we talk business. We no be bad tief. We no like for make trouble. Trouble done finish. War done finish and all the katakata wey de for inside. No Civil War again. This time na Civil Peace. No be so?"

"Na so!" answered the horrible chorus.

"What do you want from me? I am a poor man. Everything I had went with this war. Why do you come to me? You know people who have money. We . . ."

"Awright! We know say you no get plenty money. But we sef no get even anini. So derefore make you open dis window and give us one hundred pound and we go commot. Orderwise we de come for inside now to show you guitar-boy like dis . . ."

A volley of automatic fire rang through the sky. Maria and the children began to weep aloud again.

"Ah, missisi de cry again. No need for dat. We done talk say we na good tief. We just take our small money and go nwayorly. No molest. Abi we de molest?"

"At all!" sang the chorus.

"My friends," began Jonathan hoarsely. "I hear what you say and I thank you. If I had one hundred pounds . . ."

"Lookia my frien, no be play we come play for your house. If we make mistake and step for inside you no go like am-o. So derefore . . ."

"To God who made me; if you come inside and find one hundred pounds, take it and shoot me and shoot my wife and children. I swear to God. The only money I have in this life is this twenty-pounds *egg-rasher* they gave me today . . ."

"OK. Time de go. Make you open dis window and bring the twenty pound. We go manage am like dat."

There were now loud murmurs of dissent among the chorus: "Na lie de man de lie; e get plenty money . . . Make we go inside and search properly well . . . Wetin be twenty pound? . . ."

"Shurrup!" rang the leader's voice like a lone shot in the sky and silenced the murmuring at once. "Are you dere? Bring the money quick!"

"I am coming," said Jonathan fumbling in the darkness with the key of the small wooden box he kept by his side on the mat.

At the first sign of light as neighbours and others assembled to commiserate with him he was already strapping his five-gallon demijohn to his bicycle carrier and his wife, sweating in the open fire, was turning over akara balls in a wide clay bowl of boiling oil. In the corner his eldest son was rinsing out dregs of yesterday's palm wine from old beer bottles.

"I count it as nothing," he told his sympathizers, his eyes on the rope he was tying. "What is *egg-rasher?* Did I depend on it last week? Or is it greater than other things that went with the war? I say, let *egg-rasher* perish in the flames! Let it go where everything else has gone. Nothing puzzles God."

QUESTIONS

1. What is Jonathan Iwegbu's general attitude toward life? How would you characterize his personality? What aspects of the story lead you to your views?
2. What type of country does Jonathan Iwegbu live in? How would you characterize it economically, politically, geographically, and socially?

3. Why don't the thieves merely enter Iwegbu's house rather than negotiate with him? What tactics does he use to keep them at bay?
4. Does Iwegbu's character undergo a transformation during the course of the story, or does he maintain the same outlook on life? Explain your view.

Isaac Babel

MY FIRST GOOSE

Savitsky, Commander of the VI Division, rose when he saw me, and I wondered at the beauty of his giant's body. He rose, the purple of his riding-breeches and the crimson of his little tilted cap and the decorations stuck on his chest cleaving the hut as a standard cleaves the sky. A smell of scent and sickly sweet freshness of soap emanated from him. His long legs were like girls sheathed to the neck in shining riding-boots.

He smiled at me, struck his riding-whip on the table, and drew toward him an order that the Chief of Staff had just finished dictating. It was an order for Ivan Chesnokov to advance on Chugunov-Dobryvodka with the regiment entrusted to him, to make contact with the enemy and destroy the same.

"For which destruction," the Commander began to write, smearing the whole sheet, "I make this same Chesnokov entirely responsible, up to and including the supreme penalty, and will if necessary strike him down on the spot; which you, Chesnokov, who have been working with me at the front for some months now, cannot doubt."

The Commander signed the order with a flourish, tossed it to his orderlies, and turned upon me grey eyes that danced with merriment.

I handed him a paper with my appointment to the Staff of the Division.

"Put it down in the Order of the Day," said the Commander. "Put him down for every satisfaction save the front one. Can you read and write?"

"Yes, I can read and write," I replied, envying the flower and iron of that youthfulness. "I graduated in law from St. Petersburg University."

"Oh, are you one of those grinds?" he laughed. "Specs on your nose, too! What a nasty little object! They've sent you along without making any inquiries; and this is a hot place for specs. Think you'll get on with us?"

"I'll get on all right," I answered, and went off to the village with the quartermaster to find a billet for the night.

The quartermaster carried my trunk on his shoulder. Before us stretched the village street. The dying sun, round and yellow as a pumpkin, was giving up its roseate ghost to the skies.

We went up to a hut painted over with garlands. The quartermaster stopped, and said suddenly, with a guilty smile:

"Nuisance with specs. Can't do anything to stop it, either. Not a life for the brainy type here. But you go and mess up a lady, and a good lady too, and you'll have the boys patting you on the back."

He hesitated, my little trunk on his shoulder; then he came quite close to me, only to dart away again despairingly and run to the nearest yard. Cossacks were sitting there, shaving one another.

"Here, you soldiers," said the quartermaster, setting my little trunk down on the ground. "Comrade Savitsky's orders are that you're to take this chap in your billets, so no nonsense about it, because the chap's been through a lot in the learning line."

The quartermaster, purple in the face, left us without looking back. I raised my hand to my cap and saluted the Cossacks. A lad with long straight flaxen hair and the handsome face of the Ryazan Cossacks went over to my little trunk and tossed it out at the gate. Then he turned his back on me and with remarkable skill emitted a series of shameful noises.

"To your guns—number double-zero!" an older Cossack shouted at him, and burst out laughing. "Running fire!"

His guileless art exhausted, the lad made off. Then, crawling over the ground, I began to gather together the manuscripts and tattered garments that had fallen out of the trunk. I gathered them up and carried them to the other end of the yard. Near the hut, on a brick stove, stood a cauldron in which pork was cooking. The steam that rose from it was like the far-off smoke of home in the village, and it mingled hunger with desperate loneliness in my head. Then I covered my little broken trunk with hay, turning it into a pillow, and lay down on the ground to read in *Pravda* Lenin's speech at the Second Congress of the Comintern. The sun fell upon me from behind the toothed hillocks, the Cossacks trod on my feet, the lad made fun of me untiringly, the beloved lines came toward me along a thorny path and could not reach me. Then I put aside the paper and went out to the landlady, who was spinning on the porch.

"Landlady," I said, "I've got to eat."

The old woman raised to me the diffused whites of her purblind eyes and lowered them again.

"Comrade," she said, after a pause, "what with all this going on, I want to go and hang myself."

"Christ!" I muttered, and pushed the old woman in the chest with my fist. "You don't suppose I'm going to go into explanations with you, do you?"

And turning around I saw somebody's sword lying within reach. A severe-looking goose was waddling about the yard, inoffensively preening its feathers. I overtook it and pressed it to the ground. Its head cracked beneath my boot, cracked and emptied itself. The white neck lay stretched out in the dung, the wings twitched.

"Christ!" I said, digging into the goose with my sword. "Go and cook it for me, landlady."

Her blind eyes and glasses glistening, the old woman picked up the slaughtered bird, wrapped it in her apron, and started to bear it off toward the kitchen.

"Comrade," she said to me, after a while. "I want to go and hang myself." And she closed the door behind her.

The Cossacks in the yard were already sitting around their cauldron. They sat motionless, stiff as heathen priests at a sacrifice, and had not looked at the goose.

"The lad's all right," one of them said, winking and scooping up the cabbage soup with his spoon.

The Cossacks commenced their supper with all the elegance and restraint of peasants who respect one another. And I wiped the sword with sand, went out at the gate, and came in again, depressed. Already the moon hung above the yard like a cheap earring.

"Hey, you," suddenly said Surovkov, an older Cossack. "Sit down and feed with us till your goose is done."

He produced a spare spoon from his boot and handed it to me. We supped up the cabbage soup they had made, and ate the pork.

"What's in the newspaper?" asked the flaxen-haired lad, making room for me.

"Lenin writes in the paper," I said, pulling out *Pravda*. "Lenin writes that there's a shortage of everything."

And loudly, like a triumphant man hard of hearing, I read Lenin's speech out to the Cossacks.

Evening wrapped about me the quickening moisture of its twilight sheets; evening laid a mother's hand upon my burning forehead. I read on and rejoiced, spying out exultingly the secret curve of Lenin's straight line.

"Truth tickles everyone's nostrils," said Surovkov, when I had come to the end. "The question is, how's it to be pulled from the heap. But he goes and strikes at it straight off like a hen pecking at a grain!"

This remark about Lenin was made by Surovkov, platoon commander of the Staff Squadron; after which we lay down to sleep in the hayloft. We slept, all six of us, beneath a wooden roof that let in the stars, warming one another, our legs intermingled. I dreamed: and in my dreams saw women. But my heart, stained with bloodshed, grated and brimmed over.

Translated by Walter Morison

QUESTIONS

1. What is the significance of the title?
2. What sort of transformation does the narrator go through during the course of the story? What is the cause of this transformation? What is the narrator's attitude toward the transformation?
3. How does the narrator's ability to read give him power?
4. Why and how has he earned the respect of the Cossacks?

Jorge Luis Borges

THE SOUTH

The man who landed in Buenos Aires in 1871 bore the name of Johannes Dahlmann and he was a minister in the Evangelical Church. In 1939, one of his grandchildren, Juan Dahlmann, was secretary of a municipal library on Calle Córdoba, and he considered himself profoundly Argentinian. His maternal grandfather had been that Francisco Flores, of the Second Line-Infantry Division, who had died on the frontier of Buenos Aires, run through with a lance by Indians from Catriel; in the discord inherent between his two lines of descent, Juan Dahlmann (perhaps driven to it by his Germanic blood) chose the line represented by his romantic ancestor, his ancestor of the romantic death. An old sword, a leather frame containing the daguerreotype of a blank-faced man with a beard, the dash and grace of certain music, the familiar strophes of *Martin Fierro*, the passing years, boredom and solitude, all went to foster this voluntary, but never ostentatious nationalism. At the cost of numerous small privations, Dahlmann had managed to save the empty shell of a ranch in the South which had belonged to the Flores family: he continually recalled the image of the balsamic eucalyptus trees and the great rose-colored house which had once been crimson. His duties, perhaps even indolence, kept him in the city. Summer after summer he contented himself with the abstract idea of possession and with the certitude that his ranch was waiting for him on a precise site in the middle of the plain. Late in February, 1939, something happened to him.

Blind to all fault, destiny can be ruthless at one's slightest distraction. Dahlmann had succeeded in acquiring, on that very afternoon, an imperfect copy of Weil's edition of *The Thousand and One Nights*. Avid to examine this find, he did not wait for the elevator but hurried up the stairs. In the obscurity, something brushed by his forehead: a bat, a bird? On the face of the woman who opened the door to him he saw horror engraved, and the hand he wiped across his face came away red with blood. The edge of a recently painted door which someone had forgotten to close had caused this wound. Dahlmann was able to fall asleep, but from the moment he awoke at dawn the savor of all things was atrociously poignant. Fever wasted him and the pictures in *The Thousand and One Nights* served to illustrate nightmares. Friends and relatives paid him visits and, with exaggerated smiles, assured him that they thought he looked fine. Dahlmann listened to them with a kind of feeble stupor and he marveled at their not knowing that he was in hell. A week, eight days passed, and they were like eight centuries. One afternoon, the usual doctor appeared, accompanied by a new doctor, and they carried him off to a sanitarium on the Calle Ecuador, for it was necessary to X-ray him. Dahlmann, in the hackney coach which bore them away, thought that he would, at last, be able to sleep in a room different from his own. He felt happy and communicative. When he arrived at his destination, they undressed him, shaved his head, bound him with metal fastenings to a stretcher; they shone bright lights on him until he was blind and dizzy, auscultated him, and a masked man stuck a needle into his arm. He awoke with a feeling of nausea, covered with a bandage, in a cell with something of a well about it; in the days and nights which followed the operation he came to realize that he had merely been, up until then, in a suburb of hell. Ice in his mouth did not leave the least trace of freshness. During these days Dahlmann hated himself in minute detail; he hated his identity, his bodily necessities, his humiliation, the beard which bristled upon his face. He stoically endured the curative measures, which were painful, but when the surgeon told him he had been on the point of death from septicemia, Dahlmann dissolved in tears of self-pity for his fate. Physical wretchedness and the incessant anticipation of horrible nights had not allowed him time to think of anything so abstract as death. On another day, the surgeon told him he was healing and that, very soon, he would be able to go to his ranch for convalescence. Incredibly enough, the promised day arrived.

Reality favors symmetries and slight anachronisms: Dahlmann had arrived at the sanitarium in a hackney coach and now a hackney coach was to take him to the Constitución station. The first fresh tang of autumn, after the summer's oppressiveness, seemed like a symbol in nature of his rescue and release from fever and death. The city, at seven in the morning, had not lost that air of an old house lent it by the night; the streets seemed like long vestibules, the plazas were like patios. Dahlmann recognized the city with joy on the edge of vertigo: a second before his eyes registered the phenomena themselves, he recalled the corners, the billboards, the modest variety of Buenos Aires. In the yellow light of the new day, all things returned to him.

Every Argentine knows that the South begins at the other side of Rivadavia. Dahlmann was in the habit of saying that this was no mere convention, that whoever crosses this street enters a more ancient and sterner world. From inside the carriage he sought out, among the new buildings, the iron grille window, the brass knocker, the arched door, the entranceway, the intimate patio.

At the railroad station he noted that he still had thirty minutes. He quickly recalled that in a café on the Calle Brazil (a few dozen feet from Yrigoyen's house) there was an enormous cat which allowed itself to be caressed as if it were a disdainful divinity. He entered the café. There was the cat, asleep. He ordered a cup of coffee, slowly stirred the sugar, sipped it (this pleasure had been denied him in the clinic), and thought, as he smoothed the cat's black coat, that this contact was an illusion and that the two beings, man and cat, were as good as separated by a glass, for man lives in time, in succession, while the magical animal lives in the present, in the eternity of the instant.

Along the next to the last platform the train lay waiting. Dahlmann walked through the coaches until he found one almost empty. He arranged his baggage in the network rack. When the train started off, he took down his valise and extracted, after some hesitation, the first volume of *The Thousand and One Nights*. To travel with this book, which was so much a part of the history of his ill-fortune, was a kind of affirmation that his ill-fortune had been annulled; it was a joyous and secret defiance of the frustrated forces of evil.

Along both sides of the train the city dissipated into suburbs; this sight, and then a view of the gardens and villas, delayed the beginning of his reading. The truth was that Dahlmann read very little. The magnetized mountain and the genie who swore to kill his benefactor are—who would deny it?—marvelous, but not so much more than the morning itself and the mere fact of being. The joy of life distracted him from paying attention to Scheherazade and her superfluous miracles. Dahlmann closed his book and allowed himself to live.

Lunch—the bouillon served in shining metal bowls, as in the remote summers of childhood—was one more peaceful and rewarding delight.

Tomorrow I'll wake up at the ranch, he thought, and it was as if he was two men at a time: the man who traveled through the autumn day and across the geography of the fatherland, the other one, locked up in a sanitarium and subject to methodical servitude. He saw unplastered brick houses, long and angled, timelessly watching the trains go by; he saw horsemen along the dirt roads; he saw gullies and lagoons and ranches; he saw great luminous clouds that resembled marble; and all these things were accidental, casual, like dreams of the plain. He also thought he recognized trees and crop fields; but he would not have been able to name them, for his actual knowledge of the countryside was quite inferior to his nostalgic and literary knowledge.

From time to time he slept, and his dreams were animated by the impetus of the train. The intolerable white sun of high noon had already become the yellow sun which precedes nightfall, and it would not be long before it would turn red. The railroad car was now also different; it was not the same as the one which had quit the station siding at Constitución; the plain and the hours had transfigured it. Outside, the moving shadow of the railroad car stretched toward the horizon. The elemental earth was not perturbed either by settlements or other signs of humanity. The country was vast but at the same time intimate and, in some measure, secret. The limitless country sometimes contained only a solitary bull. The solitude was perfect, perhaps hostile, and it might have occurred to Dahlmann that he was traveling into the past and not merely south. He was distracted from these considerations by the railroad inspector who, on reading his ticket, advised him that the train would not let him off at the regular station but at another: an earlier stop, one scarcely known to Dahlmann. (The man added an explanation which Dahlmann did not attempt to understand, and which he hardly heard, for the mechanism of events did not concern him.)

The train laboriously ground to a halt, practically in the middle of the plain. The station lay on the other side of the tracks; it was not much more than a siding and a shed. There was no means of conveyance to be seen, but the station chief supposed that the traveler might secure a vehicle from a general store and inn to be found some ten or twelve blocks away.

Dahlmann accepted the walk as a small adventure. The sun had already disappeared from view, but a final splendor exalted the vivid and silent plain, before the night erased its color. Less to avoid fatigue than to draw out his enjoyment of these sights, Dahlmann walked slowly, breathing in the odor of clover with sumptuous joy.

The general store at one time had been painted a deep scarlet, but the years had tempered this violent color for its own good. Something in its poor architecture recalled a steel engraving, perhaps one from an old edition of *Paul et Virginie.* A number of horses were hitched up to the paling. Once inside, Dahlmann thought he recognized the shopkeeper. Then he realized that he had been deceived by the man's resemblance to one of the male nurses in the sanitarium. When the shopkeeper heard Dahlmann's request, he said he would have the shay made up. In order to add one more event to that day and to kill time, Dahlmann decided to eat at the general store.

Some country louts, to whom Dahlmann did not at first pay any attention, were eating and drinking at one of the tables. On the floor, and hanging on to the bar, squatted an old man, immobile as an object. His years had reduced and polished him as water does a stone or the generations of men do a sentence. He was dark, dried up, diminutive, and seemed outside time, situated in eternity. Dahlmann noted with satisfaction the kerchief, the thick poncho, the long *chiripá,* and the colt boots, and told himself, as he recalled futile discussions with people from the Northern counties or from the province of Entre Rios, that gauchos like this no longer existed outside the South.

Dahlmann sat down next to the window. The darkness began overcoming the plain, but the odor and sound of the earth penetrated the iron bars of the window. The shop owner brought him sardines, followed by some roast meat. Dahlmann washed the meal down with several glasses of red wine. Idling, he relished the tart savor of the wine, and let his gaze, now grown somewhat drowsy, wander over the shop. A kerosene lamp hung from a beam. There were three customers at the other table: two of them appeared to be farm workers; the third man, whose features hinted at Chinese blood, was drinking with his hat on. Of a sudden, Dahlmann felt something brush lightly against his face. Next to the heavy glass of turbid wine, upon one of the stripes in the tablecloth, lay a spit ball of breadcrumb. That was all: but someone had thrown it there.

The men at the other table seemed totally cut off from him. Perplexed, Dahlmann decided that nothing had happened, and he opened the volume of *The Thousand and One Nights,* by way of suppressing reality. After a few moments another little ball landed on his table, and now the *peones* laughed outright. Dahlmann said to himself that he was not frightened, but he reasoned that it would be a major blunder if he, a convalescent, were to allow himself to be dragged by strangers into some chaotic quarrel. He determined to leave, and had already gotten to his feet when the owner came up and exhorted him in an alarmed voice:

"*Señor* Dahlmann, don't pay any attention to those lads; they're half high."

Dahlmann was not surprised to learn that the other man, now, knew his name. But he felt that these conciliatory words served only to aggravate the situation. Previously to this moment, the *peones'* provocation was directed against an unknown face, against no one in particular, almost against no one at all. Now it was an attack against him, against his name, and his neighbors knew it. Dahlmann pushed the owner aside, confronted the *peones,* and demanded to know what they wanted of him.

The tough with the Chinese look staggered heavily to his feet. Almost in Juan Dahlmann's face he shouted insults, as if he had been a long way off. His game was to exaggerate his drunkenness, and this extravagance constituted a ferocious mockery. Between curses and obscenities, he threw a long knife into the air, followed it with his eyes, caught and juggled it, and challenged Dahlmann to a knife fight. The owner objected in a tremulous voice, pointing out that Dahlmann was unarmed. At this point, something unforeseeable occurred.

From a corner of the room, the old ecstatic gaucho—in whom Dahlmann saw a summary and cipher of the South (his South)—threw him a naked dagger, which landed at his feet. It was as if the South had resolved that Dahlmann should accept the duel. Dahlmann bent over to pick up the dagger, and felt two things. The first, that this almost instinctive act bound him to fight. The second, that the weapon, in his torpid hand, was no defense at all, but would merely serve to justify his murder. He had once played with a poniard, like all men, but his idea of fencing and knife-play did not go

further than the notion that all strokes should be directed upward, with the cutting edge held inward. *They would not have allowed such things to happen to me in the sanitarium,* he thought.

"Let's get on our way," said the other man.

They went out and if Dahlmann was without hope, he was also without fear. As he crossed the threshold, he felt that to die in a knife fight, under the open sky, and going forward to the attack, would have been a liberation, a joy, and a festive occasion, on the first night in the sanitarium, when they stuck him with the needle. He felt that if he had been able to choose, then, or to dream his death, this would have been the death he would have chosen or dreamt.

Firmly clutching his knife, which he perhaps would not know how to wield, Dahlmann went out into the plain.

QUESTIONS

1. At the beginning of the story which one of his grandfathers does Johannes Dahlmann appear to be emulating? Explain.
2. At what point in the story does the routine of Dahlmann's life change? When do events begin to seem unreal?
3. In what ways does his reading of *The Thousand and One Nights* coincide with Dahlmann's experience?
4. Who does the "old ecstatic gaucho" who throws Dahlmann a knife resemble? What inspires Dahlmann to take up the challenge made by the drunken tough? How does this challenge transform Dahlmann's perception of himself? How can Dahlmann's evolution be considered a metaphor for a larger transformation? What is the nature of this other transformation?
5. The structure of Borges's stories often resembles the genres of fantasy, science fiction, and mystery. Which if any of these forms of writing appear to have influenced this story?

Raymond Carver

CATHEDRAL

This blind man, an old friend of my wife's, he was on his way to spend the night. His wife had died. So he was visiting the dead wife's relatives in Connecticut. He called my wife from his in-laws'. Arrangements were made. He would come by train, a five-hour trip, and my wife would meet him at the station. She hadn't seen him since she worked for him one summer in Seattle ten years ago. But she and the blind man had kept in touch. They made tapes and mailed them back and forth. I wasn't enthusiastic about his visit. He was no one I knew. And his being blind bothered me. My idea of blindness came from the movies. In the movies, the blind moved slowly and never laughed. Sometimes they were led by seeing-eye dogs. A blind man in my house was not something I looked forward to.

That summer in Seattle she had needed a job. She didn't have any money. The man she was going to marry at the end of the summer was in officers' training school. He didn't have any money, either. But she was in love with the guy, and he was in love with her, etc. She'd seen something in the paper: HELP WANTED—*Reading to Blind Man*, and a telephone number. She phoned and went over, was hired on the spot. She'd worked with this blind man all summer. She read stuff to him, case studies, reports, that sort of thing. She helped him organize his little office in the county social-service department. They'd become good friends, my wife and the blind man. How do I know these things? She told me. And she told me something else. On her last day in the office, the blind man asked if he could touch her face. She agreed to this. She told me he touched his fingers to every part of her face, her nose—even her neck! She never forgot it. She even tried to write a poem about it. She was always trying to write a poem. She wrote a poem or two every year, usually after something really important had happened to her.

When we first started going out together, she showed me the poem. In the poem, she recalled his fingers and the way they had moved around over her face. In the poem, she talked about what she had felt at the time, about what went through her mind when the blind man touched her nose and lips. I can remember I didn't think much of the poem. Of course, I didn't tell her that. Maybe I just don't understand poetry. I admit it's not the first thing I reach for when I pick up something to read.

Anyway, this man who'd first enjoyed her favors, the officer-to-be, he'd been her childhood sweetheart. So okay. I'm saying that at the end of the summer she let the blind man run his hands over her face, said goodbye to him, married her childhood etc., who was now a commissioned officer, and she moved away from Seattle. But they'd kept in touch, she and the blind man. She made the first contact after a year or so. She called him up one night from an Air Force base in Alabama. She wanted to talk. They talked. He asked her to send him a tape and tell him about her life. She did this. She sent the tape. On the tape, she told the blind man about her husband and about their life together in the military. She told the blind man she loved her husband but she didn't like it where they lived and she didn't like it that he was a part of the military-industrial thing. She told the blind man she'd written a poem and he was in it. She told him that she was writing a poem about what it was like to be an Air Force officer's wife. The poem wasn't finished yet. She was still writing it. The blind man made a tape. He sent her the tape. She made a tape. This went on for years. My wife's officer was posted to one base and then another. She sent tapes from Moody AFB, McGuire, McConnell, and finally Travis, near Sacramento, where one night she got to feeling lonely and cut off from people she kept losing in that moving-around life. She got to feeling she couldn't go it another step. She went in and swallowed all the pills and capsules in the medicine chest and washed them down with a bottle of gin. Then she got into a hot bath and passed out.

But instead of dying, she got sick. She threw up. Her officer—why should he have a name? he was the childhood sweetheart, and what more does he want?—came home from somewhere, found her, and called the ambulance. In time, she put it all on a tape and sent the tape to the blind man. Over the years, she put all kinds of stuff on tapes and sent the tapes off lickety-split. Next to writing a poem every year, I think it was her chief means of recreation. On one tape, she told the blind man she'd decided to live away from her officer for a time. On another tape, she told him about her divorce. She and I began going out, and of course she told her blind man about it. She told him everything, or so it seemed to me. Once she asked me if I'd like to hear the latest tape from the blind man. This was a year ago. I was on the tape, she said. So I said okay, I'd listen to it. I got us drinks and we settled down in the living room. We made ready to listen. First she inserted the tape into the player and adjusted a couple of dials. Then she pushed a lever. The tape squeaked and someone began to talk in this loud voice. She lowered the volume. After a few minutes of harmless chitchat, I heard my own name in the mouth of this stranger, this blind man I didn't even know! And then this: "From all you've said about him, I can only conclude—" But we were interrupted, a knock at the door, something, and we didn't ever get back to the tape. Maybe it was just as well. I'd heard all I wanted to.

Now this same blind man was coming to sleep in my house.

"Maybe I could take him bowling," I said to my wife. She was at the draining board doing scalloped potatoes. She put down the knife she was using and turned around.

"If you love me," she said, "you can do this for me. If you don't love me, okay. But if you had a friend, any friend, and the friend came to visit, I'd make him feel comfortable." She wiped her hands with the dish towel.

"I don't have any blind friends," I said.

"You don't have *any* friends," she said. "Period. Besides," she said, "goddamn it, his wife's just died! Don't you understand that? The man's lost his wife!"

I didn't answer. She'd told me a little about the blind man's wife. Her name was Beulah. Beulah! That's a name for a colored woman.

"Was his wife a Negro?" I asked.

"Are you crazy?" my wife said. "Have you just flipped or something?" She picked up a potato. I saw it hit the floor, then roll under the stove. "What's wrong with you?" she said. "Are you drunk?"

"I'm just asking," I said.

Right then my wife filled me in with more detail than I cared to know. I made a drink and sat at the kitchen table to listen. Pieces of the story began to fall into place.

Beulah had gone to work for the blind man the summer after my wife had stopped working for him. Pretty soon Beulah and the blind man had themselves a church wedding. It was a little wedding—who'd want to go to such a wedding in the first place?—just the two of them, plus the minister and the minister's wife. But it was a church wedding just the same. It was what Beulah had wanted, he'd said. But even then Beulah must have been carrying the cancer in her glands. After they had been insepara-ble for eight years—my wife's word, *inseparable*—Beulah's health went into a rapid decline. She died in a Seattle hospital room, the blind man sitting beside the bed and holding on to her hand. They'd married, lived and worked together, slept together—

had sex, sure—and then the blind man had to bury her. All this without his having ever seen what the goddamned woman looked like. It was beyond my understanding. Hearing this, I felt sorry for the blind man for a little bit. And then I found myself thinking what a pitiful life this woman must have led. Imagine a woman who could never see herself as she was seen in the eyes of her loved one. A woman who could go on day after day and never receive the smallest compliment from her beloved. A woman whose husband could never read the expression on her face, be it misery or something better. Someone who could wear makeup or not—what difference to him? She could, if she wanted, wear green eyeshadow around one eye, a straight pin in her nostril, yellow slacks and purple shoes, no matter. And then to slip off into death, the blind man's hand on her hand, his blind eyes streaming tears—I'm imagining now—her last thought maybe this: that he never even knew what she looked like, and she on an express to the grave. Robert was left with a small insurance policy and half of a twenty-peso Mexican coin. The other half of the coin went into the box with her. Pathetic.

So when the time rolled around, my wife went to the depot to pick him up. With nothing to do but wait—sure, I blamed him for that—I was having a drink and watching the TV when I heard the car pull into the drive. I got up from the sofa with my drink and went to the window to have a look.

I saw my wife laughing as she parked the car. I saw her get out of the car and shut the door. She was still wearing a smile. Just amazing. She went around to the other side of the car to where the blind man was already starting to get out. This blind man, feature this, he was wearing a full beard! A beard on a blind man! Too much, I say. The blind man reached into the back seat and dragged out a suitcase. My wife took his arm, shut the car door, and, talking all the way, moved him down the drive and then up the steps to the front porch. I turned off the TV. I finished my drink, rinsed the glass, dried my hands. Then I went to the door.

My wife said, "I want you to meet Robert. Robert, this is my husband. I've told you all about him." She was beaming. She had this blind man by his coat sleeve.

The blind man let go of his suitcase and up came his hand. I took it. He squeezed hard, held my hand, and then he let it go.

"I feel like we've already met," he boomed.

"Likewise," I said. I didn't know what else to say. Then I said. "Welcome. I've heard a lot about you." We began to move then, a little group, from the porch into the living room, my wife guiding him by the arm. The blind man was carrying his suitcase in his other hand. My wife said things like, "To your left here, Robert. That's right. Now watch it, there's a chair. That's it. Sit down right here. This is the sofa. We just bought this sofa two weeks ago."

I started to say something about the old sofa. I'd liked that old sofa. But I didn't say anything. Then I wanted to say something else, small-talk, about the scenic ride along the Hudson. How going *to* New York, you should sit on the right-hand side of the train, and coming *from* New York, the left-hand side.

"Did you have a good train ride?" I said, "Which side of the train did you sit on, by the way?"

"What a question, which side!" my wife said. "What's it matter which side?" she said.

"I just asked," I said.

"Right side," the blind man said. "I hadn't been on a train in nearly forty years. Not since I was a kid. With my folks. That's been a long time. I'd nearly forgotten the sensation. I have winter in my beard now," he said. "So I've been told, anyway. Do I look distinguished, my dear?" the blind man said to my wife.

"You look distinguished, Robert," she said. "Robert," she said. "Robert, it's just so good to see you."

My wife finally took her eyes off the blind man and looked at me. I had the feeling she didn't like what she saw. I shrugged.

I've never met, or personally known, anyone who was blind. This blind man was late forties, a heavy-set, balding man with stooped shoulders, as if he carried a great weight there. He wore brown slacks, brown shoes, a light-brown shirt, a tie, a sports coat. Spiffy. He also had this full beard. But he didn't use a cane and he didn't wear dark glasses. I'd always thought dark glasses were a must for the blind. Fact was, I wished he had a pair. At first glance, his eyes looked like anyone else's eyes. But if you looked close, there was something different about them. Too much white in the iris, for one thing, and the pupils seemed to move round in the sockets without his knowing it or being able to stop it. Creepy. As I stared at his face, I saw the left pupil turn in toward his nose while the other made an effort to keep in one place. But it was only an effort, for that eye was on the roam without knowing it or wanting it to be.

I said, "Let me get you a drink. What's your pleasure? We have a little of everything. It's one of our pastimes."

"Bub, I'm a Scotch man myself," he said fast enough in this big voice.

"Right," I said. Bub! "Sure you are. I knew it."

He let his fingers touch his suitcase, which was sitting alongside the sofa. He was taking his bearings. I didn't blame him for that.

"I'll move that up to your room," my wife said.

"No, that's fine," the blind man said loudly. "It can go up when I go up."

"A little water with the Scotch?" I said.

"Very little," he said.

"I knew it," I said.

He said, "Just a tad. The Irish actor, Barry Fitzgerald? I'm like that fellow. When I drink water, Fitzgerald said, I drink water. When I drink whiskey, I drink whiskey." My wife laughed. The blind man brought his hand up under his beard. He lifted his beard slowly and let it drop.

I did the drinks, three big glasses of Scotch with a splash of water in each. Then we made ourselves comfortable and talked about Robert's travels. First the long flight from the West Coast to Connecticut, we covered that. Then from Connecticut up here by train. We had another drink concerning that leg of the trip.

I remembered having read somewhere that the blind didn't smoke because, as speculation had it, they couldn't see the smoke they exhaled. I thought I knew that much and that much only about blind people. But this blind man smoked his cigarette down to the nubbin and then lit another one. This blind man filled his ashtray and my wife emptied it.

When we sat down at the table for dinner, we had another drink. My wife heaped Robert's plate with cube steak, scalloped potatoes, green beans. I buttered him up two slices of bread. I said, "Here's bread and butter for you." I swallowed some of my drink. "Now let us pray," I said, and the blind man lowered his head. My wife looked at me, her mouth agape. "Pray the phone won't ring and the food doesn't get cold," I said.

We dug in. We ate everything there was to eat on the table. We ate like there was no tomorrow. We didn't talk. We ate. We scarfed. We grazed that table. We were into serious eating. The blind man had right away located his foods, he knew just where everything was on his plate. I watched with admiration as he used his knife and fork on the meat. He'd cut two pieces of meat, fork the meat into his mouth, and then go all out for the scalloped potatoes, the beans next, and then he'd tear off a hunk of buttered bread and eat that. He'd follow this up with a big drink of milk. It didn't seem to bother him to use his fingers once in a while, either.

We finished everything, including half a strawberry pie. For a few moments, we sat as if stunned. Sweat beaded on our faces. Finally, we got up from the table and left the dirty plates. We didn't look back. We took ourselves into the living room and sank into our places again. Robert and my wife sat on the sofa. I took the big chair. We had us two or three more drinks while they talked about the major things that had come to pass for them in the past ten years. For the most part, I just listened. Now and then I joined in. I didn't want him to think I'd left the room, and I didn't want her to think I was feeling left out. They talked of things that had happened to them—to them!—these past ten years. I waited in vain to hear my name on my wife's sweet lips: "And then my dear husband came into my life"—something like that. But I heard nothing of the sort. More talk of Robert. Robert had done a little of everything, it seemed, a regular blind jack-of-all trades. But most recently he and his wife had had an Amway distributorship, from which, I gathered, they'd earned their living, such as it was. The blind man was also a ham radio operator. He talked in his loud voice about conversations he'd had with fellow operators in Guam, in the Philippines, in Alaska, and even in Tahiti. He said he'd have a lot of friends there if he ever wanted to go visit those places. From time to time, he'd turn his blind face toward me, put his hand under his beard, ask me something. How long had I been in my present position? (Three years.) Did I like my work? (I didn't.) Was I going to stay with it? (What were the options?) Finally, when I thought he was beginning to run down, I got up and turned on the TV.

My wife looked at me with irritation. She was heading toward a boil. Then she looked at the blind man and said, "Robert, do you have a TV?"

The blind man said, "My dear, I have two TVs. I have a color set and a black-and-white thing, an old relic. It's funny, but if I turn the TV on, and I'm always turning it on, I turn on the color set. It's funny, don't you think?"

I didn't know what to say to that. I had absolutely nothing to say to that. No opinion. So I watched the news program and tried to listen to what the announcer was saying.

"This is a color TV," the blind man said. "Don't ask me how, but I can tell."

"We traded up a while ago," I said.

The blind man had another taste of his drink. He lifted his beard, sniffed it, and let it fall. He leaned forward on the sofa. He positioned his ashtray on the coffee table, then put the lighter to his cigarette. He leaned back on the sofa and crossed his legs at the ankles.

My wife covered her mouth, and then she yawned. She stretched. She said, "I think

I'll go upstairs and put on my robe. I think I'll change into something else. Robert, you make yourself comfortable," she said.

"I'm comfortable," the blind man said.

"I want you to feel comfortable in this house," she said.

"I am comfortable," the blind man said.

After she'd left the room, he and I listened to the weather report and then to the sports roundup. By that time, she'd been gone so long I didn't know if she was going to come back. I thought she might have gone to bed. I wished she'd come back downstairs. I didn't want to be left alone with a blind man. I asked him if he wanted another drink, and he said sure. Then I asked if he wanted to smoke some dope with me. I said I'd just rolled a number. I hadn't, but I planned to do so in about two shakes.

"I'll try some with you," he said.

"Damn right," I said. "That's the stuff."

I got our drinks and sat down on the sofa with him. Then I rolled us two fat numbers. I lit one and passed it. I brought it to his fingers. He took it and inhaled.

"Hold it as long as you can," I said. I could tell he didn't know the first thing.

My wife came back downstairs wearing her pink robe and her pink slippers.

"What do I smell?" she said.

"We thought we'd have us some cannabis," I said.

My wife gave me a savage look. Then she looked at the blind man and said, "Robert, I didn't know you smoked."

He said, "I do now, my dear. There's a first time for everything. But I don't feel anything yet."

"This stuff is pretty mellow," I said. "This stuff is mild. It's dope you can reason with," I said. "It doesn't mess you up."

"Not much it doesn't, bub," he said, and laughed.

My wife sat on the sofa between the blind man and me. I passed her the number. She took it and toked and then passed it back to me. "Which way is this going?" she said. Then she said, "I shouldn't be smoking this. I can hardly keep my eyes open as it is. That dinner did me in. I shouldn't have eaten so much."

"It was the strawberry pie," the blind man said. "That's what did it," he said, and he laughed his big laugh. Then he shook his head.

"There's more strawberry pie," I said.

"Do you want some more, Robert?" my wife said.

"Maybe in a little while," he said.

We gave our attention to the TV. My wife yawned again. She said, "Your bed is made up when you feel like going to bed, Robert. I know you must have had a long day. When you're ready to go to bed, say so." She pulled his arm. "Robert?"

He came to and said, "I've had a real nice time. This beats tapes, doesn't it?"

I said, "Coming at you," and I put the number between his fingers. He inhaled, held the smoke, and then let it go. It was like he'd been doing it since he was nine years old.

"Thanks, bub," he said. "But I think this is all for me. I think I'm beginning to feel it," he said. He held the burning roach out for my wife.

"Same here," she said. "Ditto. Me, too." She took the roach and passed it to me.

"I may just sit here for a while between you two guys with my eyes closed. But don't let me bother you, okay? Either one of you. If it bothers you, say so. Otherwise, I may just sit here with my eyes closed until you're ready to go to bed," she said. "Your bed's made up, Robert, when you're ready. It's right next to our room at the top of the stairs. We'll show you up when you're ready. You wake me up now, you guys, if I fall asleep." She said that and then she closed her eyes and went to sleep.

The news program ended. I got up and changed the channel. I sat back down on the sofa. I wished my wife hadn't pooped out. Her head lay across the back of the sofa, her mouth open. She'd turned so that her robe had slipped away from her legs, exposing a juicy thigh. I reached to draw her robe back over her, and it was then that I glanced at the blind man. What the hell! I flipped the robe open again.

"You say when you want some strawberry pie," I said.

"I will," he said.

I said, "Are you tired? Do you want me to take you up to your bed? Are you ready to hit the hay?"

"Not yet," he said. "No, I'll stay up with you, bub. If that's all right. I'll stay up until you're ready to turn in. We haven't had a chance to talk. Know what I mean? I feel like me and her monopolized the evening." He lifted his beard and he let it fall. He picked up his cigarettes and his lighter.

"That's all right," I said. Then I said, "I'm glad for the company."

And I guess I was. Every night I smoked dope and stayed up as long as I could before I fell asleep. My wife and I hardly ever went to bed at the same time. When I did go to sleep, I had these dreams. Sometimes I'd wake up from one of them, my heart going crazy.

Something about the church and the Middle Ages was on the TV. Not your run-of-the-mill TV fare. I wanted to watch something else. I turned to the other channels. But there was nothing on them, either. So I turned back to the first channel and apologized.

"Bub, it's all right," the blind man said. "It's fine with me. Whatever you want to watch is okay. I'm always learning something. Learning never ends. It won't hurt me to learn something tonight. I got ears," he said.

We didn't say anything for a time. He was leaning forward with his head turned at me, his right ear aimed in the direction of the set. Very disconcerting. Now and then his eyelids drooped and then they snapped open again. Now and then he put his fingers into his beard and tugged, like he was thinking about something he was hearing on the television.

On the screen, a group of men wearing cowls was being set upon and tormented by men dressed in skeleton costumes and men dressed as devils. The men dressed as devils wore devil masks, horns, and long tails. This pageant was part of a procession. The Englishman who was narrating the thing said it took place in Spain once a year. I tried to explain to the blind man what was happening.

"Skeletons," he said. "I know about skeletons," he said, and he nodded.

The TV showed this one cathedral. Then there was a long, slow look at another one. Finally, the picture switched to the famous one in Paris, with its flying buttresses and

its spires reaching up to the clouds. The camera pulled away to show the whole of the cathedral rising above the skyline.

There were times when the Englishman who was telling the thing would shut up, would simply let the camera move around over the cathedrals. Or else the camera would tour the countryside, men in fields walking behind oxen. I waited as long as I could. Then I felt I had to say something. I said, "They're showing the outside of this cathedral now. Gargoyles. Little statues carved to look like monsters. Now I guess they're in Italy. Yeah, they're in Italy. There's paintings on the walls of this one church."

"Are those fresco paintings, bub?" he asked, and he sipped from his drink.

I reached for my glass. But it was empty. I tried to remember what I could remember. "You're asking me are those frescoes?" I said. "That's a good question. I don't know."

The camera moved to a cathedral outside Lisbon. The differences in the Portuguese cathedral compared with the French and Italian were not that great. But they were there. Mostly the interior stuff. Then something occurred to me, and I said, "Something has occurred to me. Do you have any idea what a cathedral is? What they look like, that is? Do you follow me? If somebody says cathedral to you, do you have any notion what they're talking about? Do you know the difference between that and a Baptist church, say?"

He let the smoke dribble from his mouth. "I know they took hundreds of workers fifty or a hundred years to build," he said. "I just heard the man say that, of course. I know generations of the same families worked on a cathedral. I heard him say that, too. The men who began their life's work on them, they never lived to see the completion of their work. In that wise, bub, they're no different from the rest of us, right?" He laughed. Then his eyelids drooped again. His head nodded. He seemed to be snoozing. Maybe he was imagining himself in Portugal. The TV was showing another cathedral now. This one was in Germany. The Englishman's voice droned on. "Cathedrals," the blind man said. He sat up and rolled his head back and forth. "If you want the truth, bub, that's about all I know. What I just said. What I heard him say. But maybe you could describe one to me? I wish you'd do it. I'd like that. If you want to know, I really don't have a good idea."

I stared hard at the shot of the cathedral on the TV. How could I even begin to describe it? But say my life depended on it. Say my life was being threatened by an insane guy who said I had to do it or else.

I stared some more at the cathedral before the picture flipped off into the countryside. There was no use. I turned to the blind man and said, "To begin with, they're very tall." I was looking around the room for clues. "They reach way up. Up and up. Toward the sky. They're so big, some of them, they have to have these supports. To help hold them up, so to speak. These supports are called buttresses. They remind me of viaducts, for some reason. But maybe you don't know viaducts, either? Sometimes the cathedrals have devils and such carved into the front. Sometimes lords and ladies. Don't ask me why this is," I said.

He was nodding. The whole upper part of his body seemed to be moving back and forth.

"I'm not doing so good, am I?" I said.

He stopped nodding and leaned forward on the edge of the sofa. As he listened to me, he was running his fingers through his beard. I wasn't getting through to him, I could see that. But he waited for me to go on just the same. He nodded, like he was trying to encourage me. I tried to think what else to say. "They're really big," I said. "They're massive. They're built of stone. Marble, too, sometimes. In those olden days, when they built cathedrals, men wanted to be close to God. In those olden days, God was an important part of everyone's life. You could tell this from their cathedral-building. I'm sorry," I said, "but it looks like that's the best I can do for you. I'm just no good at it."

"That's all right, bub," the blind man said. "Hey, listen. I hope you don't mind my asking you. Can I ask you something? Let me ask you a simple question, yes or no. I'm just curious and there's no offense. You're my host. But let me ask if you are in any way religious? You don't mind my asking?"

I shook my head. He couldn't see that, though. A wink is the same as a nod to a blind man. "I guess I don't believe in it. In anything. Sometimes it's hard. You know what I'm saying?"

"Sure, I do," he said.

"Right," I said.

The Englishman was still holding forth. My wife sighed in her sleep. She drew a long breath and went on with her sleeping.

"You'll have to forgive me," I said. "But I can't tell you what a cathedral looks like. It just isn't in me to do it. I can't do any more than I've done."

The blind man sat very still, his head down, as he listened to me.

I said, "The truth is, cathedrals don't mean anything special to me. Nothing. Cathedrals. They're something to look at on late-night TV. That's all they are."

It was then that the blind man cleared his throat. He brought something up. He took a handkerchief from his back pocket. Then he said. "I get it, bub. It's okay. It happens. Don't worry about it," he said. "Hey, listen to me. Will you do me a favor? I got an idea. Why don't you find us some heavy paper? And a pen. We'll do something. We'll draw one together. Get us a pen and some heavy paper. Go on, bub, get the stuff," he said.

So I went upstairs. My legs felt like they didn't have any strength in them. They felt like they did after I'd done some running. In my wife's room, I looked around. I found some ballpoints in a little basket on her table. And then I tried to think where to look for the kind of paper he was talking about.

Downstairs, in the kitchen, I found a shopping bag with onion skins in the bottom of the bag. I emptied the bag and shook it. I brought it into the living room and sat down with it near his legs. I moved some things, smoothed the wrinkles from the bag, spread it out on the coffee table.

The blind man got down from the sofa and sat next to me on the carpet.

He ran his fingers over the paper. He went up and down the sides of the paper. The edges, even the edges. He fingered the corners.

"All right," he said. "All right, let's do her."

He found my hand, the hand with the pen. He closed his hand over my hand. "Go ahead, bub, draw," he said. "Draw. You'll see. I'll follow along with you. It'll be okay. Just begin now like I'm telling you. You'll see. Draw," the blind man said.

So I began. First I drew a box that looked like a house. It could have been the house I lived in. Then I put a roof on it. At either end of the roof, I drew spires. Crazy.

"Swell," he said. "Terrific. You're doing fine," he said. "Never thought anything like this could happen in your lifetime, did you, bub? Well, it's a strange life, we all know that. Go on now. Keep it up."

I put in windows with arches. I drew flying buttresses. I hung great doors. I couldn't stop. The TV station went off the air. I put down the pen and closed and opened my fingers. The blind man felt around over the paper. He moved the tips of his fingers over the paper, all over what I had drawn, and he nodded.

"Doing fine," the blind man said.

I took up the pen again, and he found my hand. I kept at it. I'm no artist. But I kept drawing just the same.

My wife opened up her eyes and gazed at us. She sat up on the sofa, her robe hanging open. She said, "What are you doing? Tell me, I want to know."

I didn't answer her.

The blind man said, "We're drawing a cathedral. Me and him are working on it. Press hard," he said to me. "That's right. That's good," he said. "Sure. You got it, bub. I can tell. You didn't think you could. But you can, can't you? You're cooking with gas now. You know what I'm saying? We're going to really have us something here in a minute. How's the old arm?" he said. "Put some people in there now. What's a cathedral without people?"

My wife said, "What's going on? Robert, what are you doing? What's going on?"

"It's all right," he said to her. "Close your eyes now," the blind man said to me.

I did it. I closed them just like he said.

"Are they closed?" he said. "Don't fudge."

"They're closed," I said.

"Keep them that way," he said. He said, "Don't stop now. Draw."

So we kept on with it. His fingers rode my fingers as my hand went over the paper. It was like nothing else in my life up to now.

Then he said, "I think that's it. I think you got it," he said. "Take a look. What do you think?"

But I had my eyes closed. I thought I'd keep them that way for a little longer. I thought it was something I ought to do.

"Well?" he said. "Are you looking?"

My eyes were still closed. I was in my house. I knew that. But I didn't feel like I was inside anything.

"It's really something," I said.

QUESTIONS

1. What is the narrator's initial attitude toward the blind man? Is his attitude based on observation, jealousy, prejudice, or a combination of these? Explain.
2. What type of personality does the narrator have? What about what he says and thinks leads you to your conclusion?

3. The blind man says while they're preparing to watch educational television that "Learning never ends. It won't hurt me to learn something tonight. I got ears." How does this remark reflect the personality of the blind man in general? How does it complement the narrator's general attitude about learning? What irony, if any, is there in their viewpoints?
4. Why do you suppose the wife enjoys the company of the blind man?
5. What insight does the husband have at the end of the story? What instigates this insight? How does it make him change as a person?
6. Carver has often been said to write about the "voiceless" people of America. What do you suppose this means? How does this story demonstrate this quality in his writing?

Isak Dinesen

THE BLUE JAR

There was once an immensely rich old Englishman who had been a courtier and a councillor to the Queen and who now, in his old age, cared for nothing but collecting ancient blue china. To that end he travelled to Persia, Japan, and China, and he was everywhere accompanied by his daughter, the Lady Helena. It happened, as they sailed in the Chinese Sea, that the ship caught fire on a still night, and everybody went into the lifeboats and left her. In the dark and the confusion the old peer was separated from his daughter. Lady Helena got up on deck late, and found the ship quite deserted. In the last moment a young English sailor carried her down into a lifeboat that had been forgotten. To the two fugitives it seemed as if fire was following them from all sides, for the phosphorescence played in the dark sea, and, as they looked up, a falling star ran across the sky, as if it was going to drop into the boat. They sailed for nine days, till they were picked up by a Dutch merchantman, and came home to England.

The old lord had believed his daughter to be dead. He now wept with joy, and at once took her off to a fashionable watering-place so that she might recover from the hardships she had gone through. And as he thought it must be unpleasant to her that a young sailor, who made his bread in the merchant service, should tell the world that he had sailed for nine days alone with a peer's daughter, he paid the boy a fine sum, and made him promise to go shipping in the other hemisphere and never come back. "For what," said the old nobleman, "would be the good of that?"

When Lady Helena recovered, and they gave her the news of the Court and of her family, and in the end also told her how the young sailor had been sent away never to come back, they found that her mind had suffered from her trials, and that she cared for nothing in all the world. She would not go back to her father's castle in its park, nor go to Court, nor travel to any gay town of the continent. The only thing which she now

wanted to do was to go, like her father before her, to collect rare blue china. So she began to sail, from one country to the other, and her father went with her.

In her search she told the people, with whom she dealt, that she was looking for a particular blue color, and would pay any price for it. But although she bought many hundred blue jars and bowls, she would always after a time put them aside and say: "Alas, alas, it is not the right blue." Her father, when they had sailed for many years, suggested to her that perhaps the color which she sought did not exist. "O God, Papa," said she, "how can you speak so wickedly? Surely there must be some of it left from the time when all the world was blue."

Her two old aunts in England implored her to come back, still to make a great match. But she answered them: "Nay, I have got to sail. For you must know, dear aunts, that it is all nonsense when learned people tell you that the seas have got a bottom to them. On the contrary, the water, which is the noblest of the elements, does, of course, go all through the earth, so that our planet really floats in the ether, like a soapbubble. And there, on the other hemisphere, a ship sails, with which I have got to keep pace. We two are like the reflection of one another, in the deep sea, and the ship of which I speak is always exactly beneath my own ship, upon the opposite side of the globe. You have never seen a big fish swimming underneath a boat, following it like a dark-blue shade in the water. But in that way this ship goes, like the shadow of my ship, and I draw it to and fro wherever I go, as the moon draws the tides, all through the bulk of the earth. If I stopped sailing, what would these poor sailors who make their bread in the merchant service do? But I shall tell you a secret," she said. "In the end my ship will go down, to the center of the globe, and at the very same hour the other ship will sink as well—for people call it sinking, although I can assure you that there is no up and down in the sea—and there, in the midst of the world, we two shall meet."

Many years passed, the old lord died, and Lady Helena became old and deaf, but she still sailed. Then it happened, after the plunder of the summer palace of the Emperor of China, that a merchant brought her a very old blue jar. The moment she set eyes on it she gave a terrible shriek. "There it is!" she cried. "I have found it at last. This is the true blue. Oh, how light it makes one. Oh, it is as fresh as a breeze, as deep as a deep secret, as full as I say not what." With trembling hands she held the jar to her bosom, and sat for six hours sunk in contemplation of it. Then she said to her doctor and her lady-companion: "Now I can die. And when I am dead you will cut out my heart and lay it in the blue jar. For then everything will be as it was then. All shall be blue round me, and in the midst of the blue world my heart will be innocent and free, and will beat gently, like a wake that sings, like the drops that fall from an oar blade." A little later she asked them: "Is it not a sweet thing to think that, if only you have patience, all that has ever been, will come back to you?" Shortly afterwards the old lady died.

QUESTIONS

1. What stylistic conventions does the author use to signal that this story has similarities to a fairy tale?

2. Does the lack of description of the young sailor help or hinder our sympathizing with the loss felt by Lady Helena?
3. What social strictures exist in the story that doom the relationship between Lady Helena and the sailor?
4. How does the direct, spare diction of the story contribute to its emotional tenor?
5. Does this story seem hopelessly outdated given contemporary mores, or does it carry a relevant message about romantic relationships today? Explain.

Louise Erdrich

SNARES

It began after church with Margaret and her small granddaughter, Lulu, and was not to end until the long days of Lent and a hard-packed snow. There were factions on the reservation, a treaty settlement in the Agent's hands. There were Chippewa who signed their names in the year 1924, and there were Chippewa who saw the cash offered as a flimsy bait. I was one and Fleur Pillager, Lulu's mother, was another who would not lift her hand to sign. It was said that all the power to witch, harm, or cure lay in Fleur, the lone survivor of the old Pillager clan. But as much as people feared Fleur, they listened to Margaret Kashpaw. She was the ringleader of the holdouts, a fierce, one-minded widow with a vinegar tongue.

Margaret Kashpaw had knots of muscles in her arms. Her braids were thin, gray as iron, and usually tied strictly behind her back so they wouldn't swing. She was plump as a basket below and tough as roots on top. Her face was gnarled around a beautiful sharp nose. Two shell earrings caught the light and flashed whenever she turned her head. She had become increasingly religious in the years after her loss, and finally succeeded in dragging me to the Benediction Mass, where I was greeted by Father Damien, from whom I occasionally won small sums at dice.

"Grandfather Nanapush," he smiled, "at last."

"These benches are a hardship for an old man," I complained. "If you spread them with soft pine-needle cushions I'd have come before."

Father Damien stared thoughtfully at the rough pews, folded his hands inside the sleeves of his robe.

"You must think of their unyielding surfaces as helpful," he offered. "God sometimes enters the soul through the humblest parts of our anatomies, if they are sensitized to suffering."

"A god who enters through the rear door," I countered, "is no better than a thief."

Father Damien was used to me, and smiled as he walked to the altar. I adjusted my old bones, longing for some relief, trying not to rustle for fear of Margaret's jabbing elbow. The time was long. Lulu probed all my pockets with her fingers until she found

a piece of hard candy. I felt no great presence in this cold place and decided, as my back end ached and my shoulders stiffened, that our original gods were better, the Chippewa characters who were not exactly perfect but at least did not require sitting on hard boards.

When Mass was over and the smell of incense was thick in all our clothes, Margaret, Lulu, and I went out into the starry cold, the snow and stubble fields, and began the long walk to our homes. It was dusk. On either side of us the heavy trees stood motionless and blue. Our footsteps squeaked against the dry snow, the only sound to hear. We spoke very little, and even Lulu ceased her singing when the moon rose to half, poised like a balanced cup. We knew the very moment someone else stepped upon the road.

We had turned a bend and the footfalls came unevenly, just out of sight. There were two men, one mixed-blood or white, from the drop of his hard boot soles, and the other one quiet, an Indian. Not long and I heard them talking close behind us. From the rough, quick tension of the Indian's language, I recognized Lazarre. And the mixed-blood must be Clarence Morrissey. The two had signed the treaty and spoke in its favor to anyone they could collar at the store. They even came to people's houses to beg and argue that this was our one chance, our good chance, that the government would withdraw the offer. But wherever Margaret was, she slapped down their words like mosquitoes and said the only thing that lasts life to life is land. Money burns like tinder, flows like water. And as for promises, the wind is steadier. It is no wonder that, because she spoke so well, Lazarre and Clarence Morrissey wished to silence her. I sensed their bad intent as they passed us, an unpleasant edge of excitement in their looks and greetings.

They went on, disappeared in the dark brush.

"Margaret," I said, "we are going to cut back." My house was close, but Margaret kept walking forward as if she hadn't heard.

I took her arm, caught the little girl close, and started to turn, but Margaret would have none of this and called me a coward. She grabbed the girl to her. Lulu, who did not mind getting tossed between us, laughed, tucked her hand into her grandma's pocket, and never missed a step. Two years ago she had tired of being carried, got up, walked. She had the balance of a little mink. She was slippery and clever, too, which was good because when the men jumped from the darkest area of brush and grappled with us half a mile on, Lulu slipped free and scrambled into the trees.

They were occupied with Margaret and me, at any rate. We were old enough to snap in two, our limbs dry as dead branches, but we fought as though our enemies were the Nadouissouix kidnappers of our childhood. Margaret uttered a war cry that had not been heard for fifty years, and bit Lazarre's hand to the bone, giving a wound which would later prove the death of him. As for Clarence, he had all he could do to wrestle me to the ground and knock me half unconscious. When he'd accomplished that, he tied me and tossed me into a wheelbarrow, which was hidden near the road for the purpose of lugging us to the Morrissey barn.

I came to my senses trussed to a manger, sitting on a bale. Margaret was roped to another bale across from me, staring straight forward in a rage, a line of froth caught between her lips. On either side of her, shaggy cows chewed and shifted their thumping hooves. I rose and staggered, the weight of the manger on my back. I planned on Margaret biting through my ropes with her strong teeth, but then the two men entered.

I'm a talker, a fast-mouth who can't keep his thoughts straight, but lets fly with words and marvels at what he hears from his own mouth. I'm a smart one. I always was a devil for convincing women. And I wasn't too bad a shot, in other ways, at convincing men. But I had never been tied up before.

"Booshoo," I said. "Children, let us loose, your game is too rough!"

They stood between us, puffed with their secrets.

"Empty old windbag," said Clarence.

"I have a bargain for you," I said, looking for an opening. "Let us go and we won't tell Pukwan." Edgar Pukwan was the tribal police. "Boys get drunk sometimes and don't know what they're doing."

Lazarre laughed once, hard and loud. "We're not drunk," he said. "Just wanting what's coming to us, some justice, money out of it."

"Kill us," said Margaret. "We won't sign."

"Wait," I said. "My cousin Pukwan will find you boys, and have no mercy. Let us go. I'll sign and get it over with, and I'll persuade the old widow."

I signaled Margaret to keep her mouth shut. She blew air into her cheeks. Clarence looked expectantly at Lazarre, as if the show were over, but Lazarre folded his arms and was convinced of nothing.

"You lie when it suits, skinny old dog," he said, wiping at his lips as if in hunger. "It's her we want, anyway. We'll shame her so she shuts her mouth."

"Easy enough," I said, smooth, "now that you've got her tied. She's plump and good looking. Eyes like a doe! But you forget that we're together, almost man and wife."

This wasn't true at all, and Margaret's face went rigid with tumbling fury and confusion. I kept talking.

"So of course if you do what you're thinking of doing you'll have to kill me afterward, and that will make my cousin Pukwan twice as angry, since I owe him a fat payment for a gun which he lent me and I never returned. All the same," I went on—their heads were spinning—"I'll forget you bad boys ever considered such a crime, something so terrible that Father Damien would nail you on boards just like in the example on the wall in church."

"Quit jabbering." Lazarre stopped me in a deadly voice.

It was throwing pebbles in a dry lake. My words left no ripple. I saw in his eyes that he intended us great harm. I saw his greed. It was like watching an ugly design of bruises come clear for a moment and reconstructing the evil blows that made them.

I played my last card.

"Whatever you do to Margaret you are doing to the Pillager woman!" I dropped my voice. "The witch, Fleur Pillager, is her own son's wife."

Clarence was too young to be frightened, but his mouth hung in interested puzzle-ment. My words had a different effect on Lazarre, as a sudden light shone, a conse-quence he hadn't considered.

I cried out, seeing this, "Don't you know she can think about you hard enough to

stop your heart?" Lazarre was still deciding. He raised his fist and swung it casually and tapped my face. It was worse not to be hit full on.

"Come near!" crooned Margaret in the old language. "Let me teach you how to die."

But she was trapped like a fox. Her earrings glinted and spun as she hissed her death song over and over, which signaled something to Lazarre, for he shook himself angrily and drew a razor from his jacket. He stropped it with fast, vicious movements while Margaret sang shriller, so full of hate that the ropes should have burned, shriveled, fallen from her body. My struggle set the manger cracking against the barn walls and further confused the cows, who bumped each other and complained. At a sign from Lazarre, Clarence sighed, rose, and smashed me. The last I saw before I blacked out, through the tiny closing pinhole of light, was Lazarre approaching Margaret with the blade.

When I woke, minutes later, it was to worse shock. For Lazarre had sliced Margaret's long braids off and was now, carefully, shaving her scalp. He started almost tenderly at the wide part, and then pulled the edge down each side of her skull. He did a clean job. He shed not one drop of her blood.

And I could not even speak to curse them. For pressing my jaw down, thick above my tongue, her braids, never cut in this life till now, were tied to silence me. Powerless, I tasted their flat, animal perfume.

It wasn't much later, or else it was forever, that we walked out into the night again. Speechless, we made our way in fierce pain down the road. I was damaged in spirit, more so than Margaret. For now she tucked her shawl over her naked head and forgot her own bad treatment. She called out in dread each foot of the way, for Lulu. But the smart, bold girl had hidden till all was clear and then run to Margaret's house. We opened the door and found her sitting by the stove in a litter of scorched matches and kindling. She had not the skill to start a fire, but she was dry-eyed. Though very cold, she was alert and then captured with wonder when Margaret slipped off her shawl.

"Where is your hair?" she asked.

I took my hand from my pocket. "Here's what's left of it. I grabbed this when they cut me loose." I was shamed by how pitiful I had been, relieved when Margaret snatched the thin gray braids from me and coiled them round her fist.

"I knew you would save them, clever man!" There was satisfaction in her voice.

I set the fire blazing. It was strange how generous this woman was to me, never blaming me or mentioning my failure. Margaret stowed her braids inside a birchbark box and merely instructed me to lay it in her grave, when that time occurred. Then she came near the stove with a broken mirror from beside her washstand and looked at her own image.

"My," she pondered, "my." She put the mirror down. "I'll take a knife to them."

And I was thinking too. I was thinking I would have to kill them.

But how does an aching and half-starved grandfather attack a young, well-fed Morrissey and a tall, sly Lazarre? Later, I rolled up in blankets in the corner by Margaret's stove, and I put my mind to this question throughout that night until, exhausted, I slept. And I thought of it first thing next morning, too, and still nothing came. It was only after we had some hot *gaulette* and walked Lulu back to her mother that an idea began to grow.

Fleur let us in, hugged Lulu into her arms, and looked at Margaret, who took off her scarf and stood bald, face burning again with smoldered fire. She told Fleur all of what happened, sparing no detail. The two women's eyes held, but Fleur said nothing. She put Lulu down, smoothed the front of her calico shirt, flipped her heavy braids over her shoulders, tapped one finger on her perfect lips. And then, calm, she went to the washstand and scraped the edge of her hunting knife keen as glass. Margaret and Lulu and I watched as Fleur cut her braids off, shaved her own head, and folded the hair into a quilled skin pouch. Then she went out, hunting, and didn't bother to wait for night to cover her tracks.

I would have to go out hunting too.

I had no gun, but anyway that was a white man's revenge. I knew how to wound with barbs of words, but had never wielded a skinning knife against a human, much less two young men. Whomever I missed would kill me, and I did not want to die by their lowly hands.

In fact, I didn't think that after Margaret's interesting kindness I wanted to leave this life at all. Her head, smooth as an egg, was ridged delicately with bone, and gleamed as if it had been buffed with a flannel cloth. Maybe it was the strangeness that attracted me. She looked forbidding, but the absence of hair also set off her eyes, so black and full of lights. She reminded me of that queen from England, of a water snake or a shrewd young bird. The earrings, which seemed part of her, mirrored her moods like water, and when they were still rounds of green lights against her throat I seemed, again, to taste her smooth, smoky braids in my mouth.

I had better things to do than fight. So I decided to accomplish revenge as quickly as possible. I was a talker who used my brains as my weapon. When I hunted, I preferred to let my game catch itself.

Snares demand clever fingers and a scheming mind, and snares had never failed me. Snares are quiet, and best of all snares are slow. I wanted to give Lazarre and Morrissey time to consider why they had to strangle. I thought hard. One- or two-foot deadfalls are required beneath a snare so that a man can't put his hand up and loosen the knot. The snares I had in mind also required something stronger than a cord, which could be broken, and finer than a rope, which even Lazarre might see and avoid. I pondered this closely, yet even so I might never have found the solution had I not gone to Mass with Margaret and grown curious about the workings of Father Damien's pride and joy, the piano in the back of the church, the instrument whose keys he breathed on, polished, then played after services, and sometimes alone. I had noticed that his hands usually stayed near the middle of the keyboard, so I took the wires from either end.

In the meantime, I was not the only one concerned with punishing Lazarre and Clarence Morrissey. Fleur was seen in town. Her thick skirts brushed the snow into clouds behind her. Though it was cold she left her head bare so everyone could see the frigid sun glare off her skull. The light reflected in the eyes of Lazarre and Clarence, who were standing at the door of the pool hall. They dropped their cue sticks in the slush and ran back to Morrissey land. Fleur walked the four streets, once in each direction, then followed.

The two men told of her visit, how she passed through the Morrissey house touching

here, touching there, sprinkling powders that ignited and stank on the hot stove. How Clarence swayed on his feet, blinked hard, and chewed his fingers. How Fleur stepped up to him, drew her knife. He smiled foolishly and asked her for supper. She reached forward and trimmed off a hank of his hair. Then she stalked from the house, leaving a taste of cold wind, and then chased Lazarre to the barn.

She made a black silhouette against the light from the door. Lazarre pressed against the wood of the walls, watching, hypnotized by the sight of Fleur's head and the quiet blade. He did not defend himself when she approached, reached for him, gently and efficiently cut bits of his hair, held his hands, one at a time, and trimmed the nails. She waved the razor-edged knife before his eyes and swept a few eyelashes into a white square of flour sacking that she then carefully folded into her blouse.

For days after, Lazarre babbled and wept. Fleur was murdering him by use of bad medicine, he said. He showed his hand, the bite that Margaret had dealt him, and the dark streak from the wound, along his wrist and inching up his arm. He even used that bound hand to scratch his name from the treaty, but it did no good.

I figured that the two men were doomed at least three ways now. Margaret won the debate with her Catholic training and decided to damn her soul by taking up the ax, since no one else had destroyed her enemies. I begged her to wait for another week, all during which it snowed and thawed and snowed again. It took me that long to arrange the snare to my satisfaction, near Lazarre's shack, on a path both men took to town.

I set it out one morning before anyone stirred, and watched from an old pine twisted along the ground. I waited while the smoke rose in a silky feather from the tiny tin spout on Lazarre's roof. I had to sit half a day before Lazarre came outside, and even then it was just for wood, nowhere near the path. I had a hard time to keep my blood flowing, my stomach still. I ate a handful of dry berries Margaret had given me, and a bit of pounded meat. I doled it to myself and waited until finally Clarence showed. He walked the trail like a blind ghost and stepped straight into my noose.

It was perfect, or would have been if I had made the deadfall two inches wider, for in falling Clarence somehow managed to spread his legs and straddle the deep hole I'd cut. It had been invisible, covered with snow, and yet in one foot-pedaling instant, the certain knowledge of its construction sprang into Clarence's brain and told his legs to reach for the sides. I don't know how he did it, but there he was poised. I waited, did not show myself. The noose jerked enough to cut slightly into the fool's neck, a too-snug fit. He was spread-eagled and on tiptoe, his arms straight out. If he twitched a finger, lost the least control, even tried to yell, one foot would go, the noose constrict.

But Clarence did not move. I could see from behind my branches that he didn't even dare to change the expression on his face. His mouth stayed frozen in shock. Only his eyes shifted, darted fiercely and wildly, side to side, showing all the agitation he must not release, searching desperately for a means of escape. They focused only when I finally stepped toward him, quiet, from the pine.

We were in full view of Lazarre's house, face to face. I stood before the boy. Just a touch, a sudden kick, perhaps no more than a word, was all that it would take. But I looked into his eyes and saw the knowledge of his situation. Pity entered me. Even for Margaret's shame, I couldn't do the thing I might have done.

I turned away and left Morrissey still balanced on the ledge of snow.

· · ·

What money I did have, I took to the trading store next day. I bought the best bonnet on the reservation. It was black as a coal scuttle, large, and shaped the same.

"It sets off my doe eyes," Margaret said and stared me down.

She wore it every day, and always to Mass. Not long before Lent and voices could be heard: "There goes Old Lady Coalbucket." Nonetheless, she was proud, and softening day by day, I could tell. By the time we got our foreheads crossed with ashes, she consented to be married.

"I hear you're thinking of exchanging the vows," said Father Damien as I shook his hand on our way out the door.

"I'm having relations with Margaret already," I told him, "that's the way we do things."

This had happened to him before, so he was not even stumped as to what remedy he should use.

"Make a confession, at any rate," he said, motioning us back into the church.

So I stepped into the little box and knelt. Father Damien slid aside the shadowy door. I told him what I had been doing with Margaret and he stopped me partway through.

"No more details. Pray to Our Lady."

"There is one more thing."

"Yes?"

"Clarence Morrissey, he wears a scarf to church around his neck each week. I snared him like a rabbit."

Father Damien let the silence fill him.

"And the last thing," I went on. "I stole the wire from your piano."

The silence spilled over into my stall, and I was held in its grip until the priest spoke.

"Discord is hateful to God. You have offended his ear." Almost as an afterthought, Damien added, "And his commandment. The violence among you must cease."

"You can have the wire back," I said. I had used only one long strand. I also agreed that I would never use my snares on humans, an easy promise. Lazarre was already caught.

Just two days later, while Margaret and I stood with Lulu and her mother inside the trading store, Lazarre entered, gesturing, his eyes rolled to the skull. He stretched forth his arm and pointed along its deepest black vein and dropped his jaw wide. Then he stepped backward into a row of traps that the trader had set to show us how they worked. Fleur's eye lit, her white scarf caught the sun as she turned. All the whispers were true. Fleur had scratched Lazarre's figure into a piece of birchbark, drawn his insides, and rubbed a bit of rouge up his arm until the red stain reached his heart. There was no sound as he fell, no cry, no word, and the traps of all types that clattered down around his body jumped and met for a long time, snapping air.

QUESTIONS

1. How would you summarize Grandfather Nanapush's personality? What aspects of his personality do you ascribe to his cultural heritage as a Native American?

2. This story is filled with figurative language. Identify at least five metaphors and similes. What qualities do they have in common? How do they reflect the ethnic culture and life-style of the characters?

3. What elements of the story appear fantastic or magical? How do they contribute to the mood of the story? How do they effect the story's outcome?

4. What is Grandfather Nanapush's reaction to Margaret's having her head shaven? What does this reveal about his personality? How does he respond to this event?

5. What are the figurative and literal "snares" that are described or implied in the story? How do they relate to the story's theme?

Gabriel García Márquez

A VERY OLD MAN WITH ENORMOUS WINGS
A Tale for Children

On the third day of rain they had killed so many crabs inside the house that Pelayo had to cross his drenched courtyard and throw them into the sea, because the newborn child had a temperature all night and they thought it was due to the stench. The world had been sad since Tuesday. Sea and sky were a single ash-gray thing and the sands of the beach, which on March nights glimmered like powdered light, had become a stew of mud and rotten shellfish. The light was so weak at noon that when Pelayo was coming back to the house after throwing away the crabs, it was hard for him to see what it was that was moving and groaning in the rear of the courtyard. He had to go very close to see that it was an old man, a very old man, lying face down in the mud, who, in spite of his tremendous efforts, couldn't get up, impeded by his enormous wings.

Frightened by that nightmare, Pelayo ran to get Elisenda, his wife, who was putting compresses on the sick child, and he took her to the rear of the courtyard. They both looked at the fallen body with mute stupor. He was dressed like a ragpicker. There were only a few faded hairs left on his bald skull and very few teeth in his mouth, and his pitiful condition of a drenched great-grandfather had taken away any sense of grandeur he might have had. His huge buzzard wings, dirty and half-plucked, were forever entangled in the mud. They looked at him so long and so closely that Pelayo and Elisenda very soon overcame their surprise and in the end found him familiar. Then they dared speak to him, and he answered in an incomprehensible dialect with a strong sailor's voice. That was how they skipped over the inconvenience of the wings and quite intelligently concluded that he was a lonely castaway from some foreign ship wrecked by the storm. And yet, they called in a neighbor woman who knew everything about life and death to see him, and all she needed was one look to show them their mistake.

"He's an angel," she told them. "He must have been coming for the child, but the poor fellow is so old that the rain knocked him down."

On the following day everyone knew that a flesh-and-blood angel was held captive in Pelayo's house. Against the judgment of the wise neighbor woman, for whom angels in those times were the fugitive survivors of a celestial conspiracy, they did not have the heart to club him to death. Pelayo watched over him all afternoon from the kitchen, armed with his bailiff's club, and before going to bed he dragged him out of the mud and locked him up with the hens in the wire chicken coop. In the middle of the night, when the rain stopped, Pelayo and Elisenda were still killing crabs. A short time afterward the child woke up without a fever and with a desire to eat. Then they felt magnanimous and decided to put the angel on a raft with fresh water and provisions for three days and leave him to his fate on the high seas. But when they went out into the courtyard with the first light of dawn, they found the whole neighborhood in front of the chicken coop having fun with the angel, without the slightest reverence, tossing him things to eat through the openings in the wire as if he weren't a supernatural creature but a circus animal.

Father Gonzaga arrived before seven o'clock, alarmed at the strange news. By that time onlookers less frivolous than those at dawn had already arrived and they were making all kinds of conjectures concerning the captive's future. The simplest among them thought that he should be named mayor of the world. Others of sterner mind felt that he should be promoted to the rank of five-star general in order to win all wars. Some visionaries hoped that he could be put to stud in order to implant on earth a race of winged wise men who could take charge of the universe. But Father Gonzaga, before becoming a priest, had been a robust woodcutter. Standing by the wire, he reviewed his catechism in an instant and asked them to open the door so that he could take a close look at that pitiful man who looked more like a huge decrepit hen among the fascinated chickens. He was lying in a corner drying his open wings in the sunlight among the fruit peels and breakfast leftovers that the early risers had thrown him. Alien to the impertinences of the world, he only lifted his antiquarian eyes and murmured something in his dialect when Father Gonzaga went into the chicken coop and said good morning to him in Latin. The parish priest had his first suspicion of an imposter when he saw that he did not understand the language of God or know how to greet His ministers. Then he noticed that seen close up he was much too human: he had an unbearable smell of the outdoors, the back side of his wings was strewn with parasites and his main feathers had been mistreated by terrestrial winds, and nothing about him measured up to the proud dignity of angels. Then he came out of the chicken coop and in a brief sermon warned the curious against the risks of being ingenuous. He reminded them that the devil had the bad habit of making use of carnival tricks in order to confuse the unwary. He argued that if wings were not the essential element in determining the difference between a hawk and an airplane, they were even less so in the recognition of angels. Nevertheless, he promised to write a letter to his bishop so that the latter would write to his primate so that the latter would write to the Supreme Pontiff in order to get the final verdict from the highest courts.

His prudence fell on sterile hearts. The news of the captive angel spread with such rapidity that after a few hours the courtyard had the bustle of a marketplace and they

had to call in troops with fixed bayonets to disperse the mob that was about to knock the house down. Elisenda, her spine all twisted from sweeping up so much marketplace trash, then got the idea of fencing in the yard and charging five cents admission to see the angel.

The curious came from far away. A traveling carnival arrived with a flying acrobat who buzzed over the crowd several times, but no one paid any attention to him because his wings were not those of an angel but, rather, those of a sidereal bat. The most unfortunate invalids on earth came in search of health: a poor woman who since childhood had been counting her heartbeats and had run out of numbers; a Portuguese man who couldn't sleep because the noise of the stars disturbed him; a sleepwalker who got up at night to undo the things he had done while awake; and many others with less serious ailments. In the midst of that shipwreck disorder that made the earth tremble, Pelayo and Elisenda were happy with fatigue, for in less than a week they had crammed their rooms with money and the line of pilgrims waiting their turn to enter still reached beyond the horizon.

The angel was the only one who took no part in his own act. He spent his time trying to get comfortable in his borrowed nest, befuddled by the hellish heat of the oil lamps and sacramental candles that had been placed along the wire. At first they tried to make him eat some mothballs, which, according to the wisdom of the wise neighbor woman, were the food prescribed for angels. But he turned them down, just as he turned down the papal lunches that the penitents brought him, and they never found out whether it was because he was an angel or because he was an old man that in the end he ate nothing but eggplant mush. His only supernatural virtue seemed to be patience. Especially during the first days, when the hens pecked at him, searching for the stellar parasites that proliferated in his wings, and the cripples pulled out feathers to touch their defective parts with, and even the most merciful threw stones at him, trying to get him to rise so they could see him standing. The only time they succeeded in arousing him was when they burned his side with an iron for branding steers, for he had been motionless for so many hours that they thought he was dead. He awoke with a start, ranting in his hermetic language and with tears in his eyes, and he flapped his wings a couple of times, which brought on a whirlwind of chicken dung and lunar dust and a gale of panic that did not seem to be of this world. Although many thought that his reaction had been one not of rage but of pain, from then on they were careful not to annoy him, because the majority understood that his passivity was not that of a hero taking his ease but that of a cataclysm in repose.

Father Gonzaga held back the crowd's frivolity with formulas of maidservant inspiration while awaiting the arrival of a final judgment on the nature of the captive. But the mail from Rome showed no sense of urgency. They spent their time finding out if the prisoner had a navel, if his dialect had any connection with Aramaic, how many times he could fit on the head of a pin, or whether he wasn't just a Norwegian with wings. Those meager letters might have come and gone until the end of time if a providential event had not put an end to the priest's tribulations.

It so happened that during those days, among so many other carnival attractions, there arrived in town the traveling show of the woman who had been changed into a spider for having disobeyed her parents. The admission to see her was not only less than the admission to see the angel, but people were permitted to ask her all manner of questions about her absurd state and to examine her up and down so that no one would ever doubt the truth of her horror. She was a frightful tarantula the size of a ram and with the head of a sad maiden. What was most heart-rending, however, was not her outlandish shape but the sincere affliction with which she recounted the details of her misfortune. While still practically a child she had sneaked out of her parents' house to go to a dance, and while she was coming back through the woods after having danced all night without permission, a fearful thunderclap rent the sky in two and through the crack came the lightning bolt of brimstone that changed her into a spider. Her only nourishment came from the meatballs that charitable souls chose to toss into her mouth. A spectacle like that, full of so much human truth and with such a fearful lesson, was bound to defeat without even trying that of a haughty angel who scarcely deigned to look at mortals. Besides, the few miracles attributed to the angel showed a certain mental disorder, like the blind man who didn't recover his sight but grew three new teeth, or the paralytic who didn't get to walk but almost won the lottery, and the leper whose sores sprouted sunflowers. Those consolation miracles, which were more like mocking fun, had already ruined the angel's reputation when the woman who had been changed into a spider finally crushed him completely. That was how Father Gonzaga was cured forever of his insomnia and Pelayo's courtyard went back to being as empty as during the time it had rained for three days and crabs walked through the bedrooms.

The owners of the house had no reason to lament. With the money they saved they built a two-story mansion with balconies and gardens and high netting so that crabs wouldn't get in during the winter, and with iron bars on the windows so that angels wouldn't get in. Pelayo also set up a rabbit warren close to town and gave up his job as bailiff for good, and Elisenda bought some satin pumps with high heels and many dresses of iridescent silk, the kind worn on Sunday by the most desirable women in those times. The chicken coop was the only thing that didn't receive any attention. If they washed it down with creolin and burned tears of myrrh inside it every so often, it was not in homage to the angel but to drive away the dungheap stench that still hung everywhere like a ghost and was turning the new house into an old one. At first, when the child learned to walk, they were careful that he not get too close to the chicken coop. But then they began to lose their fears and got used to the smell, and before the child got his second teeth he'd gone inside the chicken coop to play, where the wires were falling apart. The angel was no less standoffish with him than with other mortals, but he tolerated the most ingenious infamies with the patience of a dog who had no illusions. They both came down with chicken pox at the same time. The doctor who took care of the child couldn't resist the temptation to listen to the angel's heart, and he found so much whistling in the heart and so many sounds in his kidneys that it seemed impossible for him to be alive. What surprised him most, however, was the logic of his wings. They seemed so natural on that completely human organism that he couldn't understand why other men didn't have them too.

When the child began school it had been some time since the sun and rain had caused the collapse of the chicken coop. The angel went dragging himself about here and there like a stray dying man. They would drive him out of the bedroom with a broom and a moment later find him in the kitchen. He seemed to be in so many places

at the same time that they grew to think that he'd been duplicated, that he was reproducing himself all through the house, and the exasperated and unhinged Elisenda shouted that it was awful living in that hell full of angels. He could scarcely eat and his antiquarian eyes had also become so foggy that he went about bumping into posts. All he had left were the bare cannulae of his last feathers. Pelayo threw a blanket over him and extended him the charity of letting him sleep in the shed, and only then did they notice that he had a temperature at night, and was delirious with the tongue twisters of an old Norwegian. That was one of the few times they became alarmed, for they thought he was going to die and not even the wise neighbor woman had been able to tell them what to do with dead angels.

And yet he not only survived his worst winter, but seemed improved with the first sunny days. He remained motionless for several days in the farthest corner of the courtyard, where no one would see him, and at the beginning of December some large, stiff feathers began to grow on his wings, the feathers of a scarecrow, which looked more like another misfortune of decrepitude. But he must have known the reason for those changes, for he was quite careful that no one should notice them, that no one should hear the sea chanteys that he sometimes sang under the stars. One morning Elisenda was cutting some bunches of onions for lunch when a wind that seemed to come from the high seas blew into the kitchen. Then she went to the window and caught the angel in his first attempts at flight. They were so clumsy that his fingernails opened a furrow in the vegetable patch and he was on the point of knocking the shed down with the ungainly flapping that slipped on the light and couldn't get a grip on the air. But he did manage to gain altitude. Elisenda let out a sigh of relief, for herself and for him, when she saw him pass over the last houses, holding himself up in some way with the risky flapping of a senile vulture. She kept watching him even when she was through cutting the onions and she kept on watching until it was no longer possible for her to see him, because then he was no longer an annoyance in her life but an imaginary dot on the horizon of the sea.

Translated by Gregory Rabassa

QUESTIONS

1. Is there any indication in the story of why the angel has come to earth? What do think is the purpose of his mission?
2. What is the general attitude of the townspeople when the man with enormous wings lands? Why do they have this attitude?
3. What is the attitude of the church in Rome toward the angel? Compare and contrast it with the attitude of the town.
4. How would you characterize the faith of Pelayo and Elisenda? What actions do they take that demonstrate the nature of their faith?

Yussef Idriss

A HOUSE OF FLESH

*The ring beside the lamp . . . silence hangs heavy, ears grow blind. Fingers move
stealthily, in silence grasp the ring and put out the light. Darkness reigns and
in darkness eyes grow blind. The woman, her three daughters, and their house,
a mere room.*

The beginning is silence. The widow is tall, fair-skinned, willowy, about thirty-five. Her
daughters are also tall and full-bodied. They continue to wear their long black mourning
dresses. The youngest is sixteen, the eldest in her twenties, all three unattractive, having
inherited the father's dark, badly proportioned body, corpulent and flabby; retaining
their mother's build. The room, in spite of its size, holds them during the daytime.
Despite its extreme poverty, the room is neatly arranged in an intimate, cozy atmosphere which reflects a feminine touch. When night falls, their bodies are scattered all
over the room. Huge piles of warm throbbing flesh, sprawled on the single bed or on
the couch: breathing, heaving, deeply insomniac.

Silence has hovered over the home since the man's death two years ago after a long
illness. The mourning period was over, but the habits of those in mourning remained,
most predominantly the habit of silence. It was in fact a silence of waiting, for the girls
were growing older and the period of waiting was weighing upon them. No suitors were
knocking on their doors. What man would dare to knock on the door of poor unattractive girls, particularly if they happened to be fatherless? But hope still lived of course
(wine can remain in the barrels until the right buyer comes along), and each girl believed
her luck would change. (No matter how poor one may be, there will always be someone
else yet poorer, and if ugliness prevails there will always be someone even uglier . . . and
dreams are fulfilled if one has enough patience. . . .)

That silence was occasionally interrupted by the sound of a voice reciting the Koran,
a voice rising monotonously, emotionless. A recitation by a *muqri*.[1] The *muqri* is blind,
but the prayers are for the soul of the deceased, always delivered at the same time. Every
Friday afternoon, he comes poking his stick at their door. He abandons himself to the
extended hand that leads him inside. There he sits cross-legged on the mat and recites.
When it is over, he gropes for his sandals and pronounces a greeting that no one bothers
to reciprocate, and then leaves. Out of habit he comes, out of habit he recites, and out
of habit he leaves. No one notices him any more.

Forever this silence . . . even when the Friday afternoon recitation disturbs it. It is
as if silence is broken only with silence. Waiting is forever, like hope, little hope but
constant hope, for there is hope for every insignificant being, there is somewhere one
who is even more insignificant. And they do not aspire to much, no, they do not aspire.

Silence persisted until something happened, until one Friday when the *muqri* did not
show up. Every agreement comes to an end, no matter how long it has lasted, and it
seemed this agreement had come to its end. Only then did the widow and her daughters

---

[1] *muqri*—reader of Koranic verses.

realize that not only was he the sole male voice that broke their silence once a week, but also that he was the only man who ever knocked at their door. Other things began to dawn upon them. True, he was as poor as they were, but his outfits were always clean, his sandals always shone, his headdress was wrapped meticulously (putting to shame any man with eyes), and above all, his voice was strong, deep and melodious. The proposition hovered in the air: why not renew the agreement, and why not summon him immediately? Could he be busy elsewhere? They could wait, for waiting was an old game they were very good at.

Evening was drawing to its end, and he recited as if for the first time. Then the proposition came up: why shouldn't one of them marry a man whose voice would fill the house?

He was a bachelor with a sprouting moustache, a young man. Words generate words, and he too was looking for the right woman. The girls confer about the matter and the mother scans their faces trying to figure who the lucky one would be. But their faces evade her searching looks and seem to say: Is this how we are to be rewarded for our long wait? Shall we break our fast with a blind man? For they still dreamt of suitors, and suitors are usually young men with eyes. Poor things, they have yet to know the world of men. Impossible for them to perceive at this stage in their lives that a man is not to be judged by sight alone.

"Mother, you marry him . . . marry him."

"Me? What shame, what will people say!"

"Let them say what they will, no matter what. It will be better than living in a house without a man, the resounding voice of a man."

"Do you want me to marry before you? Never . . ."

"Wouldn't it be better if you marry before us, so that our house becomes a treading ground for men? Then we can marry after you."

"Marry him, mother. O marry him . . ."

And she married him . . . and one more breath was added to the air and their income grew just a little bit more, and a much greater problem arose. True, they survived their first night, but they didn't dare come close to each other, even inadvertently. The girls were sleeping, or pretending to do so, but the mother could feel pairs of searching beams inspecting the space that lay between them, searching lights of human eyes, prospecting antennas. The girls are old enough to understand, and the room is suddenly transformed into sentient throbbing presences, vibrating in the light of day.

One by one, each left the house when morning set in, only to return by sunset, hesitant, embarrassed. Dragging their feet, they came back to a house filled with laughter, occasionally interrupted by faint noises of a woman. It must be the mother laughing, and the dignified *muqri* they had known was now laughing too. Their mother greeted them, bareheaded, hair wet and with a comb in hand, still laughing. They looked at her face and realized that it had been for all those years like an unlit lamp in whose corners spiders and cobwebs had taken refuge. Now suddenly that face had burst into light, electrified, glistening tearful eyes, with laughter lodged there instead. The silence dissipated completely. Suppertime bustled with loud voices, jokes, highlighted by the *muqri's* imitation of Umm Kulthum and Abd al-Wahab in his gushing, whining, beautiful voice.

Well done, mother. Soon this gaiety and laughter will draw more men to the house, for the presence of men attracts other men.

Be confident, girls. Soon men will be coming and suitors will make their calls. But in fact what was preoccupying her was that young man, not the suitors. True, he was blind, but how often are we blinded ourselves from seeing others, just because they happen to be blind? Yes, she was seeing this healthy young man. His overflowing vitality had made up for those years of sickness, impotence, and early old age.

The silence was gone, never to return, and the beat of life was there to stay. The man is her legal husband; she married him according to the law of God and his Prophet, and according to his Sunna.[2] No, nothing will make her feel ashamed, for all that she does is legitimate, even when she makes no effort to hide or keep the secret, or when night creeps up and they are all huddled together, and the power of the body and soul takes over, even with the girls there aware and awake in their observation posts, fighting to control sighs and groans.

Her mornings were spent washing clothes in rich people's homes, and his days were whiled away by reciting the Quran in homes of the poor.

At the beginning, he didn't return home for a break during the day, but as his nights grew longer, he started coming home to rest his exhausted body, to regain strength for the night to come.

And once, after they had had their fill of the night, and the night had had its fill of them, he suddenly asked her what had been the matter with her during the lunch hour. Why was it that she was now so voluble and eager to talk, but then had adopted total silence? Why was she now wearing his cherished ring, the ring that was all he had given her in form of dowry, gift, wedding band? Why hadn't she been wearing it during the lunch hour?

She could have torn herself away distraught, screaming. She could have lost her senses. He could have gotten himself killed. For there could be but one meaning to what he was saying, a horrible, atrocious meaning. A choking sob kept everything back. She held her breath and kept her peace. With her ears, which she transformed into noses, eyes, and other organs of sense, she strained her every fibre to find out who the culprit was. For some reason she was positive it was the middle one, because in her eyes had grown a certain daring look that only a bullet could check. But she listened. The breathing of the three grew louder, deeper and feverish, flaming hot, hesitant and intermittent, growling in youthful dreams which would be sinful to interrupt!

Heavings turn into burning flames, into lava vomited by thirsty lands. The knots in her throat deepen and choke her. There are hungry breaths. With all her straining she cannot differentiate between one vibrant, hot pile of flesh and another. All are hungry. All groan and scream. And the groans are not just groans. They are pleas, supplications perhaps, perhaps something more.

She has totally immersed herself in her second legitimate right, and forgotten all about her first legitimate duty, her girls. Patience has become myrrh. Even the mirage of suitors is no more. Suddenly, as if bitten, as though awakened to a secret call, the girls are hungry. The food is forbidden, but hunger is yet more sinful. There exists nothing

[2]Sunna—traditional teachings of Islam, according to the Prophet.

more sinful than this hunger. How well she has known it. And how well it has known her, freed her spirit, searched her bones. She has known it. Now that she has had her fill, it is impossible for her to forget.

Hungry ones! She who took the bread from her own mouth to feed them, she whose only preoccupation was to feed them even if she were to go hungry, she the mother— has she forgotten?

And no matter how insistent his demands, her pain was changed into silence. The mother became silent, and from that moment onwards, silence never left her. At breakfast, just as she had thought, the middle girl was silent and was to remain silent from then onwards. At suppertime, the young man was gay and jovial, blind and happy, singing and laughing, with only the youngest and eldest tuning in.

Patience is tried and its bitterness becomes a sickness and no one comes knocking on their door. One day the eldest looks at the mother's ring and expresses her admiration, and the mother's heart sinks; and its beating grows louder when the daughter begs to wear the ring just for the day. In silence the mother takes it off her finger, and in silence the girl slips it onto her own.

And that evening the eldest girl keeps silent, refusing to utter a word.

And the blind man is singing and laughing boisterously with only the youngest tuning in.

With unrewarded patience, and luck that has never turned with her worrying, the youngest grows older, and asks for her turn in the ring game, and in silence her turn comes.

The ring lies beside the lamp and silence sets in and ears become blind, and in silence the finger whose turn comes gropes stealthily for the ring and turns off the light.

Darkness prevails, and in darkness eyes grow blind. Only the blind young man remains happy. Yet behind his loudness and happiness he is tormented by this silence, he is tortured by uncertainty. At the beginning he would say to himself, it must be a woman's nature to be ever-changing. One time she is fresh as the morning dew, at another time she is worn out, exhausted like swampy waters. At times satiny like rose leaves, at others prickly like cacti. True, the ring is always there, but each time the finger it encircles seems to be different. He was almost positive that they knew for sure. So why doesn't silence speak, why doesn't it speak? The mere thought made him choke on his bread. And from that moment on, he never uttered a word. He lived in fear of the violation of that collapse. This time the silence was different, respected by all. A conscious silence, not caused by poverty, nor patience, nor despair, but the most profound kind of silence, the most binding of all, a silence implemented without formal agreement. The widow and her three daughters, and the house which was a room. This was a new kind of silence. The blind reciter brought along this silence, with silence convincing himself that his companion in bed was always his legitimate wife, bearer of his ring, ever changing, unpredictable. Young and old, silken soft or callous and scaly, sometimes fat, at other times thin, whatever, this really was her business. Actually, all this was the business of those with sight and their sole responsibility.

For *they* alone possess the grace of certainty; *they* are capable of discernment; but the most *he* can know is doubt, doubt that can be removed only through the blessing of sight.

So long as he is deprived of it, he will be denied certainty, for he is the one who is blind and there is no shame for the blind.

Or is there shame for the blind?

Translated by Mona Mikhail

QUESTIONS

1. What transformations does the household undergo after the mother remarries? How do the daughters respond after this marriage?
2. How is blindness central to the plot and theme of the story? What are the different ways the author uses blindness in conveying the physical and emotional life of the characters?
3. What is the significance of the continual reference to silence? How does the import of silence change during the course of the story?
4. Explain the significance of the title.

Franz Kafka

A HUNGER ARTIST

During these last decades the interest in professional fasting has markedly diminished. It used to pay very well to stage such great performances under one's own management, but today that is quite impossible. We live in a different world now. At one time the whole town took a lively interest in the hunger artist; from day to day of his fast the excitement mounted; everybody wanted to see him at least once a day; there were people who bought season tickets for the last few days and sat from morning till night in front of his small barred cage; even in the nighttime there were visiting hours, when the whole effect was heightened by torch flares; on fine days the cage was set out in the open air, and then it was the children's special treat to see the hunger artist; for their elders he was often just a joke that happened to be in fashion, but the children stood open-mouthed, holding each other's hands for greater security, marveling at him as he sat there pallid in black tights, with his ribs sticking out so prominently, not even on a seat but down among straw on the ground, sometimes giving a courteous nod, answering questions with a constrained smile, or perhaps stretching an arm through the bars so that one might feel how thin it was, and then again withdrawing deep into himself, paying no attention to anyone or anything, not even to the all-important striking of the clock that was the only piece of furniture in his cage, but merely staring into vacancy with half shut eyes, now and then taking a sip from a tiny glass of water to moisten his lips.

Besides casual onlookers there were also relays of permanent watchers selected by the public, usually butchers, strangely enough, and it was their task to watch the hunger artist day and night, three of them at a time, in case he should have some secret recourse to nourishment. This was nothing but a formality, instituted to reassure the masses, for the initiates knew well enough that during his fast the artist would never in any circumstances, not even under forcible compulsion, swallow the smallest morsel of food; the honor of his profession forbade it. Not every watcher, of course, was capable of understanding this, there were often groups of night watchers who were very lax in carrying out their duties and deliberately huddled together in a retired corner to play cards with great absorption, obviously intending to give the hunger artist the chance of a little refreshment, which they supposed he could draw from some private hoard. Nothing annoyed the artist more than such watchers; they made him miserable; they made his fast seem unendurable; sometimes he mastered his feebleness sufficiently to sing during their watch for as long as he could keep going, to show them how unjust their suspicions were. But that was of little use; they only wondered at his cleverness in being able to fill his mouth even while singing. Much more to his taste were the watchers who sat close up to the bars, who were not content with the dim night lighting of the hall but focused him in the full glare of the electric pocket torch given them by the impresario. The harsh light did not trouble him at all, in any case he could never sleep properly, and he could always drowse a little, whatever the light, at any hour, even when the hall was thronged with noisy onlookers. He was quite happy at the prospect of spending a sleepless night with such watchers; he was ready to exchange jokes with them, to tell them stories out of his nomadic life, anything at all to keep them awake and demonstrate to them again that he had no eatables in his cage and that he was fasting as not one of them could fast. But his happiest moment was when the morning came and an enormous breakfast was brought them, at his expense, on which they flung themselves with the keen appetite of healthy men after a weary night of wakefulness. Of course there were people who argued that this breakfast was an unfair attempt to bribe the watchers, but that was going rather too far, and when they were invited to take on a night's vigil without a breakfast, merely for the sake of the cause, they made themselves scarce, although they stuck stubbornly to their suspicions.

Such suspicions, anyhow, were a necessary accompaniment to the profession of fasting. No one could possibly watch the hunger artist continuously, day and night, and so no one could produce first-hand evidence that the fast had really been rigorous and continuous; only the artist himself could know that, he was therefore bound to be the sole completely satisfied spectator of his own fast. Yet for other reasons he was never satisfied; it was not perhaps mere fasting that had brought him to such skeleton thinness that many people had regretfully to keep away from his exhibitions, because the sight of him was too much for them, perhaps it was dissatisfaction with himself that had worn him down. For he alone knew, what no other initiate knew, how easy it was to fast. It was the easiest thing in the world. He made no secret of this, yet people did not believe him; at the best they set him down as modest, most of them, however, thought he was out for publicity or else was some kind of cheat who found it easy to fast because he had discovered a way of making it easy, and then had the impudence to admit the fact, more or less. He had to put up with all that, and in the course of time had got used to it, but his inner dissatisfaction always rankled, and never yet, after any term of fasting—this must be granted to his credit—had he left the cage of his own free will. The longest period of fasting was fixed by his impresario at forty days, beyond that term he was not allowed to go, not even in great cities, and there was good reason for it, too. Experience had proved that for about forty days the interest of the public could be stimulated by a steadily increasing pressure of advertisement, but after that the town began to lose interest, sympathetic support began notably to fall off; there were of course local variations as between one town and another or one country and another, but as a general rule forty days marked the limit. So on the fortieth day the flower-bedecked cage was opened, enthusiastic spectators filled the hall, a military band played, two doctors entered the cage to measure the results of the fast, which were announced through a megaphone, and finally two young ladies appeared, blissful at having been selected for the honor, to help the hunger artist down the few steps leading to a small table on which was spread a carefully chosen invalid repast. And at this very moment the artist always turned stubborn. True, he would entrust his bony arms to the outstretched helping hands of the ladies bending over him, but stand up he would not. Why stop fasting at this particular moment, after forty days of it? He had held out for a long time, an illimitably long time; why stop now, when he was in his best fasting form, or rather, not yet quite in his best fasting form? Why should he be cheated of the fame he would get for fasting longer, for being not only the record hunger artist of all time, which presumably he was already, but for beating his own record by a performance beyond human imagination, since he felt that there were no limits to his capacity for fasting? His public pretended to admire him so much, why should it have so little patience with him; if he could endure fasting longer, why shouldn't the public endure it? Besides, he was tired, he was comfortable sitting in the straw, and now he was supposed to lift himself to his full height and go down to a meal the very thought of which gave him a nausea that only the presence of the ladies kept him from betraying, and even that with an effort. And he looked up into the eyes of the ladies who were apparently so friendly and in reality so cruel, and shook his head, which felt too heavy on its strengthless neck. But then there happened yet again what always happened. The impresario came forward, without a word—for the band made speech impossible— lifted his arms in the air above the artist, as if inviting Heaven to look down upon its creature here in the straw, this suffering martyr, which indeed he was, although in quite another sense; grasped him round the emaciated waist, with exaggerated caution, so that the frail condition he was in might be appreciated; and committed him to the care of the blenching ladies, not without secretly giving him a shaking so that his legs and body tottered and swayed. The artist now submitted completely; his head lolled on his breast as if it had landed there by chance; his body was hollowed out; his legs in a spasm of self-preservation clung close to each other at the knees, yet scraped on the ground as if it were not really solid ground, as if they were only trying to find solid ground; and the whole weight of his body, a feather-weight after all, relapsed onto one of the ladies, who, looking round for help and panting a little—this post of honor was not at all what she had expected it to be—first stretched her neck as far as she could to keep her face at least free from contact with the artist, when finding this impossible, and her more fortunate companion not coming to her aid but merely holding extended on her own

trembling hand the little bunch of knucklebones that was the artist's, to the great delight of the spectators burst into tears and had to be replaced by an attendant who had long been stationed in readiness. Then came the food, a little of which the impresario managed to get between the artist's lips, while he sat in a kind of half-fainting trance, to the accompaniment of cheerful patter designed to distract the public's attention from the artist's condition; after that, a toast was drunk to the public, supposedly prompted by a whisper from the artist in the impresario's ear; the band confirmed it with a mighty flourish, the spectators melted away, and no one had any cause to be dissatisfied with the proceedings, no one except the hunger artist himself, he only, as always.

So he lived for many years, with small regular intervals of recuperation, in visible glory, honored by the world, yet in spite of that troubled in spirit, and all the more troubled because no one would take his trouble seriously. What comfort could he possibly need? What more could he possibly wish for? And if some good-natured person, feeling sorry for him, tried to console him by pointing out that his melancholy was probably caused by fasting, it could happen, especially when he had been fasting for some time, that he reacted with an outburst of fury and to the general alarm began to shake the bars of his cage like a wild animal. Yet the impresario had a way of punishing these outbreaks which he rather enjoyed putting into operation. He would apologize publicly for the artist's behavior, which was only to be excused, he admitted, because of the irritability caused by fasting; a condition hardly to be understood by well-fed people; then by natural transition he went on to mention the artist's equally incomprehensible boast that he could fast for much longer than he was doing; he praised the high ambition, the good will, the great self-denial undoubtedly implicit in such a statement; and then quite simply countered it by bringing out photographs, which were also on sale to the public, showing the artist on the fortieth day of a fast lying in bed almost dead from exhaustion. This perversion of the truth, familiar to the artist though it was, always unnerved him afresh and proved too much for him. What was a consequence of the premature ending of his fast was here presented as the cause of it! To fight against this lack of understanding, against a whole world of nonunderstanding, was impossible. Time and again in good faith he stood by the bars listening to the impresario, but as soon as the photographs appeared he always let go and sank with a groan back on to his straw, and the reassured public could once more come close and gaze at him.

A few years later when the witnesses of such scenes called them to mind, they often failed to understand themselves at all. For meanwhile the aforementioned change in public interest had set in; it seemed to happen almost overnight; there may have been profound causes for it, but who was going to bother about that; at any rate the pampered hunger artist suddenly found himself deserted one fine day by the amusement seekers, who went streaming past him to other more favored attractions. For the last time the impresario hurried him over half Europe to discover whether the old interest might still survive here and there; all in vain; everywhere, as if by secret agreement, a positive revulsion from professional fasting was in evidence. Of course it could not really have sprung up so suddenly as all that, and many premonitory symptoms which had not been sufficiently remarked or suppressed during the rush and glitter of success now came retrospectively to mind, but it was now too late to take any countermeasures. Fasting would surely come into fashion again at some future date, yet that was no comfort for those living in the present. What, then, was the hunger artist to do? He had been applauded by thousands in his time and could hardly come down to showing himself in a street booth at village fairs, and as for adopting another profession, he was not only too old for that but too fanatically devoted to fasting. So he took leave of the impresario, his partner in an unparalleled career, and hired himself to a large circus; in order to spare his own feelings he avoided reading the conditions of his contract.

A large circus with its enormous traffic in replacing and recruiting men, animals and apparatus can always find a use for people at any time, even for a hunger artist, provided of course that he does not ask too much, and in this particular case anyhow it was not only the artist who was taken on but his famous and long-known name as well, indeed considering the peculiar nature of his performance, which was not impaired by advancing age, it could not be objected that here was an artist past his prime, no longer at the height of his professional skill, seeking a refuge in some quiet corner of a circus; on the contrary, the hunger artist averred that he could fast as well as ever, which was entirely credible, he even alleged that if he were allowed to fast as he liked, and this was at once promised him without more ado, he could astound the world by establishing a record never yet achieved, a statement which certainly provoked a smile among the other professionals, since it left out of account the change in public opinion, which the hunger artist in his zeal conveniently forgot.

He had not, however, actually lost his sense of the real situation and took it as a matter of course that he and his cage should be stationed, not in the middle of the ring as a main attraction, but outside, near the animal cages, on a site that was after all easily accessible. Large and gaily painted placards made a frame for the cage and announced what was to be seen inside it. When the public came thronging out in the intervals to see the animals, they could hardly avoid passing the hunger artist's cage and stopping there for a moment, perhaps they might even have stayed longer had not those pressing behind them in the narrow gangway, who did not understand why they should be held up on their way toward the excitements of the menagerie, made it impossible for anyone to stand gazing quietly for any length of time. And that was the reason why the hunger artist, who had of course been looking forward to these visiting hours as the main achievement of his life, began instead to shrink from them. At first he could hardly wait for the intervals; it was exhilarating to watch the crowds come streaming his way, until only too soon—not even the most obstinate self-deception, clung to almost consciously, could hold out against the fact—the conviction was borne in upon him that these people, most of them, to judge from their actions, again and again, without exception, were all on their way to the menagerie. And the first sight of them from the distance remained the best. For when they reached his cage he was at once deafened by the storm of shouting and abuse that arose from the two contending factions, which renewed themselves continuously, of those who wanted to stop and stare at him—he soon began to dislike them more than the others—not out of real interest but only out of obstinate self-assertiveness, and those who wanted to go straight on to the animals. When the first great rush was past, the stragglers came along, and these, whom nothing could have prevented from stopping to look at him as long as they had breath, raced past with long strides, hardly even glancing at him, in their haste to get to the menagerie in time. And all too rarely did it happen that he had a stroke of luck, when some father of a family fetched up before him with his children, pointed a finger at the hunger artist and explained at length what the phenomenon meant, telling stories of earlier years when he himself had watched similar but much more thrilling performances, and the children, still rather uncomprehending, since neither inside nor outside school had they been sufficiently prepared for this lesson—what did they care about fasting?—yet showed by the brightness of their intent eyes that new and better times might be coming. Perhaps, said the hunger artist to himself many a time, things would be a little better if his cage were set not quite so near the menagerie. That made it too easy for people to make their choice, to say nothing of what he suffered from the stench of the menagerie, the animals' restlessness by night, the carrying past of raw lumps of flesh for the beasts of prey, the roaring at feeding times, which depressed him continually. But he did not dare to lodge a complaint with the management; after all, he had the animals to thank for the troops of people who passed his cage, among whom there might always be one here and there to take an interest in him, and who could tell where they might seclude him if he called attention to his existence and thereby to the fact that, strictly speaking, he was only an impediment on the way to the menagerie.

A small impediment, to be sure, one that grew steadily less. People grew familiar with the strange idea that they could be expected, in times like these, to take an interest in a hunger artist, and with this familiarity the verdict went out against him. He might fast as much as he could, and he did so; but nothing could save him now, people passed him by. Just try to explain to anyone the art of fasting! Anyone who has no feeling for it cannot be made to understand it. The fine placards grew dirty and illegible, they were torn down; the little notice board telling the number of fast days achieved, which at first was changed carefully every day, had long stayed at the same figure, for after the first few weeks even this small task seemed pointless to the staff; and so the artist simply fasted on and on, as he had once dreamed of doing, and it was no trouble to him, just as he had always foretold, but no one counted the days, no one, not even the artist himself, knew what records he was already breaking, and his heart grew heavy. And when once in a time some leisurely passer-by stopped, made merry over the old figure on the board and spoke of swindling, that was in its way the stupidest lie ever invented by indifference and inborn malice, since it was not the hunger artist who was cheating; he was working honestly, but the world was cheating him of his reward.

Many more days went by, however, and that too came to an end. An overseer's eye fell on the cage one day and he asked the attendants why this perfectly good cage should be left standing there unused with dirty straw inside it; nobody knew, until one man, helped out by the notice board, remembered about the hunger artist. They poked into the straw with sticks and found him in it. "Are you still fasting?" asked the overseer. "When on earth do you mean to stop?" "Forgive me, everybody," whispered the hunger artist; only the overseer, who had his ear to the bars, understood him. "Of course," said the overseer, and tapped his forehead with a finger to let the attendants know what state the man was in, "we forgive you." "I always wanted you to admire my fasting," said the hunger artist. "We do admire it," said the overseer, affably. "But you shouldn't admire it," said the hunger artist. "Well, then we don't admire it," said the overseer, "but why shouldn't we admire it?" "Because I have to fast, I can't help it," said the hunger artist. "What a fellow you are," said the overseer, "and why can't you help it?" "Because," said the hunger artist, lifting his head a little and speaking, with his lips pursed, as if for a kiss, right into the overseer's ear, so that no syllable might be lost, "because I couldn't find the food I liked. If I had found it, believe me, I should have made no fuss and stuffed myself like you or anyone else." These were his last words, but in his dimming eyes remained the firm though no longer proud persuasion that he was still continuing to fast.

"Well, clear this out now!" said the overseer, and they buried the hunger artist, straw and all. Into the cage they put a young panther. Even the most insensitive felt it refreshing to see this wild creature leaping around the cage that had so long been dreary. The panther was all right. The food he liked was brought him without hesitation by the attendants; he seemed not even to miss his freedom; his noble body, furnished almost to the bursting point with all that it needed, seemed to carry freedom around with it too; somewhere in his jaws it seemed to lurk; and the joy of life streamed with such ardent passion from his throat that for the onlookers it was not easy to stand the shock of it. But they braced themselves, crowded round the cage, and did not want ever to move away.

QUESTIONS

1. What figure or figures in real life could the Hunger Artist represent? What aspect of society might the impresario represent?
2. Why doesn't the public take the Hunger Artist seriously in spite of his suffering? Why does the public grow weary of the Hunger Artist and refuse to pay to observe him?
3. At the end of the story, the Hunger Artist claims he never ate "because I couldn't find the food I liked." What does he mean by this?
4. Compare and contrast the public's attitude toward the panther and the Hunger Artist.

Doris Lessing

FLIGHT

Above the old man's head was the dovecote, a tall wire-netted shelf on stilts, full of strutting, preening birds. The sunlight broke on their gray breasts into small rainbows. His ears were lulled by their crooning; his hands stretched up toward his favorite, a homing pigeon, a young plump-bodied bird, which stood still when it saw him and cocked a shrewd bright eye.

"Pretty, pretty, pretty," he said, as he grasped the bird and drew it down, feeling the cold coral claws tighten around his finger. Content, he rested the bird lightly on his chest and leaned against a tree, gazing out beyond the dovecote into the landscape of a late afternoon. In folds and hollows of sunlight and shade, the dark red soil, which was broken into great dusty clods, stretched wide to a tall horizon. Trees marked the course of the valley; a stream of rich green grass the road.

His eyes traveled homeward along this road until he saw his granddaughter swinging on the gate underneath a frangipani tree. Her hair fell down her back in a wave of sunlight; and her long bare legs repeated the angles of the frangipani stems, bare, shining brown stems among patterns of pale blossoms.

She was gazing past the pink flowers, past the railway cottage where they lived, along the road to the village.

His mood shifted. He deliberately held out his wrist for the bird to take flight, and caught it again at the moment it spread its wings. He felt the plump shape strive and strain under his fingers; and, in a sudden access of troubled spite, shut the bird into a small box and fastened the bolt. "Now you stay there," he muttered and turned his back on the shelf of birds. He moved warily along the hedge, stalking his granddaughter, who was now looped over the gate, her head loose on her arms, singing. The light happy sound mingled with the crooning of the birds, and his anger mounted.

"Hey!" he shouted, and saw her jump, look back, and abandon the gate. Her eyes veiled themselves, and she said in a pert, neutral voice, "Hullo, Grandad." Politely she moved toward him, after a lingering backward glance at the road.

"Waiting for Steven, hey?" he said, his fingers curling like claws into his palm.

"Any objection?" she asked lightly, refusing to look at him.

He confronted her, his eyes narrowed, shoulders hunched, tight in a hard knot of pain that included the preening birds, the sunlight, the flowers, herself. He said, "Think you're old enough to go courting, hey?"

The girl tossed her head at the old-fashioned phrase and sulked, "Oh, Grandad!"

"Think you want to leave home, hey? Think you can go running around the fields at night?"

Her smile made him see her, as he had every evening of this warm end-of-summer month, swinging hand in hand along the road to the village with that red-handed, red-throated, violent-bodied youth, the son of the postmaster. Misery went to his head and he shouted angrily: "I'll tell your mother!"

"Tell away!" she said, laughing, and went back to the gate.

He heard her singing, for him to hear:

"I've got you under my skin,
I've got you deep in the heart of . . ."

"Rubbish," he shouted. "Rubbish. Impudent little bit of rubbish!"

Growling under his breath, he turned toward the dovecote, which was his refuge from the house he shared with his daughter and her husband and their children. But now the house would be empty. Gone all the young girls with their laughter and their squabbling and their teasing. He would be left, uncherished and alone, with that square-fronted, calm-eyed woman, his daughter.

He stopped, muttering, before the dovecote, resenting the absorbed, cooing birds. From the gate the girl shouted: "Go and tell! Go on, what are you waiting for?"

Obstinately he made his way to the house, with quick, pathetic, persistent glances of appeal back at her. But she never looked around. Her defiant but anxious young body stung him into love and repentance. He stopped. "But I never meant. . . ." he muttered, waiting for her to turn and run to him. "I didn't mean. . . ."

She did not turn. She had forgotten him. Along the road came the young man Steven, with something in his hand. A present for her? The old man stiffened as he watched the gate swing back and the couple embrace. In the brittle shadows of the frangipani tree his granddaughter, his darling, lay in the arms of the postmaster's son, and her hair flowed back over his shoulder.

"I see you!" shouted the old man spitefully. They did not move. He stumped into the little whitewashed house, hearing the wooden veranda creak angrily under his feet. His daughter was sewing in the front room, threading a needle held to the light.

He stopped again, looking back into the garden. The couple were now sauntering among the bushes, laughing. As he watched he saw the girl escape from the youth with a sudden mischievous movement and run off through the flowers with him in pursuit. He heard shouts, laughter, a scream, silence.

"But it's not like that at all," he muttered miserably. "It's not like that. Why can't you see? Running and giggling, and kissing and kissing. You'll come to something quite different."

He looked at his daughter with sardonic hatred, hating himself. They were caught and finished, both of them, but the girl was still running free.

"Can't you *see*?" he demanded of his invisible granddaughter, who was at that moment lying in the thick green grass with the postmaster's son.

His daughter looked at him and her eyebrows went up in tired forbearance.

"Put your birds to bed?" she asked, humoring him.

"Lucy," he said urgently. "Lucy. . . ."

"Well, what is it now?"

"She's in the garden with Steven."

"Now you just sit down and have your tea."

He stumped his feet alternately, thump, thump, on the hollow wooden floor and shouted: "She'll marry him. I'm telling you, she'll be marrying him next!"

His daughter rose swiftly, brought him a cup, set him a plate.

"I don't want any tea. I don't want it, I tell you."

"Now, now," she crooned. "What's wrong with it? Why not?"

"She's eighteen. Eighteen!"

"I was married at seventeen, and I never regretted it."

"Liar," he said. "Liar. Then you should regret it. Why do you make your girls marry? It's you who do it. What do you do it for? Why?"

"The other three have done fine. They've three fine husbands. Why not Alice?"

"She's the last," he mourned. "Can't we keep her a bit longer?"

"Come, now, Dad. She'll be down the road, that's all. She'll be here every day to see you."

"But it's not the same." He thought of the other three girls, transformed inside a few months from charming, petulant, spoiled children into serious young matrons.

"You never did like it when we married," she said. "Why not? Every time, it's the same. When I got married you made me feel like it was something wrong. And my girls the same. You get them all crying and miserable the way you go on. Leave Alice alone. She's happy." She sighed, letting her eyes linger on the sunlit garden. "She'll marry next month. There's no reason to wait."

"You've said they can marry?" he said incredulously.

"Yes, Dad. Why not?" she said coldly and took up her sewing.

His eyes stung, and he went out on to the veranda. Wet spread down over his chin, and he took out a handkerchief and mopped his whole face. The garden was empty.

From around the corner came the young couple; but their faces were no longer set against him. On the wrist of the postmaster's son balanced a young pigeon, the light gleaming on its breast.

"For me?" said the old man, letting the drops shake off his chin. "For me?"

"Do you like it?" The girl grabbed his hand and swung on it. "It's for you, Grandad. Steven brought it for you." They hung about him, affectionate, concerned, trying to charm away his wet eyes and his misery. They took his arms and directed him to the shelf of birds, one on each side, enclosing him, petting him, saying wordlessly that nothing would be changed, nothing could change, and that they would be with him always. The bird was proof of it, they said, from their lying happy eyes, as they thrust it on him. "There, Grandad, it's yours. It's for you."

They watched him as he held it on his wrist, stroking its soft, sun-warmed back, watching the wings lift and balance.

"You must shut it up for a bit," said the girl intimately, "until it knows this is its home."

"Teach your grandmother to suck eggs," growled the old man.

Released by his half-deliberate anger, they fell back, laughing at him. "We're glad you like it." They moved off, now serious and full of purpose, to the gate, where they hung, backs to him, talking quietly. More than anything could, their grown-up serious-ness shut him out, making him alone; also, it quietened him, took the sting out of their tumbling like puppies on the grass. They had forgotten him again. Well, so they should, the old man reassured himself, feeling his throat clotted with tears, his lips trembling. He held the new bird to his face, for the caress of its silken feathers. Then he shut it in a box and took out his favorite.

"*Now* you can go," he said aloud. He held it poised, ready for flight, while he looked down the garden toward the boy and the girl. Then, clenched in the pain of loss, he lifted the bird on his wrist and watched it soar. A whirr and a spatter of wings, and a cloud of birds rose into the evening from the dovecote.

At the gate Alice and Steven forgot their talk and watched the birds.

On the veranda, that woman, his daughter, stood gazing, her eyes shaded with a hand that still held her sewing.

It seemed to the old man that the whole afternoon had stilled to watch his gesture of self-command, that even the leaves of the trees had stopped shaking.

Dry-eyed and calm, he let his hands fall to his sides and stood erect, staring up into the sky.

The cloud of shining silver birds flew up and up, with a shrill cleaving of wings, over the dark ploughed land and the darker belts of trees and the bright folds of grass, until they floated high in the sunlight, like a cloud of motes of dust.

They wheeled in a wide circle, tilting their wings so there was flash after flash of light, and one after another they dropped from the sunshine of the upper sky to shadow, one after another, returning to the shadowed earth over trees and grass and field, returning to the valley and the shelter of night.

The garden was all a fluster and a flurry of returning birds. Then silence, and the sky was empty.

The old man turned, slowly, taking his time; he lifted his eyes to smile proudly down the garden at his granddaughter. She was staring at him. She did not smile. She was wide-eyed and pale in the cold shadow, and he saw the tears run shivering off her face.

QUESTIONS

1. How does the relationship between the grandfather, his daughter, and his granddaughter define the many conflicts in this story?
2. Why does Lessing devote so much attention to a description of the setting—and especially to the birds? What do the birds symbolize?
3. What is the connection between the first episode involving the old man and his birds and the last one?

Bobbie Ann Mason

BIG BERTHA STORIES

Donald is home again, laughing and singing. He comes home from Central City, near the strip mines, only when he feels like it, like an absentee landlord checking on his property. He is always in such a good humor when he returns that Jeannette forgives him. She cooks for him—ugly, pasty things she gets with food stamps. Sometimes he brings steaks and ice cream, occasionally money. Rodney, their child, hides in the closet when he arrives, and Donald goes around the house talking loudly about the little boy named Rodney who used to live there—the one who fell into a septic tank, or the one stolen by gypsies. The stories change. Rodney usually stays in the closet until he has to pee, and then he hugs his father's knees, forgiving him, just as Jeannette does. The way Donald saunters through the door, swinging a six-pack of beer, with a big grin on his face, takes her breath away. He leans against the door facing, looking sexy in his baseball cap and his shaggy red beard and his sunglasses. He wears sunglasses to be like the Blues Brothers, but he in no way resembles either of the Blues Brothers. I should have my head examined, Jeannette thinks.

The last time Donald was home, they went to the shopping center to buy Rodney some shoes advertised on sale. They stayed at the shopping center half the afternoon, just looking around. Donald and Rodney played video games. Jeannette felt they were a normal family. Then, in the parking lot, they stopped to watch a man on a platform demonstrating snakes. Children were petting a twelve-foot python coiled around the man's shoulders. Jeannette felt faint.

"Snakes won't hurt you unless you hurt them," said Donald as Rodney stroked the snake.

"It feels like chocolate," he said.

The snake man took a tarantula from a plastic box and held it lovingly in his palm. He said, "If you drop a tarantula, it will shatter like a Christmas ornament."

"I hate this," said Jeannette.

"Let's get out of here," said Donald.

Jeannette felt her family disintegrating like a spider shattering as Donald hurried them away from the shopping center. Rodney squalled and Donald dragged him along. Jeannette wanted to stop for ice cream. She wanted them all to sit quietly together in a booth, but Donald rushed them to the car, and he drove them home in silence, his face growing grim.

"Did you have bad dreams about the snakes?" Jeannette asked Rodney the next morning at breakfast. They were eating pancakes made with generic pancake mix. Rodney slapped his fork in the pond of syrup on his pancakes. "The black racer is the farmer's friend," he said soberly, repeating a fact learned from the snake man.

"Big Bertha kept black racers," said Donald. "She trained them for the 500." Donald doesn't tell Rodney ordinary children's stories. He tells him a series of strange stories he makes up about Big Bertha. Big Bertha is what he calls the huge strip-mining machine in Muhlenberg County, but he has Rodney believing that Big Bertha is a female version of Paul Bunyan.

"Snakes don't run in the 500," said Rodney.

"This wasn't the Indy 500 or the Daytona 500—none of your well-known 500s," said Donald. "This was the Possum Trot 500, and it was a long time ago. Big Bertha started the original 500, with snakes. Black racers and blue racers mainly. Also some red-and-white-striped racers, but those are rare."

"We always ran for the hoe if we saw a black racer," Jeannette said, remembering her childhood in the country.

In a way, Donald's absences are a fine arrangement, even considerate. He is sparing them his darkest moods, when he can't cope with his memories of Vietnam. Vietnam had never seemed such a meaningful fact until a couple of years ago, when he grew depressed and moody, and then he started going away to Central City. He frightened Jeannette, and she always said the wrong thing in her efforts to soothe him. If the welfare people find out he is spending occasional weekends at home, and even bringing some money, they will cut off her assistance. She applied for welfare because she can't depend on him to send money, but she knows he blames her for losing faith in him. He isn't really working regularly at the strip mines. He is mostly just hanging around there, watching the land being scraped away, trees coming down, bushes flung in the air.

Sometimes he operates a steam shovel, and when he comes home his clothes are filled with the clay and it is caked on his shoes. The clay is the color of butterscotch pudding.

At first, he tried to explain to Jeannette. He said, "If we could have had tanks over there as big as Big Bertha, we wouldn't have lost the war. Strip mining is just like what we were doing over there. We were stripping off the top. The topsoil is like the culture and the people, the best part of the land and the country. America was just stripping off the top, the best. We ruined it. Here, at least the coal companies have to plant vetch and loblolly pines and all kinds of trees and bushes. If we'd done that in Vietnam, maybe we'd have left that country in better shape."

"Wasn't Vietnam a long time ago?" Jeannette asked.

She didn't want to hear about Vietnam. She thought it was unhealthy to dwell on it so much. He should live in the present. Her mother is afraid Donald will do something violent, because she once read in the newspaper that a veteran in Louisville held his little girl hostage in their apartment until he had a shootout with the police and was killed. But Jeannette can't imagine Donald doing anything so extreme. When she first met him, several years ago, at her parents' pit-barbecue luncheonette, where she was working then, he had a good job at a lumberyard and he dressed nicely. He took her out to eat at a fancy restaurant. They got plastered and ended up in a motel in Tupelo, Mississippi, on Elvis Presley Boulevard. Back then, he talked nostalgically about his year in Vietnam, about how beautiful it was, how different the people were. He could never seem to explain what he meant. "They're just different," he said.

They went riding around in a yellow 1957 Chevy convertible. He drives too fast now, but he didn't then, maybe because he was so protective of the car. It was a classic. He sold it three years ago and made a good profit. About the time he sold the Chevy, his moods began changing, his even-tempered nature shifting, like driving on a smooth interstate and then switching to a secondary road. He had headaches and bad dreams. But his nightmares seemed trivial. He dreamed of riding a train through the Rocky Mountains, of hijacking a plane to Cuba, of stringing up barbed wire around the house. He dreamed he lost a doll. He got drunk and rammed the car, the Chevy's successor, into a Civil War statue in front of the courthouse. When he got depressed over the meaninglessness of his job, Jeannette felt guilty about spending money on something nice for the house, and she tried to make him feel his job had meaning by reminding him that, after all, they had a child to think of. "I don't like his name," Donald said once. "What a stupid name. Rodney. I never did like it."

Rodney has dreams about Big Bertha, echoes of his father's nightmare, like TV cartoon versions of Donald's memories of the war. But Rodney loves the stories, even though they are confusing, with lots of loose ends. The latest in the Big Bertha series is "Big Bertha and the Neutron Bomb." Last week it was "Big Bertha and the MX Missile." In the new story, Big Bertha takes a trip to California to go surfing with Big Mo, her male counterpart. On the beach, corn dogs and snow cones are free and the surfboards turn into dolphins. Everyone is having fun until the neutron bomb comes. Rodney loves the part where everyone keels over dead. Donald acts it out, collapsing on the rug. All the dolphins and the surfers keel over, everyone except Big Bertha. Big Bertha is so big she is immune to the neutron bomb.

"Those stories aren't true," Jeannette tells Rodney.

Rodney staggers and falls down on the rug, his arms and legs akimbo. He gets the giggles and can't stop. When his spasms finally subside, he says, "I told Scottie Bidwell about Big Bertha and he didn't believe me."

Donald picks Rodney up under the armpits and sets him upright. "You tell Scottie Bidwell if he saw Big Bertha he would pee in his pants on the spot, he would be so impressed."

"Are you scared of Big Bertha?"

"No, I'm not. Big Bertha is just like a wonderful woman, a big fat woman who can sing the blues. Have you ever heard Big Mama Thornton?"

"No."

"Well, Big Bertha's like her, only she's the size of a tall building. She's slow as a turtle and when she crosses the road they have to reroute traffic. She's big enough to straddle a four-lane highway. She's so tall she can see all the way to Tennessee, and when she belches, there's a tornado. She's really something. She can even fly."

"She's too big to fly," Rodney says doubtfully. He makes a face like a wadded-up washrag and Donald wrestles him to the floor again.

Donald has been drinking all evening, but he isn't drunk. The ice cubes melt and he pours the drink out and refills it. He keeps on talking. Jeannette cannot remember him talking so much about the war. He is telling her about an ammunitions dump. Jeannette had the vague idea that an ammo dump is a mound of shotgun shells, heaps of cartridge casings and bomb shells, or whatever is left over, a vast waste pile from the war, but Donald says that is wrong. He has spent an hour describing it in detail, so that she will understand.

He refills the glass with ice, some 7-Up, and a shot of Jim Beam. He slams doors and drawers, looking for a compass. Jeannette can't keep track of the conversation. It doesn't matter that her hair is uncombed and her lipstick eaten away. He isn't seeing her.

"I want to draw the compound for you," he says, sitting down at the table with a sheet of Rodney's tablet paper.

Donald draws the map in red and blue ballpoint, with asterisks and technical labels that mean nothing to her. He draws some circles with the compass and measures some angles. He makes a red dot on an oblique line, a patch that leads to the ammo dump.

"That's where I was. Right there," he says. "There was a water buffalo that tripped a land mine and its horn just flew off and stuck in the wall of the barracks like a machete thrown backhanded." He puts a dot where the land mine was, and he doodles awhile with the red ballpoint pen, scribbling something on the edge of the map that looks like feathers. "The dump was here and I was there and over there was where we piled the sandbags. And here were the tanks." He draws tanks, a row of squares with handles—guns sticking out.

"Why are you going to so much trouble to tell me about a buffalo horn that got stuck in a wall?" she wants to know.

But Donald just looks at her as though she has asked something obvious.

"Maybe I *could* understand if you'd let me," she says cautiously.

"You could never understand." He draws another tank.

In bed, it is the same as it has been since he started going away to Central City—the way he claims his side of the bed, turning away from her. Tonight, she reaches for him and he lets her be close to him. She cries for a while and he lies there, waiting for her to finish, as though she were merely putting on makeup.

"Do you want me to tell you a Big Bertha story?" he asks playfully.

"You act like you're in love with Big Bertha."

He laughs, breathing on her. But he won't come closer.

"You don't care what I look like anymore," she says. "What am I supposed to think?"

"There's nobody else. There's not anybody but you."

Loving a giant machine is incomprehensible to Jeannette. There must be another woman, someone that large in his mind. Jeannette has seen the strip-mining machine. The top of the crane is visible beyond a rise along the parkway. The strip mining is kept just out of sight of travelers because it would give them a poor image of Kentucky.

For three weeks, Jeannette has been seeing a psychologist at the free mental health clinic. He's a small man from out of state. His name is Dr. Robinson, but she calls him The Rapist, because the word *therapist* can be divided into two words, *the rapist*. He doesn't think her joke is clever, and he acts as though he has heard it a thousand times before. He has a habit of saying, "Go with that feeling," the same way Bob Newhart did on his old TV show. It's probably the first lesson in the textbook, Jeannette thinks.

She told him about Donald's last days on his job at the lumberyard—how he let the stack of lumber fall deliberately and didn't know why, and about how he went away soon after that, and how the Big Bertha stories started. Dr. Robinson seems to be waiting for her to make something out of it all, but it's maddening that he won't tell her what to do. After three visits, Jeannette has grown angry with him, and now she's holding back things. She won't tell him whether Donald slept with her or not when he came home last. Let him guess, she thinks.

"Talk about yourself," he says.

"What about me?"

"You speak so vaguely about Donald that I get the feeling that you see him as somebody larger than life. I can't quite picture him. That makes me wonder what that says about you." He touches the end of his tie to his nose and sniffs it.

When Jeannette suggests that she bring Donald in, the therapist looks bored and says nothing.

"He had another nightmare when he was home last," Jeannette says. "He dreamed he was crawling through tall grass and people were after him."

"How do *you* feel about that?" The Rapist asks eagerly.

"I didn't have the nightmare," she says coldly. "Donald did. I came to you to get advice about Donald, and you're acting like I'm the one who's crazy. I'm not crazy. But I'm lonely."

Jeannette's mother, behind the counter of the luncheonette, looks lovingly at Rodney pushing buttons on the jukebox in the corner. "It's a shame about that youngun," she says tearfully. "That boy needs a daddy."

"What are you trying to tell me? That I should file for divorce and get Rodney a new daddy?"

Her mother looks hurt. "No, honey," she says. "You need to get Donald to seek the Lord. And you need to pray more. You haven't been going to church lately."

"Have some barbecue," Jeannette's father booms, as he comes in from the back kitchen. "And I want you to take a pound home with you. You've got a growing boy to feed."

"I want to take Rodney to church," Mama says. "I want to show him off, and it might do some good."

"People will think he's an orphan," Dad says.

"I don't care," Mama says. "I just love him to pieces and I want to take him to church. Do you care if I take him to church, Jeannette?"

"No. I don't care if you take him to church." She takes the pound of barbecue from her father. Grease splotches the brown wrapping paper. Dad has given them so much barbecue that Rodney is burned out on it and won't eat it anymore.

Jeannette wonders if she would file for divorce if she could get a job. It is a thought—for the child's sake, she thinks. But there aren't many jobs around. With the cost of a baby-sitter, it doesn't pay her to work. When Donald first went away, her mother kept Rodney and she had a good job, waitressing at a steak house, but the steak house burned down one night—a grease fire in the kitchen. After that, she couldn't find a steady job, and she was reluctant to ask her mother to keep Rodney again because of her bad hip. At the steak house, men gave her tips and left their telephone numbers on the bill when they paid. They tucked dollar bills and notes in the pockets of her apron. One note said, "I want to hold your muffins." They were real-estate developers and businessmen on important missions for the Tennessee Valley Authority. They were boisterous and they drank too much. They said they'd take her for a cruise on the *Delta Queen,* but she didn't believe them. She knew how expensive that was. They talked about their speedboats and invited her for rides on Lake Barkley, or for spins in their private planes. They always used the word *spin.* The idea made her dizzy. Once, Jeannette let an electronics salesman take her for a ride in his Cadillac, and they breezed down the wilderness road through the Land Between the Lakes. His car had automatic windows and a stereo system and lighted computer-screen numbers on the dash that told him how many miles to the gallon he was getting and other statistics. He said the numbers distracted him and he had almost had several wrecks. At the restaurant, he had been flamboyant, admired by his companions. Alone with Jeannette in the Cadillac, on The Trace, he was shy and awkward, and really not very interesting. The most interesting thing about him, Jeannette thought, was all the lighted numbers on his dashboard. The Cadillac had everything but video games. But she'd rather be riding around with Donald, no matter where they ended up.

While the social worker is there, filling out her report, Jeannette listens for Donald's car. When the social worker drove up, the flutter and wheeze of her car sounded like Donald's old Chevy, and for a moment Jeannette's mind lapsed back in time. Now she listens, hoping he won't drive up. The social worker is younger than Jeannette and has been to college. Her name is Miss Bailey, and she's excessively cheerful, as though in her line of work she has seen hardships that make Jeannette's troubles seem like a trip to Hawaii.

"Is your little boy still having those bad dreams?" Miss Bailey asks, looking up from her clipboard.

Jeannette nods and looks at Rodney, who has his finger in his mouth and won't speak.

"Has the cat got your tongue?" Miss Bailey asks.

"Show her your pictures, Rodney." Jeannette explains, "He won't talk about the dreams, but he draws pictures of them."

Rodney brings his tablet of pictures and flips through them silently. Miss Bailey says, "Hmm." They are stark line drawings, remarkably steady lines for his age. "What is this one?" she asks. "Let me guess. Two scoops of ice cream?"

The picture is two huge circles, filling the page, with three tiny stick people in the corner.

"These are Big Bertha's titties," says Rodney.

Miss Bailey chuckles and winks at Jeannette. "What do you like to read, hon?" she asks Rodney.

"Nothing."

"He can read," says Jeannette. "He's smart."

"Do you like to read?" Miss Bailey asks Jeannette. She glances at the pile of paperbacks on the coffee table. She is probably going to ask where Jeannette got the money for them.

"I don't read," says Jeannette. "If I read, I just go crazy."

When she told The Rapist she couldn't concentrate on anything serious, he said she read romance novels in order to escape from reality. "Reality, hell!" she had said. "Reality's my whole problem."

"It's too bad Rodney's not here," Donald is saying. Rodney is in the closet again. "Santa Claus has to take back all these toys. Rodney would love this bicycle! And this Pac-Man game. Santa has to take back so many things he'll have to have a pickup truck!"

"You didn't bring him anything. You never bring him anything," says Jeannette.

He has brought doughnuts and dirty laundry. The clothes he is wearing are caked with clay. His beard is lighter from working out in the sun, and he looks his usual joyful self, the way he always is before his moods take over, like migraine headaches, which some people describe as storms.

Donald coaxes Rodney out of the closet with the doughnuts.

"Were you a good boy this week?"

"I don't know."

"I hear you went to the shopping center and showed out." It is not true that Rodney made a big scene. Jeannette has already explained that Rodney was upset because she wouldn't buy him an Atari. But she didn't blame him for crying. She was tired of being unable to buy him anything.

Rodney eats two doughnuts and Donald tells him a long, confusing story about Big Bertha and a rock-and-roll band. Rodney interrupts him with dozens of questions. In

the story, the rock-and-roll band gives a concert in a place that turns out to be a toxic-waste dump and the contamination is spread all over the country. Big Bertha's solution to this problem is not at all clear. Jeannette stays in the kitchen, trying to think of something original to do with instant potatoes and leftover barbecue.

"We can't go on like this," she says that evening in bed. "We're just hurting each other. Something has to change."

He grins like a kid. "Coming home from Muhlenberg County is like R and R—rest and recreation. I explain that in case you think R and R means rock and roll. Or maybe rumps and rears. Or rust and rot." He laughs and draws a circle in the air with his cigarette.

"I'm not that dumb."

"When I leave, I go back to the mines." He sighs, as though the mines were some eternal burden.

Her mind skips ahead to the future: Donald locked away somewhere, coloring in a coloring book and making clay pots, her and Rodney in some other town, with another man—someone dull and not at all sexy. Summoning up her courage, she says, "I haven't been through what you've been through and maybe I don't have a right to say this, but sometimes I think you act superior because you went to Vietnam, like nobody can ever know what you know. Well, maybe not. But you've still got your legs, even if you don't know what to do with what's between them anymore." Bursting into tears of apology, she can't help adding, "You can't go on telling Rodney those awful stories. He has nightmares when you're gone."

Donald rises from bed and grabs Rodney's picture from the dresser, holding it as he might have held a hand grenade. "Kids betray you," he says, turning the picture in his hand.

"If you cared about him, you'd stay here." As he sets the picture down, she asks, "What can I do? How can I understand what's going on in your mind? Why do you go there? Strip mining's bad for the ecology and you don't have any business strip mining."

"My job is serious, Jeannette. I run that steam shovel and put the topsoil back on. I'm reclaiming the land." He keeps talking, in a gentler voice, about strip mining, the same old things she has heard before, comparing Big Bertha to a supertank. If only they had had Big Bertha in Vietnam. He says, "When they strip off the top, I keep looking for those tunnels where the Viet Cong hid. They had so many tunnels it was unbelievable. Imagine Mammoth Cave going all the way across Kentucky."

"Mammoth Cave's one of the natural wonders of the world," says Jeannette brightly. She is saying the wrong thing again.

At the kitchen table at 2 A.M., he's telling about C-5A's. A C-5A is so big it can carry troops and tanks and helicopters, but it's not big enough to hold Big Bertha. Nothing could hold Big Bertha. He rambles on, and when Jeannette shows him Rodney's drawings of the circles, Donald smiles. Dreamily, he begins talking about women's breasts and thighs—the large, round thighs and big round breasts of American women, contrasted with the frail, delicate beauty of the Orientals. It is like comparing oven broilers and banties, he says. Jeannette relaxes. A confession about another lover from long ago is not so hard to take. He seems stuck on the breasts and thighs of American women—insisting that she understand how small and delicate the Orientals are, but then he abruptly returns to tanks and helicopters.

"A Bell Huey Cobra—my God, what a beautiful machine. So efficient!" Donald takes the food processor blade from the drawer where Jeannette keeps it. He says, "A rotor blade from a chopper could just slice anything to bits."

"Don't do that," Jeannette says.

He is trying to spin the blade on the counter, like a top. "Here's what would happen when a chopper blade hits a power line—not many of those over there!—or a tree. Not many trees, either, come to think of it, after all the Agent Orange." He drops the blade and it glances off the open drawer and falls to the floor, spiking the vinyl.

At first, Jeannette thinks the screams are hers, but they are his. She watches him cry. She has never seen anyone cry so hard, like an intense summer thundershower. All she knows to do is shove Kleenex at him. Finally, he is able to say, "You thought I was going to hurt you. That's why I'm crying."

"Go ahead and cry," Jeannette says, holding him close.

"Don't go away."

"I'm right here. I'm not going anywhere."

In the night, she still listens, knowing his monologue is being burned like a tattoo into her brain. She will never forget it. His voice grows soft and he plays with a ballpoint pen, jabbing holes in a paper towel. Bullet holes, she thinks. His beard is like a bird's nest, woven with dark corn silks.

"This is just a story," he says. "Don't mean nothing. Just relax." She is sitting on the hard edge of the kitchen chair, her toes cold on the floor, waiting. His tears have dried up and left a slight catch in his voice.

"We were in a big camp near a village. It was pretty routine and kind of soft there for a while. Now and then we'd go into Da Nang and whoop it up. We had been in the jungle for several months, so the two months at this village was a sort of rest—an R and R almost. Don't shiver. This is just a little story. Don't mean nothing! This is nothing, compared to what I could tell you. Just listen. We lost our fear. At night there would be some incoming and we'd see these tracers in the sky, like shooting stars up close, but it was all pretty minor and we didn't take it seriously, after what we'd been through. In the village I knew this Vietnamese family—a woman and her two daughters. They sold Cokes and beer to GIs. The oldest daughter was named Phan. She could speak a little English. She was really smart. I used to go see them in their hooch in the afternoons—in the siesta time of day. It was so hot there. Phan was beautiful, like the country. The village was ratty, but the country was pretty. And she was beautiful, just like she had grown up out of the jungle, like one of those flowers that bloomed high up in the trees and freaked us out sometimes, thinking it was a sniper. She was so gentle, with these eyes shaped like peach pits, and she was no bigger than a child of maybe thirteen or fourteen. I felt funny about her size at first, but later it didn't matter. It was just some wonderful feature about her, like a woman's hair, or her breasts."

He stops and listens, the way they used to listen for crying sounds when Rodney was a baby. He says, "She'd take those big banana leaves and fan me while I lay there in the heat."

"I didn't know they had bananas over there."

"There's a lot you don't know! Listen! Phan was twenty-three, and her brothers were off fighting. I never even asked which side they were fighting on." He laughs. "She got a kick out of the word *fan*. I told her that *fan* was the same word as her name. She thought I meant her name was banana. In Vietnamese the same word can have a dozen different meanings, depending on your tone of voice. I bet you didn't know that, did you?"

"No. What happened to her?"

"I don't know."

"Is that the end of the story?"

"I don't know." Donald pauses, then goes on talking about the village, the girl, the banana leaves, talking in a monotone that is making Jeannette's flesh crawl. He could be the news radio from the next room.

"You must have really liked that place. Do you wish you could go back there to find out what happened to her?"

"It's not there anymore," he says. "It blew up."

Donald abruptly goes to the bathroom. She hears the water running, the pipes in the basement shaking.

"It was so pretty," he says when he returns. He rubs his elbow absentmindedly. "That jungle was the most beautiful place in the world. You'd have thought you were in paradise. But we blew it sky-high."

In her arms, he is shaking, like the pipes in the basement, which are still vibrating. Then the pipes let go, after a long shudder, but he continues to tremble.

They are driving to the Veterans Hospital. It was Donald's idea. She didn't have to persuade him. When she made up the bed that morning—with a finality that shocked her, as though she knew they wouldn't be in it again together—he told her it would be like R and R. Rest was what he needed. Neither of them had slept at all during the night. Jeannette felt she had to stay awake, to listen for more.

"Talk about strip mining," she says now. "That's what they'll do to your head. They'll dig out all those ugly memories, I hope. We don't need them around here." She pats his knee.

It is a cloudless day, not the setting for this sober journey. She drives and Donald goes along obediently, with the resignation of an old man being taken to a rest home. They are driving through southern Illinois, known as Little Egypt, for some obscure reason Jeannette has never understood. Donald still talks, but very quietly, without urgency. When he points out the scenery, Jeannette thinks of the early days of their marriage, when they would take a drive like this and laugh hysterically. Now Jeannette points out funny things they see. The Little Egypt Hot Dog World, Pharaoh Cleaners, Pyramid Body Shop. She is scarcely aware that she is driving, and when she sees a sign, LITTLE EGYPT STARLITE CLUB, she is confused for a moment, wondering where she has been transported.

As they part, he asks, "What will you tell Rodney if I don't come back? What if they keep me here indefinitely?"

"You're coming back. I'm telling him you're coming back soon."

"Tell him I went off with Big Bertha. Tell him she's taking me on a sea cruise, to the South Seas."

"No. You can tell him that yourself."

He starts singing "Sea Cruise." He grins at her and pokes her in the ribs.

"You're coming back," she says.

Donald writes from the VA Hospital, saying that he is making progress. They are running tests, and he meets in a therapy group in which all the veterans trade memories. Jeannette is no longer on welfare because she now has a job waitressing at Fred's Family Restaurant. She waits on families, waits for Donald to come home so they can come here and eat together like a family. The fathers look at her with downcast eyes, and the children throw food. While Donald is gone, she rearranges the furniture. She reads some books from the library. She does a lot of thinking. It occurs to her that even though she loved him, she has thought of Donald primarily as a husband, a provider, someone whose name she shared, the father of her child, someone like the fathers who come to the Wednesday night all-you-can-eat fish fry. She hasn't thought of him as himself. She wasn't brought up that way, to examine someone's soul. When it comes to something deep inside, nobody will take it out and examine it, the way they will look at clothing in a store for flaws in the manufacturing. She tries to explain all this to The Rapist, and he says she's looking better, got sparkle in her eyes. "Big deal," says Jeannette. "Is that all you can say?"

She takes Rodney to the shopping center, their favorite thing to do together, even though Rodney always begs to buy something. They go to Penney's perfume counter. There, she usually hits a sample bottle of cologne—Chantilly or Charlie or something strong. Today she hits two or three and comes out of Penney's smelling like a flower garden.

"You stink!" Rodney cries, wrinkling his nose like a rabbit.

"Big Bertha smells like this, only a thousand times worse, she's so big," says Jeannette impulsively. "Didn't Daddy tell you that?"

"Daddy's a messenger from the devil."

This is an idea he must have gotten from church. Her parents have been taking him every Sunday. When Jeannette tries to reassure him about his father, Rodney is skeptical. "He gets that funny look on his face like he can see through me," the child says.

"Something's missing," Jeannette says, with a rush of optimism, a feeling of recognition. "Something happened to him once and took out the part that shows how much he cares about us."

"The way we had the cat fixed?"

"I guess. Something like that." The appropriateness of his remark stuns her, as though, in a way, her child has understood Donald all along. Rodney's pictures have been more peaceful lately, pictures of skinny trees and airplanes flying low. This morning he drew pictures of tall grass, with creatures hiding in it. The grass is tilted at an angle, as though a light breeze is blowing through it.

With her paycheck, Jeannette buys Rodney a present, a miniature trampoline they have seen advertised on television. It is called Mr. Bouncer. Rodney is thrilled about the trampoline, and he jumps on it until his face is red. Jeannette discovers that she enjoys it, too. She puts it out on the grass, and they take turns jumping. She has an image of herself on the trampoline, her sailor collar flapping, at the moment when Donald returns and sees her flying. One day a neighbor driving by slows down and calls out to

Jeannette as she is bouncing on the trampoline, "You'll tear your insides loose!" Jeannette starts thinking about that, and the idea is so horrifying she stops jumping so much. That night, she has a nightmare about the trampoline. In her dream, she is jumping on soft moss, and then it turns into a springy pile of dead bodies.

QUESTIONS

1. Why does Donald tell his "Big Bertha stories"? What function do they serve in his life?
2. How does Jeannette think and feel about her husband? Would she have gotten divorced sooner had she been financially independent?
3. There are many references to strip-mining in the story. And Donald himself makes reference to his work stating, "I'm reclaiming the land." What symbolic significance might these references have?
4. Toward the end of the story, Jeannette says about Donald, "Something's missing. . . . Something happened to him once and took out the part that shows how much he cares about us." What is she referring to? What in Donald's behavior makes her reach this conclusion?

Bharati Mukherjee

HINDUS

I ran into Pat at Sotheby's on a Friday morning two years ago. Derek and I had gone to view the Fraser Collection of Islamic miniatures at the York Avenue galleries. It bothered Derek that I knew so little about my heritage. Islam is nothing more than a marauder's faith to me, but the Mogul emperors stayed a long time in the green delta of the Ganges, flattening and reflattening a fort in the village where I was born, and forcing my priestly ancestors to prove themselves brave. Evidence on that score is still inconclusive. That village is now in Bangladesh.

Derek was a filmmaker, lightly employed at that time. We had been married three hundred and thirty-one days.

"So," Pat said, in his flashy, plummy, drawn-out intonation, "you finally made it to the States!"

It was one of those early November mornings when the woodsy smell of overheated bodies in cloth coats clogged the public stairwells. Everywhere around me I detected the plaintive signs of over-preparedness.

"Whatever are you doing here?" He engulfed me in a swirl of Liberty scarf and cashmere lapels.

"Trying to get the woman there to sell me the right catalog," I said.

The woman, a very young thing with slippery skin, ate a lusty Granny Smith apple and ignored the dark, hesitant miniature-lovers hanging about like bats in daytime.

"They have more class in London," Pat said.

"I wouldn't know. I haven't been back since that unfortunate year at Roedean."

"It was always New York you wanted," Pat laughed. "Don't say I didn't warn you. The world is full of empty promises."

I didn't remember his having warned me about life and the inevitability of grief. It was entirely possible that he had—he had always been given to clowning pronouncements—but I had not seen him in nine years and in Calcutta he had never really broken through the fortifications of my shyness.

"Come have a drink with me," Pat said.

It was my turn to laugh. "You must meet Derek," I said.

Derek had learned a great deal about India. He could reel off statistics of Panchayati Raj and the electrification of villages and the introduction of mass media, though he reserved his love for birds migrating through the wintry deserts of Jaisalmer. Knowledge of India made Derek more sympathetic than bitter, a common trait of decent outsiders. He was charmed by Pat's heedless, old-world insularity.

"Is this the lucky man?" he said to Derek. He did not hold out his hand. He waved us outside; a taxi magically appeared. "Come have a drink with me tomorrow. At my place."

He gave Derek his card. It was big and would not fit into a wallet made to hold Visa and American Express. Derek read it with his usual curiosity.

H.R.H. Maharajah Patwant Singh
of
Gotlah
Purveyor and Exporter

He tucked the card in the pocket of his raincoat. "I'll be shooting in Toronto tomorrow," he said, "but I'm sure Leela would like to keep it."

There was, in the retention of those final "h's"—even Indian maps and newspapers now referred to Gotla and to maharajas, and I had dropped the old "Leelah" in my first month in America—something of the reclusive mountebank. "I'm going to the Patels for dinner tomorrow," I said, afraid that Pat would misread the signs of healthy unpossessiveness in our marriage.

"Come for a drink before. What's the matter, Leela? Turning a prude in your old age?" To Derek he explained, "I used to rock her on my knee when she was four. She was gorgeous then, but I am no lecher."

It is true that I was very pretty at four and that Pat spent a lot of time in our house fondling us children. He brought us imported chocolates in beautiful tins and made a show of giving me the biggest. In my family, in every generation, one infant seems destined to be the repository of the family's comeliness. In my generation, I inherited the looks, like an heirloom, to keep in good condition and pass on to the next. Beauty

teaches humility and responsibility in the culture I came from. By marrying well, I could have seen to the education of my poorer cousins.

Pat was in a third floor sublet in Gramercy Park South. A West Indian doorman with pendulous cheeks and an unbuttoned jacket let me into the building. He didn't give me a chance to say where I was going as I moved toward the elevator.

"The Maharaja is third floor, to the right. All the way down."

I had misunderstood the invitation. It was not to be an hour of wit and nostalgia among exotic knick-knacks squirreled into New York from the Gotla Palace. I counted thirty guests in the first quarter hour of my short stay. Plump young men in tight-fitting suits scuttled from living room to kitchen, balancing overfull glasses of gin and tonic. The women were mostly blondes, with luridly mascaraed, brooding eyes, blonde the way South Americans are blonde, with deep residual shading. I tried to edge into a group of three women. One of them said, "I thought India was spellbinding. Naresh's partner managed to get us into the Lake Palace Hotel."

"I don't think I could take the poverty," said her friend, as I retreated.

The living room walls were hung with prints of British East India Company officials at work and play, the vestibule with mirror-images of Hindu gods and goddesses.

"Take my advice," a Gujarati man said to Pat in the dim and plantless kitchen. "Get out of diamonds—emeralds *won't* bottom out. These days it *has* to be rubies and emeralds."

In my six years in Manhattan I had not entered a kitchen without plants. There was not even a straggly avocado pushing its nervous way out of a shrivelling seed.

I moved back into the living room where the smell of stale turmeric hung like yellow fog from the ceiling. A man rose from the brocade-covered cushions of a banquette near me and plumped them, smiling, to make room for me.

"You're Pat's niece, no?" The man was francophone, a Lebanese. "Pat has such pretty nieces. You have just come from Bombay? I love Bombay. Personally, Bombay to me is like a jewel. Like Paris, like Beirut before, now like Bombay. You agree?"

I disclaimed all kinship to H.R.H. I was a Bengali Brahmin; maharajas—not to put too sharp a point on it—were frankly beneath me, by at least one caste, though some of them, like Pat, would dispute it. Before my marriage to Derek no one in my family since our initial eruption from Vishnu's knee had broken caste etiquette. I disclaimed any recent connection with India. "I haven't been home in ages," I told the Lebanese. "I am an American citizen."

"I too am. I am American," he practically squealed. He rinsed his glass with a bit of gin still left in the bottom, as though he were trying to dislodge lemon pulp stuck and drying on its sides. "You want to have dinner with me tonight, yes? I know Lebanese places, secret and intimate. Food and ambiance very romantic."

"She's going to the Patels." It was Pat. The Gujarati with advice on emeralds was still lodged in the kitchen, huddling with a stocky blonde in a fuschia silk sari.

"Oh, the Patels," said the Lebanese. "You did not say. Super guy, no? He's doing all right for himself. Not as well as me, of course. I own ten stores and he only has four."

Why, I often asked myself, was Derek never around to share these intimacies? Derek would have drawn out the suave, French-speaking, soulful side of this Seventh Avenue *shmattiste.*

It shouldn't have surprised me that the Lebanese man in the ruffled shirt should have known Mohan and Motibehn Patel. For immigrants in similar trades, Manhattan is still a village. Mohan had been in the States for eighteen years and last year had become a citizen. They'd been fortunate in having only sons, now at Cal Tech and Cornell; with daughters there would have been pressure on them to return to India for a proper, arranged marriage.

"Is he still in Queens?"

"No," I told him. "They've moved to a biggish old place on Central Park West."

"Very foolish move," said the Lebanese. "They will only spend their money now." He seemed genuinely appalled.

Pat looked at me surprised. "I can't believe it," he exclaimed. "Leela Lahiri actually going crosstown at night by herself. I remember when your Daddy wouldn't let you walk the two blocks from school to the house without that armed Nepali, what was his name, dogging your steps."

"Gulseng," I said. "He was run over by a lorry three years ago. I think his name was really something-or-other-Rana, but he never corrected us."

"Short, nasty and brutal," said Pat. "They don't come that polite and loyal these days. Just as likely to slit your throat as anyone else, these days."

The Lebanese, sensing the end of brave New World overtures, the gathering of the darknesses we shared, drifted away.

"The country's changed totally, you know," Pat continued. "Crude rustic types have taken over. The *dhotiwallahs*, you know what I mean, they would wrap themselves in loincloths if it got them more votes. No integrity, no finesse. The country's gone to the dogs, I tell you."

"That whole life's outmoded, Pat. Obsolete. All over the world."

"They tried to put me in jail," he said. His face was small with bitterness and alarm. "They didn't like my politics, I tell you. Those Communists back home arrested me and threw me in jail. Me. Like a common criminal."

"On what charges?"

"Smuggling. For selling family heirlooms to Americans who understand them. No one at home understands their value. Here, I can sell off a little Pahari painting for ten thousand dollars. Americans understand our things better than we do ourselves. India wants me to starve in my overgrown palace."

"Did you really spend a night in jail?" I couldn't believe that modernization had finally come to India and that even there, no one was immune from consequences.

"Three nights!" he fumed. "Like a common *dacoit*. The country has no respect anymore. The country has nothing. It has driven us abroad with whatever assets we could salvage."

"You did well, I take it." I did not share his perspective; I did not feel my country owed me anything. Comfort, perhaps, when I was there; a different comfort when I left it. India teaches her children: you have seen the worst. Now go out and don't be afraid.

"I have nothing," he spat. "They've stripped me of everything. At night I hear the jackals singing in the courtyard of my palace."

But he had recovered by the time I left for the crosstown cab ride to the Patels. I saw him sitting on the banquette where not too long before the Lebanese had invited me to share an evening of unwholesomeness. On his knee he balanced, a tall, silver-haired

woman who looked like Candice Bergen. She wore a pink cashmere sweater which she must have put through the washing machine. Creases, like worms, curled around her sweatered bosom.

I didn't see Pat for another two years. In those two years I did see a man who claimed to have bounced the real Candice Bergen on his knee. He had been a juggler at one time, had worked with Edgar Bergen on some vaudeville act and could still pull off card tricks and walk on his hands up and down my dining table. I kept the dining table when Derek and I split last May. He went back to Canada which we both realized too late he should never have left and the table was too massive to move out of our West 11th Street place and into his downtown Toronto, chic renovated apartment. The ex-juggler is my boss at a publishing house. My job is menial but I have a soothing title. I am called an Administrative Assistant.

In the two years I have tried to treat the city not as an island of dark immigrants but as a vast sea in which new Americans like myself could disappear and resurface at will. I did not avoid Indians, but without Derek's urging for me to be proud of my heritage, I did not seek them out. The Patels did invite me to large dinners where all the guests seemed to know with the first flick of their eyes in my direction that I had married a white man and was now separated, and there our friendships hit rock. I was a curiosity, a novel and daring element in the community; everyone knew my name. After a while I began to say I was busy to Motibehn Patel.

Pat came to the office with my boss, Bill Haines, the other day. "I wanted you to meet one of our new authors, Leela," Bill said.

"Leela, *dar-ling*!" Pat cried. His voice was shrill with enthusiasm, and he pressed me histrionically against his Burberry raincoat. I could feel a button tap my collarbone. "It's been years! Where have you been hiding your gorgeous self?"

"I didn't realize you two knew each other," Bill said.

All Indians in America, I could have told him, constitute a village.

"Her father bailed me out when the Indian government sought to persecute me," he said with a pout. "If it hadn't been for courageous friends like her daddy, I and my poor subjects might just as well have kicked the bucket."

"She's told me nothing about India," said Bill Haines. "No accent, Western clothes—"

"Yes, a shame, that. By the way, Leela, I just found a picture of Lahiri-*sahab* on an elephant when I was going through my official papers for Bill. If you come over for drinks—after getting out of those ridiculous clothes, I must insist—I can give it to you. Lahiri-*sahab* looks like Ernest Hemingway in that photo. You tell him I said he looks like Hemingway."

"Daddy's in Ranikhet this month," I said. "He's been bedridden for a while. Arthritis. He's just beginning to move around a bit again."

"I have hundreds of good anecdotes, Bill, about her Daddy and me doing *shikar* in the Sundarban forest. Absolutely *huge* Bengal tigers. I want to balance the politics— which as you rightly say are central—with some stirring bits about what it was like in the good old days."

"What are you writing?" I asked.

"I thought you'd never ask, my dear. My memoirs. At night I leave a Sony by my bed. Night is the best time for remembering. I hear the old sounds and voices. You remember, Leela, how the palace ballroom used to hum with dancing feet on my birthdays?"

"Memoirs of a Modern Maharajah," Bill Haines said.

"I seem to remember the singing of jackals," I said, not unkindly, though he chose to ignore it.

"Writing is what keeps me from going through death's gate. There are nights . . ." He didn't finish. His posture had stiffened with self-regard; he communicated great oceans of anguish. He'd probably do well. It was what people wanted to hear.

"The indignities," he said suddenly. "The atrocities." He stared straight ahead, at a watercooler. "The nights in jail, the hyenas sniffing outside your barred window. I will never forget their smell, never! It is the smell of death, Leela. The new powers-that-be are peasants. Peasants! They cannot know, they cannot suspect how they have made me suffer. The country is in the hands of tyrannical peasants!"

"Look, Pat," Bill Haines said, leading the writer toward his office, "I have to see Bob Savage, the sub-rights man one floor down. Make yourself at home. Just pull down any book you want to read. I'll be back in a minute."

"Don't worry about me. I shall be all right, Bill. I have my Sony in my pocket. I shall just sit in a corner beside the daughter of my oldest friend, this child I used to bounce on my knee, and I shall let my mind skip into the nooks and crannies of Gotlah Palace. Did I tell you, when I was a young lad my mother kept pet crocs? Big, huge gents and ladies with ugly jaws full of nasty teeth. They were her pets. She gave them names and fed them chickens every day. Come to me, Padma. Come to me, Prem."

"It'll be dynamite," Bill Haines said. "The whole project's dynamite." He pressed my hand as he eased his stubby, muscular body past the stack of dossiers on my desk. "And *you'll* be a godsend in developing this project."

"And what's with you?" Pat asked me. I could tell he already knew the essentials.

"Nothing much." But he wasn't listening anyway.

"You remember the thief my security men caught in the early days of your father's setting up a factory in my hills? You remember how the mob got excited and poured acid on his face?"

I remembered. Was the Sony recording it? Was the memory an illustration of swift and righteous justice in a collapsed Himalayan princely state, or was it the savage and disproportionate fury of a people resisting change?

"Yes, certainly I do. Can I get you a cup of coffee? Or tea?" That, of course, was an important part of my job.

"No thanks," he said with a flutter of his wrinkled hands. "I have given up all stimulants. I've even given up bed-tea. It interferes with my writing. Writing is everything to me nowadays. It has been my nirvana."

"The book sounds dynamite," I assured him. An Indian woman is brought up to please. No matter how passionately we link bodies with our new countries, we never escape the early days.

Pat dropped his voice, and, stooping conspiratorially, said to me in Hindi, "There's

one big favor you can do for me, though. Bill has spoken of a chap I should be knowing. Who is this Edgar Bergen?"

"I think he was the father of a movie actress," I said. I, too, had gone through the same contortion of recognition with Bill Haines. Fortunately, like most Americans, he could not conceive of a world in which Edgar Bergen had no currency. Again in Hindi, Pat asked me for directions to the facilities, and this time I could give a full response. He left his rolled-slim umbrella propped against my desk and walked toward the fountain.

"Is he really a maharaja?" Lisa leaned over from her desk to ask me. She is from Rhode Island. Brown hasn't cured her of responding too enthusiastically to each call or visit from a literary personage. "He's terrific. So suave and distinguished! Have you known him from way back when?"

"Yes," I said, all the way from when.

"I had no idea you spoke Hindu. It's eerie to think you can speak such a hard language. I'm having trouble enough with French. I keep forgetting that you haven't lived here always."

I keep forgetting it too. I was about to correct her silly mistake—I'd learned from Derek to be easily incensed over ignorant confusions between Hindi and Hindu—but then I thought, why bother? Maybe she's right. That slight undetectable error, call it an accent, isn't part of language at all. I speak Hindu. No matter what language I speak it will come out slightly foreign, no matter how perfectly I mouth it. There's a whole world of us now, speaking Hindu.

The manuscript of *Memoirs* was not dynamite, but I stayed up all night to finish it. In spite of the arch locutions and the aggrieved posture that Pat had stubbornly clung to, I knew I was reading about myself, blind and groping conquistador who had come to the New World too late.

QUESTIONS

1. Compare and contrast the attitude the narrator has toward India with that of Pat. How do they differ? How are they alike?
2. How would you characterize the narrator's personality and values?
3. The story is divided into two parts. What is the purpose of this division? What changes has the narrator undergone during the time dividing them? What changes has Pat undergone?
4. In the last line of the story, the narrator says she is a "blind and groping conquistador who had come to the New World too late." What does she mean by this? What behaviors or actions does she show in the story that reflect this description?

R. K. Narayan

MOTHER AND SON

Ramu's mother waited till he was halfway through dinner and then introduced the subject of marriage. Ramu merely replied, "So you are at it again!" He appeared more amused than angry, and so she brought out her favourite points one by one: her brother's daughter was getting on to fourteen, the girl was good-looking and her brother was prepared to give a handsome dowry; she (Ramu's mother) was getting old and wanted a holiday from housekeeping: she might die any moment and then who would cook Ramu's food and look after him? And the most indisputable argument: a man's luck changed with marriage. "The harvest depends not on the hand that holds the plough but on the hand which holds the pot." Earlier in the evening Ramu's mother had decided that if he refused again or exhibited the usual sullenness at the mention of marriage, she would leave him to his fate; she would leave him absolutely alone even if she saw him falling down before a coming train. She would never more interfere in his affairs. She realized what a resolute mind she possessed, and felt proud of the fact. That was the kind of person one ought to be. It was all very well having a mother's heart and so on, but even a mother could have a limit to her feelings. If Ramu thought he could do what he pleased just because she was only a mother, she would show him he was mistaken. If he was going to slight her judgement and feelings, she was going to show how indifferent she herself could be. . . .

With so much preparation she broached the subject of marriage and presented a formidable array of reasons. But Ramu just brushed them aside and spoke slightingly of the appearance of her brother's daughter. And then she announced, "This is the last time I am speaking about this. Hereafter I will leave you alone. Even if I see you drowning I will never ask why you are drowning. Do you understand?"

"Yes." Ramu brooded. He could not get through his Intermediate even at the fourth attempt; he could not get a job, even at twenty rupees a month. And here was Mother worrying him to marry. Of all girls, his uncle's! That protruding tooth alone would put off any man. It was incredible that he should be expected to marry that girl. He had always felt that when he married he would marry a girl like Rezia, whom he had seen in two or three Hindi films. Life was rusty and sterile, and Ramu lived in a stage of perpetual melancholia and depression; he loafed away his time, or slept, or read old newspapers in a free reading room. . . .

He now sat before his dining leaf and brooded. His mother watched him for a moment and said, "I hate your face. I hate anyone who sits before his leaf with that face. A woman only ten days old in widowhood would put on a more cheerful look."

"You are saying all sorts of things because I refuse to marry your brother's daughter," he replied.

"What do I care? She is a fortunate girl and will get a really decent husband." Ramu's mother hated him for his sullenness. It was this gloomy look that she hated in people. It was unbearable. She spoke for a few minutes, and he asked, "When are you going to shut up?"

"My life is nearly over," said the mother. "You will see me shutting up once and for all very soon. Don't be impatient. You ask me to shut up! Has it come to this?"

"Well, I only asked you to give me some time to eat."

"Oh, yes. You will have it soon, my boy. When I am gone you will have plenty of time, my boy."

Ramu did not reply. He ate his food in silence. "I only want you to look a little more human when you eat," she said.

"How is it possible with this food?" asked Ramu.

"What do you say?" screamed the mother. "If you are so fastidious, work and earn like all men. Throw down the money and demand what you want. Don't command when you are a pauper."

When the meal was over, Ramu was seen putting on his sandals. "Where are you going?" asked the mother.

"Going out," he curtly replied, and walked out, leaving the street door ajar.

Her duties for the day were over. She had scrubbed the floor of the kitchen, washed the vessels and put them in a shining row on the wooden shelf, returned the short scrubbing broom to its corner and closed the kitchen window.

Taking the lantern and closing the kitchen door, she came to the front room. The street door stood ajar. She became indignant at her son's carelessness. The boy was indifferent and irresponsible and didn't feel bound even to shut the street door. Here she was wearing out her palm scrubbing the floor night after night. Why should she slave if he was indifferent? He was old enough to realize his responsibilities in life.

She took out her small wooden box and put into her mouth a clove, a cardamom and a piece of areca nut. Chewing these, she felt more at peace with life. She shut the door without bolting it and lay down to sleep.

Where could Ramu have gone? She began to feel uneasy. She rolled her mat, went out, spread it on the *pyol* and lay down. She muttered to herself the holy name of Sri Rama in order to keep out disturbing thoughts. She went on whispering, "Sita Rama Rama . . ." But she ceased unconsciously. Her thoughts returned to Ramu. What did he say before going out? "I am just going out for a stroll, Mother. Don't worry. I shall be back soon." No, it was not that. Not he. Why was the boy so secretive about his movements? That was impudent and exasperating. But, she told herself, she deserved no better treatment with that terrible temper and cutting tongue of hers. There was no doubt that she had conducted herself abominably during the meal. All her life this had been her worst failing: this tendency, while in a temper, to talk without restraint. She even felt that her husband would have lived for a few more years if she had spoken to him less. . . . Ramu had said something about the food. She would include more vegetables and cook better from tomorrow. Poor boy . . .

She fell asleep. Somewhere a gong sounded one, and she woke up. One o'clock? She called, "Ramu, Ramu."

She did not dare to contemplate what he might have done with himself. Gradually she came to believe that her words during the meal had driven him to suicide. She sat up and wept. She was working herself up to a hysterical pitch. When she closed her eyes to press out the gathering tears, the vision of her son's body floating in Kukanahalli Tank came before her. His striped shirt and mill dhoti were sodden and clung close to his body. His sandals were left on one of the tank steps. His face was bloated beyond all recognition.

She screamed aloud and jumped down from the *pyol*. She ran along the whole length of Old Agrahar Street. It was deserted. Electric lights twinkled here and there. Far away a *tonga* was rattling on, the *tonga*-driver's song faintly disturbing the silence; the blast of a night constable's whistle came to her ears, and she stopped running. She realized that after all it might be only her imagination. He might have gone away to the drama, which didn't usually close before three in the morning. She rapidly uttered the holy name of Sri Rama in order to prevent the picture of Kukanahalli Tank coming before her mind.

She had a restless night. Unknown to herself, she slept in snatches and woke up with a start every time the gong boomed. The gong struck six through the chill morning.

Tears streaming down her face, she started for Kukanahalli Tank. Mysore was just waking to fresh life. Milkmen with slow cows passed along. Municipal sweepers were busy with their long brooms. One or two cycles passed her.

She reached the tank, not daring even once to look at the water. She found him sleeping on one of the benches that lined the bund. For just a second she wondered if it might be his corpse. She shook him vigorously, crying "Ramu!" She heaved a tremendous sigh of relief when he stirred.

He sat up, rubbing his eyes. "Why are you here, Mother?"

"What a place to sleep in!"

"Oh, I just fell asleep," he said.

"Come home," she said. She walked on and he followed her. She saw him going down the tank steps. "Where are you going?"

"Just for a wash," Ramu explained.

She clung to his arm and said vehemently, "No, don't go near the water."

He obeyed her, though he was slightly baffled by her vehemence.

QUESTIONS

1. Describe the lives of Ramu and his mother in this story. Where do they live? What are their social and economic backgrounds? What cultural implications about family life and marriage are advanced?
2. Explain the author's handling of time as a structuring or plotting device in the story.
3. How might the last sentence predict whether or not Ramu will marry his first cousin?

Gloria Naylor

KISWANA BROWNE

From the window of her sixth-floor studio apartment, Kiswana could see over the wall at the end of the street to the busy avenue that lay just north of Brewster Place. The late-afternoon shoppers looked like brightly clad marionettes as they moved between the congested traffic, clutching their packages against their bodies to guard them from sudden bursts of the cold autumn wind. A portly mailman had abandoned his cart and was bumping into indignant window-shoppers as he puffed behind the cap that the wind had snatched from his head. Kiswana leaned over to see if he was going to be successful, but the edge of the building cut him off from her view.

A pigeon swept across her window, and she marveled at its liquid movements in the air waves. She placed her dreams on the back of the bird and fantasized that it would glide forever in transparent silver circles until it ascended to the center of the universe and was swallowed up. But the wind died down, and she watched with a sigh as the bird beat its wings in awkward, frantic movements to land on the corroded top of a fire escape on the opposite building. This brought her back to earth.

Humph, it's probably sitting over there crapping on those folks' fire escape, she thought. Now, that's a safety hazard. . . . And her mind was busy again, creating flames and smoke and frustrated tenants whose escape was being hindered because they were slipping and sliding in pigeon shit. She watched their cussing, haphazard descent on the fire escapes until they had all reached the bottom. They were milling around, oblivious to their burning apartments, angrily planning to march on the mayor's office about the pigeons. She materialized placards and banners for them, and they had just reached the corner, boldly sidestepping fire hoses and broken glass, when they all vanished.

A tall copper-skinned woman had met this phantom parade at the corner, and they had dissolved in front of her long, confident strides. She plowed through the remains of their faded mists, unconscious of the lingering wisps of their presence on her leather bag and black fur-trimmed coat. It took a few seconds for this transfer from one realm to another to reach Kiswana, but then suddenly she recognized the woman.

"Oh, God, it's Mama!" She looked down guiltily at the forgotten newspaper in her lap and hurriedly circled random job advertisements.

By this time Mrs. Browne had reached the front of Kiswana's building and was checking the house number against a piece of paper in her hand. Before she went into the building she stood at the bottom of the stoop and carefully inspected the condition of the street and the adjoining property. Kiswana watched this meticulous inventory with growing annoyance but she involuntarily followed her mother's slowly rotating head, forcing herself to see her new neighborhood through the older woman's eyes. The brightness of the unclouded sky seemed to join forces with her mother as it highlighted every broken stoop railing and missing brick. The afternoon sun glittered and cascaded across even the tiniest fragments of broken bottle, and at that very moment the wind chose to rise up again, sending unswept grime flying into the air, as a stray tin can left by careless garbage collectors went rolling noisily down the center of the street.

Kiswana noticed with relief that at least Ben wasn't sitting in his usual place on the old garbage can pushed against the far wall. He was just a harmless old wino, but Kiswana knew her mother only needed one wino or one teenager with a reefer within a twenty-block radius to decide that her daughter was living in a building seething with dope factories and hang-outs for derelicts. If she had seen Ben, nothing would have made her believe that practically every apartment contained a family, a Bible, and a dream that one day enough could be scraped from those meager Friday night paychecks to make Brewster Place a distant memory.

As she watched her mother's head disappear into the building, Kiswana gave silent thanks that the elevator was broken. That would give her at least five minutes' grace to straighten up the apartment. She rushed to the sofa bed and hastily closed it without smoothing the rumpled sheets and blanket or removing her nightgown. She felt that somehow the tangled bedcovers would give away the fact that she had not slept alone last night. She silently apologized to Abshu's memory as she heartlessly crushed his spirit between the steel springs of the couch. Lord, that man was sweet. Her toes curled involuntarily at the passing thought of his full lips moving slowly over her instep. Abshu was a foot man, and he always started his lovemaking from the bottom up. For that reason Kiswana changed the color of the polish on her toenails every week. During the course of their relationship she had gone from shades of red to brown and was now into the purples. I'm gonna have to start mixing them soon, she thought aloud as she turned from the couch and raced into the bathroom to remove any traces of Abshu from there. She took up his shaving cream and razor and threw them into the bottom drawer of her dresser beside her diaphragm. Mama wouldn't dare pry into my drawers right in front of me, she thought as she slammed the drawer shut. Well, at least not the *bottom* drawer. She may come up with some sham excuse for opening the top drawer, but never the bottom one.

When she heard the first two short raps on the door, her eyes took a final flight over the small apartment, desperately seeking out any slight misdemeanor that might have to be defended. Well, there was nothing she could do about the crack in the wall over that table. She had been after the landlord to fix it for two months now. And there had been no time to sweep the rug, and everyone knew that off-gray always looked dirtier than it really was. And it was just too damn bad about the kitchen. How was she expected to be out job-hunting every day and still have time to keep a kitchen that looked like her mother's, who didn't even work and still had someone come in twice a month for general cleaning. And besides . . .

Her imaginary argument was abruptly interrupted by a second series of knocks, accompanied by a penetrating, "Melanie, Melanie, are you there?"

Kiswana strode toward the door. She's starting before she even gets in here. She knows that's not my name anymore.

She swung the door open to face her slightly flushed mother. "Oh, hi, Mama. You know, I thought I heard a knock, but I figured it was for the people next door, since no one hardly ever calls me Melanie." Score one for me, she thought.

"Well, it's awfully strange you can forget a name you answered to for twenty-three years," Mrs. Browne said, as she moved past Kiswana into the apartment. "My, that was a long climb. How long has your elevator been out? Honey, how do you manage

with your laundry and groceries up all those steps? But I guess you're young, and it wouldn't bother you as much as it does me." This long string of questions told Kiswana that her mother had no intentions of beginning her visit with another argument about her new African name.

"You know I would have called before I came, but you don't have a phone yet. I didn't want you to feel that I was snooping. As a matter of fact, I didn't expect to find you home at all. I thought you'd be out looking for a job." Mrs. Browne had mentally covered the entire apartment while she was talking and taking off her coat.

"Well, I got up late this morning. I thought I'd buy the afternoon paper and start early tomorrow."

"That sounds like a good idea." Her mother moved toward the window and picked up the discarded paper and glanced over the hurriedly circled ads. "Since when do you have experience as a fork-lift operator?"

Kiswana caught her breath and silently cursed herself for her stupidity. "Oh, my hand slipped—I meant to circle file clerk." She quickly took the paper before her mother could see that she had also marked cutlery salesman and chauffeur.

"You're sure you weren't sitting here moping and daydreaming again?" Amber specks of laughter flashed in the corner of Mrs. Browne's eyes.

Kiswana threw her shoulders back and unsuccessfully tried to disguise her embarrassment with indignation.

"Oh, God, Mama! I haven't done that in years—it's for kids. When are you going to realize that I'm a woman now?" She sought desperately for some womanly thing to do and settled for throwing herself on the couch and crossing her legs in what she hoped looked like a nonchalant arc.

"Please, have a seat," she said, attempting the same tones and gestures she'd seen Bette Davis use on the late movies.

Mrs. Browne, lowering her eyes to hide her amusement, accepted the invitation and sat at the window, also crossing her legs. Kiswana saw immediately how it should have been done. Her celluloid poise clashed loudly against her mother's quiet dignity, and she quickly uncrossed her legs. Mrs. Browne turned her head toward the window and pretended not to notice.

"At least you have a halfway decent view from here. I was wondering what lay beyond that dreadful wall—it's the boulevard. Honey, did you know that you can see the trees in Linden Hills from here?"

Kiswana knew that very well, because there were many lonely days that she would sit in her gray apartment and stare at those trees and think of home, but she would rather have choked than admit that to her mother.

"Oh, really, I never noticed. So how is Daddy and things at home?"

"Just fine. We're thinking of redoing one of the extra bedrooms since you children have moved out, but Wilson insists that he can manage all that work alone. I told him that he doesn't really have the proper time or energy for all that. As it is, when he gets home from the office, he's so tired he can hardly move. But you know you can't tell your father anything. Whenever he starts complaining about how stubborn you are, I tell him the child came by it honestly. Oh, and your brother was by yesterday," she added, as if it had just occurred to her.

So that's it, thought Kiswana. That's why she's here.

Kiswana's brother, Wilson, had been to visit her two days ago, and she had borrowed twenty dollars from him to get her winter coat out of layaway. That son-of-a-bitch probably ran straight to Mama—and after he swore he wouldn't say anything. I should have known, he was always a snotty-nosed sneak, she thought.

"Was he?" she said aloud. "He came by to see me, too, earlier this week. And I borrowed some money from him because my unemployment checks hadn't cleared in the bank, but now they have and everything's just fine." There, I'll beat you to that one.

"Oh, I didn't know that," Mrs. Browne lied. "He never mentioned you. He had just heard that Beverly was expecting again, and he rushed over to tell us."

Damn. Kiswana could have strangled herself.

"So she's knocked up again, huh?" she said irritably.

Her mother started. "Why do you always have to be so crude?"

"Personally, I don't see how she can sleep with Willie. He's such a dishrag."

Kiswana still resented the stance her brother had taken in college. When everyone at school was discovering their blackness and protesting on campus, Wilson never took part; he had even refused to wear an Afro. This had outraged Kiswana because, unlike her, he was dark-skinned and had the type of hair that was thick and kinky enough for a good "Fro." Kiswana had still insisted on cutting her own hair, but it was so thin and fine-textured, it refused to thicken even after she washed it. So she had to brush it up and spray it with lacquer to keep it from lying flat. She never forgave Wilson for telling her that she didn't look African, she looked like an electrocuted chicken.

"Now that's some way to talk. I don't know why you have an attitude against your brother. He never gave me a restless night's sleep, and now he's settled with a family and a good job."

"He's an assistant to an assistant junior partner in a law firm. What's the big deal about that?"

"The job has a future, Melanie. And at least he finished school and went on for his law degree."

"In other words, not like me, huh?"

"Don't put words into my mouth, young lady. I'm perfectly capable of saying what I mean."

Amen, thought Kiswana.

"And I don't know why you've been trying to start up with me from the moment I walked in. I didn't come here to fight with you. This is your first place away from home, and I just wanted to see how you were living and if you're doing all right. And I must say, you've fixed this apartment up very nicely."

"Really, Mama?" She found herself softening in the light of her mother's approval.

"Well, considering what you had to work with." This time she scanned the apartment openly.

"Look, I know it's not Linden Hills, but a lot can be done with it. As soon as they come and paint, I'm going to hang my Ashanti print over the couch. And I thought a big Boston Fern would go well in that corner, what do you think?"

"That would be fine, baby. You always had a good eye for balance."

Kiswana was beginning to relax. There was little she did that attracted her mother's

approval. It was like a rare bird, and she had to tread carefully around it lest it fly away.

"Are you going to leave that statue out like that?"

"Why, what's wrong with it? Would it look better somewhere else?"

There was a small wooden reproduction of a Yoruba goddess with large protruding breasts on the coffee table.

"Well," Mrs. Browne was beginning to blush, "it's just that it's a bit suggestive, don't you think? Since you live alone now, and I know you'll be having male friends stop by, you wouldn't want to be giving them any ideas. I mean, uh, you know, there's no point in putting yourself in any unpleasant situations because they may get the wrong impressions and uh, you know, I mean, well . . ." Mrs. Browne stammered on miserably.

Kiswana loved it when her mother tried to talk about sex. It was the only time she was at a loss for words.

"Don't worry, Mama." Kiswana smiled. "That wouldn't bother the type of men I date. Now maybe if it had big feet . . ." And she got hysterical, thinking of Abshu.

Her mother looked at her sharply. "What sort of gibberish is that about feet? I'm being serious, Melanie."

"I'm sorry, Mama." She sobered up. "I'll put it away in the closet," she said, knowing that she wouldn't.

"Good," Mrs. Browne said, knowing that she wouldn't either. "I guess you think I'm too picky, but we worry about you over here. And you refuse to put in a phone so we can call and see about you."

"I haven't refused, Mama. They want seventy-five dollars for a deposit, and I can't swing that right now."

"Melanie, I can give you the money."

"I don't want you to be giving me money—I've told you that before. Please, let me make it by myself."

"Well, let me lend it to you, then."

"No!"

"Oh, so you can borrow money from your brother, but not from me."

Kiswana turned her head from the hurt in her mother's eyes. "Mama, when I borrow from Willie, he makes me pay him back. You never let me pay you back," she said into her hands.

"I don't care. I still think it's downright selfish of you to be sitting over here with no phone, and sometimes we don't hear from you in two weeks—anything could happen—especially living among these people."

Kiswana snapped her head up. "What do you mean, *these people.* They're my people and yours, too, Mama—we're all black. But maybe you've forgotten that over in Linden Hills."

"That's not what I'm talking about, and you know it. These streets—this building—it's so shabby and rundown. Honey, you don't have to live like this."

"Well, this is how poor people live."

"Melanie, you're not poor."

"No, Mama, *you're* not poor. And what you have and I have are two totally different things. I don't have a husband in real estate with a five-figure income and a home in

Linden Hills—*you* do. What I have is a weekly unemployment check and an overdrawn checking account at United Federal. So this studio on Brewster is all I can afford."

"Well, you could afford a lot better," Mrs. Browne snapped, "if you hadn't dropped out of college and had to resort to these dead-end clerical jobs."

"Uh-huh, I knew you'd get around to that before long." Kiswana could feel the rings of anger begin to tighten around her lower backbone, and they sent her forward onto the couch. "You'll never understand, will you? Those bourgie schools were counterrevolutionary. My place was in the streets with my people, fighting for equality and a better community."

"Counterrevolutionary!" Mrs. Browne was raising her voice. "Where's your revolution now, Melanie? Where are all those black revolutionaries who were shouting and demonstrating and kicking up a lot of dust with you on that campus? Huh? They're sitting in wood-paneled offices with their degrees in mahogany frames, and they won't even drive their cars past this street because the city doesn't fix potholes in this part of town."

"Mama," she said, shaking her head slowly in disbelief, "how can you—a black woman—sit there and tell me that what we fought for during the Movement wasn't important just because some people sold out?"

"Melanie, I'm not saying it wasn't important. It was damned important to stand up and say that you were proud of what you were and to get the vote and other social opportunities for every person in this country who had it due. But you kids thought you were going to turn the world upside down, and it just wasn't so. When all the smoke had cleared, you found yourself with a fistful of new federal laws and a country still full of obstacles for black people to fight their way over—just because they're black. There was no revolution, Melanie, and there will be no revolution."

"So what am I supposed to do, huh? Just throw up my hands and not care about what happens to my people? I'm not supposed to keep fighting to make things better?"

"Of course, you can. But you're going to have to fight within the system, because it and these so-called 'bourgie' schools are going to be here for a long time. And that means that you get smart like a lot of your old friends and get an important job where you can have some influence. You don't have to sell out, as you say, and work for some corporation, but you could become an assemblywoman or a civil liberties lawyer or open a freedom school in this very neighborhood. That way you could really help the community. But what help are you going to be to these people on Brewster while you're living hand-to-mouth on file-clerk jobs waiting for a revolution? You're wasting your talents, child."

"Well, I don't think they're being wasted. At least I'm here in day-to-day contact with the problems of my people. What good would I be after four or five years of a lot of white brainwashing in some phony, prestige institution, huh? I'd be like you and Daddy and those other educated blacks sitting over there in Linden Hills with a terminal case of middle-class amnesia."

"You don't have to live in a slum to be concerned about social conditions, Melanie. Your father and I have been charter members of the NAACP for the last twenty-five years."

"Oh, God!" Kiswana threw her head back in exaggerated disgust. "That's being

concerned? That middle-of-the-road, Uncle Tom dumping ground for black Republicans!"

"You can sneer all you want, young lady, but that organization has been working for black people since the turn of the century, and it's still working for them. Where are all those radical groups of yours that were going to put a Cadillac in every garage and Dick Gregory in the White House? I'll tell you where."

I knew you would, Kiswana thought angrily.

"They burned themselves out because they wanted too much too fast. Their goals weren't grounded in reality. And that's always been your problem."

"What do you mean, my problem? I know exactly what I'm about."

"No, you don't. You constantly live in a fantasy world—always going to extremes—turning butterflies into eagles, and life isn't about that. It's accepting what is and working from that. Lord, I remember how worried you had me, putting all that lacquered hair spray on your head. I thought you were going to get lung cancer—trying to be what you're not."

Kiswana jumped up from the couch. "Oh, God, I can't take this anymore. Trying to be something I'm not—trying to be something I'm not, Mama! Trying to be proud of my heritage and the fact that I was of African descent. If that's being what I'm not, then I say fine. But I'd rather be dead than be like you—a white man's nigger who's ashamed of being black!"

Kiswana saw streaks of gold and ebony light follow her mother's flying body out of the chair. She was swung around by the shoulders and made to face the deadly stillness in the angry woman's eyes. She was too stunned to cry out from the pain of the long fingernails that dug into her shoulders, and she was brought so close to her mother's face that she saw her reflection, distorted and wavering, in the tears that stood in the older woman's eyes. And she listened in that stillness to a story she had heard from a child.

"My grandmother," Mrs. Browne began slowly in a whisper, "was a full-blooded Iroquois, and my grandfather a free black from a long line of journeymen who had lived in Connecticut since the establishment of the colonies. And my father was a Bajan who came to this country as a cabin boy on a merchant mariner."

"I know all that," Kiswana said, trying to keep her lips from trembling.

"Then, know this." And the nails dug deeper into her flesh. "I am alive because of the blood of proud people who never scraped or begged or apologized for what they were. They lived asking only one thing of this world—to be allowed to be. And I learned through the blood of these people that black isn't beautiful and it isn't ugly—black is! It's not kinky hair and it's not straight hair—it just is.

"It broke my heart when you changed your name. I gave you my grandmother's name, a woman who bore nine children and educated them all, who held off six white men with a shotgun when they tried to drag one of her sons to jail for 'not knowing his place.' Yet you needed to reach into an African dictionary to find a name to make you proud.

"When I brought my babies home from the hospital, my ebony son and my golden daughter, I swore before whatever gods would listen—those of my mother's people or those of my father's people—that I would use everything I had and could ever get to see that my children were prepared to meet this world on its own terms, so that no one could sell them short and make them ashamed of what they were or how they looked—whatever they were or however they looked. And Melanie, that's not being white or red or black—that's being a mother."

Kiswana followed her reflection in the two single tears that moved down her mother's cheeks until it blended with them into the woman's copper skin. There was nothing and then so much that she wanted to say, but her throat kept closing up every time she tried to speak. She kept her head down and her eyes closed, and thought, Oh, God, just let me die. How can I face her now?

Mrs. Browne lifted Kiswana's chin gently. "And the one lesson I wanted you to learn is not to be afraid to face anyone, not even a crafty old lady like me who can outtalk you." And she smiled and winked.

"Oh, Mama, I . . ." and she hugged the woman tightly.

"Yeah, baby." Mrs. Browne patted her back. "I know."

She kissed Kiswana on the forehead and cleared her throat. "Well, now, I better be moving on. It's getting late, there's dinner to be made, and I have to get off my feet—these new shoes are killing me."

Kiswana looked down at the beige leather pumps. "Those are really classy. They're English, aren't they?"

"Yes, but, Lord, do they cut me right across the instep." She removed the shoe and sat on the couch to massage her foot.

Bright red nail polish glared at Kiswana through the stockings. "Since when do you polish your toenails?" she gasped. "You never did that before."

"Well . . ." Mrs. Browne shrugged her shoulders, "your father sort of talked me into it, and, uh, you know, he likes it and all, so I thought, uh, you know, why not, so . . ." And she gave Kiswana an embarrassed smile.

I'll be damned, the young woman thought, feeling her whole face tingle. Daddy's into feet! And she looked at the blushing woman on her couch and suddenly realized that her mother had trod through the same universe that she herself was now traveling. Kiswana was breaking no new trails and would eventually end up just two feet away on that couch. She stared at the woman she had been and was to become.

"But I'll never be a Republican," she caught herself saying aloud.

"What are you mumbling about, Melanie?" Mrs. Browne slipped on her shoe and got up from the couch.

She went to get her mother's coat. "Nothing, Mama. It's really nice of you to come by. You should do it more often."

"Well, since it's not Sunday, I guess you're allowed at least one lie."

They both laughed.

After Kiswana had closed the door and turned around, she spotted an envelope sticking between the cushions of her couch. She went over and opened it up; there was seventy-five dollars in it.

"Oh, Mama, darn it!" She rushed to the window and started to call to the woman, who had just emerged from the building, but she suddenly changed her mind and sat down in the chair with a long sigh that caught in the upward draft of the autumn wind and disappeared over the top of the building.

QUESTIONS

1. What kind of neighborhood does Kiswana live in? How does it compare to the neighborhood her parents live in?
2. Mrs. Browne tells Kiswana, "You constantly live in a dream world." Is this true? Support your view.
3. Is Kiswana rebelling against her family? If so, how? Why does her mother think she is rebelling?
4. What are the major conflicts between Kiswana and her mother? Are they resolved by the end of the story? Explain.

Grace Paley

A CONVERSATION WITH MY FATHER

My father is eighty-six years old and in bed. His heart, that bloody motor, is equally old and will not do certain jobs any more. It still floods his head with brainy light. But it won't let his legs carry the weight of his body around the house. Despite my metaphors, this muscle failure is not due to his old heart, he says, but to a potassium shortage. Sitting on one pillow, leaning on three, he offers last-minute advice and makes a request.

"I would like you to write a simple story just once more," he says, "the kind de Maupassant wrote, or Chekhov, the kind you used to write. Just recognizable people and then write down what happened to them next."

I say, "Yes, why not? That's possible." I want to please him, though I don't remember writing that way. I *would* like to try to tell such a story, if he means the kind that begins: "There was a woman . . . ." followed by plot, the absolute line between two points which I've always despised. Not for literary reasons, but because it takes all hope away. Everyone, real or invented, deserves the open destiny of life.

Finally I thought of a story that had been happening for a couple of years right across the street. I wrote it down, then read it aloud. "Pa," I said, "how about this? Do you mean something like this?"

Once in my time there was a woman and she had a son. They lived nicely, in a small apartment in Manhattan. This boy at about fifteen became a junkie, which is not unusual in our neighborhood. In order to maintain her close friendship with him, she became a junkie too. She said it was part of the youth culture, with which she felt very much at home. After a while, for a number of reasons, the boy gave it all up and left the city and his mother in disgust. Hopeless and alone, she grieved. We all visit her.

"O.K., Pa, that's it," I said, "An unadorned and miserable tale."

"But that's not what I mean," my father said. "You misunderstood me on purpose. You know there's a lot more to it. You know that. You left everything out. Turgenev wouldn't do that. Chekhov wouldn't do that. There are in fact Russian writers you never heard of, you don't have an inkling of, as good as anyone, who can write a plain ordinary story, who would not leave out what you have left out. I object not to facts but to people sitting in trees talking senselessly, voices from who knows where. . . ."

"Forget that one, Pa, what have I left out now? In this one?"

"Her looks, for instance."

"Oh. Quite handsome, I think. Yes."

"Her hair?"

"Dark, with heavy braids, as though she were a girl or a foreigner."

"What were her parents like, her stock? That she became such a person. It's interesting, you know."

"From out of town. Professional people. The first to be divorced in their county. How's that? Enough?" I asked.

"With you, it's all a joke," he said. "What about the boy's father? Why didn't you mention him? Who was he? Or was the boy born out of wedlock?"

"Yes," I said. "He was born out of wedlock."

"For Godsakes, doesn't anyone in your stories get married? Doesn't anyone have the time to run down to City Hall before they jump into bed?"

"No," I said. "In real life, yes. But in my stories, no."

"Why do you answer me like that?"

"Oh, Pa, this is a simple story about a smart woman who came to N.Y.C. full of interest love trust excitement very up to date, and about her son, what a hard time she had in this world. Married or not, it's of small consequence."

"It is of great consequence," he said.

"O.K.," I said.

"O.K. O.K. yourself," he said, "but listen. I believe you that she's good-looking, but I don't think she was so smart."

"That's true," I said. "Actually that's the trouble with stories. People start out fantastic. You think they're extraordinary, but it turns out as the work goes along, they're just average with a good education. Sometimes the other way around, the person's kind of dumb innocent, but he outwits you and you can't even think of an ending good enough."

"What do you do then?" he asked. He had been a doctor for a couple of decades and he's still interested in details, craft, technique.

"Well, you just have to let the story lie around till some agreement can be reached between you and the stubborn hero."

"Aren't you talking silly now?" he asked. "Start again," he said. "It so happens I'm not going out this evening. Tell the story again. See what you can do this time."

"O.K.," I said. "But it's not a five-minute job." Second attempt:

Once, across the street from us, there was a fine handsome woman, our neighbor. She had a son whom she loved because she'd known him since birth (in helpless chubby infancy, and in the wrestling, hugging ages, seven to ten, as well as earlier and later). This boy, when he fell into the fist of adolescence, became a junkie. He was not a hopeless one. He was in fact hopeful, an ideologue and successful converter. With his busy brilliance, he wrote persuasive articles for his high-school newspaper. Seeking a wider audience, using important connections, he drummed into Lower Manhattan newsstand distribution a periodical called *Oh! Golden Horse!*

In order to keep him from feeling guilty (because guilt is the stony heart of nine tenths of all clinically diagnosed cancers in America today, she said), and because she had always believed in giving bad habits room at home where one could keep an eye on them, she too became a junkie. Her kitchen was famous for a while—a center for intellectual addicts who knew what they were doing. A few felt artistic like Coleridge and others were scientific and revolutionary like Leary. Although she was often high herself, certain good mothering reflexes remained, and she saw to it that there was lots of orange juice around and honey and milk and vitamin pills. However, she never cooked anything but chili, and that no more than once a week. She explained, when we talked to her, seriously, with neighborly concern, that it was her part in the youth culture and she would rather be with the young, it was an honor, than with her own generation.

One week, while nodding through an Antonioni film, this boy was severely jabbed by the elbow of a stern and proselytizing girl, sitting beside him. She offered immediate apricots and nuts for his sugar level, spoke to him sharply, and took him home.

She had heard of him and his work and she herself published, edited, and wrote a competitive journal called *Man Does Live by Bread Alone*. In the organic heat of her continuous presence he could not help but become interested once more in his muscles, his arteries, and nerve connections. In fact he began to love them, treasure them, praise them with funny little songs in *Man Does Live*. . . .

> the fingers of my flesh transcend
> my transcendental soul
> the tightness in my shoulders end
> my teeth have made me whole

To the mouth of his head (that glory of will and determination) he brought hard apples, nuts, wheat germ, and soybean oil. He said to his old friends, From now on, I guess I'll keep my wits about me. I'm going on the natch. He said he was about to begin a spiritual deep-breathing journey. How about you too, Mom? he asked kindly.

His conversion was so radiant, splendid, that neighborhood kids his age began to say that he had never been a real addict at all, only a journalist along for the smell of the story. The mother tried several times to give up what had become without her son and his friends a lonely habit. This effort only brought it to supportable levels. The boy and his girl took their electronic mimeograph and moved to the bushy edge of another borough. They were very strict. They said they would not see her again until she had been off drugs for sixty days.

At home alone in the evening, weeping, the mother read and reread the seven issues of *Oh! Golden Horse!* They seemed to her as truthful as ever. We often crossed the street to visit and console. But if we mentioned any of our children who were at college or in the hospital or dropouts at home, she would cry out, My baby! My baby! and burst into terrible, face-scarring, time-consuming tears. The End.

First my father was silent, then he said, "Number One: You have a nice sense of humor. Number Two: I see you can't tell a plain story. So don't waste time." Then he said sadly, "Number Three: I suppose that means she was alone, she was left like that, his mother. Alone. Probably sick?"

I said, "Yes."

"Poor woman. Poor girl, to be born in a time of fools, to live among fools, The end. The end. You were right to put that down. The end."

I didn't want to argue, but I had to say, "Well, it is not necessarily the end, Pa."

"Yes," he said, "what a tragedy. The end of a person."

"No, Pa," I begged him. "It doesn't have to be. She's only about forty. She could be a hundred different things in this world as time goes on. A teacher or a social worker. An ex-junkie! Sometimes it's better than having a master's in education."

"Jokes," he said. "As a writer that's your main trouble. You don't want to recognize it. Tragedy! Plain tragedy! Historical tragedy! No hope. The end."

"Oh, Pa," I said. "She could change."

"In your own life, too, you have to look it in the face." He took a couple of nitroglycerin. "Turn to five," he said, pointing to the dial on the oxygen tank. He inserted the tubes into his nostrils and breathed deep. He closed his eyes and said, "No."

I had promised the family to always let him have the last word when arguing, but in this case I had a different responsibility. That woman lives across the street. She's my knowledge and my invention. I'm sorry for her. I'm not going to leave her there in that house crying. (Actually neither would Life, which unlike me has no pity.)

Therefore: She did change. Of course her son never came home again. But right now, she's the receptionist in a storefront community clinic in the East Village. Most of the customers are young people, some old friends. The head doctor has said to her, "If we only had three people in this clinic with your experiences. . . ."

"The doctor said that?" My father took the oxygen tubes out of his nostrils and said, "Jokes. Jokes again."

"No, Pa, it could really happen that way, it's a funny world nowadays."

"No," he said. "Truth first. She will slide back. A person must have character. She does not."

"No, Pa," I said. "That's it. She's got a job. Forget it. She's in that storefront working."

"How long will it be?" he asked. "Tragedy! You too. When will you look it in the face?"

QUESTIONS

1. The author has written: "Everyone, real or invented, deserves the open destiny of life." How is this observation reflected in the story?

2. Why does the father believe his daughter should write stories like Maupassant, Chekhov, and Turgenev? Who were these writers? How do they reflect the father's philosophy?

3. Why is "filling out" the story important to the father? Why does the daughter refuse to do more with the story? What does the struggle between father and daughter actually represent?

Edgar Allan Poe

THE MASQUE OF
THE RED DEATH

The "Red Death" has long devastated the country. No pestilence had ever been so fatal, or so hideous. Blood was its Avatar and its seal—the redness and the horror of blood. There were sharp pains, and sudden dizziness, and then profuse bleeding at the pores, with dissolution. The scarlet stains upon the body and especially upon the face of the victim, were the pest ban which shut him out from the aid and from the sympathy of his fellow-men. And the whole seizure, progress and termination of the disease, were the incidents of half an hour.

But the Prince Prospero was happy and dauntless and sagacious. When his dominions were half depopulated, he summoned to his presence a thousand hale and light-hearted friends from among the knights and dames of his court, and with these retired to the deep seclusion of one of his castellated abbeys. This was an extensive and magnificent structure, the creation of the prince's own eccentric yet august taste. A strong and lofty wall girdled it in. This wall had gates of iron. The courtiers, having entered, brought furnaces and massy hammers and welded the bolts. They resolved to leave means neither of ingress or egress to the sudden impulses of despair or of frenzy from within. The abbey was amply provisioned. With such precautions the courtiers might bid defiance to contagion. The external world could take care of itself. In the meantime it was folly to grieve, or to think. The prince had provided all the appliances of pleasure. There were buffoons, there were improvisatori, there were ballet-dancers, there were musicians, there was Beauty, there was wine. All these and security were within. Without was the "Red Death."

It was toward the close of the fifth or sixth month of his seclusion, and while the pestilence raged most furiously abroad, that the Prince Prospero entertained his thousand friends at a masked ball of the most unusual magnificence.

It was a voluptuous scene, that masquerade. But first let me tell of the rooms in which it was held. There were seven—an imperial suite. In many palaces, however, such suites form a long and straight vista, while the folding doors slide back nearly to the walls on either hand, so that the view of the whole extent is scarcely impeded. Here the case was very different; as might have been expected from the duke's love of the *bizarre*. The apartments were so irregularly disposed that the vision embraced but little more than one at a time. There was a sharp turn at every twenty or thirty yards, and at each turn a novel effect. To the right and left, in the middle of each wall, a tall and narrow Gothic window looked out upon a closed corridor which pursued the windings of the suite. These windows were of stained glass whose color varied in accordance with the prevailing hue of the decorations of the chamber into which it opened. That at the eastern extremity was hung, for example, in blue—and vividly blue were its windows. The second chamber was purple in its ornaments and tapestries, and here the panes were purple. The third was green throughout, and so were the casements. The fourth was furnished and lighted with orange—the fifth with white—the sixth with violet. The seventh apartment was closely shrouded in black velvet tapestries that hung all over the ceiling and down the walls, falling in heavy folds upon a carpet of the same material and hue. But in this chamber only, the color of the windows failed to correspond with the decorations. The panes here were scarlet—a deep blood color. Now in no one of the seven apartments was there any lamp or candelabrum, amid the profusion of golden ornaments that lay scattered to and fro or depended from the roof. There was no light of any kind emanating from lamp or candle within the suite of chambers. But in the corridors that followed the suite, there stood, opposite to each window, a heavy tripod, bearing a brazier of fire that projected its rays through the tinted glass and so glaringly illumined the room. And thus were produced a multitude of gaudy and fantastic appearances. But in the western or black chamber the effect of the fire-light that streamed upon the dark hangings through the blood-tinted panes, was ghastly in the extreme, and produced so wild a look upon the countenances of those who entered, that there were few of the company bold enough to set foot within its precincts at all.

It was in this apartment, also, that there stood against the western wall, a gigantic clock of ebony. Its pendulum swung to and fro with a dull, heavy, monotonous clang; and when the minute-hand made the circuit of the face, and the hour was to be stricken, there came from the brazen lungs of the clock a sound which was clear and loud and deep and exceedingly musical, but of so peculiar a note and emphasis that, at each lapse of an hour, the musicians of the orchestra were constrained to pause, momentarily, in their performance, to hearken to the sound; and thus the waltzers perforce ceased their evolutions; and there was a brief disconcert of the whole gay company; and, while the chimes of the clock yet rang, it was observed that the giddiest grew pale, and the more aged and sedate passed their hands over their brows as if in confused reverie or meditation. But when the echoes had fully ceased, a light laughter at once pervaded the assembly; the musicians looked at each other and smiled as if at their own nervousness and folly, and made whispering vows, each to the other, that the next chiming of the clock should produce in them no similar emotion; and then, after the lapse of sixty minutes, (which embrace three thousand and six hundred seconds of the Time that flies), there came yet another chiming of the clock, and then were the same disconcert and tremulousness and meditation as before.

But, in spite of these things, it was a gay and magnificent revel. The tastes of the duke were peculiar. He had a fine eye for colors and effects. He disregarded the *decora* of mere fashion. His plans were bold and fiery, and his conceptions glowed with barbaric lustre. There are some who would have thought him mad. His followers felt that he was not. It was necessary to hear and see and touch him to be *sure* that he was not.

He had directed, in great part, the moveable embellishments of the seven chambers, upon occasion of this great *fête;* and it was his own guiding taste which had given character to the masqueraders. Be sure they were grotesque. There were much glare and glitter and piquancy and phantasm—much of what has been since seen in "Hernani." There were arabesque figures with unsuited limbs and appointments. There were delirious fancies such as the madman fashions. There was much of the beautiful, much of the woman, much of the *bizarre,* something of the terrible, and not a little of that which might have excited disgust. To and fro in the seven chambers there stalked, in fact, a multitude of dreams. And these—the dreams—writhed in and about, taking hue from the rooms, and causing the wild music of the orchestra to seem as the echo of their steps. And, anon, there strikes the ebony clock which stands in the hall of the velvet. And then, for a moment, all is still, and all is silent save the voice of the clock. The dreams are stiff-frozen as they stand. But the echoes of the chime die away—they have endured but an instant—and a light, half-subdued laughter floats after them as they depart. And now again the music swells, and the dreams live, and writhe to and fro more merrily than ever, taking hue from the many-tinted windows through which stream the rays from the tripods. But to the chamber which lies most westwardly of the seven, there are now none of the maskers who venture; for the night is waning away; and there flows a ruddier light through the blood-colored panes; and the blackness of the sable drapery appals; and to him whose foot falls upon the sable carpet, there comes from the near clock of ebony a muffled peal more solemnly emphatic than any which reaches *their* ears who indulge in the more remote gaieties of the other apartments.

But these other apartments were densely crowded, and in them beat feverishly the heart of life. And the revel went whirlingly on, until at length there commenced the sounding of midnight upon the clock. And then the music ceased, as I have told; and the evolutions of the waltzers were quieted; and there was an uneasy cessation of all things as before. But now there were twelve strokes to be sounded by the bell of the clock; and thus it happened, perhaps, that more of thought crept, with more of time, into the meditations of the thoughtful among those who revelled. And thus, too, it happened, perhaps, that before the last echoes of the last chime had utterly sunk into silence, there were many individuals in the crowd who had found leisure to become aware of the presence of a masked figure which had arrested the attention of no single individual before. And the rumor of this new presence having spread itself whisperingly around, there arose at length from the whole company a buzz, or murmur, expressive of disapprobation and surprise—then, finally, of terror, of horror, and of disgust.

In an assembly of phantasms such as I have painted, it may well be supposed that no ordinary appearance could have excited such sensation. In truth the masquerade license of the night was nearly unlimited; but the figure in question had out-Heroded Herod, and gone beyond the bounds of even the prince's indefinite decorum. There are chords in the hearts of the most reckless which cannot be touched without emotion. Even with the utterly lost, to whom life and death are equally jests, there are matters of which no jest can be made. The whole company, indeed, seemed now deeply to feel that in the costume and bearing of the stranger neither wit nor propriety existed. The figure was tall and gaunt, and shrouded from head to foot in the habiliments of the grave. The mask which concealed the visage was made so nearly to resemble the countenance of a stiffened corpse that the closest scrutiny must have had difficulty in detecting the cheat. And yet all this might have been endured, if not approved, by the mad revellers around. But the mummer had gone so far as to assume the type of the Red Death. His vesture was dabbled in *blood*—and his broad brow, with all the features of the face, was besprinkled with the scarlet horror.

When the eyes of Prince Prospero fell upon this spectral image (which with a slow and solemn movement, as if more fully to sustain its *rôle*, stalked to and fro among the waltzers) he was seen to be convulsed, in the first moment with a strong shudder either of terror or distaste; but, in the next, his brow reddened with rage.

"Who dares?" he demanded hoarsely of the courtiers who stood near him—"who dares insult us with this blasphemous mockery? Seize him and unmask him—that we may know whom we have to hang at sunrise, from the battlements!"

It was in the eastern or blue chamber in which stood the Prince Prospero as he uttered these words. They rang throughout the seven rooms loudly and clearly—for the prince was a bold and robust man, and the music had become hushed at the waving of his hand.

It was in the blue room where stood the prince, with a group of pale courtiers by his side. At first, as he spoke, there was a slight rushing movement of this group in the direction of the intruder, who at the moment was also near at hand, and now, with deliberate and stately step, made closer approach to the speaker. But from a certain nameless awe with which the mad assumptions of the mummer had inspired the whole party, there were found none who put forth hand to seize him; so that, unimpeded, he passed within a yard of the prince's person; and, while the vast assembly, as if with one impulse, shrank from the centres of the rooms to the walls, he made his way uninterruptedly, but with the same solemn and measured step which had distinguished him from the first, through the blue chamber to the purple— through the purple to the green—through the green to the orange—through this again to the white—and even thence to the violet, ere a decided movement had been made to arrest him. It was then, however, that the Prince Prospero, maddening with rage and the shame of his own momentary cowardice, rushed hurriedly through the six chambers, while none followed him on account of a deadly terror that had seized upon all. He bore aloft a drawn dagger, and had approached, in rapid impetuosity, to within three or four feet of the retreating figure, when the latter, having attained the extremity of the velvet apartment, turned suddenly and confronted his pursuer. There was a sharp cry—and the dagger dropped gleaming upon the sable carpet, upon which, instantly afterwards fell prostrate in death the Prince Prospero. Then, summoning the wild courage of despair, a throng of the revellers at once threw themselves into the black apartment, and, seizing the mummer, whose tall figure stood erect and motionless within the shadow of the ebony clock, gasped in unutterable horror at finding the grave-cerements and corpselike mask which they handled with so violent a rudeness, untenanted by any tangible form.

And now was acknowledged the presence of the Red Death. He had come like a thief in the night. And one by one dropped the revellers in the blood-bedewed halls of their revel, and died each in the despairing posture of his fall. And the life of the ebony clock went out with that of the last of the gay. And the flames of the tripods expired. And Darkness and Decay and the Red Death held illimitable dominion over all.

QUESTIONS

1. How does Poe's syntax and word choice determine the diction of the story? How would you characterize the diction? How does it help create the atmosphere of the story?
2. The author spends a lot of time describing the physical details of the Prince's domain.

What do they suggest about the Prince's life-style and personality? What is the quality of his surroundings?

3. Poe describes the clock in great detail. What might the clock symbolize and foreshadow?

4. At what point in the story does the tone shift? How does the author create tension once the mummer in red reveals himself?

Leslie Marmon Silko

THE MAN TO SEND RAIN CLOUDS

ONE

They found him under a big cottonwood tree. His Levi jacket and pants were faded light blue so that he had been easy to find. The big cottonwood tree stood apart from a small grove of winterbare cottonwoods which grew in the wide, sandy arroyo. He had been dead for a day or more, and the sheep had wandered and scattered up and down the arroyo. Leon and his brother-in-law, Ken, gathered the sheep and left them in the pen at the sheep camp before they returned to the cottonwood tree. Leon waited under the tree while Ken drove the truck through the deep sand to the edge of the arroyo. He squinted up at the sun and unzipped his jacket—it sure was hot for this time of year. But high and northwest the blue mountains were still deep in snow. Ken came sliding down the low, crumbling bank about fifty yards down, and he was bringing the red blanket.

Before they wrapped the old man, Leon took a piece of string out of his pocket and tied a small gray feather in the old man's long white hair. Ken gave him the paint. Across the brown wrinkled forehead he drew a streak of white, and along the high cheekbones he drew a strip of blue paint. He paused and watched Ken throw pinches of corn meal and pollen into the wind that fluttered the small gray feather. Then Leon painted with yellow under the old man's broad nose; and finally, when he had painted green across the chin, he smiled.

"Send us rain clouds, Grandfather." They laid the bundle in the back of the pickup and covered it with a heavy tarp before they started back to the pueblo.

They turned off the highway onto the sandy pueblo road. Not long after they passed the store and post office they saw Father Paul's car coming toward them. When he recognized their faces he slowed his car and waved for them to stop. The young priest rolled down the car window.

"Did you find old Teofilo?" he asked loudly.

Leon stopped the truck. "Good morning, Father. We were just out to the sheep camp. Everything is O.K. now."

"Thank God for that. Teofilo is a very old man. You really shouldn't allow him to stay at the sheep camp alone."

"No, he won't do that any more now."

"Well, I'm glad you understand. I hope I'll be seeing you at Mass this week—we missed you last Sunday. See if you can get old Teofilo to come with you." The priest smiled and waved at them as they drove away.

TWO

Louise and Teresa were waiting. The table was set for lunch, and the coffee was boiling on the black iron stove. Leon looked at Louise and then at Teresa.

"We found him under a cottonwood tree in the big arroyo near sheep camp. I guess he sat down to rest in the shade and never got up again." Leon walked toward the old man's bed. The red plaid shawl had been shaken and spread carefully over the bed, and a new brown flannel shirt and pair of stiff new Levis were arranged neatly beside the pillow. Louise held the screen door open while Leon and Ken carried in the red blanket. He looked small and shriveled, and after they dressed him in the new shirt and pants he seemed more shrunken.

It was noontime now because the church bells rang the Angelus. They ate the beans with hot bread, and nobody said anything until after Teresa poured the coffee.

Ken stood up and put on his jacket. "I'll see about the gravediggers. Only the top layer of soil is frozen. I think it can be ready before dark."

Leon nodded his head and finished his coffee. After Ken had been gone for a while, the neighbors and clanspeople came quietly to embrace Teofilo's family and to leave food on the table because the gravediggers would come to eat when they were finished.

THREE

The sky in the west was full of pale-yellow light. Louise stood outside with her hands in the pockets of Leon's green army jacket that was too big for her. The funeral was over, and the old men had taken their candles and medicine bags and were gone. She waited until the body was laid into the pickup before she said anything to Leon. She touched his arm, and he noticed that her hands were still dusty from the corn meal that she had sprinkled around the old man. When she spoke, Leon could not hear her.

"What did you say? I didn't hear you."

"I said that I had been thinking about something."

"About what?"

"About the priest sprinkling holy water for Grandpa. So he won't be thirsty."

Leon stared at the new moccasins that Teofilo had made for the ceremonial dances in the summer. They were nearly hidden by the red blanket. It was getting colder, and the wind pushed gray dust down the narrow pueblo road. The sun was approaching the long mesa where it disappeared during the winter. Louise stood there shivering and watching his face. Then he zipped up his jacket and opened the truck door. "I'll see if he's there."

FOUR

Ken stopped the pickup at the church, and Leon got out; and then Ken drove down the hill to the graveyard where people were waiting. Leon knocked at the old carved door with its symbols of the Lamb. While he waited he looked up at the twin bells from the king of Spain with the last sunlight pouring around them in their tower.

The priest opened the door and smiled when he saw who it was. "Come in! What brings you here this evening?"

The priest walked toward the kitchen, and Leon stood with his cap in his hand, playing with the earflaps and examining the living room—the brown sofa, the green armchair, and the brass lamp that hung down from the ceiling by links of chain. The priest dragged a chair out of the kitchen and offered it to Leon.

"No thank you, Father. I only came to ask you if you would bring your holy water to the graveyard."

The priest turned away from Leon and looked out the window at the patio full of shadows and the dining-room windows of the nuns' cloister across the patio. The curtains were heavy, and the light from within faintly penetrated; it was impossible to see the nuns inside eating supper. "Why didn't you tell me he was dead? I could have brought the Last Rites anyway."

Leon smiled. "It wasn't necessary, Father."

The priest stared down at his scuffed brown loafers and the worn hem of his cassock. "For a Christian burial it was necessary."

His voice was distant, and Leon thought that his blue eyes looked tired.

"It's O.K. Father, we just want him to have plenty of water."

The priest sank down into the green chair and picked up a glossy missionary magazine. He turned the colored pages full of lepers and pagans without looking at them.

"You know I can't do that, Leon. There should have been the Last Rites and a funeral Mass at the very least."

Leon put on his green cap and pulled the flaps down over his ears. "It's getting late, Father. I've got to go."

When Leon opened the door Father Paul stood up and said, "Wait." He left the room and came back wearing a long brown overcoat. He followed Leon out the door and across the dim churchyard to the adobe steps in front of the church. They both stooped to fit through the low adobe entrance. And when they started down the hill to the graveyard only half of the sun was visible above the mesa.

The priest approached the grave slowly, wondering how they had managed to dig into the frozen ground; and then he remembered that this was New Mexico, and saw the pile of cold loose sand beside the hole. The people stood close to each other with little clouds of steam puffing from their faces. The priest looked at them and saw a pile of jackets, gloves, and scarves in the yellow, dry tumbleweeds that grew in the graveyard. He looked at the red blanket, not sure that Teofilo was so small, wondering if it wasn't some perverse Indian trick—something they did in March to ensure a good harvest—wondering if maybe old Teofilo was actually at sheep camp corralling the sheep for the night. But there he was, facing into a cold dry wind and squinting at the last sunlight, ready to bury a red wool blanket while the faces of his parishioners were in shadow with the last warmth of the sun on their backs.

His fingers were stiff, and it took him a long time to twist the lid off the holy water. Drops of water fell on the red blanket and soaked into dark icy spots. He sprinkled the grave and the water disappeared almost before it touched the dim, cold sand; it reminded him of something—he tried to remember what it was, because he thought if he could remember he might understand this. He sprinkled more water; he shook the container until it was empty, and the water fell through the light from sundown like August rain that fell while the sun was still shining, almost evaporating before it touched the wilted squash flowers.

The wind pulled at the priest's brown Franciscan robe and swirled away the corn meal and pollen that had been sprinkled on the blanket. They lowered the bundle into the ground, and they didn't bother to untie the stiff pieces of new rope that were tied around the ends of the blanket. The sun was gone, and over on the highway the eastbound lane was full of headlights. The priest walked away slowly. Leon watched him climb the hill, and when he had disappeared within the tall, thick walls, Leon turned to look up at the high blue mountains in the deep snow that reflected a faint red light from the west. He felt good because it was finished, and he was happy about the sprinkling of the holy water; now the old man could send them big thunderclouds for sure.

QUESTIONS

1. There appears to be quite a cross-cultural mixture of daily life and religious tradition. What elements in the story demonstrate this blend of cultures?

2. Although the entire story is rather short, it is divided into even shorter sections. How do these sections function in the story? How does this structural element contribute to the pacing and action of the story?

3. Leon and the priest have different perspectives concerning the use of the holy water for Teofilo's burial. Explain each one's view of the role of the holy water. How are their attitudes reconciled?

4. How can the conflict and resolution in this story be viewed as a metaphor for social and cultural life in America?

James Thurber

THE CATBIRD SEAT

Mr. Martin bought the pack of Camels on Monday night in the most crowded cigar store on Broadway. It was theater time and seven or eight men were buying cigarettes. The clerk didn't even glance at Mr. Martin, who put the pack in his overcoat pocket and went out. If any of the staff at F & S had seen him buy the cigarettes, they would have been astonished, for it was generally known that Mr. Martin did not smoke, and never had. No one saw him.

It was just a week to the day since Mr. Martin had decided to rub out Mrs. Ulgine Barrows. The term "rub out" pleased him because it suggested nothing more than the correction of an error—in this case an error of Mr. Fitweiler. Mr. Martin had spent each night of the past week working out his plan and examining it. As he walked home now he went over it again. For the hundredth time he resented the element of imprecision, the margin of guesswork that entered into the business. The project as he had worked it out was casual and bold, the risks were considerable. Something might go wrong anywhere along the line. And therein lay the cunning of his scheme. No one would ever see in it the cautious, painstaking hand of Erwin Martin, head of the filing department at F & S, of whom Mr. Fitweiler had once said, "Man is fallible but Martin isn't." No one would see his hand, that is, unless it were caught in the act.

Sitting in his apartment, drinking a glass of milk, Mr. Martin reviewed his case against Mrs. Ulgine Barrows, as he had every night for seven nights. He began at the beginning. Her quacking voice and braying laugh had first profaned the halls of F & S on March 7, 1941 (Mr. Martin had a head for dates). Old Roberts, the personnel chief, had introduced her as the newly appointed special adviser to the president of the firm, Mr. Fitweiler. The woman had appalled Mr. Martin instantly, but he hadn't shown it. He had given her his dry hand, a look of studious concentration, and a faint smile. "Well," she had said, looking at the papers on his desk, "are you lifting the oxcart out of the ditch?" As Mr. Martin recalled that moment, over his milk, he squirmed slightly. He must keep his mind on her crimes as a special adviser, not on her peccadillos as a personality. This he found difficult to do, in spite of entering an objection and sustaining it. The faults of the woman as a woman kept chattering on in his mind like an unruly witness. She had, for almost two years now, baited him. In the halls, in the elevator, even in his own office, into which she romped now and then like a circus horse, she was constantly shouting these silly questions at him. "Are you lifting the oxcart out of the ditch? Are you tearing up the pea patch? Are you hollering down the rain barrel? Are you scraping around the bottom of the pickle barrel? Are you sitting in the catbird seat?"

It was Joey Hart, one of Mr. Martin's two assistants, who had explained what the gibberish meant. "She must be a Dodger fan," he had said. "Red Barber announces the Dodger games over the radio and he uses those expressions—picked 'em up down South." Joey had gone on to explain one or two. "Tearing up the pea patch" meant going on a rampage; "sitting in the catbird seat" meant sitting pretty, like a batter with three balls and no strikes on him. Mr. Martin dismissed all this with an effort. It had been annoying, it had driven him near to distraction, but he was too solid a man to be moved to murder by anything so childish. It was fortunate, he reflected as he passed on to the important charges against Mrs. Barrows, that he had stood up under it so well. He had maintained always an outward appearance of polite tolerance. "Why, I even believe you like the woman," Miss Paird, his other assistant, had once said to him. He had simply smiled.

A gavel rapped in Mr. Martin's mind and the case proper was resumed. Mrs. Ulgine Barrows stood charged with willful, blatant, and persistent attempts to destroy the efficiency and system of F & S. It was competent, material, and relevant to review her advent and rise to power. Mr. Martin had got the story from Miss Paird, who seemed always able to find things out. According to her, Mrs. Barrows had met Mr. Fitweiler at a party, where she had rescued him from the embraces of a powerfully built drunken man who had mistaken the president of F & S for a famous retired Middle Western football coach. She had led him to a sofa and somehow worked upon him a monstrous magic. The aging gentleman had jumped to the conclusion there and then that this was a woman of singular attainments, equipped to bring out the best in him and in the firm. A week later he had introduced her into F & S as his special adviser. On that day confusion got its foot in the door. After Miss Tyson, Mr. Brundage, and Mr. Bartlett had been fired and Mr. Munson had taken his hat and stalked out, mailing his resignation later, old Roberts had been emboldened to speak to Mr. Fitweiler. He mentioned that Mr. Munson's department had been "a little disrupted" and hadn't they perhaps better resume the old system there? Mr. Fitweiler had said certainly not. He had the greatest faith in Mrs. Barrows' ideas. "They require a little seasoning, a little seasoning, is all," he had added. Mr. Roberts had given it up. Mr. Martin reviewed in detail all the changes wrought by Mrs. Barrows. She had begun chipping at the cornices of the firm's edifice and now she was swinging at the foundation stones with a pickaxe.

Mr. Martin came now, in his summing up, to the afternoon of Monday, November 2, 1942—just one week ago. On that day, at 3 P.M., Mrs. Barrows had bounced into his office. "Boo!" she had yelled. "Are you scraping around the bottom of the pickle barrel?" Mr. Martin had looked at her from under his green eyeshade, saying nothing. She had begun to wander about the office, taking it in with her great, popping eyes. "Do you really need *all* these filing cabinets?" she had demanded suddenly. Mr. Martin's heart had jumped. "Each of these files," he had said, keeping his voice even, "plays an indispensable part in the system of F & S." She had brayed at him, "Well, don't tear up the pea patch!" and gone to the door. From there she had bawled, "But you sure have got a lot of fine scrap in here!" Mr. Martin could no longer doubt that the finger was on his beloved department. Her pickaxe was on the upswing, poised for the first blow. It had not come yet; he had received no blue memo from the enchanted Mr. Fitweiler bearing nonsensical instructions deriving from the obscene woman. But there was no doubt in Mr. Martin's mind that one would be forthcoming. He must act quickly. Already a precious week had gone by. Mr. Martin stood up in his living room, still holding his milk glass. "Gentlemen of the jury," he said to himself, "I demand the death penalty for this horrible person."

The next day Mr. Martin followed his routine, as usual. He polished his glasses more often and once sharpened an already sharp pencil, but not even Miss Paird noticed.

Only once did he catch sight of his victim; she swept past him in the hall with a patronizing "Hi!" At five-thirty he walked home, as usual, and had a glass of milk, as usual. He had never drunk anything stronger in his life—unless you could count ginger ale. The late Sam Schlosser, the S of F & S, had praised Mr. Martin at a staff meeting several years before for his temperate habits. "Our most efficient worker neither drinks nor smokes," he had said. "The results speak for themselves." Mr. Fitweiler had sat by, nodding approval.

Mr. Martin was still thinking about that red-letter day as he walked over to the Schrafft's on Fifth Avenue near Forty-sixth Street. He got there, as he always did, at eight o'clock. He finished his dinner and the financial page of the *Sun* at a quarter to nine, as he always did. It was his custom after dinner to take a walk. This time he walked down Fifth Avenue at a casual pace. His gloved hands felt moist and warm, his forehead cold. He transferred the Camels from his overcoat to a jacket pocket. He wondered, as he did so, if they did not represent an unnecessary note of strain. Mrs. Barrows smoked only Luckies. It was his idea to puff a few puffs on a Camel (after the rubbing-out), stub it out in the ashtray holding her lipstick-stained Luckies, and thus drag a small red herring across the trail. Perhaps it was not a good idea. It would take time. He might even choke, too loudly.

Mr. Martin had never seen the house on West Twelfth Street where Mrs. Barrows lived, but he had a clear enough picture of it. Fortunately, she had bragged to everybody about her ducky first-floor apartment in the perfectly darling three-story red-brick. There would be no doorman or other attendants; just the tenants of the second and third floors. As he walked along, Mr. Martin realized that he would get there before nine-thirty. He had considered walking north on Fifth Avenue from Schrafft's to a point from which it would take him until ten o'clock to reach the house. At that hour people were less likely to be coming in or going out. But the procedure would have made an awkward loop in the straight thread of his casualness, and he had abandoned it. It was impossible to figure when people would be entering or leaving the house, anyway. There was a great risk at any hour. If he ran into anybody, he would simply have to place the rubbing-out of Ulgine Barrows in the inactive file forever. The same thing would hold true if there were someone in her apartment. In that case he would just say that he had been passing by, recognized her charming house, and thought to drop in.

It was eighteen minutes after nine when Mr. Martin turned into Twelfth Street. A man passed him, and a man and a woman, talking. There was no one within fifty paces when he came to the house, halfway down the block. He was up the steps and in the small vestibule in no time, pressing the bell under the card that said "Mrs. Ulgine Barrows." When the clicking in the lock started, he jumped forward against the door. He got inside fast, closing the door behind him. A bulb in a lantern hung from the hall ceiling on a chain seemed to give a monstrously bright light. There was nobody on the stair, which went up ahead of him along the left wall. A door opened down the hall in the wall on the right. He went toward it swiftly, on tiptoe.

"Well, for God's sake, look who's here!" bawled Mrs. Barrows, and her braying laugh rang out like the report of a shotgun. He pushed past her like a football tackle, bumping her. "Hey, quit shoving!" she said, closing the door behind them. They were in her living room, which seemed to Mr. Martin to be lighted by a hundred lamps.

"What's after you?" she said. "You're as jumpy as a goat." He found he was unable to speak. His heart was wheezing in his throat. "I—yes," he finally brought out. She was jabbering and laughing as she started to help him off with his coat. "No, no," he said. "I'll put it here." He took it off and put it on a chair near the door. "Your hat and gloves, too," she said. "You're in a lady's house." He put his hat on top of the coat. Mrs. Barrows seemed larger than he had thought. He kept his gloves on. "I was passing by," he said. "I recognized—is there anyone here?" She laughed louder than ever. "No," she said, "we're all alone. You're as white as a sheet, you funny man. Whatever *has* come over you? I'll mix you a toddy." She started toward a door across the room. "Scotch-and-soda be all right? But say, you don't drink, do you?" She turned and gave him her amused look. Mr. Martin pulled himself together. "Scotch-and-soda will be all right," he heard himself say. He could hear her laughing in the kitchen.

Mr. Martin looked quickly around the living room for the weapon. He had counted on finding one there. There were andirons and a poker and something in a corner that looked like an Indian club. None of them would do. It couldn't be that way. He began to pace around. He came to a desk. On it lay a metal paper knife with an ornate handle. Would it be sharp enough? He reached for it and knocked over a small brass jar. Stamps spilled out of it and it fell to the floor with a clatter. "Hey," Mrs. Barrows yelled from the kitchen, "are you tearing up the pea patch?" Mr. Martin gave a strange laugh. Picking up the knife, he tried its point against his left wrist. It was blunt. It wouldn't do.

When Mrs. Barrows reappeared, carrying two highballs, Mr. Martin, standing there with his gloves on, became acutely conscious of the fantasy he had wrought. Cigarettes in his pocket, a drink prepared for him—it was all too grossly improbable. It was more than that; it was impossible. Somewhere in the back of his mind a vague idea stirred, sprouted. "For heaven's sake, take off those gloves," said Mrs. Barrows. "I always wear them in the house," said Mr. Martin. The idea began to bloom, strange and wonderful. She put the glasses on a coffee table in front of a sofa and sat on the sofa. "Come over here, you odd little man," she said. Mr. Martin went over and sat beside her. It was difficult getting a cigarette out of the pack of Camels, but he managed it. She held a match for him, laughing. "Well," she said, handing him his drink, "this is perfectly marvelous. You with a drink and a cigarette."

Mr. Martin puffed, not too awkwardly, and took a gulp of the highball. "I drink and smoke all the time," he said. He clinked his glass against hers. "Here's nuts to that old windbag, Fitweiler," he said, and gulped again. The stuff tasted awful, but he made no grimace. "Really, Mr. Martin," she said, her voice and posture changing, "you are insulting our employer." Mrs. Barrows was now all special adviser to the president. "I am preparing a bomb," said Mr. Martin, "which will blow the old goat higher than hell." He had only had a little of the drink, which was not strong. It couldn't be that. "Do you take dope or something?" Mrs. Barrows asked coldly. "Heroin," said Mr. Martin. "I'll be coked to the gills when I bump that old buzzard off." "Mr. Martin!" she shouted, getting to her feet. "That will be all of that. You must go at once." Mr. Martin took another swallow of his drink. He tapped his cigarette out in the ashtray and put the pack of Camels on the coffee table. Then he got up. She stood glaring at him. He walked over and put on his hat and coat. "Not a word about this," he said, and laid an index finger against his lips. All Mrs. Barrows could bring out was "Really!" Mr.

Martin put his hand on the doorknob. "I'm sitting in the catbird seat," he said. He stuck his tongue out at her and left. Nobody saw him go.

Mr. Martin got to his apartment, walking, well before eleven. No one saw him go in. He had two glasses of milk after brushing his teeth, and he felt elated. It wasn't tipsiness, because he hadn't been tipsy. Anyway, the walk had worn off all effects of the whiskey. He got in bed and read a magazine for a while. He was asleep before midnight.

Mr. Martin got to the office at eight-thirty the next morning, as usual. At a quarter to nine, Ulgine Barrows, who had never before arrived at work before ten, swept into his office. "I'm reporting to Mr. Fitweiler now!" she shouted. "If he turns you over to the police, it's no more than you deserve!" Mr. Martin gave her a look of shocked surprise. "I beg your pardon?" he said. Mrs. Barrows snorted and bounced out of the room, leaving Miss Paird and Joey staring after her. "What's the matter with that old devil now?" asked Miss Paird. "I have no idea," said Mr. Martin, resuming his work. The other two looked at him and then at each other. Miss Paird got up and went out. She walked slowly past the closed door of Mr. Fitweiler's office. Mrs Barrows was yelling inside, but she was not braying. Miss Paird could not hear what the woman was saying. She went back to her desk.

Forty-five minutes later, Mrs. Barrows left the president's office and went into her own, shutting the door. It wasn't until half an hour later that Mr. Fitweiler sent for Mr. Martin. The head of the filing department, neat, quiet, attentive, stood in front of the old man's desk. Mr. Fitweiler was pale and nervous. He took his glasses off and twiddled them. He made a small, bruffing sound in his throat. "Martin," he said, "you have been with us more than twenty years." "Twenty-two, sir," said Mr. Martin. "In that time," pursued the president, "your work and your—uh—manner have been exemplary." "I trust so, sir," said Mr. Martin. "I have understood, Martin," said Mr. Fitweiler, "that you have never taken a drink or smoked." "That is correct, sir," said Mr. Martin. "Ah, yes." Mr. Fitweiler polished his glasses. "You may describe what you did after leaving the office yesterday, Martin," he said. Mr. Martin allowed less than a second for his bewildered pause. "Certainly, sir," he said. "I walked home. Then I went to Schrafft's for dinner. Afterward I walked home again. I went to bed early, sir, and read a magazine for a while. I was asleep before eleven." "Ah, yes," said Mr. Fitweiler again. He was silent for a moment, searching for the proper words to say to the head of the filing department. "Mrs. Barrows," he said finally, "Mrs. Barrows has worked hard, Martin, very hard. It grieves me to report that she has suffered a severe breakdown. It has taken the form of a persecution complex accompanied by distressing hallucinations." "I am very sorry, sir," said Mr. Martin. "Mrs. Barrows is under the delusion," continued Mr. Fitweiler, "that you visited her last evening and behaved yourself in an—uh—unseemly manner." He raised his hand to silence Mr. Martin's little pained outcry. "It is the nature of these psychological diseases," Mr. Fitweiler said, "to fix upon the least likely and most innocent party as the—uh—source of persecution. These matters are not for the lay mind to grasp, Martin. I've just had my psychiatrist, Dr. Fitch, on the phone. He would not, of course, commit himself, but I suggested to Mrs. Barrows, when she had completed her—uh—story to me this morning, that she visit Dr. Fitch, for I suspected a condition at once. She flew, I regret to say, into a rage, and demanded—uh—requested that I call you on the carpet. You may not know, Martin, but Mrs.

Barrows had planned a reorganization of your department—subject to my approval, of course, subject to my approval. This brought you, rather than anyone else, to her mind—but again that is a phenomenon for Dr. Fitch and not for us. So, Martin, I am afraid Mrs. Barrows' usefulness here is at an end." "I am dreadfully sorry, sir," said Mr. Martin.

It was at this point that the door to the office blew open with the suddenness of a gas-main explosion and Mrs. Barrows catapulted through it. "Is the little rat denying it?" she screamed. "He can't get away with that!" Mr. Martin got up and moved discreetly to a point beside Mr. Fitweiler's chair. "You drank and smoked at my apartment," she bawled at Mr. Martin, "and you know it! You called Mr. Fitweiler an old windbag and said you were going to blow him up when you got coked to the gills on your heroin!" She stopped yelling to catch her breath and a new glint came into her popping eyes. "If you weren't such a drab, ordinary little man," she said, "I'd think you'd planned it all. Sticking your tongue out, saying you were sitting in the catbird seat, because you thought no one would believe me when I told it! My God, it's really too perfect!" She brayed loudly and hysterically, and the fury was on her again. She glared at Mr. Fitweiler. "Can't you see how he has tricked us, you old fool? Can't you see his little game?" But Mr. Fitweiler had been surreptitiously pressing all the buttons under the top of his desk and employees of F & S began pouring into the room. "Stockton," said Mr. Fitweiler, "you and Fishbein will take Mrs. Barrows to her home. Mrs. Powell, you will go with them." Stockton, who had played a little football in high school, blocked Mrs. Barrows as she made for Mr. Martin. It took him and Fishbein together to force her out of the door into the hall, crowded with stenographers and office boys. She was still screaming imprecations at Mr. Martin, tangled and contradictory imprecations. The hubbub finally died out down the corridor.

"I regret that this has happened," said Mr. Fitweiler. "I shall ask you to dismiss it from your mind, Martin." "Yes, sir," said Mr. Martin, anticipating his chief's "That will be all" by moving to the door. "I will dismiss it." He went out and shut the door, and his step was light and quick in the hall. When he entered his department he had slowed down to his customary gait, and he walked quietly across the room to the W20 file, wearing a look of studious concentration.

QUESTIONS

1. When did you first realize the story was comic? What devices does Thurber use to maintain the comic aspect of the story?
2. What are some of the things about Mrs. Barrows that irritate Mr. Martin? How does Martin express this irritation?
3. Thurber is satirizing an aspect of modern life. What aspect is it? Which character or characters seem to embody it the most, and why?
4. The success of the story's conclusion resides in its irony. How does Thurber effectively create this irony?

Luisa Valenzuela

THE CENSORS

Poor Juan! One day they caught him with his guard down before he could even realize that what he had taken as a stroke of luck was really one of fate's dirty tricks. These things happen the minute you're careless, as one often is. Juancito let happiness—a feeling you can't trust—get the better of him when he received from a confidential source Mariana's new address in Paris and knew that she hadn't forgotten him. Without thinking twice, he sat down at his table and wrote her a letter. *The* letter that now keeps his mind off his job during the day and won't let him sleep at night (what had he scrawled, what had he put on that sheet of paper he sent to Mariana?).

Juan knows there won't be a problem with the letter's contents, that it's irreproachable, harmless. But what about the rest? He knows that they examine, sniff, feel, and read between the lines of each and every letter, and check its tiniest comma and most accidental stain. He knows that all letters pass from hand to hand and go through all sorts of tests in the huge censorship offices and that, in the end, very few continue on their way. Usually it takes months, even years, if there aren't any snags; all this time the freedom, maybe even the life, of both sender and receiver is in jeopardy. And that's why Juan's so troubled: thinking that something might happen to Mariana because of his letters. Of all people, Mariana, who must finally feel safe there where she always dreamt she'd live. But he knows that the *Censor's Secret Command* operates all over the world and cashes in on the discount in air fares; there's nothing to stop them from going as far as that hidden Paris neighborhood, kidnapping Mariana, and returning to their cozy homes, certain of having fulfilled their noble mission.

Well, you've got to beat them to the punch, do what everyone tries to do: sabotage the machinery, throw sand in its gears, get to the bottom of the problem so as to stop it.

This was Juan's sound plan when he, like many others, applied for a censor's job—not because he had a calling or needed a job: no, he applied simply to intercept his own letter, a consoling albeit unoriginal idea. He was hired immediately, for each day more and more censors are needed and no one would bother to check on his references.

Ulterior motives couldn't be overlooked by the *Censorship Division*, but they needn't be too strict with those who applied. They knew how hard it would be for the poor guys to find the letter they wanted and even if they did, what's a letter or two when the new censor would snap up so many others? That's how Juan managed to join the *Post Office's Censorship Division*, with a certain goal in mind.

The building had a festive air on the outside that contrasted with its inner staidness. Little by little, Juan was absorbed by his job, and he felt at peace since he was doing everything he could to get his letter for Mariana. He didn't even worry when, in his first month, he was sent to *Section K* where envelopes are very carefully screened for explosives.

It's true that on the third day, a fellow worker had his right hand blown off by a letter, but the division chief claimed it was sheer negligence on the victim's part. Juan and the other employees were allowed to go back to their work, though feeling less secure. After work, one of them tried to organize a strike to demand higher wages for unhealthy work, but Juan didn't join in; after thinking it over, he reported the man to his superiors and thus got promoted.

You don't form a habit by doing something once, he told himself as he left his boss's office. And when he was transferred to *Section F*, where letters are carefully checked for poison dust, he felt he had climbed a rung in the ladder.

By working hard, he quickly reached *Section E* where the job became more interesting, for he could now read and analyze the letters' contents. Here he could even hope to get hold of his letter, which, judging by the time that had elapsed, had gone through the other sections and was probably floating around in this one.

Soon his work became so absorbing that his noble mission blurred in his mind. Day after day he crossed out whole paragraphs in red ink, pitilessly chucking many letters into the censored basket. These were horrible days when he was shocked by the subtle and conniving ways employed by people to pass on subversive messages; his instincts were so sharp that he found behind a simple "the weather's unsettled" or "prices continue to soar" the wavering hand of someone secretly scheming to overthrow the Government.

His zeal brought him swift promotion. We don't know if this made him happy. Very few letters reached him in *Section B*—only a handful passed the other hurdles—so he read them over and over again, passed them under a magnifying glass, searched for microprint with an electronic microscope, and tuned his sense of smell so that he was beat by the time he made it home. He'd barely manage to warm up his soup, eat some fruit, and fall into bed, satisfied with having done his duty. Only his darling mother worried, but she couldn't get him back on the right track. She'd say, though it wasn't always true: Lola called, she's at the bar with the girls, they miss you, they're waiting for you. Or else she'd leave a bottle of red wine on the table. But Juan wouldn't overdo it: any distraction could make him lose his edge and the perfect censor had to be alert, keen, attentive, and sharp to nab cheats. He had a truly patriotic task, both self-denying and uplifting.

His basket for censored letters became the best fed as well as the most cunning basket in the whole *Censorship Division*. He was about to congratulate himself for having finally discovered his true mission, when his letter to *Mariana* reached his hands. Naturally, he censored it without regret. And just as naturally, he couldn't stop them from executing him the following morning, another victim of his devotion to his work.

Translated by David Unger

QUESTIONS

1. How can this story be viewed as a metaphor for the average individual's role in society?
2. The author says that Juan's idea to become a censor was an "unoriginal idea." What does this reflect about Juan's personality? What does it say about citizens in general?

3. The Censorship Department seems omnipotent and omnipresent. What agency or agencies could it symbolize in real life?
4. This story is marked by a scarcity of physical detail. Would precise detail have added to or distracted from the impact of the story?

John A. Williams

SON IN THE AFTERNOON

It was hot. I tend to be a bitch when it's hot. I goosed the little Ford over Sepulveda Boulevard toward Santa Monica until I got stuck in the traffic that pours from L.A. into the surrounding towns. I'd had a very lousy day at the studio.

I was—still am—a writer and this studio had hired me to check scripts and films with Negroes in them to make sure the Negro moviegoer wouldn't be offended. The signs were already clear that one day the whole of American industry would be racing pell-mell to get a Negro, showcase a spade. I was kind of a pioneer. I'm a *Negro* writer, you see. The day had been tough because of a couple of verbs—slink and walk. One of those Hollywood hippies had done a script calling for a Negro waiter to slink away from the table where a dinner party was glaring at him. I said the waiter should walk, not slink, because later on he becomes a hero. The Hollywood hippie, who understood it all because he had some colored friends, said that it was essential to the plot that the waiter slink. I said you don't slink one minute and become a hero the next; there has to be some consistency. The Negro actor I was standing up for said nothing either way. He had played Uncle Tom roles so long that he had become Uncle Tom. But the director agreed with me.

Anyway . . . hear me out now. I was on my way to Santa Monica to pick up my mother, Nora. It was a long haul for such a hot day. I had planned a quiet evening: a nice shower, fresh clothes, and then I would have dinner at the Watkins and talk with some of the musicians on the scene for a quick taste before they cut to their gigs. After, I was going to the Pigalle down on Figueroa and catch Earl Grant at the organ, and still later, if nothing exciting happened, I'd pick up Scottie and make it to the Lighthouse on the Beach or to the Strollers and listen to some of the white boys play. I liked the long drive, especially while listening to Sleepy Stein's show on the radio. Later, much later of course, it would be home, back to Watts.

So you see, this picking up Nora was a little inconvenient. My mother was a maid for the Couchmans. Ronald Couchman was an architect, a good one I understood from Nora who has a fine sense for this sort of thing; you don't work in some hundred-odd houses during your life without getting some idea of the way a house should be laid out. Couchman's wife, Kay, was a playgirl who drove a white Jaguar from one party to another. My mother didn't like her too much; she didn't seem to care much for her son,

Ronald, junior. There's something wrong with a parent who can't really love her own child, Nora thought. The Couchmans lived in a real fine residential section, of course. A number of actors lived nearby, character actors, not really big stars.

Somehow it is very funny. I mean that the maids and butlers knew everything about these people, and these people knew nothing at all about the help. Through Nora and her friends I knew who was laying whose wife; who had money and who *really* had money; I knew about the wild parties hours before the police, and who smoked marijuana, when, and where they got it.

To get to Couchman's driveway I had to go three blocks up one side of a palm-planted center strip and back down the other. The driveway bent gently, then swept back out of sight of the main road. The house, sheltered by slim palms, looked like a transplanted New England Colonial. I parked and walked to the kitchen door, skirting the growling Great Dane who was tied to a tree. That was the route to the kitchen door.

I don't like kitchen doors. Entering people's houses by them, I mean. I'd done this thing most of my life when I called at places where Nora worked to pick up the patched or worn sheets or the half-eaten roasts, the battered, tarnished silver—the fringe benefits of a housemaid. As a teen-ager I'd told Nora I was through with that crap; I was not going through anyone's kitchen door. She only laughed and said I'd learn. One day soon after, I called for her and without knocking walked right through the front door of this house and right on through the living room. I was almost out of the room when I saw feet behind the couch. I leaned over and there was Mr. Jorgensen and his wife making out like crazy. I guess they thought Nora had gone and it must have hit them sort of suddenly and they went at it like the hell-bomb was due to drop any minute. I've been that way too, mostly in the spring. Of course, when Mr. Jorgensen looked over his shoulder and saw me, you know what happened. I was thrown out and Nora right behind me. It was the middle of winter, the old man was sick and the coal bill three months overdue. Nora was right about those kitchen doors: I learned.

My mother saw me before I could ring the bell. She opened the door. "Hello," she said. She was breathing hard, like she'd been running or something. "Come in and sit down. I don't know *where* that Kay is. Little Ronald is sick and she's probably out gettin' drunk again." She left me then and trotted back through the house, I guess to be with Ronnie. I hated the combination of her white nylon uniform, her dark brown face and the wide streaks of gray in her hair. Nora had married this guy from Texas a few years after the old man had died. He was all right. He made out okay. Nora didn't have to work, but she just couldn't be still; she always had to be doing something. I suggested she quit work, but I had as much luck as her husband. I used to tease her about liking to be around those white folks. It would have been good for her to take an extended trip around the country visiting my brothers and sisters. Once she got to Philadelphia, she could go right out to the cemetery and sit awhile with the old man.

I walked through the Couchman home. I liked the library. I thought if I knew Couchman I'd like him. The room made me feel like that. I left it and went into the big living room. You could tell that Couchman had let his wife do that. Everything in it was fast, dart-like, with no sense of ease. But on the walls were several of Couchman's conceptions of buildings and homes. I guess he was a disciple of Wright. My mother

walked rapidly through the room without looking at me and said, "Just be patient, Wendell. She should be here real soon."

"Yeah," I said, "with a snootful." I had turned back to the drawings when Ronnie scampered into the room, his face twisted with rage.

"Nora!" he tried to roar, perhaps the way he'd seen the parents of some of his friends roar at their maids. I'm quite sure Kay didn't shout at Nora, and I don't think Couchman would. But then no one shouts at Nora. "Nora, you come right back here this minute!" the little bastard shouted and stamped and pointed to a spot on the floor where Nora was supposed to come to roost. I have a nasty temper. Sometimes it lies dormant for ages and at other times, like when the weather is hot and nothing seems to be going right, it's bubbling and ready to explode. "Don't talk to *my* mother like that, you little—!" I said sharply, breaking off just before I cursed. I wanted him to be large enough for me to strike. "How'd you like for me to talk to *your* mother like that?"

The nine-year-old looked up at me in surprise and confusion. He hadn't expected me to say anything. I was just another piece of furniture. Tears rose in his eyes and spilled out onto his pale cheeks. He put his hands behind him, twisted them. He moved backwards, away from me. He looked at my mother with a "Nora, come help me" look. And sure enough, there was Nora, speeding back across the room, gathering the kid in her arms, tucking his robe together. I was too angry to feel hatred for myself.

Ronnie was the Couchman's only kid. Nora loved him. I suppose that was the trouble. Couchman was gone ten, twelve hours a day. Kay didn't stay around the house any longer than she had to. So Ronnie had only my mother. I think kids should have someone to love, and Nora wasn't a bad sort. But somehow when the six of us, her own children, were growing up we never had her. She was gone, out scuffling to get those crumbs to put into our mouths and shoes for our feet and praying for something to happen so that all the space in between would be taken care of. Nora's affection for us took the form of rushing out into the morning's five o'clock blackness to wake some silly bitch and get her coffee; took form in her trudging five miles home every night instead of taking the streetcar to save money to buy tablets for us, to use at school, we said. But the truth was that all of us liked to draw and we went through a writing tablet in a couple of hours every day. Can you imagine? There's not a goddamn artist among us. We never had the physical affection, the pat on the head, the quick, smiling kiss, the "gimmee a hug" routine. All of this Ronnie was getting.

Now he buried his little blond head in Nora's breast and sobbed. "There, there now," Nora said. "Don't you cry, Ronnie. Ol' Wendell is just jealous, and he hasn't much sense either. He didn't mean nuthin'."

I left the room. Nora had hit it of course, hit it and passed on. I looked back. It didn't look so incongruous, the white and black together, I mean. Ronnie was still sobbing. His head bobbed gently on Nora's shoulder. The only time I ever got that close to her was when she trapped me with a bearhug so she could whale the daylights out of me after I put a snowball through Mrs. Grant's window. I walked outside and lit a cigarette. When Ronnie was in the hospital the month before, Nora got me to run her way over to Hollywood every night to see him. I didn't like that worth a damn. All right, I'll admit it: it did upset me. All that affection I didn't get nor my brothers and sisters going to that little white boy who, without a doubt, when away from her called her the names he'd learned from adults. Can you imagine a nine-year-old kid calling Nora a "girl," "our girl?" I spat at the Great Dane. He snarled and then I bounced a rock off his fanny. "Lay down, you bastard," I muttered. It was a good thing he was tied up.

I heard the low cough of the Jaguar slapping against the road. The car was throttled down, and with a muted roar it swung into the driveway. The woman aimed it for me. I was evil enough not to move. I was tired of playing with these people. At the last moment, grinning, she swung the wheel over and braked. She bounded out of the car like a tennis player vaulting over a net.

"Hi," she said, tugging at her shorts.

"Hello."

"You're Nora's boy?"

"I'm Nora's son." Hell, I was as old as she was; besides, I can't stand "boy."

"Nora tells us you're working in Hollywood. Like it?"

"It's all right."

"You must be pretty talented."

We stood looking at each other while the dog whined for her attention. Kay had a nice body and it was well tanned. She was high, boy, was she high. Looking at her, I could feel myself going into my sexy bastard routine; sometimes I can swing it great. Maybe it all had to do with the business inside. Kay took off her sunglasses and took a good look at me. "Do you have a cigarette?"

I gave her one and lit it. "Nice tan," I said. Most white people I know think it's a great big deal if a Negro compliments them on their tans. It's a large laugh. You have all this volleyball about color and come summer you can't hold the white folks back from the beaches, anyplace where they can get some sun. And of course the blacker they get, the more pleased they are. Crazy. If there is ever a Negro revolt, it will come during the summer and Negroes will descend upon the beaches around the nation and paralyze the country. You can't conceal cattle prods and bombs and pistols and police dogs when you're showing your birthday suit to the sun.

"You like it?" she asked. She was pleased. She placed her arm next to mine. "Almost the same color," she said.

"Ronnie isn't feeling well," I said.

"Oh, the poor kid. I'm so glad we have Nora. She's such a charm. I'll run right in and look at him. Do have a drink in the bar. Fix me one too, will you?" Kay skipped inside and I went to the bar and poured out two strong drinks. I made hers stronger than mine. She was back soon. "Nora was trying to put him to sleep and she made me stay out." She giggled. She quickly tossed off her drink. "Another, please?" While I was fixing her drink she was saying how amazing it was for Nora to have such a talented son. What she was really saying was that it was amazing for a servant to have a son who was not also a servant. "Anything can happen in a democracy," I said. "Servants' sons drink with madames and so on."

"Oh, Nora isn't a servant," Kay said. "She's part of the family."

Yeah, I thought. Where and how many times had I heard *that* before?

In the ensuing silence, she started to admire her tan again. "You think it's pretty good, do you? You don't know how hard I worked to get it." I moved close to her and

held her arm. I placed my other arm around her. She pretended not to see or feel it, but she wasn't trying to get away either. In fact she was pressing closer and the register in my brain that tells me at the precise moment when I'm in, went off. Kay was very high. I put both arms around her and she put both hers around me. When I kissed her, she responded completely.

"Mom!"

"Ronnie, come back to bed," I heard Nora shout from the other room. We could hear Ronnie running over the rug in the outer room. Kay tried to get away from me, push me to one side, because we could tell that Ronnie knew where to look for his Mom: he was running right for the bar, where we were. "Oh, please," she said, "don't let him see us." I wouldn't let her push me away. "Stop!" she hissed. "He'll *see* us!" We stopped struggling just for an instant, and we listened to the echoes of the word *see*. She gritted her teeth and renewed her efforts to get away.

Me? I had the scene laid right out. The kid breaks into the room, see, and sees his mother in this real wriggly clinch with this colored guy who's just shouted at him, see, and no matter how his mother explains it away, the kid has the image—the colored guy and his mother—for the rest of his life, see?

That's the way it happened. The kid's mother hissed under her breath, *"You're crazy!"* and she looked at me as though she were seeing me or something about me for the very first time. I'd released her as soon as Ronnie, romping into the bar, saw us and came to a full, open-mouthed halt. Kay went to him. He looked first at me, then at his mother. Kay turned to me, but she couldn't speak.

Outside in the living room my mother called, "Wendell, where are you? We can go now."

I started to move past Kay and Ronnie. I felt many things, but I made myself think mostly, *There you little bastard, there.*

My mother thrust her face inside the door and said, "Good-bye, Mrs. Couchman. See you tomorrow. 'Bye, Ronnie."

"Yes," Kay said, sort of stunned. "Tomorrow." She was reaching for Ronnie's hand as we left, but the kid was slapping her hand away. I hurried quickly after Nora, hating the long drive back to Watts.

QUESTIONS

1. What kind of man is the narrator? What different emotions does he display during the story? How do his race and race relations affect his point of view?
2. What does the narrator feel about Ronnie? What injustice exists in the way the narrator's mother treats her own son in comparison to the way she treats Ronnie?
3. What is the effect of telling the story in the first person? How would it have been different had it been told in the third person or from the viewpoint of one of the other characters?
4. At the end of the story, the narrator says "I felt many things." What might some of these things be?

Richard Wright

THE MAN WHO WAS ALMOST A MAN

Dave struck out across the fields, looking homeward through paling light. Whut's the use talkin wid 'em niggers in the field? Anyhow, his mother was putting supper on the table. Them niggers can't understan nothing. One of these days he was going to get a gun and practice shooting, then they couldn't talk to him as though he were a little boy. He slowed, looking at the ground. Shucks, Ah ain scareda them even ef they are biggern me! Aw, ah know whut Ahma do. Ahm going by ol Joe's sto n git that Sears Roebuck catlog n look at them guns. Mebbe Ma will lemme buy one when she gits mah pay from ol man Hawkins. Ahma beg her t gimme some money. Ahm ol ernough to hava gun. Ahm seventeen. Almost a man. He strode, feeling his long loose-jointed limbs. Shucks, a man oughta hava little gun aftah he done worked hard all day.

He came in sight of Joe's store. A yellow lantern glowed on the front porch. He mounted steps and went through the screen door, hearing it bang behind him. There was a strong smell of coal oil and mackerel fish. He felt very confident until he saw fat Joe walk in through the rear door, then his courage began to ooze.

"Howdy, Dave! Whutcha want?"

"How yuh, Mistah Joe? Aw, Ah don wanna buy nothing. Ah jus wanted t see ef yuhd lemme look at tha catlog erwhile."

"Sure! You wanna see it here?"

"Nawsuh, Ah wans t take it home wid me. Ah'll bring it back termorrow when Ah come in from the fiels."

"You plannin on buying something?"

"Yessuh."

"Your ma lettin you have your own money now?"

"Shucks. Mistah Joe, Ahm gittin t be a man like anybody else!"

Joe laughed and wiped his greasy white face with a red bandanna.

"Whut you plannin on buyin?"

Dave looked at the floor, scratched his head, scratched his thigh, and smiled. Then he looked up shyly.

"Ah'll tell yuh, Mistah Joe, ef yuh promise yuh won't tell."

"I promise."

"Waal, Ahma buy a gun."

"A gun? Whut you want with a gun?"

"Ah wanna keep it."

"You ain't nothing but a boy. You don't need a gun."

"Aw, lemme have the catlog, Mistah Joe. Ah'll bring it back."

Joe walked through the rear door. Dave was elated. He looked around at barrels of sugar and flour. He heard Joe coming back. He craned his neck to see if he was bringing the book. Yeah, he's got it. Gawddog, he's got it!

"Here, but be sure you bring it back. It's the only one I got."

"Sho, Mistah Joe."

"Say, if you wanna buy a gun, why don't you buy one from me? I gotta gun to sell."

"Will it shoot?"

"Sure it'll shoot."

"Whut kind is it?"

"Oh, it's kinda old . . . a left-handed Wheeler. A pistol. A big one."

"Is it got bullets in it?"

"It's loaded."

"Kin Ah see it?"

"Where's your money?"

"Whut yuh wan fer it?"

"I'll let you have it for two dollars."

"Just two dollahs? Shucks, Ah could buy tha when Ah git mah pay."

"I'll have it here when you want it."

"Awright, suh. Ah be in fer it."

He went through the door, hearing it slam again behind him. Ahma git some money from Ma n buy me a gun! Only two dollahs! He tucked the thick catalogue under his arm and hurried.

"Where yuh been, boy?" His mother held a steaming dish of black-eyed peas.

"Aw, Ma, ah jus stopped down the road to talk wid the boys."

"Yuh know bettah t keep suppah waitin."

He sat down, resting the catalogue on the edge of the table.

"Yuh git up from there and git to the well n wash yosef! Ah ain feedin no hogs in mah house!"

She grabbed his shoulder and pushed him. He stumbled out of the room, then came back to get the catalogue.

"Whut this?"

"Aw, Ma, it's jusa catlog."

"Who yuh git it from?"

"From Joe, down at the sto."

"Waal, thas good. We kin use it in the outhouse."

"Naw, Ma." He grabbed for it. "Gimme ma catlog, Ma."

She held onto it and glared at him.

"Quit hollerin at me! Whut's wrong wid yuh? Yuh crazy?"

"But Ma, please. It ain mine! It's Joe's! He tol me to bring it back t im termorrow."

She gave up the book. He stumbled down the back steps, hugging the thick book under his arm. When he had splashed water on his face and hands, he groped back to the kitchen and fumbled in a corner for the towel. He bumped into a chair; it clattered to the floor. The catalogue sprawled at his feet. When he had dried his eyes he snatched up the book and held it again under his arm. His mother stood watching him.

"Now, ef yuh gonna act a fool over that ol book, Ah'll take it n burn it up."

"Naw, Ma, please."

"Waal, set down n be still!"

He sat down and drew the oil lamp close. He thumbed page after page, unaware of the food his mother set on the table. His father came in. Then his small brother.

"Whutcha got there, Dave?" his father asked.

"Jusa catlog," he answered, not looking up.

"Yeah, here they is!" His eyes glowed at blue-and-black revolvers. He glanced up, feeling sudden guilt. His father was watching him. He eased the book under the table and rested it on his knees. After the blessing was asked, he ate. He scooped up peas and swallowed fat meat without chewing. Buttermilk helped to wash it down. He did not want to mention money before his father. He would do much better by cornering his mother when she was alone. He looked at his father uneasily out of the edge of his eye.

"Boy, how come yuh don quit foolin wid tha book n eat yo suppah?"

"Yessuh."

"How you n old man Hawkins gitten erlong?"

"Suh?"

"Can't yuh hear? Why don yuh lissen? As ast yu how wuz yuh n ol man Hawkins gittin erlong?"

"Oh, swell, Pa. Ah plows mo lan than anybody over there."

"Waal, yuh oughta keep yo mind on whut yuh doin."

"Yessuh."

He poured his plate full of molasses and sopped it up slowly with a chunk of cornbread. When his father and brother had left the kitchen, he still sat and looked again at the guns in the catalogue, longing to muster courage enough to present his case to his mother. Lawd, ef Ah only had tha pretty one! He could almost feel the slickness of the weapon with his fingers. If he had a gun like that he would polish it and keep it shining so it would never rust. N Ah'd keep it loaded, by Gawd!

"Ma?" His voice was hesitant.

"Hunh?"

"Ol man Hawkins give yuh mah money yit?"

"Yeah, but ain no usa yuh thinking bout throwin nona it erway. Ahme keeping tha money sos yuh kin have cloes t go to school this winter."

He rose and went to her side with the open catalogue in his palms. She was washing dishes, her head bent low over a pan. Shyly he raised the book. When he spoke, his voice was husky, faint.

"Ma, Gawd knows Ah wans one of these."

"One of whut?" she asked, not raising her eyes.

"One of these," he said again, not daring even to point. She glanced up at the page, then at him with wide eyes.

"Nigger, is yuh gone plumb crazy?"

"Aw, Ma—"

"Git outta here! Don yuh talk to me bout no gun! Yuh a fool!"

"Ma, Ah kin buy one fer two dollahs."

"Not ef Ah knows it, yuh ain!"

"But yuh promised me one—"

"Ah don care whut Ah promised! Yuh ain nothing but a boy yit!"

"Ma, ef yuh lemme buy one Ah'll *never* ast yuh fer nothing no mo."

"Ah tol yuh t git outta here! Yuh ain gonna toucha penny of tha money fer no gun!

Thas how come Ah has Mistah Hawkins t pay yo wages t me, cause Ah knows yuh ain got no sense."

"But, Ma, we needa gun. Pa ain got no gun. We needa gun in the house. Yuh kin never tell whut might happen."

"Now don yuh try to maka fool outta me, boy! Ef we did hava gun, yuh wouldn't have it!"

He laid the catalogue down and slipped his arm around her waist.

"Aw, Ma, Ah done worked hard alla summer n ain ast yuh fer nothin, is Ah, now?"

"Thas whut yuh spose t do!"

"But Ma, Ah wans a gun. Yuh kin lemme have two dollahs outta mah money. Please, Ma. I kin give it to Pa . . . Please, Ma! Ah loves yuh, Ma."

When she spoke her voice came soft and low.

"Whut yu wan wida gun, Dave? Yuh don need no gun. Yuh'll git in trouble. N ef yo pa jus thought Ah let yuh have money to buy a gun he'd hava fit."

"I'll hide it, Ma. It ain but two dollahs."

"Lawd, chil, whut's wrong wid yuh?"

"Ain nothin wrong, Ma. Ahm almos a man now. Ah wans a gun."

"Who gonna sell yuh a gun?"

"Ol Joe at the sto."

"N it don cos but two dollahs?"

"Thas all, Ma. Jus two dollahs. Please, Ma."

She was stacking the plates away; her hands moved slowly, reflectively. Dave kept an anxious silence. Finally, she turned to him.

"Ah'll let yuh git tha gun ef yuh promise me one thing."

"Whut's tha, Ma?"

"Yuh bring it straight back t me, yuh hear? It be fer Pa."

"Yessum! Lemme go now, Ma."

She stooped, turned slightly to one side, raised the hem of her dress, rolled down the top of her stocking, and came up with a slender wad of bills.

"Here," she said. "Lawd knows yuh don need no gun. But yer pa does. Yuh bring it right back to me, yuh hear? Ahma put it up. Now ef yuh don, Ahma have yuh pa lick yuh so hard yuh won fergit it."

"Yessum."

He took the money, ran down the steps, and across the yard.

"Dave! Yuuuuuh Daaaaave!"

He heard, but he was not going to stop now. "Naw, Lawd!"

The first movement he made the following morning was to reach under his pillow for the gun. In the gray light of dawn he held it loosely, feeling a sense of power. Could kill a man with a gun like this. Kill anybody, black or white. And if he were holding his gun in his hand, nobody could run over him; they would have to respect him. It was a big gun, with a long barrel and a heavy handle. He raised and lowered it in his hand, marveling at its weight.

He had not come straight home with it as his mother had asked; instead he had stayed out in the fields, holding the weapon in his hand, aiming it now and then at some imaginary foe. But he had not fired it; he had been afraid that his father might hear. Also he was not sure he knew how to fire it.

To avoid surrendering the pistol he had not come into the house until he knew that they were all asleep. When his mother had tiptoed to his bedside late that night and demanded the gun, he had first played possum; then he had told her that the gun was hidden outdoors, that he would bring it to her in the morning. Now he lay turning it slowly in his hands. He broke it, took out the cartridges, felt them, and then put them back.

He slid out of bed, got a long strip of old flannel from a trunk, wrapped the gun in it, and tied it to his naked thigh while it was still loaded. He did not go in to breakfast. Even though it was not yet daylight, he started for Jim Hawkins' plantation. Just as the sun was rising he reached the barns where the mules and plows were kept.

"Hey! That you, Dave?"

He turned. Jim Hawkins stood eying him suspiciously.

"What're yuh doing here so early?"

"Ah didn't know Ah wuz gittin up so early, Mistah Hawkins. Ah wuz fixin t hitch up ol Jenny n take her t the fiels."

"Good. Since you're so early, how about plowing that stretch down by the woods?"

"Suits me, Mistah Hawkins."

"O.K. Go to it!"

He hitched Jenny to a plow and started across the fields. Hot dog! This was just what he wanted. If he could get down by the woods, he could shoot his gun and nobody would hear. He walked behind the plow, hearing the traces creaking, feeling the gun tied tight to his thigh.

When he reached the woods, he plowed two whole rows before he decided to take out the gun. Finally, he stopped, looked in all directions, then untied the gun and held it in his hand. He turned to the mule and smiled.

"Know whut this is, Jenny? Naw, yuh wouldn know! Yuhs jusa ol mule! Anyhow, this is a gun, n it kin shoot, by Gawd!"

He held the gun at arm's length. Whut t hell, Ahma shoot this thing! He looked at Jenny again.

"Lissen here, Jenny! When Ah pull this ol trigger, Ah don wan yuh t run n acka fool now!"

Jenny stood with head down, her short ears pricked straight. Dave walked off about twenty feet, held the gun far out from him at arm's length, and turned his head. Hell, he told himself, Ah ain afraid. The gun felt loose in his fingers; he waved it wildly for a moment. Then he shut his eyes and tightened his forefinger. Bloom! A report half deafened him and he thought his right hand was torn from his arm. He heard Jenny whinnying and galloping over the field, and he found himself on his knees, squeezing his fingers hard between his legs. His hand was numb; he jammed it into his mouth, trying to warm it, trying to stop the pain. The gun lay at his feet. He did not quite know what had happened. He stood up and stared at the gun as though it were a living thing. He gritted his teeth and kicked the gun. Yuh almos broke mah arm! He turned to look for Jenny; she was far over the fields, tossing her head and kicking wildly.

"Hol on there, ol mule!"

When he caught up with her she stood trembling, walling her big white eyes at him. The plow was far away; the traces had broken. Then Dave stopped short, looking, not believing. Jenny was bleeding. Her left side was red and wet with blood. He went closer. Lawd, have mercy! Wondah did Ah shoot this mule? He grabbed for Jenny's mane. She flinched, snorted, whirled, tossing her head.

"Hol on now! Hol on."

Then he saw the hole in Jenny's side, right between the ribs. It was round, wet, red. A crimson stream streaked down the front leg, flowing fast, Good Gawd! Ah wuzn't shootin at tha mule. He felt panic. He knew he had to stop that blood, or Jenny would bleed to death. He had never seen so much blood in all his life. He chased the mule for half a mile, trying to catch her. Finally she stopped, breathing hard, stumpy tail half arched. He caught her mane and led her back to where the plow and gun lay. Then he stooped and grabbed handfuls of damp black earth and tried to plug the bullet hole. Jenny shuddered, whinnied, and broke from him.

"Hol on! Hol on now!"

He tried to plug it again, but blood came anyhow. His fingers were hot and sticky. He rubbed dirt into his palms, trying to dry them. Then again he attempted to plug the bullet hole, but Jenny shied away, kicking her heels high. He stood helpless. He had to do something. He ran at Jenny; she dodged him. He watched a red stream of blood flow down Jenny's leg and form a bright pool at her feet.

"Jenny . . . Jenny," he called weakly.

His lips trembled. She's bleeding t death! He looked in the direction of home, wanting to go back, wanting to get help. But he saw the pistol lying in the damp black clay. He had a queer feeling that if he only did something, this would not be; Jenny would not be there bleeding to death.

When he went to her this time, she did not move. She stood with sleepy, dreamy eyes; and when he touched her she gave a low-pitched whinny and knelt to the ground, her front knees slopping in blood.

"Jenny . . . Jenny . . ." he whispered.

For a long time she held her neck erect; then her head sank, slowly. Her ribs swelled with a mighty heave and she went over.

Dave's stomach felt empty, very empty. He picked up the gun and held it gingerly between his thumb and forefinger. He buried it at the foot of a tree. He took a stick and tried to cover the pool of blood with dirt—but what was the use? There was Jenny lying with her mouth open and her eyes walled and glassy. He could not tell Jim Hawkins he had shot his mule. But he had to tell something. Yeah, Ah'll tell en Jenny started gittin wil n fell on the joint of the plow. . . . But that would hardly happen to a mule. He walked across the field slowly, head down.

It was sunset. Two of Jim Hawkins' men were over near the edge of the woods digging a hole in which to bury Jenny. Dave was surrounded by a knot of people, all of whom were looking down at the dead mule.

"I don't see how in the world it happened," said Jim Hawkins for the tenth time.

The crowd parted and Dave's mother, father, and small brother pushed into the center.

"Where Dave?" his mother called.

"There he is," said Jim Hawkins.

His mother grabbed him.

"What happened, Dave? Whut yuh done?"

"Nothin."

"C mon, boy, talk," his father said.

Dave took a deep breath and told the story he knew nobody believed.

"Waal," he drawled. "Ah brung ol Jenny down here sos Ah could do mah plowin. Ah plowed bout two rows, just like yuh see." He stopped and pointed at the long rows of upturned earth. "Then somethin musta been wrong wid ol Jenny. She wouldn ack right a-tall. She started snortin n kickin her heels. Ah tried t hol her, but she pulled erway, rearin n goin in. Then when the point of the plow was stickin up in the air, she swung erroun n twisted herself back on it . . . She stuck herself n started t bleed. N fo Ah could do anything, she wuz dead."

"Did you ever hear of anything like that in all your life?" asked Jim Hawkins.

There were white and black standing in the crowd. They murmured. Dave's mother came close to him and looked hard into his face. "Tell the truth, Dave," she said.

"Looks like a bullet hole to me," said one man.

"Dave, whut yuh do wid the gun?" his mother asked.

The crowd surged in, looking at him. He jammed his hands into his pockets, shook his head slowly from left to right, and backed away. His eyes were wide and painful.

"Did he hava gun?" asked Jim Hawkins.

"By Gawd, Ah tol yuh that wuz a gun wound," said a man, slapping his thigh.

His father caught his shoulders and shook him till his teeth rattled.

"Tell whut happened, yuh rascal! Tell whut . . ."

Dave looked at Jenny's stiff legs and began to cry.

"Whut yuh do wid tha gun?" his mother asked.

"Whut wuz he doin wida gun?" his father asked.

"Come on and tell the truth." said Hawkins. "Ain't nobody going to hurt you . . ."

His mother crowded close to him.

"Did yuh shoot tha mule, Dave?"

Dave cried, seeing blurred white and black faces.

"Ahh ddinn gggo tt sshooot hher . . . Ah ssswear ffo Gawd Ahh ddin. . . . Ah wuz a-tryin t sssee ef the old gggun would sshoot—"

"Where yuh git the gun from?" his father asked.

"Ah got it from Joe, at the sto."

"Where yuh git the money?"

"Ma give it t me."

"He kept worryin me, Bob. Ah had t. Ah tol im t bring the gun right back t me . . . It was fer yuh, the gun."

"But how yuh happen to shoot that mule?" asked Jim Hawkins.

"Ah wuzn shootin at the mule, Mistah Hawkins. The gun jumped when Ah pulled the trigger . . . N fo Ah knowed anythin Jenny was there a-bleedin."

Somebody in the crowd laughed. Jim Hawkins walked close to Dave and looked into his face.

"Well, looks like you have bought you a mule, Dave."

"Ah swear fo Gawd, Ah didn go t kill the mule, Mistah Hawkins!"

"But you killed her!"

All the crowd was laughing now. They stood on tiptoe and poked heads over one another's shoulders.

"Well, boy, look like yuh done bought a dead mule! Hahaha!"

"Ain tha ershame."

"Hohohohoho."

Dave stood, head down, twisting his feet in the dirt.

"Well, you needn't worry about it, Bob," said Jim Hawkins to Dave's father. "Just let the boy keep on working and pay me two dollars a month."

"Whut yuh wan fer yo mule, Mistah Hawkins?"

Jim Hawkins screwed up his eyes.

"Fifty dollars."

"Whut yuh do wid tha gun?" Dave's father demanded.

Dave said nothing.

"Yuh wan me t take a tree n beat yuh till yuh talk!"

"Nawsuh!"

"Whut yuh do wid it?"

"Ah throwed it erway."

"Where?"

"Ah . . . Ah throwed it in the creek."

"Waal, c mon home. N firs thing in the mawnin git to tha creek n fin tha gun."

"Yessuh."

"What yuh pay fer it?"

"Two dollahs."

"Take tha gun n git yo money back n carry it t Mistah Hawkins, yuh hear? N don fergit Ahma lam you black bottom good fer this! Now march yosef on home, suh!"

Dave turned and walked slowly. He heard people laughing. Dave glared, his eyes welling with tears. Hot anger bubbled in him. Then he swallowed and stumbled on.

That night Dave did not sleep. He was glad that he had gotten out of killing the mule so easily, but he was hurt. Something hot seemed to turn over inside him each time he remembered how they laughed. He tossed on his bed, feeling his hard pillow. N Pa says he's gonna beat me . . . He remembered other beatings, and his back quivered. Naw, naw, Ah sho don wan im t beat me tha way no mo. Dam em all! Nobody ever gave him anything. All he did was work. They treat me like a mule, n then they beat me. He gritted his teeth. N Ma had t tell on me.

Well, if he had to, he would take old man Hawkins that two dollars. But that meant selling the gun. And he wanted to keep that gun. Fifty dollars for a dead mule.

He turned over, thinking how he had fired the gun. He had an itch to fire it again. Ef other men kin shoota gun, by Gawd, Ah kin! He was still, listening. Mebbe they all sleepin now. The house was still. He heard the soft breathing of his brother. Yes, now! He would go down and get that gun and see if he could fire it! He eased out of bed and slipped into overalls.

The moon was bright. He ran almost all the way to the edge of the woods. He stumbled over the ground, looking for the spot where he had buried the gun. Yeah, here it is. Like a hungry dog scratching for a bone, he pawed it up. He puffed his black cheeks and blew dirt from the trigger and barrel. He broke it and found four cartridges unshot. He looked around; the fields were filled with silence and moonlight. He clutched the gun stiff and hard in his fingers. But, as soon as he wanted to pull the trigger, he shut his eyes and turned his head. Naw, Ah can't shoot wid mah eyes closed n mah head turned. With effort he held his eyes open; then he squeezed. *Blooooom!* He was stiff, not breathing. The gun was still in his hands. Dammit, he'd done it. He fired again. *Blooooom!* He smiled. *Blooooom! Blooooom! Click, click.* There! It was empty. If anybody could shoot a gun, he could. He put the gun into his hip pocket and started across the fields.

When he reached the top of a ridge he stood straight and proud in the moonlight, looking at Jim Hawkins' big white house, feeling the gun sagging in his pocket. Lawd, ef Ah had just one mo bullet Ah'd taka shot at tha house. Ah'd like t scare ol man Hawkins jusa little . . . Jusa enough t let im know Dave Saunders is a man.

To his left the road curved, running to the tracks of the Illinois Central. He jerked his head, listening. From far off came a faint *hoooof-hoooof; hoooof-hoooof; hoooof-hoooof.* . . . He stood rigid. Two dollahs a mont. Les see now . . . Tha means it'll take bout two years. Shucks! Ah'll be dam!

He started down the road, toward the tracks. Yeah, here she comes! He stood beside the track and held himself stiffly. Here she comes, erroun the ben . . . C mon, yuh slow poke! C mon! He had his hand on his gun; something quivered in his stomach. Then the train thundered past, the gray and brown box cars rumbling and clinking. He gripped the gun tightly; then he jerked his hand out of his pocket. Ah betcha Bill wouldn't do it! Ah betcha . . . The cars slid past, steel grinding upon steel. Ahm ridin yuh ternight, so hep me Gawd! He was hot all over. He hesitated just a moment; then he grabbed, pulled atop of a car, and lay flat. He felt his pocket; the gun was still there. Ahead the long rails were glinting in the moonlight, stretching away, away to some-where, somewhere where he could be a man . . .

QUESTIONS

1. Why does Dave want to buy a gun? Do you feel he is justified in his desire?
2. Critics have said Richard Wright has a good ear for dialogue. Does this story confirm this view? Explain.
3. How much of Dave's desire to become more manly is a result of being a typical adolescent? How much can be attributed to his race and class?
4. Why does Dave leave town at the end of the story? Is this an act of courage or cowardice? Does it make him more of a "man" or less of one?

P o e t r y

Isaac Grünewald. *The Singing Tree*. 1915. Norrköpings Konstmseum, Norköpping.

UNDERSTANDING POETRY

Perhaps the oldest kind of literature known to humanity, poetry in its earliest stages was told or sung, but during its long and continuing evolution it has become part of the written tradition and has been used for several purposes. Poetry springs from that time when humankind "discovered in fear and rapture the throbbing newness of the world. Poets have always known. All the legends of antiquity attest to it," writes Aimé Césaire.

Foremost among the many uses of poetry has been its ability as lyric, narrative, and epic to pay homage to the gods and to recount the history of specific groups of people. The Egyptian "utterances," pyramid texts, and demotic literatures; the Indian vedas; the Greek epics; the Norse sagas; sections of the Old Testament; the Japanese "Record of Ancient Things;" *Kojiki* (which derives from the more ancient Chinese writings); and the Sacred Book of the Quiche Maya, the *Popol Vuh*—these are but a few examples of group history. We easily recognize form, rhythm, imagery, and compression in the writings of the cultures of these peoples.

Americans, however, like Europeans, have been most influenced by Greek culture, in which the writers were known as poets, a title that carried both responsibility and praise. Greek literature consisted in large measure of plays that were written in poetry, a convention of the time. Aristotle's *Poetics*, therefore, touches on both playwrighting and poetry. Roman poets adopted most of the rules of the Greeks, but these fell into decline, later to be revived during the Renaissance. Beginning with Geoffrey Chaucer (1340?–1400), poetry in England flowered and spread throughout the English-speaking world and far beyond, though English was in turn influenced by a host of other languages. These enriched the English language and helped to establish new and enlarge old themes that were not merely English, but universal. Today the language is so wealthy that poets continually explore it for new or different ways to express themselves. Rita Dove, poet laureate of the United States, writes, "Poetry, for me, must explore the felicities of language," as she combines "historical occurrences [like the one in 'Parsley'] with the epiphanal quality of the lyric poem."

During the evolution of poetry there has been the enduring discussion about what it *is*. Strabo (58 B.C.–24 A.D.), along with many before and after him, believed poetry was a mask for historical and scientific truths. Emily Dickinson's quatrain, written about two thousand years later, alludes to the same thing:

> To clothe the fiery thought
> In simple words succeeds,
> For still the craft of genius is
> To mask a king in weeds.

The major role of poetry, however, according to Wordsworth, Coleridge, and others of their time, was to stand in opposition to science. "Poetry," Coleridge wrote, "is not the proper antithesis to prose, but to science. Poetry is opposed to science, and prose to meter." Leigh Hunt (1784–1859), an influential figure of the Romantic period, declared, "Poetry begins where matter of fact or science ceases. . . ." Césaire in our own time says that science "is a lion without antelope and without zebras . . . It is gnawed by hunger, the hunger of feeling, the hunger of life." And Omar Salinas in "Quetzacoatle" takes the impersonal "Big Bang" scientific theory of the origin of the universe and turns it into an exciting, vivid image:

> You lunged and caught fire
> flowers falling from a disenchanted
> sky

The Korean poet So Chongju (1915–) also joins the opposition against science with this statement: "What must cause the poet to worry is not the anxiety drawn out of that which cannot be completed, but the anxiety and longing instilled by that which is completed too readily." Science fixes rules, insists on the veracity of its computations beyond which the poet must always travel.

The question of what poetry is or does remains open, and perhaps that is the wisest way to perceive poetry: as not being static. While we presume that poetry and prose differ, Thomas Mann (1875–1955) and Ezra Pound agree that it would be a "fruitless and futile mania" to probe for those differences.

Nevertheless, commonly accepted as differences between poetry and prose is that poetry may be written in meter, thus creating rhythm, and prose is not; that poetry may use rhyme (though it is not required to), while prose does not. Poetry distills, compresses, and refines knowledge from bulk to universal essences through rigorous and selective use of language. Prose, in contrast, is not necessarily concerned with those processes. Prose has long been considered "ordinary" language, even though the best prose may contain quite extraordinary language. It is worth noting that a number of poets also write prose fiction, like Alice Walker, Shirley Lim, Alexander Pushkin, Gwendolyn Brooks, Louise Erdrich, Raymond Carver, Rita Dove, Ishmael Reed, Margaret Atwood, Wole Soyinka, Sandra Cisneros, Al Young, and others. This suggests that the differences between the genres may be in the eye of the beholder.

The poet may be like Houdini, binding himself or herself in the chains of traditional poetic forms and then creating interaction between theme, tone, imagery, simile, metaphor, personification, apostrophe, rhythm, meter, sound, and structure. Then the poet is tossed into the sea of creativity. The poet is further expected to miraculously escape, that escape being a poetic rendering of universal truth, vision, or beauty. When all is said and done, poetry should surprise us as much as Houdini's escapes surprised and delighted his audiences.

Some poetry may appear to be difficult to read (and some of it really is). But, like other forms of literature, it should be placed in perspective. We should know, for example, when the poem was written, because that helps to tell us what kind of tradition it has inherited. Maybe the title of a poem will supply the clues we need to understand its theme, like W. H. Auden's "The Unknown Citizen," or Gwendolyn Brooks' "The Bean Eaters." We should not try to bring more to a poem than is really there; if we anticipate, we cannot be surprised or delighted. Above all, the reader should have confidence in his or her ability to both understand and enjoy poetry, whatever its form. The more traditional structures, such as the sonnet or the villanelle, were the result of convention or poetic challenge; poetry is always changing, but every poem challenges the reader to get inside it.

Nothing about a poem is as important as the way it makes us feel—usually, the way the poet *wants* us to feel—and this is a reminder that it is *imagination* or *invention* and not profound meaning that is the most important gift the poet can bring us, for the poet always and ultimately wants us to understand the poem. Gwendolyn Brooks says quite pointedly, "I don't want [my work] to misrepresent the way I look at life to my readers."

Like Houdini, who kept seeking new ways to escape new inventions for detention, poetry evolved from the confinement of rigid structures and sometimes content, to what we now call *free verse*. This kind of poetry was fired by a new kind of poet, epitomized by Walt Whitman, in a relatively new nation. This was a poetry freed from the old rules. It introduced *cadence,* a sometimes stuttering kind of rhythm, and relied heavily on imagery. Free verse imagined the ordinary to be universal.

The new forms that were to spark the imagination, however, were not by any means acceptable to all poets. In this collection, for example, a number of twentieth century poets are as comfortable with the sonnet as were the poets of sixteenth century England. Auden, who remained a disciple of traditional structures, wrote of such devices as rhyme, meter, and stanza, that they "are like servants. If the master poet is fair enough to win their affection and firm enough to command their respect, the result is an orderly, happy household." Still, form changes to reflect contemporary sensibilities. Thus, we include among poets the legions of blues, folk, rock, and others who sing story-poems which, in the poetic tradition, are also reduced to shimmering, universal essences.

In the sections that follow, we examine the strategies employed by poets to frame their visions of human experience in verse. Brief essays introduce key elements of poetic technique: theme, diction, tone, imagery, symbolism, simile and metaphor, personification and apostrophe, meter, rhythm and sound, structure, and form. Within each chapter, the work of several poets appears, followed by questions for comprehension and writing. By carefully reading and discussing the selections in each chapter, we might come to agree with Gwendolyn Brooks' assessment that poetry is, in the final analysis, "life distilled."

9. Theme

A poem, as Robert Frost once suggested, might very well begin in delight and end in wisdom, but before a poem can even be written the poet needs—if only subconsciously—to have a subject in mind. Any subject might inspire the poet. Nevertheless, we do tend to think of traditional subjects for poetry—love, death, nature, religion, and war, for example—and to place many poems in such categories; we place poems in conventional categories far more frequently than we place fiction or drama in subject groups. Moreover, poets often become identified, sometimes misleadingly or simplistically, with specific subjects. Thus Shakespeare becomes a love poet because of his sonnets; Donne a poet preoccupied with God; Langston Hughes an urban poet; Robert Frost a nature poet; Emily Dickinson and Anne Sexton poets dwelling on death.

Poetry is the most complex, intense, and condensed of literary forms, but we can respond to much of it by understanding each poem's subject. We cannot extrapolate a theme from a poem until we identify and understand the subject. Theme, discussed initially in Chapter 1 of this text (pages 8–10), is a general statement the poet wants to make about a specific subject. Until the modern period, the subjects, themes, and forms acceptable to poetic culture were fairly uniform and conventional. However, in the twentieth century, the range of content, ideas, and forms—broadened by everything from psychoanalysis to thermodynamics to jazz—has led to a greater complexity of expression. Often technique—notably image and diction—obscures content in contemporary poetry, a phenomenon that confirms paradoxically our pressing need to know what a poem is about before we can know what it means.

Because poetry, as the American poet and critic Ivor Winters was fond of stating, is a statement in words about a human experience, we know that a poet will attempt to communicate through language some aspect of experience. But we must also ask about the purpose behind the speaker's presentation of the subject. The purpose might be to offer a definition, to express an emotion, to describe something objectively, to reveal something about human nature, or to project an idea or attitude. In a poem like Countee Cullen's "Incident" (see page 384), we sense all of these purposes. By establishing the central purpose of the poem, we move closer to understanding its meaning, or theme. In Shakespeare's "Let me not to the marriage of true minds," the purpose is relatively clear: the poet wants to state (perhaps dogmatically) the nature of true love. A poet's deepest purpose, however, might seem simple when it is actually quite subtle. Andrew Marvell in "To His Coy Mistress" apparently takes as his central purpose the seduction of his mistress, but perhaps he has larger philosophical intentions to convey. If we determine that Marvell's purpose embraces not just love and sexuality but also ethics and morality, then our final understanding of the poem, growing as it does from our perception of subject, speaker, and purpose, might be at odds with other interpretations.

Diverging interpretations and evaluations of poems are commonplace, even when readers establish a consensus on the general subject, purpose, speaker, and context of the poem. Ultimately, each of us is forced back to the language of the poem for meaning. "Language," declared Shelley, "is given to us to express our ideas." Thus, to understand a poem we often have recourse to paraphrase—to restating the poem in our own words, often line by line or stanza by stanza. We also look for poetic techniques—for the methods discussed in subsequent chapters in this section—to both help us in detecting meaning and aid us in our appreciation of the poem and the poet's craft. We seek in a poem the illumination of experience and, often, revelations about it. We turn to poets expecting from them a vision of life that contains the power to offer both delight and wisdom.

William Shakespeare

LET ME NOT TO THE MARRIAGE OF TRUE MINDS

Let me not to the marriage of true minds
Admit impediments. Love is not love
Which alters when it alteration finds,
Or bends with the remover to remove:
O, no; it is an ever-fixèd mark,   5
That looks on tempests and is never shaken:
It is the star to every wandering bark,
Whose worth's unknown, although his height be taken.
Love's not Time's fool, though rosy lips and cheeks
Within his bending sickle's compass come;   10
Love alters not with his brief hours and weeks,
But bears it out even to the edge of doom.
    If this be error and upon me proved,
    I never writ, nor no man ever loved.

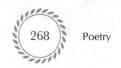

QUESTIONS

1. What familiar part of the standard Christian marriage ceremony does Shakespeare's first sentence echo? Why does Shakespeare use "marriage" as a word at the outset of the poem?
2. A sonnet is based on certain poetic conventions (see pages 346–348). One key convention of a Shakespearean sonnet is the division of the fourteen lines of the poem into four groups: lines 1–4, 5–8, 9–12, and 13–14. Analyze the organization of the poem according to these divisions, showing the way that Shakespeare advances his theme from stage to stage.
3. What two comparisons does Shakespeare draw in lines 5–8? What is the connection between "mark" and "star"? Explain the meaning of the eighth line. How does Shakespeare establish the conflict between love and time in lines 9–12?
4. What is the meaning and the tone of the last two rhymed lines? State the general theme that emerges from the poem.

Andrew Marvell

TO HIS COY MISTRESS

    Had we but world enough, and time,
This coyness, lady, were no crime.
We would sit down, and think which way
To walk, and pass our long love's day.
Thou by the Indian Ganges' side   5
Should'st rubies find: I by the tide
Of Humber would complain. I would
Love you ten years before the Flood,
And you should, if you please, refuse
Till the conversion of the Jews,   10
My vegetable love should grow
Vaster than empires, and more slow,
An hundred years should go to praise
Thine eyes, and on thy forehead gaze:
Two hundred to adore each breast: 15
But thirty thousand to the rest;
An age at least to every part,
And the last age should show your heart.
For, lady, you deserve this state,
Nor would I love at lower rate.   20
    But at my back I always hear

Time's wingèd chariot hurrying near;
And yonder all before us lie
Deserts of vast eternity.
Thy beauty shall no more be found,   25
Nor in thy marble vault shall sound
My echoing song; then worms shall try
That long preserved virginity,
And your quaint honor turn to dust,
And into ashes all my lust.   30
The grave's a fine and private place,
But none, I think, do there embrace.
    Now therefore, while the youthful hue
Sits on thy skin like morning dew,
And while thy willing soul transpires   35
At every pore with instant fires,
Now let us sport us while we may;
And now, like am'rous birds of prey,
Rather at once our time devour,
Than languish in his slow-chapped power.   40
Let us roll all our strength, and all
Our sweetness, up into one ball;
And tear our pleasures with rough strife
Thorough the iron gates of life.
Thus, though we cannot make our sun   45
Stand still, yet we will make him run.

QUESTIONS

1. Marvell builds a cogent argument to persuade his love in this poem, employing in the first two stanzas what debaters call a *straw man* (that is, an idea that is easy to knock down). What idea does he advance and then demolish in the first stanza? What related idea does he present and then destroy in the second stanza? With these possible objections to his argument eliminated, what is left for the lady to accept in the third stanza?

2. Many critics state that "To His Coy Mistress" is in the *carpe diem* tradition, in which the poet states that we should "seize the day," or do things immediately rather than postpone them. Here, Marvell relates the *carpe diem* motif to the need to enjoy love while one is still young. Evaluate the importance of this concept to your understanding of the poem.

3. The imagery, or vivid description, is very effective in this poem. Examine each stanza and explain the types or patterns of description that you detect. How does the description contribute to Marvell's argument?

4. How skillful is Marvell's argument? Is the poet interested only in seducing a woman, or are deeper ideas involved? For example, why does he refer to time and death?

WILD NIGHTS—
WILD NIGHTS!

Wild Nights—Wild Nights!
Were I with thee
Wild Nights should be
Our Luxury!

Futile—the Winds—   5
To a Heart in port—
Done with the Compass—
Done with the Chart!

Rowing in Eden—
Ah, the Sea!   10
Might I but moor—Tonight—
In Thee!

QUESTIONS

1. What emotions and tensions does the speaker project in the poem?
2. Write a psychological profile of the speaker of the poem. Point to details in the poem
   that reveal her attitudes—emotional, intellectual, and, perhaps, sexual.
3. State the theme of "Wild Nights—Wild Nights!"
4. Commenting on Dickinson's love lyrics, the critic Denis Donoghue observes: "Many
   of her poems enact certain moments on the way toward love, including desire,
   expectation, premonition, fear. But more poems still dispose certain moments on the
   other side of love, as loss, despair, terror, then death." In which category would you
   place "Wild Nights—Wild Nights!" and why?

Adrienne Rich

I COME HOME FROM YOU

I come home from you through the early light of spring
flashing off ordinary walls, the Pez Dorado,
the Discount Wares, the shoe-store. . . . I'm lugging my sack
of groceries, I dash for the elevator

where a man, taut, elderly, carefully composed   5
lets the door almost close on me.—*For god's sake hold it!*
I croak at him.—*Hysterical,*—he breathes my way.
I let myself into the kitchen, unload my bundles,
make coffee, open the window, put on Nina Simone
singing *Here comes the sun.* . . . I open the mail,   10
drinking delicious coffee, delicious music,
my body still both light and heavy with you. The mail
lets fall, a Xerox of something written by a man
aged 27, a hostage, tortured in prison:
My genitals have been the object of such a sadistic display   15
they keep me constantly awake with the pain . . .
Do whatever you can to survive.
You know, I think that men love wars . . .
And my incurable anger, my unmendable wounds
break open further with tears, I am crying helplessly,   20
And they still control the world, and you are not in my arms.

QUESTIONS

1. How is the experience of the poem framed by the "you"? What figures in the poem contrast with this "you"? What evidence, if any, exists in the poem that the "you" might be a woman? Discuss.

2. What are the speaker's various emotions in the poem? What is her attitude toward life? The speaker mentions "Delicious coffee, delicious music/my body still heavy with you." Explain the effect of these images.

3. How does the letter "written by a man" alter the speaker's frame of mind? Why is the "sadistic display" that he alludes to especially relevant to the theme of the poem? What is the theme?

4. Marge Piercy has written that Rich's poems are "taut with pain and intelligence, honed by a careful clear-eyed rage and precise compassion." Use this statement to explore the qualities and strengths of "I come home from you."

5. Rich has asserted that "we are confronted with the naked and unabashed failure of patriarchal politics and patriarchal civilization." In this context, explain why "I come home from you" could be interpreted as an assault on male-dominated society.

Rita Dove

ADOLESCENCE—II

Although it is night, I sit in the bathroom, waiting.
Sweat prickles behind my knees, the baby-breasts are alert.
Venetian blinds slice up the moon; the tiles quiver in pale strips.

Then they come, the three seal men with eyes as round
As dinner plates and eyelashes like sharpened tines.   5
They bring the scent of licorice. One sits in the washbowl,

One on the bathtub edge; one leans against the door.
"Can you feel it yet?" they whisper.
I don't know what to say, again. They chuckle,

Patting their sleek bodies with their hands.   10
"Well, maybe next time." And they rise,
Glittering like pools of ink under moonlight,

And vanish. I clutch at the ragged holes
They leave behind, here at the edge of darkness.
Night rests like a ball of fur on my tongue.   15

QUESTIONS

1. What aspect or aspects of adolescent experience is the poet suggesting? What clues
   are provided that helped you reach your conclusion?
2. Study the many images of water in the poem. What might these images symbolize?
3. Examine the way the men are described. What do they mean by "Can you feel it
   yet?" How does their presence make the narrator feel?

Cathy Song

PICTURE BRIDE

She was a year younger
than I,
twenty-three when she left Korea.
Did she simply close

the door of her father's house   5
and walk away? And
was it a long way
through the tailor shops of Pusan
to the wharf where the boat
waited to take her to an island   10
whose name she had
only recently learned,
on whose shore
a man waited,
turning her photograph   15
to the light when the lanterns
in the camp outside
Waialua Sugar Mill were lit
and the inside of his room
grew luminous   20
from the wings of moths
migrating out of the cane stalks?
What things did my grandmother
take with her? And when
she arrived to look   25
into the face of the stranger
who was her husband,
thirteen years older than she,
did she politely untie
the silk bow of her jacket,   30
her tent-shaped dress
filling with the dry wind
that blew from the surrounding fields
where the men were burning the cane?

QUESTIONS

1. What does the poem's title connote? How does it influence the theme?
2. Explain the image of the dry wind in the poem.
3. Why does Song write of her subject, "did she politely untie the silken bow of her jacket"? Why might these lines be a key to the meaning of the poem?
4. What is the tone of this poem? What is the poet's attitude toward arranged marriages?

10. Diction

"Poetry," wrote Ralph Waldo Emerson, "teaches us the enormous force of a few words." The careful selection, compression, and arrangement of language by the artist gives poetry the power to project experience vividly and memorably for the reader. Poets generally do not want to use language to convey information, argue issues, or engage in conventional forms of discourse, although these objectives might infiltrate or even dominate individual poems. Instead, they want to use the force of language to heighten our perception of some aspect of experience—to render that experience as precisely, brilliantly, and originally as possible.

Poets manipulate and control language, using a wide range of strategies that will be examined in future chapters of this anthology. They know that words appeal to the instincts, emotions, senses, intelligence, and biases of readers, and that they must select and position words effectively in a poem in order to obtain the desired effect. "Proper words in proper places," demanded Jonathan Swift, stressing this dual commitment to the selection and placement of language in poetry. If poets take such painstaking care in choosing and ordering language, then we should not rush through a poem, quickly seeking its meaning or central experience. A poem deserves our commitment to appreciating the use of language.

In this context, we begin by recognizing that words have both denotative and connotative meanings and values. The *denotative meaning* of a word is given by the dictionary definition and is largely independent of people's emotions and personal responses to the word. Of course, ordinary words—"fall," for instance—can have multiple definitions in a dictionary. Words can also change in meaning with the passage of time.

The other realm of meaning that pertains to words is *connotation*, referring to the shades of meaning and suggestive possibilities of words. In this essentially emotional, subjective realm of language, a word like "engaged" as used by Octavio Paz in a poem in this section or a word like "mothers" in a selection by Nikki Giovanni moves from the denotation of the term to a special range of meaning and suggestion that the poet wants to bring to it. Poets make conscious choices concerning the denotations and

274

connotations of words. Poets, seeking the richest possibilities of language, might be plain or ornamental, direct or indirect, witty or serious, in style and tone. Regardless of these stylistic strategies, they must always start with the denotative and connotative power of words to convey experience and meaning.

Poets, the supreme craftsmen and craftswomen of language, invariably move beyond the bare, denotative values of words to mine the rich suggestions and associations that words hold. They work magic with the core of meaning inherent in words, transforming plain metal into a rare alloy that shimmers with emotional implication and possibility. The English writer Robert Thouless, in an essay called "Emotional Meanings," took two famous lines from John Keats's poem "The Eve of St. Agnes" and reduced them from connotative splendor to denotative neutrality in order to explore some of the ways in which we respond to language. Keats wrote:

> Full on this casement shone the wintry moon,
> And threw warm gules on Madeline's fair breast.

The beauty of these lines derives in large part from the ordering and presentation of emotionally charged words—*casement, warm gules* (the name in heraldry for red), *Madeline, fair, breast*—suggesting or creating an aura of romance. Thouless reduces these beautiful lines to bare, denotative exactness:

> Full on the window shown the wintry moon,
> Making red marks on Jane's uncolored chest.

All poetic and assuredly most connotative power goes out of language in the second version. Emotional effect has been replaced by scientific effect. Fortunately, the poet moves effectively from the power of denotative meanings to the greater power of connotative meanings in the creation of poetry that appeals to the experience of readers.

Consider, for instance, the denotative and connotative value of language in the following short poem by Aphra Behn, who was the first woman in England to earn her living exclusively as a writer.

When Maidens Are Young

> When maidens are young, and in their spring,
> Of pleasure, of pleasure, let'em take their full swing,
>   Full swing, full swing,
> And love, and dance, and play, and sing,
> For Silvia, believe it, when youth is done,
> There's naught but hum-drum, hum-drum, hum-drum,
> There's naught but hum-drum, hum-drum, hum-drum.

In this poem, Aphra Behn considers the youth of maidens and urges them to enjoy themselves before the cares of adult womanhood set in. This is the theme, or general meaning, of the experience that we can abstract from the poem. Yet how does the poet arrive at this statement about experience, if not through the images, ideas, and rhythms that we associate with the language? To participate in the experience of the poem, we have to ask basic questions about the way language performs in it. What did "maidens" mean to Behn in the 1670s, and what does it mean to us today? What denotations and connotations attach themselves to the word "spring"? What words convey the joys of a woman's youth? What meanings has "hum-drum" in the last two lines, and why are certain words repeated? In considering such questions, we discover that words in "When Maidens Are Young" assuredly control the experience of the poem. Aphra Behn's selection and repetition of words convey the range of maidenly pleasure, the urgency in embracing it quickly, and the certainty that it will alter to the plodding, repetitive, and irrevocably dull state of "hum-drum" adulthood in a way that no prose statement can.

All of the poems in this section reveal striking control of diction. If words are power, then the poet who controls language also projects this power. Here we see linguistic power in the hands of women and men, and the varieties of experience that they express with it. And here we also see how each poet chooses, as Adrienne Rich said of Emily Dickinson, to have it out on her or his own premises.

Ben Jonson

ON MY FIRST DAUGHTER

Here lies, to each her parents' ruth,
Mary, the daughter of their youth;
Yet all heaven's gifts being heaven's due,
It makes the father less to rue.
At six months' end she parted hence   5
With safety of her innocence;
Whose soul heaven's queen, whose name she bears,
In comfort of her mother's tears,
Hath placed amongst her virgin train:
Where, while that severed doth remain,   10
This grave partakes the fleshly birth;
Which cover lightly, gentle earth!

QUESTIONS

1. Jonson's epitaph has been admired for the excellence of its diction and syntax. What might readers have found to praise in the features of the poem?
2. How could the tone of this poem be best described?
3. Does the poem have a dominant feeling, or mood, or is there a mixture of feelings expressed? Explain.

Aphra Behn

THE DEFIANCE

By Heaven 'tis false, I am not vain;
　　And rather would the subject be
Of your indifference, or disdain,
　　Than wit or raillery.

Take back the trifling praise you give,　　　　　　　　　　5
　　And pass it on some other fool,
Who may the injuring wit believe,
　　That turns her into ridicule.

Tell her, she's witty, fair, and gay,
　　With all the charms that can subdue:　　　　　　　　10
Perhaps she'll credit what you say;
　　But curse me if I do.

If your diversion you design,
　　On my good-nature you have prest:
Or if you do intend it mine,　　　　　　　　　　　　　　15
　　You have mistook the jest.

QUESTIONS

1. From just the title of the poem, what can you tell about the tone of the language in which it is written? What does the poet mean by "defiance" in the context of the poem?
2. What are the origins of "tis" in the first line? Consult the *Oxford English Dictionary* (OED) to answer this question. Use the OED or some other unabridged dictionary to find out how Behn would have been using these words: "wit," "raillery," "design," "prest."
3. What synonyms do "disdain," "trifling," "gay," and "diversion" suggest in the poem? What denotations exist for "wit"? Which is most appropriate in the context of the poem?
4. Paraphrase each stanza. Sum up the general meaning of the poem. Did you arrive at this statement of the theme through a consideration of the poet's use of denotation, connotation, or both? Explain.
5. How does attention to denotative and connotative aspects of language lead to an appreciation of the theme of Behn's poem? One form of such attention would be to analyze the words and phrases she uses to capture the varieties of human action and reaction.

Emily Dickinson

SHE ROSE TO HIS REQUIREMENT

She rose to his Requirement—dropt
The Playthings of Her Life
To take the honorable Work
Of Woman, and of Wife—

If ought She missed in Her new Day,   5
Of Amplitude, or Awe—
Or first Prospective—Or the Gold
In using, wear away,

It lay unmentioned—as the Sea
Develop Pearl, and Weed,   10
But only to Himself—be known
The Fathoms they abide—

QUESTIONS

1. What two words in the first stanza mean the opposite of each other? What words might be taken connotatively to be opposites? Why does Dickinson arrange key words this way?
2. What equation does Dickinson draw between "Work," "Woman," and "Wife"? What is the standard definition of "honorable"? How does Dickinson use this word in the context of the poem?
3. Explain Dickinson's use of "Amplitude," "Awe," and "Prospective" in the second stanza. What might "Gold" refer to, and what connotations are involved?
4. List the words in the third stanza that denote the life of the sea. In what way is a woman's mind like the sea? What idea does Dickinson want to draw from this frame of reference?
5. What larger meaning concerning women and marriage emerges from the poem? Analyze Dickinson's handling of the "requirements" of women's lives, concentrating on the words she uses.

Octavio Paz

ENGAGED

Stretched out on the grass
a boy and a girl.
Sucking their oranges, giving their kisses
like waves exchanging foam.

Stretched out on the beach   5
a boy and a girl.
Sucking their limes, giving their kisses,
like clouds exchanging foam.

Stretched out underground
a boy and a girl.   10
Saying nothing, never kissing,
giving silence for silence.

            Translated by Muriel Rukeyser

QUESTIONS

1. Compare and contrast the first two stanzas with the last. Do they conflict or complement or both? Explain.
2. What is suggested by the word "underground?"
3. Many phrases and words are repeated in the poem. How can you tie this use of repetition to the title?

Nikki Giovanni

MOTHERS

the last time i was home
to see my mother we kissed
exchanged pleasantries
and unpleasantries pulled a warm
comforting silence around   5
us and read separate books

i remember the first time
i consciously saw her
we were living in a three room
apartment on burns avenue
mommy always sat in the dark   10
i don't know how i knew that but she did

that night i stumbled into the kitchen
maybe because i've always been
a night person or perhaps because i had wet the bed   15
she was sitting on a chair
the room was bathed in moonlight diffused through
those thousands of panes landlords who rented
to people with children were prone to put in windows

she may have been smoking but maybe not   20
her hair was three-quarters her height
which made me a strong believer in the samson myth
and very black

i'm sure i just hung there by the door
i remember thinking: what a beautiful lady   25

she was very deliberately waiting
perhaps for my father to come home
from his night job or maybe for a dream
that had promised to come by
"come here" she said "i'll teach you   30
a poem: *i see the moon*
        the moon sees me
        god bless the moon
        and god bless me"
i taught it to my son   35
who recited it for her
just to say we must learn
to bear the pleasures
as we have borne the pains

QUESTIONS

1. What is the occasion of this poem? What does the speaker learn? Define the speaker's
   feelings in the first stanza and in succeeding stanzas.

2. Give several denotations for "pleasantries" in line 3; then select the one that is most appropriate here.
3. Does the word "home" have positive or negative connotations for Giovanni? Justify your answer.
4. What is the poet's attitude toward "mothers"? Why does she use the plural? What is the effect of "mommy" in line 11? What details does the speaker use to depict her mother?

1 1 . T o n e

Tone, as defined in the fiction section devoted to this topic (see pages 116–118), is the writer's attitude toward his or her subject. It is the *voice* of the writer that we hear—a voice that is intimately connected in most instances to theme and mood. This voice may be serious or playful, modest or arrogant, irreverent or devout. Tone may be constant, or it may shift from line to line or stanza to stanza in a poem. We trace in the tone of a poem the speaker's unique emotional and intellectual approach to a subject.

With certain subjects—for example, death—it is often easy for us to hear the tone or voice that illuminates the emotional context, the situation, the mood, and the speaker's frame of mind. Here are the opening lines from Ben Jonson's poem on the death of his first son (1616). The complete poem appears on page 410 of the anthology.

> Farewell, thou child of my right hand and joy;
> My sin was too much hope of thee, loved boy,
> Seven years thou wert lent to me, and I thee pay,
> Exacted by thy fate, on the just day.

We expect the tone of grief and loss in such a poem, but other tonalities are involved as well, notably the sense of sin and of fatalism that Jonson brings to the specific occasion of the poem. We hear the voice of a great poet coping with personal tragedy in natural and moving yet at the same time stately and noble language.

We seek in the language of a poem clues to its range of tone. Indeed, if we overlook or misinterpret these clues, we misjudge tone and as a consequence fail to understand the theme or complete meaning of a poem. Virtually all of the elements of poetic language come into play when we explore a poem's tonality: word choice, selection of details, connotations, figures of speech, imagery, rhythm, phrasing and construction of lines and sentences, irony, satire, and other conventions. With so many elements and techniques to contend with, we should avoid the temptation to reduce the tone of a poem to a single word—except if we use that word as a starting point for a more sophisticated analysis of the mingling of tones that we typically encounter in a poem.

Even very short lyrics can require us to be sensitive to the full range of poetic convention and literary tradition that a poet might exploit in the rendering of tone. Phillis Wheatley, who was born in Africa around 1753 and brought to Boston in 1761 as a slave, offers an interesting commingling of tones in her short poem, "On Being Brought From Africa to America":

> 'Twas mercy brought me from my pagan land,
> Taught my benighted soul to understand
> That there's a God, that there's a Saviour too:
> Once I redemption neither sought nor knew.
> Some view our sable race with scornful eye,
> "Their colour is a diabolic dye."
> Remember, Christians, Negroes, black as Cain,
> May be refined, and join th' angelic train.

How do we contend with tone or *tones* in this poem? Is the tone serious in the first four lines, or is Wheatley being ironic? Indeed, could the tone of the overall poem be slightly ironic and even paradoxical? Again, is Wheatley neutral and subdued in tone in lines 5–6, or is gentle criticism of the position implied? By the end of the lyric, the tone— moralistic and mildly imperative—seems to crystalize, as Wheatley offers a homily for her "Christian" audience. Nevertheless, we can approach the problem of tone in this poem from shifting perspectives, depending largely on the voice of the poet.

The contradictions of life and living, which we sense in the poem by Wheatley, provide the poet with the powerful weapons of irony, satire, and paradox; they have been used longest, it seems, against the greatest human institution, the state. Almost universal is the question inherent in her poem: Why can't my country be better than it now is?

Irony (from the Greek *eironeia*) has long been a major weapon because it is not what it seems to be; it possesses shades of meaning that run counter to the obvious sense of images and words. Satire (from the Latin *satira*) is criticism of human folly, individual or collective, but carries with it the hope that once folly is revealed, those guilty of it will quit being fools. Paradox (from the Greek *paradoxon*), may seem to be contradictory, but it carries certain truths. These tools and their many relatives are used more precisely by poets, who imaginatively compress and distill their ideas to a far greater extent than do writers of fiction or drama.

Tone is perhaps most discernible when the poet uses irony, satire, or paradox, for they largely reveal the author's attitude toward the subject he or she is writing about. The great Roman satirist Juvenal (A.D. 60–130) noted that "it is difficult not to write satire," given the follies of Roman society during his day, and that "indignation creates [his] verses." Juvenal, like many poets he influenced, did not rely on understatement, a relative of irony; he used wit like a rapier, perhaps finding that understatement was deceitful, like using a dagger.

Shelley's use of irony and paradox in "Ozymandias" in no way approaches the ironic fervor—the opposite of understatement—seen in his "Song to the Men of England":

> Men of England, wherefore plough
> For the lords who lay ye low?
> Wherefore weave with toil and care
> The rich robes your tyrants wear?
>
> Wherefore feed, and clothe, and save,
> From the cradle to the grave,
> Those ungrateful drones who would
> Drain your sweat—nay, drink your blood?

While "Ozymandias" is coolly allegorical in its irony, "Song to the Men of England" seems to have been written with uncommon urgency. It might be considered a call to revolt against the state, or it might be considered hyperbole—exaggeration for reasons having little to do with credence.

If the state is a ready target for the use of irony, then the mores and habits and practices within it, sanctioned *de facto* by the state, are equally vulnerable. It seems to be true, however, that the discrepancies between what the state says it is and what it really is are the subjects mainly of the victims of those discrepancies. It will be argued that such situations are not the stuff of art, but humanity's conflicts and its desire to be rid of conflicts often seem to be central to the ironic or satiric imagination.

We sense this interplay of ironic and satiric tonalities in another poem in this section, Claude McKay's "America," which reflects not only the racial but also the creative conflict when race becomes a factor in literature. This is a relatively recent phenomenon that is most often observed in the Western world. However, in Africa, South America, Central America, and other parts of the world where people of different cultures have merged into one civilization, the phenomenon is spreading.

One of the best modern American satirists was Melvin B. Tolson (1898–1966), whose irony is deeply rooted in history, not in the personal, as with McKay. Both share a sense of traditional poetic form and rhythm. "Dark Symphony" (1940) concretely attacks the state, while "America" deals with it in the abstract:

> None in the Land can say
> To us black men Today:
> You smash stock markets with your coined blitzkriegs,
> And make a hundred million guinea pigs.
> You counterfeit our Christianity,
> And bring contempt upon Democracy.

Tolson declares here that African Americans are not guilty of making the state what it is—that being a victim precludes the possession and exercise of power.

Irony, satire, and paradox in poetry, drama, and fiction are used to the end that

human institutions be improved. It is debatable that these weapons have been successful. Nevertheless, their continued use serves as fair warning that improvement is still much to be desired and that these well-used literary tools will be with us for some time to come.

Percy Bysshe Shelley

OZYMANDIAS

I met a traveler from an antique land
Who said: Two vast and trunkless legs of stone
Stand in the desert . . . Near them, on the sand,
Half sunk, a shattered visage lies, whose frown,
And wrinkled lip, and sneer of cold command,   5
Tell that its sculptor well those passions read
Which yet survive, stamped on these lifeless things,
The hand that mocked them, and the heart that fed;
And on the pedestal these words appear:
"My name is Ozymandias, king of kings: 10
Look on my works, ye Mighty, and despair!"
Nothing beside remains. Round the decay
Of that colossal wreck, boundless and bare
The lone and level sands stretch far away.

QUESTIONS

1. From the description in the poem, what kind of ruler was Ozymandias likely to have been?
2. What statement is Shelley making about the artist and his or her work?
3. Explain fully the irony of the shattered statue and the words chiseled on its pedestal. How does Shelley combine verbal irony, irony of situation, and dramatic irony in the poem?

Edward Arlington Robinson

RICHARD CORY

Whenever Richard Cory went down town,
We people on the pavement looked at him:
He was a gentleman from sole to crown,
Clean favored, and imperially slim.

And he was always quietly arrayed,   5
And he was always human when he talked;
But still he fluttered pulses when he said,
'Good-morning,' and he glittered when he walked.

And he was rich—yes, richer than a king—
And admirably schooled in every grace: 10
In fine, we thought that he was everything
To make us wish that we were in his place.

So on we worked, and waited for the light,
And went without the meat, and cursed the bread;
And Richard Cory, one calm summer night,   15
Went home and put a bullet through his head.

QUESTIONS

1. Why does the narrator refer to "We people" in the second line? Does he ever speak of himself as "I" or "me"? Does the narrator have a sense of self-worth?
2. Point out word choices that imply the narrator's respect for Richard Cory. How would the poem be diminished if Robinson named his creation John Smith or Luke Havergal (a character in another Robinson sketch)?
3. Does the narrator understand the suicide of Richard Cory? Is the reader better able to comprehend it? How does this affect the reader's attitude toward the poem's narrator?
4. What is the effect of the definite articles in the last stanza, "the light . . . the meat . . . the bread"? Express the sentence's meaning in more literal language. What are the religious overtones of "the light"? Would the narrator be expected to intend those overtones?
5. Analyze Robinson's use of irony and ironic contrast in this poem.

Claude McKay

AMERICA

Although she feeds me bread of bitterness,
And sinks into my throat her tiger's tooth,
Stealing my breath of life, I will confess
I love this cultured hell that tests my youth!
Her vigor flows like tides into my blood,   5
Giving me strength against her hate.
Her bigness sweeps my being like a flood.
Yet as a rebel fronts a king in state,
I stand within her walls with not a shred
Of terror, malice, not a word of jeer.   10
Darkly I gaze into the days ahead,
And see her might and granite wonders there,
Beneath the touch of Time's unerring hand,
Like priceless treasures sinking in the sand.

QUESTIONS

1. What connotations does "America" have for McKay?
2. Describe the tone and theme of "America."
3. Explain why McKay cites the paradox of his love and "her hate." What does "bread of bitterness" symbolize in biblical terms?
4. What does the author mean by the phrase "cultured hell"? Explain why, for McKay, the juxtaposition of words like these adds to the depth of his ironic lament.
5. It is implied by McKay that the same elements that brought down Ozymandias and his civilization will bring down America. Describe those elements and offer an evaluation.

Ezra Pound

THE RIVER-MERCHANT'S
WIFE: A LETTER

While my hair was still cut straight across my forehead
I played about the front gate, pulling flowers.
You came by on bamboo stilts, playing horse,
You walked about my seat, playing with blue plums.
And we went on living in the village of Chokan: 5
Two small people, without dislike or suspicion.

At fourteen I married My Lord you.
I never laughed, being bashful.
Lowering my head, I looked at the wall.
Called to, a thousand times, I never looked back.   10

At fifteen I stopped scowling,
I desired my dust to be mingled with yours
For ever and for ever and for ever.
Why should I climb the look out?
At sixteen you departed,   15
You went into far Ku-to-yen, by the river of swirling eddies,
And you have been gone five months.
The monkeys make sorrowful noise overhead.

You dragged your feet when you went out.
By the gate now, the moss is grown, the different mosses,   20
Too deep to clear them away!
The leaves fall early this autumn, in wind.
The paired butterflies are already yellow with August
Over the grass in the West garden;
They hurt me. I grow older.   25
If you are coming down through the narrows of the river Kiang,
Please let me know beforehand,
And I will come out to meet you
                    As far as Cho-fu-Sa.

QUESTIONS

1. What emotional transformation does the narrator of the poem undergo during the
   course of the poem?
2. Why does the narrator call her husband "My Lord you"? What does it reveal about
   their relationship?

3. What is the tone of the poem? What particular words and images contribute to the tone? Does the tone change during the poem or does it remain constant throughout? Explain.
4. What does the line "Why should I climb the look out" mean? Is it meant to be taken literally, figuratively, or both?

June Jordan

THE WEDDING

Tyrone married her this afternoon
not smiling as he took the aisle
and her slightly rough hand.
Dizzella listened to the minister
staring at his wrist and twice   5
forgetting her name:
Do you promise to obey?
Will you honor humility and love
as poor as you are?
Tyrone stood small but next   10
to her person
trembling. Tyrone stood
straight and bony
black alone with one key
in his pocket.   15
By marrying today
they made themselves a man
and woman
answered friends or unknown
curious about the Cadillacs   20
displayed in front of Beaulah Baptist.
Beaulah Baptist
life in general
indifferent
barely known   25

QUESTIONS

1. How would you characterize the mood of the wedding day? What images, in particular, suggest this mood? How does this mood influence the tone?

2. What is the significance of the "one key" in Tyrone's pocket?
3. What is the poet implying about the effect of poverty on the emotional life of the bride and groom? Of "life in general" in Beaulah Baptist Church?

Shirley Geok-lin Lim

AH MAH

Grandmother was smaller
than me at eight. Had she
been child forever?

Helpless, hopeless, chin sharp
as a knuckle, fan face   5
hardly half-opened, not a scrap

of fat anywhere: she tottered
in black silk, leaning on
handmaids, on two tortured

fins. At sixty, his sons all   10
married, grandfather bought her,
Soochow flower song girl.

Every bone in her feet
had been broken, bound tighter
than any neighbor's sweet   15

daughter's. Ten toes and instep
curled inwards, yellow petals
of chrysanthemum, wrapped

in gold cloth. He bought the young
face, small knobby breasts   20
he swore he'd not dress in sarong

of maternity. Each night
he held her feet in his palms,
like lotus in the tight

hollows of celestial lakes.   25
In his calloused flesh, her
weightless soles, cool and slack,

clenched in his stranger's fever.

QUESTIONS

1. The poet provides a physical description of her grandmother as well as clues to her personality and emotional life. How are all these elements similar?
2. What aspects of the poem suggest the cultural milieu of the couple? What tone does the poet seem to adopt in describing this milieu? Which words suggest it and why?
3. What is the grandmother's relationship to the world she lives in and to her husband, in particular?

12. Imagery

Poetry often helps us to visualize and experience the world by offering images or descriptive details that appeal to our senses. This collection of individual images in a poem is termed *imagery;* and imagery in turn may be defined as the verbal representation of sensory experience. The poet's most typical strategy in developing imagery is to concentrate on visual impressions—on things that we can see in the mind's eye. But forms of imagery based on other sense impressions—sound, taste, touch, smell—can also be employed. Imagery can even involve internal physical sensations like hunger, pain, and nausea, as well as a broad range of mental and emotional states. What we appreciate in imagery is the pictorial power of language to capture the world of sensory impressions.

Archibald MacLeish reveals the centrality of imagery to poetic art and to the nature of figurative language at the outset of his famous poem "Ars Poetica":

> A poem should be palpable and mute
> As a globed fruit,
>
> Dumb
> As old medallions to the thumb,
>
> Silent as the sleeve-worn stone
> Of casement ledges where the moss has grown—
>
> A poem should be wordless
> As the flight of birds.

We can readily imagine what these lines would be like without the sequence of images that heightens the ideas posited by the poem. Indeed, part of MacLeish's intention is to contrast the flat, expository, "prosaic" statement at the start of each stanza with the heightened, metaphoric, "poetic" sensory details that govern the end of each stanza. The delight of these lines comes in large part from the coincidence of ideas and images. The "art of poetry" involves the poet's ability to invent imagery that arouses sensations in readers, thereby bringing them into intimate contact with the experience of the poem and perhaps enabling them to understand that experience better.

MacLeish's images convey the idea of what a poem "should be." Similarly, imagery conveys an understanding of things, whether that imagery is literal or figurative, denotative or connotative. Even when the poem relies heavily on imagery to project a direct impression of things, as in Japanese haiku poetry or the poetry of the twentieth-century imagists, there is often a clear line of meaning traced through the images. One of the most famous haiku poems, by Taniguchi Buson (1715–1783), reveals again the coincidence of imagery and idea:

> The piercing chill I feel:
>   my dead wife's comb, in our bedroom,
>   under my heel.

This is a remarkable poem, even in translation, for it captures in a series of visceral and tactile images the sense of death a husband feels for his departed wife. The chill in the first line of the poem is existential, running to the very fiber of the speaker's being. It is reinforced in the next two lines, in which the cold sense of touch serves as a correlative of death. Even the comb and the bedroom, intimate aspects of his wife's former existence, are details that serve to intensify the sensation felt by the speaker. Here, some might say that Buson captures the sensory experience of the speaker, but that "meaning" is not involved. However, we do understand the mind and feelings of the speaker, and assuredly this is meaning enough.

Many modern poets—notably Ezra Pound, William Carlos Williams, and Amy Lowell—were influenced by earlier Japanese and Chinese poetry. They learned from this verse the power of imagery, untainted by poetic statement, to capture and convey the experience of things in this world. William Carlos Williams's "The Red Wheelbarrow" is one of the best-known imagist poems:

> So much depends
> upon
>
> a red wheel
> barrow
>
> glazed with rain
> water
>
> beside the white
> chickens.

The visual images in this poem are fixed and vivid, but what the poem seemingly lacks, in contrast to Buson's haiku, is a definable human mood or a readily comprehensible statement about experience. In short, the imagery seems too literal and too denotative, meaning exactly what it states, offering us a mental picture of a scene but nothing more. Yet we are drawn back to the poet's opening declaration; the poem actually begins with a declarative statement, forcing us to discover why "so much" depends upon the things that are described. In other words, we must probe the imagery once again to discover meaning, and various interpretations might develop. Perhaps Williams means that we do live in a physical world, in a world that we are able to apprehend with our senses, and that we depend on that world, for we are defined by our relationship to it.

Poets want us to sense vividly and to perceive the world through their images, often arranged in a pattern, but they also tend to call attention to the significance of the imagery. When the English poet and Catholic priest Gerard Manley Hopkins offers a catalogue of seasonal delights in "Spring," we know that other meaningful statements reinforce the pattern of imagery:

> Nothing is so beautiful as spring—
>   When weeds, in wheels, shoot long and lovely and lush;
>   Thrush's eggs look little low heavens, and thrush
> Through the echoing timber does so rinse and wring
> The ear, it strikes like lightnings to hear him sing;
>   The glassy peartree leaves and blooms, they brush
>   The descending blue; that blue is all in a rush
> With richness; the racing lambs too have fair their fling.
>
> What is all this juice and all this joy?
>   A strain of the earth's sweet being in the beginning
> In Eden garden.—Have, get, before it cloy,
>   Before it cloud, Christ, lord, and sour with sinning,
> Innocent mind and Mayday in girl and boy,
>   Most, O maid's child, thy choice and worthy the winning.

The visual and auditory images reinforce the poet's expository statement in the first line. In the second and third stanzas, Hopkins deepens the significance of the imagery and the poem by likening the pristine and pastoral spring landscape to Eden before the fall. He turns the poem into a delicate prayer for purity and innocence, which he associates with the purity of spring—a landscape and a time freed from another season "sour with sinning."

All of the poems in this section resemble Hopkin's "Spring" in that they contain various patterns of imagery. However, there is a wide range of intention and effect in these poems. We can imagine or visualize the landscapes offered by the poets with varying degrees of precision. More significantly, we discover through the imagery and the sensory experience—the sights, sounds, and other sensations evoked—a carefully arranged world of meaning and value.

Thomas Campion

THERE IS A GARDEN
IN HER FACE

There is a garden in her face,
Where roses and white lilies grow,
A heavenly paradise is that place,
Wherein all pleasant fruits do flow.
There cherries grow, which none may buy   5
Till "Cherry ripe!" themselves do cry.

Those cherries fairly do enclose
Of orient pearl a double row;
Which when her lovely laughter shows,
They look like rosebuds filled with snow.   10
Yet them nor peer nor prince can buy,
Till "Cherry ripe!" themselves do cry.

Her eyes like angels watch them still;
Her brows like bended bows do stand,
Threatening with piercing frowns to kill   15
All that attempt with eye or hand
Those sacred cherries to come nigh,
Till "Cherry ripe!" themselves do cry.

QUESTIONS

1. Though most madrigal writers hired poets to write verses for their songs, Campion chose to write his own. In this, perhaps his most famous, a lady is praised for her beauty. What is the religious resonance of the "roses" and "white lilies" of stanza 1? What lady is traditionally associated with these flowers?
2. Throughout the poem, images of flowers and fruit predominate. Is it, then, a fault to introduce an "orient pearl" in stanza 2? How would you explain the presence of an alien image?
3. By stanza 3, the lady has undergone a change in status. No longer merely a pleasant garden, she has been given the power to kill with a single glance those who would disturb her prerogative. Just what is this "right" of hers and how does it relate to the refrain "Cherry ripe!"?

Samuel Taylor Coleridge

KUBLA KHAN

In Xanadu did Kubla Khan
A stately pleasure dome decree:
Where Alph, the sacred river, ran
Through caverns measureless to man
   Down to a sunless sea.   5
So twice five miles of fertile ground
With walls and towers were girdled round:
And there were gardens bright with sinuous rills,
Where blossomed many an incense-bearing tree;
And here were forests ancient as the hills,   10
Enfolding sunny spots of greenery.

But oh! that deep romantic chasm which slanted
Down the green hill athwart a cedarn cover!
A savage place! as holy and enchanted
As e'er beneath a waning moon was haunted   15
By woman wailing for her demon lover!
And from this chasm, with ceaseless turmoil seething,
As if this earth in fast thick pants were breathing,
A mighty fountain momently was forced:
Amid whose swift half-intermitted burst   20
Huge fragments vaulted like rebounding hail,
Or chaffy grain beneath the thresher's flail:
And 'mid these dancing rocks at once and ever
It flung up momently the sacred river.
Five miles meandering with a mazy motion   25
Through wood and dale the sacred river ran,
Then reached the caverns measureless to man,
And sank in tumult to a lifeless ocean:
And 'mid this tumult Kubla heard from far
Ancestral voices prophesying war!   30
   The shadow of the dome of pleasure
   Floated midway on the waves;
   Where was heard the mingled measure
   From the fountain and the caves.
It was a miracle of rare device,   35
A sunny pleasure dome with caves of ice!

   A damsel with a dulcimer
   In a vision once I saw:

It was an Abyssinian maid,
And on her dulcimer she played,   40
Singing of Mount Abora.
Could I revive within me
Her symphony and song,
To such a deep delight 'twould win me,
That with music loud and long,   45
I would build that dome in air,
That sunny dome! those caves of ice!
And all who heard should see them there,
And all should cry, Beware! Beware!
His flashing eyes, his floating hair!   50
Weave a circle round him thrice,
And close your eyes with holy dread,
For he on honeydew hath fed,
And drunk the milk of Paradise.

QUESTIONS

1. Kipling called the first nine lines of this poem "the most magical in the English language." What accounts for their preternatural quality? How is the imagery "magical"?
2. What can Coleridge have in mind when he describes the chasm of line 12 as "romantic"? Why is it a "savage" place?
3. The poem's final stanza switches from third-person narrative to first person direct address. What reason can you give for this? Do the speaker's concerns hearken back to the matter of the first two stanzas?
4. Some critics claim that "Kubla Khan" is about the pleasures of art and the sinister forces that threaten it. Examine the evidence in the poem that would support this interpretation.
5. Robert Graves maintains that Coleridge is the finest poet in English in rendering the state of "entrancement." What makes the imaginative force of "Kubla Khan" so intense? How does Coleridge conceive the role of imagination in the poem?

Wallace Stevens

THE SNOW MAN

One must have a mind of winter
To regard the frost and the boughs
Of the pine-trees crusted with snow;

And have been cold a long time
To behold the junipers shagged with ice,   5
The spruces rough in the distant glitter

Of the January sun; and not to think
Of any misery in the sound of the wind,
In the sound of a few leaves,

Which is the sound of the land   10
Full of the same wind
That is blowing in the same bare place

For the listener, who listens in the snow,
And, nothing himself, beholds
Nothing that is not there and the nothing that is.   15

QUESTIONS

1. Who is the "snow man" referred to in the title?
2. What are the possible meanings of the phrase "one must have a mind of winter"?
3. The word "nothing" is referred to three times in the final stanza. What is the significance of each?
4. Describe the mood and tone of the poem. How do the sensory images in the poem contribute to its mood and tone? How do they reinforce the theme that is expressed in the final line?

Elizabeth Bishop

FILLING STATION

Oh, but it is dirty!
—this little filling station,
oil-soaked, oil-permeated
to a disturbing, over-all
black translucency.   5
Be careful with that match!

Father wears a dirty,
oil-soaked monkey suit
that cuts him under the arms,
and several quick and saucy   10
and greasy sons assist him
(it's a family filling station),
all quite thoroughly dirty.

Do they live in the station?
It has a cement porch   15
behind the pumps, and on it
a set of crushed and grease-
impregnated wickerwork;
on the wicker sofa
a dirty dog, quite comfy.   20

Some comic books provide
the only note of color—
of certain color. They lie
upon a big dim doily
draping a taboret   25
(part of the set), beside
a big hirsute begonia.

Why the extraneous plant?
Why the taboret?
Why, oh why, the doily?   30
(Embroidered in daisy stitch
with marguerites, I think,
and heavy with gray crochet.)

Somebody embroidered the doily.
Somebody waters the plant,   35

or oils it, maybe. Somebody
arranges the rows of cans
so that they softly say:
ESSO—SO—SO—SO
to high-strung automobiles.   40
Somebody loves us all.

QUESTIONS

1. What expectation is created by the exclamatory sequence at the start of the poem?
   Is the expectation fulfilled? Explain.
2. What words and images convey the dirtiness of the filling station? What details in the
   scene contrast with the dirt and grease? Why does Bishop ask so many questions
   about these contrasting details?
3. How does Bishop achieve a playful, witty tone in this poem? Why does she adopt this
   stance? What is the tone of the last line, "Somebody loves us all"?
4. Wallace Fowlie writes, "Miss Bishop's world is opulent, but in the most unexpected
   and most humble ways." How does this observation capture the spirit of "Filling
   Station"?

Margaret Atwood

GAME AFTER SUPPER

This is before electricity,
it is when there were porches.

On the sagging porch an old man
is rocking. The porch is wooden,

the house is wooden and grey;   5
in the living room which smells of
smoke and mildew, soon
the woman will light the kerosene lamp.

There is a barn but I am not in the barn;
there is an orchard too, gone bad,   10
its apples like soft cork
but I am not there either.

I am hiding in the long grass
with my two dead cousins,
the membrane grown already   15
across their throats.

We hear crickets and our own hearts
close to our ears;
though we giggle, we are afraid.

From the shadows around   20
the corner of the house
a tall man is coming to find us:

He will be an uncle,
if we are lucky.

QUESTIONS

1. Is the poet describing a memory, a dream, a fantasy, or something that really happened? On what do you base your view?
2. How does Atwood establish the time and place of the poem?
3. What is the significance of the title?
4. How does the author use details to evoke the senses of sight, smell, touch, and hearing?

Robert Hayden

THOSE WINTER SUNDAYS

Sundays too my father got up early
and put his clothes on in the blueblack cold,
then with cracked hands that ached
from labor in the weekday weather made
banked fires blaze. No one ever thanked him.   5

I'd wake and hear the cold splintering, breaking.
When the rooms were warm, he'd call,
and slowly I would rise and dress,
fearing the chronic angers of that house,

Speaking indifferently to him,   10
who had driven out the cold
and polished my good shoes as well.
What did I know, what did I know
of love's austere and lonely offices?

QUESTIONS

1. The narrator remembers his father as fluctuating between the "blueblack cold" and the fire's "blaze." How does he use this opposition between hot and cold to illustrate "love's austere and lonely offices"?
2. How does the narrator's "fearing the chronic angers of that house" and "speaking indifferently to him" affect his description of his father? What is his attitude toward his father after having "spoken" the poem?
3. Can we read this poem as a unique rendering of the black experience in America? How does Hayden's use of imagery, diction, and syntax support your conclusion? How does the use of language organize the poem's "meaning"?
4. Analyze the way Hayden controls imagery, mood, and tone in this poem in order define his attitude toward his father.

Louise Erdrich

THE STRANGE PEOPLE

The antelope are strange people . . . they are beautiful to look at, and yet they are tricky. We do not trust them. They appear and disappear; they are like shadows on the plains. Because of their great beauty, young men sometimes follow the antelope and are lost forever. Even if those foolish ones find themselves and return, they are never again right in their heads.

—Pretty Shield, Medicine Woman of the Crows
transcribed and edited by Frank Linderman (1932)

All night I am the doe, breathing
his name in a frozen field,
the small mist of the word
drifting always before me.

And again he has heard it   5
and I have gone burning

to meet him, the jacklight
fills my eyes with blue fire,
the heart in my chest
explodes like a hot stone.   10

Then slung like a sack
in the back of his pickup,
I wipe the death scum
from my mouth, sit up laughing,
and shriek in my speeding grave.   15

Safely shut in the garage,
when he sharpens his knife
and thinks to have me, like that,
I come toward him,
a lean gray witch,   20
through the bullets that enter and dissolve.

I sit in his house
drinking coffee till dawn,
and leave as frost reddens on hubcaps,
crawling back into my shadowy body.   25
All day, asleep in clean grasses,
I dream of the one who could really wound me.

QUESTIONS

1. What is the purpose of the epigraph that introduces the poem? How essential is it for your understanding of the poem's meaning?
2. Describe the relationship between the poem's narrator and the human as it is depicted in the first two stanzas. How does the imagery reinforce this relationship?
3. The narrator is apparently dead in stanzas 3 through 5. How then can he or she speak?
4. Who might be the "one who could really wound me"?

13. Symbolism

We know from an earlier section (see Chapter 7) that a symbol may be defined as something that stands for other than what it is. For example, the plumbing in Kay Boyle's "Astronomer's Wife" means more than what it literally is; it stands for the earthy, sensuous part of the main character's personality. In a similar way, symbolism in poetry radiates beyond the thing toward other levels and varieties of meaning. Often a symbol in poetry may be readily understood because it has become a part of common cultural knowledge: a cross symbolizes Christ; a rose, beauty; an American flag, patriotism. Yet symbolism in poetry also can be complex and demanding, forcing us to use our best critical faculties to discuss broader meanings in objects, persons, conditions, and things.

With a conventional poetic symbol or with symbolism that we can easily understand, we readily detect highly charged meaning in an image. This rich suggestiveness, pointing toward added meaning or value in a word, reflects the connotative power of language—the ability of words to mean more than they denote. Yet the importance of a conventional symbol is that it has a similar effect on all of us. The conventional symbol is like a sign pointing directly from the object to something else that it clearly suggests. The rose has functioned traditionally in this manner, as in Robert Burns's "A Red, Red Rose" or the following well-known poem, "Song," by Edmund Waller:

> Go, lovely rose!
> Tell her that wastes her time and me
>   That now she knows,
> When I resemble her to thee,
> How sweet and fair she seems to be.
>
>   Tell her that's young
> And shuns to have her graces spied,

That hadst thou sprung
In deserts, where no men abide,
Thou must have uncommended died.

Small is the worth
Of beauty from the light retired;
　　Bid her come forth,
Suffer herself to be desired,
And not blush so to be admired.

Then die! that she
The common fate of all things rare
　　May read in thee:
How small a part of time they share
That are so wondrous sweet and fair!

Here the fragile and transitory beauty of the rose is likened by the speaker to his beloved's beauty; and Waller apostrophizes the flower in order to advance a conventional thesis that his own rose, his beloved, should "suffer herself to be desired" before her "rare" beauty fades.

Not all symbols, however, have meanings so readily identifiable and understood. For one thing, poets can use even conventional symbols in special contexts that force us to reconsider or abandon traditional meanings. William Blake, especially, has a penchant for altering traditional symbolic meanings. In "The Sick Rose," he offers a strikingly new symbolic context for this much-used flower:

O rose, thou art sick
The invisible worm
That flies in the night
In the howling storm

Has found out thy bed
Of crimson joy,
And his dark secret love
Does thy life destroy.

Why is the rose sick? And who or what is the "invisible worm"? In this poem we are forced to mediate between two major symbols in order to arrive at any interpretation. Nevertheless, it is the overall context of the poem that permits us to fix symbolic meaning. The rose—which might symbolize love, beauty, innocence, sexual purity, or this entire constellation of ideas—is being attacked by the destructive agent or force symbolized by the worm. Violation, notably of a sexual nature, is the normative or standard context, forcing us to read the poem in a despairing, potentially tragic way.

Even when there is a *range* of meaning associated with a symbol, we can usually set this range and work within it in order to understand the poem.

Another problem involved in understanding poetic symbolism is that it often overlaps with or is reinforced by imagery, metaphors, and allusions. An image, for instance, can be repeated in a poem, forming a pattern of persistent symbolic meaning. The following poem by Emily Dickinson reflects the way in which image, metaphor, and symbolism blend within each other:

> 'Twas warm—at first—like Us—
> Until there crept upon
> A Chill—like frost upon a Glass—
> Till all the scene—be gone.
>
> The forehead copied Stone—
> The Fingers grew too cold
> To ache—and like a Skater's Brook—
> The busy eyes—congealed—
>
> It straightened—that was all—
> It crowded Cold to Cold—
> It multiplied indifference—
> As Pride were all it could—
>
> And even when with Cords—
> 'Twas lowered, like a Weight—
> It made no Signal, nor demurred,
> But dropped like Adamant.

In this remarkable tracing of the process whereby death encroaches upon life, Dickinson employs images of coldness and rocklike hardness to suggest death, reinforcing the image with metaphorical language. Yet it might be argued that the *degree* to which Dickinson stresses these qualities forces us to interpret the images symbolically. She is, of course, speaking very literally as well, but the importance that she invests in a particular portion of imagery makes us suspect that Dickinson also wants the poem to possess symbolic power.

Symbolism also can shade into allusion. We can have difficulty determining whether a reference to something in history, literature, or legend (either real or imaginary) is allusive or symbolic. Essentially, poets are willing to exploit both the allusive and symbolic dimensions of language in a single context. Ann Finch, Countess of Winchilsea (1661–1720), does this in her poem "Adam Pos'd":

> Cou'd our first father, at his toilsome plough,
> Thorns in his path, and labour on his brow,
> Cloath'd only in a rude, unpolish'd skin,

Cou'd he a vain fantastick nymph have seen,
In all her airs, in all her antick graces,
Her various fashions, and more various faces;
How had it pos'd that skill, which late assign'd
Just appellations to each several kind!
A right idea of the sight to frame;
T' have guest from what new element she came;
T' have hit the wav'ring form, and giv'n this Thing a name.

We might argue that the poet is alluding to the biblical creation myth, to Adam in the Garden of Eden, and specifically to the creation and even naming of the primal woman, Eve. And we would be correct. Yet, "our first father" and "this Thing" are also symbolic properties of a highly conventional nature. Understanding of them does not require specialized knowledge; at the symbolic level, they are part of our cultural heritage.

When dealing with the most common and obvious poetic symbols or the most unusual and complex, we must be prepared to explain and assess a symbol's contribution to the richness of meaning in a poem. The following selections are fine examples of the way in which poets employ symbolism and technical resources to vary and compress meaning.

William Blake

THE TYGER

Tyger! Tyger! burning bright
In the forests of the night,
What immortal hand or eye
Could frame thy fearful symmetry?

In what distant deeps or skies   5
Burnt the fire of thine eyes?
On what wings dare he aspire?
What the hand, dare seize the fire?

And what shoulder, & what art,
Could twist the sinews of thy heart?   10
And when thy heart began to beat,
What dread hand? & what dread feet?

What the hammer? what the chain?
In what furnace was thy brain?
What the anvil? what dread grasp   15
Dare its deadly terrors clasp?

When the stars threw down their spears,
And water'd heaven with their tears,
Did he smile his work to see?
Did he who made the Lamb make thee?   20

Tyger! Tyger! burning bright
In the forests of the night,
What immortal hand or eye
Dare frame thy fearful symmetry?

QUESTIONS

1. What is the Tyger? Is it the sole subject of the poem?
2. What Christian allusions do you find in this poem?
3. Who or what are the "stars" of line 17?
4. Bertrand Russell recounts that the first time he read this poem he became too dizzy to stand and nearly fainted. Was Russell's reaction ludicrous, or does the poem raise issues that are staggering? Explain.

Emily Dickinson

THERE'S A CERTAIN SLANT OF LIGHT

There's a certain slant of light,
On winter afternoons,
That oppresses, like the weight
Of cathedral tunes.

Heavenly hurt it gives us;   5
We can find no scar,
But internal difference
Where the meanings are.

None may teach it anything,
'Tis the seal, despair,—   10
An imperial affliction
Sent us of the air.

When it comes, the landscape listens,
Shadows hold their breath;
When it goes, 'tis like the distance   15
On the look of death.

QUESTIONS

1. Is the light in the first line a symbol? How does it become symbolic in the course of the poem?
2. Why does Dickinson liken the winter light to cathedral tunes? What is the relationship between the words "oppresses" and "weight"?
3. What contribution does the phrase "Heavenly hurt" make to the symbolic meaning of the poem?
4. Which important word from stanza 3 functions as a symbol?
5. The critic Denis Donaghue observes, "Distance and death are cousins in many of Emily Dickinson's poems." Apply this statement to this poem and to its symbolic meanings.

Robert Frost

STOPPING BY WOODS ON A SNOWY EVENING

Whose woods these are I think I know.
His house is in the village though;
He will not see me stopping here
To watch his woods fill up with snow.

My little horse must think it queer   5
To stop without a farmhouse near
Between the woods and frozen lake
The darkest evening of the year.

He gives his harness bells a shake
To ask if there is some mistake.   10
The only other sound's the sweep
Of easy wind and downy flake.

The woods are lovely, dark and deep,
But I have promises to keep,
And miles to go before I sleep,   15
And miles to go before I sleep.

QUESTIONS

1. Paraphrase what happens literally in the course of this poem.
2. What do we know about the speaker in the poem? What is his relationship to the horse and to the owner of the woods?
3. What conflict does the speaker experience in the poem? How is the conflict expressed in symbolic terms?
4. How do the various images in the poem—the snow, the "darkest" winter night, the frozen lake, the "easy wind and downy flake"—form a symbolic pattern?
5. Offer a symbolic interpretation of the last stanza. How do the dark woods and the repeated image of sleep reinforce each other symbolically?
6. What is Frost saying about the relationship between life and death, between the pursuit of beauty and pursuit of other obligations?

Denise Levertov

THE VICTORS

In June the bush we call
alder was heavy, listless,
its leaves studded with galls,

growing wherever we didn't
want it. We cut it   5
savagely, hunted it from the pasture, chopped it

away from the edge of the wood.
In July, still everywhere, it appeared
wearing green berries.

Anyway it must go. It takes   10
the light and air and the good of the earth
from flowers and young trees.

But now in August
its berries are red. Do the birds
eat them? Swinging   15

clusters of red, the hedges are full of them,
red-currant red, a graceful
ornament or a merry smile.

QUESTIONS

1. Who are "The Victors" referred to in the poem's title?
2. If we assume that the alders are symbols, what might they symbolize? Explain your view.
3. Has the speaker's attitude toward the alders changed during the course of the poem? If so, how?
4. Explain the meaning of the last sentence. Explain why it has such unusual syntax.

Nancy Morejón

CENTRAL PARK
SOME PEOPLE (3 P.M.)

he who crosses a park in great and flourishing Havana
amidst a flood of blinding white light
a white and blinding light
which would have driven that Van Gogh's sunflower mad
that blinding white light   5
which fills the Chinese eyes of the Chinese street photographers
he who crosses a park and doesn't understand
that blinding white light that almost repeats itself
he who is at a loss at that time of day
takes all kinds of roundabout and unnecessary   10
sojourns around Havana's Central Park
he who crosses a park strewn with sacred trees
who walks through it with open yet closed eyes

loving the Revolution's impact on the eyes
the impact he felt in his eyes and waist　　　　　　　　　　　　　15
he who is sustained by that light might know about the night and the wine

because in parks and in this one so central the one in Havana
old men sit on benches
light cigars look at each other
and talk about the Revolution and Fidel　　　　　　　　　　　　20
the old men who now remain on the benches
and are forever basking in the sun
it is a secret to no one
there go two men and an old worn-out briefcase
a fat bloated hand a shout wearing a grey hat　　　　　　　　　25
the old men meet next to the statue
of the Apostle Martí in 1966 in December of 1966
the year nearly over and waiting for
'the anniversary of freedom and paying tribute to the martyrs'
yes for all the men of the people who died and their blood　　　30
to bask in the afternoon sun in Havana Cuba free territory of America
he who crosses the park this world the womb of the Revolution in this
　　manner

must sigh and walk slowly and breathe
and step lightly and sigh and breathe and walk slowly　　　　　35
and forfeit his whole life
rabidly
　　　　compañeros

　　　　　　　　　　　　　Translated by Sylvia Carranza

QUESTIONS

1. Explain the image of the white light. How does it become symbolic?
2. What symbolic connection does the poet draw between religion and the Cuban revolution? Trace this motif in the poem.
3. How does the poet blend imagery, politics, and religion to render a symbolic statement?

14. Simile and Metaphor

The language of poetry typically is not literal: it does not project direct statements about experience. Instead, poets utilize numerous *figures of speech*—and there are more than 200 distinct varieties—in order to render an experience indirectly and imaginatively.

Figures of speech are ways of saying one thing and meaning another. Thus Robert Burns relies on figurative language when he declares, in one of the most famous stanzas in English poetry:

> O, my luve's like a red, red rose
> That's newly sprung in June.
> O, my luve is like the melodie
> That's sweetly played in tune.

We know that Burns's love is not literally a rose or a melody. But by using figurative language—in this case two similes that draw comparisions quickly—Burns invites us to picture the essence of his love through the rich train of associations that we bring to flowers and music.

Often the pictorial impact of figurative language, its power to make us "see," is generated by vivid comparisons known as *similes* and *metaphors*. Both similes and metaphors draw comparisons between things that are essentially unlike; in other words, we picture someone or something as if it were someone or something else. A poet who directly identifies the comparison by using such signals as "like," "as," and "resembles" is creating similes. With a metaphor, the comparison expressed is indirect, or implied, rather than stated. If Burns had written, "My luve's a red, red rose" (and forms of the verb "to be" are the clearest metaphorical signals), he would have designed a metaphor.

In both instances, poets seek compressed, imaginative likenesses of things drawn from logically different realms.

Metaphorical language (and here we include both metaphors and similes) permits poets to project ideas and emotions more vividly and eloquently than they could by literal statement. Often we are amazed by the power and originality of the metaphorical statement, for metaphorical language can transform experience for us, presenting it in unsuspected ways. Thus the American poet Langston Hughes in his poem "Harlem" likens a dream deferred to a raisin, a sore, rotten meat, a heavy load, an explosion. Note how we develop a *feeling* for the concept through metaphorical language, and also how we are controlled by the metaphors in our thinking about the subject. Why is the dream deferred a raisin? Why is it a sore? We apprehend meaning through metaphor. The poet therefore introduces metaphor to convey the subjective truth of the experience that unfolds in the rest of the poem.

In the examples from the poems by Burns and Hughes, we see how similes and metaphors can draw explicit comparisons that dominate individual lines. As a general rule, similes do not develop long or complex comparisons, although Judith Ortíz Cofer accomplishes this task in "What the Gypsy Said to Her Children" (see page 381), beginning "We are like the dead / invisible to those who do not / want to see." Certain varieties of metaphor, however, can control not just lines but major segments of a poem, or even an entire poem. The *extended metaphor* stretches over a series of lines; while the *controlling metaphor* dominates the poem. William Shakespeare in the following sonnet uses both varieties of metaphorical language to structure the content of the poem.

> My love is as a fever, longing still
> For that which longer nurseth the disease,
> Feeding on that which doth preserve the ill,
> The uncertain sickly appetite to please.
> My reason, the physician to my love,
> Angry that his prescriptions are not kept,
> Hath left me, and I desperate now approve
> Desire is death, which physic did except.
> Past cure I am, now reason is past care,
> And frantic-mad with evermore unrest;
> My thoughts and my discourse as madmen's are,
> At random from the truth vainly expressed:
> For I have sworn thee fair, and thought thee bright,
> Who art as black as hell, as dark as night.

Here the controlling metaphor likens the poet's love to a fever, while a subordinate extended metaphor compares his reason to a physician. And in the last line of the couplet at the end of the sonnet, Shakespeare shifts to striking, almost vicious similes to damn the subject that has caused him so much madness.

In dealing with metaphorical language in poetry, we must expect the unexpected and recognize that the detection of likenesses is not always as easy as in our examples. At times, there are implied metaphors in poetry—comparisons that we must infer without the aid of such grammatical connectives as "like" or "is"—that test our interpretive abilities. Here, for instance, is a short lyric by Randall Jarrell entitled "The Death of the Ball Turret Gunner":

> From my mother's sleep I fell into the State,
> And I hunched in its belly till my wet fur froze.
> Six miles from earth, loosed from its dream of life,
> I woke to black flak and the nightmare fighters.
> When I died they washed me out of the turret with a hose.

Admittedly these are not the easiest lines to interpret, for the dominant metaphor is implied; it can be known only if we examine the images that attach to it. Fortunately, Jarrell in a note on his poem has given us a clue to its metaphorical meaning. Speaking of the gunner, he observed: "hunched upside-down in his little sphere, he looked like the foetus in the womb." Armed with this revelation, we are better prepared to understand the experience of war—as painful separation from life—invoked by the metaphorical language of the poem.

Poets rely heavily on metaphorical language to capture their visions of human experience. Metaphorical statements by poets can elicit unusually sharp and precise reactions from readers. A poem, conditioned strongly by simile and metaphor, offers a compressed, emotionally intense, and highly imaginative clarification of life and its complexities.

Wilfred Owen

DULCE ET DECORUM EST

> Bent double, like old beggars under sacks,
> Knock-kneed, coughing like hags, we cursed through sludge,
> Till on the haunting flares we turned our backs
> And towards our distant rest began to trudge.
> Men marched asleep. Many had lost their boots   5
> But limped on, blood-shod. All went lame; all blind;
> Drunk with fatigue; deaf even to the hoots
> Of tired, outstripped Five-Nines that dropped behind.
>
> Gas! Gas! Quick, boys!—An ecstasy of fumbling,
> Fitting the clumsy helmets just in time,   10
> But someone still was yelling out and stumbling

And flound'ring like a man in fire or lime . . .
Dim through the misty panes and thick green light,
As under a green sea, I saw him drowning.

In all my dreams, before my helpless sight,   15
He plunges at me, guttering, choking, drowning.

If in some smothering dreams you too could pace
Behind the wagon that we flung him in,
And watch the white eyes writhing in his face,
His hanging face, like a devil's sick of sin;   20
If you could hear, at every jolt, the blood
Come gargling from the froth-corrupted lungs
Obscene as cancer, bitter as the cud
Of vile, incurable sores on innocent tongues,—
My friend, you would not tell with such high zest   25
To children ardent for some desperate glory,
The old lie: *Dulce et decorum est*
Pro patria mori.

QUESTIONS

1. Why are the troops in the first line "like old beggars under sacks"? How does this simile connect with the one in line 2?
2. What extended metaphor controls the second and third stanzas? How does the simile in line 12 successfully reinforce the larger comparison?
3. Why is the gassed soldier's face likened to a devil's in line 20? How does the comparison in lines 23–24 contribute to the effectiveness of the poem?
4. The last lines of the poem are taken from the Latin poet Horace: "It is sweet and fitting to die for one's country." What is Owen's attitude toward this idea? How does it bear on the theme of the poem?
5. The poet Ted Hughes has written of Owens, "His work is a version of old-style prophecy." What do you think Hughes meant by this?

Langston Hughes

HARLEM

What happens to a dream deferred?
    Does it dry up
    like a raisin in the sun?
    Or fester like a sore—
    And then run?   5

    Does it stink like rotten meat?
    Or crust and sugar over—
    like a syrupy sweet?

    Maybe it just sags
    like a heavy load.   10

    Or does it explode?

QUESTIONS

1. This poem consists of four progressively smaller stanzas governed by similes. What is the effect of structuring the poem this way?
2. What is the function of the repetition in punctuation in stanzas 1 and 2? How does it contribute to the poem's effect?
3. Why do you suppose Hughes ended the poem with an italicized question?
4. If you have read Lorraine Hansberry's play *A Raisin in the Sun* (included in this anthology), discuss the implication of having taken the title from Langston Hughes's poem.

Nicanor Parra

PIANO SOLO

Since man's life is nothing but an action at a distance,
A bit of froth shining on the inside of a glass,
Since the trees are nothing but fluttering furniture,
Nothing but chairs and tables in perpetual motion,
Since we ourselves are nothing but beings   5

(As god himself is nothing but god)
Since we don't talk to be heard
But to make others talk
And the echo precedes the voices that raise it,
Since we haven't even the consolation of chaos   10
In a garden that yawns and fills with air,
A puzzle we have to solve before we die
So that we can be tranquilly restored to existence
After we have overdone it with women,
Since there is also a heaven in hell   15
Allow me also to do a few things:

I want to make a noise with my feet,
I want my soul to discover its body.

Translated by W. S. Merwin

QUESTIONS

1. This poem is replete with metaphors about life. Interpret the metaphors and explain
   what the poet's general view of life is.
2. According to the poet, what does a typical life lack? What negative trait do most lives
   have? How can a healthy balance be found?
3. What is the significance of the poem's title? What part or parts of the poem are
   particularly pertinent to the title?
4. The poet is also a physicist. How does this fact influence your interpretation of the
   poem and the images that the poet uses in the poem?

Josephine Miles

HOUSEWIFE

Occasional mornings when an early fog
Not yet dispersed stands in every yard
And drips and undiscloses, she is severely
Put to the task of herself.

Usually here we have view window dawns,   5
The whole East Bay at least some spaces into the room,
Puffing the curtains, and then she is out
In the submetropolitan stir.

But when the fog at the glass pauses and closes
She is put to ponder   10
A life-line, how it chooses to run obscurely
In her hand, before her.

QUESTIONS

1. How does the title provide us with a clue to the woman's life? Would your response
    to and interpretation of the poem have been different had there been no title?
2. What is the effect of the fog on the woman? What does it reveal about the woman's
    own conception of her role in life? How does it function as an extended meta-
    phor?
3. What does the poet mean by "Put to the task of herself"? What is the woman "put
    to ponder"? How are these two lines related?
4. Compare and contrast the description of the fog and its effect on the woman with
    the description and effect of the fog in "The Love Song of J. Alfred Prufrock" (see
    pages 394–398).

Maxine Kumin

TOGETHER

The water closing
over us and the
going down is all.
Gills are given.
We convert in a   5
town of broken hulls
and green doubloons.
O you dead pirates
hear us! There is
no salvage. All   10
you know is the color
of warm caramel. All
is salt. See how
our eyes have migrated
to the uphill side?   15
Now we are new round
mouths and no spines
letting the water cover.

It happens over
and over, me in   20
your body and you
in mine.

QUESTIONS

1. What is this poem about? At what point do you discover the subject of the poem? Is there an extended metaphor? Explain.
2. How, or in what way, do the people in this poem become absorbed in nature? Why does Kumin rely so heavily on nautical imagery to convey this absorption? What is the purpose or goal?
3. Examine each sentence in the poem. Why is it difficult to establish meanings for some of these sentences? How do the sentences connect in terms of meaning?
4. Is there a "theme" in this poem, or is the poet simply trying to transcribe the specific sensation of two human beings coming together? Explain.

Sylvia Plath

DADDY

You do not do, you do not do
Any more, black shoe
in which I have lived like a foot
For thirty years, poor and white,
Barely daring to breathe or Achoo.   5

Daddy, I have had to kill you.
You died before I had time—
Marble-heavy, a bag full of God,
Ghastly statue with one grey toe
Big as a Frisco seal   10

And a head in the freakish Atlantic
Where it pours bean green over blue
In the waters off beautiful Nauset.
I used to pray to recover you.
Ach, du.   15

In the German tongue, in the Polish town
Scraped flat by the roller
Of wars, wars, wars.
But the name of the town is common.
My Polack friend   20

Says there are a dozen or two.
So I never could tell where you
Put your foot, your root,
I never could talk to you.
The tongue stuck in my jaw.   25

It stuck in a barb wire snare.
Ich, ich, ich, ich,
I could hardly speak.
I thought every German was you.
And the language obscene   30

An engine, an engine
Chuffing me off like a Jew.
A Jew to Dachau, Auschwitz, Belsen.
I began to talk like a Jew.
I think I may well be a Jew.   35

The snows of the Tyrol, the clear beer of Vienna
Are not very pure or true.
With my gypsy ancestress and my weird luck
And my Taroc pack and my Taroc pack
I may be a bit of a Jew.   40

I have always been scared of *you*,
With your Luftwaffe, your gobbledygoo.
And your neat moustache
And your Aryan eye, bright blue.
Panzer-man, panzer-man, O You—   45

Not God but a swastika
So black no sky could squeak through.
Every woman adores a Fascist,
The boot in the face, the brute
Brute heart of a brute like you.   50

You stand at the blackboard, daddy,
In the picture I have of you,
A cleft in your chin instead of your foot

But no less a devil for that, no not
Any less the black man who   55

Bit my pretty red heart in two.
I was ten when they buried you.
At twenty I tried to die
And get back, back, back at you.
I thought even the bones will do.   60

But they pulled me out of the sack,
And they stuck me together with glue.
And then I knew what to do.
I made a model of you,
A man in black with a Meinkampf look   65

And a love of the rack and the screw.
And I said I do, I do.
So daddy, I'm finally through.
The black telephone's off at the root,
The voices just can't worm through.   70

If I've killed one man, I've killed two—
The vampire who said he was you
And drank my blood for a year,
Seven years, if you want to know.
Daddy, you can lie back now.   75

There's a stake in your fat black heart
And the villagers never liked you.
They are dancing and stamping on you.
They always *knew* it was you,
Daddy, daddy, you bastard, I'm through.   80

QUESTIONS

1. What extended metaphors control the speaker's emotional responses to her father?
   To what objects and concepts does she liken her father in stanzas 2–3?
2. Explain the shift in setting in stanza 4. Why does the speaker liken language to an
   "engine" and herself to a Jew? In this context, identify the German terms and
   allusions in the poem and explain their relevance.
3. What explicit comparison does she draw in stanza 9? How do you interpret the line
   in stanza 10 "Every woman adores a Fascist"? How do the extended comparisons
   in stanzas 11–16 reinforce the dominant comparison established earlier in the poem?
4. Speaking of Plath's *Ariel,* Robert Lowell declared: "Everything in these poems is

personal, confessional, felt, but the manner of feeling is controlled hallucination, the autobiography of a fever." Relate this statement to "Daddy," examining carefully the metaphorical language.

5. Sylvia Plath wrote, "I think that personal experience is very important, but certainly it shouldn't be a kind of shut-box and mirror-looking, narcissistic experience. I believe it should be *relevant,* and relevant to larger things, the bigger things such as Hiroshima and Dachau and so on." Assess Plath's statement in the context of "Daddy."

David Mura

GRANDFATHER AND GRANDMOTHER IN LOVE

Now I will ask for one true word beyond
betrayal, that creaks and buoys like the bedsprings
used by the bodies that begot the bodies that begot me.
Now I will think of the moon bluing the white
sheets soaked in sweat, that heard him whisper   5
haiku of clover, azaleas, the cry of the cuckoo:
complaints of moles and beetles,
blight and bad debts, as the *biwa*'s[1] spirit
bubbled up between them, its song quavering.
Now I take this word and crack it, like a seed   10
between the teeth, spit it out into the world,
and let it seek the loam that nourished his greenhouse
roses, sputtering petals of chrysanthemum:
let it leave the sweet taste of *teriyaki,*
and a grain of rice lodges in my molars,   15
and the faint breath of *sake,* hot in the nostrils.
Now the drifting before writhing, now Buddha
stand back, now he bumps beside her,
otoo-san,[2] *okaa-san,*[3] calling each other.
Now there reverberates the *ran* of lovers,   20
and the bud of the past has burst through
into the other world,

[1] *biwa*—a Japanese stringed instrument
[2] *otoo-san*—grandfather
[3] *okaa-san*—grandmother

where she, teasing, pushes him away, swats
his hand, like a pesky, tickling fly,
and then turns to his face that cries out   25
laughing, and he is hauling her in, trawling
the caverns of her flesh, gathering gift
after gift from a sea that seems endless,
depths a boy dreams of, where dolphins
and fluorescent fins and fish with wings   30
suddenly spill their glittering scales
before him, and he, who was always baffled by beauty,
lets slip the net and dives under, and the night
washes over them, slipping from sight,
just the soft shushing of waves, drifting ground   35
swells, echoing the knocking tide of morning.

QUESTIONS

1. What does the poet mean by the "one true word beyond/betrayal"?
2. How does the poet use simile and metaphor, and what is the intended effect?
3. Images of nature abound in the poem. What are they, and how could you classify
   them according to type?
4. Upon whom is the poem focused—the grandfather, the grandmother, or both
   equally? How did you arrive at your conclusion?
5. The poet is a *Sansei*, a third-generation Japanese American. Explain how this might
   influence the poem.

15. Personification
and Apostrophe

One variety of figurative language is personification, which attributes human characteristics to ideas, nonhuman forms of life, and inanimate objects. As such, personification
draws comparisons in special ways, tapping the world of correspondences from a clear
technical perspective. It offers imaginative discoveries about experience and clarifica-
tions about the world by linking things from different realms. When poets personify
beauty or wisdom, a mandolin or the moon, a tree or a flower, a cat or a toad, they call
attention to those human and nonhuman connections that broaden and illuminate the
universe of experience.

   Personification humanizes and animates the universe for us. Its figurative comparisons are condensed, concrete, and often conventional, but also at times unique. At
times, personification exists in a line or two or a poem, much like a limited or minor
metaphor. The Welsh poet Dylan Thomas personifies time in these lines from "Fern
Hill":

> Time let me hail and climb
> Golden in the heydays of his eyes.

Equally fresh and inventive personification appears in Fadwa Tuquan's "After Twenty
Years":

> Here the moon
> Sells its face every night,
> For a dagger, a candle, a braid of rain.

The moon as a spectator and judge of human behavior is a conventional comparison, but Tuquan turns it nicely; much personification does operate with conventional correspondences.

Just as individual lines of a poem might be governed by personification, so an entire poem can be dominated by the technique, as in the well-known "I Wandered Lonely as a Cloud," by William Wordsworth.

> I wandered lonely as a cloud
> That floats on high o'er vales and hills,
> When all at once I saw a crowd,
> A host, of golden daffodils,
> Beside the lake, beneath the trees,
> Fluttering and dancing in the breeze.
>
> Continuous as the stars that shine
> And twinkle on the milky way,
> They stretched in never-ending line
> Along the margin of a bay;
> Ten thousand saw I at a glance,
> Tossing their heads in sprightly dance.
>
> The waves beside them danced, but they
> Outdid the sparkling waves in glee;
> A poet could not but be gay,
> In such a jocund company;
> I gazed—and gazed—but little thought
> What wealth the show to me had brought:
>
> For oft, when on my couch I lie
> In vacant or in pensive mood,
> They flash upon that inward eye
> Which is the bliss of solitude;
> And then my heart with pleasure fills,
> And dances with the daffodils.

Wordsworth does not belabor the comparison of the daffodils to a joyful band of dancers. In fact, the imaginative power of the personification lies in the poet's subdued and subtle humanization of the flowers. We can visualize the daffodils as human forms in a merry procession, as well as perceive their impact on Wordsworth's emotions.

Personification is often allied to apostrophe, in which the speaker addresses someone who is absent or something that is nonhuman and generally not spoken to, but addressed as if it were alive and present. Here, for instance, is the Renaissance poet Sir Philip Sidney, addressing one of the most traditionally personified objects in world literature.

With how sad steps, O Moon, thou climb'st the skies,
How silently, and with how wan a face!
What! may it be that even in heav'nly place
That busy archer his sharp arrows tries?
Sure, if that long-with-love-acquainted eyes
Can judge of love, thou feel'st a lover's case.
I read it in thy looks; thy languisht grace
To me, that feel the like, thy state descries.
Then, ev'n of fellowship, O Moon, tell me,
Is constant love deem'd there but want of wit?
Are beauties there as proud as here they be?
Do they above love to be lov'd, and yet
Those lovers scorn whom that love doth possess?
Do they call virtue there ungratefulness?

The moon is personified as a stricken lover, sad and silent, pallid, and languishing over unrequited love. Sidney permits this personification to dominate the first eight lines of the sonnet before drawing another set of correspondences between lunar and terrestrial love in the last six lines. Thus the moon comes alive, not for a purely fanciful purpose, but rather to serve as a vehicle for indicting ungrateful or thoughtless worldly lovers. Moreover, Sidney in the title and twice in the poem addresses his subject intimately as "O Moon" and reinforces this human bond with "thou" and "thy." Through apostrophe, the moon and Sidney become companions in a lovers' complaint.

Apostrophe as a distinct figure of speech can also exist without personification. William Wordsworth, for instance, begins one sonnet by apostrophizing a deceased poet, "Milton thou shouldst be living at this hour." And when William Blake apostrophizes the tiger in his famous poem, he does so without humanizing or personifying the beast.

Tyger! Tyger! burning bright
In the forests of the night,
What immortal hand or eye
Could frame thy fearful symmetry?

In what distant deeps or skies
Burnt the fire of thine eyes?
On what wings dare he aspire?
What the hand dare seize the fire?

And what shoulder, & what art,
Could twist the sinews of thy heart?
And when thy heart began to beat,
What dread hand? & what dread feet?

What the hammer? what the chain?
In what furnace was thy brain?
What the anvil? what dread grasp
Dare its deadly terrors clasp?

When the stars threw down their spears,
And water'd heaven with their tears,
Did he smile his work to see?
Did he who made the Lamb make thee?

Tyger! Tyger! burning bright
In the forests of the night,
What immortal hand or eye
Dare frame thy fearful symmetry?

Apostrophe in this instance heightens the life of the tiger, but that life (and the force behind it) is nonhuman, even as Blake anthropomorphizes the creator of the tiger and indulges in personification of the stars.

Both personification and apostrophe have the power to infuse life, objects, the natural world, and the realm of ideas with a humanizing impulse. As techniques, they bring us closer to the things of this world with compression and immediacy. Because personification and apostrophe tend to treat conventional subjects and rely on standard usage, they can seem stilted or all too familiar. Consequently, we must be prepared to evaluate the effectiveness and originality of personification and apostrophe when poets use these techniques in their verse.

John Keats

TO AUTUMN

I

Season of mists and mellow fruitfulness,
    Close bosom-friend of the maturing sun;
Conspiring with him how to load and bless
    With fruit the vines that round the thatch-eves run;
To bend with apples the mossed cottage-trees,
    And fill all fruit with ripeness to the core;   5
        To swell the gourd, and plump the hazel shells
With a sweet kernel; to set budding more,
    And still more, later flowers for the bees,

Until they think warm days will never cease,   10
    For Summer has o'er-brimmed their clammy cells.

II

Who hath not seen thee oft amid thy store?
    Sometimes whoever seeks abroad may find
Thee sitting careless on a granary floor,
    Thy hair soft-lifted by the winnowing wind;   15
Or on a half-reaped furrow sound asleep,
    Drowsed with the fume of poppies, while thy hook
        Spares the next swath and all its twinéd flowers:
And sometimes like a gleaner thou dost keep
    Steady thy laden head across a brook;   20
    Or by a cider-press, with patient look,
        Thou watchest the last oozings hours by hours.

III

Where are the songs of Spring? Ay, where are they?
    Think not of them, thou hast thy music too—
While barréd clouds bloom the soft-dying day,   25
    And touch the stubble-plains with rosy hue;
Then in a wailful choir the small gnats mourn
    Among the river sallows, borne aloft
        Or sinking as the light wind lives or dies;
And full-grown lambs loud bleat from hilly bourn;   30
    Hedge-crickets sing; and now with treble soft
    The red-breast whistles from a garden-croft;
        And gathering swallows twitter in the skies.

QUESTIONS

1. Why does Keats apostrophize autumn? What are his feelings about this season?
2. How does Keats personify autumn in each of the three stanzas?
3. What patterns of imagery do you detect in each stanza? What is the relationship of other seasons to the development of the imagery? Why is time important in the poem? In addition to visual imagery, what other types of sensory imagery appear in the poem? Cite examples and explain their effects. What mood is created by the various forms of imagery in the poem?
4. Is the subject of the poem simply autumn, or does Keats introduce other subjects and ideas?

Walt Whitman

I SAW IN LOUISIANA
A LIVE-OAK GROWING

I saw in Louisiana a live-oak growing,
All alone stood it and the moss hung down from the branches,
Without any companion it grew there uttering joyous leaves of dark green,
And its look, rude, unbending, lusty, made me think of myself,
But I wonder'd how it could utter joyous leaves standing alone there without
    its friend near, for I knew I could not,   5
And I broke off a twig with a certain number of leaves upon it, and twined
    around it a little moss,
And brought it away, and I have placed it in sight in my room,
It is not needed to remind me as of my own dear friends,
(For I believe lately I think of little else than of them,)
Yet it remains to me a curious token, it makes me think of manly love;   10
For all that, and though the live-oak glistens there in Louisiana solitary in a
    wide flat space,
Uttering joyous leaves all its life without a friend a lover near,
I know very well I could not.

QUESTIONS

1. The poet compares himself to the tree. In what ways are they similar? In what ways
   are they distinct?
2. What methods does the poet use to personify the tree? What might be the reason for
   this personification?
3. What sexual allusions are included in the poem? What does the poet mean by
   "manly love"?
4. The term *celebratory* is often used in describing Walt Whitman's poetry. What and
   how is the poet celebrating in this poem?

Emily Dickinson

BECAUSE I COULD NOT STOP FOR DEATH

Because I could not stop for Death—
He kindly stopped for me—

The Carriage held but just Ourselves—
And Immortality.

We slowly drove—He knew no haste   5
And I had put away
My labor and my leisure too,
For His Civility—

We passed the School, where Children strove
At Recess—in the Ring—   10
We passed the Fields of Gazing Grain—
We passed the Setting Sun—

Or rather—He passed Us—
The Dews drew quivering and chill—
For only Gossamer, my Gown—   15
My Tippet—only Tulle—

We paused before a House that seemed
A Swelling of the Ground—
The Roof was scarcely visible—
The Cornice—in the Ground—   20

Since then—'tis Centuries—and yet
Feels shorter than the Day
I first surmised the Horses' Heads
Were toward Eternity—

QUESTIONS

1. Why can't the poet stop for Death? Why must a third person be present? (Remember that Dickinson is a single woman living in Victorian New England.)
2. What is Dickinson's attitude toward Death? Is she worried? indifferent? How careful are her observations? Give examples.
3. How is Death personified in this poem?
4. How can Death and the poet come upon an unfamiliar house in the fifth stanza, after

they have passed everything else? Why do they pause? Does Dickinson distinguish between the inside and the outside of the house? Some critics have identified the house with a tomb. Why? Do you agree?

5. The poet and critic Allen Tate has said that this poem shows "love being a symbol interchangeable with death." Is this an accurate reading of the poem? Why or why not?

May Swenson

HEARING THE WIND
AT NIGHT

I heard the wind coming,
transferred from tree to tree.
I heard the leaves
swish, wishing to be free

to come with the wind, yet wanting to stay   5
with the boughs like sleeves.
The wind was a green ghost.
Possessed of tearing breath

the body of each tree
whined, a whipping post,   10
then straightened and resumed
its vegetable oath.

I heard the wind going,
and it went wild.
Somewhere the forest threw itself   15
into tantrum like a child.

I heard the trees tossing
in punishment or grief,
then sighing, and soughing,
soothing themselves to sleep.   20

QUESTIONS

1. What is the relationship of the wind to the trees? In what ways are the trees personified in the poem? Is the wind personified? Explain.

2. The poet and critic Elizabeth Bishop has stated: "Miss Swenson is one of the few good poets who write good poems about nature, and really about nature, not just comparing it to states of mind or society." Does her statement apply to "Hearing the Wind at Night"? Defend your answer.
3. Analyze Swenson's extensive use of figurative language in the poem—notably personification, simile, and metaphor—and the way that she achieves a coherent picture of certain objects in the natural world.
4. Robert Lowell has called Swenson "quick-eyed." Based on your reading of her poem, what do you think he means?

Fadwa Tuquan

AFTER TWENTY YEARS

Here the foot prints stop;
Here the moon
Lies with the wolves, the dogs, and the stones,
Behind the rocks and the tents, behind the trees.
Here the moon   5
Sells its face every night,
For a dagger, a candle, a braid of rain.
Don't throw a stone in their fire;
Don't steal the glass rings
From the gypsies' fingers.   10
They slept, and so did the fish and the stones and the trees.

Here the foot prints stop;
Here the moon was in labour.
Gypsies!
Give her then the glass rings   15
And the blue bracelets.
                    Translated from Arabic, translator unknown

QUESTIONS

1. How would you characterize the mood of the poem? What images contribute to the establishment of this mood?
2. The moon is described three times. How would you characterize these descriptions? What do they have in common?

3. The exact locale of the poem is not named. What sort of place is the poet describing? What type of atmosphere does it suggest? What goes on there? Who inhabits it?

4. Why has the poet separated the poem into two stanzas? What change, if any, has occurred between the first stanza and the second? What might be the significance of the moon "in labour?"

16. Meter, Rhythm, and Sound

Our universe is filled with rhythm. We find it in the seasonal changes, the ebb and flow of the tides, the rising and setting of the moon and sun, and the planets and stars that are most visible at regular intervals.

Our bodies, too, function as a result of rhythmic impulses sent out by the brain, which itself pulses in rhythmic waves. Sometimes we can tell who a person is not by the face—we may not be able to see the face from a distance—but by the way he or she walks; the rhythms of the walk are familiar to us.

The use of rhythm in poetry in fact may be a subconscious attempt to imitate the movements of things that control our lives. Of course the use of rhythm is also a conscious effort to emulate patterns of thought, speech, and sometimes sight.

The rhythms we find in poetry are achieved through the use of meter, and meter is produced by accentuating the sounds of certain syllables in certain words. We call this emphasis "stress" or "accent." The syllables or words that are *not* emphasized are characterized as being "unstressed" or "unaccented." If we remember that poetry was at first intended to be heard rather than read, meter and rhythm make far more sense to us. The poet, whether he or she wishes to be or not, is part of an old tradition that demands that the poet carefully select words not only for their syllabic content, but also for the power of those words to evoke in us an experience he or she wishes to share.

In traditional poetry, each line contains a number of feet, usually one to eight:

One foot	Monometer
Two feet	Dimeter
Three feet	Trimeter
Four feet	Tetrameter
Five feet	Pentameter
Six feet	Hexameter
Seven feet	Heptameter
Eight feet	Octameter

Within each foot of poetry there is usually one stressed and one or two unstressed syllables. We still use Greek terms to identify the kind of stress placed on various syllables:

Iamb (Iambic) First used by the seventh century B.C. poet Archilochus, the iamb was considered to approximate more than any other meter the rhythm and character of speech. Within a foot it is characterized by an unstressed (⌣) syllable followed by a stressed (′) syllable.

Trochee (trochaic) Used in early Greek tragedies and later replaced by the iamb, the trochee was believed useful in heightening excitement. Within a foot it is character- ized by a stressed (′) syllable followed by an unstressed (⌣) syllable. In Greek, "trochee" means "running foot."

Anapest (Anapestic) Also widely used in Greek drama, the anapest later became a favorite of generations of English poets. In Greek, "anapest" means "struck back"; anapest is recognized by its two unstressed (⌣ ⌣) beats and one stressed (′) beat.

Dactyl (Dactylic) In Greek, "dactyl" means "finger"; this meter is intended to corre- spond with its three syllables to the three joints of a finger. It is composed of one stressed (′) beat and two unstressed (⌣ ⌣) beats.

Spondee (Spondaic) Rarely used today except in so-called experimental poetry, the spondee uses two stressed (′ ′) beats. The Greeks used it with "drinking poems."

Scansion is the method of analyzing the metrical pattern—the kind of meter and number of feet used—of a poem. To scan is to analyze and measure. For example, if we scan Elinor Wylie's "Puritan Sonnet," we can readily see that the first two lines are predominantly iambic, with one trochaic and one anapestic substitution in the first line. (Substitution of one foot of a predominant pattern is a key way to vary rhythm.)

Dówn tŏ / the Púr/ĭ tăn már/rŏw óf / my bónes

There's some/thĭng ín / thĭs rích/nĕss thăt / Ĭ háte

More than 2,600 years old, the iamb continues to be the most popular metrical pattern, possibly because, as the Greeks believed, it most closely approximates the alternating short and long (or unaccented and accented) emphasis found in everyday speech.

Everyday speech, of course, has sounds, rhythms, pitches, and intonation. Used well, it is like music. If we have never heard Beethoven's Fifth Symphony, the opening notes hint that it is going to be exultant, more heroic even than his Third Symphony. We understand sound when it is made, but sometimes it escapes us when it is created in poetry. If we once again recall that originally poetry was written to be heard, we can then understand sound being a major component in the composition of it. "Music," Alexander Pope wrote in *An Essay on Criticism*, "resembles poetry."

Sound is strongly related to metrical rhythms—that is, sound created by the poet's careful selection and placement of certain words that possess the ability to evoke in the reader the sense of an echo, of lyrics to a song. "Manifest in rhythm and meter," writes Joseph Shipley, "its [sound's] power is subtlest within the word."

Much poetry reflects the marriage of meter, rhythm, and sound. Poets employ *alliteration,* which is the repetition of a *consonant* sound at the front of words or syllables; *assonance* or words that resemble each other in vowel sounds; and *onomatopoeia* or words that fortify the sense of the word used. *Rhyme,* the repetition of identical or similar sounds, is used very often in poetry because it is beautiful in and of itself, because it fulfills a rhythmically constructive function, and because it defines pauses or the end of a poem. The most widely used is *end rhyme,* but *front rhyme* and *sprung rhyme* are not unusual. (See the glossary for definitions of all terms used.)

Robert Burns's "Sweet Afton," with its repetition of lines and phrases, captures the rhythms and sounds that we associate with poetry:

> Flow gently, sweet Afton, among thy green braes!
> Flow gently, I'll sing thee a song in thy praise!
> My Mary's asleep by thy murmuring stream,
> Flow gently, sweet Afton, disturb not her dream!

> Flow gently, sweet Afton, among thy green braes!
> Flow gently, sweet river, the theme of my lays!
> My Mary's asleep by thy murmuring stream,
> Flow gently, sweet Afton, disturb not her dream!

Though not much heard in recent years, "Sweet Afton" is a good example of poetry set to music, a throwback to extremely ancient days when rhythms of instrument and poem matched perfectly and when sound was of paramount importance.

A. E. Housman stresses the importance of rhythm and sound in his definition of poetry as "not the thing said but a way of saying it." Housman, a master of verse technique, was praised by the critics and R. P. Tristram Coffin and Alexander M. Witherspoon, who wrote in 1929: "Songs are many, but the poets who have made the world's best poems for songs are few and far apart. You can count them, almost, on the fingers of one hand: Sappho, Horace, Burns and Heine. Maybe A. E. Housman will join that company in time. But Robert Herrick (1591–1674) is already there and he is not the least of them." Listen to Herrick's "Upon a Child That Died" (1648):

> Here she lies, a pretty bud,
> Lately made of flesh and blood,
> Who as soon fell fast asleep
> As her eyes did little peep.
> Give her strewings, but not stir
> The earth that lightly covers her.

By contrast, a contemporary poet, Samuel Allen, uses the "language of the people" rather than the "extraordinary" language allegedly assigned to poets in a poem dedicated to the legendary pitcher Satchel Paige. It has the ironic title "American Gothic."

To Satch

Sometimes I feel like I will *never* stop
Just go on forever
Til one fine mornin'
I'm gonna reach up and grab me a handfulla stars
Swing out my long lean leg
And whip three hot strikes burnin' down the heavens
And look over at God and say
How about that!

When we have little or no rhyme and little or no rhythm tied to traditional meter, we are required to *imagine* sound to accompany the images presented. In the case of baseball in Allen's poem, that isn't difficult to do; free, or "experimental," verse draws largely upon a more or less shared familiarity with the subject. Poetry simply would not be poetry without rhythm, cadence, and sound.

John Donne

THE BAIT

Come, live with me, and be my love,
And we will some new pleasures prove,
Of golden sands, and crystal brooks,
With silken lines, and silver hooks.

There will the river whisp'ring run,   5
Warm'd by thy eyes more than the sun;
And there the enamoured fish will stay,
Begging themselves they may betray.

When thou wilt swim in that live bath,
Each fish, which every channel hath,   10
Most amorously to thee will swim,
Gladder to catch thee, than thou him.

If thou, to be so seen, beest loath
By sun or moon, thou dark'nest both;
And if mine eyes have leave to see,   15
I need not their light, having thee.

Let others freeze with angling reeds,
And cut their legs with shells and weeds,
Or treacherously poor fish beset
With strangling snares or windowy net;   20

Let coarse bold hands, from slimy nest,
The bedded fish in banks outwrest;
Or curious traitors, sleave-silk flies,
Bewitch poor fishes' wand'ring eyes.

For thee, thou need'st no such deceit,   25
For thou thyself art thine own bait;
That fish, that is not catch'd thereby,
Is wiser far, alas, than I.

QUESTIONS

1. What is the prevailing metrical pattern in this poem? Scan the first stanza.
2. What is the theme of this poem? What varieties and patterns of sound reinforce the theme?
3. Donne tends to use words with very few syllables. What is the effect? Words in this poem of more than two syllables are crucial to the ambivalence felt in the relationship. Which words are these?
4. To what extent is "The Bait" an erotic poem? Explain.
5. Analyze the double image Donne employs here and the effectiveness of the language, sound, and imagery exercised in the use of it.

Matthew Arnold

TO MARGUERITE—
CONTINUED

Yes! in the sea of life enisled,
With echoing straits between us thrown,
Dotting the shoreless watery wild,
We mortal millions live *alone*.
The islands feel the enclasping flow,   5
And then their endless bounds they know.

But when the moon their hollows lights,
And they are swept by balms of spring,
And in their glens, on starry nights,
The nightingales divinely sing;   10
And lovely notes, from shore to shore,
Across the sounds and channels pour—

Oh! then a longing like despair
Is to their farthest caverns sent;
For surely once, they feel, we were   15
Parts of a single continent!
Now round us spreads the watery plain—
Oh might our marges meet again!

Who order'd, that their longing's fire
Should be, as soon as kindled, cool'd?   20
Who renders vain their deep desire?—
A God, a God their severance ruled!
And bade betwixt their shores to be
The unplumb'd, salt, estranging sea.

QUESTIONS

1. Paraphrase each of the four stanzas in this poem. How does Arnold advance his thesis from stanza to stanza? Which famous line best states the thesis?
2. What varieties of alliteration, rhyme, and other sound effects can you find in the poem? What is the cumulative effect?
3. Imagery of water predominates in this poem. Cite examples and their significance. What other patterns of imagery relate to the water motif?
4. What is Arnold's attitude toward God? Why?

Gwendolyn Brooks

HUNCHBACK GIRL: SHE THINKS OF HEAVEN

My Father, it is surely a blue place
And straight. Right. Regular. Where I shall find
No need for scholarly nonchalance or looks
A little to the left or guards upon the
Heart to halt love that runs without crookedness   5
Along its crooked corridors. My Father,
It is a planned place surely. Out of coils,
Unscrewed, released, no more to be marvelous,
I shall walk straightly through most proper halls
Proper myself, princess of properness.   10

QUESTIONS

1. How does the title make certain words in the poem suggest double meanings? Which words are these?
2. The poet uses assonance (repetition of vowel sound) and alliteration (repetition of consonants) in the poem. How does the rhythm these devices create add to the poem's theme and tone?
3. To whom is the poem's narrator speaking?
4. What does the narrator wish for?

Elinor Wylie

PURITAN SONNET

Down to the Puritan marrow of my bones
There's something in this richness that I hate.
I love the look, austere, immaculate,
Of landscapes drawn in pearly monotones.
There's something in my very blood that owns   5
Bare hills, cold silver on a sky of slate,
A thread of water, churned to milky spate
Streaming through slanted pastures fenced with stones.

I love those skies, thin blue or snowy gray,
Those fields sparse-planted, rendering meager sheaves;   10
That spring, briefer than apple-blossom's breath,
Summer, so much too beautiful to stay,
Swift autumn, like a bonfire of leaves,
And sleepy winter, like the sleep of death.

QUESTIONS

1. What unifying tone is there to the images and metaphors mentioned in the poem?
   What colors predominate in the poem? How do the images and metaphors reflect
   the philosophy of Puritanism?
2. Is Wylie's depiction of the Puritan life positive, negative, both, or neither? What
   aspects of the poem—especially the meter, rhythm, and rhyme—led you to your
   view?
3. In part, this poem is describing a locale. Drawing on the poem itself and your
   knowledge of Puritanism in the United States, to which geographical area of the
   country could she be referring?
4. What about the sonnet form makes it a particularly suitable one for a poem about
   Puritanism?

Allen Ginsberg

A SUPERMARKET IN CALIFORNIA

What thoughts I have of you tonight, Walt Whitman, for I walked
    down the sidestreets under the trees with a headache
    self-conscious looking at the full moon.
In my hungry fatigue, and shopping for images, I went into the
    neon fruit supermarket, dreaming of your enumerations!
What peaches and what penumbras! Whole families shopping at
    night! Aisles full of husbands! Wives in the avocados, babies in
    the tomatoes—and you, García Lorca, what were you doing
    down by the watermelons?

I saw you, Walt Whitman, childless, lonely old grubber, poking
    among the meats in the refrigerator and eyeing the grocery boys.

I heard you asking questions of each: Who killed the pork chops?
    What price bananas? Are you my Angel?   5
I wandered in and out of the brilliant stacks of cans following you,
    and followed in my imagination by the store detective.
We strode down the open corridors together in our solitary fancy
    tasting artichokes, possessing every frozen delicacy, and never
    passing the cashier.

Where are we going, Walt Whitman? The doors close in an hour.
    Which way does your beard point tonight?
(I touch your book and dream of our odyssey in the supermarket
    and feel absurd.)
Will we walk all night through solitary streets? The trees add shade
    to shade, lights out in the houses, we'll both be lonely.   10

Will we stroll dreaming of the lost America of love past blue
    automobiles in driveways, home to our silent cottage?
Ah, dear father, graybeard, lonely old courage-teacher, what
    America did you have when Charon quit poling his ferry and you
    got out on a smoking bank and stood watching the boat
    disappear on the black waters of Lethe?

QUESTIONS

1. The speaker of the poem goes "shopping for images" in the "neon fruit supermarket." What kinds of images does he "buy"? Who else is "shopping"?
2. Why is Whitman called "childless, lonely old grubber . . . eyeing the grocery boys"? What image do you get of that man in this poem? Why is it appropriate that he appear as a central figure in this poem?
3. What is "the lost America of love"? Where was it "found" before it was "lost"?
4. The poem closes with Whitman on the shores of the nether world of Greek mythology. Is this an appropriate final image? What does it suggest about the speaker's attitude toward America?
5. The poem is written as an address to Whitman and therefore appears almost conversational in style. How does this affect your reading of the poem? How would a more formal poem treat this subject? How would it be different? Be specific in your analysis of the devices that Ginsberg uses—especially consider diction, sound, rhythm, and length of lines.

Margaret Walker

POPPA CHICKEN

Poppa was a sugah daddy
Pimping in his prime;
All the gals for miles around
Walked to Poppa's time.

Poppa Chicken owned the town,   5
Give his women hell;
All the gals on Poppa's time
Said that he was swell.

Poppa's face was long and black;
Poppa's grin was broad.   10
When Poppa Chicken walked the streets
The gals cried Lawdy! Lawd!

Poppa Chicken made his gals
Toe his special line:
"Treat 'em rough and make 'em say   15
Poppa Chicken's fine!"

Poppa Chicken toted guns;
Poppa wore a knife.
One night Poppa shot a guy
Threat'ning Poppa's life.   20

Poppa done his time in jail
Though he got off light;
Bought his pardon in a year;
Come back out in might.

Poppa walked the streets this time,   25
Gals around his neck.
And everybody said the jail
Hurt him nary speck.

Poppa smoked his long cigars—
Special Poppa brands—   30
Rocks all glist'ning in his tie;
On his long black hands.

Poppa lived without a fear;
Walked without a rod.
Poppa cussed the coppers out;   35
Talked like he was God.

Poppa met a pretty gal;
Heard her name was Rose;
Took one look at her and soon
Bought her pretty clothes.   40

One night she was in his arms,
In walked her man Joe,
All he done was look and say,
"Poppa's got to go."

Poppa Chicken still is hot   45
Though he's old and gray,
Walking round here with his gals
Pimping every day.

QUESTIONS

1. What is the tone of this poem? Why doesn't Walker make any ethical judgment about Poppa's activities? Is she fond of Poppa? Explain.
2. What features of this poem give it a balladlike quality? What do we typically expect of the figures in ballads? Examine the ingredients and techniques drawn from music and folklore that make "Poppa Chicken" a special type of poem.
3. Point to instances of African-American idiom in the poem. Does this make the poem too narrow? What of Walker's intention to write inclusively about the human condition?
4. Is there a theme to this poem? Explain.

17. Structure and Form

W. H. Auden, a famous modern English poet and critic who is represented in this anthology, had very demanding criteria for judging "greatness" in poets. According to Auden, a great poet had to have a first-rate intellect; be proficient and prolific across many subject areas; and possess superior creativity and originality. Above all, any great poet must be a master of poetic form—of structures ranging from two-line stanzas (or couplets) to sonnets to longer and more intricate verse forms.

Phrased differently, a poet aspiring to greatness must submit to poetic rules and discipline. Such a poet would reflect deep understanding of traditional poetic forms in English and perhaps in other languages; and a contemporary poet would be able to transform these traditional or "closed" structures into more modern or "open" variants, most notably free verse. Nowhere is this sense of tradition and discipline more apparent than in the development of the sonnet in English and American poetry.

Poets often seem to relish discipline, so it is not strange that we have come from the flowing, imagery-filled blank verse of the Song of Solomon and the Psalms to the rigid fourteen-line sonnet with all its limitations. The sonnet is perhaps the best-known verse form in English. A sonnet must possess fourteen lines—no more, no less; it must have rhythm and meter—iambic pentameter; and it must rhyme in conformity with a traditional scheme.

From the Italian and English sonnet forms there have come, even with the limitations—challenges, some might say—new thematic approaches to writing the sonnet. (Sonnet means "little sound.") Although a short poem, the sonnet may be thematically as powerful as a longer poem, a story, or even a novel, and it may be just as satisfying. The form has lasted through seven centuries and shows no sign of falling out of favor in the late twentieth century. The sonnet reaches backward and forward, complementing past and future; John Donne probably would have admired Cullen's sonnets, as Cullen admired Keats's sonnets. Themes change, as they should, but the tradition of the form holds.

The sonnet is much like the classical essay that begins with a question; after the question, the essay is all answer. The sonnet poses a problem or asks a question in its first eight lines—the *octave*—and in the next six—the *sestet*—proposes to solve the problem or to answer the question.

The sonnet underwent changes in England, although many poets continued to use the Italian form of octave and sestet. The English, following the lead of Shakespeare, often used three four-line stanzas, or *quatrains*, and resolved any question or problem in the final two lines of the sonnet, which were called the *couplet*.

Keats's "On First Looking into Chapman's Homer" is an example of the Italian sonnet:

> Much have I travell'd in the realms of gold,
> And many goodly states and kingdoms seen;
> Round many western islands have I been
> Which bards in fealty to Apollo hold.
> Oft of one wide expanse had I been told
> That deep-brow'd Homer ruled as his demesne:
> Yet did I never breathe its pure serene
> Till I heard Chapman speak out loud and bold:
> Then I felt like some watcher of the skies
> When a new planet swims into his ken;
> Or like stout Cortez, when with eagle eyes
> He stared at the Pacific—and all his men
> Look'd at each other with a wild surmise—
> Silent, upon a peak in Darien.

Coleridge's "To the Reverend W. L. Bowles" (1794) is in the English, or Elizabethan, or Shakespearean, tradition:

> My heart has thanked thee, Bowles! for those soft strains
>   Whose sadness soothes me, like the murmuring
>   Of wild-bees in the sunny showers of spring!
> For hence not callous to the mourner's pains
>
> Through youth's gay prime and thornless paths I went:
>   And when the mightier throes of mind began,
>   And drove me forth, a thought-bewildered man,
> Their mild and manliest melancholy lent
>
> A mingled charm, such as the pang consigned
>   To slumber, though the big tear it renewed;
>   Bidding a strange mysterious pleasure brood
> Over the wavy and tumultuous mind,

As the great Spirit erst with plastic sweep
Moved on the darkness of the unformed deep.

Sonnets offer disciplined approaches to human experience, as the poems by Keats and Coleridge suggest. Precise metrical lines, clear imagery, logical and thematic clarity, and purity of language also are found in the sonnet. Any closed form demands a great deal of the poet, but it always rewards both author and reader in kind.

Aside from the sonnet, there are dozens of poetic forms, some drawn from other cultures, some rooted in popular culture. Consider this delicate haiku written by Matsuo Basho (1664–1694):

> This road:
> no one walks along it
> Dusk in autumn.

Contrast it with this limerick by an anonymous author.

> There once was a man from Nantucket
> Who kept all his cash in a bucket
>   But his daughter named Nan
>   Ran away with a man,
> And as for the bucket, Nantucket.

Poetic forms and structures are legion, often rooted in time and place. The long cadenced lines of Whitman extolling New York are never chilled by the "pure and lonely" poetics of Robert Lowell; the Beat poets mimic Langston Hughes's use of jazz in poetry. And the poets' various ethnic impulses to universality echo in the forms they adopt.

Perhaps, for example, William Blake felt that his "London" required a poetic structure different from the one used by Juvenal to describe Rome. Blake's eye sweeps through the streets of London and finds them to be just as offensive as they were a century earlier, when Swift described them in "heroic verse," a form that he used with mockery. Heroic verse, normally used in French, Latin, and Greek, was for heroic themes. But each poet feels a different need for form: for Blake the quatrain expresses division; for Swift, the forty-nine-line iambic pentameter produces an urban mass. The stanza or, in Blake's case, the quatrain, like a paragraph in fiction, may be seen as a look from another camera angle at the same subject. The stanza may also state one complete theme or idea but be linked to related ideas and stanzas.

Poetic sensibilities change with time. Today traditional sonnets and formal dramatic monologues, epics and odes, and other "closed" forms have yielded to poetic structures rooted in twentieth century life, with verse as uneven in length and form as some city blocks and as diverse. Poets today approach structure and form from complementing and conflicting backgrounds. They find structures to both lament and exalt the contemporary condition, compelled to find poetic forms—as Sonia Sanchez and Joy Harjo do—that best capture the way they live, feel, and think.

William Shakespeare

SHALL I COMPARE THEE TO A SUMMER'S DAY?

Shall I compare thee to a summer's day?
Thou art more lovely and more temperate,
Rough winds do shake the darling buds of May,
And summer's lease hath all too short a date.
Sometime too hot the eye of heaven shines,   5
And often is his gold complexion dimm'd;
And every fair from fair sometime declines,
By chance, or nature's changing course, untrimm'd;
But thy eternal summer shall not fade
Nor lose possession of that fair thou ow'st,   10
Nor shall Death brag thou wand'rest in his shade
When in eternal lines to time thou grow'st.
   So long as men can breathe or eyes can see,
   So long lives this, and this gives life to thee.

QUESTIONS

1. Shakespeare's attitude toward nature is a complex one. How would you characterize it? Does he praise or reject nature? And if not nature, what is there to admire in the beloved? How does he structure his argument?
2. The phrase "eternal summer" seems to be a contradiction in terms. What might Shakespeare be referring to?
3. What do we know about the person the poem addresses?
4. Shakespeare's response to the flux of time and the stasis of death is the same: that his art shall conquer them both. Show how he organizes this idea in terms of sonnet form.
5. Analyze the various images of limitation in the poem and their relationship to the theme of immortality.

Robert Herrick

TO THE VIRGINS,
TO MAKE MUCH OF TIME

Gather ye rosebuds while ye may,
   Old Time is still a-flying;
And this same flower that smiles today
   Tomorrow will be dying.

The glorious lamp of heaven, the Sun,   5
   The higher he's a-getting,
The sooner will his race be run,
   And nearer he's to setting.

That age is best which is the first,
   When youth and blood are warmer;   10
But being spent, the worse, and worst
   Times still succeed the former.

Then be not coy, but use your time;
   And while ye may, go marry;
For having lost but once your prime,   15
   You may forever tarry.

QUESTIONS

1. What is the theme of the poem? Is it as apt today as it was when the poet wrote it in the seventeenth century?
2. What words and syntax indicate that the poem is not contemporary? Is it a "closed" or "open" poem? Explain.
3. Read the poem aloud several times. How does the author use sound to enhance the effect of the poem? What is the effect of rhyme on the poem?

Robert Browning

MY LAST DUCHESS

Ferrara

That's my last Duchess painted on the wall,
Looking as if she were alive. I call
That piece a wonder, now: Frà Pandolf's hands
Worked busily a day, and there she stands.
Will't please you sit and look at her? I said   5
"Frà Pandolf" by design, for never read
Strangers like you that pictured countenance,
The depth and passion of its earnest glance,
But to myself they turned (since none puts by
The curtain I have drawn for you, but I)   10
And seemed as they would ask me, if they durst,
How such a glance came there; so, not the first
Are you to turn and ask thus Sir, 'twas not
Her husband's presence only, called that spot
Of joy into the Duchess' cheek: perhaps   15
Frà Pandolf chanced to say "Her mantle laps
Over my lady's wrist too much," or "Paint
Must never hope to reproduce the faint
Half-flush that dies along her throat": such stuff
Was courtesy, she thought, and cause enough   20
For calling up that spot of joy. She had
A heart—how shall I say?—too soon made glad,
Too easily impressed; she liked whate'er
She looked on, and her looks went everywhere.
Sir, 'twas all one! My favor at her breast,   25
The dropping of the daylight in the West,
The bough of cherries some officious fool
Broke in the orchard for her, the white mule
She rode with round the terrace—all and each
Would draw from her alike the approving speech,   30
Or blush, at least. She thanked men—good! but thanked
Somehow—I know not how—as if she ranked
My gift of a nine-hundred-years-old name
With anybody's gift. Who'd stoop to blame
This sort of trifling? Even had you skill   35
In speech—(which I have not)—to make your will
Quite clear to such an one, and say, "Just this
Or that in you disgusts me; here you miss,

Or there exceed the mark"—and if she let
Herself be lessoned so, nor plainly set   40
Her wits to yours, forsooth, and made excuse
—E'en then would be some stooping; and I choose
Never to stoop. Oh sir, she smiled, no doubt,
Whene'er I passed her; but who passed without
Much the same smile? This grew; I gave commands;   45
Then all smiles stopped together. There she stands
As if alive. Will't please you rise? We'll meet
The company below, then. I repeat,
The Count your master's known munificence
Is ample warrant that no just pretense   50
Of mine for dowry will be disallowed;
Though his fair daughter's self, as I avowed
At starting, is my object. Nay, we'll go
Together down, sir. Notice Neptune, though,
Taming a sea horse, thought a rarity,   55
Which Claus of Innsbruck cast in bronze for me!

QUESTIONS

1. Browning was famous for his dramatic monologues, and this is one of his best. What is the dramatic situation? How would you describe the speaker? Why do you think he values art so highly? How does he gratuitously give himself and his past actions away? Analyze the way in which this dramatic monologue is structured around the gradual revelation of the speaker's personality.
2. What is the difference between these couplets and the heroic couplets of the eighteenth century? What literary effects are achieved by Browning's use of the couplet?
3. The poem ends as it begins, with a reference to art. What significance is there to the statue of Neptune taming a seahorse? Does Browning mean this to be taken symbolically? Explain.
4. A critic, Leonard Nathanson, writes that "the Duke performs the very act he asserts to be the most repugnant to his nature; after sacrificing his wife rather than his dignity, he sacrifices that dignity." What other instances and varieties of irony do you detect in the poem?

e. e. cummings

NEXT TO OF COURSE GOD AMERICA I

"next to of course god america i
love you land of the pilgrims' and so forth oh
say can you see by the dawn's early my
country 'tis of centuries come and go
and are no more what of it we should worry   5
in every language even deafanddumb
thy sons acclaim your glorious name by gorry
by jingo by gee by gosh by gum
why talk of beauty what could be more beautiful than these heroic happy dead   10
who rushed like lions to the roaring slaughter
they did not stop to think they died instead
then shall the voice of liberty be mute?"

He spoke. And drank rapidly a glass of water

QUESTIONS

1. How does the structure of the poem differ from the "traditional" fourteen-line sonnet? Supply the rhyme scheme. Why is it that two lines do not rhyme with any other?
2. Why is the poem composed primarily of clichés, and what kind of person is generally associated with the use of them?
3. The first thirteen lines in this poem are a single sentence. Explain what effect is gained by this strategy.
4. The nouns "pilgrim" and "sons" form the basis upon which this poem is structured. What satire does Cummings intend by using them?
5. Which lines have the most alliteration? In which lines are there sound changes?
6. Why would this poem not "work" without the last line? What impression is given by the lack of a period after "water"?

Muriel Rukeyser

MYTH

Long afterward, Oedipus, old and blinded, walked the
roads.   He smelled a familiar smell.   It was
the Sphinx.   Oedipus said, "I want to ask one question.
Why didn't I recognize my mother?"   "You gave the
wrong answer," said the Sphinx.   "But that was what   5
made everything possible," said Oedipus.   "No," she said.
"When I asked, What walks on four legs in the morning,
two at noon, and three in the evening, you answered,
Man.   You didn't say anything about woman."
"When you say Man," said Oedipus, "you include women   10
too. Everyone knows that."   She said, "That's what
you think."

QUESTIONS

1. What makes this piece of writing a poem and not a work of prose?
2. The last line is ironic for several reasons. What are they?
3. The title of the poem is "Myth." What makes the poem resemble a myth?
4. Rukeyser's poetry has often addressed themes of oppression. How does this poem
   represent this choice of theme?

Sonia Sanchez

POEM AT THIRTY

it is midnight
no magical bewitching
hour for me
i know only that
i am here waiting   5
remembering that
once as a child
i walked two
miles in my sleep.
did I know   10

then where i
was going?
traveling. i'm
always traveling.
i want to tell   15
you about me
about nights on a
brown couch when
i wrapped my
bones in lint and   20
refused to move.
no one touches
me anymore.
father do not
send me out   25
among strangers.
you you black man
stretching scraping
the mold from your body
here is my hand.   30
i am not afraid
of the night.

QUESTIONS

1. At first glance this poem seems to lack what some might call the "richness" of poetic imagery; nevertheless, the poem creates a unique and moving vision of a black woman's "poetic" experience. How is this accomplished? Consider the way the poem sets out its story, the language it uses, the implied settings on which it rests. What elements do these have in common? How do they establish the tone of the poem?

2. How is the poet-persona at thirty similar to and different from the child who walked two miles in her sleep? Does she know where she is going? Does it matter?

3. Why does the poem begin at midnight? Why is it not a "magical bewitching hour"? What is it instead?

4. Why does the speaker want to tell "about nights on a brown couch . . ."? What do we learn from this story?

5. Will the "black man / stretching scraping / the mold from [his] body" take the hand of the poet-persona when "no one touches . . . anymore"? Why is the insistence on physical existence—on the importance of the body—part of "Poem at Thirty"?

Joy Harjo

FISHING

This is the longest day of the year, on the Illinois River or a similar river in
the same place. Cicadas are part of the song as they praise their invisible
ancestors while fish blinking back the relentless sun in Oklahoma circle in
the muggy river of life. They dare the fisher to come and get them. Fish too
anticipate the game of fishing. Their ancestors perfected the moves, sent   5
down stories that appear as electrical impulse when sunlight hits water.
The hook carries great symbology in the coming of age, and is crucial to
the making of warriors. The greatest warriors are those who dangle a
human for hours on a string, break sacred water for the profanity of air
then snap fiercely back into pearly molecules that describe fishness. They   10
smell me as I walk the banks with fishing pole, nightcrawlers and a
promise I made to that old friend Louis to fish with him this summer. This
is the only place I can keep that promise, inside a poem as familiar to him
as the banks of his favorite fishing place. I try not to let the fish see me see
them as they look for his tracks on the soft earth made of fossils and ashes.   15
I hear the burble of fish talk: When is that old Creek coming back? He
was the one we loved to tease most, we liked his songs and once in awhile
he gave us a good run. Last night I dreamed I tried to die, I was going to
look for Louis. It was rather comical. I worked hard to muster my last
breath, then lay down in the summer, along the banks of the last mythic   20
river, my pole and tackle box next to me. What I thought was my last
breath floated off as a cloud making an umbrella of grief over my relatives.
How embarrassing when the next breath came, and then the next. I reeled
in one after another, as if I'd caught a bucket of suckers instead of bass. I
guess it wasn't my time, I explained, and went fishing anyway as a liar   25
and I know most fishers to be liars most of the time. Even Louis when it
came to fishing, or even dying. The leap between the sacred and profane is
as thin as a fishing line, and is part of the mystery on this river of life, as is
the way our people continue to make warriors in the strangest of times. I
save this part of the poem for the fish camp next to the oldest spirits whose   30
dogs bark to greet visitors. It's near Louis's favorite spot where the wisest
and fattest fish laze. I'll meet him there.

QUESTIONS

1. How does Harjo "play" on traditional forms of nature poetry?
2. Harjo is Native American. How does the structure of the poem reflect her heritage?
3. What is the theme of this poem? How does the poem's open, experimental form
   reinforce this theme?
4. What aspects of figurative language and technique make this piece of literature a
   poem rather than an example of prose?

18. An Anthology of Poetry

Anna Akhmatova

LOT'S WIFE

The just man followed then his angel guide
Where he strode on the black highway, hulking and bright;
But a wild grief in his wife's bosom cried,
Look back, it is not too late for a last sight

Of the red towers of your native Sodom, the square   5
Where once you sang, the gardens you shall mourn,
And the tall house with empty windows where
You loved your husband and your babes were born.

She turned, and looking on the bitter view
Her eyes were welded shut by mortal pain;   10
Into transparent salt her body grew,
And her quick feet were rooted in the plain.

Who would waste tears upon her? Is she not
The least of our losses, this unhappy wife?
Yet in my heart she will not be forgot   15
Who, for a single glance, gave up her life.

Translated by Richard Wilbur

Al-Tutili

SEVILLE

I was bored with old Seville
And Seville was bored with me;
Had the city shared my skill
To invent abusive rhyme,
Rivals in invective, we   5
Would have had a lovely time.

So at last my weary heart
Could endure no more, and cried
It was time that we should part:
Water is much more purified   10
Than the dribble of a pool.

Translated by A. J. Arberry

QUESTIONS

1. Why does the poet want to leave Seville?
2. What can we infer about the personality of the poet?
3. When the poet says "Seville was bored with me," to what or whom is he referring? The city itself? Residents of the city? City life in general?
4. Al-Tutili was a Moorish poet who wrote sometime between A.D. 632–1050, in the southern Spanish city of Seville, then famous for its beauty and its arts. Poets competed with each other in poetry contests. This poem is called a *zajal*. Discuss the rhyme scheme and compare or contrast it with the sonnet.

Paula Gunn Allen

WOMANWORK

some make potteries
some weave and spin
remember
the Woman/celebrate
webs and making   5
out of own flesh

earth
bowl and urn
to hold water
and ground corn   10
balanced on heads
and springs lifted
and rivers in our eyes
brown hands shaping
earth into earth   15
food for bodies
water for fields
they use
old pots
broken   20
fragments
castaway
bits
to make new
mixed with clay   25
it makes strong
bowls, jars
new
she
brought   30
light
we remember this
as we make
the water bowl
broken   35
marks the grandmother's grave
so she will shape water
for bowls
for food growing
for bodies   40
eating
at drink
thank her

Yehuda Amichai

THE SWEET BREAKDOWN
OF ABIGAIL

We hit her with little blows
like an egg for peeling.

Desperate, perfume blows
She hits back at the world.

With pointed gigglings she takes revenge   5
For all that sadness.

And with hasty fallings-in-love,
Like hiccups of emotion.

Terrorist of sweetness,
She fills bombs   10
With despair and cinnamon, cloves and love splinters.

At night when she tears her jewelry
Off herself
There's great danger she won't know the limit
And will go on tearing and slashing away   15
All of her life.

                              Translated by Ted Hughes

Maya Angelou

SOUTHEAST ARKANASIA

After Eli Whitney's gin
brought to generations' end
bartered flesh and broken bones
Did it cleanse you of your sin
        Did you ponder?   5

Now, when farmers bury wheat
and the cow men dump the sweet

butter down on Davy Jones
Does it sanctify your street
      Do you wonder?   10

Or is guilt your nightly mare
bucking wake your evenings' share
of the stilled repair of groans
and the absence of despair
      over yonder?   15

TO A HUSBAND

Your voice at times a fist
      Tight in your throat
Jabs ceaselessly at phantoms
      In the room,
Your hand a carved and   5
      skimming boat
Goes down the Nile
      To point out Pharaoh's tomb.

You're Africa to me
      At brightest dawn.   10
The Congo's green and
      Copper's brackish hue,
A continent to build
      With Black Man's brawn.
I sit at home and see it all   15
      Through you.

Matthew Arnold

DOVER BEACH

The sea is calm tonight,
The tide is full, the moon lies fair
Upon the straits; on the French coast the light
Gleams and is gone; the cliffs of England stand,

Glimmering and vast, out in the tranquil bay.   5
Come to the window, sweet is the night-air!
Only, from the long line of spray
Where the sea meets the moon-blanched land,
Listen! you hear the grating roar
Of pebbles which the waves draw back, and fling,   10
At their return, up the high strand,
Begin, and cease, and then again begin,
With tremulous cadence slow, and bring
The eternal note of sadness in.

Sophocles long ago   15
Heard it on the Aegean, and it brought
Into his mind the turbid ebb and flow
Of human misery; we
Find also in the sound a thought,
Hearing it by this distant northern sea.   20

The Sea of Faith
Was once, too, at the full, and round earth's shore
Lay like the folds of a bright girdle furled.
But now I only hear
Its melancholy, long, withdrawing roar,   25
Retreating, to the breath
Of the night-wind, down the vast edges drear
And naked shingles of the world.

Ah, love, let us be true
To one another! for the world, which seems   30
To lie before us like a land of dreams,
So various, so beautiful, so new,
Hath really neither joy, nor love, nor light,
Nor certitude, nor peace, nor help for pain;
And we are here as on a darkling plain   35
Swept with confused alarms of struggle and flight,
Where ignorant armies clash by night.

QUESTIONS

1. What does the "eternal note of sadness" mentioned in the first stanza refer to? What does the reference to Sophocles imply?

2. What is the general mood of the poem? How do the rhythm and sound of the poem merge to create this mood? At what point does the general mood of the poem change? What does it change to?

3. To whom may Arnold refer when he states "Ah, love" in the final stanza? A real person? An imagined one? Or something else?

W. H. Auden

THE UNKNOWN CITIZEN

(TO JS/07/M/378

THIS MARBLE MONUMENT
IS ERECTED BY THE STATE)

He was found by the Bureau of Statistics to be
One against whom there was no official complaint,
And all the reports on his conduct agree
That, in the modern sense of an old-fashioned word, he was a saint.
For in everything he did he served the Greater Community.   5
Except for the War till the day he retired
He worked in a factory and never got fired,
But satisfied his employers, Fudge Motors Inc.
Yet he wasn't a scab or odd in his views,
For his Union reports that he paid his dues,   10
(Our report on his Union shows it was sound)
And our Social Psychology workers found
That he was popular with his mates and liked a drink.
The Press are convinced that he bought a paper every day
And that his reactions to advertisements were normal in every way.   15
Policies taken out in his name prove that he was fully insured,
And his Health-card shows he was once in hospital but left it cured.
Both Producers Research and High-Grade Living declare
He was fully sensible to the advantages of the Installment Plan
And had everything necessary to the Modern Man,   20
A phonograph, radio, a car and a frigidaire.
Our researchers into Public Opinion are content
That he held the proper opinions for the time of year;
When there was peace, he was for peace; when there was war, he went.
He was married and added five children to the population,   25

Which our Eugenist says was the right number for a parent of his generation,
And our teachers report that he never interfered with their education.
Was he free? Was he happy? The question is absurd:
Had anything been wrong, we should certainly have heard.

QUESTIONS

1. How would you characterize the tone and diction of the poem?
2. What specific standards and institutions of society did the citizen conform to?
3. What is the theme of the poem? How does the simple rhyme scheme of the poem contribute to its theme? In other words, how does the form support its content?
4. Many of the words in this poem are capitalized. What is the poet suggesting by this device?

Kofi Awoonor

SONG OF WAR

I shall sleep in white calico;
War has come upon the sons of men
And I shall sleep in calico;
Let the boys go forward,
Kpli and his people should go forward;   5
Let the white man's guns boom,
We are marching forward;
We all shall sleep in calico.

When we start, the ground shall shake;
The war is within our very huts;   10
Cowards should fall back
And live at home with the women;
They who go near our wives
While we are away in battle
Shall lose their calabashes when we come.   15

Where has it been heard before
That a snake has bitten a child
In front of its own mother;
The war is upon us

It is within our very huts   20
And the sons of men shall fight it
Let the white man's guns boom
And its smoke cover us
We are fighting them to die.

We shall die on the battlefield   25
We shall like death at no other place,
Our guns shall die with us
And our sharp knives shall perish with us
We shall die on the battlefield.

Ingeborg Bachmann

THE GREAT FREIGHT

The great freight of the summer has been loaded.
The sun-ship in the harbour waits the tide,
if behind you the seagull dives and cries.
The great freight of the summer has been loaded.

The sun-ship in the harbour waits the tide.   5
The unmasked smile of the lemurs treads
on the lips of the figureheads.
The sun-ship in the harbour waits the tide.

If behind you the seagull dives and cries,
from the west comes the order to sink from sight.   10
You will drown with open eyes in light,
if behind you the seagull dives and cries.
                              Translated by William Crisman

Amiri Baraka

PREFACE TO A TWENTY VOLUME SUICIDE NOTE

Lately, I've become accustomed to the way
The ground opens up and envelops me
Each time I go out to walk the dog.
Or the broad edged silly music the wind
Makes when I run for a bus—   5

Things have come to that.

And now, each night I count the stars,
And each night I get the same number.
And when they will not come to be counted
I count the holes they leave.   10

Nobody sings anymore.

And then last night, I tiptoed up
To my daughter's room and heard her
Talking to someone, and when I opened
The door, there was no one there . . .   15
Only she on her knees,
Peeking into her own clasped hands.

Ulli Beier

PRAISE-NAMES OF TWINS

Those who are woken up with a drum.
Those who have beautiful eyes.
I am glad to receive you.
You meet one who prepared cloth for you.
Two in a day!   5
Uncountable in the eyes of the co-wives,

Though only two in the eyes of the mother,
They walk together.
They do not leave one another behind.
Two joined on top of a tree.   10
Something sweet on top of the tree.

                                            from the Yoruba

John Berryman

THE BALL POEM

What is the boy now, who has lost his ball,
What, what is he to do? I saw it go
Merrily bouncing, down the street, and then
Merrily over—there it is in the water!
No use to say 'O there are other balls':   5
An ultimate shaking grief fixes the boy
As he stands rigid, trembling, staring down
All his young days into the harbour where
His ball went. I would not intrude on him,
A dime, another ball, is worthless. Now   10
He senses first responsibility
In a world of possessions. People will take balls,
Balls will be lost always, little boy,
And no one buys a ball back. Money is external.
He is learning, well behind his desperate eyes,   15
The epistemology of loss, how to stand up
Knowing what every man must one day know
And most know many days, how to stand up
And gradually light returns to the street,
A whistle blows, the ball is out of sight,   20
Soon part of me will explore the deep and dark
Floor of the harbour . . . I am everywhere,
I suffer and move, my mind and my heart move
With all that move me, under the water
Or whistling, I am not a little boy.   25

William Blake

THE LAMB

Little Lamb, who made thee?
Dost thou know who made thee?
Gave thee life & bid thee feed,
By the stream & o'er the mead;
Gave thee clothing of delight,   5
Softest clothing wooly bright;
Gave thee such a tender voice,
Making all the vales rejoice!
Little Lamb who made thee?
Dost thou know who made thee?   10
Little Lamb I'll tell thee,
Little Lamb I'll tell thee!
He is calléd by thy name,
For he calls himself a Lamb:
He is meek & he is mild,   15
He became a little child:
I a child & thou a lamb,
We are calléd by his name.
Little Lamb God bless thee.
Little Lamb God bless thee.   20

LONDON

I wander thro' each charter'd street,
Near where the charter'd Thames does flow,
And mark in every face I meet
Marks of weakness, marks of woe.

In every cry of every Man,   5
In every Infant's cry of fear,
In every voice, in every ban,
The mind-forg'd manacles I hear.

How the Chimney-sweeper's cry
Every black'ning Church appalls;   10
And the hapless Soldier's sigh
Runs in blood down Palace walls.

But most thro' midnight streets I hear
How the youthful Harlot's curse
Blasts the new born Infant's tear,   15
And blights with plagues the Marriage hearse.

Louise Bogan

CASSANDRA

To me, one silly task is like another.
I bare the shambling tricks of lust and pride.
This flesh will never give a child its mother,—
Song, like a wing, tears through my breast, my side,
And madness chooses out my voice again,   5
Again. I am the chosen no hand saves:
The shrieking heaven lifted over men,
Not the dumb earth, wherein they set their graves.

Anne Bradstreet

BEFORE THE BIRTH OF ONE OF HER CHILDREN

All things within this fading world hath end,
Adversity doth still our joyes attend;
No tyes so strong, no friends so dear and sweet,
But with deaths parting blow is sure to meet.
The sentence past is most irrevocable,   5
A common thing, yet oh inevitable;
How soon, my Dear, death may my steps attend,
How soon't may be thy Lot to lose thy friend,
We both are ignorant, yet love bids me
These farewell lines to recommend to thee,   10
That when that knot's unty'd that made us one,

I may seem thine, who in effect am none.
And if I see not half my dayes that's due,
What nature would, God grant to yours and you;
The many faults that well you know I have,   15
Let be interr'd in my oblivious grave;
If any worth or virtue were in me,
Let that live freshly in thy memory
And when thou feel'st no grief, as I no harms,
Yet love thy dead, who long lay in thine arms: 20
And when thy loss shall be repaid with gains
Look to my little babes my dear remains.
And if thou love thy self, or loved'st me
These O protect from step Dames injury.
And if chance to thine eyes shall bring this verse,   25
With some sad sighs honour my absent Herse;
And kiss this paper for thy loves dear sake,
Who with salt tears this last Farewel did take.

IN MEMORY OF MY DEAR GRAND-CHILD ELIZABETH BRADSTREET, WHO DECEASED AUGUST, 1665, BEING A YEAR AND A HALF OLD

Farewel dear babe, my hearts too much content.
Farewel sweet babe, the pleasure of mine eye,
Farewel fair flower that for a space was lent,
Then ta'en away unto Eternity.
Blest babe why should I once bewail thy fate,   5
Or sigh thy dayes so soon were terminate;
Sith thou art settled in an Everlasting state.

By nature Trees do rot when they are grown.
And Plumbs and Apples throughly ripe do fall,
And Corn and grass are in their season mown,   10
And time brings down what is both strong and tall.
But plants new set to be eradicate,
And buds new blown, to have so short a date,
Is by His hand alone that guides nature and fate.

QUESTIONS

1. What is the poem's main argument? In which lines is it most clearly expressed?
2. Where is repetition used in the poem? What is its function and effect?
3. The poem is composed of two stanzas. What makes each stanza stand as a separate unit of expression?
4. What is the mood of the poem? How does the author create this mood?

William Stanley Braithwaite

THE WATCHERS

Two women on the lone wet strand
    (The wind's out with a will to roam)
The waves wage war on rocks and sand,
    (And a ship is long due home.)

The sea sprays in the women's eyes—   5
    (Hearts can writhe like the sea's wild foam)
Lower descend the tempestuous skies,
    (For the wind's out with a will to roam.)

"O daughter, thine eyes be better than mine,"
    (The waves ascend high as yonder dome)   10
"North or south is there never a sign?"
    (And a ship is long due home.)

They watched there all the long night through—
    (The wind's out with a will to roam)
Wind and rain and sorrow for two,—   15
    (And heaven on the long reach home.)

Gwendolyn Brooks

THE BEAN EATERS

They eat beans mostly, this old yellow pair.
Dinner is a casual affair.
Plain chipware on a plain and creaking wood,
Tin flatware.

Two who are Mostly Good.   5
Two who have lived their day,
But keep on putting on their clothes
And putting things away.

And remembering . . .
Remembering, with twinklings and twinges,   10
As they lean over the beans in their rented back room that
        is full of beads and receipts and dolls and cloths,
        tobacco crumbs, vases and fringes.

WE REAL COOL

The Pool Players.
Seven at the Golden Shovel.

We real cool. We
Left school. We

Lurk late. We   5
Strike straight. We

Sing sin. We
Thin gin. We

Jazz June. We
Die soon.   10

Sterling A. Brown

SOUTHERN ROAD

Swing dat hammer—hunh—
Steady, bo';
Swing dat hammer—hunh—
Steady, bo';
Ain't no rush, bebby,   5
Long ways to go.

Burner tore his—hunh—
Black heart away;
Burner tore his—hunh—
Black heart away;   10
Got me life, bebby,
An' a day.

Gal's on Fifth Street—hunh—
Son done gone;
Gal's on Fifth Street—hunh—   15
Son done gone;
Wife's in de ward, bebby,
Babe's not bo'n.

My ole man died—hunh—
Cussin' me;   20
My ole man died—hunh—
Cussin' me;
Ole lady rocks, bebby,
Huh misery.

Doubleshackled—hunh—   25
Guard behin';
Doubleshackled—hunh—
Guard behin';
Ball an' chain, bebby,
On my min'.   30

White man tells me—hunh—
Damn yo' soul;
White man tells me—hunh—

Damn yo' soul;
Got no need, bebby,   35
To be tole.

Chain gang nevah—hunh—
Let me go;
Chain gang nevah—hunh—
Let me go;   40
Po' los' boy, bebby,
Evahmo'. . . .

QUESTIONS

1. What is the function of repetition in "Southern Road"?
2. Is this a song or poem or both? Should it be read or sung? What elements in it contribute to your definition?
3. What is the speaker of the poem protesting? What does he forecast for his future?

Elizabeth Barrett Browning

CONSOLATION

All are not taken; there are left behind
Living Belovéds, tender looks to bring
And make the daylight still a happy thing,
And tender voices, to make soft the wind.
But if it were not so—if I could find   5
No love in all the world for comforting,
Nor any path but hollowly did ring
Where "dust to dust" the love from life disjoined,
And if, before those sepulchers unmoving
I stood alone (as some forsaken lamb   10
Goes bleating up the moors in weary dearth),
Crying, "Where are ye, O my loved and loving?"—
I know a Voice would sound, "Daughter, I AM.
Can I suffice for HEAVEN and not for earth?"

IF THOU MUST LOVE ME, LET IT BE FOR NAUGHT

If thou must love me, let it be for naught
Except for love's sake only. Do not say
"I love her for her smile—her look—her way
Of speaking gently—for a trick of thought
That falls in well with mine, and certes brought   5
A sense of pleasant ease on such a day"—
For these things in themselves, Belovéd, may
Be changed, or change for thee—and love, so wrought,
May be unwrought so. Neither love me for
Thine own dear pity's wiping my cheeks dry—   10
A creature might forget to weep, who bore
Thy comfort long, and lose thy love thereby!
But love me for love's sake, that evermore
Thou mayst love on, through love's eternity.

QUESTIONS

1. How does the speaker distinguish permanent love from temporary love?
2. How would you characterize the poet's diction? What words in particular are representative of this diction?
3. How reasonable or impossible is it to love the way the poet suggests one should love?

George Gordon, Lord Byron

ON THIS DAY I COMPLETE MY THIRTY-SIXTH YEAR

Missolonghi, Jan. 22, 1824.

'Tis time this heart should be unmoved,
    Since others it hath ceased to move:
Yet, though I cannot be beloved,
    Still let me love!

My days are in the yellow leaf;   5
   The flowers and fruits of love are gone;
The worm, the canker, and the grief
   Are mine alone!

The fire that on my bosom preys
   Is lone as some volcanic isle;   10
No torch is kindled at its blaze—
   A funeral pile.

The hope, the fear, the jealous care,
   The exalted portion of the pain
And power of love, I cannot share,   15
   But wear the chain.

But 'tis not *thus*—and 'tis not *here*—
   Such thoughts should shake my soul, nor *now*,
Where glory decks the hero's bier,
   Or binds his brow.   20

The sword, the banner, and the field,
   Glory and Greece, around me see!
The Spartan, borne upon his shield,
   Was not more free.

Awake! (not Greece—she is awake!)   25
   Awake, my spirit! Think through *whom*
Thy life-blood tracks its parent lake,
   And then strike home!

Tread those reviving passions down,
   Unworthy manhood!—unto thee   30
Indifferent should the smile or frown
   Of beauty be.

If thou regrett'st thy youth, *why live?*
   The land of honourable death
Is here:—up to the field, and give   35
   Away thy breath!

Seek out—less often sought than found—
   A soldier's grave, for thee the best;
Then look around, and choose thy ground,
   And take thy rest.   40

QUESTIONS

1. This is one of the last poems that Byron wrote. What do you find that foretells his death?
2. Why does Byron declare in the first stanza, "Still let me love"? What type of love does he have in mind? Is it the same love that animates "She Walks in Beauty"? Explain.
3. What does the "fire" in stanza 3 symbolize?

SHE WALKS IN BEAUTY

1

She walks in Beauty, like the night
    Of cloudless climes and starry skies;
And all that's best of dark and bright
    Meet in her aspect and her eyes:
Thus mellowed to that tender light   5
    Which Heaven to gaudy day denies.

2

One shade the more, one ray the less,
    Had half impaired the nameless grace
Which waves in every raven tress,
    Or softly lightens o'er her face;   10
Where thoughts serenely sweet express
    How pure, how dear their dwelling-place.

3

And on that cheek, and o'er that brow,
    So soft, so calm, yet eloquent,
The smiles that win, the tints that glow,   15
    But tell of days in goodness spent,
A mind at peace with all below,
    A heart whose love is innocent!

Raymond Carver

PHOTOGRAPH OF MY FATHER IN HIS TWENTY-SECOND YEAR

October. Here in this dank, unfamiliar kitchen
I study my father's embarrassed young man's face.
Sheepish grin, he holds in one hand a string
Of spiny yellow perch, in the other
A bottle of Carlsbad beer.   5

In jeans and denim shirt, he leans
Against the front fender of a Ford *circa* 1934.
He would like to pose bluff and hearty for his posterity,
Wear his old hat cocked over his ear, stick out his
tongue . . .   10
All his life my father wanted to be bold.

But the eyes give him away, and the hands
That limply offer the string of dead perch
And the bottle of beer. Father, I loved you,
Yet how can I say thank you,   15
   I who cannot hold my liquor either
And do not even know the places to fish?

Lorna Dee Cervantes

REFUGEE SHIP

Like wet cornstarch, I slide
past my grandmother's eyes. Bible
at her side, she removes her glasses.
The pudding thickens.

Mama raised me without language.   5
I'm orphaned from my Spanish name.
The words are foreign, stumbling

on my tongue. I see in the mirror
my reflection: bronzed skin, black hair.

I feel I am a captive   10
aboard the refugee ship.
The ship that will never dock.
El barco que nunca atraca.

Aimé Césaire

SPIRALS

we ascend
braids of gallows birds from the cañafistulas
(the executioner must have forgotten the last grooming)
we ascend
beautiful hands hanging from ferns and waving farewells that no one hears   5
we ascend
the balisiers are breaking their hearts on the precise moment when the
    phoenix is reborn from its
            highest consuming flame
we ascend
we descend   10
the Cecropias hide their faces
and their dreams in the skeletons of their phosphorescent hands
the circles of the funnel now close faster and faster
it is the end of hell
we crawl we float   15
we coil the chasms of the earth
the resentments of men
the rancor of races tighter and tighter
and the abyssal undertows carry us back
in a tangle of lianas   20
of stars and shudders

Translated by Clayton Eshleman and Annette Smith

Cho Chihun

ANCIENT TEMPLE

Overcome by a stealthy slumber,
A blue boy in the upper seat,

With the wooden fish in his hands,
Closes his eyes and nods.

While Amitabha and Bodhisattva   5
Smile, smile without words,

Along the western borders,
Under the blinding red sky,
Peonies fall, peonies fall.

translated by Peter H. Lee

So Chongju

POETICS

The sea women of Cheju
    diving for abalone deep in the sea
leave the very best of the shells they find
    stuck to the rocks deep down
in the water, to pluck and gather   5
    the day their loves return.
The very best shellfish
    of poems too:
                Leave them there!
What empty, aimless wandering   10
    if every last one is gathered up.
Longing for the sea, just leave it there,
    this being a poet.

Translated by D. R. McCann

QUESTIONS

1. What is the central analogy the poet makes in the poem? Is it an apt analogy? Explain.
2. The poet says to leave one's best poems "there." Where is there?
3. What danger does the poet foresee in expressing all of oneself and holding nothing back?

Judith Ortiz Cofer

WHAT THE GYPSY SAID TO HER CHILDREN

We are like the dead
invisible to those who do not
want to see,
and color is our only protection against
the killing silence of their eyes,   5
the crimson of our tents pitched
like a scream
in the fields of our foes,
the amber warmth of our fires
where we gather to lift our voices   10
in the purple lament of our songs,
And beyond the scope of their senses
where all colors blend into one
we will build our cities of light,
we will carve them   15
out of the granite of their hatred,
with our own brown hands.

Jayne Cortez

MAKING IT

I know they want me to make it
to enter eye droppers and invade pills
turn around or get shot
I know they wanna vaccinate me with
the fear of myself   5
so i'll pull down my face and nod
I know they want me to make it
but i'm not in a hurry

Stephen Crane

WAR IS KIND

Do not weep, maiden, for war is kind.
Because your lover threw wild hands toward the sky
And the affrighted steed ran on alone,
Do not weep.
War is kind.   5

    Hoarse, booming drums of the regiment
    Little souls who thirst for fight,
    These men were born to drill and die
    The unexplained glory flies above them
    Great is the battle-god, great, and his kingdom—   10
    A field where a thousand corpses lie.

Do not weep, babe, for war is kind.
Because your father tumbled in the yellow trenches,
Raged at his breast, gulped and died,
Do not weep.   15
War is kind.

    Swift, blazing flag of the regiment
    Eagle with crest of red and gold,
    These men were born to drill and die
    Point for them the virtue of slaughter   20

Make plain to them the excellence of killing
And a field where a thousand corpses lie.

Mother whose heart hung humble as a button
On the bright splendid shroud of your son,
Do not weep.   25
War is kind.

QUESTIONS

1. What is the purpose of repetition in the poem?
2. What is the irony behind the title?
3. Crane refers to the soldiers as "little souls" who have "the unexplained glory" above them. How do these phrases contribute to the portrait Crane draws of the average soldier?
4. Compare and contrast the way the poet refers to men and women in the poem. How does he portray their relationships in terms of the effects of war?

Victor Hernandez Cruz

THE SECRETS II

This morning I move like the river
moves
Science in your eyes
Say the music elevates
passed clouds   5
Some tall legs
Encircle the river
Heads bob to the ticking
of the solar calender
Do you remember   10
the fourth floor of the pyramids
The hilarious perfume of your
feathers
The soft music of the sea flute
This morning I move like the river   15
moves
In and out of rooms like the warm
wind passing through

Countee Cullen

INCIDENT

(For Eric Walrond)

Once riding in old Baltimore,
    Heart-filled, head-filled with glee,
I saw a Baltimorean
    Keep looking straight at me.

Now I was eight and very small,   5
    And he was no whit bigger,
And so I smiled, but he poked out
    His tongue, and called me, "Nigger."

I saw the whole of Baltimore
    From May until December;   10
Of all the things that happened there
    That's all that I remember.

YET DO I MARVEL

I doubt not God is good, well-meaning, kind,
And did He stoop to quibble could tell why
The little buried mole continues blind,
Why flesh that mirrors Him must some day die,
Make plain the reason tortured Tantalus   5
Is baited by the fickle fruit, declare
If merely brute caprice dooms Sisyphus
To struggle up a never-ending stair.
Inscrutable His ways are, and immune
To catechism by a mind too strewn   10
With petty cares to slightly understand
What awful brain compels His awful hand.
Yet do I marvel at this curious thing:
To make a poet black, and bid him sing!

Roque Dalton

LOVE POEM

Those who widened the Panama Canal
(and were on the 'silver roll' not the 'gold roll')
those who repaired the Pacific fleet
in California bases,
those who rotted in prisons in Guatemala,   5
Mexico, Honduras, Nicaragua
for stealing, smuggling, swindling,
for starving,
those always suspected of everything
("Allow me to place him in your custody   10
for suspicious loitering
aggravated by the fact of being Salvadoran")
those who pack the bars and whorehouses
in every port and capital
('The Blue Grotto,' 'The G-String,' 'Happyland')   15
The sowers of corn deep in foreign forests,
the crime barons of the scandal sheets,
those who nobody ever knows where they're from,
the best artisans in the world,
those who were riddled with bullets crossing the border,   20
those who died from malaria
or scorpion bites or swarming bees
in the hell of banana plantations,
those who got drunk and wept for the national anthem
under a Pacific cyclone or up north in the snow,   25
the spongers, beggers, pot-heads,
the stupid sons of whores,
those who were barely able to get back,
those who had a little more luck,
the forever undocumented,   30
those who do anything, sell anything, eat anything,
the first ones to pull a knife,
the wretched the most wretched of the earth,
my compatriots,
my brothers.   35

Translated by Richard Schaaf

Kamala Das

AN INTRODUCTION

I don't know politics but I know the names
Of those in power, and can repeat them like
Days of the week, or names of months, beginning with
Nehru.[1] I am Indian, very brown, born in
Malabar, I speak three languages, write in   5
Two, dream in one. Don't write in English, they said,
English is not your mother-tongue. Why not leave
Me alone, critics, friends, visiting cousins,
Every one of you? Why not let me speak in
Any language I like? The language I speak   10
Becomes mine, its distortions, its queernesses
All mine, mine alone. It is half English, half
Indian, funny perhaps, but it is honest,
It is as human as I am human, don't
You see? It voices my joys, my longings, my   15
Hopes, and it is useful to me as cawing
Is to crows or roaring to the lions, it
Is human speech, the speech of the mind that is
Here and not there, a mind that sees and hears and
Is aware. Not the deaf, blind speech   20
Of trees in storm or of monsoon clouds or of rain or the
Incoherent mutterings of the blazing
Funeral pyre. I was child, and later they
Told me I grew, for I became tall, my limbs
Swelled and one or two places sprouted hair. When   25
I asked for love, not knowing what else to ask
For, he drew a youth of sixteen into the
Bedroom and closed the door. He did not beat me
But my sad woman-body felt so beaten.
The weight of my breasts and womb crushed me. I shrank   30
Pitifully. Then . . . I wore a shirt and my
Brother's trousers, cut my hair short and ignored
My womanliness. Dress in saris,[2] be girl,
Be wife, they said. Be embroiderer, be cook,
Be a quarreller with servants. Fit in. Oh,   35
Belong, cried the categorizers. Don't sit
On walls or peep in through our lace-draped windows.

[1] Jawaharlal Nehru (1889–1964), India's first prime minister after she gained independence.
[2] Traditional dress of Indian women.

Be Amy, or be Kamala. Or, better
Still, be Madhavikutty.[3] It is time to
Choose a name, a role. Don't play pretending games. 40
Don't play at schizophrenia or be a
Nympho. Don't cry embarrassingly loud when
Jilted in love . . . I met a man, loved him. Call
Him not by any name, he is every man
Who wants a woman, just as I am every 45
Woman who seeks love. In him . . . the hungry haste
Of rivers, in me . . . the ocean's tireless
Waiting. Who are you, I ask each and everyone,
The answer is, it is I. Anywhere and
Everywhere, I see the one who calls himself 50
I; in this world, he is tightly packed like the
Sword in its sheath. It is I who drink lonely
Drinks at twelve, midnight, in hotels of strange towns,
It is I who laugh, it is I who make love
And then feel shame, it is I who lie dying 55
With a rattle in my throat. I am sinner,
I am saint. I am the beloved and the
Betrayed. I have no joys which are not yours, no
Aches which are not yours. I too call myself I.

René Depestre

NOTHINGNESS

My heart
    is slowly
        sinking inside me
I feel it
    down in my belly 5
Wiggling around
      like a little
        dog
Now at last
    it has come to rest 10
      on my knee

[3] "Madhavavikutty is the pseudonym I use when I write stories in Malayalam, the language spoken here in Kerala State" [Das's note].

And in its place
emptied
and gaping
A hard little pebble shines in the sun   15
Translated by Norman R. Shapiro

QUESTIONS

1. What is the relationship between the line structure of the poem and its meaning?
2. How does the title of the poem affect your understanding of it? How would your view of the poem have been altered if there had been no title at all?
3. What experience is the poet describing?
4. Does the poem end on a positive note, a negative one, both, or neither?

Babette Deutsch

DISASTERS OF WAR

Streets opening like wounds: Madrid's. The thresh
Of resistance ends before a tumbled wall;
The coward and the cursing sprawl
Brotherly, one white heap of flesh
Char-mouthed and boneyard black.   5
A woman, dragged off, howls—a lively sack
Of loot. An infant, fallen on its back,
Scowls from the stones at the Herodian lark.
Light is the monster fattening on this dark.

If shadow takes cadavers for her chair,   10
Where fresh fires glare life lifts a wolfish snout.
Bruised and abused by hope, the rout,
Turning, is gunned across the square
And scattered. Rope, knife, lead
Slice prayer short. A lolling head   15
Grins, as with toothache. Stubbornly, the dead
Thrust forward like a beggar's senseless claw.
What is scrawled there in acid? THIS I SAW.

Beyond the Madonnas and marbles, Goya's brute
Testament pits itself against the hush   20

Of the blond halls, the urbane crush—
Against the slat-eyed, the astute,
Craning, against the guard, who yawns.
And pits itself in vain: this dark, these dawns,
Vomit of an old war, things the nightmare spawns   25
Are pictures at an exhibition. We
Look, having viewed too much, and cannot see.

Emily Dickinson

FROM ALL THE JAILS

From all the Jails the Boys and Girls
Ecstatically leap—
Beloved only Afternoon
That Prison doesn't keep

They storm the Earth and stun the Air,   5
A Mob of solid Bliss—
Alas—that Frowns should lie in wait
For such a Foe as this—

A LIGHT EXISTS IN SPRING

A Light exists in Spring
Not present on the Year
At any other period—
When March is scarcely here

A Color stands abroad   5
On Solitary Fields
That Science cannot overtake
But Human Nature feels.

It waits upon the Lawn,
It shows the furthest Tree   10
Upon the furthest Slope you know
It almost speaks to you.

Then as Horizons step
Or Noons report away
Without the Formula of sound   15
It passes and we stay—

A quality of loss
Affecting our Content
As Trade had suddenly encroached
Upon a Sacrament.   20

John Donne

HOLY SONNET 7

At the round earth's imagined corners, blow
Your trumpets, angels; and arise, arise
From death, you numberless infinities
Of souls, and to your scattered bodies go;
All whom the flood did, and fire shall, o'erthrow,   5
All whom war, dearth, age, agues, tyrannies,
Despair, law, chance hath slain, and you whose eyes
Shall behold God, and never taste death's woe.
But let them sleep, Lord, and me mourn a space;
For, if above all these, my sins abound,   10
'Tis late to ask abundance of Thy grace
When we are there. Here on this lowly ground,
Teach me how to repent; for that's as good
As if Thou hadst sealed my pardon with Thy blood.

QUESTIONS

1. How does the imperative mood of the poem influence its overall effect?
2. To whom does the word "you" refer in line 7?
3. How did you respond to the unusually long series in lines 5 through 8? What might have been the poet's purpose in using this device?
4. What change in tone occurs in line 9? What is the narrator of the poem entreating God to do?

HOLY SONNET 14

Batter my heart, three-personed God; for you
As yet but knock, breathe, shine, and seek to mend.
That I may rise and stand, o'erthrow me and bend
Your force to break, blow, burn, and make me new.
I, like an usurped town, to another due,   5
Labor to admit you, but, oh, to no end;
Reason, your viceroy in me, me should defend,
But is captived and proves weak or untrue.
Yet dearly I love you and would be lovèd fain,
But am betrothed unto your enemy: 10
Divorce me, untie or break that knot again,
Take me to you, imprison me, for I,
Except you enthrall me, never shall be free,
Nor ever chaste, except you ravish me.

Rita Dove

FIFTH GRADE AUTOBIOGRAPHY

I was four in this photograph fishing
with my grandparents at a lake in Michigan.
My brother squats in poison ivy.
His Davy Crockett cap
sits squared on his head so the raccoon tail   5
flounces down the back of his sailor suit.

My grandfather sits to the far right
in a folding chair,
and I know his left hand is on
the tobacco in his pants pocket   10
because I used to wrap it for him
every Christmas. Grandmother's hips
bulge from the brush, she's leaning
into the ice chest, sun through the trees
printing her dress with soft   15
luminous paws.

I am staring jealously at my brother;
the day before he rode his first horse, alone.
I was strapped in a basket
behind my grandfather.   20
He smelled of lemons. He's died—

but I remember his hands.

PARSLEY*

1. The Cane Fields

There is a parrot imitating spring
in the palace, its feathers parsley green.
Out of the swamp the cane appears

to haunt us, and we cut it down. El General
searches for a word; he is all the world   5
there is. Like a parrot imitating spring,

we lie down screaming as rain punches through
and we come up green. We cannot speak an R—
out of the swamp, the cane appears

and then the mountain we call in whispers *Katalina*.   10
The children gnaw their teeth to arrowheads.
There is a parrot imitating spring.

El General has found his word: *perejil*.
Who says it, lives. He laughs, teeth shining
out of the swamp. The cane appears   15

in our dreams, lashed by wind and streaming.
And we lie down. For every drop of blood
there is a parrot imitating spring.
Out of the swamp the cane appears.

2. The Palace

The word the general's chosen is parsley.   20
It is fall, when thoughts turn
to love and death; the general thinks

---

*On October 2, 1957, Rafael Trujillo (1891–1961), dictator of the Dominican Republic, ordered 20,000 blacks killed because they could not pronounce the letter "r" in *perejil*, the Spanish word for parsley.

of his mother, how she died in the fall
and he planted her walking cane at the grave
and it flowered, each spring stolidly forming   25
four-star blossoms. The general

pulls on his boots, he stomps to
her room in the palace, the one without
curtains, the one with a parrot
in a brass ring. As he paces he wonders   30
Who can I kill today. And for a moment
the little knot of screams
is still. The parrot, who has traveled

all the way from Australia in an ivory
cage, is, coy as a widow, practising   35
spring. Ever since the morning
his mother collapsed in the kitchen
while baking skull-shaped candies
for the Day of the Dead, the general
has hated sweets. He orders pastries   40
brought up for the bird; they arrive
dusted with sugar on a bed of lace.
The knot in his throat starts to twitch;
he sees his boots the first day in battle
splashed with mud and urine   45
as a soldier falls at his feet amazed—
how stupid he looked!—at the sound
of artillery. *I never thought it would sing*
the soldier said, and died. Now

the general sees the fields of sugar   50
cane, lashed by rain and streaming.
He sees his mother's smile, the teeth
gnawed to arrowheads. He hears
the Haitians sing without R's
as they swing the great machetes: 55
Katalina, they sing, *Katalina,*

mi madle, mi amol en muelte. God knows
his mother was no stupid woman; she
could roll an R like a queen. Even
a parrot can roll an R! In the bare room   60
the bright feathers arch in a parody
of greenery, as the last pale crumbs
disappear under the blackened tongue. Someone

calls out his name in a voice
so like his mother's, a startled tear   65
splashes the tip of his right boot.
My mother, my love in death.
The general remembers the tiny green sprigs
men of his village wore in their capes
to honor the birth of a son. He will   70
order many, this time, to be killed

for a single, beautiful word.

T. S. Eliot

THE LOVE SONG OF
J. ALFRED PRUFROCK

S'io credessi che mia risposta fosse
a persona che mai tornasse al mondo,
questa fiamma staria senza più scosse.
Ma per ció che giammai di questo fondo
non tornó vivo alcun, s'i'odo il vero,
*senza tema d'infamia ti rispondo.**

Let us go then, you and I,
When the evening is spread out against the sky
Like a patient etherised upon a table;
Let us go, through certain half-deserted streets,
The muttering retreats   5
Of restless nights in one-night cheap hotels
And sawdust restaurants with oyster-shells:
Streets that follow like a tedious argument
Of insidious intent
To lead you to an overwhelming question . . .   10
Oh, do not ask, 'What is it?'
Let us go and make our visit.

In the room the women come and go
Talking of Michelangelo.

*Epigraph: "If I thought my answer were to one who would never return to the world, this flame would shake no more; but since no one did ever return alive from this depth, if what I hear be true, without fear of infamy I answer you." (Inferno 27:61–66)

The yellow fog that rubs its back upon the window-panes,   15
The yellow smoke that rubs its muzzle on the window-panes,
Licked its tongue into the corners of the evening,
Lingered upon the pools that stand in drains,
Let fall upon its back the soot that falls from chimneys,
Slipped by the terrace, made a sudden leap,   20
And seeing that it was a soft October night,
Curled once about the house, and fell asleep.

And indeed there will be time
For the yellow smoke that slides along the street
Rubbing its back upon the window-panes;   25
There will be time, there will be time
To prepare a face to meet the faces that you meet;
There will be time to murder and create,
And time for all the works and days of hands
That lift and drop a question on your plate;   30
Time for you and time for me,
And time yet for a hundred indecisions,
And for a hundred visions and revisions,
Before the taking of a toast and tea.

In the room the women come and go   35
Talking of Michelangelo.

And indeed there will be time
To wonder, 'Do I dare?' and, 'Do I dare?'
Time to turn back and descend the stair,
With a bald spot in the middle of my hair—   40
(They will say: 'How his hair is growing thin!')
My morning coat, my collar mounting firmly to the chin,
My necktie rich and modest, but asserted by a simple pin—
(They will say: "But how his arms and legs are thin!")
Do I dare   45
Disturb the universe?
In a minute there is time
For decisions and revisions which a minute will reverse.

For I have known them all already, known them all—
Have known the evenings, mornings, afternoons,   50
I have measured out my life with coffee spoons;
I know the voices dying with a dying fall
Beneath the music from a farther room.
    So how should I presume?

And I have known the eyes already, known them all—   55
The eyes that fix you in a formulated phrase,
And when I am formulated, sprawling on a pin,
When I am pinned and wriggling on the wall,
Then how should I begin
To spit out all the butt-ends of my days and ways?   60
    And how should I presume?

And I have known the arms already, known them all—
Arms that are braceleted and white and bare
(But in the lamplight, downed with light brown hair!)
Is it perfume from a dress   65
That makes me so digress?
Arms that lie along a table, or wrap about a shawl.
    And should I then presume?
    And how should I begin?

    . . . . . .

Shall I say, I have gone at dusk through narrow streets   70
And watched the smoke that rises from the pipes
Of lonely men in shirt-sleeves, leaning out of windows? . . .
I should have been a pair of ragged claws
Scuttling across the floors of silent seas.

    . . . . . .

And the afternoon, the evening, sleeps so peacefully!   75
Smoothed by long fingers,
Asleep . . . tired . . . or it malingers,
Stretched on the floor, here beside you and me.
Should I, after tea and cakes and ices,
Have the strength to force the moment to its crisis?   80
But though I have wept and fasted, wept and prayed,
Though I have seen my head (grown slightly bald) brought in upon a platter,
I am no prophet—and here's no great matter;
I have seen the moment of my greatness flicker,
And I have seen the eternal Footman hold my coat, and snicker,   85
And in short, I was afraid.

And would it have been worth it, after all,
After the cups, the marmalade, the tea,
Among the porcelain, among some talk of you and me,
Would it have been worth while,   90
To have bitten off the matter with a smile,
To have squeezed the universe into a ball
To roll it towards some overwhelming question,
To say: 'I am Lazarus, come from the dead,

Come back to tell you all, I shall tell you all'—   95
If one, settling a pillow by her head,
   Should say: 'That is not what I meant at all.
   That is not it, at all.'
And would it have been worth it, after all,
Would it have been worth while,   100
After the sunsets and the dooryards and the sprinkled streets,
After the novels, after the teacups, after the skirts that trail along the floor—
And this, and so much more?—
It is impossible to say just what I mean!
But as if a magic lantern threw the nerves in patterns on a screen: 105
Would it have been worth while
If one, settling a pillow or throwing off a shawl,
And turning toward the window, should say:
   'That is not it at all,
   That is not what I meant, at all.'   110
   . . . . .

No! I am not Prince Hamlet, nor was meant to be;
Am an attendant lord, one that will do
To swell a progress, start a scene or two,
Advise the prince; no doubt, an easy tool,
Deferential, glad to be of use,   115
Politic, cautious, and meticulous;
Full of high sentence, but a bit obtuse;
At times, indeed, almost ridiculous—
Almost, at times, the Fool.

I grow old . . . I grow old . . .   120
I shall wear the bottoms of my trousers rolled.

Shall I part my hair behind? Do I dare to eat a peach?
I shall wear white flannel trousers, and walk upon the beach.
I have heard the mermaids singing, each to each.

I do not think that they will sing to me.   125

I have seen them riding seaward on the waves
Combing the white hair of the waves blown back
When the wind blows the water white and black.

We have lingered in the chambers of the sea
By sea-girls wreathed with seaweed red and brown   130
Till human voices wake us, and we drown.

QUESTIONS

1. What is the irony in the title? What seems to be the narrator's attitude toward love?
2. What emotional tone pervades the poem? What are some salient images that reflect this tone?
3. What type of man is the narrator? What is his outlook on his own life? What clues do we get from the line "I am not Prince Hamlet, nor was meant to be"? What is the narrator's outlook on human existence in general?
4. There are two sections of the poem that employ animal imagery. What kind of animals are being suggested? What is the effect of using these two images?
5. At the time of its publication, this poem caused quite a stir in the literary world, owing to the way the narrator depicts and evaluates his life. Why might this be?

Lawrence Ferlinghetti

IN GOYA'S GREATEST SCENES

In Goya's greatest scenes we seem to see
                      the people of the world
     exactly at the moment when
        they first attained the title of
               'suffering humanity'   5
    They writhe upon the page
             in a veritable rage
             of adversity
  Heaped up
      groaning with babies and bayonets   10
           under cement skies
    in an abstract landscape of blasted trees
      bent statues bats wings and beaks
         slippery gibbets
      cadavers and carnivorous cocks   15
   and all the final hollering monsters
     of the
           'imagination of disaster'
  they are so bloody real
         it is as if they really still existed   20

And they do

  Only the landscape is changed
They still are ranged along the roads
  plagued by legionaires
     false windmills and demented roosters   25

They are the same people
    only further from home
  on freeways fifty lanes wide
   on a concrete continent
    spaced with bland billboards   30
   illustrating imbecile illusions of happiness

  The scene shows fewer tumbrils
     but more maimed citizens
      in painted cars
    and they have strange license plates 35
  and engines
    that devour America

QUESTIONS

1. What is the central comparison that the poet is making? What details exist between the two things being compared?
2. The first stanza describes a work of visual art. What purpose might the author have for choosing to describe a work of art using words? Does the author assume the reader is familiar with the art being described?
3. Ferlinghetti's line structure is quite unusual. What is unusual about it? What do you think his purpose is in structuring the poem this way? What relationship is there between the line structure of the poem and the way the poem is intended to be read?

Anne Finch

TRAIL ALL YOUR PIKES

Trail all your pikes, dispirit every drum,
March in a slow procession from afar,
Ye silent, ye dejected, men of war.
Be still the hautboys, and the flute be dumb!
Display no more, in vain, the lofty banner;   5
For see where on the bier before ye lies
The pale, the fall'n, the untimely sacrifice
To your mistaken shrine, to your false idol Honour.

Gisele Fong

CORROSION

Ashamed of you
    woman pushing her way rudely to the snowpeas
    Loud restaurants and the slurpings, accents,
        the strange animal parts
        that show up in your soup   5
    Old man sitting on a corner
        slowly rocking, slowly rocking,
        ranting of old days,
        as the pigeons
            clutter   10
            by his feet
You are not a part of me.

I am
    a normal teenager
    eat pizza, go roller skating, listen to top 40   15
    flirt with boys, go to the beach;
    fit in.

"Are you Chinese, Japanese, Korean, Filipino, Hawaiian?
    Do you eat lice . . . Do you know Bruce?
        Oh AAAAH So, Sukiyaki!   20
            Sahlee, Chalee!"
You are not a part of me.

Immigrant, sweatshop woman,
    kung fu man, laundry worker,
        Chinese waiter, computer nerd.   25
You are not a part of me.

Eyes, tongue,
  leg, breast,
    heart
You are not a part of me.   30

Carolyn Forché

DULCIMER MAKER

Calf-deep in spruce dust
wood curls off his knife
blade wet bare bulb light.

The finish of his hands
shows oil, grain, knots   5
where his growth scarred him.

Planing black oak
thin to flow sounds.
Tones of wind filling
bottle lips.   10

It is his work tying strings
across fresh-cut pine.

He sings into wood, listens:
tree rings, water!

The wood drinks his cloth,   15
its roots going to the depths of him,
spreading.

He wants to build a lute for music
carved on Sumerian stones, a music
no one has heard for three thousand years.   20

For this he will work
the oldest wood he can find.
It will not be as far away,
as unfamiliar.

Robert Frost

MENDING WALL

Something there is that doesn't love a wall,
That sends the frozen-ground-swell under it,
And spills the upper boulders in the sun;
And makes gaps even two can pass abreast.
The work of hunters is another thing: 5
I have come after them and made repair
Where they have left not one stone on a stone,
But they would have the rabbit out of hiding,
To please the yelping dogs. The gaps I mean,
No one has seen them made or heard them made,   10
But at spring mending-time we find them there.
I let my neighbor know beyond the hill;
And on a day we meet to walk the line
And set the wall between us once again.
We keep the wall between us as we go.   15
To each the boulders that have fallen to each.
And some are loaves and some so nearly balls
We have to use a spell to make them balance:
'Stay where you are until our backs are turned!'
We wear our fingers rough with handling them.   20
Oh, just another kind of outdoor game,
One on a side. It comes to little more:
There where it is we do not need the wall:
He is all pine and I am apple orchard.
My apple trees will never get across   25
And eat the cones under his pines, I tell him.
He only says, 'Good fences make good neighbors.'
Spring is the mischief in me, and I wonder
If I could put a notion in his head:
'*Why* do they make good neighbors? Isn't it   30

Where there are cows? But here there are no cows.
Before I built a wall I'd ask to know
What I was walling in or walling out,
And to whom I was like to give offense.
Something there is that doesn't love a wall,   35
That wants it down.' I could say 'Elves' to him,
But it's not elves exactly, and I'd rather
He said it for himself. I see him there
Bringing a stone grasped firmly by the top
In each hand, like an old-stone savage armed.   40
He moves in darkness as it seems to me,
Not of woods only and the shade of trees.
He will not go behind his father's saying,
And he likes having thought of it so well
He says again, 'Good fences make good neighbors.'   45

ONCE BY THE PACIFIC

The shattered water made a misty din.
Great waves looked over others coming in,
And thought of doing something to the shore
That water never did to land before.
The clouds were low and hairy in the skies,   5
Like locks blown forward in the gleam of eyes.
You could not tell, and yet it looked as if
The shore was lucky in being backed by cliff,
The cliff in being backed by continent;
It looked as if a night of dark intent   10
Was coming, and not only a night, an age.
Someone had better be prepared for rage.
There would be more than ocean-water broken
Before God's last *Put out the Light* was spoken.

Anthony Grooms

HOMESPACE

My mother did not know me when I knocked.
She said her son was killed in the war.
It was only when I blurted my tears
That she opened the screen and fell

Into my arms. My father welcomed me as a hero.   5
They gave a cookout. No one my age came.
I made myself busy with the fire
So I wouldn't have to talk. When the fuel

Exploded on the coals, I heard screams.
In the evening the orange sun dropped   10
Into the haze of the blue ridges. August seemed cool.
Women and children laughed from the porch.

Men sat under the elms.
I watched the sky for the enemy.

Joy Harjo

I GIVE YOU BACK

I release you, my beautiful and terrible
fear. I release you. You were my beloved
and hated twin, but now, I don't know you
as myself. I release you with all the
pain I would know at the death of   5
my daughters.

You are not my blood anymore.

I give you back to the white soldiers
who burned down my home, beheaded my children,
raped and sodomized my brothers and sisters.   10
I give you back to those who stole the
food from our plates when we were starving.

I release you, fear, because you hold
these scenes in front of me and I was born
with eyes that can never close.   15

I release you, fear, so you can no longer
keep me naked and frozen in the winter,
or smothered under blankets in the summer.

I release you
I release you   20
I release you
I release you

I am not afraid to be angry.
I am not afraid to rejoice.
I am not afraid to be black.   25
I am not afraid to be white.
I am not afraid to be hungry.
I am not afraid to be full.
I am not afraid to be hated.
I am not afraid to be loved.   30

to be loved, to be loved, fear.

Oh, you have choked me, but I gave you the leash.
You have gutted me but I gave you the knife.
You have devoured me, but I laid myself across the fire.
You held my mother down and raped her,   35
              but I gave you the heated thing.

I take myself back, fear.
You are not my shadow any longer.
I won't hold you in my hands.
You can't live in my eyes, my ears, my voice   40
my belly, or in my heart my heart
my heart my heart

But come here, fear
I am alive and you are so afraid
                        of dying.   45

George Herbert

CHURCH-MONUMENTS

While that my soul repairs to her devotion,
Here I intomb my flesh, that it betimes
May take acquaintance of this heap of dust;
To which the blast of death's incessant motion,
Fed with the exhalation of our crimes,   5
Drives all at last. Therefore I gladly trust

My body to this school, that it may learn
To spell his elements, and find his birth
Written in dusty heraldry and lines;
Which dissolution sure doth best discern,   10
Comparing dust with dust, and earth with earth.
These laugh at jet and marble put for signs,

To sever the good fellowship of dust,
And spoil the meeting. What shall point out them,
When they shall bow, and kneel, and fall down flat   15
To kiss those heaps, which now they have in trust?
Dear flesh, while I do pray, learn here thy stem
And true descent: that when thou shalt grow fat

And wanton in thy cravings, thou mayst know,
That flesh is but the glass, which holds the dust   20
That measures all our time; which also shall
Be crumbled into dust. Mark here below
How tame these ashes are, how free from lust,
That thou mayst fit thy self against thy fall.

Gerard Manley Hopkins

PIED BEAUTY

Glory be to God for dappled things—
    For skies of couple-colour as a brinded cow;
        For rose-moles all in stipple upon trout that swim;
Fresh-firecoal chestnut-falls; finches' wings;

Landscape plotted and pieced—fold, fallow, and plough;   5
  And áll trádes, their gear and tackle and trim.

All things counter, original, spare, strange;
  Whatever is fickle, freckled (who knows how?)
    With swift, slow; sweet, sour; adazzle, dim;
He fathers-forth whose beauty is past change: 10
              Praise him.

Henry Howard

TO HIS LADY

Set me whereas the sun doth parch the green,
  Or where his beams may not dissolve the ice,
In temperate heat, where he is felt and seen,
  With proud people, in presence sad and wise;
Set me in base, or yet in high degree,   5
  In the long night, or in the shortest day,
In clear weather, or where mists thickest be,
  In lofty youth, or when my hairs be gray;
Set me in earth, in heaven, or yet in hell,
  In hill, in dale, or in the foaming flood,   10
Thrall, or at large, alive whereso I dwell,
  Sick, or in health, in ill fame, or in good;
    Yours will I be, and with that only thought
    Comfort myself when that my hap is nought.

Langston Hughes

EVENIN' AIR BLUES

Folks, I come up North
Cause they told me de North was fine.
I come up North
Cause they told me de North was fine.

Been up here six months—   5
I'm about to lose my mind.

This mornin' for breakfast
I chawed de mornin' air.
This mornin' for breakfast
Chawed de mornin' air.   10
But this evenin' for supper,
I got evenin' air to spare.

Believe I'll do a little dancin'
Just to drive my blues away—
A little dancin'   15
To drive my blues away,
Cause when I'm dancin'
De blues forgets to stay.

But if you was to ask me
How de blues they come to be,   20
Says if you was to ask me
How de blues they come to be—
You wouldn't need to ask me:
Just look at me and see!

MOTHER TO SON

Well, Son, I'll tell you
Life for me ain't been no crystal stair
It's had tacks in it,
And splinters,
And boards torn up,   5
And places with no carpets on the floor,

Bare.
But all the time
I'se been climbin' on
and reachin' landin's   10
And turning corners
And sometimes goin' on in the dark
Where there ain't been no light.
So, Boy, don't you turn back.
Don't you set down on the steps   15

'Cause you find it's kinder hard.
Don't you fall now—
For I'se still goin', Honey,
I'se still climbin'
And life for me ain't been   20
                    no crystal stair.

THE NEGRO SPEAKS
OF RIVERS

I've known rivers:
I've known rivers ancient as the world and older than the flow of human
    blood in human veins.

My soul has grown deep like the rivers.

I bathed in the Euphrates when dawns were young.   5
I built my hut near the Congo and it lulled me to sleep.
I looked upon the Nile and raised the pyramids above it.
I heard the singing of the Mississippi when Abe Lincoln went down to New
    Orleans, and I've seen its muddy bosom turn all golden in the sunset.

I've known rivers: 10
Ancient, dusky rivers.

My soul has grown deep like the rivers.

SHARE-CROPPERS

Just a herd of Negroes
Driven to the field,
Plowing, planting, hoeing,
To make the cotton yield.

When the cotton's picked   5
And the work is done
Boss man takes the money
And we get none,

Leaves us hungry, ragged
As we were before.   10
Year by year goes by
And we are nothing more

Than a herd of Negroes
Driven to the field—
Plowing life away   15
To make the cotton yield.

VAGABONDS

We are the desperate
Who do not care,
The hungry
Who have nowhere
To eat,   5
No place to sleep,
The tearless
Who cannot
Weep.

Lawson Fusao Inada

NIGHTSONG IN ASIAN AMERICA

**For the living memory of
John Okada, pioneer, novelist:
No-No Boy, 1957**

The sky fits perfectly on all matter.
Nothing is jagged enough: volcanic
mass of the Cascades; structures of Seattle.

To come upon disaster at Cottage Grove—
the smashed front end of a Chevrolet,   5
occupants and lights strewn in order . . .

Which is why the moon hides
half of itself over Roseburg, or beacons
seek and find in the cracks of cliffs.

Napa tsukemono in the back seat   10
spreads its lovely, abundant musk

Everything we eat needs rice.
These supplies must reach the people.

Randall Jarrell

THE DEATH OF THE BALL TURRET GUNNER

From my mother's sleep I fell into the State,
And I hunched in its belly till my wet fur froze.
Six miles from earth, loosed from its dream of life,
I woke to black flak and the nightmare fighters.
When I died they washed me out of the turret with a hose.   5

Ben Jonson

ON MY FIRST SON

Farewell, thou child of my right hand, and joy;
My sin was too much hope of thee, loved boy:
Seven years thou wert lent to me, and I thee pay,
Exacted by thy fate, on the just day.
O could I lose all father now! for why   5
Will man lament the state he should envy,
To have so soon 'scaped world's and flesh's rage,
And, if no other misery, yet age?
Rest in soft peace, and asked, say, "Here doth lie
Ben Jonson his best piece of poetry."   10
For whose sake henceforth all his vows be such
As what he loves may never like too much.

TO CELIA

Come my *Celia*, let us prove,
While we may, the sports of love;
Time will not be ours, for ever:
He, at length, our good will sever.
Spend not then his gifts in vain.   5
Sunnes, that set, may rise again:
But if once we lose this light,
'Tis, with us, perpetual night.
Why should we defer our joys?
Fame, and rumor are but toys.   10
Cannot we delude the eyes
Of a few poor houshold spys?
Or his easier ears beguile,
So removed by our wile?

June Jordan

SAFE

The Río Escondido at night
in between
jungle growing down to the muddy
edges of deep water possibilities
        helicopter attack   5
        alligator assault
        contra confrontations
        blood sliding into the silent scenery
where I sat cold and wet
but surrounded by five   10
compañeros
in a dugout canoe

John Keats

WRITTEN IN DISGUST OF VULGAR SUPERSTITION

The church bells toll a melancholy round,
  Calling the people to some other prayers,
  Some other gloominess, more dreadful cares,
More hearkening to the sermon's horrid sound.
Surely the mind of man is closely bound   5
  In some black spell; seeing that each one tears
  Himself from fireside joys, and Lydian airs,
And converse high of those with glory crown'd.
Still, still they toll, and I should feel a damp—
  A chill as from a tomb, did I not know   10
That they are going like an outburnt lamp;
  That 'tis their sighing, wailing ere they go
  Into oblivion;—that fresh flowers will grow,
And many glories of immortal stamp.

QUESTIONS

1. How many allusions to sadness, horror, and death can you find in the poem? How do these contribute to its tone?
2. What is the poet's attitude toward religion in the poem? What is his attitude toward religious ritual?
3. In line 2, he says the bells are "calling the people to some other prayers." What prayers are they being taken from?
4. The last two lines provide an optimistic message contrary to the rest of the poem. What is this message?

Maurice Kenny

CORN-PLANTER

I plant corn four years:
ravens steal it;
rain drowns it;
August burns it;
locusts ravage leaves.   5

I stand in a circle and throw seed.
Old men laugh because they know the wind
will carry the seed to my neighbor.

I stand in a circle on planted seed.
Moles burrow through the earth   10
and harvest my crop.

I throw seed to the wind
and wind drops it on the desert.

The eighth year I spend planting corn;
I tend my fields all season.   15
After September's harvest I take it to the market.
The people of my village are too poor to buy it.

The ninth spring I make chicken-feather headdresses,
plastic tom-toms and beaded belts.
I grow rich,   20
buy an old Ford,
drive to Chicago,
and get drunk
on Welfare checks.

D. H. Lawrence

PIANO

Softly, in the dusk, a woman is singing to me;
Taking me back down the vista of years, till I see
A child sitting under the piano, in the boom of the tingling strings
And pressing the small, poised feet of a mother who smiles as she sings

In spite of myself, the insidious mastery of song   5
Betrays me back, till the heart of me weeps to belong
To the old Sunday evenings at home, with winter outside
And hymns in the cosy parlour, the tinkling piano our guide.

So now it is vain for the singer to burst into clamour
With the great black piano appassionato. The glamour   10
Of childish days is upon me, my manhood is cast
Down in the flood of remembrance, I weep like a child for the past.

Denise Levertov

THE ACHE OF MARRIAGE

The ache of marriage:

thigh and tongue, beloved,
are heavy with it,
it throbs in the teeth

We look for communion   5
and are turned away, beloved,
each and each

It is leviathan and we
in its belly
looking for joy, some joy   10
not to be known outside it

two by two in the ark of
the ache of it.

LIVING WHILE IT MAY

The young elm that must be cut
because its roots push at the house wall

taps and scrapes my window
urgently—but when I look round at it

remains still. Or if I turn by chance,   5
it seems its leaves are eyes, or the whole spray
of leaves and twigs a face flattening
its nose against the glass, breathing a cloud,

longing to see clearly my life whose term
is not yet known.   10

Philip Levine

SPRING IN THE OLD WORLD

In the central terminal rain pouring
through the broken glass on the trains below,
loading and unloading. Above the gray dome
the great sky twisting in from the North Sea.
Cold, wet, wondering, I stood in the corner.   5
A dark boy walked in off the streets, a shepherd
born of shepherds. At 14 come to Tetuan
for work, then to Ceuta, Algeciras, Amsterdam.
His robes black now with rain, he cracks
sunflower seeds between his teeth, *pipas*   10
he calls them, and spits the shells and laughs.
In the lower Atlas the hills are green
where his brothers and he raced
through the long grass and wildflowers,
shouting to the air, their skirts   15
flared out around them, open and burning.

QUESTIONS

1. What irony exists in the title?
2. In what two continents does the action described in the poem take place?
3. How does the poet create mood and atmosphere in describing the train terminal?
   How are they contrasted in the final five lines of the poem?

Shirley Geok-lin Lim

MODERN SECRETS

Last night I dreamt in Chinese.
Eating Yankee shredded wheat
I said it in English
To a friend who answered
In monosyllables: 5
All of which I understood.

The dream shrank to its fiction.
I had understood its end
Many years ago. The sallow child
Ate rice from its ricebowl   10
And hides still in the cupboard
With the china and tea-leaves.

Audre Lorde

OYA

God of my father discovered at midnight
my mother asleep on her thunders
my father
returning at midnight
out of tightening circles of anger   5
out of days' punishment
the inelegant safety of power
Now midnight empties your house of bravado
and passion sleeps like a mist
outside desire   10
your strength splits like a melon
dropped on our prisoners floor
midnight glows
like a jeweled love
at the core of the broken fruit.   15

My mother is sleeping.
Hymns of dream lie like bullets
in her nights weapons
the sacred steeples
of nightmare are secret and hidden   20
in the disguise of fallen altars
I too shall learn how to conquer yes
Yes yes god
damned
I love you   25
now free me
quickly
before I destroy us.

Amy Lowell

THE TAXI

When I go away from you
The world beats dead
Like a slackened drum.
I call out for you against the jutted stars
And shout into the ridges of the wind.   5
Streets coming fast,
One after the other,
Wedge you away from me,
And the lamps of the city prick my eyes
So that I can no longer see your face.   10
Why should I leave you,
To wound myself upon the sharp edges of the night?

Robert Lowell

CHILDREN OF LIGHT

Our fathers wrung their bread from stocks and stones
And fenced their gardens with the Redman's bones;
Embarking from the Nether Land of Holland,
Pilgrims unhouseled by Geneva's night,
They planted here the Serpent's seeds of light;   5
And here the pivoting searchlights probe to shock
The riotous glass houses built on rock,
And candles gutter by an empty altar,
And light is where the landless blood of Cain
Is burning, burning the unburied grain.   10

Mairi MacInnes

VJ DAY

This minute you're in Japan
   Lecturing the enemy
That thirty odd years ago
   Aimed at your little ship
Rocket, torpedo and bomb.   5
   Now you confer over poetry.

Tonight I seem to hear
   Lorries whine and rumble
Over the crossing in town
   In convoy from factory,   10
And then the far-off hum
   Of raiders coming to bomb.

In fact we both got off
   With the rest of our lives.
Why do I dream of blood   15
   Instead of your nightingales?
This clearing of my sight
   Makes me grope for you in bed—

The mind so denies you're there
   While I am here; or you fought,   20
I stayed at home; or war
   Brought you the fuller peace;
Or you survive by fate,
   I only because I'm a woman.

Annette M'Baye

SILHOUETTE

for Henriette Bathily

Behind, sun, before, shadow!
A watergourd on a stately head,
A breast, a strip of loincloth fluttering,
Two feet that erase the pattern on the sand.

                              Translated by Kathleen Weaver

Claude McKay

OUTCAST

For the dim regions whence my fathers came
My spirit, bondaged by the body, longs.
Words felt, but never heard, my lips would frame;
My soul would sing forgotten jungle songs.
I would go back to darkness and to peace,   5
But the great western world holds me in fee,
And I may never hope for full release
While to its alien gods I bend my knee.
Something in me is lost, forever lost,
Some vital thing has gone out of my heart,   10
And I must walk the way of life a ghost
Among the sons of earth, a thing apart.

For I was born, far from my native clime,
Under the white man's menace, out of time.

Ifeanyi Menkiti

VETERANS DAY

And because somebody
fired a gun
at somebody else
at Sarajevo;
but more because   5
of a man named Darwin,
who said his daddy
was an ape,
and proved it in a book;

therefore did the nations   10
fight amongst themselves
to decide who was fittest to survive
and killed a few million people
among whom were Africans
conscripted to serve;   15

bloodied, that is, to prove a point
concerning civilization's
monkey-mongering ways.

Czeslaw Milosz

ON PRAYER

You ask me how to pray to someone who is not.
All I know is that prayer constructs a velvet bridge
And walking it we are aloft, as on a springboard,
Above landscapes the color of ripe gold
Transformed by a magic stopping of the sun.   5
That bridge leads to the shore of Reversal
Where everything is just the opposite and the word *is*
Unveils a meaning we hardly envisioned.
Notice: I say *we;* there, every one, separately,
Feels compassion for others entangled in the flesh   10
And knows that if there is no other shore
They will walk that aerial bridge all the same.

Translated from Polish by the author

John Milton

WHEN I CONSIDER HOW MY LIGHT IS SPENT

When I consider how my light is spent
   Ere half my days, in this dark world and wide,
   And that one talent which is death to hide
   Lodged with me useless, though my soul more bent
To serve therewith my Maker, and present   5
   My true account, lest he returning chide;
   "Doth God exact day-labor, light denied?"
   I fondly ask: but Patience to prevent
That murmur, soon replies, "God doth not need
   Either man's work or his own gifts; who best   10
   Bear his mild yoke, they serve him best. His state
Is kingly. Thousands at his bidding speed
   And post o'er land and ocean without rest:
   They also serve who only stand and wait."

Janice Mirikitani

PRISONS OF SILENCE

1.

The strongest prisons are built
with walls of silence.

2.

Morning light falls between us
like a wall.
We have laid beside each other   5
as we have for years.
Before the war, when life
would clamor through our windows,
we woke joyfully to the work.

I keep those moments   10
like a living silent seed.

After day's work, I would
smell the damp soil in his hands,
his hands that felt the outlines
of my body in the velvet   15
night of summers.

I hold his warm hands to this
cold wall of flesh
as I have for years.

      3.

Jap!   20
Filthy Jap!

Who lives within me?

Abandoned homes, confiscated land,
loyalty oaths, barbed wire prisons
in a strange wasteland.   25

Go home, Jap!
Where is home?

A country of betrayal.
No one speaks to us.

We would not speak to each other.   30

We were accused.

Hands in our hair,
hands that spread our legs
and searched our thighs for secret weapons,
hands that knit barbed wire   35
to cripple our flight.

Giant hot hands flung me,
fluttering, speechless into
barbed wire, thorns in a broken wing.

The strongest prisons are built   40
with walls of silence.

   4.

I watched him depart that day
from the tedious wall of wire,

the humps of barracks,
handsome in his uniform.   45

I would look each day for letters
from a wall of time,
waiting for approach of my deliverance
from a wall of dust.

I do not remember   50
reading about his death
only the wall of wind
that encased me, as I turned my head.

> 5.

U.S. Japs hailed as heroes!

I do not know the face of this country   55
it is inhabited by strangers
who call me obscene names.

Jap. Go home.
Where is home?

I am alone wandering   60
in this desert.

Where is home?
Who lives within me?

A stranger with a knife in her tongue
and broken wing,
mad from separations and losses cruel   65
as hunger.

Walls suffocate her as a tomb,
encasing history.

> 6.

I have kept myself contained   70
within these walls shaped to my body
and buried my rage.
I rebuilt my life
like a wall, unquestioning.
Obeyed their laws . . . their laws.   75

7.

All persons of Japanese ancestry
   filthy jap.
Both alien and non-alien
   japs are enemy aliens.
To be incarcerated   80
   for their own good
A military necessity
   The army to handle only the japs
Where is home?
A country of betrayal.   85

8.

This wall of silence crumbles
from the bigness of their crimes.
This silent wall
crushed by living memory.

He awakens from the tomb   90
I have made for myself
and unearths my rage.

I must speak.

9.

He faces me in this small
room of myself.   95
I find the windows
where light escapes.

From this cell of history
this mute grave,
we birth our rage.   100

We heal our tongues.

We listen to ourselves

   Korematsu, Hirabayashi, Yasui.

We ignite the syllables of our names.

We give testimony.   105

We hear the bigness of our sounds freed
like many clapping hands,
thundering for reparations.

We give testimony.

Our noise is dangerous.   110

10.

We beat our hands
like wings healed.

We soar
from these walls of silence.

SING WITH YOUR BODY

To my daughter, Tianne Tsukiko

We love with great difficulty
spinning in one place
afraid to create

         spaces

                 new/rhythm   5

the beat of a child
dangled by her own inner ear
takes Aretha with her

         upstairs,   somewhere.

go quickly, Tsukiko,   10

         into your circled dance

go quickly

         before your steps are
         halted by who you are not

go quickly   15

         to learn the mixed
         rhythm of your tongue,

> go quickly
>
> to who you are
>
> before   20
>
>
> your mother swallows
> what she has lost.

Pat Mora

ELENA

My Spanish isn't enough.
I remember how I'd smile
listening to my little ones,
understanding every word they'd say,
their jokes, their songs, their plots.   5
Vamos a pedirle dulces a mamá. Vamos.
But that was in Mexico.
Now my children go to American high schools.
They speak English. At night they sit around
the kitchen table, laugh with one another.   10
I stand by the stove and feel dumb, alone.
I bought a book to learn English.
My husband frowned, drank more beer.
My oldest said, *"Mamá,* he doesn't want you
to be smarter than he is." I'm forty,   15
embarrassed at mispronouncing words,
embarrassed at the laughter of my children,
the grocer, the mailman. Sometimes I take
my English book and lock myself in the bathroom,
say the thick words softly,   20
for if I stop trying, I will be deaf
when my children need my help.

QUESTIONS

1. What are the main problems the narrator has developed after having moved to the
   United States? How does she try to rectify them? How successful is she?

2. What does the narrator fear when she says "I will be deaf when my children need my help"?
3. The narrator contends that she does not speak English well. Does the way she uses English in the poem reinforce this or refute it?

Carlos Nejar

OIL LAMPS

Jesualdo Monte,
when you are free
there will be no bundle
on your back.

Today you rip away   5
the paper wrap
that set the fence on fire
around your master's land.

When you are free
there will be no bundle   10
on your back.
No more stables
no more ration cards
no more laughing whips
that punish your belly   15
that punish your dreams.

When you are free
there will be no bundle
on your back.

Pablo Neruda

THE UNITED FRUIT CO.

When the trumpet sounded, it was
all prepared on the earth,
and Jehovah parceled out the earth
to Coca-Cola, Inc., Anaconda,
Ford Motors, and other entities: 5
The Fruit Company, Inc.
reserved for itself the most succulent,
the central coast of my own land,
the delicate waist of America.
It rechristened its territories   10
as the "Banana Republics"
and over the sleeping dead,
over the restless heroes
who brought about the greatness,
the liberty and the flags,   15
it established the comic opera:
abolished the independencies,
presented crowns of Caesar,
unsheathed envy, attracted
the dictatorship of the flies,   20
Trujillo flies, Tacho flies,
Carias flies, Martinez flies,
Ubico flies, damp flies
of modest blood and marmalade,
drunken flies who zoom   25
over the ordinary graves,
circus flies, wise flies
well trained in tyranny.

Among the bloodthirsty flies
the Fruit Company lands its ships,   30
taking off the coffee and the fruit;
the treasure of our submerged
territories flows as though
on plates into the ships.

Meanwhile Indians are falling   35
into the sugared chasms
of the harbors, wrapped
for burial in the mist of the dawn:

a body rolls, a thing
that has no name, a fallen cipher, 40
a cluster of dead fruit
thrown down on the dump.

Translated by Robert Bly

Simon J. Ortiz

SPEAKING

I take him outside
under the trees,
have him stand on the ground.
We listen to the crickets,
cicadas, million years old sound. 5
Ants come by us.
I tell them,
"This is he, my son.
This boy is looking at you.
I am speaking for him." 10

The crickets, cicadas,
the ants, the millions of years
are watching us,
hearing us.
My son murmurs infant words, 15
speaking, small laughter
bubbles from him.
Tree leaves tremble.
They listen to this boy
speaking for me. 20

Wilfred Owen

ANTHEM FOR DOOMED YOUTH

What passing-bells for these who die as cattle?
    Only the monstrous anger of the guns.

    Only the stuttering rifles' rapid rattle
Can patter out their hasty orisons.
No mockeries now for them; no prayers nor bells,   5
    Nor any voice of mourning save the choirs,—
The shrill, demented choirs of wailing shells;
    And bugles calling for them from sad shires.

What candles may be held to speed them all?
    Not in the hands of boys, but in their eyes   10
Shall shine the holy glimmers of good-byes.
    The pallor of girls' brows shall be their pall;
Their flowers the tenderness of patient minds,
And each slow dusk a drawing-down of blinds.

QUESTIONS

1. How would you summarize the nature of the "anthem" to which the poet is referring?
2. What appears to be the poet's attitude toward war? What evidence does he provide to support your view?
3. While the poet describes responses to the doomed soldiers, he does not depict nor describe the soldiers themselves. How does this affect the mood of the poem? How does it contribute to the theme?

Papyrus Harris 500

BEGINNING OF THE SONGS OF DELIGHT

1

Portulaca: apportioned to you is my heart,
I do for you what it desires,
When I am in your arms.
My longing for you is my eye-paint,
When I see you my eyes shine;   5
I press close to you to look at you,
Beloved of men, who rules my heart!
O happiness of this hour,
Let the hour go on forever!
Since I have lain with you,   10
You raised up my heart;
Be it sad or gay,
Do not leave me!

2

Saam-plants here summon us,
I am your sister, your best one;   15
I belong to you like this plot of ground
That I planted with flowers
And sweet-smelling herbs.
Sweet is its stream,
Dug by your hand,   20
Refreshing in the northwind.
A lovely place to wander in,
Your hand in my hand.
My body thrives, my heart exults
At our walking together;   25
Hearing your voice is pomegranate wine,
I live by hearing it.
Each look with which you look at me
Sustains me more than food and drink.

          Translated by Miriam Lichtheim

Pepi I Pyramid Texts

UTTERANCE 432
The king prays to the sky-goddess

Sarcophagus Chamber, West Wall

O Great One who became Sky,
You are strong, you are mighty,
You fill every place with your beauty,
The whole earth is beneath you, you possess it!
As you enfold earth and all things in your arms,   5
So have you taken this Pepi to you,
An indestructible star within you![1]

Translated by Miriam Lichtheim

Katherine Philips

AGAINST LOVE

Hence, Cupid! with your cheating toys,
Your real Griefs, and painted Joys,
Your Pleasure which itself destroys.
Lovers like men in fevers burn and rave,
And only what will injure them do crave.   5
Men's weakness makes Love so severe,
They give him power by their fear,
And make the shackles which they wear.
Who to another does his heart submit;
Makes his own Idol, and then worships it.   10
Him whose heart is all his own,
Peace and liberty does crown;
He apprehends no killing frown.
He feels no raptures which are joys diseas'd,
And is not much transported, but still pleas'd.   15

---

[1] By ornamenting the ceiling of the sarcophagus chamber with stars, the chamber was made to represent the night sky; and the prayers addressed to the sky-goddess Nut ask her, as mother of the dead king, to take him in her arms and transform him into a star.

Ezra Pound

A VIRGINAL

No, no! Go from me. I have left her lately.
I will not spoil my sheath with lesser brightness,
For my surrounding air hath a new lightness;
Slight are her arms, yet they have bound me straitly
And left me cloaked as with a gauze of aether;   5
As with sweet leaves; as with subtle clearness.
Oh, I have picked up magic in her nearness
To sheathe me half in half the things that sheathe her.
No, no! Go from me. I have still the flavour,
Soft as spring wind that's come from birchen bowers.   10
Green come the shoots, aye April in the branches,
As winter's wound with her sleight hand she staunches,
Hath of the trees a likeness of the savour;
As white their bark, so white this lady's hours.

Alexander Pushkin

A SOWER WENT OUT
TO SOW HIS SEED

The seeds of freedom freely sowing
I rose betimes, before the sun.
In faith and innocence unknowing
I plied the furrows, one by one.
The fruits I sowed were never tasted,   5
My labour lost, my fervour wasted.
For strength expended—nothing won!

Graze on, ye peaceful sheep and cattle.
The call of honour cannot grip
Or charm you into freedom's battle.   10
For you—the knife, the shearer's clip!
Your heritage—the herdsman's rattle,
The yoke, the chain, the drover's whip!

Interpreted by Henry Jones

QUESTIONS

1. What is the speaker's attitude toward work? What is the fruit of his labor?
2. Compare and contrast the lives of the farm animals as the speaker describes them with the life of the worker. How are they similar? How are they different?
3. Does the poem have a metaphoric quality, does it refer to only the narrator, or both? Explain your view.

TO MY OLD NURSE

Faithful friend in years of sorrow,
Frail and aged nurse of mine,
Expecting me with every morrow,
Lonely in the woods of pine.
Waiting in your attic lowly,   5
Sadly watching, as on guard.
Knitting needles clicking slowly,
Fingers wrinkled, withered, hard.
Peering at deserted portal—
Dark and distant is the road—   10
Grief and care, unhappy mortal,
These are now thy bosom's load.
And still you dream. . . . .

        Interpreted by Henry Jones

Ibn Quzman

THE RADISH

The radish is a good
And doubtless wholesome food,
But proves, to vex the eater,
A powerful repeater.

This only fault I find: 5
What should be left behind
Comes issuing instead
Right from the eater's head!
       Translated by A. J. Arberry

Rahel

TO MY COUNTRY

I haven't sung your praise,
nor glorified your name
in tales of bravery
and the spoils of war.
I only plant a tree   5
on Jordan's quiet banks.
I only wear a path
over the fields.
Surely very meagre,
Mother, I know.   10
Surely very meagre,
your daughter's offering:
Only a joyous shout
on a radiant day,
only secret weeping   15
over your barrenness.
      Translated from Hebrew
        by Diane Mintz

Ishmael Reed

SERMONETTE

a poet was busted by a topless judge
his friends went to morristwn nj & put
black powder on his honah's doorstep
black powder into his honah's car
black powder on his honah's briefs   5
tiny dolls into his honah's mind

by nightfall his honah could a go go no mo
his dog went crazy & ran into a crocodile
his widow fell from a wall &
hanged herself   10
his daughter was run over by a black man
cming home for the wakes the two boys
skidded into mourning
all the next of kin's teeth fell out

gimmie dat ol time   15
               religion
it's good enough
       for me!

QUESTIONS

1. In what dialect is the poem written? What effect does the dialect have on the tone
   of the poem? Of what significance is the fact that the poem is written in lower-case
   letters?
2. What does the poet mean by "topless judge." What is the irony behind this image?
3. What has the poet actually done to the judge? Why do the series of calamities occur
   in the second stanza?
4. What is the significance of the title? What is the moral of this "sermonette"?

Roberto Fernandez Retamar

A MOTTO FROM POETS:
LEAVE STONE

A motto from poets: leave stone
alone, it won't grow; try
trees, working their way up
and up into air.
And there they inscribe their names magnificent   5
in the sun as banners
But its rock keeps when trees
are ash, or furniture; you eat, or sleep, or lie
dead among the painted detritus of trees.
And all the time there's some stone   10
somewhere, planted, not
bigger, not
smaller, carrying still
across its livid frontage some savage
scrawl, some few letters   15
of someone long gone who,
one afternoon, graved them there,
laughing, dreaming, remembering.

Translated by Tim Reynolds

Adrienne Rich

AUGUST

Two horses in yellow light
eating windfall apples under a tree

as summer tears apart   milkweeds stagger
and grasses grow more ragged

They say there are ions in the sun   5
neutralizing magnetic fields on earth

Some way to explain
what this week has been, and the one before it!

If I am flesh sunning on rock
if I am brain burning in fluorescent light   10

if I am dream like a wire with fire
throbbing along it

if I am death to man
I have to know it

His mind is too simple, I cannot go on   15
sharing his nightmares

My own are becoming clearer, they open
into prehistory

which looks like a village lit with blood
where all the fathers are crying: *My son is mine!*   20

Theodore Roethke

MY PAPA'S WALTZ

The whiskey on your breath
Could make a small boy dizzy;
But I hung on like death:
Such waltzing was not easy.

We romped until the pans   5
Slid from the kitchen shelf;
My mother's countenance
Could not unfrown itself.

The hand that held my wrist
Was battered on one knuckle;   10
At every step you missed
My right ear scraped a buckle.

You beat time on my head
With a palm caked hard by dirt,
Then waltzed me off to bed   15
Still clinging to your shirt.

Christina Rossetti

UPHILL

Does the road wind uphill all the way?
   Yes, to the very end.
Will the day's journey take the whole long day?
   From morn to night, my friend.

But is there for the night a resting place?   5
   A roof for when the slow dark hours begin.
May not the darkness hide it from my face?
   You cannot miss that inn.

Shall I meet other wayfarers at night?
   Those who have gone before.   10
Then must I knock, or call when just in sight?
   They will not keep you standing at that door.

Shall I find comfort, travel-sore and weak?
   Of labor you shall find the sum.
Will there be beds for me and all who seek?   15
   Yea, beds for all who come.

Muriel Rukeyser

THE LOST ROMANS

Where are they, not those young men, not those
   young women
Who walked among the bullet-headed Romans with their
   roads, their symmetry, their iron rule—

We know the dust and bones they are gone to, those   5
        young Romans
Who stood against the bitter imperial, their young
        green life with its poems—
Where are the poems made music against the purple
Setting their own purple up for a living sign,   10
Bright fire of some forgotten future against empire,
Their poems in the beautiful Roman tongue
Sex-songs, love-poems, freedom-songs?
Not only the young, but the old and in chains,
The slaves in their singing, the fierce northern   15
        gentle blond rhythms,
The Judean cantillations, lullabies of Carthage,
Gaul with her cries, all the young Roman rebels,
Where are their songs? Who will unlock them,
Who will find them for us, in some undiscovered   20
        painted cave
For we need you, sisters, far brothers, poems
        of our lost Rome.

Luis Omar Salinas

QUETZALCOATLE

You lunged and caught fire
    flowers falling from a disenchanted
sky
You made your move
    and caught the world   5
by your nostrils
and escaped half god
        demolished

You appear in our nightmares
      sad and brave   10
your descendants
        drinking peyote

Your fingers dig into clouds
    as memory burns

and you embrace your land   15
     and disappear
                         into the vapor
                         of dream

Bert Schierbeek

THE BICYCLE REPAIRMAN

in his cave
dimly lit
one door open
he sits
kneels   5
and hunkers
before his umpteenth
bicycle

you say hi
he says hi   10
a twinkling in
his eyes and he sees
upon all these pedals
illuminated all over all
those legs and from the saddle   15
all those thighs those dresses
blowing up and what's under them
and he has to imagine

then he stands up
clasps the handlebar   20
can see all those hands
round the handgrip
and gives a tug

then he mumbles:
                    one day   25
                    at noon Mount Mola drifted
                    into the mist
                    and became totally invisible

Translated by Charles McGeehan

Léopold Sédar Senghor

PRAYER TO THE MASKS

Masks! O Masks!
Black mask, red mask, you white-and-black masks
Masks of the four cardinal points where the Spirit blows
I greet you in silence!
And you, not the least of all, Ancestor with the lion head.   5
You keep this place safe from women's laughter
And any wry, profane smiles
You exude the immortal air where I inhale
The breath of my Fathers.
Masks with faces without masks, stripped of every dimple   10
And every wrinkle
You created this portrait, my face leaning
On an altar of blank paper
And in your image, listen to me!
The Africa of empires is dying—it is the agony   15
Of a sorrowful princess
And Europe, too, tied to us at the navel.
Fix your steady eyes on your oppressed children
Who give their lives like the poor man his last garment.
Let us answer "present" at the rebirth of the World   20
As white flour cannot rise without the leaven.
Who else will teach rhythm to the world
Deadened by machines and cannons?
Who will sound the shout of joy at daybreak to wake
    orphans and the dead?   25
Tell me, who will bring back the memory of life
To the man of gutted hopes?
They call us men of cotton, coffee, and oil
They call us men of death.
But we are men of dance, whose feet get stronger   30
As we pound upon firm ground.

                         Translated by Melvin Dixon

QUESTIONS

1. What makes this piece a poem? What makes it a prayer?
2. What is the "place" referred to in the sixth line? Why must it be "safe from women's laughter"?
3. Who is the implied audience of this poem? Who is the stated audience of the poem? What is the significance of each to the poet?

4. What does the poet imply about the relationship between Africa and Europe? What does the poet imply concerning the difference between Africans and Europeans? What images does the poet use to illuminate these differences?
5. What does the poet predict will be the effect on the world of the liberation of Africa?

Anne Sexton

THE BLACK ART

A woman who writes feels too much,
those trances and portents!
As if cycles and children and islands
weren't enough; as if mourners and gossips
and vegetables were never enough.   5
She thinks she can warn the stars.
A writer is essentially a spy.
Dear love, I am that girl.

A man who writes knows too much,
such spells and fetiches!   10
As if erections and congresses and products
weren't enough; as if machines and galleons
and wars were never enough.
With used furniture he makes a tree.
A writer is essentially a crook.   15
Dear love, you are that man.

Never loving ourselves,
hating even our shoes and our hats,
we love each other, *precious, precious.*
Our hands are light blue and gentle.   20
Our eyes are full of terrible confessions.
But when we marry,
the children leave in disgust
There is too much food and no one left over
to eat up all the weird abundance.   25

QUESTIONS

1. According to the poet, what is the primary difference between a female poet and a male poet? Between men and women in general?

2. To whom does the line "Never loving ourselves" refer?
3. Why do "the children leave in disgust"? What is the "food" in the last sentence?
4. What seems to be the poet's general view of marriage?

THE FURY OF FLOWERS
AND WORMS

Let the flowers make a journey
on Monday so that I can see
ten daisies in a blue vase
with perhaps one red ant
crawling to the gold center.   5
A bit of the field on my table,
close to the worms
who struggle blindly,
moving deep into their slime,
moving deep into God's abdomen,   10
moving like oil through water,
sliding through the good brown.

The daisies grow wild
like popcorn.
They are God's promise to the field.   15
How happy I am, daisies, to love you.
How happy you are to be loved
and found magical, like a secret
from the sluggish field.
If all the world picked daisies   20
wars would end, the common cold would stop,
unemployment would end, the monetary market
would hold steady and no money would float.
Listen world,
if you'd just take the time to pick   25
the white fingers, the penny heart,
all would be well.
They are so unexpected.

They are as good as salt.
If someone had brought them   30
to van Gogh's room daily
his ear would have stayed on.

I would like to think that no one would die anymore
if we all believed in daisies
but the worms know better, don't they?   35
They slide into the ear of a corpse
and listen to his great sigh.

Percy Bysshe Shelley

SONG

To the Men of England

I

Men of England, wherefore plough
For the lords who lay ye low?
Wherefore weave with toil and care
The rich robes your tyrants wear?

II

Wherefore feed, and clothe, and save,   5
From the cradle to the grave,
Those ungrateful drones who would
Drain your sweat—nay, drink your blood?

III

Wherefore, Bees of England, forge
Many a weapon, chain, and scourge,   10
That these stingless drones may spoil
The forced produce of your toil?

IV

Have ye leisure, comfort, calm,
Shelter, food, love's gentle balm?
Or what is it ye buy so dear   15
With your pain and with your fear?

V

The seed ye sow, another reaps;
The wealth ye find, another keeps;
The robes ye weave, another wears;
The arms ye forge, another bears.   20

VI

Sow seed,—but let no tyrant reap;
End wealth,—let no impostor heap;
Weave robes,—let not the idle wear;
Forge arms,—in your defence to bear.

VII

Shrink to your cellars, holes, and cells;   25
In halls ye deck, another dwells.
Why shake the chains ye wrought? Ye see
The steel ye tempered glance on ye.

VIII

With plough and spade, and hoe and loom,
Trace your grave, and build your tomb,   30
And weave your winding-sheet, till fair
England be your sepulchre.

Sir Philip Sidney

WITH HOW SAD STEPS, O MOON

With how sad steps, O Moon, thou climb'st the skies,
How silently, and with how wan a face!
What! may it be that even in heav'nly place
That busy archer his sharp arrows tries?
Sure, if that long-with-love-acquainted eyes   5
Can judge of love, thou feel'st a lover's case.

I read it in thy looks; thy languisht grace
To me, that feel the like, thy state descries.
Then, ev'n of fellowship, O Moon, tell me,
Is constant love deem'd there but want of wit?   10
Are beauties there as proud as here they be?
Do they above love to be lov'd, and yet
Those lovers scorn whom that love doth possess?
Do they call virtue there ungratefulness?

Mohan Singh

EVENING

The sun horse panting and snorting
Reaches the shores of evening
Kicking his hoofs and flicking red dust
His vermilion mane wet with perspiration
He throws red foam from his mouth   5

The mellow-colored Evening comes
And places her hand between his pricked ears
Her long fingers
Feel the hot breath from his nostrils
And take off the bridle from his mouth   10

The restive animal
Tamed and quietened
Walks behind the Evening slowly
And goes into the stable of darkness

Translated by Balwant Gargi

QUESTIONS

1. Images of redness occur three times in the first stanza. What mood do they create?
   What is the effect of their contrast with the "mellow-colored Evening" that occurs
   in the first line of the second stanza?
2. How is evening personified? Why does the poet capitalize the word?
3. What progression in mood occurs from the first to the final stanza? What progression
   in time occurs?

Stevie Smith

THE WEAK MONK

The monk sat in his den,
He took the mighty pen
And wrote "Of God and Men."

One day the thought struck him
It was not according to Catholic doctrine;   5
His blood ran dim.

He wrote till he was ninety years old,
Then he shut the book with a clasp of gold
And buried it under the sheep fold.

He'd enjoyed it so much, he loved to plod,   10
And he thought he'd a right to expect that God
Would rescue his book alive from the sod.

Of course it rotted in the snow and rain;
No one will ever know now what he wrote of God and men.
For this the monk is to blame.   15

Gary Snyder

NOT LEAVING THE HOUSE

When Kai is born
I quit going out

Hang around the kitchen——make cornbread
Let nobody in.
Mail is flat.   5
     Masa lies on her side, Kai sighs,
     Non washes and sweeps
We sit and watch
     Masa nurse, and drink green tea.

Navajo turquoise beads over the bed   10
A peacock tail feather at the head

A badger pelt from Nagano-ken
For a mattress; under the sheet;
A pot of yogurt setting
Under the blankets, at his feet.   15

Masa, Kai,
And Non, our friend
In the green garden light reflected in
Not leaving the house.
From dawn til late at night   20
     making a new world of ourselves
     around this life.

Edith Sodergran

HOPE

I want to forget my manners—
I couldn't care less about noble styles,
I roll up my sleeves.
The dough of poetry is rising . . .
Oh, what a sorrow—   5
I can't bake cathedrals . . .
The soaring high forms—
The goal of persistent yearning.
Child of our time—
doesn't your soul have its right shell?   10
Before I die
I'll bake a cathedral.

         Translated by Jaakko A. Ahokas

Gary Soto

DAYBREAK

In this moment when the light starts up
In the east and rubs
The horizon until it catches fire,

We enter the fields to hoe,
Row after row, among the small flags of onion,   5
Waving off the dragonflies
That ladder the air.

And tears the onions raise
Do not begin in your eyes but in ours,
In the salt blown   10
From one blister into another;

They begin in knowing
You will never waken to bear
The hour timed to a heart beat,
The wind pressing us closer to the ground.   15

When the season ends,
And the onions are unplugged from their sleep,
We won't forget what you failed to see,
And nothing will heal
Under the rain's broken fingers.   20

LEARNING TO BARGAIN

Summer. Flies knitting
Filth on the window,
A mother calling a son home . . . .
I'm at that window, looking
Onto the street: dusk,   5
A neighbor kid sharpening
A stick at the curb.
I go outside and sit
Next to him without saying
A word. When he looks   10
Up, his eyes dark as flies,

I ask about the cat, the one
Among weeds in the alley.
"It's mine," he admits
And stares down at his feet,   15
Then my feet. "What do you want?"
"A dime," I say. Without
Looking at me, he gets
Up, goes behind his house,
And returns with two coke bottles.   20
"These make a dime." He sits
At the curb, his shoulders
So bony they could be wings
To lift him so far. "Don't tell."
He snaps a candy in halves   25
And we eat in silence.

Wole Soyinka

TELEPHONE
CONVERSATION

The price seemed reasonable, location
Indifferent. The landlady swore she lived
Off premises. Nothing remained
But self-confession. 'Madam,' I warned,
'I hate a wasted journey—I am African.'   5
Silence. Silenced transmission of
Pressurized good-breeding. Voice, when it came,
Lipstick coated, long gold-rolled
Cigarette-holder pipped. Caught I was, foully.
'HOW DARK?' . . . I had not misheard. . . . 'ARE YOU LIGHT 10
OR VERY DARK?' Button B. Button A. Stench
Of rancid breath of public hide-and-speak.
Red booth. Red pillar-box. Red double-tiered
Omnibus squelching tar. It *was* real! Shamed
By ill-mannered silence, surrender   15
Pushed dumbfoundment to beg simplification.
Considerate she was, varying the emphasis—
'ARE YOU DARK? OR VERY LIGHT?' Revelation came.
'You mean—like plain or milk chocolate?'

Her assent was clinical, crushing in its light   20
Impersonality. Rapidly, wave-length adjusted,
I chose. 'West African sepia'—and as afterthought,
'Down in my passport.' Silence for spectroscopic
Flight of fancy, till truthfulness changed her accent
Hard on the mouthpiece. 'WHAT'S THAT?' conceding   25
'DON'T KNOW WHAT THAT IS.' 'Like brunette.'
'THAT'S DARK, ISN'T IT?' 'Not altogether.
Facially, I am brunette, but madam, you should see
The rest of me. Palm of my hand, soles of my feet
Are a peroxide blonde. Friction, caused—   30
Foolishly madam—by sitting down, has turned
My bottom raven black—One moment madam!'—sensing
Her receiver rearing on the thunderclap
About my ears—'Madam,' I pleaded, 'wouldn't you rather
See for yourself?'   35

Stephen Spender

AN ELEMENTARY SCHOOL CLASSROOM IN A SLUM

Far far from gusty waves, these children's faces.
Like rootless weeds the torn hair round their paleness.
The tall girl with her weighed-down head. The paper-
seeming boy with rat's eyes. The stunted unlucky heir
Of twisted bones, reciting a father's gnarled disease,   5
His lesson from his desk. At back of the dim class,
One unnoted, sweet and young: his eyes live in a dream
Of squirrels' game, in tree room, other than this.

On sour cream walls, donations. Shakespeare's head
Cloudless at dawn, civilized dome riding all cities.   10
Belled, flowery, Tyrolese valley. Open-handed map
Awarding the world its world. And yet, for these
Children, these windows, not this world, are world,
Where all their future's painted with a fog,
A narrow street sealed in with a lead sky,   15
Far far from rivers, capes, and stars of words.

Surely Shakespeare is wicked, the map a bad example
With ships and sun and love tempting them to steal—
For lives that slyly turn in their cramped holes
From fog to endless night? On their slag heap, these children   20
Wear skins peeped through by bones and spectacles of steel
With mended glass, like bottle bits on stones.
All of their time and space are foggy slum
So blot their maps with slums as big as doom.

Unless, governor, teacher, inspector, visitor,   25
This map becomes their window and these windows
That open on their lives like crouching tombs
Break, O break open, till they break the town
And show the children to the fields and all their world
Azure on their sands, to let their tongues   30
Run naked into books, the white and green leaves open
The history theirs whose language is the sun.

Wallace Stevens

THE IRISH CLIFFS OF MOHER

Who is my father in this world, in this house,
At the spirit's base?

My father's father, his father's father, his—
Shadows like winds

Go back to a parent before thought, before speech,   5
At the head of the past.

They go to the cliffs of Moher rising out of the mist,
Above the real,

Rising out of present time and place, above
The wet, green grass.   10

This is not landscape, full of the somnambulations
Of poetry

And the sea. This is my father or, maybe,
It is as he was,

A likeness, one of the race of fathers: earth   15
And sea and air.

Jonathan Swift

A DESCRIPTION
OF A CITY SHOWER

Careful observers may foretell the hour
(By sure prognostics) when to dread a shower:
While rain depends, the pensive cat gives o'er
Her frolics, and pursues her tail no more.
Returning home at night, you'll find the sink   5
Strike your offended sense with double stink.
If you be wise, then go not far to dine;
You'll spend in coach hire more than save in wine.
A coming shower your shooting corns presage,
Old aches throb, your hollow tooth will rage.   10
Sauntering in coffeehouse is Dulman seen;
He damns the climate and complains of spleen.
    Meanwhile the South, rising with dabbled wings,
A sable cloud athwart the welkin flings,
That swilled more liquor than it could contain,   15
And, like a drunkard, gives it up again.
Brisk Susan whips her linen from the rope,
While the first drizzling shower is borne aslope:
Such is that sprinkling which some careless quean
Flirts on you from her mop, but not so clean: 20
You fly, invoke the gods; then turning, stop
To rail; she singing, still whirls on her mop.
Not yet the dust had shunned the unequal strife,
But, aided by the wind, fought still for life,
And wafted with its foe by violent gust,   25
Twas doubtful which was rain and which was dust.
Ah! where must needy poet seek for aid,
When dust and rain at once his coat invade?
Sole coat, where dust cemented by the rain

Erects the nap, and leaves a mingled stain.   30
   Now in contiguous drops the flood comes down,
Threatening with deluge this devoted town.
To shops in crowds the daggled females fly,
Pretend to cheapen goods, but nothing buy.
The Templar spruce, while every spout's abroach,   35
Stays till 'tis fair, yet seems to call a coach.
The tucked-up sempstress walks with hasty strides,
While streams run down her oiled umbrella's sides.
Here various kinds, by various fortunes led,
Commence acquaintance underneath a shed.   40
Triumphant Tories and desponding Whigs
Forget their feuds, and join to save their wigs.
Boxed in a chair the beau impatient sits,
While spouts run clattering o'er the roof by fits,
And ever and anon with frightful din   45
The leather sounds, he trembles from within.
So when Troy chairmen bore the wooden steed,
Pregnant with Greeks impatient to be freed
(Those bully Greeks, who, as the moderns do,
Instead of paying chairmen, run them through),   50
Laocoön struck the outside with his spear,
And each imprisoned hero quaked for fear.
   Now from all parts the swelling kennels flow,
And bear their trophies with them as they go:
Filth of all hues and odors seem to tell   55
What street they sailed from, by their sight and smell.
They, as each torrent drives with rapid force,
From Smithfield or St. Pulchre's shape their course,
And in huge confluence joined at Snow Hill ridge,
Fall from the conduit prone to Holborn Bridge.   60
Sweepings from butchers' stalls, dung, guts, and blood,
Drowned puppies, stinking sprats, all drenched in mud,
Dead cats, and turnip tops, come tumbling down the flood.

Sara Teasdale

BARTER

Life has loveliness to sell—
    All beautiful and splendid things,
Blue waves whitened on a cliff,
    Climbing fire that sways and sings,
And children's faces looking up   5
Holding wonder like a cup.

Life has loveliness to sell—
    Music like a curve of gold,
Scent of pine trees in the rain,
    Eyes that love you, arms that hold,   10
And for your spirit's still delight,
Holy thoughts that star the night.

Spend all you have for loveliness,
    Buy it and never count the cost,
For one white singing hour of peace   15
    Count many a year of strife well lost,
And for a breath of ecstasy
Give all you have been or could be.

Dylan Thomas

FERN HILL

Now as I was young and easy under the apple boughs
About the lilting house and happy as the grass was green,
    The night above the dingle starry,
      Time let me hail and climb
    Golden in the heydays of his eyes,   5
And honoured among wagons I was prince of the apple towns
And once below a time I lordly had the trees and leaves
      Trail with daisies and barley
    Down the rivers of the windfall light.

And as I was green and carefree, famous among the barns   10
About the happy yard and singing as the farm was home,

In the sun that is young once only,
    Time let me play and be
  Golden in the mercy of his means,
And green and golden I was huntsman and herdsman, the calves   15
Sang to my horn, the foxes on the hills barked clear and cold,
    And the sabbath rang slowly
    In the pebbles of the holy streams.

All the sun long it was running, it was lovely, the hay
Fields high as the house, the tunes from the chimneys, it was air   20
    And playing, lovely and watery
      And fire green as grass.
    And nightly under the simple stars
As I rode to sleep the owls were bearing the farm away,
All the moon long I heard, blessed among stables, the night-jars   25
    Flying with the ricks, and the horses
      Flashing into the dark.

And then to awake, and the farm, like a wanderer white
With the dew, come back, the cock on his shoulder: it was all
    Shining, it was Adam and maiden,   30
      The sky gathered again
    And the sun grew round that very day.
So it must have been after the birth of the simple light
In the first, spinning place, the spellbound horses walking warm
    Out of the whinnying green stable   35
    On to the fields of praise.

And honoured among foxes and pheasants by the gay house
Under the new made clouds and happy as the heart was long,
  In the sun born over and over,
    I ran my heedless ways,   40
  My wishes raced through the house high hay
And nothing I cared, at my sky blue trades, that time allows
In all his tuneful turning so few and such morning songs
  Before the children green and golden
    Follow him out of grace.   45

Nothing I cared, in the lamb white days, that time would take me
Up to the swallow thronged loft by the shadow of my hand,
  In the moon that is always rising,
    Nor that riding to sleep
  I should hear him fly with the high fields   50
And wake to the farm forever fled from the childless land.
Oh as I was young and easy in the mercy of his means,
    Time held me green and dying
    Though I sang my chains like the sea.

Joyce Carol Thomas

BLACK CHILD

My mother says I am
Still honey in sassafras tea
My father calls me the
Brown sugar of his days
Yet they warn   5
There are those who
Have brewed a
Bitter potion for
Children kissed long by the sun
Therefore I approach   10
The cup slowly
But first I ask
Who has set this table

Mohamud S. Togane

ARFAYE

A man without a nickname is like a goat without horns.
a Somali proverb

Arfaye: the sweet-smelling one,
fattest Somali in the city of Mogadishu,
city without deodorants.
Everybody knows his nickname and the irony
that sweetens the truth. Nobody knows his real name.   5
I can see him now in my mind's eye
in the middle of Main Street
in the frying sun
melting away
about to drown in his sweaty khaki uniform   10
flinging sweat away from his eyes
trying to direct a traffic of stubborn donkeys,
skittish camels (impatient drivers poking their behinds)
hauling grass and milk;
donkey-carts driven by heedless drivers   15

who claim the city belongs to their tribe and donkeys;
goats, sheep, and cattle on their way to the slaughter-house;
jay walkers, paraplegic beggars scuttling on all fours
(an American nicknamed them spidermen);
beeping Fiats and thunder-farting ancient trucks without mufflers.   20
Out of this medley sometimes a relief would appear:
quivering ripe breasts of a careless bushwoman
or some undulating steatopygous behind
then Arfaye would pause, tilt his head in worshipful wonder,
flash a smile, and throw darts of desire.   25

Melvin B. Tolson

A LEGEND OF VERSAILLES

Lloyd George and Woodrow Wilson and Clemenceau—
The Big Three: England, America, and France—
Met at Versailles. The Tiger ached to know
About the myth to end war's dominance.

"One moment, gentlemen," the Tiger said,   5
"Do you really want a lasting peace?" And then
Lloyd George assented with his shaggy head
And Woodrow Wilson, nodding, chafed his chin.

"The price of such a peace is great. We must give
Up secret cartels, spheres of power and trade;   10
Tear down our tariff walls; let lesser breeds live
As equals; scrap the empires we have made."

The gentlemen protested, "You go too far."
The Tiger shouted, "You don't mean peace, but war!"

Gerald Vizenor

FAMILY PHOTOGRAPH

among trees
my father was a spruce

corded for tribal pulp
he left the white earth reservation
colonial genealogies   5
taking up the city at twenty-three

telling stories
sharing dreams from a mason jar
running
low through the stumps at night   10
was his line

at twenty-three
he waited with the old men
colorless
dressed in their last uniforms   15
reeling on the nicollet island bridge

arm bands adrift
wooden limbs
men too civilized by war
thrown back to evangelists and charity   20

no reservation superintendents there
no indian agents
pacing off allotments twenty acres short
only family photographs ashore

no catholics on the wire   25
tying treaty money to confirmations

in the city
my father was an immigrant
hanging paper flowers
painting ceilings white for a union boss
disguising saint louis park   30

his weekend women
listened to him measuring my blood at night

downtown rooms were cold
half truths   35
peeling like blisters of history
two sizes too small

he smiles
holding me in a photograph then
the new spruce   40
half white
half immigrant
taking up the city and losing at cards

David Wagoner

A VALEDICTORY
TO STANDARD OIL
OF INDIANA

In the darkness east of Chicago, the sky burns over the plumbers'
   nightmares
Red and blue, and my hometown lies there loaded with gasoline.
Registers ring like gas-pumps, pumps like pinballs, pinballs like broken alarm
   clocks,
And it's time for morning, but nothing's going to work.
From cat-cracker to candle-shop, from grease-works along the pipeline,   5
Over storage tanks like kings on a checkerboard ready to jump the county,
The word goes out: With refined regrets
We suggest you sleep all day in your houses shaped like lunch buckets
And don't show up at the automated gates.
Something else will tap the gauges without yawning   10
And check the valves at the feet of the cooling-towers without complaining.
Standard Oil is canning my high school classmates
And the ones who fell out of junior high or slipped in the grades.
What should they do, gassed up in their Tempests and Comets, raring to go
Somewhere with their wives scowling in front and kids stuffed in the back,   15
Past drive-ins jammed like car-lots, trying to find the beaches
But blocked by freights for hours, stopped dead in their tracks
Where the rails, as thick as thieves along the lakefront,
Lower their crossing gates to shut the frontier? What can they think about

As they stare at the sides of boxcars for a sign,   20
And Lake Michigan drains slowly into Lake Huron,
The mills level the Dunes, and the eels go sailing through the trout,
And mosquitoes inherit the evening, while toads no bigger than horseflies
Hop crazily after them over the lawns and sidewalks, and the rainbows fall
Flat in the oil they came from? There are two towns now,   25
One dark, one going to be dark, divided by cyclone fences:
One pampered and cared for like pillboxes and cathedrals,
The other vanishing overnight in the dumps and swamps like a struck
    sideshow.
As the Laureate of the Class of '44—which doesn't know it has one—
I offer this poem, not from hustings or barricades   30
Or the rickety stage where George Rogers Clark stood glued to the wall,
But from another way out, like Barnum's "This Way to the Egress,"
Which moved the suckers when they'd seen enough. Get out of town.

Diane Wakoski

TO AN AUTOCRAT

Today you told me
you kicked the first lady
you lived with
out
because she washed her underwear,   5
blue silky things,
and hung them in the bathroom to dry.

A few days ago
you told me
another girl got kicked out   10
for mentioning
grandchildren.

These anecdotes
about taboos
begin to extend from telephone calls   15
to toothbrushing
and leave me trembling
as I suppose you think a lady should

afraid to make any independent move.
There is no doubt   20
you possess this house
and everything in it.
You can move me out or in
at will;
have done so to prove your power.   25
My only weapon
is logic
which salts you like a withering garden snail.
                                                    Because
it is you   30
who give me lectures
about the hang-ups of marriage,
and of people wanting to possess each other.
Save your stories for men,
I ought to tell you,   35
because any woman who buys them
is a guerrilla fighter who believes you've been master
of your house too long.
When you move all us silly ones
with our dripping underwear out   40
and install this one liberated lady with her fine panties
and spider-web bras,
her short icy slips,
and satin garters that draw your eyes up her legs
like filings following a magnet,   45
and you never see a vestige of how she launders them,
and she follows all your rules
and makes no demands,
while we poor offenders are always needing things
and trying to live our own lives too,   50
then,
sir,
I tremble for you
for real.
Will she cut your throat one night as you sleep   55
or take off your balls?
Will she steal you blind
and leave with your stockbroker
or debilitate you with your own weaknesses
and jump in to mastery after   60
she's spoiled you for anything but drink and talk?
She is your fate,
anyway,

if you don't realize
that living together   65
is what makes us human and decent.
We give in to others' needs, their rights,
making a fair division of privileges
and chores.
Our dog finds a long beam of sunshine   70
coming in an afternoon window
and she stretches her doberman body
to fit it.
        She follows the sunshine around the house
from morning to late afternoon,   75
stretching or curling into the patterns it makes
on the floor.
She is not perfect,
but she fits
the hours of the day.   80
            She understands
living/
    loving what you have,
making
the fit.   85

Margaret Walker

LINEAGE

My grandmothers were strong.
They followed plows and bent to toil.
They moved through fields sowing seed.

They touched earth and grain grew.
They were full of sturdiness and singing.   5
My grandmothers were strong.

My grandmothers are full of memories.
Smelling of soap and onions and wet clay
With veins rolling roughly over quick hands
They have many clean words to say.   10
My grandmothers were strong.
Why am I not as they?

Chad Walsh

PORT AUTHORITY
TERMINAL:
9 A.M. MONDAY

From buses beached like an invasion fleet
They fill the waiting room with striding feet.

Their faces, white, and void of hate or pity,
Move on tall bodies toward the conquered city.

Among the lesser breeds of black and brown   5
They board their taxis with an absent frown,

Each to his concrete citadel,
To rule the city and to buy and sell.

At five o'clock they ride the buses back,
Leaving their Irish to guard the brown and black.   10

At six a drink, at seven dinner's served.
At ten or twelve, depressed, undressed, unnerved,

They mount their wives, dismount, they doze and dream
Apocalyptic Negroes in a stream

Of moving torches, marching from the slums,   15
Beating a band of garbage pails for drums,

Marching, with school-age children in their arms,
Advancing on the suburbs and the farms,

To integrate the schools and burn the houses . . .
The normal morning comes, the clock arouses   20

Junior and senior executive alike.
Back on the bus, and down the usual pike.

From buses beached like an invasion fleet
They fill the waiting room with striding feet.

Phillis Wheatley

TO THE RIGHT HONORABLE WILLIAM, EARL OF DARTMOUTH

Hail, happy day, when, smiling like the morn,
Fair Freedom rose New England to adorn:
The northern clime beneath her genial ray,
Dartmouth, congratulates thy blissful sway:
Elate with hope her race no longer mourns,   5
Each soul expands, each grateful bosom burns,
While in thine hand with pleasure we behold
The silken reins, and Freedom's charms unfold.
Long lost to realms beneath the northern skies
She shines supreme, while hated faction dies: 10
Soon as appear'd the Goddess long desir'd,
Sick as the view, she languish'd and expir'd;
Thus from the splendors of the morning light
The owl in sadness seeks the caves of night.
    No more America in mournful strain   15
Of wrongs, and grievance unredress'd complain,
No longer shalt thou dread the iron chain,
Which wanton Tyranny with lawless hand
Had made, and which it meant t' enslave the land.

    Should you, my lord, while you peruse my song,   20
Wonder from whence my love of Freedom sprung,
Whence flow these wishes for the common good,
By feeling hearts alone best understood,
I, young in life, by seeming cruel fate
Was snatch'd from Afric's fancy'd happy seat: 25
What pangs excruciating must molest,
What sorrows labour in my parent's breast!
Steel'd was the soul and by no misery mov'd
That from a father seiz'd his babe belov'd.
Such, such my case. And can I then but pray   30
Others may never feel tyrannic sway?
    For favours past, great Sir, our thanks are due,
And thee we ask thy favours to renew,
Since in thy pow'r, as in thy will before,
To sooth the griefs, which thou did'st once deplore.   35
May heav'nly grace the sacred sanction give

To all thy works, and thou for ever live
Not only on the wings of fleeting Fame,
Though praise immortal crowns the patriot's name,
But to conduct to heav'n's refulgent fane,   40
May fiery courses sweep th' ethereal plain,
And bear thee upwards to that blest abode,
Where, like prophet, thou shalt find thy God.

QUESTIONS

1. What central metaphor does the poet use to describe the idea of freedom?
2. Describe the diction in the poem. What words and phrases contribute to the diction? Which words seem archaic or out of fashion?
3. What was the narrator's personal experience? What seems to be her attitude regarding this experience?

Walt Whitman

CAVALRY CROSSING A FORD

A line in long array, where they wind betwixt green islands;
They take a serpentine course—their arms flash in the sun—Hark to the
  musical clank;
Behold the silvery river—in it the splashing horses, loitering, stop to drink;
Behold the brown-faced men—each group, each person, a picture—the   5
  negligent rest on the saddles;
Some emerge on the opposite bank—others are just entering the
  ford—while,
Scarlet, and blue, and snowy white,
The guidon flags flutter gaily in the wind.   10

I HEAR AMERICA SINGING

I hear America singing, the varied carols I hear,
Those of mechanics, each one singing his as it should be blithe
    and strong,
The carpenter singing his as he measures his plank or beam,
The mason singing his as he makes ready for work, or leaves off   5
    work,
The boatman singing what belongs to him in his boat, the deck-
    hand singing on the steamboat deck,
The shoemaker singing as he sits on his bench, the hatter singing
    as he stands,   10
The wood-cutter's song, the ploughboy's on his way in the
    morning, or at noon intermission or at sundown,
The delicious singing of the mother, or of the young wife at work,
    or of the girl sewing or washing,
Each singing what belongs to him or her and to none else,   15
The day what belongs to the day—at night the party of young
    fellows, robust, friendly,
Singing with open mouths their strong melodious songs.

THERE WAS A CHILD
WENT FORTH

There was a child went forth every day,
And the first object he look'd upon, that object he became,
And that object became part of him for the day or a certain part of the day,
Or for many years or stretching cycles of years.

The early lilacs became part of this child,   5
And grass and white and red morning-glories, and white and red clover,
    and the song of the phœbe-bird,
And the Third-month lambs and the sow's pink-faint litter,
    and the mare's foal and the cow's calf,
And the noisy brood of the barnyard or by the mire of the pond-side,   10
And the fish suspending themselves so curiously below there,
    and the beautiful curious liquid,
And the water-plants with their graceful flat heads, all became part of him.

The field-sprouts of Fourth-month and Fifth-month became part of him,
Winter-grain sprouts and those of the light-yellow corn,   15
    and the esculent roots of the garden,
And the apple-trees cover'd with blossoms and the fruit afterward,
    and wood-berries, and the commonest weeds by the road,
And the old drunkard staggering home from the outhouse of the tavern
    whence he had lately risen,   20
And the schoolmistress that pass'd on her way to the school,
And the friendly boys that pass'd, and the quarrelsome boys,
And the tidy and fresh-cheek'd girls, and the barefoot negro boy and girl,
And all the changes of city and country wherever he went.

His own parents, he that had father'd him and she that had conceiv'd him   25
    in her womb and birth'd him,
They give this child more of themselves than that,
They gave him afterward every day, they became part of him.

The mother at home quietly placing the dishes on the supper-table,
The mother with mild words, clean her cap and gown,   30
    a wholesome odor falling off her person and clothes as she walks by,
The father, strong, self-sufficient, manly, mean, anger'd, unjust,
The blow, the quick loud word, the tight bargain, the crafty lure,
The family usages, the language, the company, the furniture,
    the yearning and swelling heart,   35
Affection that will not be gainsay'd, the sense of what is real,
    the thought if after all it should prove unreal,
The doubts of day-time and the doubts of night-time,
    the curious whether and how,
Whether that which appears so is so, or is it all flashes and specks?   40
Men and women crowding fast in the streets,
    if they are not flashes and specks what are they?
The streets themselves and the façades of houses, and goods in the windows,
Vehicles, teams, the heavy-plank'd wharves, the huge crossing at the ferries,
The village on the highland seen from afar at sunset, the river between,   45
Shadows, aureola and mist, the light falling on roofs and gables
    of white or brown two miles off,
The schooner near by sleepily dropping down the tide,
    the little boat slack-tow'd astern,
The hurrying tumbling waves, quick-broken crests, slapping,   50
The strata of color'd clouds, the long bar of maroon-tint away solitary
    by itself, the spread of purity it lies motionless in,
The horizon's edge, the flying sea-crow, the fragrance of salt marsh and
    shore mud,
These became part of that child who went forth every day,   55
    and who now goes, and will always go forth every day.

William Carlos Williams

DANSE RUSSE

If when my wife is sleeping
and the baby and Kathleen
are sleeping
and the sun is a flame-white disc
in silken mists   5
above shining trees,—
if I in my north room
dance naked, grotesquely
before my mirror
waving my shirt round my head   10
and singing softly to myself:
"I am lonely, lonely.
I was born to be lonely,
I am best so!"
If I admire my arms, my face,   15
my shoulders, flanks, buttocks
against the yellow drawn shades,—

Who shall say I am not
the happy genius of my household?

QUESTIONS

1. The title is an early twentieth-century term in ballet that connoted scandal and exoticism. How do the narrator's behavior and the poet's imagery make this title apt?
2. What pleasure does the poet derive from his dance? Why is it only possible for him to feel this pleasure when he is alone?
3. How can the poet be "lonely" and happy at the same time?
4. Concentrate on the line structure of the poem and the rhythm it creates as you read the poem aloud. How does its rhythm contribute to the mood of the poem?

TO WAKEN AN OLD LADY

Old age is
a flight of small
cheeping birds
skimming

bare trees   5
above a snow glaze.
Gaining and failing
they are buffeted
by a dark wind—
But what?   10
On harsh weedstalks
the flock has rested,
the snow
is covered with broken
seedhusks   15
and the wind tempered
by a shrill
piping of plenty.

James Wright

AUTUMN BEGINS IN MARTINS FERRY, OHIO

In the Shreve High football stadium,
I think of Polacks nursing long beers in Tiltonsville,
And gray faces of Negroes in the blast furnace at Benwood,
And the ruptured night watchman of Wheeling Steel,
Dreaming of heroes.   5

All the proud fathers are ashamed to go home.
Their women cluck like starved pullets,
Dying for love.

Therefore,
Their sons grow suicidally beautiful   10
At the beginning of October,
And gallop terribly against each other's bodies.

QUESTIONS

1. To which economic class does the poet refer in paragraph 1?
2. Why are the "proud fathers . . . ashamed to go home"?

3. What does the phrase "Their sons grow suicidally beautiful" mean? What is the psychological relationship between the sons and their fathers?
4. James Wright's father was a coal miner, and his youth was spent in a blue-collar environment in the Midwest. How does the poem demonstrate his knowledge of this aspect of America?

Sir Thomas Wyatt

THEY FLEE FROM ME

They flee from me, that sometime did me seek,
With naked foot stalking in my chamber.
I have seen them, gentle, tame, and meek,
That now are wild, and do not remember
That sometime they put themselves in danger   5
To take bread at my hand; and now they range,
Busily seeking with a continual change.

Thankéd be fortune it hath been otherwise,
Twenty times better; but once in special,
In thin array, after a pleasant guise,   10
When her loose gown from her shoulders did fall,
And she me caught in her arms long and small,
And therewithall sweetly did me kiss
And softly said, "Dear heart, how like you this?"

It was no dream, I lay broad waking.   15
But all is turned, thorough my gentleness,
Into a strange fashion of forsaking;
And I have leave to go, of her goodness,
And she also to use newfangleness.
But since that I so kindely am servéd,   20
I fain would know what she hath deservéd.

Mitsuye Yamada

DESERT RUN

I

I return to the desert
where criminals
were abandoned to wander
away to their deaths
where scorpions   5
spiders
snakes
lizards
and rats
live in outcast harmony   10
where the sculptor's wreck
was reclaimed
by the gentle drifting sands.

We approach the dunes while
the insistent flies bother our ears   15
the sound of crunching gravel under
our shoes cracks the desolate stillness
and opens our way.

Everything is done in silence here:
the wind fingers fluted stripes   20
over mounds and mounds of sand
the swinging grasses sweep
patterns on the slopes
the sidewinder passes out of sight.
I was too young to hear silence before.   25

II

I spent 547 sulking days here
in my own dreams
there was not much to marvel at
I thought
only miles of sagebrush and   30
lifeless sand.

I watched the most beautiful
sunsets in the world and saw nothing

forty years ago
I wrote my will here   35
my fingers moved slowly in the
hot sand the texture of whole wheat flour
three words: I died here
the winds filed them away.

I am back to claim my body   40
my carcass lies
between the spiny branches
of two creosote bushes
it looks strangely like a small calf
left to graze and die   45
half of its bones are gone
after all these years

but no matter
I am satisfied
I take a dry stick   50
and give myself
a ritual burial.

III

Like the bull snakes brought
into this desert by the soldiers
we were transported here   55
to drive away rattlers
in your nightmares
we were part of some one's plan
to spirit away spies
in your peripheral vision.   60

My skin turned pink brown
in the bright desert light
I slithered in the matching sand
doing what you put me here to do
we were predators at your service   65
I put your mind at ease.

I am that odd creature
the female bull snake
I flick my tongue in your face
an image trapped in your mirror.   70
You will use me or

you will honor me in a shrine
to keep me pure.

IV

At night the outerstellar darkness
above is only an arm's length away   75
I am pressed by the silence around me
the stars are bold as big as quarters
against the velvet blue sky
their beams search for the marrow
of my bones   80
I shiver as I stumble my way to
the outhouse.

In the morning we find
kangaroo rats
have built mounds of messy homes   85
out of dry sticks and leavings
behind our wagon
They have accepted our alien presence.
The night creatures keep a discreet
distance.   90

V

The desert is the lungs of the world.
This land of sudden lizards and nappy ants
is only useful when not used
We must leave before we feel we can
change it.   95

When we leave the dirt roads
my body is thankful for the
paved ride the rest of the way
home.
Rows of yucca trees with spiked crowns   100
wave stiffly at us
Some watch us arms akimbo.

I cannot stay in the desert
where you will have me nor
will I be brought back in a cage   105
to grace your need for exotica.
I write these words at night

for I am still a night creature
but I will not keep a discreet distance
If you must fit me to your needs   110
I will die
and so will you.

William Butler Yeats

LEDA AND THE SWAN

A sudden blow; the great wings beating still
Above the staggering girl, her thighs caressed
By the dark webs, her nape caught in his bill,
He holds her helpless breast upon his breast.

How can those terrified vague fingers push   5
The feathered glory from her loosening thighs?
And how can body, laid in that white rush,
But feel the strange heart beating where it lies?

A shudder in the loins engenders there
The broken wall, the burning roof and tower   10
And Agamemnon dead.
                                        Being so caught up,
So mastered by the brute blood of the air,
Did she put on his knowledge with his power
Before the indifferent beak could let her drop?   15

Al Young

A POEM FOR WILLARD MOTLEY

Sometimes at the mouth of this river,
from the far right side of my brain,
I fish all night
in Mexican remembrance
of you, Willard Motley; your elegant   5
hoodlums, your cinematic wops
trapped by themselves between midnight and dawn inside air bubbles
no fish could ever fill
with sly, spicy cartoon talk.   10
I don't suppose you had to be
womanless or manless to cast
such virulent lines into the mouths
of your violent, somnolent characters,
but I'd be willing to bet   15
a Kentucky Derby to a Frank Yerby
that fearlessness helped.

Your forget-me-not bohemian ways
live on in the slow memory
of someone who only heard   20
about your private, festive outbursts
in a sea-surrounded salt & tequila land
the abrupt & unnameable color
of the fathomless dreams of our race.
And so sometimes at the muddy banks   25
of these waters I stand & unreel
my own knotted lines; a knucklehead
shadowed in silver light & weary
as Bogart of knocking at doors.

Again & again I picture John Derek,   30
the way he was: your first-born
prettyboy screen-heroic victim
whose latest wife Bo played Jane
to a Tarzan I couldn't even stick
around the theater long enough to see.   35
My eyes were too lidded with sad, rusting
ironies to stay open in the heavy-colored

dark. Somehow I couldn't stop
thinking about Fred Astaire,
that agile, singing step-dancer   40
the whole world loved up there.
After all the riches Negroes paved
his way with, how could he go &
marry that frisky young jockey
of a wife who openly championed the KKK?   45

It's a very old story, you know;
washed out, wish-defying; so fishy
& predictable you could chart it
on a graph. What waters were you
treading when you realized no man could   50
write your epitaph? What Chicago,
what Sicily possessed you at that point?

Bernice Zamora

NOTES FROM A CHICANA "COED"

for P.H.

To cry that the *gabacho*
is our oppressor is to shout
in abstraction, *carnal.*
He no more oppresses us
than you do now as you tell me   5
"It's the gringo who oppresses you, Babe."
You cry "The gringo is our oppressor!"
to the tune of $20,000 to $30,000
a year, brother, and I wake up
alone each morning and ask,   10
"Can I feed my children today?"

To make the day easier
I write poems about
pájaros, mariposas,
and the fragrance   15

of perfume I
smell on your collar;
you're quick to point out
that I must write
about social reality,   20
about "the gringo who
oppresses you, Babe."
And so I write about
how I worked in beet fields
as a child, about how I   25
worked as a waitress
eight hours at night to
get through high school,
about working as a
seamstress, typist, and field clerk   30
to get through college, and
about how, in graduate school
I held two jobs, seven days
a week, still alone, still asking,
"Can I feed my children today?"   35

To give meaning to my life
you make love to me in alleys,
in back seats of borrowed Vegas,
in six-dollar motel rooms
after which you talk about   40
your five children and your wife
who writes poems at home
about *pájaros, mariposas,*
and the fragrance of perfume
she smells on your collar.   45
Then you tell me how you
bear the brunt of the
gringo's oppression for me,
and how you would go
to prison for me, because   50
"The gringo is oppressing you, Babe!"

And when I mention
your G.I. Bill, your
Ford Fellowship, your
working wife, your   55
three *gabacha guisás*
when you ask me to
write your thesis,

you're quick to shout,
"Don't give me that   60
Women's Lib trip, *mujer,*
that only divides us,
and we have to work
together for the *movimiento;*
the *gabacho* is oppressing us!"   65

Oye carnal, you may as well
tell me that moon water
cures constipation, that
penguin soup prevents *crudas,*
or that the Arctic Ocean is *menudo,*   70
because we both learned in the barrios,
man, that pigeon shit slides easier.

Still, because of the *gabacho,*
I must write poems about
pájaros, mariposas, and the fragrance   75
of oppressing perfume I smell somewhere.

Cyn. Zarco

ASPARAGUS

There's a washcloth
with a picture of asparagus
in my bathroom.

Did you know
that Pilipinos were picked   5
to grow asparagus in the West
because they were short
and built closer to the ground?

I'm 5'3". I don't use
that washcloth anymore.   10

D r a m a

Romare Bearden. *The Piano Lesson*. 1983. Collage and watercolor. 29″ X 22″.
Courtesy Estate of Romare Bearden.

UNDERSTANDING DRAMA

"All the world's a stage," wrote Shakespeare in one of the most famous lines in drama, "and all the men and women merely players." Indeed our human drama is persistent and universal, probably as old as the earliest hunters who disguised themselves and tried to act like those animals they were trying to lure into a trap and kill. The hunt and other crucial activities became ongoing dramas reflecting human conflict and the struggle for survival; and these dramas lent themselves to the creation of stories about bravery and cowardice, endurance and extinction, tragedy and comedy.

From its beginnings, drama (which Aristotle called "imitated human action"), like other forms of literature, was meant to tell the story of humankind in conflict with its world. In the acting out of events, drama often invested the most ancient and sometimes the most ordinary rituals with pomp and mystery. Western drama, in fact, grew from religious rituals; comedy derived from the Dionysian rites celebrating fertility and growth, and tragedy from the goat songs (again embedded in Dionysian rituals) that stressed the sacrificial nature of existence and the reality of death. Drama in all ages is, as William Archer stated aptly in *Play-making* (1926), "a representation of the will of man in conflict with the mysterious powers of natural forces which limit and belittle us: it is one of us thrown living upon the stage there to struggle against fatality, against social law, against one of his fellow mortals, against himself if need be, against the ambitions, the interests, the prejudices, the folly, the malevolence of those around him." There could be no drama without that universal picture, on stage, of human beings confronting physical, mental, and spiritual obstacles.

Drama differs from other forms of literature in that it demands a stage and performances. The drama critic Eric Bentley is correct when he declares that drama enjoys a double life—that it can be enjoyed by both spectator and reader. But the fact remains that most plays are written to be produced. Most critics stress this obvious but also subtle truth, that drama must be performed; in fact, performance is an element of drama. Professor J. M. Manly, for one, states that drama requires a story, told in action, by actors who impersonate the characters of the story. Similarly, Elder Olson speculates: "If we think about the things a dramatist must do, as a *minimum,* to make a play, it becomes clear that he must (1) devise some sort of action, together with characters who can appropriately carry it out, (2) contrive a scenario which shows what actions are to be enacted on the stage in what order, and (3) compose the dialog, or at least indicate roughly what sort of thing shall be said by the actors." In both definitions of drama there is, as we shall see, the relentless ghost of Aristotle dominating the various elements. Yet what is most revealing about these definitions, and all other useful explanations of the nature of drama, is that they stress the theatrical perspective.

It is the theatrical perspective that forces us to focus on drama's need for producers and directors, playwright and actors, theater and stage, audience and, alas, critics. A

play, after all, is human action or human experience dramatized for stage production, and this theatrical reality offers both possibilities and constraints. Playwrights have always been aware of the special environment of theater. George Bernard Shaw, writing for *The New York Times* in 1912, listed in several paragraphs the many factors that dictate the playwright's methods. Here is a typical paragraph:

> I do not select my methods: they are imposed on me by a hundred considerations: by the physical considerations of theatrical representation, by the laws devised by the municipality to guard against fires and other accidents to which theatres are liable, by the economies of theatrical commerce, by the nature and limits of the art of acting, by the capacity of the spectators for understanding what they see and hear, and by the accidental circumstances of the particular production in hand.

Shakespeare knew about these theatrical constraints three hundred years before Shaw, just as Broadway playwrights and producers understand them more than half a century after Shaw. Theater depends on numerous art forms, and it is assuredly an expensive literary art.

The playwright, unlike the poet or fiction writer, creates for a mass audience, not for individuals. In classical times, the distinction between poet and dramatist was not so marked. In ancient Greece, playwrights were called poets, for drama was written in verse; and poets often competed in state-sponsored contests. Greek dramatic presentations (the word "drama" comes from the Greek word meaning "a thing done") were civic occasions; sometimes the performances lasted for days. Eventually, drama and poetry went their separate ways, although at times they would again merge significantly, as in works by Shakespeare, Ibsen (notably *Brand* and *Peer Gynt*), Brecht, and Archibald MacLeish. Drama can incorporate poetry while still being fiction in an imaginative sense; it shares with these major genres a telling about humankind and the world. Nevertheless, its elements ultimately contrast with those of poetry and fiction because those elements must be made visible. We go to the theater to *see;* that is its essence.

The question of exactly *what* we see has been a subject of critical debate ever since Aristotle formulated his ideas about drama, especially tragedy, in his *Poetics.* What we should see, to follow Aristotle's *Poetics,* is plot, the most important part of drama. The ancients liked to compare plot to the tying and untying of a knot. Plot should be organized, according to Aristotle, in such a way as to present the good or just hero or heroine who must suffer because of some inherent personal defect. Plot is the entire action and sequence of events in a play—all the movement arranged as an organic whole. As Aristotle explained, speaking specifically of tragedy:

> A whole is that which has a beginning, a middle, and an end. A beginning is that which does not itself follow anything by causal necessity, but after which something naturally is or comes to be. An end, on the contrary, is that which itself naturally follows some other thing, either by necessity, or as a rule, but has nothing following it. A middle is that which follows something, as some other thing follows it.

Through plot, a playwright "imitates" the cause-and-effect movement of existence, adjusting the rhythm to fit the mode of presentation, whether that mode is comedy or farce, tragedy or melodrama, tragicomedy or pantomime. Through plot, characters reach out to us in language and action, melody and spectacle (to invoke once again some key Aristotelian categories), in order to illuminate their confrontations with time and the world.

Ideally we must feel and vicariously *live* through these confrontations and the larger human experience of the play, if we are spectators, or bring an equal sensitivity to our solitary reading of the play. A playwright normally has only two to three hours to create this special magic of drama, to bring us into the theatrical universe. As the noted philosopher Susanne K. Langer states in *Feeling and Form*, drama confronts us with "the semblance of events lived and felt . . . so that they constitute a purely and completely experienced reality, a piece of *virtual life.*" Perhaps we invest the characters with ourselves, sharing their pity and fear, their joy and laughter, within the enchanted context of the play. However, when it is over, we feel pleasure because our emotions have been manipulated—as we wished them to be—and we are ourselves once again. Aristotle, again referring to tragedy, termed this emotional response *catharsis*, the purging of pity and fear in the very being of an audience.

Aristotle has had such a pervasive influence on the conventions of drama that playwrights and critics have been honoring, modifying, or attempting to abandon his rules ever since they were formulated in the *Poetics*. Of course, Aristotle based his formulations about the elements of drama (for instance, the structural elements of fable, character, and thought; and the stylistic elements of language, melody, and spectacle) and about the dramatic unities of time, place, and action upon the earlier Greek drama of Sophocles, Aeschylus, Euripides, and Aristophanes. Two of these great Greek dramatists—Sophocles and Aristophanes—are represented in this anthology, including the *Oedipus Rex* of Sophocles, which Aristotle considered the perfect example of tragedy. Aristotle, in other words, based his critical theories on living drama. In *Oedipus Rex,* the perfectly "Aristotelian" play, the characters come to destruction more from their own defects than from the wrath of the gods that Aeschylus used in an earlier time. Moreover, the plot embodied the rules of dramatic unity—that the action of the play be a unified whole, that the scene remain unchanged or be confined to a specific area, and that the action of the play be limited to 24 hours—that Aristotle esteemed.

Dramatists and critics have had to deal with Aristotle's ghost. Lost for a time, the Aristotelian concepts of drama's form and content surged back into Renaissance drama in the sixteenth century. Shakespeare, for one, modified Aristotle's conceptions of plot by creating double plots in many of his plays, notably in *King Lear;* while in *Othello,* presented in this text, there is a "violation" of the concept of unity of place. Historically, then, as drama has evolved, dramatists have questioned Aristotle's ghost. In 1663, Molière declared that "the great rule of all rules is not to please." He was not comfortable with Aristotle's influence during the neoclassical period. One of his characters in *School for Wives* (1663) echoes the wish of Molière to be free from old restraints: "When I see a play I look only whether the points strike me; and when I am well entertained, I do not ask whether I have been wrong, or whether the rules of Aristotle would forbid me to laugh." In the twentieth century, the great dramatist Bertolt Brecht would still be trying to expiate Aristotle's ghost. In his anti-Aristotelian essay, "Theatre for Pleasure or Theatre for Instruction," Brecht insists that we must not only be amused by theater and be drawn into it, but also be detached, or alienated, from the theatrical event to

such an extent that we can learn from the dramatic representation on stage and feel urged to act militantly because of this detached understanding of the human drama. We can never make too much of Aristotle, but eventually we do come back to the play itself; and a play, as Thornton Wilder observed in 1941, "visibly represents pure existing."

How playwrights recreate or reproduce "pure existing" is a matter that varies from dramatist to dramatist and age to age. Shakespeare and his Elizabethan contemporaries used plot conventions that did not exist in Aristotle's time; while Brecht, in a play like *Mother Courage*, works wonders with the sort of episodic plot that Aristotle despised. Again, historical progress results in revolutions in stage-setting techniques. Devices far more complicated than those used by the Greeks were common in Renaissance drama. The Renaissance produced the modern proscenium arch, instead of the usual two or three arches, and stage setting became an art in its own right. Some playwrights, seeking maximum popularity, devised plots to utilize the spectacular: fireworks, water fountains, trapdoors, flying machines, and the like.

A play—that visible representation of pure existing—derives from the artistry of the dramatist and the values of the age. For example, Shakespeare's tragedy *Othello* is usually discussed without reference to the question of racism, but in discussions of *The Merchant of Venice* the question of anti-Semitism often arises. Was Shakespeare interested in the issue of racism in *Othello?* Textual analysis of the play and the treatment on which Shakespeare based his tragedy indicate that racism is an issue, adding yet another dimension to this extraordinary drama. Margaret Webster, producer of the play starring Paul Robeson and Uta Hagen, wrote: "One fact stands in sharp relief. The difference in race between Othello and every other character in the play is, indeed, the heart of the matter. This is the cause of Othello's terrible vulnerability on which Iago fastens so pitilessly; because of this, the conduct of which Desdemona is accused seems to Othello only too horribly possible; this is Iago's first and most powerful weapon, twisted to every conceivable use. . . ."

Major dramatists—Sophocles, Shakespeare, Ibsen, Miller, Hansberry, Hwang—probe the values of their age in an effort to seek the individual's importance in the world. What William Rose Benet said of Ibsen, that he "brought the problems and ideas of his day onto the stage," is true of all significant playwrights looking for affirmations of life itself. Drama might very well have begun in imitation of life with only remembered or told events as guidelines, but today it is firmly wedded to the written word, or script. A script is composed of the dialogue and stage directions designed to set "pure existing" in motion, with the acts and scenes that structure this action—all of which, of course, are not to be found in a work of fiction or poetry as we know them today.

Fiction and poetry make us imagine, make us create paths that lead us into the writer's world. On stage, however, all is spoken or couched in movement. The sets and machinery visibly present us a place and a time that we do not have to imagine. The characters "play" before us: real, palpable, and, one hopes, as true to life or the spirit of life as the playwright wished them to be. Theme, symbol, tone, plot—indeed, all dramatic convention—unfold and evolve before us. The dramatic elements evolve from the written to the spoken word, defining and giving depth to the characters and action we see. The dramatist, like a demigod, literally *speaks* Creation into existence; and in this process the dramatist teaches the human heart, as Shelley suggested, the knowledge of itself.

Perhaps what some saw and others did not is the beginning and the essence of drama; those who had had singular experiences wished to share them, to tell a tale, to act out a story. In drama the entire process of telling stories has come full circle. The oral traditions mark our beginnings as literate peoples. Then came the signs, symbols, glyphs, and alphabets, followed by extended writing and printing. It is the combination of how well the playwright has perceived and written and how well the actor conveys the meanings of his or her words—the double utilization of language—that provides us with the most successful drama.

As you explore the rich diversity of drama in the following sections, you will find brief essays exploring theme, character, plot, and dramatic form, followed by major plays for discussion and evaluation. You will also see the interplay of many cultures that has shaped plays around the world, and be encouraged to identify those shared experiences that make for great universal drama.

19. Theme

A play transmits signals from the dramatist to both the actors and the audience about the nature of its subject, the range of experience that it contains, the nature and form of that experience, and what that experience ultimately means. When Maurya in John Millington Synge's *Riders to the Sea* declares at the end of the play, "No man at all can be living forever, and we must be satisfied," we see how the playwright can telegraph through one character a partial or complete theme deriving from the action of the play. We look to characters and their speeches, and to setting, action, plot, tone, mood, and figurative range of language—in short, to the total context and all the conventions of drama—in order to discover what a play means.

When we observe drama in production or read a dramatic script, we see the signs that guide us toward an appreciation and understanding of the experience being enacted. Good playwrights know the value of theme and the value of stage time, so they orchestrate their signals in order to advance action, subject, and theme in as effective and significant a manner as possible. Playwrights also know their audience. Whether it is Sophocles writing for a Greek audience more than two thousand years ago, Shakespeare writing for an Elizabethan audience, or Arthur Miller writing for us today, all great dramatists communicate what they want to say about human experience by creating, ordering, and tailoring a theatrical world in such a way that it will offer an image of the real world that we inhabit. Today we can understand the dramatic world of Sophocles and Shakespeare, because the meanings contained within the dramatic conventions that they manipulate are universal. But we can also misinterpret plays of other nations and periods. The Russians have a tendency to laugh at *Hamlet,* while we offer more sympathy in modern times to Shylock in *The Merchant of Venice* than Shakespeare probably intended. Nevertheless, we must always enter the "imaginary" world of any play, try to catch quickly the major signals (Is this going to be a comedy, a tragedy, a tragicomedy, a "problem" play, or something else?), locate other important signals, and determine finally the playwright's controlling vision of life, of human relationships, of the contours and complexities of society, and of the ultimate mysteries of the cosmos.

At times, the meaning of a play will be so baldly stated that there can be no misunderstanding, but at other times we must be prepared to bring considerable interpretative powers to bear on the drama in order to understand and appreciate it. The morality plays that were popular in Western Europe during the fourteenth to sixteenth centuries offered transparent ethical and spiritual truths. At the outset of *Everyman*, written around 1500 and the most famous English morality play, a Messenger offers the following overview of the subject and meaning of the drama.

> I pray you give all your audience
> And hear this matter with reverence
> By figure a moral play:
> The *Summoning of Everyman* called it is,
> That of our lives and ending shows
> How transitory we be all day.

The Messenger then offers a series of Christian axioms on the vanity of human pleasures, the inevitability of death, and the certainty that "our Heaven King/Calleth Everyman to a general reckoning." The audience of the later Middle Ages and, indeed, the audience today would have little trouble in detecting in *Everyman* the highly moralistic theme of the play, for it has been spelled out.

Often the very form of a play—a morality play, a Greek tragedy, a neoclassical comedy—will alert us to possible meanings. Yet few significant plays surrender all their meaning readily, and in many instances the meaning or theme of a play can prove elusive and open to debate. Whereas Aristotle in his *Poetics* asserted that drama is the "imitation of an action," we sometimes have difficulty determining exactly *what* is being imitated and why. At times, the dramatist will provide instructions on how the subject and action of a play should be interpreted. Thus Ibsen in his notes for *A Doll's House* wrote: "A woman cannot be herself in the society of the present day, which is an exclusively masculine society, with laws framed by men and with a judicial system that judges feminine conduct from a masculine point of view." However, more typically a playwright does not provide so explicit a controlling idea for a play, thereby forcing the director to be the interpretative medium, or forcing readers themselves to be the interpreters.

Readers know that most plays work toward a clarification of some aspect of human experience. A play might concern itself with love, revenge, the fate of kings, jealousy, political or psychological oppression, and so forth. Such subjects may be universal or fairly topical. The treatment of the subjects may be tragic, farcical, fantastic, or anything in between. Above all, it is the theme of the play that lends unity and consistency to the production. For example, the general subject of the two short plays in this section, Synge's *Riders to the Sea* and Hughes's *Soul Gone Home,* is the loss of sons by their mothers. Yet what the dramatists *say* about the subject varies, as we shall see, with the vision of the playwright. Each play seeks to dramatize specific lives and to illuminate social conditions. Each play is "universal" in that it concentrates on death in the family—a subject and a reality that shall persist as long as humanity itself lasts. What is so striking about any comparative assessment of these two plays is not so much their commonality

in subject as their divergence in characterization, action, tone, mood, and theme. In other words, the signals created by Synge and Hughes are different. As you read these plays, try to locate the important signals in order to discover how each work acquires from a common subject its own meaning.

John Millington Synge

RIDERS TO THE SEA

CHARACTERS

MAURYA, an old woman	BARTLEY, her son
CATHLEEN, her daughter	NORA, a younger daughter
MEN AND WOMEN	

An island off the west of Ireland.

    Cottage kitchen, with nets, oil-skins, spinning-wheel, some new boards standing by the wall, etc. CATHLEEN, *a girl of about twenty, finishes kneading cake, and puts it down on the pot-oven by the fire; then wipes her hands, and begins to spin at the wheel.* NORA, *a young girl, puts her head in at the door.*

NORA [*in a low voice*]: Where is she?

CATHLEEN: She's lying down, God help her, and may be sleeping, if she's able.

[NORA *comes in softly, and takes a bundle from under her shawl.*]

CATHLEEN [*spinning the wheel rapidly*]: What is it you have?

NORA: The young priest is after bringing them. It's a shirt and a plain stocking were got off a drowned man in Donegal.

[CATHLEEN *stops her wheel with a sudden movement, and leans out to listen.*]

NORA: We're to find out if it's Michael's they are, some time herself will be down looking by the sea.

CATHLEEN: How would they be Michael's, Nora? How would he go the length of that way to the Far North?

NORA: The young priest says he's known the like of it. "If it's Michael's they are," says he, "you can tell herself he's got a clean burial by the grace of God, and if they're not his, let no one say a word about them, for she'll be getting her death," says he, "with crying and lamenting."

[*The door which* NORA *half closed is blown open by a gust of wind.*]

CATHLEEN [*looking out anxiously*]: Did you ask him would he stop Bartley going this day with the horses to the Galway fair?

NORA: "I won't stop him," says he, "but let you not be afraid. Herself does be saying prayers half through the night, and the Almighty God won't leave her destitute," says he, "with no son living."

CATHLEEN: Is the sea bad by the white rocks, Nora?

NORA: Middling bad, God help us. There's a great roaring in the west, and it's worse it'll be getting when the tide's turned to the wind. [*She goes over to the table with the bundle.*] Shall I open it now?

CATHLEEN: Maybe she'd wake up on us, and come in before we'd done. [*Coming to the table.*] It's a long time we'll be, and the two of us crying.

NORA [*goes to the inner door and listens*]: She's moving about on the bed. She'll be coming in a minute.

CATHLEEN: Give me the ladder, and I'll put them up in the turf-loft, the way she won't know of them at all, and maybe when the tide turns she'll be going down to see would he be floating from the east.

[*They put the ladder against the gable of the chimney;* CATHLEEN *goes up a few steps and hides the bundle in the turf-loft.* MAURYA *comes from the inner room.*]

MAURYA [*looking up at* CATHLEEN *and speaking querulously*]: Isn't it turf enough you have for this day and evening?

CATHLEEN: There's a cake baking at the fire for a short space [*throwing down the turf*] and Bartley will want it when the tide turns if he goes to Connemara.

[NORA *picks up the turf and puts it round the pot-oven.*]

MAURYA [*sitting down on a stool at the fire*]: He won't go this day with the wind rising from the south and west. He won't go this day, for the young priest will stop him surely.

NORA: He'll not stop him, Mother, and I heard Eamon Simon and Stephen Pheety and Colum Shawn saying he would go.

MAURYA: Where is he itself?

NORA: He went down to see would there be another boat sailing in the week, and I'm thinking it won't be long till he's here now, for the tide's turning at the green head, and the hooker's tacking from the east.

CATHLEEN: I hear some one passing the big stones.

NORA [*looking out*]: He's coming now, and he in a hurry.

BARTLEY [*comes in and looks round the room; speaking sadly and quietly*]: Where is the bit of new rope, Cathleen, was bought in Connemara?

CATHLEEN [*coming down*]: Give it to him, Nora; it's on a nail by the white boards. I hung it up this morning, for the pig with the black feet was eating it.

NORA [*giving him a rope*]: Is that it, Bartley?

MAURYA: You'd do right to leave that rope, Bartley, hanging by the boards. [BARTLEY *takes the rope.*] It will be wanting in this place, I'm telling you, if Michael is washed up tomorrow morning, or the next morning, or any morning in the week, for it's a deep grave we'll make him by the grace of God.

BARTLEY [*beginning to work with the rope*]: I've no halter the way I can ride down on the mare, and I must go now quickly. This is the one boat going for two weeks or beyond it, and the fair will be a good fair for horses I heard them saying below.

MAURYA: It's a hard thing they'll be saying below if the body is washed up and there's no man in it to make the coffin, and I after giving a big price for the finest white boards you'd find in Connemara. [*She looks round at the boards.*]

BARTLEY: How would it be washed up, and we after looking each day for nine days, and a strong wind blowing a while back from the west and south?

MAURYA: If it wasn't found itself, that wind is raising the sea, and there was a star up against the moon, and it rising in the night. If it was a hundred horses, or a thousand horses you had itself, what is the price of a thousand horses against a son where there is one son only?

BARTLEY [*working at the halter, to* CATHLEEN]: Let you go down each day, and see the sheep aren't jumping in on the rye, and if the jobber comes you can sell the pig with the black feet if there is a good price going.

MAURYA: How would the like of her get a good price for a pig?

BARTLEY [*to* CATHLEEN]: If the west wind holds with the last bit of the moon let you and Nora get up weed enough for another cock for the kelp. It's hard set we'll be from this day with no one in it but one man to work.

MAURYA: It's hard set we'll be surely the day you're drownd'd with the rest. What way will I live and the girls with me, and I an old woman looking for the grave?

[BARTLEY *lays down the halter, takes off his old coat and puts on a newer one of the same flannel.*]

BARTLEY [*to* NORA]: Is she coming to the pier?

NORA [*looking out*]: She's passing the green head and letting fall her sails.

BARTLEY [*getting his purse and tobacco*]: I'll have half an hour to go down, and you'll see me coming again in two days, or in three days, or maybe in four days if the wind is bad.

MAURYA [*turning round to the fire, and putting her shawl over her head*]: Isn't it a hard and cruel man won't hear a word from an old woman, and she holding him from the sea?

CATHLEEN: It's the life of a young man to be going on the sea, and who would listen to an old woman with one thing and she saying it over?

BARTLEY [*taking the halter*]: I must go now quickly. I'll ride down on the red mare, and the gray pony'll run behind me. . . . The blessing of God on you. [*He goes out.*]

MAURYA [*crying out as he is in the door*]: He's gone now, God spare us, and we'll not see him again. He's gone now, and when the black night is falling I'll have no son left me in the world.

CATHLEEN: Why wouldn't you give him your blessing and he looking round in the door? Isn't it sorrow enough is on every one in this house without your sending him out with an unlucky word behind him, and a hard word in his ear?

[MAURYA *takes up the tongs and begins raking the fire aimlessly without looking round.*]

NORA [*turning toward her*]: You're taking away the turf from the cake.

CATHLEEN [*crying out*]: The Son of God forgive us, Nora, we're after forgetting his bit of bread. [*She comes over to the fire.*]

NORA: And it's destroyed he'll be going till dark night, and he after eating nothing since the sun went up.

CATHLEEN [*turning the cake out of the oven*]: It's destroyed he'll be, surely. There's no sense left on any person in a house where an old woman will be talking forever.

[MAURYA *sways herself on her stool.*]

CATHLEEN [*cutting off some of the bread and rolling it in a cloth; to* MAURYA]: Let you go down now to the spring well and give him this and he passing. You'll see him then and the dark word will be broken, and you can say "God speed you," the way he'll be easy in his mind.

MAURYA [*taking the bread*]: Will I be in it as soon as himself?

CATHLEEN: If you go now quickly.

MAURYA [*standing up unsteadily*]: It's hard set I am to walk.

CATHLEEN [*looking at her anxiously*]: Give her the stick, Nora, or maybe she'll slip on the big stones.

NORA: What stick?

CATHLEEN: The stick Michael brought from Connemara.

MAURYA [*taking a stick* NORA *gives her*]: In the big world the old people do be leaving things after them for their sons and children, but in this place it is the young men do be leaving things behind for them that do be old.

[*She goes out slowly.* NORA *goes over to the ladder.*]

CATHLEEN: Wait, Nora, maybe she'd turn back quickly. She's that sorry, God help her, you wouldn't know the thing she'd do.

NORA: Is she gone round by the bush?

CATHLEEN [*looking out*]: She's gone now. Throw it down quickly, for the Lord knows when she'll be out of it again.

NORA [*getting the bundle from the loft*]: The young priest said he'd be passing to-morrow, and we might go down and speak to him below if it's Michael's they are surely.

CATHLEEN [*taking the bundle*]: Did he say what way they were found?

NORA [*coming down*]: "There were two men," says he, "and they rowing round with poteen before the cocks crowed, and the oar of one of them caught the body, and they passing the black cliffs of the north."

CATHLEEN [*trying to open the bundle*]: Give me a knife, Nora, the strings perished with the salt water, and there's a black knot on it you wouldn't loosen in a week.

NORA [*giving her a knife*]: I've heard tell it was a long way to Donegal.

CATHLEEN [*cutting the string*]: It is surely. There was a man in here a while ago—the man sold us that knife—and he said if you set off walking from the rock beyond, it would be seven days you'd be in Donegal.

NORA: And what time would a man take, and he floating?

[CATHLEEN *opens the bundle and takes out a bit of a stocking. They look at them eagerly.*]

CATHLEEN [*in a low voice*]: The Lord spare us, Nora! isn't it a queer hard thing to say if it's his they are surely?

NORA: I'll get his shirt off the hook the way we can put the one flannel on the other. [*She looks through some clothes hanging in the corner.*] It's not with them, Cathleen, and where will it be?

CATHLEEN: I'm thinking Bartley put it on him in the morning, for his own shirt was heavy with the salt in it. [*Pointing to the corner.*] There's a bit of a sleeve was of the same stuff. Give me that and it will do.

[NORA *brings it to her and they compare the flannel.*]

CATHLEEN: It's the same stuff, Nora; but if it is itself aren't there great rolls of it in the shops of Galway, and isn't it many another man may have a shirt of it as well as Michael himself?

NORA [*who has taken up the stocking and counted the stiches, crying out*]: It's Michael, Cathleen, it's Michael; God spare his soul, and what will herself say when she hears this story, and Bartley on the sea?

CATHLEEN [*taking the stocking*]: It's a plain stocking.

NORA: It's the second one of the third pair I knitted, and I put up three score stiches, and I dropped four of them.

CATHLEEN [*counts the stitches*]: It's that number is in it. [*Crying out.*] Ah, Nora, isn't it a bitter thing to think of him floating that way to the far north, and no one to keen him but the black hags that do be flying on the sea?

NORA [*swinging herself round, and throwing out her arms on the clothes*]: And isn't it a pitiful thing when there is nothing left of a man who was a great rower and fisher, but a bit of an old shirt and a plain stocking?

CATHLEEN [*after an instant*]: Tell me is herself coming, Nora? I hear a little sound on the path.

NORA [*looking out*]: She is, Cathleen. She's coming up to the door.

CATHLEEN: Put these things away before she'll come in. Maybe it's easier she'll be after giving her blessing to Bartley, and we won't let on we've heard anything the time he's on the sea.

NORA [*helping* CATHLEEN *to close the bundle*]: We'll put them here in the corner.

[*They put them into a hole in the chimney corner.* CATHLEEN *goes back to the spinning-wheel.*]

NORA: Will she see it was crying I was?

CATHLEEN: Keep your back to the door the way the light'll not be on you.

[NORA *sits down at the chimney corner, with her back to the door.* MAURYA *comes in very slowly, without looking at the girls, and goes over to her stool at the other side of the fire. The cloth with the bread is still in her hand. The girls look at each other, and* NORA *points to the bundle of bread.*]

[*After spinning for a moment.*] You didn't give him his bit of bread?

[MAURYA *begins to keen softly, without turning round.*]

Did you see him riding down?

[MAURYA *goes on keening.*]

[*A little impatient.*] God forgive you; isn't it a better thing to raise your voice and tell what you seen, than to be making lamentation for a thing that's done? Did you see Bartley, I'm saying to you.

MAURYA [*with a weak voice*]: My heart's broken from this day.

CATHLEEN [*as before*]: Did you see Bartley?

MAURYA: I seen the fearfulest thing.

CATHLEEN [*leaves her wheel and looks out*]: God forgive you; he's riding the mare now over the green head, and the gray pony behind him.

MAURYA [*starts, so that her shawl falls back from her head and shows her white tossed hair. With a frightened voice*]: The gray pony behind him.

CATHLEEN [*coming to the fire*]: What is it ails you, at all?

MAURYA [*speaking very slowly*]: I've seen the fearfulest thing any person has seen, since the day Bride Dara seen the dead man with a child in his arms.

CATHLEEN AND NORA: Uah.

[*They crouch down in front of the old woman at the fire.*]

NORA: Tell us what it is you seen.

MAURYA: I went down to the spring well, and I stood there saying a prayer to myself. Then Bartley came along, and he riding on the red mare with the gray pony behind him. [*She puts up her hands, as if to hide something from her eyes.*] The Son of God spare us, Nora!

CATHLEEN: What is it you seen?

MAURYA: I seen Michael himself.

CATHLEEN [*speaking softly*]: You did not, Mother; it wasn't Michael you seen, for his body is after being found in the Far North, and he's got a clean burial by the grace of God.

MAURYA [*a little defiantly*]: I'm after seeing him this day, and he riding and galloping. Bartley came first on the red mare; and I tried to say, "God speed you," but something choked the words in my throat. He went by quickly; and "the blessing of God on you," says he, and I could say nothing. I looked up then, and I crying, at the gray pony, and there was Michael upon it—with fine clothes on him, and new shoes on his feet.

CATHLEEN [*begins to keen*]: It's destroyed we are from this day. It's destroyed, surely.

NORA: Didn't the young priest say the Almighty God wouldn't leave her destitute with no son living?

MAURYA [*in a low voice, but clearly*]: It's little the like of him knows of the sea. . . . Bartley

will be lost now, and let you call in Eamon and make me a good coffin out of the white boards, for I won't live after them. I've had a husband, and a husband's father, and six sons in this house—six fine men, though it was a hard birth I had with every one of them and they coming to the world—and some of them were found and some of them were not found, but they're gone now the lot of them. . . . There were Stephen, and Shawn, were lost in the great wind, and found after in the Bay of Gregory of the Golden Mouth, and carried up the two of them on the one plank, and in by that door.

[*She pauses for a moment, the girls start as if they heard something through the door that is half open behind them.*]

NORA [*in a whisper*]: Did you hear that, Cathleen? Did you hear a noise in the northeast?

CATHLEEN [*in a whisper*]: There's some one after crying out by the seashore.

MAURYA [*continues without hearing anything*]: There was Sheamus and his father, and his own father again, were lost in a dark night, and not a stick or sign was seen of them when the sun went up. There was Patch after was drowned out of a curagh that turned over. I was sitting here with Bartley, and he a baby, lying on my two knees, and I seen two women, and three women, and four women coming in, and they crossing themselves, and not saying a word. I looked out then, and there were men coming after them, and they holding a thing in the half of a red sail, and water dripping out of it—it was a dry day, Nora—and leaving a track to the door.

[*She pauses again with her head stretched out toward the door. It opens softly and old women begin to come in, crossing themselves on the threshold, and kneeling down in front of the stage with red petticoats over their heads.*]

MAURYA [*half in a dream, to* CATHLEEN]: Is it Patch or Michael, or what is it at all?

CATHLEEN: Michael is after being found in the Far North and when he is found there how could he be here in this place?

MAURYA: There does be a power of young men floating round in the sea, and what way would they know if it was Michael they had, or another man like him, for when a man is nine days in the sea, and the wind blowing, it's hard set his own mother would be to say what man was it.

CATHLEEN: It's Michael, God spare him, for they're after sending us a bit of his clothes from the Far North.

[*She reaches out and hands* MAURYA *the clothes that belonged to* MICHAEL. MAURYA *stands up slowly, and takes them in her hands.* NORA *looks out.*]

NORA: They're carrying a thing among them and there's water dripping out of it and leaving a track by the big stones.

CATHLEEN [*in a whisper to the women who have come in*]: Is it Bartley it is?

ONE OF THE WOMEN: It is surely, God rest his soul.

[*Two younger women come in and pull out the table. Then men carry in the body of* BARTLEY, *laid on a plank, with a bit of a sail over it, and lay it on the table.*]

CATHLEEN [*to the women, as they are doing so*]: What way was he drowned?

ONE OF THE WOMEN: The gray pony knocked him into the sea, and he was washed out where there is a great surf on the white rocks.

[MAURYA *has gone over and knelt down at the head of the table. The women are keening softly and swaying themselves with a slow movement.* CATHLEEN *and* NORA *kneel at the other end of the table. The men kneel near the door.*]

MAURYA [*raising her head and speaking as if she did not see the people around her*]: They're all gone now, and there isn't anything more the sea can do to me. . . . I'll have no call now to be crying and praying when the wind breaks from the south, and you can hear the surf is in the east, and the surf is in the west, making a great stir with the two noises, and they hitting one on the other. I'll have no call now to be going down and getting Holy Water in the dark nights after Samhain, and I won't care what way the sea is when the other women will be keening. [*To* NORA.] Give me the Holy Water, Nora, there's a small sup still on the dresser.

[NORA *gives it to her.*]

MAURYA [*drops* MICHAEL's *clothes across* BARTLEY's *feet, and sprinkles the Holy Water over him*]: It isn't that I haven't prayed for you, Bartley, to the Almighty God. It isn't that I haven't said prayers in the dark night till you wouldn't know what I'd be saying; but it's a great rest I'll have now, and it's time surely. It's a great rest I'll have now, and great sleeping in the long nights after Samhain, if it's only a bit of wet flour we do have to eat, and maybe a fish that would be stinking. [*She kneels down again, crossing herself, and saying prayers under her breath.*]

CATHLEEN [*to an old man*]: Maybe yourself and Eamon would make a coffin when the sun rises. We have fine white boards herself bought, God help her, thinking Michael would be found, and I have a new cake you can eat while you'll be working.

THE OLD MAN [*looking at the boards*]: Are there nails with them?

CATHLEEN: There are not, Colum; we didn't think of the nails.

ANOTHER MAN: It's a great wonder she wouldn't think of the nails, and all the coffins she's seen made already.

CATHLEEN: It's getting old she is, and broken.

[MAURYA *stands up again very slowly and spreads out the pieces of* MICHAEL's *clothes beside the body, sprinkling them with the last of the Holy Water.*]

NORA [*in a whisper to* CATHLEEN]: She's quiet now and easy; but the day Michael was drowned you could hear her crying out from this to the spring well. It's fonder she was of Michael, and would any one have thought that?

CATHLEEN [*slowly and clearly*]: An old woman will be soon tired with anything she will

do, and isn't it nine days herself is after crying and keening, and making great sorrow in the house?

MAURYA [*puts the empty cup mouth downwards on the table, and lays her hands together on* BARTLEY'*s feet*]: They're all together this time, and the end is come. May the Almighty God have mercy on Bartley's soul, and on Michael's soul, and on the souls of Sheamus and Patch, and Stephen and Shawn; [*bending her head*] and may He have mercy on my soul, Nora, and on the soul of every one is left living in the world.

[*She pauses, and the keen rises a little more loudly from the women, then sinks away.*]

Michael has a clean burial in the Far North, by the grace of the Almighty God. Bartley will have a fine coffin out of the white boards, and a deep grave surely. What more can we want than that? No man at all can be living forever, and we must be satisfied.

[*She kneels down again and the curtain falls slowly.*]

QUESTIONS

1. How does the title alert us to the play's subject and theme? How is the sea described in the play? Who are the "riders" to the sea? In what way is nature the protagonist in the play?
2. Synge learned on Aran that a drowned, headless man could be identified only by his clothing. How does Synge incorporate this fact into the structure of the play? Is his method effective?
3. How does Synge present and develop the basic conflict in the play?
4. Action and dialogue are clearly dominated by women. What bearing does this have on the theme of the play? Some critics have charged that Maurya (whose name means "goddess of fate") is too passive in her suffering at the end of this tragedy. Support or refute this assertion.
5. What is a *keen?* Synge wrote, "The keen reveals the mood of beings who feel their isolation in the face of a universe that wars on them with winds and seas." How does this statement inform the subject and theme of the play?
6. Synge once declared, "We should unite stoicism, asceticism, and ecstasy." How does this statement inform the theme of *Riders to the Sea?*
7. William Butler Yeats wrote of Synge: "He loves all that has edge, all that is salt in the mouth, all that is rough in the hand, all that heightens the emotions by contest, all that stings into life the sense of tragedy." How does Yeats's observation capture the strength and brilliance of *Riders to the Sea?*

Langston Hughes

SOUL GONE HOME

CHARACTERS

THE MOTHER
THE SON
TWO MEN

Night.

> *A tenement room, bare, ugly, dirty. An unshaded electric-light bulb. In the middle of the room a cot on which the body of a Negro youth is lying. His hands are folded across his chest. There are pennies on his eyes. He is a soul gone home.*
>
> *As the curtain rises, his mother, a large, middle-aged woman in a red sweater, kneels weeping beside the cot, loudly simulating grief.*

MOTHER: Oh, Gawd! Oh Lawd! Why did you take my son from me? Oh, Gawd, why did you do it? He was all I had! Oh, Lawd, what am I gonna do? [*Looking at the dead boy and stroking his head.*] Oh, son! Oh, Ronnie! Oh, my boy, speak to me! Ronnie, say something to me! Son, why don't you talk to your mother? Can't you see she's bowed down in sorrow? Son, speak to me, just a word! Come back from the spirit-world and speak to me! Ronnie, come back from the dead and speak to your mother!

SON [*lying there dead as a doornail, speaking loudly*]: I wish I wasn't dead, so I could speak to you. You been a hell of a mama!

MOTHER [*falling back from the cot in astonishment, but still on her knees*]: Ronnie! Ronnie! What's that you say? What you sayin' to your mother? [*Wild-eyed.*] Is you done opened your mouth and spoke to me?

SON: I said you a hell of a mama!

MOTHER [*rising suddenly and backing away, screaming loudly*]: Awo-oo-o! Ronnie, that ain't you talkin'!

SON: Yes, it is me talkin', too! I say you been a no-good mama.

MOTHER: What for you talkin' to me like that, Ronnie? You ain't never said nothin' like that to me before.

SON: I know it, but I'm dead now—and I can say what I want to say. [*Stirring.*] You done called on me to talk, ain't you? Lemme take these pennies off my eyes so I can see. [*He takes the coins off his eyes, throws them across the room, and sits up in bed. He is a very dark boy in a torn white shirt. He looks hard at his mother.*] Mama, you know you ain't done me right.

MOTHER: What you mean, I ain't done you right? [*She is rooted in horror.*] What you mean, huh?

SON: You know what I mean.

MOTHER: No, I don't neither. [*Trembling violently.*] What you mean comin' back to haunt your poor old mother? Ronnie, what does you mean?

SON [*leaning forward*]: I'll tell you just what I mean! You been a bad mother to me.

MOTHER: Shame! Shame! Shame, talkin' to your mama that away. Damn it! Shame! I'll slap your face. [*She starts toward him, but he rolls his big white eyes at her, and she backs away.*] Me, what borned you! Me, what suffered the pains o' death to bring you into this world! Me, what raised you up, what washed your dirty didies. [*Sorrowfully.*] And now I'm left here mighty nigh prostrate 'cause you gone from me! Ronnie, what you mean talkin' to *me* like that—what brought you into this world?

SON: You never did feed me good, that's what I mean! Who wants to come into the world hongry, and go out the same way?

MOTHER: What you mean hongry? When I had money, ain't I fed you?

SON [*sullenly*]: Most of the time you ain't had no money.

MOTHER: Twarn't my fault then.

SON: Twarn't *my* fault neither.

MOTHER [*defensively*]: You always was so weak and sickly, you couldn't earn nothin' sellin' papers.

SON: I know it.

MOTHER: You never was no use to me.

SON: So you just lemme grow up in the street, and I ain't had no manners nor morals, neither.

MOTHER: Manners and morals? Ronnie, where'd you learn all them big words?

SON: I learnt 'em just now in the spirit-world.

MOTHER [*coming nearer*]: But you ain't been dead no more'n an hour.

SON: That's long enough to learn a lot.

MOTHER: Well, what else did you find out?

SON: I found out you was a hell of a mama puttin' me out in the cold to sell papers soon as I could even walk.

MOTHER: What? You little liar!

SON: If I'm lyin', I'm dyin'! And lettin' me grow up all bowlegged and stunted from undernourishment.

MOTHER: Under-nurse-mint?

SON: Undernourishment. You heard what the doctor said last week?

MOTHER: Naw, what'd he say?

SON: He said I was dyin' o' undernourishment, that's what he said. He said I had TB 'cause I didn't have enough to eat never when I were a child. And he said I couldn't get well, nohow eating nothin' but beans ever since I been sick. Said I needed milk and eggs. And you said you ain't got no money for milk and eggs, which I know you ain't. [*Gently.*] We never had no money, mama, not even since you took up hustlin' on the streets.

MOTHER: Son, money ain't everything.

SON: Naw, but when you got TB you have to have milk and eggs.

MOTHER [*advancing sentimentally*]: Anyhow, I love you, Ronnie!

SON [*rudely*]: Sure you love me—but here I am dead.

MOTHER [*angrily*]: Well, damn your hide, you ain't even decent dead. If you was, you wouldn't be sittin' there jawin' at your mother when she's sheddin' every tear she's got for you tonight.

SON: First time you ever did cry for me, far as I know.

MOTHER: Tain't! You's a liar! I cried when I borned you—you was such a big child—ten pounds.

SON: Then *I* did the cryin' after that, I reckon.

MOTHER [*proudly*]: Sure, I could of let you die, but I didn't. Naw, I kept you with me—off and on. And I lost the chance to marry many a good man, too—if it weren't for you. No man wants to take care o' nobody else's child. [*Self-pityingly.*] You been a burden to me, Randolph.

SON [*angrily*]: What did you have me for then, in the first place?

MOTHER: How could I help havin' you, you little bastard? Your father ruint me—and you's the result. And I been worried with you for sixteen years. [*Disgustedly.*] Now, just when you get big enough to work and do me some good, you have to go and die.

SON: I sure am dead!

MOTHER: But you ain't decent dead! Here you come back to haunt your poor old mama, and spoil her cryin' spell, and spoil the mournin'. [*There is the noise of an ambulance going outside. The mother goes to the window and looks down into the street. Turns to son.*] Ronnie, lay down quick! Here comes the city's ambulance to take you to the undertaker's. Don't let them white men see you dead, sitting up here quarrelin' with your mother. Lay down and fold your hands back like I had 'em.

SON [*passing his hand across his head*]: All right, but gimme that comb yonder and my stocking cap. I don't want to go out of here with my hair standin' straight up in front, even if I is dead. [*The mother hands him a comb and his stocking cap. The son combs his hair and puts the cap on. Noise of men coming up the stairs.*]

MOTHER: Hurry up, Ronnie, they'll be here in no time.

SON: Aw, they got another flight to come yet. Don't rush me, ma!

MOTHER: Yes, but I got to put these pennies back on your eyes, boy! [*She searches in a corner for the coins as her son lies down and folds his hands, stiff in death. She finds the coins and puts them nervously on his eyes, watching the door meanwhile. A knock.*] Come in.

[*Enter two men in the white coats of city health employees.*]

MAN: Somebody sent for us to get the body of Ronnie Bailey? Third floor, apartment five.

MOTHER: Yes, sir, here he is! [*Weeping loudly.*] He's my boy! Oh, Lawd, he's done left me! Oh, Lawdy, he's done gone home! His soul's gone home! Oh, what am I gonna do? Mister! Mister! Mister, the Lawd's done took him home! [*As the men unfold the stretchers, she continues to weep hysterically. They place the boy's thin body on the stretchers and cover it with a rubber cloth. Each man takes his end of the stretchers. Silently, they walk out the door as the mother wails.*] Oh, my son! Oh, my boy! Come back, come back, come back! Ronnie, come back! [*One loud scream as the door closes.*] Awo-ooo-o!

[*As the footsteps of the men die down on the stairs, the mother becomes suddenly quiet. She goes to a broken mirror and begins to rouge and powder her face. In the street the ambulance gong sounds fainter and fainter in the distance. The mother takes down an old fur coat from a nail and puts it*

on. Before she leaves, she smooths back the quilts on the cot from which the dead boy has been removed. She looks into the mirror again, and once more whitens her face with powder. She dons a red hat. From a handbag she takes a cigarette, lights it, and walks slowly out the door. At the door she switches off the light. The hallway is dimly illuminated. She turns before closing the door, looks back into the room, and speaks.]

MOTHER: Tomorrow, Ronnie, I'll buy you some flowers—if I can pick up a dollar tonight. You was a hell of a no-good son, I swear!

Curtain.

QUESTIONS

1. Would you characterize the tone of the play as comic, tragic, tragicomic, or something else? Explain your answer.
2. Hughes describes the mother as "loudly simulating grief." What does this imply about the relationship of the mother to her son? What might Hughes be implying in this stage direction about the black experience in America in general?
3. The son makes the ironic remark that "I'm dead now—and I can say what I want to say." What does he mean by this? Find other ironies in the characters' actions and statements, and explain their meaning.
4. Why does the author write in "stock" black dialect? For naturalism? To make a statement? For humor? Explain.
5. Hughes stated that he was a "propaganda writer: my main material is the race problem." How is his statement connected to the theme of *Soul Gone Home*?
6. Compare and contrast the themes of *Riders to the Sea* and *Soul Gone Home*.

---

20. Character

When the stage opens before us—either as spectators or as readers—we are confronted first and immediately with characters in the world of the play. We want to know about these characters: What are they like? What motivates them? What are their problems and conflicts? What are their destinies? As participants in the dramatic experience, we seem to be interested first and foremost in the people set in motion by the play.

Aristotle might have been correct in terming plot the "soul" of drama, yet it is equally true that there could be no "soul" in drama without character. Character is revealed through plot, the total structure of the play. As Santayana states in *The Sense of Beauty:* "Plot is the synthesis of actions, and is a reproduction of those experiences from which our notion of things is originally derived; for character can never be observed in the world except as manifested in action." Yet it is character that looms out of that plotted action. Through our interest in the characters on the stage, we learn about human nature, the characters' relationship to the world, and the dramatist's vision of the world. Put simply, as playwright and novelist Arnold Bennett once did, the foundation of both drama and fiction is "character creating and nothing else."

Unlike fiction and poetry, drama gives us *living* images of people on stage. Characterization in fiction can create memorable figures, but it is clear that playwrights have other stylistic and technical resources, as well as formal constraints, to deal with in their "invention" of human figures. A dramatist, preoccupied with stage time, does not have the leisure of the novelist in developing character. He or she must get us to "see" and "hear" characters from the outset of a script. We understand the characters' motives through what they say and do and through the responses of other characters to them. Othello would not be the tragic figure we know without Iago's view of him or without Iago's reaction to him. We know something about Maurya's pain before we see her through Cathleen and Nora in *Riders to the Sea.*

Playwrights use many techniques and conventions to make their dramatic characters stand out on the stage. Characters do not just talk idly, as we do in common speech. Their dialogues and monologues are rooted in *thought,* as in Hamlet's famous "To be

or not to be." Making thought the basis of a dramatic figure's speech is a common technique of character development. With drama, we are also interested in the very rhythms of the characters' speech. Again, Shakespeare affords a brilliant example of rhythmic dialogue in Macbeth's lines,

> Tomorrow, and tomorrow, and tomorrow
> Creeps in this petty pace from day to day
> To the last syllable of recorded time,

This is pure poetry transmuted into spoken lines. Closely related to this procedure of establishing rhythmic patterns for dialogue is the playwright's revelation of character through imagery; another technique is the vivid reproduction of sense experience. Iago's fondness for lacing his speech with violent and distasteful animal imagery reveals much about himself, his motives, and the world of *Othello*.

At an equally basic theatrical level, character is a composite of the physical appearance, the voices, the gestures, the clothing and costumes, the setting—all created by the playwright, director, designers and technicians, and the actors themselves. The crooked, humpbacked figure of the protagonist in Shakespeare's *Richard III* is a vivid reflection of Richard's twisted character. Willy Loman's fondness for gardens, and his own sterile garden "prop" (indeed all the stage props that comprise setting in *Death of a Salesman*), reveals his dreams and inner conflicts. The costumes in *A Doll's House* help to make visible the characters' essence and their lives. We get to "know" characters through a broad range of theatrical conventions.

Yet determining exactly how a great playwright "discovers" a character is a more difficult task than recognizing the dramatic methods involved in the creation of character. Ibsen tells us as much as any modern dramatist about the art of character invention:

> Before I write down one word I have to have the character in mind through and through. I must penetrate to the last wrinkle of his soul. I always proceed from the individual. The stage setting, the dramatic ensemble, all *that* comes naturally and does not cause me any worry, as soon as I am certain of the individual in every aspect of his humanity. I have to have his exterior in mind also, down to the last button, how he stands and walks, his behavior, what his voice sounds like.

A character must come to life in the author's imagination. Then, as William Faulkner once said of his characters, the writer must pursue his or her character down the road and into the action or field of conflict and existence.

It would be difficult for great drama—any drama—to exist without tension and conflict. These elements arise through the use of characters who tend to be opposites (e.g., good and bad) or through the use of protagonists and antagonists. Sometimes characters are rounded, or strongly drawn; sometimes, as in most comedy, they are flat "types"; sometimes characters may possess a bit of both the rogue and the hero; and sometimes, as in Ibsen's *The Wild Duck* (1855), it may be difficult to find a protagonist. Characters in classical tragedies are three dimensional and monumental, but their sense of "doom" makes them ultimately a little mysterious and elusive in their characterization. In modern drama, character can defy all theatrical norms; a modern play such as Hecht and MacArthur's *The Front Page* (1928), a comedy, utilizes heroes with somewhat unsavory characteristics and villains with rather likeable characteristics. Frequently in contemporary drama, the antagonist is not another character at all, but society and its systems.

In the modern era of drama, no one has had a greater impact on the revelation of character against both social and psychological backdrops than Henrik Ibsen. In *A Doll's House,* there is clear dramatic tension between the characters Nora and Helmer; she is the protagonist, and he the antagonist. This tension between the sexes engages us today as much as it was involved in the works of Aristophanes and Shakespeare. Moreover, in the Ibsen play multiple tensions are brewing between the characters: Nora and Krogstad; Krogstad and Mrs. Linde (apparently); Helmer and Krogstad. With each confrontation, the characters take on new dimensions for us, until the theme begins to emerge, arising as it must directly out of the actions of each of the characters.

The best drama is created upon those themes that endure through human experience and are revealed through human nature. Location, dialogue, and even society may change, but somehow the conditions that perpetuate universal themes continue. Lorraine Hansberry's *A Raisin in the Sun,* set in a specific place and among a particular American people, uses in dialogue the vernacular of those people and the streets from which some of them have come. In Ibsen's play, the major characters come from the same struggling middle class. In Hansberry's play, there is a meeting of several classes— and memorable characters from each of these backgrounds. In both plays, women dominate the action and carry forward the theme.

A theme present in both is that if society is going to be changed for the better, women will change it since men don't seem to have noticed that there is anything wrong. The women in these plays are characters who accomplish their ends and realize their destinies. Hansberry would agree with Ibsen, who wrote of his characters: "I finally stand at the limit of knowledge: I know my people from close and long association— they are my intimate friends, they will not disappoint me, I shall always see them as I do now."

Henrik Ibsen

A DOLL'S HOUSE

Translated by Otto Reinert

LIST OF CHARACTERS

TORVALD HELMER, a lawyer
NORA, his wife
DR. RANK
MRS. LINDE
KROGSTAD
THE HELMERS' THREE SMALL CHILDREN
ANNE-MARIE, the children's nurse
A HOUSEMAID
A PORTER

Scene: The Helmers' living room

ACT I

A pleasant, tastefully but not expensively furnished, living room. A door on the rear wall, right, leads to the front hall, another door, left, to HELMER's *study. Between the two doors a piano. A third door in the middle of the left wall; further front a window. Near the window a round table and a small couch. Towards the rear of the right wall a fourth door; further front a tile stove with a rocking chair and a couple of armchairs in front of it. Between the stove and the door a small table. Copperplate etchings on the walls. A whatnot with porcelain figurines and other small objects. A small bookcase with de luxe editions. A rug on the floor; fire in the stove. Winter day.*

The doorbell rings, then the sound of the front door opening. NORA, *dressed for outdoors, enters, humming cheerfully. She carries several packages, which she puts down on the table, right. She leaves the door to the front hall open; there a* PORTER *is seen holding a Christmas tree and a basket. He gives them to the* MAID, *who has let them in.*

NORA: Be sure to hide the Christmas tree, Helene. The children mustn't see it before tonight when we've trimmed it. [*Opens her purse; to the* PORTER.] How much?
PORTER: Fifty ore.
NORA: Here's a crown. No, keep the change. [*The* PORTER *thanks her, leaves.* NORA *closes the door. She keeps laughing quietly to herself as she takes off her coat, etc. She takes a bag of macaroons from her pocket and eats a couple. She walks cautiously over to the door to the study and listens.*] Yes, he's home. [*Resumes her humming, walks over to the table, right.*]
HELMER [*in his study*]: Is that my little lark twittering out there?
NORA [*opening some of the packages*]: That's right.

HELMER: My squirrel bustling about?

NORA: Yes.

HELMER: When did squirrel come home?

NORA: Just now. [*Puts the bag of macaroons back in her pocket, wipes her mouth.*] Come out here, Torvald. I want to show you what I've bought.

HELMER: I'm busy! [*After a little while he opens the door and looks in, pen in hand.*] Bought, eh? All that? So little wastrel has been throwing money around again?

NORA: Oh but Torvald, this Christmas we can be a little extravagant, can't we? It's the first Christmas we don't have to scrimp.

HELMER: I don't know about that. We certainly don't have money to waste.

NORA: Yes, Torvald, we do. A little, anyway. Just a tiny little bit? Now that you're going to get that big salary and make lots and lots of money.

HELMER: Starting at New Year's, yes. But payday isn't till the end of the quarter.

NORA: That doesn't matter. We can always borrow.

HELMER: Nora! [*Goes over to her and playfully pulls her ear.*] There you go being irresponsible again. Suppose I borrowed a thousand crowns today and you spent it all for Christmas and on New Year's Eve a tile hit me in the head and laid me out cold.

NORA [*putting her hand over his mouth*]: I won't have you say such horrid things.

HELMER: But suppose it happened. Then what?

NORA: If it did, I wouldn't care whether we owed money or not.

HELMER: But what about the people I had borrowed from?

NORA: Who cares about them! They are strangers.

HELMER: Nora, Nora, you *are* a woman. No, really! You know how I feel about that. No debts! A home in debt isn't a free home, and if it isn't free it isn't beautiful. We've managed nicely so far, you and I, and that's the way we'll go on. It won't be for much longer.

NORA [*walks over toward the stove*]: All right, Torvald. Whatever you say.

HELMER [*follows her*]: Come, come, my little songbird mustn't droop her wings. What's this? Can't have a pouty squirrel in the house, you know. [*Takes out his wallet.*] Nora, what do you think I have here?

NORA [*turns around quickly*]: Money!

HELMER: Here. [*Gives her some bills.*] Don't you think I know Christmas is expensive?

NORA [*counting*]: Ten—twenty—thirty—forty. Thank you, thank you, Torvald. This helps a lot.

HELMER: I certainly hope so.

NORA: It does, it does. But I want to show you what I got. It was cheap, too. Look. New clothes for Ivar. And a sword. And a horse and trumpet for Bob. And a doll and a little bed for Emmy. It isn't any good, but it wouldn't last, anyway. And here's some dress material and scarves for the maids. I feel bad about old Anne-Marie, though. She really should be getting much more.

HELMER: And what's in here?

NORA [*cries*]: Not till tonight!

HELMER: I see. But now what does my little prodigal have in mind for herself?

NORA: Oh, nothing. I really don't care.

HELMER: Of course you do. Tell me what you'd like. Within reason.

NORA: Oh, I don't know. Really, I don't. The only thing—

HELMER: Well?

NORA [*fiddling with the buttons without looking at him*]: If you really want to give me something, you might—you could—

HELMER: All right, let's have it.

NORA [*quickly*]: Some money, Torvald. Just as much as you think you can spare. Then I'll buy myself something one of these days.

HELMER: No, really Nora—

NORA: Oh yes, please, Torvald. Please? I'll wrap the money in pretty gold paper and hang it on the tree. Won't that be nice?

HELMER: What's the name for little birds that are always spending money?

NORA: Wastrels, I know. But please let's do it my way, Torvald. Then I'll have time to decide what I need most. Now that's sensible, isn't it?

HELMER [*smiling*]: Oh, very sensible. That is, if you really bought yourself something you could use. But it all disappears in the household expenses or you buy things you don't need. And then you come back to me for more.

NORA: Oh, but Torvald—

HELMER: That's the truth, dear little Nora, and you know it. [*Puts his arm around her.*] My wastrel is a little sweetheart, but she *does* go through an awful lot of money awfully fast. You've no idea how expensive it is for a man to keep a wastrel.

NORA: That's not fair, Torvald. I really save all I can.

HELMER [*laughs*]: Oh, I believe that. All you can. Meaning, exactly nothing!

NORA [*hums, smiles mysteriously*]: You don't know all the things we songbirds and squirrels need money for, Torvald.

HELMER: You know, you're funny. Just like your father. You're always looking for ways to get money, but as soon as you do it runs through your fingers and you can never say what you spent it for. Well, I guess I'll just have to take you the way you are. It's in your blood. Yes, that sort of thing is hereditary, Nora.

NORA: In that case, I wish I had inherited many of Daddy's qualities.

HELMER: And I don't want you any different from just what you are—my own sweet little songbird. Hey!—I think I just noticed something. Aren't you looking what's the word?—a little—sly—?

NORA: I am?

HELMER: You definitely are. Look at me.

NORA [*looks at him*]: Well?

HELMER [*wagging a finger*]: Little sweet-tooth hasn't by any chance been on a rampage today, has she?

NORA: Of course not. Whatever makes you think that?

HELMER: A little detour by the pastryshop maybe?

NORA: No, I assure you, Torvald—

HELMER: Nibbled a little jam?

NORA: Certainly not!

HELMER: Munched a macaroon or two?

NORA: No, really, Torvald, I honestly—

HELMER: All right. Of course I was only joking.

NORA [*walks toward the table, right*]: You know I wouldn't do anything to displease you.

HELMER: I know. And I have your promise. [*Over to her.*] All right, keep your little Christmas secrets to yourself, Nora darling. They'll all come out tonight, I suppose, when we light the tree.

NORA: Did you remember to invite Rank?

HELMER: No, but there's no need to. He knows he'll have dinner with us. Anyway, I'll see him later this morning. I'll ask him then. I did order some good wine. Oh Nora, you've no idea how much I'm looking forward to tonight!

NORA: Me too. And the children, Torvald! They'll have such a good time!

HELMER: You know, it *is* nice to have a good, safe job and a comfortable income. Feels good just thinking about it. Don't you agree?

NORA: Oh, it's wonderful!

HELMER: Remember last Christmas? For three whole weeks you shut yourself up every evening till long after midnight, making ornaments for the Christmas tree and I don't know what else. Some big surprise for all of us, anyway. I'll be damned if I've ever been so bored in my whole life!

NORA: I wasn't bored at all.

HELMER [*smiling*]: But you've got to admit you didn't have much to show for it in the end.

NORA: Oh, don't tease me again about that! Could I help it that the cat got in and tore up everything?

HELMER: Of course you couldn't, my poor little Nora. You just wanted to please the rest of us, and that's the important thing. But I *am* glad the hard times are behind us. Aren't you?

NORA: Oh yes. I think it's just wonderful.

HELMER: This year I won't be bored and lonely. And you won't have to strain your dear eyes and your delicate little hands—

NORA [*claps her hands*]: No I won't, will I, Torvald? Oh, how wonderful, how lovely, to hear you say that! [*Puts her arm under his.*] Let me tell you how I think we should arrange things, Torvald. Soon as Christmas is over—[*The doorbell rings.*] Someone's at the door. [*Straightens things up a bit.*] A caller, I suppose. Bother!

HELMER: Remember, I'm not home for visitors.

MAID [*in the door to the front hall*]: Ma'am, there's a lady here—

NORA: All right. Ask her to come in.

MAID [*to* HELMER]: And the Doctor just arrived.

HELMER: Is he in the study?

MAID: Yes, sir.

[HELMER *exits into his study. The* MAID *shows* MRS. LINDE *in and closes the door behind her as she leaves.* MRS. LINDE *is in travel dress.*]

MRS. LINDE [*timid and a little hesitant*]: Good morning, Nora.

NORA [*uncertainly*]: Good morning.

MRS. LINDE: I don't believe you know who I am.

NORA: No—I'm not sure—Though I know I should—Of course! Kristine! It's you!

MRS. LINDE: Yes, it's me.

NORA: And I didn't even recognize you! I had no idea! [*In a lower voice.*] You've changed, Kristine.

MRS. LINDE: I'm sure I have. It's been nine or ten long years.

NORA: Has it really been that long? Yes, you're right. I've been so happy these last eight years. And now you're here. Such a long trip in the middle of winter. How brave!

MRS. LINDE: I got in on the steamer this morning.

NORA: To have some fun over the holidays, of course. That's lovely. For we *are* going to have fun. But take off your coat! You aren't cold, are you? [*Helps her.*] There, now! Let's sit down here by the fire and just relax and talk. No, you sit there. I want the rocking chair. [*Takes her hands.*] And now you've got your old face back. It was just for a minute, right at first—Though you are a little more pale, Kristine. And maybe a little thinner.

MRS. LINDE: And much, much older, Nora.

NORA: Maybe a little older. Just a teeny-weeny bit, not much. [*Interrupts herself, serious.*] Oh, but how thoughtless of me, chatting away like this! Sweet, good Kristine, can you forgive me?

MRS. LINDE: Forgive you what, Nora?

NORA [*in a low voice*]: You poor dear, you lost your husband, didn't you?

MRS. LINDE: Three years ago, yes.

NORA: I know. I saw it in the paper. Oh please believe me, Kristine. I really meant to write you, but I never got around to it. Something was always coming up.

MRS. LINDE: Of course, Nora. I understand.

NORA: No, that wasn't very nice of me. You poor thing, all you must have been through. And he didn't leave you much, either, did he?

MRS. LINDE: No.

NORA: And no children?

MRS. LINDE: No.

NORA: Nothing at all, in other words?

MRS. LINDE: Not so much as a sense of loss—a grief to live on—

NORA [*incredulous*]: But Kristine, how can that *be?*

MRS. LINDE [*with a sad smile, strokes* NORA*'s hair*]: That's the way it sometimes is, Nora.

NORA: All alone. How awful for you. I have three darling children. You can't see them right now, though; they're out with their nurse. But now you must tell me everything—

MRS. LINDE: No, no; I'd rather listen to you.

NORA: No, you begin. Today I won't be selfish. Today I'll think only of you. Except there's one thing I've just got to tell you first. Something marvelous that's happened to us just these last few days. You haven't heard, have you?

MRS. LINDE: No; tell me.

NORA: Just think. My husband's been made manager of the Mutual Bank.

MRS. LINDE: Your husband—! Oh, I'm so glad!

NORA: Yes, isn't that great? You see, private law practice is so uncertain, especially when you won't have anything to do with cases that aren't—you know—quite nice. And of course Torvald won't do that, and I quite agree with him. Oh, you've no idea how delighted we are! He takes over at New Year's, and he'll be getting a big salary and all sorts of extras. From now on we'll be able to live in quite a different way—exactly as we like. Oh, Kristine! I feel so carefree and happy! It's lovely to have lots and lots of money and not have to worry about a thing! Don't you agree?

MRS. LINDE: It would be nice to have enough, at any rate.

NORA: No, I don't mean just enough. I mean lots and lots!

MRS. LINDE [*smiles*]: Nora, Nora, when are you going to be sensible? In school you spent a great deal of money.

NORA [*quietly laughing*]: Yes, and Torvald says I still do. [*Raises her finger at* MRS. LINDE.] But "Nora, Nora" isn't so crazy as you all think. Believe me, we've had nothing to be extravagant with. We've both had to work.

MRS. LINDE: You too?

NORA: Yes. Oh, it's been little things mostly—sewing, crocheting, embroidery—that sort of thing. [*Casually.*] And other things too. You know, of course, that Torvald left government service when we got married? There was no chance of promotion in his department, and of course he had to make more money than he had been making. So for the first few years he worked altogether too hard. He had to take jobs on the side and work night and day. It turned out to be too much for him. He became seriously ill. The doctors told him he needed to go south.

MRS. LINDE: That's right; you spent a year in Italy, didn't you?

NORA: Yes, we did. But you won't believe how hard it was to get away. Ivar had just been born. But of course we had to go. Oh, it was a wonderful trip. And it saved Torvald's life. But it took a lot of money, Kristine.

MRS. LINDE: I'm sure it did.

NORA: Twelve hundred specie dollars. Four thousand eight hundred crowns. That's a lot of money.

MRS. LINDE: Yes. So it's lucky you have it when something like that happens.

NORA: Well, actually we got the money from Daddy.

MRS. LINDE: I see. That was about the time your father died, I believe.

NORA: Yes, just about then. And I couldn't even go and take care of him. I was expecting little Ivar any day. And I had poor Torvald to look after, desperately sick and all. My dear, good Daddy! I never saw him again, Kristine. That's the saddest thing that's happened to me since I got married.

MRS. LINDE: I know you were very fond of him. But then you went to Italy?

NORA: Yes, for now we had the money, and the doctors urged us to go. So we left about a month later.

MRS. LINDE: And when you came back your husband was well again?

NORA: Healthy as a horse!

MRS. LINDE: But—the doctor?

NORA: What do you mean?

MRS. LINDE: I thought the maid said it was the doctor, that gentleman who came the same time I did.

NORA: Oh, that's Dr. Rank. He doesn't come as a doctor. He's our closest friend. He looks in at least once every day. No, Torvald hasn't been sick once since then. And the children are strong and healthy, too, and so am I. [*Jumps up and claps her hands.*]

Oh God, Kristine! Isn't it wonderful to be alive and happy! Isn't it just lovely!—But now I'm being mean again, talking only about myself and my things. [*Sits down on a footstool close to* MRS. LINDE *and puts her arms on her lap.*] Please, don't be angry with me! Tell me, is it really true that you didn't care for your husband? Then why did you marry him?

MRS. LINDE: Mother was still alive then, but she was bedridden and helpless. And I had my two younger brothers to look after. I didn't think I had the right to turn him down.

NORA: No, I suppose not. So he had money then?

MRS. LINDE: He was quite well off, I think. But it was an uncertain business, Nora. When he died, the whole thing collapsed and there was nothing left.

NORA: And then—?

MRS. LINDE: Well, I had to manage as best I could. With a little store and a little school and anything else I could think of. The last three years have been one long work day for me, Nora, without any rest. But now it's over. My poor mother doesn't need me any more. She passed away. And the boys are on their own too. They've both got jobs and support themselves.

NORA: What a relief for you—

MRS. LINDE: No, not relief. Just a great emptiness. Nobody to live for any more. [*Gets up, restlessly.*] That's why I couldn't stand it any longer in that little hole. Here in town it has to be easier to find something to keep me busy and occupy my thoughts. With a little luck I should be able to find a permanent job, something in an office—

NORA: Oh but Kristine, that's exhausting work, and you look worn out already. It would be much better for you to go to a resort.

MRS. LINDE [*walks over to the window*]: I don't have a Daddy who can give me the money, Nora.

NORA [*getting up*]: Oh, don't be angry with me.

MRS. LINDE [*over to her*]: Dear Nora, don't *you* be angry with *me*. That's the worst thing about my kind of situation: you become so bitter. You've nobody to work for, and yet you have to look out for yourself, somehow. You've got to keep on living, and so you become selfish. Do you know—when you told me about your husband's new position I was delighted not so much for your sake as for my own.

NORA: Why was that? Oh, I see. You think maybe Torvald can give you a job?

MRS. LINDE: That's what I had in mind.

NORA: And he will too, Kristine. Just leave it to me. I'll be ever so subtle about it. I'll think of something nice to tell him, something he'll like. Oh I so much want to help you.

MRS. LINDE: That's very good of you, Nora—making an effort like that for me. Especially since you've known so little trouble and hardship in your own life.

NORA: I—?—have known so little—?

MRS. LINDE [*smiling*]: Oh well, a little sewing or whatever it was. You're still a child, Nora.

NORA [*with a toss of her head, walks away*]: You shouldn't sound so superior.

MRS. LINDE: I shouldn't?

NORA: You're just like all the others. None of you think I'm good for anything really serious.

MRS. LINDE: Well, now—

NORA: That I've never been through anything difficult.

MRS. LINDE: But Nora! You just told me all your troubles!

NORA: That's nothing [*Lowers her voice.*] I haven't told you about *it.*

MRS. LINDE: It? What's that? What do you mean?

NORA: You patronize me, Kristine, and that's not fair. You're proud that you worked so long and so hard for your mother.

MRS. LINDE: I don't think I patronize anyone. But it *is* true that I'm both proud and happy that I could make mother's last years comparatively easy.

NORA: And you're proud of all you did for your brothers.

MRS. LINDE: I think I have the right to be.

NORA: And so do I. But now I want to tell you something, Kristine. I have something to be proud and happy about too.

MRS. LINDE: I don't doubt that for a moment. But what exactly do you mean?

NORA: Not so loud! Torvald mustn't hear—not for anything in the world. Nobody must know about this, Kristine. Nobody but you.

MRS. LINDE: But what is it?

NORA: Come here. [*Pulls her down on the couch beside her.*] You see, I *do* have something to be proud and happy about. I've saved Torvald's life.

MRS. LINDE: Saved—? How do you mean—"saved"?

NORA: I told you about our trip to Italy. Torvald would have died if he hadn't gone.

MRS. LINDE: I understand that. And so your father gave you the money you needed.

NORA [*smiles*]: Yes, that's what Torvald and all the others think. But—

MRS. LINDE: But what?

NORA: Daddy didn't give us a penny. *I* raised that money.

MRS. LINDE: *You* did? That whole big amount?

NORA: Twelve hundred specie dollars. Four thousand eight hundred crowns. *Now* what do you say?

MRS. LINDE: But Nora, how could you? Did you win in the state lottery?

NORA [*contemptuously*]: State lottery! [*Snorts.*] What is so great about that?

MRS. LINDE: Where did it come from then?

NORA [*humming and smiling, enjoying her secret*]: Hmmm. Tra-la-la-la-la!

MRS. LINDE: You certainly couldn't have borrowed it.

NORA: Oh? And why not?

MRS. LINDE: A wife can't borrow money without her husband's consent.

NORA [*with a toss of her head*]: Oh, I don't know—take a wife with a little bit of a head for business—a wife who knows how to manage things—

MRS. LINDE: But Nora, I don't understand at all—

NORA: You don't have to. I didn't say I borrowed the money, did I? I could have gotten it some other way. [*Leans back.*] An admirer may have given it to me. When you're as tolerably goodlooking as I am—

MRS. LINDE: Oh, you're crazy.

NORA: I think you're dying from curiosity, Kristine.

MRS. LINDE: I'm beginning to think you've done something very foolish, Nora.

NORA [*sits up*]: Is it foolish to save your husband's life?

MRS. LINDE: I say it's foolish to act behind his back.

NORA: But don't you see: he couldn't be told! You're missing the whole point, Kristine. We couldn't even let him know how seriously ill he was. The doctors came to *me* and told me his life was in danger, that nothing could save him but a stay in the south. Don't you think I tried to work on him? I told him how lovely it would be if I could go abroad like other young wives. I cried and begged. I said he'd better remember what condition I was in, that he had to be nice to me and do what I wanted. I even hinted he could borrow the money. But that almost made him angry with me. He told me I was being irresponsible and that it was his duty as my husband not to give in to my moods and whims—I think that's what he called it. All right, I said to myself, you've got to be saved somehow, and so I found a way—

MRS. LINDE: And your husband never learned from your father that the money didn't come from him?

NORA: Never. Daddy died that same week. I thought of telling him all about it and ask him not to say anything. But since he was so sick—It turned out I didn't have to—

MRS. LINDE: And you've never told your husband?

NORA: Of course not! Good heavens, how could I? He, with his strict principles! Besides, you know how men are. Torvald would find it embarrassing and humiliating to learn that he owed me anything. It would upset our whole relationship. Our happy, beautiful home would no longer be what it is.

MRS. LINDE: Aren't you ever going to tell him?

NORA [*reflectively, half smiling*]: Yes—one day, maybe. Many, many years from now, when I'm no longer young and pretty. Don't laugh! I mean when Torvald no longer feels about me the way he does now, when he no longer thinks it's fun when I dance for him and put on costumes and recite for him. Then it will be good to have something in reserve—[*Interrupts herself.*] Oh, I'm just being silly! That day will never come.—Well, now, Kristine, what do you think of my great secret? Don't you think I'm good for something too?—By the way, you wouldn't believe all the worry I've had because of it. It's been very hard to meet my obligations on schedule. You see, in business there's something called quarterly interest and something called install-ments on the principal, and those are terribly hard to come up with. I've had to save a little here and a little there, whenever I could. I couldn't use much of the house-keeping money, for Torvald has to eat well. And I couldn't use what I got for clothes for the children. They have to look nice, and I didn't think it would be right to spend less than I got—the sweet little things!

MRS. LINDE: Poor Nora! So you had to take it from your own allowance?

NORA: Yes, of course. After all, it was my affair. Every time Torvald gave me money for a new dress and things like that, I never used more than half of it. I always bought the cheapest, simplest things for myself. Thank God, everything looks good on me, so Torvald never noticed. But it was hard many times, Kristine, for it's fun to have pretty clothes. Don't you think?

MRS. LINDE: Certainly.

NORA: Anyway, I had other ways of making money too. Last winter I was lucky enough to get some copying work. So I locked the door and sat up writing every night till quite late. God! I often got so tired—! But it was great fun, too, working and making money. It was almost like being a man.

MRS. LINDE: But how much have you been able to pay off this way?

NORA: I couldn't tell you exactly. You see, it's very difficult to keep track of business like that. All I know is I have been paying off as much as I've been able to scrape together. Many times I just didn't know what to do. [*Smiles.*] Then I used to imagine a rich old gentleman had fallen in love with me—

MRS. LINDE: What! What old gentleman?

NORA: Phooey! And now he was dead and they were reading his will, and there it said in big letters, "All my money is to be paid in cash immediately to the charming Mrs. Nora Helmer."

MRS. LINDE: But dearest Nora—who *was* this old gentleman?

NORA: For heaven's sake, Kristine, don't you see! There *was* no old gentleman. He was just somebody I made up when I couldn't think of any way to raise the money. But never mind him. The old bore can be anyone he likes to for all I care. I have no use for him or his last will, for now I don't have a single worry in the world. [*Jumps up.*] Dear God, what a lovely thought that is! To be able to play and have fun with the children, to have everything nice and pretty in the house, just the way Torvald likes it! Not a care! And soon spring will be here, and the air will be blue and high. Maybe we can travel again. Maybe I'll see the ocean again! Oh, yes, yes!—It's wonderful to be alive and happy!

[*The doorbell rings.*]

MRS. LINDE [*getting up*]: There's the doorbell. Maybe I better be going.

NORA: No, please stay. I'm sure it's just someone for Torvald—

MAID [*in the hall door*]: Excuse me, ma'am. There's a gentleman here who'd like to see Mr. Helmer.

NORA: You mean the bank manager.

MAID: Sorry, ma'am; the bank manager. But I didn't know—since the Doctor is with him—

NORA: Who is the gentleman?

KROGSTAD [*appearing in the door*]: It's just me, Mrs. Helmer.

[MRS. LINDE *starts, looks, turns away toward the window.*]

NORA [*takes a step toward him, tense, in a low voice*]: You? What do you want? What do you want with my husband?

KROGSTAD: Bank business—in a way. I have a small job in the Mutual, and I understand your husband is going to be our new boss—

NORA: So it's just—

KROGSTAD: Just routine business, ma'am. Nothing else.

NORA: All right. In that case, why don't you go through the door to the office.

[*Dismisses him casually as she closes the door. Walks over to the stove and tends the fire.*]

MRS. LINDE: Nora—who was that man?

NORA: His name's Krogstad. He's a lawyer.

MRS. LINDE: So it *was* him.

NORA: Do you know him?

MRS. LINDE: I used to—many years ago. For a while he clerked in our part of the country.

NORA: Right. He did.

MRS. LINDE: He has changed a great deal.

NORA: I believe he had a very unhappy marriage.

MRS. LINDE: And now he's a widower, isn't he?

NORA: With many children. There now; it's burning nicely again. [*Closes the stove and moves the rocking chair a little to the side.*]

MRS. LINDE: They say he's into all sorts of business.

NORA: Really? Maybe so. I wouldn't know. But let's not think about business. It's such a bore.

DR. RANK [*appears in the door to* HELMER*'s study*]: No, I don't want to be in the way. I'd rather talk to your wife a bit. [*Closes the door and notices* MRS. LINDE.] Oh, I beg your pardon. I believe I'm in the way here too.

NORA: No, not at all. [*Introduces them.*] Dr. Rank. Mrs. Linde.

RANK: Aha. A name often heard in this house. I believe I passed you on the stairs coming up.

MRS. LINDE: Yes. I'm afraid I climb stairs very slowly. They aren't good for me.

RANK: I see. A slight case of inner decay, perhaps?

MRS. LINDE: Overwork, rather.

RANK: Oh, is that all? And now you've come to town to relax at all the parties?

MRS. LINDE: I have come to look for a job.

RANK: A proven cure for overwork, I take it?

MRS. LINDE: One has to live, Doctor.

RANK: Yes, that seems to be the common opinion.

NORA: Come on, Dr. Rank—you want to live just as much as the rest of us.

RANK: Of course I do. Miserable as I am, I prefer to go on being tortured as long as possible. All my patients feel the same way. And that's true of the moral invalids too. Helmer is talking with a specimen right this minute.

MRS. LINDE [*in a low voice*]: Ah!

NORA: What do you mean?

RANK: Oh, this lawyer, Krogstad. You don't know him. The roots of his character are decayed. But even he began by saying something about having to *live*—as if it were a matter of the highest importance.

NORA: Oh? What did he want with Torvald?

RANK: I don't really know. All I heard was something about the bank.

NORA: I didn't know that Krog—that this Krogstad had anything to do with the Mutual Bank.

RANK: Yes, he seems to have some kind of job there. [*To* MRS. LINDE.] I don't know if you are familiar in your part of the country with the kind of person who is always running around trying to sniff out cases of moral decrepitude and as soon as he finds

one puts the individual under observation in some excellent position or other. All the healthy ones are left out in the cold.

MRS. LINDE: I should think it's the sick who need looking after the most.

RANK [*shrugs his shoulders*]: There we are. That's the attitude that turns society into a hospital.

[NORA, *absorbed in her own thoughts, suddenly starts giggling and clapping her hands.*]

RANK: What's so funny about that? Do you even know what society is?

NORA: What do I care about your stupid society! I laughed at something entirely different—something terribly amusing. Tell me, Dr. Rank—all the employees in the Mutual Bank, from now on they'll all be dependent on Torvald, right?

RANK: Is that what you find so enormously amusing?

NORA [*smiles and hums*]: That's my business, that's my business! [*Walks around.*] Yes, I do think it's fun that we—that Torvald is going to have so much influence on so many people's lives. [*Brings out the bag of macaroons.*] Have a macaroon, Dr. Rank.

RANK: Well, well—macaroons. I thought they were banned around here.

NORA: Yes, but these were some that Kristine gave me.

MRS. LINDE: What! I?

NORA: That's all right. Don't look so scared. You couldn't know that Torvald won't let me have them. He's afraid they'll ruin my teeth. But who cares! Just once in a while—! Right, Dr. Rank? Have one! [*Puts a macaroon into his mouth.*] You too, Kristine. And one for me. A very small one. Or at most two. [*Walks around again.*] Yes, I really feel very, very happy. Now there's just one thing I'm dying to do.

RANK: Oh? And what's that?

NORA: Something I'm dying to say so Torvald could hear.

RANK: And why can't you?

NORA: I don't dare to, for it's not nice.

MRS. LINDE: Not nice?

RANK: In that case, I guess you'd better not. But surely to the two of us—? What is it you'd like to say for Helmer to hear?

NORA: I want to say, "Goddammit!"

RANK: Are you out of your mind!

MRS. LINDE: For heaven's sake, Nora!

RANK: Say it. Here he comes.

NORA [*hiding the macaroons*]: Shhh!

[HELMER *enters from his study, carrying his hat and overcoat.*]

NORA [*going to him*]: Well, dear, did you get rid of him?

HELMER: Yes, he just left.

NORA: Torvald, I want you to meet Kristine. She's just come to town.

HELMER: Kristine—? I'm sorry; I don't think—

NORA: Mrs. Linde, Torvald dear. Mrs. Kristine Linde.

HELMER: Ah, yes. A childhood friend of my wife's, I suppose.

MRS. LINDE: Yes, we've known each other for a long time.

NORA: Just think; she has come all this way just to see you.

HELMER: I'm not sure I understand—

MRS. LINDE: Well, not really—

NORA: You see, Kristine is an absolutely fantastic secretary, and she would so much like to work for a competent executive and learn more than she knows already—

HELMER: Very sensible, I'm sure, Mrs. Linde.

NORA: So when she heard about your appointment—there was a wire—she came here as fast as she could. How about it, Torvald? Couldn't you do something for Kristine? For my sake. Please?

HELMER: Quite possibly. I take it you're a widow, Mrs. Linde?

MRS. LINDE: Yes.

HELMER: And you've had office experience?

MRS. LINDE: Some—yes.

HELMER: In that case I think it's quite likely that I'll be able to find you a position.

NORA [claps her hands]: I knew it! I knew it!

HELMER: You've arrived at a most opportune time, Mrs. Linde.

MRS. LINDE: Oh, how can I ever thank you—

HELMER: Not at all, not at all. [Puts his coat on.] But today you'll have to excuse me—

RANK: Wait a minute; I'll come with you. [Gets his fur coat from the front hall, warms it by the stove.]

NORA: Don't be long, Torvald.

HELMER: An hour or so; no more.

NORA: Are you leaving, too, Kristine?

MRS. LINDE [putting on her things]: Yes, I'd better go and find a place to stay.

HELMER: Good. Then we'll be going the same way.

NORA [helping her]: I'm sorry this place is so small, but I don't think we very well could—

MRS. LINDE: Of course! Don't be silly, Nora. Goodbye, and thank you for everything.

NORA: Goodbye. We'll see you soon. You'll be back this evening, of course. And you too, Dr. Rank; right? If you feel well enough? Of course you will. Just wrap yourself up.

[General small talk as all exit into the hall. Children's voices are heard on the stairs.]

NORA: There they are! There they are! [She runs and opens the door. The nurse ANNE-MARIE enters with the children.]

NORA: Come in! Come in! [Bends over and kisses them.] Oh, you sweet, sweet darlings! Look at them, Kristine! Aren't they beautiful?

RANK: No standing around in the draft!

HELMER: Come along, Mrs. Linde. This place isn't fit for anyone but mothers right now.

[DR. RANK, HELMER, and MRS. LINDE go down the stairs. The NURSE enters the living room with the children. NORA follows, closing the door behind her.]

NORA: My, how nice you all look! Such red cheeks! Like apples and roses. [*The children all talk at the same time.*] You've had so much fun? I bet you have. Oh, isn't that nice! You pulled both Emmy and Bob on your sleigh? Both at the same time? That's very good, Ivar. Oh, let me hold her for a minute, Anne-Marie. My sweet little doll baby! [*Takes the smallest of the children from the* NURSE *and dances with her.*] Yes, yes, of course; Mama'll dance with you too, Bob. What? You threw snowballs? Oh, I wish I'd been there! No, no; I want to take their clothes off, Anne-Marie. Please let me; I think it's so much fun. You go on in. You look frozen. There's hot coffee on the stove.

[*The* NURSE *exits into the room to the left.* NORA *takes the children's wraps off and throws them all around. They all keep telling her things at the same time.*]

NORA: Oh, really? A big dog ran after you? But it didn't bite you. Of course not. Dogs don't bite sweet little doll babies. Don't peek at the packages, Ivar! What's in them? Wouldn't you like to know! No, no; that's something terrible! Play? You want to play? What do you want to play? Okay, let's play hide-and-seek. Bob hides first. You want *me* to? All right. I'll go first.

[*Laughing and shouting,* NORA *and the children play in the living room and in the adjacent room, right. Finally,* NORA *hides herself under the table; the children rush in, look for her, can't find her. They hear her low giggle, run to the table, lift the rug that covers it, see her. General hilarity. She crawls out, pretends to scare them. New delight. In the meantime there has been a knock on the door between the living room and the front hall, but nobody has noticed. Now the door is opened halfway;* KROGSTAD *appears. He waits a little. The play goes on.*]

KROGSTAD: Pardon me, Mrs. Helmer—

NORA [*with a muted cry turns around, jumps up*]: Ah! What do you want?

KROGSTAD: I'm sorry. The front door was open. Somebody must have forgotten to close it—

NORA [*standing up*]: My husband isn't here, Mr. Krogstad.

KROGSTAD: I know.

NORA: So what do you want?

KROGSTAD: I'd like a word with you.

NORA: With—? [*To the children.*] Go in to Anne-Marie. What? No, the strange man won't do anything bad to Mama. When he's gone we'll play some more.

[*She takes the children into the room to the left and closes the door.*]

NORA [*tense, troubled*]: You want to speak with me?

KROGSTAD: Yes I do.

NORA: Today—? It isn't the first of the month yet.

KROGSTAD: No, it's Christmas Eve. It's up to you what kind of holiday you'll have.

NORA: What do you want? I can't possibly—

KROGSTAD: Let's not talk about that just yet. There's something else. You do have a few minutes, don't you?

NORA: Yes. Yes, of course. That is,—

KROGSTAD: Good. I was sitting in Olsen's restaurant when I saw your husband go by.

NORA: Yes—?

KROGSTAD: —with a lady.

NORA: What of it?

KROGSTAD: May I be so free as to ask: wasn't that lady Mrs. Linde?

NORA: Yes.

KROGSTAD: Just arrived in town?

NORA: Yes, today.

KROGSTAD: She's a good friend of yours, I understand?

NORA: Yes, she is. But I fail to see—

KROGSTAD: I used to know her myself.

NORA: I know that.

KROGSTAD: So you know about that. I thought as much. In that case, let me ask you a simple question. Is Mrs. Linde going to be employed in the bank?

NORA: What makes you think you have the right to cross-examine me like this, Mr. Krogstad—you, one of my husband's employees? But since you ask, I'll tell you. Yes, Mrs. Linde is going to be working in the bank. And it was I who recommended her, Mr. Krogstad. Now you know.

KROGSTAD: So I was right.

NORA [*walks up and down*]: After all, one does have a little influence, you know. Just because you're a woman, it doesn't mean that—Really, Mr. Krogstad, people in a subordinate position should be careful not to offend someone who—oh well—

KROGSTAD: —has influence?

NORA: Exactly.

KROGSTAD [*changing his tone*]: Mrs. Helmer, I must ask you to be good enough to use your influence on my behalf.

NORA: What do you mean?

KROGSTAD: I want you to make sure that I am going to keep my subordinate position in the bank.

NORA: I don't understand. Who is going to take your position away from you?

KROGSTAD: There's no point in playing ignorant with me, Mrs. Helmer. I can very well appreciate that your friend would find it unpleasant to run into me. So now I know who I can thank for my dismissal.

NORA: But I assure you—

KROGSTAD: Never mind. Just want to say you still have time. I advise you to use your influence to prevent it.

NORA: But Mr. Krogstad, I don't have any influence—none at all.

KROGSTAD: No? I thought you just said—

NORA: Of course I didn't mean it that way. I! Whatever makes you think that I have any influence of that kind on my husband?

KROGSTAD: I went to law school with your husband. I have no reason to think that the bank manager is less susceptible than other husbands.

NORA: If you're going to insult my husband, I'll ask you to leave.

KROGSTAD: You're brave, Mrs. Helmer.

NORA: I'm not afraid of you any more. After New Year's I'll be out of this thing with you.

KROGSTAD [*more controlled*]: Listen, Mrs. Helmer. If necessary, I'll fight as for my life to keep my little job in the bank.

NORA: So it seems.

KROGSTAD: It isn't just the money; that's really the smallest part of it. There is something else—Well, I guess I might as well tell you. It's like this. I'm sure you know, like everybody else, that some years ago I committed—an impropriety.

NORA: I believe I've heard it mentioned.

KROGSTAD: The case never came to court, but from that moment all doors were closed to me. So I took up the kind of business you know about. I had to do something, and I think I can say about myself that I have not been among the worst. But now I want to get out of all that. My sons are growing up. For their sake I must get back as much of my good name as I can. This job in the bank was like the first rung on the ladder. And now your husband wants to kick me down and leave me back in the mud again.

NORA: But I swear to you, Mr. Krogstad; it's not at all in my power to help you.

KROGSTAD: That's because you don't want to. But I have the means to force you.

NORA: You don't mean you're going to tell my husband I owe you money?

KROGSTAD: And if I did?

NORA: That would be a mean thing to do. [*Almost crying.*] That secret, which is my joy and my pride—for him to learn about it in such a coarse and ugly manner—to learn it from *you*—! It would be terribly unpleasant for me.

KROGSTAD: Just unpleasant?

NORA [*heatedly*]: But go ahead! Do it! It will be worse for you than for me. When my husband realizes what a bad person you are, you'll be sure to lose your job.

KROGSTAD: I asked you if it was just domestic unpleasantness you were afraid of?

NORA: When my husband finds out, of course he'll pay off the loan, and then we won't have anything more to do with you.

KROGSTAD [*stepping closer*]: Listen, Mrs. Helmer—either you have a very bad memory, or you don't know much about business. I think I had better straighten you out on a few things.

NORA: What do you mean?

KROGSTAD: When your husband was ill, you came to me to borrow twelve hundred dollars.

NORA: I knew nobody else.

KROGSTAD: I promised to get you the money—

NORA: And you did.

KROGSTAD: I promised to get you the money on certain conditions. At the time you were so anxious about your husband's health and so set on getting him away that I doubt very much that you paid much attention to the details of our transaction. That's why I remind you of them now. Anyway, I promised to get you the money if you would sign an I.O.U., which I drafted.

NORA: And which I signed.

KROGSTAD: Good. But below your signature I added a few lines, making your father security for the loan. Your father was supposed to put his signature to those lines.

NORA: Supposed to—? He did.

KROGSTAD: I had left the date blank. That is, your father was to date his own signature. You recall that, don't you, Mrs. Helmer?

NORA: I guess so—

KROGSTAD: I gave the note to you. You were to mail it to your father. Am I correct?

NORA: Yes.

KROGSTAD: And of course you did so right away, for no more than five or six days later you brought the paper back to me, signed by your father. Then I paid you the money.

NORA: Well? And haven't I been keeping up with the payments?

KROGSTAD: Fairly well, yes. But to get back to what we were talking about—those were difficult days for you, weren't they, Mrs. Helmer?

NORA: Yes, they were.

KROGSTAD: Your father was quite ill, I believe.

NORA: He was dying.

KROGSTAD: And died shortly afterwards?

NORA: That's right.

KROGSTAD: Tell me, Mrs. Helmer; do you happen to remember the date of your father's death? I mean the exact day of the month?

NORA: Daddy died on September 29.

KROGSTAD: Quite correct. I have ascertained that fact. That's why there is something peculiar about this [*takes out a piece of paper*], which I can't account for.

NORA: Peculiar? How? I don't understand—

KROGSTAD: It seems very peculiar, Mrs. Helmer, that your father signed this promissory note three days after his death.

NORA: How so? I don't see what—

KROGSTAD: Your father died on September 29. Now look. He has dated his signature October 2. Isn't that odd?

[NORA *remains silent.*]

KROGSTAD: Can you explain it?

[NORA *is still silent.*]

KROGSTAD: I also find it striking that the date and the month and the year are not in your father's handwriting but in a hand I think I recognize. Well, that might be explained. Your father may have forgotten to date his signature and somebody else may have done it here, guessing at the date before he had learned of your father's death. That's all right. It's only the signature itself that matters. And that is genuine, isn't it, Mrs. Helmer? You father *did* put his name to this note?

NORA [*after a brief silence tosses her head back and looks defiantly at him*]: No, he didn't. I wrote
   Daddy's name.

KROGSTAD: Mrs. Helmer—do you realize what a dangerous admission you just
   made?

NORA: Why? You'll get your money soon.

KROGSTAD: Let me ask you something. Why didn't you mail this note to your father?

NORA: Because it was impossible. Daddy was sick—you know that. If I had asked him
   to sign it, I would have had to tell him what the money was for. But I couldn't tell
   him, as sick as he was, that my husband's life was in danger. That was impossible.
   Surely you can see that.

KROGSTAD: Then it would have been better for you if you had given up your trip
   abroad.

NORA: No, that was impossible! That trip was to save my husband's life. I couldn't give
   it up.

KROGSTAD: But didn't you realize that what you did amounted to fraud against me?

NORA: I couldn't let that make any difference. I didn't care about you at all. I hated
   the way you made all those difficulties for me, even though you knew the danger my
   husband was in. I thought you were cold and unfeeling.

KROGSTAD: Mrs. Helmer, obviously you have no clear idea of what you have done.
   Let me tell you that what I did that time was no more and no worse. And it ruined
   my name and reputation.

NORA: You! Are you trying to tell me that you did something brave once in order to
   save your wife's life?

KROGSTAD: The law doesn't ask about motives.

NORA: Then it's a bad law.

KROGSTAD: Bad or not—if I produce this note in court you'll be judged according
   to the law.

NORA: I refuse to believe you. A daughter shouldn't have the right to spare her dying
   old father worry and anxiety? A wife shouldn't have the right to save her husband's
   life? I don't know the laws very well, but I'm sure that somewhere they make
   allowance for cases like that. And you, a lawyer, don't know that? I think you must
   be a bad lawyer, Mr. Krogstad.

KROGSTAD: That may be. But business—the kind of business you and I have with
   one another—don't you think I know something about that? Very well. Do what you
   like. But let me tell you this: if I'm going to be kicked out again, you'll keep me
   company. [*He bows and exits through the front hall.*]

NORA [*pauses thoughtfully; then, with a defiant toss of her head*]: Oh, nonsense! Trying to scare
   me like that! I'm not all that silly. [*Starts picking up the children's clothes; soon stops.*] But—?
   No! That's impossible! I did it for love!

CHILDREN [*in the door to the left*]: Mama, the strange man just left. We saw him.

NORA: Yes, yes; I know. But don't tell anybody about the strange man. Do you hear?
   Not even Daddy.

CHILDREN: We won't. But now you'll play with us again, won't you, Mama?

NORA: No, not right now.

CHILDREN: But Mama—you promised.

NORA: I know, but I can't just now. Go to your own room. I've so much to do. Be nice now, my little darlings. Do as I say. [*She nudges them gently into the other room and closes the door. She sits down on the couch, picks up a piece of embroidery, makes a few stitches, then stops.*] No! [*Throws the embroidery down, goes to the hall door and calls out.*] Helene! Bring the Christmas tree in here, please! [*Goes to the table, left, opens the drawer, halts.*] No—that's impossible!

MAID [*with the Christmas tree*]: Where do you want it, ma'am?

NORA: There. The middle of the floor.

MAID: You want anything else?

NORA: No, thanks. I have everything I need. [*The* MAID *goes out.* NORA *starts trimming the tree.*] I want candles—and flowers—That awful man! Oh, nonsense! There's nothing wrong. This will be a lovely tree. I'll do everything you want me to, Torvald. I'll sing for you—dance for you—

[HELMER, *a bundle of papers under his arm, enters from outside.*]

NORA: Ah—you're back already?

HELMER: Yes. Has anybody been here?

NORA: Here? No.

HELMER: That's funny. I saw Krogstad leaving just now.

NORA: Oh? Oh yes, that's right. Krogstad was here for just a moment.

HELMER: I can tell from your face that he came to ask you to put in a word for him.

NORA: Yes.

HELMER: And it was supposed to be your own idea, wasn't it? You were not to tell me he'd been here. He asked you that too, didn't he?

NORA: Yes, Torvald, but—

HELMER: Nora, Nora, how could you! Talk to a man like that and make him promises! And lying to me about it afterwards—!

NORA: Lying—?

HELMER: Didn't you say nobody had been here? [*Shakes his finger at her.*] My little songbird must never do that again. Songbirds are supposed to have clean beaks to chirp with—no false notes. [*Puts his arm around her waist.*] Isn't that so? Of course it is. [*Lets her go.*] And that's enough about that. [*Sits down in front of the fireplace.*] Ah, it's nice and warm in here. [*Begins to leaf through his papers.*]

NORA [*busy with the tree; after a brief pause*]: Torvald.

HELMER: Yes.

NORA: I'm looking forward so much to the Stenborgs' costume party day after tomorrow.

HELMER: And I can't wait to find out what you're going to surprise me with.

NORA: Oh, that silly idea!

HELMER: Oh?

NORA: I can't think of anything. It all seems so foolish and pointless.

HELMER: Ah, my little Nora admits that?

NORA [*behind his chair, her arms on the back of the chair*]: Are you very busy, Torvald?

HELMER: Well—

NORA: What are all those papers?

HELMER: Bank business.

NORA: Already?

HELMER: I've asked the board to give me the authority to make certain changes in organization and personnel. That's what I'll be doing over the holidays. I want it all settled before New Year's.

NORA: So that's why this poor Krogstad—

HELMER: Hm.

NORA [leisurely playing with the hair on his neck]: If you weren't so busy, Torvald, I'd ask you for a great big favor.

HELMER: Let's hear it, anyway.

NORA: I don't know anyone with better taste than you, and I want so much to look nice at the party. Couldn't you sort of take charge of me, Torvald, and decide what I'll wear—Help me with my costume?

HELMER: Aha! Little Lady Obstinate is looking for someone to rescue her?

NORA: Yes, Torvald. I won't get anywhere without your help.

HELMER: All right. I'll think about it. We'll come up with something.

NORA: Oh, you *are* nice! [Goes back to the Christmas tree. A pause.] Those red flowers look so pretty.—Tell me, was it really all that bad what this Krogstad fellow did?

HELMER: He forged signatures. Do you have any idea what that means?

NORA: Couldn't it have been because he felt he had to?

HELMER: Yes, or like so many others he may simply have been thoughtless. I'm not so heartless as to condemn a man absolutely because of a single imprudent act.

NORA: Of course not, Torvald!

HELMER: People like him can redeem themselves morally by openly confessing their crime and taking their punishment.

NORA: Punishment—?

HELMER: But that was not the way Krogstad chose. He got out of it with tricks and evasions. That's what has corrupted him.

NORA: So you think that if—?

HELMER: Can't you imagine how a guilty person like that has to lie and fake and dissemble wherever he goes—putting on a mask before everybody he's close to, even his own wife and children. It's this thing with the children that's the worst part of it, Nora.

NORA: Why is that?

HELMER: Because when a man lives inside such a circle of stinking lies he brings infection into his own home and contaminates his whole family. With every breath of air his children inhale the germs of something ugly.

NORA [moving closer behind him]: Are you so sure of that?

HELMER: Of course I am. I have seen enough examples of that in my work. Nearly all young criminals have had mothers who lied.

NORA: Why mothers—particularly?

HELMER: Most often mothers. But of course fathers tend to have the same influence. Every lawyer knows that. And yet, for years this Krogstad has been poisoning his own children in an atmosphere of lies and deceit. That's why I call him a lost soul morally. [*Reaches out for her hands.*] And that's why my sweet little Nora must promise me never to take his side again. Let's shake on that.—What? What's this? Give me your hand. There! Now that's settled. I assure you, I would find it impossible to work in the same room with that man. I feel literally sick when I'm around people like that.

NORA [*withdraws her hand and goes to the other side of the Christmas tree*]: It's so hot in here. And I have so much to do.

HELMER [*gets up and collects his papers*]: Yes, and I really should try to get some of this reading done before dinner. I must think about your costume too. And maybe just possibly I'll have something to wrap in gilt paper and hang on the Christmas tree. [*Puts his hand on her head.*] Oh my adorable little songbird! [*Enters his study and closes the door.*]

NORA [*after a pause, in a low voice*]: It's all a lot of nonsense. It's not that way at all. It's impossible. It has to be impossible.

NURSE [*in the door, left*]: The little ones are asking ever so nicely if they can't come in and be with their mama.

NORA: No, no, no! Don't let them in here! You stay with them, Anne-Marie.

NURSE: If you say so, ma'am. [*Closes the door.*]

NORA [*pale with terror*]: Corrupt my little children—! Poison my home—? [*Brief pause; she lifts her head.*] That's not true. Never. Never in a million years.

ACT II

The same room. The Christmas tree is in the corner by the piano, stripped, shabby-looking, with burnt-down candles. NORA's outside clothes are on the couch. NORA is alone. She walks around restlessly. She stops by the couch and picks up her coat.

NORA [*drops the coat again*]: There's somebody now! [*Goes to the door, listens.*] No. Nobody. Of course not—not on Christmas. And not tomorrow either.—But perhaps—[*Opens the door and looks.*] No, nothing in the mailbox. All empty. [*Comes forward.*] How silly I am! Of course he isn't serious. Nothing like that could happen. After all, I have three small children.

[*The NURSE enters from the room, left, carrying a big carton.*]

NURSE: Well, at last I found it—the box with your costume.

NORA: Thanks. Just put it on the table.

NURSE [*does so*]: But it's all a big mess, I'm afraid.

NORA: Oh, I wish I could tear the whole thing to little pieces!

NURSE: Heavens! It's not as bad as all that. It can be fixed all right. All it takes is a little patience.

NORA: I'll go over and get Mrs. Linde to help me.

NURSE: Going out again? In this awful weather? You'll catch a cold.

NORA: That might not be such a bad thing. How are the children?

NURSE: The poor little dears are playing with their presents, but—

NORA: Do they keep asking for me?

NURSE: Well, you know; they're used to being with their mamma.

NORA: I know. But Anne-Marie, from now on I can't be with them as much as before.

NURSE: Oh well. Little children get used to everything.

NORA: You think so? Do you think they'll forget their mamma if I were gone altogether?

NURSE: Goodness me—gone altogether?

NORA: Listen, Anne-Marie—something I've wondered about. How could you bring yourself to leave your child with strangers?

NURSE: But I had to, if I were to nurse you.

NORA: Yes, but how could you *want* to?

NURSE: When I could get such a nice place? When something like that happens to a poor young girl, she'd better be grateful for whatever she gets. For *he* didn't do a thing for me—the louse!

NORA: But your daughter has forgotten all about you, hasn't she?

NURSE: Oh no! Not at all! She wrote to me both when she was confirmed and when she got married.

NORA [*putting her arms around her neck*]: You dear old thing—you were a good mother to me when I was little.

NURSE: Poor little Nora had no one else, you know.

NORA: And if my little ones didn't, I know you'd—oh, I'm being silly! [*Opens the carton.*] Go in to them, please. I really should—. Tomorrow you'll see how pretty I'll be.

NURSE: I know. There won't be anybody at that party half as pretty as you, ma'am. [*Goes out, left.*]

NORA [*begins to take clothes out of the carton; in a moment she throws it all down*]: If only I dared to go out. If only I knew nobody would come. That nothing would happen while I was gone.—How silly! Nobody'll come. Just don't think about it. Brush the muff. Beautiful gloves. Beautiful gloves. Forget it. Forget it. One, two, three, four, five, six—[*Cries out.*] There they are! [*Moves toward the door, stops irresolutely.*]

[MRS. LINDE *enters from the hall. She has already taken off her coat.*]

NORA: Oh, it's you, Kristine. There's no one else out there, is there? I'm so glad you're here.

MRS. LINDE: They told me you'd asked for me.

NORA: I just happened to walk by. I need your help with something—badly. Let's sit here on the couch. Look. Torvald and I are going to a costume party tomorrow night—at Consul Stenborg's upstairs—and Torvald wants me to go as a Neapolitan fisher girl and dance the tarantella. I learned it when we were on Capri.

MRS. LINDE: Well, well! So you'll be putting on a whole show?

NORA: Yes. Torvald thinks I should. Look, here's the costume. Torvald had it made for me while we were there. But it's all so torn and everything. I just don't know—

MRS. LINDE: Oh, that can be fixed. It's not that much. The trimmings have come loose in a few places. Do you have needle and thread? Oh, here we are. All set.

NORA: I really appreciate it, Kristine.

MRS. LINDE [*sewing*]: So you'll be in disguise tomorrow night, eh? You know—I may come by for just a moment, just to look at you.—Oh dear. I haven't even thanked you for the nice evening last night.

NORA [*gets up, moves around*]: Oh, I don't know. I don't think last night was as nice as it usually is.—You should have come to town a little earlier, Kristine.—Yes, Torvald knows how to make it nice and pretty around here.

MRS. LINDE: You too, I should think. After all, you're your father's daughter. By the way, is Dr. Rank always as depressed as he was last night?

NORA: No, last night was unusual. He's a very sick man, you know—very sick. Poor Rank, his spine is rotting away. Tuberculosis, I think. You see, his father was a nasty old man with mistresses and all that sort of thing. Rank has been sickly ever since he was a little boy.

MRS. LINDE [*dropping her sewing to her lap*]: But dearest Nora, where have you learned about things like that?

NORA [*still walking about*]: Oh, you know—with three children you sometimes get to talk with—other wives. Some of them know quite a bit about medicine. So you pick up a few things.

MRS. LINDE [*resumes her sewing; after a brief pause*]: Does Dr. Rank come here every day?

NORA: Every single day. He's Torvald's oldest and best friend, after all. And my friend too, for that matter. He's part of the family, almost.

MRS. LINDE: But tell me, is he quite sincere? I mean, isn't he the kind of man who likes to say nice things to people?

NORA: No, not at all. Rather the opposite, in fact. What makes you say that?

MRS. LINDE: When you introduced us yesterday, he told me he'd often heard my name mentioned in this house. But later on it was quite obvious that your husband really had no idea who I was. So how could Dr. Rank—?

NORA: You're right, Kristine, but I can explain that. You see, Torvald loves me so very much that he wants me all to himself. That's what he says. When we were first married he got almost jealous when I as much as mentioned anybody from back home that I was fond of. So of course I soon stopped doing that. But with Dr. Rank I often talk about home. You see, he likes to listen to me.

MRS. LINDE: Look here, Nora. In many ways you're still a child. After all, I'm quite a bit older than you and have had more experience. I want to give you a piece of advice. I think you should get out of this thing with Dr. Rank.

NORA: Get out of what thing?

MRS. LINDE: Several things in fact, if you want my opinion. Yesterday you said something about a rich admirer who was going to give you money—

NORA: One who doesn't exist, unfortunately. What of it?

MRS. LINDE: Does Dr. Rank have money?

NORA: Yes, he does.

MRS. LINDE: And no dependents?

NORA: No. But—?

MRS. LINDE: And he comes here every day?

NORA: Yes, I told you that already.

MRS. LINDE: But how can that sensitive man be so tactless?

NORA: I haven't the slightest idea what you're talking about.

MRS. LINDE: Don't play games with me, Nora. Don't you think I know who you borrowed the twelve hundred dollars from?

NORA: Are you out of your mind! The very idea—! A friend of both of us who sees us every day—! What a dreadfully uncomfortable position that would be!

MRS. LINDE: So it really isn't Dr. Rank?

NORA: Most certainly not! I would never have dreamed of asking him—not for a moment. Anyway, he didn't have any money then. He inherited it afterwards.

MRS. LINDE: Well, I still think it may have been lucky for you, Nora dear.

NORA: The idea! It would never have occurred to me to ask Dr. Rank—. Though I'm sure that if I *did* ask him—

MRS. LINDE: But of course you wouldn't.

NORA: Of course not. I can't imagine that that would ever be necessary. But I am quite sure that if I told Dr. Rank—

MRS. LINDE: Behind your husband's back?

NORA: I must get out of—this other thing. That's also behind his back. I *must* get out of it.

MRS. LINDE: That's what I told you yesterday. But—

NORA [*walking up and down*]: A man manages these things so much better than a woman—

MRS. LINDE: One's husband, yes.

NORA: Silly, silly! [*Stops.*] When you've paid off all you owe, you get your I.O.U. back; right?

MRS. LINDE: Yes, of course.

NORA: And you can tear it into a hundred thousand little pieces and burn it—that dirty, filthy paper!

MRS. LINDE [*looks hard at her, puts down her sewing, rises slowly*]: Nora—you're hiding something from me.

NORA: Can you tell?

MRS. LINDE: Something's happened to you, Nora, since yesterday morning. What is it?

NORA [*going to her*]: Kristine! [*Listens.*] Shhh. Torvald just came back. Listen. Why don't you go in to the children for a while. Torvald can't stand having sewing around. Get Anne-Marie to help you.

MRS. LINDE [*gathers some of the sewing things together*]: All right, but I'm not leaving here till you and I have talked.

[*She goes out left, just as* HELMER *enters from the front hall.*]

NORA [*towards him*]: I have been waiting and waiting for you, Torvald.

HELMER: Was that the dressmaker?

NORA: No, it was Kristine. She's helping me with my costume. Oh Torvald, just wait till you see how nice I'll look!

HELMER: I told you. Pretty good idea I had, wasn't it?

NORA: Lovely! And wasn't it nice of me to go along with it?

HELMER [*his hand under her chin*]: Nice? To do what your husband tells you? All right, you little rascal; I know you didn't mean it that way. But don't let me interrupt you. I suppose you want to try it on.

NORA: And you'll be working?

HELMER: Yes. [*Shows her a pile of papers.*] Look. I've been down to the bank. [*Is about to enter his study.*]

NORA: Torvald.

HELMER [*halts*]: Yes?

NORA: What if your little squirrel asked you ever so nicely—

HELMER: For what?

NORA: Would you do it?

HELMER: Depends on what it is.

NORA: Squirrel would run around and do all sorts of fun tricks if you'd be nice and agreeable.

HELMER: All right. What is it?

NORA: Lark would chirp and twitter in all the rooms, up and down—

HELMER: So what? Lark does that anyway.

NORA: I'll be your elfmaid and dance for you in the moonlight, Torvald.

HELMER: Nora, don't tell me it's the same thing you mentioned this morning?

NORA [*closer to him*]: Yes, Torvald. I beg you!

HELMER: You really have the nerve to bring that up again?

NORA: Yes. You've just got to do as I say. You *must* let Krogstad keep his job.

HELMER: My dear Nora. It's his job I intend to give to Mrs. Linde.

NORA: I know. And that's ever so nice of you. But can't you just fire somebody else?

HELMER: This is incredible! You just don't give up, do you? Because you make some foolish promise, I am supposed to—!

NORA: That's not the reason, Torvald. It's for your own sake. That man writes for the worst newspapers. You've said so yourself. There's no telling what he may do to you. I'm scared to death of him.

HELMER: Ah, I understand. You're afraid because of what happened before.

NORA: What do you mean?

HELMER: You're thinking of your father, of course.

NORA: Yes. Yes, you're right. Remember the awful things they wrote about Daddy in the newspapers. I really think they might have forced him to resign if the ministry hadn't sent you to look into the charges and if you hadn't been so helpful and understanding.

HELMER: My dear little Nora, there is a world of difference between your father and me. Your father's official conduct was not above reproach. Mine is, and I intend for it to remain that way as long as I hold my position.

NORA: Oh, but you don't know what vicious people like that may think of. Oh, Torvald! Now all of us could be so happy together here in our own home, peaceful and carefree. Such a good life, Torvald, for you and me and the children! That's why I implore you—

HELMER: And it's exactly because you plead for him that you make it impossible for me to keep him. It's already common knowledge in the bank that I intend to let Krogstad go. If it gets out that the new manager has changed his mind because of his wife—

NORA: Yes? What then?

HELMER: No, of course, that wouldn't matter at all as long as little Mrs. Pighead here got her way! Do you want me to make myself look ridiculous before my whole staff—make people think I can be swayed by just anybody—by outsiders? Believe me, I would soon enough find out what the consequences would be! Besides, there's another thing that makes it absolutely impossible for Krogstad to stay on in the bank now that I'm in charge.

NORA: What's that?

HELMER: I suppose in a pinch I could overlook his moral shortcomings—

NORA: Yes, you could; couldn't you, Torvald?

HELMER: And I understand he's quite a good worker, too. But we've known each other for a long time. It's one of those imprudent relationships you get into when you're young that embarrass you for the rest of your life. I guess I might as well be frank with you: he and I are on a first name basis. And that tactless fellow never hides the fact even when other people are around. Rather, he seems to think it entitles him to be familiar with me. Every chance he gets he comes out with his damn "Torvald, Torvald." I'm telling you, I find it most awkward. He would make my position in the bank intolerable.

NORA: You don't really mean any of this, Torvald.

HELMER: Oh? I don't? And why not?

NORA: No, for it's all so petty.

HELMER: What! Petty? You think I'm being petty!

NORA: No, I *don't* think you are petty, Torvald dear. That's exactly why I—

HELMER: Never mind. You think my reasons are petty, so it follows that I must be petty too. Petty! Indeed! By God, I'll put an end to this right now! [*Opens the door to the front hall and calls out.*] Helene!

NORA: What are you doing?

HELMER [*searching among his papers*]: Making a decision. [*The* MAID *enters.*] Here. Take this letter. Go out with it right away. Find somebody to deliver it. But quick. The address is on the envelope. Wait. Here's money.

MAID: Very good, sir. [*She takes the letter and goes out.*]

HELMER [*collecting his papers*]: There now, little Mrs. Obstinate!

NORA [*breathless*]: Torvald—what was that letter?

HELMER: Krogstad's dismissal.

NORA: Call it back, Torvald! There's still time! Oh Torvald, please—call it back! For my sake, for your own sake, for the sake of the children! Listen to me, Torvald! Do it! You don't know what you're doing to all of us!

HELMER: Too late.

NORA: Yes. Too late.

HELMER: Dear Nora, I forgive you this fear you're in, although it really is an insult to me. Yes, it is! It's an insult to think that I am scared of a shabby scrivener's revenge. But I forgive you, for it's such a beautiful proof how much you love me.

[*Takes her in his arms.*] And that's the way it should be, my sweet darling. Whatever happens, you'll see that when things get really rough I have both strength and courage. You'll find out that I am man enough to shoulder the whole burden.

NORA [*terrified*]: What do you mean by that?

HELMER: All of it, I tell you—

NORA [*composed*]: You'll never have to do that.

HELMER: Good. Then we'll share the burden, Nora—like husband and wife, the way it ought to be. [*Caresses her.*] Now are you satisfied? There, there, there. Not that look in your eyes—like a frightened dove. It's all your own foolish imagination.—Why don't you practice the tarantella—and your tambourine, too. I'll be in the inner office and close both doors, so I won't hear you. You can make as much noise as you like. [*Turning in the doorway.*] And when Rank comes, tell him where to find me. [*He nods to her, enters his study carrying his papers, and closes the door.*]

NORA [*transfixed by terror, whispers*]: He would do it. He'll do it. He'll do it in spite of the whole world.—No, this mustn't happen. Anything rather than that! There must be a way—! [*The doorbell rings.*] Dr. Rank! Anything rather than that! Anything—anything at all!

[*She passes her hand over her face, pulls herself together, and opens the door to the hall.* DR. RANK *is out there, hanging up his coat. Darkness begins to fall during the following scene.*]

NORA: Hello there, Dr. Rank. I recognized your ringing. Don't go in to Torvald yet. I think he's busy.

RANK: And you?

NORA [*as he enters and she closes the door behind him*]: You know I always have time for you.

RANK: Thanks. I'll make use of that as long as I can.

NORA: What do you mean by that—As long as you can?

RANK: Does that frighten you?

NORA: Well, it's a funny expression. As if something was going to happen.

RANK: Something is going to happen that I've long been expecting. But I admit I hadn't thought it would come quite so soon.

NORA [*seizes his arm*]: What is it you've found out? Dr. Rank—tell me!

RANK [*sits down by the stove*]: I'm going downhill fast. There's nothing to do about that.

NORA [*with audible relief*]: So it's *you*—

RANK: Who else? No point in lying to myself. I'm in worse shape than any of my other patients, Mrs. Helmer. These last few days I've been making up my inner status. Bankrupt. Chances are that within a month I'll be rotting up in the cemetery.

NORA: Shame on you! Talking that horrid way!

RANK: The thing itself is horrid—damn horrid. The worst of it, though, is all that other horror that comes first. There is only one more test I need to make. After that I'll have a pretty good idea when I'll start coming apart. There is something I want to say to you. Helmer's refined nature can't stand anything hideous. I don't want him in my sick room.

NORA: Oh, but Dr. Rank—

RANK: I don't want him there. Under no circumstance. I'll close my door to him. As soon as I have full certainty that the worst is about to begin I'll give you my card with a black cross on it. Then you'll know the last horror of destruction has started.

NORA: Today you're really quite impossible. And I had hoped you'd be in a particularly good mood.

RANK: With death on my hands? Paying for someone else's sins? Is there justice in that? And yet there isn't a single family that isn't ruled by that same law of ruthless retribution, in one way or another.

NORA [*puts her hands over her ears*]: Poppycock! Be fun! Be fun!

RANK: Well, yes. You may just as well laugh at the whole thing. My poor, innocent spine is suffering for my father's frolics as a young lieutenant.

NORA [*over by the table, left*]: Right. He was addicted to asparagus and goose liver paté, wasn't he?

RANK: And truffles.

NORA: Of course. Truffles. And oysters too, I think.

RANK: And oysters. Obviously.

NORA: And all the port and champagne that go with it. It's really too bad that goodies like that ruin your backbone.

RANK: Particularly an unfortunate backbone that never enjoyed any of it.

NORA: Ah yes, that's the saddest part of it all.

RANK [*looks searchingly at her*]: Hm—

NORA [*after a brief pause*]: Why did you smile just then?

RANK: No, it was you that laughed.

NORA: No, it was you that smiled, Dr. Rank!

RANK [*gets up*]: You're more of a mischief-maker than I thought.

NORA: I feel in the mood for mischief today.

RANK: So it seems.

NORA [*with both her hands on his shoulders*]: Dear, dear Dr. Rank, don't you go and die and leave Torvald and me.

RANK: Oh, you won't miss me for very long. Those who go away are soon forgotten.

NORA [*with an anxious look*]: Do you believe that?

RANK: You'll make new friends, and then—

NORA: Who'll make new friends?

RANK: Both you and Helmer, once I'm gone. You yourself seem to have made a good start already. What was this Mrs. Linde doing here last night?

NORA: Aha—Don't tell me you're jealous of poor Kristine?

RANK: Yes, I am. She'll be my successor in this house. As soon as I have made my excuses, that woman is likely to—

NORA: Shh—not so loud. She's in there.

RANK: Today too? There you are!

NORA: She's mending my costume. My God, you really *are* unreasonable. [*Sits down on the couch.*] Now be nice, Dr. Rank. Tomorrow you'll see how beautifully I'll dance, and then you are to pretend I'm dancing just for you—and for Torvald too, of course. [*Takes several items out of the carton.*] Sit down, Dr. Rank; I want to show you something.

RANK [*sitting down*]: What?

NORA: Look.

RANK: Silk stockings.

NORA: Flesh-colored. Aren't they lovely? Now it's getting dark in here, but tomorrow—No, no. You only get to see the foot. Oh well, you might as well see all of it.

RANK: Hmm.

NORA: Why do you look so critical? Don't you think they'll fit?

RANK: That's something I can't possibly have a reasoned opinion about.

NORA [*looks at him for a moment*]: Shame on you. [*Slaps his ear lightly with the stocking.*] That's what you get. [*Puts the things back in the carton.*]

RANK: And what other treasures are you going to show me?

NORA: Nothing at all, because you're naughty. [*She hums a little and rummages in the carton.*]

RANK [*after a brief silence*]: When I sit here like this, talking confidently with you, I can't imagine—I can't possibly imagine what would have become of me if I hadn't had you and Helmer.

NORA [*smiles*]: Well, yes—I do believe you like being with us.

RANK [*in a lower voice, lost in thought*]: And then to have to go away from it all—

NORA: Nonsense. You are not going anywhere.

RANK [*as before*]: —and not to leave behind as much as a poor little token of gratitude, hardly a brief memory of someone missed, nothing but a vacant place that anyone can fill.

NORA: And what if I were to ask you—? No—

RANK: Ask me what?

NORA: For a great proof of your friendship—

RANK: Yes, yes—?

NORA: No, I mean—for an enormous favor—

RANK: Would you really for once make me as happy as all that?

NORA: But you don't even know what it is.

RANK: Well, then; tell me.

NORA: Oh, but I can't, Dr. Rank. It's altogether too much to ask—It's advice and help and a favor—

RANK: So much the better. I can't even begin to guess what it is you have in mind. So for heaven's sake tell me! Don't you trust me?

NORA: Yes, I trust you more than anyone else I know. You are my best and most faithful friend. I know that. So I will tell you. All right, Dr. Rank. There is something you can help me prevent. You know how much Torvald loves me—beyond all words. Never for a moment would he hesitate to give his life for me.

RANK [*leaning over to her*]: Nora—do you really think he's the only one—?

NORA [*with a slight start*]: Who—?

RANK: —would gladly give his life for you.

NORA [*heavily*]: I see.

RANK: I have sworn an oath to myself to tell you before I go. I'll never find a better occasion.—All right, Nora; now you know. And now you also know that you can confide in me more than in anyone else.

NORA [*gets up; in a calm, steady voice*]: Let me get by.

RANK [*makes room for her but remains seated*]: Nora—

NORA [*in the door to the front hall*]: Helene, bring the lamp in here, please. [*Walks over to the stove.*] Oh, dear Dr. Rank. That really wasn't very nice of you.

RANK [*gets up*]: That I have loved you as much as anybody—was that not nice?

NORA: No, not that. But that you told me. There was no need for that.

RANK: What do you mean? Have you known—?

[*The* MAID *enters with the lamp, puts it on the table, and goes out.*]

RANK: Nora—Mrs. Helmer—I'm asking you: did you know?

NORA: Oh, how can I tell what I knew and didn't know! I really can't say—But that you could be so awkward, Dr. Rank! Just when everything was so comfortable.

RANK: Well, anyway, now you know that I'm at your service with my life and soul. And now you must speak.

NORA [*looks at him*]: After what just happened?

RANK: I beg of you—let me know what it is.

NORA: There is nothing I can tell you now.

RANK: Yes, yes. You mustn't punish me this way. Please let me do for you whatever anyone *can* do.

NORA: Now there is nothing you can do. Besides, I don't think I really need any help, anyway. It's probably just my imagination. Of course that's all it is. I'm sure of it! [*Sits down in the rocking chair, looks at him, smiles.*] Well, well, well, Dr. Rank! What a fine gentleman you turned out to be! Aren't you ashamed of yourself, now that we have light?

RANK: No, not really. But perhaps I ought to leave—and not come back?

NORA: Don't be silly; of course not! You'll come here exactly as you have been doing. You know perfectly well that Torvald can't do without you.

RANK: Yes, but what about you?

NORA: Oh, I always think it's perfectly delightful when you come.

RANK: That's the very thing that misled me: You are a riddle to me. It has often seemed to me that you'd just as soon be with me as with Helmer.

NORA: Well, you see, there are people you love, and then there are other people you'd almost rather be with.

RANK: Yes, there is something in that.

NORA: When I lived at home with Daddy, of course I loved him most. But I always thought it was so much fun to sneak off down to the maids' room, for they never gave me good advice and they always talked about such fun things.

RANK: Aha! So it's *their* place I have taken.

NORA [*jumps up and goes over to him*]: Oh dear, kind Dr. Rank, you know very well I didn't mean it that way. Can't you see that with Torvald it is the way it used to be with Daddy?

[*The* MAID *enters from the front hall.*]

MAID: Ma'am! [*Whispers to her and gives her a caller's card.*]

NORA [*glances at the card*]: Ah! [*Puts it in her pocket.*]

RANK: Anything wrong?

NORA: No, no; not at all. It's nothing—just my new costume—

RANK: But your costume is lying right there!

NORA: Oh yes, that one. But this is another one. I ordered it. Torvald mustn't know—

RANK: Aha. So that's the great secret.

NORA: That's it. Why don't you go in to him, please. He's in the inner office. And keep him there for a while—

RANK: Don't worry. He won't get away. [*Enters* HELMER*'s study.*]

NORA [*to the* MAID]: You say he's waiting in the kitchen?

MAID: Yes. He came up the back stairs.

NORA: But didn't you tell him there was somebody with me?

MAID: Yes, but he wouldn't listen.

NORA: He won't leave?

MAID: No, not till he's had a word with you, ma'am.

NORA: All right. But try not to make any noise. And, Helene—don't tell anyone he's here. It's supposed to be a surprise for my husband.

MAID: I understand, ma'am—[*She leaves.*]

NORA: The terrible is happening. It's happening, after all. No, no, no. It can't happen. It won't happen. [*She bolts the study door.*]

[*The* MAID *opens the front hall door for* KROGSTAD *and closes the door behind him. He wears a fur coat for traveling, boots, and a fur hat.*]

NORA [*toward him*]: Keep your voice down. My husband's home.

KROGSTAD: That's all right.

NORA: What do you want?

KROGSTAD: To find out something.

NORA: Be quick, then. What is it?

KROGSTAD: I expect you know I've been fired.

NORA: I couldn't prevent it, Mr. Krogstad. I fought for you as long and as hard as I could, but it didn't do any good.

KROGSTAD: Your husband doesn't love you any more than that? He knows what I can do to you, and yet he runs the risk—

NORA: Surely you didn't think I'd tell him?

KROGSTAD: No, I really didn't. It wouldn't be like Torvald Helmer to show that kind of guts—

NORA: Mr. Krogstad, I insist that you show respect for my husband.

KROGSTAD: By all means. All due respect. But since you're so anxious to keep this a secret, may I assume that you are a little better informed than yesterday about exactly what you have done?

NORA: Better than *you* could ever teach me.

KROGSTAD: Of course. Such a bad lawyer as I am—

NORA: What do you want of me?

KROGSTAD: I just wanted to find out how you are, Mrs. Helmer. I've been thinking about you all day. You see, even a bill collector, a pen pusher, a—anyway, someone like me—even he has a little of what they call a heart.

NORA: Then show it. Think of my little children.

KROGSTAD: Have you and your husband thought of mine? Never mind. All I want to tell you is that you don't need to take this business too seriously. I have no intention of bringing charges right away.

NORA: Oh no, you wouldn't; would you? I knew you wouldn't.

KROGSTAD: The whole thing can be settled quite amiably. Nobody else needs to know anything. It will be between the three of us.

NORA: My husband must never find out about this.

KROGSTAD: How are you going to prevent that? Maybe you can pay me the balance on the loan?

NORA: No, not right now.

KROGSTAD: Or do you have a way of raising the money one of these next few days?

NORA: None I intend to make use of.

KROGSTAD: It wouldn't do you any good, anyway. Even if you had the cash in your hand right this minute, I wouldn't give you your note back. It wouldn't make any difference *how* much money you offered me.

NORA: Then you'll have to tell me what you plan to use the note *for.*

KROGSTAD: Just keep it; that's all. Have it on hand, so to speak. I won't say a word to anybody else. So if you've been thinking about doing something desperate—

NORA: I have.

KROGSTAD: —like leaving house and home—

NORA: I have!

KROGSTAD: —or even something worse—

NORA: How did you know?

KROGSTAD: —then: don't.

NORA: How did you know I was thinking of *that?*

KROGSTAD: Most of us do, right at first. I did, too, but when it came down to it I didn't have the courage—

NORA [*tonelessly*]: Nor do I.

KROGSTAD [*relieved*]: See what I mean? I thought so. You don't either.

NORA: I don't. I don't.

KROGSTAD: Besides, it would be very silly of you. Once that first domestic blow-up is behind you—. Here in my pocket is a letter for your husband.

NORA: Telling him everything?

KROGSTAD: As delicately as possible.

NORA [*quickly*]: He mustn't get that letter. Tear it up. I'll get you the money somehow.

KROGSTAD: Excuse me, Mrs. Helmer. I thought I just told you—

NORA: I'm not talking about the money I owe you. Just let me know how much money you want from my husband, and I'll get it for you.

KROGSTAD: I want no money from your husband.

NORA: Then, what *do* you want?

KROGSTAD: I'll tell you, Mrs. Helmer. I want to rehabilitate myself; I want to get up in the world; and your husband is going to help me. For a year and a half I haven't done anything disreputable. All that time I have been struggling with the most miserable circumstances. I was content to work my way up step by step. Now I've been kicked out, and I'm no longer satisfied just getting my old job back. I want more than that; I want to get to the top. I'm being quite serious. I want the bank to take me back but in a higher position. I want your husband to create a new job for me—

NORA: He'll never do that!

KROGSTAD: He will. I know him. He won't dare not to. And once I'm back inside and he and I are working together, you'll see! Within a year I'll be the manager's right hand. It will be Nils Krogstad and not Torvald Helmer who'll be running the Mutual Bank!

NORA: You'll never see that happen!

KROGSTAD: Are you thinking of—?

NORA: Now I *do* have the courage.

KROGSTAD: You can't scare me. A fine, spoiled lady like you—

NORA: You'll see, you'll see!

KROGSTAD: Under the ice, perhaps? Down into that cold, black water? Then spring comes, and you float up again—hideous, can't be identified, hair all gone—

NORA: You don't frighten me.

KROGSTAD: Nor you me. One doesn't do that sort of thing, Mrs. Helmer. Besides, what good would it do? He'd still be in my power.

NORA: Afterwards? When I'm no longer—?

KROGSTAD: Aren't you forgetting that your reputation would be in my hands?

[NORA *stares at him, speechless.*]

KROGSTAD: All right; now I've told you what to expect. So don't do anything foolish. When Helmer gets my letter I expect to hear from him. And don't you forget that it's your husband himself who forces me to use such means again. That I'll never forgive him. Goodbye, Mrs. Helmer. [*Goes out through the hall.*]

NORA [*at the door, opens it a little, listens*]: He's going. And no letter. Of course not! That would be impossible! [*Opens the door more.*] What's he doing? He's still there. Doesn't go down. Having second thoughts—? Will he—?

[*The sound of a letter dropping into the mailbox. Then* KROGSTAD's *steps are heard going down the stairs, gradually dying away.*]

NORA [*with a muted cry runs forward to the table by the couch; brief pause*]: In the mailbox. [*Tiptoes back to the door to the front hall.*] There it is. Torvald, Torvald—now we're lost!

MRS. LINDE [*enters from the left, carrying* NORA's *Capri costume*]: There now. I think it's all fixed. Why don't we try it on you—

NORA [*in a low, hoarse voice*]: Kristine, come here.

MRS. LINDE: What's wrong with you? You look quite beside yourself.

NORA: Come over here. Do you see that letter? There, look—through the glass in the mailbox.

MRS. LINDE: Yes, yes; I see it.

NORA: That letter is from Krogstad.

MRS. LINDE: Nora—it was Krogstad who lent you the money!

NORA: Yes, and now Torvald will find out about it.

MRS. LINDE: Oh believe me, Nora. That's the best thing for both of you.

NORA: There's more to it than you know. I forged a signature—

MRS. LINDE: Oh my God—!

NORA: I just want to tell you this, Kristine, that you must be my witness.

MRS. LINDE: Witness? How? Witness to what?

NORA: If I lose my mind—and that could very well happen—

MRS. LINDE: Nora!

NORA: —or if something were to happen to me—something that made it impossible for me to be here—

MRS. LINDE: Nora, Nora! You're not yourself!

NORA: —and if someone were to take all the blame, assume the whole responsibility— Do you understand—?

MRS. LINDE: Yes, yes; but how can you think—!

NORA: —then you are to witness that that's not so, Kristine. I am not beside myself. I am perfectly rational, and what I'm telling you is that nobody else has known about this. I've done it all by myself, the whole thing. Just remember that.

MRS. LINDE: I will. But I don't understand any of it.

NORA: Oh, how could you! For it's the wonderful that's about to happen.

MRS. LINDE: The wonderful?

NORA: Yes, the wonderful. But it's so terrible, Kristine. It mustn't happen for anything in the whole world!

MRS. LINDE: I'm going over to talk to Krogstad right now.

NORA: No, don't. Don't go to him. He'll do something bad to you.

MRS. LINDE: There was a time when he would have done anything for me.

NORA: He!

MRS. LINDE: Where does he live?

NORA: Oh, I don't know—Yes, wait a minute—[Reaches into her pocket.] here's his card.—But the letter, the letter—!

HELMER [in his study, knocks on the door]: Nora!

NORA [cries out in fear]: Oh, what is it? What do you want?

HELMER: That's all right. Nothing to be scared about. We're not coming in. For one thing, you've bolted the door, you know. Are you modeling your costume?

NORA: Yes, yes; I am. I'm going to be so pretty, Torvald.

MRS. LINDE [having looked at the card]: He lives just around the corner.

NORA: Yes, but it's no use. Nothing can save us now. The letter is in the mailbox.

MRS. LINDE: And your husband has the key?

NORA: Yes. He always keeps it with him.

MRS. LINDE: Krogstad must ask for his letter back, unread. He's got to think up some pretext or other—

NORA: But this is just the time of day when Torvald—

MRS. LINDE: Delay him. Go in to him. I'll be back as soon as I can. [She hurries out through the hall door.]

NORA [walks over to HELMER's door, opens it, and peeks in]: Torvald!

HELMER [*still offstage*]: Well, well! So now one's allowed in one's own living room again. Come on, Rank. Now we'll see—[*In the doorway.*] But what's this?

NORA: What, Torvald dear?

HELMER: Rank prepared me for a splendid metamorphosis.

RANK [*in the doorway*]: That's how I understood it. Evidently I was mistaken.

NORA: Nobody gets to admire me in my costume before tomorrow.

HELMER: But, dearest Nora—you look all done in. Have you been practicing too hard?

NORA: No, I haven't practiced at all.

HELMER: But you'll have to, you know.

NORA: I know it, Torvald. I simply must. But I can't do a thing unless you help me. I have forgotten everything.

HELMER: Oh it will all come back. We'll work on it.

NORA: Oh yes, please, Torvald. You just have to help me. Promise? I am so nervous. That big party—. You mustn't do anything else tonight. Not a bit of business. Don't even touch a pen. Will you promise, Torvald?

HELMER: I promise. Tonight I'll be entirely at your service—you helpless little thing.—Just a moment, though. First I want to—[*Goes to the door to the front hall.*]

NORA: What are you doing out there?

HELMER: Just looking to see if there's any mail.

NORA: No, no! Don't, Torvald!

HELMER: Why not?

NORA: Torvald, I beg you. There is no mail.

HELMER: Let me just look, anyway. [*Is about to go out.*]

[NORA *by the piano, plays the first bars of the tarantella dance.*]

HELMER [*halts at the door*]: Aha!

NORA: I won't be able to dance tomorrow if I don't get to practice with you.

HELMER [*goes to her*]: Are you really all that scared, Nora dear?

NORA: Yes, so terribly scared. Let's try it right now. There's still time before we eat. Oh please, sit down and play for me, Torvald. Teach me, coach me, the way you always do.

HELMER: Of course I will, my darling, if that's what you want. [*Sits down at the piano.*]

[NORA *takes the tambourine out of the carton, as well as a long, many-colored shawl. She quickly drapes the shawl around herself, then leaps into the middle of the floor.*]

NORA: Play for me! I want to dance!

[HELMER *plays and* NORA *dances.* DR. RANK *stands by the piano behind* HELMER *and watches.*]

HELMER [*playing*]: Slow down, slow down!

NORA: Can't!

HELMER: Not so violent, Nora!

NORA: It has to be this way.

HELMER [*stops playing*]: No, no. This won't do at all.

NORA [*laughing, swinging her tambourine*]: What did I tell you?

RANK: Why don't you let me play?

HELMER [*getting up*]: Good idea. Then I can direct her better.

[RANK *sits down at the piano and starts playing.* NORA *dances more and more wildly.* HELMER *stands over by the stove, repeatedly correcting her. She doesn't seem to hear. Her hair comes loose and falls down over her shoulders. She doesn't notice but keeps on dancing.* MRS. LINDE *enters.*]

MRS. LINDE [*stops by the door, dumbfounded*]: Ah—!

NORA [*dancing*]: We're having such fun, Kristine!

HELMER: My dearest Nora, you're dancing as if it were a matter of life and death!

NORA: It is! It is!

HELMER: Rank, stop. This is sheer madness. Stop, I say!

[RANK *stops playing;* NORA *suddenly stops dancing.*]

HELMER [*goes over to her*]: If I hadn't seen it I wouldn't have believed it. You've forgotten every single thing I ever taught you.

NORA [*tosses away the tambourine*]: See? I told you.

HELMER: Well! You certainly need coaching.

NORA: Didn't I tell you I did? Now you've seen for yourself. I'll need your help till the very minute we're leaving for the party. Will you promise, Torvald?

HELMER: You can count on it.

NORA: You're not to think of anything except me—not tonight and not tomorrow. You're not to read any letters—not to look in the mailbox—

HELMER: Ah, I see. You're still afraid of that man.

NORA: Yes—yes, that too.

HELMER: Nora, I can tell from looking at you. There's a letter from him out there.

NORA: I don't know. I think so. But you're not to read it now. I don't want anything ugly to come between us before it's all over.

RANK [*to* HELMER *in a low voice*]: Better not argue with her.

HELMER [*throws his arm around her*]: The child shall have her way. But tomorrow night, when you've done your dance—

NORA: Then you'll be free.

MAID [*in the door, right*]: Dinner can be served any time, ma'am.

NORA: We want champagne, Helene.

MAID: Very good, ma'am. [*Goes out.*]

HELMER: Aha! Having a party, eh?

NORA: Champagne from now till sunrise! [*Calls out.*] And some macaroons, Helene. Lots!—just this once.

HELMER [*taking her hands*]: There, there—I don't like this wild—frenzy—Be my own sweet little lark again, the way you always are.

NORA: Oh, I will. But you go on in. You too, Dr. Rank. Kristine, please help me put up my hair.

RANK [*in a low voice to* HELMER *as they go out*]: You don't think she is—you know—expecting—?

HELMER: Oh no. Nothing like that. It's just this childish fear I was telling you about. [*They go out, right.*]

NORA: Well?

MRS. LINDE: Left town.

NORA: I saw it in your face.

MRS. LINDE: He'll be back tomorrow night. I left him a note.

NORA: You shouldn't have. I don't want you to try to stop anything. You see, it's a kind of ecstasy, too, this waiting for the wonderful.

MRS. LINDE: But what is it you're waiting *for?*

NORA: You wouldn't understand. Why don't you go in to the others. I'll be there in a minute.

[MRS. LINDE *enters the dining room, right.*]

NORA [*stands still for a little while, as if collecting herself; she looks at her watch*]: Five o'clock. Seven hours till midnight. Twenty-four more hours till next midnight. Then the tarantella is over. Twenty-four plus seven—thirty-one more hours to live.

HELMER [*in the door, right*]: What's happening to my little lark?

NORA [*to him, with open arms*]: Here's your lark!

ACT III

The same room. The table by the couch and the chairs around it have been moved to the middle of the floor. A lighted lamp is on the table. The door to the front hall is open. Dance music is heard from upstairs.

MRS. LINDE *is seated by the table, idly leafing through the pages of a book. She tries to read but seems unable to concentrate. Once or twice she turns her head in the direction of the door, anxiously listening.*

MRS. LINDE [*looks at her watch*]: Not yet. It's almost too late. If only he hasn't—[*Listens again.*] Ah! There he is. [*She goes to the hall and opens the front door carefully. Quiet footsteps on the stairs. She whispers.*] Come in. There's nobody here.

KROGSTAD [*in the door*]: I found your note when I got home. What's this all about?

MRS. LINDE: I've got to talk to you.

KROGSTAD: Oh? And it has to be here?

MRS. LINDE: It couldn't be at my place. My room doesn't have a separate entrance. Come in. We're quite alone. The maid is asleep and the Helmers are at a party upstairs.

KROGSTAD [*entering*]: Really? The Helmers are dancing tonight, are they?

MRS. LINDE: And why not?

KROGSTAD: You're right. Why not, indeed.

MRS. LINDE: All right, Krogstad. Let's talk, you and I.

KROGSTAD: I didn't know we had anything to talk about.

MRS. LINDE: We have much to talk about.

KROGSTAD: I didn't think so.

MRS. LINDE: No, because you've never really understood me.

KROGSTAD: What was there to understand? What happened was perfectly common-place. A heartless woman jilts a man when she gets a more attractive offer.

MRS. LINDE: Do you think I'm all that heartless? And do you think it was easy for me to break with you?

KROGSTAD: No?

MRS. LINDE: You really thought it was?

KROGSTAD: If it wasn't, why did you write the way you did that time?

MRS. LINDE: What else could I do? If I had to make a break, I also had the duty to destroy whatever feelings you had for me.

KROGSTAD [*clenching his hands*]: So that's the way it was. And you did—*that*—just for money!

MRS. LINDE: Don't forget I had a helpless mother and two small brothers. We couldn't wait for you, Krogstad. You know yourself how uncertain your prospects were then.

KROGSTAD: All right. But you still didn't have the right to throw me over for some-body else.

MRS. LINDE: I don't know. I have asked myself that question many times. Did I have that right?

KROGSTAD [*in a lower voice*]: When I lost you I lost my footing. Look at me now. A shipwrecked man on a raft.

MRS. LINDE: Rescue may be near.

KROGSTAD: It *was* near. Then you came between.

MRS. LINDE: I didn't know that, Krogstad. Only today did I find out it's your job I'm taking over in the bank.

KROGSTAD: I believe you when you say so. But now that you *do* know, aren't you going to step aside?

MRS. LINDE: No, for it wouldn't do you any good.

KROGSTAD: Whether it would or not—*I* would do it.

MRS. LINDE: I have learned common sense. Life and hard necessity have taught me that.

KROGSTAD: And life has taught me not to believe in pretty speeches.

MRS. LINDE: Then life has taught you a very sensible thing. But you do believe in actions, don't you?

KROGSTAD: How do you mean?

MRS. LINDE: You referred to yourself just now as a shipwrecked man.

KROGSTAD: It seems to me I had every reason to do so.

MRS. LINDE: And I am a shipwrecked woman. No one to grieve for, no one to care for.

KROGSTAD: You made your choice.

MRS. LINDE: I had no other choice that time.

KROGSTAD: Let's say you didn't. What then?

MRS. LINDE: Krogstad, how would it be if we two shipwrecked people got together?

KROGSTAD: What's this!

MRS. LINDE: Two on one wreck are better off than each on his own.

KROGSTAD: Kristine!

MRS. LINDE: Why do you think I came to town?

KROGSTAD: Surely not because of me?

MRS. LINDE: If I'm going to live at all I must work. All my life, for as long as I can remember, I have worked. That's been my one and only pleasure. But now that I'm all alone in the world I feel nothing but this terrible emptiness and desolation. There is no joy in working just for yourself. Krogstad—give me someone and something to work for.

KROGSTAD: I don't believe this. Only hysterical females go in for that kind of high-minded self-sacrifice.

MRS. LINDE: Did you ever know me to be hysterical?

KROGSTAD: You really could do this? Listen—do you know about my past? All of it?

MRS. LINDE: Yes, I do.

KROGSTAD: Do you also know what people think of me around here?

MRS. LINDE: A little while ago you sounded as if you thought that together with me you might have become a different person.

KROGSTAD: I'm sure of it.

MRS. LINDE: Couldn't that still be?

KROGSTAD: Kristine—do you know what you are doing? Yes, I see you do. And you think you have the courage—?

MRS. LINDE: I need someone to be a mother to, and your children need a mother. You and I need one another. Nils, I believe in you—in the real you. Together with you I dare to do anything.

KROGSTAD [*seizes her hands*]: Thanks, thanks, Kristine—now I know I'll raise myself in the eyes of others.—Ah, but I forget—!

MRS. LINDE [*listening*]: Shh!—There's the tarantella. You must go; hurry!

KROGSTAD: Why? What is it?

MRS. LINDE: Do you hear what they're playing up there? When that dance is over they'll be down.

KROGSTAD: All right. I'm leaving. The whole thing is pointless, anyway. Of course you don't know what I'm doing to the Helmers.

MRS. LINDE: Yes, Krogstad; I do know.

KROGSTAD: Still, you're brave enough—?

MRS. LINDE: I very well understand to what extremes despair can drive a man like you.

KROGSTAD: If only it could be undone!

MRS. LINDE: It could, for your letter is still out there in the mailbox.

KROGSTAD: Are you sure?

MRS. LINDE: Quite sure. But—

KROGSTAD [*looks searchingly at her*]: Maybe I'm beginning to understand. You want to save your friend at any cost. Be honest with me. That's it, isn't it?

MRS. LINDE: Krogstad, you may sell yourself once for somebody else's sake, but you don't do it twice.

KROGSTAD: I'll demand my letter back.

MRS. LINDE: No, no.

KROGSTAD: Yes, of course. I'll wait here till Helmer comes down. Then I'll ask him for my letter. I'll tell him it's just about my dismissal—that he shouldn't read it.

MRS. LINDE: No, Krogstad. You are not to ask for that letter back.

KROGSTAD: But tell me—wasn't that the real reason you wanted to meet me here?

MRS. LINDE: At first it was, because I was so frightened. But that was yesterday. Since then I have seen the most incredible things going on in this house. Helmer must learn the whole truth. This miserable secret must come out in the open; those two must come to a full understanding. They simply can't continue with all this concealment and evasion.

KROGSTAD: All right; if you want to take that chance. But there is one thing I *can* do, and I'll do that right now.

MRS. LINDE [*listening*]: But hurry! Go! The dance is over. We aren't safe another minute.

KROGSTAD: I'll be waiting for you downstairs.

MRS. LINDE: Yes, do. You must see me home.

KROGSTAD: I've never been so happy in my whole life. [*He leaves through the front door. The door between the living room and the front hall remains open.*]

MRS. LINDE [*straightens up the room a little and gets her things ready*]: What a change! Oh yes!—what a change! People to work for—to live for—a home to bring happiness to. I can't wait to get to work—! If only they'd come soon—[*Listens.*] Ah, there they are. Get my coat on—[*Puts on her coat and hat.*]

[HELMER'S *and* NORA'S *voices are heard outside. A key is turned in the lock, and* HELMER *almost forces* NORA *into the hall. She is dressed in her Italian costume, with a big black shawl over her shoulders. He is in evening dress under an open black cloak.*]

NORA [*in the door, still resisting*]: No, no, no! I don't want to! I want to go back upstairs. I don't want to leave so early.

HELMER: But dearest Nora—

NORA: Oh please, Torvald—please! I'm asking you as nicely as I can—just another hour!

HELMER: Not another minute, sweet. You know we agreed. There now. Get inside. You'll catch a cold out here. [*She still resists, but he guides her gently into the room.*]

MRS. LINDE: Good evening.

NORA: Kristine!

HELMER: Ah, Mrs. Linde. Still here?

MRS. LINDE: I know. I really should apologize, but I so much wanted to see Nora in her costume.

NORA: You've been waiting up for me?

MRS. LINDE: Yes, unfortunately I didn't get here in time. You were already upstairs, but I just didn't feel like leaving till I had seen you.

HELMER [*removing* NORA'S *shawl*]: Yes, do take a good look at her, Mrs. Linde. I think I may say she's worth looking at. Isn't she lovely?

MRS. LINDE: She certainly is—

HELMER: Isn't she a miracle of loveliness, though? That was the general opinion at the party, too. But dreadfully obstinate—that she is, the sweet little thing. What can we do about that? Will you believe it—I practically had to use force to get her away.

NORA: Oh Torvald, you're going to be sorry you didn't give me even half an hour more.

HELMER: See what I mean, Mrs. Linde? She dances the tarantella—she is a tremendous success—quite deservedly so, though perhaps her performance was a little too natural—I mean, more than could be reconciled with the rules of art. But all right! The point is: she's a success, a tremendous success. So should I let her stay after that? Weaken the effect? Of course not. So I take my lovely little Capri girl—I might say, my capricious little Capri girl—under my arm—a quick turn around the room—a graceful bow in all directions, and—as they say in the novels—the beautiful apparition is gone. A finale should always be done for effect, Mrs. Linde, but there doesn't seem to be any way of getting that into Nora's head. Poooh—! It's hot in here. [*Throws his cloak down on a chair and opens the door to his room.*] Why, it's dark in here! Of course. Excuse me—[*Goes inside and lights a couple of candles.*]

NORA [*in a hurried, breathless whisper*]: Well?

MRS. LINDE [*in a low voice*]: I have talked to him.

NORA: And—?

MRS. LINDE: Nora—you've got to tell your husband everything.

NORA [*no expression in her voice*]: I knew it.

MRS. LINDE: You have nothing to fear from Krogstad. But you must speak.

NORA: I'll say nothing.

MRS. LINDE: Then the letter will.

NORA: Thank you, Kristine. Now I know what I have to do. Shh!

HELMER [*returning*]: Well, Mrs. Linde, have you looked your fill?

MRS. LINDE: Yes. And now I'll say goodnight.

HELMER: So soon? Is that your knitting?

MRS. LINDE [*takes it*]: Yes, thank you. I almost forgot.

HELMER: So you knit, do you?

MRS. LINDE: Oh yes.

HELMER: You know—you ought to take up embroidery instead.

MRS. LINDE: Oh? Why?

HELMER: Because it's so much more beautiful. Look. You hold the embroidery so—in your left hand. Then with your right you move the needle—like this—in an easy, elongated arc—you see?

MRS. LINDE: Maybe you're right—

HELMER: Knitting, on the other hand, can never be anything but ugly. Look here: arms pressed close to the sides—the needles going up and down—there's something Chinese about it somehow—. That really was an excellent champagne they served us tonight.

MRS. LINDE: Well, goodnight, Nora. And don't be obstinate any more.

HELMER: Well said, Mrs. Linde!

MRS. LINDE: Goodnight, sir.

HELMER [*sees her to the front door*]: Goodnight, goodnight. I hope you'll get home all right? I'd be very glad to—but of course you don't have far to walk, do you? Goodnight, goodnight. [*She leaves. He closes the door behind her and returns to the living room.*] There! At last we got rid of her. She really is an incredible bore, that woman.

NORA: Aren't you very tired, Torvald?

HELMER: No, not in the least.

NORA: Not sleepy either?

HELMER: Not at all. Quite the opposite. I feel enormously—animated. How about you? Yes, you do look tired and sleepy.

NORA: Yes, I am very tired. Soon I'll be asleep.

HELMER: What did I tell you? I was right, wasn't I? Good thing I didn't let you stay any longer.

NORA: Everything you do is right.

HELMER [*kissing her forehead*]: Now my little lark is talking like a human being. But did you notice what splendid spirits Rank was in tonight?

NORA: Was he? I didn't notice. I didn't get to talk with him.

HELMER: Nor did I—hardly. But I haven't seen him in such a good mood for a long time. [*Looks at her, comes closer to her.*] Ah! It does feel good to be back in our own home again, to be quite alone with you—my young, lovely, ravishing woman!

NORA: Don't look at me like that, Torvald!

HELMER: Am I not to look at my most precious possession? All that loveliness that is mine, nobody's but mine, all of it mine.

NORA [*walks to the other side of the table*]: I won't have you talk to me like that tonight.

HELMER [*follows her*]: The tarantella is still in your blood. I can tell. That only makes you all the more alluring. Listen! The guests are beginning to leave. [*Softly.*] Nora— soon the whole house will be quiet.

NORA: Yes, I hope so.

HELMER: Yes, don't you, my darling? Do you know—when I'm at a party with you, like tonight—do you know why I hardly ever talk to you, why I keep away from you, only look at you once in a while—a few stolen glances—do you know why I do that? It's because I pretend that you are my secret love, my young, secret bride-to-be, and nobody has the slightest suspicion that there is anything between us.

NORA: Yes, I know. All your thoughts are with me.

HELMER: Then when we're leaving and I lay your shawl around your delicate young shoulders—around that wonderful curve of your neck—then I imagine you're my young bride, that we're coming away from the wedding, that I am taking you to my home for the first time—that I am alone with you for the first time—quite alone with you, you young, trembling beauty! I have desired you all evening—there hasn't been a longing in me that hasn't been for you. When you were dancing the tarantella, chasing, inviting—my blood was on fire; I couldn't stand it any longer—that's why I brought you down so early—

NORA: Leave me now, Torvald. Please! I don't want all this.

HELMER: What do you mean? You're only playing your little teasing bird game with me; aren't you, Nora? Don't want to? I'm your husband, aren't I?

[*There is a knock on the front door.*]

NORA [*with a start*]: Did you hear that—?

HELMER [*on his way to the hall*]: Who is it?

RANK [*outside*]: It's me. May I come in for a moment?

HELMER [*in a low voice, annoyed*]: Oh, what does he want now? [*Aloud.*] Just a minute. [*Opens the door.*] Well! How good of you not to pass by our door.

RANK: I thought I heard your voice, so I felt like saying hello. [*Looks around.*] Ah yes—this dear, familiar room. What a cozy, comfortable place you have here, you two.

HELMER: Looked to me as if you were quite comfortable upstairs too.

RANK: I certainly was. Why not? Why not enjoy all you can in this world? As much as you can for as long as you can, anyway. Excellent wine.

HELMER: The champagne, particularly.

RANK: You noticed that too? Incredible how much I managed to put away.

NORA: Torvald drank a lot of champagne tonight, too.

RANK: Did he?

NORA: Yes, he did, and then he's always so much fun afterwards.

RANK: Well, why not have some fun in the evening after a well spent day?

HELMER: Well spent? I'm afraid I can't claim that.

RANK [*slapping him lightly on the shoulder*]: But you see, I can!

NORA: Dr. Rank, I believe you must have been conducting a scientific test today.

RANK: Exactly.

HELMER: What do you know—little Nora talking about scientific tests!

NORA: May I congratulate you on the result?

RANK: You may indeed.

NORA: It was a good one?

RANK: The best possible for both doctor and patient—certainty.

NORA [*a quick query*]: Certainty?

RANK: Absolute certainty. So why shouldn't I have myself an enjoyable evening afterwards?

NORA: I quite agree with you, Dr. Rank. You should.

HELMER: And so do I. If only you don't pay for it tomorrow.

RANK: Oh well—you get nothing for nothing in this world.

NORA: Dr. Rank—you are fond of costume parties, aren't you?

RANK: Yes, particularly when there is a reasonable number of amusing disguises.

NORA: Listen—what are the two of us going to be the next time?

HELMER: You frivolous little thing! Already thinking about the next party!

RANK: You and I? That's easy. You'll be Fortune's Child.

HELMER: Yes, but what is a fitting costume for that?

RANK: Let your wife appear just the way she always is.

HELMER: Beautiful. Very good indeed. But how about yourself? Don't you know what you'll go as?

RANK: Yes, my friend. I know precisely what I'll be.

HELMER: Yes?

RANK: At the next masquerade I'll be invisible.

HELMER: That's a funny idea.

RANK: There's a certain black hat—you've heard about the hat that makes you invisible, haven't you? You put that on, and nobody can see you.

HELMER [*suppressing a smile*]: I guess that's right.

RANK: But I'm forgetting what I came for. Helmer, give me a cigar—one of your dark Havanas.

HELMER: With the greatest pleasure. [*Offers him his case.*]

RANK [*takes one and cuts off the tip*]: Thanks.

NORA [*striking a match*]: Let me give you a light.

RANK: Thanks. [*She holds the match; he lights his cigar.*] And now goodbye!

HELMER: Goodbye, goodbye, my friend.

NORA: Sleep well, Dr. Rank.

RANK: I thank you.

NORA: Wish me the same.

RANK: You? Well, if you really want me to—. Sleep well. And thanks for the light. [*He nods to both of them and goes out.*]

HELMER [*in a low voice*]: He had had quite a bit to drink.

NORA [*absently*]: Maybe so.

[HELMER *takes out his keys and goes out into the hall.*]

NORA: Torvald—what are you doing out there?

HELMER: Emptying the mailbox. It is quite full. There wouldn't be room for the newspapers in the morning—

NORA: Are you going to work tonight?

HELMER: You know very well I won't.—Say! What's this? Somebody's been at the lock.

NORA: The lock—?

HELMER: Yes. Why, I wonder. I hate to think that any of the maids—. Here's a broken hairpin. It's one of yours, Nora.

NORA [*quickly*]: Then it must be one of the children.

HELMER: You better make damn sure they stop that. Hm, hm.—There! I got it open, finally. [*Gathers up the mail, calls out to the kitchen.*] Helene?—Oh Helene—turn out the light here in the hall, will you? [*He comes back into the living room and closes the door.*] Look how it's been piling up. [*Shows her the bundle of letters. Starts leafing through it.*] What's this?

NORA [*by the window*]: The letter! Oh no, no, Torvald!

HELMER: Two calling cards—from Rank.

NORA: From Dr. Rank?

HELMER [*looking at them*]: "Doctor medicinae Rank." They were on top. He must have put them there when he left just now.

NORA: Anything written on them?

HELMER: A black cross above the name. What a macabre idea. Like announcing his own death.

NORA: That's what it is.

HELMER: Hm? You know about this? Has he said anything to you?

NORA: That card means he has said goodbye to us. He'll lock himself up to die.

HELMER: My poor friend. I knew of course he wouldn't be with me very long. But so soon—. And hiding himself away like a wounded animal—

NORA: When it has to be, it's better it happens without words. Don't you think so, Torvald?

HELMER [*walking up and down*]: He'd grown so close to us. I find it hard to think of him as gone. With his suffering and loneliness he was like a clouded background for our happy sunshine. Well, it may be better this way. For him, at any rate. [*Stops.*] And perhaps for us, too, Nora. For now we have nobody but each other. [*Embraces her.*] Oh you—my beloved wife! I feel I just can't hold you close enough. Do you know, Nora—many times I have wished some great danger threatened you, so I could risk my life and blood and everything—everything, for your sake.

NORA [*frees herself and says in a strong and firm voice*]: I think you should go and read your letters now, Torvald.

HELMER: No, no—not tonight. I want to be with you, my darling.

NORA: With the thought of your dying friend—?

HELMER: You are right. This has shaken both of us. Something not beautiful has come between us. Thoughts of death and dissolution. We must try to get over it—out of it. Till then—we'll each go to our own room.

NORA [*her arms around his neck*]: Torvald—goodnight! Goodnight!

HELMER [*kisses her forehead*]: Goodnight, my little songbird. Sleep well, Nora. Now I'll read my letters. [*He goes into his room, carrying the mail. Closes the door.*]

NORA [*her eyes desperate, her hands groping, finds* HELMER*'s black cloak and throws it around her; she whispers, quickly, brokenly, hoarsely*]. Never see him again. Never. Never. Never. [*Puts her shawl over her head.*] And never see the children again, either. Never; never.—The black, icy water—fathomless—this—! If only it was all over.—Now he has it. Now he's reading it. No, no; not yet. Torvald—goodbye—you—the children—

[*She is about to hurry through the hall, when* HELMER *flings open the door to his room and stands there with an open letter in his hand.*]

HELMER: Nora!

NORA [*cries out*]: Ah—!

HELMER: What is it? You know what's in this letter?

NORA: Yes, I do! Let me go! Let me out!

HELMER [*holds her back*]: Where do you think you're going?

NORA [*trying to tear herself loose from him*]: I won't let you save me, Torvald!

HELMER [*tumbles back*]: True! Is it true what he writes? Oh my God! No, no—this can't possibly be true.

NORA: It is true. I have loved you more than anything else in the whole world.

HELMER: Oh, don't give me any silly excuses.

NORA [*taking a step towards him*]: Torvald—!

HELMER: You wretch! What have you done!

NORA: Let me go. You are not to sacrifice yourself for me. You are not to take the blame.

HELMER: No more playacting. [*Locks the door to the front hall.*] You'll stay here and answer me. Do you understand what you have done? Answer me! Do you understand?

NORA [*gazes steadily at him with an increasingly frozen expression*]: Yes. Now I'm beginning to understand.

HELMER [*walking up and down*]: What a dreadful awakening. All these years—all these eight years—she, my pride and my joy—a hypocrite, a liar—oh worse! worse!—a criminal! Oh, the bottomless ugliness in all this! Damn! Damn! Damn!

[NORA, *silent, keeps gazing at him.*]

HELMER [*stops in front of her*]: I ought to have guessed that something like this would happen. I should have expected it. All your father's loose principles—Silence! You have inherited every one of your father's loose principles. No religion, no morals, no sense of duty—. Now I am being punished for my leniency with him. I did it for your sake, and this is how you pay me back.

NORA: Yes. This is how.

HELMER: You have ruined all my happiness. My whole future—that's what you have destroyed. Oh, it's terrible to think about. I am at the mercy of an unscrupulous man. He can do with me whatever he likes, demand anything of me, command me and dispose of me just as he pleases—I dare not say a word! To go down so miserably, to be destroyed—all because of an irresponsible woman!

NORA: When I am gone from the world, you'll be free.

HELMER: No noble gestures, please. Your father was always full of such phrases too. What good would it do me if you were gone from the world, as you put it? Not the slightest good at all. He could still make the whole thing public, and if he did, people would be likely to think I had been your accomplice. They might even think it was my idea—that it was I who urged you to do it! And for all this I have you to thank—you, whom I've borne on my hands through all the years of our marriage. *Now* do you understand what you've done to me?

NORA [*with cold calm*]: Yes.

HELMER: I just can't get it into my head that this is happening; it's all so incredible. But we have to come to terms with it somehow. Take your shawl off. Take it off, I say! I have to satisfy him one way or another. The whole affair must be kept quiet at whatever cost.—And as far as you and I are concerned, nothing must seem to have changed. I'm talking about appearances, of course. You'll go on living here; that goes without saying. But I won't let you bring up the children; I dare not trust you with them.—Oh! Having to say this to one I have loved so much, and whom I still—! But all that is past. It's not a question of happiness any more but of hanging on to what can be salvaged—pieces, appearances—[*The doorbell rings.*]

HELMER [*jumps*]: What's that? So late. Is the worst—? Has he—! Hide, Nora! Say you're sick.

[NORA *doesn't move.* HELMER *opens the door to the hall.*]

MAID [*half dressed, out in the hall*]: A letter for your wife, sir.

HELMER: Give it to me. [*Takes the letter and closes the door.*] Yes, it's from him. But I won't let you have it. I'll read it myself.

NORA: Yes—you read it.

HELMER [*by the lamp*]: I hardly dare. Perhaps we're lost, both you and I. No; I've got to know. [*Tears the letter open, glances through it, looks at an enclosure; a cry of joy.*] Nora!

[NORA *looks at him with a question in her eyes.*]

HELMER: Nora!—No, I must read it again.—Yes, yes; it is so! I'm saved! Nora, I'm saved!

NORA: And I?

HELMER: You too, of course; we're both saved, both you and I. Look! He's returning your note. He writes that he's sorry, he regrets, a happy turn in his life—oh, it doesn't matter what he writes. We're saved, Nora! Nobody can do anything to you now. Oh Nora, Nora—. No, I want to get rid of this disgusting thing first. Let me see—[*Looks at the signature.*] No, I don't want to see it. I don't want it to be more than a bad dream, the whole thing. [*Tears up the note and both letters, throws the pieces in the stove, and watches them burn.*] There! Now it's gone.—He wrote that ever since Christmas Eve—. Good God, Nora, these must have been three terrible days for you.

NORA: I have fought a hard fight these last three days.

HELMER: And been in agony and seen no other way out than—. No, we won't think of all that ugliness. We'll just rejoice and tell ourselves it's over, it's all over! Oh, listen to me, Nora. You don't seem to understand. It's over. What *is* it? Why do you look like that—that frozen expression on your face? Oh my poor little Nora, don't you think I know what it is? You can't make yourself believe that I have forgiven you. But I have, Nora; I swear to you, I have forgiven you for everything. Of course I know that what you did was for love of me.

NORA: That is true.

HELMER: You have loved me the way a wife ought to love her husband. You just didn't have the wisdom to judge the means. But do you think I love you any less because you don't know how to act on your own? Of course not. Just lean on me. I'll advise you; I'll guide you. I wouldn't be a man if I didn't find you twice as attractive because of your womanly helplessness. You mustn't pay any attention to the hard words I said to you right at first. It was just that first shock when I thought everything was collapsing all around me. I have forgiven you, Nora. I swear to you—I really have forgiven you.

NORA: I thank you for your forgiveness. [*She goes out through the door, right.*]

HELMER: No, stay—[*Looks into the room she entered.*] What are you doing in there?

NORA [*within*]: Getting out of my costume.

HELMER [*by the open door*]: Good, good. Try to calm down and compose yourself, my poor little frightened songbird. Rest safely; I have broad wings to cover you with. [*Walks around near the door.*] What a nice and cozy home we have, Nora. Here's shelter for you. Here I'll keep you safe like a hunted dove I have rescued from the hawk's talons. Believe me: I'll know how to quiet your beating heart. It will happen by and by, Nora; you'll see. Why, tomorrow you'll look at all this in quite a different light. And soon everything will be just the way it was before. I won't need to keep reassuring you that I have forgiven you; you'll feel it yourself. Did you really think I could have abandoned you, or even reproached you? Oh, you don't know a real man's heart, Nora. There is something unspeakably sweet and satisfactory for a man to know deep in himself that he has forgiven his wife—forgiven her in all the fullness of his honest heart. You see, that way she becomes his very own all over again—in a double sense, you might say. He has, so to speak, given her a second birth; it is as if she had become his wife and his child, both. From now on that's what you'll be to me, you lost and helpless creature. Don't worry about a thing, Nora. Only be frank with me, and I'll be your will and your conscience.—What's this? You're not in bed? You've changed your dress—!

NORA [*in an everyday dress*]: Yes, Torvald. I have changed my dress.

HELMER: But why—now—this late—?

NORA: I'm not going to sleep tonight.

HELMER: But my dear Nora—

NORA [*looks at her watch*]: It isn't all that late. Sit down here with me, Torvald. You and I have much to talk about. [*Sits down at the table.*]

HELMER: Nora—what is this all about? That rigid face—

NORA: Sit down. This will take a while. I have much to say to you.

HELMER [*sits down, facing her across the table*]: You worry me, Nora. I don't understand you.

NORA: No, that's just it. You don't understand me. And I have never understood you—not till tonight. No, don't interrupt me. Just listen to what I have to say.—This is a settling of accounts, Torvald.

HELMER: What do you mean by that?

NORA [*after a brief silence*]: Doesn't one thing strike you, now that we are sitting together like this?

HELMER: What would that be?

NORA: We have been married for eight years. Doesn't it occur to you that this is the first time that you and I, husband and wife, are having a serious talk?

HELMER: Well—serious—. What do you mean by that?

NORA: For eight whole years—longer, in fact—ever since we first met, we have never talked seriously to each other about a single serious thing.

HELMER: You mean I should forever have been telling you about worries you couldn't have helped me with anyway?

NORA: I am not talking about worries. I'm saying we have never tried seriously to get to the bottom of anything together.

HELMER: But dearest Nora, I hardly think that would have been something *you—*

NORA: That's the whole point. You have never understood me. Great wrong has been done to me, Torvald. First by Daddy and then by you.

HELMER: What! By us two? We who have loved you more deeply than anyone else?

NORA [*shakes her head*]: You never loved me—neither Daddy nor you. You only thought it was fun to be in love with me.

HELMER: But, Nora—what an expression to use!

NORA: That's the way it has been, Torvald. When I was home with Daddy, he told me all his opinions, and so they became my opinions too. If I disagreed with him I kept it to myself, for he wouldn't have liked that. He called me his little doll baby, and he played with me the way I played with my dolls. Then I came to your house—

HELMER: What a way to talk about our marriage!

NORA [*imperturbably*]: I mean that I passed from Daddy's hands into yours. You arranged everything according to your taste, and so I came to share it—or I pretended to; I'm not sure which. I think it was a little of both, now one and now the other. When I look back on it now, it seems to me I've been living here like a pauper—had a hand-to-mouth kind of existence. I have earned my keep by doing tricks for you, Torvald. But that's the way you wanted it. You have great sins against me to answer for, Daddy and you. It's your fault that nothing has become of me.

HELMER: Nora, you're being both unreasonable and ungrateful. Haven't you been happy here?

NORA: No, never. I thought I was, but I wasn't.

HELMER: Not—not happy!

NORA: No; just having fun. And you have always been very good to me. But our home has never been more than a playroom. I have been your doll wife here, just the way I used to be Daddy's doll child. And the children have been my dolls. I thought it was fun when you played with me, just as they thought it was fun when I played with them. That's been our marriage, Torvald.

HELMER: There is something in what you are saying—exaggerated and hysterical though it is. But from now on things will be different. Playtime is over; it's time for growing up.

NORA: Whose growing up—mine or the children's?

HELMER: Both yours and the children's, Nora darling.

NORA: Oh Torvald, you're not the man to bring me up to be the right kind of wife for you.

HELMER: How can you say that?

NORA: And I—? What qualifications do I have for bringing up the children?

HELMER: Nora!

NORA: You said so yourself a minute ago—that you didn't dare to trust me with them.

HELMER: In the first flush of anger, yes. Surely, you're not going to count that.

NORA: But you were quite right. I am *not* qualified. Something else has to come first. Somehow I have to grow up myself. And you are not the man to help me do that. That's a job I have to do by myself. And that's why I'm leaving you.

HELMER [*jumps up*]: What did you say!

NORA: I have to be by myself if I am to find out about myself and about all the other things too. So I can't stay here with you any longer.

HELMER: Nora, Nora!

NORA: I'm leaving now. I'm sure Kristine will put me up for tonight.

HELMER: You're out of your mind! I won't let you! I forbid you!

NORA: You can't forbid me anything any more; it won't do any good. I'm taking my own things with me. I won't accept anything from you, either now or later.

HELMER: But this is madness!

NORA: Tomorrow I'm going home—I mean back to my old hometown. It will be easier for me to find some kind of job there.

HELMER: Oh, you blind, inexperienced creature—!

NORA: I must see to it that I get experience, Torvald.

HELMER: Leaving your home, your husband, your children! Not a thought of what people will say!

NORA: I can't worry about that. All I know is that I have to leave.

HELMER: Oh, this is shocking! Betraying your most sacred duties like this!

NORA: And what do you consider my most sacred duties?

HELMER: Do I need to tell you that? They are your duties to your husband and your children.

NORA: I have other duties equally sacred.

HELMER: You do not. What duties would they be?

NORA: My duties to myself.

HELMER: You are a wife and a mother before you are anything else.

NORA: I don't believe that any more. I believe I am first of all a human being, just as much as you—or at any rate that I must try to become one. Oh, I know very well that most people agree with you, Torvald, and that it says something like that in all the books. But what people say and what the books say is no longer enough for me. I have to think about these things myself and see if I can't find the answers.

HELMER: You mean to tell me you don't know what your proper place in your own home is? Don't you have a reliable guide in such matters? Don't you have religion?

NORA: Oh but Torvald—I don't really know what religion is.

HELMER: What are you saying!

NORA: All I know is what the Reverend Hansen told me when he prepared me for confirmation. He said that religion was *this* and it was *that*. When I get by myself, away from here, I'll have to look into that, too. I have to decide if what the Reverend Hansen said was right, or anyway if it is right for *me*.

HELMER: Oh, this is unheard of in a young woman! If religion can't guide you, let me appeal to your conscience. For surely you have moral feelings? Or—answer me— maybe you don't?

NORA: Well, you see, Torvald, I don't really know what to say. I just don't know. I am confused about these things. All I know is that my ideas are quite different from yours. I have just found out that the laws are different from what I thought they were, but in no way can I get it into my head that those laws are right. A woman shouldn't have the right to spare her dying old father or save her husband's life! I just can't believe that.

HELMER: You speak like a child. You don't understand the society you live in.

NORA: No, I don't. But I want to find out about it. I have to make up my mind who is right, society or I.

HELMER: You are sick, Nora; you have a fever. I really don't think you are in your right mind.

NORA: I have never felt so clearheaded and sure of myself as I do tonight.

HELMER: And clearheaded and sure of yourself you're leaving your husband and children?

NORA: Yes.

HELMER: Then there is only one possible explanation.

NORA: What?

HELMER: You don't love me any more.

NORA: No, that's just it.

HELMER: Nora! Can you say that?

NORA: I am sorry, Torvald, for you have always been so good to me. But I can't help it. I don't love you any more.

HELMER [*with forced composure*]: And this too is a clear and sure conviction?

NORA: Completely clear and sure. That's why I don't want to stay here any more.

HELMER: And are you ready to explain to me how I came to forfeit your love?

NORA: Certainly I am. It was tonight, when the wonderful didn't happen. That was when I realized you were not the man I thought you were.

HELMER: You have to explain. I don't understand.

NORA: I have waited patiently for eight years, for I wasn't such a fool that I thought the wonderful is something that happens any old day. Then this—thing—came crashing in on me, and then there wasn't a doubt in my mind that now—now comes the wonderful. When Krogstad's letter was in that mailbox, never for a moment did it even occur to me that you would submit to his conditions. I was so absolutely certain that you would say to him: make the whole thing public—tell everybody. And when that had happened—

HELMER: Yes, then what? When I had surrendered my wife to shame and disgrace—!

NORA: When that had happened, I was absolutely certain that you would stand up and take the blame and say, "I'm the guilty one."

HELMER: Nora!

NORA: You mean I never would have accepted such a sacrifice from you? Of course not. But what would my protests have counted against yours? *That* was the wonderful I was hoping for in terror. And to prevent that I was going to kill myself.

HELMER: I'd gladly work nights and days for you, Nora—endure sorrow and want for your sake. But nobody sacrifices his *honor* for his love.

NORA: A hundred thousand women have done so.

HELMER: Oh, you think and talk like a silly child.

NORA: All right. But you don't think and talk like the man I can live with. When you had gotten over your fright—not because of what threatened *me* but because of the risk to *you*—and the whole danger was past, then you acted as if nothing at all had happened. Once again I was your little songbird, your doll, just as before, only now you had to handle her even more carefully, because she was so frail and weak. [*Rises.*] Torvald—that moment I realized that I had been living here for eight years with a stranger and had borne him three children—Oh, I can't stand thinking about it! I feel like tearing myself to pieces!

HELMER [*heavily*]: I see it, I see it. An abyss has opened up between us.—Oh but Nora—surely it can be filled?

NORA: The way I am now I am no wife for you.

HELMER: I have it in me to change.

NORA: Perhaps—if your doll is taken from you.

HELMER: To part—to part from you! No, no, Nora! I can't grasp that thought!

NORA [*goes out, right*]: All the more reason why it has to be. [*She returns with her outdoor clothes and a small bag, which she sets down on the chair by the table.*]

HELMER: Nora, Nora! Not now! Wait till tomorrow.

NORA [*putting on her coat*]: I can't spend the night in a stranger's rooms.

HELMER: But couldn't we live here together like brother and sister—?

NORA [*tying on her hat*]: You know very well that wouldn't last long—. [*Wraps her shawl around her.*] Goodbye, Torvald. I don't want to see the children. I know I leave them in better hands than mine. The way I am now I can't be anything to them.

HELMER: But some day, Nora—some day—?

NORA: How can I tell? I have no idea what's going to become of me.

HELMER: But you're still my wife, both as you are now and as you will be.

NORA: Listen, Torvald—when a wife leaves her husband's house, the way I am doing now, I have heard he has no more legal responsibilities for her. At any rate, I now release you from all responsibility. You are not to feel yourself obliged to me for anything, and I have no obligations to you. There has to be full freedom on both sides. Here is your ring back. Now give me mine.

HELMER: Even this?

NORA: Even this.

HELMER: Here it is.

NORA: There. So now it's over. I'm putting the keys here. The maids know everything about the house—better than I. Tomorrow, after I'm gone, Kristine will come over and pack my things from home. I want them sent after me.

HELMER: Over! It's all over! Nora, will you never think of me?

NORA: I'm sure I'll often think of you and the children and this house.

HELMER: May I write to you, Nora?

NORA: No—never. I won't have that.

HELMER: But send you things—? You must let me.

NORA: Nothing, nothing.

HELMER: —help you, when you need help—

NORA: I told you, no; I won't have it. I'll accept nothing from strangers.

HELMER: Nora—can I never again be more to you than a stranger?

NORA [*picks up her bag*]: Oh Torvald—then the most wonderful of all would have to happen—

HELMER: Tell me what that would be—!

NORA: For that to happen, both you and I would have to change so that—Oh Torvald, I no longer believe in the wonderful.

HELMER: But I *will* believe. Tell me! Change, so that—?

NORA: So that our living together would become a true marriage. Goodbye. [*She goes out through the hall.*]

HELMER [*sinks down on a chair near the door and covers his face with his hands*]: Nora! Nora! [*Looks around him and gets up.*] All empty. She's gone. [*With sudden hope.*] The most wonderful—?!

[*From downstairs comes the sound of a heavy door slamming shut.*]

QUESTIONS

Act I

1. Describe Nora's behavior during her first appearance. How does this contrast to Helmer's behavior during his first appearance? What is the initial, overriding concern of both Nora and Helmer very early in the play? What behavior of Nora's indicates a latent rebelliousness? What else does this behavior indicate?
2. Explain why Mrs. Linde doesn't feel even "a grief to live on" (page 512). Why would this be so? Describe the similarities in the lives of Nora and Mrs. Linde, and tell what this mutual situation symbolizes.
3. What in Mrs. Linde's statements makes Nora reveal some information about how she got the money to take Helmer to Italy when he was sick? What is Nora trying to prove? What are we allowed to believe she had done to earn the money?
4. Why would Helmer be embarrassed and humiliated to learn that he owed his wife anything? Why does Nora feel that she must have something, if only a secret?
5. What dramatic devices does Ibsen use to heighten tension?
6. Krogstad says, "what I did that time was no more and no worse" than the fraud Nora has committed (page 525). In light of what's happened to Krogstad, what does this imply about Ibsen's society? Is sex discrimination the only issue?

Act II

1. What irony is revealed in this act, and who is involved?
2. What does Nora reveal during the scene with Rank that for the first time relates to the title of the play?
3. What manner of person does Rank seem to be?
4. What does Krogstad ultimately contribute to Nora's rebirth? What does Rank contribute? From what disease, more fully developed in a later play by Ibsen, is Rank really dying? What is meant by his remark, "my poor innocent spine is suffering for my father's frolics as a young lieutenant"? How does this belief square with Helmer's that certain behavioral traits are also transmitted from generation to generation?
5. Does Rank's impending death influence Nora's decision to leave? Explain.

Act III

1. Does Mrs. Linde's initiative with Krogstad deepen her as a character? How?
2. How does Mrs. Linde's previous situation with her family and late husband compare to Nora's crisis with Helmer's illness and her father's death?
3. With Krogstad is Mrs. Linde being "hysterical" or realistic?
4. Why does Mrs. Linde insist that the "concealment and evasion" of Nora and Helmer be brought to an end?
5. In earlier times the tarantella dance was believed to be a remedy for tarantism, which results from the bite of a tarantula. Explain the symbolism of the spider. Who or what

would be the spider, and who would have been bitten? What mood does talk of the dance and the dance itself evoke in Nora? in Rank? in Helmer?
6. What is the symbolism behind Helmer's talk of knitting versus embroidery?
7. At what point in this act does Nora truly perceive Helmer's self-centered concern for convention?

Lorraine Hansberry

A RAISIN IN THE SUN

CHARACTERS

RUTH YOUNGER
TRAVIS YOUNGER
WALTER LEE YOUNGER (Brother)
BENEATHA YOUNGER
LENA YOUNGER (Mama)

JOSEPH ASAGAI
GEORGE MURCHISON
KARL LINDNER
BOBO
MOVING MEN

The action of the play is set in Chicago's Southside, sometime between World War II and the present.

ACT I

SCENE I: *Friday morning.*
SCENE II: *The following morning.*

ACT II

SCENE I: *Later, the same day.*
SCENE II: *Friday night, a few weeks later.*
SCENE III: *Moving day, one week later.*

ACT III

An hour later.

What happens to a dream deferred?
Does it dry up
Like a raisin in the sun?
Or fester like a sore—
And then run?
Does it stink like rotten meat?
Or crust and sugar over—
Like a syrupy sweet?

Maybe it just sags
Like a heavy load.

Or does it explode?
—Langston Hughes

ACT I

SCENE I

The YOUNGER *living room would be a comfortable and well-ordered room if it were not for a number of indestructible contradictions to this state of being. Its furnishings are typical and undistinguished and their primary feature now is that they have clearly had to accommodate the living of too many people for too many years—and they are tired. Still, we can see that at some time, a time probably no longer remembered by the family [except perhaps for* MAMA], *the furnishings of this room were actually selected with care and love and even hope—and brought to this apartment and arranged with taste and pride.*

That was a long time ago. Now the once loved pattern of the couch upholstery has to fight to show itself from under acres of crocheted doilies and couch covers which have themselves finally come to be more important than the upholstery. And here a table or a chair has been moved to disguise the worn places in the carpet: but the carpet has fought back by showing its weariness, with depressing uniformity, elsewhere on its surface.

Weariness has, in fact, won in this room. Everything has been polished, washed, sat on, used, scrubbed too often. All pretenses but living itself have long since vanished from the very atmosphere of this room.

Moreover, a section of this room, for it is not really a room unto itself, though the landlord's lease would make it seem so, slopes backward to provide a small kitchen area, where the family prepares the meals that are eaten in the living room proper, which must also serve as dining room. The single window that has been provided for these "two" rooms is located in this kitchen area. The sole natural light the family may enjoy in the course of a day is only that which fights its way through this little window.

At left, a door leads to a bedroom which is shared by MAMA *and her daughter,* BENEATHA. *At right, opposite, is a second room (which in the beginning of the life of this apartment was probably a breakfast room) which serves as a bedroom for* WALTER *and his wife,* RUTH.

Time: Sometime between World War II and the present.

Place: Chicago's Southside.

At Rise: It is morning dark in the living room. WALTER *is asleep on the make-down bed at center. An alarm clock sounds from within the bedroom at right, and presently* RUTH *enters from that room and closes the door behind her. She crosses sleepily toward the window. As she passes her sleeping son she reaches down and shakes him a little. At the window she raises the shade and a dusky Southside morning light comes in feebly. She fills a pot with water and puts it on to boil. She calls to the boy between yawns, in a slightly muffled voice.*

RUTH *is about thirty. We can see that she was a pretty girl, even exceptionally so, but now it is apparent that life has been little that she expected, and disappointment has already begun to hang in her face. In a few years, before thirty-five even, she will be known among her people as a "settled woman." She crosses to her son and gives him a good, final, rousing shake.*

RUTH: Come on now, boy, it's seven thirty! [*Her son sits up at last, in a stupor of sleepiness.*] I say hurry up, Travis! You ain't the only person in the world got to use a bathroom! [*The child, a sturdy, handsome little boy of ten or eleven, drags himself out of the bed and almost blindly takes his towels and "today's clothes" from drawers and a closet and goes out to the bathroom, which is in an outside hall and which is shared by another family or families on the same floor.* RUTH *crosses to the bedroom door at right and opens it and calls in to her husband.*] Walter Lee! . . . It's after seven thirty! Lemme see you do some waking up in there now! [*She waits.*] You better get up from there, man! It's after seven thirty I tell you. [*She waits again.*] All right, you just go ahead and lay there and next thing you know Travis be finished and Mr. Johnson'll be in there and you'll be fussing and cussing round here like a mad man! And be late too! [*She waits, at the end of patience.*] *Walter Lee*—it's time for you to get up!

[*She waits another second and then starts to go into the bedroom, but is apparently satisfied that her husband has begun to get up. She stops, pulls the door to, and returns to the kitchen area. She wipes her face with a moist cloth and runs her fingers through her sleep-disheveled hair in a vain effort and ties an apron around her housecoat. The bedroom door at right opens and her husband stands in the doorway in his pajamas, which are rumpled and mismated. He is a lean, intense young man in his middle thirties, inclined to quick nervous movements and erratic speech habits—and always in his voice there is a quality of indictment.*]

WALTER: Is he out yet?

RUTH: What you mean *out?* He ain't hardly got in there good yet.

WALTER [*wandering in, still more oriented to sleep than to a new day*]: Well, what was you doing all that yelling for if I can't even get in there yet? [*Stopping and thinking.*] Check coming today?

RUTH: They *said* Saturday and this is just Friday and I hopes to God you ain't going to get up here first thing this morning and start talking to me 'bout no money— 'cause I 'bout don't want to hear it.

WALTER: Something the matter with you this morning?

RUTH: No—I'm just sleepy as the devil. What kind of eggs you want?

WALTER: Not scrambled. [RUTH *starts to scramble eggs.*] Paper come? [RUTH *points impatiently to the rolled up* Tribune *on the table, and he gets it and spreads it out and vaguely reads the front page.*] Set off another bomb yesterday.

RUTH [*maximum indifference*]: Did they?

WALTER [*looking up*]: What's the matter with you?

RUTH: Ain't nothing the matter with me. And don't keep asking me that this morning.

WALTER: Ain't nobody bothering you. [*Reading the news of the day absently again.*] Say Colonel McCormick is sick.

RUTH [*affecting tea-party interest*]: Is he now? Poor thing.

WALTER [*sighing and looking at his watch*]: Oh, me. [*He waits.*] Now what is that boy doing in that bathroom all this time? He just going to have to start getting up earlier. I can't be being late to work on account of him fooling around in there.

RUTH [*turning on him*]: Oh, no he ain't going to be getting up no earlier no such thing! It ain't his fault that he can't get to bed no earlier nights 'cause he got a bunch of crazy good-for-nothing clowns sitting up running their mouths in what is supposed to be his bedroom after ten o'clock at night . . .

WALTER: That's what you mad about, ain't it? The things I want to talk about with my friends just couldn't be important in your mind, could they?

[*He rises and finds a cigarette in her handbag on the table and crosses to the little window and looks out, smoking and deeply enjoying this first one.*]

RUTH [*almost matter of factly, a complaint too automatic to deserve emphasis*]: Why you always got to smoke before you eat in the morning?

WALTER [*at the window*]: Just look at 'em down there . . . Running and racing to work . . . [*He turns and faces his wife and watches her a moment at the stove, and then, suddenly.*] You look young this morning, baby.

RUTH [*indifferently*]: Yeah?

WALTER: Just for a second—stirring them eggs. It's gone now—just for a second it was—you looked real young again. [*Then, drily.*] It's gone now—you look like yourself again.

RUTH: Man, if you don't shut up and leave me alone.

WALTER [*looking out to the street again*]: First thing a man ought to learn in life is not to make love to no colored woman first thing in the morning. You all some evil people at eight o'clock in the morning.

[TRAVIS *appears in the hall doorway, almost fully dressed and quite wide awake now, his towels and pajamas across his shoulders. He opens the door and signals for his father to make the bathroom in a hurry.*]

TRAVIS [*watching the bathroom*]: Daddy, come on!

[WALTER *gets his bathroom utensils and flies out to the bathroom.*]

RUTH: Sit down and have your breakfast, Travis.

TRAVIS: Mama, this is Friday. [*Gleefully.*] Check coming tomorrow, huh?

RUTH: You get your mind off money and eat your breakfast.

TRAVIS [*eating*]: This is the morning we supposed to bring the fifty cents to school.

RUTH: Well, I ain't got no fifty cents this morning.

TRAVIS: Teacher say we have to.

RUTH: I don't care what teacher say. I ain't got it. Eat your breakfast, Travis.

TRAVIS: I *am* eating.

RUTH: Hush up now and just eat!

[*The boy gives her an exasperated look for her lack of understanding, and eats grudgingly.*]

TRAVIS: You think Grandmama would have it?

RUTH: No! And I want you to stop asking your grandmother for money, you hear me?

TRAVIS [*outraged*]: Gaaaleee! I don't ask her, she just gimme it sometimes!

RUTH: Travis Willard Younger—I got so much on me this morning to be—

TRAVIS: Maybe Daddy—

RUTH: *Travis!*

[*The boy hushes abruptly. They are both quiet and tense for several seconds.*]

TRAVIS [*presently*]: Could I maybe go carry some groceries in front of the supermarket for a little while after school then?

RUTH: Just hush, I said. [TRAVIS *jabs his spoon into his cereal bowl viciously, and rests his head in anger upon his fists.*] If you through eating, you can get over there and make up your bed.

[*The boy obeys stiffly and crosses the room, almost mechanically, to the bed and more or less carefully folds the covering. He carries the bedding into his mother's room and returns with his books and cap.*]

TRAVIS [*sulking and standing apart from her unnaturally*]: I'm gone.

RUTH [*looking up from the stove to inspect him automatically*]: Come here. [*He crosses to her and she studies his head.*] If you don't take this comb and fix this here head, you better! [TRAVIS *puts down his books with a great sigh of oppression, and crosses to the mirror. His mother mutters under her breath about his "slubbornness".*] 'Bout to march out of here with that head looking just like chickens slept in it! I just don't know where you get your slubborn ways . . . And get your jacket, too. Looks chilly out this morning.

TRAVIS [*with conspicuously brushed hair and jacket*]: I'm gone.

RUTH: Get carfare and milk money—[*Waving one finger.*]—and not a single penny for no caps, you hear me?

TRAVIS [*with sullen politeness*]: Yes'm.

[*He turns in outrage to leave. His mother watches after him as in his frustration he approaches the door almost comically. When she speaks to him, her voice has become a very gentle tease.*]

RUTH [*mocking; as she thinks he would say it*]: Oh, Mama makes me so mad sometimes, I don't know what to do! [*She waits and continues to his back as he stands stock-still in front of the door.*] I wouldn't kiss that woman good-bye for nothing in this world this morning! [*The boy finally turns around and rolls his eyes at her, knowing the mood has changed and he is vindicated; he does not, however, move toward her yet.*] Not for nothing in this world! [*She finally laughs aloud at him and holds out her arms to him and we see that it is a way between them, very old and practiced. He crosses to her and allows her to embrace him warmly but keeps his face fixed with masculine rigidity. She holds him back from her presently and looks at him and runs her fingers over the features of his face. With utter gentleness—.*] Now—whose little old angry man are you?

TRAVIS [*the masculinity and gruffness start to fade at last*]: Aw gaalee—Mama . . .

RUTH [*mimicking*]: Aw—gaaaaalleeeee, Mama! [*She pushes him, with rough playfulness and finality, toward the door.*] Get on out of here or you going to be late.

TRAVIS [*in the face of love, new aggressiveness*]: Mama, could I *please* go carry groceries?

RUTH: Honey, it's starting to get so cold evenings.

WALTER [*coming in from the bathroom and drawing a make-believe gun from a make-believe holster and shooting at his son*]: What is it he wants to do?

RUTH: Go carry groceries after school at the supermarket.

WALTER: Well, let him go . . .

TRAVIS [*quickly, to the ally*]: I *have* to—she won't gimme the fifty cents . . .

WALTER [*to his wife only*]: Why not?

RUTH [*simply, and with flavor*]: 'Cause we don't have it.

WALTER [*to* RUTH *only*]: What you tell the boy things like that for? [*Reaching down into his pants with a rather important gesture.*] Here, son—

[*He hands the boy the coin, but his eyes are directed to his wife's.* TRAVIS *takes the money happily.*]

TRAVIS: Thanks, Daddy.

[*He starts out.* RUTH *watches both of them with murder in her eyes.* WALTER *stands and stares back at her with defiance, and suddenly reaches into his pocket again on an afterthought.*]

WALTER [*without even looking at his son, still staring hard at his wife*]: In fact, here's another fifty cents . . . Buy yourself some fruit today—or take a taxi cab to school or something!

TRAVIS: Whoopee—

[*He leaps up and clasps his father around the middle with his legs, and they face each other in mutual appreciation; slowly* WALTER LEE *peeks around the boy to catch the violent rays from his wife's eyes and draws his head back as if shot.*]

WALTER: You better get down now—and get to school, man.

TRAVIS [*at the door*]: O.K. Good-bye. [*He exits.*]

WALTER [*after him, pointing with pride*]: That's *my* boy. [*She looks at him in disgust and turns back to her work.*] You know what I was thinking 'bout in the bathroom this morning?

RUTH: No.

WALTER: How come you always try to be so pleasant!

RUTH: What is there to be pleasant 'bout!

WALTER: You want to know what I was thinking 'bout in the bathroom or not!

RUTH: I know what you was thinking 'bout.

WALTER [*ignoring her*]: 'Bout what me and Willy Harris was talking about last night.

RUTH [*immediately—a refrain*]: Willy Harris is a good-for-nothing loud mouth.

WALTER: Anybody who talks to me has got to be a good-for-nothing loud mouth, ain't he? And what you know about who is just a good-for-nothing loud mouth? Charlie Atkins was just a "good-for-nothing loud mouth" too, wasn't he! When he wanted me to go in the dry-cleaning business with him. And now—he's grossing a hundred thousand a year. A hundred thousand dollars a year! You still call *him* a loud mouth!

RUTH [*bitterly*]: Oh, Walter Lee . . .

[*She folds her head on her arms over on the table.*]

WALTER [*rising and coming to her and standing over her*]: You tired, ain't you? Tired of everything. Me, the boy, the way we live—this beat-up hole—everything. Ain't you? [*She doesn't look up, doesn't answer.*] So tired—moaning and groaning all the time, but you wouldn't do nothing to help, would you? You couldn't be on my side that long for nothing, could you?

RUTH: Walter, please leave me alone.

WALTER: A man needs for a woman to back him up . . .

RUTH: Walter—

WALTER: Mama would listen to you. You know she listen to you more than she do me and Bennie. She think more of you. All you have to do is just sit down with her when you drinking your coffee one morning and talking 'bout things like you do and—[*He sits down beside her and demonstrates graphically what he thinks her methods and tone should be.*]—you just sip your coffee, see, and say easy like that you been thinking 'bout that deal Walter Lee is so interested in, 'bout the store and all, and sip some more coffee, like what you saying ain't really that important to you—And the next thing you know, she be listening good and asking you questions and when I come home—I can tell her the details. This ain't no fly-by-night proposition, baby. I mean we figured it out, me and Willy and Bobo.

RUTH [*with a frown*]: Bobo?

WALTER: Yeah. You see, this little liquor store we got in mind cost seventy-five thousand and we figured the initial investment on the place be 'bout thirty thousand, see. That be ten thousand each. Course, there's a couple of hundred you got to pay so's you don't spend your life just waiting for them clowns to let your license get approved—

RUTH: You mean graft?

WALTER [*frowning impatiently*]: Don't call it that. See there, that just goes to show you what women understand about the world. Baby, don't *nothing* happen for you in this world 'less you pay *somebody* off!

RUTH: Walter, leave me alone! [*She raises her head and stares at him vigorously—then says, more quietly.*] Eat your eggs, they gonna be cold.

WALTER [*straightening up from her and looking off*]: That's it. There you are. Man say to his woman: I got me a dream. His woman say: Eat your eggs. [*Sadly, but gaining in power.*] Man say: I got to take hold of this here world, baby! And a woman will say: Eat your eggs and go to work. [*Passionately now.*] Man say: I got to change my life, I'm choking to death, baby! And his woman say—[*In utter anguish as he brings his fists down on his thighs.*]—Your eggs is getting cold!

RUTH [*softly*]: Walter, that ain't none of our money.

WALTER [*not listening at all or even looking at her*]: This morning, I was lookin' in the mirror and thinking about it . . . I'm thirty-five years old; I been married eleven years and

I got a boy who sleeps in the living room—[*Very, very quietly.*]—and all I got to give him is stories about how rich white people live . . .

RUTH: Eat your eggs, Walter.

WALTER: *Damn my eggs . . . damn all the eggs that ever was!*

RUTH: Then go to work.

WALTER [*looking up at her*]: See—I'm trying to talk to you 'bout myself—[*Shaking his head with the repetition.*]—and all you can say is eat them eggs and go to work.

RUTH [*wearily*]: Honey, you never say nothing new. I listen to you every day, every night and every morning and you never say nothing new. [*Shrugging.*] So you would rather *be* Mr. Arnold than be his chauffeur. So—I would *rather* be living in Bucking-ham Palace.

WALTER: That is just what is wrong with the colored woman in this world . . . Don't understand about building their men up and making 'em feel like they somebody. Like they can do something.

RUTH [*drily, but to hurt*]: There *are* colored men who do things.

WALTER: No thanks to the colored woman.

RUTH: Well, being a colored woman, I guess I can't help myself none.

[*She rises and gets the ironing board and sets it up and attacks a huge pile of rough-dried clothes, sprinkling them in preparation for the ironing and then rolling them into tight fat balls.*]

WALTER [*mumbling*]: We one group of men tied to a race of women with small minds.

[*His sister* BENEATHA *enters. She is about twenty, as slim and intense as her brother. She is not as pretty as her sister-in-law, but her lean, almost intellectual face has a handsomeness of its own. She wears a bright-red flannel nightie, and her thick hair stands wildly about her head. Her speech is a mixture of many things; it is different from the rest of the family's insofar as education has permeated her sense of English—and perhaps the Midwest rather than the South has finally—at last—won out in her inflection; but not altogether, because over all of it is a soft slurring and transformed use of vowels which is the decided influence of the Southside. She passes through the room without looking at either* RUTH *or* WALTER *and goes to the outside door and looks, a little blindly, out to the bathroom. She sees that it has been lost to the Johnsons. She closes the door with a sleepy vengeance and crosses to the table and sits down a little defeated.*]

BENEATHA: I am going to start timing those people.

WALTER: You should get up earlier.

BENEATHA [*her face in her hands. She is still fighting the urge to go back to bed*]: Really—would you suggest dawn? Where's the paper?

WALTER [*pushing the paper across the table to her as he studies her almost clinically, as though he has never seen her before*]: You a horrible-looking chick at this hour.

BENEATHA [*drily*]: Good morning everybody.

WALTER [*senselessly*]: How is school coming?

BENEATHA [*in the same spirit*]: Lovely. Lovely. And you know, biology is the greatest. [*Looking up at him.*] I dissected something that looked just like you yesterday.

WALTER: I just wondered if you've made up your mind and everything.

BENEATHA [*gaining in sharpness and impatience*]: And what did I answer yesterday morning—and the day before that?

RUTH [*from the ironing board, like someone disinterested and old*]: Don't be so nasty, Bennie.

BENEATHA [*still to her brother*]: And the day before that and the day before that!

WALTER [*defensively*]: I'm interested in you. Something wrong with that? Ain't many girls who decide—

WALTER *and* BENEATHA [*in unison*]: —"to be a doctor."

[*Silence.*]

WALTER: Have we figured out yet just exactly how much medical school is going to cost?

RUTH: Walter Lee, why don't you leave that girl alone and get out of here to work?

BENEATHA [*exits to the bathroom and bangs on the door*]: Come on out of there, please! [*She comes back into the room.*]

WALTER [*looking at his sister intently*]: You know the check is coming tomorrow.

BENEATHA [*turning on him with a sharpness all her own*]: That money belongs to Mama, Walter, and it's for her to decide how she wants to use it. I don't care if she wants to buy a house or a rocket ship or just nail it up somewhere and look at it. It's hers. Not ours—*hers.*

WALTER [*bitterly*]: Now ain't that fine! You just got your mother's interest at heart, ain't you, girl? You such a nice girl—but if Mama got that money she can always take a few thousand and help you through school too—can't she?

BENEATHA: I have never asked anyone around here to do anything for me!

WALTER: No! And the line between asking and just accepting when the time comes is big and wide—ain't it!

BENEATHA [*with fury*]: What do you want from me, Brother—that I quit school or just drop dead, which!

WALTER: I don't want nothing but for you to stop acting holy 'round here. Me and Ruth done made some sacrifices for you—why can't you do something for the family?

RUTH: Walter, don't be dragging me in it.

WALTER: You are in it—Don't you get up and go work in somebody's kitchen for the last three years to help put clothes on her back?

RUTH: Oh, Walter—that's not fair . . .

WALTER: It ain't that nobody expects you to get on your knees and say thank you, Brother; thank you, Ruth; thank you Mama—and thank you, Travis, for wearing the same pair of shoes for two semesters—

BENEATHA [*dropping to her knees*]: Well—I *do*—all right?—thank everybody . . . and forgive me for ever wanting to be anything at all . . . forgive me, forgive me!

RUTH: Please stop it! Your mama'll hear you.

WALTER: Who the hell told you you had to be a doctor? If you so crazy 'bout messing 'round with sick people—then go be a nurse like other women—or just get married and be quiet . . .

BENEATHA: Well—you finally got it said . . . It took you three years but you finally got it said. Walter, give up; leave me alone—it's Mama's money.

WALTER: *He was my father, too!*

BENEATHA: So what? He was mine, too—and Travis' grandfather—but the insurance money belongs to Mama. Picking on me is not going to make her give it to you to invest in any liquor stores—[*Underbreath, dropping into a chair.*]—and I for one say, God bless Mama for that!

WALTER [*to* RUTH]: See—did you hear? Did you hear!

RUTH: Honey, please go to work.

WALTER: Nobody in this house is ever going to understand me.

BENEATHA: Because you're a nut.

WALTER: Who's a nut?

BENEATHA: You—you are a nut. Thee is mad, boy.

WALTER [*looking at his wife and his sister from the door, very sadly*]: The world's most backward race of people, and that's a fact.

BENEATHA [*turning slowly in her chair.*]: And then there are all those prophets who would lead us out of the wilderness—[WALTER *slams out of the house.*]—into the swamps!

RUTH: Bennie, why you always gotta be pickin' on your brother? Can't you be a little sweeter sometimes? [*Door opens.* WALTER *walks in.*]

WALTER [*to* RUTH]: I need some money for carfare.

RUTH [*looks at him, then warms; teasing, but tenderly*]: Fifty cents? [*She goes to her bag and gets money.*] Here, take a taxi.

[WALTER *exits.* MAMA *enters. She is a woman in her early sixties, full-bodied and strong. She is one of those women of a certain grace and beauty who wear it so unobtrusively that it takes a while to notice. Her dark-brown face is surrounded by the total whiteness of her hair, and, being a woman who has adjusted to many things in life and overcome many more, her face is full of strength. She has, we can see, wit and faith of a kind that keep her eyes lit and full of interest and expectancy. She is, in a word, a beautiful woman. Her bearing is perhaps most like the noble bearing of the women of the Hereros of Southwest Africa—rather as if she imagines that as she walks she still bears a basket or a vessel upon her head. Her speech, on the other hand, is as careless as her carriage is precise—she is inclined to slur everything—but her voice is perhaps not so much quiet as simply soft.*]

MAMA: Who that 'round here slamming doors at this hour?

[*She crosses through the room, goes to the window, opens it, and brings in a feeble little plant growing doggedly in a small pot on the window sill. She feels the dirt and puts it back out.*]

RUTH: That was Walter Lee. He and Bennie was at it again.

MAMA: My children and they tempers. Lord, if this little old plant don't get more sun than it's been getting it ain't never going to see spring again. [*She turns from the window.*] What's the matter with you this morning, Ruth? You looks right peaked. You aiming to iron all them things? Leave some for me. I'll get to 'em this afternoon. Bennie honey, it's too drafty for you to be sitting 'round half dressed. Where's your robe?

BENEATHA: In the cleaners.

MAMA: Well, go get mine and put it on.

BENEATHA: I'm not cold, Mama, honest.

MAMA: I know—but you so thin . . .

BENEATHA [*irritably*]: Mama, I'm not cold.

MAMA [*seeing the make-down bed as* TRAVIS *has left it*]: Lord have mercy, look at that poor bed. Bless his heart—he tries, don't he? [*She moves to the bed* TRAVIS *has sloppily made up.*]

RUTH: No—he don't half try at all 'cause he knows you going to come along behind him and fix everything. That's just how come he don't know how to do nothing right now—you done spoiled that boy so.

MAMA: Well—he's a little boy. Ain't supposed to know 'bout housekeeping. My baby, that's what he is. What you fix for his breakfast this morning?

RUTH [*angrily*]: I feed my son, Lena!

MAMA: I ain't meddling—[*Underbreath; busybodyish.*]I just noticed all last week he had cold cereal, and when it starts getting this chilly in the fall a child ought to have some hot grits or something when he goes out in the cold—

RUTH [*furious*]: I gave him hot oats—is that all right!

MAMA: I ain't meddling. [*Pause.*] Put a lot of nice butter on it? [RUTH *shoots her an angry look and does not reply.*] He likes lots of butter.

RUTH [*exasperated*]: Lena—

MAMA [*to* BENEATHA. MAMA *is inclined to wander conversationally sometimes*]: What was you and your brother fussing 'bout this morning?

BENEATHA: It's not important, Mama. [*She gets up and goes to look out at the bathroom, which is apparently free, and she picks up her towels and rushes out.*]

MAMA: What was they fighting about?

RUTH: Now you know as well as I do.

MAMA [*shaking her head*]: Brother still worrying hisself sick about that money?

RUTH: You know he is.

MAMA: You had breakfast?

RUTH: Some coffee.

MAMA: Girl, you better start eating and looking after yourself better. You almost thin as Travis.

RUTH: Lena—

MAMA: Uh-hunh?

RUTH: What are you going to do with it?

MAMA: Now don't you start, child. It's too early in the morning to be talking about money. It ain't Christian.

RUTH: It's just that he got his heart set on that store—

MAMA: You mean that liquor store that Willy Harris want him to invest in?

RUTH: Yes—

MAMA: We ain't no business people, Ruth. We just plain working folks.

RUTH: Ain't nobody business people till they go into business. Walter Lee say colored people ain't never going to start getting ahead till they start gambling on some different kinds of things in the world—investments and things.

MAMA: What done got into you, girl? Walter Lee done finally sold you on investing.

RUTH: No. Mama, something is happening between Walter and me. I don't know what it is—but he needs something—something I can't give him any more. He needs this chance, Lena.

MAMA [*frowning deeply*]: But liquor, honey—

RUTH: Well—like Walter say—I spec people going to always be drinking themselves some liquor.

MAMA: Well—whether they drinks it or not ain't none of my business. But whether I go into business selling it to 'em *is*, and I don't want that on my ledger this late in life. [*Stopping suddenly and studying her daughter-in-law.*] Ruth Younger, what's the matter with you today? You look like you could fall over right there.

RUTH: I'm tired.

MAMA: Then you better stay home from work today.

RUTH: I can't stay home. She'd be calling up the agency and screaming at them, "My girl didn't come in today—send me somebody! My girl didn't come in!" Oh, she just have a fit . . .

MAMA: Well, let her have it. I'll just call her up and say you got the flu—

RUTH [*laughing*]: Why the flu?

MAMA: 'Cause it sounds respectable to 'em. Something white people get, too. They know 'bout the flu. Otherwise they think you been cut up or something when you tell 'em you sick.

RUTH: I got to go in. We need the money.

MAMA: Somebody would of thought my children done all but starved to death the way they talk about money here late. Child, we got a great big old check coming tomorrow.

RUTH [*sincerely, but also self-righteously*]: Now that's your money. It ain't got nothing to do with me. We all feel like that—Walter and Bennie and me—even Travis.

MAMA [*thoughtfully, and suddenly very far away*]: Ten thousand dollars—

RUTH: Sure is wonderful.

MAMA: Ten thousand dollars.

RUTH: You know what you should do, Miss Lena? You should take yourself a trip somewhere. To Europe or South America or someplace—

MAMA [*throwing up her hands at the thought*]: Oh child!

RUTH: I'm serious. Just pack up and leave! Go on away and enjoy yourself some. Forget about the family and have yourself a ball for once in your life—

MAMA [*drily*]: You sound like I'm just about ready to die. Who'd go with me? What I look like wandering 'round Europe by myself?

RUTH: Shoot—these here rich white women do it all the time. They don't think nothing of packing up they suitcases and piling on one of them big steamships and—swoosh!—they gone, child.

MAMA: Something always told me I wasn't no rich white woman.

RUTH: Well—what are you going to do with it then?

MAMA: I ain't rightly decided. [*Thinking. She speaks now with emphasis.*] Some of it got to be put away for Beneatha and her schoolin'—and ain't nothing going to touch that part of it. Nothing. [*She waits several seconds, trying to make up her mind about something, and looks at* RUTH *a little tentatively before going on.*] Been thinking that we maybe could meet the notes on a little old two-story somewhere, with a yard where Travis could play in the summertime, if we use part of the insurance for a down payment and everybody kind of pitch in. I could maybe take on a little day work again, few days a week—

RUTH [*studying her mother-in-law furtively and concentrating on her ironing, anxious to encourage without seeming to*]: Well, Lord knows, we've put enough rent into this here rat trap to pay for four houses by now . . .

MAMA [*looking up at the words "rat trap" and then looking around and leaning back and sighing—in a suddenly reflective mood—*]: "Rat trap"—yes, that's all it is. [*Smiling.*] I remember just as well the day me and Big Walter moved in here. Hadn't been married but two weeks and wasn't planning on living here no more than a year. [*She shakes her head at the dissolved dream.*] We was going to set away, little by little, don't you know, and buy a little place out in Morgan Park. We had even picked out the house. [*Chuckling a little.*] Looks right dumpy today. But Lord, child, you should know all the dreams I had 'bout buying that house and fixing it up and making me a little garden in the back—[*She waits and stops smiling.*] And didn't none of it happen. [*Dropping her hands in a futile gesture.*]

RUTH [*keeps her head down, ironing*]: Yes, life can be a barrel of disappointments, sometimes.

MAMA: Honey, Big Walter would come in here some nights back then and slump down on that couch there and just look at the rug, and look at me and look at the rug and then back at me—and I'd know he was down then . . . really down. [*After a second very long and thoughtful pause; she is seeing back to times that only she can see.*] And then, Lord, when I lost that baby—little Claude—I almost thought I was going to lose Big Walter too. Oh, that man grieved hisself! He was one man to love his children.

RUTH: Ain't nothin' can tear at you like losin' your baby.

MAMA: I guess that's how come that man finally worked hisself to death like he done. Like he was fighting his own war with this here world that took his baby from him.

RUTH: He sure was a fine man, all right. I always liked Mr. Younger.

MAMA: Crazy 'bout his children! God knows there was plenty wrong with Walter Younger—hard-headed, mean, kind of wild with women—plenty wrong with him. But he sure loved his children. Always wanted them to have something—be something. That's where Brother gets all these notions, I reckon. Big Walter used to say, he'd get right wet in the eyes sometimes, lean his head back with the water standing in his eyes and say, "Seem like God didn't see fit to give the black man nothing but dreams—but He did give us children to make them dreams seem worth while." [*She smiles.*] He could talk like that, don't you know.

RUTH: Yes, he sure could. He was a good man, Mr. Younger.

MAMA: Yes, a fine man—just couldn't never catch up with his dreams, that's all.

[BENEATHA *comes in, brushing her hair and looking up to the ceiling, where the sound of a vacuum cleaner has started up.*]

BENEATHA: What could be so dirty on that woman's rugs that she has to vacuum them every single day?

RUTH: I wish certain young women 'round here who I could name would take inspiration about certain rugs in a certain apartment I could also mention.

BENEATHA [*shrugging*]: How much cleaning can a house need, for Christ's sakes.

MAMA [*not liking the Lord's name used thus*]: Bennie!

RUTH: Just listen to her—just listen!

BENEATHA: Oh, God!

MAMA: If you use the Lord's name just one more time—

BENEATHA [*a bit of a whine*]: Oh, Mama—

RUTH: Fresh—just fresh as salt, this girl!

BENEATHA [*drily*]: Well—if the salt loses its savor—

MAMA: Now that will do. I just ain't going to have you 'round here reciting the scriptures in vain—you hear me?

BENEATHA: How did I manage to get on everybody's wrong side by just walking into a room?

RUTH: If you weren't so fresh—

BENEATHA: Ruth, I'm twenty years old.

MAMA: What time you be home from school today?

BENEATHA: Kind of late. [*With enthusiasm.*] Madeline is going to start my guitar lessons today.

[MAMA *and* RUTH *look up with the same expression.*]

MAMA: Your *what* kind of lessons?

BENEATHA: Guitar.

RUTH: Oh, Father!

MAMA: How come you done taken it in your mind to learn to play the guitar?

BENEATHA: I just want to, that's all.

MAMA [*smiling*]: Lord, child, don't you know what to do with yourself? How long it going to be before you get tired of this now—like you got tired of that little play-acting group you joined last year? [*Looking at* RUTH.] And what was it the year before that?

RUTH: The horseback-riding club for which she bought that fifty-five-dollar riding habit that's been hanging in the closet ever since!

MAMA [*to* BENEATHA]: Why you got to flit so from one thing to another, baby?

BENEATHA [*sharply*]: I just want to learn to play the guitar. Is there anything wrong with that?

MAMA: Ain't nobody trying to stop you. I just wonders sometimes why you has to flit so from one thing to another all the time. You ain't never done nothing with all that camera equipment you brought home—

BENEATHA: I don't flit! I—I experiment with different forms of expression—

RUTH: Like riding a horse?

BENEATHA: —People have to express themselves one way or another.

MAMA: What is it you want to express?

BENEATHA [*angrily*]: Me! [MAMA *and* RUTH *look at each other and burst into raucous laughter.*] Don't worry—I don't expect you to understand.

MAMA [*to change the subject*]: Who you going out with tomorrow night?

BENEATHA [*with displeasure*]: George Murchison again.

MAMA [*pleased*]: Oh—you getting a little sweet on him?

RUTH: You ask me, this child ain't sweet on nobody but herself—[*Underbreath.*] Express herself!

[*They laugh.*]

BENEATHA: Oh—I like George all right, Mama. I mean I like him enough to go out with him and stuff, but—

RUTH [*for devilment*]: What does *and stuff* mean?

BENEATHA: Mind your own business.

MAMA: Stop picking at her now, Ruth. [*A thoughtful pause, and then a suspicious sudden look at her daughter as she turns in her chair for emphasis.*] What *does* it mean?

BENEATHA [*wearily*]: Oh, I just mean I couldn't ever really be serious about George. He's—he's so shallow.

RUTH: Shallow—what do you mean he's shallow? He's *Rich!*

MAMA: Hush, Ruth.

BENEATHA: I know he's rich. He knows he's rich, too.

RUTH: Well—what other qualities a man got to have to satisfy you, little girl?

BENEATHA: You wouldn't even begin to understand. Anybody who married Walter could not possibly understand.

MAMA [*outraged*]: What kind of way is that to talk about your brother?

BENEATHA: Brother is a flip—let's face it.

MAMA [*to* RUTH, *helplessly*]: What's a flip?

RUTH [*glad to add kindling*]: She's saying he's crazy.

BENEATHA: Not crazy. Brother isn't really crazy yet—he—he's an elaborate neurotic.

MAMA: Hush your mouth!

BENEATHA: As for George. Well. George looks good—he's got a beautiful car and he takes me to nice places and, as my sister-in-law says, he is probably the richest boy I will ever get to know and I even like him sometimes—but if the Youngers are sitting around waiting to see if their little Bennie is going to tie up the family with the Murchisons, they are wasting their time.

RUTH: You mean you wouldn't marry George Murchison if he asked you someday? That pretty, rich thing? Honey, I knew you was odd—

BENEATHA: No I would not marry him if all I felt for him was what I feel now. Besides, George's family wouldn't really like it.

MAMA: Why not?

BENEATHA: Oh, Mama—the Murchisons are honest-to-God-real-*live*-rich colored people, and the only people in the world who are more snobbish than rich white people are rich colored people. I thought everybody knew that. I've met Mrs. Murchison. She's a scene!

MAMA: You must not dislike people 'cause they well off, honey.

BENEATHA: Why not? It makes just as much sense as disliking people 'cause they are poor, and lots of people do that.

RUTH [*a wisdom-of-the-ages manner. To* MAMA]: Well, she'll get over some of this—

BENEATHA: Get over it? What are you talking about, Ruth? Listen, I'm going to be a doctor. I'm not worried about who I'm going to marry yet—if I ever get married.

MAMA *and* RUTH: *If!*

MAMA: Now, Bennie—

BENEATHA: Oh, I probably will . . . but first I'm going to be a doctor, and George, for one, still thinks that's pretty funny. I couldn't be bothered with that. I am going to be a doctor and everybody around here better understand that!

MAMA [*kindly*]: 'Course you going to be a doctor, honey, God willing.

BENEATHA [*drily*]: God hasn't got a thing to do with it.

MAMA: Beneatha—that just wasn't necessary.

BENEATHA: Well—neither is God. I get sick of hearing about God.

MAMA: Beneatha!

BENEATHA: I mean it! I'm just tired of hearing about God all the time. What has He got to do with anything? Does He pay tuition?

MAMA: You 'bout to get your fresh little jaw slapped!

RUTH: That's just what she needs, all right!

BENEATHA: Why? Why can't I say what I want to around here, like everybody else?

MAMA: It don't sound nice for a young girl to say things like that—you wasn't brought up that way. Me and your father went to trouble to get you and Brother to church every Sunday.

BENEATHA: Mama, you don't understand. It's all a matter of ideas, and God is just one idea I don't accept. It's not important. I am not going out and be immoral or commit crimes because I don't believe in God. I don't even think about it. It's just that I get tired of Him getting credit for all the things the human race achieves through its own stubborn effort. There simply is no blasted God—there is only man and it is he who makes miracles!

[MAMA *absorbs this speech, studies her daughter and rises slowly and crosses to* BENEATHA *and slaps her powerfully across the face. After, there is only silence and the daughter drops her eyes from her mother's face, and* MAMA *is very tall before her.*]

MAMA: Now—you say after me, in my mother's house there is still God. [*There is a long pause and* BENEATHA *stares at the floor wordlessly.* MAMA *repeats the phrase with precision and cool emotion.*] In my mother's house there is still God.

BENEATHA: In my mother's house there is still God. [*A long pause.*]

MAMA [*walking away from* BENEATHA, *too disturbed for triumphant posture. Stopping and turning back to her daughter*]: There are some ideas we ain't going to have in this house. Not long as I am at the head of this family.

BENEATHA: Yes, ma'am.

[MAMA *walks out of the room.*]

RUTH [*almost gently, with profound understanding*]: You think you a woman, Bennie—but you still a little girl. What you did was childish—so you got treated like a child.

BENEATHA: I see. [*Quietly.*] I also see that everybody thinks it's all right for Mama to be a tyrant. But all the tyranny in the world will never put a God in the heavens!

[*She picks up her books and goes out.*]

RUTH [*goes to* MAMA's *door*]: She said she was sorry.

MAMA [*coming out, going to her plant*]: They frightens me, Ruth. My children.

RUTH: You got good children, Lena. They just a little off sometimes—but they're good.

MAMA: No—there's something come down between me and them that don't let us understand each other and I don't know what it is. One done almost lost his mind thinking 'bout money all the time and the other done commence to talk about things I can't seem to understand in no form or fashion. What is it that's changing, Ruth?

RUTH [*soothingly, older than her years*]: Now . . . you taking it all too seriously. You just got strong-willed children and it takes a strong woman like you to keep 'em in hand.

MAMA [*looking at her plant and sprinkling a little water on it*]: They spirited all right, my children. Got to admit they got spirit—Bennie and Walter. Like this little old plant that ain't never had enough sunshine or nothing—and look at it . . .

[*She has her back to* RUTH, *who has had to stop ironing and lean against something and put the back of her hand to her forehead.*]

RUTH [*trying to keep* MAMA *from noticing*]: You . . . sure . . . loves that little old thing, don't you? . . .

MAMA: Well, I always wanted me a garden like I used to see sometimes at the back of the houses down home. This plant is close as I ever got to having one. [*She looks out of the window as she replaces the plant.*] Lord, ain't nothing as dreary as the view from this window on a dreary day, is there? Why ain't you singing this morning, Ruth? Sing that "No Ways Tired." That song always lifts me up so—[*She turns at last to see that* RUTH *has slipped quietly into a chair, in a state of semiconsciousness.*] Ruth! Ruth honey—what's the matter with you . . . Ruth!

SCENE II

It is the following morning; a Saturday morning and house cleaning is in progress at the YOUNGERS. *Furniture has been shoved hither and yon and* MAMA *is giving the kitchen-area walls a washing down.* BENEATHA, *in dungarees, with a handkerchief tied around her face, is spraying insecticide into the cracks in the walls. As they work, the radio is on and a Southside disk-jockey program is inappropriately filling the house with a rather exotic saxophone blues.* TRAVIS, *the sole idle one, is leaning on his arms, looking out of the window.*

TRAVIS: Grandmama, that stuff Bennie is using smells awful. Can I go downstairs, please?

MAMA: Did you get all them chores done already? I ain't seen you doing much.

TRAVIS: Yes'm—finished early. Where did Mama go this morning?

MAMA [*looking at* BENEATHA]: She had to go on a little errand.

TRAVIS: Where?

MAMA: To tend to her business.

TRAVIS: Can I go outside then?

MAMA: Oh, I guess so. You better stay right in front of the house, though . . . and keep a good lookout for the postman.

TRAVIS: Yes'm [*He starts out and decides to give his* AUNT BENEATHA *a good swat on the legs as he passes her.*] Leave them poor little old cockroaches alone, they ain't bothering you none.

[*He runs as she swings the spray gun at him both viciously and playfully.* WALTER *enters from the bedroom and goes to the phone.*]

MAMA: Look out there, girl, before you be spilling some of that stuff on that child!

TRAVIS [*teasing*]: That's right—look out now!

[*He exits.*]

BENEATHA [*drily*]: I can't imagine that it would hurt him—it has never hurt the roaches.

MAMA: Well, little boys' hides ain't as tough as Southside roaches.

WALTER [*into phone*]: Hello—Let me talk to Willy Harris.

MAMA: You better get over there behind the bureau. I seen one marching out of there like Napoleon yesterday.

WALTER: Hello, Willy? It ain't come yet. It'll be here in a few minutes. Did the lawyer give you the papers?

BENEATHA: There's really only one way to get rid of them, Mama—

MAMA: How?

BENEATHA: Set fire to this building.

WALTER: Good. Good. I'll be right over.

BENEATHA: Where did Ruth go, Walter?

WALTER: I don't know. [*He exits abruptly.*]

BENEATHA: Mama, where did Ruth go?

MAMA [*looking at her with meaning*]: To the doctor, I think.

BENEATHA: The doctor? What's the matter. [*They exchange glances.*] You don't think—

MAMA [*with her sense of drama*]: Now I ain't saying what I think. But I ain't never been wrong 'bout a woman neither.

[*The phone rings.*]

BENEATHA [*at the phone*]: Hay-lo . . . [*Pause, and a moment of recognition.*] Well—when did you get back! . . . And how was it? . . . Of course I've missed you—in my way . . . This morning? No . . . house cleaning and all that and Mama hates it if

I let people come over when the house is like this . . . You *have?* Well, that's different . . . What is it—Oh, what the hell, come on over . . . Right, see you then. [*She hangs up.*]

MAMA [*who has listened vigorously, as is her habit*]: Who is that you inviting over here with this house looking like this? You ain't got the pride you was born with!

BENEATHA: Asagai doesn't care how houses look, Mama—he's an intellectual.

MAMA: *Who?*

BENEATHA: Asagai—Joseph Asagai. He's an African boy I met on campus. He's been studying in Canada all summer.

MAMA: What's his name?

BENEATHA: Asagai, Joseph. Ah-sah-guy . . . He's from Nigeria.

MAMA: Oh, that's the little country that was founded by slaves way back . . .

BENEATHA: No, Mama—that's Liberia.

MAMA: I don't think I never met no African before.

BENEATHA: Well, do me a favor and don't ask him a whole lot of ignorant questions about Africans. I mean, do they wear clothes and all that—

MAMA: Well, now, I guess if you think we so ignorant 'round here maybe you shouldn't bring your friends here—

BENEATHA: It's just that people ask such crazy things. All anyone seems to know about when it comes to Africa is Tarzan—

MAMA [*indignantly*]: Why should I know anything about Africa?

BENEATHA: Why do you give money at church for the missionary work?

MAMA: Well, that's to help save people.

BENEATHA: You mean save them from *heathenism*—

MAMA [*innocently*]: Yes.

BENEATHA: I'm afraid they need more salvation from the British and the French.

[RUTH *comes in forlornly and pulls off her coat with dejection. They both turn to look at her.*]

RUTH [*dispiritedly*]: Well, I guess from all the happy faces—everybody knows.

BENEATHA: You pregnant?

MAMA: Lord have mercy, I sure hope it's a little old girl. Travis ought to have a sister.

[BENEATHA *and* RUTH *give her a hopeless look for this grandmotherly enthusiasm.*]

BENEATHA: How far along are you?

RUTH: Two months.

BENEATHA: Did you mean to? I mean did you plan it or was it an accident?

MAMA: What do you know about planning or not planning?

BENEATHA: Oh, Mama.

RUTH [*wearily*]: She's twenty years old, Lena.

BENEATHA: Did you plan it, Ruth?

RUTH: Mind your own business.

BENEATHA: It is my business—where is he going to live, on the *roof?* [*There is silence*

following the remark as the three women react to the sense of it.] Gee—I didn't mean that,
   Ruth, honest. Gee, I don't feel like that at all. I—I think it is wonderful.
RUTH [*dully*]: Wonderful.
BENEATHA: Yes—really.
MAMA [*looking at* RUTH, *worried*]: Doctor say everything going to be all right?
RUTH [*far away*]: Yes—she says everything is going to be fine . . .
MAMA [*immediately suspicious*]: "She"—What doctor you went to?

[RUTH *folds over, near hysteria.*]

MAMA [*worriedly hovering over* RUTH]: Ruth honey—what's the matter with you—you
   sick?

[RUTH *has her fists clenched on her thighs and is fighting hard to suppress a scream that seems to
be rising in her.*]

BENEATHA: What's the matter with her, Mama?
MAMA [*working her fingers in* RUTH's *shoulder to relax her*]: She be all right. Women gets right
   depressed sometimes when they get her way. [*Speaking softly, expertly, rapidly.*] Now you
   just relax. That's right . . . just lean back, don't think 'bout nothing at all . . . nothing
   at all—
RUTH: I'm all right . . .

[*The glassy-eyed look melts and then she collapses into a fit of heavy sobbing. The bell rings.*]

BENEATHA: Oh, my God—that must be Asagai.
MAMA [*To* RUTH]: Come on now, honey. You need to lie down and rest awhile . . . then
   have some nice hot food.

[*They exit,* RUTH's *weight on her mother-in-law.* BENEATHA, *herself profoundly disturbed, opens
the door to admit a rather dramatic-looking young man with a large package.*]

ASAGAI: Hello, Alaiyo—
BENEATHA [*holding the door open and regarding him with pleasure*]: Hello . . . [*Long pause.*]
   Well—come in. And please excuse everything. My mother was very upset about my
   letting anyone come here with the place like this.
ASAGAI [*coming into the room*]: You look disturbed too . . . Is something wrong?
BENEATHA [*still at the door, absently*]: Yes . . . we've all got acute ghetto-itus. [*She smiles
   and comes toward him, finding a cigarette and sitting.*] So—sit down! How was Canada?
ASAGAI [*a sophisticate*]: Canadian.
BENEATHA [*looking at him*]: I'm very glad you are back.
ASAGAI [*looking back at her in turn*]: Are you really?
BENEATHA: Yes—very.
ASAGAI: Why—you were quite glad when I went away. What happened?
BENEATHA: You went away.

ASAGAI: Ahhhhhhhh.

BENEATHA: Before—you wanted to be so serious before there was time.

ASAGAI: How much time must there be before one knows what one feels?

BENEATHA [*stalling this particular conversation; her hands pressed together, in a deliberately childish gesture*]: What did you bring me?

ASAGAI [*handing her the package*]: Open it and see.

BENEATHA [*eagerly opening the package and drawing out some records and the colorful robes of a Nigerian woman*]: Oh, Asagai! . . . You got them for me! . . . How beautiful . . . and the records too! [*She lifts out the robes and runs to the mirror with them and holds the drapery up in front of herself.*]

ASAGAI [*coming to her at the mirror*]: I shall have to teach you how to drape it properly. [*He flings the material about her for the moment and stands back to look at her.*] Ah—Oh-pay-pay-day oh-gbah-mu-shay. [*A Yoruba exclamation for admiration.*] You wear it well . . . very well . . . mutilated hair and all.

BENEATHA [*turning suddenly*]: My hair—what's wrong with my hair?

ASAGAI [*shrugging*]: Were you born with it like that?

BENEATHA [*reaching up to touch it*]: No . . . of course not. [*She looks back to the mirror, disturbed.*]

ASAGAI [*smiling*]: How then?

BENEATHA: You know perfectly well how . . . as crinkly as yours . . . that's how.

ASAGAI: And it is ugly to you that way?

BENEATHA [*quickly*]: Oh, no—not ugly . . . [*More slowly, apologetically.*] But it's so hard to manage when it's well—raw.

ASAGAI: And so to accommodate that—you mutilate it every week?

BENEATHA: It's not mutilation!

ASAGAI [*laughing aloud at her seriousness*]: Oh . . . please! I am only teasing you because you are so very serious about these things. [*He stands back from her and folds his arms across his chest as he watches her pulling at her hair and frowning in the mirror.*] Do you remember the first time you met me at school? . . . [*He laughs.*] You came up to me and you said—and I thought you were the most serious little thing I had ever seen—you said: [*He imitates her.*] "Mr. Asagai—I want very much to talk with you. About Africa. You see, Mr. Asagai, I am looking for my *identity!*" [*He laughs.*]

BENEATHA [*turning to him, not laughing*]: Yes—[*Her face is quizzical, profoundly disturbed.*]

ASAGAI [*still teasing and reaching out and taking her face in his hands and turning her profile to him*]: Well . . . it is true that this is not so much a profile of a Hollywood queen as perhaps a queen of the Nile—[*A mock dismissal of the importance of the question.*] But what does it matter? Assimilationism is so popular in your country.

BENEATHA [*wheeling, passionately, sharply*]: I am not an assimilationist!

ASAGAI [*the protest hangs in the room for a moment and* ASAGAI *studies her, his laughter fading*]: Such a serious one. [*There is a pause.*] So—you like the robes? You must take excellent care of them—they are from my sister's personal wardrobe.

BENEATHA [*with incredulity*]: You—you sent all the way home—for me?

ASAGAI [*with charm*]: For you—I would do much more . . . Well, that is what I came for. I must go.

BENEATHA: Will you call me Monday?

ASAGAI: Yes . . . We have a great deal to talk about. I mean about identity and time and all that.

BENEATHA: Time?

ASAGAI: Yes. About how much time one needs to know what one feels.

BENEATHA: You never understood that there is more than one kind of feeling which can exist between a man and a woman—or, at least, there should be.

ASAGAI [*shaking his head negatively but gently*]: No. Between a man and a woman there need be only one kind of feeling. I have that for you . . . Now even . . . right this moment . . .

BENEATHA: I know—and by itself—it won't do. I can find that anywhere.

ASAGAI: For a woman it should be enough.

BENEATHA: I know—because that's what it says in all the novels that men write. But it isn't. Go ahead and laugh—but I'm not interested in being someone's little episode in America or—[*With feminine vengeance.*]—one of them! [ASAGAI *has burst into laughter again.*] That's funny as hell, huh!

ASAGAI: It's just that every American girl I have known has said that to me. White—black—in this you are all the same. And the same speech, too!

BENEATHA [*angrily*]: Yuk, yuk, yuk!

ASAGAI: It's how you can be sure that the world's most liberated women are not liberated at all. You all talk about it too much!

[MAMA *enters and is immediately all social charm because of the presence of a guest.*]

BENEATHA: Oh—Mama—this is Mr. Asagai.

MAMA: How do you do?

ASAGAI [*total politeness to an elder*]: How do you do, Mrs. Younger. Please forgive me for coming at such an outrageous hour on a Saturday.

MAMA: Well, you are quite welcome. I just hope you understand that our house don't always look like this. [*Chatterish.*] You must come again. I would love to hear all about—[*Not sure of the name.*]—your country. I think it's so sad the way our American Negroes don't know nothing about Africa 'cept Tarzan and all that. And all that money they pour into these churches when they ought to be helping you people over there drive out them French and Englishmen done taken away your land. [*The mother flashes a slightly superior look at her daughter upon completion of the recitation.*]

ASAGAI [*taken aback by this sudden and acutely unrelated expression of sympathy*]: Yes . . . yes . . .

MAMA [*smiling at him suddenly and relaxing and looking him over*]: How many miles is it from here to where you come from?

ASAGAI: Many thousands.

MAMA [*looking at him as she would* WALTER]: I bet you don't half look after yourself, being away from your mama either. I spec you better come 'round here from time to time and get yourself some decent home-cooked meals . . .

ASAGAI [*moved*]: Thank you. Thank you very much. [*They are all quiet, then—.*] Well . . . I must go. I will call you Monday, Alaiyo.

MAMA: What's that he call you?

ASAGAI: Oh—"Alaiyo." I hope you don't mind. It is what you would call a nickname, I think. It is a Yoruba word. I am a Yoruba.

MAMA [*looking at* BENEATHA]: I—I thought he was from—

ASAGAI [*understanding*]: Nigeria is my country. Yoruba is my tribal origin—

BENEATHA: You didn't tell us what Alaiyo means . . . for all I know, you might be calling me Little Idiot or something . . .

ASAGAI: Well . . . let me see . . . I do not know how just to explain it . . . The sense of a thing can be so different when it changes languages.

BENEATHA: You're evading.

ASAGAI: No—really it is difficult . . . [*Thinking.*] It means . . . it means One for Whom Bread—Food—Is Not Enough. [*He looks at her.*] Is that all right?

BENEATHA [*understanding, softly*]: Thank you.

MAMA [*looking from one to the other and not understanding any of it*]: Well . . . that's nice . . . You must come see us again—Mr.—

ASAGAI: Ah-sah-guy . . .

MAMA: Yes . . . Do come again.

ASAGAI: Good-bye. [*He exits.*]

MAMA [*after him*]: Lord, that's a pretty thing just went out here! [*Insinuatingly, to her daughter.*] Yes, I guess I see why we done commence to get so interested in Africa 'round here. Missionaries my aunt Jenny! [*She exits.*]

BENEATHA: Oh, Mama! . . . [*She picks up the Nigerian dress and holds it up to her in front of the mirror again. She sets the headdress on haphazardly and then notices her hair again and clutches at it and then replaces the headdress and frowns at herself. Then she starts to wriggle in front of the mirror as she thinks a Nigerian woman might.* TRAVIS *enters and regards her.*]

TRAVIS: You cracking up?

BENEATHA: Shut up. [*She pulls the headdress off and looks at herself in the mirror and clutches at her hair again and squinches her eyes as if trying to imagine something. Then, suddenly, she gets her raincoat and kerchief and hurriedly prepares for going out.*]

MAMA [*coming back into the room*]: She's resting now. Travis, baby, run next door and ask Miss Johnson to please let me have a little kitchen cleanser. This here can is empty as Jacob's kettle.

TRAVIS: I just came in.

MAMA: Do as you told. [*He exits and she looks at her daughter.*] Where you going?

BENEATHA [*halting at the door*]: To become a queen of the Nile! [*She exits in a breathless blaze of glory.* RUTH *appears in the bedroom doorway.*]

MAMA: Who told you to get up?

RUTH: Ain't nothing wrong with me to be lying in no bed for. Where did Bennie go?

MAMA [*drumming her fingers*]: Far as I could make out—to Egypt. [RUTH *just looks at her.*] What time is it getting to?

RUTH: Ten twenty. And the mailman going to ring that bell this morning just like he done every morning for the last umpteen years.

[TRAVIS *comes in with the cleanser can.*]

TRAVIS: She say to tell you that she don't have much.

MAMA [*angrily*]: Lord, some people I could name sure is tight-fisted! [*Directing her grandson.*] Mark two cans of cleanser down on the list there. If she that hard up for kitchen cleanser, I sure don't want to forget to get her none!

RUTH: Lena—maybe the woman is just short on cleanser—

MAMA [*not listening*]: —Much baking powder as she done borrowed from me all these years, she could of done gone into the baking business!

[*The bell sounds suddenly and sharply and all three are stunned—serious and silent—mid-speech. In spite of all the other conversations and distractions of the morning, this is what they have been waiting for, even* TRAVIS, *who looks helplessly from his mother to his grandmother.* RUTH *is the first to come to life again.*]

RUTH [*to* TRAVIS]: *Get down them steps, boy!*

[TRAVIS *snaps to life and flies out to get the mail.*]

MAMA [*her eyes wide, her hand to her breast*]: You mean it done really come?

RUTH [*excited*]: Oh, Miss Lena!

MAMA [*collecting herself*]: Well . . . I don't know what we all so excited about 'round here for. We known it was coming for months.

RUTH: That's a whole lot different from hoping it come and being able to hold it in your hands . . . a piece of paper worth ten thousand dollars . . . [TRAVIS *bursts back into the room. He holds the envelope high above his head, like a little dancer, his face is radiant and he is breathless. He moves to his grandmother with sudden slow ceremony and puts the envelope into her hands. She accepts it, and then merely holds it and looks at it.*] Come on! Open it . . . Lord have mercy, I wish Walter Lee was here!

TRAVIS: Open it, Grandmama!

MAMA [*staring at it*]: Now you all be quiet. It's just a check.

RUTH: Open it . . .

MAMA [*still staring at it*]: Now don't act silly . . . We ain't never been no people to act silly 'bout no money—

RUTH [*swiftly*]: We ain't never had none before—*open it!*

[MAMA *finally makes a good strong tear and pulls out the thin blue slice of paper and inspects it closely. The boy and his mother study it raptly over* MAMA's *shoulders.*]

MAMA: *Travis!* [*She is counting off with doubt.*] Is that the right number of zeros?

TRAVIS: Yes'm . . . ten thousand dollars. Gaalee, Grandmama, you rich.

MAMA [*she holds the check away from her, still looking at it; slowly her face sobers into a mask of unhappiness*]: Ten thousand dollars. [*She hands it to* RUTH.] Put it away somewhere, Ruth. [*She does not look at* RUTH; *her eyes seem to be seeing something somewhere very far off.*] Ten thousand dollars they give you. Ten thousand dollars.

TRAVIS [*to his mother, sincerely*]: What's the matter with Grandmama—don't she want to be rich?

RUTH [*distractedly*]: You go on out and play now, baby. [TRAVIS *exits.* MAMA *starts wiping dishes absently, humming intently to herself.* RUTH *turns to her, with kind exasperation.*] You've gone and got yourself upset.

MAMA [*not looking at her*]: I spec if it wasn't for you all . . . I would just put that money away or give it to the church or something.

RUTH: Now what kind of talk is that. Mr. Younger would just be plain mad if he could hear you talking foolish like that.

MAMA [*stopping and staring off*]: Yes . . . he sure would. [*Sighing.*] We got enough to do with that money, all right. [*She halts then, and turns and looks at her daughter-in-law hard; * RUTH *avoids her eyes and* MAMA *wipes her hands with finality and turns to speak firmly to* RUTH.] Where did you go today, girl?

RUTH: To the doctor.

MAMA [*impatiently*]: Now, Ruth . . . you know better than that. Old Doctor Jones is strange enough in his way but there ain't nothing 'bout him make somebody slip and call him "she"—like you done this morning.

RUTH: Well, that's what happened—my tongue slipped.

MAMA: You went to see that woman, didn't you?

RUTH [*defensively, giving herself away*]: What woman you talking about?

MAMA [*angrily*]: That woman who—

[WALTER *enters in great excitement.*]

WALTER: Did it come?

MAMA [*quietly*]: Can't you give people a Christian greeting before you start asking about money?

WALTER [*to* RUTH]: Did it come? [RUTH *unfolds the check and lays it quietly before him, watching him intently with thoughts of her own.* WALTER *sits down and grasps it close and counts off the zeros.*] Ten thousand dollars—[*He turns suddenly, frantically to his mother and draws some papers out of his breast pocket.*] Mama—look. Old Willy Harris put everything on paper—

MAMA: Son—I think you ought to talk to your wife . . . I'll go on out and leave you alone if you want—

WALTER: I can talk to her later—Mama, look—

MAMA: Son—

WALTER: WILL SOMEBODY PLEASE LISTEN TO ME TODAY!

MAMA [*quietly*]: I don't 'low no yellin' in this house, Walter Lee, and you know it—[WALTER *stares at them in frustration and starts to speak several times.*] And there ain't going to be no investing in no liquor stores. I don't aim to have to speak on that again.

[*A long pause.*]

WALTER: Oh—so you don't aim to have to speak on that again? So *you* have decided . . . [*Crumpling his papers.*] Well, *you* tell that to my boy tonight when you put him to sleep on the living-room couch . . . [*Turning to* MAMA *and speaking directly to her.*]

Yeah—and tell it to my wife, Mama, tomorrow when she has to go out of here to look after somebody else's kids. And tell it to *me*, Mama, every time we need a new pair of curtains and I have to watch *you* go out and work in somebody's kitchen. Yeah, you tell me then! [WALTER *starts out.*]

RUTH: Where you going?

WALTER: I'm going out!

RUTH: Where?

WALTER: Just out of this house somewhere—

RUTH [*getting her coat*]: I'll come too.

WALTER: I don't want you to come!

RUTH: I got something to talk to you about, Walter.

WALTER: That's too bad.

MAMA [*still quietly*]: Walter Lee—[*She waits and he finally turns and looks at her.*] Sit down.

WALTER: I'm a grown man, Mama.

MAMA: Ain't nobody said you wasn't grown. But you still in my house and my presence. And as long as you are—you'll talk to your wife civil. Now sit down.

RUTH [*suddenly*]: Oh, let him go on out and drink himself to death! He makes me sick to my stomach! [*She flings her coat against him.*]

WALTER [*violently*]: And you turn mine too, baby! [RUTH *goes into their bedroom and slams the door behind her.*] That was my greatest mistake—

MAMA [*still quietly*]: Walter, what is the matter with you?

WALTER: Matter with me? Ain't nothing the matter with *me!*

MAMA: Yes there is. Something eating you up like a crazy man. Something more than me not giving you this money. The past few years I been watching it happen to you. You get all nervous acting and kind of wild in the eyes—[WALTER *jumps up impatiently at her words.*] I said sit there now, I'm talking to you!

WALTER: Mama—I don't need no nagging at me today.

MAMA: Seem like you getting to a place where you always tied up in some kind of knot about something. But if anybody ask you 'bout it you just yell at 'em and bust out the house and go out and drink somewheres. Walter Lee, people can't live with that. Ruth's a good, patient girl in her way—but you getting to be too much. Boy, don't make the mistake of driving that girl away from you.

WALTER: Why—what she do for me?

MAMA: She loves you.

WALTER: Mama—I'm going out. I want to go off somewhere and be by myself for a while.

MAMA: I'm sorry 'bout your liquor store, son. It just wasn't the thing for us to do. That's what I want to tell you about—

WALTER: I got to go out, Mama—[*He rises.*]

MAMA: It's dangerous, son.

WALTER: What's dangerous?

MAMA: When a man goes outside his home to look for peace.

WALTER [*beseechingly*]: Then why can't there never be no peace in this house then?

MAMA: You done found it in some other house?

WALTER: No—there ain't no woman! Why do women always think there's a woman somewhere when a man gets restless. [*Coming to her.*] Mama—Mama—I want so many things . . .

MAMA: Yes, son—

WALTER: I want so many things that they are driving me kind of crazy . . . Mama— look at me.

MAMA: I'm looking at you. You a good-looking boy. You got a job, a nice wife, a fine boy and—

WALTER: A job. [*Looks at her.*] Mama, a job? I open and close car doors all day long. I drive a man around in his limousine and I say, "Yes, sir; no, sir; very good, sir; shall I take the Drive, sir?" Mama, that ain't no kind of job . . . that ain't nothing at all. [*Very quietly.*] Mama, I don't know if I can make you understand.

MAMA: Understand what, baby?

WALTER [*quietly*]: Sometimes it's like I can see the future stretched out in front of me—just plain as day. The future, Mama. Hanging over there at the edge of my days. Just waiting for me—a big, looming blank space—full of *nothing.* Just waiting for *me.* [*Pause.*] Mama—sometimes when I'm downtown and I pass them cool, quiet-looking restaurants where them white boys are sitting back and talking 'bout things . . . sitting there turning deals worth millions of dollars . . . sometimes I see guys don't look much older than me—

MAMA: Son—how come you talk so much 'bout money?

WALTER [*with immense passion*]: Because it is life, Mama!

MAMA [*quietly*]: Oh—[*Very quietly.*] So now it's life. Money is life. Once upon a time freedom used to be life—now it's money. I guess the world really do change . . .

WALTER: No—it was always money, Mama. We just didn't know about it.

MAMA: No. . . . something has changed. [*She looks at him.*] You something new, boy. In my time we was worried about not being lynched and getting to the North if we could and how to stay alive and still have a pinch of dignity too . . . Now here come you and Beneatha—talking 'bout things we ain't never even thought about hardly, me and your daddy. You ain't satisfied or proud of nothing we done. I mean that you had a home; that we kept you out of trouble till you was grown; that you don't have to ride to work on the back of nobody's streetcar—You my children—but how different we done become.

WALTER: You just don't understand, Mama, you just don't understand.

MAMA: Son—do you know your wife is expecting another baby? [WALTER *stands, stunned, and absorbs what his mother has said.*] That's what she wanted to talk to you about. [WALTER *sinks down into a chair.*] This ain't for me to be telling—but you ought to know. [*She waits.*] I think Ruth is thinking 'bout getting rid of that child.

WALTER [*slowly understanding*]: No—no—Ruth wouldn't do that.

MAMA: When the world gets ugly enough—a woman will do anything for her family. *The part that's already living.*

WALTER: You don't know Ruth, Mama, if you think she would do that.

[RUTH *opens the bedroom door and stands there a little limp.*]

RUTH [*beaten*]: Yes I would too, Walter. [*Pause.*] I gave her a five-dollar down payment.

[*There is total silence as the man stares at his wife and the mother stares at her son.*]

MAMA [*presently*]: Well—[*Tightly.*] Well—son, I'm waiting to hear you say something
. . . I'm waiting to hear how you be your father's son. Be the man he was . . . [*Pause.*]
Your wife say she going to destroy your child. And I'm waiting to hear you talk like
him and say we a people who give children life, not who destroys them—[*She rises.*]
I'm waiting to see you stand up and look like your daddy and say we done give up
one baby to poverty and that we ain't going to give up nary another one . . . I'm
waiting.

WALTER: Ruth—

MAMA: If you a son of mine, tell her! [WALTER *turns, looks at her and can say nothing. She
continues, bitterly.*] You . . . you are a disgrace to your father's memory. Somebody get
me my hat.

ACT II

SCENE I

Time: Later the same day.

At rise: RUTH *is ironing again. She has the radio going. Presently* BENEATHA'*s bedroom door opens
and* RUTH'*s mouth falls and she puts down the iron in fascination.*

RUTH: What have we got on tonight!

BENEATHA [*emerging grandly from the doorway so that we can see her thoroughly robed in the costume
Asagai brought*]: You are looking at what a well-dressed Nigerian woman wears—[*She
parades for* RUTH, *her hair completely hidden by the headdress; she is coquettishly fanning herself
with an ornate oriental fan, mistakenly more like Butterfly than any Nigerian that ever was.*] Isn't
it beautiful? [*She promenades to the radio and, with an arrogant flourish, turns off the good loud
blues that is playing.*] Enough of this assimilationist junk! [RUTH *follows her with her eyes
as she goes to the phonograph and puts on a record and turns and waits ceremoniously for the music
to come up. Then, with a shout*—] OCOMOGOSIAY!

[RUTH *jumps. The music comes up, a lovely Nigerian melody.* BENEATHA *listens, enraptured, her
eyes far away*—"*back to the past.*" *She begins to dance.* RUTH *is dumbfounded.*]

RUTH: What kind of dance is that?

BENEATHA: A folk dance.

RUTH [*Pearl Bailey*]: What kind of folks do that, honey?

BENEATHA: It's from Nigeria. It's a dance of welcome.

RUTH: Who you welcoming?

BENEATHA: The men back to the village.

RUTH: Where they been?

BENEATHA: How should I know—out hunting or something. Anyway, they are coming back now . . .

RUTH: Well, that's good.

BENEATHA [*with the record*]:

Alundi, alundi
Alundi alunya
Jop pu a jeepua
Ang gu sooooooooooo

Ai yai yae . . .
Ayehaye—alundi . . .

[WALTER *comes in during this performance; he has obviously been drinking. He leans against the door heavily and watches his sister, at first with distaste. Then his eyes look off—"back to the past"—as he lifts both his fists to the roof, screaming.*]

WALTER: YEAH . . . AND ETHIOPIA STRETCH FORTH HER HANDS AGAIN! . . .

RUTH [*drily, looking at him*]: Yes—and Africa sure is claiming her own tonight. [*She gives them both up and starts ironing again.*]

WALTER [*all in a drunken, dramatic shout*]: Shut up! . . . I'm digging them drums . . . them drums move me! . . . [*He makes his weaving way to his wife's face and leans in close to her.*] In my *heart of hearts*— [*He thumps his chest.*]—I am much warrior!

RUTH [*without even looking up*]: In your heart of hearts you are much drunkard.

WALTER [*coming away from her and starting to wander around the room, shouting*]: Me and Jomo . . . [*Intently, in his sister's face. She has stopped dancing to watch him in this unknown mood.*] That's my man, Kenyatta. [*Shouting and thumping his chest.*] FLAMING SPEAR! HOT DAMN! [*He is suddenly in possession of an imaginary spear and actively spearing enemies all over the room.*] OCOMOGOSIAY . . . THE LION IS WAKING . . . OWIMOWEH! [*He pulls his shirt open and leaps up on a table and gestures with his spear. The bell rings.* RUTH *goes to answer.*]

BENEATHA [*to encourage* WALTER, *thoroughly caught up with this side of him*]: OCOMOGO-SIAY, FLAMING SPEAR!

WALTER [*on the table, very far gone, his eyes pure glass sheets. He sees what we cannot, that he is a leader of his people, a great chief, a descendant of Chaka, and that the hour to march has come*]: Listen, my black brothers—

BENEATHA: OCOMOGOSIAY!

WALTER: —Do you hear the waters rushing against the shores of the coastlands—

BENEATHA: OCOMOGOSIAY!

WALTER: —Do you hear the screeching of the cocks in yonder hills beyond where the chiefs meet in council for the coming of the mighty war—

BENEATHA: OCOMOGOSIAY!

WALTER: —Do you hear the beating of the wings of the birds flying low over the mountains and the low places of our land—

[RUTH *opens the door.* GEORGE MURCHISON *enters.*]

BENEATHA: OCOMOGOSIAY!

WALTER: —Do you hear the singing of the women, singing the war songs of our fathers to the babies in the great houses . . . singing the sweet war songs? OH, DO YOU HEAR, MY BLACK BROTHERS!

BENEATHA [*completely gone*]: We hear you, Flaming Spear—

WALTER: Telling us to prepare for the greatness of the time—[*To* GEORGE.] Black Brother! [*He extends his hand for the fraternal clasp.*]

GEORGE: Black Brother, hell!

RUTH [*having had enough, and embarrassed for the family*]: Beneatha, you got company— what's the matter with you? Walter Lee Younger, get down off that table and stop acting like a fool . . .

[WALTER *comes down off the table suddenly and makes a quick exit to the bathroom.*]

RUTH: He's had a little to drink . . . I don't know what her excuse is.

GEORGE [*to* BENEATHA]: Look honey, we're going *to* the theatre—we're not going to be *in* it . . . so go change, huh?

RUTH: You expect this boy to go out with you looking like that?

BENEATHA [*looking at* GEORGE]: That's up to George. If he's ashamed of his heritage—

GEORGE: Oh, don't be so proud of yourself, Bennie—just because you look eccentric.

BENEATHA: How can something that's natural be eccentric?

GEORGE: That's what being eccentric means—being natural. Get dressed.

BENEATHA: I don't like that, George.

RUTH: Why must you and your brother make an argument out of everything people say?

BENEATHA: Because I hate assimilationist Negroes!

RUTH: Will somebody please tell me what assimila-whoever means!

GEORGE: Oh, it's just a college girl's way of calling people Uncle Toms—but that isn't what it means at all.

RUTH: Well, what does it mean?

BENEATHA [*cutting* GEORGE *off and staring at him as she replies to* RUTH]: It means someone who is willing to give up his own culture and submerge himself completely in the dominant, and in this case, *oppressive* culture!

GEORGE: Oh, dear, dear, dear! Here we go! A lecture on the African past! On our Great West African Heritage! In one second we will hear all about the great Ashanti empires; the great Songhay civilizations; and the great sculpture of Benth—and then some poetry in the Bantu—and the whole monologue will end with the word *bondage!* [*Nastily*] Let's face it, baby, your heritage is nothing but a bunch of raggedy-assed spirituals and some grass huts!

BENEATHA: *Grass huts!* [RUTH *crosses to her and forcibly pushes her toward the bedroom.*] See there . . . you are standing there in your splendid ignorance talking about people who were the first to smelt iron on the face of the earth! [RUTH *is pushing her through the door.*] The Ashanti were performing surgical operations when the English—[RUTH *pulls the door to, with* BENEATHA *on the other side, and smiles graciously at* GEORGE. BENEATHA *opens the door and shouts the end of the sentence defiantly at* GEORGE.]—were still tatooing themselves with blue dragons . . . [*She goes back inside.*]

RUTH: Have a seat, George. [*They both sit.* RUTH *folds her hands rather primly on her lap, determined to demonstrate the civilization of the family.*] Warm, ain't it? I mean for September. [*Pause.*] Just like they always say about Chicago weather: If it's too hot or cold for you, just wait a minute and it'll change. [*She smiles happily at this cliché of clichés.*] Everybody say it's got to do with them bombs and things they keep setting off. [*Pause.*] Would you like a nice cold beer?

GEORGE: No, thank you. I don't care for beer. [*He looks at his watch.*] I hope she hurries up.

RUTH: What time is the show?

GEORGE: It's an eight-thirty curtain. That's just Chicago though. In New York standard curtain time is eight forty. [*He is rather proud of this knowledge.*]

RUTH [*properly appreciating it*]: You get to New York a lot?

GEORGE [*offhand*]: Few times a year.

RUTH: Oh—that's nice. I've never been to New York.

[WALTER *enters. We feel he has relieved himself, but the edge of unreality is still with him.*]

WALTER: New York ain't got nothing Chicago ain't. Just a bunch of hustling people all squeezed up together—being "Eastern." [*He turns his face into a screw of displeasure.*]

GEORGE: Oh—you've been?

WALTER: *Plenty* of times.

RUTH [*shocked at the lie*]: Walter Lee Younger!

WALTER [*staring her down*]: Plenty! [*Pause.*] What we got to drink in this house? Why don't you offer this man some refreshment. [*To* GEORGE.] They don't know how to entertain people in this house, man.

GEORGE: Thank you—I don't really care for anything.

WALTER [*feeling his head; sobriety coming*]: Where's Mama?

RUTH: She ain't come back yet.

WALTER [*looking* MURCHISON *over from head to toe, scrutinizing his carefully casual tweed sports jacket over cashmere V-neck sweater over soft eyelet shirt and tie, and soft slacks, finished off with white buckskin shoes*]: Why all you college boys wear them fairyish-looking white shoes?

RUTH: Walter Lee!

[GEORGE MURCHISON *ignores the remark.*]

WALTER [*to* RUTH]: Well, they look crazy as hell—white shoes, cold as it is.

RUTH [*crushed*]: You have to excuse him—

WALTER: No he don't! Excuse me for what? What you always excusing me for! I'll excuse myself when I needs to be excused! [*A pause.*] They look as funny as them black knee socks Beneatha wears out of here all the time.

RUTH: It's the college *style*, Walter.

WALTER: Style, hell. She looks like she got burnt legs or something!

RUTH: Oh, Walter—

WALTER [*an irritable mimic*]: Oh, Walter! Oh, Walter! [*To* MURCHISON.] How's your old man making out? I understand you all going to buy that big hotel on the Drive? [*He finds a beer in the refrigerator, wanders over to* MURCHISON, *sipping and wiping his lips with the back of his hand, and straddling a chair backwards to talk to the other man.*] Shrewd move. Your old man is all right, man. [*Tapping his head and half winking for emphasis.*] I mean he knows how to operate. I mean he thinks *big*, you know what I mean, I mean for a *home*, you know? But I think he's kind of running out of ideas now. I'd like to talk to him. Listen, man, I got some plans that could turn this city upside down. I mean I think like he does. *Big.* Invest big, gamble big, hell, lose *big* if you have to, you know what I mean. It's hard to find a man on this whole Southside who understands my kind of thinking—you dig? [*He scrutinizes* MURCHISON *again, drinks his beer, squints his eyes and leans in close, confidential, man to man.*] Me and you ought to sit down and talk sometimes, man. Man, I got me some ideas . . .

MURCHISON [*with boredom*]: Yeah—sometimes we'll have to do that, Walter.

WALTER [*understanding the indifference, and offended*]: Yeah—well, when you get the time, man. I know you a busy little boy.

RUTH: Walter, please—

WALTER [*bitterly, hurt*]: I know ain't nothing in this world as busy as you colored college boys with your fraternity pins and white shoes . . .

RUTH [*covering her face with humiliation*]: Oh, Walter Lee—

WALTER: I see you all the time—with the books tucked under your arms—going to your [*British A—a mimic.*] "clahsses." And for what! What the hell you learning over there? Filling up your heads—[*Counting off on his fingers.*]—with the sociology and the psychology—but they teaching you how to be a man? How to take over and run the world? They teaching you how to run a rubber plantation or a steel mill? Naw—just to talk proper and read books and wear white shoes . . .

GEORGE [*looking at him with distaste, a little above it all*]: You're all wacked up with bitterness, man.

WALTER [*intently, almost quietly, between the teeth, glaring at the boy*]: And you—ain't you bitter, man? Ain't you just about had it yet? Don't you see no stars gleaming that you can't reach out and grab? You happy?—you contented son-of-a-bitch—you happy? You got it made? Bitter? Man, I'm a volcano. Bitter? Here I am a giant—surrounded by ants! Ants who can't even understand what it is the giant is talking about.

RUTH [*passionately and suddenly*]: Oh, Walter—ain't you with nobody!

WALTER [*violently*]: No! 'Cause ain't nobody with me! Not even my own mother!

RUTH: Walter, that's a terrible thing to say!

[BENEATHA *enters, dressed for the evening in a cocktail dress and earrings.*]

GEORGE: Well—hey, you look great.

BENEATHA: Let's go, George. See you all later.

RUTH: Have a nice time.

GEORGE: Thanks. Good night. [*To* WALTER, *sarcastically.*] Good night, *Prometheus.*

[BENEATHA *and* GEORGE *exit.*]

WALTER [*to* RUTH]: Who is Prometheus?

RUTH: I don't know. Don't worry about it.

WALTER [*in fury, pointing after* GEORGE]: See there—they get to a point where they can't insult you man to man—they got to go talk about something ain't nobody never heard of!

RUTH: How you know it was an insult? [*To humor him.*] Maybe Prometheus is a nice fellow.

WALTER: Prometheus! I bet there ain't even no such thing! I bet that simple-minded clown—

RUTH: Walter—[*She stops what she is doing and looks at him.*]

WALTER [*yelling*]: Don't start!

RUTH: Start what?

WALTER: Your nagging! Where was I? Who was I with? How much money did I spend?

RUTH [*plaintively*]: Walter Lee—why don't we just try to talk about it . . .

WALTER [*not listening*]: I been out talking with people who understand me. People who care about the things I got on my mind.

RUTH [*wearily*]: I guess that means people like Willy Harris.

WALTER: Yes, people like Willy Harris.

RUTH [*with a sudden flash of impatience*]: Why don't you all just hurry up and go into the banking business and stop talking about it!

WALTER: Why? You want to know why? 'Cause we all tied up in a race of people that don't know how to do nothing but moan, pray and have babies! [*The line is too bitter even for him and he looks at her and sits down.*]

RUTH: Oh, Walter . . . [*Softly*] Honey, why can't you stop fighting me?

WALTER [*without thinking*]: Who's fighting you? Who even cares about you? [*This line begins the retardation of his mood.*]

RUTH: Well—[*She waits a long time, and then with resignation starts to put away her things.*] I guess I might as well go on to bed . . . [*More or less to herself.*] I don't know where we lost it . . . but we have . . . [*Then, to him.*] I—I'm sorry about this new baby, Walter. I guess maybe I better go on and do what I started . . . I guess I just didn't realize how bad things was with us . . . I guess I just didn't really realize—[*She starts out to the bedroom and stops.*] You want some hot milk?

WALTER: Hot milk?

RUTH: Yes—hot milk.

WALTER: Why hot milk?

RUTH: 'Cause after all that liquor you come home with you ought to have something hot in your stomach.

WALTER: I don't want no milk.

RUTH: You want some coffee then?

WALTER: No, I don't want no coffee. I don't want nothing hot to drink. [*Almost plaintively.*] Why you always trying to give me something to eat?

RUTH [*standing and looking at him helplessly*]: What else can I give you, Walter Lee Younger?

[*She stands and looks at him and presently turns to go out again. He lifts his head and watches her going away from him in a new mood which began to emerge when he asked her "Who cares about you?"*]

WALTER: It's been rough, ain't it, baby? [*She hears and stops but does not turn around and he continues to her back.*] I guess between two people there ain't never as much understood as folks generally thinks there is. I mean like between me and you—[*She turns to face him.*] How we gets to the place where we scared to talk softness to each other. [*He waits, thinking hard himself.*] Why you think it got to be like that? [*He is thoughtful, almost as a child would be.*] Ruth, what is it gets into people ought to be close?

RUTH: I don't know, honey. I think about it a lot.

WALTER: On account of you and me, you mean? The way things are with us. The way something done come down between us.

RUTH: There ain't so much between us, Walter . . . Not when you come to me and try to talk to me. Try to be with me . . . a little even.

WALTER [*total honesty*]: Sometimes . . . sometimes . . . I don't even know how to try.

RUTH: Walter—

WALTER: Yes?

RUTH [*coming to him, gently and with misgiving, but coming to him*]: Honey . . . life don't have to be like this. I mean sometimes people can do things so that things are better . . . You remember how we used to talk when Travis was born . . . about the way we were going to live . . . the kind of house . . . [*She is stroking his head.*] Well, it's all starting to slip away from us . . .

[MAMA *enters, and* WALTER *jumps up and shouts at her.*]

WALTER: Mama, where have you been?

MAMA: My—them steps is longer than they used to be. Whew! [*She sits down and ignores him.*] How you feeling this evening, Ruth?

[RUTH *shrugs, disturbed some at having been prematurely interrupted and watching her husband knowingly.*]

WALTER: Mama, where have you been all day?

MAMA [*still ignoring him and leaning on the table and changing to more comfortable shoes*]: Where's Travis?

RUTH: I let him go out earlier and he ain't come back yet. Boy, is he going to get it!

WALTER: Mama!

MAMA [*as if she has heard for the first time*]: Yes, son?

WALTER: Where did you go this afternoon?

MAMA: I went down town to tend to some business that I had to tend to.

WALTER: What kind of business?

MAMA: You know better than to question me like a child, Brother.

WALTER [*rising and bending over the table*]: Where were you, Mama? [*Bringing his fists down and shouting.*] Mama, you didn't go do something with that insurance money, something crazy?

[*The front door opens slowly, interrupting him, and* TRAVIS *peeks his head in, less than hopefully.*]

TRAVIS [*to his mother*]: Mama, I—

RUTH: "Mama I" nothing! You're going to get it, boy! Get on in that bedroom and get yourself ready!

TRAVIS: But I—

MAMA: Why don't you all never let the child explain hisself.

RUTH: Keep out of it now, Lena.

[MAMA *clamps her lips together, and* RUTH *advances toward her son menacingly.*]

RUTH: A thousand times I have told you not to go off like that—

MAMA [*holding out her arms to her grandson*]: Well—at least let me tell him something. I want him to be the first one to hear . . . Come here, Travis. [*The boy obeys, gladly.*] Travis—[*She takes him by the shoulders and looks into his face.*]—you know that money we got in the mail this morning?

TRAVIS: Yes'm—

MAMA: Well—what you think your grandmama gone and done with that money?

TRAVIS: I don't know, Grandmama.

MAMA [*putting her finger on his nose for emphasis*]: She went out and she bought you a house! [*The explosion comes from* WALTER *at the end of the revelation and he jumps up and turns away from all of them in a fury.* MAMA *continues, to* TRAVIS.] You glad about the house? It's going to be yours when you get to be a man.

TRAVIS: Yeah—I always wanted to live in a house.

MAMA: All right, gimme some sugar then—[TRAVIS *puts his arms around her neck as she watches her son over the boy's shoulder. Then, to* TRAVIS, *after the embrace.*] Now when you say your prayers tonight, you thank God and your grandfather—'cause it was him who give you the house—in his way.

RUTH [*taking the boy from* MAMA *and pushing him toward the bedroom*]: Now you get out of here and get ready for your beating.

TRAVIS: Aw, Mama—

RUTH: Get on in there—[*Closing the door behind him and turning radiantly to her mother-in-law.*] So you went and did it!

MAMA [*quietly, looking at her son with pain*]: Yes, I did.

RUTH [*raising both arms classically*]: *Praise God!* [*Looks at* WALTER *a moment, who says nothing. She crosses rapidly to her husband.*] Please, honey—let me be glad . . . you be glad too. [*She has laid her hands on his shoulders, but he shakes himself free of her roughly, without turning to face her.*] Oh, Walter . . . a home . . . a home. [*She comes back to* MAMA.] Well—where is it? How big is it? How much it going to cost?

MAMA: Well—

RUTH: When we moving?

MAMA [*smiling at her*]: First of the month.

RUTH [*throwing back her head with jubilance*]: *Praise God!*

MAMA [*tentatively, still looking at her son's back turned against her and* RUTH]: It's—it's a nice house too . . . [*She cannot help speaking directly to him. An imploring quality in her voice, her manner, makes her almost like a girl now.*] Three bedrooms—nice big one for you and Ruth. . . . Me and Beneatha still have to share our room, but Travis have one of his

own—and—[*With difficulty.*] I figures if the—new baby—is a boy, we could get one
of them double-decker outfits . . . And there's a yard with a little patch of dirt where
I could maybe get to grow me a few flowers . . . And a nice big basement . . .

RUTH: Walter honey, be glad—

MAMA [*still to his back, fingering things on the table*]: 'Course I don't want to make it sound
fancier than it is . . . It's just a plain little old house—but it's made good and
solid—and it will be *ours*. Walter Lee—it makes a difference in a man when he can
walk on floors that belong to *him* . . .

RUTH: Where is it?

MAMA [*frightened at this telling*]: Well—well—it's out there in Clybourne Park—

[RUTH's *radiance fades abruptly, and* WALTER *finally turns slowly to face his mother with
incredulity and hostility.*]

RUTH: Where?

MAMA [*matter-of-factly*]: Four o six Clybourne Street, Clybourne Park.

RUTH: Clybourne Park? Mama, there ain't no colored people living in Clybourne
Park.

MAMA [*almost idiotically*]: Well, I guess there's going to be some now.

WALTER [*bitterly*]: So that's the peace and comfort you went out and bought for us
today!

MAMA [*raising her eyes to meet his finally*]: Son—I just tried to find the nicest place for the
least amount of money for my family.

RUTH [*trying to recover from the shock*]: Well—well—'course I ain't one never been 'fraid
of no crackers, mind you—but—well, wasn't there no other houses nowhere?

MAMA: Them houses they put up for colored in them areas way out all seem to cost
twice as much as other houses. I did the best I could.

RUTH [*struck senseless with the news, in its various degrees of goodness and trouble, she sits a moment,
her fists propping her chin in thought, and then she starts to rise, bringing her fists down with vigor,
the radiance spreading from cheek to cheek again*]: Well—well!—All I can say is—if this is
my time in life—*my time*—to say good-bye—[*and she builds with momentum as she starts
to circle the room with an exuberant, almost tearfully happy release*]—to these God-damned
cracking walls!—[*she pounds the walls*]—and these marching roaches!—[*she wipes at an
imaginary army of marching roaches*]—and this cramped little closet which ain't now or
never was no kitchen! . . . then I say it loud and good, *Hallelujah! and good-bye misery*
. . . *I don't never want to see your ugly face again!* [*She laughs joyously, having practically destroyed
the apartment, and flings her arms up and lets them come down happily, slowly, reflectively, over her
abdomen, aware for the first time perhaps that the life therein pulses with happiness and not despair.*]
Lena?

MAMA [*moved, watching her happiness*]: Yes, honey?

RUTH [*looking off*]: Is there—is there a whole lot of sunlight?

MAMA [*understanding*]: Yes, child, there's a whole lot of sunlight.

[*Long pause.*]

RUTH [*collecting herself and going to the door of the room* TRAVIS *is in*]: Well—I guess I better see 'bout Travis. [*To* MAMA.] Lord, I sure don't feel like whipping nobody today! [*She exits.*]

MAMA [*the mother and son are left alone now and the mother waits a long time, considering deeply, before she speaks*]: Son—you—you understand what I done, don't you? [WALTER *is silent and sullen.*] I—I just seen my family falling apart today . . . just falling to pieces in front of my eyes . . . We couldn't of gone on like we was today. We was going backwards 'stead of forwards—talking 'bout killing babies and wishing each other was dead . . . When it gets like that in life—you just got to do something different, push on out and do something bigger . . . [*She waits.*] I wish you say something, son . . . I wish you'd say how deep inside you you think I done the right thing—

WALTER [*crossing slowly to his bedroom door and finally turning there and speaking measuredly*]: What you need me to say you done right for? *You* the head of this family. You run our lives like you want to. It was your money and you did what you wanted with it. So what you need for me to say it was all right for? [*Bitterly, to hurt her as deeply as he knows is possible.*] So you butchered up a dream of mine—you—who always talking 'bout your children's dreams . . .

MAMA: Walter Lee—

[*He just closes the door behind him.* MAMA *sits alone, thinking heavily.*]

SCENE II

Time: Friday night. A few weeks later.

    At rise: Packing crates mark the intention of the family to move. BENEATHA *and* GEORGE *come in, presumably from an evening out again.*

GEORGE: O.K. . . . O.K., whatever you say . . . [*They both sit on the couch. He tries to kiss her. She moves away.*] Look, we've had a nice evening; let's not spoil it, huh? . . .

[*He again turns her head and tries to nuzzle in and she turns away from him, not with distaste but with momentary lack of interest; in a mood to pursue what they were talking about.*]

BENEATHA: I'm *trying* to talk to you.

GEORGE: We always talk.

BENEATHA: Yes—and I love to talk.

GEORGE [*exasperated; rising*]: I know it and I don't mind it sometimes . . . I want you to cut it out, see—The moody stuff, I mean. I don't like it. You're a nice-looking girl . . . all over. That's all you need, honey, forget the atmosphere. Guys aren't going to go for the atmosphere—they're going to go for what they see. Be glad for that. Drop the Garbo routine. It doesn't go with you. As for myself, I want a nice— [*Groping.*]—simple—[*Thoughtfully.*]—sophisticated girl . . . not a poet—O.K.?

[*She rebuffs him again and he starts to leave.*]

BENEATHA: Why are you angry?

GEORGE: Because this is stupid! I don't go out with you to discuss the nature of "quiet desperation" or to hear all about your thoughts—because the world will go on thinking what it thinks regardless—

BENEATHA: Then why read books? Why go to school?

GEORGE [*with artificial patience, counting on his fingers*]: It's simple. You read books—to learn facts—to get grades—to pass the course—to get a degree. That's all—it has nothing to do with thoughts.

[*A long pause.*]

BENEATHA: I see. [*A longer pause as she looks at him.*] Good night, George.

[GEORGE *looks at her a little oddly, and starts to exit. He meets* MAMA *coming in.*]

GEORGE: Oh—hello, Mrs. Younger.

MAMA: Hello, George, how you feeling?

GEORGE: Fine—fine, how are you?

MAMA: Oh, a little tired. You know them steps can get you after a day's work. You all have a nice time tonight?

GEORGE: Yes—a fine time. Well, good night.

MAMA: Good night. [*He exits.* MAMA *closes the door behind her.*] Hello, honey. What you sitting like that for?

BENEATHA: I'm just sitting.

MAMA: Didn't you have a nice time?

BENEATHA: No.

MAMA: No? What's the matter?

BENEATHA: Mama, George is a fool—honest. [*She rises.*]

MAMA [*hustling around unloading the packages she has entered with; she stops*]: Is he, baby?

BENEATHA: Yes. [BENEATHA *makes up* TRAVIS' *bed as she talks.*]

MAMA: You sure?

BENEATHA: Yes.

MAMA: Well—I guess you better not waste your time with no fools.

[BENEATHA *looks up at her mother, watching her put groceries in the refrigerator. Finally she gathers up her things and starts into the bedroom. At the door she stops and looks back at her mother.*]

BENEATHA: Mama—

MAMA: Yes, baby—

BENEATHA: Thank you.

MAMA: For what?

BENEATHA: For understanding me this time.

[*She exits quickly and the mother stands, smiling a little, looking at the place where* BENEATHA *just stood.* RUTH *enters.*]

RUTH: Now don't you fool with any of this stuff, Lena—

MAMA: Oh, I just thought I'd sort a few things out.

[*The phone rings.* RUTH *answers.*]

RUTH [*at the phone*]: Hello—Just a minute. [*Goes to door.*] Walter, it's Mrs. Arnold. [*Waits. Goes back to the phone. Tense.*] Hello. Yes, this is his wife speaking . . . He's lying down now. Yes . . . well, he'll be in tomorrow. He's been very sick. Yes—I know we should have called, but we were so sure he'd be able to come in today. Yes—yes, I'm very sorry. Yes . . . Thank you very much. [*She hangs up.* WALTER *is standing in the doorway of the bedroom behind her.*] That was Mrs. Arnold.

WALTER [*indifferently*]: Was it?

RUTH: She said if you don't come in tomorrow that they are getting a new man . . .

WALTER: Ain't that sad—ain't that crying sad.

RUTH: She said Mr. Arnold has had to take a cab for three days . . . Walter, you ain't been to work for three days! [*This is a revelation to her.*] Where you been, Walter Lee Younger? [WALTER *looks at her and starts to laugh.*] You're going to lose your job.

WALTER: That's right . . .

RUTH: Oh, Walter, and with your mother working like a dog every day—

WALTER: That's sad too—Everything is sad.

MAMA: What you been doing for these three days, son?

WALTER: Mama—you don't know all the things a man what got leisure can find to do in this city . . . What's this—Friday night? Well—Wednesday I borrowed Willy Harris' car and I went for a drive . . . just me and myself and I drove and drove . . . Way out . . . way past South Chicago, and I parked the car and I sat and looked at the steel mills all day long. I just sat in the car and looked at them big black chimneys for hours. Then I drove back and I went to the Green Hat. [*Pause.*] And Thursday—Thursday I borrowed the car again and I got in it and I pointed it the other way and I drove the other way—four hours—way, way up to Wisconsin, and I looked at the farms. I just drove and looked at the farms. Then I drove back and I went to the Green Hat. [*Pause.*] And today—today I didn't get the car. Today I just walked. All over the Southside. And I looked at the Negroes and they looked at me and finally I just sat down on the curb at Thirty-ninth and South Parkway and I just sat there and watched the Negroes go by. And then I went to the Green Hat. You all sad? You all depressed? And you know where I am going right now—

[RUTH *goes out quietly.*]

MAMA: Oh, Big Walter, is this the harvest of our days?

WALTER: You know what I like about the Green Hat? [*He turns the radio on and a steamy, deep blues pours into the room.*] I like this little cat they got there who blows a sax . . . He blows. He talks to me. He ain't but 'bout five feet tall and he's got a conked head and his eyes is always closed and he's all music—

MAMA [*rising and getting some papers out of her handbag*]: Walter—

WALTER: And there's this other guy who plays the piano . . . and they got a sound. I mean they can work on some music . . . They got the best little combo in the world in the Green Hat . . . You can just sit there and drink and listen to them three men play and you realize that don't nothing matter worth a damn, but just being there—

MAMA: I've helped do it to you, haven't I, son? Walter, I been wrong.

WALTER: Naw—you ain't never been wrong about nothing, Mama.

MAMA: Listen to me, now. I say I been wrong, son. That I been doing to you what the rest of the world been doing to you. [*She stops and he looks up slowly at her and she meets his eyes pleadingly.*] Walter—what you ain't never understood is that I ain't got nothing, don't own nothing, ain't never really wanted nothing that wasn't for you. There ain't nothing as precious to me . . . There ain't nothing worth holding on to, money, dreams, nothing else—if it means—if it means it's going to destroy my boy. [*She puts her papers in front of him and he watches her without speaking or moving.*] I paid the man thirty-five hundred dollars down on the house. That leaves sixty-five hundred dollars. Monday morning I want you to take this money and take three thousand dollars and put it in a savings account for Beneatha's medical schooling. The rest you put in a checking account—with your name on it. And from now on any penny that come out of it or that go in it is for you to look after. For you to decide. [*She drops her hands a little helplessly.*] It ain't much, but it's all I got in the world and I'm putting in your hands. I'm telling you to be the head of this family from now on like you supposed to be.

WALTER [*stares at the money*]: You trust me like that, Mama?

MAMA: I ain't never stop trusting you. Like I ain't never stop loving you.

[*She goes out, and* WALTER *sits looking at the money on the table as the music continues in its idiom, pulsing in the room. Finally, in a decisive gesture, he gets up, and, in mingled joy and desperation, picks up the money. At the same moment,* TRAVIS *enters for bed.*]

TRAVIS: What's the matter, Daddy? You drunk?

WALTER [*sweetly, more sweetly than we have ever known him*]: No, Daddy ain't drunk. Daddy ain't going to never be drunk again. . . .

TRAVIS: Well, good night, Daddy.

[*The* FATHER *has come from behind the couch and leans over, embracing his son.*]

WALTER: Son, I feel like talking to you tonight.

TRAVIS: About what?

WALTER: Oh, about a lot of things. About you and what kind of man you going to be when you grow up. . . . Son—son, what do you want to be when you grow up?

TRAVIS: A bus driver.

WALTER [*laughing a little*]: A what? Man, that ain't nothing to want to be!

TRAVIS: Why not?

WALTER: 'Cause, man—it ain't big enough—you know what I mean.

TRAVIS: I don't know then. I can't make up my mind. Sometimes Mama asks me that too. And sometimes when I tell you I just want to be like you—she says she don't want me to be like that and sometimes she says she does. . . .

WALTER [*gathering him up in his arms*]: You know what, Travis? In seven years you going to be seventeen years old. And things is going to be very different with us in seven years, Travis. . . . One day when you are seventeen I'll come home—home from my office downtown somewhere—

TRAVIS: You don't work in no office, Daddy.

WALTER: No—but after tonight. After what your daddy gonna do tonight, there's going to be offices—a whole lot of offices. . . .

TRAVIS: What you gonna do tonight, Daddy?

WALTER: You wouldn't understand yet, son, but your daddy's gonna make a transaction . . . a business transaction that's going to change our lives. . . . That's how come one day when you 'bout seventeen years old I'll come home and I'll be pretty tired, you know what I mean, after a day of conferences and secretaries getting things wrong the way they do . . . 'cause an executive's life is hell, man—[*The more he talks the farther away he gets.*] And I'll pull the car up on the driveway . . . just a plain black Chrysler, I think, with white walls—no—black tires. More elegant. Rich people don't have to be flashy . . . though I'll have to get something a little sportier for Ruth—maybe a Cadillac convertible to do her shopping in. . . . And I'll come up the steps to the house and the gardener will be clipping away at the hedges and he'll say, "Good evening, Mr. Younger." And I'll say, "Hello, Jefferson, how are you this evening?" And I'll go inside and Ruth will come downstairs and meet me at the door and we'll kiss each other and she'll take my arm and we'll go up to your room to see you sitting on the floor with the catalogues of all the great schools in America around you. . . . All the great schools in the world! And—and I'll say, all right son—it's your seventeenth birthday, what is it you've decided? . . . Just tell me where you want to go to school and you'll *go*. Just tell me, what it is you want to be—and you'll *be* it. . . . Whatever you want to be—Yessir! [*He holds his arms open for* TRAVIS.] You just name it, son . . . [TRAVIS *leaps into them.*] and I hand you the world! [WALTER's *voice has risen in pitch and hysterical promise and on the last line he lifts* TRAVIS *high.*]

SCENE III

Time: Saturday, moving day, one week later.

Before the curtain rises, RUTH's *voice, a strident, dramatic church alto, cuts through the silence.*

It is, in the darkness, a triumphant surge, a penetrating statement of expectation: "Oh, Lord, I don't feel no ways tired! Children, oh, glory hallelujah!"

As the curtain rises we see that RUTH *is alone in the living room, finishing up the family's packing. It is moving day. She is nailing crates and tying cartons.* BENEATHA *enters, carrying a guitar case, and watches her exuberant sister-in-law.*

RUTH: Hey!

BENEATHA [*putting away the case*]: Hi.

RUTH [*pointing at a package*]: Honey—look in that package there and see what I found on sale this morning at the South Center. [RUTH *gets up and moves to the package and draws out some curtains.*] Lookahere—hand-turned hems!

BENEATHA: How do you know the window size out there?

RUTH [*who hadn't thought of that*]: Oh—Well, they bound to fit something in the whole

house. Anyhow, they was too good a bargain to pass us. [RUTH *slaps her head, suddenly remembering something.*] Oh, Bennie—I meant to put a special note on that carton over there. That's your mama's good china and she wants 'em to be very careful with it.

BENEATHA: I'll do it. [BENEATHA *finds a piece of paper and starts to draw large letters on it.*]

RUTH: You know what I'm going to do soon as I get in that new house?

BENEATHA: What?

RUTH: Honey—I'm going to run me a tub of water up to here . . . [*With her fingers practically up to her nostrils.*] And I'm going to get in it—and I am going to sit . . . and sit . . . and sit in that hot water and the first person who knocks to tell *me* to hurry up and come out—

BENEATHA: Gets shot at sunrise.

RUTH [*laughing happily*]: You said it, sister! [*Noticing how large* BENEATHA *is absent-mindedly making the note.*] Honey, they ain't going to read that from no airplane.

BENEATHA [*laughing herself*]: I guess I always think things have more emphasis if they are big, somehow.

RUTH [*looking up at her and smiling*]: You and your brother seem to have that as a philosophy of life. Lord, that man—done changed so 'round here. You know—you know what we did last night? Me and Walter Lee?

BENEATHA: What?

RUTH [*smiling to herself*]: We went to the movies. [*Looking at* BENEATHA *to see if she understands.*] We went to the movies. You know the last time me and Walter went to the movies together?

BENEATHA: No.

RUTH: Me neither. That's how long it been. [*Smiling again.*] But we went last night. The picture wasn't much good, but that didn't seem to matter. We went—and we held hands.

BENEATHA: Oh, Lord!

RUTH: We held hands—and you know what?

BENEATHA: What?

RUTH: When we come out of the show it was late and dark and all the stores and things was closed up . . . and it was kind of chilly and there wasn't many people on the streets . . . and we was still holding hands, me and Walter.

BENEATHA: You're killing me.

[WALTER *enters with a large package. His happiness is deep in him; he cannot keep still with his newfound exuberance. He is singing and wiggling and snapping his fingers. He puts his package in a corner and puts a phonograph record, which he has brought in with him, on the record player. As the music comes up he dances over to* RUTH *and tries to get her to dance with him. She gives in at last to his raunchiness and in a fit of giggling allows herself to be drawn into his mood and together they deliberately burlesque an old social dance of their youth.*]

BENEATHA [*regarding them a long time as they dance, then drawing in her breath for a deeply exaggerated comment which she does not particularly mean*]: Talk about—olddddddddddfashioned-ddddddd—Negroes!

WALTER [*stopping momentarily*]: What kind of Negroes?

[*He says this in fun. He is not angry with her today, nor with anyone. He starts to dance with his wife again.*]

BENEATHA: Old-fashioned.

WALTER [*as he dances with* RUTH]: You know, when these *New Negroes* have their convention—[*pointing at his sister*]—that is going to be the chairman of the Committee on Unending Agitation. [*He goes on dancing, then stops.*] Race, race, race! . . . Girl, I do believe you are the first person in the history of the entire human race to successfully brainwash yourself. [BENEATHA *breaks up and he goes on dancing. He stops again, enjoying his tease.*] Damn, even the N double A C P takes a holiday sometimes! [BENEATHA *and* RUTH *laugh. He dances with* RUTH *some more and starts to laugh and stops and pantomimes someone over an operating table.*] I can just see that chick someday looking down at some poor cat on an operating table before she starts to slice him, saying . . . [*Pulling his sleeves back maliciously.*] "By the way, what are your views on civil rights down there? . . ." [*He laughs at her again and starts to dance happily. The bell sounds.*]

BENEATHA: Sticks and stones may break my bones but . . . words will never hurt me! [BENEATHA *goes to the door and opens it as* WALTER *and* RUTH *go on with the clowning.* BENEATHA *is somewhat surprised to see a quiet-looking middle-aged white man in a business suit holding his hat and a briefcase in his hand and consulting a small piece of paper.*]

MAN: Uh—how do you do, miss. I am looking for a Mrs.—[*He looks at the slip of paper.*] Mrs. Lena Younger?

BENEATHA [*smoothing her hair with slight embarrassment*]: Oh—yes, that's my mother. Excuse me. [*She closes the door and turns to quiet the other two.*] Ruth! Brother! Somebody's here. [*Then she opens the door. The man casts a curious quick glance at all of them.*] Uh—come in please.

MAN [*coming in*]: Thank you.

BENEATHA: My mother isn't here just now. Is it business?

MAN: Yes . . . well, of a sort.

WALTER [*freely, the Man of the House*]: Have a seat. I'm Mrs. Younger's son. I look after most of her business matters.

[RUTH *and* BENEATHA *exchange amused glances.*]

MAN [*regarding* WALTER, *and sitting*]: Well—My name is Karl Lindner . . .

WALTER [*stretching out his hand*]: Walter Younger. This is my wife—[RUTH *nods politely.*]—and my sister.

LINDNER: How do you do.

WALTER [*amiably, as he sits himself easily on a chair, leaning with interest forward on his knees and looking expectantly into the newcomer's face*]: What can we do for you, Mr. Lindner!

LINDNER [*some minor shuffling of the hat and briefcase on his knees*]: Well—I am a representative of the Clybourne Park Improvement Association—

WALTER [*pointing*]: Why don't you sit your things on the floor?

LINDNER: Oh—yes. Thank you. [*He slides the briefcase and hat under the chair.*] And as I was saying—I am from the Clybourne Park Improvement Association and we have had it brought to our attention at the last meeting that you people—or at least your

mother—has bought a piece of residential property at—[*He digs for the slip of paper again.*]—four o six Clybourne Street . . .

WALTER: That's right. Care for something to drink? Ruth, get Mr. Lindner a beer.

LINDNER [*upset for some reason*]: Oh—no, really. I mean thank you very much, but no thank you.

RUTH [*innocently*]: Some coffee?

LINDNER: Thank you, nothing at all.

[BENEATHA *is watching the man carefully.*]

LINDNER: Well, I don't know how much you folks know about our organization. [*He is a gentle man; thoughtful and somewhat labored in his manner.*] It is one of these community organizations set up to look after—Oh, you know, things like block upkeep and special projects and we also have what we call our New Neighbors Orientation Committee . . .

BENEATHA [*drily*]: Yes—and what do they do?

LINDNER [*turning a little to her and then returning the main force to* WALTER]: Well—it's what you might call a sort of welcoming committee, I guess. I mean they, we, I'm the chairman of the committee—go around and see the new people who move into the neighborhood and sort of give them the lowdown on the way we do things out in Clybourne Park.

BENEATHA [*with appreciation of the two meanings, which escape* RUTH *and* WALTER]: Un-huh.

LINDNER: And we also have the category of what the association calls—[*He looks elsewhere.*]—uh—special community problems . . .

BENEATHA: Yes—and what are some of those?

WALTER: Girl, let the man talk.

LINDNER [*with understated relief*]: Thank you. I would sort of like to explain this thing in my own way. I mean I want to explain to you in a certain way.

WALTER: Go ahead.

LINDNER: Yes. Well. I'm going to try to get right to the point. I'm sure we'll all appreciate that in the long run.

BENEATHA: Yes.

WALTER: Be still now!

LINDNER: Well—

RUTH [*still innocently*]: Would you like another chair—you don't look comfortable.

LINDNER [*more frustrated than annoyed*]: No, thank you very much. Please. Well—to get right to the point I—[*A great breath, and he is off at last.*] I am sure you people must be aware of some of the incidents which have happened in various parts of the city when colored people have moved into certain areas—[BENEATHA *exhales heavily and starts tossing a piece of fruit up and down in the air.*] Well—because we have what I think is going to be a unique type of organization in American community life—not only do we deplore that kind of thing—but we are trying to do something about it. [BENEATHA *stops tossing and turns with a new and quizzical interest to the man.*] We feel—[*Gaining confidence in his mission because of the interest in the faces of the people he is talking to.*]—we feel that most of the trouble in this world, when you come right down to it—[*He hits his knee for emphasis.*]—most of the trouble exists because people just don't sit down and talk to each other.

RUTH [*nodding as she might in church, pleased with the remark*]: You can say that again, mister.

LINDNER [*more encouraged by such affirmation*]: That we don't try hard enough in this world to understand the other fellow's problem. The other guy's point of view.

RUTH: Now that's right.

[BENEATHA *and* WALTER *merely watch and listen with genuine interest.*]

LINDNER: Yes—that's the way we feel out in Clybourne Park. And that's why I was elected to come here this afternoon and talk to you people. Friendly like, you know, the way people should talk to each other and see if we couldn't find some way to work this thing out. As I say, the whole business is a matter of *caring* about the other fellow. Anybody can see that you are a nice family of folks, hard working and honest I'm sure. [BENEATHA *frowns slightly, quizzically, her head tilted regarding him.*] Today everybody knows what it means to be on the outside of *something*. And of course, there is always somebody who is out to take the advantage of people who don't always understand.

WALTER: What do you mean?

LINDNER: Well—you see our community is made up of people who've worked hard as the dickens for years to build up that little community. They're not rich and fancy people; just hardworking, honest people who don't really have much but those little homes and a dream of the kind of community they want to raise their children in. Now, I don't say we are perfect and there is a lot wrong in some of the things they want. But you've got to admit that a man, right or wrong, has the right to want to have the neighborhood he lives in a certain kind of way. And at the moment the overwhelming majority of our people out there feel that people get along better, take more of a common interest in the life of the community, when they share a common background. I want you to believe me when I tell you that race prejudice simply doesn't enter into it. It is a matter of the people of Clybourne Park believing, rightly or wrongly, as I say, that for the happiness of all concerned that our Negro families are happier when they live in their *own* communities.

BENEATHA [*with a grand and bitter gesture*]: This, friends, is the Welcoming Committee!

WALTER [*dumfounded, looking at* LINDNER]: Is this what you came marching all the way over here to tell us?

LINDNER: Well, now we've been having a fine conversation. I hope you'll hear me all the way through.

WALTER [*tightly*]: Go ahead, man.

LINDNER: You see—in the face of all things I have said, we are prepared to make your family a very generous offer . . .

BENEATHA: Thirty pieces and not a coin less!

WALTER: Yeah?

LINDNER [*putting on his glasses and drawing a form out of the briefcase*]: Our association is

prepared, through the collective effort of our people, to buy the house from you at a financial gain to your family.

RUTH: Lord have mercy, ain't this the living gall!

WALTER: All right, you through?

LINDNER: Well, I want to give you the exact terms of the financial arrangement—

WALTER: We don't want to hear no exact terms of no arrangements. I want to know if you got any more to tell us 'bout getting together?

LINDNER [*taking off his glasses*]: Well—I don't suppose that you feel . . .

WALTER: Never mind how I feel—you got any more to say 'bout how people ought to sit down and talk to each other? . . . Get out of my house, man. [*He turns his back and walks to the door.*]

LINDNER [*looking around at the hostile faces and reaching and assembling his hat and briefcase*]: Well—I don't understand why you people are reacting this way. What do you think you are going to gain by moving into a neighborhood where you just aren't wanted and where some elements—well—people can get awful worked up when they feel that their whole way of life and everything they've ever worked for is threatened.

WALTER: Get out.

LINDNER [*at the door, holding a small card*]: Well—I'm sorry it went like this.

WALTER: Get out.

LINDNER [*almost sadly regarding* WALTER]: You just can't force people to change their hearts, son. [*He turns and puts his card on a table and exits.* WALTER *pushes the door to with stinging hatred, and stands looking at it.* RUTH *just sits and* BENEATHA *just stands. They say nothing.* MAMA *and* TRAVIS *enter.*]

MAMA: Well—this all the packing got done since I left out of here this morning. I testify before God that my children got all the energy of the dead. What time the moving men due?

BENEATHA: Four o'clock. You had a caller, Mama. [*She is smiling, teasingly.*]

MAMA: Sure enough—who?

BENEATHA [*her arms folded saucily*]: The Welcoming Committee.

[WALTER *and* RUTH *giggle.*]

MAMA [*innocently*]: Who?

BENEATHA: The Welcoming Committee. They said they're sure going to be glad to see you when you get there.

WALTER [*devilishly*]: Yeah, they said they can't hardly wait to see your face.

[*Laughter.*]

MAMA [*sensing their facetiousness*]: What's the matter with you all?

WALTER: Ain't nothing the matter with us. We just telling you 'bout the gentleman who came to see you this afternoon. From the Clybourne Park Improvement Association.

MAMA: What he want?

RUTH [*in the same mood as* BENEATHA *and* WALTER]: To welcome you, honey.

WALTER: He said they can't hardly wait. He said the one thing they don't have, that they just *dying* to have out there is a fine family of colored people! [*To* RUTH *and* BENEATHA.] Ain't that right!

RUTH *and* BENEATHA [*mockingly*]: Yeah! He left his card in case—[*They indicate the card, and* MAMA *picks it up and throws it on the floor—understanding and looking off as she draws her chair up to the table on which she has put her plant and some sticks and some cord.*]

MAMA: Father, give us strength. [*Knowingly—and without fun.*] Did he threaten us?

BENEATHA: Oh—Mama—they don't do it like that any more. He talked Brotherhood. He said everybody ought learn how to sit down and hate each other with good Christian fellowship.

[*She and* WALTER *shake hands to ridicule the remark.*]

MAMA [*Sadly*]: Lord, protect us . . .

RUTH: You should hear the money those folks raised to buy the house from us. All we paid and then some.

BENEATHA: What they think we going to do—eat 'em?

RUTH: No, honey, marry 'em.

MAMA [*shaking her head*]: Lord, Lord, Lord . . .

RUTH: Well—that's the way the crackers crumble. Joke.

BENEATHA [*laughingly noticing what her mother is doing*]: Mama, what are you doing?

MAMA: Fixing my plant so it won't get hurt none on the way . . .

BENEATHA: Mama, you going to take *that* to the new house?

MAMA: Un-huh—

BENEATHA: That raggedy-looking old thing?

MAMA [*stopping and looking at her*]: It expresses me.

RUTH [*with delight, to* BENEATHA]: So, there, Miss Thing!

[WALTER *comes to* MAMA *suddenly and bends down behind her and squeezes her in his arms with all his strength. She is overwhelmed by the suddenness of it and, though delighted, her manner is like that of* RUTH *with* TRAVIS.]

MAMA: Look out now, boy! You make me mess up my thing here!

WALTER [*his face lit, he slips down on his knees beside her, his arms still about her*]: Mama . . . you know what it means to climb up in the chariot?

MAMA [*gruffly, very happy*]: Get on away from me now . . .

RUTH [*near the gift-wrapped package, trying to catch* WALTER's *eye*]: Psst—

WALTER: What the old song say, Mama . . .

RUTH: Walter—Now? [*She is pointing at the package.*]

WALTER [*speaking the lines, sweetly, playfully, in his mother's face*]:
    I got wings . . . you got wings . . .
    All God's children got wings . . .

MAMA: Boy—get out of my face and do some work . . .

WALTER:

When I get to heaven gonna put on my wings,
Gonna fly all over God's heaven . . .

BENEATHA [*teasingly, from across the room*]: Everybody talking 'bout heaven ain't going there!

WALTER [*to* RUTH, *who is carrying the box across to them*]: I don't know, you think we ought to give her that . . . Seems to me she ain't been very appreciative around here.

MAMA [*eyeing the box, which is obviously a gift*]: What is that?

WALTER [*taking it from* RUTH *and putting it on the table in front of* MAMA]: Well—what you all think. Should we give it to her?

RUTH: Oh—she was pretty good today.

MAMA: I'll good you—[*She turns her eyes to the box again.*]

BENEATHA: Open it, Mama.

[*She stands up, looks at it, turns and looks at all of them, and then presses her hands together and does not open the package.*]

WALTER [*sweetly*]: Open it, Mama. It's for you. [MAMA *looks in his eyes. It is the first present in her life without its being Christmas. Slowly she opens her package and lifts out, one by one, a brand-new sparkling set of gardening tools.* WALTER *continues, prodding.*] Ruth made up the note—read it . . .

MAMA [*picking up the card and adjusting her glasses*]: "To our own Mrs. Miniver—Love from Brother, Ruth and Beneatha." Ain't that lovely . . .

TRAVIS [*tugging at his father's sleeve*]: Daddy, can I give her mine now?

WALTER: All right, son. [TRAVIS *flies to get his gift.*] Travis didn't want to go in with the rest of us, Mama. He got his own. [*Somewhat amused.*] We don't know what it is . . .

TRAVIS [*racing back in the room with a large hatbox and putting it in front of his grandmother*]: Here!

MAMA: Lord have mercy, baby. You done gone and bought your grandmother a hat?

TRAVIS [*very proud*]: Open it!

[*She does and lifts out an elaborate, but very elaborate, wide gardening hat, and all the adults break up at the sight of it.*]

RUTH: Travis, honey, what is that?

TRAVIS [*who thinks it is beautiful and appropriate*]: It's a gardening hat! Like the ladies always have on in the magazines when they work in their gardens.

BENEATHA [*giggling fiercely*]: Travis—we were trying to make Mama Mrs. Miniver— not Scarlett O'Hara!

MAMA [*indignantly*]: What's the matter with you all! This here is a beautiful hat! [*Absurdly.*] I always wanted me one just like it! [*She pops it on her head to prove it to her grandson, and the hat is ludicrous and considerably oversized.*]

RUTH: Hot dog! Go, Mama!

WALTER [*doubled over with laughter*]: I'm sorry, Mama—but you look like you ready to go out and chop you some cotton sure enough!

[*They all laugh except* MAMA, *out of deference to* TRAVIS' *feelings.*]

MAMA [*gathering the boy up to her*]: Bless your heart—this is the prettiest hat I ever owned—[WALTER, RUTH *and* BENEATHA *chime in—noisily, festively and insincerely congratulating* TRAVIS *on his gift.*] What are we all standing around here for? We ain't finished packin' yet. Bennie, you ain't packed one book.

[*The bell rings.*]

BENEATHA: That couldn't be the movers . . . it's not hardly two good yet—

[BENEATHA *goes into her room.* MAMA *starts for door.*]

WALTER [*turning, stiffening*]: Wait—wait—I'll get it. [*He stands and looks at the door.*]
MAMA: You expecting company, son?
WALTER [*just looking at the door*]: Yeah—yeah . . .

[MAMA *looks at* RUTH, *and they exchange innocent and unfrightened glances.*]

MAMA [*not understanding*]: Well, let them in, son.
BENEATHA [*from her room*]: We need some more string.
MAMA: Travis—you run to the hardware and get me some string cord.

[MAMA *goes out and* WALTER *turns and looks at* RUTH. TRAVIS *goes to a dish for money.*]

RUTH: Why don't you answer the door, man?
WALTER [*suddenly bounding across the floor to her*]: 'Cause sometimes it hard to let the future begin! [*Stooping down in her face.*]

I got wings! You got wings!
All God's children got wings!

[*He crosses to the door and throws it open. Standing there is a very slight little man in a not too prosperous business suit and with haunted frightened eyes and a hat pulled down tightly, brim up, around his forehead.* TRAVIS *passes between the men and exits.* WALTER *leans deep in the man's face, still in his jubilance.*]

When I get to heaven gonna put on my wings,
Gonna fly all over God's heaven . . .

[*The little man just stares at him.*]

Heaven—

[*Suddenly he stops and looks past the little man into the empty hallway.*]

Where's Willy, man?

BOBO: He ain't with me.

WALTER [*not disturbed*]: Oh—come on in. You know my wife.

BOBO [*dumbly, taking off his hat*]: Yes—h'you, Miss Ruth.

RUTH [*quietly, a mood apart from her husband already, seeing* BOBO]: Hello, Bobo.

WALTER: You right on time today . . . Right on time. That's the way! [*He slaps* BOBO *on his back.*] Sit down . . . lemme hear.

[RUTH *stands stiffly and quietly in back of them, as though somehow she senses death, her eyes fixed on her husband.*]

BOBO [*his frightened eyes on the floor, his hat in his hands*]: Could I please get a drink a water, before I tell you about it, Walter Lee?

[WALTER *does not take his eyes off the man,* RUTH *goes blindly to the tap and gets a glass of water and brings it to* BOBO.]

WALTER: There ain't nothing wrong, is there?

BOBO: Lemme tell you—

WALTER: Man—didn't nothing go wrong?

BOBO: Lemme tell you—Walter Lee. [*Looking at* RUTH *and talking to her more than to* WALTER.] You know how it was. I got to tell you how it was. I mean first I got to tell you how it was all the way . . . I mean about the money I put in, Walter Lee . . .

WALTER [*with taut agitation now*]: What about the money you put in?

BOBO: Well—it wasn't much as we told you—me and Willy—[*He stops.*] I'm sorry, Walter. I got a bad feeling about it. I got a real bad feeling about it . . .

WALTER: Man, what you telling me about all this for? . . . Tell me what happened in Springfield . . .

BOBO: Springfield.

RUTH [*like a dead woman*]: What was supposed to happen in Springfield?

BOBO [*to her*]: This deal that me and Walter went into with Willy—Me and Willy was going to go down to Springfield and spread some money 'round so's we wouldn't have to wait so long for the liquor license . . . That's what we were going to do. Everybody said that was the way you had to do, you understand, Miss Ruth?

WALTER: Man—what happened down there?

BOBO [*a pitiful man, near tears*]: I'm trying to tell you, Walter.

WALTER [*screaming at him suddenly*]: THEN TELL ME, GODDAMNIT . . . WHAT'S THE MATTER WITH YOU?

BOBO: Man . . . I didn't go to no Springfield, yesterday.

WALTER [*halted, life hanging in the moment*]: Why not?

BOBO [*the long way, the hard way to tell*]: 'Cause I didn't have no reasons to . . .

WALTER: Man, what are you talking about!

BOBO: I'm talking about the fact that when I got to the train station yesterday morning—eight o'clock like we planned . . . Man—*Willy didn't never show up.*

WALTER: Why . . . where was he . . . where is he?

BOBO: That's what I'm trying to tell you . . . I don't know . . . I waited six hours . . . I called his house . . . and I waited . . . six hours . . . I waited in that train station six hours . . . [*Breaking into tears.*] That was all the extra money I had in the world . . . [*Looking up at* WALTER *with the tears running down his face.*] Man, *Willy is gone.*

WALTER: Gone, what you mean Willy is gone? Gone where? You mean he went by himself. You mean he went off to Springfield by himself—to take care of getting the license—[*Turns and looks anxiously at* RUTH.] You mean maybe he didn't want too many people in on the business down there? [*Looks to* RUTH *again, as before.*] You know Willy got his own ways. [*Looks back to* BOBO.] Maybe you was late yesterday and he just went on down there without you. Maybe—maybe—he's been callin' you at home tryin' to tell you what happened or something. Maybe—maybe—he just got sick. He's somewhere—he's got to be somewhere. We just got to find him—me and you got to find him. [*Grabs* BOBO *senselessly by the collar and starts to shake him.*] We got to!

BOBO [*in sudden angry, frightened agony*]: What's the matter with you, Walter! *When a cat take off with your money he don't leave you no maps!*

WALTER [*turning madly, as though he is looking for* WILLY *in the very room*]: Willy! . . . Willy . . . don't do it . . . Please don't do it . . . Man, not with that money . . . Man, please, not with that money . . . Oh, God . . . Don't let it be true . . . [*He is wandering around, crying out for* Willy *and looking for him or perhaps for help from God.*] Man . . . I trusted you . . . Man, I put my life in your hands . . . [*He starts to crumple down on the floor as* RUTH *just covers her face in horror.* MAMA *opens the door and comes into the room, with* BENEATHA *behind her.*] Man . . . [*He starts to pound the floor with his fists, sobbing wildly.*] *That money is made out of my father's flesh* . . .

BOBO [*standing over him helplessly*]: I'm sorry, Walter . . . [*Only* WALTER'S *sobs reply.* BOBO *puts on his hat.*] I had my life staked on this deal, too . . . [*He exits.*]

MAMA [*to* WALTER]: Son—[*She goes to him, bends down to him, talks to his bent head.*] Son . . . Is it gone? Son, I gave you sixty-five hundred dollars. Is it gone? All of it? Beneatha's money too?

WALTER [*lifting his head slowly*]: Mama . . . I never . . . went to the bank at all . . .

MAMA [*not wanting to believe him*]: You mean . . . your sister's school money . . . you used that too . . . Walter? . . .

WALTER: Yessss! . . . All of it . . . It's all gone . . .

[*There is total silence.* RUTH *stands with her face covered with her hands;* BENEATHA *leans forlornly against a wall, fingering a piece of red ribbon from the mother's gift.* MAMA *stops and looks at her son without recognition and then, quite without thinking about it, starts to beat him senselessly in the face.* BENEATHA *goes to them and stops it.*]

BENEATHA: Mama!

[MAMA *stops and looks at both of her children and rises slowly and wanders vaguely, aimlessly away from them.*]

MAMA: I seen . . . him . . . night after night . . . come in . . . and look at that rug . . . and then look at me . . . the red showing in his eyes . . . the veins moving in his head . . . I seen him grow thin and old before he was forty . . . working and working and working like somebody's old horse . . . killing himself . . . and you—you give it all away in a day . . .

BENEATHA: Mama—

MAMA: Oh, God . . . [*She looks up to Him.*] Look down here—and show me the strength.

BENEATHA: Mama—

MAMA [*folding over*]: Strength . . .

BENEATHA [*plaintively*]: Mama . . .

MAMA: Strength!

ACT III

An hour later.

   At curtain, there is a sullen light of gloom in the living room, gray light not unlike that which began the first scene of Act One. At left we can see WALTER *within his room, alone with himself. He is stretched out on the bed, his shirt out and open, his arms under his head. He does not smoke, he does not cry out, he merely lies there, looking up at the ceiling, much as if he were alone in the world.*

   In the living room BENEATHA *sits at the table, still surrounded by the now almost ominous packing crates. She sits looking off. We feel that this is a mood struck perhaps an hour before, and it lingers now, full of the empty sound of profound disappointment. We see on a line from her brother's bedroom the sameness of their attitudes. Presently the bell rings and* BENEATHA *rises without ambition or interest in answering. It is* ASAGAI, *smiling broadly, striding into the room with energy and happy expectation and conversation.*

ASAGAI: I came over . . . I had some free time. I thought I might help with the packing. Ah, I like the look of packing crates! A household in preparation for a journey! It depresses some people . . . but for me . . . it is another feeling. Something full of the flow of life, do you understand? Movement, progress . . . It makes me think of Africa.

BENEATHA: Africa!

ASAGAI: What kind of a mood is this? Have I told you how deeply you move me?

BENEATHA: He gave away the money, Asagai . . .

ASAGAI: Who gave away what money?

BENEATHA: The insurance money. My brother gave it away.

ASAGAI: Gave it away?

BENEATHA: He made an investment! With a man even Travis wouldn't have trusted.

ASAGAI: And it's gone?

BENEATHA: Gone!

ASAGAI: I'm very sorry . . . And you, now?

BENEATHA: Me? . . . Me? . . . Me I'm nothing . . . Me. When I was very small

. . . we used to take our sleds out in the wintertime and the only hills we had were the ice-covered stone steps of some houses down the street. And we used to fill them in with snow and make them smooth and slide down them all day . . . and it was very dangerous you know . . . far too steep . . . and sure enough one day a kid named Rufus came down too fast and hit the sidewalk . . . and we saw his face just split open right there in front of us . . . And I remember standing there looking at his bloody open face thinking that was the end of Rufus. But the ambulance came and they took him to the hospital and they fixed the broken bones and they sewed it all up . . . and the next time I saw Rufus he just had a little line down the middle of his face . . . I never got over that . . .

ASAGAI: What?

BENEATHA: That that was what one person could do for another, fix him up—sew up the problem, make him all right again. That was the most marvelous thing in the world . . . I wanted to do that. I always thought it was the one concrete thing in the world that a human being could do. Fix up the sick, you know—and make them whole again. This was truly being God. . . .

ASAGAI: You wanted to be God?

BENEATHA: No—I wanted to cure. It used to be so important to me. I wanted to cure. It used to matter. I used to care. I mean about people and how their bodies hurt . . .

ASAGAI: And you've stopped caring?

BENEATHA: Yes—I think so.

ASAGAI: Why?

[WALTER *rises, goes to the door of his room and is about to open it, then stops and stands listening, leaning on the door jamb.*]

BENEATHA: Because it doesn't seem deep enough, close enough to what ails mankind—I mean this thing of sewing up bodies or administering drugs. Don't you understand? It was a child's reaction to the world. I thought that doctors had the secret to all the hurts. . . . That's the way a child sees things—or an idealist.

ASAGAI: Children see things very well sometimes—and idealists even better.

BENEATHA: I know that's what you think. Because you are still where I left off—you still care. This is what you see for the world, for Africa. You with the dreams of the future will patch up all Africa—you are going to cure the Great Sore of colonialism with Independence—

ASAGAI: Yes!

BENEATHA: Yes—and you think that one word is the penicillin of the human spirit: "Independence!" But then what?

ASAGAI: That will be the problem for another time. First we must get there.

BENEATHA: And where does it end?

ASAGAI: End? Who even spoke of an end? To life? To living?

BENEATHA: An end to misery!

ASAGAI [*smiling*]: You sound like a French intellectual.

BENEATHA: No! I sound like a human being who just had her future taken right out of her hands! While I was sleeping in my bed in there, things were happening in this world that directly concerned me—and nobody asked me, consulted me—they just went out and did things—and changed my life. Don't you see there isn't any real progress, Asagai, there is only one large circle that we march in, around and around, each of us with our own little picture—in front of us—our own little mirage that we think is the future.

ASAGAI: That is the mistake.

BENEATHA: What?

ASAGAI: What you just said—about the circle. It isn't a circle—it is simply a long line—as in geometry, you know, one that reaches into infinity. And because we cannot see the end—we also cannot see how it changes. And it is very odd but those who see the changes are called "idealists"—and those who cannot, or refuse to think, they are the "realists." It is very strange, and amusing too, I think.

BENEATHA: You—you are almost religious.

ASAGAI: Yes . . . I think I have the religion of doing what is necessary in the world—and of worshipping man—because he is so marvelous, you see.

BENEATHA: Man is foul! And the human race deserves its misery!

ASAGAI: You see: *you* have become the religious one in the old sense. Already, and after such a small defeat, you are worshipping despair.

BENEATHA: From now on, I worship the truth—and the truth is that people are puny, small and selfish. . . .

ASAGAI: Truth? Why is it that you despairing ones always think that only you have the truth? I never thought to see *you* like that. Your brother made a stupid, childish mistake—and you are grateful to him. So that now you can give up the ailing human race on account of it. You talk about what good is struggle; what good is anything? Where are we all going? And why are we bothering?

BENEATHA: *And you cannot answer it!* All your talk and dreams about Africa and Independence. Independence and then what? What about all the crooks and petty thieves and just plain idiots who will come into power to steal and plunder the same as before—only now they will be black and do it in the name of the new Independence—You cannot answer that.

ASAGAI [*shouting over her*]: *I live the answer!* [*Pause.*] In my village at home it is the exceptional man who can even read a newspaper . . . or who ever *sees* a book at all. I will go home and much of what I will have to say will seem strange to the people of my village . . . But I will teach and work and things will happen, slowly and swiftly. At times it will seem that nothing changes at all . . . and then again . . . the sudden dramatic events which make history leap into the future. And then quiet again. Retrogression even. Guns, murder, revolution. And I even will have moments when I wonder if the quiet was not better than all that death and hatred. But I will look about my village at the illiteracy and disease and ignorance and I will not wonder long. And perhaps . . . perhaps I will be a great man . . . I mean perhaps I will hold on to the substance of truth and find my way always with the right course . . . and perhaps for it I will be butchered in my bed some night by the servants of empire . . .

BENEATHA: *The martyr!*

ASAGAI: . . . or perhaps I shall live to be a very old man respected and esteemed in my new nation . . . And perhaps I shall hold office and this is what I'm trying to tell you, Alaiyo; perhaps the things I believe now for my country will be wrong and outmoded, and I will not understand and do terrible things to have things my way or merely to keep my power. Don't you see that there will be young men and women, not British soldiers then, but my own black countrymen . . . to step out of the shadows some evening and slit my then useless throat? Don't you see they have always been there . . . that they always will be. And that such a thing as my own death will be an advance? They who might kill me even . . . actually replenish me!

BENEATHA: Oh, Asagai, I know all that.

ASAGAI: Good! Then stop moaning and groaning and tell me what you plan to do.

BENEATHA: Do?

ASAGAI: I have a bit of a suggestion.

BENEATHA: What?

ASAGAI [*rather quietly for him*]: That when it is all over—that you come home with me—

BENEATHA [*slapping herself on the forehead with exasperation born of misunderstanding*]: Oh— Asagai—at this moment you decide to be romantic!

ASAGAI [*quickly understanding the misunderstanding*]: My dear, young creature of the New World—I do not mean across the city—I mean across the ocean; home—to Africa.

BENEATHA [*slowly understanding and turning to him with murmured amazement*]: To—to Nigeria?

ASAGAI: Yes! . . . [*Smiling and lifting his arms playfully.*] Three hundred years later the African Prince rose up out of the seas and swept the maiden back across the middle passage over which her ancestors had come—

BENEATHA [*unable to play*]: Nigeria?

ASAGAI: Nigeria. Home. [*Coming to her with genuine romantic flippancy.*] I will show you our mountains and our stars; and give you cool drinks from gourds and teach you the old songs and the ways of our people—and, in time, we will pretend that—[*Very softly.*]—you have only been away for a day—

[*She turns her back to him, thinking. He swings her around and takes her full in his arms in a long embrace which proceeds to passion.*]

BENEATHA [*pulling away*]: You're getting me all mixed up—

ASAGAI: Why?

BENEATHA: Too many things—too many things have happened today. I must sit down and think. I don't know what I feel about anything right this minute. [*She promptly sits down and props her chin on her fist.*]

ASAGAI [*charmed*]: All right, I shall leave you. No—don't get up. [*Touching her, gently sweetly.*] Just sit awhile and think . . . Never be afraid to sit awhile and think. [*He goes to door and looks at her.*] How often I have looked at you and said, "Ah—so this is what the New World hath finally wrought . . ."

[*He exits. BENEATHA sits on alone. Presently WALTER enters from his room and starts to rummage through things, feverishly looking for something. She looks up and turns in her seat.*]

BENEATHA [*hissingly*]: Yes—just look at what the New World hath wrought! . . . Just look! [*She gestures with bitter disgust.*] There he is! *Monsieur le petit bourgeois noir*—himself! There he is—Symbol of a Rising Class! Entrepreneur! Titan of the system! [WALTER *ignores her completely and continues frantically and destructively looking for something and hurling things to floor and tearing things out of their place in his search.* BENEATHA *ignores the eccentricity of his actions and goes on with the monologue of insult.*] Did you dream of yachts on Lake Michigan, Brother? Did you see yourself on that Great Day sitting down at the Conference Table, surrounded by all the mighty baldheaded men in America? All halted, waiting, breathless, waiting for your pronouncements on industry? Waiting for you—Chairman of the Board? [WALTER *finds what he is looking for—a small piece of white paper—and pushes it in his pocket and puts on his coat and rushes out without ever having looked at her. She shouts after him.*] I look at you and I see the final triumph of stupidity in the world!

[*The door slams and she returns to just sitting again.* RUTH *comes quickly out of* MAMA's *room.*]

RUTH: Who was that?

BENEATHA: Your husband.

RUTH: Where did he go?

BENEATHA: Who knows—maybe he has an appointment at U.S. Steel.

RUTH [*anxiously, with frightened eyes*]: You didn't say nothing bad to him, did you?

BENEATHA: Bad? Say anything bad to him? No—I told him he was a sweet boy and full of dreams and everything is strictly peachy keen, as the ofay kids say!

[MAMA *enters from her bedroom. She is lost, vague, trying to catch hold, to make some sense of her former command of the world, but it still eludes her. A sense of waste overwhelms her gait; a measure of apology rides on her shoulders. She goes to her plant, which has remained on the table, looks at it, picks it up and takes it to the window sill and sits it outside, and she stands and looks at it a long moment. Then she closes the window, straightens her body with effort and turns around to her children.*]

MAMA: Well—ain't it a mess in here, though? [*A false cheerfulness, a beginning of something.*] I guess we all better stop moping around and get some work done. All this unpacking and everything we got to do. [RUTH *raises her head slowly in response to the sense of the line; and* BENEATHA *in similar manner turns very slowly to look at her mother.*] One of you all better call the moving people and tell 'em not to come.

RUTH: Tell 'em not to come?

MAMA: Of course, baby. Ain't no need in 'em coming all the way here and having to go back. They charges for that too. [*She sits down, fingers to her brow, thinking.*] Lord, ever since I was a little girl, I always remembers people saying, "Lena—Lena Eggleston, you aims too high all the time. You needs to slow down and see life a little more like it is. Just slow down some." That's what they always used to say down home— "Lord, that Lena Eggleston is a high-minded thing. She'll get her due one day!"

RUTH: No, Lena . . .

MAMA: Me and Big Walter just didn't never learn right.

RUTH: Lena, no! We gotta go. Bennie—tell her . . . [*She rises and crosses to* BENEATHA *with her arms outstretched.* BENEATHA *doesn't respond.*] Tell her we can still move . . . the notes ain't but a hundred and twenty five a month. We got four grown people in this house—we can work . . .

MAMA [*to herself*]: Just aimed too high all the time—

RUTH [*turning and going to* MAMA *fast—the words pouring out with urgency and desperation*]: Lena—I'll work . . . I'll work twenty hours a day in all the kitchens in Chicago . . . I'll strap my baby on my back if I have to and scrub all the floors in America and wash all the sheets in America if I have to—but we got to move . . . We got to get out of here.

[MAMA *reaches out absently and pats* RUTH's *hand.*]

MAMA: No—I sees things differently now. Been thinking 'bout some of the things we could do to fix this place up some. I seen a second-hand bureau over on Maxwell Street just the other day that could fit right there. [*She points to where the new furniture might go.* RUTH *wanders away from her.*] Would need some new handles on it and then a little varnish and then it look like something brand-new. And—we can put up them new curtains in the kitchen . . . Why this place be looking fine. Cheer us all up so that we forget trouble ever came . . . [*To* RUTH.] And you could get some nice screens to put up in your room round the baby's basinet . . . [*She looks at both of them, pleadingly.*] Sometimes you just got to know when to give up some things . . . and hold on to what you got.

[WALTER *enters from the outside, looking spent and leaning against the door, his coat hanging from him.*]

MAMA: Where you been, son?

WALTER [*breathing hard*]: Made a call.

MAMA: To who, son?

WALTER: To The Man.

MAMA: What man, baby?

WALTER: The Man, Mama. Don't you know who The Man is?

RUTH: Walter Lee?

WALTER: *The Man.* Like the guys in the streets say—The Man. Captain Boss—Mistuh Charley . . . Old Captain Please Mr. Bossman . . .

BENEATHA [*suddenly*]: Lindner!

WALTER: That's right! That's good. I told him to come right over.

BENEATHA [*fiercely, understanding*]: For what? What do you want to see him for!

WALTER [*looking at his sister*]: We going to do business with him.

MAMA: What you talking 'bout, son?

WALTER: Talking 'bout life, Mama. You all always telling me to see life like it is. Well—I laid in there on my back today . . . and I figured it out. Life just like it is. Who gets and who don't get. [*He sits down with his coat on and laughs.*] Mama, you know it's all divided up. Life is. Sure enough. Between the takers and the "tooken." [*He laughs.*] I've figured it out finally. [*He looks around at them.*] Yeah. Some of us always getting "tooken." [*He laughs.*] People like Willy Harris, they don't never get "tooken." And you know why the rest of us do? 'Cause we all mixed up. Mixed up bad. We get to looking 'round for the right and the wrong; and we worry about it and cry about it and stay up nights trying to figure out 'bout the wrong and the right of things all the time . . . And all the time, man, them takers is out there operating, just taking and taking. Willy Harris? Shoot—Willy Harris don't even count. He don't even count in the big scheme of things. But I'll say one thing for old Willy Harris . . . he's taught me something. He's taught me to keep my eye on what counts in this world. Yeah—[*Shouting out a little.*] Thanks, Willy!

RUTH: What did you call that man for, Walter Lee?

WALTER: Called him to tell him to come on over to the show. Gonna put on a show for the man. Just what he wants to see. You see, Mama, the man came here today and he told us that them people out there where you want us to move—well they so upset they willing to pay us not to move out there. [*He laughs again.*] And—and oh, Mama—you would of been proud of the way me and Ruth and Bennie acted. We told him to get out . . . Lord have mercy! We told the man to get out. Oh, we was some proud folks this afternoon, yeah. [*He lights a cigarette.*] We were still full of that old-time stuff . . .

RUTH [*coming toward him slowly*]: You talking 'bout taking them people's money to keep us from moving in that house?

WALTER: I ain't just talking 'bout it, baby—I'm telling you that's what's going to happen.

BENEATHA: Oh, God! Where is the bottom! Where is the real honest-to-God bottom so he can't go any farther!

WALTER: See—that's the old stuff. You and that boy that was here today. You all want everybody to carry a flag and a spear and sing some marching songs, huh? You wanna spend your life looking into things and trying to find the right and the wrong part, huh? Yeah. You know what's going to happen to that boy someday—he'll find himself sitting in a dungeon, locked in forever—and the takers will have the key! Forget it, baby! There ain't no causes—there ain't nothing but taking in this world, and he who takes most is smartest—and it don't make a damn bit of difference *how.*

MAMA: You making something inside me cry, son. Some awful pain inside me.

WALTER: Don't cry, Mama. Understand. That white man is going to walk in that door able to write checks for more money than we ever had. It's important to him and I'm going to help him . . . I'm going to put on the show, Mama.

MAMA: Son—I come from five generations of people who was slaves and sharecroppers—but ain't nobody in my family never let nobody pay 'em no money that was a way of telling us we wasn't fit to walk the earth. We ain't never been that poor. [*Raising her eyes and looking at him.*] We ain't never been that dead inside.

BENEATHA: Well—we are dead now. All the talk about dreams and sunlight that goes on in this house. All dead.

WALTER: What's the matter with you all! I didn't make this world! It was give to me this way! Hell, yes, I want me some yachts someday! Yes, I want to hang some real pearls 'round my wife's neck. Ain't she supposed to wear no pearls? Somebody tell me—tell me, who decides which women is suppose to wear pearls in this world. I tell you I am a *man*—and I think my wife should wear some pearls in this world!

[*This last line hangs a good while and* WALTER *begins to move about the room. The word "Man" has penetrated his consciousness; he mumbles it to himself repeatedly between strange agitated pauses as he moves about.*]

MAMA: Baby, how you going to feel on the inside?

WALTER: Fine! . . . Going to feel fine . . . a man . . .

MAMA: You won't have nothing left then, Walter Lee.

WALTER [*coming to her*]: I'm going to feel fine, Mama. I'm going to look that son-of-a-bitch in the eyes and say—[*He falters.*]—and say, "All right, Mr. Lindner—[*He falters even more.*]—that's your neighborhood out there. You got the right to keep it like you want. You got the right to have it like you want. Just write the check and—the house is yours." And, and I am going to say—[*His voice almost breaks.*] And you—you people just put the money in my hand and you won't have to live next to this bunch of stinking niggers! . . . [*He straightens up and moves away from his mother, walking around the room.*] Maybe—maybe I'll just get down on my black knees . . . [*He does so;* RUTH *and* BENNIE *and* MAMA *watch him in frozen horror.*] Captain, Mistuh, Bossman. [*He starts crying.*] A-hee-hee-hee! [*Wringing his hands in profoundly anguished imitation.*] Yasssssuh! Great White Father, just gi' ussen de money, fo' God's sake, and we's ain't gwine come out deh and dirty up yo' white folks neighborhood . . . [*He breaks down completely, then gets up and goes into the bedroom.*]

BENEATHA: That is not a man. That is nothing but a toothless rat.

MAMA: Yes—death done come in this here house. [*She is nodding, slowly, reflectively.*] Done come walking in my house. On the lips of my children. You what supposed to be my beginning again. You—what supposed to be my harvest. [*To* BENEATHA.] You—you mourning your brother?

BENEATHA: He's no brother of mine.

MAMA: What you say?

BENEATHA: I said that that individual in that room is no brother of mine.

MAMA: That's what I thought you said. You feeling like you better than he is today? [BENEATHA *does not answer.*] Yes? What you tell him a minute ago? That he wasn't a man? Yes? You give him up for me? You done wrote his epitaph too—like the rest of the world? Well, who give you the privilege?

BENEATHA: Be on my side for once! You saw what he just did, Mama! You saw him—down on his knees. Wasn't it you who taught me—to despise any man who would do that? Do what he's going to do.

MAMA: Yes—I taught you that. Me and your daddy. But I thought I taught you something else too . . . I thought I taught you to love him.

BENEATHA: Love him? There is nothing left to love.

MAMA: There is always something left to love. And if you ain't learned that, you ain't learned nothing. [*Looking at her.*] Have you cried for that boy today? I don't mean for yourself and for the family 'cause we lost the money. I mean for him; what he been through and what it done to him. Child, when do you think is the time to love somebody the most; when they done good and made things easy for everybody? Well then, you ain't through learning—because that ain't the time at all. It's when he's at his lowest and can't believe in hisself 'cause the world done whipped him so. When you starts measuring somebody, measure him right, child, measure him right. Make sure you done taken into account what hills and valleys he come through before he got to wherever he is.

[TRAVIS *bursts into the room at the end of the speech, leaving the door open.*]

TRAVIS: Grandmama—the moving men are downstairs! The truck just pulled up.
MAMA [*turning and looking at him*]: Are they, baby? They downstairs?

[*She sighs and sits. Lindner appears in the doorway. He peers in and knocks lightly, to gain attention, and comes in. All turn to look at him.*]

LINDNER [*hat and briefcase in hand*]: Uh—hello . . .

[RUTH *crosses mechanically to the bedroom door and opens it and lets it swing open freely and slowly as the lights come up on* WALTER *within, still in his coat, sitting at the far corner of the room. He looks up and out through the room to* LINDNER.]

RUTH: He's here.

[*A long minute passes and* WALTER *slowly gets up.*]

LINDNER [*coming to the table with efficiency, putting his briefcase on the table and starting to unfold papers and unscrew fountain pens*]: Well, I certainly was glad to hear from you people. [WALTER *has begun the trek out of the room, slowly and awkwardly, rather like a small boy, passing the back of his sleeve across his mouth from time to time.*] Life can really be so much simpler than people let it be most of the time. Well—with whom do I negotiate? You, Mrs. Younger, or your son here? [MAMA *sits with her hands folded on her lap and her eyes closed as* WALTER *advances.* TRAVIS *goes close to* LINDNER *and looks at the papers curiously.*] Just some official papers, sonny.
RUTH: Travis, you go downstairs.
MAMA [*opening her eyes and looking into* WALTER's]: No. Travis, you stay right here. And you make him understand what you doing, Walter Lee. You teach him good. Like Willy Harris taught you. You show where our five generations done come to. Go ahead, son—
WALTER [*looks down into his boy's eyes.* TRAVIS *grins at him merrily and* WALTER *draws him beside him with his arm lightly around his shoulder*]: Well, Mr. Lindner. [BENEATHA *turns away.*] We called you—[*There is a profound, simple groping quality in his speech.*]—because, well, me and my family [*He looks around and shifts from one foot to the other.*] Well—we are very plain people . . .
LINDNER: Yes—
WALTER: I mean—I have worked as a chauffeur most of my life—and my wife here,

she does domestic work in people's kitchens. So does my mother. I mean—we are plain people . . .

LINDNER: Yes, Mr. Younger—

WALTER [*really like a small boy, looking down at his shoes and then up at the man*]: And—uh—well, my father, well, he was a laborer most of his life.

LINDNER [*absolutely confused*]: Uh, yes—

WALTER [*looking down at his toes once again*]: My father almost beat a man to death once because this man called him a bad name or something, you know what I mean?

LINDNER: No, I'm afraid I don't.

WALTER [*finally straightening up*]: Well, what I mean is that we come from people who had a lot of pride. I mean—we are very proud people. And that's my sister over there and she's going to be a doctor—and we are very proud—

LINDNER: Well—I am sure that is very nice, but—

WALTER [*starting to cry and facing the man eye to eye*]: What I am telling you is that we called you over here to tell you that we are very proud and that this is—this is my son, who makes the sixth generation of our family in this country, and that we have all thought about your offer and we have decided to move into our house because my father—my father—he earned it. [MAMA *has her eyes closed and is rocking back and forth as though she were in church, with her head nodding the amen yes.*] We don't want to make no trouble for nobody or fight no causes—but we will try to be good neighbors. That's all we got to say. [*He looks the man absolutely in the eyes.*] We don't want your money. [*He turns and walks away from the man.*]

LINDNER [*looking around at all of them*]: I take it then that you have decided to occupy.

BENEATHA: That's what the man said.

LINDNER [*to* MAMA *in her reverie*]: Then I would like to appeal to you, Mrs. Younger. You are older and wiser and understand things better I am sure . . .

MAMA [*rising*]: I am afraid you don't understand. My son said we was going to move and there ain't nothing left for me to say. [*Shaking her head with double meaning.*] You know how these young folks is nowadays, mister. Can't do a thing with 'em. Good-bye.

LINDNER [*folding up his materials*]: Well—if you are that final about it . . . There is nothing left for me to say. [*He finishes. He is almost ignored by the family, who are concentrating on* WALTER LEE. *At the door* LINDNER *halts and looks around.*] I sure hope you people know what you're doing. [*He shakes his head and exits.*]

RUTH [*looking around and coming to life*]: Well, for God's sake—if the moving men are here—LET'S GET THE HELL OUT OF HERE!

MAMA [*into action*]: Ain't it the truth! Look at all this here mess. Ruth put Travis' good jacket on him . . . Walter Lee, fix your tie and tuck your shirt in, you look just like somebody's hoodlum. Lord have mercy, where is my plant? [*She flies to get it amid the general bustling of the family, who are deliberately trying to ignore the nobility of the past moment.*] You all start on down . . . Travis child, don't go empty-handed . . . Ruth, where did I put that box with my skillets in it? I want to be in charge of it myself . . . I'm going to make us the biggest dinner we ever ate tonight . . . Beneatha, what's the matter with them stockings? Pull them things up, girl . . .

[*The family starts to file out as two moving men appear and begin to carry out the heavier pieces of furniture, bumping into the family as they move about.*]

BENEATHA: Mama, Asagai—asked me to marry him today and go to Africa—

MAMA [*in the middle of her getting-ready activity*]: He did? You ain't old enough to marry nobody—[*Seeing the moving men lifting one of her chairs precariously.*] Darling, that ain't no bale of cotton, please handle it so we can sit in it again. I had that chair twenty-five years . . .

[*The movers sigh with exasperation and go on with their work.*]

BENEATHA [*girlishly and unreasonably trying to pursue the conversation*]: To go to Africa, Mama—be a doctor in Africa . . .

MAMA [*distracted*]: Yes, baby—

WALTER: Africa! What he want you to go to Africa for?

BENEATHA: To practice there . . .

WALTER: Girl, if you don't get all them silly ideas out your head! You better marry yourself a man with some loot . . .

BENEATHA [*angrily, precisely as in the first scene of the play*]: What have you got to do with who I marry!

WALTER: Plenty. Now I think George Murchison—

[*He and* BENEATHA *go out yelling at each other vigorously;* BENEATHA *is heard saying that she would not marry* GEORGE MURCHISON *if he were Adam and she were Eve, etc. The anger is loud and real till their voices diminish.* RUTH *stands at the door and turns to* MAMA *and smiles knowingly.*]

MAMA [*fixing her hat at last*]: Yeah—they something all right, my children . . .

RUTH: Yeah—they're something. Let's go, Lena.

MAMA [*stalling, starting to look around at the house*]: Yes—I'm coming. Ruth—

RUTH: Yes?

MAMA [*quietly, woman to woman*]: He finally come into his manhood today, didn't he? Kind of like a rainbow after the rain . . .

RUTH [*biting her lip lest her own pride explode in front of* MAMA]: Yes, Lena.

[WALTER's *voice calls for them raucously.*]

MAMA [*waving* RUTH *out vaguely*]: All right, honey—go on down. I be down directly.

[RUTH *hesitates, then exits.* MAMA *stands, at last alone in the living room, her plant on the table before her as the lights start to come down. She looks around at all the walls and ceilings and suddenly, despite herself, while the children call below, a great heaving thing rises in her and she puts her fist to her mouth, takes a final desperate look, pulls her coat about her, pats her hat and goes out. The lights dim down. The door opens and she comes back in, grabs her plant, and goes out for the last time.*]

Curtain

QUESTIONS

1. The playwright introduces her description of the Younger home by saying it has a "number of indestructible contradictions." Explain what she means by this. Select one of the characters introduced in Act I, and explain his or her "contradictions."

2. What is the first major conflict that occurs in Act I? How does it foreshadow a major event that occurs in the latter part of the play?

3. Based on Act I, which of the characters do you find most appealing? Least appealing? Explain why.

4. What is the chief conflict between George Murchison and Beneatha? Between George Murchison and Walter?

5. Compare Walter's feelings at the end of Act II, scene II, with his reaction to what Bobo reveals to him at the end of Act II, scene III. How does the contrast between these two dramatic moments contribute to the dramatic tension of the play?

6. Asagai and Beneatha have an argument at the beginning of Act III. What is each one's main contention? Do you take sides with either of them? If so, which one, and why?

7. In Act III, Walter explains to Mama what he plans to tell Lindner about moving into the new house. But what he actually tells him when he arrives is quite different. How do you account for this change of heart? How does it heighten the intensity of the drama?

21. Plot

A plot in drama, as in fiction, is a causally connected series of events arranged in such a way as to advance various conflicts and to achieve internal unity. George Santayana observed that the dramatist "allows us to see other men's minds through the medium of events." The dramatist orders events into scenes and acts, structuring elements and action according to any number of patterns. He or she ties and unties the knot of conflict in order to afford us insights not only into the human mind but also into human destiny.

Our own lives and destinies do not, of course, conform to well-defined "plots," except in the vaguest sense of the word. Dramatic plots, by contrast, impose artificial order on human actions—and typically on extremes of human action. In the spirit of Aristotle, who wrote that "the plot is the imitation of the Action," playwrights impose artistic order on existence, giving form or design to life, so that the spectator or reader can experience it intelligibly. Plot governs everything in a play, perhaps more so than in fiction. E. M. Forster acknowledges this possibility in *Aspects of the Novel* when he comments: "In the drama all human happiness and misery must take the form of action. Otherwise its existence remains unknown, and this is the great difference between the drama and the novel." If playwrights have a passion for plot, it is only because they recognize that carefully structured action is the soul of drama.

Plot asks that we remember the action and what that action implies when we finally consider what the play is "saying" to us. Plot, and there may be more than one, should quickly grip us and move us directly into the action of the drama. All plots within a single play, whether major or minor, are related, and all must be resolved to our emotional and intellectual satisfaction.

How dramatists plan their plots—their series of interrelated actions—cannot be oversimplified or rendered by a single formula. Such plot formulations as the one developed by Freytag in the nineteenth century (see the diagram on page 33) can be useful when analyzing the structures of certain types of plays. A well-built tragedy, like *Oedipus Rex* or *Hamlet*, might very well reflect the famous five-part dramatic structure outlined in our discussion of plot in fiction: the introduction or exposition; the rising action or complication; the climax or turning point; the falling action; and the resolution or catastrophe. Yet much Shakespearean and Elizabethan drama does not conform readily to this conception of plot. And with the development of modern drama by Ibsen, the many faces of dramatic plot change radically as action follows new social and psychological, as well as artistic, channels of development.

What we do look for in all dramatic plots is a series of interrelated actions that are tied together by the interplay of opposing and, typically, antagonistic forces. Without conflict, without that "itch of suspense" (as Eric Bentley terms it) fostered by clashing forces, drama would be dull indeed. In part, the function of dramatic plot is to reveal character in conflict and action. With an economy far greater than that which can be attempted by a writer of fiction, a dramatist makes every gesture, every action, every bit of dialogue advance major and minor conflicts. And through these patterned conflicts, often divided into segments defined as scenes and acts, the dramatist also uses plot to illuminate a vision of life. In *Oedipus Rex*, for example, a play containing six sections and five choral odes (a plot structure common in Greek tragedy), Sophocles structures the action so as to pile question upon question: Why have disasters overtaken Thebes? What happened when King Laius was murdered? Who murdered him and why? The answer to each question succeeds only in raising more questions, all with growing apprehension and finally horror. For all along, plot has been revealing the theme of a protagonist, or main character, in the hands of fate. Discovering this, what is Oedipus— any man or woman—to do? These are questions that force a person into psychological, physical, and ultimately spiritual conflict.

Just as Oedipus struggles with questions of destiny, or fate, seemingly written in both personal and cosmic terms (for Apollo, that ambiguous god of vengeance, penance, and prophecy, delivers to Oedipus his awful fate), the great figures of modern drama are caught in equally appropriate conflicts that define their destinies. No contemporary dramatic protagonist is more famous than Willy Loman in Arthur Miller's *Death of a Salesman*. As a caveat, we must acknowledge that the essential structure of Miller's play, with its flashbacks and rapid shifts in time, its expressionistic settings and lighting (in which the stage environment is "distorted" so that external reality reflects the internal psychological condition of the protagonist), could never have been duplicated within the plot conventions of earlier theater. Technology, the American business ethic (replacing the pantheon of Greek gods), and Freud, among other considerations, contribute to the modernity of plot in Miller's play. Nevertheless, the essence of the plots centering on Oedipus and Willy Loman are strikingly alike—confirmations in their own ways of Aristotle's dictum that plot is the "soul" of tragedy.

The questions governing plot development in *Oedipus Rex* are replaced by statements—all of which lead, as elements of plot should, to theme. Furthermore, in *Death of a Salesman*, many of the plots could have been made dramas of their own: the tension and pretension between Biff and Happy; the love-hate relationship between Biff and Willy; the obvious differences that could lead to conflict between Ben and Willy. These subplots swirl around Willy Loman, who, however, commands center stage. The tantalizing, connecting question in *Death of a Salesman* is why Biff (a reflection of his father) has become such an abominable failure. Miller supplies the answer late in Act II—but then that answer is supplied from the point of view of both father and son.

It is the burden of both Oedipus and Willy to discover the motives behind their own destinies and for us to understand those motives through plot. Both Oedipus and Willy, victims of fate and of themselves, playthings of the material and spiritual worlds, in the end become arbiters of how the last moments of their lives will be spent. While Willy may not be the inheritor of a grand history or myth-story, it is his determination to control some aspect of his life that connects him down through the generations to Oedipus and makes us consider that despite the divergent plots, a common tragic theme is as much the domain of the pauper as it is of the prince.

Sophocles

OEDIPUS REX

English translation by
Dudley Fitts and Robert Fitzgerald

CHARACTERS

OEDIPUS	MESSENGER
A PRIEST	SHEPHERD OF LAÏOS
CREON	SECOND MESSENGER
TEIRESIAS	CHORUS OF THEBAN ELDERS
IOCASTÊ	

Scene   Before the palace of OEDIPUS, *king of Thebes. A central door and two lateral doors open onto a platform which runs the length of the façade. On the platform, right and left, are altars; and three steps lead down into the "orchestra," or chorus-ground. At the beginning of the action these steps are crowded by suppliants who have brought branches and chaplets of olive leaves and who lie in various attitudes of despair.* OEDIPUS *enters.*

PROLOGUE

OEDIPUS: My children, generations of the living
   In the line of Kadmos, nursed at his ancient hearth:
   Why have you strewn yourselves before these altars
   In supplication, with your boughs and garlands?
   The breath of incense rises from the city   5
   With a sound of prayer and lamentation.

                     Children,
   I would not have you speak through messengers,

And therefore I have come myself to hear you—
I, Oedipus, who bear the famous name.
[*To a Priest.*] You, there, since you are eldest in the company,   10
Speak for them all, tell me what preys upon you,
Whether you come in dread, or crave some blessing:
Tell me, and never doubt that I will help you
In every way I can; I should be heartless
Were I not moved to find you suppliant here.   15
PRIEST: Great Oedipus, O powerful King of Thebes!
    You see how all the ages of our people
    Cling to your altar steps: here are boys
    Who can barely stand alone, and here are priests
    By weight of age, as I am a priest of God,   20
    And young men chosen from those yet unmarried;
    As for the others, all that multitude,
    They wait with olive chaplets in the squares,
    At the two shrines of Pallas, and where Apollo
    Speaks in the glowing embers.

                          Your own eyes   25
    Must tell you: Thebes is in her extremity
    And cannot lift her head from the surge of death.
    A rust consumes the buds and fruits of the earth;
    The herds are sick; children die unborn,
    And labor is vain. The god of plague and pyre   30
    Raids like detestable lightning through the city,
    And all the house of Kadmos is laid waste,
    All emptied, and all darkened: Death alone
    Battens upon the misery of Thebes.
    You are not one of the immortal gods, we know;   35
    Yet we have come to you to make our prayer
    As to the man of all men best in adversity
    And wisest in the ways of God. You saved us
    From the Sphinx, that flinty singer, and the tribute
    We paid to her so long; yet you were never   40
    Better informed than we, nor could we teach you:
    It was some god breathed in you to set us free.

    Therefore, O mighty King, we turn to you:
    Find us our safety, find us a remedy,
    Whether by counsel of the gods or the men.   45
    A king of wisdom tested in the past
    Can act in a time of troubles, and act well.
    Noblest of men, restore
    Life to your city! Think how all men call you
    Liberator for your triumph long ago;   50
    Ah, when your years of kingship are remembered,

Let them not say *We rose, but later fell*—
Keep the State from going down in the storm!
Once, years ago, with happy augury,
You brought us fortune; be the same again!   55
No man questions your power to rule the land:
But rule over men, not over a dead city!
Ships are only hulls, citadels are nothing,
When no life moves in the empty passageways.

OEDIPUS: Poor children! You may be sure I know   60
   All that you longed for in your coming here.
   I know that you are deathly sick; and yet,
   Sick as you are, not one is as sick as I.
   Each of you suffers in himself alone
   His anguish, not another's; but my spirit   65
   Groans for the city, for myself, for you.

   I was not sleeping, you are not waking me.
   No, I have been in tears for a long while
   And in my restless thought walked many ways.
   In all my search, I found one helpful course,   70
   And that I have taken: I have sent Creon,
   Son of Menoikeus, brother of the Queen,
   To Delphi, Apollo's place of revelation,
   To learn there, if he can,
   What act or pledge of mine may save the city.   75
   I have counted the days, and now, this very day,
   I am troubled, for he has overstayed his time.
   What is he doing? He has been gone too long.
   Yet whenever he comes back, I should do ill
   To scant whatever hint the god may give.   80

PRIEST: It is a timely promise. At this instant
   They tell me Creon is here.

OEDIPUS: O Lord Apollo!
   May his news be fair as his face is radiant!

PRIEST: It could not be otherwise: he is crowned with bay,
   The chaplet is thick with berries.

OEDIPUS: We shall soon know;   85
   He is near enough to hear us now.

   [*Enter* CREON]

                    O Prince:
   Brother: son of Menoikeus:
   What answer do you bring us from the god?

CREON: It is favorable. I can tell you, great afflictions
   Will turn out well, if they are taken well.   90

OEDIPUS: What was the oracle? These vague words
   Leave me still hanging between hope and fear.
CREON: Is it your pleasure to hear me with all these
   Gathered around us? I am prepared to speak,
   But should we not go in?
OEDIPUS: Let them all hear it.   95
   It is for them I suffer, more than myself.
CREON: Then I will tell you what I heard at Delphi.

   In plain words
   The god commands us to expel from the land of Thebes
   And old defilement that it seems we shelter.   100
   It is a deathly thing, beyond expiation.
   We must not let it feed upon us longer.
OEDIPUS: What defilement? How shall we rid ourselves of it?
CREON: By exile or death, blood for blood. It was
   Murder that brought the plague-wind on the city.   105
OEDIPUS: Murder of whom? Surely the god has named him?
CREON: My lord: long ago Laïos was our king,
   Before you came to govern us.
OEDIPUS: I know;
   I learned of him from others; I never saw him.
CREON: He was murdered; and Apollo commands us now   110
   To take revenge upon whoever killed him.
OEDIPUS: Upon whom? Where are they? Where shall we find a clue
   To solve that crime, after so many years?
CREON: Here in this land, he said.
                  If we make enquiry,
   We may touch things that otherwise escape us.   115
OEDIPUS: Tell me: Was Laïos murdered in his house,
   Or in the fields, or in some foreign country?
CREON: He said he planned to make a pilgrimage.
   He did not come home again.
OEDIPUS: And was there no one,
   No witness, no companion, to tell what happened?   120
CREON: They were all killed but one, and he got away
   So frightened that he could remember one thing only.
OEDIPUS: What was that one thing? One may be the key
   To everything, if we resolve to use it.
CREON: He said that a band of highwaymen attacked them,   125
   Outnumbered them, and overwhelmed the King.
OEDIPUS: Strange, that a highwayman should be so daring—
   Unless some faction here bribed him to do it.
CREON: We thought of that. But after Laïos' death
   New troubles arose and we had no avenger.   130
OEDIPUS: What troubles could prevent your hunting down the killers?

CREON: The riddling Sphinx's song
    Made us deaf to all mysteries but her own.
OEDIPUS: Then once more I must bring what is dark to light.
    It is most fitting that Apollo shows,   135
    As you do, this compunction for the dead.
    You shall see how I stand by you, as I should,
    To avenge the city and the city's god.
    And not as though it were for some distant friend,
    But for my own sake, to be rid of evil.   140
    Whoever killed King Laïos might—who knows?—
    Decide at any moment to kill me as well.
    By avenging the murdered king I protect myself.
    Come then, my children: leave the altar steps,
    Lift up your olive boughs!
                        One of you go   145
    And summon the people of Kadmos to gather here.
    I will do all that I can; you may tell them that.   [*Exit a* PAGE.]
    So, with the help of God,
    We shall be saved—or else indeed we are lost.
PRIEST: Let us rise, children. It was for this we came,   150
    And now the King has promised it himself.
    Phoibos has sent us an oracle; may he descend
    Himself to save us and drive out the plague.

[*Exeunt* OEDIPUS *and* CREON *into the palace by the central door. The priest and the suppliants disperse right and left. After a short pause the* CHORUS *enters the orchestra.*]

PÁRODOS

Strophe 1

CHORUS: What is God singing in his profound
    Delphi of gold and shadow?
    What oracle for Thebes, the sunwhipped city?
    Fear unjoints me, the roots of my heart tremble.
    Now I remember, O Healer, your power, and wonder;   5
    Will you send doom like a sudden cloud, or weave it
    Like nightfall of the past?
    Speak, speak to us, issue of holy sound:
    Dearest to our expectancy: be tender!

Antistrophe 1

    Let me pray to Athenê, the immortal daughter of Zeus,   10
    And to Artemis her sister

Who keeps her famous throne in the market ring,
And to Apollo, bowman at the far butts of heaven—

O gods, descend! Like three streams leap against
The fires of our grief, the fires of darkness;   15
Be swift to bring us rest!

As in the old time from the brilliant house
Of air you stepped to save us, come again!

Strophe 2

Now our afflictions have no end,
Now all our stricken host lies down   20
And no man fights off death with his mind;

The noble plowland bears no grain,
And groaning mothers cannot bear—
See, how our lives like birds take wing,
Like sparks that fly when a fire soars,   25
To the shore of the god of evening.

Antistrophe 2

The plague burns on, it is pitiless,
Though pallid children laden with death
Lie unwept in the stony ways,
And old gray women by every path   30
Flock to the strand about the altars

There to strike their breasts and cry
Worship of Phoibos in wailing prayers:
Be kind, God's golden child!

Strophe 3

There are no swords in this attack by fire,   35
No shields, but we are ringed with cries.
Send the besieger plunging from our homes
Into the vast sea-room of the Atlantic
Or into the waves that foam eastward of Thrace—
For the day ravages what the night spares—   40

Destroy our enemy, lord of the thunder!
Let him be riven by lightning from heaven!

Antistrophe 3

Phoibos Apollo, stretch the sun's bowstring,
That golden cord, until it sing for us,
Flashing arrows in heaven!
                          Artemis, Huntress,   45
Race with flaring lights upon our mountains!
O scarlet god, O golden-banded brow,
O Theban Bacchos in a storm of Maenads,

[*Enter* OEDIPUS, *center.*]

Whirl upon Death, that all the Undying hate!
Come with blinding cressets, come in joy!   50

SCENE I

OEDIPUS: Is this your prayer? It may be answered. Come,
    Listen to me, act as the crisis demands,
    And you shall have relief from all these evils.
    Until now I was a stranger to this tale,
    As I had been a stranger to the crime.   5
    Could I track down the murderer without a clue?
    But now, friends,
    As one who became a citizen after the murder,
    I make this proclamation to all Thebans:
    If any man knows by whose hand Laïos, son of Labdakos,   10
    Met his death, I direct that man to tell me everything,
    No matter what he fears for having so long withheld it.
    Let it stand as promised that no further trouble
    Will come to him, but he may leave the land in safety.

    Moreover: If anyone knows the murderer to be foreign,   15
    Let him not keep silent: he shall have his reward from me.
    However, if he does conceal it; if any man
    Fearing for his friend or for himself disobeys this edict,
    Hear what I propose to do:

    I solemnly forbid the people of this country,   20
    Where power and throne are mine, ever to receive that man
    Or speak to him, no matter who he is, or let him
    Join in sacrifice, lustration, or in prayer.
    I decree that he be driven from every house,

Being, as he is, corruption itself to us: the Delphic   25
Voice of Zeus has pronounced this revelation.
Thus I associate myself with the oracle
And take the side of the murdered king.

As for the criminal, I pray to God—
Whether it be a lurking thief, or one of a number—   30
I pray that that man's life be consumed in evil and wretchedness.
And as for me, this curse applies no less
If it should turn out that the culprit is my guest here,
Sharing my hearth.
         You have heard the penalty.
I lay it on you now to attend to this   35
For my sake, for Apollo's, for the sick
Sterile city that heaven has abandoned.
Suppose the oracle had given you no command:
Should this defilement go uncleansed for ever?
You should have found the murderer: your king,   40
A noble king, had been destroyed!
         Now I,
Having the power that he held before me,
Having his bed, begetting children there
Upon his wife, as he would have, had he lived—
Their son would have been my children's brother,   45
If Laïos had had luck in fatherhood!
(But surely ill luck rushed upon his reign)—
I say I take the son's part, just as though
I were his son, to press the fight for him
And see it won! I'll find the hand that brought   50
Death to Labdakos' and Polydoros' child,
Heir of Kadmos' and Agenor's line.
And as for those who fail me,
May the gods deny them the fruit of the earth,
Fruit of the womb, and may they rot utterly!   55
Let them be wretched as we are wretched, and worse!

For you, for loyal Thebans, and for all
Who find my actions right, I pray the favor
Of justice, and of all the immortal gods.
CHORAGOS: Since I am under oath, my lord, I swear   60
I did not do the murder, I cannot name
The murderer. Might not the oracle
That has ordained the search tell where to find him?
OEDIPUS: An honest question. But no man in the world
Can make the gods do more than the gods will.   65

CHORAGOS: There is one last expedient—
OEDIPUS: Tell me what it is.
    Though it seem slight, you must not hold it back.
CHORAGOS: A lord clairvoyant to the lord Apollo,
    As we all know, is the skilled Teiresias.
    One might learn much about this from him, Oedipus.   70
OEDIPUS: I am not wasting time:
    Creon spoke of this, and I have sent for him—
    Twice, in fact; it is strange that he is not here.
CHORAGOS: The other matter—that old report—seems useless.
OEDIPUS: Tell me. I am interested in all reports.   75
CHORAGOS: The King was said to have been killed by highwaymen.
OEDIPUS: I know. But we have no witness to that.
CHORAGOS: If the killer can feel a particle of dread,
    Your curse will bring him out of hiding!
OEDIPUS: No.
    The man who dared that act will fear no curse.   80

[*Enter the blind seer* TEIRESIAS, *led by a page.*]

CHORAGOS: But there is one man who may detect the criminal.
    This is Teiresias, this is the holy prophet
    In whom, alone of all men, truth was born.
OEDIPUS: Teiresias: seer: student of mysteries,
    Of all that's taught and all that no man tells,   85
    Secrets of Heaven and secrets of the earth:
    Blind though you are, you know the city lies
    Sick with plague; and from this plague, my lord,
    We find that you alone can guard or save us.

    Possibly you did not hear the messengers?   90
    Apollo, when we sent to him,
    Sent us back word that this great pestilence
    Would lift, but only if we established clearly
    The identity of those who murdered Laïos.
    They must be killed or exiled.
                      Can you use   95
    Birdflight or any art of divination
    To purify yourself, and Thebes, and me
    From this contagion? We are in your hands.
    There is no fairer duty
    Than that of helping others in distress.   100
TEIRESIAS: How dreadful knowledge of the truth can be
    When there's no help in truth! I knew this well,
    But did not act on it: else I should not have come.

OEDIPUS: What is troubling you? Why are your eyes so cold?

TEIRESIAS: Let me go home. Bear your own fate, and I'll   105
    Bear mine. It is better so: trust what I say.

OEDIPUS: What you say is ungracious and unhelpful
    To your native country. Do not refuse to speak.

TEIRESIAS: When it comes to speech, your own is neither temperate
    Nor opportune. I wish to be more prudent.   110

OEDIPUS: In God's name, we all beg you—

TEIRESIAS: You are all ignorant.
    No; I will never tell you what I know.
    Now it is my misery; then, it would be yours.

OEDIPUS: What! You do know something, and will not tell us?
    You would betray us all and wreck the State?   115

TEIRESIAS: I do not intend to torture myself, or you.
    Why persist in asking? You will not persuade me.

OEDIPUS: What a wicked old man you are! You'd try a stone's
    Patience! Out with it! Have you no feeling at all?

TEIRESIAS: You call me unfeeling. If you could only see   120
    The nature of your own feelings . . .

OEDIPUS: Why,
    Who would not feel as I do? Who could endure
    Your arrogance toward the city?

TEIRESIAS: What does it matter!
    Whether I speak or not, it is bound to come.

OEDIPUS: Then, if "it" is bound to come, you are bound to tell me.   125

TEIRESIAS: No, I will not go on. Rage as you please.

OEDIPUS: Rage? Why not!
               And I'll tell you what I think:
    You planned it, you had it done, you all but
    Killed him with your own hands: if you had eyes,
    I'd say the crime was yours and yours alone.   130

TEIRESIAS: So? I charge you, then.
    Abide by the proclamation you have made:
    From this day forth
    Never speak again to these men or to me;
    You yourself are the pollution of this country.   135

OEDIPUS: You dare say that! Can you possibly think you have
    Some way of going free, after such insolence?

TEIRESIAS: I have gone free. It is the truth sustains me.

OEDIPUS: Who taught you shamelessness? It was not your craft.

TEIRESIAS: You did. You made me speak. I did not want to.   140

OEDIPUS: Speak what? Let me hear it again more clearly.

TEIRESIAS: Was it not clear before? Are you tempting me?

OEDIPUS: I did not understand it. Say it again.

TEIRESIAS: I say that you are the murderer whom you seek.

OEDIPUS: Now twice you have spat out infamy. You'll pay for it!   145
TEIRESIAS: Would you care for more? Do you wish to be really angry?
OEDIPUS: Say what you will. Whatever you say is worthless.
TEIRESIAS: I say you live in hideous shame with those
   Most dear to you. You cannot see the evil.
OEDIPUS: It seems you can go on mouthing like this for ever.   150
TEIRESIAS: I can, if there is power in truth.
OEDIPUS: There is:
   But not for you, not for you,
   You sightless, witless, senseless, mad old man!
TEIRESIAS: You are the madman. There is no one here
   Who will not curse you soon, as you curse me.   155
OEDIPUS: You child of endless night! You cannot hurt me
   Or any other man who sees the sun.
TEIRESIAS: True: it is not from me your fate will come.
   That lies within Apollo's competence,
   As it is his concern.
OEDIPUS: Tell me: 160
   Are you speaking for Creon, or for yourself?
TEIRESIAS: Creon is no threat. You weave your own doom.
OEDIPUS: Wealth, power, craft of statesmanship!
   Kingly position, everywhere admired!
   What savage envy is stored up against these,   165
   If Creon, whom I trusted, Creon my friend,
   For this great office which the city once
   Put in my hands unsought—if for this power
   Creon desires in secret to destroy me!

   He has brought this decrepit fortune-teller, this   170
   Collector of dirty pennies, this prophet fraud—
   Why, he is no more clairvoyant than I am!
                    Tell us:
   Has your mystic mummery ever approached the truth?
   When that hellcat the Sphinx was performing here,
   What help were you to these people?   175
   Her magic was not for the first man who came along:
   It demanded a real exorcist. Your birds—
   What good were they? or the gods, for the matter of that?
   But I came by,
   Oedipus, the simple man, who knows nothing—   180
   I thought it out for myself, no birds helped me!
   And this is the man you think you can destroy,
   That you may be close to Creon when he's king!
   Well, you and your friend Creon, it seems to me,
   Will suffer most. If you were not an old man,   185
   You would have paid already for your plot.

CHORAGOS: We cannot see that his words or yours
    Have been spoken except in anger, Oedipus,
    And of anger we have no need. How can God's will
    Be accomplished best? That is what most concerns us.   190
TEIRESIAS: You are a king. But where argument's concerned
    I am your man, as much a king as you.
    I am not your servant, but Apollo's.
    I have no need of Creon to speak for me.

    Listen to me. You mock my blindness, do you?   195
    But I say that you, with both your eyes, are blind:
    You cannot see the wretchedness of your life,
    Nor in whose house you live, no, nor with whom.
    Who are your father and mother? Can you tell me?
    You do not even know the blind wrongs   200
    That you have done them, on earth and in the world below.
    But the double lash of your parents' curse will whip you
    Out of this land some day, with only night
    Upon your precious eyes.
    Your cries then—where will they not be heard?   205
    What fastness of Kithairon will not echo them?
    And that bridal-descant of yours—you'll know it then,
    The song they sang when you came here to Thebes
    And found your misguided berthing.
    All this, and more, that you cannot guess at now,   210
    Will bring you to yourself among your children.
    Be angry, then. Curse Creon. Curse my words.
    I tell you, no man that walks upon the earth
    Shall be rooted out more horribly than you.
OEDIPUS: Am I to bear this from him?—Damnation   215
    Take you! Out of this place! Out of my sight!
TEIRESIAS: I would not have come at all if you had not asked me.
OEDIPUS: Could I have told that you'd talk nonsense, that
    You'd come here to make a fool of yourself, and of me?
TEIRESIAS: A fool? Your parents thought me sane enough.   220
OEDIPUS: My parents again!—Wait: who were my parents?
TEIRESIAS: This day will give you a father, and break your heart.
OEDIPUS: Your infantile riddles! Your damned abracadabra!
TEIRESIAS: You were a great man once at solving riddles.
OEDIPUS: Mock me with that if you like; you will find it true.   225
TEIRESIAS: It was true enough. It brought about your ruin.
OEDIPUS: But if it saved this town?
TEIRESIAS [to the page]: Boy, give me your hand.
OEDIPUS: Yes, boy; lead him away.
                —While you are here
    We can do nothing. Go; leave us in peace.

TEIRESIAS: I will go when I have said what I have to say.   230
   How can you hurt me? And I tell you again:
   The man you have been looking for all this time,
   The damned man, the murderer of Laïos,
   That man is in Thebes. To your mind he is foreignborn,
   But it will soon be shown that he is a Theban,   235
   A revelation that will fail to please.
                    A blind man,
   Who has his eyes now; a penniless man, who is rich now;
   And he will go tapping the strange earth with his staff;
   To the children with whom he lives now he will be
   Brother and father—the very same; to her   240
   Who bore him, son and husband—the very same
   Who came to his father's bed, wet with his father's blood.

   Enough. Go think that over.
   If later you find error in what I have said,
   You may say that I have no skill in prophecy.   245

[*Exit* TEIRESIAS, *led by his page.* OEDIPUS *goes into the palace.*]

ODE I

Strophe 1

CHORUS: The Delphic stone of prophecies
   Remembers ancient regicide
   And a still bloody hand.
   That killer's hour of flight has come.
   He must be stronger than riderless   5
   Coursers of untiring wind,
   For the son of Zeus armed with his father's thunder
   Leaps in lightning after him;
   And the Furies follow him, the sad Furies.

Antistrophe 1

   Holy Parnossos' peak of snow   10
   Flashes and blinds that secret man,
   That all shall hunt him down:
   Though he may roam the forest shade
   Like a bull gone wild from pasture
   To rage through glooms of stone.   15
   Doom comes down on him; flight will not avail him;

For the world's heart calls him desolate,
And the immortal Furies follow, for ever follow.

Strophe 2

But now a wilder thing is heard
From the old man skilled at hearing Fate in the wingbeat of a bird.   20
Bewildered as a blown bird, my soul hovers and cannot find
Foothold in this debate, or any reason or rest of mind.
But no man ever brought—none can bring
Proof of strife between Thebes' royal house,
Labdakos' line, and the son of Polybos;   25
And never until now has any man brought word
Of Laïos' dark death staining Oedipus the King.

Antistrophe 2

Divine Zeus and Apollo hold
Perfect intelligence alone of all tales ever told;
And well though this diviner works, he works in his own night;   30
No man can judge that rough unknown or trust in second sight,
For wisdom changes hands among the wise.
Shall I believe my great lord criminal
At a raging word that a blind old man let fall?
I saw him, when the carrion woman faced him of old,   35
Prove his heroic mind! These evil words are lies.

SCENE II

CREON: Men of Thebes:
　　I am told that heavy accusations
　　Have been brought against me by King Oedipus.
　　I am not the kind of man to bear this tamely.

　　If in these present difficulties   5
　　He holds me accountable for any harm to him
　　Through anything I have said or done—why, then,
　　I do not value life in this dishonor.
　　It is not as though this rumor touched upon
　　Some private indiscretion. The matter is grave.   10
　　The fact is that I am being called disloyal
　　To the State, to my fellow citizens, to my friends.
CHORAGOS: He may have spoken in anger, not from his mind.

CREON: But did you not hear him say I was the one
    Who seduced the old prophet into lying?   15
CHORAGOS: The thing was said; I do not know how seriously.
CREON: But you were watching him! Were his eyes steady?
    Did he look like a man in his right mind?
CHORAGOS: I do not know.
    I cannot judge the behavior of great men.
    But here is the King himself.

    [*Enter* OEDIPUS.]

OEDIPUS: So you dared come back.   20
    Why? How brazen of you to come to my house,
    You murderer!
                 Do you think I do not know
    That you plotted to kill me, plotted to steal my throne?
    Tell me, in God's name: am I coward, a fool,
    That you should dream you could accomplish this?   25
    A fool who could not see your slippery game?
    A coward, not to fight back when I saw it?
    You are the fool, Creon, are you not? hoping
    Without support or friends to get a throne?
    Thrones may be won or bought: you could do neither.   30
CREON: Now listen to me. You have talked; let me talk, too.
    You cannot judge unless you know the facts.
OEDIPUS: You speak well: there is one fact; but I find it hard
    To learn from the deadliest enemy I have.
CREON: That above all I must dispute with you.   35
OEDIPUS: That above all I will not hear you deny.
CREON: If you think there is anything good in being stubborn
    Against all reason, then I say you are wrong.
OEDIPUS: If you think a man can sin against his own kind
    And not be punished for it, I say you are mad.   40
CREON: I agree. But tell me: what have I done to you?
OEDIPUS: You advised me to send for that wizard, did you not?
CREON: I did. I should do it again.
OEDIPUS: Very well. Now tell me:
    How long has it been since Laïos—
CREON: What of Laïos?
OEDIPUS: Since he vanished in that onset by the road?   45
CREON: It was long ago, a long time.
OEDIPUS: And this prophet,
    Was he practicing here then?
CREON: He was; and with honor, as now.
OEDIPUS: Did he speak of me at that time?

CREON: He never did;
   At least, not when I was present.
OEDIPUS: But . . . the enquiry?
   I suppose you held one?
CREON: We did, but we learned nothing.   50
OEDIPUS: Why did the prophet not speak against me then?
CREON: I do not know; and I am the kind of man
   Who holds his tongue when he has no facts to go on.
OEDIPUS: There's one fact that you know, and you could tell it.
CREON: What fact is that? If I know it, you shall have it.   55
OEDIPUS: If he were not involved with you, he could not say
   That it was I who murdered Laïos.
CREON: If he says that, you are the one that knows it!—
   But now it is my turn to question you.
OEDIPUS: Put your questions. I am no murderer.   60
CREON: First, then: You married my sister?
OEDIPUS: I married your sister.
CREON: And you rule the kingdom equally with her?
OEDIPUS: Everything that she wants she has from me.
CREON: And I am the third, equal to both of you?
OEDIPUS: That is why I call you a bad friend.   65
CREON: No. Reason it out, as I have done.
   Think of this first. Would any sane man prefer
   Power, with all a king's anxieties,
   To that same power and the grace of sleep?
   Certainly not I.   70
   I have never longed for the king's power—only his rights.
   Would any wise man differ from me in this?
   As matters stand, I have my way in everything
   With your consent, and no responsibilities.
   If I were king, I should be a slave to policy.   75
   How could I desire a scepter more
   Than what is now mine—untroubled influence?
   No, I have not gone mad; I need no honors,
   Except those with the perquisites I have now.
   I am welcome everywhere; every man salutes me,   80
   And those who want your favor seek my ear,
   Since I know how to manage what they ask.
   Should I exchange this ease for that anxiety?
   Besides, no sober mind is treasonable.
   I hate anarchy   85
   And never would deal with any man who likes it.

   Test what I have said. Go to the priestess
   At Delphi, ask if I quoted her correctly.

And as for this other thing: if I am found
Guilty of treason with Teiresias,   90
Then sentence me to death! You have my word
It is a sentence I should cast my vote for—
But not without evidence!
                              You do wrong
When you take good men for bad, bad men for good.
A true friend thrown aside—why, life itself   95
Is not more precious!
                        In time you will know this well:
For time, and time alone, will show the just man,
Though scoundrels are discovered in a day.
CHORAGOS: This is well said, and a prudent man would ponder it.
    Judgments too quickly formed are dangerous.   100
OEDIPUS: But is he not quick in his duplicity?
    And shall I not be quick to parry him?
    Would you have me stand still, hold my peace, and let
    This man win everything, through my inaction?
CREON: And you want—what is it, then? To banish me?   105
OEDIPUS: No, not exile. It is your death I want,
    So that all the world may see what treason means.
CREON: You will persist, then? You will not believe me?
OEDIPUS: How can I believe you?
CREON: Then you are a fool.
OEDIPUS: To save myself?
CREON: In justice, think of me.   110
OEDIPUS: You are evil incarnate.
CREON: But suppose that you are wrong?
OEDIPUS: Still I must rule.
CREON: But not if you rule badly.
OEDIPUS: O city, city!
CREON: It is my city, too!
CHORAGOS: Now, my lords, be still. I see the Queen,
    Iocastê, coming from her palace chambers;   115
    And it is time she came, for the sake of you both.
    This dreadful quarrel can be resolved through her.

[*Enter* IOCASTÊ.]

IOCASTÊ: Poor foolish men, what wicked din is this?
    With Thebes sick to death, is it not shameful
    That you should rake some private quarrel up?   120
    [*To* OEDIPUS.] Come into the house.
                        —And you, Creon, go now:
    Let us have no more of this tumult over nothing.

CREON: Nothing? No, sister: what your husband plans for me
   Is one of two great evils: exile or death.
OEDIPUS: He is right.
                       Why, woman, I have caught him squarely   125
   Plotting against my life.
CREON: No! Let me die
   Accurst if ever I have wished you harm!
IOCASTÊ: Ah, believe it, Oedipus!
   In the name of the gods, respect this oath of his
   For my sake, for the sake of these people here!   130

Strophe 1

CHORAGOS: Open your mind to her, my lord. Be ruled by her, I beg you!
OEDIPUS: What would you have me do?
CHORAGOS: Respect Creon's word. He has never spoken like a fool,
   And now he has sworn an oath.
OEDIPUS: You know what you ask?
CHORAGOS: I do.
OEDIPUS: Speak on, then.
CHORAGOS: A friend so sworn should not be baited so,   135
   In blind malice, and without final proof.
OEDIPUS: You are aware, I hope, that what you say
   Means death for me, or exile at the least.

Strophe 2

CHORAGOS: No, I swear by Helios, first in Heaven!
   May I die friendless and accurst,   140
   The worst of deaths, if ever I meant that!
      It is the withering fields
          That hurt my sick heart:
      Must we bear all these ills,
                And now your bad blood as well?   145
OEDIPUS: Then let him go. And let me die, if I must,
   Or be driven by him in shame from the land of Thebes.
   It is your unhappiness, and not his talk,
   That touches me.
                 As for him—
   Wherever he is, I will hate him as long as I live.   150
CREON: Ugly in yielding, as you were ugly in rage!
   Natures like yours chiefly torment themselves.
OEDIPUS: Can you not go? Can you not leave me?
CREON: I can.

You do not know me; but the city knows me,
And in its eyes I am just, if not in yours.   [*Exit* CREON.]   155

Antistrophe 1

CHORAGOS: Lady Iocastê, did you not ask the King to go to his chambers?
IOCASTÊ: First tell me what has happened.
CHORAGOS: There was suspicion without evidence; yet it rankled
　　As even false charges will.
IOCASTÊ:　　　　　　　　　On both sides?
CHORAGOS:　　　　　　　　　　　On both.
IOCASTÊ:　　　　　　　　　　　　But what was said?
CHORAGOS: Oh let it rest, let it be done with!   160
　　Have we not suffered enough?
OEDIPUS: You see to what your decency has brought you:
　　You have made difficulties where my heart saw none.

Antistrophe 2

CHORAGOS: Oedipus, it is not once only I have told you—
　　You must know I should count myself unwise   165
　　To the point of madness, should I now forsake you—
　　　　You, under whose hand,
　　　　　　In the storm of another time,
　　　　Our dear land sailed out free.
　　　　　　But now stand fast at the helm!   170
IOCASTÊ: In God's name, Oedipus, inform your wife as well:
　　Why are you so set in this hard anger?
OEDIPUS: I will tell you, for none of these men deserves
　　My confidence as you do. It is Creon's work,
　　His treachery, his plotting against me.   175
IOCASTÊ: Go on, if you can make this clear to me.
OEDIPUS: He charges me with the murder of Laïos.
IOCASTÊ: Has he some knowledge? Or does he speak from hearsay?
OEDIPUS: He would not commit himself to such a charge,
　　But he has brought in that damnable soothsayer   180
　　To tell his story.
IOCASTÊ:　　　　Set your mind at rest.
　　If it is a question of soothsayers, I tell you
　　That you will find no man whose craft gives knowledge
　　Of the unknowable.
　　　　　　　　Here is my proof:

An oracle was reported to Laïos once   185
(I will not say from Phoibos himself, but from

His appointed ministers, at any rate)
That his doom would be death at the hands of his own son—
His son, born of his flesh and of mine!

Now, you remember the story: Laïos was killed   190
By marauding strangers where three highways meet;
But his child had not been three days in this world
Before the King had pierced the baby's ankles
And left him to die on a lonely mountainside.

Thus, Apollo never caused that child   195
To kill his father, and it was not Laïos' fate
To die at the hands of his son, as he had feared.
This is what prophets and prophecies are worth!
Have no dread of them.
      It is God himself
Who can show us what he wills, in his own way.   200
OEDIPUS: How strange a shadowy memory crossed my mind,
  Just now while you were speaking; it chilled my heart.
IOCASTÊ: What do you mean? What memory do you speak of?
OEDIPUS: If I understand you, Laïos was killed
  At a place where three roads meet.
IOCASTÊ: So it was said;   205
  We have no later story.
OEDIPUS: Where did it happen?
IOCASTÊ: Phokis, it is called: at a place where the Theban Way
  Divides into the roads towards Delphi and Daulia.
OEDIPUS: When?
IOCASTÊ: We had the news not long before you came
  And proved the right to your succession here.   210
OEDIPUS: Ah, what net has God been weaving for me?
IOCASTÊ: Oedipus! Why does this trouble you?
OEDIPUS: Do not ask me yet.
  First, tell me how Laïos looked, and tell me
  How old he was.
IOCASTÊ: He was tall, his hair just touched
  With white; his form was not unlike your own.   215
OEDIPUS: I think that I myself may be accurst
  By my own ignorant edict.
IOCASTÊ: You speak strangely.
  It makes me tremble to look at you, my King.
OEDIPUS: I am not sure that the blind man cannot see.
  But I should know better if you were to tell me—   220
IOCASTÊ: Anything—though I dread to hear you ask it.
OEDIPUS: Was the King lightly escorted, or did he ride
  With a large company, as a ruler should?

IOCASTÊ: There were five men with him in all: one was a herald;
  And a single chariot, which he was driving.   225
OEDIPUS: Alas, that makes it plain enough!
                                        But who—
  Who told you how it happened?
IOCASTÊ: A household servant,
  The only one to escape.
OEDIPUS: And is he still
  A servant of ours?
IOCASTÊ: No; for when he came back at last
  And found you enthroned in the place of the dead king,   230
  He came to me, touched my hand with his, and begged
  That I would send him away to the frontier district
  Where only the shepherds go—
  As far away from the city as I could send him.
  I granted his prayer; for although the man was a slave,   235
  He had earned more than this favor at my hands.
OEDIPUS: Can he be called back quickly?
IOCASTÊ: Easily.
  But why?
OEDIPUS: I have taken too much upon myself
  Without enquiry; therefore I wish to consult him.
IOCASTÊ: Then he shall come.
                            But am I not one also   240
  To whom you might confide these fears of yours!
OEDIPUS: That is your right; it will not be denied you,
  Now least of all; for I have reached a pitch
  Of wild foreboding. Is there anyone
  To whom I should sooner speak?   245
  Polybos of Corinth is my father.
  My mother is a Dorian: Meropê.
  I grew up chief among the men of Corinth
  Until a strange thing happened—
  Not worth my passion, it may be, but strange.   250

  At a feast, a drunken man maundering in his cups
  Cries out that I am not my father's son!

  I contained myself that night, though I felt anger
  And a sinking heart. The next day I visited
  My father and mother, and questioned them. They stormed,   255
  Calling it all the slanderous rant of a fool;
  And this relieved me. Yet the suspicion
  Remained always aching in my mind;
  I knew there was talk; I could not rest;

And finally, saying nothing to my parents,   260
I went to the shrine at Delphi.
The god dismissed my question without reply;
He spoke of other things.
                    Some were clear,
Full of wretchedness, dreadful, unbearable:
As, that I should lie with my own mother, breed   265
Children from whom all men would turn their eyes;
And that I should be my father's murderer.

I heard all this, and fled. And from that day
Corinth to me was only in the stars
Descending in that quarter of the sky,   270
As I wandered farther and farther on my way
To a land where I should never see the evil
Sung by the oracle. And I came to this country
Where, so you say, King Laïos was killed.
I will tell you all that happened there, my lady.   275

There were three highways
Coming together at a place I passed;
And there a herald came towards me, and a chariot
Drawn by horses, with a man such as you describe
Seated in it. The groom leading the horses   280
Forced me off the road at his lord's command;
But as this charioteer lurched over towards me
I struck him in my rage. The old man saw me
And brought his double goad down upon my head
As I came abreast.
                  He was paid back, and more!   285
Swinging my club in this right hand I knocked him
Out of his car, and he rolled on the ground.
                         I killed him.

I killed them all.
Now if that stranger and Laïos were—kin,
Where is a man more miserable than I?   290
More hated by the gods? Citizen and alien alike
Must never shelter me or speak to me—
I must be shunned by all.
                  And I myself
Pronounced this malediction upon myself!

Think of it: I have touched you with these hands,   295
These hands that killed your husband. What defilement!

Am I all evil, then? It must be so,
Since I must flee from Thebes, yet never again
See my own countrymen, my own country,
For fear of joining my mother in marriage   300
And killing Polybos, my father.
                              Ah,
If I was created so, born to this fate,
Who could deny the savagery of God?

O holy majesty of heavenly powers!
May I never see that day! Never!   305
Rather let me vanish from the race of men
Than know the abomination destined me!
CHORAGOS: We too, my lord, have felt dismay at this.
    But there is hope: you have yet to hear the shepherd.
OEDIPUS: Indeed, I fear no other hope is left me.   310
IOCASTÊ: What do you hope from him when he comes?
OEDIPUS: This much:
    If his account of the murder tallies with yours,
    Then I am cleared.
IOCASTÊ: —What was it that I said
    Of such importance?
OEDIPUS: Why, "marauders," you said,
    Killed the King, according to this man's story.   315
    If he maintains that still, if there were several,
    Clearly the guilt is not mine: I was alone.
    But if he says one man, singlehanded, did it,
    Then the evidence all points to me.
IOCASTÊ: You may be sure that he said there were several;   320
    And can he call back that story now? He cannot.
    The whole city heard it as plainly as I.
    But suppose he alters some detail of it:
    He cannot ever show that Laïos' death
    Fulfilled the oracle: for Apollo said   325
    My child was doomed to kill him; and my child—
    Poor baby!—it was my child that died first.

    No. From now on, where oracles are concerned,
    I would not waste a second thought on any.
OEDIPUS: You may be right.
                         But come: let someone go   330
    For the shepherd at once. This matter must be settled.
IOCASTÊ: I will send for him.
    I would not wish to cross you in anything,
    And surely not in this.—Let us go in.

                              [*Exeunt into the palace.*]

ODE II

Strophe 1

CHORUS: Let me be reverent in the ways of right,
　　Lowly the paths I journey on;
　　Let all my words and actions keep
　　The laws of the pure universe
　　From highest Heaven handed down.　　　　　　　5
　　For Heaven is their bright nurse,
　　Those generations of the realms of light;
　　Ah, never of mortal kind were they begot,
　　Nor are they slaves of memory, lost in sleep:
　　Their Father is greater than Time, and ages not.　　10

Antistrophe 1

　　The tyrant is a child of Pride
　　Who drinks from his great sickening cup
　　Recklessness and vanity,
　　Until from his high crest headlong
　　He plummets to the dust of hope.　　　　　　　15
　　That strong man is not strong.
　　But let no fair ambition be denied;
　　May God protect the wrestler for the State
　　In government, in comely policy,
　　Who will fear God, and on His ordinance wait.　　20

Strophe 2

　　Haughtiness and the high hand of disdain
　　Tempt and outrage God's holy law;
　　And any mortal who dares hold
　　No immortal Power in awe
　　Will be caught up in a net of pain:　　　　　　25
　　The price for which his levity is sold.
　　Let each man take due earnings, then,
　　And keep his hands from holy things,
　　And from blasphemy stand apart—
　　Else the crackling blast of heaven　　　　　　　30
　　Blows on his head, and on his desperate heart;
　　Though fools will honor impious men,
　　In their cities no tragic poet sings.

Antistrophe 2

Shall we lose faith in Delphi's obscurities,
We who have heard the world's core   35
Discredited, and the sacred wood
Of Zeus at Elis praised no more?
The deeds and the strange prophecies
Must make a pattern yet to be understood.
Zeus, if indeed you are lord of all,   40
Throned in light over night and day,
Mirror this in your endless mind:
Our masters call the oracle
Words on the wind, and the Delphic vision blind!
Their hearts no longer know Apollo,   45
And reverence for the gods has died away.

SCENE III

[*Enter* IOCASTÊ.]

IOCASTÊ: Princes of Thebes, it has occurred to me
    To visit the altars of the gods, bearing
    These branches as a suppliant, and this incense.
    Our King is not himself: his noble soul
    Is overwrought with fantasies of dread,   5
    Else he would consider
    The new prophecies in the light of the old.
    He will listen to any voice that speaks disaster,
    And my advice goes for nothing.

[*She approaches the altar, right.*]

                            To you, then, Apollo,
    Lycean lord, since you are nearest, I turn in prayer.   10
    Receive these offerings, and grant us deliverance
    From defilement. Our hearts are heavy with fear
    When we see our leader distracted, as helpless sailors
    Are terrified by the confusion of their helmsman.

[*Enter* MESSENGER.]

MESSENGER: Friends, no doubt you can direct me: 15
    Where shall I find the house of Oedipus,
    Or, better still, where is the King himself?

CHORAGOS: It is this very place, stranger; he is inside.
    This is his wife and mother of his children.
MESSENGER: I wish her happiness in a happy house,   20
    Blest in all the fulfillment of her marriage.
IOCASTÊ: I wish as much for you: your courtesy
    Deserves a like good fortune. But now, tell me:
    Why have you come? What have you to say to us?
MESSENGER: Good news, my lady, for your house and your husband.   25
IOCASTÊ: What news? Who sent you here?
MESSENGER: I am from Corinth.
    The news I bring ought to mean joy for you,
    Though it may be you will find some grief in it.
IOCASTÊ: What is it? How can it touch us in both ways?
MESSENGER: The people of Corinth, they say,   30
    Intend to call Oedipus to be their king.
IOCASTÊ: But old Polybos—is he not reigning still?
MESSENGER: No. Death holds him in his sepulchre.
IOCASTÊ: What are you saying? Polybos is dead?
MESSENGER: If I am not telling the truth, may I die myself.   35
IOCASTÊ [to a maidservant]: Go in, go quickly; tell this to your master.

    O riddlers of God's will, where are you now!
    This was the man whom Oedipus, long ago,
    Feared so, fled so, in dread of destroying him—
    But it was another fate by which he died.   40

[Enter OEDIPUS, center.]

OEDIPUS: Dearest Iocastê, why have you sent for me?
IOCASTÊ: Listen to what this man says, and then tell me
    What has become of the solemn prophecies.
OEDIPUS: Who is this man? What is his news for me?
IOCASTÊ: He has come from Corinth to announce your father's death!   45
OEDIPUS: Is it true, stranger? Tell me in your own words.
MESSENGER: I cannot say it more clearly: the King is dead.
OEDIPUS: Was it by treason? Or by an attack of illness?
MESSENGER: A little thing brings old men to their rest.
OEDIPUS: It was sickness, then?
MESSENGER: Yes, and his many years.   50
OEDIPUS: Ah!
    Why should a man respect the Pythian hearth, or
    Give heed to the birds that jangle above his head?
    They prophesied that I should kill Polybos,
    Kill my own father; but he is dead and buried,   55
    And I am here—I never touched him, never,

Unless he died in grief for my departure,
And thus, in a sense, through me. No. Polybos
Has packed the oracles off with him underground.
They are empty words.
IOCASTÊ: Had I not told you so?   60
OEDIPUS: You had; it was my faint heart that betrayed me.
IOCASTÊ: From now on never think of those things again.
OEDIPUS: And yet—must I not fear my mother's bed?
IOCASTÊ: Why should anyone in this world be afraid,
Since Fate rules us and nothing can be foreseen?   65
A man should live only for the present day.
Have no more fear of sleeping with your mother:
How many men, in dreams, have lain with their mothers!
No reasonable man is troubled by such things.
OEDIPUS: That is true; only—   70
If only my mother were not still alive!
But she is alive. I cannot help my dread.
IOCASTÊ: Yet this news of your father's death is wonderful.
OEDIPUS: Wonderful. But I fear the living woman.
MESSENGER: Tell me, who is this woman that you fear?   75
OEDIPUS: It is Meropê, man; the wife of King Polybos.
MESSENGER: Meropê? Why should you be afraid of her?
OEDIPUS: An oracle of the gods, a dreadful saying.
MESSENGER: Can you tell me about it or are you sworn to silence?
OEDIPUS: I can tell you, and I will.   80
Apollo said through his prophet that I was the man
Who should marry his own mother, shed his father's blood
With his own hands. And so, for all these years
I have kept clear of Corinth, and no harm has come—
Though it would have been sweet to see my parents again.   85
MESSENGER: And is this the fear that drove you out of Corinth?
OEDIPUS: Would you have me kill my father?
MESSENGER: As for that
You must be reassured by the news I gave you.
OEDIPUS: If you could reassure me, I would reward you.
MESSENGER: I had that in mind, I will confess: I thought   90
I could count on you when you returned to Corinth.
OEDIPUS: No: I will never go near my parents again.
MESSENGER: Ah, son, you still do not know what you are doing—
OEDIPUS: What do you mean? In the name of God tell me!
MESSENGER: —If these are your reasons for not going home.   95
OEDIPUS: I tell you, I fear the oracle may come true.
MESSENGER: And guilt may come upon you through your parents?
OEDIPUS: That is the dread that is always in my heart.
MESSENGER: Can you not see that all your fears are groundless?
OEDIPUS: How can you say that? They are my parents, surely?   100

MESSENGER: Polybos was not your father.

OEDIPUS: Not my father?

MESSENGER: No more your father than the man speaking to you.

OEDIPUS: But you are nothing to me!

MESSENGER: Neither was he.

OEDIPUS: Then why did he call me son?

MESSENGER: I will tell you:

   Long ago he had you from my hands, as a gift.   105

OEDIPUS: Then how could he love me so, if I was not his?

MESSENGER: He had no children, and his heart turned to you.

OEDIPUS: What of you? Did you buy me? Did you find me by chance?

MESSENGER: I came upon you in the crooked pass of Kithairon.

OEDIPUS: And what were you doing there?

MESSENGER: Tending my flocks.   110

OEDIPUS: A wandering shepherd?

MESSENGER: But your savior, son, that day.

OEDIPUS: From what did you save me?

MESSENGER: Your ankles should tell you that.

OEDIPUS: Ah, stranger, why do you speak of that childhood pain?

MESSENGER: I cut the bonds that tied your ankles together.

OEDIPUS: I have had the mark as long as I can remember.   115

MESSENGER: That was why you were given the name you bear.

OEDIPUS: God! Was it my father or my mother who did it?

   Tell me!

MESSENGER: I do not know. The man who gave you to me

   Can tell you better than I.   120

OEDIPUS: It was not you that found me, but another?

MESSENGER: It was another shepherd gave you to me.

OEDIPUS: Who was he? Can you tell me who he was?

MESSENGER: I think he was said to be one of Laïos' people.

OEDIPUS: You mean the Laïos who was king here years ago?   125

MESSENGER: Yes; King Laïos; and the man was one of his herdsmen.

OEDIPUS: Is he still alive? Can I see him?

MESSENGER: These men here

   Know best about such things.

OEDIPUS: Does anyone here

   Know this shepherd that he is talking about?

   Have you seen him in the fields, or in the town?   130

   If you have, tell me. It is time things were made plain.

CHORAGOS: I think the man he means is that same shepherd

   You have already asked to see. Iocastê perhaps

   Could tell you something.

OEDIPUS: Do you know anything

   About him, Lady? Is he the man we have summoned?   135

   Is that the man this shepherd means?

IOCASTÊ: Why think of him?

Forget this herdsman. Forget it all.
This talk is a waste of time.

OEDIPUS: How can you say that,
When the clues to my true birth are in my hands?

IOCASTÊ: For God's love, let us have no more questioning!   140
Is your life nothing to you?
My own is pain enough for me to bear.

OEDIPUS: You need not worry. Suppose my mother a slave,
And born of slaves: no baseness can touch you.

IOCASTÊ: Listen to me, I beg you: do not do this thing!   145

OEDIPUS: I will not listen; the truth must be made known.

IOCASTÊ: Everything that I say is for your own good!

OEDIPUS: My own good
Snaps my patience, then: I want none of it.

IOCASTÊ: You are fatally wrong! May you never learn who you are!

OEDIPUS: Go, one of you, and bring the shepherd here.   150
Let us leave this woman to brag of her royal name.

IOCASTÊ: Ah, miserable!
That is the only word I have for you now.
That is the only word I can ever have.

                                   [*Exit into the palace.*]

CHORAGOS: Why has she left us, Oedipus? Why has she gone   155
In such a passion of sorrow? I fear this silence:
Something dreadful may come of it.

OEDIPUS: Let it come!
However base my birth, I must know about it.
The Queen, like a woman, is perhaps ashamed
To think of my low origin. But I   160
Am a child of luck; I cannot be dishonored.
Luck is my mother; the passing months, my brothers,
Have seen me rich and poor.
                   If this is so,
How could I wish that I were someone else?
How could I not be glad to know my birth?   165

ODE III

Strophe

CHORUS: If ever the coming time were known
     To my heart's pondering,
     Kithairon, now by Heaven I see the torches
     At the festival of the next full moon,

And see the dance, and hear the choir sing   5
A grace to your gentle shade:
Mountain where Oedipus was found,
O mountain guard of a noble race!
May the god who heals us lend his aid,
And let that glory come to pass   10
For our king's cradling-ground.

Antistrophe

Of the nymphs that flower beyond the years,
Who bore you, royal child,
To Pan of the hills or the timberline Apollo,
Cold in delight where the upland clears,   15
Or Hermês for whom Kyllenê's heights are piled?
Or flushed as evening cloud,
Great Dionysos, roamer of mountains,
He—was it he who found you there,
And caught you up in his own proud   20
Arms from the sweet god-ravisher
Who laughed by the Muses' fountains?

SCENE IV

OEDIPUS: Sirs: though I do not know the man,
   I think I see him coming, this shepherd we want:
   He is old, like our friend here, and the men
   Bringing him seem to be servants of my house.
   But you can tell, if you have ever seen him.   5

[*Enter shepherd escorted by servants.*]

CHORAGOS: I know him, he was Laïos' man. You can trust him.
OEDIPUS: Tell me first, you from Corinth: is this the shepherd
   We were discussing?
MESSENGER: This is the very man.
OEDIPUS [*to shepherd*]: Come here. No, look at me. You must answer
   Everything I ask.—You belonged to Laïos?   10
SHEPHERD: Yes: born his slave, brought up in his house.
OEDIPUS: Tell me: what kind of work did you do for him?
SHEPHERD: I was a shepherd of his, most of my life.
OEDIPUS: Where mainly did you go for pasturage?
SHEPHERD: Sometimes Kithairon, sometimes the hills near-by.   15
OEDIPUS: Do you remember ever seeing this man out there?

SHEPHERD: What would he be doing there? This man?
OEDIPUS: This man standing here. Have you ever seen him before?
SHEPHERD: No. At least, not to my recollection.
MESSENGER: And that is not strange, my lord, But I'll refresh   20
  His memory: he must remember when we two
  Spent three whole seasons together, March to September,
  On Kithairon or thereabouts. He had two flocks;
  I had one. Each autumn I'd drive mine home
  And he would go back with his to Laïos' sheepfold.—   25
  Is this not true, just as I have described it?
SHEPHERD: True, yes; but it was all so long ago.
MESSENGER: Well, then: so you remember, back in those days
  That you gave me a baby boy to bring up as my own?
SHEPHERD: What if I did? What are you trying to say?   30
MESSENGER: King Oedipus was once that little child.
SHEPHERD: Damn you, hold your tongue!
OEDIPUS: No more of that!
  It is your tongue needs watching, not this man's.
SHEPHERD: My King, my Master, what is it I have done wrong?
OEDIPUS: You have not answered his question about the boy.   35
SHEPHERD: He does not know . . . He is only making trouble . . .
OEDIPUS: Come, speak plainly, or it will go hard with you.
SHEPHERD: In God's name, do not torture an old man!
OEDIPUS: Come here, one of you; bind his arms behind him.
SHEPHERD: Unhappy king! What more do you wish to learn?   40
OEDIPUS: Did you give this man the child he speaks of?
SHEPHERD: I did.
  And I would to God I had died that very day.
OEDIPUS: You will die now unless you speak the truth.
SHEPHERD: Yet if I speak the truth, I am worse than dead.
OEDIPUS: Very well; since you insist upon delaying—   45
SHEPHERD: No! I have told you already that I gave him the boy.
OEDIPUS: Where did you get him? From your house?
  From somewhere else?
SHEPHERD: Not from mine, no. A man gave him to me.
OEDIPUS: Is that man here? Do you know whose slave he was?
SHEPHERD: For God's love, my King, do not ask me
  any more!   50
OEDIPUS: You are a dead man if I have to ask you again.
SHEPHERD: Then . . . Then the child was from the palace of Laïos.
OEDIPUS: A slave child? or a child of his own line?
SHEPHERD: Ah, I am on the brink of dreadful speech!
OEDIPUS: And I of dreadful hearing. Yet I must hear.   55
SHEPHERD: If you must be told, then . . .
                      They said it was Laïos' child,
  But it is your wife who can tell you about that.

OEDIPUS: My wife!—Did she give it to you?
SHEPHERD: My lord, she did.
OEDIPUS: Do you know why?
SHEPHERD: I was told to get rid of it.
OEDIPUS: An unspeakable mother!
SHEPHERD: There had been prophecies . . .   60
OEDIPUS: Tell me.
SHEPHERD: It was said that the boy would kill his own father.
OEDIPUS: Then why did you give him over to this old man?
SHEPHERD: I pitied the baby, my King,
    And I thought that this man would take him far away
    To his own country.
                              He saved him—but for what a fate!   65
    For if you are what this man says you are,
    No man living is more wretched than Oedipus.
OEDIPUS: Ah God!
    It was true!
              All the prophecies!
                         —Now,
    O Light, may I look on you for the last time!   70
    I, Oedipus,
    Oedipus, damned in his birth, in his marriage damned,
    Damned in the blood he shed with his own hand!

[*He rushes into the palace.*]

ODE IV

Strophe 1

CHORUS: Alas for the seed of men.
    What measure shall I give these generations
    That breathe on the void and are void
    And exist and do not exist?

    Who bears more weight of joy   5
    Than mass of sunlight shifting in images,
    Or who shall make his thought stay on
    That down time drifts away?

    Your splendor is all fallen.

    O naked brow of wrath and tears,   10
    O change of Oedipus!

I who saw your days call no man blest—
Your great days like ghosts gone.

Antistrophe 1

That mind was a strong bow.
Deep, how deep you drew it then, hard archer,   15
At a dim fearful range,
And brought dear glory down!

You overcame the stranger—
The virgin with her hooking lion claws—
And though death sang, stood like a tower   20
To make pale Thebes take heart.

Fortress against our sorrow!

Divine king, giver of laws,
Majestic Oedipus!
No prince in Thebes had ever such renown,   25
No prince won such grace of power.

Strophe 2

And now of all men ever known
Most pitiful is this man's story:
His fortunes are most changed, his state
Fallen to a low slave's   30
Ground under bitter fate.

O Oedipus, most royal one!
The great door that expelled you to the light
Gave at night—ah, gave night to your glory:
As to the father, to the fathering son.   35

All understood too late,

How could that queen whom Laïos won,
The garden that he harrowed at his height,
Be silent when that act was done?

Antistrophe 2

But all eyes fail before time's eye,   40
All actions come to justice there.

Though never willed, though far down the deep past,
Your bed, your dread sirings,
Are brought to book at last.
Child by Laïos doomed to die,   45
Then doomed to lose that fortunate little death,
Would God you never took breath in this air
That with my wailing lips I take to cry:

For I weep the world's outcast.

I was blind, and now I can tell why: 50
Asleep, for you had given ease of breath
To Thebes, while the false years went by.

EXODOS

[*Enter, from the palace, second messenger.*]

SECOND MESSENGER: Elders of Thebes, most honored in this land,
    What horrors are yours to see and hear, what weight
    Of sorrow to be endured, if, true to your birth,
    You venerate the line of Labdakos!
    I think neither Istros nor Phasis, those great rivers,   5
    Could purify this place of the corruption
    It shelters now, or soon must bring to light—
    Evil not done unconsciously, but willed.

    The greatest griefs are those we cause ourselves.
CHORAGOS: Surely, friend, we have grief enough already;   10
    What new sorrow do you mean?
SECOND MESSENGER: The Queen is dead.
CHORAGOS: Iocastê? Dead? But at whose hand?
SECOND MESSENGER: Her own.
    The full horror of what happened you cannot know,
    For you did not see it; but I, who did, will tell you
    As clearly as I can how she met her death.   15

    When she had left us,
    In passionate silence, passing through the court,
    She ran to her apartment in the house,
    Her hair clutched by the fingers of both hands.
    She closed the doors behind her; then, by that bed   20
    Where long ago the fatal son was conceived—
    That son who should bring about his father's death—

We heard her call upon Laïos, dead so many years,
And heard her wail for the double fruit of her marriage,
A husband by her husband, children by her child.   25

Exactly how she died I do not know:
For Oedipus burst in moaning and would not let us
Keep vigil to the end: it was by him
As he stormed about the room that our eyes were caught.
From one to another of us he went, begging a sword,   30
Cursing the wife who was not his wife, the mother
Whose womb had carried his own children and himself.
I do not know: it was none of us aided him,
But surely one of the gods was in control!
For with a dreadful cry   35
He hurled his weight, as though wrenched out of himself,
At the twin doors: the bolts gave, and he rushed in.
And there we saw her hanging, her body swaying
From the cruel cord she had noosed about her neck.
A great sob broke from him heartbreaking to hear,   40
As he loosed the rope and lowered her to the ground.
I would blot out from my mind what happened next!
For the King ripped from her gown the golden brooches
That were her ornament, and raised them, and plunged them down
Straight into his own eyeballs, crying, "No more,   45
No more shall you look on the misery about me,
The horrors of my own doing! Too long you have known
The faces of those whom I should never have seen,
Too long been blind to those for whom I was searching!
From this hour, go in darkness!" And as he spoke,   50
He struck at his eyes—not once, but many times;
And the blood spattered his beard,
Bursting from his ruined sockets like red hail.

So from the unhappiness of two this evil has sprung,
A curse on the man and woman alike. The old   55
Happiness of the house of Labdakos
Was happiness enough: where is it today?
It is all wailing and ruin, disgrace, death—all
The misery of mankind that has a name—
And it is wholly and for ever theirs.   60
CHORAGOS: Is he in agony still? Is there no rest for him?
SECOND MESSENGER: He is calling for someone to lead him to the gates
     So that all the children of Kadmos may look upon
     His father's murderer, his mother's—no,

I cannot say it!
     And then he will leave Thebes,   65
Self-exiled, in order that the curse
Which he himself pronounced may depart from the house.
He is weak, and there is none to lead him,
So terrible is his suffering.
      But you will see:
Look, the doors are opening; in a moment   70
You will see a thing that would crush a heart of stone.

[*The central door is opened;* OEDIPUS, *blinded, is led in.*]

CHORAGOS: Dreadful indeed for men to see,
 Never have my own eyes
 Looked on a sight so full of fear.

 Oedipus!   75
 What madness came upon you, what daemon
 Leaped on your life with heavier
 Punishment than a mortal man can bear?
 No: I cannot even
 Look at you, poor ruined one.   80
 And I would speak, question, ponder,
 If I were able. No.
 You make me shudder.
OEDIPUS: God. God.
 Is there a sorrow greater?   85
 Where shall I find harbor in this world?
 My voice is hurled far on a dark wind.
 What has God done to me?
CHORAGOS: Too terrible to think of, or to see.

Strophe 1

OEDIPUS: O cloud of night,   90
 Never to be turned away: night coming on,
 I cannot tell how: night like a shroud!
 My fair winds brought me here.
      Oh God. Again
 The pain of the spikes where I had sight,
 The flooding pain   95
 Of memory, never to be gouged out.
CHORAGOS: This is not strange.
 You suffer it all twice over, remorse in pain,
 Pain in remorse.

Antistrophe 1

OEDIPUS: Ah dear friend   100
   Are you faithful even yet, you alone?
   Are you still standing near me, will you stay here,
   Patient, to care for the blind?
                        The blind man!
   Yet even blind I know who it is attends me,
   By the voice's tone—   105
   Though my new darkness hide the comforter.
CHORAGOS: O fearful act!
   What god was it drove you to rake black
   Night across your eyes?
OEDIPUS: Apollo. Apollo. Dear   110
   Children, the god was Apollo.
   He brought my sick, sick fate upon me.
   But the blinding hand was my own!
   How could I bear to see
   When all my sight was horror everywhere?   115
CHORAGOS: Everywhere; that is true.
OEDIPUS: And now what is left?
   Images? Love? A greeting even,
   Sweet to the senses? Is there anything?
   Ah, no, friends: lead me away.   120
   Lead me away from Thebes.
                    Lead the great wreck
   And hell of Oedipus, whom the gods hate.
CHORAGOS: Your fate is clear, you are not blind to that.
   Would God you had never found it out!

Antistrophe 2

OEDIPUS: Death take the man who unbound   125
   My feet on that hillside
   And delivered me from death to life! What life?
   If only I had died,
   This weight of monstrous doom
   Could not have dragged me and my darlings down.   130
CHORAGOS: I would have wished the same.
OEDIPUS: Oh never to have come here
   With my father's blood upon me! Never
   To have been the man they call his mother's husband!
   Oh accurst! Oh child of evil,   135
   To have entered that wretched bed—
                    the selfsame one!
   More primal than sin itself, this fell to me.

CHORAGOS: I do not know how I can answer you.
    You were better dead than alive and blind.
OEDIPUS: Do not counsel me any more. This punishment   140
    That I have laid upon myself is just.
    If I had eyes,
    I do not know how I could bear the sight
    Of my father, when I came to the house of Death,
    Or my mother: for I have sinned against them both   145
    So vilely that I could not make my peace
    By strangling my own life.
                    Or do you think my children,
    Born as they were born, would be sweet to my eyes?
    Ah never, never! Nor this town with its high walls,
    Nor the holy images of the gods.
                    For I,   150
    Thrice miserable—Oedipus, noblest of all the line
    Of Kadmos, have condemned myself to enjoy
    These things no more, by my own malediction
    Expelling that man whom the gods declared
    To be a defilement in the house of Laïos.   155
    After exposing the rankness of my own guilt,
    How could I look men frankly in the eyes?
    No, I swear it,
    If I could have stifled my hearing at its source,
    I would have done it and made all this body   160
    A tight cell of misery, blank to light and sound:
    So I should have been safe in a dark agony
    Beyond all recollection.
                Ah Kithairon!
    Why did you shelter me? When I was cast upon you,
    Why did I not die? Then I should never   165
    Have shown the world my execrable birth.
    Ah Polybos! Corinth, city that I believed
    The ancient seat of my ancestors: how fair
    I seemed, your child! And all the while this evil
    Was cancerous within me!
                For I am sick   170
    In my daily life, sick in my origin.

    O three roads, dark ravine, woodland and way
    Where three roads met: you, drinking my father's blood,
    My own blood, spilled by my own hand: can you remember
    The unspeakable things I did there, and the things   175
    I went on from there to do?
                O marriage, marriage!
    The act that engendered me, and again the act

Performed by the son in the same bed—

     —Ah, the net
Of incest, mingling fathers, brothers, sons,
With brides, wives, mothers: the last evil   180
That can be known by men: no tongue can say
How evil!
    No. For the love of God, conceal me
Somewhere far from Thebes; or kill me; or hurl me
Into the sea, away from men's eyes for ever.
Come, lead me. You need not fear to touch me.   185
Of all men, I alone can bear this guilt.

[*Enter* CREON.]

CHORAGOS: We are not the ones to decide; but Creon here
 May fitly judge of what you ask. He only
 Is left to protect the city in your place.
OEDIPUS: Alas, how can I speak to him? What right have I   190
 To beg his courtesy whom I have deeply wronged?
CREON: I have not come to mock you, Oedipus,
 Or to reproach you, either.
 [*To attendants.*]   —You, standing there:
 If you have lost all respect for man's dignity,
 At least respect the flame of Lord Helios: 195
 Do not allow this pollution to show itself
 Openly here, an affront to the earth
 And Heaven's rain and the light of day. No, take him
 Into the house as quickly as you can.
 For it is proper   200
 That only the close kindred see his grief.
OEDIPUS: I pray you in God's name, since your courtesy
 Ignores my dark expectation, visiting
 With mercy this man of all men most execrable:
 Give me what I ask—for your good, not for mine.   205
CREON: And what is it that you would have me do?
OEDIPUS: Drive me out of this country as quickly as may be
 To a place where no human voice can ever greet me.
CREON: I should have done that before now—only,
 God's will had not been wholly revealed to me.   210
OEDIPUS: But his command is plain: the parricide
 Must be destroyed. I am that evil man.
CREON: That is the sense of it, yes; but as things are,
 We had best discover clearly what is to be done.
OEDIPUS: You would learn more about a man like me?   215
CREON: You are ready now to listen to the god.

OEDIPUS: I will listen. But it is to you
    That I must turn for help. I beg you, hear me.

    The woman in there—
    Give her whatever funeral you think proper: 220
    She is your sister.
                —But let me go, Creon!
    Let me purge my father's Thebes of the pollution
    Of my living here, and go out to the wild hills,
    To Kithairon, that has won such fame with me,
    The tomb my mother and father appointed for me,   225
    And let me die there, as they willed I should.
    And yet I know
    Death will not ever come to me through sickness
    Or in any natural way: I have been preserved
    For some unthinkable fate. But let that be.   230
    As for my sons, you need not care for them.
    They are men, they will find some way to live.
    But my poor daughters, who have shared my table,
    Who never before have been parted from their father—
    Take care of them, Creon; do this for me.   235
    And will you let me touch them with my hands
    A last time, and let us weep together?
    Be kind, my lord,
    Great prince, be kind!
                  Could I but touch them,
    They would be mine again, as when I had my eyes.   240

    [*Enter* ANTIGONÊ *and* ISMENÊ, *attended.*]

    Ah, God!
    Is it my dearest children I hear weeping?
    Has Creon pitied me and sent my daughters?
CREON: Yes, Oedipus: I knew that they were dear to you
    In the old days, and know you must love them still.   245
OEDIPUS: May God bless you for this—and be a friendlier
    Guardian to you than he has been to me!

    Children, where are you?
    Come quickly to my hands: they are your brother's—
    Hands that have brought your father's once clear eyes   250
    To this way of seeing—
                Ah dearest ones,
    I had neither sight nor knowledge then, your father
    By the woman who was the source of his own life!

And I weep for you—having no strength to see you—,
I weep for you when I think of the bitterness   255
That men will visit upon you all your lives.
What homes, what festivals can you attend
Without being forced to depart again in tears?
And when you come to marriageable age,
Where is the man, my daughters, who would dare   260
Risk the bane that lies on all my children?
Is there any evil wanting? Your father killed
His father; sowed the womb of her who bore him;
Engendered you at the fount of his own existence!
That is what they will say of you.

                                      Then, whom   265
Can you ever marry? There are no bridegrooms for you,
And your lives must wither away in sterile dreaming.
O Creon, son of Menoikeus!
You are the only father my daughters have,
Since we, their parents, are both of us gone for ever.   270
They are your own blood: you will not let them
Fall into beggary and loneliness;
You will keep them from the miseries that are mine!
Take pity on them; see, they are only children,
Friendless except for you. Promise me this,   275
Great Prince, and give me your hand in token of it.

[CREON *clasps his right hand.*]

Children:
I could say much, if you could understand me,
But as it is, I have only this prayer for you:
Live where you can, be as happy as you can—   280
Happier, please God, than God has made your father!
CREON: Enough. You have wept enough. Now go within.
OEDIPUS: I must; but it is hard.
CREON: Time eases all things.
OEDIPUS: But you must promise—
CREON: Say what you desire.
OEDIPUS: Send me from Thebes!
CREON: God grant that I may!   285
OEDIPUS: But since God hates me . . .
CREON: No, he will grant your wish.
OEDIPUS: You promise?
CREON: I cannot speak beyond my knowledge.
OEDIPUS: Then lead me in.
CREON: Come now, and leave your children.

OEDIPUS: No! Do not take them from me!

CREON: Think no longer

That you are in command here, but rather think   290
How, when you were, you served your own destruction.

[*Exeunt into the house all but the* CHORUS; *the* CHORAGOS *chants directly to the audience.*]

CHORAGOS: Men of Thebes: look upon Oedipus.
This is the king who solved the famous riddle
And towered up, most powerful of men.
No mortal eyes but looked on him with envy,   295
Yet in the end ruin swept over him.
Let every man in mankind's frailty
Consider his last day; and let none
Presume on his good fortune until he find
Life, at his death, a memory without pain.   300

QUESTIONS

1. What kind of ruler does Oedipus seem to be when we first meet him? Why does he address his people as children?
2. What incidents have happened in this country? Why has Oedipus sent Creon to Delphi?
3. What *is* Delphi? How can it be related to a modern institution?
4. Why is revenge such a political-philosophical imperative? Which Old Testament saying supports revenge?
5. What function does the Chorus serve in the play? What is the relation of the choral odes to the scenes? How do they help to advance the plot?
6. In *Oedipus* how has kindness developed into evil, and what is the message in this development?
7. How does Oedipus's own power entrap him?
8. Explain how Sophocles has observed the unities of time, place, and action in *Oedipus.*
9. Analyze the ironic elements in the play.
10. What does Sophocles say, ultimately, about fate and human nature in this play?

Arthur Miller

DEATH OF A SALESMAN

LIST OF CHARACTERS

WILLY LOMAN	UNCLE BEN
LINDA	HOWARD WAGNER
BIFF	JENNY
HAPPY	STANLEY
BERNARD	MISS FORSYTHE
THE WOMAN	LETTA
CHARLEY	

Scene: The action takes place in WILLY LOMAN'*s house and yard and in various places he visits in the New York and Boston of today.*

ACT I

Scene A melody is heard, played upon a flute. It is small and fine, telling of grass and trees and the horizon. The curtain rises.

Before us is the SALESMAN'*s house. We are aware of towering, angular shapes behind it, surrounding it on all sides. Only the blue light of the sky falls upon the house and forestage; the surrounding area shows an angry glow of orange. As more light appears, we see a solid vault of apartment houses around the small, fragile-seeming home. An air of the dream clings to the place, a dream rising out of reality. The kitchen at center seems actual enough, for there is a kitchen table with three chairs, and a refrigerator. But no other fixtures are seen. At the back of the kitchen there is a draped entrance, which leads to the living room. To the right of the kitchen, on a level raised two feet, is a bedroom furnished only with a brass bedstead and a straight chair. On a shelf over the bed a silver athletic trophy stands. A window opens onto the apartment house at the side.*

Behind the kitchen, on a level raised six and a half feet, is the boys' bedroom, at present barely visible. Two beds are dimly seen, and at the back of the room a dormer window. (This bedroom is above the unseen living room.) At the left a stairway curves up to it from the kitchen.

The entire setting is wholly or, in some places, partially transparent. The roof-line of the house is one-dimensional; under and over it we see the apartment buildings. Before the house lies an apron, curving beyond the forestage into the orchestra. This forward area serves as the back yard as well as the locale of all WILLY'*s imaginings and of his city scenes. Whenever the action is in the present the actors observe the imaginary wall-lines, entering the house only through its door at the left. But in the scenes of the past these boundaries are broken, and characters enter or leave a room by stepping "through" a wall onto the forestage.*

From the right, WILLY LOMAN, THE SALESMAN, *enters, carrying two large sample cases. The flute plays on. He hears but is not aware of it. He is past sixty years of age, dressed quietly. Even as he crosses the stage to the doorway of the house, his exhaustion is apparent. He unlocks the door, comes into the kitchen, and thankfully lets his burden down, feeling the soreness of his palms. A word-sigh escapes his lips—it might be "Oh, boy, oh, boy." He closes the door, then carries his cases out into the living room, through the draped kitchen doorway.*

LINDA, *his wife, has stirred in her bed at the right. She gets out and puts on a robe, listening. Most often jovial, she has developed an iron repression of her exceptions to* WILLY*'s behavior—she more than loves him, she admires him, as though his mercurial nature, his temper, his massive dreams and little cruelties, served her only as sharp reminders of the turbulent longings within him, longings which she shares but lacks the temperament to utter and follow to their end.*

LINDA [*hearing* WILLY *outside the bedroom, calls with some trepidation*]: Willy!

WILLY: It's all right. I came back.

LINDA: Why? What happened? [*Slight pause.*] Did something happen, Willy?

WILLY: No, nothing happened.

LINDA: You didn't smash the car, did you?

WILLY [*with casual irritation*]: I said nothing happened. Didn't you hear me?

LINDA: Don't you feel well?

WILLY: I'm tired to the death. [*The flute has faded away. He sits on the bed beside her, a little numb.*] I couldn't make it. I just couldn't make it, Linda.

LINDA [*very carefully, delicately*]: Where were you all day? You look terrible.

WILLY: I got as far as a little above Yonkers. I stopped for a cup of coffee. Maybe it was the coffee.

LINDA: What?

WILLY [*after a pause*]: I suddenly couldn't drive any more. The car kept going off onto the shoulder, y'know?

LINDA [*helpfully*]: Oh. Maybe it was the steering again. I don't think Angelo knows the Studebaker.

WILLY: No, it's me, it's me. Suddenly I realize I'm goin' sixty miles an hour and I don't remember the last five minutes. I'm—I can't seem to—keep my mind to it.

LINDA: Maybe it's your glasses. You never went for your new glasses.

WILLY: No, I see everything. I came back ten miles an hour. It took me nearly four hours from Yonkers.

LINDA [*resigned*]: Well, you'll just have to take a rest, Willy, you can't continue this way.

WILLY: I just got back from Florida.

LINDA: But you didn't rest your mind. Your mind is overactive, and the mind is what counts, dear.

WILLY: I'll start out in the morning. Maybe I'll feel better in the morning. [*She is taking off his shoes.*] These goddam arch supports are killing me.

LINDA: Take an aspirin. Should I get you an aspirin? It'll soothe you.

WILLY [*with wonder*]: I was driving along, you understand? And I was fine. I was even observing the scenery. You can imagine, me looking at scenery, on the road every week of my life. But it's so beautiful up there, Linda, the trees are so thick, and the sun is warm. I opened the windshield and just let the warm air bathe over me. And then all of a sudden I'm goin' off the road! I'm tellin' ya, I absolutely forgot I was driving. If I'd've gone the other way over the white line I might've killed somebody. So I went on again—and five minutes later I'm dreamin' again, and I

nearly . . . [*He presses two fingers against his eyes.*] I have such thoughts, I have such strange thoughts.

LINDA: Willy, dear. Talk to them again. There's no reason why you can't work in New York.

WILLY: They don't need me in New York. I'm the New England man. I'm vital in New England.

LINDA: But you're sixty years old. They can't expect you to keep traveling every week.

WILLY: I'll have to send a wire to Portland. I'm supposed to see Brown and Morrison tomorrow morning at ten o'clock to show the line. Goddammit, I could sell them! [*He starts putting on his jacket.*]

LINDA [*taking the jacket from him*]: Why don't you go down to the place tomorrow and tell Howard you've simply got to work in New York? You're too accommodating, dear.

WILLY: If old man Wagner was alive I'd a been in charge of New York now! That man was a prince, he was a masterful man. But that boy of his, that Howard, he don't appreciate. When I went north the first time, the Wagner Company didn't know where New England was!

LINDA: Why don't you tell those things to Howard, dear?

WILLY [*encouraged*]: I will, I definitely will. Is there any cheese?

LINDA: I'll make you a sandwich.

WILLY: No, go to sleep. I'll take some milk. I'll be up right away. The boys in?

LINDA: They're sleeping. Happy took Biff on a date tonight.

WILLY [*interested*]: That so?

LINDA: It was so nice to see them shaving together, one behind the other, in the bathroom. And going out together. You notice? The whole house smells of shaving lotion.

WILLY: Figure it out. Work a lifetime to pay off a house. You finally own it, and there's nobody to live in it.

LINDA: Well, dear, life is a casting off. It's always that way.

WILLY: No, no, some people—some people accomplish something. Did Biff say anything after I went this morning?

LINDA: You shouldn't have criticized him, Willy, especially after he just got off the train. You mustn't lose your temper with him.

WILLY: When the hell did I lose my temper? I simply asked him if he was making any money. Is that a criticism?

LINDA: But, dear, how could he make any money?

WILLY [*worried and angered*]: There's such an undercurrent in him. He became a moody man. Did he apologize when I left this morning?

LINDA: He was crestfallen, Willy. You know how he admires you. I think if he finds himself, then you'll both be happier and not fight any more.

WILLY: How can he find himself on a farm? Is that a life? A farmhand? In the beginning, when he was young, I thought, well, a young man, it's good for him to tramp around, take a lot of different jobs. But it's more than ten years now and he has yet to make thirty-five dollars a week!

LINDA: He's finding himself, Willy.

WILLY: Not finding yourself at the age of thirty-four is a disgrace!

LINDA: Shh!

WILLY: The trouble is he's lazy, goddammit!

LINDA: Willy, please!

WILLY: Biff is a lazy bum!

LINDA: They're sleeping. Get something to eat. Go on down.

WILLY: Why did he come home? I would like to know what brought him home.

LINDA: I don't know. I think he's still lost, Willy. I think he's very lost.

WILLY: Biff Loman is lost. In the greatest country in the world a young man with such—personal attractiveness, gets lost. And such a hard worker. There's one thing about Biff—he's not lazy.

LINDA: Never.

WILLY [*with pity and resolve*]: I'll see him in the morning; I'll have a nice talk with him. I'll get him a job selling. He could be big in no time. My God! Remember how they used to follow him around in high school? When he smiled at one of them their faces lit up. When he walked down the street . . . [*He loses himself in reminiscences.*]

LINDA [*trying to bring him out of it*]: Willy, dear, I got a new kind of American-type cheese today. It's whipped.

WILLY: Why do you get American when I like Swiss?

LINDA: I just thought you'd like a change . . .

WILLY: I don't want a change! I want Swiss cheese. Why am I always being contradicted?

LINDA [*with a covering laugh*]: I thought it would be a surprise.

WILLY: Why don't you open a window in here, for God's sake?

LINDA [*with infinite patience*]: They're all open, dear.

WILLY: The way they boxed us in here. Bricks and windows, windows and bricks.

LINDA: We should've bought the land next door.

WILLY: The street is lined with cars. There's not a breath of fresh air in the neighborhood. The grass don't grow any more, you can't raise a carrot in the back yard. They should've had a law against apartment houses. Remember those two beautiful elm trees out there? When I and Biff hung the swing between them?

LINDA: Yeah, like being a million miles from the city.

WILLY: They should've arrested the builder for cutting those down. They massacred the neighborhood. [*Lost.*] More and more I think of those days, Linda. This time of year it was lilac and wisteria. And then the peonies would come out, and the daffodils. What fragrance in this room!

LINDA: Well, after all, people had to move somewhere.

WILLY: No, there's more people now.

LINDA: I don't think there's more people. I think . . .

WILLY: There's more people! That's what's ruining this country! Population is getting out of control. The competition is maddening! Smell the stink from that apartment house! And another one on the other side . . . How can they whip cheese?

[*On* WILLY's *last line,* BIFF *and* HAPPY *raise themselves up in their beds, listening.*]

LINDA: Go down, try it. And be quiet.

WILLY [*turning to* LINDA, *guiltily*]: You're not worried about me, are you, sweetheart?

BIFF: What's the matter?

HAPPY: Listen!

LINDA: You've got too much on the ball to worry about.

WILLY: You're my foundation and my support, Linda.

LINDA: Just try to relax, dear. You make mountains out of molehills.

WILLY: I won't fight with him any more. If he wants to go back to Texas, let him go.

LINDA: He'll find his way.

WILLY: Sure. Certain men just don't get started till later in life. Like Thomas Edison, I think. Or B.F. Goodrich. One of them was deaf. [*He starts for the bedroom doorway.*] I'll put my money on Biff.

LINDA: And Willy—if it's warm Sunday we'll drive in the country. And we'll open the windshield, and take lunch.

WILLY: No, the windshields don't open on the new cars.

LINDA: But you opened it today.

WILLY: Me? I didn't. [*He stops.*] Now isn't that peculiar! Isn't that a remarkable . . . [*He breaks off in amazement and fright as the flute is heard distantly.*]

LINDA: What, darling?

WILLY: That is the most remarkable thing.

LINDA: What, dear?

WILLY: I was thinking of the Chevvy. [*Slight pause.*] Nineteen twenty-eight . . . when I had that red Chevvy . . . [*Breaks off.*] That funny? I coulda sworn I was driving that Chevvy today.

LINDA: Well, that's nothing. Something must've reminded you.

WILLY: Remarkable. Ts. Remember those days? The way Biff used to simonize that car? The dealer refused to believe there was eighty thousand miles on it. [*He shakes his head.*] Heh! [*To* LINDA.] Close your eyes, I'll be right up. [*He walks out of the bedroom.*]

HAPPY [*to* BIFF]: Jesus, maybe he smashed up the car again!

LINDA [*calling after* WILLY]: Be careful on the stairs, dear! The cheese is on the middle shelf. [*She turns, goes over to the bed, takes his jacket, and goes out of the bedroom.*]

[*Light has risen on the boys' room. Unseen,* WILLY *is heard talking to himself, "Eighty thousand miles," and a little laugh.* BIFF *gets out of bed, comes downstage a bit, and stands attentively.* BIFF *is two years older than his brother* HAPPY, *well built, but in these days bears a worn air and seems less self-assured. He has succeeded less, and his dreams are stronger and less acceptable than* HAPPY'*s.* HAPPY *is tall, powerfully made. Sexuality is like a visible color on him, or a scent that many women have discovered. He, like his brother, is lost, but in a different way, for he has never allowed himself to turn his face toward defeat and is thus more confused and hard-skinned, although seemingly more content.*]

HAPPY [*getting out of bed*]: He's going to get his license taken away if he keeps that up. I'm getting nervous about him, y'know, Biff?

BIFF: His eyes are going.

HAPPY: I've driven with him. He sees all right. He just doesn't keep his mind on it. I drove into the city with him last week. He stops at a green light and then it turns red and he goes. [*He laughs.*]

BIFF: Maybe he's color-blind.

HAPPY: Pop? Why he's got the finest eye for color in the business. You know that.

BIFF [*sitting down on his bed*]: I'm going to sleep.

HAPPY: You're not still sour on Dad, are you, Biff?

BIFF: He's all right, I guess.

WILLY [*underneath them, in the living room*]: Yes, sir, eighty thousand miles—eighty-two thousand!

BIFF: You smoking?

HAPPY [*holding out a pack of cigarettes*]: Want one?

BIFF [*taking a cigarette*]: I can never sleep when I smell it.

WILLY: What a simonizing job, heh?

HAPPY [*with deep sentiment*]: Funny, Biff, y'know? Us sleeping in here again? The old beds. [*He pats his bed affectionately.*] All the talk that went across those two beds, huh? Our whole lives.

BIFF: Yeah. Lotta dreams and plans.

HAPPY [*with a deep and masculine laugh*]: About five hundred women would like to know what was said in this room. [*They share a soft laugh.*]

BIFF: Remember that big Betsy something—what the hell was her name—over on Bushwick Avenue?

HAPPY [*combing his hair*]: With the collie dog!

BIFF: That's the one. I got you in there, remember?

HAPPY: Yeah, that was my first time—I think. Boy, there was a pig. [*They laugh, almost crudely.*] You taught me everything I know about women. Don't forget that.

BIFF: I bet you forgot how bashful you used to be. Especially with girls.

HAPPY: Oh, I still am, Biff.

BIFF: Oh, go on.

HAPPY: I just control it, that's all. I think I got less bashful and you got more so. What happened, Biff? Where's the old humor, the old confidence? [*He shakes* BIFF'*s knee.* BIFF *gets up and moves restlessly about the room.*] What's the matter?

BIFF: Why does Dad mock me all the time?

HAPPY: He's not mocking you, he . . .

BIFF: Everything I say there's a twist of mockery on his face. I can't get near him.

HAPPY: He just wants you to make good, that's all. I wanted to talk to you about Dad for a long time, Biff. Something's—happening to him. He—talks to himself.

BIFF: I noticed that this morning. But he always mumbled.

HAPPY: But not so noticeable. It got so embarrassing I sent him to Florida. And you know something? Most of the time he's talking to you.

BIFF: What's he say about me?

HAPPY: I can't make it out.

BIFF: What's he say about me?

HAPPY: I think the fact that you're not settled, that you're still kind of up in the air . . .

BIFF: There's one or two other things depressing him, Happy.

HAPPY: What do you mean?

BIFF: Never mind. Just don't lay it all to me.

HAPPY: But I think if you just got started—I mean—is there any future for you out there?

BIFF: I tell ya, Hap, I don't know what the future is. I don't know—what I'm supposed to want.

HAPPY: What do you mean?

BIFF: Well, I spent six or seven years after high school trying to work myself up. Shipping clerk, salesman, business of one kind or another. And it's a measly manner of existence. To get on that subway on the hot mornings in summer. To devote your whole life to keeping stock, or making phone calls, or selling or buying. To suffer fifty weeks of the year for the sake of a two-week vacation, when all you really desire is to be outdoors, with your shirt off. And always to have to get ahead of the next fella. And still—that's how you build a future.

HAPPY: Well, you really enjoy it on a farm? Are you content out there?

BIFF [*with rising agitation*]: Hap, I've had twenty or thirty different kinds of jobs since I left home before the war, and it always turns out the same. I just realized it lately. In Nebraska when I herded cattle, and the Dakotas, and Arizona, and now in Texas. It's why I came home now, I guess, because I realized it. This farm I work on, it's spring there now, see? And they've got about fifteen new colts. There's nothing more inspiring or—beautiful than the sight of a mare and a new colt. And it's cool there now, see? Texas is cool now, and it's spring. And whenever spring comes to where I am, I suddenly get the feeling, my God, I'm not gettin' anywhere! What the hell am I doing, playing around with horses, twenty-eight dollars a week! I'm thirty-four years old, I oughta be makin' my future. That's when I come running home. And now, I get here, and I don't know what to do with myself. [*After a pause.*] I've always made a point of not wasting my life, and everytime I come back here I know that all I've done is to waste my life.

HAPPY: You're a poet, you know that, Biff? You're a—you're an idealist!

BIFF: No, I'm mixed up very bad. Maybe I oughta get married. Maybe I oughta get stuck into something. Maybe that's my trouble. I'm like a boy. I'm not married, I'm not in business, I just—I'm like a boy. Are you content, Hap? You're a success, aren't you? Are you content?

HAPPY: Hell, no!

BIFF: Why? You're making money, aren't you?

HAPPY [*moving about with energy, expressiveness*]: All I can do now is wait for the merchandise manager to die. And suppose I get to be merchandise manager? He's a good friend of mine, and he just built a terrific estate on Long Island. And he lived there about two months and sold it, and how he's building another one. He can't enjoy it once it's finished. And I know that's just what I would do. I don't know what the hell I'm workin' for. Sometimes I sit in my apartment—all alone. And I think of the rent I'm paying. And it's crazy. But then, it's what I always wanted. My own apartment, a car, and plenty of women. And still, goddammit, I'm lonely.

BIFF [*with enthusiasm*]: Listen, why don't you come out West with me?

HAPPY: You and I, heh?

BIFF: Sure, maybe we could buy a ranch. Raise cattle, use our muscles. Men built like we are should be working out in the open.

HAPPY [*avidly*]: The Loman Brothers, heh?

BIFF [*with vast affection*]: Sure, we'd be known all over the counties!

HAPPY [*enthralled*]: That's what I dream about, Biff. Sometimes I want to just rip my clothes off in the middle of the store and outbox that goddam merchandise manager. I mean I can outbox, outrun, and outlift anybody in that store, and I have to take orders from those common, petty sons-of-bitches till I can't stand it any more.

BIFF: I'm tellin' you, kid, if you were with me I'd be happy out there.

HAPPY [*enthused*]: See, Biff, everybody around me is so false that I'm constantly lowering my ideals . . .

BIFF: Baby, together we'd stand up for one another, we'd have someone to trust.

HAPPY: If I were around you . . .

BIFF: Hap, the trouble is we weren't brought up to grub for money. I don't know how to do it.

HAPPY: Neither can I!

BIFF: Then let's go!

HAPPY: The only thing is—what can you make out there?

BIFF: But look at your friend. Builds an estate and then hasn't the peace of mind to live in it.

HAPPY: Yeah, but when he walks into the store the waves part in front of him. That's fifty-two thousand dollars a year coming through the revolving door, and I got more in my pinky finger than he's got in his head.

BIFF: Yeah, but you just said . . .

HAPPY: I gotta show some of those pompous, self-important executives over there that Hap Loman can make the grade. I want to walk into the store the way he walks in. Then I'll go with you, Biff. We'll be together yet, I swear. But take those two we had tonight. Now weren't they gorgeous creatures?

BIFF: Yeah, yeah, most gorgeous I've had in years.

HAPPY: I get that any time I want, Biff. Whenever I feel disgusted. The only trouble is, it gets like bowling or something. I just keep knockin' them over and it doesn't mean anything. You still run around a lot?

BIFF: Naa. I'd like to find a girl—steady, somebody with substance.

HAPPY: That's what I long for.

BIFF: Go on! You'd never come home.

HAPPY: I would! Somebody with character, with resistance! Like Mom, y'know? You're gonna call me a bastard when I tell you this. That girl Charlotte I was with tonight is engaged to be married in five weeks. [*He tries on his new hat.*]

BIFF: No kiddin'!

HAPPY: Sure, the guy's in line for the vice-presidency of the store. I don't know what gets into me, maybe I just have an overdeveloped sense of competition or something, but I went and ruined her, and furthermore I can't get rid of her. And he's the third executive I've done that to. Isn't that a crummy characteristic? And to top it all, I go to their weddings! [*Indignantly, but laughing.*] Like I'm not supposed to take bribes. Manufacturers offer me a hundred-dollar bill now and then to throw an order their

way. You know how honest I am, but it's like this girl, see. I hate myself for it. Because I don't want the girl, and still, I take it and—I love it!

BIFF: Let's go to sleep.

HAPPY: I guess we didn't settle anything, heh?

BIFF: I just got one idea that I think I'm going to try.

HAPPY: What's that?

BIFF: Remember Bill Oliver?

HAPPY: Sure, Oliver is very big now. You want to work for him again?

BIFF: No, but when I quit he said something to me. He put his arm on my shoulder, and he said, "Biff, if you ever need anything, come to me."

HAPPY: I remember that. That sounds good.

BIFF: I think I'll go to see him. If I could get ten thousand or even seven or eight thousand dollars I could buy a beautiful ranch.

HAPPY: I bet he'd back you. 'Cause he thought highly of you, Biff. I mean, they all do. You're well liked, Biff. That's why I say to come back here, and we both have the apartment. And I'm tellin' you, Biff, any babe you want . . .

BIFF: No, with a ranch I could do the work I like and still be something. I just wonder though. I wonder if Oliver still thinks I stole that carton of basketballs.

HAPPY: Oh, he probably forgot that long ago. It's almost ten years. You're too sensitive. Anyway, he didn't really fire you.

BIFF: Well, I think he was going to. I think that's why I quit. I was never sure whether he knew or not. I know he thought the world of me, though. I was the only one he'd let lock up the place.

WILLY [below]: You gonna wash the engine, Biff?

HAPPY: Shh!

[BIFF *looks at* HAPPY, *who is gazing down, listening.* WILLY *is mumbling in the parlor.*]

HAPPY: You hear that?

[*They listen.* WILLY *laughs warmly.*]

BIFF [growing angry]: Doesn't he know Mom can hear that?

WILLY: Don't get your sweater dirty, Biff!

[*A look of pain crosses* BIFF's *face.*]

HAPPY: Isn't that terrible? Don't leave again, will you? You'll find a job here. You gotta stick around. I don't know what to do about him, it's getting embarrassing.

WILLY: What a simonizing job!

BIFF: Mom's hearing that!

WILLY: No kiddin', Biff, you got a date? Wonderful!

HAPPY: Go on to sleep. But talk to him in the morning, will you?

BIFF [reluctantly getting into bed]: With her in the house. Brother!

HAPPY [getting into bed]: I wish you'd have a good talk with him.

[*The light on their room begins to fade.*]

BIFF [*to himself in bed*]: That selfish, stupid . . .
HAPPY: Sh . . . Sleep, Biff.

[*Their light is out. Well before they have finished speaking,* WILLY*'s form is dimly seen below in the darkened kitchen. He opens the refrigerator, searches in there, and takes out a bottle of milk. The apartment houses are fading out, and the entire house and surroundings become covered with leaves. Music insinuates itself as the leaves appear.*]

WILLY: Just wanna be careful with those girls, Biff, that's all. Don't make any promises. No promises of any kind. Because a girl, y'know, they always believe what you tell 'em, and you're very young, Biff, you're too young to be talking seriously to girls.

[*Light rises on the kitchen.* WILLY, *talking, shuts the refrigerator door and comes downstage to the kitchen table. He pours milk into a glass. He is totally immersed in himself, smiling faintly.*]

WILLY: Too young entirely, Biff. You want to watch your schooling first. Then when you're all set, there'll be plenty of girls for a boy like you. [*He smiles broadly at a kitchen chair.*] That so? The girls pay for you? [*He laughs*] Boy, you must really be makin' a hit.

[WILLY *is gradually addressing—physically—a point offstage, speaking through the wall of the kitchen, and his voice has been rising in volume to that of a normal conversation.*]

WILLY: I been wondering why you polish the car so careful. Ha! Don't leave the hubcaps, boys. Get the chamois to the hubcaps. Happy, use newspaper on the windows, it's the easiest thing. Show him how to do it Biff! You see, Happy? Pad it up, use it like a pad. That's it, that's it, good work. You're doin' all right, Hap. [*He pauses, then nods in approbation for a few seconds, then looks upward.*] Biff, first thing we gotta do when we get time is clip that big branch over the house. Afraid it's gonna fall in a storm and hit the roof. Tell you what. We get a rope and sling her around, and then we climb up there with a couple of saws and take her down. Soon as you finish the car, boys, I wanna see ya. I got a surprise for you, boys.
BIFF [*offstage*]: Whatta ya got, Dad?
WILLY: No, you finish first. Never leave a job till you're finished—remember that. [*Looking toward the "big trees."*] Biff, up in Albany I saw a beautiful hammock. I think I'll buy it next trip, and we'll hang it right between those two elms. Wouldn't that be something? Just swingin' there under those branches. Boy, that would be . . .

[YOUNG BIFF *and* YOUNG HAPPY *appear from the direction* WILLY *was addressing.* HAPPY *carries rags and a pail of water.* BIFF, *wearing a sweater with a block "S," carries a football.*]

BIFF [*pointing in the direction of the car offstage*]: How's that, Pop, professional?
WILLY: Terrific. Terrific job, boys. Good work, Biff.

HAPPY: Where's the surprise, Pop?

WILLY: In the back seat of the car.

HAPPY: Boy! [*He runs off.*]

BIFF: What is it, Dad? Tell me, what'd you buy?

WILLY [*laughing, cuffs him*]: Never mind, something I want you to have.

BIFF [*turns and starts off*]: What is it, Hap?

HAPPY [*offstage*]: It's a punching bag!

BIFF: Oh, Pop!

WILLY: It's got Gene Tunney's signature on it!

[HAPPY *runs onstage with a punching bag.*]

BIFF: Gee, how'd you know we wanted a punching bag?

WILLY: Well, it's the finest thing for the timing.

HAPPY [*lies down on his back and pedals with his feet*]: I'm losing weight, you notice, Pop?

WILLY [*to* HAPPY]: Jumping rope is good too.

BIFF: Did you see the new football I got?

WILLY [*examining the ball*]: Where'd you get a new ball?

BIFF: The coach told me to practice my passing.

WILLY: That so? And he gave you the ball, heh?

BIFF: Well, I borrowed it from the locker room. [*He laughs confidentially.*]

WILLY [*laughing with him at the theft*]: I want you to return that.

HAPPY: I told you he wouldn't like it!

BIFF [*angrily*]: Well, I'm bringing it back!

WILLY [*stopping the incipient argument, to* HAPPY]: Sure, he's gotta practice with a regulation ball, doesn't he? [*To* BIFF.] Coach'll probably congratulate you on your initiative!

BIFF: Oh, he keeps congratulating my initiative all the time, Pop.

WILLY: That's because he likes you. If somebody else took that ball there'd be an uproar. So what's the report, boys, what's the report?

BIFF: Where'd you go this time, Dad? Gee we were lonesome for you.

WILLY [*pleased, puts an arm around each boy and they come down to the apron*]: Lonesome, heh?

BIFF: Missed you every minute.

WILLY: Don't say? Tell you a secret, boys. Don't breathe it to a soul. Someday I'll have my own business, and I'll never have to leave home any more.

HAPPY: Like Uncle Charley, heh?

WILLY: Bigger than Uncle Charley! Because Charley is not—liked. He's liked, but he's not—well liked.

BIFF: Where'd you go this time, Dad?

WILLY: Well, I got on the road, and I went north to Providence. Met the Mayor.

BIFF: The Mayor of Providence!

WILLY: He was sitting in the hotel lobby.

BIFF: What'd he say?

WILLY: He said, "Morning!" And I said, "You got a fine city here, Mayor." And then he had coffee with me. And then I went to Waterbury. Waterbury is a fine city. Big clock city, the famous Waterbury clock. Sold a nice bill there. And then Boston—

Boston is the cradle of the Revolution. A fine city. And a couple of other towns in Mass., and on to Portland and Bangor and straight home!

BIFF: Gee, I'd love to go with you sometime, Dad.

WILLY: Soon as summer comes.

HAPPY: Promise?

WILLY: You and Hap and I, and I'll show you all the towns. America is full of beautiful towns and fine, upstanding people. And they know me, boys, they know me up and down New England. The finest people. And when I bring you fellas up, there'll be open sesame for all of us, 'cause one thing, boys: I have friends. I can park my car in any street in New England, and the cops protect it like their own. This summer, heh?

BIFF AND HAPPY [*together*]: Yeah! You bet!

WILLY: We'll take our bathing suits.

HAPPY: We'll carry your bags, Pop!

WILLY: Oh, won't that be something! Me comin' into the Boston stores with you boys carryin' my bags. What a sensation!

[BIFF *is prancing around, practicing passing the ball.*]

WILLY: You nervous, Biff, about the game?

BIFF: Not if you're gonna be there.

WILLY: What do they say about you in school, now that they made you captain?

HAPPY: There's a crowd of girls behind him everytime the classes change.

BIFF [*taking* WILLY'*s hand*]: This Saturday, Pop, this Saturday—just for you, I'm going to break through for a touchdown.

HAPPY: You're supposed to pass.

BIFF: I'm takin' one play for Pop. You watch me, Pop, and when I take off my helmet, that means I'm breakin' out. Then you watch me crash through that line!

WILLY [*kisses* BIFF]: Oh, wait'll I tell this in Boston!

[BERNARD *enters in knickers. He is younger than* BIFF, *earnest and loyal, a worried boy.*]

BERNARD: Biff, where are you? You're supposed to study with me today.

WILLY: Hey, looka Bernard. What're you lookin' so anemic about, Bernard?

BERNARD: He's gotta study, Uncle Willy. He's got Regents next week.

HAPPY [*tauntingly, spinning* BERNARD *around*]: Let's box, Bernard!

BERNARD: Biff! [*He gets away from* HAPPY.] Listen, Biff, I heard Mr. Birnbaum say that if you don't start studyin' math he's gonna flunk you, and you won't graduate. I heard him!

WILLY: You better study with him, Biff. Go ahead now.

BERNARD: I heard him!

BIFF: Oh, Pop, you didn't see my sneakers! [*He holds up a foot for* WILLY *to look at.*]

WILLY: Hey, that's a beautiful job of printing!

BERNARD [*wiping his glasses*]: Just because he printed University of Virginia on his sneakers doesn't mean they've got to graduate him. Uncle Willy!

WILLY [*angrily*]: What're you talking about? With scholarships to three universities they're gonna flunk him?

BERNARD: But I heard Mr. Birnbaum say . . .

WILLY: Don't be a pest, Bernard! [*To his boys.*] What an anemic!

BERNARD: Okay, I'm waiting for you in my house, Biff.

[BERNARD *goes off. The* LOMANS *laugh.*]

WILLY: Bernard is not well liked, is he?

BIFF: He's liked, but he's not well liked.

HAPPY: That's right, Pop.

WILLY: That's just what I mean. Bernard can get the best marks in school, y'understand, but when he gets out in the business world, y'understand, you are going to be five times ahead of him. That's why I thank Almighty God you're both built like Adonises. Because the man who makes an appearance in the business world, the man who creates personal interest, is the man who gets ahead. Be liked and you will never want. You take me, for instance. I never have to wait in line to see a buyer. "Willy Loman is here!" That's all they have to know, and I go right through.

BIFF: Did you knock them dead, Pop?

WILLY: Knocked 'em cold in Providence, slaughtered 'em in Boston.

HAPPY [*on his back, pedaling again*]: I'm losing weight, you notice, Pop?

[LINDA *enters as of old, a ribbon in her hair, carrying a basket of washing.*]

LINDA [*with youthful energy*]: Hello, dear!

WILLY: Sweetheart!

LINDA: How'd the Chevvy run?

WILLY: Chevrolet, Linda, is the greatest car ever built. [*To the boys.*] Since when do you let your mother carry wash up the stairs?

BIFF: Grab hold there, boy!

HAPPY: Where to, Mom?

LINDA: Hang them up on the line. And you better go down to your friends, Biff. The cellar is full of boys. They don't know what to do with themselves.

BIFF: Ah, when Pop comes home they can wait!

WILLY [*laughs appreciatively*]: You better go down and tell them what to do, Biff.

BIFF: I think I'll have them sweep out the furnace room.

WILLY: Good work, Biff.

BIFF [*goes through wall-line of kitchen to doorway at back and calls down*]: Fellas! Everybody sweep out the furnace room! I'll be right down!

VOICES: All right! Okay, Biff.

BIFF: George and Sam and Frank, come out back! We're hangin' up the wash! Come on, Hap, on the double! [*He and* HAPPY *carry out the basket.*]

LINDA: The way they obey him!

WILLY: Well, that's training, the training. I'm tellin' you, I was sellin' thousands and thousands, but I had to come home.

LINDA: Oh, the whole block'll be at that game. Did you sell anything?

WILLY: I did five hundred gross in Providence and seven hundred gross in Boston.

LINDA: No! Wait a minute, I've got a pencil. [*She pulls pencil and paper out of her apron pocket.*] That makes your commission . . . Two hundred—my God! Two hundred and twelve dollars!

WILLY: Well, I didn't figure it yet, but . . .

LINDA: How much did you do?

WILLY: Well, I—I did—about a hundred and eighty gross in Providence. Well, no—it came to—roughly two hundred gross on the whole trip.

LINDA [*without hesitation*]: Two hundred gross. That's . . . [*She figures.*]

WILLY: The trouble was that three of the stores were half-closed for inventory in Boston. Otherwise I woulda broke records.

LINDA: Well, it makes seventy dollars and some pennies. That's very good.

WILLY: What do we owe?

LINDA: Well, on the first there's sixteen dollars on the refrigerator——

WILLY: Why sixteen?

LINDA: Well, the fan belt broke, so it was a dollar eighty.

WILLY: But it's brand new.

LINDA: Well, the man said that's the way it is. Till they work themselves in, y'know.

[*They move through the wall-line into the kitchen.*]

WILLY: I hope we didn't get stuck on that machine.

LINDA: They got the biggest ads of any of them!

WILLY: I know, it's a fine machine. What else?

LINDA: Well, there's nine-sixty for the washing machine. And for the vacuum cleaner there's three and a half due on the fifteenth. Then the roof, you got twenty-one dollars remaining.

WILLY: It don't leak, does it?

LINDA: No, they did a wonderful job. Then you owe Frank for the carburetor.

WILLY: I'm not going to pay that man! That goddam Chevrolet, they ought to prohibit the manufacture of that car!

LINDA: Well, you owe him three and a half. And odds and ends, comes to around a hundred and twenty dollars by the fifteenth.

WILLY: A hundred and twenty dollars! My God, if business don't pick up I don't know what I'm gonna do!

LINDA: Well, next week you'll do better.

WILLY: Oh, I'll knock 'em dead next week. I'll go to Hartford. I'm very well liked in Hartford. You know, the trouble is, Linda, people don't seem to take to me.

[*They move onto the forestage.*]

LINDA: Oh, don't be foolish.

WILLY: I know it when I walk in. They seem to laugh at me.

LINDA: Why? Why would they laugh at you? Don't talk that way, Willy.

[WILLY *moves to the edge of the stage.* LINDA *goes into the kitchen and starts to darn stockings.*]

WILLY: I don't know the reason for it, but they just pass me by. I'm not noticed.

LINDA: But you're doing wonderful, dear. You're making seventy to a hundred dollars a week.

WILLY: But I gotta be at it ten, twelve hours a day. Other men—I don't know—they do it easier. I don't know why—I can't stop myself—I talk too much. A man oughta come in with a few words. One thing about Charley. He's a man of few words, and they respect him.

LINDA: You don't talk too much, you're just lively.

WILLY [*smiling*]: Well, I figure, what the hell, life is short, a couple of jokes. [*To himself.*] I joke too much! [*The smile goes.*]

LINDA: Why? You're . . .

WILLY: I'm fat. I'm very—foolish to look at, Linda. I didn't tell you, but Christmas time I happened to be calling on F. H. Stewarts, and a salesman I know, as I was going in to see the buyer I heard him say something about—walrus. And I—I cracked him right across the face. I won't take that. I simply will not take that. But they do laugh at me. I know that.

LINDA: Darling . . .

WILLY: I gotta overcome it. I know I gotta overcome it. I'm not dressing to advantage, maybe.

LINDA: Willy, darling, you're the handsomest man in the world . . .

WILLY: Oh, no, Linda.

LINDA: To me you are. [*Slight pause.*] The handsomest.

[*From the darkness is heard the laughter of a woman.* WILLY *doesn't turn to it, but it continues through* LINDA'*s lines.*]

LINDA: And the boys, Willy. Few men are idolized by their children the way you are.

[*Music is heard as behind a scrim, to the left of the house;* THE WOMAN, *dimly seen, is dressing.*]

WILLY [*with great feeling*]: You're the best there is, Linda, you're a pal, you know that? On the road—on the road I want to grab you sometimes and just kiss the life outa you.

[*The laughter is loud now, and he moves into a brightening area at the left, where* THE WOMAN *has come from behind the scrim and is standing, putting on her hat, looking into a "mirror" and laughing.*]

WILLY: Cause I get so lonely—especially when business is bad and there's nobody to talk to. I get the feeling that I'll never sell anything again, that I won't make a living for you, or a business, a business for the boys. [*He talks through* THE WOMAN'*s subsiding laughter;* THE WOMAN *primps at the "mirror."*] There's so much I want to make for . . .

THE WOMAN: Me? You didn't make me, Willy. I picked you.

WILLY [*pleased*]: You picked me?

THE WOMAN [*who is quite proper-looking,* WILLY*'s age*]: I did. I've been sitting at that desk watching all the salesmen go by, day in, day out. But you've got such a sense of humor, and we do have such a good time together, don't we?

WILLY: Sure, sure. [*He takes her in his arms.*] Why do you have to go now?

THE WOMAN: It's two o'clock . . .

WILLY: No, come on in! [*He pulls her.*]

THE WOMAN: . . . my sisters 'll be scandalized. When'll you be back?

WILLY: Oh, two weeks about. Will you come up again?

THE WOMAN: Sure thing. You do make me laugh. It's good for me. [*She squeezes his arm, kisses him.*] And I think you're a wonderful man.

WILLY: You picked me, heh?

THE WOMAN: Sure. Because you're so sweet. And such a kidder.

WILLY: Well, I'll see you next time I'm in Boston.

THE WOMAN: I'll put you right through to the buyers.

WILLY [*slapping her bottom*]: Right. Well, bottoms up!

THE WOMAN [*slaps him gently and laughs*]: You just kill me, Willy. [*He suddenly grabs her and kisses her roughly.*] You kill me. And thanks for the stockings. I love a lot of stockings. Well, good night.

WILLY: Good night. And keep your pores open!

THE WOMAN: Oh, Willy!

[THE WOMAN *bursts out laughing, and* LINDA*'s laughter blends in.* THE WOMAN *disappears into the dark. Now the area at the kitchen table brightens.* LINDA *is sitting where she was at the kitchen table, but now is mending a pair of her silk stockings.*]

LINDA: You are, Willy. The handsomest man. You've got no reason to feel that . . .

WILLY [*coming out of* THE WOMAN*'s dimming area and going over to* LINDA]: I'll make it all up to you, Linda, I'll . . .

LINDA: There's nothing to make up, dear. You're doing fine, better than . . .

WILLY [*noticing her mending*]: What's that?

LINDA: Just mending my stockings. They're so expensive . . .

WILLY [*angrily, taking them from her*]: I won't have you mending stockings in this house! Now throw them out!

[LINDA *puts the stockings in her pocket.*]

BERNARD [*entering on the run*]: Where is he? If he doesn't study!

WILLY [*moving to the forestage, with great agitation*]: You'll give him the answers!

BERNARD: I do, but I can't on a Regents! That's a state exam! They're liable to arrest me!

WILLY: Where is he? I'll whip him, I'll whip him!

LINDA: And he'd better give back that football, Willy, it's not nice.

WILLY: Biff! Where is he? Why is he taking everything?

LINDA: He's too rough with the girls, Willy. All the mothers are afraid of him!

WILLY: I'll whip him!

BERNARD: He's driving the car without a license!

[THE WOMAN's *laugh is heard*.]

WILLY: Shut up!

LINDA: All the mothers . . .

WILLY: Shut up!

BERNARD [*backing quietly away and out*]: Mr. Birnbaum says he's stuck up.

WILLY: Get outa here!

BERNARD: If he doesn't buckle down he'll flunk math! [*He goes off*.]

LINDA: He's right, Willy, you've gotta . . .

WILLY [*exploding at her*]: There's nothing the matter with him! You want him to be a worm like Bernard? He's got spirit, personality . . .

[*As he speaks*, LINDA, *almost in tears, exits into the living room*. WILLY *is alone in the kitchen, wilting and staring. The leaves are gone. It is night again, and the apartment houses look down from behind*.]

WILLY: Loaded with it. Loaded! What is he stealing? He's giving it back, isn't he? Why is he stealing? What did I tell him? I never in my life told him anything but decent things.

[HAPPY *in pajamas has come down the stairs*; WILLY *suddenly becomes aware of* HAPPY's *presence*.]

HAPPY: Let's go now, come on.

WILLY [*sitting down at the kitchen table*]: Huh! Why did she have to wax the floors herself? Everytime she waxes the floors she keels over. She knows that!

HAPPY: Shh! Take it easy. What brought you back tonight?

WILLY: I got an awful scare. Nearly hit a kid in Yonkers. God! Why didn't I go to Alaska with my brother Ben that time! Ben! That man was a genius, that man was success incarnate! What a mistake! He begged me to go.

HAPPY: Well, there's no use in . . .

WILLY: You guys! There was a man started with the clothes on his back and ended up with diamond mines!

HAPPY: Boy, someday I'd like to know how he did it.

WILLY: What's the mystery? The man knew what he wanted and went out and got it! Walked into a jungle, and comes out, the age of twenty-one, and he's rich! The world is an oyster, but you don't crack it open on a mattress!

HAPPY: Pop, I told you I'm gonna retire you for life.

WILLY: You'll retire me for life on seventy goddam dollars a week? And your women and your car and your apartment, and you'll retire me for life! Christ's sake, I couldn't get past Yonkers today! Where are you guys, where are you? The woods are burning! I can't drive a car!

[CHARLEY *has appeared in the doorway. He is a large man, slow of speech, laconic, immovable. In all he says, despite what he says, there is pity, and, now, trepidation. He has a robe over pajamas, slippers on his feet. He enters the kitchen.*]

CHARLEY: Everything all right?

HAPPY: Yeah, Charley, everything's . . .

WILLY: What's the matter?

CHARLEY: I heard some noise. I thought something happened. Can't we do something about the walls? You sneeze in here, and in my house hats blow off.

HAPPY: Let's go to bed, Dad. Come on.

[CHARLEY *signals to* HAPPY *to go.*]

WILLY: You go ahead, I'm not tired at the moment.

HAPPY [*to* WILLY]: Take it easy, huh? [*He exits.*]

WILLY: What're you doin' up?

CHARLEY [*sitting down at the kitchen table opposite* WILLY]: Couldn't sleep good. I had a heartburn.

WILLY: Well, you don't know how to eat.

CHARLEY: I eat with my mouth.

WILLY: No, you're ignorant. You gotta know about vitamins and things like that.

CHARLEY: Come on, let's shoot. Tire you out a little.

WILLY [*hesitantly*]: All right. You got cards?

CHARLEY [*taking a deck from his pocket*]: Yeah, I got them. Someplace. What is it with those vitamins?

WILLY [*dealing*]: They build up your bones. Chemistry.

CHARLEY: Yeah, but there's no bones in a heartburn.

WILLY: What are you talkin' about? Do you know the first thing about it?

CHARLEY: Don't get insulted.

WILLY: Don't talk about something you don't know anything about.

[*They are playing. Pause.*]

CHARLEY: What're you doin' home?

WILLY: A little trouble with the car.

CHARLEY: Oh. [*Pause.*] I'd like to take a trip to California.

WILLY: Don't say.

CHARLEY: You want a job?

WILLY: I got a job, I told you that. [*After a slight pause.*] What the hell are you offering me a job for?

CHARLEY: Don't get insulted.

WILLY: Don't insult me.

CHARLEY: I don't see no sense in it. You don't have to go on this way.

WILLY: I got a good job. [*Slight pause.*] What do you keep comin' in here for?

CHARLEY: You want me to go?

WILLY [*after a pause, withering*]: I can't understand it. He's going back to Texas again. What the hell is that?

CHARLEY: Let him go.

WILLY: I got nothin' to give him, Charley, I'm clean, I'm clean.

CHARLEY: He won't starve. None a them starve. Forget about him.

WILLY: Then what have I got to remember?

CHARLEY: You take it too hard. To hell with it. When a deposit bottle is broken you don't get your nickel back.

WILLY: That's easy enough for you to say.

CHARLEY: That ain't easy for me to say.

WILLY: Did you see the ceiling I put up in the living room?

CHARLEY: Yeah, that's a piece of work. To put up a ceiling is a mystery to me. How do you do it?

WILLY: What's the difference?

CHARLEY: Well, talk about it.

WILLY: You gonna put up a ceiling?

CHARLEY: How could I put up a ceiling?

WILLY: Then what the hell are you bothering me for?

CHARLEY: You're insulted again.

WILLY: A man who can't handle tools is not a man. You're disgusting.

CHARLEY: Don't call me disgusting, Willy.

[UNCLE BEN, *carrying a valise and an umbrella, enters the forestage from around the right corner of the house. He is a stolid man, in his sixties, with a mustache and an authoritative air. He is utterly certain of his destiny, and there is an aura of far places about him. He enters exactly as* WILLY *speaks.*]

WILLY: I'm getting awfully tired, Ben.

[BEN'*s music is heard.* BEN *looks around at everything.*]

CHARLEY: Good, keep playing; you'll sleep better. Did you call me Ben?

[BEN *looks at his watch.*]

WILLY: That's funny. For a second there you reminded me of my brother Ben.

BEN: I only have a few minutes. [*He strolls, inspecting the place.* WILLY *and* CHARLEY *continue playing.*]

CHARLEY: You never heard from him again, heh? Since that time?

WILLY: Didn't Linda tell you? Couple of weeks ago we got a letter from his wife in Africa. He died.

CHARLEY: That so.

BEN [*chuckling*]: So this is Brooklyn, eh?

CHARLEY: Maybe you're in for some of his money.

WILLY: Naa, he had seven sons. There's just one opportunity I had with that man . . .

BEN: I must make a train, William. There are several properties I'm looking at in Alaska.

WILLY: Sure, sure! If I'd gone with him to Alaska that time, everything would've been totally different.

CHARLEY: Go on, you'd froze to death up there.

WILLY: What're you talking about?

BEN: Opportunity is tremendous in Alaska, William. Surprised you're not up there.

WILLY: Sure, tremendous.

CHARLEY: Heh?

WILLY: There was the only man I ever met who knew the answers.

CHARLEY: Who?

BEN: How are you all?

WILLY [taking a pot, smiling]: Fine, fine.

CHARLEY: Pretty sharp tonight.

BEN: Is Mother living with you?

WILLY: No, she died a long time ago.

CHARLEY: Who?

BEN: That's too bad. Fine specimen of a lady, Mother.

WILLY [to CHARLEY]: Heh?

BEN: I'd hoped to see the old girl.

CHARLEY: Who died?

BEN: Heard anything from Father, have you?

WILLY [unnerved]: What do you mean, who died?

CHARLEY [taking a pot]: What're you talkin' about?

BEN [looking at his watch]: William, it's half-past eight!

WILLY [as though to dispel his confusion he angrily stops CHARLEY's hand]: That's my build!

CHARLEY: I put the ace . . .

WILLY: If you don't know how to play the game I'm not gonna throw my money away on you!

CHARLEY [rising]: It was my ace, for God's sake!

WILLY: I'm through, I'm through!

BEN: When did Mother die?

WILLY: Long ago. Since the beginning you never knew how to play cards.

CHARLEY [picks up the cards and goes to the door]: All right! Next time I'll bring a deck with five aces.

WILLY: I don't play that kind of game!

CHARLEY [turning to him]: You ought to be ashamed of yourself!

WILLY: Yeah?

CHARLEY: Yeah! [He goes out.]

WILLY [slamming the door after him]: Ignoramus!

BEN [as WILLY comes toward him through the wall-line of the kitchen]: So you're William.

WILLY [shaking BEN's hand]: Ben! I've been waiting for you so long! What's the answer? How did you do it?

BEN: Oh, there's a story in that.

[LINDA *enters the forestage, as of old, carrying the wash basket.*]

LINDA: Is this Ben?

BEN [*gallantly*]: How do you do, my dear.

LINDA: Where've you been all these years? Willy's always wondered why you . . .

WILLY [*pulling* BEN *away from her impatiently*]: Where is Dad? Didn't you follow him? How did you get started?

BEN: Well, I don't know how much you remember.

WILLY: Well, I was just a baby, of course, only three or four years old . . .

BEN: Three years and eleven months.

WILLY: What a memory, Ben!

BEN: I have many enterprises, William, and I have never kept books.

WILLY: I remember I was sitting under the wagon in—was it Nebraska?

BEN: It was South Dakota, and I gave you a bunch of wild flowers.

WILLY: I remember you walking away down some open road.

BEN [*laughing*]: I was going to find Father in Alaska.

WILLY: Where is he?

BEN: At that age I had a very faulty view of geography, William. I discovered after a few days that I was heading due south, so instead of Alaska, I ended up in Africa.

LINDA: Africa!

WILLY: The Gold Coast!

BEN: Principally diamond mines.

LINDA: Diamond mines!

BEN: Yes, my dear. But I've only a few minutes . . .

WILLY: No! Boys! Boys! [YOUNG BIFF *and* HAPPY *appear.*] Listen to this. This is your Uncle Ben, a great man! Tell my boys, Ben!

BEN: Why, boys, when I was seventeen I walked into the jungle, and when I was twenty-one I walked out. [*He laughs.*] And by God I was rich.

WILLY [*to the boys*]: You see what I been talking about? The greatest things can happen!

BEN [*glancing at his watch*]: I have an appointment in Ketchikan Tuesday week.

WILLY: No, Ben! Please tell about Dad. I want my boys to hear. I want them to know the kind of stock they spring from. All I remember is a man with a big beard, and I was in Mamma's lap, sitting around a fire, and some kind of high music.

BEN: His flute. He played the flute.

WILLY: Sure, the flute, that's right!

[*New music is heard, a high, rollicking tune.*]

BEN: Father was a very great and a very wild-hearted man. We would start in Boston, and he'd toss the whole family into the wagon, and then he'd drive the team right across the country; through Ohio, and Indiana, Michigan, Illinois, and all the Western states. And we'd stop in the towns and sell the flutes that he'd made on the way. Great inventor, Father. With one gadget he made more in a week than a man like you could make in a lifetime.

WILLY: That's just the way I'm bringing them up, Ben—rugged, well liked, all-around.

BEN: Yeah? [*To* BIFF.] Hit that, boy—hard as you can. [*He pounds his stomach.*]

BIFF: Oh, no, sir!

BEN [*taking boxing stance*]: Come on, get to me! [*He laughs.*]

WILLY: Go to it, Biff! Go ahead, show him!

BIFF: Okay! [*He cocks his fists and starts in.*]

LINDA [*to* WILLY]: Why must he fight, dear?

BEN [*sparring with* BIFF]: Good boy! Good boy!

WILLY: How's that, Ben, heh?

HAPPY: Give him the left, Biff!

LINDA: Why are you fighting?

BEN: Good boy! [*Suddenly comes in, trips* BIFF, *and stands over him, the point of his umbrella poised over* BIFF's *eye.*]

LINDA: Look out, Biff!

BIFF: Gee!

BEN [*Patting* BIFF's *knee*]: Never fight fair with a stranger, boy. You'll never get out of the jungle that way. [*Taking* LINDA's *hand and bowing.*] It was an honor and a pleasure to meet you, Linda.

LINDA [*withdrawing her hand coldly, frightened*]: Have a nice—trip.

BEN [*to* WILLY]: And good luck with your—what do you do?

WILLY: Selling.

BEN: Yes. Well . . . [*He raises his hand in farewell to all.*]

WILLY: No, Ben, I don't want you to think . . . [*He takes* BEN's *arm to show him.*] It's Brooklyn, I know, but we hunt too.

BEN: Really, now.

WILLY: Oh, sure, there's snakes and rabbits and—that's why I moved out here. Why Biff can fell any one of these trees in no time! Boys! Go right over to where they're building the apartment house and get some sand. We're gonna rebuild the entire front stoop right now! Watch this, Ben!

BIFF: Yes, sir! On the double, Hap!

HAPPY [*as he and* BIFF *run off*]: I lost weight, Pop, you notice?

[CHARLEY *enters in knickers, even before the boys are gone.*]

CHARLEY: Listen, if they steal any more from that building the watchman'll put the cops on them!

LINDA [*to* WILLY]: Don't let Biff . . .

[BEN *laughs lustily.*]

WILLY: You shoulda seen the lumber they brought home last week. At least a dozen six-by-tens worth all kinds a money.

CHARLEY: Listen, if that watchman . . .

WILLY: I gave them hell, understand. But I got a couple of fearless characters there.

CHARLEY: Willy, the jails are full of fearless characters.

BEN [*clapping* WILLY *on the back, with a laugh at* CHARLEY]: And the stock exchange, friend!

WILLY [*joining in* BEN's *laughter*]: Where are the rest of your pants?

CHARLEY: My wife bought them.

WILLY: Now all you need is a golf club and you can go upstairs and go to sleep. [*To* BEN.] Great athlete! Between him and his son Bernard they can't hammer a nail!

BERNARD [*rushing in*]: The watchman's chasing Biff!

WILLY [*angrily*]: Shut up! He's not stealing anything!

LINDA [*alarmed, hurrying off left*]: Where is he? Biff, dear! [*She exits.*]

WILLY [*moving toward the left, away from* BEN]: There's nothing wrong. What's the matter with you?

BEN: Nervy boy. Good!

WILLY [*laughing*]: Oh, nerves of iron, that Biff!

CHARLEY: Don't know what it is. My New England man comes back and he's bleedin', they murdered him up there.

WILLY: It's contacts, Charley, I got important contacts!

CHARLEY [*sarcastically*]: Glad to hear it, Willy. Come in later, we'll shoot a little casino. I'll take some of your Portland money. [*He laughs at* WILLY *and exits.*]

WILLY [*turning to* BEN]: Business is bad, it's murderous. But not for me, of course.

BEN: I'll stop by on my way back to Africa.

WILLY [*longingly*]: Can't you stay a few days? You're just what I need, Ben, because I—I have a fine position here, but I—well, Dad left when I was such a baby and I never had a chance to talk to him and I still feel—kind of temporary about myself.

BEN: I'll be late for my train.

[*They are at opposite ends of the stage:*]

WILLY: Ben, my boys—can't we talk? They'd go into the jaws of hell for me, see, but I . . .

BEN: William, you're being first-rate with your boys. Outstanding, manly chaps!

WILLY [*hanging on to his words*]: Oh, Ben, that's good to hear! Because sometimes I'm afraid that I'm not teaching them the right kind of—Ben, how should I teach them?

BEN [*giving great weight to each word, and with a certain vicious audacity*]: William, when I walked into the jungle, I was seventeen. When I walked out I was twenty-one. And, by God, I was rich! [*He goes off into darkness around the right corner of the house.*]

WILLY: . . . was rich! That's just the spirit I want to imbue them with! To walk into a jungle! I was right! I was right! I was right!

[BEN *is gone, but* WILLY *is still speaking to him as* LINDA, *in nightgown and robe, enters the kitchen, glances around for* WILLY, *then goes to the door of the house, looks out and sees him. Comes down to his left. He looks at her.*]

LINDA: Willy, dear? Willy?

WILLY: I was right!

LINDA: Did you have some cheese? [*He can't answer.*] It's very late, darling. Come to bed, heh?

WILLY [*looking straight up*]: Gotta break your neck to see a star in this yard.

LINDA: You coming in?

WILLY: Whatever happened to that diamond watch fob? Remember? When Ben came from Africa that time? Didn't he give me a watch fob with a diamond in it?

LINDA: You pawned it, dear. Twelve, thirteen years ago. For Biff's radio correspondence course.

WILLY: Gee, that was a beautiful thing. I'll take a walk.

LINDA: But you're in your slippers.

WILLY [*starting to go around the house at the left*]: I was right! I was! [*Half to* LINDA, *as he goes, shaking his head.*] What a man! There was a man worth talking to. I was right!

LINDA [*calling after* WILLY]: But in your slippers, Willy!

[WILLY *is almost gone when* BIFF, *in his pajamas, comes down the stairs and enters the kitchen.*]

BIFF: What is he doing out there?

LINDA: Sh!

BIFF: God Almighty, Mom, how long has he been doing this?

LINDA: Don't, he'll hear you.

BIFF: What the hell is the matter with him?

LINDA: It'll pass by morning.

BIFF: Shouldn't we do anything?

LINDA: Oh, my dear, you should do a lot of things, but there's nothing to do, so go to sleep.

[HAPPY *comes down the stair and sits on the steps.*]

HAPPY: I never heard him so loud, Mom.

LINDA: Well, come around more often; you'll hear him. [*She sits down at the table and mends the lining of* WILLY'S *jacket.*]

BIFF: Why didn't you ever write me about this, Mom?

LINDA: How would I write to you? For over three months you had no address.

BIFF: I was on the move. But you know I thought of you all the time. You know that, don't you, pal?

LINDA: I know, dear, I know. But he likes to have a letter. Just to know that there's still a possibility for better things.

BIFF: He's not like this all the time, is he?

LINDA: It's when you come home he's always the worst.

BIFF: When I come home?

LINDA: When you write you're coming, he's all smiles, and talks about the future, and—he's just wonderful. And then the closer you seem to come, the more shaky he gets, and then, by the time you get here, he's arguing, and he seems angry at you. I think it's just that maybe he can't bring himself to—to open up to you. Why are you so hateful to each other? Why is that?

BIFF [*evasively*]: I'm not hateful, Mom.

LINDA: But you no sooner come in the door than you're fighting!

BIFF: I don't know why. I mean to change. I'm tryin', Mom, you understand?

LINDA: Are you home to stay now?

BIFF: I don't know. I want to look around, see what's doin'.

LINDA: Biff, you can't look around all your life, can you?

BIFF: I just can't take hold, Mom. I can't take hold of some kind of a life.

LINDA: Biff, a man is not a bird, to come and go with the springtime.

BIFF: Your hair . . . [*He touches her hair.*] Your hair got so gray.

LINDA: Oh, it's been gray since you were in high school. I just stopped dyeing it, that's all.

BIFF: Dye it again, will ya? I don't want my pal looking old. [*He smiles.*]

LINDA: You're such a boy! You think you can go away for a year and . . . You've got to get it into your head now that one day you'll knock on this door and there'll be strange people here . . .

BIFF: What are you talking about? You're not even sixty, Mom.

LINDA: But what about your father?

BIFF [*lamely*]: Well, I meant him too.

HAPPY: He admires Pop.

LINDA: Biff, dear, if you don't have any feeling for him, then you can't have any feeling for me.

BIFF: Sure I can, Mom.

LINDA: No. You can't just come to see me, because I love him. [*With a threat, but only a threat, of tears.*] He's the dearest man in the world to me, and I won't have anyone making him feel unwanted and low and blue. You've got to make up your mind now, darling, there's no leeway any more. Either he's your father and you pay him that respect, or else you're not to come here. I know he's not easy to get along with—nobody knows that better than me—but . . .

WILLY [*from the left, with a laugh*]: Hey, hey, Biffo!

BIFF [*starting to go out after* WILLY]: What the hell is the matter with him? [HAPPY *stops him.*]

LINDA: Don't—don't go near him!

BIFF: Stop making excuses for him! He always, always wiped the floor with you. Never had an ounce of respect for you.

HAPPY: He's always had respect for . . .

BIFF: What the hell do you know about it?

HAPPY [*surlily*]: Just don't call him crazy!

BIFF: He's got no character—Charley wouldn't do this. Not in his own house—spewing out that vomit from his mind.

HAPPY: Charley never had to cope with what he's got to.

BIFF: People are worse off than Willy Loman. Believe me, I've seen them!

LINDA: Then make Charley your father, Biff. You can't do that, can you? I don't say he's a great man. Willy Loman never made a lot of money. His name was never in the paper. He's not the finest character that ever lived. But he's a human being, and a terrible thing is happening to him. So attention must be paid. He's not to be allowed to fall into his grave like an old dog. Attention, attention must be finally paid to such a person. You called him crazy . . .

BIFF: I didn't mean . . .

LINDA: No, a lot of people think he's lost his—balance. But you don't have to be very smart to know what his trouble is. The man is exhausted.

HAPPY: Sure!

LINDA: A small man can be just as exhausted as a great man. He works for a company thirty-six years this March, opens up unheard-of territories to their trademark, and now in his old age they take his salary away.

HAPPY [*indignantly*]: I didn't know that, Mom.

LINDA: You never asked, my dear! Now that you get your spending money someplace else you don't trouble your mind with him.

HAPPY: But I gave you money last . . .

LINDA: Christmas time, fifty dollars! To fix the hot water it cost ninety-seven fifty! For five weeks he's been on straight commission, like a beginner, an unknown!

BIFF: Those ungrateful bastards!

LINDA: Are they any worse than his sons? When he brought them business, when he was young, they were glad to see him. But now his old friends, the old buyers that loved him so and always found some order to hand him in a pinch—they're all dead, retired. He used to be able to make six, seven calls a day in Boston. Now he takes his valises out of the car and puts them back and takes them out again and he's exhausted. Instead of walking he talks now. He drives seven hundred miles, and when he gets there no one knows him any more, no one welcomes him. And what goes through a man's mind, driving seven hundred miles home without having earned a cent? Why shouldn't he talk to himself? Why? When he has to go to Charley and borrow fifty dollars a week and pretend to me that it's his pay? How long can that go on? How long? You see what I'm sitting here and waiting for? And you tell me he has no character? The man who never worked a day but for your benefit? When does he get the medal for that? Is this his reward—to turn around at the age of sixty-three and find his sons, who he loved better than his life, one a philandering bum . . .

HAPPY: Mom!

LINDA: That's all you are, my baby! [*To* BIFF.] And you! What happened to the love you had for him? You were such pals! How you used to talk to him on the phone every night! How lonely he was till he could come home to you!

BIFF: All right, Mom. I'll live here in my room, and I'll get a job. I'll keep away from him, that's all.

LINDA: No, Biff. You can't stay here and fight all the time.

BIFF: He threw me out of this house, remember that.

LINDA: Why did he do that? I never knew why.

BIFF: Because I know he's a fake and he doesn't like anybody around who knows!

LINDA: Why a fake? In what way? What do you mean?

BIFF: Just don't lay it all at my feet. It's between me and him—that's all I have to say. I'll chip in from now on. He'll settle for half my pay check. He'll be all right. I'm going to bed. [*He starts for the stairs.*]

LINDA: He won't be all right.

BIFF [*turning on the stairs, furiously*]: I hate this city and I'll stay here. Now what do you want?

LINDA: He's dying, Biff.

[HAPPY *turns quickly to her, shocked.*]

BIFF [*after a pause*]: Why is he dying?

LINDA: He's been trying to kill himself.

BIFF [*with great horror*]: How?

LINDA: I live from day to day.

BIFF: What're you talking about?

LINDA: Remember I wrote you that he smashed up the car again? In February?

BIFF: Well?

LINDA: The insurance inspector came. He said that they have evidence. That all these accidents in the last year—weren't—weren't—accidents.

HAPPY: How can they tell that? That's a lie.

LINDA: It seems there's a woman . . . [*She takes a breath as:*]

BIFF [*sharply but contained*]: What woman?

LINDA [*simultaneously*]: . . . and this woman . . .

LINDA: What?

BIFF: Nothing. Go ahead.

LINDA: What did you say?

BIFF: Nothing, I just said what woman?

HAPPY: What about her?

LINDA: Well, it seems she was walking down the road and saw his car. She says that he wasn't driving fast at all, and that he didn't skid. She says he came to that little bridge, and then deliberately smashed into the railing, and it was only the shallowness of the water that saved him.

BIFF: Oh, no, he probably just fell asleep again.

LINDA: I don't think he fell asleep.

BIFF: Why not?

LINDA: Last month . . . [*With great difficulty.*] Oh, boys, it's so hard to say a thing like this! He's just a big stupid man to you, but I tell you there's more good in him than in many other people. [*She chokes, wipes her eyes.*] I was looking for a fuse. The lights blew out, and I went down the cellar. And behind the fuse box—it happened to fall out—was a length of rubber pipe—just short.

HAPPY: No kidding!

LINDA: There's a little attachment on the end of it. I knew right away. And sure enough, on the bottom of the water heater there's a new little nipple on the gas pipe.

HAPPY [*angrily*]: That—jerk.

BIFF: Did you have it taken off?

LINDA: I'm—I'm ashamed to. How can I mention it to him? Every day I go down and take away that little rubber pipe. But, when he comes home, I put it back where it was. How can I insult him that way? I don't know what to do. I live from day to day, boys. I tell you, I know every thought in his mind. It sounds so old-fashioned and silly, but I tell you he put his whole life into you and you've turned your backs on him. [*She is bent over in the chair, weeping, her face in her hands.*] Biff, I swear to God! Biff, his life is in your hands!

HAPPY [*to* BIFF]: How do you like that damned fool!

BIFF [*kissing her*]: All right, pal, all right. It's all settled now. I've been remiss. I know that, Mom. But now I'll stay, and I swear to you, I'll apply myself. [*Kneeling in front of her, in a fever of self-reproach.*] It's just—you see, Mom, I don't fit in business. Not that I won't try. I'll try, and I'll make good.

HAPPY: Sure you will. The trouble with you in business was you never tried to please people.

BIFF: I know, I . . .

HAPPY: Like when you worked for Harrison's. Bob Harrison said you were tops, and then you go and do some damn fool thing like whistling whole songs in the elevator like a comedian.

BIFF [*against* HAPPY]: So what? I like to whistle sometimes.

HAPPY: You don't raise a guy to a responsible job who whistles in the elevator!

LINDA: Well, don't argue about it now.

HAPPY: Like when you'd go off and swim in the middle of the day instead of taking the line around.

BIFF [*his resentment rising*]: Well, don't you run off? You take off sometimes, don't you? On a nice summer day?

HAPPY: Yeah, but I cover myself!

LINDA: Boys!

HAPPY: If I'm going to take a fade the boss can call any number where I'm supposed to be and they'll swear to him that I just left. I'll tell you something that I hate to say, Biff, but in the business world some of them think you're crazy.

BIFF [*angered*]: Screw the business world!

HAPPY: All right, screw it! Great, but cover yourself!

LINDA: Hap, Hap!

BIFF: I don't care what they think! They've laughed at Dad for years, and you know why? Because we don't belong in this nuthouse of a city! We should be mixing cement on some open plain or—or carpenters. A carpenter is allowed to whistle!

[WILLY *walks in from the entrance of the house, at left.*]

WILLY: Even your grandfather was better than a carpenter. [*Pause. They watch him.*] You never grew up. Bernard does not whistle in the elevator, I assure you.

BIFF [*as though to laugh* WILLY *out of it*]: Yeah, but you do, Pop.

WILLY: I never in my life whistled in an elevator! And who in the business world thinks I'm crazy?

BIFF: I didn't mean it like that, Pop. Now don't make a whole thing out of it, will ya?

WILLY: Go back to the West! Be a carpenter, a cowboy, enjoy yourself!

LINDA: Willy, he was just saying . . .

WILLY: I heard what he said!

HAPPY [*trying to quiet* WILLY]: Hey, Pop, come on now . . .

WILLY [*continuing over* HAPPY'*s line*]: They laugh at me, heh? Go to Filene's, go to the Hub, go to Slattery's, Boston. Call out the name Willy Loman and see what happens! Big shot!

BIFF: All right, Pop.

WILLY: Big!

BIFF: All right!

WILLY: Why do you always insult me?

BIFF: I didn't say a word. [*To* LINDA.] Did I say a word?

LINDA: He didn't say anything, Willy.

WILLY [*going to the doorway of the living room*]: All right, good night, good night.

LINDA: Willy, dear, he just decided . . .

WILLY [*to* BIFF]: If you get tired hanging around tomorrow, paint the ceiling I put up in the living room.

BIFF: I'm leaving early tomorrow.

HAPPY: He's going to see Bill Oliver, Pop.

WILLY [*interestedly*]: Oliver? For what?

BIFF [*with reserve, but trying, trying*]: He always said he'd stake me. I'd like to go into business, so maybe I can take him up on it.

LINDA: Isn't that wonderful?

WILLY: Don't interrupt. What's wonderful about it? There's fifty men in the City of New York who'd stake him. [*To* BIFF.] Sporting goods?

BIFF: I guess so. I know something about it and . . .

WILLY: He knows something about it! You know sporting goods better than Spalding, for God's sake! How much is he giving you?

BIFF: I don't know, I didn't even see him yet, but . . .

WILLY: Then what're you talkin' about?

BIFF [*getting angry*]: Well, all I said was I'm gonna see him, that's all!

WILLY [*turning away*]: Ah, you're counting your chickens again.

BIFF [*starting left for the stairs*]: Oh, Jesus, I'm going to sleep!

WILLY [*calling after him*]: Don't curse in this house!

BIFF [*turning*]: Since when did you get so clean?

HAPPY [*trying to stop them*]: Wait a . . .

WILLY: Don't use that language to me! I won't have it!

HAPPY [*grabbing* BIFF, *shouts*]: Wait a minute! I got an idea. I got a feasible idea. Come here, Biff, let's talk this over now, let's talk some sense here. When I was down in Florida last time, I thought of a great idea to sell sporting goods. It just came back to me. You and I, Biff—we have a line, the Loman Line. We train a couple of weeks, and put on a couple of exhibitions, see?

WILLY: That's an idea!

HAPPY: Wait! We form two basketball teams, see? Two water-polo teams. We play each other. It's a million dollars' worth of publicity. Two brothers, see? The Loman Brothers. Displays in the Royal Palms—all the hotels. And banners over the ring and the basketball court: "Loman Brothers." Baby, we could sell sporting goods!

WILLY: That is a one-million-dollar idea!

LINDA: Marvelous!

BIFF: I'm in great shape as far as that's concerned.

HAPPY: And the beauty of it is, Biff, it wouldn't be like a business. We'd be out playin' ball again . . .

BIFF [*enthused*]: Yeah, that's . . .

WILLY: Million-dollar . . .

HAPPY: And you wouldn't get fed up with it, Biff. It'd be the family again. There'd be the old honor, and comradeship, and if you wanted to go off for a swim or some-thin'—well, you'd do it! Without some smart cooky gettin' up ahead of you!

WILLY: Lick the world! You guys together could absolutely lick the civilized world.

BIFF: I'll see Oliver tomorrow. Hap, if we could work that out . . .

LINDA: Maybe things are beginning to . . .

WILLY [*wildly enthused, to* LINDA]: Stop interrupting! [*To* BIFF.] But don't wear sport jacket and slacks when you see Oliver.

BIFF: No, I'll . . .

WILLY: A business suit, and talk as little as possible, and don't crack any jokes.

BIFF: He did like me. Always liked me.

LINDA: He loved you!

WILLY [*to* LINDA]: Will you stop! [*To* BIFF.] Walk in very serious. You are not applying for a boy's job. Money is to pass. Be quiet, fine, and serious. Everybody likes a kidder, but nobody lends him money.

HAPPY: I'll try to get some myself, Biff. I'm sure I can.

WILLY: I see great things for you kids, I think your troubles are over. But remember, start big and you'll end big. Ask for fifteen. How much you gonna ask for?

BIFF: Gee, I don't know . . .

WILLY: And don't say "Gee." "Gee" is a boy's word. A man walking in for fifteen thousand dollars does not say "Gee!"

BIFF: Ten, I think, would be top though.

WILLY: Don't be so modest. You always started too low. Walk in with a big laugh. Don't look worried. Start off with a couple of your good stories to lighten things up. It's not what you say, it's how you say it—because personality always wins the day.

LINDA: Oliver always thought the highest of him . . .

WILLY: Will you let me talk?

BIFF: Don't yell at her, Pop, will ya?

WILLY [*angrily*]: I was talking, wasn't I?

BIFF: I don't like you yelling at her all the time, and I'm tellin' you, that's all.

WILLY: What're you, takin' over this house?

LINDA: Willy . . .

WILLY [*turning to her*]: Don't take his side all the time, goddammit!

BIFF [*furiously*]: Stop yelling at her!

WILLY [*suddenly pulling on his cheek, beaten down, guilt ridden*]: Give my best to Bill Oliver— he may remember me. [*He exits through the living room doorway.*]

LINDA [*her voice subdued*]: What'd you have to start that for? [BIFF *turns away.*] You see how sweet he was as soon as you talked hopefully? [*She goes over to* BIFF.] Come up and say good night to him. Don't let him go to bed that way.

HAPPY: Come on, Biff, let's buck him up.

LINDA: Please, dear. Just say good night. It takes so little to make him happy. Come. [*She goes through the living room doorway, calling upstairs from within the living room.*] Your pajamas are hanging in the bathroom, Willy!

HAPPY [*looking toward where* LINDA *went out*]: What a woman! They broke the mold when they made her. You know that, Biff?

BIFF: He's off salary. My God, working on commission!

HAPPY: Well, let's face it: he's no hot-shot selling man. Except that sometimes, you have to admit, he's a sweet personality.

BIFF [*deciding*]: Lend me ten bucks, will ya? I want to buy some new ties.

HAPPY: I'll take you to a place I know. Beautiful stuff. Wear one of my striped shirts tomorrow.

BIFF: She got gray. Mom got awful old. Gee, I'm gonna go in to Oliver tomorrow and knock him for a . . .

HAPPY: Come on up. Tell that to Dad. Let's give him a whirl. Come on.

BIFF [*steamed up*]: You know, with ten thousand bucks, boy!

HAPPY [*as they go into the living room*]: That's the talk, Biff, that's the first time I've heard the old confidence out of you! [*From within the living room, fading off.*] You're gonna live with me, kid, and any babe you want just say the word . . . [*The last lines are hardly heard. They are mounting the stairs to their parents' bedroom.*]

LINDA [*entering her bedroom and addressing* WILLY, *who is in the bathroom. She is straightening the bed for him*]. Can you do anything about the shower? It drips.

WILLY [*from the bathroom*]: All of a sudden everything falls to pieces. Goddam plumbing, oughta be sued, those people. I hardly finished putting it in and the thing . . . [*His words rumble off.*]

LINDA: I'm just wondering if Oliver will remember him. You think he might?

WILLY [*coming out of the bathroom in his pajamas*]: Remember him? What's the matter with you, you crazy? If he'd've stayed with Oliver he'd be on top by now! Wait'll Oliver gets a look at him. You don't know the average caliber any more. The average young man today—[*he is getting into bed*]—is got a caliber of zero. Greatest thing in the world for him was to bum around.

[BIFF *and* HAPPY *enter the bedroom. Slight pause.*]

WILLY [*stops short, looking at* BIFF]: Glad to hear it, boy.

HAPPY: He wanted to say good night to you, sport.

WILLY [*to* BIFF]: Yeah. Knock him dead, boy. What'd you want to tell me?

BIFF: Just take it easy, Pop. Good night. [*He turns to go.*]

WILLY [*unable to resist*]: And if anything falls off the desk while you're talking to him—like a package or something—don't you pick it up. They have office boys for that.

LINDA: I'll make a big breakfast . . .

WILLY: Will you let me finish? [*To* BIFF.] Tell him you were in the business in the West. Not farm work.

BIFF: All right, Dad.

LINDA: I think everything . . .

WILLY [*going right through her speech*]: And don't undersell yourself. No less than fifteen thousand dollars.

BIFF [*unable to bear him*]: Okay. Good night, Mom. [*He starts moving.*]

WILLY: Because you got a greatness in you, Biff, remember that. You got all kinds a greatness . . . [*He lies back, exhausted.* BIFF *walks out.*]

LINDA [*calling after* BIFF]: Sleep well, darling!

HAPPY: I'm gonna get married, Mom. I wanted to tell you.

LINDA: Go to sleep, dear.

HAPPY [*going*]: I just wanted to tell you.

WILLY: Keep up the good work. [HAPPY *exits.*] God . . . remember that Ebbets Field game? The championship of the city?

LINDA: Just rest. Should I sing to you?

WILLY: Yeah. Sing to me. [LINDA *hums a soft lullaby.*] When that team came out—he was the tallest, remember?

LINDA: Oh, yes. And in gold.

[BIFF *enters the darkened kitchen, takes a cigarette, and leaves the house. He comes downstage into a golden pool of light. He smokes, staring at the night.*]

WILLY: Like a young god. Hercules—something like that. And the sun, the sun all around him. Remember how he waved to me? Right up from the field, with the representatives of three colleges standing by? And the buyers I brought, and the cheers when he came out—Loman, Loman, Loman! God Almighty, he'll be great yet. A star like that, magnificent, can never really fade away!

[*The light on* WILLY *is fading. The gas heater begins to glow through the kitchen wall, near the stairs, a blue flame beneath red coils.*]

LINDA [*timidly*]: Willy dear, what has he got against you?

WILLY: I'm so tired. Don't talk any more.

[BIFF *slowly returns to the kitchen. He stops, stares toward the heater.*]

LINDA: Will you ask Howard to let you work in New York?

WILLY: First thing in the morning. Everything'll be all right.

[BIFF *reaches behind the heater and draws out a length of rubber tubing. He is horrified and turns his head toward* WILLY's *room, still dimly lit, from which the strains of* LINDA's *desperate but monotonous humming rise.*]

WILLY [*staring through the window into the moonlight*]: Gee, look at the moon moving between the buildings!

[BIFF *wraps the tubing around his hand and quickly goes up the stairs.*]

ACT II

Scene Music is heard, gay and bright. The curtain rises as the music fades away. WILLY, *in shirt sleeves, is sitting at the kitchen table, sipping coffee, his hat in his lap.* LINDA *is filling his cup when she can.*

WILLY: Wonderful coffee. Meal in itself.

LINDA: Can I make you some eggs?

WILLY: No. Take a breath.

LINDA: You look so rested, dear.

WILLY: I slept like a dead one. First time in months. Imagine, sleeping till ten on a Tuesday morning. Boys left nice and early, heh?

LINDA: They were out of here by eight o'clock.

WILLY: Good work!

LINDA: It was so thrilling to see them leaving together. I can't get over the shaving lotion in this house!

WILLY [*smiling*]: Mmm . . .

LINDA: Biff was very changed this morning. His whole attitude seemed to be hopeful. He couldn't wait to get downtown to see Oliver.

WILLY: He's heading for a change. There's no question, there simply are certain men that take longer to get—solidified. How did he dress?

LINDA: His blue suit. He's so handsome in that suit. He could be a—anything in that suit!

[WILLY *gets up from the table.* LINDA *holds his jacket for him.*]

WILLY: There's no question, no question at all. Gee, on the way home tonight I'd like to buy some seeds.

LINDA [*laughing*]: That'd be wonderful. But not enough sun gets back there. Nothing'll grow any more.

WILLY: You wait, kid, before it's all over we're gonna get a little place out in the country, and I'll raise some vegetables, a couple of chickens . . .

LINDA: You'll do it yet, dear.

[WILLY *walks out of his jacket.* LINDA *follows him.*]

WILLY: And they'll get married, and come for a weekend. I'd build a little guest house. 'Cause I got so many fine tools, all I'd need would be a little lumber and some peace of mind.

LINDA [*joyfully*]: I sewed the lining . . .

WILLY: I could build two guest houses, so they'd both come. Did he decide how much he's going to ask Oliver for?

LINDA [*getting him into the jacket*]: He didn't mention it, but I imagine ten or fifteen thousand. You going to talk to Howard today?

WILLY: Yeah. I'll put it to him straight and simple. He'll just have to take me off the road.

LINDA: And Willy, don't forget to ask for a little advance, because we've got the insurance premium. It's the grace period now.

WILLY: That's a hundred . . . ?

LINDA: A hundred and eight, sixty-eight. Because we're a little short again.

WILLY: Why are we short?

LINDA: Well, you had the motor job on the car . . .

WILLY: That goddam Studebaker!

LINDA: And you got one more payment on the refrigerator . . .

WILLY: But it just broke again!

LINDA: Well, it's old, dear.

WILLY: I told you we should've bought a well-advertised machine. Charley bought a General Electric and it's twenty years old and it's still good, that son-of-a-bitch.

LINDA: But, Willy . . .

WILLY: Whoever heard of a Hastings refrigerator? Once in my life I would like to own something outright before it's broken! I'm always in a race with the junkyard! I just finished paying for the car and it's on its last legs. The refrigerator consumes belts like a goddam maniac. They time those things. They time them so when you finally paid for them, they're used up.

LINDA [*buttoning up his jacket as he unbuttons it*]: All told, about two hundred dollars would carry us, dear. But that includes the last payment on the mortgage. After this payment, Willy, the house belongs to us.

WILLY: It's twenty-five years!

LINDA: Biff was nine years old when we bought it.

WILLY: Well, that's a great thing. To weather a twenty-five year mortgage is . . .

LINDA: It's an accomplishment.

WILLY: All the cement, the lumber, the reconstruction I put in this house! There ain't a crack to be found in it any more.

LINDA: Well, it served its purpose.

WILLY: What purpose? Some stranger'll come along, move in, and that's that. If only Biff would take this house, and raise a family . . . [*He starts to go.*] Good-by, I'm late.

LINDA [*suddenly remembering*]: Oh, I forgot! You're supposed to meet them for dinner.

WILLY: Me?

LINDA: At Frank's Chop House on Forty-eighth near Sixth Avenue.

WILLY: Is that so! How about you?

LINDA: No, just the three of you. They're gonna blow you to a big meal!

WILLY: Don't say! Who thought of that?

LINDA: Biff came to me this morning, Willy, and he said, "Tell Dad, we want to blow him to a big meal." Be there six o'clock. You and your two boys are going to have dinner.

WILLY: Gee whiz! That's really somethin'. I'm gonna knock Howard for a loop, kid. I'll get an advance, and I'll come home with a New York job. Goddammit, now I'm gonna do it!

LINDA: Oh, that's the spirit, Willy!

WILLY: I will never get behind a wheel the rest of my life!

LINDA: It's changing, Willy, I can feel it changing!

WILLY: Beyond a question. G'by, I'm late. [*He starts to go again.*]

LINDA [*calling after him as she runs to the kitchen table for a handkerchief*]: You got your glasses?

WILLY [*feels for them, then comes back in*]: Yeah, yeah, got my glasses.

LINDA [*giving him the handkerchief*]: And a handkerchief.

WILLY: Yeah, handkerchief.

LINDA: And your saccharine?

WILLY: Yeah, my saccharine.

LINDA: Be careful on the subway stairs.

[*She kisses him, and a silk stocking is seen hanging from her hand.* WILLY *notices it.*]

WILLY: Will you stop mending stockings? At least while I'm in the house. It gets me nervous. I can't tell you. Please.

[LINDA *hides the stocking in her hand as she follows* WILLY *across the forestage in front of the house.*]

LINDA: Remember, Frank's Chop House.

WILLY [*passing the apron*]: Maybe beets would grow out there.

LINDA [*laughing*]: But you tried so many times.

WILLY: Yeah. Well, don't work hard today. [*He disappears around the right corner of the house.*]

LINDA: Be careful!

[*As* WILLY *vanishes,* LINDA *waves to him. Suddenly the phone rings. She runs across the stage and into the kitchen and lifts it.*]

LINDA: Hello? Oh, Biff! I'm so glad you called, I just . . . Yes, sure, I just told him. Yes, he'll be there for dinner at six o'clock, I didn't forget. Listen, I was just dying to tell you. You know that little rubber pipe I told you about? That he connected to the gas heater? I finally decided to go down the cellar this morning and take it away and destroy it. But it's gone! Imagine? he took it away himself, it isn't there! [*She listens.*] When? Oh, then you took it. Oh—nothing, it's just that I'd hoped he'd taken it away himself. Oh, I'm not worried, darling, because this morning he left in such high spirits, it was like the old days! I'm not afraid any more. Did Mr. Oliver see you? . . . Well, you wait there then. And make a nice impression on him, darling. Just don't perspire too much before you see him. And have a nice time with Dad. He may have big news too! . . . That's right, a New York job. And be sweet to him tonight, dear. Be loving to him. Because he's only a little boat looking for a harbor. [*She is trembling with sorrow and joy.*] Oh, that's wonderful, Biff, you'll save his life. Thanks, darling. Just put your arm around him when he comes into the restaurant. Give him a smile. That's the boy . . . Good-by, dear . . . You got your comb? . . . That's fine. Good-by, Biff dear.

[*In the middle of her speech,* HOWARD WAGNER, *thirty-six, wheels on a small typewriter table on which is a wire-recording machine and proceeds to plug it in. This is on the left forestage. Light slowly fades on* LINDA *as it rises on* HOWARD. HOWARD *is intent on threading the machine and only glances over his shoulder as* WILLY *appears.*]

WILLY: Pst! Pst!

HOWARD: Hello, Willy, come in.

WILLY: Like to have a little talk with you, Howard.

HOWARD: Sorry to keep you waiting. I'll be with you in a minute.

WILLY: What's that, Howard?

HOWARD: Didn't you ever see one of these? Wire recorder.

WILLY: Oh. Can we talk a minute?

HOWARD: Records things. Just got delivery yesterday. Been driving me crazy, the most terrific machine I ever saw in my life. I was up all night with it.

WILLY: What do you do with it?

HOWARD: I bought it for dictation, but you can do anything with it. Listen to this. I had it home last night. Listen to what I picked up. The first one is my daughter. Get this. [*He flicks the switch and "Roll out the Barrel" is heard being whistled.*] Listen to that kid whistle.

WILLY: That is lifelike, isn't it?

HOWARD: Seven years old. Get that tone.

WILLY: Ts, ts. Like to ask a little favor if you . . .

[*The whistling breaks off, and the voice of* HOWARD's *daughter is heard.*]

HIS DAUGHTER: "Now you, Daddy."

HOWARD: She's crazy for me! [*Again the same song is whistled.*] That's me! Ha! [*He winks.*]

WILLY: You're very good!

[*The whistling breaks off again. The machine runs silent for a moment.*]

HOWARD: Sh! Get this now, this is my son.

HIS SON: "The capital of Alabama is Montgomery; the capital of Arizona is Phoenix; the capital of Arkansas is Little Rock; the capital of California is Sacramento . . ." [*and on, and on.*]

HOWARD [*holding up five fingers*]: Five years old, Willy!

WILLY: He'll make an announcer some day!

HIS SON [*continuing*]: "The capital . . ."

HOWARD: Get that—alphabetical order! [*The machine breaks off suddenly.*] Wait a minute. The maid kicked the plug out.

WILLY: It certainly is a . . .

HOWARD: Sh, for God's sake!

HIS SON: "It's nine o'clock, Bulova watch time. So I have to go to sleep."

WILLY: That really is . . .

HOWARD: Wait a minute! The next is my wife.

[*They wait.*]

HOWARD'S VOICE: "Go on, say something." [*Pause.*] "Well, you gonna talk?"

HIS WIFE: "I can't think of anything."

HOWARD'S VOICE: "Well, talk—it's turning."

HIS WIFE [*shyly, beaten*]: "Hello." [*Silence.*] "Oh, Howard, I can't talk into this . . ."

HOWARD [*snapping the machine off*]: That was my wife.

WILLY: That is a wonderful machine. Can we . . .

HOWARD: I tell you, Willy, I'm gonna take my camera, and my bandsaw, and all my hobbies, and out they go. This is the most fascinating relaxation I ever found.

WILLY: I think I'll get one myself.

HOWARD: Sure, they're only a hundred and a half. You can't do without it. Supposing you wanna hear Jack Benny, see? But you can't be at home at that hour. So you tell the maid to turn the radio on when Jack Benny comes on, and this automatically goes on with the radio . . .

WILLY: And when you come home you . . .

HOWARD: You can come home twelve o'clock, one o'clock, any time you like, and you get yourself a Coke and sit yourself down, throw the switch, and there's Jack Benny's program in the middle of the night!

WILLY: I'm definitely going to get one. Because lots of times I'm on the road, and I think to myself, what I must be missing on the radio!

HOWARD: Don't you have a radio in the car?

WILLY: Well, yeah, but who ever thinks of turning it on?

HOWARD: Say, aren't you supposed to be in Boston?

WILLY: That's what I want to talk to you about, Howard. You got a minute? [*He draws a chair in from the wing.*]

HOWARD: What happened? What're you doing here?

WILLY: Well . . .

HOWARD: You didn't crack up again, did you?

WILLY: Oh, no. No . . .

HOWARD: Geez, you had me worried there for a minute. What's the trouble?

WILLY: Well, tell you the truth, Howard. I've come to the decision that I'd rather not travel any more.

HOWARD: Not travel! Well, what'll you do?

WILLY: Remember, Christmas time, when you had the party here? You said you'd try to think of some spot for me here in town.

HOWARD: With us?

WILLY: Well, sure.

HOWARD: Oh, yeah, yeah. I remember. Well, I couldn't think of anything for you, Willy.

WILLY: I tell ya, Howard. The kids are all grown up, y'know. I don't need much any more. If I could take home—well, sixty-five dollars a week, I could swing it.

HOWARD: Yeah, but Willy, see I . . .

WILLY: I tell ya why, Howard. Speaking frankly and between the two of us, y'know—I'm just a little tired.

HOWARD: Oh, I could understand that, Willy. But you're a road man, Willy, and we do a road business. We've only got a half-dozen salesmen on the floor here.

WILLY: God knows, Howard. I never asked a favor of any man. But I was with the firm when your father used to carry you in here in his arms.

HOWARD: I know that, Willy, but . . .

WILLY: Your father came to me the day you were born and asked me what I thought of the name of Howard, may he rest in peace.

HOWARD: I appreciate that, Willy, but there just is no spot here for you. If I had a spot I'd slam you right in, but I just don't have a single solitary spot.

[*He looks for his lighter.* WILLY *has picked it up and gives it to him. Pause.*]

WILLY [*with increasing anger*]: Howard, all I need to set my table is fifty dollars a week.
HOWARD: But where am I going to put you, kid?
WILLY: Look, it isn't a question of whether I can sell merchandise, is it?
HOWARD: No, but it's a business, kid, and everybody's gotta pull his own weight.
WILLY [*desperately*]: Just let me tell you a story, Howard . . .
HOWARD: 'Cause you gotta admit, business is business.
WILLY [*angrily*]: Business is definitely business, but just listen for a minute. You don't understand this. When I was a boy—eighteen, nineteen—I was already on the road. And there was a question in my mind as to whether selling had a future for me. Because in those days I had a yearning to go to Alaska. See, there were three gold strikes in one month in Alaska, and I felt like going out. Just for the ride, you might say.
HOWARD [*barely interested*]: Don't say.
WILLY: Oh, yeah, my father lived many years in Alaska. He was an adventurous man. We've got quite a little streak of self-reliance in our family. I thought I'd go out with my older brother and try to locate him, and maybe settle in the North with the old man. And I was almost decided to go, when I met a salesman in the Parker House. His was Dave Singleman. And he was eighty-four years old, and he'd drummed merchandise in thirty-one states. And old Dave, he'd go up to his room, y'understand, put on his green velvet slippers—I'll never forget—and pick up his phone and call the buyers, and without ever leaving his room, at the age of eighty-four, he made his living. And when I saw that, I realized that selling was the greatest career a man could want. 'Cause what could be more satisfying than to be able to go, at the age of eighty-four, into twenty or thirty different cities, and pick up a phone, and be remembered and loved and helped by so many different people? Do you know? when he died—and by the way he died the death of a salesman, in his green velvet slippers in the smoker of the New York, New Haven and Hartford, going into Boston—when he died, hundreds of salesmen and buyers were at his funeral. Things were sad on a lotta trains for months after that. [*He stands up.* HOWARD *has not looked at him.*] In those days there was personality in it, Howard. There was respect, and comradeship, and gratitude in it. Today, it's all cut and dried, and there's no chance for bringing friendship to bear—or personality. You see what I mean? They don't know me any more.
HOWARD [*moving away, to the right*]: That's just the thing, Willy.
WILLY: If I had forty dollars a week—that's all I'd need. Forty dollars, Howard.
HOWARD: Kid, I can't take blood from a stone, I . . .
WILLY [*desperation is on him now*]: Howard, the year Al Smith was nominated, your father came to me and . . .
HOWARD [*starting to go off*]: I've got to see some people, kid.
WILLY [*stopping him*]: I'm talking about your father! There were promises made across this desk! You mustn't tell me you've got people to see—I put thirty-four years into

this firm, Howard, and now I can't pay my insurance! You can't eat the orange and throw the peel away—a man is not a piece of fruit! [*After a pause.*] Now pay attention. Your father—in 1928 I had a big year. I averaged a hundred and seventy dollars a week in commissions.

HOWARD [*impatiently*]: Now, Willy, you never averaged . . .

WILLY [*banging his hand on the desk*]: I averaged a hundred and seventy dollars a week in the year of 1928! And your father came to me—or rather, I was in the office here—it was right over this desk—and he put his hand on my shoulder . . .

HOWARD [*getting up*]: You'll have to excuse me, Willy, I gotta see some people. Pull yourself together. [*Going out.*] I'll be back in a little while.

[*On* HOWARD's *exit, the light on his chair grows very bright and strange.*]

WILLY: Pull myself together! What the hell did I say to him? My God, I was yelling at him! How could I? [WILLY *breaks off, staring at the light, which occupies the chair, animating it. He approaches this chair, standing across the desk from it.*] Frank, Frank, don't you remember what you told me that time? How you put your hand on my shoulder, and Frank . . . [*He leans on the desk and as he speaks the dead man's name he accidentally switches on the recorder, and instantly*]

HOWARD'S SON: ". . . of New York is Albany. The capital of Ohio is Cincinnati, the capital of Rhode Island is . . ." [*The recitation continues.*]

WILLY [*leaping away with fright, shouting*]: Ha! Howard! Howard! Howard!

HOWARD [*rushing in*]: What happened?

WILLY [*pointing at the machine, which continues nasally, childishly, with the capital cities*]: Shut it off! Shut it off!

HOWARD [*pulling the plug out*]: Look, Willy . . .

WILLY [*pressing his hands to his eyes*]: I gotta get myself some coffee. I'll get some coffee . . .

[WILLY *starts to walk out.* HOWARD *stops him.*]

HOWARD [*rolling up the cord*]: Willy, look . . .

WILLY: I'll go to Boston.

HOWARD: Willy, you can't go to Boston for us.

WILLY: Why can't I go?

HOWARD: I don't want you to represent us. I've been meaning to tell you for a long time now.

WILLY: Howard, are you firing me?

HOWARD: I think you need a good long rest, Willy.

WILLY: Howard . . .

HOWARD: And when you feel better, come back, and we'll see if we can work something out.

WILLY: But I gotta earn money, Howard. I'm in no position to . . .

HOWARD: Where are your sons? Why don't your sons give you a hand?

WILLY: They're working on a very big deal.

HOWARD: This is no time for false pride, Willy. You go to your sons and you tell them that you're tired. You've got two great boys, haven't you?

WILLY: Oh, no question, no question, but in the meantime . . .

HOWARD: Then that's that, heh?

WILLY: All right, I'll go to Boston tomorrow.

HOWARD: No, no.

WILLY: I can't throw myself on my sons. I'm not a cripple!

HOWARD: Look, kid, I'm busy this morning.

WILLY [*grasping* HOWARD's *arm*]: Howard, you've got to let me go to Boston!

HOWARD [*hard, keeping himself under control*]: I've got a line of people to see this morning. Sit down, take five minutes, and pull yourself together, and then go home, will ya? I need the office, Willy. [*He starts to go, turns, remembering the recorder, starts to push off the table holding the recorder.*] Oh, yeah. Whenever you can this week, stop by and drop off the samples. You'll feel better, Willy, and then come back and we'll talk. Pull yourself together, kid, there's people outside.

[HOWARD *exits, pushing the table off left.* WILLY *stares into space, exhausted. Now the music is heard*—BEN's *music—first distantly, then closer, closer. As* WILLY *speaks,* BEN *enters from the right. He carries valise and umbrella.*]

WILLY: Oh, Ben, how did you do it? What is the answer? Did you wind up the Alaska deal already?

BEN: Doesn't take much time if you know what you're doing. Just a short business trip. Boarding ship in an hour. Wanted to say good-by.

WILLY: Ben, I've got to talk to you.

BEN [*glancing at his watch*]: Haven't the time, William.

WILLY [*crossing the apron to* BEN]: Ben, nothing's working out. I don't know what to do.

BEN: Now, look here, William. I've bought timberland in Alaska and I need a man to look after things for me.

WILLY: God, timberland! Me and my boys in those grand outdoors!

BEN: You've a new continent at your doorstep, William. Get out of these cities, they're full of talk and time payments and courts of law. Screw on your fists and you can fight for a fortune up there.

WILLY: Yes, yes! Linda, Linda!

[LINDA *enters as of old, with the wash.*]

LINDA: Oh, you're back?

BEN: I haven't much time.

WILLY: No, wait! Linda, he's got a proposition for me in Alaska.

LINDA: But you've got . . . [*To* BEN.] He's got a beautiful job here.

WILLY: But in Alaska, kid, I could . . .

LINDA: You're doing well enough, Willy!

BEN [*to* LINDA]: Enough for what, my dear?

LINDA [*frightened of* BEN *and angry at him*]: Don't say those things to him! Enough to be

happy right here, right now. [*To* WILLY, *while* BEN *laughs.*] Why must everybody conquer the world? You're well liked, and the boys love you, and someday—[*To* BEN]—why, old man Wagner told him just the other day that if he keeps it up he'll be a member of the firm, didn't he, Willy?

WILLY: Sure, sure. I am building something with this firm, Ben, and if a man is building something he must be on the right track, mustn't he?

BEN: What are you building? Lay your hand on it. Where is it?

WILLY [*hesitantly*]: That's true, Linda, there's nothing.

LINDA: Why? [*To* BEN.] There's a man eighty-four years old—

WILLY: That's right, Ben, that's right. When I look at that man I say, what is there to worry about?

BEN: Bah!

WILLY: It's true, Ben. All he has to do is go into any city, pick up the phone, and he's making his living and you know why?

BEN [*picking up his valise*]: I've got to go.

WILLY [*holding* BEN *back*]: Look at this boy!

[BIFF, *in his high school sweater, enters carrying suitcase.* HAPPY *carries* BIFF'*s shoulder guards, gold helmet, and football pants.*]

WILLY: Without a penny to his name, three great universities are begging for him, and from there the sky's the limit, because it's not what you do, Ben. It's who you know and the smile on your face! It's contacts, Ben, contacts! The whole wealth of Alaska passes over the lunch table at the Commodore Hotel, and that's the wonder, the wonder of this country, that a man can end with diamonds here on the basis of being liked! [*He turns to* BIFF.] And that's why when you get out on that field today it's important. Because thousands of people will be rooting for you and loving you. [*To* BEN, *who has again begun to leave.*] And Ben! when he walks into a business office his name will sound out like a bell and all the doors will open to him! I've seen it, Ben, I've seen it a thousand times! You can't feel it with your hand like timber, but it's there!

BEN: Good-by, William.

WILLY: Ben, am I right? Don't you think I'm right? I value your advice.

BEN: There's a new continent at your doorstep, William. You could walk out rich. Rich! [*He is gone.*]

WILLY: We'll do it here, Ben! You hear me? We're gonna do it here!

[YOUNG BERNARD *rushes in. The gay music of the* BOYS *is heard.*]

BERNARD: Oh, gee, I was afraid you left already!

WILLY: Why? What time is it?

BERNARD: It's half-past one!

WILLY: Well, come on, everybody! Ebbets Field next stop! Where's the pennants? [*He rushes through the wall-line of the kitchen and out into the living room.*]

LINDA [*to* BIFF]: Did you pack fresh underwear?

BIFF [*who has been limbering up*]: I want to go!

BERNARD: Biff, I'm carrying your helmet, ain't I?

HAPPY: No, I'm carrying the helmet.

BERNARD: Oh, Biff, you promised me.

HAPPY: I'm carrying the helmet.

BERNARD: How am I going to get in the locker room?

LINDA: Let him carry the shoulder guards. [*She puts her coat and hat on in the kitchen.*]

BERNARD: Can I, Biff? 'Cause I told everybody I'm going to be in the locker room.

HAPPY: In Ebbets Field it's the clubhouse.

BERNARD: I meant the clubhouse. Biff!

HAPPY: Biff!

BIFF [*grandly, after a slight pause*]: Let him carry the shoulder guards.

HAPPY [*as he gives* BERNARD *the shoulder guards*]: Stay close to us now.

[WILLY *rushes in with the pennants.*]

WILLY [*handing them out*]: Everybody wave when Biff comes out on the field. [HAPPY *and* BERNARD *run off.*] You set now, boy?

[*The music has died away.*]

BIFF: Ready to go, Pop. Every muscle is ready.

WILLY [*at the edge of the apron*]: You realize what this means?

BIFF: That's right, Pop.

WILLY [*feeling* BIFF'*s muscles*]: You're comin' home this afternoon captain of the All-Scholastic Championship Team of the City of New York.

BIFF: I got it, Pop. And remember, pal, when I take off my helmet, that touchdown is for you.

WILLY: Let's go! [*He is starting out, with his arm around* BIFF, *when* CHARLEY *enters, as of old, in knickers.*] I got no room for you, Charley.

CHARLEY: Room? For what?

WILLY: In the car.

CHARLEY: You goin' for a ride? I wanted to shoot some casino.

WILLY [*furiously*]: Casino! [*Incredulously.*] Don't you realize what today is?

LINDA: Oh, he knows, Willy. He's just kidding you.

WILLY: That's nothing to kid about!

CHARLEY: No, Linda, what's goin on?

LINDA: He's playing in Ebbets Field.

CHARLEY: Baseball in this weather?

WILLY: Don't talk to him. Come on, come on! [*He is pushing them out.*]

CHARLEY: Wait a minute, didn't you hear the news?

WILLY: What?

CHARLEY: Don't you listen to the radio? Ebbets Field just blew up.

WILLY: You go to hell! [CHARLEY *laughs. Pushing them out.*] Come on, come on! We're late.

CHARLEY [*as they go*]: Knock a homer, Biff, knock a homer!

WILLY [*the last to leave, turning to* CHARLEY]: I don't think that was funny, Charley. This is the greatest day of his life.

CHARLEY: Willy, when are you going to grow up?

WILLY: Yeah, heh? When this game is over, Charley, you'll be laughing out of the other side of your face. They'll be calling him another Red Grange. Twenty-five thousand a year.

CHARLEY [*kidding*]: Is that so?

WILLY: Yeah, that's so.

CHARLEY: Well, then, I'm sorry, Willy. But tell me something.

WILLY: What?

CHARLEY: Who is Red Grange?

WILLY: Put up your hands. Goddam you, put up your hands!

[CHARLEY, *chuckling, shakes his head and walks away, around the left corner of the stage.* WILLY *follows him. The music rises to a mocking frenzy.*]

WILLY: Who the hell do you think you are, better than everybody else? You don't know everything, you big, ignorant, stupid . . . Put up your hands!

[*Light rises, on the right side of the forestage, on a small table in the reception room of* CHARLEY'S *office. Traffic sounds are heard.* BERNARD, *now mature, sits whistling to himself. A pair of tennis rackets and an overnight bag are on the floor beside him.*]

WILLY [*offstage*]: What are you walking away for? Don't walk away! If you're going to say something say it to my face! I know you laugh at me behind my back. You'll laugh out of the other side of your goddam face after this game. Touchdown! Touchdown! Eighty thousand people! Touchdown! Right between the goal posts.

[BERNARD *is a quiet, earnest, but self-assured young man.* WILLY'S *voice is coming from right upstage now.* BERNARD *lowers his feet off the table and listens.* JENNY, *his father's secretary, enters.*]

JENNY [*distressed*]: Say, Bernard, will you go out in the hall?

BERNARD: What is that noise? Who is it?

JENNY: Mr. Loman. He just got off the elevator.

BERNARD [*getting up*]: Who's he arguing with?

JENNY: Nobody. There's nobody with him. I can't deal with him any more, and your father gets all upset everytime he comes. I've got a lot of typing to do, and your father's waiting to sign it. Will you see him?

WILLY [*entering*]: Touchdown! Touch—[*He sees* JENNY.] Jenny, Jenny, good to see you. How're ya? Workin'? Or still honest?

JENNY: Fine. How've you been feeling?

WILLY: Not much any more, Jenny. Ha, ha! [*He is surprised to see the rackets.*]

BERNARD: Hello, Uncle Willy.

WILLY [*almost shocked*]: Bernard! Well, look who's here! [*He comes quickly, guiltily, to* BERNARD *and warmly shakes his hand.*]

BERNARD: How are you? Good to see you.

WILLY: What are you doing here?

BERNARD: Oh, just stopped by to see Pop. Get off my feet till my train leaves. I'm going to Washington in a few minutes.

WILLY: Is he in?

BERNARD: Yes, he's in his office with the accountant. Sit down.

WILLY [*sitting down*]: What're you going to do in Washington?

BERNARD: Oh, just a case I've got there, Willy.

WILLY: That so? [*Indicating the rackets.*] You going to play tennis there?

BERNARD: I'm staying with a friend who's got a court.

WILLY: Don't say. His own tennis court. Must be fine people, I bet.

BERNARD: They are, very nice. Dad tells me Biff's in town.

WILLY [*with a big smile*]: Yeah, Biff's in. Working on a very big deal, Bernard.

BERNARD: What's Biff doing?

WILLY: Well, he's been doing very big things in the West. But he decided to establish himself here. Very big. We're having dinner. Did I hear your wife had a boy?

BERNARD: That's right. Our second.

WILLY: Two boys! What do you know!

BERNARD: What kind of a deal has Biff got?

WILLY: Well, Bill Oliver—very big sporting-goods man—he wants Biff very badly. Called him in from the West. Long distance, carte blanche, special deliveries. Your friends have their own private tennis court?

BERNARD: You still with the old firm, Willy?

WILLY [*after a pause*]: I'm—I'm overjoyed to see how you made the grade, Bernard, overjoyed. It's an encouraging thing to see a young man really—really . . . Looks very good for Biff—very . . . [*He breaks off, then.*] Bernard . . . [*He is so full of emotion, he breaks off again.*]

BERNARD: What is it, Willy?

WILLY [*small and alone*]: What—what's the secret?

BERNARD: What secret?

WILLY: How—how did you? Why didn't he ever catch on?

BERNARD: I wouldn't know that, Willy.

WILLY [*confidentially, desperately*]: You were his friend, his boyhood friend. There's something I don't understand about it. His life ended after that Ebbets Field game. From the age of seventeen nothing good ever happened to him.

BERNARD: He never trained himself for anything.

WILLY: But he did, he did. After high school he took so many correspondence courses. Radio mechanics; television; God knows what, and never made the slightest mark.

BERNARD [*taking off his glasses*]: Willy, do you want to talk candidly?

WILLY [*rising, faces* BERNARD]: I regard you as a very brilliant man, Bernard. I value your advice.

BERNARD: Oh, the hell with the advice, Willy. I couldn't advise you. There's just one

thing I've always wanted to ask you. When he was supposed to graduate, and the math teacher flunked him . . .

WILLY: Oh, that son-of-a-bitch ruined his life.

BERNARD: Yeah, but, Willy, all he had to do was go to summer school and make up that subject.

WILLY: That's right, that's right.

BERNARD: Did you tell him not to go to summer school?

WILLY: Me? I begged him to go. I ordered him to go!

BERNARD: Then why wouldn't he go?

WILLY: Why? Why! Bernard, that question has been trailing me like a ghost for the last fifteen years. He flunked the subject, and laid down and died like a hammer hit him!

BERNARD: Take it easy, kid.

WILLY: Let me talk to you—I got nobody to talk to. Bernard, Bernard, was it my fault? Y'see? It keeps going around in my mind, maybe I did something to him. I got nothing to give him.

BERNARD: Don't take it so hard.

WILLY: Why did he lay down? What is the story there? You were his friend!

BERNARD: Willy, I remember, it was June, and our grades came out. And he'd flunked math.

WILLY: That son-of-a-bitch!

BERNARD: No, it wasn't right then. Biff just got very angry, I remember, and he was ready to enroll in summer school.

WILLY [surprised]: He was?

BERNARD: He wasn't beaten by it at all. But then, Willy, he disappeared from the block for almost a month. And I got the idea that he'd gone up to New England to see you. Did he have a talk with you then?

[WILLY stares in silence.]

BERNARD: Willy?

WILLY [with a strong edge of resentment in his voice]: Yeah, he came to Boston. What about it?

BERNARD: Well, just that when he came back—I'll never forget this, it always mystifies me. Because I'd thought so well of Biff, even though he'd always taken advantage of me. I loved him, Willy, y'know? And he came back after that month and took his sneakers—remember those sneakers with "University of Virginia" printed on them? He was so proud of those, wore them every day. And he took them down in the cellar, and burned them up in the furnace. We had a fist fight. It lasted at least half an hour. Just the two of us, punching each other down the cellar, and crying right through it. I've often thought of how strange it was that I knew he'd given up his life. What happened in Boston, Willy?

[WILLY looks at him as at an intruder.]

BERNARD: I just bring it up because you asked me.

WILLY [*angrily*]: Nothing. What do you mean, "What happened?" What's that got to do with anything?

BERNARD: Well, don't get sore.

WILLY: What are you trying to do, blame it on me? If a boy lays down is that my fault?

BERNARD: Now, Willy, don't get . . .

WILLY: Well, don't—don't talk to me that way! What does that mean, "What happened?"

[CHARLEY *enters. He is in his vest, and he carries a bottle of bourbon.*]

CHARLEY: Hey; you're going to miss that train. [*He waves the bottle.*]

BERNARD: Yeah, I'm going. [*He takes the bottle.*] Thanks, Pop. [*He picks up his rackets and bag.*] Good-by, Willy, and don't worry about it. You know, "If at first you don't succeed . . ."

WILLY: Yes, I believe in that.

BERNARD: But sometimes, Willy, it's better for a man just to walk away.

WILLY: Walk away?

BERNARD: That's right.

WILLY: But if you can't walk away?

BERNARD [*after a slight pause*]: I guess that's when it's tough. [*Extending his hand.*] Good-by, Willy.

WILLY [*shaking* BERNARD*'s hand*]: Good-by, boy.

CHARLEY [*an arm on* BERNARD*'s shoulder*]: How do you like this kid? Gonna argue a case in front of the Supreme Court.

BERNARD [*protesting*]: Pop!

WILLY [*genuinely shocked, pained, and happy*]: No! The Supreme Court!

BERNARD: I gotta run. 'By, Dad!

CHARLEY: Knock 'em dead, Bernard!

[BERNARD *goes off.*]

WILLY [*as* CHARLEY *takes out his wallet*]: The Supreme Court! And he didn't even mention it!

CHARLEY [*counting out money on the desk*]: He don't have to—he's gonna do it.

WILLY: And you never told him what to do, did you? You never took any interest in him.

CHARLEY: My salvation is that I never took any interest in anything. There's some money—fifty dollars. I got an accountant inside.

WILLY: Charley, look . . . [*With difficulty.*] I got my insurance to pay. If you can manage it—I need a hundred and ten dollars.

[CHARLEY *doesn't reply for a moment; merely stops moving.*]

WILLY: I'd draw it from my bank but Linda would know, and I . . .

CHARLEY: Sit down, Willy.

WILLY [*moving toward the chair*]: I'm keeping an account of everything, remember. I'll pay every penny back. [*He sits.*]

CHARLEY: Now listen to me, Willy.

WILLY: I want you to know I appreciate . . .

CHARLEY [*sitting down on the table*]: Willy, what're you doin'? What the hell is going on in your head?

WILLY: Why? I'm simply . . .

CHARLEY: I offered you a job. You make fifty dollars a week, and I won't send you on the road.

WILLY: I've got a job.

CHARLEY: Without pay? What kind of a job is a job without pay? [*He rises.*] Now, look, kid, enough is enough. I'm no genius but I know when I'm being insulted.

WILLY: Insulted!

CHARLEY: Why don't you want to work for me?

WILLY: What's the matter with you? I've got a job.

CHARLEY: Then what're you walkin' in here every week for?

WILLY [*getting up*]: Well, if you don't want me to walk in here. . . .

CHARLEY: I'm offering you a job.

WILLY: I don't want your goddam job!

CHARLEY: When the hell are you going to grow up?

WILLY [*furiously*]: You big ignoramus, if you say that to me again I'll rap you one! I don't care how big you are! [*He's ready to fight.*]

[*Pause.*]

CHARLEY [*kindly, going to him*]: How much do you need, Willy?

WILLY: Charley, I'm strapped. I'm strapped. I don't know what to do. I was just fired.

CHARLEY: Howard fired you?

WILLY: That snotnose. Imagine that? I named him. I named him Howard.

CHARLEY: Willy, when're you gonna realize that them things don't mean anything? You named him Howard, but you can't sell that. The only thing you got in this world is what you can sell. And the funny thing is that you're a salesman, and you don't know that.

WILLY: I've always tried to think otherwise, I guess. I always felt that if a man was impressive, and well liked, that nothing . . .

CHARLEY: Why must everybody like you? Who liked J. P. Morgan? Was he impressive? In a Turkish bath he'd look like a butcher. But with his pockets on he was very well liked. Now listen, Willy, I know you don't like me, and nobody can say I'm in love with you, but I'll give you a job because—just for the hell of it, put it that way. Now what do you say?

WILLY: I—I just can't work for you, Charley.

CHARLEY: What're you, jealous of me?

WILLY: I can't work for you, that's all, don't ask me why.

CHARLEY [*angered, takes out more bills*]: You been jealous of me all your life, you damned fool! Here, pay your insurance. [*He puts the money in* WILLY's *hand.*]

WILLY: I'm keeping strict accounts.

CHARLEY: I've got some work to do. Take care of yourself. And pay your insurance.

WILLY [*moving to the right*]: Funny, y'know? After all the highways, and the trains, and the appointments, and the years, you end up worth more dead than alive.

CHARLEY: Willy, nobody's worth nothin' dead. [*After a slight pause.*] Did you hear what I said?

[WILLY *stands still, dreaming.*]

CHARLEY: Willy!

WILLY: Apologize to Bernard for me when you see him. I didn't mean to argue with him. He's a fine boy. They're all fine boys, and they'll end up big—all of them. Someday they'll all play tennis together. Wish me luck, Charley. He saw Bill Oliver today.

CHARLEY: Good luck.

WILLY [*on the verge of tears*]: Charley, you're the only friend I got. Isn't that a remarkable thing? [*He goes out.*]

CHARLEY: Jesus!

[CHARLEY *stares after him a moment and follows. All light blacks out. Suddenly raucous music is heard, and a red glow rises behind the screen at right.* STANLEY, *a young waiter, appears, carrying a table, followed by* HAPPY, *who is carrying two chairs.*]

STANLEY [*putting the table down*]: That's all right, Mr. Loman, I can handle it myself. [*He turns and takes the chairs from* HAPPY *and places them at the table.*]

HAPPY [*glancing around*]: Oh, this is better.

STANLEY: Sure, in the front there you're in the middle of all kinds of noise. Whenever you got a party, Mr. Loman, you just tell me and I'll put you back here. Y'know, there's a lotta people they don't like it private, because when they go out they like to see a lotta action around them because they're sick and tired to stay in the house by theirself. But I know you, you ain't from Hackensack. You know what I mean?

HAPPY [*sitting down*]: So how's it coming, Stanley?

STANLEY: Ah, it's a dog's life. I only wish during the war they'd a took me in the Army. I coulda been dead by now.

HAPPY: My brother's back, Stanley.

STANLEY: Oh, he come back, heh? From the Far West.

HAPPY: Yeah, big cattle man, my brother, so treat him right. And my father's coming too.

STANLEY: Oh, your father too!

HAPPY: You got a couple of nice lobsters?

STANLEY: Hundred per cent, big.

HAPPY: I want them with the claws.

STANLEY: Don't worry, I don't give you no mice. [HAPPY *laughs.*] How about some wine? It'll put a head on the meal.

HAPPY: No. You remember, Stanley, that recipe I brought you from overseas? With the champagne in it?

STANLEY: Oh, yeah, sure. I still got it tacked up yet in the kitchen. But that'll have to cost a buck apiece anyways.

HAPPY: That's all right.

STANLEY: What'd you, hit a number or somethin'?

HAPPY: No, it's a little celebration. My brother is—I think he pulled off a big deal today. I think we're going into business together.

STANLEY: Great! That's the best for you. Because a family business, you know what I mean?—that's the best.

HAPPY: That's what I think.

STANLEY: 'Cause what's the difference? Somebody steals? It's in the family. Know what I mean? [*Sotto voce*.] Like this bartender here. The boss is goin' crazy what kinda leak he's got in the cash register. You put it in but it don't come out.

HAPPY [*raising his head*]: Sh!

STANLEY: What?

HAPPY: You notice I wasn't lookin' right or left, was I?

STANLEY: No.

HAPPY: And my eyes are closed.

STANLEY: So what's the . . . ?

HAPPY: Strudel's comin'.

STANLEY [*catching on, looks around*]: Ah, no, there's no . . .

[*He breaks off as a furred, lavishly dressed girl enters and sits at the next table. Both follow her with their eyes.*]

STANLEY: Geez, how'd ya know?

HAPPY: I got radar or something. [*Staring directly at her profile.*] Oooooooo . . . Stanley.

STANLEY: I think that's for you, Mr. Loman.

HAPPY: Look at that mouth. Oh, God. And the binoculars.

STANLEY: Geez, you got a life, Mr. Loman.

HAPPY: Wait on her.

STANLEY [*going to the GIRL's table*]: Would you like a menu, ma'am?

GIRL: I'm expecting someone, but I'd like a . . .

HAPPY: Why don't you bring her—excuse me, miss, do you mind? I sell champagne, and I'd like you to try my brand. Bring her a champagne, Stanley.

GIRL: That's awfully nice of you.

HAPPY: Don't mention it. It's all company money. [*He laughs.*]

GIRL: That's a charming product to be selling, isn't it?

HAPPY: Oh, gets to be like everything else. Selling is selling, y'know.

GIRL: I suppose.

HAPPY: You don't happen to sell, do you?

GIRL: No, I don't sell.

HAPPY: Would you object to a compliment from a stranger? You ought to be on a magazine cover.

GIRL [*looking at him a little archly*]: I have been.

[STANLEY *comes in with a glass of champagne.*]

HAPPY: What'd I say before, Stanley? You see? She's a cover girl.

STANLEY: Oh, I could see, I could see.

HAPPY [*to the* GIRL]: What magazine?

GIRL: Oh, a lot of them. [*She takes the drink.*] Thank you.

HAPPY: You know what they say in France, don't you? "Champagne is the drink of the complexion"—Hya, Biff!

[BIFF *has entered and sits with* HAPPY.]

BIFF: Hello, kid. Sorry I'm late.

HAPPY: I just got here. Uh, Miss . . . ?

GIRL: Forsythe.

HAPPY: Miss Forsythe, this is my brother.

BIFF: Is Dad here?

HAPPY: His name is Biff. You might've heard of him. Great football player.

GIRL: Really? What team?

HAPPY: Are you familiar with football?

GIRL: No, I'm afraid I'm not.

HAPPY: Biff is quarterback with the New York Giants.

GIRL: Well, that is nice, isn't it? [*She drinks.*]

HAPPY: Good health.

GIRL: I'm happy to meet you.

HAPPY: That's my name. Hap. It's really Harold, but at West Point they called me Happy.

GIRL [*now really impressed*]: Oh, I see. How do you do? [*She turns her profile.*]

BIFF: Isn't Dad coming?

HAPPY: You want her?

BIFF: Oh, I could never make that.

HAPPY: I remember the time that idea would never come into your head. Where's the old confidence, Biff?

BIFF: I just saw Oliver . . .

HAPPY: Wait a minute. I've got to see that old confidence again. Do you want her? She's on call.

BIFF: Oh, no. [*He turns to look at the* GIRL.]

HAPPY: I'm telling you. Watch this. [*Turning to the* GIRL.] Honey? [*She turns to him.*] Are you busy?

GIRL: Well, I am . . . but I could make a phone call.

HAPPY: Do that, will you, honey? And see if you can get a friend. We'll be here for a while. Biff is one of the greatest football players in the country.

GIRL [*standing up*]: Well, I'm certainly happy to meet you.

HAPPY: Come back soon.

GIRL: I'll try.

HAPPY: Don't try, honey, try hard.

[*The* GIRL *exits.* STANLEY *follows, shaking his head in bewildered admiration.*]

HAPPY: Isn't that a shame now? A beautiful girl like that? That's why I can't get married. There's not a good woman in a thousand. New York is loaded with them, kid!

BIFF: Hap, look . . .

HAPPY: I told you she was on call!

BIFF [*strangely unnerved*]: Cut it out, will ya? I want to say something to you.

HAPPY: Did you see Oliver?

BIFF: I saw him all right. Now look, I want to tell Dad a couple of things and I want you to help me.

HAPPY: What? Is he going to back you?

BIFF: Are you crazy? You're out of your goddam head, you know that?

HAPPY: Why? What happened?

BIFF [*breathlessly*]: I did a terrible thing today, Hap. It's been the strangest day I ever went through. I'm all numb, I swear.

HAPPY: You mean he wouldn't see you?

BIFF: Well, I waited six hours for him, see? All day. Kept sending my name in. Even tried to date his secretary so she'd get me to him, but no soap.

HAPPY: Because you're not showin' the old confidence, Biff. He remembered you, didn't he?

BIFF [*stopping* HAPPY *with a gesture*]: Finally, about five o'clock, he comes out. Didn't remember who I was or anything. I felt like such an idiot, Hap.

HAPPY: Did you tell him my Florida idea?

BIFF: He walked away. I saw him for one minute. I got so mad I could've torn the walls down! How the hell did I ever get the idea I was a salesman there? I even believed myself that I'd been a salesman for him! And then he gave me one look and—I realized what a ridiculous lie my whole life has been! We've been talking in a dream for fifteen years. I was a shipping clerk.

HAPPY: What'd you do?

BIFF [*with great tension and wonder*]: Well, he left, see. And the secretary went out. I was all alone in the waiting room. I don't know what came over me, Hap. The next thing I know I'm in his office—paneled walls, everything. I can't explain it. I—Hap, I took his fountain pen.

HAPPY: Geez, did he catch you?

BIFF: I ran out. I ran down all eleven flights. I ran and ran and ran.

HAPPY: That was an awful dumb—what'd you do that for?

BIFF [*agonized*]: I don't know, I just—wanted to take something, I don't know. You gotta help me, Hap, I'm gonna tell Pop.

HAPPY: You crazy? What for?

BIFF: Hap, he's got to understand that I'm not the man somebody lends that kind of money to. He thinks I've been spiting him all these years and it's eating him up.

HAPPY: That's just it. You tell him something nice.

BIFF: I can't.

HAPPY: Say you got a lunch date with Oliver tomorrow.

BIFF: So what do I do tomorrow?

HAPPY: You leave the house tomorrow and come back at night and say Oliver is thinking it over. And he thinks it over for a couple of weeks, and gradually it fades away and nobody's the worse.

BIFF: But it'll go on forever!

HAPPY: Dad is never so happy as when he's looking forward to something!

[WILLY *enters.*]

HAPPY: Hello, scout!

WILLY: Gee, I haven't been here in years!

[STANLEY *has followed* WILLY *in and sets a chair for him.* STANLEY *starts off but* HAPPY *stops him.*]

HAPPY: Stanley!

[STANLEY *stands by, waiting for an order.*]

BIFF [*going to* WILLY *with guilt, as to an invalid*]: Sit down, Pop. You want a drink?

WILLY: Sure, I don't mind.

BIFF: Let's get a load on.

WILLY: You look worried.

BIFF: N-no. [*To* STANLEY.] Scotch all around. Make it doubles.

STANLEY: Doubles, right. [*He goes.*]

WILLY: You had a couple already, didn't you?

BIFF: Just a couple, yeah.

WILLY: Well, what happened, boy? [*Nodding affirmatively, with a smile.*] Everything go all right?

BIFF [*takes a breath, then reaches out and grasps* WILLY*'s hand*]: Pal . . . [*He is smiling bravely, and* WILLY *is smiling too.*] I had an experience today.

HAPPY: Terrific, Pop.

WILLY: That so? What happened?

BIFF [*high, slightly alcoholic, above the earth*]: I'm going to tell you everything from first to last. It's been a strange day. [*Silence. He looks around, composes himself as best he can, but his breath keeps breaking the rhythm of his voice.*] I had to wait quite a while for him, and . . .

WILLY: Oliver?

BIFF: Yeah, Oliver. All day, as a matter of cold fact. And a lot of—instances—facts, Pop, facts about my life came back to me. Who was it, Pop? Who ever said I was a salesman with Oliver?

WILLY: Well, you were.

BIFF: No, Dad, I was shipping clerk.

WILLY: But you were practically . . .

BIFF [*with determination*]: Dad, I don't know who said it first, but I was never a salesman for Bill Oliver.

WILLY: What're you talking about?

BIFF: Let's hold on to the facts tonight, Pop. We're not going to get anywhere bullin' around. I was a shipping clerk.

WILLY [*angrily*]: All right, now listen to me . . .

BIFF: Why don't you let me finish?

WILLY: I'm not interested in stories about the past or any crap of that kind because the woods are burning, boys, you understand? There's a big blaze going on all around. I was fired today.

BIFF [*shocked*]: How could you be?

WILLY: I was fired, and I'm looking for a little good news to tell your mother, because the woman has waited and the woman has suffered. The gist of it is that I haven't got a story left in my head, Biff. So don't give me a lecture about facts and aspects. I am not interested. Now what've you got to say to me?

[STANLEY *enters with three drinks. They wait until he leaves.*]

WILLY: Did you see Oliver?

BIFF: Jesus, Dad!

WILLY: You mean you didn't go up there?

HAPPY: Sure he went up there.

BIFF: I did. I—saw him. How could they fire you?

WILLY [*on the edge of his chair*]: What kind of a welcome did he give you?

BIFF: He won't even let you work on commission?

WILLY: I'm out! [*Driving.*] So tell me, he gave you a warm welcome?

HAPPY: Sure, Pop, sure!

BIFF [*driven*]: Well, it was kind of . . .

WILLY: I was wondering if he'd remember you. [*To* HAPPY.] Imagine, man doesn't see him for ten, twelve years and gives him that kind of a welcome!

HAPPY: Damn right!

BIFF [*trying to return to the offensive*]: Pop, look . . .

WILLY: You know why he remembered you, don't you? Because you impressed him in those days.

BIFF: Let's talk quietly and get this down to the facts, huh?

WILLY [*as though* BIFF *had been interrupting*]: Well, what happened? It's great news, Biff. Did he take you into his office or'd you talk in the waiting room?

BIFF: Well, he came in, see, and . . .

WILLY [*with a big smile*]: What'd he say? Betcha he threw his arm around you.

BIFF: Well, he kinda . . .

WILLY: He's a fine man. [*To* HAPPY.] Very hard man to see, y'know.

HAPPY [*agreeing*]: Oh, I know.

WILLY [*to* BIFF]: Is that where you had the drinks?

BIFF: Yeah, he gave me a couple of—no, no!

HAPPY [*cutting in*]: He told him my Florida idea.

WILLY: Don't interrupt. [*To* BIFF.] How'd he react to the Florida idea?

BIFF: Dad, will you give me a minute to explain?

WILLY: I've been waiting for you to explain since I sat down here! What happened? He took you into his office and what?

BIFF: Well—I talked. And—and he listened, see.

WILLY: Famous for the way he listens, y'know. What was his answer?

BIFF: His answer was—[*He breaks off, suddenly angry.*] Dad, you're not letting me tell you what I want to tell you!

WILLY [*accusing, angered*]: You didn't see him, did you?

BIFF: I did see him!

WILLY: What'd you insult him or something? You insulted him, didn't you?

BIFF: Listen, will you let me out of it, will you just let me out of it!

HAPPY: What the hell!

WILLY: Tell me what happened!

BIFF [*to* HAPPY]: I can't talk to him!

[*A single trumpet note jars the ear. The light of green leaves stains the house, which holds the air of night and a dream.* YOUNG BERNARD *enters and knocks on the door of the house.*]

YOUNG BERNARD [*frantically*]: Mrs. Loman, Mrs. Loman!

HAPPY: Tell him what happened!

BIFF [*to* HAPPY]: Shut up and leave me alone!

WILLY: No, no! You had to go and flunk math!

BIFF: What math? What're you talking about?

YOUNG BERNARD: Mrs. Loman, Mrs. Loman!

[LINDA *appears in the house, as of old.*]

WILLY [*wildly*]: Math, math, math!

BIFF: Take it easy, Pop!

YOUNG BERNARD: Mrs. Loman!

WILLY [*furiously*]: If you hadn't flunked you'd've been set by now!

BIFF: Now, look, I'm gonna tell you what happened, and you're going to listen to me.

YOUNG BERNARD: Mrs. Loman!

BIFF: I waited six hours . . .

HAPPY: What the hell are you saying?

BIFF: I kept sending in my name but he wouldn't see me. So finally he . . .[*He continues unheard as light fades low on the restaurant.*]

YOUNG BERNARD: Biff flunked math!

LINDA: No!

YOUNG BERNARD: Birnbaum flunked him! They won't graduate him!

LINDA: But they have to. He's gotta go to the university. Where is he? Biff! Biff!

YOUNG BERNARD: No, he left. He went to Grand Central.

LINDA: Grand—You mean he went to Boston!

YOUNG BERNARD: Is Uncle Willy in Boston?

LINDA: Oh, maybe Willy can talk to the teacher. Oh, the poor, poor boy!

[Light on house area snaps out.]

BIFF [*at the table, now audible, holding up a gold fountain pen*]: . . . so I'm washed up with Oliver, you understand? Are you listening to me?

WILLY [*at a loss*]: Yeah, sure. If you hadn't flunked . . .

BIFF: Flunked what? What're you talking about?

WILLY: Don't blame everything on me! I didn't flunk math—you did! What pen?

HAPPY: That was awful dumb, Biff, a pen like that is worth—

WILLY [*seeing the pen for the first time*]: You took Oliver's pen?

BIFF [*weakening*]: Dad, I just explained it to you.

WILLY: You stole Bill Oliver's fountain pen!

BIFF: I didn't exactly steal it! That's just what I've been explaining to you!

HAPPY: He had it in his hand and just then Oliver walked in, so he got nervous and stuck it in his pocket!

WILLY: My God, Biff!

BIFF: I never intended to do it, Dad!

OPERATOR'S VOICE: Standish Arms, good evening!

WILLY [*shouting*]: I'm not in my room!

BIFF [*frightened*]: Dad, what's the matter? [*He and* HAPPY *stand up.*]

OPERATOR: Ringing Mr. Loman for you!

WILLY: I'm not there, stop it!

BIFF [*horrified, gets down on one knee before* WILLY]: Dad, I'll make good, I'll make good. [WILLY *tries to get to his feet.* BIFF *holds him down.*] Sit down now.

WILLY: No, you're no good, you're no good for anything.

BIFF: I am, Dad, I'll find something else, you understand? Now don't worry about anything. [*He holds up* WILLY'*s face.*] Talk to me, Dad.

OPERATOR: Mr. Loman does not answer. Shall I page him?

WILLY [*attempting to stand, as though to rush and silence the* OPERATOR]: No, no, no!

HAPPY: He'll strike something, Pop.

WILLY: No, no . . .

BIFF [*desperately, standing over* WILLY]: Pop, listen! Listen to me! I'm telling you something good. Oliver talked to his partner about the Florida idea. You listening? He—he talked to his partner, and he came to me . . . I'm going to be all right, you hear? Dad, listen to me, he said it was just a question of the amount!

WILLY: Then you . . . got it?

HAPPY: He's gonna be terrific, Pop!

WILLY [*trying to stand*]: Then you got it, haven't you? You got it! You got it!

BIFF [*agonized, holds* WILLY *down*]: No, no. Look, Pop. I'm supposed to have lunch with them tomorrow. I'm just telling you this so you'll know that I can still make an impression, Pop. And I'll make good somewhere, but I can't go tomorrow, see?

WILLY: Why not? You simply . . .

BIFF: But the pen, Pop!

WILLY: You give it to him and tell him it was an oversight!

HAPPY: Sure, have lunch tomorrow!

BIFF: I can't say that . . .

WILLY: You were doing a crossword puzzle and accidentally used his pen!

BIFF: Listen, kid, I took those balls years ago, now I walk in with his fountain pen? That clinches it, don't you see? I can't face him like that! I'll try elsewhere.

PAGE'S VOICE: Paging Mr. Loman!

WILLY: Don't you want to be anything?

BIFF: Pop, how can I go back?

WILLY: You don't want to be anything, is that what's behind it?

BIFF [*now angry at* WILLY *for not crediting his sympathy*]: Don't take it that way! You think it was easy walking into that office after what I'd done to him? A team of horses couldn't have dragged me back to Bill Oliver!

WILLY: Then why'd you go?

BIFF: Why did I go? Why did I go! Look at you! Look at what's become of you!

[*Off left,* THE WOMAN *laughs.*]

WILLY: Biff, you're going to go to that lunch tomorrow, or . . .

BIFF: I can't go. I've got no appointment!

HAPPY: Biff, for . . . !

WILLY: Are you spiting me?

BIFF: Don't take it that way! Goddammit!

WILLY [*strikes* BIFF *and falters away from the table*]: You rotten little louse! Are you spiting me?

THE WOMAN: Someone's at the door, Willy!

BIFF: I'm no good, can't you see what I am?

HAPPY [*separating them*]: Hey, you're in a restaurant! Now cut it out, both of you! [*The girls enter.*] Hello, girls, sit down.

[THE WOMAN *laughs, off left.*]

MISS FORSYTHE: I guess we might as well. This is Letta.

THE WOMAN: Willy, are you going to wake up?

BIFF [*ignoring* WILLY]: How're ya, miss, sit down. What do you drink?

MISS FORSYTHE: Letta might not be able to stay long.

LETTA: I gotta get up very early tomorrow. I got jury duty. I'm so excited! Were you fellows ever on a jury?

BIFF: No, but I been in front of them! [*The girls laugh.*] This is my father.

LETTA: Isn't he cute? Sit down with us, Pop.

HAPPY: Sit him down, Biff!

BIFF [*going to him*]: Come on, slugger, drink us under the table. To hell with it! Come on, sit down, pal.

[*On* BIFF'*s last insistence,* WILLY *is about to sit.*]

THE WOMAN [*now urgently*]: Willy, are you going to answer the door!

[THE WOMAN's *call pulls* WILLY *back. He starts right, befuddled.*]

BIFF: Hey, where are you going?

WILLY: Open the door.

BIFF: The door?

WILLY: The washroom . . . the door . . . where's the door?

BIFF [*leading* WILLY *to the left*]: Just go straight down.

[WILLY *moves left.*]

THE WOMAN: Willy, Willy, are you going to get up, get up, get up, get up?

[WILLY *exits left.*]

LETTA: I think it's sweet you bring your daddy along.

MISS FORSYTHE: Oh, he isn't really your father!

BIFF [*at left, turning to her resentfully*]: Miss Forsythe, you've just seen a prince walk by. A fine, troubled prince. A hard-working, unappreciated prince. A pal, you understand? A good companion. Always for his boys.

LETTA: That's so sweet.

HAPPY: Well, girls, what's the program? We're wasting time. Come on, Biff. Gather round. Where would you like to go?

BIFF: Why don't you do something for him?

HAPPY: Me!

BIFF: Don't you give a damn for him, Hap?

HAPPY: What're you talking about? I'm the one who—

BIFF: I sense it, you don't give a good goddam about him. [*He takes the rolled-up hose from his pocket and puts it on the table in front of* HAPPY.] Look what I found in the cellar, for Christ's sake. How can you bear to let it go on?

HAPPY: Me? Who goes away? Who runs off and—

BIFF: Yeah, but he doesn't mean anything to you. You could help him—I can't! Don't you understand what I'm talking about? He's going to kill himself, don't you know that?

HAPPY: Don't I know it! Me!

BIFF: Hap, help him! Jesus . . . help him . . . Help me, help me, I can't bear to look at his face! [*Ready to weep, he hurries out, up right.*]

HAPPY [*starting after him*]: Where are you going?

MISS FORSYTHE: What's he so mad about?

HAPPY: Come on, girls, we'll catch up with him.

MISS FORSYTHE [*as* HAPPY *pushes her out*]: Say, I don't like that temper of his!

HAPPY: He's just a little overstrung, he'll be all right!

WILLY [*off left, as* THE WOMAN *laughs*]: Don't answer! Don't answer!

LETTA: Don't you want to tell your father . . .

HAPPY: No, that's not my father. He's just a guy. Come on, we'll catch Biff, and, honey, we're going to paint this town! Stanley, where's the check! Hey, Stanley!

[*They exit.* STANLEY *looks toward left.*]

STANLEY [*calling to* HAPPY *indignantly*]: Mr. Loman! Mr. Loman!

[STANLEY *picks up a chair and follows them off. Knocking is heard off left.* THE WOMAN *enters, laughing.* WILLY *follows her. She is in a black slip; he is buttoning his shirt. Raw, sensuous music accompanies their speech:*]

WILLY: Will you stop laughing? Will you stop?

THE WOMAN: Aren't you going to answer the door? He'll wake the whole hotel.

WILLY: I'm not expecting anybody.

THE WOMAN: Whyn't you have another drink, honey, and stop being so damn self-centered?

WILLY: I'm so lonely.

THE WOMAN: You know you ruined me, Willy? From now on, whenever you come to the office, I'll see that you go right through to the buyers. No waiting at my desk anymore, Willy. You ruined me.

WILLY: That's nice of you to say that.

THE WOMAN: Gee, you are self-centered! Why so sad? You are the saddest, self-centeredest soul I ever did see-saw. [*She laughs. He kisses her.*] Come on inside, drummer boy. It's silly to be dressing in the middle of the night. [*As knocking is heard.*] Aren't you going to answer the door?

WILLY: They're knocking on the wrong door.

THE WOMAN: But I felt the knocking. And he heard us talking in here. Maybe the hotel's on fire!

WILLY [*his terror rising*]: It's a mistake.

THE WOMAN: Then tell him to go away!

WILLY: There's nobody there.

THE WOMAN: It's getting on my nerves, Willy. There's somebody standing out there and it's getting on my nerves!

WILLY [*pushing her away from him*]: All right, stay in the bathroom here, and don't come out. I think there's a law in Massachusetts about it, so don't come out. It may be that new room clerk. He looked very mean. So don't come out. It's a mistake, there's no fire.

[*The knocking is heard again. He takes a few steps away from her, and she vanishes into the wing. The light follows him, and now he is facing* YOUNG BIFF, *who carries a suitcase.* BIFF *steps toward him. The music is gone.*]

BIFF: Why didn't you answer?

WILLY: Biff! What are you doing in Boston?

BIFF: Why didn't you answer? I've been knocking for five minutes, I called you on the phone . . .

WILLY: I just heard you. I was in the bathroom and had the door shut. Did anything happen at home?

BIFF: Dad—I let you down.

WILLY: What do you mean?

BIFF: Dad . . .

WILLY: Biffo, what's this about? [*Putting his arm around* BIFF.] Come on, let's go downstairs and get you a malted.

BIFF: Dad, I flunked math.

WILLY: Not for the term?

BIFF: The term. I haven't got enough credits to graduate.

WILLY: You mean to say Bernard wouldn't give you the answers?

BIFF: He did, he tried, but I only got a sixty-one.

WILLY: And they wouldn't give you four points?

BIFF: Birnbaum refused absolutely. I begged him, Pop, but he won't give me those points. You gotta talk to him before they close the school. Because if he saw the kind of man you are, and you just talked to him in your way, I'm sure he'd come through for me. The class came right before practice, see, and I didn't go enough. Would you talk to him? He's like you, Pop. You know the way you could talk.

WILLY: You're on. We'll drive right back.

BIFF: Oh, Dad, good work! I'm sure he'll change it for you!

WILLY: Go downstairs and tell the clerk I'm checkin' out. Go right down.

BIFF: Yes, sir! See, the reason he hates me, Pop—one day he was late for class so I got up at the blackboard and imitated him. I crossed my eyes and talked with a lithp.

WILLY [*laughing*]: You did? The kids like it?

BIFF: They nearly died laughing!

WILLY: Yeah? What'd you do?

BIFF: The thquare root of thixthy twee is . . . [WILLY *bursts out laughing;* BIFF *joins.*] And in the middle of it he walked in!

[WILLY *laughs and* THE WOMAN *joins in offstage.*]

WILLY [*without hesitation*]: Hurry downstairs and . . .

BIFF: Somebody in there?

WILLY: No, that was next door.

[THE WOMAN *laughs offstage.*]

BIFF: Somebody got in your bathroom!

WILLY: No, it's the next room, there's a party—

THE WOMAN [*enters, laughing; she lisps this*]: Can I come in? There's something in the bathtub, Willy, and it's moving!

[WILLY *looks at* BIFF, *who is staring open-mouthed and horrified at* THE WOMAN.]

WILLY: Ah—you better go back to your room. They must be finished painting by now. They're painting her room so I let her take a shower here. Go back, go back . . . [*He pushes her.*]

THE WOMAN [*resisting*]: But I've got to get dressed, Willy, I can't—

WILLY: Get out of here! Go back, go back . . . [*Suddenly striving for the ordinary.*] This is Miss Francis, Biff, she's a buyer. They're painting her room. Go back, Miss Francis, go back . . .

THE WOMAN: But my clothes, I can't go out naked in the hall!

WILLY [*pushing her offstage*]: Get outa here! Go back, go back!

[BIFF *slowly sits down on his suitcase as the argument continues offstage.*]

THE WOMAN: Where's my stockings? You promised me stockings, Willy!

WILLY: I have no stockings here!

THE WOMAN: You had two boxes of size nine sheers for me, and I want them!

WILLY: Here, for God's sake, will you get outa here!

THE WOMAN [*enters holding a box of stockings*]: I just hope there's nobody in the hall. That's all I hope. [*To* BIFF.] Are you football or baseball?

BIFF: Football.

THE WOMAN [*angry, humiliated*]: That's me too. G'night. [*She snatches her clothes from* WILLY, *and walks out.*]

WILLY [*after a pause*]: Well, better get going. I want to get to the school first thing in the morning. Get my suits out of the closet. I'll get my valise. [BIFF *doesn't move.*] What's the matter! [BIFF *remains motionless, tears falling.*] She's a buyer. Buys for J. H. Simmons. She lives down the hall—they're painting. You don't imagine—[*He breaks off. After a pause.*] Now listen, pal, she's just a buyer. She sees merchandise in her room and they have to keep it looking just so . . . [*Pause. Assuming command.*] All right, get my suits. [BIFF *doesn't move.*] Now stop crying and do as I say. I gave you an order. Biff, I gave you an order! Is that what you do when I give you an order? How dare you cry! [*Putting his arm around* BIFF.] Now look, Biff, when you grow up you'll understand about these things. You mustn't—you mustn't overemphasize a thing like this. I'll see Birnbaum first thing in the morning.

BIFF: Never mind.

WILLY [*getting down beside* BIFF]: Never mind! He's going to give you those points. I'll see to it.

BIFF: He wouldn't listen to you.

WILLY: He certainly will listen to me. You need those points for the U. of Virginia.

BIFF: I'm not going there.

WILLY: Heh? If I can't get him to change that mark you'll make it up in summer school. You've got all summer to—

BIFF [*his weeping breaking from him*]: Dad . . .

WILLY [*infected by it*]: Oh, my boy . . .

BIFF: Dad . . .

WILLY: She's nothing to me, Biff. I was lonely, I was terribly lonely.

BIFF: You—you gave her Mama's stockings! [*His tears break through and he rises to go.*]

WILLY [*grabbing for* BIFF]: I gave you an order!

BIFF: Don't touch me, you—liar!

WILLY: Apologize for that!

BIFF: You fake! You phony little fake! You fake! [*Overcome, he turns quickly and weeping fully goes out with his suitcase.* WILLY *is left on the floor on his knees.*]

WILLY: I gave you an order! Biff, come back here or I'll beat you! Come back here! I'll whip you!

[STANLEY *comes quickly in from the right and stands in front of* WILLY.]

WILLY [*shouts at* STANLEY]: I gave you an order . . .

STANLEY: Hey, let's pick it up, pick it up, Mr. Loman. [*He helps* WILLY *to his feet.*] Your boys left with the chippies. They said they'll see you home.

[*A second waiter watches some distance away.*]

WILLY: But we were supposed to have dinner together.

[*Music is heard,* WILLY's *theme.*]

STANLEY: Can you make it?

WILLY: I'll—sure, I can make it. [*Suddenly concerned about his clothes.*] Do I—I look all right?

STANLEY: Sure, you look all right. [*He flicks a speck off* WILLY's *lapel.*]

WILLY: Here—here's a dollar.

STANLEY: Oh, your son paid me. It's all right.

WILLY [*putting it in* STANLEY's *hand*]: No, take it. You're a good boy.

STANLEY: Oh, no, you don't have to . . .

WILLY: Here—here's some more, I don't need it any more. [*After a slight pause*] me—is there a seed store in the neighborhood?

STANLEY: Seeds? You mean like to plant?

[*As* WILLY *turns,* STANLEY *slips the money back into his jacket pocket.*]

WILLY: Yes. Carrots, peas . . .

STANLEY: Well, there's hardware stores on Sixth Avenue, but it may be too late now.

WILLY [*anxiously*]: Oh, I'd better hurry. I've got to get some seeds. [*He starts off to the right.*] I've got to get some seeds, right away. Nothing's planted. I don't have a thing in the ground.

[WILLY *hurries out as the light goes down.* STANLEY *moves over to the right after him, watches him off. The other waiter has been staring at* WILLY.]

STANLEY [*to the waiter*]: Well, whatta you looking at?

[*The waiter picks up the chairs and moves off right.* STANLEY *takes the table and follows him. The light fades on this area. There is a long pause, the sound of the flute coming over. The light gradually rises on the kitchen, which is empty.* HAPPY *appears at the door of the house, followed by* BIFF.]

HAPPY *is carrying a large bunch of long-stemmed roses. He enters the kitchen, looks around for* LINDA. *Not seeing her, he turns to* BIFF, *who is just outside the house door, and makes a gesture with his hands, indicating "Not here, I guess." He looks into the living room and freezes. Inside,* LINDA, *unseen is seated,* WILLY'*s coat on her lap. She rises ominously and quietly and moves toward* HAPPY, *who backs up into the kitchen, afraid.*]

HAPPY: Hey, what're you doing up? [LINDA *says nothing but moves toward him implacably.*] Where's Pop? [*He keeps backing to the right and now* LINDA *is in full view in the doorway to the living room.*] Is he sleeping?

LINDA: Where were you?

HAPPY [*trying to laugh it off*]: We met two girls, Mom, very fine types. Here, we brought you some flowers. [*Offering them to her.*] Put them in your room, Ma.

[*She knocks them to the floor at* BIFF'*s feet. He has now come inside and closed the door behind him. She stares at* BIFF, *silent.*]

HAPPY: Now what'd you do that for? Mom, I want you to have some flowers . . .

LINDA [*cutting* HAPPY *off, violently to* BIFF]: Don't you care whether he lives or dies?

HAPPY [*going to the stairs*]: Come upstairs, Biff.

BIFF [*with a flare of disgust, to* HAPPY]: Go away from me! [*To* LINDA.] What do you mean, lives or dies? Nobody's dying around here, pal.

LINDA: Get out of my sight! Get out of here!

BIFF: I wanna see the boss.

LINDA: You're not going near him!

BIFF: Where is he? [*He moves into the living room and* LINDA *follows.*]

LINDA [*shouting after* BIFF]: You invite him for dinner. He looks forward to it all day—[BIFF *appears in his parents' bedroom, looks around, and exits*]—and then you desert him there. There's no stranger you'd do that to!

HAPPY: Why? He had a swell time with us. Listen, when I—[LINDA *comes back into the kitchen*]—desert him I hope I don't outlive the day!

LINDA: Get out of here!

HAPPY: Now look, Mom . . .

LINDA: Did you have to go to women tonight? You and your lousy rotten whores!

[BIFF *re-enters the kitchen.*]

HAPPY: Mom, all we did was follow Biff around trying to cheer him up! [*To* BIFF.] Boy, what a night you gave me!

LINDA: Get out of here, both of you, and don't come back! I don't want you tormenting him any more. Go on now, get your things together! [*To* BIFF.] You can sleep in his apartment. [*She starts to pick up the flowers and stops herself.*] Pick up this stuff, I'm not your maid any more. Pick it up, you bum, you!

[HAPPY *turns his back to her in refusal.* BIFF *slowly moves over and gets down on his knees, picking up the flowers.*]

LINDA: You're a pair of animals! Not one, not another living soul would have had the cruelty to walk out on the man in a restaurant!

BIFF [*not looking at her*]: Is that what he said?

LINDA: He didn't have to say anything. He was so humiliated he nearly limped when he came in.

HAPPY: But, Mom, he had a great time with us . . .

BIFF [*cutting him off violently*]: Shut up!

[*Without another word,* HAPPY *goes upstairs.*]

LINDA: You! You didn't even go in to see if he was all right!

BIFF [*still on the floor in front of* LINDA, *the flowers in his hand; with self-loathing*]: No. Didn't. Didn't do a damned thing. How do you like that, heh? Left him babbling in a toilet.

LINDA: You louse. You . . .

BIFF: Now you hit it on the nose! [*He gets up, throws the flowers in the wastebasket.*] The scum of the earth, and you're looking at him!

LINDA: Get out of here!

BIFF: I gotta talk to the boss, Mom. Where is he?

LINDA: You're not going near him. Get out of this house!

BIFF [*with absolute assurance, determination*]: No. We're gonna have an abrupt conversation, him and me.

LINDA: You're not talking to him.

[*Hammering is heard from outside the house, off right.* BIFF *turns toward the noise.*]

LINDA [*suddenly pleading*]: Will you please leave him alone?

BIFF: What's he doing out there?

LINDA: He's planting the garden!

BIFF [*quietly*]: Now? Oh, my God!

[BIFF *moves outside,* LINDA *following. The light dies down on them and comes up on the center of the apron as* WILLY *walks into it. He is carrying a flashlight, a hoe, and a handful of seed packets. He raps the top of the hoe sharply to fix it firmly, and then moves to the left, measuring off the distance with his foot. He holds the flashlight to look at the seed packets, reading off the instructions. He is in the blue of night.*]

WILLY: Carrots . . . quarter-inch apart. Rows . . . one-foot rows. [*He measures it off.*] One foot. [*He puts down a package and measures off.*] Beets. [*He puts down another package and measures again.*] Lettuce. [*He reads the package, puts it down.*] One foot—[*He breaks off as* BEN *appears at the right and moves slowly down to him.*] What a proposition, ts, ts. Terrific, terrific. 'Cause she's suffered, Ben, the woman has suffered. You understand me? A man can't go out the way he came in, Ben, a man has got to add up to something. You can't, you can't—[BEN *moves toward him as though to interrupt.*] You gotta consider, now. Don't answer so quick. Remember, it's a guaranteed twenty-thousand-dollar proposition. Now look, Ben, I want you to go through the ins and outs of this thing with me. I've got nobody to talk to, Ben, and the woman has suffered, you hear me?

BEN [*standing still, considering*]: What's the proposition?

WILLY: It's twenty thousand dollars on the barrelhead. Guaranteed, gilt-edged, you understand?

BEN: You don't want to make a fool of yourself. They might not honor the policy.

WILLY: How can they dare refuse? Didn't I work like a coolie to meet every premium on the nose? And now they don't pay off? Impossible!

BEN: It's called a cowardly thing, William.

WILLY: Why? Does it take more guts to stand here the rest of my life ringing up a zero?

BEN [*yielding*]: That's a point, William. [*He moves, thinking, turns.*] And twenty thousand—that is something one can feel with the hand, it is there.

WILLY [*now assured, with rising power*]: Oh, Ben, that's the whole beauty of it! I see it like a diamond, shining in the dark, hard and rough, that I can pick up and touch in my hand. Not like—like an appointment! This would not be another damned-fool appointment, Ben, and it changes all the aspects. Because he thinks I'm nothing, see, and so he spites me. But the funeral . . . [*Straightening up.*] Ben, that funeral will be massive! They'll come from Maine, Massachusetts, Vermont, New Hampshire! All the oldtimers with the strange license plates—that boy will be thunderstruck, Ben, because he never realized—I am known! Rhode Island, New York, New Jersey—I am known, Ben, and he'll see it with his eyes once and for all. He'll see what I am, Ben! He's in for a shock, that boy!

BEN [*coming down to the edge of the garden*]: He'll call you a coward.

WILLY [*suddenly fearful*]: No, that would be terrible.

BEN: Yes. And a damned fool.

WILLY: No, no, he mustn't, I won't have that! [*He is broken and desperate.*]

BEN: He'll hate you, William.

[*The gay music of the* BOYS *is heard.*]

WILLY: Oh, Ben, how do we get back to all the great times? Used to be so full of light, and comradeship, the sleigh-riding in winter, and the ruddiness on his cheeks. And always some kind of good news coming up, always something nice coming up ahead. And never even let me carry the valises in the house, and simonizing, simonizing that little red car! Why, why can't I give him something and not have him hate me?

BEN: Let me think about it. [*He glances at his watch.*] I still have a little time. Remarkable proposition, but you've got to be sure you're not making a fool of yourself.

[BEN *drifts off upstage and goes out of sight.* BIFF *comes down from the left.*]

WILLY [*suddenly conscious of* BIFF, *turns and looks up at him, then begins picking up the packages of seeds in confusion.*]: Where the hell is that seed? [*Indignantly.*] You can't see nothing out here! They boxed in the whole goddam neighborhood!

BIFF: There are people all around here. Don't you realize that?

WILLY: I'm busy. Don't bother me.

BIFF [*taking the hoe from* WILLY]: I'm saying good-by to you, Pop. [WILLY *looks at him, silent, unable to move.*] I'm not coming back any more.

WILLY: You're not going to see Oliver tomorrow?

BIFF: I've got no appointment, Dad.

WILLY: He put his arm around you, and you've got no appointment?

BIFF: Pop, get this now, will you? Everytime I've left it's been a fight that sent me out of here. Today I realized something about myself and I tried to explain it to you and I—I think I'm just not smart enough to make any sense out of it for you. To hell with whose fault it is or anything like that. [*He takes* WILLY's *arm.*] Let's just wrap it up, heh? Come on in, we'll tell Mom. [*He gently tries to pull* WILLY *to left.*]

WILLY [*frozen, immobile, with guilt in his voice*]: No, I don't want to see her.

BIFF: Come on! [*He pulls again, and* WILLY *tries to pull away.*]

WILLY [*highly nervous*]: No, no, I don't want to see her.

BIFF [*tries to look into* WILLY's *face, as if to find the answer there*]: Why don't you want to see her?

WILLY [*more harshly now*]: Don't bother me, will you?

BIFF: What do you mean, you don't want to see her? You don't want them calling you yellow, do you? This isn't your fault; it's me, I'm a bum. Now come inside! [WILLY *strains to get away.*] Did you hear what I said to you?

[WILLY *pulls away and quickly goes by himself into the house.* BIFF *follows.*]

LINDA [*to* WILLY]: Did you plant, dear?

BIFF [*at the door, to* LINDA]: All right, we had it out. I'm going and I'm not writing any more.

LINDA [*going to* WILLY *in the kitchen*]: I think that's the best way, dear. 'Cause there's no use drawing it out, you'll just never get along.

[WILLY *doesn't respond.*]

BIFF: People ask where I am and what I'm doing, you don't know, and you don't care. That way it'll be off your mind and you can start brightening up again. All right? That clears it, doesn't it? [WILLY *is silent, and* BIFF *goes to him.*] You gonna wish me luck, scout? [*He extends his hand.*] What do you say?

LINDA: Shake his hand, Willy.

WILLY [*turning to her, seething with hurt*]: There's no necessity to mention the pen at all, y'know.

BIFF [*gently*]: I've got no appointment, Dad.

WILLY [*erupting fiercely*]: He put his arm around . . . ?

BIFF: Dad, you're never going to see what I am, so what's the use of arguing? If I strike oil I'll send you a check. Meantime forget I'm alive.

WILLY [*to* LINDA]: Spite, see?

BIFF: Shake hands, Dad.

WILLY: Not my hand.

BIFF: I was hoping not to go this way.

WILLY: Well, this is the way you're going. Good-by.

[BIFF *looks at him a moment, then turns sharply and goes to the stairs.*]

WILLY [*stops him with*]: May you rot in hell if you leave this house!

BIFF [*turning*]: Exactly what is it that you want from me?

WILLY: I want you to know, on the train, in the mountains, in the valleys, wherever you go, that you cut down your life for spite!

BIFF: No, no.

WILLY: Spite, spite, is the word of your undoing! And when you're down and out, remember what did it. When you're rotting somewhere beside the railroad tracks, remember, and don't you dare blame it on me!

BIFF: I'm not blaming it on you!

WILLY: I won't take the rap for this, you hear?

[HAPPY *comes down the stairs and stands on the bottom step, watching.*]

BIFF: That's just what I'm telling you!

WILLY [*sinking into a chair at a table, with full accusation*]: You're trying to put a knife in me—don't think I don't know what you're doing!

BIFF: All right, phony! Then let's lay it on the line. [*He whips the rubber tube out of his pocket and puts it on the table.*]

HAPPY: You crazy . . .

LINDA: Biff! [*She moves to grab the hose, but* BIFF *holds it down with his hand.*]

BIFF: Leave it there! Don't move it!

WILLY [*not looking at it*]: What is that?

BIFF: You know goddam well what that is.

WILLY [*caged, wanting to escape*]: I never saw that.

BIFF: You saw it. The mice didn't bring it into the cellar! What is this supposed to do, make a hero out of you? This supposed to make me sorry for you?

WILLY: Never heard of it.

BIFF: There'll be no pity for you, you hear it? No pity!

WILLY [*to* LINDA]: You hear the spite!

BIFF: No, you're going to hear the truth—what you are and what I am!

LINDA: Stop it!

WILLY: Spite!

HAPPY [*coming down toward* BIFF]: You cut it now!

BIFF [*to* HAPPY]: The man don't know who we are! The man is gonna know! [*To* WILLY.] We never told the truth for ten minutes in this house!

HAPPY: We always told the truth!

BIFF [*turning on him*]: You big blow, are you the assistant buyer? You're one of the two assistants to the assistant, aren't you?

HAPPY: Well, I'm practically—

BIFF: You're practically full of it! We all are! And I'm through with it [*to* WILLY.] Now hear this, Willy, this is me.

WILLY: I know you!

BIFF: You know why I had no address for three months? I stole a suit in Kansas City and I was in jail. [*To* LINDA, *who is sobbing.*] Stop crying. I'm through with it.

[LINDA *turns away from them, her hands covering her face.*]

WILLY: I suppose that's my fault!

BIFF: I stole myself out of every good job since high school!

WILLY: And whose fault is that?

BIFF: And I never got anywhere because you blew me so full of hot air I could never stand taking orders from anybody! That's whose fault it is!

WILLY: I hear that!

LINDA: Don't, Biff!

BIFF: It's goddam time you heard that! I had to be boss big shot in two weeks, and I'm through with it!

WILLY: Then hang yourself! For spite, hang yourself!

BIFF: No! Nobody's hanging himself, Willy! I ran down eleven flights with a pen in my hand today. And suddenly I stopped, you hear me? And in the middle of that office building, do you hear this? I stopped in the middle of that building and I saw—the sky. I saw the things that I love in this world. The work and the food and time to sit and smoke. And I looked at the pen and said to myself, what the hell am I grabbing this for? Why am I trying to become what I don't want to be? What am I doing in an office, making a contemptuous, begging fool of myself, when all I want is out there, waiting for me the minute I say I know who I am! Why can't I say that, Willy? [*He tries to make* WILLY *face him, but* WILLY *pulls away and moves to the left.*]

WILLY [*with hatred, threateningly*]: The door of your life is wide open!

BIFF: Pop! I'm a dime a dozen, and so are you!

WILLY [*turning on him now in an uncontrolled outburst*]: I am not a dime a dozen! I am Willy Loman, and you are Biff Loman!

[BIFF *starts for* WILLY, *but is blocked by* HAPPY. *In his fury,* BIFF *seems on the verge of attacking his father.*]

BIFF: I am not a leader of men, Willy, and neither are you. You were never anything but a hard-working drummer who landed in the ash can like all the rest of them! I'm one dollar an hour, Willy I tried seven states and couldn't raise it. A buck an hour! Do you gather my meaning? I'm not bringing home any prizes any more, and you're going to stop waiting for me to bring them home!

WILLY [*directly to* BIFF]: You vengeful, spiteful mut!

[BIFF *breaks from* HAPPY. WILLY, *in fright, starts up the stairs.* BIFF *grabs him.*]

BIFF [*at the peak of his fury*]: Pop, I'm nothing! I'm nothing, Pop. Can't you understand that? There's no spite in it any more. I'm just what I am, that's all.

[BIFF*'s fury has spent itself, and he breaks down, sobbing, holding on to* WILLY, *who dumbly fumbles for* BIFF*'s face.*]

WILLY [*astonished*]: What're you doing? What're you doing? [*To* LINDA.] Why is he crying?

BIFF [*crying, broken*]: Will you let me go, for Christ's sake? Will you take that phony dream and burn it before something happens? [*Struggling to contain himself, he pulls away and moves to the stairs.*] I'll go in the morning. Put him—put him to bed. [*Exhausted,* BIFF *moves up the stairs to his room.*]

WILLY [*after a long pause, astonished, elevated*]: Isn't that—isn't that remarkable? Biff—he likes me!

LINDA: He loves you, Willy!

HAPPY [*deeply moved*]: Always did, Pop.

WILLY: Oh, Biff! [*staring wildly.*] He cried! Cried to me. [*He is choking with his love, and now cries out his promise.*] That boy—that boy is going to be magnificent!

[BEN *appears in the light just outside the kitchen.*]

BEN: Yes, outstanding, with twenty thousand behind him.

LINDA [*sensing the racing of his mind, fearfully, carefully*]: Now come to bed, Willy. It's all settled now.

WILLY [*finding it difficult not to rush out of the house*]: Yes, we'll sleep. Come on. Go to sleep, Hap.

BEN: And it does take a great kind of a man to crack the jungle.

[*In accents of dread,* BEN's *idyllic music starts up.*]

HAPPY [*his arm around* LINDA]: I'm getting married, Pop, don't forget it. I'm changing everything. I'm gonna run that department before the year is up. You'll see, Mom. [*He kisses her.*]

BEN: The jungle is dark but full of diamonds, Willy.

[WILLY *turns, moves, listening to* BEN.]

LINDA: Be good. You're both good boys, just act that way, that's all.

HAPPY: 'Night, Pop. [*He goes upstairs.*]

LINDA [*to* WILLY]: Come, dear.

BEN [*with greater force*]: One must go in to fetch a diamond out.

WILLY [*to* LINDA, *as he moves slowly along the edge of kitchen, toward the door*]: I just want to get settled down, Linda. Let me sit alone for a little.

LINDA [*almost uttering her fear*]: I want you upstairs.

WILLY [*taking her in his arms*]: In a few minutes, Linda. I couldn't sleep right now. Go on, you look awful tired. [*He kisses her.*]

BEN: Not like an appointment at all. A diamond is rough and hard to the touch.

WILLY: Go on now. I'll be right up.

LINDA: I think this is the only way, Willy.

WILLY: Sure, it's the best thing.

BEN: Best thing!

WILLY: The only way. Everything is gonna be—go on, kid, get to bed. You look so tired.

LINDA: Come right up.

WILLY: Two minutes.

[LINDA *goes into the living room, then reappears in her bedroom.* WILLY *moves just outside the kitchen door.*]

WILLY: Loves me. [*Wonderingly.*] Always loved me. Isn't that a remarkable thing? Ben, he'll worship me for it!

BEN [*with promise*]: It's dark there, but full of diamonds.

WILLY: Can you imagine that magnificence with twenty thousand dollars in his pocket?

LINDA [*calling from her room*]: Willy! Come up!

WILLY [*calling into the kitchen*]: Yes! yes. Coming! It's very smart, you realize that, don't you, sweetheart? Even Ben sees it. I gotta go, baby. 'By! 'By! [*Going over to* BEN, *almost dancing.*] Imagine? When the mail comes he'll be ahead of Bernard again!

BEN: A perfect proposition all around.

WILLY: Did you see how he cried to me? Oh, if I could kiss him, Ben!

BEN: Time, William, time!

WILLY: Oh, Ben, I always knew one way or another we were gonna make it, Biff and I!

BEN [*looking at his watch*]: The boat. We'll be late. [*He moves slowly off into the darkness.*]

WILLY [*elegiacally, turning to the house*]: Now when you kick off, boy, I want a seventy-yard boot, and get right down the field under the ball, and when you hit, hit low and hit hard, because it's important, boy. [*He swings around and faces the audience.*] There's all kinds of important people in the stands, and the first thing you know . . . [*Suddenly realizing he is alone.*] Ben! Ben, where do I . . . ? [*He makes a sudden movement of search.*] Ben, how do I . . . ?

LINDA [*calling*]: Willy, you coming up?

WILLY [*uttering a gasp of fear, whirling about as if to quiet her*]: Sh! [*He turns around as if to find his way; sounds, faces, voices, seem to be swarming in upon him and he flicks at them, crying.*] Sh! Sh! [*Suddenly music, faint and high, stops him. It rises in intensity, almost to an unbearable scream. He goes up and down on his toes, and rushes off around the house.*] Shhh!

LINDA: Willy?

[*There is no answer.* LINDA *waits.* BIFF *gets up off his bed. He is still in his clothes.* HAPPY *sits up.* BIFF *stands listening.*]

LINDA [*with real fear*]: Willy, answer me! Willy!

[*There is the sound of a car starting and moving away at full speed.*]

LINDA: No!

BIFF [*rushing down the stairs*]: Pop!

[*As the car speeds off, the music crashes down in a frenzy of sound, which becomes the soft pulsation of a single cello string.* BIFF *slowly returns to his bedroom. He and* HAPPY *gravely don their jackets.* LINDA *slowly walks out of her room. The music has developed into a dead march. The leaves of day are appearing over everything.* CHARLEY *and* BERNARD, *somberly dressed, appear and knock on the kitchen door.* BIFF *and* HAPPY *slowly descend the stairs to the kitchen as* CHARLEY *and* BERNARD *enter. All stop a moment when* LINDA, *in clothes of mourning, bearing a little bunch of roses, comes through the draped doorway into the kitchen. She goes to* CHARLEY *and takes his arm. Now all move toward the audience, through the wall-line of the kitchen. At the limit of the apron,* LINDA *lays down the flowers, kneels, and sits back on her heels. All stare down at the grave.*]

REQUIEM

CHARLEY:　It's getting dark, Linda.

[LINDA *doesn't react. She stares at the grave.*]

BIFF:　How about it, Mom? Better get some rest, heh? They'll be closing the gate soon.

[LINDA *makes no move. Pause.*]

HAPPY [*deeply angered*]:　He had no right to do that. There was no necessity for it. We would've helped him.
CHARLEY [*grunting*]:　Hmmm.
BIFF:　Come along, Mom.
LINDA:　Why didn't anybody come?
CHARLEY:　It was a very nice funeral.
LINDA:　But where are all the people he knew? Maybe they blame him.
CHARLEY:　Naa. It's a rough world, Linda. They wouldn't blame him.
LINDA:　I can't understand it. At this time especially. First time in thirty-five years we were just about free and clear. He only needed a little salary. He was even finished with the dentist.
CHARLEY:　No man only needs a little salary.
LINDA:　I can't understand it.
BIFF:　There were a lot of nice days. When he'd come home from a trip; or on Sundays, making the stoop; finishing the cellar; putting on the new porch; when he built the extra bathroom; and put up the garage. You know something, Charley, there's more of him in that front stoop than in all the sales he ever made.
CHARLEY:　Yeah. He was a happy man with a batch of cement.
LINDA:　He was so wonderful with his hands.
BIFF:　He had the wrong dreams. All, all, wrong.
HAPPY [*almost ready to fight* BIFF]:　Don't say that!
BIFF:　He never knew who he was.
CHARLEY [*stopping* HAPPY'*s movement and reply. To* BIFF]:　Nobody dast blame this man. You don't understand: Willy was a salesman. And for a salesman, there is no rock bottom to the life. He don't put a bolt to a nut, he don't tell you the law or give you medicine. He's a man way out there in the blue, riding on a smile and a shoeshine. And when they start not smiling back—that's an earthquake. And then you get

yourself a couple of spots on your hat, and you're finished. Nobody dast blame this man. A salesman is got to dream, boy. It comes with the territory.

BIFF: Charley, the man didn't know who he was.

HAPPY [*infuriated*]: Don't say that!

BIFF: Why don't you come with me, Happy?

HAPPY: I'm not licked that easily. I'm staying right in this city, and I'm gonna beat this racket! [*He looks at* BIFF, *his chin set.*] The Loman Brothers!

BIFF: I know who I am, kid.

HAPPY: All right, boy. I'm gonna show you and everybody else that Willy Loman did not die in vain. He had a good dream. It's the only dream you can have—to come out number-one man. He fought it out here, and this is where I'm gonna win it for him.

BIFF [*with a hopeless glance at* HAPPY, *bends toward his mother*]: Let's go, Mom.

LINDA: I'll be with you in a minute. Go on, Charley. [*He hesitates.*] I want to, just for a minute. I never had a chance say good-by.

[CHARLEY *moves away, followed by* HAPPY. BIFF *remains a slight distance up and left of* LINDA. *She sits there, summoning herself. The flute begins, not far away, playing behind her speech.*]

LINDA: Forgive me, dear. I can't cry. I don't know what it is, I can't cry. I don't understand it. Why did you ever do that? Help me Willy, I can't cry. It seems to me that you're just on another trip. I keep expecting you. Willy, dear, I can't cry. Why did you do it? I search and search and I search, and I can't understand it, Willy. I made the last payment on the house today. Today, dear. And there'll be nobody home. [*A sob rises in her throat.*] We're free and clear. [*Sobbing more fully, released.*] We're free. [BIFF *comes slowly toward her.*] We're free . . . We're free . . .

[BIFF *lifts her to her feet and moves out up right with her in his arms.* LINDA *sobs quietly.* BERNARD *and* CHARLEY *come together and follow them, followed by* HAPPY. *Only the music of the flute is left on the darkening stage as over the house the hard towers of the apartment buildings rise into sharp focus, and the curtain falls.*]

QUESTIONS

Act I

1. What is unusual about the staging of *Death of a Salesman?* What is the function of such staging?

2. How does Miller foreshadow coming conflicts with the Wagner company, with Biff, and with the environment?

3. Describe the impasse that confronts Biff and Happy. Why has it developed?

4. Miller has established graphic dramatic contrasts. Which ones stand out most vividly? How do they serve to structure the play?

5. Discuss Willy's faith in things: cars, refrigerators, advertised products. Why do they all seem to be worthless, betrayers of his confidence? How does this motif help to structure the plot?

6. Linda knows that Willy's not earning, but borrowing money from Charlie. Why does she remain silent?
7. What does it say about Willy that he hasn't left the Wagner company on his own? Relate this to his failure to use the rubber tubing.

Act II and Requiem
1. Act II opens with rising action, filled with optimism. Explain why.
2. Describe how revelations about Willy and the business deepen the plot of the play.
3. Explain how Biff is a reflection of Willy and why that intensifies the hostility between them. Why does Biff take or steal things of no consequence?
4. What does the Requiem contribute to plot and theme?
5. One of the ingredients of tragedy is that the protagonist himself is instrumental in the misadventures that befall him. How is this true of both Oedipus and Willy Loman?
6. We feel different kinds of sympathy for Oedipus and Willy. Why? Oedipus begins as a king and ends a blind man leaving his country, his wife a suicide. Willy has only dreamed of being on top. He kills himself while his wife lives. Where are the similarities in their lives? the differences?
7. Compare and contrast how Sophocles and Miller have observed the Aristotelian unities. How does Miller manage to escape them while preserving them?

22. Form

The two major types of dramatic composition are comedy and tragedy. There are, of course, other forms of drama: tragicomedy (which we saw in Hughes's *Soul Gone Home* in Chapter 19), farce, allegory, melodrama, burlesque, social and political drama, and so forth. Nevertheless, tragedy is the purest form of drama that we would term "serious," while comedy is that form of drama that provokes amusement or laughter.

Pure tragedy and comedy are among our oldest dramatic forms. Aristotle defined tragedy as the "imitation of an action that is serious, complete, and of a certain magnitude," basing his prescription largely on the classic Greek theater of the fifth century B.C. Classic Greek theater—that of Aeschylus, Sophocles, and Euripides—offers some of the finest examples of tragedy. Other periods recognized for the flourishing of pure tragedy are the late Renaissance (which includes the theater of Shakespeare) and the neoclassical age of late-seventeenth-century France, which produced a great tragedian, Jean Racine. Obviously, technical and structural differences exist between the tragic dramas of different periods. For example, action in Greek tragedy develops through an alternating rhythm of dramatic scene and choral interlude, while action in a Shakespearean tragedy flows—often surges—from event to event, often ignoring the Greek obsession with the "unities" of time, place, and action. Similarly, a contemporary tragedy such as Arthur Miller's *Death of a Salesman* does not deal with the heroic and noble figures of Greek and Shakespearean tragedy but instead with ordinary men and women. Yet the sense of tragedy radiating from the great dramas of various ages remains constant, for in pure tragedy we witness individuals at war with society, the world, and themselves; caught in that universal conflict between good and evil; subjected to pain, suffering, and often death; the victims of what the Greeks termed "moira," or fate. We identify with the intense world of tragedy, sensing perhaps our own proximity to the suffering and catastrophe enacted.

In fact, it is the *experience* of tragedy that illuminates for us its essential nature. The power of tragedy lies in its ability to involve the audience in the destiny of its characters. With tragedy, we witness, typically, chief characters, or protagonists, who are immersed in suffering—not arbitrary suffering or suffering for its own sake, but suffering caused by the protagonists' painful efforts to make sense out of life and to order their destiny. These figures seek moral and spiritual certainties in a fallen world. They are noble in their quest, often grander than us in passion and purpose, but like us in their key faults, which the Greeks termed *hamartia*. As they embrace their inevitably disastrous destiny, we come to fear for their fate, because we know that we could be overtaken by similar events, and to pity them for their misfortunes. Aristotle called this audience response to tragedy *catharsis*—the purging of emotion that permits a deeper wisdom to emerge. Thus we share with the tragic character a hard-earned wisdom about the inevitability of suffering and about the trials of life. But we also share with the tragic character a paradoxically affirmative insight into the potential greatness and nobility of men and women. In tragedy, Arthur Miller has written, "lies the belief—optimistic if you will—in the perfectability of man."

By contrast, the rhythm of comedy removes the audience from characters, objectifies the dramatic experience of the play, and permits us to look in a detached and often critical manner at the vices and virtues of social creatures. The world of comedy is typically a social landscape that is susceptible to order and improvement if only human beings would suppress their foibles and vices and seek to improve or reform themselves. Whereas the world of tragedy is a relatively closed universe in which an affirmative vision can emerge only after genuine suffering and loss, the world of comedy is open, joyful, often overflowing with life, and delightfully ritualistic. There is potential disaster and ruination in comedy, but comic action moves—whether farcically, amusingly, ironically, satirically, fantastically, or boisterously—toward rebirth, regeneration, and improvement.

The Greeks called comedy *komoidia*—a joyful song of celebration, a form of play that often blended the sacred, secular, and profane. The element of play is central to our enjoyment of comedy, for in the comic world we witness characters who play at being in love (or not in love) or at being warlike, who are miserly, or foolish, or pompous, or tyrannical, or villainous. These characters tend to be caricatures—simplified embodiments of specific foibles and vices. By extension, the conflicts that these ridiculous figures enmesh themselves in might be real and potentially disastrous, but we are amused by their antics and problems, rather than awed or frightened by them. At the same time, the value of comedy goes beyond our ability to laugh at characters. Comedy contains its own cathartic, or therapeutic, value, enlightening us about human weaknesses and delusions, objectifying our criticism of social and political sham and exploitation, holding the mirror of nature up to our own ridiculous behavior, and perhaps curing us of any temptation to take our problems too seriously.

In the world of comedy, fortune is a kind mediator between potential diaster and eventual triumph for individuals. Thus comedy defuses conflict, even as it offers quirky and unpredictable surprises in the advancement of the action. Despite these surprises, the comic world is known and manageable, populated with equally well-known social types. Moreover, there are fairly standard plot variations in comedy, notably on the theme of love or on one's position in society or on the battle of the sexes. Governing the comic plot is the happy or favorable ending—that celebration of youth over age, goodness over wickedness, common sense over dogmatism or downright mindlessness,

understanding over misunderstanding, life over death. Comedy's conclusion invokes balance, harmony, and renewal; it is an affirmation of the sheer abundance that is possible in human existence.

In this section, two of the world's greatest dramatists—Aristophanes and Shakespeare—treat the subjects of love and war from the opposing perspectives of comedy and tragedy. Aristophanes's *Lysistrata* is a boisterous, satirical, and often farcical comedy about the battle of the sexes, set against the very real backdrop of the Peloponnesian War (431–404 B.C.), which pitted Athens against Sparta. He ridicules and holds up for laughter what Othello calls the "Pride, pomp, and circumstance of glorious war," while exposing the farcical nature of human sexuality. By contrast, Shakespeare's *Othello* is a profound and intricate study of the destructive element that undermines the substance of love, human sexuality, life, and civilization itself. In the words of the critic Alvin Kernan, *Othello* captures through a rich symbology "those qualities of being and universal forces that are forever at war in the universe and between which tragic man is always in movement." Both plays assert their own versions of comic and tragic order at the end of the action in an attempt to show how the world should be ordered properly. Yet the divergences in these plays are equally significant. In these departures, we can discover the antithetical energies that animate comic and tragic drama.

Aristophanes

LYSISTRATA

Translated by Dudley Fitts

PERSONS REPRESENTED

LYSISTRATA, ⎫	SPARTAN HERALD
KALONIKE, ⎬ Athenian women	SPARTAN AMBASSADOR
MYRRHINE, ⎭	A SENTRY
LAMPITO, a Spartan woman	[BABY SON OF KINESIAS
CHORUS	STRATYLLIS
COMMISSIONER	SPARTANS
KINESIAS, husband of Myrrhine	ATHENIANS]

Scene: Athens. First, a public square; later, beneath the walls of the Akropolis;° later, a courtyard within the Akropolis.

Akropolis: Fortress of Athens, sacred to the goddess Athena.

PROLOGUE°

Athens; a public square; early morning; Lysistrata alone.

LYSISTRATA: If someone had invited them to a festival—
    of Bacchos,° say; or to Pan's° shrine, or to Aphrodite's°
    over at Kolias—, you couldn't get through the streets,
    what with the drums and the dancing. But now,
    not a woman in sight!
                  Except—oh, yes!   5

[*Enter* KALONIKE.]

    Here's one of my neighbors, at last. Good
        morning, Kalonike.
KALONIKE: Good morning, Lysistrata.
                              Darling,
    don't frown so! You'll ruin your face!
LYSISTRATA: Never mind my face.
    Kalonike,
    the way we women behave! Really, I don't blame the men   10
    for what they say about us.
KALONIKE: No; I imagine they're right.
LYSISTRATA: For example: I call a meeting
    to think out a most important matter—and what happens?
    The women all stay in bed!
KALONIKE: Oh, they'll be along.
    It's hard to get away, you know: a husband, a cook,
    a child . . . Home life can be *so* demanding!   15
LYSISTRATA: What I have in mind is even more demanding.
KALONIKE: Tell me: what is it?
LYSISTRATA: It's big.
KALONIKE: Goodness! *How* big?
LYSISTRATA: Big enough for all of us.
KALONIKE: But we're not all here!
LYSISTRATA: We would be, if *that's* what was up!
                        No, Kalonike,   20
    this is something I've been turning over for nights,
    long sleepless nights.
KALONIKE: It must be getting worn down, then,
    if you've spent so much time on it.

Prologue: Portion of the play explaining the background and current action. **Bacchos:** (Bacchus) God of wine and the object of wild, orgiastic ritual and celebration; also called Dionysus. **Pan:** God of nature, forests, flocks, and shepherds, depicted as half-man and half-goat. Pan was considered playful and lecherous. **Aphrodite:** Goddess of love.

LYSISTRATA: Worn down or not,
  it comes to this: Only we women can save Greece!
KALONIKE: Only we women? Poor Greece!
LYSISTRATA: Just the same,   25
  it's up to us. First, we must liquidate
  the Peloponnesians—
KALONIKE: Fun, fun!
LYSISTRATA: —and then the Boiotians.°
KALONIKE: Oh! But not those heavenly eels!
LYSISTRATA: You needn't worry.
  I'm not talking about eels.—But here's the point:
  If we can get the women from those places—   30
  all those Boiotians and Peloponnesians—
  to join us women here, why, we can save
  all Greece!
KALONIKE: But dearest Lysistrata!
  How can women do a thing so austere, so
  political? We belong at home. Our only armor's   35
  our perfumes, our saffron dresses and
  our pretty little shoes!
LYSISTRATA: Exactly. Those
  transparent dresses, the saffron, the
     perfume, those pretty shoes—
KALONIKE: Oh?
LYSISTRATA: Not a single man would lift
  his spear—
KALONIKE: I'll send my dress to the dyer's tomorrow!   40
LYSISTRATA: —or grab a shield—
KALONIKE: The sweetest little negligee—
LYSISTRATA: —or haul out his sword.
KALONIKE: I know where
  I can buy the dreamiest sandals!
LYSISTRATA: Well, so you see. Now, shouldn't
  the women have come?
KALONIKE: Come? They should have *flown!*
LYSISTRATA: Athenians are always late.
                              But imagine!   45
  There's no one here from the South Shore, or from Salamis.
KALONIKE: Things are hard over in Salamis, I swear.
  They have to get going at dawn.
LYSISTRATA: And nobody from Acharnai.
  I thought they'd be here hours ago.
KALONIKE: Well, you'll get

Boiotians: Crude-mannered inhabitants of Boiotia, which was noted for its seafood.

that awful Theagenes woman: she'll be   50
a sheet or so in the wind.
                 But look!
Someone at last! Can you see who they are?

[*Enter* MYRRHINE *and other women.*]

LYSISTRATA: They're from Anagyros.
KALONIKE: They certainly are.
You'd know them anywhere, by the scent.
MYRRHINE: Sorry to be late, Lysistrata.
                        Oh come,   55
don't scowl so. Say something!
LYSISTRATA: My dear Myrrhine,
what is there to say? After all,
you've been pretty casual about the whole thing.
MYRRHINE: Couldn't find
my girdle in the dark, that's all.
                  But what *is*
"the whole thing"?
KALONIKE: No, we've got to wait   60
for those Boiotians and Peloponnesians.
LYSISTRATA: That's more like it.—But, look!
Here's Lampito!

[*Enter* LAMPITO *with women from Sparta.*]

LYSISTRATA: Darling Lampito,
how pretty you are today! What a nice color!
Goodness, you look as though you could strangle a bull!   65
LAMPITO: Ah think Ah could! It's the work-out
in the gym every day; and, of co'se that dance of ahs
where y' kick yo' own tail.
KALONIKE: What an adorable figure!
LAMPITO: Lawdy, when y' touch me lahk that,
Ah feel lahk a heifer at the altar!
LYSISTRATA: And this young lady?   70
Where is she from?
LAMPITO: Boiotia. Social-Register type.
LYSISTRATA: Ah. "Boiotia of the fertile plain."
KALONIKE: And if you look,
you'll find the fertile plain has just been mowed.
LYSISTRATA: And this lady?
LAMPITO: Hagh, wahd, handsome.
She comes from Korinth.

KALONIKE: High and wide's the word for it.

LAMPITO: Which one of you   75
  called this heah meeting, and why?

LYSISTRATA: I did.

LAMPITO: Well, then, tell us:
  What's up?

MYRRHINE: Yes, darling, what *is* on your mind, after all?

LYSISTRATA: I'll tell you.—But first, one little question.

MYRRHINE: Well?

LYSISTRATA: It's your husbands. Fathers of your children. Doesn't it
    bother you
  that they're always off with the Army? I'll stake my life,   80
  not one of you has a man in the house this minute!

KALONIKE: Mine's been in Thrace the last five months, keeping an eye
  on that General.

MYRRHINE: Mine's been in Pylos for seven.

LAMPITO: And mahn,
  whenever he gets a *dis*charge, he goes raht back
  with that li'l ole shield of his, and enlists again!   85

LYSISTRATA: And not the ghost of a lover to be found!
  From the very day the war began—
                              those Milesians!
  I could skin them alive!
                    —I've not seen so much, even,
  as one of those leather consolation prizes.—
  But there! What's important is: If I've found a way   90
  to end the war, are you with me?

MYRRHINE: I should *say* so!
  Even if I have to pawn my best dress and
  drink up the proceeds.

KALONIKE: Me, too! Even if they split me
  right up the middle, like a flounder.

LAMPITO: Ah'm shorely with you.
  Ah'd crawl up Taygetos° on mah knees   95
  if that'd bring peace.

LYSISTRATA: All right, then; here it is:
  Women! Sisters!
  If we really want our men to make peace,
  we must be ready to give up—

MYRRHINE: Give up what?
  Quick, tell us!

LYSISTRATA: But *will* you?

Taygetos: A mountain range.

MYRRHINE: We will, even if it kills us.   100
LYSISTRATA: Then we must give up going to bed with our men.

[*Long silence.*]

Oh? So now you're sorry? Won't look at me?
Doubtful? Pale? All teary-eyed?
                              But come: be frank with me.
Will you do it, or not? Well? Will you do it?
MYRRHINE: I couldn't. No.
Let the war go on.
KALONIKE: Nor I. Let the war go on.   105
LYSISTRATA: You, you little flounder,
ready to be split up the middle?
KALONIKE: Lysistrata, no!
I'd walk through fire for you—you *know* I would!—but don't
ask us to give up *that!* Why, there's nothing like it!
LYSISTRATA: And you?
BOIOTIAN: No. I must say *I'd* rather walk through fire.   110
LYSISTRATA: What an utterly perverted sex we women are!
No wonder poets write tragedies about us.
There's only one thing we can think of.
                              But you from Sparta:
if you stand by me, we may win yet! Will you?
It means so much!
LAMPITO: Ah sweah, it means *too* much!   115
By the Two Goddesses,° it does! Asking a girl
to sleep—Heaven knows how long!—in a great big bed
with nobody there but herself! But Ah'll stay with you!
Peace comes first!
LYSISTRATA: Spoken like a true Spartan!
KALONIKE: But if—
                    oh dear!
                              —if we give up what you tell us to,   120
will there *be* any peace?
LYSISTRATA: Why, mercy, of course there will!
We'll just sit snug in our very thinnest gowns,
perfumed and powdered from top to bottom, and those men
simply won't stand still! And when we say No,
they'll go out of their minds! And there's your peace.   125
You can take my word for it.

Two Goddesses: A woman's oath referring to Demeter, the earth goddess, and her daughter Persephone, who was associated with seasonal cycles of fertility.

LAMPITO: Ah seem to remember
　　that Colonel Menelaos threw his sword away
　　when he saw Helen's breast all bare.°
KALONIKE: But, goodness me!
　　What if they just get up and leave us?
LYSISTRATA: In that case
　　we'll have to fall back on ourselves, I suppose.   130
　　But they won't.
KALONIKE: I must say that's not much help. But
　　what if they drag us into the bedroom?
LYSISTRATA: Hang on to the door.
KALONIKE: What if they slap us?
LYSISTRATA: If they do, you'd better give in.
　　But be sulky about it. Do I have to teach you how?
　　You know there's no fun for men when they have to force you.   135
　　There are millions of ways of getting them to see reason.
　　Don't you worry: a man
　　doesn't like it unless the girl cooperates.
KALONIKE: I suppose so. Oh, all right. We'll go along.
LAMPITO: Ah imagine us Spahtans can arrange a peace. But you   140
　　Athenians! Why, you're just war-mongerers!
LYSISTRATA: Leave that to me.
　　I know how to make them listen.
LAMPITO: Ah don't see how.
　　After all, they've got their boats; and there's lots of money
　　piled up in the Akropolis.
LYSISTRATA: The Akropolis? Darling,
　　we're taking over the Akropolis today!   145
　　That's the older women's job. All the rest of us
　　are going to the Citadel to sacrifice—you understand me?
　　And once there, we're in for good!
LAMPITO: Whee! Up the rebels!
　　Ah can see you're a good strateegist.
LYSISTRATA: Well, then, Lampito,
　　what we have to do now is take a solemn oath.   150
LAMPITO: Say it. We'll sweah.
LYSISTRATA: This is it.
　　—But where's our Inner Guard?
　　　　—Look, Guard: you see this shield?
　　Put it down here. Now bring me the victim's entrails.
KALONIKE: But the oath?

Colonel Menelaos . . . Helen's breast: Helen, wife of King Menelaos of Sparta, was abducted by Paris and taken to Troy. The incident led to the Trojan War.

LYSISTRATA: You remember how in Aischylos' *Seven*°
  they killed a sheep and swore on a shield? Well, then?   155
KALONIKE: But I don't see how you can swear for peace on a shield.
LYSISTRATA: What else do you suggest?
KALONIKE: Why not a white horse?
  We could swear by that.
LYSISTRATA: And where will you get a white horse?
KALONIKE: I never thought of that. *What* can we do?
LYSISTRATA: I have it!
  Let's set this big black wine-bowl on the ground   160
  and pour in a gallon or so of Thasian,° and swear
  not to add one drop of water.
LAMPITO: Ah lahk *that* oath!
LYSISTRATA: Bring the bowl and the wine-jug.
KALONIKE: Oh, what a simply *huge* one!
LYSISTRATA: Set it down. Girls, place your hands on the gift-offering.
  O Goddess of Persuasion! And thou, O Loving-cup: 165
  Look upon this our sacrifice, and
  be gracious!
KALONIKE: See the blood spill out. How red and pretty it is!
LAMPITO: And Ah must say it smells good.
MYRRHINE: Let me swear first!
KALONIKE: No, by Aphrodite, we'll match for it!   170
LYSISTRATA: Lampito: all of you women: come, touch the bowl,
  and repeat after me—remember, this is an oath—:
  I WILL HAVE NOTHING TO DO WITH MY HUSBAND OR MY
      LOVER
KALONIKE: *I will have nothing to do with my husband or my lover*
LYSISTRATA: THOUGH HE COME TO ME IN PITIABLE CONDITION   175
KALONIKE: *Though he come to me in pitiable condition*
  (Oh Lysistrata! This is killing me!)
LYSISTRATA: IN MY HOUSE I WILL BE UNTOUCHABLE
KALONIKE: *In my house I will be untouchable*
LYSISTRATA: IN MY THINNEST SAFFRON SILK   180
KALONIKE: *In my thinnest saffron silk*
LYSISTRATA: AND MAKE HIM LONG FOR ME.
KALONIKE: *And make him long for me.*
LYSISTRATA: I WILL NOT GIVE MYSELF
KALONIKE: *I will not give myself*   185
LYSISTRATA: AND IF HE CONSTRAINS ME
KALONIKE: *And if he constrains me*

Seven: Aeschylus's *Seven Against Thebes,* which deals with the war between the sons of Oedipus for the throne of Thebes. **Thasian:** Wine from Thasos.

LYSISTRATA: I WILL BE COLD AS ICE AND NEVER MOVE
KALONIKE: *I will be cold as ice and never move*
LYSISTRATA: I WILL NOT LIFT MY SLIPPERS TOWARD THE
       CEILING   190
KALONIKE: *I will not lift my slippers toward the ceiling*
LYSISTRATA: OR CROUCH ON ALL FOURS LIKE THE LIONESS IN
       THE CARVING
KALONIKE: *Or crouch on all fours like the lioness in the carving*
LYSISTRATA: AND IF I KEEP THIS OATH LET ME DRINK FROM
       THIS BOWL
KALONIKE: *And if I keep this oath let me drink from this bowl*   195
LYSISTRATA: IF NOT, LET MY OWN BOWL BE FILLED WITH
       WATER.
KALONIKE: *If not, let my own bowl be filled with water.*
LYSISTRATA: You have all sworn?
MYRRHINE: We have.
LYSISTRATA: Then thus
   I sacrifice the victim.

   [*Drinks largely.*]

KALONIKE: Save some for us!
   Here's to you, darling, and to you, and to you!   200

   [*Loud cries offstage.*]

LAMPITO: What's all *that* whoozy-goozy?
LYSISTRATA: Just what I told you.
   The older women have taken the Akropolis.
   Now you, Lampito,
   rush back to Sparta. We'll take care of things here. Leave
   these girls here for hostages.
                      The rest of you,   205
   up to the Citadel: and mind you push in the bolts.
KALONIKE: But the men? Won't they be after us?
LYSISTRATA: Just you leave
   the men to me. There's not fire enough in the world,
   or threats either, to make me open these doors
   except on my own terms.
KALONIKE: I hope not, by Aphrodite!   210
   After all,
   we've got a reputation for bitchiness to live up to.   [*Exeunt.*°]

Exeunt: Latin for "they go out."

PARODOS:°
CHORAL EPISODE

The hillside just under the Akropolis. Enter Chorus of Old Men with burning torches and braziers; much puffing and coughing.

KORYPHAIOS^(man):° Forward march, Drakes, old friend: never you mind
   that damn big log banging hell down on your back.

Strophe° 1

CHORUS^(men): There's this to be said for longevity:
   You see things you thought that you'd never see.
     Look, Strymodoros, who would have thought it?   5
     We've caught it—
               the New Femininity!
   The wives of our bosom, our board, our bed—
   Now, by the gods, they've gone ahead
   And taken the Citadel (Heaven knows why!),
   Profanèd the sacred statuar-y,   10
           And barred the doors,
           The subversive whores!
KORYPHAIOS^(m): Shake a leg there, Philurgos, man: The Akropolis or bust!
   Put the kindling around here. We'll build one almighty big
   bonfire for the whole bunch of bitches, every last one;   15
   and the first we fry will be old Lykon's woman.

Antistrophe° 1

CHORUS^(m): They're not going to give me the old horse-laugh!
   No, by Demeter, they won't pull this off!
     Think of Kleomenes: even he
     Didn't go free
             till he brought me his stuff.   20
   A good man he was, all stinking and shaggy,
   Bare as an eel except for the bag he
   Covered his rear with. God, what a mess!
   Never a bath in six years, I'd guess.
           Pure Sparta, man!   25
           He also ran.
KORYPHAIOS^(m): That was a siege, friends! Seventeen ranks strong

---

Parodos: The song or ode chanted by the Chorus on their entry. **Koryphaios:** Leader of the Chorus; also called *Choragos*. There are two Choruses and two Koryphaioi, one male and one female. **Strophe:** Song sung by the Chorus as they danced from stage right to stage left. **Antistrophe:** Song sung by the Chorus following the Strophe, as they danced back from stage left to stage right.

we slept at the Gate. And shall we not do as much
against these women, whom God and Euripides hate?
If we don't, I'll turn in my medals from Marathon.   30

Strophe 2

CHORUS⁽ᵐ⁾: Onward and upward! A little push,
    And we're there.
Ouch, my shoulders! I could wish
    For a pair
Of good strong oxen. Keep your eye   35
    On the fire there, it mustn't die.
                    Akh! Akh!
    The smoke would make a cadaver cough!

Antistrophe 2

Holy Herakles, a hot spark
    Bit my eye!
Damn this hellfire, damn this work!   40
    So say I.
Onward and upward just the same.
(Laches, remember the Goddess: for shame!)
                    Akh! Akh!   45
    The smoke would make a cadaver cough!
KORYPHAIOS⁽ᵐ⁾: At last (and let us give suitable thanks to God
    for his infinite mercies) I have managed to bring
    my personal flame to the common goal. It breathes, it lives.
    Now, gentlemen, let us consider. Shall we insert   50
    the torch, say, into the brazier, and thus extract
    a kindling brand? And shall we then, do you think,
    push on to the gate like valiant sheep? On the whole yes.
    But I would have you consider this, too: if they—
    I refer to the women—should refuse to open,   55
    what then? Do we set the doors afire
    and smoke them out? At ease, men. Meditate.
    Akh, the smoke! Woof! What we really need
    is the loan of a general or two from the Samos Command.°
    At least we've got this lumber off our backs.   60
    That's something. And now let's look to our fire.

    O Pot, brave Brazier, touch my torch with flame!
    Victory, Goddess, I invoke thy name!

Samos Command: Headquarters of the Athenian military.

Strike down these paradigms of female pride,
And we shall hang our trophies up inside.   65

[*Enter* CHORUS OF OLD WOMEN *on the walls of the Akropolis, carrying jars of water.*]

KORYPHAIOS^(woman): Smoke, girls, smoke! There's smoke all over the place!
   Probably fire, too. Hurry, girls! Fire! Fire!

Strophe 1

CHORUS^(women): Nikodike, run!
   Or Kalyke's done
   To a turn, and poor Kritylla's   70
   Smoked like a ham.
                    Damn
   These old men! Are we too late?
   I nearly died down at the place
   Where we fill our jars:
       Slaves pushing and jostling—   75
       Such a hustling
   I never saw in all my days.

Antistrophe 1

   But here's water at last.
   Haste, sisters, haste!
   Slosh it on them, slosh it down,
   the silly old wrecks!   80
                    Sex
   Almighty! What they want's
   A hot bath? Good. Send one down.
   Athena of Athens town,
       Trito-born!° Helm of Gold!   85
       Cripple the old
   Firemen! Help us help them drown!

[*The old men capture a woman,* STRATYLLIS.]

STRATYLLIS: Let me go! Let me go!
KORYPHAIOS^(w):   You walking corpses,
   have you no shame?
KORYPHAIOS^(m):   I wouldn't have believed it!
   An army of women in the Akropolis!   90

Trito-born: Athena, goddess of wisdom, was said to have been born near Lake Tritonis, in Libya.

KORYPHAIOS^(w): So we scare you, do we? Grandpa, you've seen
  only our pickets yet!

KORYPHAIOS^(m):   Hey, Phaidrias!
  Help me with the necks of these jabbering hens!

KORYPHAIOS^(w): Down with your pots, girls! We'll need both hands
  if these antiques attack us!

KORYPHAIOS^(m):   Want your face kicked in?   95

KORYPHAIOS^(w): Want your balls chewed off?

KORYPHAIOS^(m):   Look out! I've got a stick!

KORYPHAIOS^(w): You lay a half-inch of your stick on Stratyllis,
  and you'll never stick again!

KORYPHAIOS^(m): Fall apart!

KORYPHAIOS^(w):   I'll spit up your guts!

KORYPHAIOS^(m):   Euripides! Master!
  How well you knew women!

KORYPHAIOS^(w):   Listen to him, Rhodippe,   100
  up with the pots!

KORYPHAIOS^(m):   Demolition of God,
  what good are your pots?

KORYPHAIOS^(w):   You refugee from the tomb,
  what good is your fire?

KORYPHAIOS^(m):   Good enough to make a pyre
  to barbecue you!

KORYPHAIOS^(w): We'll squizzle your kindling!

KORYPHAIOS^(m): You think so?

KORYPHAIOS^(w):   Yah! Just hang around a while!   105

KORYPHAIOS^(m): Want a touch of my torch?

KORYPHAIOS^(w):   It needs a good soaping.

KORYPHAIOS^(m): How about you?

KORYPHAIOS^(w):   Soap for a senile bridegroom!

KORYPHAIOS^(m): Senile? Hold your trap

KORYPHAIOS^(w):   Just *you* try to hold it!

KORYPHAIOS^(m): The yammer of women!

KORYPHAIOS^(w):   Oh is that so?
  You're not in the jury room now, you know.   110

KORYPHAIOS^(m): Gentlemen, I beg you, burn off that woman's hair!

KORYPHAIOS^(w): Let it come down!

[*They empty their pots on the men.*]

KORYPHAIOS^(m): What a way to drown!

KORYPHAIOS^(w):   Hot, hey?

KORYPHAIOS^(m):   Say,
  enough!

KORYPHAIOS^(w): Dandruff

needs watering. I'll make you   115
nice and fresh.
KORYPHAIOS^(m): For God's sake, you,
hold off!

SCENE I

[*Enter a Commissioner accompanied by four constables.*]

COMMISSIONER: These degenerate women! What a racket of little drums,
what a yapping for Adonis° on every house-top!
It's like the time in the Assembly when I was listening
to a speech—out of order, as usual—by that fool
Demostratos,° all about troops for Sicily,°   5
that kind of nonsense—
              and there was his wife
trotting around in circles howling
Alas for Adonis!—
          and Demostratos insisting
we must draft every last Zakynthian that can walk—
and his wife up there on the roof,   10
drunk as an owl, yowling
Oh weep for Adonis!—
          and that damned ox Demostratos
mooing away through the rumpus. That's what we get
for putting up with this wretched woman-business!
KORYPHAIOS^(m): Sir, you haven't heard the half of it. They laughed at us!   15
Insulted us! They took pitchers of water
and nearly drowned us! We're still wringing out our clothes,
for all the world like unhousebroken brats.
COMMISSIONER: Serves you right, by Poseidon!
Whose fault is it if these women-folk of ours   20
get out of hand? We coddle them,
we teach them to be wasteful and loose. You'll see a husband
go into a jeweler's. "Look," he'll say,
"jeweler," he'll say, "you remember that gold choker
you made for my wife? Well, she went to a dance last night   25
and broke the clasp. Now, I've got to go to Salamis,
and can't be bothered. Run over to my house tonight,
will you, and see if you can put it together for her."
Or another one

Adonis: Fertility god, loved by Aphrodite. **Demostratos:** Athenian orator and politician. **Sicily:** Reference to the Sicilian Expedition (415–413 B.C.) in which Athens was decisively defeated.

goes to a cobbler—a good strong workman, too,   30
with an awl that was never meant for child's play. "Here,"
he'll tell him, "one of my wife's shoes is pinching
her little toe. Could you come up about noon
and stretch it out for her?"
               Well, what do you expect?
Look at me, for example, I'm a Public Officer,   35
and it's one of my duties to pay off the sailors.
And where's the money? Up there in the Akropolis!
And those blasted women slam the door in my face!
But what are we waiting for?
              —Look here, constable,
stop sniffing around for a tavern, and get us   40
some crowbars. We'll force their gates! As a matter of fact,
I'll do a little forcing myself.

[*Enter* LYSISTRATA, *above, with* MYRRHINE, KALONIKE, *and the* BOIOTIAN.]

LYSISTRATA: No need of forcing.
  Here I am, of my own accord. And all this talk
  about locked doors—! We don't need locked doors,
  but just the least bit of common sense.   45
COMMISSIONER: Is that so, ma'am!
               —Where's my constable?
               —Constable,
  arrest that woman, and tie her hands behind her.
LYSISTRATA: If he touches me, I swear by Artemis
  there'll be one scamp dropped from the public pay-roll tomorrow!
COMMISSIONER: Well, constable? You're not afraid, I suppose? Grab her,   50
  two of you, around the middle!
KALONIKE: No, by Pandrosos!°
  Lay a hand on her, and I'll jump on you so hard
  your guts will come out the back door!
COMMISSIONER: That's what *you* think!
  Where's the sergeant?—Here, you: tie up that trollop first,
  the one with the pretty talk!
MYRRHINE: By the Moon-Goddess,°   55
  just try! They'll have to scoop you up with a spoon!
COMMISSIONER: Another one!
              Officer, seize that woman!
                  I swear
  I'll put an end to this riot!

Pandrosos: A woman's oath referring to one of the daughters of the founder of Athens. **Moon-Goddess:**
Artemis, goddess of the hunt and of fertility, daughter of Zeus.

BOIOTIAN: By the Taurian,°
  one inch closer, you'll be one screaming bald-head!
COMMISSIONER: Lord, what a mess! And my constables seem ineffective.   60
  But—women get the best of us? By God, no!
                      —Skythians!°
  Close ranks and forward march!
LYSISTRATA: "Forward," indeed!
  By the Two Goddesses, what's the sense in *that?*
  They're up against four companies of women
  armed from top to bottom.
COMMISSIONER: Forward, my Skythians!   65
LYSISTRATA: Forward, yourselves, dear comrades!
  You grainlettucebeanseedmarket girls!
  You garlicandonionbreadbakery girls!
  Give it to 'em! Knock 'em down! Scratch 'em!
  Tell 'em what you think of 'em!

[*General melee, the* SKYTHIANS *yield.*]

                  —Ah, that's enough!   70
  Sound a retreat: good soldiers don't rob the dead.
COMMISSIONER: A nice day *this* has been for the police!
LYSISTRATA: Well, there you are.—Did you really think we women
  would be driven like slaves? Maybe now you'll admit
  that a woman knows something about spirit.
COMMISSIONER: Spirit enough,   75
  especially spirits in bottles! Dear Lord Apollo!
KORYPHAIOS [m]: Your Honor, there's no use talking to them. Words
  mean nothing whatever to wild animals like these.
  Think of the sousing they gave us! and the water
  was not, I believe, of the purest.   80
KORYPHAIOS [w]: You shouldn't have come after us. And if you try it again,
  you'll be one eye short!—Although, as a matter of fact,
  what I like best is just to stay at home and read,
  like a sweet little bride: never hurting a soul, no,
  never going out. But if you *must* shake hornets' nests,   85
  look out for the hornets.

Strophe 1

CHORUS [m]: Of all the beasts that God hath wrought
    What monster's worse than woman?

Taurian: Reference to Artemis, who was said to have been worshiped in a cult at Taurica Chersonesos.
Skythians: Athenian archers.

Who shall encompass with his thought
   Their guile unending? No man.   90

They've seized the Heights, the Rock, the Shrine—
   But to what end? I wot not.
Sure there's some clue to their design!
   Have you the key? I thought not.
KORYPHAIOS^(m): We might question them, I suppose. But I warn you, sir,   95
   don't believe anything you hear! It would be un-Athenian
   not to get to the bottom of this plot.
COMMISSIONER: Very well.
   My first question is this: Why, so help you God,
   did you bar the gates of the Akropolis?
LYSISTRATA: Why?
   To keep the money, of course. No money, no war.   100
COMMISSIONER: You think that money's the cause of war?
LYSISTRATA: I do.
   Money brought about that Peisandros° business
   and all the other attacks on the State. Well and good!
   They'll not get another cent here!
COMMISSIONER: And what will you do?
LYSISTRATA: What a question! From now on, we intend   105
   to control the Treasury.
COMMISSIONER: Control the Treasury!
LYSISTRATA: Why not? Does that seem strange? After all,
   we control our household budgets.
COMMISSIONER: But that's different!
LYSISTRATA: "Different"? What do you mean?
COMMISSIONER: I mean simply this:
   it's the Treasury that pays for National Defense.   110
LYSISTRATA: Unnecessary. We propose to abolish war.
COMMISSIONER: Good God.—And National Security?
LYSISTRATA: Leave that to us.
COMMISSIONER: You?
LYSISTRATA: Us.
COMMISSIONER: We're done for, then!
LYSISTRATA: Never mind.
   We women will save you in spite of yourselves.
COMMISSIONER: What nonsense!
LYSISTRATA: If you like. But you must accept it, like it or not.   115
COMMISSIONER: Why, this is downright subversion!
LYSISTRATA: Maybe it is.
   But we're going to save you, Judge.
COMMISSIONER: I don't *want* to be saved.

Peisandros: A politician who plotted against the Athenian democracy.

LYSISTRATA: Tut. The death-wish. All the more reason.

COMMISSIONER: But the idea of women bothering
     themselves about peace and war!

LYSISTRATA: Will you listen to me?

COMMISSIONER: Yes. But be brief, or I'll—   120

LYSISTRATA: This is no time for stupid threats.

COMMISSIONER: By the gods,
   I can't stand any more!

AN OLD WOMAN: Can't stand? Well, well.

COMMISSIONER: That's enough out of you, you old buzzard!
   Now, Lysistrata: tell me what you're thinking.

LYSISTRATA: Glad to.
                Ever since this war began   125
We women have been watching you men, agreeing with you,
keeping our thoughts to ourselves. That doesn't mean
we were happy: we weren't, for we saw how things were going;
but we'd listen to you at dinner
arguing this way and that.
              —Oh you, and your big   130
Top Secrets!—
         And then we'd grin like little patriots
(though goodness knows we didn't feel like grinning) and ask you:
"Dear, did the Armistice come up in Assembly today?"
And you'd say, "None of your business! Pipe down!" you'd say.
And so we would.

AN OLD WOMAN: *I* wouldn't have, by God!   135

COMMISSIONER: You'd have taken a beating, then!
                 —Go on.

LYSISTRATA: Well, we'd be quiet. But then, you know, all at once
you men would think up something worse than ever.
Even *I* could see it was fatal. And, "Darling," I'd say,
"have you gone completely mad?" And my husband would look at me   140
and say, "Wife, you've got your weaving to attend to.
Mind your tongue, if you don't want a slap. 'War's
a man's affair!' "°

COMMISSIONER: Good words, and well pronounced.

LYSISTRATA: You're a fool if you think so.
              It was hard enough
to put up with all this banquet-hall strategy.   145
But then we'd hear you out in the public square:
"Nobody left for the draft-quota here in Athens?"
you'd say; and, "No," someone else would say, "not a man!"
And so we women decided to rescue Greece.
You might as well listen to us now: you'll have to, later.   150

'War's a man's affair!': Quoted from Homer's *Iliad*, VI, 492, Hector's farewell to his wife, Andromache.

COMMISSIONER: *You* rescue Greece? Absurd.
LYSISTRATA: You're the absurd one.
COMMISSIONER: You expect me to take orders from a woman?
            I'd die first!
LYSISTRATA: Heavens, if that's what's bothering you, take my veil,
    here, and wrap it around your poor head.
KALONIKE: Yes,
    and you can have my market-basket, too.   155
    Go home, tighten your girdle, do the washing, mind
    your beans! "War's a woman's affair!"
KORYPHAIOS⁽ʷ⁾:   Ground pitchers! Close ranks!

Antistrophe

CHORUS⁽ʷ⁾: This is a dance that I know well,
        My knees shall never yield.   160
    Wobble and creak I may, but still
        I'll keep the well-fought field.
    Valor and grace march on before,
        Love prods us from behind.
    Our slogan is EXCELSIOR,   165
        Our watchword SAVE MANKIND.
KORYPHAIOS⁽ʷ⁾: Women, remember your grandmothers! Remember
    that little old mother of yours, what a stinger she was!
    On, on, never slacken. There's a strong wind astern!
LYSISTRATA: O Eros of delight! O Aphrodite! Kyprian!°   170
    If ever desire has drenched our breasts or dreamed
    in our thighs, let it work so now on the men of Hellas°
    that they shall tail us through the land, slaves, slaves
    to Woman, Breaker of Armies!
COMMISSIONER: And if we do?
LYSISTRATA: Well, for one thing, we shan't have to watch you   175
    going to market, a spear in one hand, and heaven knows
    what in the other.
KALONIKE: Nicely said, by Aphrodite!
LYSISTRATA: As things stand now, you're neither men nor women.
    Armor clanking with kitchen pans and pots—
    You sound like a pack of Korybantes!°   180
COMMISSIONER: A man must do what a man must do.
LYSISTRATA: So I'm told.
    But to see a General, complete with Gorgon-shield,
    jingling along the dock to buy a couple of herrings!

Kyprian: Reference to Aphrodite's association with Cyprus (Kyprus), a place sacred to her and a center for
her worship.   **Hellas:** Greece.   **Korybantes:** Priestesses of Cybele, a fertility goddess, who was celebrated
in frenzied rituals accompanied by the beating of cymbals.

KALONIKE: *I* saw a Captain the other day—lovely fellow he was,
  nice curly hair—sitting on his horse; and—can you believe it?— 185
  he'd just bought some soup, and was pouring it into his helmet!
  And there was a soldier from Thrace
  swishing his lance like something out of Euripides,
  and the poor fruit-store woman got so scared
  that she ran away and let him have his figs free! 190
COMMISSIONER: All this is beside the point.
                    Will you be so kind
  as to tell me how you mean to save Greece?
LYSISTRATA:
                    Of course.
  Nothing could be simpler.
COMMISSIONER: I assure you, I'm all ears.
LYSISTRATA: Do you know anything about weaving?
  Say the yarn gets tangled: we thread it 195
  this way and that through the skein, up and down,
  until it's free. And it's like that with war.
  We'll send our envoys
  up and down, this way and that, all over Greece,
  until it's finished.
COMMISSIONER: Yarn? Thread? Skein? 200
  Are you out of your mind? I tell you,
  war is a serious business.
LYSISTRATA: So serious
  that I'd like to go on talking about weaving.
COMMISSIONER: All right. Go ahead.
LYSISTRATA: The first thing we have to do
  is to wash our yarn, get the dirt out of it. 205
  You see? Isn't there too much dirt here in Athens?
  You must wash those men away.
              Then our spoiled wool—
  that's like your job-hunters, out for a life
  of no work and big pay. Back to the basket,
  citizens or not, allies or not, 210
  or friendly immigrants.
           And your colonies?
  Hanks of wool lost in various places. Pull them
  together, weave them into one great whole,
  and our voters are clothed for ever.
COMMISSIONER: It would take a woman
  to reduce state questions to a matter of carding and weaving. 215
LYSISTRATA: You fool! Who were the mothers whose sons sailed off
  to fight for Athens in Sicily?
COMMISSIONER: Enough!
  I beg you, do not call back those memories.
LYSISTRATA: And then,

instead of the love that every woman needs,
we have only our single beds, where we can dream   220
of our husbands off with the Army.
                              Bad enough for wives!
But what about our girls, getting older every day,
and older, and no kisses?
COMMISSIONER: Men get older, too.
LYSISTRATA: Not in the same sense.
                        A soldier's discharged,
and he may be bald and toothless, yet he'll find   225
a pretty young thing to go to bed with.
                              But a woman!
Her beauty is gone with the first gray hair.
She can spend her time
consulting the oracles and the fortune-tellers,
but they'll never send her a husband.   230
COMMISSIONER: Still, if a man can rise to the occasion—
LYSISTRATA: Rise? Rise, yourself!

[*Furiously*]

Go invest in a coffin!
                    You've money enough.
                              I'll bake you
a cake for the Underworld.
                        And here's your funeral
wreath!

[*She pours water upon him.*]

MYRRHINE: And here's another!

[*More water.*]

KALONIKE: And here's   235
    my contribution!

[*More water.*]

LYSISTRATA: What are you waiting for?
   All aboard Styx Ferry!
                      Charon's° calling for you!
   It's sailing-time: don't disrupt the schedule!

Charon: The god who ferried the souls of the newly dead across the river Styx to Hades.

COMMISSIONER: The insolence of women! And to me!
  No, by God, I'll go back to town and show   240
  the rest of the Commission what might happen
     to them.   [*Exit* COMMISSIONER.]
LYSISTRATA: Really, I suppose we should have laid out his corpse
  on the doorstep, in the usual way.
                        But never mind.
We'll give him the rites of the dead tomorrow morning.
        [*Exit* LYSISTRATA *with* MYRRHINE *and* KALONIKE.]

PARABASIS:° CHORAL EPISODE

Ode° 1

KORYPHAIOS^(m): Sons of Liberty, awake! The day of glory is at hand.
CHORUS^(m): I smell tyranny afoot, I smell it rising from the land.
  I scent a trace of Hippias,° I sniff upon the breeze
  A dismal Spartan hogo that suggests King Kleisthenes.°
    Strip, strip for action, brothers!   5
    Our wives, aunts, sisters, mothers
  Have sold us out: the streets are full of godless female rages.
  Shall we stand by and let our women confiscate our wages?
                              [Epirrhema° 1]
KORYPHAIOS^(m): Gentlemen, it's a disgrace to Athens, a disgrace
  to all that Athens stands for, if we allow these grandmas   10
  to jabber about spears and shields and making friends
  with the Spartans. What's a Spartan? Give me a wild wolf
  any day. No. They want the Tyranny back, I suppose.
  Are we going to take that? No. Let us look like
  the innocent serpent, but be the flower under it,   15
  as the poet sings. And just to begin with,
  I propose to poke a number of teeth
  down the gullet of that harridan over there.

Antode° 1

KORYPHAIOS^(w): Oh, is that so? When you get home, your own mamma
    won't know you!
CHORUS^(w): Who do you think we are, you senile bravos? Well, I'll show you.   20

Parabasis: Section of the play in which the author presented his own views through the Koryphaios directly to the audience. The parabasis in *Lysistrata* is shorter than those in Aristophanes' other works and unusual in that the Koryphaios does not speak directly for the author. **Ode:** Song sung by the Chorus. **Hippias:** An Athenian tyrant. **Kleisthenes:** A bisexual Athenian. **Epirrhema:** A part of the parabasis spoken by the Koryphaios following an ode delivered by his or her half of the Chorus. **Antode:** Lyric song sung by half of the Chorus in response to the Ode sung by the other half.

I bore the sacred vessels in my eighth year,° and at ten
I was pounding out the barley for Athena Goddess;° then
   They made me Little Bear
   At the Brauronian Fair;°
I'd held the Holy Basket° by the time I was of age,   25
The Blessed Dry Figs had adorned my plump decolletage.

                           [Antepirrhema° 1]

KORYPHAIOS⁽ʷ⁾: A "disgrace to Athens," and I, just at the moment
I'm giving Athens the best advice she ever had?
Don't I pay taxes to the State? Yes, I pay them
in baby boys. And what do you contribute,   30
you impotent horrors? Nothing but waste: all
our Treasury,° dating back to the Persian Wars,
gone! rifled! And not a penny out of your pockets!
Well, then? Can you cough up an answer to that?
Look out for your own gullet, or you'll get a crack   35
from this old brogan that'll make your teeth see stars!

Ode 2

CHORUS⁽ᵐ⁾: Oh insolence!
  Am I unmanned?
  Incontinence!
  Shall my scarred hand   40
  Strike never a blow
  To curb this flow-
  ing female curse?

  Leipsydrion!°
  Shall I betray   45
  The laurels won
  On that great day?
  Come, shake a leg,
  Shed old age, beg
  The years reverse!   50

                           [Epirrhema 2]

KORYPHAIOS⁽ᵐ⁾: Give them an inch, and we're done for! We'll have them
launching boats next and planning naval strategy,

---

eighth year: Young girls between the ages of seven and eleven served in the temple of Athena in the Akropolis. **pounding out the barley for Athena Goddess:** At age ten a girl could be chosen to grind the sacred grain of Athena. **Brauronian Fair:** A ritual in the cult of Artemis, who is associated with wild beasts, in which young girls dressed up as bears and danced for the goddess. **Holy Basket:** In one ritual to Athena, young girls carried baskets of objects sacred to the goddess. **Antepirrhema:** The speech delivered by the second Koryphaios after the second half of the Chorus had sung an ode. **Treasury:** Athenian politicians were raiding the funds that were collected by Athens to finance a war against Persia. **Leipsydrion:** A place where Athenian patriots had heroically fought.

sailing down on us like so many Artemisias.
Or maybe they have ideas about the cavalry.
That's fair enough, women are certainly good   55
in the saddle. Just look at Mikon's paintings,
all those Amazons wrestling with all those men!
On the whole, a straitjacket's their best uniform.

Antode 2

CHORUS^(w): Tangle with me,
   And you'll get cramps.
   Ferocity   60
   's no use now, Gramps!
   By the Two,
   I'll get through
   To you wrecks yet!   65

   I'll scramble your eggs,
   I'll burn your beans,
   With my two legs.
   You'll see such scenes
   As never yet   70
   Your two eyes met.
   A curse? You bet!

                                  [Antepirrhema 2]

KORYPHAIOS^(w): If Lampito stands by me, and that delicious Theban girl,
Ismenia—what good are *you?* You and your seven
Resolutions! Resolutions? Rationing Boiotian eels   75
and making our girls go without them at Hekate's° Feast!
That was statesmanship! And we'll have to put up with it
and all the rest of your decrepit legislation
until some patriot—God give him strength!—
grabs you by the neck and kicks you off the Rock.   80

SCENE II

[*Reenter* LYSISTRATA *and her lieutenants.*]

KORYPHAIOS^(w) *(tragic tone): Great Queen, fair Architect of our emprise,*
  Why lookst thou on us with foreboding eyes?
LYSISTRATA: The behavior of these idiotic women!
  There's something about the female temperament
  that I can't bear!

Hekate: Patron of successful wars, object of a Boiotian cult (later associated with sorcery).

KORYPHAIOS^(w):⠀⠀⠀What in the world do you mean?

LYSISTRATA: Exactly what I say.

KORYPHAIOS^(w): What dreadful thing has happened?
⠀⠀Come, tell us: we're all your friends.

LYSISTRATA:⠀⠀⠀⠀⠀⠀⠀⠀⠀⠀⠀It isn't easy
⠀⠀to say it; yet, God knows, we can't hush it up.

KORYPHAIOS^(w): Well, then? Out with it!

LYSISTRATA:⠀⠀⠀⠀⠀⠀⠀⠀⠀⠀To put it bluntly,
⠀⠀we're dying to get laid.

KORYPHAIOS^(w):⠀⠀⠀⠀Almighty God!⠀⠀⠀⠀⠀⠀⠀⠀⠀⠀⠀10

LYSISTRATA: Why bring God into it?—No, it's just as I say.
⠀⠀I can't manage them any longer: they've gone man-crazy,
⠀⠀they're all trying to get out.
⠀⠀⠀⠀⠀⠀⠀⠀⠀⠀⠀⠀Why, look:
⠀⠀one of them was sneaking out the back door
⠀⠀over there by Pan's cave; another⠀⠀⠀⠀⠀⠀⠀⠀⠀⠀15
⠀⠀was sliding down the walls with rope and tackle;
⠀⠀another was climbing aboard a sparrow, ready to take off
⠀⠀for the nearest brothel—I dragged *her* back by the hair!
⠀⠀They're all finding some reason to leave.
⠀⠀⠀⠀⠀⠀⠀⠀⠀⠀⠀⠀⠀Look there!
⠀⠀There goes another one.
⠀⠀⠀⠀⠀⠀⠀⠀⠀⠀—Just a minute, you!⠀⠀⠀⠀⠀⠀⠀20
⠀⠀Where are you off to so fast?

FIRST WOMAN:⠀⠀⠀⠀⠀⠀I've got to get home.
⠀⠀I've a lot of Milesian wool, and the worms are spoiling it.

LYSISTRATA: Oh bother you and your worms! Get back inside!

FIRST WOMAN: I'll be back right away, I swear I will.
⠀⠀I just want to get it stretched out on my bed.⠀⠀⠀⠀⠀25

LYSISTRATA: You'll do no such thing. You'll stay right here.

FIRST WOMAN:⠀⠀⠀⠀⠀⠀⠀⠀And my wool?
⠀⠀⠀⠀You want it ruined?

LYSISTRATA:⠀⠀⠀⠀⠀⠀Yes, for all I care.

SECOND WOMAN: Oh dear! My lovely new flax from Amorgos—
⠀⠀I left it at home, all uncarded!

LYSISTRATA:⠀⠀⠀⠀⠀⠀⠀⠀Another one!
⠀⠀And all she wants is someone to card her flax.⠀⠀⠀⠀⠀30
⠀⠀Get back in there!

SECOND WOMAN:⠀⠀But I swear by the Moon-Goddess,
⠀⠀the minute I get it done, I'll be back!

LYSISTRATA:⠀⠀⠀⠀⠀⠀⠀⠀⠀⠀I say No.
⠀⠀If you, why not all the other women as well?

THIRD WOMAN: O Lady Eileithyia!° Radiant goddess! Thou

Eileithyia: Goddess of childbirth.

intercessor for women in childbirth! Stay, I pray thee,   35
oh stay this parturition. Shall I pollute
a sacred spot?°

LYSISTRATA: And what's the matter with *you?*

THIRD WOMAN: I'm having a baby—any minute now.

LYSISTRATA: But you weren't pregnant yesterday.

THIRD WOMAN: Well, I am today.
Let me go home for a midwife, Lysistrata: 40
there's not much time.

LYSISTRATA: I never heard such nonsense.
What's that bulging under your cloak?

THIRD WOMAN: A little baby boy.

LYSISTRATA: It certainly isn't. But it's something hollow,
like a basin or—Why, it's the helmet of Athena!
And you said you were having a baby.

THIRD WOMAN: Well, I am! So there!   45

LYSISTRATA: Then why the helmet?

THIRD WOMAN: I was afraid that my pains
might begin here in the Akropolis; and I wanted
to drop my chick into it, just as the dear doves do.

LYSISTRATA: Lies! Evasions!—But at least one thing's clear:
you can't leave the place before your purification.°   50

THIRD WOMAN: But I can't stay here in the Akropolis! Last night I dreamed
of the Snake.

FIRST WOMAN: And those horrible owls, the noise they make!
I can't get a bit of sleep; I'm just about dead.

LYSISTRATA: You useless girls, that's enough: Let's have no more lying.
Of course you want your men. But don't you imagine   55
that they want you just as much? I'll give you my word,
their nights must be pretty hard.
                              Just stick it out!
A little patience, that's all, and our battle's won.
I have heard an Oracle. Should you like to hear it?

FIRST WOMAN: An Oracle? Yes, tell us!

LYSISTRATA: Here is what it says: 60
WHEN SWALLOWS SHALL THE HOOPOE SHUN
    AND SPURN HIS HOT DESIRE,
ZEUS WILL PERFECT WHAT THEY'VE BEGUN
    AND SET THE LOWER HIGHER.

FIRST WOMAN: Does that mean we'll be on top?   65

LYSISTRATA: BUT IF THE SWALLOWS SHALL FALL OUT
    AND TAKE THE HOOPOE'S BAIT,

---

pollute a sacred spot: Giving birth on the Akropolis was forbidden because it was sacred ground. **purification:** A ritual cleansing of a woman after childbirth.

A CURSE MUST MARK THEIR HOUR OF DOUBT,
   INFAMY SEAL THEIR FATE.

THIRD WOMAN: I swear, *that* Oracle's all too clear.

FIRST WOMAN: Oh the dear gods!   70

LYSISTRATA: Let's not be downhearted, girls. Back to our places!
   The god has spoken. How can we possibly fail him?

                    [*Exit* LYSISTRATA *with the dissident women.*]

CHORAL EPISODE

Strophe

CHORUS [m]: I know a little story that I learned way back in school
   Goes like this:
   Once upon a time there was a young man—and no fool—
   Named Melanion; and his
   One aversi-on was marriage. He loathed the very thought.   5
   So he ran off to the hills, and in a special grot
   Raised a dog, and spent his days
   Hunting rabbits. And it says
   That he never never never did come home.
   It might be called a refuge *from* the womb.   10
   All right,
           all right,
                   all right!
   We're as bright as young Melanion, and we hate
   the very sight
   Of you women!

A MAN: How about a kiss, old lady?

A WOMAN: Here's an onion for your eye!   15

A MAN: A kick in the guts, then?

A WOMAN: Try, old bristle-tail, just try!

A MAN: Yet they say Myronides
   On hands and knees
   Looked just as shaggy fore and aft as I!   20

Antistrophe

CHORUS [w]: Well, *I* know a little story, and it's just as good as yours.
   Goes like this:
   Once there was a man named Timon—a rough diamond, of course,
   And that whiskery face of his
   Looked like murder in the shrubbery. By God, he was a son   25
   Of the Furies, let me tell you! And what did he do but run
   From the world and all its ways,

Cursing mankind! And it says
That his choicest execrations as of then
Were leveled almost wholly at *old* men.   30
All right,
      all right,
            all right!
But there's one thing about Timon: he could always stand the sight
of us women.
A WOMAN: How about a crack in the jaw, Pop?
A MAN: I can take it, Ma—no fear!   35
A WOMAN: How about a kick in the face?
A MAN: You'd reveal your old caboose?
A WOMAN: What I'd show,
   I'll have you know,
   Is an instrument you're too far gone to use.   40

SCENE III

[*Reenter* LYSISTRATA.]

LYSISTRATA: Oh, quick, girls, quick! Come here!
A WOMAN: What is it?
LYSISTRATA: A man.
   A man simply bulging with love.
                        O Kyprian Queen,°
   O Paphian, O Kythereian! Hear us and aid us!
A WOMAN: Where is this enemy?
LYSISTRATA: Over there, by Demeter's shrine.
A WOMAN: Damned if he isn't. But who *is* he?
MYRRHINE: My husband.   5
   Kinesias.
LYSISTRATA: Oh then, get busy! Tease him! Undermine him!
   Wreck him! Give him everything—kissing, tickling, nudging,
   whatever you generally torture him with—: give him everything
   except what we swore on the wine we would not give.
MYRRHINE: Trust me.
LYSISTRATA: I do. But I'll help you get him started.   10
   The rest of you women, stay back.

[*Enter* KINESIAS.]

Kyprian Queen: Aphrodite.

KINESIAS: Oh God! Oh my God!
   I'm stiff from lack of exercise. All I can do to stand up.
LYSISTRATA: Halt! Who are you, approaching our lines?
KINESIAS: Me? I.
LYSISTRATA: A man?
KINESIAS: You have eyes, haven't you?
LYSISTRATA: Go away.
KINESIAS: Who says so?
LYSISTRATA: Officer of the Day.
KINESIAS: Officer, I beg you,   15
   by all the gods at once, bring Myrrhine out.
LYSISTRATA: Myrrhine? And who, my good sir, are you?
KINESIAS: Kinesias. Last name's Pennison. Her husband.
LYSISTRATA: Oh, of course. I beg your pardon. We're glad to see you.
   We've heard so much about you. Dearest Myrrhine   20
   is always talking about Kinesias—never nibbles an egg
   or an apple without saying
   "Here's to Kinesias!"
KINESIAS: Do you really mean it?
LYSISTRATA: I do.
   When we're discussing men, she always says
   "Well, after all, there's nobody like Kinesias!"   25
KINESIAS: Good God.—Well, then, please send her down here.
LYSISTRATA: And what do *I* get out of it?
KINESIAS: A standing promise.
LYSISTRATA: I'll take it up with her.

                         [*Exit* LYSISTRATA.]

KINESIAS: But be quick about it!
   Lord, what's life without a wife? Can't eat. Can't sleep.
   Every time I go home, the place is so empty, so   30
   insufferably sad. Love's killing me, Oh,
   hurry!

[*Enter* MANES, *a slave, with* KINESIAS's *baby; the voice of* MYRRHINE *is heard offstage.*]

MYRRHINE: But of course I love him! Adore him—But no,
   he hates love. No. I won't go down.

[*Enter* MYRRHINE, *above.*]

KINESIAS: Myrrhine!
   Darlingest Myrrhinette! Come down quick!
MYRRHINE: Certainly not.
KINESIAS: Not? But why, Myrrhine?   35
MYRRHINE: Why? You don't need me.

KINESIAS: Need you? My God, *look* at me!
MYRRHINE: So long!

[*Turns to go.*]

KINESIAS: Myrrhine, Myrrhine, Myrrhine!
If not for my sake, for our child!

[*Pinches Baby.*]

                —All right, you: pipe up!
BABY: Mummie! Mummie! Mummie!
KINESIAS: You hear that?
Pitiful, I call it. Six days now   40
with never a bath; no food; enough to break your heart!
MYRRHINE: My darlingest child! What a father *you* acquired!
KINESIAS: At least come down for his sake.
MYRRHINE: I suppose I must.
Oh, this mother business!   [*Exit.*]
KINESIAS: How pretty she is! And younger!
The harder she treats me, the more bothered I get.

[MYRRHINE *enters, below.*]

MYRRHINE: Dearest child,   45
you're as sweet as your father's horrid. Give me a kiss.
KINESIAS: Now don't you see how wrong it was to get involved
in this scheming League of women? It's bad
for us both.
MYRRHINE: Keep your hands to yourself!
KINESIAS: But our house
going to rack and ruin?
MYRRHINE: *I* don't care.
KINESIAS: And your knitting   50
all torn to pieces by the chickens? Don't you care?
MYRRHINE: Not at all.
KINESIAS: And our debt to Aphrodite?
Oh, *won't* you come back?
MYRRHINE: No.—At least, not until you men
make a treaty and stop this war.
KINESIAS: Why, I suppose
that might be arranged.
MYRRHINE: Oh? Well, I suppose   55
I might come down then. But meanwhile,
I've sworn not to.

KINESIAS: Don't worry.—Now let's have fun.
MYRRHINE: No! Stop it! I said no!
                                —Although, of course,
    I *do* love you.
KINESIAS: I know you do. Darling Myrrhine:
        come, shall we?
MYRRHINE: Are you out of your mind? In front of the child?   60
KINESIAS: Take him home, Manes.

                                [*Exit* MANES *with* BABY.]
                        There. He's gone.
                                Come on!
    There's nothing to stop us now.
MYRRHINE: You devil! But where?
KINESIAS: In Pan's cave. What could be snugger than that?
MYRRHINE: But my purification before I go back to the Citadel?
KINESIAS: Wash in the Klepsydra.°
MYRRHINE: And my oath?
KINESIAS: Leave the oath to me.   65
    After all, I'm the man.
MYRRHINE: Well . . . if you say so.
                        I'll go find a bed.
KINESIAS: Oh, bother a bed! The ground's good enough for me.
MYRRHINE: No. You're a bad man, but you deserve something better
        than dirt.
                                        [*Exit* MYRRHINE.]

KINESIAS: What a love she is! And how thoughtful!

[*Reenter* MYRRHINE.]

MYRRHINE: Here's your bed.
    Now let me get my clothes off.
                                But, good horrors!   70
    We haven't a mattress.
KINESIAS: Oh, forget the mattress!
MYRRHINE: No.
    Just lying on blankets? Too sordid.
KINESIAS: Give me a kiss.
MYRRHINE: Just a second.   [*Exit* MYRRHINE.]
KINESIAS: I swear, I'll explode!

[*Reenter* MYRRHINE.]

Klepsydra: A water clock beneath the walls of the Akropolis. Kinesias's suggestion borders on blasphemy.

MYRRHINE: Here's your mattress.
  I'll just take my dress off.
                             But look—
where's our pillow?
KINESIAS: I don't *need* a pillow!
MYRRHINE: Well, *I* do.   75
                             [*Exit* MYRRHINE.]
KINESIAS: I don't suppose even Herakles°
  would stand for this!

[*Reenter* MYRRHINE.]

MYRRHINE: There we are. Ups-a-daisy!
KINESIAS: So we are. Well, come to bed.
MYRRHINE: But I wonder:
  is everything ready now?
KINESIAS: I can swear to that. Come, darling!
MYRRHINE: Just getting out of my girdle.
                             But remember, now,   80
  what you promised about the treaty.
KINESIAS: Yes, yes, yes!
MYRRHINE: But no coverlet!
KINESIAS: Damn it, I'll be
  your coverlet!
MYRRHINE: Be right back.   [*Exit* MYRRHINE.]
KINESIAS: This girl and her coverlets
  will be the death of me.

[*Reenter* MYRRHINE.]

MYRRHINE: Here we are. Up you go!
KINESIAS: Up? I've been up for ages.
MYRRHINE: Some perfume?   85
KINESIAS: No, by Apollo!
MYRRHINE: Yes, by Aphrodite!
  I don't care whether you want it or not.
                             [*Exit* MYRRHINE.]
KINESIAS: For love's sake, hurry!

[*Reenter* MYRRHINE.]

Herakles: Greek hero (Hercules) known for his Twelve Labors.

MYRRHINE: Here, in your hand. Rub it right in.
KINESIAS: Never cared for perfume.
    And this is particularly strong. Still, here goes.   90
MYRRHINE: What a nitwit I am! I brought you the Rhodian bottle.
KINESIAS: Forget it.
MYRRHINE: No trouble at all. You just wait here.

                                                    [*Exit* MYRRHINE.]

KINESIAS: God damn the man who invented perfume!

[*Reenter* MYRRHINE.]

MYRRHINE: At last! The right bottle!
KINESIAS: I've got the rightest
    bottle of all, and it's right here waiting for you.   95
    Darling, forget everything else. Do come to bed.
MYRRHINE: Just let me get my shoes off.
                            —And, by the way,
    you'll vote for the treaty?
KINESIAS: I'll think about it.

                                            [MYRRHINE *runs away.*]

    There! That's done it! The damned woman,
    she gets me all bothered, she half kills me,   100
    and off she runs! What'll I do? Where
    can I get laid?
                    —And you, little prodding pal,
    who's going to take care of *you?* No, you and I
    had better get down to old Foxdog's Nursing Clinic.
CHORUS (m): Alas for the woes of man, alas   105
    Specifically for you.
    She's brought you to a pretty pass:
        What are you going to do?
    Split, heart! Sag, flesh! Proud spirit, crack!
    Myrrhine's got you on your back.   110
KINESIAS: The agony, the protraction!
KORYPHAIOS (m):   Friend,
    What woman's worth a damn?
    They bitch us all, world without end.
KINESIAS: Yet they're so damned sweet, man!
KORYPHAIOS (m): Calamitous, that's what I say.   115
    You should have learned that much today.
CHORUS (m): O blessed Zeus, roll womankind.
    Up into one great ball;
    Blast them aloft on a high wind,
        And once there, let them fall.   120

Down, down they'll come, the pretty dears,
And split themselves on our thick spears.

[*Exit* KINESIAS.]

SCENE IV

[*Enter a Spartan Herald.*]

HERALD: Gentlemen, Ah beg you will be so kind
as to direct me to the Central Committee.
Ah have a communication.

[*Reenter* COMMISSIONER.]

COMMISSIONER: Are you a man,
or a fertility symbol?
HERALD: Ah refuse to answer that question!
Ah'm a certified Herald from Spahta, and Ah've come   5
to talk about an ahmistice.
COMMISSIONER: Then why
that spear under your cloak?
HERALD: Ah have no speah!
COMMISSIONER: You don't walk naturally, with your tunic
poked out so. You have a tumor, maybe,
or a hernia?
HERALD: You lost yo' mahnd, man?
COMMISSIONER: Well,   10
something's up, I can see that. And I don't like it.
HERALD: Colonel, Ah resent this.
COMMISSIONER: So I see. But what *is* it?
HERALD: A staff
with a message from Spahta.
COMMISSIONER: Oh, I know about those staffs.
Well, then, man, speak out: How are things in Sparta?
HERALD: Hahd, Colonel, hahd! We're at a standstill.   15
Cain't seem to think of anything but women.
COMMISSIONER: How curious! Tell me, do you Spartans think
that maybe Pan's to blame?
HERALD: Pan? No, Lampito and her little naked friends.
They won't let a man come nigh them.   20
COMMISSIONER: How are you handling it?
HERALD: Losing our mahnds,
if y' want to know, and walking around hunched over
lahk men carrying candles in a gale.

The women have swohn they'll have nothing to do with us
until we get a treaty.
COMMISSIONER: Yes. I know.   25
It's a general uprising, sir, in all parts of Greece.
But as for the answer—
                        Sir: go back to Sparta
and have them send us your Armistice Commission.
I'll arrange things in Athens.
                        And I may say
that my standing is good enough to make them listen.   30
HERALD: A man after mah own haht! Seh, Ah thank you.   [*Exit* HERALD.]

CHORAL EPISODE

Strophe

CHORUS⁽ᵐ⁾: Oh these women! Where will you find
  A slavering beast that's more unkind?
    Where's a hotter fire?
  Give me a panther, any day.
  He's not so merciless as they,   5
    And panthers don't conspire.

Antistrophe

CHORUS⁽ʷ⁾: We may be hard, you silly old ass,
  But who brought you to this stupid pass?
    You're the ones to blame.
  Fighting with us, your oldest friends,   10
  Simply to serve your selfish ends—
    Really, you have no shame!
KORYPHAIOS⁽ᵐ⁾: No, I'm through with women for ever.
KORYPHAIOS⁽ʷ⁾: If you say so.
  Still, you might put some clothes on. You look too absurd
  standing around naked. Come, get into this cloak.   15
KORYPHAIOS⁽ᵐ⁾: Thank you; you're right. I merely took it off
  because I was in such a temper.
KORYPHAIOS⁽ʷ⁾:   That's much better.
  Now you resemble a man again.
                Why have you been so horrid?
  And look: there's some sort of insect in your eye.
  Shall I take it out?
KORYPHAIOS⁽ᵐ⁾:   An insect, is it? So that's   20
  what's been bothering me. Lord, yes: take it out!

KORYPHAIOS [w]: You might be more polite.
—But, heavens!

What an enormous mosquito!
KORYPHAIOS [m]:   You've saved my life.
That mosquito was drilling an artesian well
in my left eye.
KORYPHAIOS [w]:   Let me wipe   25
those tears away.—And now: one little kiss?
KORYPHAIOS [m]: No, no kisses.
KORYPHAIOS [w]: You're so difficult.
KORYPHAIOS [m]: You impossible women! How you do get around us!
The poet was right: Can't live with you, or without you.
But let's be friends.   30
And to celebrate, you might join us in an Ode.

Strophe 1

CHORUS [m and w]: Let it never be said
    That my tongue is malicious:
    Both by word and by deed
I would set an example that's noble and gracious.   35
    We've had sorrow and care
    Till we're sick of the tune.
    Is there anyone here
    Who would like a small loan?
        My purse is crammed,   40
        As you'll soon find;
And you needn't pay me back if the Peace gets signed.

Strophe 2

    I've invited to lunch
    Some Karystian rips°—
    An esurient bunch,   45
But I've ordered a menu to water their lips.
    I can still make soup
    And slaughter a pig.
    You're all coming, I hope?
    But a bath first, I beg!   50
        Walk right up
        As though you owned the place,
And you'll get the front door slammed to in your face.

Karystian rips: The Karystians were allies of Athens but were scorned for their primitive ways and loose morals.

SCENE V

[*Enter* SPARTAN AMBASSADOR, *with entourage.*]

KORYPHAIOS⁽ᵐ⁾: The Commission has arrived from Sparta.
                How oddly they're walking!
                         Gentlemen, welcome to Athens!
    How is life in Lakonia?
AMBASSADOR: Need we discuss that?
    Simply use your eyes.
CHORUS⁽ᵐ⁾:   The poor man's right:
                         What a sight!
AMBASSADOR: Words fail me.   5
    But come, gentlemen, call in your Commissioners,
    and let's get down to a Peace.
CHORAGOS⁽ᵐ⁾:   The state we're in! Can't bear
    a stitch below the waist. It's a kind of pelvic
    paralysis.
COMMISSIONER: Won't somebody call
         Lysistrata?—Gentlemen,
    we're no better off than you.
AMBASSADOR: So I see.   10
A SPARTAN: Seh, do y'all feel a certain strain
    early in the morning?
AN ATHENIAN: I do, sir. It's worse than a strain.
    A few more days, and there's nothing for us but Kleisthenes,
    that broken blossom.
CHORAGOS⁽ᵐ⁾: But you'd better get dressed again.
    You know these people going around Athens with chisels,   15
    looking for statues of Hermes.°
ATHENIAN: Sir, you are right.
SPARTAN: He certainly is! Ah'll put mah own clothes back on.

    [*Enter* ATHENIAN COMMISSIONERS.]

COMMISSIONER: Gentlemen from Sparta, welcome. This is a sorry business.
SPARTAN [*to one of his own group*]: Colonel, we got dressed just in time. Ah
    sweah, if they'd seen us the way we were, there'd have been a new wah   20
    between the states.
COMMISSIONER: Shall we call the meeting to order?
                         Now, Lakonians,
    what's your proposal?

---

statues of Hermes: The usual representation of Hermes was with an erect phallus. Statues of Hermes
were scattered through Athens and were attacked by vandals just before the Sicilian Expedition.

AMBASSADOR: We propose to consider peace.
COMMISSIONER: Good. That's on our minds, too.
                         —Summon Lysistrata.
We'll never get anywhere without her.
AMBASSADOR: Lysistrata?   25
Summon Lysis-*any*body! Only, summon!
KORYPHAIOS [(m)]:   No need to summon:
here she is, herself.

[*Enter* LYSISTRATA.]

COMMISSIONER: Lysistrata! Lion of women!
This is your hour to be
hard and yielding, outspoken and shy, austere and
gentle. You see here   30
the best brains of Hellas (confused, I admit,
by your devious charming) met as one man
to turn the future over to you.
LYSISTRATA: That's fair enough,
unless you men take it into your heads
to turn to each other instead of to us. But I'd know   35
soon enough if you did.
                    —Where is Reconciliation?
Go, some of you: bring her here.

                                          [*Exeunt two women.*]
                    And now, women,
lead the Spartan delegates to me: not roughly
or insultingly, as our men handle them, but gently,
politely, as ladies should. Take them by the hand,   40
or by anything else if they won't give you their hands.

[*The* SPARTANS *are escorted over.*]

There.—The Athenians next, by any convenient handle.

[*The* ATHENIANS *are escorted.*]

Stand there, please.—Now, all of you, listen to me.

[*During the following speech the two women reenter, carrying an enormous statue of a
naked girl; this is Reconciliation.*]

I'm only a woman, I know; but I've a mind,
and, I think, not a bad one: I owe it to my father   45

and to listening to the local politicians.
So much for that.
                    Now, gentlemen,
since I have you here, I intend to give you a scolding.
We are all Greeks.
Must I remind you of Thermopylai,° of Olympia,   50
of Delphoi? names deep in all our hearts?
Are they not a common heritage?
                              Yet you men
go raiding through the country from both sides,
Greek killing Greek, storming down Greek cities—
and all the time the Barbarian across the sea   55
is waiting for his chance!
                    —That's my first point.
AN ATHENIAN: Lord! I can hardly contain myself.
LYSISTRATA: As for you Spartans:
Was it so long ago that Perikleides°
came here to beg our help? I can see him still,
his gray face, his sombre gown. And what did he want?   60
An army from Athens. All Messene
was hot at your heels, and the sea-god splitting your land.
Well, Kimon and his men,
four thousand strong, marched out and saved all Sparta.
And what thanks do we get? You come back to murder us.   65
AN ATHENIAN: They're aggressors, Lysistrata!
A SPARTAN: Ah admit it.
When Ah look at those laigs, Ah sweah Ah'll aggress mahself!
LYSISTRATA: And you, Athenians: do you think you're blameless?
Remember that bad time when we were helpless,   70
and an army came from Sparta, and that was the end of the Thessalian
    menace,
the end of Hippias and his allies.
                    And that was Sparta,
and only Sparta; but for Sparta, we'd be
cringing slaves today, not free Athenians.

[*From this point, the male responses are less to* LYSISTRATA *than to the statue.*]

A SPARTAN: A well shaped speech.
AN ATHENIAN: Certainly it has its points.   75
LYSISTRATA: Why are we fighting each other? With all this history

---

Thermopylai: A narrow pass where, in 480 B.C., an army of three hundred Spartans held out for three days against a superior Persian force.   **Perikleides:** Spartan ambassador to Athens who successfully urged Athenians to aid Sparta in quelling a rebellion.

of favors given and taken, what stands in the way
of making peace?
AMBASSADOR: Spahta is ready, ma'am,
so long as we get that place back.
LYSISTRATA: What place, man?
AMBASSADOR: Ah refer to Pylos.
COMMISSIONER: Not a chance, by God!   80
LYSISTRATA: Give it to them, friend.
COMMISSIONER: But—what shall we have to bargain with?
LYSISTRATA: Demand something in exchange.
COMMISSIONER: Good idea.—Well, then:
Cockeville first, and the Happy Hills, and the country
between the Legs of Megara.
AMBASSADOR: Mah government objects.
LYSISTRATA: Overruled. Why fuss about a pair of legs?   85

[*General assent. The statue is removed.*]

AN ATHENIAN: I want to get out of these clothes and start my plowing.
A SPARTAN: Ah'll fertilize mahn first, by the Heavenly Twins!
LYSISTRATA: And so you shall,
once you've made peace. If you are serious,
go, both of you, and talk with your allies.   90
COMMISSIONER: Too much talk already. No, we'll stand together.
We've only one end in view. All that we want
is our women; and I speak for our allies.
AMBASSADOR: Mah government concurs.
AN ATHENIAN: So does Karystos.
LYSISTRATA: Good—But before you come inside   95
to join your wives at supper, you must perform
the usual lustration. Then we'll open
our baskets for you, and all that we have is yours.
But you must promise upright good behavior
from this day on. Then each man home with his woman!   100
AN ATHENIAN: Let's get it over with.
A SPARTAN: Lead on. Ah follow.
AN ATHENIAN: Quick as a cat can wink!

[*Exeunt all but the* CHORUSES.]

Antistrophe 1

CHORUS [w]: Embroideries and
Twinkling ornaments and
Pretty dresses—I hand   105
them all over to you, and with never a qualm.

They'll be nice for your daughters
On festival days
When the girls bring the Goddess
The ritual prize.   110
Come in, one and all:
Take what you will.
I've nothing here so tightly corked that you can't make it spill.

Antistrophe 2

You may search my house,
But you'll not find   115
The least thing of use,
Unless your two eyes are keener than mine.
Your numberless brats
Are half starved? And your slaves?
Courage, grandpa! I've lots   120
Of grain left, and big loaves.
I'll fill your guts,
I'll go the whole hog;
But if you come too close to me, remember:
'ware the dog!   [*Exeunt* CHORUSES.]

EXODOS°

[*A* DRUNKEN CITIZEN *enters, approaches the gate, and is halted by a sentry.*]

CITIZEN: Open. The. Door.
SENTRY: Now, friend, just shove along!
—So you want to sit down. If it weren't such an old joke,
I'd tickle your tail with this torch. Just the sort of gag
this audience appreciates.
CITIZEN: I. Stay. Right. Here.
SENTRY: Get away from there, or I'll scalp you! The gentlemen from Sparta   5
are just coming back from dinner.

[*Exit* CITIZEN; *the general company reenters; the two* CHORUSES *now represent* SPAR-
TANS *and* ATHENIANS.]

A SPARTAN: Ah must say,
Ah never tasted better grub.
AN ATHENIAN: And those Lakonians!

Exodos: Final scene.

They're gentlemen, by the Lord! Just goes to show,
a drink to the wise is sufficient.
COMMISSIONER: And why not?
A sober man's an ass.   10
Men of Athens, mark my words: the only efficient
Ambassador's a drunk Ambassador. Is that clear?
Look: we go to Sparta,
and when we get there we're dead sober. The result?
Everyone cackling at everyone else. They make speeches;   15
and even if we understand, we get it all wrong
when we file our reports in Athens. But today—!
Everybody's happy. Couldn't tell the difference
between *Drink to Me Only* and
The Star-spangled Athens.
                    What's a few lies,   20
washed down in good strong drink?

[*Reenter the* DRUNKEN CITIZEN.]

SENTRY: God almighty,
he's back again!
CITIZEN: I. Resume. My. Place.
A SPARTAN [*to an Athenian*]: Ah beg yo', seh,
take yo' instrument in yo' hand and play for us.
Ah'm told   25
yo' understand the in*tri*cacies of the floot?
Ah'd lahk to execute a song and dance
in honor of Athens,
                    and, of cohse, of Spahta.
CITIZEN: Toot. On. Your. Flute.

[*The following song is a solo—an aria—accompanied by the flute. The* CHORUS OF
SPARTANS *begins a slow dance.*]

A SPARTAN: O memory,   30
Let the Muse speak once more
In my young voice. Sing glory.
Sing Artemision's shore,
Where Athens fluttered the Persians. *Alalai,*°
Sing glory, that great   35
Victory! Sing also
Our Leonidas and his men,
Those wild boars, sweat and blood

Alalai: War cry.

Down in a red drench. Then, then
The barbarians broke, though they had stood   40
Numberless as the sands before!

O Artemis,
Virgin Goddess, whose darts
Flash in our forests: approve
This pact of peace and join our hearts,   45
From this day on, in love.
Huntress, descend!

LYSISTRATA: All that will come in time.
                              But now, Lakonians,
take home your wives. Athenians, take yours.
Each man be kind to his woman; and you, women   50
be equally kind. Never again, pray God,
shall we lose our way in such madness.

KORYPHAIOS (Athenian):   And now
     let's dance our joy.

[*From this point the dance becomes general.*]

CHORUS (Athenian): Dance, you Graces
                              Artemis, dance
          Dance, Phoibos,° Lord of dancing
                              Dance,   55
          In a scurry of Maenads,° Lord Dionysos
                              Dance, Zeus Thunderer
                    Dance, Lady Hera°
          Queen of the sky
                         Dance, dance, all you gods
          Dance witness everlasting of our pact
     Evohi Evohe°   60
          Dance for the dearest
                         the Bringer of Peace
          Deathless Aphrodite!

COMMISSIONER: Now let us have another song from Sparta.

CHORUS (Spartan): From Taygetos, from Taygetos,
     Lakonian Muse, come down.   65
          Sing to the Lord Apollo
               Who rules Amyklai Town.

Phoibos: Apollo, god of the sun. **Maenads:** Female worshipers of Bacchus (Dionysus). **Hera:** Wife of Zeus. *Evohi Evohe:* "Come forth! Come forth!" An orgiastic cry associated with rituals of Bacchus.

Sing Athena of the House of Brass!°
Sing Leda's Twins,° that chivalry
    Resplendent on the shore
Of our Eurotas; sing the girls
    That dance along before:

    Sparkling in dust their gleaming feet,
        Their hair a Bacchant fire,
    And Leda's daughter, thyrsos° raised,
        Leads their triumphant choir.
CHORUS (S and A): *Evohé!*
        Evohaí!
          Evohé!
            We pass
        Dancing
            dancing
                to greet
Athena of the House of Brass.

70

75

QUESTIONS

1. How does Aristophanes build dramatic suspense at the beginning of the play? What characters and action account for the suspense? What are the two main comic crises in the play?
2. Describe Lysistrata's personality. Does she bear any resemblance to comic characters we find today on TV or in the movies?
3. What are the main traits Aristophanes draws in depicting the women in the play? What traits does he draw in depicting the men? Which of the two sexes appears the stronger willed? How does the contrast between the two sexes create comedy?
4. There are quite a few references to sex during the play. How does Aristophanes incorporate these references into the dialogue? Into the action on stage?
5. Lysistrata has a prolonged argument with the Magistrate. Who wins the argument? Who has the better argument? Explain.
6. The sources of classical Greek comedy are earlier religious rituals and festivals. In these festivals, participants in processions often engaged in wild, suggestive antics, employed jokes and insults, and dressed in erotic costumes. How does *Lysistrata* reflect this cultural background? Why is this ritualistic movement the reverse of tragic movement?

House of Brass: Temple to Athena on the Akropolis of Sparta.   **Leda's Twins:** Leda, raped by Zeus, bore quadruplets, two daughters (one of whom was Helen) and two sons.   **thyrsos:** A staff twined with ivy and carried by Bacchus and his followers.

William Shakespeare

THE TRAGEDY OF OTHELLO, THE MOOR OF VENICE

CHARACTERS

OTHELLO, the Moor
BRABANTIO, (a Venetian senator), father to Desdemona
CASSIO, an honorable lieutenant (to Othello)
IAGO (Othello's ancient), a villain
RODERIGO, a gulled gentleman
DUKE OF VENICE
SENATORS (of Venice)
MONTANO, governor of Cyprus
LODOVICO AND GRATIANO (kinsmen to Brabantio), two noble Venetians
SAILORS
CLOWN
DESDEMONA, wife to Othello
EMILIA, wife to Iago
BIANCA, a courtesan
MESSENGER, HERALD, OFFICERS, VENETIAN GENTLEMEN, MUSICIANS,
    ATTENDANTS

Scene: Venice and Cyprus

ACT I

SCENE I

[*Enter* RODERIGO *and* IAGO.]

RODERIGO:
    Tush, never tell me! I take it much unkindly
    That thou, Iago, who has had my purse
    As if the strings were thine, shouldst know of this.   3
IAGO:
    'Sblood, but you'll not hear me!   4
    If ever I did dream of such a matter,
    Abhor me.
RODERIGO:
    Thou told'st me thou didst hold him in thy hate.

Scene i A street in Venice   **3** *this* i.e. Desdemona's elopement   **4** *'Sblood* by God's blood

IAGO:

>Despise me if I do not. Three great ones of the city,
>In personal suit to make me his lieutenant,
>Off-capped to him; and, by the faith of man,   10
>I know my price; I am worth no worse a place.
>But he, as loving his own pride and purposes,
>Evades them with a bombast circumstance.   13
>Horribly stuffed with epithets of war;
>[And, in conclusion,]
>Nonsuits my mediators; for, "Certes," says he,   16
>"I have already chose my officer."
>And what was he?
>Forsooth, a great arithmetician,   19
>One Michael Cassio, a Florentine
>(A fellow almost damned in a fair wife)   21
>That never set a squadron in the field,
>Nor the division of a battle knows
>More than a spinster; unless the bookish theoric,
>Wherein the tongued consuls can propose
>As masterly as he. Mere prattle without practice
>Is all his soldiership. But he, sir, had th' election;
>And I (of whom his eyes had seen the proof
>At Rhodes, at Cyprus, and on other grounds
>Christian and heathen) must be belee'd and calmed   30
>By debitor and creditor; this counter-caster,   31
>He, in good time, must his lieutenant be,
>And I—God bless the mark!—his Moorship's ancient.   33

RODERIGO:

>By heaven, I rather would have been his hangman.

IAGO:

>Why, there's no remedy; 'tis the curse of service.
>Preferment goes by letter and affection,   36
>And not by old gradation, where each second
>Stood heir to th'first. Now, sir, be judge yourself,
>Whether I in any just term am affined   39
>To love the Moor.

RODERIGO: I would not follow him then.

IAGO:

>O, sir, content you;
>I follow him to serve my turn upon him.
>We cannot all be masters, nor all masters

---

10 *him* i.e. Othello   **13** *a bombast circumstance* pompous circumlocutions   **16** *Nonsuits* rejects   **19** *arithmetician* theoretician   **21** *almost . . . wife* (an obscure allusion: Cassio is unmarried, but see IV,i, 123)   **30** *belee'd and calmed* left in the lurch   **31** *counter-caster* bookkeeper   **33** *ancient* ensign   **36** *affection* favoritism   **39** *affined* obliged

Cannot be truly followed. You shall mark
Many a duteous and knee-crooking knave
That, doting on his own obsequious bondage,
Wears out his time, much like his master's ass,
For naught but provender; and when he's old, cashiered. 48
Whip me such honest knaves! Others there are
Who, trimmed in forms and visages of duty, 50
Keep yet their hearts attending on themselves;
And, throwing but shows of service on their lords,
Do well thrive by them, and when they have lined their coats,
Do themselves homage. These fellows have some soul;
And such a one do I profess myself. For, sir,
It is as sure as you are Roderigo,
Were I the Moor, I would not be Iago.
In following him, I follow but myself;
Heaven is my judge, not I for love and duty,
But seeming so, for my peculiar end;
For when my outward action doth demonstrate
The native act and figure of my heart 62
In compliment extern, 'tis not long after 63
But I will wear my heart upon my sleeve
For daws to peck at; I am not what I am.

RODERIGO:
What a full fortune does the thick-lips owe 66
If he can carry't thus!

IAGO:　　　　　　　Call up her father,
Rouse him. Make after him, poison his delight,
Proclaim him in the streets. Incense her kinsmen,
And though he in a fertile climate dwell,
Plague him with flies; though that his joy be joy,
Yet throw such changes of vexation on't
As it may lose some color.

RODERIGO:
Here is her father's house. I'll call aloud.

IAGO:
Do, with like timorous accent and dire yell 75
As when, by night and negligence, the fire
Is spied in populous cities.

RODERIGO:
What, ho, Brabantio! Signior Brabantio, ho!

IAGO:
Awake! What, ho, Brabantio! Thieves! thieves! thieves!

---

48 *cashiered* turned off　**50** *trimmed* dressed up　**62** *The . . . heart* what I really believe and intend
63 *compliment extern* outward appearance　**66** *thick-lips* (Elizabethans made no clear distinction between
Moors and Negroes); *owe* own　**75** *timorous* terrifying

Look to your house, your daughter, and your bags!
Thieves! thieves!   81

[BRABANTIO *at a window*.]

BRABANTIO [*above*]:
   What is the reason of this terrible summons?
   What is the matter there?
RODERIGO:
   Signior, is all your family within?
IAGO:
   Are your doors locked?
BRABANTIO: Why, wherefore ask you this?
IAGO:
   Zounds, sir, y' are robbed! For shame, put on your gown!
   Your heart is burst; you have lost half your soul.
   Even now, now, very now, an old black ram
   Is tupping your white ewe. Arise, arise!
   Awake the snorting citizens with the bell,   90
   Or else the devil will make a grandsire of you.
   Arise, I say!
BRABANTIO: What, have you lost your wits?
RODERIGO:
   Most reverend signior, do you know my voice?
BRABANTIO:
   Not I. What are you?
RODERIGO:
   My name is Roderigo.
BRABANTIO: The worser welcome!
   I have charged thee not to haunt about my doors.
   In honest plainness thou hast heard me say
   My daughter is not for thee; and now, in madness,
   Being full of supper and distemp'ring draughts,
   Upon malicious knavery dost thou come
   To start my quiet.
RODERIGO:
   Sir, sir, sir—
BRABANTIO: But thou must needs be sure
   My spirit and my place have in them power
   To make this bitter to thee.
RODERIGO: Patience, good sir.
BRABANTIO:
   What tell'st thou me of robbing? This is Venice;
   My house is not a grange.   106

---

81 s.d. *Brabantio at a window* (added from quarto)   **90** *snorting* snoring   **106** *grange* isolated farmhouse

RODERIGO: Most grave Brabantio,
  In simple and pure soul I come to you.
IAGO: Zounds, sir, you are one of those that will not serve God if the devil
  bid you. Because we come to do you service, and you think we are
  ruffians, you'll have your daughter covered with a Barbary horse; you'll
  have your nephews neigh to you; you'll have coursers for cousins, and   112
  gennets for germans.   113
BRABANTIO:
  What profane wretch art thou?
IAGO: I am one, sir, that comes to tell you your daughter and the Moor are
  now making the beast with two backs.
BRABANTIO:
  Thou art a villain.
IAGO: You are—a senator.
BRABANTIO:
  This thou shalt answer. I know thee, Roderigo.
RODERIGO:
  Sir, I will answer anything. But I beseech you,
  If't be your pleasure and most wise consent,
  As partly I find it is, that your fair daughter,
  At this odd-even and dull watch o' the' night,   123
  Transported, with no worse nor better guard
  But with a knave of common hire, a gondolier,
  To the gross clasps of a lascivious Moor—
  If this be known to you, and your allowance,   127
  We then have done you bold and saucy wrongs;
  But if you know not this, my manners tell me
  We have your wrong rebuke. Do not believe
  That, from the sense of all civility,   131
  I thus would play and trifle with your reverence.
  Your daughter, if you have not given her leave,
  I say again, hath made a gross revolt,
  Tying her duty, beauty, wit, and fortunes
  In an extravagant and wheeling stranger   136
  Of here and everywhere. Straight satisfy yourself.
  If she be in her chamber, or your house,
  Let loose on me the justice of the state
  For thus deluding you.
BRABANTIO: Strike on the tinder, ho!
  Give me a taper! Call up all my people!
  This accident is not unlike my dream.   143

---

112 *nephews* i.e. grandsons   **113** *gennets for germans* Spanish horses for near kinsmen   **123** *odd-even* between
night and morning   **127** *allowance* approval   **131** *from the sense* in violation   **136** *extravagant and wheeling*
expatriate and roving   **143** *accident* occurrence

Belief of it oppresses me already
Light, I say! light! [*Exit (above).*]
IAGO: Farewell, for I must leave you.
It seems not meet, nor wholesome to my place,
To be produced—as, if I stay, I shall—
Against the Moor. For I do know the state,
However, this may gall him with some check, 149
Cannot with safety cast him; for he's embarked 150
With such loud reason to the Cyprus wars,
Which even now stand in act, that for their souls 152
Another of his fathom they have none 153
To lead their business; in which regard,
Though I do hate him as I do hell-pains,
Yet, for necessity of present life,
I must show out a flag and sign of love,
Which is indeed but sign. That you shall surely find him,
Lead to the Sagittary the raised search; 159
And there will I be with him. So farewell. [*Exit.*] 160

[*Enter (below)* BRABANTIO *in his nightgown, and servants with torches.*]

BRABANTIO:
It is too true an evil. Gone she is;
And what's to come of my despisèd time
Is naught but bitterness. Now, Roderigo,
Where didst thou see her?—O unhappy girl!—
With the Moor, say'st thou?—Who would be a father?—
How didst thou know 'twas she?—O, she deceives me
Past thought!—What said she to you?—Get moe tapers! 167
Raise all my kindred!—Are they married, think you?
RODERIGO:
Truly I think they are.
BRABANTIO:
O heaven! How got she out? O treason of the blood!
Fathers, from hence trust not your daughters' minds
By what you see them act. Is there not charms
By which the property of youth and maidhood 173
May be abused? Have you not read, Roderigo,
Of some such thing?
RODERIGO: Yes, sir, I have indeed.
BRABANTIO:
Call up my brother.—O, would you had had her!—

---

149 *check* reprimand **150** *cast* discharge **152** *stand in act* are going on **153** *fathom* capacity **159** *Sagittary* an inn **160 s.d.** *nightgown* dressing gown **167** *moe* more **173** *property* nature

Some one way, some another.—Do you know
Where we may apprehend her and the Moor?

RODERIGO:
I think I can discover him, if you please
To get good guard and go along with me.

BRABANTIO:
Pray you lead on. At every house I'll call;
I may command at most.—Get weapons, ho!
And raise some special officers of night.—
On, good Roderigo; I'll deserve your pains.   [*Exeunt.*]   185

SCENE II

[*Enter* OTHELLO, IAGO, *and attendants with torches.*]

IAGO:
Though in the trade of war I have slain men,
Yet do I hold it very stuff o' th' conscience
To do no contrived murther. I lack iniquity
Sometimes to do me service. Nine or ten times
I had thought t' have yerked him here under the ribs.   5

OTHELLO:
'Tis better as it is.

IAGO: Nay, but he prated,
And spoke such scurvy and provoking terms
Against your honor
That with the little godliness I have
I did full hard forbear him. But I pray you, sir,
Are you fast married? Be assured of this,   11
That the magnifico is much beloved,   12
And hath in his effect a voice potential   13
As double as the Duke's. He will divorce you,   14
Or put upon you what restraint and grievance
The law, with all his might to enforce it on,
Will give him cable.

OTHELLO: Let him do his spite.
My services which I have done the signiory   18
Shall out-tongue his complaints. 'Tis yet to know—   19
Which, when I know that boasting is an honor,
I shall promulgate—I fetch my life and being
From men of royal siege; and my demerits   22

---

185 *deserve* show gratitude for
Scene ii Before the lodgings of Othello   **5** *yerked* stabbed   **11** *fast* securely   **12** *magnifico* grandee (Brabantio)   **13** *potential* powerful   **14** *double* doubly influential   **18** *signiory* Venetian government   **19** *yet to
know* still not generally known   **22** *siege* rank; *demerits* deserts

May speak unbonneted to as proud a fortune   23
As this that I have reached. For know, Iago,
But that I love the gentle Desdemona,
I would not my unhousèd free condition   26
Put into circumscription and confine
For the sea's worth. But look, what lights come yond?

IAGO:

Those are the raisèd father and his friends.
You were best go in.

OTHELLO: Not I; I must be found.
My parts, my title, and my perfect soul   31
Shall manifest me rightly. Is it they?

IAGO:

By Janus, I think no.

[*Enter* CASSIO, *with torches, officers.*]

OTHELLO:

The servants of the Duke, and my lieutenant.
The goodness of the night upon you, friends!
What is the news?

CASSIO: The Duke does greet you, general;
And he requires your haste-post-haste appearance
Even on the instant.

OTHELLO: What's the matter, think you?

CASSIO:

Something from Cyprus, as I may divine.
It is a business of some heat. The galleys
Have sent a dozen sequent messengers   41
This very night at one another's heels,
And many of the consuls, raised and met,
Are at the Duke's already. You have been hotly called for;
When, being not at your lodging to be found,
The Senate hath sent about three several quests
To search you out.

OTHELLO: 'Tis well I am found by you.
I will but spend a word here in the house,
And go with you.   [*Exit.*]

CASSIO: Ancient, what makes he here?

IAGO:

Faith, he to-night hath boarded a land carack.   50
If it prove lawful prize, he's made for ever.

23-24 *May speak . . . reached* are equal, I modestly assert, to those of Desdemona's family   **26** *unhoused* unrestrained   **31** *perfect soul* stainless conscience   **41** *sequent* consecutive   **50** *carack* treasure ship

CASSIO:

I do not understand.

IAGO: He's married.

CASSIO: To who?

[*Enter* OTHELLO.]

IAGO:

Marry, to—Come, captain, will you go?

OTHELLO: Have with you.

CASSIO:

Here comes another troop to seek for you.

[*Enter* BRABANTIO, RODERIGO, *and others with lights and weapons.*]

IAGO:

It is Brabantio. General, be advised.

He comes to bad intent.

OTHELLO: Holla! stand there!

RODERIGO:

Signior, it is the Moor.

BRABANTIO: Down with him, thief!

[*They draw on both sides.*]

IAGO:

You, Roderigo! Come, sir, I am for you.

OTHELLO:

Keep up your bright swords, for the dew will rust them.   59

Good signior, you shall more command with years

Than with your weapons.

BRABANTIO:

O thou foul thief, where hast thou stowed my daughter?

Damned as thou art, thou hast enchanted her!

For I'll refer me to all things of sense,

If she in chains of magic were not bound,

Whether a maid so tender, fair, and happy,

So opposite to marriage that she shunned

The wealthy curlèd darlings of our nation,

Would ever have, t'incur a general mock,

Run from her guardage to the sooty bosom

Of such a thing as thou—to fear, not to delight.

Judge me the world if 'tis not gross in sense   72

59 *Keep up* i.e. sheath   **72** *gross in sense* obvious

That thou hast practiced on her with foul charms,
Abused her delicate youth with drugs or minerals
That weaken motion. I'll have't disputed on;   75
'Tis probable, and palpable to thinking.
I therefore apprehend and do attach thee   77
For an abuser of the world, a practicer
Of arts inhibited and out of warrant.
Lay hold upon him. If he do resist,
Subdue him at his peril.

OTHELLO: Hold your hands,
Both you of my inclining and the rest.
Were it my cue to fight, I should have known it
Without a prompter. Where will you that I go
To answer this your charge?

BRABANTIO: To prison, till fit time
Of law and course of direct session   86
Call thee to answer.

OTHELLO: What if I do obey?
How may the Duke be therewith satisfied,
Whose messengers are here about my side
Upon some present business of the state
To bring me to him?

OFFICER: 'Tis true, most worthy signior.
The Duke's in council, and your noble self
I am sure is sent for.

BRABANTIO: How? The Duke in council?
In this time of the night? Bring him away.
Mine's not an idle cause. The Duke himself,   95
Or any of my brothers of state,
Cannot but feel this wrong as 'twere their own;
For if such actions may have passage free,
Bondslaves and pagans shall our statesmen be.   [*Exeunt.*]

SCENE III

[*Enter* DUKE *and senators, set at a table, with lights and attendants.*]

DUKE:
There is no composition in these news   1
That gives them credit.

1 SENATOR: Indeed they are disporportioned.
My letters say a hundred and seven galleys.

---

75 *motion* perception   **77** *attach* arrest   **86** *direct session* regular trial   **95** *idle* trifling
Scene iii The Venetian Senate Chamber   **1** *composition* consistency

DUKE:
  And mine a hundred forty.
2 SENATOR: And mine two hundred.
  But though they jump not on a just account—   5
  As in these cases where the aim reports   6
  'Tis oft with difference—yet do they all confirm
  A Turkish fleet, and bearing up to Cyprus.
DUKE:
  Nay, it is possible enough to judgement.
  I do not so secure me in the error   10
  But the main article I do approve   11
  In fearful sense.
SAILOR [*within*]: What, ho! what, ho! what, ho!
OFFICER:
  A messenger from the galleys.

  [*Enter* SAILOR]

DUKE: Now, what's the business?
SAILOR:
  The Turkish preparation makes for Rhodes.
  So was I bid report here to the state
  By Signior Angelo.
DUKE:
  How say you by this change?
1 SENATOR: This cannot be
  By no assay of reason. 'Tis a pageant   18
  To keep us in false gaze. When we consider   19
  Th'importancy of Cyprus to the Turk,
  And let ourselves again but understand
  That, as it more concerns the Turk than Rhodes,
  So may he with more facile question bear it,   23
  For that it stands not in such warlike brace,   24
  But altogether lacks th' abilities
  That Rhodes is dressed in—if we make thought of this,
  We must not think the Turk is so unskillful
  To leave that latest which concerns him first,
  Neglecting an attempt of ease and gain
  To wake and wage a danger profitless.   30

5 *jump* agree   **6** *aim* conjecture   **10** *so secure me* take such comfort   **11** *article* substance; *approve* accept
18 *assay* test   **19** *in false gaze* looking the wrong way   **23** *with . . . bear* more easily capture   **24** *brace* posture
of defense   **30** *wake and wage* rouse and risk

DUKE:

Nay, in all confidence, he's not for Rhodes.

OFFICER:

Here is more news.

[*Enter a messenger.*]

MESSENGER:

The Ottomites, reverend and gracious,
Steering with due course toward the isle of Rhodes,
Have there injointed them with an after fleet.

1 SENATOR:

Ay, so I thought. How many, as you guess?

MESSENGER:

Of thirty sail; and now they do restem   37
Their backward course, bearing with frank appearance
Their purposes toward Cyprus. Signior Montano,
Your trusty and most valiant servitor,
With his free duty recommends you thus,
And prays you to believe him.

DUKE:

'Tis certain then for Cyprus.
Marcus Luccicos, is not he in town?   44

1 SENATOR:

He's now in Florence.

DUKE:

Write from us to him; post, post-haste dispatch.

1 SENATOR:

Here comes Brabantio and the valiant Moor.

[*Enter* BRABANTIO, OTHELLO, CASSIO, IAGO, RODERIGO, *and officers.*]

DUKE:

Valiant Othello, we must straight employ you
Against the general enemy Ottoman.
[*To* BRABANTIO]
I did not see you. Welcome, gentle signior.
We lacked your counsel and your help to-night.

BRABANTIO:

So did I yours. Good your grace, pardon me.
Neither my place, nor aught I heard of business,
Hath raised me from my bed; nor doth the general care

---

37 *restem* steer again   **44** *Marcus Luccicos* (presumably a Venetian envoy)

Take hold on me; for my particular grief
Is of so floodgate and o'erbearing nature   56
That it engluts and swallows other sorrows,   57
And it is still itself.

DUKE: Why, what's the matter?

BRABANTIO:
My daughter! O, my daughter!

ALL: Dead?

BRABANTIO: Ay, to me.
She is abused, stol'n from me, and corrupted
By spells and medicines bought of mountebanks;
For nature so prepost'rously to err,
Being not deficient, blind, or lame of sense,   63
Sans witchcraft could not.

DUKE:
Who'er he be that in this foul proceeding
Hath thus beguiled your daughter of herself,
And you of her, the bloody book of law
You shall yourself read in the bitter letter
After your own sense; yea, though our proper son   69
Stood in your action.   70

BRABANTIO: Humbly I thank your grace.
Here is the man—this Moor, whom now, it seems,
Your special mandate for the state affairs
Hath hither brought.

ALL: We are very sorry for't.

DUKE [*to* OTHELLO]:
What, in your own part, can you say to this?

BRABANTIO:
Nothing, but this is so.

OTHELLO:
Most potent, grave, and reverend signiors,
My very noble, and approved good masters,   77
That I have ta'en away this old man's daughter,
It is most true; true I have married her.
The very head and front of my offending
Hath this extent, no more. Rude am I in my speech,   81
And little blessed with the soft phrase of peace;
For since these arms of mine had seven years' pith   83
Till now some nine moons wasted, they have used
Their dearest action in the tented field;

56 *floodgate* torrential   **57** *engluts* devours   **63** *deficient* feeble-minded   **69** *our proper* my own   **70** *stood in your action* were accused by you   **77** *approved* tested by experience   **81** *rude* unpolished   **83** *pith* strength

And little of this great world can I speak
More than pertains to feats of broil and battle;
And therefore little shall I grace my cause
In speaking for myself. Yet, by your gracious patience,
I will a round unvarnished tale deliver   90
Of my whole course of love—what drugs, what charms,
What conjuration, and what mighty magic
(For such proceeding am I charged withal)
I won his daughter.

BRABANTIO: A maiden never bold;
Of spirit so still and quiet that her motion   95
Blushed at herself; and she—in spite of nature,
Of years, of country, credit, everything—
To fall in love with what she feared to look on!
It is a judgment maimed and most imperfect
That will confess perfection so could err
Against all rules of nature, and must be driven
To find out practices of cunning hell   102
Why this should be. I therefore vouch again   103
That with some mixtures pow'rful o'er the blood,   104
Or with some dram, conjured to this effect,
He wrought upon her.

DUKE: To vouch this is no proof,
Without more certain and more overt test
Than these thin habits and poor likelihoods   108
Of modern seeming do prefer against him.   109

1 SENATOR:
But, Othello, speak.
Did you by indirect and forcèd courses   111
Subdue and poison this young maid's affections?
Or came it by request, and such fair question   113
As soul to soul affordeth?

OTHELLO: I do beseech you,
Send for the lady to the Sagittary
And let her speak of me before her father.
If you do find me foul in her report,
The trust, the office, I do hold of you
Not only take away, but let your sentence
Even fall upon my life.

DUKE: Fetch Desdemona hither.

---

90 *round* plain   **95–96** *her motion Blushed* her own emotions caused her to blush   **102** *practices* plots   **103** *vouch* assert   **104** *blood* passions   **108** *thin habits* slight appearances   **109** *modern seeming* everyday supposition   **111** *forced* violent   **113** *question* conversation

OTHELLO:

Ancient, conduct them; you best know the place.

[*Exit* IAGO, *with two or three attendants.*]

And still she come, as truly as to heaven

I do confess the vices of my blood,

So justly to your grave ears I'll present

How I did thrive in this fair lady's love,

And she in mine.

DUKE:

Say it, Othello.

OTHELLO:

Her father loved me, oft invited me;

Still questioned me the story of my life   129

From year to year—the battles, sieges, fortunes

That I have passed.

I ran it through, even from my boyish days

To th' very moment that he bade me tell it.

Wherein I spoke of most disastrous chances,

Of moving accidents by flood and field;

Of hairbreadth scapes i' th' imminent deadly breach;

Of being taken by the insolent foe

And sold to slavery; of my redemption thence

And portance in my travels' history;   139

Wherin of anters vast and deserts idle,   140

Rough quarries, rocks, and hills whose heads touch heaven,

It was my hint to speak—such was the process;   142

And of the Cannibals that each other eat,

The Anthropophagi, and men whose heads   144

Do grow beneath their shoulders. This to hear

Would Desdemona seriously incline;

But still the house affairs would draw her thence;

Which ever as she could with haste dispatch,

She'd come again, and with a greedy ear

Devour up my discourse. Which I observing,

Took once a pliant hour, and found good means   151

To draw from her a prayer of earnest heart

That I would all my pilgrimage dilate,   153

Whereof by parcels she had something heard,   154

But not intentively. I did consent,   155

And often did beguile her of her tears

When I did speak of some distressful stroke

---

129 *Still* continually　**139** *portance* behavior　**140** *anters* caves　**142** *hint* occasion　**144** *Anthropophagi* man-eaters　**151** *pliant* propitious　**153** *dilate* recount in full　**154** *parcels* portions　**155** *intentively* with full attention

That my youth suffered. My story being done,
She gave me for my pains a world of sighs.
She swore, i' faith, 'twas strange, 'twas passing strange;
'Twas pitiful, 'twas wondrous pitiful.
She wished she had not heard it; yet she wished
That heaven had made her such a man. She thanked me;
And bade me, if I had a friend that loved her,
I should but teach him how to tell my story,
And that would woo her. Upon this hint I spake.   166
She loved me for the dangers I had passed,
And I loved her that she did pity them.
This only is the witchcraft I have used.
Here comes the lady. Let her witness it.

[*Enter* DESDEMONA, IAGO, *attendants.*]

DUKE:
I think this tale would win my daughter too.
Good Brabantio,
Take up this mangled matter at the best.
Men do their broken weapons rather use
Than their bare hands.
BRABANTIO: I pray you hear her speak.
If she confess that she was half the wooer,
Destruction on my head if my bad blame
Light on the man! Come hither, gentle mistress.
Do you perceive in all this noble company
Where most you owe obedience?
DESDEMONA: My noble father,
I do perceive here a divided duty.
To you I am bound for life and education;   182
My life and education both do learn me
How to respect you: you are the lord of duty;
I am hitherto your daughter. But here's my husband;
And so much duty as my mother showed
To you, preferring you before her father,
So much I challenge that I may profess   188
Due to the Moor my lord.
BRABANTIO: God be with you! I have done.
Please it your grace, on to the state affairs.
I had rather to adopt a child than get it.   191
Come hither, Moor.
I here do give thee that with all my heart

166 *hint* opportunity   **182** *education* upbringing   **188** *challenge* claim the right   **191** *get* beget

Which, but thou hast already, with all my heart
I would keep from thee. For your sake, jewel,   195
I am glad at soul I have no other child;
For thy escape would teach me tyranny,   197
To hang clogs on them. I have done, my lord.

DUKE:
Let me speak like yourself and lay a sentence   199
Which, as a grise or step, may help these lovers   200
Into your favor.
When remedies are past, the griefs are ended
By seeing the worst, which late on hopes depended.
To mourn a mischief that is past and gone
Is the next way to draw new mischief on.
What cannot be preserved when fortune takes,
Patience her injury a mock'ry makes.
The robbed that smiles steals something from the thief;
He robs himself that spends a bootless grief.

BRABANTIO:
So let the Turk of Cyprus us beguile: 210
We lose it not so long as we can smile.
He bears the sentence well that nothing bears
But the free comfort which from thence he hears;
But he bears both the sentence and the sorrow
That to pay grief must of poor patience borrow.
These sentences, to sugar, or to gall,
Being strong on both sides, are equivocal.
But words are words. I never yet did hear
That the bruisèd heart was piercèd through the ear.
I humbly beseech you, now to the affairs of state.

DUKE: The Turk with a most mighty preparation makes
for Cyprus. Othello, the fortitude of the place is best   222
known to you; and though we have there a substitute
of most allowed sufficiency, yet opinion, a more sover-   224
eign mistress of effects, throws a more safer voice on you.
You must therefore be content to slubber the gloss of   226
your new fortunes with this more stubborn and
boist'rous expedition.

OTHELLO:
The tyrant custom, most grave senators,
Hath made the flinty and steel couch of war
My thrice-driven bed of down. I do agnize   231

---

195 *For your sake* because of you   **197** *escape* escapade   **199** *like yourself* as you should; *sentence* maxim
200 *grise* step   **222** *fortitude* fortification   **224** *allowed* acknowledged; *opinion* public opinion   **226** *slubber*
sully   **231–33** *agnize . . . hardness* recognize in myself a natural and easy response to hardship

A natural and prompt alacrity
I find in hardness; and do undertake
These present wars against the Ottomites.
Most humbly, therefore, bending to your state,
I crave fit disposition for my wife,
Due reference of place, and exhibition,   237
With such accommodation and besort   238
As levels with her breeding.   239

DUKE: If you please,
Be't at her father's.

BRABANTIO: I will not have it so.

OTHELLO:
Nor I.

DESDEMONA: Nor I. I would not there reside,
To put my father in impatient thoughts
By being in his eye. Most gracious Duke,
To my unfolding lend your prosperous ear,   244
And let me find a charter in your voice,
T' assist my simpleness.   246

DUKE:
What would you, Desdemona?

DESDEMONA:
That I did love the Moor to live with him,
My downright violence, and storm of fortunes,
May trumpet to the world. My heart's subdued
Even to the very quality of my lord.
I saw Othello's visage in his mind,
And to his honors and his valiant parts
Did I my soul and fortunes consecrate.
So that, dear lords, if I be left behind,
A moth of peace, and he go to the war,
The rites for which I love him are bereft me,
And I a heavy interim shall support
By his dear absence. Let me go with him.

OTHELLO:
Let her have your voice.
Vouch with me, heaven, I therefore beg it not
To please the palate of my appetite,
Not to comply with heat—the young affects   263
In me defunct—and proper satisfaction;
But to be free and bounteous to her mind;
And heaven defend your good souls that you think

237 *exhibition* allowance of money   238 *besort* suitable company   239 *levels* corresponds   244 *prosperous*
favorable   246 *simpleness* lack of skill   263 *heat* passions; *young affects* tendencies of youth

I will your serious and great business scant
When she is with me. No, when light-winged toys
Of feathered Cupid seel with wanton dullness   269
My speculative and officed instruments,   270
That my disports corrupt and taint my business,   271
Let housewives make a skillet of my helm,
And all indign and base adversities   273
Make head against my estimation!   274

DUKE:
Be it as you shall privately determine,
Either for her stay or going. Th' affair cries haste,
And speed must answer it.

1 SENATOR:
You must away to-night.

OTHELLO: With all my heart.

DUKE:
At nine i' th' morning here we'll meet again.
Othello, leave some officer behind,
And he shall our commission bring to you,
With such things else of quality and respect
As doth import you.   283

OTHELLO: So please your grace, my ancient;
A man he is of honesty and trust.
To his conveyance I assign my wife,
With what else needful your good grace shall think
To be sent after me.

DUKE: Let it be so.
Good night to every one.
[To BRABANTIO]   And, noble signior,
If virtue no delighted beauty lack,
Your son-in-law is far more fair than black.   289

1 SENATOR:
Adieu, brave Moor. Use Desdemona well.

BRABANTIO:
Look to her, Moor, if thou hast eyes to see:
She has deceived her father, and may thee.

                    [Exeunt DUKE, senators, officers, etc.]

OTHELLO:
My life upon her faith!—Honest Iago,
My Desdemona must I leave to thee.
I prithee let thy wife attend on her,
And bring them after in the best advantage.   297

---

269 *seel* blind **270** *My . . . instruments* my perceptive and responsible faculties **271** *That* so that **273** *indign* unworthy **274** *estimation* reputation **283** *import* concern **289** *delighted* delightful **297** *in the best advantage* at the best opportunity

Come, Desdemona. I have but an hour
Of love, of worldly matters and direction,
To spend with thee. We must obey the time.

[*Exit* MOOR *and* DESDEMONA.]

RODERIGO: Iago,—

IAGO: What say'st thou, noble heart?

RODERIGO: What will I do, think'st thou?

IAGO: Why, go to bed and sleep.

RODERIGO: I will incontinently drown myself. 305

IAGO: If thou dost, I shall never love thee after. Why, thou silly gentleman!

RODERIGO: It is silliness to live when to live is torment; and then have we a
prescription to die when death is our physician.

IAGO: O villainous! I have looked upon the world for four times seven
years; and since I could distinguish betwixt a benefit and an injury, I
never found man that knew how to love himself. Ere I would say I would
drown myself for the love of a guinea hen, I would change my humanity
with a baboon.

RODERIGO: What should I do? I confess it is my shame to be so fond, but it
is not in my virtue to amend it.

IAGO: Virtue? a fig! 'Tis in ourselves that we are thus or,
thus. Our bodies are our gardens, to the which our wills
are gardeners; so that if we will plant nettles or sow
lettuce, set hyssop and weed up thyme, supply it with
one gender of herbs or distract it with many—either to 320
have it sterile with idleness or manured with industry—
why, the power and corrigible authority of this lies in 322
our wills. If the balance of our lives had not one scale
of reason to poise another of sensuality, the blood and 324
baseness of our natures would conduct us to most
preposterous conclusions. But we have reason to cool our
raging motions, our carnal stings, our unbitted lusts; 327
whereof I take this that you call love to be a sect or scion. 328

RODERIGO: It cannot be.

IAGO: It is merely a lust of the blood and a permission of
the will. Come, be a man! Drown thyself? Drown cats
and blind puppies! I have professed me thy friend, and I
confess me knit to thy deserving with cables of perdurable
toughness. I could never better stead thee than now. Put
money in thy purse. Follow thou the wars; defeat thy 335
favor with an usurped beard. I say, put money in thy
purse. It cannot be that Desdemona should long continue her love to the Moor—put money in thy purse—nor

---

305 *incontinently* forthwith   **320** *gender* species   **322** *corrigible authority* corrective power   **324** *poise* counter-balance   **324–25** *blood and baseness* animal instincts   **327** *motions* appetites; *unbitted* uncontrolled   **328** *sect or scion* offshoot, cutting   **335–36** *defeat thy favor* spoil thy appearance

he his to her. It was a violent commencement in her, and
thou shalt see an answerable sequestration—put but   340
money in thy purse. These Moors are changeable in their
wills—fill thy purse with money. The food that to him
now is as luscious as locusts shall be to him shortly as bitter as coloquintida. She must change for youth: when she   344
is sated with his body, she will find the error of her choice.
She must have change, she must. Therefore put money
in thy purse. If thou wilt needs damn thyself, do it a more
delicate way than drowning. Make all the money thou   348
canst. If sanctimony and a frail vow betwixt an erring   349
barbarian and a supersubtle Venetian be not too hard for
my wits and all the tribe of hell, thou shalt enjoy her.
Therefore make money. A pox of drowning thyself! 'Tis
clean out of the way. Seek thou rather to be hanged in
compassing thy joy than to be drowned and go without
her.

RODERIGO: Wilt thou be fast to my hopes, if I depend on
the issue?

IAGO: Thou art sure of me. Go, make money. I have told,
thee often, and I retell thee again and again, I hate the
Moor. My cause is hearted; thine hath no less reason.   360
Let us be conjunctive in our revenge against him. If
thou canst cuckold him, thou dost thyself a pleasure, me
a sport. There are many events in the womb of time,
which will be delivered. Traverse, go, provide thy   364
money! We will have more of this to-morrow. Adieu.

RODERIGO: Where shall we meet i' th' morning?

IAGO: At my lodging.

RODERIGO: I'll be with thee betimes.

IAGO: Go to, farewell.—Do you hear, Roderigo?

RODERIGO: What say you?

IAGO: No more of drowning, do you hear?

RODERIGO: I am changed.

IAGO: Go to, farewell. Put money enough in your purse.

RODERIGO: I'll sell all my land.   [*Exit.*]

IAGO:
Thus do I ever make my fool my purse;
For I mine own gained knowledge should profane
If I would time expend with such a snipe   377
But for my sport and profit. I hate the Moor;
And it is thought abroad that 'twixt my sheets

---

340 *sequestration* estrangement   **344** *coloquintida* a medicine   **348** *Make* raise   **349** *erring* wandering
360 *My cause is hearted* my heart is in it   **364** *Traverse* forward march   **377** *snipe* fool

H'as done my office. I know not if't be true;
But I, for mere suspicion in that kind,
Will do as if for surety. He holds me well;   382
The better shall my purpose work on him.
Cassio's a proper man. Let me see now:
To get his place, and to plume up my will   385
In double knavery—How, how?—Let's see:—
After some time, to abuse Othello's ears
That he is too familiar with his wife.
He hath a person and a smooth dispose   389
To be suspected—framed to make women false.
The Moor is of a free and open nature   391
That thinks men honest that but seem to be so;
And will as tenderly be led by th' nose
As asses are.
I have't! It is engend'red! Hell and night
Must bring this monstrous birth to the world's light.

                                                    [*Exit.*]

ACT II

SCENE I

[*Enter* MONTANO *and two gentlemen.*]

MONTANO:
  What from the cape can you discern at sea?
1 GENTLEMAN:
  Nothing at all: it is a high-wrought flood.
  I cannot 'twixt the heaven and the main
  Descry a sail.
MONTANO:
  Methinks the wind hath spoke aloud at land;
  A fuller blast ne'er shook our battlements.
  If it hath ruffianed so upon the sea,
  What ribs of oak, when mountains melt on them,
  Can hold the mortise? What shall we hear of this?   9
2 GENTLEMAN:
  A segregation of the Turkish fleet.   10
  For do but stand upon the foaming shore,

382 *well* in high regard   **385** *plume up* gratify   **389** *dispose* manner   **391** *free* frank
Scene i An open place in Cyprus, near the harbor   **9** *hold the mortise* hold their joints together   **10** *segregation* scattering

The chidden billow seems to pelt the clouds;
The wind-shaked surge, with high and monstrous mane,
Seems to cast water on the burning Bear
And quench the Guards of th' ever-fixèd pole.   15
I never did like molestation view   16
On the enchafèd flood.
MONTANO: If that the Turkish fleet
Be not ensheltered and embayed, they are drowned;
It is impossible to bear it out.

[Enter a third gentleman.]

3 GENTLEMAN:
News, lads! Our wars are done.
The desperate tempest hath so banged the Turks
That their designment halts. A noble ship of Venice   22
Hath seen a grievous wrack and sufferance   23
On most part of their fleet.
MONTANO:
How? Is this true?
3 GENTLEMAN: The ship is here put in,
A Veronesa; Michael Cassio,   26
Lieutenant to the warlike Moor Othello,
Is come on shore; the Moor himself at sea,
And is in full commission here for Cyprus.
MONTANO:
I am glad on't. 'Tis a worthy governor.
3 GENTLEMAN:
But this same Cassio, though he speak of comfort
Touching the Turkish loss, yet he looks sadly
And prays the Moor be safe, for they were parted
With foul and violent tempest.
MONTANO: Pray heaven he be;
For I have served him, and the man commands
Like a full soldier. Let's to the seaside, ho!
As well to see the vessel that's come in
As to throw out our eyes for brave Othello,
Even till we make the main and th' aerial blue
An indistinct regard.   40
3 GENTLEMAN: Come, let's do so;
For every minute is expectancy
Of more arrivance.

15 *Guards* stars near the North Star; *pole* polestar   16 *molestation* tumult   22 *desegment halts* plan is crippled
23 *sufferance* disaster   26 *Veronesa* ship furnished by Verona   40 *An indistinct regard* indistinguishable

[*Enter* CASSIO.]

CASSIO:

Thanks, you the valiant of this warlike isle,
That so approve the Moor! O, let the heavens
Give him defense against the elements,
For I have lost him on a dangerous sea!

MONTANO:

Is he well shipped?

CASSIO:

His bark is stoutly timbered, and his pilot
Of very expert and approved allowance;
Therefore my hopes, not surfeited to death,   50
Stand in bold cure.   51

[*Within.*] A sail, a sail, a sail!

[*Enter a messenger.*]

CASSIO:

What noise?

1 GENTLEMAN:

The town is empty; on the brow o' th' sea
Stand ranks of people, and they cry "A sail!"

CASSIO:

My hopes do shape him for the governor.

[*A shot.*]

2 GENTLEMAN:

They do discharge their shot of courtesy:
Our friends at least.

CASSIO: I pray you, sir, go forth

And give us truth who 'tis that is arrived.

2 GENTLEMAN:

I shall.   [*Exit.*]

MONTANO:

But, good lieutenant, is your general wived?

CASSIO:

Most fortunately. He hath achieved a maid
That paragons description and wild fame;   62
One that excels the quirks of blazoning pens,   63

---

50 *surfeited to death* over indulged **51** *in bold cure* a good chance of fulfillment **62** *paragons* surpasses
63 *quirks* ingenuities; *blazoning* describing

And in th' essential vesture of creation   64
Does tire the ingener.

[*Enter second gentleman.*]

                    How now? Who has put in?

2 GENTLEMAN:
'Tis one Iago, ancient to the general.

CASSIO:
H'as had most favorable and happy speed:
Tempests themselves, high seas, and howling winds,
The guttered rocks and congregated sands,   69
Traitors ensteeped to clog the guiltless keel,   70
As having sense of beauty, do omit
Their mortal natures, letting go safely by   72
The divine Desdemona.

MONTANO: What is she?

CASSIO:
She that I spake of, our great captain's captain,
Left in the conduct of the bold Iago,
Whose footing here anticipates our thoughts   76
A se'nnight's speed. Great Jove, Othello guard,   77
And swell his sail with thine own pow'rful breath,
That he may bless this bay with his tall ship,
Make love's quick pants in Desdemona's arms,
Give renewed fire to our extincted spirits,
And bring all Cyprus comfort!

[*Enter* DESDEMONA, IAGO, RODERIGO, *and* EMILIA *with attendants.*]

                    O, behold!
The riches of the ship is come on shore!
You men of Cyprus, let her have your knees.   84
Hail to thee, lady! and the grace of heaven,
Before, behind thee, and on every hand,
Enwheel thee round!

DESDEMONA: I thank you, valiant Cassio.
What tidings can you tell me of my lord?

CASSIO:
He is not yet arrived; nor know I aught
But that he's well and will be shortly here.

64–65 *And . . . ingener* merely to describe her as God made her exhausts her praiser **69** *guttered* jagged
70 *ensteeped* submerged **72** *mortal* deadly **76** *footing* landing **77** *sen'night's* week's **84** *knees* i.e. kneeling

DESDEMONA:

O but I fear! How lost you company?

CASSIO:

The great contention of the sea and skies
Parted our fellowship.

[*Within.*]   A sail, a sail! [*A shot.*]

But hark. A sail!

2 GENTLEMAN:

They give their greeting to the citadel;
This likewise is a friend.

CASSIO: See for the news.

[*Exit gentleman.*]

Good ancient, you are welcome.

[*To* EMILIA.]   Welcome, mistress.—

Let it not gall your patience, good Iago,
That I extend my manners. 'Tis my breeding
That gives me this bold show of courtesy.   99

[*Kisses* EMILIA.]

IAGO:

Sir, would she give you so much of her lips
As of her tongue she oft bestows on me,
You would have enough.

DESDEMONA: Alas, she has no speech!

IAGO:

In faith, too much.
I find it still when I have list to sleep.
Marry, before your ladyship, I grant,
She puts her tongue a little in her heart
And chides with thinking.

EMILIA:

You have little cause to say so.

IAGO:

Come on, come on! You are pictures out of doors,
Bells in your parlors, wildcats in your kitchens,
Saints in your injuries, devils being offended,
Players in your housewifery, and housewives in your
   beds.   112

DESDEMONA:

O, fie upon thee, slanderer!

99 s.d. *Kisses* EMILIA (kissing was a common Elizabethan form of social courtesy)   **112** *housewifery* housekeeping; *housewives* hussies

IAGO:
  Nay, it is true, or else I am a Turk:
  You rise to play, and go to bed to work.
EMILIA:
  You shall not write my praise.
IAGO: No, let me not.
DESDEMONA:
  What wouldst thou write of me, if thou shouldst praise me?
IAGO:
  O gentle lady, do not put me to't,
  For I am nothing if not critical.
DESDEMONA:
  Come on, assay.—There's one gone to the harbor?   120
IAGO:
  Ay, madam.
DESDEMONA:
  I am not merry; but I do beguile
  The thing I am by seeming otherwise.—
  Come, how wouldst thou praise me?
IAGO:
  I am about it; but indeed my invention
  Comes from my pate as birdlime does from frieze—   126
  It plucks out brains and all. But my Muse labors,
  And thus she is delivered:
  If she be fair and wise, fairness and wit—
  The one's for use, the other useth it.
DESDEMONA:
  Well praised! How if she be black and witty?   131
IAGO:
  If she be black, and thereto have a wit,
  She'll find a white that shall her blackness fit.
DESDEMONA:
  Worse and worse!
EMILIA:
  How if fair and foolish?
IAGO:
  She never yet was foolish that was fair,
  For even her folly helped her to an heir.   137
DESDEMONA: These are old fond paradoxes to make fools   138
  laugh i' th' alehouse. What miserable praise hast thou
  for her that's foul and foolish?   140

---

120 *assay* try   **126** *birdlime* a sticky paste; *frieze* rough cloth   **131** *black* brunette   **137** *folly* wantonness
138 *fond* foolish   **140** *foul* ugly

IAGO:

> There's none so foul, and foolish thereunto,
> But does foul pranks which fair and wise ones do.

DESDEMONA: O heavy ignorance! Thou praisest the worst best. But what praise couldst thou bestow on a deserving woman indeed—one that in the authority of her merit did justly put on the vouch of very malice itself?   145

IAGO:

> She that was ever fair, and never proud;
> Had tongue at will, and yet was never loud;
> Never lacked gold, and yet went never gay;
> Fled from her wish, and yet said "Now I may";
> She that, being ang'red, her revenge being nigh,
> Bade her wrong stay, and her displeasure fly;
> She that in wisdom never was so frail
> To change the cod's head for the salmon's tail;   154
> She that could think, and ne'er disclose her mind;
> See suitors following, and not look behind:
> She was a wight (if ever such wight were)—

DESDEMONA: To do what?

IAGO:

> To suckle fools and chronicle small beer.   159

DESDEMONA: O most lame and impotent conclusion! Do not learn of him, Emilia, though he be thy husband. How say you, Cassio? Is he not a most profane and liberal counsellor?   162

CASSIO: He speaks home, madam. You may relish him more in the soldier than in the scholar.   163

IAGO [aside]: He takes her by the palm. Ay, well said, whisper! With as little a web as this will I ensnare as great a fly as Cassio. Ay, smile upon her, do! I will gyve thee in thine own courtship.—You say true; 'tis so, indeed!—If such tricks as these strip you out of your lieutenantry, it   167 had been better you had not kissed your three fingers so oft—which now again you are most apt to play the sir in. Very good! well kissed! an   170 excellent courtesy! 'Tis so, indeed. Yet again your fingers to your lips? Would they were clyster pipes for your sake! [*Trumpet within.*] The   172 Moor! I know his trumpet.

CASSIO: 'Tis truly so.

DESDEMONA: Let's meet him and receive him.

CASSIO: Lo, where he comes.

---

145 *put on the vouch* compel the approval   **154** *To . . . tail* i.e. to exchange the good for poor but expensive
159 *chronicle small beer* keep petty household accounts   **162** *profane and liberal* worldly and licentious
163 *home* bluntly   **167** *gyve . . . courtship* manacle you by your courtly manners   **170** *sir* courtly gentleman
172 *clyster pipes* syringes

[*Enter* OTHELLO *and attendants.*]

OTHELLO:
O my fair warrior!
DESDEMONA: My dear Othello!
OTHELLO:
It gives me wonder great as my content
To see you here before me. O my soul's joy!
If after every tempest come such calms,
May the winds blow till they have wakened death!
And let the laboring bark climb hills of seas
Olympus-high, and duck again as low
As hell's from heaven! If it were now to die,
'Twere now to be most happy; for I fear   185
My soul hath her content so absolute
That not another comfort like to this
Succeeds in unknown fate.
DESDEMONA: The heavens forbid
But that our loves and comforts should increase
Even as our days do grow.
OTHELLO: Amen to that, sweet powers!
I cannot speak enough of this content;
It stops me here; it is too much of joy.
And this, and this, the greatest discords be
[*They kiss.*]
That e'er our hearts shall make!
IAGO [*aside*]:   O, you are well tuned now!
But I'll set down the pegs that make this music,   195
As honest as I am.
OTHELLO: Come, let us to the castle.
News, friends! Our wars are done; the Turks are drowned.
How does my old acquaintance of this isle?—
Honey, you shall be well desired in Cyprus;   199
I have found great love amongst them. O my sweet,
I prattle out of fashion, and I dote
In mine own comforts. I prithee, good Iago,
Go to the bay and disembark my coffers.
Bring thou the master to the citadel;   204
He is a good one, and his worthiness
Does challenge much respect.—Come, Desdemona,   206
Once more well met at Cyprus.
                    [*Exit* OTHELLO *(with all but* IAGO *and* RODERIGO.*)*]

185 *happy* fortunate   **195** *set down* loosen   **199** *well desired* warmly welcomed   **204** *master* ship captain
206 *challenge* deserve

IAGO [*to an attendant, who goes out*]: Do thou meet me presently at the
harbor. [*to* RODERIGO] Come hither. If you be'st valiant (as they say base
men being in love have then a nobility in their natures more than is
native to them), list me. The lieutenant to-night watches on the court of   211
guard. First, I must tell thee this: Desdemona is directly in love with
him.

RODERIGO: With him? Why, 'tis not possible.

IAGO: Lay thy finger thus, and let thy soul be instructed. Mark me with   215
what violence she first loved the Moor, but for bragging and telling her
fantastical lies; and will she love him still for prating? Let not thy
discreet heart think it. Her eye must be fed; and what delight shall she
have to look on the devil? When the blood is made dull with the act of
sport, there should be, again to inflame it and to give satiety a fresh
appetite, loveliness in favor, sympathy in years, manners, and beauties;
all which the Moor is defective in. Now for want of these required
conveniences, her delicate tenderness will find itself abused, begin to   223
heave the gorge, disrelish and abhor the Moor. Very nature will instruct   224
her in it and compel her to some second choice. Now sir, this
granted—as it is a most pregnant and unforced position—who stands   226
so eminent in the degree of this fortune as Cassio does? A knave very
voluble; no further conscionable than in putting on the mere form of   228
civil and humane seeming for the better compassing of his salt and   229
most hidden loose affection? Why, none! why, none! A slipper and   230
subtle knave; a finder-out of occasions; that has an eye can stamp and
counterfeit advantages, though true advantage never present itself; a
devilish knave! Besides, the knave is handsome, young, and hath all
those requisites in him that folly and green minds look after. A pestilent
complete knave! and the woman hath found him already.

RODERIGO: I cannot believe that in her; she's full of most blessed condition.   236

IAGO: Blessed fig's-end! The wine she drinks is made of grapes. If she had
been blessed, she would never have loved the Moor. Blessed pudding!
Didst thou not see her paddle with the palm of his hand? Didst not
mark that?

RODERIGO: Yes, that I did; but that was but courtesy.

IAGO: Lechery, by this hand! an index and obscure prologue to the history
of lust and foul thoughts. They met so near with their lips that their
breaths embraced together. Villainous thoughts, Roderigo! When these
mutualities so marshal the way, hard at hand comes the master and   245
main exercise, th' incorporate conclusion. Pish! But, sir, be you ruled by   246
me: I have brought you from Venice. Watch you to-night; for the
command, I'll lay't upon you. Cassio knows you not. I'll not be far from

---

211–12 *court of guard* headquarters   **215** *thus* i.e. on your lips   **223** *conveniences* compatibilities   **224** *heave the gorge* be nauseated   **226** *pregnant* evident   **228** *conscionable* conscientious   **229** *humane* polite; *salt* lecherous   **230** *slipper* slippery   **236** *condition* character   **245** *mutualities* exchanges   **246** *incorporate* carnal

you: do you find some occasion to anger Cassio, either by speaking too
loud, or tainting his discipline, or from what other course you please   250
which the time shall more favorably minister.

RODERIGO: Well.

IAGO: Sir, he's rash and very sudden in choler, and haply with his   253
truncheon may strike at you. Provoke him that he may; for even out of
that will I cause these of Cyprus to mutiny; whose qualification shall   255
come into no true taste again but by the displanting of Cassio. So shall   256
you have a shorter journey to your desires by the means I shall then
have to prefer them; and the impediment most profitably removed   258
without the which there were no expectation of our prosperity.

RODERIGO: I will do this if you can bring it to any opportunity.

IAGO: I warrant thee. Meet me by and by at the citadel; I must fetch his
necessaries ashore. Farewell.

RODERIGO: Adieu.   [*Exit.*]

IAGO:
    That Cassio loves her, I do well believe't;
    That she loves him, 'tis apt and of great credit.   265
    The Moor, howbeit that I endure him not,
    Is of a constant, loving, noble nature,
    And I dare think he'll prove to Desdemona
    A most dear husband. Now I do love her too;
    Not out of absolute lust, though peradventure
    I stand accountant for as great a sin,   271
    But partly led to diet my revenge,   272
    For that I do suspect the lusty Moor
    Hath leaped into my seat; the thought whereof
    Doth, like a poisonous mineral, gnaw my inwards;
    And nothing can or shall content my soul
    Till I am evened with him, wife for wife;
    Of failing so, yet that I put the Moor
    At least into a jealousy so strong
    That judgment cannot cure. Which think to do,
    If this poor trash of Venice, whom I trash   281
    For his quick hunting, stand the putting on,   282
    I'll have our Michael Cassio on the hip,   283
    Abuse him to the Moor in the rank garb   284
    (For I fear Cassio with my nightcap too),
    Make the Moor thank me, love me, and reward me
    For making him egregiously an ass

---

250 *tainting* discrediting   **253** *sudden in choler* violent in anger   **255** *qualification* appeasement   **256** *true taste*
satisfactory state   **258** *prefer* advance   **265** *apt* probable   **271** *accountant* accountable   **272** *diet* feed
281 *I trash* I weight down (in order to keep under control)   **282** *For* in order to develop; *stand the putting on*
responds to my inciting   **283** *on the hip* at my mercy   **284** *rank barb* gross manner

And practicing upon his peace and quiet
Even to madness. 'Tis here, but yet confused:
Knavery's plain face is never seen till used.   [*Exit.*]

288

SCENE II

[*Enter* OTHELLO's *herald, with a proclamation.*]

HERALD: It is Othello's pleasure, our noble and valiant general, that, upon
certain tidings now arrived, importing the mere perdition of the
Turkish fleet, every man put himself into triumph; some to dance, some
to make bonfires, each man to what sport and revels his addiction leads
him. For, besides these beneficial news, it is the celebration of his
nuptial. So much was his pleasure should be proclaimed. All offices are
open, and there is full liberty of feasting from the present hour of five
till the bell have told eleven. Heaven bless the isle of Cyprus and our
noble general Othello!

2

6

[*Exit.*]

SCENE III

[*Enter* OTHELLO, DESDEMONA, CASSIO, *and attendants.*]

OTHELLO:
Good Michael, look you to the guard to-night.
Let's teach ourselves that honorable stop,
Not to outsport discretion.
CASSIO:
Iago hath direction what to do;
But not withstanding, with my personal eye
Will I look to't.
OTHELLO: Iago is most honest.
Michael, good night. To-morrow with your earliest
Let me have speech with you.
[*To* DESDEMONA]   Come, my dear love.
The purchase made, the fruits are to ensue;
That profit's yet to come 'tween me and you.—
Good night.

[*Exit* OTHELLO *with* DESDEMONA *and attendants.*]
[*Enter* IAGO.]

288 *practicing upon* plotting against
Scene ii A street in Cyprus   **2** *mere perdition* complete destruction   **6** *offices* kitchens and storerooms
Scene iii The Cyprian castle

CASSIO: Welcome, Iago. We must to the watch.

IAGO: Not this hour, lieutenant; 'tis not yet ten o' th' clock. Our general cast   13
us thus early for the love of his Desdemona; who let us not therefore
blame. He hath not yet made wanton the night with her, and she is
sport for Jove.

CASSIO: She's a most exquisite lady.

IAGO: And, I'll warrant her, full of game.

CASSIO: Indeed, she's a most fresh and delicate creature.

IAGO: What an eye she has! Methinks it sounds a parley to provocation.

CASSIO: An inviting eye; and yet methinks right modest:

IAGO: And when she speaks, is it not an alarum to love?

CASSIO: She is indeed perfection.

IAGO: Well, happiness to their sheets! Come, lieutenant, I have a stoup of   24
wine, and here without are a brace of Cyprus gallants that would fain
have a measure to the health of black Othello.

CASSIO: Not to-night, good Iago. I have very poor and unhappy brains for
drinking; I could well wish courtesy would invent some other custom of
entertainment.

IAGO: O, they are our friends. But one cup! I'll drink for you.

CASSIO: I have drunk but one cup to-night, and that was craftily qualified
too; and behold what innovation it makes here. I am unfortunate in the   32
infirmity and dare not task my weakness with any more.

IAGO: What, man! 'Tis a night of revels: the gallants desire it.

CASSIO: Where are they?

IAGO: Here at the door; I pray you call them in.

CASSIO: I'll do't, but it dislikes me.   [Exit.]

IAGO:
    If I can fasten but one cup upon him
    With that which he hath drunk to-night already,
    He'll be as full of quarrel and offense
    As my young mistress' dog. Now my sick fool Roderigo,
    Whom love hath turned almost the wrong side out,
    To Desdemona hath to-night caroused
    Potations pottle-deep; and he's to watch.   44
    Three lads of Cyprus—noble swelling spirits,
    That hold their honors in a wary distance,   46
    The very elements of this warlike isle—   47
    Have I to-night flustered with flowing cups,
    And they watch too. Now, 'mongst this flock of drunkards
    Am I to put our Cassio in some action
    That may offend the isle.

---

13 *cast* dismissed   **24** *stoup* two-quart tankard   **32** *qualified* diluted; *innovation* disturbance   **44** *pottle-deep*
bottoms up   **46** *That . . . distance* very sensitive about their honor   **47** *very elements* true representatives

[*Enter* CASSIO, MONTANO, *and gentleman servants following with wine.*]

But here they come.
If consequence do but approve my dream,
My boat sails freely, both with wind and stream.

CASSIO: 'Fore God, they have given me a rouse already.   54

MONTANO: Good faith, a little one; not past a pint, as I
am a soldier.

IAGO: Some wine, ho!
[*Sings.*]   And let me the canakin clink, clink;
And let me the canakin clink.
A soldier's a man;
A life's but a span,
Why then, let a soldier drink.
Some wine boys!

CASSIO: Fore God, an excellent song!

IAGO: I learned it in England, where indeed they are most potent in potting.
Your Dane, your German, and your swag-bellied Hollander—Drink,
ho!—are nothing to your English.

CASSIO: Is your Englishman so expert in his drinking?

IAGO: Why, he drinks you with facility your Dane dead drunk; he sweats not
to overthrow your Almain; he gives your Hollander a vomit ere the next
pottle can be filled.

CASSIO: To the health of our general!

MONTANO: I am for it, lieutenant, and I'll do you justice.

IAGO: O sweet England!
[*Sings.*]   King Stephen was a worthy peer;
His breeches cost him but a crown;
He held 'em sixpence all too dear,
With that he called the tailor lown.   78
He was a wight of high renown,
And thou art but of low degree.
'Tis pride that pulls the country down;
Then take thine auld cloak about thee.
Some wine, ho!

CASSIO: 'Fore God, this is a more exquisite song than the other.

IAGO: Will you hear 't again?

CASSIO: No, for I hold him to be unworthy of his place that does those   86
things. Well, God's above all; and there be souls must be saved, and
there be souls must not be saved.

IAGO: It's true, good lieutenant.

CASSIO: For mine own part—no offense to the general,
nor any man of quality—I hope to be saved.

---

54 *rouse* bumper   **78** *lown* rascal   **86–7** *does . . . things* i.e. behaves in this fashion

IAGO: And so do I too, lieutenant.

CASSIO: Ay, but, by your leave, not before me. The lieutenant is to be saved before the ancient. Let's have no
more of this; let's to our affairs.—God forgive us our
sins!—Gentlemen, let's look to our business. Do not
think, gentlemen, I am drunk. This is my ancient; this
is my right hand, and this is my left. I am not drunk now.
I can stand well enough, and I speak well enough.

ALL: Excellent well!

CASSIO: Why, very well then. You must not think then
that I am drunk.   [*Exit.*]

MONTANO:
To th' platform, masters, Come, let's set the watch.

IAGO:
You see this fellow that is gone before.
He's a soldier fit to stand by Caesar
And give direction; and do but see his vice.
'Tis to his virtue a just equinox,   107
The one as long as th'other. 'Tis pity of him.
I fear the trust Othello puts him in,
On some odd time of his infirmity,
Will shake this island.

MONTANO: But is he often thus?

IAGO:
'Tis evermore his prologue to his sleep:
He'll watch the horologe a double set   113
If drink rock not his cradle.

MONTANO: It were well
The general were put in mind of it.
Perhaps he sees it not, or his good nature
Prizes the virtue that appears in Cassio
And looks not on his evils. Is not this true?

[*Enter* RODERIGO.]

IAGO [*aside to him*]:
How now, Roderigo?
I pray you after the lieutenant, go!   [*Exit* RODERIGO.]

MONTANO:
And 'tis great pity that the noble Moor
Should hazard such a place as his own second
With one of an ingraft infirmity.   123

107 *just equinox* exact equivalent   **113** *watch . . . set* stay awake twice around the clock   **123** *ingraft* i.e.
ingrained

It were an honest action to say
So to the Moor.

IAGO: Not I, for this fair island!
I do love Cassio well and would do much
To cure him of this evil.
[*Within*]   Help! help!
                            But hark! What noise?

[*Enter* CASSIO, *driving in* RODERIGO.]

CASSIO:
Zounds, you rogue! you rascal!

MONTANO:
What's the matter, lieutenant?

CASSIO: A knave teach me my duty?
I'll beat the knave into a twiggen bottle.   130

RODERIGO:
Beat me?

CASSIO: Dost thou prate, rogue?
[*Strikes him.*]

MONTANO: Nay, good lieutenant!
[*Stays him.*]
I pray you, sir, hold your hand.

CASSIO: Let me go, sir,
Or I'll knock you o'er the mazzard.   133

MONTANO: Come, come, you're drunk!

CASSIO: Drunk?

[*They fight.*]

IAGO [*aside to* RODERIGO]:
Away, I say! Go out and cry a mutiny!   [*Exit* RODERIGO.]
Nay, good lieutenant. God's will, gentlemen!
Help, ho!—lieutenant—sir—Montano—sir—
Help, masters!—Here's a goodly watch indeed!

[*A bell rung.*]

Who's that which rings the bell? Diablo, ho!
The town will rise. God's will, lieutenant, hold!   140
You'll be shamed for ever.

[*Enter* OTHELLO *and gentlemen with weapons.*]

130 *twiggen* wicker-covered   **133** *mazzard* head   **140** *rise* grow riotous

OTHELLO: What is the matter here?
MONTANO:
Zounds, I bleed still, I am hurt to th' death.
He dies!
OTHELLO:
Hold for your lives!
IAGO:
Hold, hold! Lieutenant—sir—Montano—gentlemen!
Have you forgot all sense of place and duty?
Hold! The general speaks to you. Hold, for shame!
OTHELLO:
Why, how now, ho? From whence ariseth this?
Are we turned Turks, and to ourselves do that
Which heaven hath forbid the Ottomites?
For Christian shame put by this barbarous brawl!
He that stirs next to carve for his own rage   151
Holds his soul light; he dies upon his motion.
Silence that dreadful bell! It frights the isle
From her propriety. What is the matter, masters?   154
Honest Iago, that looks dead with grieving,
Speak. Who began this? On thy love, I charge thee.
IAGO:
I do not know. Friends, all, but now, even now,
In quarter, and in terms like bride and groom   158
Devesting them for bed; and then, but now—
As if some planet had unwitted men—
Swords out, and tilting one at other's breast
In opposition bloody. I cannot speak
Any beginning to this peevish odds,   163
And would in action glorious I had lost
Those legs that brought me to a part of it!
OTHELLO:
How comes it, Michael, you are thus forgot?
CASSIO:
I pray you pardon me; I cannot speak.
OTHELLO:
Worthy Montano, you were wont to be civil;
The gravity and stillness of your youth
The world hath noted, and your name is great
In mouths of wisest censure. What's the matter   171
That you unlace your reputation thus   172
And spend your rich opinion for the name   173
Of a night-brawler? Give me answer to it.

---

151 *carve for* indulge   **154** *propriety* proper self   **158** *quarter* friendliness   **163** *peevish odds* childish quarrel
171 *censure* judgment   **172** *unlace* undo   **173** *rich opinion* high reputation

MONTANO:

    Worthy Othello, I am hurt to danger.

    Your officer, Iago, can inform you,

    While I spare speech, which something now offends me,   177

    Of all that I do know; nor know I aught

    By me that's said or done amiss this night,

    Unless self-charity be sometimes a vice,

    And to defend ourselves it be a sin

    When violence assails us.

OTHELLO: Now, by heaven,

    My blood begins my safer guides to rule,   183

    And passion, having my best judgement collied,   184

    Assays to lead the way. If I once stir   185

    Or do but lift this arm, the best of you

    Shall sink in my rebuke. Give me to know

    How this foul rout began, who set it on;

    And he that is approved in this offense,   189

    Though he had twinned with me, both at a birth,

    Shall lose me. What! in a town of war,

    Yet wild, the people's hearts brimful of fear,

    To manage private and domestic quarrel?   193

    In night, and on the court and guard of safety?

    'Tis monstrous. Iago, who began't?

MONTANO:

    If partially affined, or leagued in office,   196

    Thou dost deliver more or less than truth,

    Thou art no soldier.

IAGO: Touch me not so near.

    I had rather have this tongue cut from my mouth

    Than it should do offense to Michael Cassio;

    Yet I persuade myself, to speak the truth

    Shall nothing wrong him. This it is, general.

    Montano and myself being in speech,

    There comes a fellow crying out for help,

    And Cassio following him with determined sword

    To execute upon him. Sir, this gentleman   206

    Steps in to Cassio and entreats his pause.

    Myself the crying fellow did pursue,

    Lest by his clamor—as it so fell out—

    The town might fall in fright. He, swift of foot,

    Outran my purpose; and I returned then rather

    For that I heard the clink and fall of swords,

---

177 *offends* pains **183** *blood* passion **184** *collied* darkened **185** *Assays* tries **189** *approved in* proved guilty of **193** *manage* carry on **196** *partially . . . office* prejudiced by comradeship or official relations **206** *execute* work his will

And Cassio high in oath; which till to-night   213
I ne'er might say before. When I came back—
For this was brief—I found them close together
At blow and thrust, even as again they were
When you yourself did part them.
More of this matter cannot I report;
But men are men; the best sometimes forget.
Though Cassio did some little wrong to him,
As men in rage strike those that wish them best,
Yet surely Cassio I believe received
From him that fled some strange indignity,
Which patience could not pass.   224
OTHELLO: I know, Iago,
Thy honesty and love doth mince this matter,
Making it light to Cassio. Cassio, I love thee;
But never more be officer of mine.

[*Enter* DESDEMONA, *attended.*]

Look if my gentle love be not raised up!
I'll make thee an example.
DESDEMONA: What's the matter?
OTHELLO:
All's well now, sweeting; come away to bed.
[*To* MONTANO.]
Sir, for your hurts, myself will be your surgeon.
Lead him off.
[MONTANO *is led off.*]
Iago, look with care about the town
And silence those whom this vile brawl distracted.   234
Come, Desdemona; 'tis the soldiers' life
To have their balmy slumbers waked with strife.
                           [*Exit, with all but* IAGO *and* CASSIO.]
IAGO: What, are you hurt, lieutenant?
CASSIO: Ay, past all surgery.
IAGO: Marry, God forbid!
CASSIO: Reputation, reputation, reputation! O, I have lost my reputation! I
have lost the immortal part of myself, and what remains is bestial. My
reputation, Iago, my reputation!
IAGO: As I am an honest man, I thought you had received some bodily
wound. There is more sense in that than in reputation. Reputation is an
idle and most false imposition; oft got without merit and lost without
deserving. You have lost no reputation at all unless you repute yourself
such a loser. What, man! there are ways to recover the general again.   247

213 *high in oath* cursing   **224** *pass* pass over, ignore   **234** *distracted* excited   **247** *recover* regain favor with

You are but now cast in his mood—a punishment more in policy than in 248
malice, even so as one would beat his offenseless dog to affright an
imperious lion. Sue to him again, and he's yours.

CASSIO: I will rather sue to be despised than to deceive so good a
commander with so slight, so drunken, and so indiscreet an officer.
Drunk! and speak parrot! and squabble! swagger! swear! and discourse 253
fustian with one's own shadow! O thou invisible spirit of wine, if thou 254
hast no name to be known by, let us call thee devil!

IAGO: What was he that you followed with your sword? What had he done to
you?

CASSIO: I know not.

IAGO: Is't possible?

CASSIO: I remember a mass of things, but nothing distinctly; a quarrel, but
nothing wherefore. O God, that men should put an enemy in their
mouths to steal away their brains! that we should with joy, pleasance,
revel, and applause transform ourselves into beasts! 263

IAGO: Why, but you are now well enough. How came you thus recovered?

CASSIO: It hath pleased the devil drunkenness to give place to the devil
wrath. One unperfectness shows me another, to make me frankly
despise myself.

IAGO: Come, you are too severe a moraler. As the time, the place, and the
condition of this country stands, I could heartily wish this had not so
befall'n; but since it is as it is, mend it for your own good.

CASSIO: I will ask him for my place again: he shall tell me I am a drunkard!
Had I as many mouths as Hydra, such an answer would stop them all. 272
To be now a sensible man, by and by a fool, and presently a beast! O
strange! Every inordinate cup is unblest, and the ingredient is a devil. 274

IAGO: Come, come, good wine is a good familiar creature if it be well used.
Exclaim no more against it. And, good lieutenant, I think you think I
love you.

CASSIO: I have well approved it, sir. I drunk! 278

IAGO: You or any man living may be drunk at some time, man. I'll tell you
what you shall do. Our general's wife is now the general. I may say so in
this respect, for that he hath devoted and given up himself to the
contemplation, mark, and denotement of her parts and graces. Confess
yourself freely to her; importune her help to put you in your place again.
She is of so free, so kind, so apt, so blessed a disposition she holds it a 284
vice in her goodness not to do more than she is requested. This broken
joint between you and her husband entreat her to splinter; and my 286
fortunes against any lay worth naming, this crack of your love shall 287
grow stronger than it was before.

CASSIO: You advise me well.

---

248 *cast in his mood* dismissed because of his anger **253** *parrot* meaningless phrases **254** *fustian* bombastic
nonsense **263** *applause* desire to please **272** *Hydra* monster with many heads **274** *ingredient* contents
278 *approved* proved **284** *free* bounteous **286** *splinter* bind up with splints **287** *lay* wager

IAGO: I protest, in the sincerity of love and honest kindness.

CASSIO: I think if freely; and betimes in the morning will I beseech the
virtuous Desdemona to undertake for me. I am desperate of my fortunes
if they check me here.

IAGO: You are in the right. Good night, lieutenant; I must to the watch.

CASSIO: Good night, honest Iago.   [*Exit* CASSIO.]

IAGO:

And what's he then that says I play the villain,
When this advice is free I give and honest,
Probal to thinking, and indeed the course   298
To win the Moor again? For 'tis most easy
Th' inclining Desdemona to subdue   300
In any honest suit; she's framed as fruitful
As the free elements. And then for her
To win the Moor—were't to renounce his baptism,
All seals and symbols of redeemèd sin—
His soul is so enfettered to her love
That she may make, unmake, do what she list,
Even as her appetite shall play the god
With his weak function. How am I then a villain
To counsel Cassio to this parallel course,   309
Directly to his good? Divinity of hell!   310
When devils will the blackest sins put on,   311
They do suggest at first with heavenly shows,
As I do now. For whiles this honest fool
Plies Desdemona to repair his fortunes,
And she for him pleads strongly to the Moor,
I'll pour this pestilence into his ear,
That she repeals him for her body's lust;   317
And by how much she strives to do him good,
She shall undo her credit with the Moor.
So will I turn her virtue into pitch,
And out of her own goodness make the net
That shall enmesh them all.
    [*Enter* RODERIGO.]   How, now, Roderigo?

RODERIGO: I do follow here in the chase, not like a hound that hunts, but
one that fills up the cry. My money is almost spent; I have been to-night   324
exceedingly well cudgelled; and I think the issue will be—I shall have so
much experience for my pains; and so, with no money at all, and a little
more wit, return again to Venice.

IAGO:

How poor are they that have not patience!
What wound did ever heal but by degrees?

---

298 *Probal* probable   **300** *subdue* persuade   **309** *parallel* corresponding   **310** *Divinity* theology   **311** *put on*
incite   **317** *repeals him* seeks his recall   **324** *cry* pack

Thou know'st we work by wit, and not by witchcraft;
And wit depends on dilatory time.
Does't not go well? Cassio hath beaten thee,
And thou by that small hurt hast cashiered Cassio. 333
Though other things grow fair against the sun,
Yet fruits that blossom first will first be ripe.
Content thyself awhile. By the mass, 'tis morning!
Pleasure and action make the hours seem short.
Retire thee; go where thou art billeted.
Away, I say! Thou shalt know more hereafter.
Nay, get thee gone! [*Exit* RODERIGO.]
    Two things are to be done:
My wife must move for Cassio to her mistress;
I'll set her on;
Myself the while to draw the Moor apart
And bring him jump when he may Cassio find 344
Soliciting his wife. Ay, that's the way!
Dull not device by coldness and delay. [*Exit.*]

ACT III

SCENE I

[*Enter* CASSIO, *with musicians and the* CLOWN.]

CASSIO:
 Masters, play here, I will content your pains: 1
 Something that's brief; and bid "Good morrow, general."
 [*They play.*]
CLOWN: Why, masters, ha' your instruments been in Naples, that they speak 3
 i' th' nose thus?
MUSICIAN: How, sir, how?
CLOWN: Are these, I pray you, called wind instruments?
MUSICIAN: Ay, marry, are they, sir.
CLOWN: O, thereby hangs a tail.
MUSICIAN: Whereby hangs a tale, sir?
CLOWN: Marry, sir, by many a wind instrument that I know. But, masters,
 here's money for you; and general so likes your music that he desires
 you, for love's sake, to make no more noise with it.
MUSICIAN: Well, sir, we will not.

---

333 *cashiered Cassio* maneuvered Cassio's discharge   **344** *jump* at the exact moment
Scene i Before the chamber of Othello and Desdemona   **1** *content* reward   **3** *Naples* (notorious for its
association with venereal disease)

CLOWN: If you have any music that may not be heard, to't again: but, as they
say, to hear music the general does not greatly care.

MUSICIAN: We have none such, sir.

CLOWN: Then put up your pipes in your bag, for I'll away.
Go, vanish into air, away!

[*Exit* MUSICIAN *(with his fellows)*.]

CASSIO: Dost thou hear, my honest friend?

CLOWN: No, I hear not your honest friend. I hear you.

CASSIO: Prithee keep up thy quillets. There's a poor piece of gold for thee. If   21
the gentlewoman that attends the general's wife be stirring, tell her there's
one Cassio entreats her a little favor of speech. Wilt thou do this?

CLOWN: She is stirring sir. If she will stir hither, I shall
seem to notify unto her.

CASSIO:
Do, good my friend.   [*Exit* CLOWN.]

[*Enter* IAGO.]   In happy time, Iago.   27

IAGO:
You have not been abed then?

CASSIO:
Why, no; the day had broke
Before we parted. I have made bold, Iago,
To send in to your wife: my suit to her
Is that she will to virtuous Desdemona
Procure me some access.

IAGO: I'll send her to you presently;
And I'll devise a mean to draw the Moor
Out of the way, that your converse and business
May be more free.

CASSIO:
I humbly thank you for't.   [*Exit* IAGO.]
                    I never knew
A Florentine more kind and honest.   38

[*Enter* EMILIA.]

EMILIA:
Good morrow, good lieutenant. I am sorry
For your displeasure; but all will sure be well.
The general and his wife are talking of it,
And she speaks for you stoutly. The Moor replies
That he you hurt is of great fame in Cyprus
And great affinity, and that in wholesome wisdom   44

---

21 *quillets* quips **27** *In happy time* well met **38** *Florentine* i.e. even a Florentine (like Cassio; Iago was a
Venetian) **44** *affinity* family connections

He might not but refuse you; but he protests he loves you,
And needs no other suitor but his likings
To take the safest occasion by the front   47
To bring you in again.
CASSIO: Yet I beseech you,
If you think fit, or that it may be done,
Give me advantage of some brief discourse
With Desdemona alone.
EMILIA: Pray you come in.
I will bestow you where you shall have time
To speak your bosom freely.   53
CASSIO: I am much bound to you.

                                                [*Exeunt.*]

SCENE II

[*Enter* OTHELLO, IAGO, *and gentlemen.*]

OTHELLO:
These letters given Iago, to the pilot
And by him do my duties to the Senate.
That done, I will be walking on the works;   3
Repair there to me.
IAGO: Well, my good lord, I'll do't.
OTHELLO:
This fortification, gentlemen, shall we see't?
GENTLEMEN:
We'll wait upon your lordship.   [*Exeunt.*]

SCENE III

[*Enter* DESDEMONA, CASSIO, *and* EMILIA.]

DESDEMONA:
Be thou assured, good Cassio, I will do
All my abilities in thy behalf.
EMILIA:
Good madam, do. I warrant it grieves my husband
As if the cause were his.

---

47 *occasion* opportunity; *front* forelock   **53** *your bosom* your inmost thoughts
Scene ii The castle   **3** *works* fortifications
Scene iii The castle grounds

DESDEMONA:
    O, that's an honest fellow. Do not doubt, Cassio,
    But I will have my lord and you again
    As friendly as you were.
CASSIO: Bounteous madam,
    Whatever shall become of Michael Cassio,
    He's never anything but your true servant.
DESDEMONA:
    I know't; I thank you. You do love my lord;
    You have known him long; and be you well assured
    He shall in strangeness stand no farther off   12
    Than in a politic distance.   13
CASSIO: Ay, but, lady,
    That policy may either last so long,
    Or feed upon such nice and waterish diet,   15
    Or breed itself so out of circumstance,
    That, I being absent, and my place supplied,
    My general will forget my love and service.
DESDEMONA:
    Do not doubt that; before Emilia here   19
    I give thee warrant of thy place. Assure thee,
    If I do vow a friendship, I'll perform it
    To the last article. My lord shall never rest;
    I'll watch him tame and talk him out of patience;   23
    His bed shall seem a school, his board a shrift;   24
    I'll intermingle everything he does
    With Cassio's suit. Therefore be merry, Cassio,
    For thy solicitor shall rather die
    Than give thy cause away.

    [*Enter* OTHELLO *and* IAGO *(at a distance).*]

EMILIA:
    Madam, here comes my lord.
CASSIO:
    Madam, I'll take my leave.
DESDEMONA:
    Why, stay, and hear me speak.
CASSIO:
    Madam, not now: I am very ill at ease,
    Unfit for mine own purposes.

---

12 *strangeness* aloofness   13 *Than . . . distance* than wise policy requires   15 *Or . . . diet* or be continued for
such slight reasons   19 *doubt* fear   23 *watch him tame* keep him awake until he gives in   24 *shrift* confessional

DESDEMONA:

Well, do your descretion. [*Exit* CASSIO.]

IAGO:

Ha! I like not that.

OTHELLO: What dost thou say?

IAGO:

Nothing, my lord; or if—I know not what.

OTHELLO:

Was not that Cassio parted from my wife?

IAGO:

Cassio, my lord? No, sure, I cannot think it,
That he would steal away so guilty-like,
Seeing your coming.

OTHELLO: I do believe 'twas he.

DESDEMONA:

How now, my lord?
I have been talking with a suitor here,
A man that languishes in your displeasure.

OTHELLO:

Who is't you mean?

DESDEMONA:

Why, your lieutenant, Cassio. Good my lord,
If I have any grace or power to move you,
His present reconciliation take; 47
For if he be not one that truly loves you,
That errs in ignorance, and not in cunning,
I have no judgment in an honest face.
I prithee call him back.

OTHELLO: Went he hence now?

DESDEMONA:

Yes, faith; so humbled
That he hath left part of his grief with me
To suffer with him. Good love, call him back.

OTHELLO:

Not now, sweet Desdemon; some other time.

DESDEMONA:

But shall't be shortly?

OTHELLO: The sooner, sweet, for you.

DESDEMONA:

Shall't be to-night at supper?

OTHELLO: No, not to-night.

DESDEMONA:

To-morrow dinner then?

47 *present* immediate

OTHELLO: I shall not dine at home;
   I meet the captains at the citadel.
DESDEMONA:
   Why, then, to-morrow night, or Tuesday morn,
   On Tuesday noon or night, or Wednesday morn.
   I prithee name the time, but let it not
   Exceed three days. I' faith, he's penitent;
   And yet his trespass, in our common reason
   (Save that, they say, the wars must make examples
   Out of their best), is not almost a fault   66
   T'incur a private check. When shall he come?   67
   Tell me, Othello. I wonder in my soul
   What you could ask me that I should deny
   Or stand so mamm'ring on. What? Michael Cassio,   70
   That came a-wooing with you, and so many a time,
   When I have spoke of you dispraisingly,
   Hath ta'en your part—to have so much to do
   To bring him in? By'r Lady, I could do much—
OTHELLO:
   Prithee no more. Let him come when he will!
   I will deny thee nothing.
DESDEMONA: Why, this is not a boon;
   'Tis as I should entreat you wear your gloves,
   Or feed on nourishing dishes, or keep you warm,
   Or sue to you to do a peculiar profit
   To your own person. Nay, when I have a suit
   Wherein I mean to touch your love indeed,
   It shall be full of poise and difficult weight,
   And fearful to be granted.   83
OTHELLO: I will deny thee nothing!
   Whereon I do beseech thee grant me this,
   To leave me but a little to myself.
DESDEMONA:
   Shall I deny you? No. Farewell, my lord.
OTHELLO:
   Farewell, my Desdemon: I'll come to thee straight.
DESDEMONA:
   Emilia, come.—Be as your fancies teach you;
   Whate'er you be, I am obedient.   *[Exit (with* EMILIA*).]*
OTHELLO:
   Excellent wretch! Perdition catch my soul   90
   But I do love thee! and when I love thee not,
   Chaos is come again.

---

66 *not almost* hardly   **67** *a private check* even a private reprimand   **70** *mamm'ring on* hesitating about
83 *fearful* dangerous   **90** *wretch* (a term of endearment)

IAGO:

My noble lord—

OTHELLO: What dost thou say, Iago?

IAGO:

Did Michael Cassio, when you wooed my lady,
Know of your love?

OTHELLO:

He did, from first to last. Why dost thou ask?

IAGO:

But for a satisfaction of my thought;
No further harm.

OTHELLO: Why of thy thought, Iago?

IAGO:

I did not think he had been acquainted with her.

OTHELLO:

O, yes, and went between us very oft.   100

IAGO:

Indeed?

OTHELLO:

Indeed? Ay, indeed! Discern'st thou aught in that?
Is he not honest?

IAGO: Honest, my lord?

OTHELLO: Honest. Ay, honest.

IAGO:

My lord, for aught I know.

OTHELLO:

What dost thou think?

IAGO: Think, my lord?

OTHELLO: Think, my lord?
By heaven, he echoes me,
As if there were some monster in his thought
Too hideous to be shown. Thou dost mean something:
I heard thee say even now, thou lik'st not that,
When Cassio left my wife. What didst not like?
And when I told thee he was of my counsel
In my whole course of wooing, thou cried'st "Indeed?"
And didst contract and purse thy brow together,
As if you then hadst shut up in thy brain
Some horrible conceit. If thou dost love me,   115
Show me thy thought.

IAGO:

My lord, you know I love you.

OTHELLO: I think thou dost;
And, for I know thou'rt full of love and honesty

100 _went . . . us_ (i.e. as messenger)   115 _conceit_ fancy

And weigh'st thy words before thou giv'st them breath,
Therefore these stops of thine fright me the more;
For such things in a false disloyal knave
Are tricks of custom; but in a man that's just
They are close dilations, working from the heart   123
That passion cannot rule.
IAGO: For Michael Cassio,
I dare be sworn I think that he is honest.
OTHELLO:
I think so too.
IAGO: Men should be what they seem;
Or those that be not, would they might seem none!   127
OTHELLO:
Certain, men should be what they seem.
IAGO:
Why then, I think Cassio's an honest man.
OTHELLO:
Nay, yet there's more in this.
I prithee speak to me as to thy thinkings,
As thou dost ruminate, and give thy worst of thoughts
The worst of words.
IAGO: Good my lord, pardon me:
Though I am bound to every act of duty,
I am not bound to that all slaves are free to.   135
Utter my thoughts? Why, say they are vile and false,
As where's that palace whereinto foul things
Sometimes intrude not? Who has a breast so pure
But some uncleanly apprehensions
Keep leets and law days, and in Sessions sit   140
With meditations lawful?
OTHELLO:
Thou dost conspire against thy friend, Iago,
If thou but think'st him wronged, and mak'st his ear
A stranger to thy thoughts.
IAGO: I do beseech you—
Though I perchance am vicious in my guess
(As I confess it is my nature's plague
To spy into abuses, and oft my jealousy   147
Shapes faults that are not), that your wisdom yet
From one that so imperfectly conjects   149

123–24 *close dilations . . . rule* secret emotions which well up in spite of restraint   **127** *seem none* i.e. not pretend
to be men when they are really monsters   **135** *bound . . . free to* bound to tell that which even slaves are allowed
to keep to themselves   **140** *leets and law days* sittings of the courts   **147** *jealousy* suspicion   **149** *conjects*
conjectures

Would take no notice, nor build yourself a trouble
Out of his scattering and unsure observance.
It were not for your quiet nor your good,
Nor for my manhood, honesty, and wisdom,
To let you know my thoughts.

OTHELLO: What dost thou mean?

IAGO:

Good name in man and woman, dear my lord,
Is the immediate jewel of their souls.   156
Who steals my purse steals trash; 'tis something, nothing;
'Twas mine, 'tis his, and has been slave to thousands;
But he that filches from me my good name
Robs me of that which not enriches him
And makes me poor indeed.

OTHELLO:

By heaven, I'll know thy thoughts!

IAGO:

You cannot, if my heart were in your hand;
Nor shall not whilst 'tis in my custody.

OTHELLO:

Ha!

IAGO: O, beware, my lord, of jealousy!
It is the green-eyed monster, which doth mock   166
The meat it feeds on. That cuckold lives in bliss
Who, certain of his fate, loves not his wronger;
But O, what damnèd minutes tells he o'er
Who dotes, yet doubts—suspects, yet strongly loves!

OTHELLO:

O misery!

IAGO:

Poor and content is rich, and rich enough;
But riches fineless is as poor as winter   173
To him that ever fears he shall be poor.
Good God, the souls of all my tribe defend
From jealousy!

OTHELLO: Why, why is this?
Think'st thou I'd make a life of jealousy,
To follow still the changes of the moon
With fresh suspicions? No! To be once in doubt
Is once to be resolved. Exchange me for a goat
When I shall turn the business of my soul
To such exsufflicate and blown surmises,   182

156 *immediate* nearest the heart   **166** *mock* play with, like a cat with a mouse   **173** *fineless* unlimited
182 *exsufficate and blown* spat out and flyblown

Matching this inference. 'Tis not to make me jealous
To say my wife is fair, feeds well, loves company,
Is free of speech, sings, plays, and dances;
Where virtue is, these are more virtuous.
Nor from mine own weak merits will I draw
The smallest fear or doubt of her revolt,   188
For she had eyes, and chose me. No, Iago;
I'll see before I doubt; when I doubt, prove;
And on the proof there is no more but this—
Away at once with love or jealousy!

IAGO:
I am glad of this; for now I shall have reason
To show the love and duty that I bear you
With franker spirit. Therefore, as I am bound,
Receive it from me. I speak not yet of proof.
Look to your wife; observe her well with Cassio;
Wear your eyes thus, not jealous nor secure: 198
I would not have your free and noble nature,
Out of self-bounty, be abused. Look to't.   200
I know our country disposition well:
In Venice they do let God see the pranks
They dare not show their husbands; their best conscience
Is not to leav't undone, but keep't unknown.

OTHELLO:
Dost thou say so?

IAGO:
She did deceive her father, marrying you;
And when she seemed to shake and fear your looks,
She loved them most.

OTHELLO: And so she did.

IAGO: Why, go to then!
She that, so young, could give out such a seeming
To seel her father's eyes up close as oak—   210
He thought 'twas witchcraft—but I am much to blame.
I humbly do beseech you of your pardon
For too much loving you.

OTHELLO: I am bound to thee for ever.

IAGO:
I see this hath a little dashed your spirits.

OTHELLO:
Not a jot, not a jot.

IAGO: I' faith, I fear it has.

188 *revolt* unfaithfulness   **198** *secure* overconfident   **200** *self-bounty* natural goodness   **210** *seel* close; *oak* oak grain

I hope you will consider what is spoke
Comes from my love. But I do see y' are moved.
I am to pray you not to strain my speech
To grosser issues nor to larger reach   219
Than to suspicion.

OTHELLO:
I will not.

IAGO: Should you do so, my lord,
My speech should fall into such vile success   222
As my thoughts aim not at. Cassio's my worthy friend—
My lord, I see y' are moved.

OTHELLO: No, not much moved:
I do not think but Desdemona's honest.   225

IAGO:
Long live she so! and long live you to think so!

OTHELLO:
And yet, how nature erring from itself—

IAGO:
Ay, there's the point! as (to be bold with you)
Not to affect many proposèd matches
Of her own clime, complexion, and degree,
Whereto we see in all things nature tends—
Foh! one may smell in such a will most rank,
Foul disproportions, thoughts unnatural—
But pardon me—I do not in position   234
Distinctly speak of her; though I may fear
Her will, recoiling to her better judgment,   236
May fall to match you with her country forms,   237
And happily repent.   238

OTHELLO: Farewell, farewell!
If more thou dost perceive, let me know more.
Set on thy wife to observe. Leave me, Iago.

IAGO:
My lord, I take my leave.   [Going.]

OTHELLO:
Why did I marry? This honest creature doubtless
Sees and knows more, much more, than he unfolds.

IAGO [returns]:
My lord, I would I might entreat your honor
To scan this thing no further: leave it to time.
Although 'tis fit that Cassio have his place,

---

219 *To grosser issues* to mean something more monstrous **222** *vile success* evil outcome **225** *honest* chaste
234 *position* definite assertion **236** *recoiling* reverting **237** *fall to match* happen to compare **238** *happily*
haply, perhaps

For sure he fills it up with great ability,
Yet, if you please to hold him off awhile,
You shall by that perceive him and his means.
Note if your lady strain his entertainment   250
With any strong or vehement importunity;
Much will be seen in that. In the mean time
Let me be thought too busy in my fears   253
(As worthy cause I have to fear I am)
And hold her free, I do beseech your honor.   255
OTHELLO:
    Fear not my government.   256
IAGO:
    I once more take my leave.   [*Exit.*]
OTHELLO:
    This fellow's of exceeding honesty,
And knows all qualities, with a learned spirit   259
Of human dealings. If I do prove her haggard,   260
Though that her jesses were my dear heartstrings,   261
I'd whistle her off and let her down the wind   262
To prey at fortune. Haply, for I am black
And have not those soft parts of conversation   264
That chamberers have, or for I am declined   265
Into the vale of years—yet that's not much—
She's gone. I am abused, and my relief
Must be to loathe her. O curse of marriage,
That we can call these delicate creatures ours,
And not their appetites! I had rather be a toad
And live upon the vapor of a dungeon
Than keep a corner in the thing I love
For others' uses. Yet 'tis the plague of great ones;   273
Prerogatived are they less than the base.   274
'Tis destiny unshunnable, like death.
Even then this forkèd plague is fated to us   276
When we do quicken. Look where she comes.   277

[*Enter* DESDEMONA *and* EMILIA.]

If she be false, O, then heaven mocks itself!
I'll not believe't.
DESDEMONA: How now, my dear Othello?

250 *strain his entertainment* urge his recall   253 *busy* meddlesome   255 *hold her free* consider her guiltless   256 *government* self-control   259 *qualities* natures   259–60 *learned spirit Of* mind informed about   260 *haggard* a wild hawk   261 *jesses* thongs for controlling a hawk   262–63 *whistle . . . fortune* turn her out and let her take care of herself   264 *soft . . . conversation* ingratiating manners   265 *chamberers* courtiers   273 *great ones* prominent men   274 *Prerogatived* privileged   276 *forkèd plague* i.e. horns of a cuckold   277 *do quicken* are born

Your dinner, and the generous islanders　　　　　　　　　　280
By you invited, do attend your presence.
OTHELLO:
I am to blame.
DESDEMONA:　　Why do you speak so faintly?
Are you not well?
OTHELLO:
I have a pain upon my forehead, here.
DESDEMONA:
Faith, that's with watching; 'twill away again.　　　　285
Let me but bind it hard, within this hour
It will be well.
OTHELLO:　　　Your napkin is too little;　　　　　　　287
[*He pushes the handkerchief from him, and it falls unnoticed.*]
Let it alone. Come, I'll go in with you.　　　　　　　288
DESDEMONA:
I am very sorry that you are not well.　　　[*Exit (with* OTHELLO*).*]
EMILIA:
I am glad I have found this napkin;
This was her first remembrance from the Moor,
My wayward husband hath a hundred times
Wooed me to steal it; but she so loves the token
(For he conjured her she should ever keep it)
That she reserves it evermore about her
To kiss and talk to. I'll have the work ta'en out　　　296
And give't Iago.
What he will do with it heaven knows, not I;
I nothing but to please his fantasy.　　　　　　　　299

[*Enter* IAGO.]

IAGO:
How now? What do you here alone?
EMILIA:
Do not you chide; I have a thing for you.
IAGO:
A thing for me? It is a common thing—
EMILIA: Ha?
IAGO:
To have a foolish wife.
EMILIA:
O, is that all? What will you give me now
For that same handkerchief?

280 *generous* noble　**285** *watching* working late　**287** *napkin* handkerchief　**288** *it* i.e. his forehead
296 *work ta'en out* pattern copied　**299** *fantasy* whim

IAGO: What handkerchief?
EMILIA:
What handkerchief!
Why, that the Moor first gave to Desdemona;
That which so often you did bid me steal.
IAGO:
Hast stol'n it from her?
EMILIA:
No, faith; she let it drop by negligence,
And to th' advantage, I, being here, took't up.   312
Look, here it is.
IAGO: A good wench! Give it me.
EMILIA:
What will you do with't, that you have been so earnest
To have me filch it?
IAGO: Why, what is that to you?
[Snatches it.]
EMILIA:
If it be not for some purpose of import,   316
Give't me again. Poor lady, she'll run mad
When she shall lack it.
IAGO:
Be not acknown on't; I have use for it.   319
Go, leave me.   [Exit EMILIA.]
I will in Cassio's lodgings lose this napkin
And let him find it. Trifles light as air
Are to the jealous confirmations strong
As proofs of holy writ. This may do something.
The Moor already changes with my poison:
Dangerous conceits are in their natures poisons,   326
Which at the first are scarce found to distaste,
But with a little act upon the blood
Burn like the mines of sulphur.
[Enter OTHELLO.]   I did say so.
Look where he comes! Not poppy nor mandragora,   330
Nor all the drowsy syrups of the world,
Shall ever med'cine thee to that sweet sleep
Which thou owedst yesterday.
OTHELLO: Ha! ha! false to me?
IAGO:
Why, how now, general? No more of that!
OTHELLO:
Avaunt! be gone! Thou hast set me on the rack.

312 *to th' advantage* opportunely   **316** *import* importance   **319** *Be . . . on't* do not acknowledge it   **326** *conceits* ideas   **330** *mandragora* a narcotic

I swear 'tis better to be much abused
Than but to know't a little.

IAGO: How now, my lord?

OTHELLO:

What sense had I of her stol'n hours of lust?
I saw't not, thought it not, it harmed not me;
I slept the next night well, fed well, was free and merry;   340
I found not Cassio's kisses on her lips.
He that is robbed, not wanting what is stol'n,   342
Let him not know't, and he's not robbed at all.

IAGO:

I am sorry to hear this.

OTHELLO:

I had been happy if the general camp,
Pioners and all, had tasted her sweet body,   346
So I had nothing known. O, now for ever
Farewell the tranquil mind! farewell content!
Farewell the plumèd troop, and the big wars   349
That make ambition virtue! O, farewell!
Farewell the neighing steed and the shrill trump,
The spirit-stirring drum, th' ear-piercing fife,
The royal banner, and all quality,
Pride, pomp, and circumstance of glorious war!   354
And O you mortal engines whose rude throats   355
Th' immortal Jove's dread clamors counterfeit,   356
Farewell! Othello's occupation's gone!

IAGO:

Is't possible, my lord?

OTHELLO:

Villain, be sure thou prove my love a whore!
Be sure of it; give me the ocular proof;
Or, by the worth of mine eternal soul,
Thou hadst been better have been born a dog
Than answer my waked wrath!

IAGO: Is't come to this?

OTHELLO:

Make me to see't; or at the least so prove it
That the probation bear no hinge nor loop   365
To hang a doubt on—or woe upon thy life!

IAGO:

My noble lord—

OTHELLO:

If thou dost slander her and torture me,

---

340 *free* carefree   **342** *wanting* missing   **346** *Pioners* sappers, laborers   **349** *big* stately   **354** *circumstance*
pageantry   **355** *mortal engines* deadly artillery   **356** *counterfeit* imitate   **365** *probation* proof

Never pray more; abandon all remorse;
On horror's head horrors accumulate;
Do deeds to make heaven weep, all earth amazed;
For nothing canst thou to damnation add
Greater than that.

IAGO: O grace! O heaven forgive me!
Are you a man? Have you a soul or sense?—
God b' wi' you! take mine office. O wretched fool,
That liv'st to make thine honesty a vice!
O monstrous would! Take note, take note, O world,
To be direct and honest is not safe.
I thank you for this profit; and from hence   379
I'll love no friend, sith love breeds such offense.

OTHELLO:
  Nay stay. Thou shouldst be honest.

IAGO:
  I should be wise; for honesty's a fool
  And loses that it works for.

OTHELLO: By the world,
I think my wife be honest, and think she is not;
I think that thou art just, and think thou art not.
I'll have some proof. Her name, that was as fresh
As Dian's visage, is now begrimed and black
As mine own face. If there be cords, or knives,
Poison, or fire, or suffocating streams,
I'll not endure it. Would I were satisfied!   390

IAGO:
I see, sir, you are eaten up with passion:
I do repent me that I put it to you.
You would be satisfied?

OTHELLO: Would? Nay, I will.

IAGO:
And may; but how? how satisfied, my lord?
Would you, the supervisor, grossly gape on?   395
Behold her topped?

OTHELLO: Death and damnation! O!

IAGO:
It were a tedious difficulty, I think,
To bring them to that prospect. Damn them then,
If ever mortal eyes do see them bolster   399
More than their own! What then? How then?
What shall I say? Where's satisfaction?

---

379 *profit* profitable lesson   **390** *satisfied* completely informed   **395** *supervisor* spectator   **399** *bolster* lie together

It is impossible you should see this,
Were they as prime as goats, as hot as monkeys,   403
As salt as wolves in pride, and fools as gross   404
As ignorance made drunk. But yet, I say,
If imputation and strong circumstances
Which lead directly to the door of truth
Will give you satisfaction, you may have't.

OTHELLO:
Give me a living reason she's disloyal.

IAGO:
I do not like the office.
But sith I am ent'red in this cause so far,
Pricked to't by foolish honesty and love,
I will go on. I lay with Cassio lately,
And being troubled with a raging tooth,
I could not sleep.
There are a kind of men so loose of soul
That in their sleeps will mutter their affairs.
One of this kind is Cassio.
In sleep I heard him say, "Sweet Desdemona,
Let us be wary, let us hide our loves!"
And then, sir, would he gripe and wring my hand,
Cry "O sweet creature!" and then kiss me hard,
As if he plucked up kisses by the roots
That grew upon my lips; then laid his leg
Over my thigh, and sighed, and kissed, and then
Cried "Cursèd fate that gave thee to the Moor!"

OTHELLO:
O monstrous! monstrous!

IAGO: Nay, this was but his dream.

OTHELLO:
But this denoted a foregone conclusion: 428
'Tis a shrewd doubt, though it be but a dream.   429

IAGO:
And this may help to thicken other proofs
That do demonstrate thinly.

OTHELLO: I'll tear her all to pieces!

IAGO:
Nay, but be wise. Yet we see nothing done;
She may be honest yet. Tell me but this—
Have you not sometimes seen a handkerchief
Spotted with strawberries in your wife's hand?

---

403 *prime* lustful   **404** *salt* lecherous; *pride* heat   **428** *foregone conclusion* previous experience   **429** *a shrewd
doubt* cursedly suspicious

OTHELLO:

I gave her such a one; 'twas my first gift.

IAGO:

I know not that; but such a handkerchief—
I am sure it was your wife's—did I to-day
See Cassio wipe his beard with.

OTHELLO: If it be that—

IAGO:

If it be that, or any that was hers,
It speaks against her with the other proofs.

OTHELLO:

O, that the slave had forty thousand lives!
One is too poor, too weak for my revenge.
Now do I see 'tis true. Look here, Iago:
All my fond love thus do I blow to heaven.
'Tis gone.
Arise, black vengeance, from the hollow hell!
Yield up, O love, thy crown and hearted throne
To tyrannous hate! Swell, bosom, with thy fraught,   449
For 'tis of aspics' tongues!   450

IAGO: Yet be content.

OTHELLO:

O, blood, blood, blood!

IAGO:

Patience, I say. Your mind perhaps may change.

OTHELLO:

Never, Iago. Like to the Pontic sea,   453
Whose icy current and compulsive course
Ne'er feels retiring ebb, but keeps due on
To the Propontic and the Hellespont,
Even so my bloody thoughts, with violent pace,
Shall ne'er look back, ne'er ebb to humble love,
Till that a capable and wide revenge   459
Swallow them up.
[*He kneels.*]   Now, by yond marble heaven,
In the due reverence of a sacred vow
I here engage my words.

IAGO: Do not rise yet.

[IAGO *kneels.*]

Witness, you ever-burning lights above,
You elements that clip us round about,   464

449 *fraught* burden   **450** *aspics* deadly poisonous snakes   **453** *Pontic sea* Black Sea   **459** *capable* all-embrac-
ing   **464** *clip* encompass

Witness that here Iago doth give up
The execution of his wit, hands, heart   466
To wrongèd Othello's service! Let him command,
And to obey shall be in me remorse,   468
What bloody business ever.
    [*They rise.*]
OTHELLO: I greet thy love,
Not with vain thanks but with acceptance bounteous,
And will upon the instant put thee to't.
Within these three days let me hear thee say
That Cassio's not alive.
IAGO:
My friend is dead; 'tis done at your request
But let her live.
OTHELLO:
Damn her, lewd minx! O, damn her! damn her!
Come, go with me apart. I will withdraw
To furnish me with some swift means of death
For the fair devil. Now art thou my lieutenant.
IAGO:
I am your own for ever.   [*Exeunt.*]

SCENE IV

[*Enter* DESDEMONA, EMILIA, *and* CLOWN.]

DESDEMONA: Do you know, sirrah, where Lieutenant Cassio lies?   2
CLOWN: I dare not say he lies anywhere.
DESDEMONA: Why, man?
CLOWN: He's a soldier, and for me to say a soldier lies is
    stabbing.
DESDEMONA: Go to. Where lodges he?
CLOWN: To tell you where he lodges is to tell you where I lie.
DESDEMONA: Can anything be made of this?
CLOWN: I know not where he lodges; and for me to devise
    a lodging, and say he lies here or he lies there, were to
    lie in mine own throat.
DESDEMONA: Can you enquire him out, and be edified by
    report?
CLOWN: I will catechize the world for him; that is, make
    questions, and by them answer.

466 *execution* activities; *wit* mind   **468** *remorse* pity
Scene iv The environs of the castle   **2** *lies* lives, lodges

DESDEMONA: Seek him, bid him come hither. Tell him I
  have moved my lord on his behalf and hope all will be   19
  well.
CLOWN: To do this is within the compass of man's wit,
  and therefore I'll attempt the doing of it.   [*Exit.*]
DESDEMONA:
  Where should I lose that handkerchief, Emilia?
EMILIA:
  I know not, madam.
DESDEMONA:
  Believe me, I had rather have lost my purse
  Full of crusadoes; and but my noble Moor   26
  Is true of mind, and made of no such baseness
  As jealous creatures are, it were enough
  To put him to ill thinking.
EMILIA: Is he not jealous?
DESDEMONA:
  Who? he? I think the sun where he was born
  Drew all such humors from him.   31

[*Enter* OTHELLO.]

EMILIA: Look where he comes.
DESDEMONA:
  I will not leave him now till Cassio
  Be called to him.—How is't with you, my lord?
OTHELLO:
  Well, my good lady. [*aside*] O, hardness to dissemble!—
  How do you, Desdemona?
DESDEMONA: Well, my good lord.
OTHELLO:
  Give me your hand. This hand is moist, my lady.
DESDEMONA:
  It yet hath felt no age nor known no sorrow.
OTHELLO:
  This argues fruitfulness and liberal heart.
  Hot, hot, and moist. This hand of yours requires
  A sequester from liberty, fasting and prayer,   40
  Much castigation, exercise devout;
  For here's a young and sweating devil here
  That commonly rebels. 'Tis a good hand,
  A frank one.

19 *moved* made proposals **26** *crusadoes* Portuguese gold coins **31** *humors* inclinations **40** *sequester* removal

DESDEMONA: You may, indeed, say so;
For 'twas that hand that gave away my heart.
OTHELLO:
A liberal hand! The hearts of old gave hands;
But our new heraldry is hands, not hearts. 47
DESDEMONA:
I cannot speak of this. Come now, your promise!
OTHELLO:
What promise, chuck?
DESDEMONA:
I have sent to bid Cassio come speak with you.
OTHELLO:
I have a salt and sorry rheum offends me. 51
Lend me thy handkerchief.
DESDEMONA: Here, my lord.
OTHELLO:
That which I gave you.
DESDEMONA: I have it not about me.
OTHELLO:
Not?
DESDEMONA: No, faith, my lord.
OTHELLO: That's a fault.
That handkerchief
Did an Egyptian to my mother give. 56
She was a charmer, and could almost read 57
The thoughts of people. She told her, while she kept it,
'Twould make her amiable and subdue my father 59
Entirely to her love; but if she lost it
Or made a gift of it, my father's eye
Should hold her loathèd, and his spirits should hunt
After new fancies. She, dying, gave it me,
And bid me, when my fate would have me wive,
To give it her. I did so; and take heed on't;
Make it a darling like your precious eye.
To lose't or give't away were such perdition 67
As nothing else could match.
DESDEMONA: Is't possible?
OTHELLO:
'Tis true. There's magic in the web of it.
A sibyl that had numb'red in the world
The sun to course two hundred compasses, 71
In her prophetic fury sewed the work;

---

47 *heraldry* heraldic symbolism **51** *salt . . . rheum* distressing head-cold **56** *Egyptian* gypsy **57** *charmer* sorceress **59** *amiable* lovable **67** *perdition* disaster **71** *compasses* annual rounds

The worms were hallowed that did breed the silk;
And it was dyed in mummy which the skillful   74
Conserved of maiden's hearts.

DESDEMONA: I' faith? Is't true?

OTHELLO:

Most veritable. Therefore look to't well.

DESDEMONA:

Then would to God that I had never seen't!

OTHELLO: Ha! Wherefore?

DESDEMONA:

Why do you speak so startingly and rash?

OTHELLO:

Is't lost? Is't gone? Speak, is it out o' th' way?

DESDEMONA: Heaven bless us!

OTHELLO: Say you?

DESDEMONA:

It is not lost. But what an if it were?

OTHELLO: How?

DESDEMONA:

I say it is not lost.

OTHELLO: Fetch't, let me see't!

DESDEMONA:

Why, so I can, sir; but I will not now.
This is a trick to put me from my suit: 87
Pray you let Cassio be received again.

OTHELLO:

Fetch me the handkerchief! My mind misgives.

DESDEMONA:

Come, come!
You'll never meet a more sufficient man.

OTHELLO:

The handkerchief!

DESDEMONA: I pray talk me of Cassio.

OTHELLO:

The handkerchief!

DESDEMONA: A man that all his time   93
Hath founded his good fortunes on your love,
Shared dangers with you—

OTHELLO:

The handkerchief!

DESDEMONA:

I' faith, you are to blame.

OTHELLO: Zounds!   [*Exit* OTHELLO.]

---

74 *mummy* a drug made from mummies **87** *put* divert **93** *all . . . time* during his whole career

EMILIA: Is not this man jealous?

DESDEMONA:

I ne'er saw this before.
Sure there's some wonder in this handkerchief;
I am most unhappy in the loss of it.

EMILIA:

'Tis not a year or two shows us a man.
They are all but stomachs, and we all but food;
They eat us hungerly, and when they are full,
They belch us.

[*Enter* IAGO *and* CASSIO.]

Look you—Cassio and my husband!

IAGO:

There is no other way; 'tis she must do't.
And lo the happiness! Go and importune her.   108

DESDEMONA:

How now, good Cassio? What's the news with you?

CASSIO:

Madam, my former suit. I do beseech you
That by your virtuous means I may again
Exist, and be a member of his love
Whom I with all the office of my heart
Entirely honor. I would not be delayed.
If my offense be of such mortal kind
That neither service past, nor present sorrows,
Nor purposed merit in futurity,
Can ransom me into his love again,
But to know so must be my benefit.
So shall I clothe me in a forced content,
And shut myself up in some other course,   121
To fortune's alms.

DESDEMONA: Alas, thrice-gentle Cassio!
My advocation is not now in tune.   123
My lord is not my lord; nor should I know him,
Were he in favor as in humor altered.   125
So help me every spirit sanctified
As I have spoken for you all my best
And stood within the blank of his displeasure   128
For my free speech! You must awhile be patient.

---

108 *happiness* good luck   **121** *shut myself up in* confine myself to   **123** *advocation* advocacy   **125** *favor* appearance   **128** *blank* bull's-eye of the target

What I can do I will; and more I will
Than for myself I dare. Let that suffice you.

IAGO:
Is my lord angry?

EMILIA: He went hence but now,
And certainly in strange unquietness.

IAGO:
Can he be angry? I have seen the cannon
When it hath blown his ranks into the air
And, like the devil, from his very arm
Puffed his own brother—and is he angry?
Something of moment then. I will go meet him.
There's matter in't indeed if he be angry.

DESDEMONA:
I prithee do so.   [*Exit* IAGO.]
                    Something sure of state,   140
Either from Venice or some unhatched practice   141
Made demonstrable here in Cyprus to him,
Hath puddled his clear spirit; and in such cases   143
Men's natures wrangle with inferior things,
Though great ones are their object. 'Tis even so;
For let our finger ache, and it endues   146
Our other, healthful members even to a sense
Of pain. Nay, we must think men are not gods,
Nor of them look for such observancy
As fits the bridal. Beshrew me much, Emilia,
I was, unhandsome warrior as I am,   151
Arraigning his unkindness with my soul;   152
But now I find I had suborned the witness,
And he's indicted falsely.

EMILIA:
Pray heaven it be state matters, as you think,
And no conception nor no jealous toy   156
Concerning you.

DESDEMONA:
Alas the day! I never gave him cause.

EMILIA:
But jealous souls will not be answered so;
They are not ever jealous for the cause,
But jealous for they're jealous. 'Tis a monster
Begot upon itself, born on itself.   162

---

140 *state* public affairs   **141** *unhatched practice* budding plot   **143** *puddled* muddied   **146** *endues* brings
151 *unhandsome warrior* inadequate soldier   **152** *Arraigning . . . soul* indicting his unkindness before the bar of
my soul   **156** *toy* fancy   **162** *Begot . . . itself* self-engendered

DESDEMONA:

Heaven keep that monster from Othello's mind!

EMILIA: Lady, amen.

DESDEMONA:

I will go seek him. Cassio, walk here about:

If I do find him fit, I'll move your suit

And seek to effect it to my uttermost.

CASSIO:

I humbly thank your ladyship.

[*Exeunt* DESDEMONA *and* EMILIA.]

[*Enter* BIANCA.]

BIANCA:

Save you, friend Cassio!

CASSIO: What make you from home?

How is't with you, my most fair Bianca?

I' faith, sweet love, I was coming to your house.

BIANCA:

And I was going to your lodging, Cassio.

What, keep a week away? seven days and nights?

Eightscore eight hours? and lovers' absent hours,

More tedious than the dial eightscore times?   175

O weary reck'ning!

CASSIO: Pardon me, Bianca:

I have this while with leaden thoughts been pressed;

But I shall in a more continuate time   178

Strike off this score of absence. Sweet Bianca,

[*Gives her* DESDEMONA's *handkerchief.*]

Take me this work out.   180

BIANCA: O Cassio, whence came this?

This is some token from a newer friend.

To the felt absence now I feel a cause.

Is't come to this? Well, well.

CASSIO: Go to, woman!

Throw your vile guesses in the devil's teeth,

From whence you have them. You are jealous now

That this is from some mistress, some remembrance.

No, by my faith, Bianca.

BIANCA: Why, whose is it?

CASSIO:

I know not, sweet; I found it in my chamber.

175 *dial* clock **178** *continuate* uninterrupted **180** *Take . . . out* copy this embroidery for me

I like the work well; ere it be demanded,　　　　　　　　　　189
As like enough it will, I'd have it copied.
Take it and do't, and leave me for this time.

BIANCA:
Leave you? Wherefore?

CASSIO:
I do attend here on the general
And think it no addition, nor my wish,
To have him see me womaned.

BIANCA:　　　　　　　　　　Why, I pray you?

CASSIO:
Not that I love you not.

BIANCA:　　　　　　　But that you do not love me!
I pray you bring me on the way a little,
And say if I shall see you soon at night.

CASSIO:
'Tis but a little way that I can bring you,
For I attend here; but I'll see you soon.

BIANCA:
'Tis very good. I must be circumstanced.　　　　　　*[Exeunt.]*　　201

ACT IV

SCENE I

[*Enter* OTHELLO *and* IAGO.]

IAGO:
Will you think so?

OTHELLO:　　　　Think so, Iago?

IAGO:　　　　　　　　　What,
To kiss in private?

OTHELLO:　　　An unauthorized kiss.

IAGO:
Or to be naked with her friend in bed
An hour or more, not meaning any harm?

OTHELLO:
Naked in bed, Iago, and not mean harm?
It is hypocrisy against the devil.　　　　　　　　　　　　　　6
They that mean virtuously, and yet do so,
The devil their virtue tempts, and they tempt heaven.

---

189 *work* needlework　**201** *circumstanced* governed by circumstances
Scene i The environs of the castle　**6** *hypocrisy . . . devil* i.e. feigned sin instead of feigned virtue

IAGO:

So they do nothing, 'tis a venial slip.
But if I give my wife a handkerchief—

OTHELLO:

What then?

IAGO:

Why, then 'tis hers, my lord; and being hers,
She may, I think, bestow't on any man.

OTHELLO:

She is protectress of her honor too;
May she give that?

IAGO:

Her honor is an essence that's not seen;
They have it very oft that have it not.
But for the handkerchief—

OTHELLO:

By heaven, I would most gladly have forgot it!
Thou said'st—O, it comes o'er my memory
As doth the raven o'er the infected house,   21
Boding to all!—he had my handkerchief.

IAGO:

Ay, what of that?

OTHELLO: That's not so good now.

IAGO: What
If I had said I had seen him do you wrong?
Or heard him say—as knaves be such abroad
Who having, by their own importunate suit,
Or voluntary dotage of some mistress,
Convincèd or supplied them, cannot choose   28
But they must blab—

OTHELLO: Hath he said anything?

IAGO:

He hath, my lord; but be you well assured,
No more than he'll unswear.

OTHELLO: What hath he said?

IAGO:

Faith, that he did—I know not what he did.

OTHELLO: What? what?

IAGO:

Lie—

OTHELLO: With her?

IAGO: With her, on her; what you will.

OTHELLO: Lie with her? lie on her?—We say lie on her when they belie

---

21 *infected* plague-stricken   **28** *Convincèd or supplied* overcome or gratified

her.—Lie with her! Zounds, that's fulsome.—Handkerchief—
confessions—handkerchief!—To confess, and be hanged for his
labor—first to be hanged, and then to confess! I tremble at it. Nature   38
would not invest herself in such shadowing passion without some
instruction. It is not words that shakes me thus.—Pish! Noses, ears,
and lips? Is't possible?—Confess?—Handkerchief?—O devil!

[*Falls in a trance.*]

IAGO: Work on,
My med'cine, work! Thus credulous fools are caught,
And many worthy and chaste dames even thus,
All guiltless, meet reproach.—What, ho! my lord!
My lord, I say! Othello!
[*Enter* CASSIO.]   How now, Cassio?
CASSIO:
What's the matter?
IAGO:
My lord is fall'n into an epilepsy.
This is his second fit; he had one yesterday.
CASSIO:
Rub him about the temples.
IAGO: No, forbear.
The lethargy must have his quiet course.   51
If not, he foams at mouth, and by and by
Breaks out to savage madness. Look, he stirs.
Do you withdraw yourself a little while.
He will recover straight. When he is gone,
I would on great occasion speak with you.   [*Exit* CASSIO.]
How is it, general? Have you not hurt your head?
OTHELLO:
Dost thou mock me?
IAGO: I mock you? No, by heaven.
Would you would bear your fortune like a man!
OTHELLO:
A hornèd man's a monster and a beast.   60
IAGO:
There's many a beast then in a populous city,
And many a civil monster.
OTHELLO:
Did he confess it?
IAGO: Good sir, be a man.

38–40 *Nature . . . instruction* my natural faculties would not be so overcome by passion without reason
51 *lethargy* coma   **60** *hornèd man* cuckold

Think every bearded fellow that's but yoked
May draw with you. There's millions now alive
That nightly lie in those unproper beds   66
Which they dare swear peculiar: your case is better.   67
O, 'tis the spite of hell, the fiend's arch-mock,
To lip a wanton in a secure couch,   69
And to suppose her chaste! No, let me know;
And knowing what I am, I know what she shall be.

OTHELLO:
O, thou art wise! 'Tis certain.

IAGO: Stand you awhile apart;
Confine yourself but in a patient list.   73
Whilst you were here, o'erwhelmèd with your grief—
A passion most unsuiting such a man—
Cassio came hither. I shifted him away
And laid good'scuse upon your ecstasy;   77
Bade him anon return, and he speak with me;
The which he promised. Do but encave yourself   79
And mark the fleers, the gibes, and notable scorns
That dwell in every region of his face;
For I will make him tell the tale anew—
Where, how, how oft, how long ago, and when
He hath, and is again to cope your wife.   84
I say, but mark his gesture. Marry, patience!
Or I shall say y'are all in all in spleen,   86
And nothing of a man.

OTHELLO: Dost thou hear, Iago?
I will be found most cunning in my patience;
But—dost thou hear?—most bloody.

IAGO: That's not amiss;
But yet keep time in all. Will you withdraw?
[OTHELLO retires.]
Now will I question Cassio of Bianca,
A huswife that by selling her desires   92
Buys herself bread and clothes. It is a creature
That dotes on Cassio, as 'tis the strumpet's plague
To beguile many and be beguiled by one.
He, when he hears of her, cannot refrain
From the excess of laughter. Here he comes.

[*Enter* CASSIO.]

---

66 *unproper* not exclusively their own   **67** *peculiar* exclusively their own   **69** *secure* free from fear of rivalry
73 *in a patient list* within the limits of self-control   **77** *ecstasy* trance   **79** *encave* conceal   **84** *cope* meet
86 *all in all in spleen* wholly overcome by your passion   **92** *huswif* hussy

As he shall smile, Othello shall go mad;
And his unbookish jealousy must conster   99
Poor Cassio's smiles, gestures, and light behavior
Quite in the wrong. How do you now, lieutenant?

CASSIO:
The worser that you give me the addition   102
Whose want even kills me.

IAGO:
Ply Desdemona well, and you are sure on't.
Now, if this suit lay in Bianca's power,
How quickly should you speed!

CASSIO: Alas, poor caitiff!   106

OTHELLO:
Look how he laughs already!

IAGO:
I never knew a woman love man so.

CASSIO:
Alas, poor rogue! I think, i' faith, she loves me.

OTHELLO:
Now he denies it faintly, and laughs it out.

IAGO:
Do you hear, Cassio?

OTHELLO: Now he importunes him
To tell it o'er. Go to! Well said, well said!

IAGO:
She gives it out that you shall marry her.
Do you intend it?

CASSIO: Ha, ha, ha!

OTHELLO:
Do you triumph, Roman? Do you triumph?

CASSIO: I marry her? What, a customer? Prithee bear some charity to my   117
wit; do not think it so unwholesome. Ha, ha, ha!

OTHELLO: So, so, so, so! They laugh that win!

IAGO:
Faith, the cry goes that you shall marry her.

CASSIO: Prithee say true.

IAGO: I am a very villain else.

OTHELLO: Have you scored me? Well.   123

CASSIO: This is the monkey's own giving out. She is persuaded I will marry
her out of her own love and flattery, not out of my promise.

OTHELLO: Iago beckons me; now he begins the story.   126

---

99 *unbookish* uninstructed; *conster* construe, interpret   **102** *addition* title   **106** *caitiff* wretch   **117** *customer* prostitute   **123** *scored me* settled my account (?)   **126** *beckons* signals

CASSIO: She was here even now; she haunts me in every place. I was t' other day talking on the sea bank with certain Venetians, and thither comes the bauble, and, by this hand, she falls me thus about my neck—   129

OTHELLO: Crying "O dear Cassio!" as it were. His gesture imports it.

CASSIO: So hangs, and lolls, and weeps upon me; so shakes and pulls me! Ha, ha, ha!

OTHELLO: Now he tells how she plucked him to my chamber. O, I see that nose of yours, but not that dog I shall throw it to.

CASSIO: Well, I must leave her company.

[*Enter* BIANCA.]

IAGO: Before me! Look where she comes.

CASSIO: 'Tis such another fitchew! marry, a perfumed one. What do you   137
mean by this haunting of me?

BIANCA: Let the devil and his dam haunt you! What did you mean by that same handkerchief you gave me even now? I was a fine fool to take it. I must take out the whole work? A likely piece of work that you should find it in your chamber and know not who left it there! This is some minx's token, and I must take out the work? There! Give it your hobby-horse. Wheresoever you had it, I'll take out no work on't.   144

CASSIO: How now, my sweet Bianca? How now? how now?

OTHELLO: By heaven, that should be my handkerchief!

BIANCA: An you'll come to supper to-night, you may; an you will not, come when you are next prepared for.   [*Exit.*]

IAGO: After her, after her!

CASSIO: Faith, I must; she'll rail in the street else.

IAGO: Will you sup there?

CASSIO: Yes, I intend so.

IAGO: Well, I may chance to see you; for I would very fain speak with you.

CASSIO: Prithee come. Will you?

IAGO: Go to! say no more.   [*Exit* CASSIO.]

OTHELLO [*comes forward*]: How shall I murder him, Iago?

IAGO: Did you perceive how he laughed at his vice?   158

OTHELLO: O Iago!

IAGO: And did you see the handkerchief?

OTHELLO: Was that mine?

IAGO: Yours, by this hand! And to see how he prizes the foolish woman your   162
wife! She gave it him, and he hath giv'n it his whore.

---

129 *bauble* plaything   **137** *fitchew* polecat (slang for whore)   **144** *hobby-horse* harlot   **158** *vice* i.e. vicious conduct   **162** *prizes* values

OTHELLO: I would have him nine years a-killing!—A fine woman! a fair woman! a sweet woman!

IAGO: Nay, you must forget that.

OTHELLO: Ay, let her rot, and perish, and be damned to-night; for she shall not live. No, my heart is turned to stone; I strike it, and it hurts my hand. O, the world hath not a sweeter creature! She might lie by an emperor's side and command him tasks.

IAGO: Nay, that's not your way.

OTHELLO: Hang her! I do but say what she is. So delicate with her needle! an admirable musician! O, she will sing the savageness out of a bear! Of so high and plenteous wit and invention—   174

IAGO: She's the worse for all this.

OTHELLO: O, a thousand thousand times! And then, of so gentle a condition!   176

IAGO: Ay, too gentle.

OTHELLO: Nay, that's certain. But yet the pity of it, Iago! O Iago, the pity of it, Iago!

IAGO: If you are so fond over her iniquity, give her patent to offend; for if it touch not you, it comes near nobody.   180

OTHELLO: I will chop her into messes! Cuckold me!

IAGO: O, 'tis foul in her.

OTHELLO: With mine officer!

IAGO: That's fouler.

OTHELLO: Get me some poison, Iago, this night. I'll not expostulate with her, lest her body and beauty un- provide my mind again. This night, Iago!   187

IAGO: Do it not with poison. Strangle her in her bed, even the bed she hath contaminated.

OTHELLO: Good, good! The justice of it pleases. Very good!

IAGO: And for Cassio, let me be his undertaker: you shall hear more by midnight.   192

OTHELLO:
Excellent good!
[*A trumpet.*] What trumpet is that same?

IAGO:
I warrant something from Venice.

[*Enter* LODOVICO, DESDEMONA, *and attendants.*]

            'Tis Lodovico.
This comes from the Duke; and see, your wife is with him.

LODOVICO:
God save you, worthy general!

174 *invention* imagination **176** *condition* disposition **180** *patent* license **187–88** *unprovide* disarm
192 *be his undertaker* undertake to deal with him

OTHELLO: With all my heart, sir.
LODOVICO:

    The Duke and senators of Venice greet you.
    [*Gives him a letter.*]

OTHELLO:

    I kiss the instrument of their pleasures.
    [*Opens the letter and reads.*]

DESDEMONA:

    And what's the news, good cousin Lodovico?

IAGO:

    I am very glad to see you, signior.
    Welcome to Cyprus.

LODOVICO:

    I thank you. How does Lieutenant Cassio?

IAGO: Lives, sir.

DESDEMONA:

    Cousin, there's fall'n between him and my lord
    An unkind breach; but you shall make all well.

OTHELLO: Are you sure of that?

DESDEMONA: My lord?

OTHELLO [*reads*]: "This fail you not to do, as you will—"

LODOVICO:

    He did not call; he's busy in the paper.
    Is there division 'twixt thy lord and Cassio?

DESDEMONA:

    A most unhappy one. I would do much
    T'atone them, for the love I bear to Cassio?   212

OTHELLO:

    Fire and brimstone!

DESDEMONA: My lord?

OTHELLO: Are you wise?

DESDEMONA:

    What, is he angry?

LODOVICO: May be the letter moved him;
    For, as I think, they do command him home,
    Deputing Cassio in his government.

DESDEMONA:

    By my troth, I am glad on't.

OTHELLO: Indeed?

DESDEMONA: My lord?

OTHELLO:

    I am glad to see you mad.   218

DESDEMONA: Why, sweet Othello—

212 *atone* reconcile   **218** *mad* i.e. waggish

OTHELLO: Devil!

   [*Strikes her.*]

DESDEMONA: I have not deserved this.

LODOVICO:

   My lord, this would not be believed in Venice,

   Though I should swear I saw't. 'Tis very much.

   Make her amends; she weeps.

OTHELLO: O devil, devil!

   If that the earth could teem with woman's tears,   224

   Each drop she falls would prove a crocodile.   225

   Out of my sight!

DESDEMONA: I will not stay to offend you.   [*Going.*]

LODOVICO:

   Truly, an obedient lady.

   I do beseech your lordship call her back.

OTHELLO:

   Mistress!

DESDEMONA: My lord?

OTHELLO: What would you with her, sir?

LODOVICO:

   Who? I, my lord?

OTHELLO:

   Ay! You did wish that I would make her turn.

   Sir, she can turn, and turn, and yet go on

   And turn again; and she can weep, sir, weep;

   And she's obedient; as you say, obedient,

   Very obedient.—Proceed you in your tears.—

   Concerning this, sir—O well-painted passion!—   236

   I am commanded home.—Get you away;

   I'll send for you anon.—Sir, I obey the mandate

   And will return to Venice.—Hence, avaunt!   [*Exit* DESDEMONA.]

   Cassio shall have my place. And, sir, to-night

   I do entreat that we may sup together.

   You are welcome, sir, to Cyprus.—Goats and monkeys!   [*Exit.*]

LODOVICO:

   Is this the noble Moor whom our full Senate

   Call all in all sufficient? Is this the nature

   Whom passion could not shake? whose solid virtue

   The shot of accident nor dart of chance

   Could neither graze nor pierce?

IAGO: He is much changed.

LODOVICO:

   Are his wits safe? Is he not light of brain?

---

224 *teem* breed   **225** *crocodile* (crocodiles were supposed to shed hypocritical tears to lure men to destruction)
236 *passion* grief

IAGO:

He's that he is; I may not breath my censure.
What he might be—if what he might he is not—
I would to heaven he were!

LODOVICO: What, strike his wife?

IAGO:

Faith, that was not so well; yet would I knew
That stroke would prove the worst!

LODOVICO: Is it his use?   253
Or did the letters work upon his blood
And new-create this fault?

IAGO: Alas, alas!
It is not honesty in me to speak.
What I have seen and known. You shall observe him,
And his own courses will denote him so
That I may save my speech. Do but go after
And mark how he continues.

LODOVICO:

I am sorry that I am deceived in him.   [*Exeunt.*]

SCENE II

[*Enter* OTHELLO *and* EMILIA.]

OTHELLO:

You have seen nothing then?

EMILIA:

Nor ever heard, nor ever did suspect.

OTHELLO:

Yes, you have seen Cassio and she together.

EMILIA:

But then I saw no harm, and then I heard
Each syllable that breath made up between them.

OTHELLO:

What, did they never whisper?

EMILIA: Never, my lord.

OTHELLO:

Nor send you out o' th' way?

EMILIA: Never.

OTHELLO:

To fetch her fan, her gloves, her mask, nor nothing?

EMILIA: Never, my lord.

253 *use* custom
Scene ii Within the castle

OTHELLO: That's strange.

EMILIA:
I durst, my lord, to wager she is honest,
Lay down my soul as stake. If you think other,
Remove your thought; it doth abuse your bosom.   14
If any wretch have put this in your head,
Let heaven requite it with the serpent's curse!   16
For if she be not honest, chaste, and true,
There's no man happy; the purest of their wives
Is foul as slander.

OTHELLO: Bid her come hither. Go.   [*Exit* EMILIA.]
She says enough; yet she's a simple bawd
That cannot say as much. This is a subtle whore,
A closet lock and key of villanous secrets;
And yet she'll kneel and pray; I have seen her do't.

[*Enter* DESDEMONA *and* EMILIA.]

DESDEMONA:
My lord, what is you will?

OTHELLO: Pray, chuck, come hither.

DESDEMONA:
What is your pleasure?

OTHELLO: Let me see your eyes.
Look in my face.

DESDEMONA: What horrible fancy's this?

OTHELLO [*to* EMILIA]:
Some of your function, mistress.
Leave procreants alone and shut the door;   28
Cough or cry hem if anybody come.
Your mystery, your mystery! Nay, dispatch!   [*Exit* EMILIA.]   30

DESDEMONA:
Upon my knees, what doth your speech import?
I understand a fury in your words,
(But not the words.)

OTHELLO:
Why, what art thou?

DESDEMONA: Your wife, my lord; your true
And loyal wife.

OTHELLO: Come, swear it, damn thyself;
Lest, being like one of heaven, the devils themselves   36

14 *abuse . . . bosom* deceive your heart **16** *serpent's curse* (cf. Genesis iii, 14) **28** *procreants* mating couples **30** *mystery* trade, occupation **36** *being . . . heaven* looking like an angel

Should fear to seize thee. Therefore be double-damned—
Swear thou art honest.   38

DESDEMONA: Heaven doth truly know it.

OTHELLO:

Heaven truly knows that thou art false as hell.

DESDEMONA:

To whom, my lord? With whom? How am I false?

OTHELLO:

Ah, Desdemona! away! away! away!

DESDEMONA:

Alas the heavy day! Why do you weep?
Am I the motive of these tears, my lord?
If haply you my father do suspect
An instrument of this your calling back,   45
Lay not your blame on me. If you have lost him,
Why, I have lost him too.

OTHELLO: Had it pleased heaven
To try me with affliction, had they rained
All kinds of sores and shames on my bare head,
Steeped me in poverty to the very lips,
Given to captivity me and my utmost hopes,
I should have found in some place of my soul
A drop of patience. But, alas, to make me
A fixèd figure for the time of scorn   54
To point his slow unmoving finger at!
Yet could I bear that too; well, very well.
But there where I have garnered up my heart,
Where either I must live or bear no life,
The fountain from the which my current runs
Or else dries up—to be discarded thence,
Or keep it as a cistern for fouls toads
To knot and gender in—turn thy complexion there,   62
Patience, thou young and rose-lipped cherubin!
Ay, there look grim as hell!

DESDEMONA:

I hope my noble lord esteems me honest.

OTHELLO:

O, ay; as summer flies are in the shambles,   66
That quicken even with blowing. O thou weed,   67
Who art so lovely fair, and smell'st so sweet,
That the sense aches at thee, would thou hadst ne'er
    been born!

---

38 *honest* chaste   **45** *An instrument* to be the cause   **54** *time of scorn* scornful world   **62** *turn thy complexion there*
change thy color at that point   **66** *shambles* slaughterhouse   **67** *quicken* come to life

DESDEMONA:
   Alas, what ignorant sin have I committed?
OTHELLO:
   Was this fair paper, this most goodly book,
   Made to write "whore" upon? What committed?
   Committed? O thou public commoner!   73
   I should make very forges of my cheeks
   That would to cinders burn up modesty,
   Did I but speak thy deeds. What committed?
   Heaven stops the nose at it, and the moon winks;   77
   The bawdy wind, that kisses all it meets,
   Is hushed within the hollow mine of earth
   And will not hear it. What committed?
   Impudent strumpet!
DESDEMONA: By heaven, you do me wrong!
OTHELLO:
   Are not you a strumpet?
DESDEMONA: No, as I am a Christian!
   If to preserve this vessel for my lord
   From any other foul unlawful touch
   Be not to be a strumpet, I am none.
OTHELLO:
   What, not a whore?
DESDEMONA: No, as I shall be saved!
OTHELLO: Is't possible?
DESDEMONA:
   O, heaven forgive us!
OTHELLO: I cry you mercy then.   88
   I took you for that cunning whore of Venice
   That married with Othello.—[calling] You, mistress,
   That have the office opposite to Saint Peter
   And keep the gate of hell!
   [Enter EMILIA.]   You, you, ay, you!
   We have done our course; there's money for your pains:
   I pray you turn the key, and keep our counsel.   [Exit.]
EMILIA:
   Alas, what does this gentleman conceive?
   How do you, madam? How do you, my good lady?
DESDEMONA: Faith, half asleep.   97
EMILIA:
   Good madam, what's the matter with my lord?
DESDEMONA: With who?
EMILIA: Why, with my lord, madam.

73 *commoner* harlot   **77** *winks* closes her eyes   **88** *cry you mercy* beg your pardon   **97** *half asleep* i.e. stunned

DESDEMONA:

Who is thy lord?

EMILIA: He that is yours, sweet lady.

DESDEMONA:

I have none. Do not talk to me, Emilia.

I cannot weep; nor answers have I none

But what should go by water. Prithee to-night

Lay on my bed my wedding sheets, remember;

And call thy husband hither.

EMILIA: Here's a change indeed!   [*Exit.*]

DESDEMONA:

'Tis meet I should be used so, very meet.

How have I been behaved, that he might stick

The small'st opinion on my least misuse?   109

[*Enter* IAGO *and* EMILIA.]

IAGO:

What is your pleasure, madam? How is't with you?

DESDEMONA:

I cannot tell. Those that do teach young babes

Do it with gentle means and easy tasks:

He might have chid me so; for, in good faith,

I am a child to chiding.

IAGO: What is the matter, lady?

EMILIA:

Alas, Iago, my lord hath so bewhored her,

Thrown such despite and heavy terms upon her

As true hearts cannot bear.

DESDEMONA:

Am I that name, Iago?

IAGO: What name, fair lady?

DESDEMONA:

Such as she said my lord did say I was.

EMILIA:

He called her whore. A beggar in his drink

Could not have laid such terms upon his callet.   121

IAGO:

Why did he so?

DESDEMONA:

I do not know; I am sure I am none such.

IAGO:

Do not weep, do not weep. Alas the day!

109 *small'st opinion* least suspicion; *least misuse* slightest misconduct   **121** *callet* whore

EMILIA:

Hath she forsook so many noble matches,

Her father and her country, and her friends,

To be called whore? Would it not make one weep?

DESDEMONA:

It is my wretched fortune.

IAGO: Beshrew him for't!

How comes this trick upon him?   129

DESDEMONA: Nay, heaven doth know.

EMILIA:

I will be hanged if some eternal villain,

Some busy and insinuating rogue,

Some cogging, cozening slave, to get some office,   132

Have not devised this slander. I'll be hanged else.

IAGO:

Fie, there is no such man! It is impossible.

DESDEMONA:

If any such there be, heaven pardon him!

EMILIA:

A halter pardon him! and hell gnaw his bones!

Why should he call her whore? Who keeps her company?

What place? what time? what form? what likelihood?

The Moor's abused by some most villainous knave,

Some base notorious knave, some scurvy fellow.

O heaven, that such companions thou'dst unfold,   141

And put in every honest hand a whip

To lash the rascals naked through the world

Even from the east to th' west!

IAGO: Speak within door.   144

EMILIA:

O, fie upon them! Some such squire he was

That turned your wit the seamy side without

And made you to suspect me with the Moor.

IAGO:

You are a fool. Go to.

DESDEMONA: Alas, Iago,

What shall I do to win my lord again?

Good friend, go to him; for, by this light of heaven,

I know not how I lost him. Here I kneel:

If e'er my will did trespass 'gainst his love

Either in discourse of thought or actual deed,   153

Or that mine eyes, mine ears, or any sense

---

129 *trick* freakish behavior   **132** *cogging, cozening* cheating, defrauding   **141** *companions* rogues; *unfold* expose
144 *within door* with restraint   **153** *discourse* course

Delighted them in any other form,
Or that I do not yet, and ever did,
And ever will (though he do shake me off
To beggarly divorcement) love him dearly,
Comfort forswear me! Unkindness may do much;   159
And his unkindness may defeat my life,   160
But never taint my love. I cannot say "whore."
It does abhor me now I speak the word;
To do the act that might the addition earn
Not the world's mass of vanity could make me.

IAGO:
I pray you be content. 'Tis but his humor.
The business of the state does him offense,
And he does chide with you.

DESDEMONA:
If 'twere no other

IAGO: 'Tis but so, I warrant.
[Trumpets within.]
Hark how these instruments summon you to supper.
The messengers of Venice stay the meat:
Go in, and weep not. All things shall be well.

[Exeunt DESDEMONA and EMILIA.]

[Enter RODERIGO.]

How now, Roderigo?
RODERIGO: I do not find that thou deal'st justly with me.
IAGO: What in the contrary?
RODERIGO: Every day thou daff'st me with some device, Iago, and rather, as   175
it seems to me now, keep'st from me all conveniency than suppliest me   176
with the least advantage of hope. I will indeed no longer endure it; nor
am I yet persuaded to put up in peace what already I have foolishly
suffered.
IAGO: Will you hear me, Roderigo?
RODERIGO: Faith, I have heard too much; for your words and performances
are no kin together.
IAGO: You charge me most unjustly.
RODERIGO: With naught but truth. I have wasted myself out of my means.
The jewels you have had from me to deliver to Desdemona would half
have corrupted a votarist. You have told me she hath received them, and   186
returned me expectations and comforts of sudden respect and   187
acquaintance; but I find none.

159 *Comfort forswear* happiness forsake   **160** *defeat* destroy   **175** *thou . . . device* you put me off with some trick
176 *conveniency* favorable opportunities   **186** *votarist* nun   **187** *sudden respect* immediate notice

IAGO: Well, go to; very well.

RODERIGO: Very well! go to! I cannot go to, man; nor 'tis not very well. By
    this hand, I say 'tis very scurvy, and begin to find myself fopped in it.   191

IAGO: Very well.

RODERIGO: I tell you 'tis not very well. I will make myself known to
    Desdemona. If she will return me my jewels, I will give over my suit and
    repent my unlawful solicitation; if not, assure yourself I will seek
    satisfaction of you.

IAGO: You have said now.

RODERIGO: Ay, and said nothing but what I protest intendment of doing.

IAGO: Why, now I see there's mettle in thee; and even from this instant do
    build on thee a better opinion than ever before. Give me thy hand,
    Roderigo. Thou hast taken against me a most just exception; but yet I
    protest I have dealt most directly in thy affair.   202

RODERIGO: It hath not appeared.

IAGO: I grant indeed it hath not appeared, and your suspicion is not
    without wit and judgment. But, Roderigo, if thou hast that in thee
    indeed which I have greater reason to believe now than ever, I mean
    purpose, courage, and valor, this night show it. If thou the next night
    following enjoy not Desdemona, take me from this world with treachery
    and devise engines for my life.   209

RODERIGO: Well, what is it? Is it within reason and compass?

IAGO: Sir, there is especial commission come from Venice to depute Cassio
    in Othello's place.

RODERIGO: Is that true? Why, then Othello and Desdemona return again to
    Venice.

IAGO: O, no; he goes into Mauritania and takes away with him the fair
    Desdemona, unless his abode be lingered here by some accident;   216
    wherein none can be so determinate as the removing of Cassio.   217

RODERIGO: How do you mean removing of him?

IAGO: Why, by making him uncapable of Othello's place—knocking out his
    brains.

RODERIGO: And that you would have me to do?

IAGO: Ay, if you dare do yourself a profit and a right. He sups to-night with
    a harlotry, and thither will I go to him. He knows not yet of his
    honorable fortune. If you will watch his going thence, which I will
    fashion to fall out between twelve and one, you may take him at your
    pleasure. I will be near to second your attempt, and he shall fall between
    us. Come, stand not amazed at it, but go along with me. I will show you
    such a necessity in his death that you shall think yourself bound to put
    it on him. It is now high supper time, and the night grows to waste.
    About it!

191 *fopped* duped   **202** *directly* straightforwardly   **209** *engines for* plots against   **216** *abode . . . here* stay here
be extended   **217** *determinate* effective

RODERIGO: I will hear further reason for this.

IAGO: And you shall be satisfied.   *[Exeunt.]*

SCENE III

[Enter OTHELLO, LODOVICO, DESDEMONA, EMILIA, *and attendants.]*

LODOVICO:

   I do beseech you, sir, trouble yourself no further.

OTHELLO:

   O, pardon me; 'twill do me good to walk.

LODOVICO:

   Madam, good night, I humbly thank your ladyship.

DESDEMONA:

   Your honor is most welcome.

OTHELLO: Will you walk, sir?

   O, Desdemona—

DESDEMONA: My lord?

OTHELLO: Get you to bed on th' instant; I will be returned forthwith. Dismiss

   your attendant there. Look't be done.

DESDEMONA: I will, my lord.

             [Exit OTHELLO, *with* LODOVICO *and attendants.]*

EMILIA: How goes it now? He looks gentler than he did.

DESDEMONA:

   He says he will return incontinent.   11

   He hath commanded me to go to bed,

   And bade me to dismiss you.

EMILIA: Dismiss me?

DESDEMONA:

   It was his bidding; therefore, good Emilia,

   Give me my nightly wearing, and adieu.

   We must not now displease him.

EMILIA: I would you had never seen him!

DESDEMONA:

   So would not I. My love doth so approve him

   That even his stubbornness, his checks, his frowns—   19

   Prithee unpin me—have grace and favor in them.

EMILIA: I have laid those sheets you bade me on the bed.

DESDEMONA:

   All's one. Good faith, how foolish our minds!

   If I do die before thee, prithee shroud me

   In one of those same sheets.

Scene iii Within the castle   **11** *incontinent* at once   **19** *stubbornness* roughness; *checks* rebukes

EMILIA: Come, come! You talk.
DESDEMONA:
My mother had a maid called Barbary.
She was in love; and he she loved proved mad   26
And did forsake her. She had a song of "Willow";
An old thing 'twas; but it expressed her fortune,
And she died singing it. That song to-night
Will not go from my mind; I have much to do
But to go hang my head all at one side
And sing it like poor Barbary. Prithee dispatch.
EMILIA:
Shall I go fetch your nightgown?   33
DESDEMONA: No, unpin me here.
This Lodovico is a proper man.
EMILIA: A very handsome man.
DESDEMONA: He speaks well.
EMILIA: I know a lady in Venice would have walked bare-
foot to Palestine for a touch of his nether lip.
DESDEMONA [*sings*]:
"The poor soul sat sighing by a sycamore tree,
    Sing all a green willow;
Her hand on her bosom, her head on her knee,
    Sing willow, willow, willow.
The fresh streams ran by her and murmured her moans;
    Sing willow, willow, willow;
Her salt tears fell from her, and soft'ned the stones"—
Lay by these.
    "Sing willow, willow, willow"—
Prithee hie thee; he'll come anon.   48
    "Sing all a green willow must be my garland.
    Let nobody blame him; his scorn I approve"—
Nay, that's not next. Hark! who is't that knocks?
EMILIA: It's the wind.
DESDEMONA [*sings*]:
"I called my love false love; but what said he then?
    Sing willow, willow, willow:
If I court moe women, you'll couch with moe men."
So, get thee gone; good night. Mine eyes do itch.
Doth that bode weeping?
EMILIA: 'Tis neither here nor there.
DESDEMONA:
I have heard it said so. O, these men, these men!
Dost thou in conscience think—tell me, Emilia—

26 *mad* wild, faithless **33** *nightgown* dressing gown **48** *hie thee* hurry

That there be women do abuse their husbands
In such gross kind?
EMILIA: There be some such, no question.
DESDEMONA:
Wouldst thou do such a deed for all the world?
EMILIA:
Why, would not you?
DESDEMONA: No, by this heavenly light!
EMILIA:
Nor I neither by this heavenly light.
I might do't as well i' th' dark.
DESDEMONA:
Wouldst thou do such as deed for all the world?
EMILIA: The world's a huge thing; it is a great price for a small vice.
DESDEMONA:
In troth, I think thou wouldst not.
EMILIA: In troth, I think I should; and undo't when I had done it. Marry, I
    would not do such a thing for a joint-ring, nor for measures of lawn,   70
    nor for gowns, petticoats, nor caps, nor any petty exhibition; but, for all   71
    the whole world—'Ud's pity! who would not make her husband a
    cuckold to make him a monarch? I should venture purgatory for't.
DESDEMONA:
Beshrew me if I would do such a wrong
For the whole world.
EMILIA: Why, the wrong is but a wrong i' th' world; and having the world for
    your labor, 'tis a wrong in your own world, and you might quickly make
    it right.
DESDEMONA: I do not think there is any such woman.
EMILIA: Yes, a dozen; and as many to th' vantage as would store the world   80
    they played for.
But I do think it is their husbands' faults
If wives do fall. Say that they slack their duties
And pour our treasures into foreign laps;
Or else break out in peevish jealousies,   85
Throwing restraint upon us; or say they strike us,
Or scant our former having in despite—   87
Why, we have galls; and though we have some grace,   88
Yet have we some revenge. Let husbands know
Their wives have sense like them. They see, and smell,
And have their palates both for sweet and sour,
As husbands have. What is it that they do
When they change us for others? Is it sport?

70 *joint-ring* ring made in separable halves **71** *exhibition* gift **80** *to th' vantage* besides; *store* populate
85 *peevish* senseless **87** *having* allowance **88** *galls* spirits to resent

I think it is. And doth affection breed it?
I think it doth. Is't frailty that thus errs?
It is so too. And have not we affections,
Desires for sport, and frailty, as men have?
Then let them use us well; else let them know,
The ills we do, their ills instruct us so.

DESDEMONA:
Good night, good night. God me such usage send,   100
Not to pick from bad, but by bad mend!   [*Exeunt.*]

ACT V

SCENE I

[*Enter* IAGO *and* RODERIGO.]

IAGO:
Here, stand behind this bulk; straight will he come.   1
Wear thy good rapier bare, and put it home.
Quick, quick! Fear nothing; I'll be at thy elbow.
It makes us, or it mars us—think on that,
And fix most firm thy resolution.

RODERIGO:
Be near at hand; I may miscarry in't.

IAGO:
Here, at thy hand. Be bold, and take thy stand.
[*Stands aside.*]

RODERIGO:
I have no great devotion to the deed,
And yet he hath given me satisfying reasons.
'Tis but a man gone. Forth my sword! He dies!

IAGO:
I have rubbed this young quat almost to the sense,   11
And he grows angry. Now whether he kill Cassio,
Or Cassio him, or each do kill the other,
Every way makes by gain. Live Roderigo,
He calls me to a restitution large
Of gold and jewels that I bobbed from him   16
As gifts to Desdemona.
It must not be. If Cassio do remain,
He hath a daily beauty in his life.

100 *usage* habits
Scene i A street in Cyprus   **1** *bulk* projecting shop-front   **11** *quat* pimple; *sense* quick   **16** *bobbed* swindled

That makes me ugly; and besides, the Moor
May unfold me to him; there stand I in much peril.
No, he must die. Be't so! I hear him coming.

[*Enter* CASSIO.]

RODERIGO:
I know his gait. 'Tis he. Villain, thou diest!
[*Makes a pass at* CASSIO.]
CASSIO:
That thrust had been mine enemy indeed
But that my coat is better than thou know'st.   25
I will make proof of thine.
[*Draws, and wounds* RODERIGO.]
RODERIGO: O, I am slain!
[IAGO *darts from concealment behind* CASSIO,
wounds him in the leg, and exits.]
CASSIO:
I am maimed for ever. Help, ho! Murder! murder!
[*Falls.*]

[*Enter* OTHELLO.]

OTHELLO:
The voice of Cassio. Iago keeps his word.
RODERIGO:
O, villain that I am!
OTHELLO: It is even so.
CASSIO:
O, help, ho! light! a surgeon!
OTHELLO:
'Tis he. O brave Iago, honest and just,
That hast such noble sense of thy friend's wrong!
Thou teachest me. Minion, your dear lies dead,   33
And your unblest fate hies. Strumpet, I come.   34
Forth or my heart those charms, thine eyes, are blotted.
Thy bed, lust-stained, shall with lust's blood be spotted.
[*Exit* OTHELLO.]

[*Enter* LODOVICO *and* GRATIANO.]

CASSIO:
What, ho? No watch? No passage? Murder! murder!   37

---

25 *coat* under-shirt of mail   **33** *Minion* mistress   **34** *hies* hurries on   **37** *passage* passers-by

GRATIANO:

'Tis some mischance. The cry is very direful.

CASSIO: O, help!

LODOVICO: Hark!

RODERIGO: O wretched villain!

LODOVICO:

Two or three groan. It is a heavy night.   42

These may be counterfeits. Let's think't unsafe

To come in to the cry without more help.

RODERIGO:

Nobody come? Then shall I bleed to death.

LODOVICO: Hark!

[*Enter* IAGO, *with a light.*]

GRATIANO:

Here's one comes in his shirt, with light and weapons.

IAGO:

Who's there? Whose noise is this that cries on murder?   48

LODOVICO:

We do not know.

IAGO: Did not you hear a cry?

CASSIO:

Here, here! For heaven's sake, help me!

IAGO: What's the matter?

GRATIANO:

This is Othello's ancient, as I take it.

LODOVICO:

The same indeed, a very valiant fellow.

IAGO:

What are you here that cry so grievously?

CASSIO:

Iago? O, I am spoiled, undone by villains!

Give me some help.

IAGO:

O me, lieutenant! What villains have done this?

CASSIO:

I think that one of them is hereabout

And cannot make away.   58

IAGO: O treacherous villains!

[*To* LODOVICO *and* GRATIANO.]

What are you there? Come in, and give some help.

42 *heavy* cloudy, dark   **48** *cries on* raises the cry of   **58** *make* get

RODERIGO:

O, help me here!

CASSIO:

That's one of them.

IAGO: O mur'drous slave! O villain!

[*Stabs* RODERIGO.]

RODERIGO:

O damned Iago! O inhuman dog!

IAGO:

Kill men i' th' dark?—Where be these bloody thieves?—
How silent is this town!—Ho! murder! murder!—
What may you be? Are you of good or evil?

LODOVICO:

As you shall prove us, praise us.

IAGO: Signior Lodovico?

LODOVICO: He, sir.

IAGO:

I cry you mercy. Here's Cassio hurt by villains.

GRATIANO: Cassio?

IAGO: How is't, brother?

CASSIO:

My leg is cut in two.

IAGO: Marry, heaven forbid!   72

Light, gentleman. I'll bind it with my shirt.

[*Enter* BIANCA.]

BIANCA:

What is the matter, ho? Who is't that cried?

IAGO:

Who is't that cried?

BIANCA:

O my dear Cassio! my sweet Cassio!
O Cassio, Cassio, Cassio!

IAGO:

O notable strumpet!—Cassio, may you suspect
Who they should be that have thus mangled you?

CASSIO: No.

GRATIANO: I am sorry to find you thus. I have been to seek you.

IAGO:

Lend me a garter. So. O for a chair
To bear him easily hence!   82

72 *Marry* (from By Mary)   **82** *chair* litter

BIANCA:

Alas, he faints! O Cassio, Cassio, Cassio!

IAGO:

Gentlemen all, I do suspect this trash

To be a party in this injury.—

Patience awhile, good Cassio.—Come, come!

Lend me a light. Know we this face or no?

Alas, my friend and my dear countryman

Roderigo? No.—Yes, sure.—O heaven, Roderigo!

GRATIANO: What, of Venice?

IAGO:

Even he, sir. Did you know him?

GRATIANO: Know him? Ay.

IAGO:

Signior Gratiano? I cry your gentle pardon.

These bloody accidents must excuse my manners

That so neglected you.

GRATIANO: I am glad to see you.

IAGO:

How do you, Cassio?—O, a chair, a chair!

GRATIANO: Roderigo?

IAGO:

He, he, 'tis he!

[*A chair brought in.*] O, that's well said; the chair.   98

Some good man bear him carefully from hence.

I'll fetch the general's surgeon.

[*To* BIANCA]   For you, mistress,

Save you your labor.—He that lies slain here, Cassio,

Was my dear friend. What malice was between you?

CASSIO:

None in the world; nor do I know the man.

IAGO [*to* BIANCA]:

What, look you pale?—O, bear him out o' th' air.

[CASSIO *and* RODERIGO *are borne off.*]

Stay you, good gentlemen.—Look you pale, mistress?—

Do you perceive the gastness of her eye?—   106

Nay, if you stare, we shall hear more anon.

Behold her well; I pray you look upon her.

Do you see, gentlemen? Nay, guiltiness will speak,

Though tongues were out of use.

[*Enter* EMILIA.]

98 *well said* well done   **106** *gastness* terror

EMILIA:
    'Las, what's the matter? What's the matter, husband?

IAGO:
    Cassio hath here been set on in the dark
    By Roderigo, and fellows that are scaped.
    He's almost slain, and Roderigo dead.

EMILIA:
    Alas, good gentleman! alas, good Cassio!

IAGO:
    This is the fruits of whoring. Prithee, Emilia,
    Go know of Cassio where he supped to-night.
    [*To* BIANCA.]
    What, do you shake at that?

BIANCA:
    He supped at my house; but I therefore shake not.

IAGO:
    O, did he so? I charge you go with me.

EMILIA:
    Fie, fie upon thee, strumpet!

BIANCA:
    I am no strumpet, but of life as honest   122
    As you that thus abuse me.

EMILIA: As I? Foh! fie upon thee!

IAGO:
    Kind gentlemen, let's go see poor Cassio dressed.
    [*To* BIANCA.]
    Come, mistress, you must tell's another tale.
    Emilia, run you to the citadel
    And tell my lord and lady what hath happed.

                                [*Exit* EMILIA.]
    Will you go on afore?   [*Exeunt (all but* IAGO*).*]
                This is the night
    That either makes me or fordoes me quite.   [*Exit.*]   129

SCENE II

[DESDEMONA *asleep in her bed. Enter* OTHELLO *with a light.*]

OTHELLO:
    It is the cause, it is the cause, my soul.   1
    Let me not name it to you, you chaste stars!

122 *honest* chaste   **129** *fordoes* destroys
Scene ii A bedchamber in the castle   **1** *cause* cause of justice

It is the cause. Yet I'll not shed her blood,
Nor scar that whiter skin of hers than snow,
And smooth as monumental alabaster.
Yet she must die, else she'll betray more men.
Put out the light, and then put out the light.
If I quench thee, thou flaming minister,   8
I can again thy former light restore,
Should I repent me; but once put out thy light,
Thou cunning'st pattern of excelling nature,
I know not where is that Promethean heat   12
That can thy light relume. When I have plucked the rose,   13
I cannot give it vital growth again;
It needs must wither. I'll smell thee on the tree.
[*He kisses her.*]
O balmy breath, that dost almost persuade
Justice to break her sword! One more, one more!
Be thus when thou art dead, and I will kill thee,
And love thee after. One more, and that's the last!
So sweet was ne'er so fatal. I must weep,
But they are cruel tears. This sorrow's heavenly;
It strikes where it doth love. She wakes.
DESDEMONA:
    Who's there? Othello?
OTHELLO: Ay, Desdemona.
DESDEMONA:
    Will you come to bed, my lord?
OTHELLO:
    Have you prayed to-night, Desdemona?
DESDEMONA: Ay, my lord.
OTHELLO:
    If you bethink yourself of any crime   26
    Unreconciled as yet to heaven and grace,
    Solicit for it straight.
DESDEMONA:
    Alack, my lord, what may you mean by that?
OTHELLO:
    Well, do it, and be brief; I will walk by.
    I would not kill thy unprepared spirit.
    No, heaven forfend! I would not kill thy soul.   32
DESDEMONA:
    Talk you of killing?
OTHELLO: Ay, I do.
DESDEMONA: Then heaven
    Have mercy on me!

8 *minister* servant   **12** *Promethean heat* divine fire   **13** *relume* relight   **26** *crime* sin   **32** *forfend* forbid

OTHELLO: Amen, with all my heart!
DESDEMONA:
  If you say so, I hope you will not kill me.
OTHELLO: Hum!
DESDEMONA:
  And yet I fear you; for you're fatal then
  When your eyes roll so. Why I should fear I know not,
  Since guiltiness I know not; but yet I feel I fear.
OTHELLO:
  Think on thy sins.
DESDEMONA: They are loves I bear to you.
OTHELLO:
  Ay, and for that thou diest.
DESDEMONA:
  That death's unnatural that kills for loving.
  Alas, why gnaw you so your nether lip?
  Some bloody passion shakes your very frame.
  These are portents; but yet I hope, I hope,   45
  They do not point on me.
OTHELLO: Peace and be still!
DESDEMONA:
  I will so. What's the matter?
OTHELLO:
  That handkerchief which I so loved and gave thee
  Thou gav'st to Cassio.
DESDEMONA: No, by my life and soul!
  Send for the man and ask him.
OTHELLO: Sweet soul, take heed,
  Take heed of perjury; thou art on thy deathbed.
DESDEMONA:
  Ay, but not yet to die.
OTHELLO: Yes, presently.   52
  Therefore confess thee freely of thy sin;
  For to deny each article with oath
  Cannot remove nor choke that strong conception   55
  That I do groan withal. Thou art to die.
DESDEMONA:
  Then Lord have mercy on me!
OTHELLO: I say amen.
DESDEMONA:
  And have you mercy too! I never did
  Offend you in my life; never loved Cassio   59
  But with such general warranty of heaven
  As I might love. I never gave him token.

45 *portents* signs of impending violence   **52** *presently* at once   **55** *conception* belief   **59** *Offend* wrong

OTHELLO:

By heaven, I saw my handkerchief in's hand!
O perjured woman! thou dost stone my heart,
And mak'st me call what I intend to do
A murder, which I thought a sacrifice.
I saw the handkerchief.

63

DESDEMONA: He found it then.

I never gave it him. Send for him hither.
Let him confess a truth.

OTHELLO: He hath confessed.

DESDEMONA:

What, my lord?

OTHELLO:

That he hath used thee.

DESDEMONA: How? unlawfully?

OTHELLO: Ay.

DESDEMONA:

He will not say so.

OTHELLO: No, his mouth is stopped.
Honest Iago hath ta'en order for't.

72

DESDEMONA:

O, my fear interprets. What, is he dead?

OTHELLO:

Had all his hairs been lives, my great revenge
Had stomach for them all.

DESDEMONA:

Alas, he is betrayed, and I undone!

OTHELLO:

Out, strumpet! Weep'st thou for him to my face?

DESDEMONA:

O, banish me, my lord, but kill me not!

OTHELLO:

Down, strumpet!

DESDEMONA:

Kill me to-morrow; let me live to-night!

OTHELLO:

Nay, if you strive—

DESDEMONA:

But half an hour!

OTHELLO: Being done, there is no pause.

DESDEMONA:

But while I say on prayer!

OTHELLO: It is too late.

63 *stone my heart* turn my heart to stone   **72** *ta'en order* taken measures

[*Smothers her.*]

DESDEMONA: O Lord, Lord, Lord!
[EMILIA *at the door.*]
EMILIA [*calls within*]:
    My lord, my lord! What, ho! my lord, my lord!
OTHELLO:
    What noise is this? Not dead? not yet quite dead?
    I that am cruel am yet merciful;
    I would not have thee linger in thy pain.
    So, so.
EMILIA [*within*]:
    What, ho! my lord, my lord!
OTHELLO: Who's there?
EMILIA [*within*]:
    O, good my lord, I would speak a word with you!
OTHELLO:
    Yes, 'tis Emilia.—By and by.—She's dead.—   92
    'Tis like she comes to speak of Cassio's death.
    The noise was here. Ha! no more moving?
    Still as the grave.—Shall she come in? Were't good?—
    I think she stirs again. No.—What's best to do?
    If she come in, she'll sure speak to my wife.
    My wife! my wife! what wife! I have no wife.
    O, insupportable! O heavy hour!
    Methinks it should be now a huge eclipse
    Of sun and moon, and that th'affrighted globe
    Should yawn at yawn at alteration.   102
EMILIA [*within*]:   I do beseech you
    That I may speak with you, O good my lord!
OTHELLO:
    I had forgot thee. O, come in, Emilia.
    Soft, by and by.—Let me the curtains draw.—
    [*Closes the bed-curtains.*]
    Where art thou?
    [*Opens the door.*]

[*Enter* EMILIA.]

                What's the matter with thee now?
EMILIA:
    O my good lord, yonder's foul murder done!
OTHELLO: What? Now?

92 *By and by* just a moment (addressed to Emilia)   **102** *yawn* open, as in an earthquake

EMILIA: But now, my lord.

OTHELLO:

 It is the very error of the moon.   110

 She comes more nearer earth than she was wont

 And makes men mad.

EMILIA:

 Cassio, my lord, hath killed a young Venetian

 Called Roderigo.

OTHELLO: Roderigo killed?

 And Cassio killed?

EMILIA: No, Cassio is not killed.

OTHELLO:

 Not Cassio killed? Then murder's out of tune,

 And sweet revenge grows harsh

DESDEMONA:

 O, falsely, falsely murdered!

EMILIA: O Lord! what cry is that?

OTHELLO: That? What?

EMILIA:

 Out and alas! that was my lady's voice.

 Help! help, ho! help! O lady, speak again!

 Sweet Desdemona! O sweet mistress, speak!

DESDEMONA:

 A guiltless death I die.

EMILIA:

 O, who hath done this deed?

DESDEMONA:

 Nobody—I myself. Farewell.

 Commend me to my kind lord. O, farewell!   126

[*She dies.*]

OTHELLO:

 Why, how should she be murd'red?

EMILIA: Alas, who knows?

OTHELLO:

 You heard her say herself, it was not I.

EMILIA:

 She said so. I must needs report the truth.

OTHELLO:

 She's like a liar gone to burning hell!

 'Twas I that killed her.

EMILIA: O, the more angel she,

 And you the blacker devil!

110 *error* straying off course **126** *Commend* remember

OTHELLO:
  She turned to folly, and she was a whore.
EMILIA:
  Thou dost belie her, and thou art a devil.
OTHELLO:
  She was false as water.
EMILIA: Thou art rash as fire to say   135
  That she was false. O, she was heavenly true!
OTHELLO:
  Cassio did top her. Ask thy husband else.
  O, I were damned beneath all depth in hell
  But that I did proceed upon just grounds
  To this extremity. Thy husband knew it all.
EMILIA: My husband?
OTHELLO: Thy husband.
EMILIA:
  That she was false to wedlock?
OTHELLO:
  Ay, with Cassio. Nay, had she been true,
  If heaven would make me such another world
  Of one entire and perfect chrysolite,   146
  I'd not have sold her for it.
EMILIA:
  My husband?
OTHELLO: Ay, 'twas he that told me first.
  An honest man he is, and hates the slime
  That sticks on filthy deeds.
EMILIA: My husband?
OTHELLO:
  What needs this iterance, woman? I say thy husband.   151
EMILIA:
  O mistress, villainy hath made mocks with love!
  My husband say that she was false?
OTHELLO: He, woman.
  I say, thy husband. Dost understand the word?
  My friend, thy husband; honest, honest Iago.
EMILIA:
  If he say so, may his pernicious soul
  Rot half a grain a day! he lies to th' heart.
  She was too fond of her most filthy bargain.
OTHELLO: Ha!
EMILIA: Do thy worst.
  This deed of thine is no more worthy heaven
  Than thou wast worthy her.

135 *water* (which is yielding) **146** *chrysolite* (precious topaz) **151** *iterance* repetition

OTHELLO: Peace, you were best.
EMILIA:

    Thou hast not half the power to do me harm
    As I have to be hurt. O gull! O dolt!   164
    As ignorant as dirt! thou hast done a deed—
    I care not for thy sword; I'll make thee known,
    Though I lost twenty lives. Help! help! Ho! help!
    The Moor hath killed my mistress! Murder! murder!

[*Enter* MONTANO, GRATIANO, IAGO, *and others.*]

MONTANO:

    What is the matter? How now, general?
EMILIA:

    O, are you come, Iago? You have done well,
    That men must lay their murders on your neck.
GRATIANO:

    What is the matter?
EMILIA:

    Disprove this villain, if thou be'st a man.
    He says thou told'st him that his wife was false.
    I know thou didst not; thou'rt not such a villain.
    Speak, for my heart is full.
IAGO:

    I told him what I thought, and told no more
    Than what he found himself was apt and true.
EMILIA:

    But did you ever tell him she was false?
IAGO: I did.
EMILIA:

    You told a lie, an odious damnèd lie!
    Upon my soul, a lie! a wicked lie!
    She false with Cassio? Did you say with Cassio?
IAGO:

    With Cassio, mistress. Go to, charm your tongue.   184
EMILIA:

    I will not charm my tongue; I am bound to speak:
    My mistress here lies murdered in her bed—
ALL:

    O heavens forfend!
EMILIA:

    And your reports have set the murder on.
OTHELLO:

    Nay, stare not, masters. It is true indeed.

164 *to be hurt* to endure hurt   **184** *charm* cast a spell on

GRATIANO:

  'Tis a strange truth.   190

MONTANO:

  O monstrous act!

EMILIA: Villainy, villainy, villainy!

  I think upon't—I think I smell't!—O villainy!

  I thought so then.—I'll kill myself for grief.—

  O villainy, villainy!

IAGO:

  What, are you mad? I charge you get you home.

EMILIA:

  Good gentlemen, let me have leave to speak.

  'Tis proper I obey him, but not now.

  Perchance, Iago, I will ne'er go home.

OTHELLO:

  O! O! O!

[Falls on the bed.]

EMILIA: Nay, lay thee down and roar!

  For thou hast killed the sweetest innocent

  That e'er lift up eye.

OTHELLO: O, she was foul!

  [Rises.]

  I scarce did know you, uncle. There lies your niece,

  Whose breath, indeed, these hands have newly stopped.

  I know this act shows horrible and grim.   204

GRATIANO:

  Poor Desdemona! I am glad thy father's dead.

  Thy match was mortal to him, and pure grief

  Shore his old thread in twain. Did he live now,

  This sight would make him do a desperate turn;   208

  Yea, curse his better angel from his side,

  And fall to reprobation.   210

OTHELLO:

  'Tis pitiful; but yet Iago knows

  That she with Cassio hath the act of shame

  A thousand times committed. Cassio confessed it;

  And she did gratify his amorous works   214

  With that recognizance and pledge of love   215

  Which I first gave her. I saw it in his hand.

  It was a handkerchief, an antique token

  My father gave my mother.

---

204 *shows* appears **208** *turn* act **210** *reprobation* rejection by God, damnation **214** *gratify* reward
215 *recognizance* token

EMILIA:

O God! O heavenly God!

IAGO:

Zounds, hold your peace!

EMILIA: 'Twill out, 'twill out! I peace?

No, I will speak as liberal as the north,   221

Let heaven and men and devils, let them all,

All, all, cry shame against me, yet I'll speak.

IAGO:

Be wise, and get you home.

EMILIA: I will not.

[IAGO *draws and threatens* EMILIA.]

GRATIANO: Fie!

Your sword upon a woman?

EMILIA:

O thou dull Moor, that handkerchief thou speak'st of

I found by fortune, and did give my husband;

For often with a solemn earnestness—

More than indeed belonged to such a trifle—

He begged of me to steal't.

IAGO: Villainous whore!

EMILIA:

She give it Cassio? No, alas, I found it,

And I did give't my husband.

IAGO: Filth, thou liest!

EMILIA:

By heaven, I do not, I do not, gentlemen.

O murd'rous coxcomb! what should such a fool

Do with so good a wife?

OTHELLO: Are there no stones in heaven   235

But what serves for the thunder? Precious villain!

[*The* MOOR *runs at* IAGO, *but is disarmed by* MONTANO. IAGO *kills his wife.*]

GRATIANO:

The woman falls. Sure he hath killed his wife.

EMILIA:

Ay, ay. O, lay me by my mistress' side.   [*Exit* IAGO.]

GRATIANO:

He's gone, but his wife's killed.

MONTANO:

'Tis a notorious villain. Take you this weapon,   240

---

221 *liberal as the north* unchecked as the north wind blows   **235** *stones* bolts like those used for thunderbolts
240 *notorious* notable

Which I have here recovered from the Moor.
Come, guard the door without. Let him not pass,
But kill him rather. I'll after that same villain,
For 'tis a damnèd slave.

[*Exit* MONTANO, *with all but* OTHELLO *and* EMILIA.]

OTHELLO: I am not valiant neither;
But every puny whipster gets my sword.   245
But why should honor outlive honesty?
Let it go all.

EMILIA: What did thy song bode, lady?
Hark, canst thou hear me? I will play the swan,
And die in music. [*Sings.*] "Willow, willow, willow."
Moor, she was chaste. She loved thee, cruel Moor:
So come my soul to bliss as I speak true.
So speaking as I think, alas, I die.

[*She dies.*]

OTHELLO:
I have another weapon in this chamber;
It is a sword of Spain, the ice brook's temper.   254
O, here it is.—Uncle, I must come forth.

GRATIANO [*within*]:
If thou attempt it, it will cost thee dear.
Thou hast no weapon, and perforce must suffer.

OTHELLO:
Look in upon me then and speak with me,
Or, naked as I am, I will assault thee.   259

[*Enter* GRATIANO.]

GRATIANO:
What is the matter?

OTHELLO: Behold, I have a weapon;
A better never did itself sustain
Upon a soldier's thigh. I have seen the day
That with this little arm and this good sword
I have made my way through more impediments
Than twenty times your stop. But O vain boast!   265
Who can control his fate? 'Tis not so now.
Be not afraid, though you do see me weaponed.
Here is my journey's end, here is my butt,   268

245 *puny whipster* top-whipping boy   254 *ice brook's* i.e. a Spanish blade, tempered in cold running water
259 *naked* disarmed   265 *stop* power to stop   268 *butt* limit

And very seamark of my utmost sail: 269
Do you go back dismayed? 'Tis a lost fear.   270
Man but a rush against Othello's breast,   271
And he retires. Where should Othello go?
Now, how dost thou look now? O ill-starred wench!
Pale as thys mock! When we shall meet at compt,   274
This look of thine will hurl my soul from heaven,
And fiends will snatch at it. Cold, cold, my girl?
Even like thy chastity.
O cursèd, cursèd slave! Whip me, ye devils,
From the possession of this heavenly sight!
Blow me about in winds! roast me in sulphur!
Wash me in steep-down gulfs of liquid fire!
Oh Desdemon! dead Desdemon! dead! Oh! Oh!

[*Enter* LODOVICO, MONTANO, IAGO *(as prisoner), and officers;* CASSIO *in a chair.*]

LODOVICO:
  Where is this rash and most unfortunate man?
OTHELLO:
  That's he that was Othello. Here I am.
LODOVICO:
  Where is that viper? Bring the villain forth.
OTHELLO:
  I look down towards his feet—but that's a fable.   286
  If that thou be'st a devil, I cannot kill thee.
  [*Wounds* IAGO.]
LODOVICO:
  Wrench his sword from him.
  [OTHELLO *is disarmed.*]
IAGO: I bleed, sir, but not killed.
OTHELLO:
  I am not sorry neither. I'd have thee live;
  For in my sense, 'tis happiness to die.
LODOVICO:
  O thou Othello that wert once so good,
  Fall'n in the practice of a damnèd slave,   292
  What shall be said to thee?
OTHELLO: Why, anything:
  An honorable murderer, if you will;
  For naught did I in hate, but all in honor.

---

269 *seamark* beacon, destination **270** *lost* wasted **271** *Man but a rush* wield only a reed **274** *compt* final
accounting, Last Judgment **286** *I . . . feet* i.e. to see if they are cloven, like the Devil's **292** *practice* plot

LODOVICO:

This wretch hath part confessed his villainy.

Did you and he consent in Cassio's death?

OTHELLO: Ay.

CASSIO:

Dear general, I never gave you cause.

OTHELLO:

I do believe it, and I ask your pardon.

Will you, I pray, demand that demi-devil

Why he hath thus ensnared my soul and body?

IAGO:

Demand me nothing. What you know, you know.

From this time forth I never will speak word.

LODOVICO:

What, not to pray?

GRATIANO: Torments will ope your lips.

OTHELLO:

Well, thou dost best.

LODOVICO:

Sir, you shall understand what hath befall'n,

Which, as I think, you know not. Here is a letter

Found in the pocket of the slain Roderigo;

And here another. The one of them imports

The death of Cassio to be undertook

By Roderigo.

OTHELLO:

O villain!

CASSIO: Most heathenish and most gross!

LODOVICO:

Now here's another discontented paper

Found in his pocket too; and this, it seems,

Roderigo meant t' have sent this damnèd villain;

But that, belike, Iago in the nick

Came in and satisfied him.

OTHELLO: O thou pernicious caitiff!—

How came you, Cassio, by that handkerchief

That was my wife's?

CASSIO: I found it in my chamber;

And he himself confessed but even now

That there he dropped it for a special purpose

Which wrought to his desire.

OTHELLO: O fool! fool! fool!

297

317

297 *consent in* agree upon   **317** *nick* nick of time

CASSIO:

 There is besides in Roderigo's letter,
 How he upbraids Iago that he made him
 Brave me upon the watch; whereon it came
 That I was cast; and even but now he spake,   327
 After long seeming dead—Iago hurt him,
 Iago set him on.

LODOVICO:

 You must forsake this room and go with us.
 Your power and your command is taken off,
 And Cassio rules Cyprus. For this slave,
 If there by any cunning cruelty
 That can torment him much and hold him long,
 It shall be his. You shall close prisoner rest
 Till that the nature of your fault be known
 To the Venetian state. Come, bring away.

OTHELLO:

 Soft you! a word or two before you go.
 I have done the state some service, and they know't.
 No more of that. I pray you, in your letters,
 When you shall these unlucky deeds relate,   341
 Speak of me as I am. Nothing extenuate,
 Nor set down aught in malice. Then must you speak
 Of one that loved not wisely, but too well;
 Of one not easily jealous, but, being wrought,
 Perplexed in the extreme; of one whose hand,   346
 Like the base Judean, threw a pearl away   347
 Richer than all his tribe; of one whose subdued eyes,   348
 Albeit unusèd to the melting mood,
 Drop tears as fast as the Arabian trees
 Their med'cinable gum. Set you down this.
 And say besides that in Aleppo once,
 Where a malignant and a turbaned Turk
 Beat a Venetian and traduced the state,
 I took by th' throat the circumcisèd dog
 And smote him—thus.

 [*He stabs himself.*]

LODOVICO:

 O bloody period!   357

GRATIANO: All that's spoke is marred.

327 *cast* dismissed   341 *unlucky* fatal   346 *Perplexed* distracted   347 *Judean* Judas Iscariot (?) (quarto reads
"Indian")   348 *subdued* i.e. conquered by grief   357 *period* ending

OTHELLO:

I kissed thee ere I killed thee. No way but this,
Killing myself, to die upon a kiss.

[He falls upon the bed and dies.]

CASSIO:

This did I fear, but thought he had no weapon;
For he was great of heart.
LODOVICO [*to* IAGO]:   O Spartan dog,
More fell than anguish, hunger, or the sea!   362
Look on the tragic loading of this bed.
This is thy work. The object poisons sight;
Let it be hid. Gratiano, keep the house,   365
And seize upon the fortunes of the Moor,   366
For they succeed on you. To you, lord governor,
Remains the censure of this hellish villain,   368
The time, the place, the torture. O, enforce it!
Myself will straight aboard, and to the state
This heavy act with heavy heart relate.   *[Exeunt.]*

QUESTIONS

Act I

1. All three scenes in Act I are set in Venice. What do we learn about the Venetian state from these scenes? What elements make up the "world" of each scene? What, especially, does the Venetian senate symbolize in terms of values?
2. We get three distinct impressions of Iago as we move through each scene in Act I. What is he like in each? Point carefully to his key speeches to support your character analysis. What composite picture of his character is formed by the end of Act I?
3. It has been noted that Othello is a dignified, noble, and heroic figure. How does this impression emerge in Act I? In this context, examine one of Othello's greatest speeches, in which he recapitulates his life (scene iii, lines 128–170). Analyze the diction, images, and tone. Comment on Othello's growing love for Desdemona, culminating in the lines, "She loved me for the dangers I had passed/And I loved her that she did pity them."
4. Why does Shakespeare delay the entrance of Desdemona until the third scene? How does she complement Othello in her speech and behavior? How does she begin to contrast with Iago?

362 *fell* cruel   **365** *Let it be hid* i.e. draw the bed curtains   **366** *seize upon* take legal possession of **368** *censure* judicial sentence

Act II

1. Act II opens on Cyprus, a shift in setting that Samuel Johnson objected to: "Had the scene [the play] opened in Cyprus and the preceeding incidents been occasionally related, there had been wanting to a drama of the most exact and scrupulous regularity." What is the critic objecting to here? Do you agree or disagree with Dr. Johnson's complaint? Explain.

2. Note that Venice, Cyprus, and the lands beyond the sea's horizon (symbolized in part by the invading Turkish fleet) seem to represent three different "worlds" in terms of values and levels of civilization. How does Shakespeare characterize each of these worlds? What is Othello's relationship to them?

3. Images of a turbulent sea—that "high-wrought flood," as Shakespeare describes it at the start of Act II—dominate the first scene. How does this sea imagery influence action, mood, and theme? For instance, why does Shakespeare contrive a triple landing? What does nature symbolize in the first scene? How does nature's "tempest" reflect the tempests brewing between various characters?

4. What is Iago's conception of women, love, and sexuality in Act II?

5. Analyze the dramatic effectiveness of Othello's reunion with Desdemona (with Iago looking on) in scene i, lines 178–207.

6. Of what new element in Othello's character do we learn from his speech in scene iii, lines 182–195?

7. Explain how Iago begins to succeed in his dark plans in the third scene of Act II. What is the significance of the fact that Othello charges that people are beginning to act like Turks (see lines 147–156)? How does the looming tragedy expand when Iago, toward the end of the act (see lines 296–322) likens himself to the devil, declaring of Desdemona, "So will I turn her virtue into pitch,/And out of her own goodness make the net/That shall enmesh them all"?

Act III

1. Why does Cassio bring musicians to play beneath Othello's window in the first scene? What is the function of this relatively lighthearted interlude? How does this action benefit Iago's ends?

2. What is Othello's state of mind in his soliloquy beginning, "This fellow's of exceeding honesty" (lines 258–277)? Why is this an unusual speech for him?

3. Contrast the relationship between Iago and Emilia in the third scene with that between Othello and Desdemona.

4. Trace the changes in the three meetings between Othello and Desdemona in Act III.

5. Explain the progression and complication of the tragic action in *Othello* through the first three acts of the play. Has the action moved too fast? Explain.

Act IV

1. How does Iago's language change at the start of Act IV? What does this change in the tone of his language tell us about the progression of the conflict?

2. What new trick does Iago devise to advance Othello's jealousy in the first scene? Why does Othello fall for such an obvious deception?

3. Analyze Desdemona's character during the episode in the second scene in which

Othello accuses her of being a whore. Why can't Othello perceive her essential goodness and innocence?

4. The second scene concludes with a confrontation between Roderigo and Iago. Summarize this scene and explain its importance in the advancement of the tragedy. Does Iago betray his true motives at this point or not? Explain.

5. Compare and contrast the minds of Desdemona and Emilia in the third scene. Why is Desdemona so passive?

Act V

1. Compare and contrast the two scenes in this act.
2. Divide the second scene into three parts, corresponding to the major stages of the action. What happens in each episode?
3. Analyze Othello's first speech at the start of the second scene. Why must he kill Desdemona quickly, rather than listening to her pleas?
4. Describe the importance of Emilia in Act V, after Desdemona has been killed.
5. How does Othello regain some of his lost stature and heroic character at the end of the play?
6. In what way is order restored at the end of the tragedy?

23. An Anthology of Drama

Woody Allen

DEATH KNOCKS

The play takes place in the bedroom of the Nat Ackermans' two-story house, somewhere in Kew Gardens. The carpeting is wall-to-wall. There is a big double bed and a large vanity. The room is elaborately furnished and curtained, and on the walls there are several paintings and a not really attractive barometer. Soft theme music as the curtain rises. Nat Ackerman, a bald, paunchy fifty-seven-year-old dress manufacturer is lying on the bed finishing off tomorrow's Daily News. *He wears a bathrobe and slippers, and reads by a bed light clipped to the white headboard of the bed. The time is near midnight. Suddenly we hear a noise, and Nat sits up and looks at the window.*

NAT: What the hell is that?

[*Climbing awkwardly through the window is a sombre, caped figure. The intruder wears a black hood and skintight black clothes. The hood covers his head but not his face, which is middle-aged and stark white. He is something like* NAT *in appearance. He huffs audibly and then trips over the windowsill and falls into the room.*]

DEATH [*for it is no one else*]: Jesus Christ. I nearly broke my neck.
NAT [*watching with bewilderment*]: Who are you?
DEATH: Death.
NAT: Who?
DEATH: Death. Listen—can I sit down? I nearly broke my neck. I'm shaking like a leaf.
NAT: Who *are* you?
DEATH: *Death.* You got a glass of water?

NAT: Death? What do you mean, Death?

DEATH: What is wrong with you? You see the black costume and the whitened face?

NAT: Yeah.

DEATH: Is it Halloween?

NAT: No.

DEATH: Then I'm Death. Now can I get a glass of water—or a Fresca?

NAT: If this is some joke—

DEATH: What kind of joke? You're fifty-seven? Nat Ackerman? One eighteen Pacific Street? Unless I blew it—where's that call sheet? [*He fumbles through pocket, finally producing a card with an address on it. It seems to check.*]

NAT: What do you want with me?

DEATH: What do I want? What do you think I want?

NAT: You must be kidding. I'm in perfect health.

DEATH [*unimpressed*]: Uh-huh. [*Looking around.*] This is a nice place. You do it yourself?

NAT: We had a decorator, but we worked with her.

DEATH [*looking at picture on the wall*]: I love those kids with the big eyes.

NAT: I don't want to go yet.

DEATH: *You* don't want to go? Please don't start in. As it is, I'm nauseous from the climb.

NAT: What climb?

DEATH: I climbed up the drainpipe. I was trying to make a dramatic entrance. I see the big windows and you're awake reading. I figure it's worth a shot. I'll climb up and enter with a little—you know . . . [*Snaps fingers.*] Meanwhile, I get my heel caught on some vines, the drainpipe breaks, and I'm hanging by a thread. Then my cape begins to tear. Look, let's just go. It's been a rough night.

NAT: You broke my drainpipe?

DEATH: Broke. It didn't break. It's a little bent. Didn't you hear anything? I slammed into the ground.

NAT: I was reading.

DEATH: You must have really been engrossed. [*Lifting newspaper* NAT *was reading.*] "NAB COEDS IN POT ORGY." Can I borrow this?

NAT: I'm not finished.

DEATH: Er—I don't know how to put this to you, pal . . .

NAT: Why didn't you just ring downstairs?

DEATH: I'm telling you, I could have, but how does it look? This way I get a little drama going. Something. Did you read *Faust?*

NAT: What?

DEATH: And what if you had company? You're sitting there with important people. I'm Death—I should ring the bell and traipse right in the front? Where's your thinking?

NAT: Listen, Mister, it's very late.

DEATH: Yeah. Well, you want to go?

NAT: Go where?

DEATH: Death. It. The Thing. The Happy Hunting Grounds. [*Looking at his own knee.*] Y'know, that's a pretty bad cut. My first job, I'm liable to get gangrene yet.

NAT: Now, wait a minute. I need time. I'm not ready to go.

DEATH: I'm sorry. I can't help you. I'd like to, but it's the moment.

NAT: How can it be the moment? I just merged with Modiste Originals.

DEATH: What's the difference, a couple of bucks more or less.

NAT: Sure, what do you care? You guys probably have all your expenses paid.

DEATH: You want to come along now?

NAT [*studying him*]: I'm sorry, but I cannot believe you're Death.

DEATH: Why? What'd you expect—Rock Hudson?

NAT: No, it's not that.

DEATH: I'm sorry if I disappointed you.

NAT: Don't get upset. I don't know, I always thought you'd be . . . uh . . . taller.

DEATH: I'm five seven. It's average for my weight.

NAT: You look a little like me.

DEATH: Who should I look like? I'm your death.

NAT: Give me some time. Another day.

DEATH: I can't. What do you want me to say?

NAT: One more day. Twenty-four hours.

DEATH: What do you need it for? The radio said rain tomorrow.

NAT: Can't we work out something?

DEATH: Like what?

NAT: You play chess?

DEATH: No, I don't.

NAT: I once saw a picture of you playing chess.

DEATH: Couldn't be me, because I don't play chess. Gin rummy, maybe.

NAT: You play gin rummy?

DEATH: Do I play gin rummy? Is Paris a city?

NAT: You're good, huh?

DEATH: Very good.

NAT: I'll tell you what I'll do—

DEATH: Don't make any deals with me.

NAT: I'll play you gin rummy. If you win, I'll go immediately. If I win, give me some more time. A little bit—one more day.

DEATH: Who's got time to play gin rummy?

NAT: Come on. If you're so good.

DEATH: Although I feel like a game . . .

NAT: Come on. Be a sport. We'll shoot for a half hour.

DEATH: I really shouldn't.

NAT: I got the cards right here. Don't make a production.

DEATH: All right, come on. We'll play a little. It'll relax me.

NAT [*getting cards, pad, and pencil*]: You won't regret this.

DEATH: Don't give me a sales talk. Get the cards and give me a Fresca and put out something. For God's sake, a stranger drops in, you don't have potato chips or pretzels.

NAT: There's M&M's downstairs in a dish.

DEATH: M&M's. What if the President came? He'd get M&M's, too?

NAT: You're not the President.

DEATH: Deal.

[NAT *deals, turns up a five.*]

NAT: You want to play a tenth of a cent a point to make it interesting?

DEATH: It's not interesting enough for you?

NAT: I play better when money's at stake.

DEATH: Whatever you say, Newt.

NAT: Nat. Nat Ackerman. You don't know my name?

DEATH: Newt, Nat—I got such a headache.

NAT: You want that five?

DEATH: No.

NAT: So pick.

DEATH [*surveying his hand as he picks*]: Jesus, I got nothing here.

NAT: What's it like?

DEATH: What's what like?

[*Throughout the following, they pick and discard.*]

NAT: Death.

DEATH: What should it be like? You lay there.

NAT: Is there anything after?

DEATH: Aha, you're saving twos.

NAT: I'm asking. Is there anything after?

DEATH [*absently*]: You'll see.

NAT: Oh, then I will actually see something?

DEATH: Well, maybe I shouldn't have put it that way. Throw.

NAT: To get an answer from you is a big deal.

DEATH: I'm playing cards.

NAT: All right, play, play.

DEATH: Meanwhile, I'm giving you one card after another.

NAT: Don't look through the discards.

DEATH: I'm not looking. I'm straightening them up. What was the knock card?

NAT: Four. You ready to knock already?

DEATH: Who said I'm ready to knock? All I asked was what was the knock card.

NAT: And all I asked was is there anything for me to look forward to.

DEATH: Play.

NAT: Can't you tell me anything? Where do we go?

DEATH: We? To tell you the truth, *you* fall in a crumpled heap on the floor.

NAT: Oh, I can't wait for that! Is it going to hurt?

DEATH: Be over in a second.

NAT: Terrific. [*Sighs.*] I needed this. A man merges with Modiste Originals . . .

DEATH: How's four points?

NAT: You're knocking?

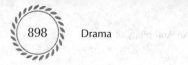

DEATH: Four points is good?

NAT: No, I got two.

DEATH: You're kidding.

NAT: No, you lose.

DEATH: Holy Christ, and I thought you were saving sixes.

NAT: No. Your deal. Twenty points and two boxes. Shoot. [*Death deals.*] I must fall on the floor, eh? I can't be standing over the sofa when it happens?

DEATH: No. Play.

NAT: Why not?

DEATH: Because you fall on the floor! Leave me alone. I'm trying to concentrate.

NAT: Why must it be on the floor? That's all I'm saying! Why can't the whole thing happen and I'll stand next to the sofa?

DEATH: I'll try my best. Now can we play?

NAT: That's all I'm saying. You remind me of Moe Lefkowitz. He's also stubborn.

DEATH: I remind him of Moe Lefkowitz. I'm one of the most terrifying figures you could possibly imagine, and him I remind of Moe Lefkowitz. What is he, a furrier?

NAT: You should be such a furrier. He's good for eighty thousand a year. Passementeries. He's got his own factory. Two points.

DEATH: What?

NAT: Two points. I'm knocking. What have you got?

DEATH: My hand is like a basketball score.

NAT: And it's spades.

DEATH: If you didn't talk so much.

[*They redeal and play on.*]

NAT: What'd you mean before when you said this was your first job?

DEATH: What does it sound like?

NAT: What are you telling me—that nobody ever went before?

DEATH: Sure they went. But I didn't take them.

NAT: So who did?

DEATH: Others.

NAT: There's others?

DEATH: Sure. Each one has his own personal way of going.

NAT: I never knew that.

DEATH: Why should you know? Who are you?

NAT: What do you mean who am I? Why—I'm nothing?

DEATH: Not nothing. You're a dress manufacturer. Where do you come to knowledge of the eternal mysteries?

NAT: What are you talking about? I make a beautiful dollar. I sent two kids through college. One is in advertising, the other's married. I got my own home. I drive a Chrysler. My wife has whatever she wants. Maids, mink coat, vacations. Right now she's at the Eden Roc. Fifty dollars a day because she wants to be near her sister. I'm supposed to join her next week, so what do you think I am—some guy off the street?

DEATH: All right. Don't be so touchy.

NAT: Who's touchy?

DEATH: How would you like it if I got insulted quickly?

NAT: Did I insult you?

DEATH: You didn't say you were disappointed in me?

NAT: What do you expect? You want me to throw you a block party?

DEATH: I'm not talking about that. I mean me personally. I'm too short, I'm this, I'm that.

NAT: I said you looked like me. It's like a reflection.

DEATH: All right, deal, deal.

[*They continue to play as music steals in and the lights dim until all is in total darkness. The lights slowly come up again, and now it is later and their game is over.* NAT *tallies.*]

NAT: Sixty-eight . . . one-fifty . . . Well, you lose.

DEATH [*dejectedly looking through the deck*]: I knew I shouldn't have thrown that nine. Damn it.

NAT: So I'll see you tomorrow.

DEATH: What do you mean you'll see me tomorrow?

NAT: I won the extra day. Leave me alone.

DEATH: You were serious?

NAT: We made a deal.

DEATH: Yeah, but—

NAT: Don't "but" me. I won twenty-four hours. Come back tomorrow.

DEATH: I didn't know we were actually playing for time.

NAT: That's too bad about you. You should pay attention.

DEATH: Where am I going to go for twenty-four hours?

NAT: What's the difference? The main thing is I won an extra day.

DEATH: What do you want me to do—walk the streets?

NAT: Check into a hotel and go to a movie. Take a *schvitz*. Don't make a federal case.

DEATH: Add the score again.

NAT: Plus you owe me twenty-eight dollars.

DEATH: *What?*

NAT: That's right, Buster. Here it is—read it.

DEATH [*going through pockets*]: I have a few singles—not twenty-eight dollars.

NAT: I'll take a check.

DEATH: From what account?

NAT: Look who I'm dealing with.

DEATH: Sue me. Where do I keep my checking account?

NAT: All right, gimme what you got and we'll call it square.

DEATH: Listen, I need that money.

NAT: Why should you need money?

DEATH: What are you talking about? You're going to the Beyond.

NAT: So?

DEATH: So—you know how far that is?

NAT: So?

DEATH: So where's gas? Where's tolls?

NAT: We're going by car!

DEATH: You'll find out. [*Agitatedly.*] Look—I'll be back tomorrow, and you'll give me a chance to win the money back. Otherwise I'm in definite trouble.

NAT: Anything you want. Double or nothing we'll play. I'm liable to win an extra week or a month. The way you play, maybe years.

DEATH: Meantime I'm stranded.

NAT: See you tomorrow.

DEATH [*being edged to the doorway*]: Where's a good hotel? What am I talking about hotel, I got no money. I'll go sit in Bickford's. [*He picks up the* News.]

NAT: Out. Out. That's my paper. [*He takes it back.*]

DEATH [*exiting*]: I couldn't just take him and go. I had to get involved in rummy.

NAT [*calling after him*]: And be careful going downstairs. On one of the steps the rug is loose.

[*And, on cue, we hear a terrific crash.* NAT *sighs, then crosses to the bedside table and makes a phone call.*]

NAT: Hello, Moe? Me. Listen, I don't know if somebody's playing a joke, or what, but Death was just here. We played a little gin . . . No, *Death*. In person. Or somebody who claims to be Death. But, Moe, he's such a *schlep!*

Curtain

QUESTIONS

1. How is humor initially established in the play? What conventions about the portrait of death has Allen broken?
2. What is Nat's attitude toward the figure he meets, claiming to be Death? How is his attitude portrayed as humorous? What does Nat's attitude toward Death reveal about his character and values?
3. Was the figure who entered Nat's home truly Death or an imposter? What are the implications in the play for either interpretation?

Brigid Brophy

THE WASTE DISPOSAL UNIT

CHARACTERS

The Waste Disposal Unit was first presented by B.B.C. Radio, Great Britain, on April 9, 1964, with the following cast:

HOMER KNOCKERBICKER   Harry Towb
VIRGIL KNOCKERBICKER   Ronald Wilson
MERRY KNOCKERBICKER   Mavis Villiers
LIA-PIA   Nicolette Bernard
ANGELO LUMACA   John Baddeley
MRS. VAN DEN MOST   Mavis Villiers

(*Note:* The roles of MERRY and her mother, MRS. VAN DEN MOST, are performed by the same actress.)

Scene: The salone *of a* palazzo *in northern Italy. The time is the present.*

The salone *of a* palazzo *in northern Italy.*

The room is marbled and splendid, but the splendour is of a cool and echoing kind because the place is simply not furnished at all, apart from a crate of Coca-Cola bottles—some full, some already used—that has been nakedly dumped in the middle of the intricately patterned floor.

Luckily there are two marble windowseats beneath the tall uncurtained windows.

On one of these VIRGIL KNOCKERBICKER *is lying reading a small black-bound notebook which is propped up on his humped knees. He is dressed in black himself—cashmere sweater, narrow trousers, black plimsolls; his soft dark hair is cropped to the point of seeming a mere continuance of the pile on his jumper. In his black costume and his complete absorption in his small volume, he resembles—no doubt on purpose—the young Lord Hamlet.*

HOMER KNOCKERBICKER, *a slightly older and considerably plumper American is walking echoingly up and down the room. He is as worried and hot as Virgil is cool and controlled—this despite the fact that his clothing, unlike Virgil's, is designed for coolness rather than picturesque effect. His light-coloured, loose cotton suit and his transparent nylon-seersucker shirt are already crumpled, though the day (some of whose brilliance spills in through the windows) is not yet far advanced. In patches, his shirt is already even more translucent than the manufacturer intended, where his sweat has affected it as grease affects paper. From time to time he takes a vast handkerchief from his breast pocket and uses it to wipe his spectacles.*

Doors to left and right of the salone *lead out to the rest of the* palazzo.

Through the window there are summer country Italian sounds: chickens, occasional cicadas, lambrettas.

HOMER: Virgil?
VIRGIL [*without looking up from his reading*]: Homer?

HOMER: Virgil, you planning on lying around all day today, the way you did yesterday?

VIRGIL: Mm-hm. [VIRGIL *thinks he has now disposed of the subject.*]

HOMER: This heat's murder. Merry says it isn't any worse than Southern California, but I tell her it is, it carries a higher degree of humidity. Southern California, you get the ocean. [*After a pause.*] Gee, it's hot. It's hot as hell.

VIRGIL: Maybe you should relax more.

HOMER: I guess one in the family is enough.

VIRGIL: One what?

HOMER: O, you know. You know what I mean, Virgil. It's hot enough so it even mists up my lenses. You're lucky you don't have to wear glasses. This heat, you wouldn't be able to see to write.

VIRGIL: I'm not writing. I'm reading back what I already did.

HOMER: That reminds me, sometime I got to talk with you—you want a drink, Virgil?

VIRGIL: Mm-hm. Whisky sour.

HOMER: I didn't mean hard liquor.

VIRGIL: O. No thanks.

HOMER: I wish we had a water cooler in this place. Guess I'll have myself a Coke. I wonder if Merry could use a Coke. You think Merry could use a Coke, Virgil?

[HOMER *alludes to the door at the left.*]

VIRGIL: How would I know? Go on in and ask her.

HOMER: O, I can't go in there right now. She isn't through fixing her face.

VIRGIL: O. Well yell.

HOMER [*as he helps himself to a bottle of Coca-Cola and removes the cap*]: What?

VIRGIL: Yell. Ask her through the bedroom door.

HOMER: Yeh, I might *do* that. [*He drinks deep, directly from the bottle.*] I might *do* that. Sure.

VIRGIL: Well go ahead.

HOMER: Sure.

MERRY [*offstage, calling cooingly in a pretty, tinkling voice*]: Ho-mer!

HOMER [*calling hastily back, towards the door at the left*]: I'll be right in, honey. I just grabbed myself a Coke. I just gotta find some place to put it down. [*He crams it into the crate and runs over to the door at the left; but as his hand turns the knob:*]

MERRY: O, don't come *in*, Homer.

[HOMER *shuts the door hastily.*]

HOMER: I certainly am sorry, Merry.

MERRY: Why, that's perfectly all right, Homer, think no more of it. Homer?

HOMER: Yes, Merry?

MERRY: Would you take a look round the *palazzo* see if I left my Kleenex some place.

HOMER: Sure, Merry. [HOMER *returns to the middle of the room.*] I don't see too well, my lenses got misted up again. [*Calling:*] I don't see them any place, honey, but I'll keep right on searching. Virgil, you seen them?

VIRGIL: See what?

HOMER: Merry's Kleenex.

VIRGIL: Sure. [VIRGIL *pulls out a box from behind his back.*]

HOMER: Now why in the world would you want to do that?

VIRGIL: This window-seat isn't too soft, Homer.

HOMER: If you wouldn't lie around all day—

VIRGIL: Don't you want them?

HOMER: What?

VIRGIL: Merry's Kleenex.

HOMER: Wait a moment, can't you, I got to wipe off these lenses again.

VIRGIL: Don't *you* get steamed up, too.

HOMER: I'm not getting steamed up, but you don't seem to understand, I got to get those Kleenex to Merry. Give here. [*He takes the box from* VIRGIL.] Why, Virgil, you crushed in one whole side of the pack. I don't know how Merry's going to—

VIRGIL: Yeh, well, these sharp-angled packs aren't really any more comfortable than marble. I guess I really took Merry's Kleenex more as a kind of talisman. You know, like a chicken sits on a china egg. To inspire my work.

HOMER: Now that's something I have to talk with you about, Virgil. I'll just go give these to Merry. I'll be right back. [*Approaching the door at the left and calling:*] Merry! I found them, honey. But I'm afraid the pack didn't stand up too well—

MERRY: Now isn't that just too bad of me, Homer. I was just going to call out I didn't need them any more.

HOMER: O.

MERRY: Homer, don't be sore. I found another pack right in here.

HOMER: O, I'm not sore, Merry. I'm certainly glad you found another pack. That's swell. You through yet, honey?

MERRY: Not yet, Homer.

HOMER: O. O.K.

VIRGIL [*as, without looking away from his book, he reaches a hand out towards the Kleenex*]: Give here.

HOMER: What?

VIRGIL: If Merry doesn't want them, I may as well sit on them a while longer. You never know what might hatch. I'll take a look round later, see if I can find a pack that isn't crushed. You don't have any scatter cushions round the place, Homer, I guess you don't have the domesticated touch, but you have to hand it to Merry, she certainly does have scatter Kleenex.

HOMER: Now see here, Virgil—

MERRY [*offstage*]: I don't hear you too well but you boys sound to be having a lot of fun out there. I'll be right along.

HOMER: That's swell, honey.

VIRGIL: I don't figure how it takes a woman that long to make up like she was twenty-five when she *is* twenty-five.

HOMER: Now wait a moment, Virgil—

VIRGIL: Mm-hm?

HOMER: Merry's a lovely person.

VIRGIL: Sure. Sure, Homer. Merry's just great. She's great material.

HOMER: What do you mean, "material"?

VIRGIL: You know how it is, Homer. I guess I have a professional attitude, that's all. I'm certainly glad you married Merry.

HOMER [*not sure whether to be angered*]: I don't know just how you mean that, Virgil. Do you mean you're glad on account of your work?

VIRGIL: O, I don't separate my work from my life.

HOMER: Now that's something we have to talk about. I'll just have myself that Coke. . . .

VIRGIL: In fact, I don't separate my work from *your* life.

[HOMER *puts the bottle abruptly back into the crate, and prepares to be angry.*]

HOMER: I didn't hear you too well, Virgil, I was kind of swallowing, but did you say my life or my wife?

VIRGIL: O, I wouldn't dare—

HOMER: Let's leave Merry out of this, Virgil. I want to talk with you.

VIRGIL: Mm-hm?

HOMER: Don't you ever look up from that book?

VIRGIL: I'm told I have very remarkable concentration.

HOMER: I guess you wouldn't break your concentration no matter what happened.

VIRGIL: Nothing does happen.

HOMER: Maybe not, but most of the time it sounds like it did. Know what I think, Virgil? I think Italy's the noisiest country I was ever in.

VIRGIL: It's no worse than Southern California.

HOMER: It is *so* worse than Southern California. Out here you got the cicadas. If it isn't the cicadas, it's the lambrettas. If it isn't the lambrettas, it's the doves. If it isn't the doves, it's those goddam chickens out there in the yard.

VIRGIL: I don't mind the chickens in the *yard* too much.

HOMER: Now see h—

VIRGIL: Cool off, Homer.

HOMER: How can I cool off, this heat? We ought to have drapes at those windows, cut out the sun, but I don't know the Italian for drapes, anyway Merry likes looking out the window. . . . I'm worried, Virgil. I don't know how Merry's going to take this kind of climatic conditions.

VIRGIL: Relax, Homer. Merry doesn't feel it at all.

HOMER: You don't know how Merry feels. Merry is a very delicate character. I don't see how I can ask Merry to live in a climate like this.

VIRGIL: You didn't ask her. It was Merry's idea.

HOMER: You know what I *mean*, Virgil. You know how it is. A guy has to look out for his wife, he has to make provision. If I'd have known there wouldn't even have been a shower in this *palazzo*—

VIRGIL: You had one fixed.

HOMER: Sure I had one fixed, and I'm going to have plenty else fixed, I'm going to make this old *palazzo* like so it won't know itself. . . . But Merry's a very sensitive person. She's delicate, Virgil, even though she doesn't make any song and dance—

MERRY [*calling musically from the next room*]: Ho-mer!

HOMER: Yes, honey?

MERRY: Could you step in here for a moment, Homer?

HOMER: Sure, Merry. I'll be right in. You through now? [*A bell rings loudly.*]

HOMER: I'll get it. [*He stops making towards the door at the left, and sets out for the door at the right; checks himself; executes a step-dance of hesitation; and finally calls, in a despairing flurry, towards the door on the left:*] I'll be right back, Merry. I just got to go see to the front door bell.

VIRGIL: Let Lia-Pia get it.

HOMER: How can I let Lia-Pia get it? She doesn't speak English.

VIRGIL: So she doesn't speak English. Maybe it was an Italian dropped by.

HOMER: Are you crazy? How would an Italian drop by?

VIRGIL: Well, we're in Italy.

HOMER: Sure, I *know* we're in Italy, but—

MERRY: Ho-mer! Would you step along to the front door. The bell just rang.

HOMER: Sure, Merry, sure. I'll get it.

[*As* HOMER *leaves by the door at the right,* MERRY *trips in by the door at the left. She tiptoes on her sneakers across the room, comes up behind* VIRGIL *as he reads, and places her hands as a blindfold over his eyes.*]

MERRY: Morning, Virgil. Guess who?

VIRGIL [*sourly*]: Merry.

MERRY [*releasing his eyes*]: You're a good guesser, Virgil.

VIRGIL [*craning round and looking at her*]: Mm-hm, Merry. Just like I thought. Morning, Merry. You look cute.

MERRY [*dropping him a mock curtsey*]: Why, thank you, Virgil.

VIRGIL [*looking her up and down*]: Sure, cute. Little pony tail, all done up in a tartan bow, and those long white kneehose, and your Bermuda shorts, and that cute little—what you call it?

MERRY: Shirtwaister?

VIRGIL: Sure, shirtwaister. O, you look cute, Merry. You look like all the college girls in Southern California rolled into one.

MERRY: Why, Virgil, that's the darlingest thing you ever said to me, I guess you must be becoming a better integrated personality. I'm going to give you a little kiss on your brow, just for saying that. [*She bends over and neatly deposits the kiss.*]

VIRGIL: O, don't take any account of me, Merry, I'm just apple-polishing. There's something I want you to tell me.

MERRY: Well, I'll certainly tell you anything I can, Virgil, but Homer says you already know 'most everything. I'm going to just curl up alongside of you on this lovely *Ren*aissance window-seat, and then you can ask me anything you want. [*Doing so.*] I guess wherever I am I find myself some corner I can curl up in. There now, Virgil. What's your problem? You know, Virgil, Homer has a very, very high regard for your intellectual integrity.

VIRGIL: Now how would he be able to judge, I wonder?

MERRY: Now, Virgil, Homer's—

VIRGIL: O sure, Homer's a lovely person.

MERRY [*subsiding*]: I'm certainly glad you appreciate it. Now what is it I can tell you?

VIRGIL: Why don't you let your husband in your bedroom, Merry?

MERRY [*rising in fury*]: Virgil Knockerbicker, how can you make such an absolutely awful insinuation? If you dare imply for one moment—

VIRGIL: Merry, I only asked—

MERRY: Virgil Knockerbicker, I'm going right back in the bou*doir* until Homer returns. [*She turns her back on* VIRGIL.]

VIRGIL: Merry, what did I do?

MERRY [*swinging on him*]: What did you *do!* You were insinuating that my relationship with Homer is not perfectly adjusted on the physical side.

VIRGIL: Merry, I only—

MERRY: You as good as called me a frigid wife!

VIRGIL: Merry, I—

MERRY [*stamping*]: I do so let him in my bedroom!

VIRGIL: He told me a while back he couldn't go in there.

MERRY [*losing all her anger, now the trouble is explained*]: O sure, but that was in the morning.

VIRGIL: What's the difference?

MERRY: Virgil, you certainly seem a little naïve for your age. Homer comes in my room nights—*of* course—and then he always goes away while it's still dark. He promised me that's how it would always be, and I know Homer won't break his promise. Then mornings he doesn't come in again before I got my face fixed.

VIRGIL: Is it that important he shouldn't see you without you got your face fixed?

MERRY: Well maybe it isn't that important right now, Virgil, but it will be. And the way Homer is, it could do a lot of damage to his feelings if I suddenly had to ask him to quit coming in when I got to be of age when it would matter. Right after Homer became my beau, I figured I ought to start right in planning for the future. It was our wedding night I asked him to give me this promise. That way I know he'll never break it.

VIRGIL [*laying his book down on his knees and surrendering himself to musing in wonder on* MERRY *'s revelation*]: And you feel you couldn't possibly let him in till you're through fixing your face?

MERRY [*with quiet resolution*]: No, I couldn't do that, Virgil. I just couldn't *do* that. [*Dreamily*] You see, Virgil, I have something I want to preserve.

VIRGIL: Your face?

MERRY [*gently*]: No, Virgil, something intangible, something that's been kind of entrusted to me. I don't know that you can understand very well, Virgil. Although you and I are pretty much of an age, I guess a woman matures faster than a man. I doubt that you have achieved sufficient maturation yet to understand. But what I feel is—well, I guess I feel that romance is a very wonderful and a very fragile thing. [*She lets these words hang like a beautiful sunset in the air for a moment. Then she trips to the door at the right.*]

MERRY: I guess I'll just go along and see who it was dropped by. Maybe I can help Homer some. [*Opening the door and pausing.*] Well . . . I'm glad you talked with me about this, Virgil. I'm not going to tell Homer we talked about it, because I believe that even within the marital framework there ought to be areas of privacy. If you have some more problems, Virgil, I hope you will talk with me about them. I have a personal conviction that relationships can only achieve a completely adjusted orientation if problems are brought right out in the open. And I sincerely hope we can all three pass a wonderful vacation in this lovely old *palazzo*.

[MERRY *leaves by the door at the right.* LIA-PIA *shuffles in by the door at the left. She is a dear old thing in a black overall and lopsided bedroom slippers. She is ushering in a smartly dressed young Italian.*]

LIA-PIA [*clucking comfortingly, like a dove*]: Si accomodi, signore, si accomodi, si accomodi.

[LIA-PIA *shuffles out, leaving the visitor, as he thinks, alone. He deposits his smart, speckled-leather briefcase against his side of the Coca-Cola crate, settles the sit of his perfectly pressed suit, puts one foot up on the side of the crate and bends to pull up one of his quite unsagging thin-nylon socks.*]

VIRGIL [*picking up his book to resume reading and speaking without looking at the stranger*]: I don't know why the old thing told you to accommodate yourself. I don't see where you can.

THE VISITOR [*whirling round in surprise*]: Ah, scusi, non avevo visto—

VIRGIL: O.K. maybe I *am* insignificant. You could sit on the Coca-Cola crate but I doubt that it's comfortable.

THE ITALIAN: Please, it is no matter. I am come to work, not sit. You are Mr. Knockerbicker?

VIRGIL: Mm-hm.

ANGELO: I am the man who is come to fix the——

VIRGIL: O, then I'm not the Mr. Knockerbicker you want. The Mr. Knockerbicker you want, the Mr. Knockerbicker who counts, will be along presently. Pardon me if I catch up on some reading while you wait. [*He begins to do so.*]

ANGELO: Please? The Mr. Knockerbicker who counts?

VIRGIL: Sure, who counts out the dough. I'm just the kid brother. The Mr. Knockerbicker who counts went to meet you, and the Mrs. Knockerbicker who counts went right after him, but the way this palace is constructed, if you miss somebody the first time round, you have to go through the whole tour of the building before you get back where you started. I guess the *Renaissance* just wasn't *onto* the principle of the corridor.

ANGELO [*with a self-introductory bow*]: Lumaca, Angelo.

VIRGIL [*with an inclination of his head, sidelong, over his book*]: Knockerbicker, Virgil.

ANGELO: You are reading?

VIRGIL [*continuing to do so*]: Mm-hm.

ANGELO: I, too, read very often. It is being very hot. I take off my coat. This is not a nuisance?

VIRGIL [*without attending*]: Go right ahead.

[ANGELO *takes off coat, folds it inside out, removes his wallet, hangs his coat on a knob of the shutters at the window not occupied by* VIRGIL *and returns to talk to* VIRGIL.]

ANGELO: Ah, that is better. You are not being too hot, dressed all in black?

VIRGIL: Black is the coolest colour there is. And I am one of the coolest characters there is.

ANGELO: I am sorry. I have been bad to ask that question.

VIRGIL: How so?

ANGELO: Probably you are wearing the black because you are being bereaved.

VIRGIL: No, I wasn't bereaved recently, but now you come to mention it I'm prepared.

ANGELO: You are reading a book which is interesting?

VIRGIL [*still reading*]: Enthralling.

ANGELO: Love story, police story, espionage, *Reader's Digest,* Science Fiction?

VIRGIL: Poetry.

ANGELO: Ah, I, too, am loving poetry. Even though I am being an engineer, I am loving poetry. You know what I am thinking, Mr. Knockerbicker junior? I am thinking in life today there is not being enough poetry. I am loving beauty in all its forms. I love poetry, music, paintings—I am loving all the arts. And you know why, Mr. Knockerbicker junior? Because they are so beautiful. To me, they are so beautiful. I am loving all the beautiful things—including the women, yes?

VIRGIL [*without interest*]: That so?

ANGELO: I think you are feeling the same, eh, Mr. Knockerbicker junior?

VIRGIL: Mm-hm. [*As an afterthought.*] All except the women.

ANGELO [*astounded*]: How is this? You are not loving the women?

VIRGIL [*without emphasis*]: I'm homosexual.

ANGELO [*completely taken aback*]: O. [*After a pause of swallowing the information.*] I am begging your pardon.

VIRGIL [*without looking up*]: Don't mention it. [*Musing.*] What a *peculiar* conversation.

ANGELO: Mr. Knockerbicker junior, this poem you read, who is the author?

[VIRGIL *reads to the end of the page before replying.*]

VIRGIL: I am.

[ANGELO *laughs politely.* VIRGIL *continues to read.*]

ANGELO: You are meaning this is true? Really you have written a poem?

VIRGIL: Am writing. I didn't finish it yet.

ANGELO: And you are beginning it when?

VIRGIL: When I was ten.

ANGELO: You are writing since you have been ten one poem? So many years, one poem?

VIRGIL: I'm not that old.

ANGELO: No, but—

VIRGIL: I guess it was the romantic movement spread the idea a poem has to be a lyric.

ANGELO: Without the lyric feeling, where is the poetry?

VIRGIL: Before romanticism was invented, there were plenty of long poems. My namesake Virgil, who was born not too far from here, wrote an extremely long poem. My brother's namesake wrote two of them. Dante and Milton also wrote long poems, but as my parents didn't have any more sons they are not commemorated in our family.

ANGELO: Dante, Milton, that was long ago. Modern life moves with more pace, Mr. Knockerbicker junior. How did you find rhymes for a long poem? It is difficult, yes?

VIRGIL: I don't use rhyme.

ANGELO: Without the rhyme, how is it poetry? You are writing the blank verses?

VIRGIL: I don't use meter.

ANGELO: What can it be like, your poem?

VIRGIL: My poem is kind of an American Song of Songs.

ANGELO: But without the rhyme, without the meter, where is the poetry?

VIRGIL: The poetry is in the subject.

ANGELO: Mr. Knockerbicker junior, what *is* the subject of your poem?

VIRGIL: The subject of my poem is the American Woman.

ANGELO: Ah, now I am understanding. The American Woman, she is poetry herself.

VIRGIL [*prosaically agreeing*]: Yes, I include her among the ideas which have a sufficient poetic content in themselves, along with the collision of planets and the copulation of dinosaurs.

ANGELO [*overwhelmed*]: You must be a very poetical person, Mr. Knockerbicker junior.

VIRGIL: Fortunately I don't have to reply to that compliment because I hear the other Mr. Knockerbicker on his way back. He has a very weighty tread. Come to think of it, Homer must weigh all of a hundred and sixty.

[HOMER *comes worriedly through the door at the left.*]

VIRGIL: Meet Mr. Homer Knockerbicker. Homer, meet Mr. Angelo Lumaca.

HOMER [*politely, but too distractedly worried to pay attention*]: Mr. Lumaca.

ANGELO: Call me Angelo.

HOMER: Sure. [*Worry bursting out of him.*] Virgil, did you see Merry any place? Lia-Pia was saying something about the *signora,* but I didn't follow her too well—

VIRGIL: Merry went right after you. She'll be back. [*Virgil resumes his reading.*]

HOMER: I certainly hope she will. This *palazzo.* . . . [*Sighs, and wipes his spectacles.*] A person as delicate as Merry could easily get lost in a *palazzo* like this. Pardon me, Angelo, I'm sorry I had to keep you waiting, I got snarled up with the hired help, she only speaks Italian, I didn't get what she was trying to tell me. . . .

[MERRY *comes through the door at the left.*]

MERRY: O, Homer, there you are. I was— [*Stopping and dimpling prettily*] Why, I didn't know we had company.

HOMER: Honey, I'd like to have you meet Mr. Angelo Lumaca.

ANGELO: Call me please Angelo.

MERRY: Angelo? Why, that must mean angel. That's a perfectly darling name. I'd certainly feel very privileged to call you by a name like that. Welcome to our *palazzo*, Angelo. I certainly never thought I'd be welcoming a real Italian to a real Italian *palazzo*.

ANGELO: Welcome to Italy, Mrs. Knockerbicker. [*He kisses her hand.*]

MERRY [*delighted*]: You certainly have *palazzo* manners.

VIRGIL: Now she'll want us all to kiss her hand every morning. It'll become a ritual, like the breakfast food.

HOMER: Now see here, Virgil—

MERRY: Now, Homer, quit picking on Virgil. You know he can't help himself.

ANGELO [*conversationally, trying to help them steer past a family row*]: You hired this *palazzo*, Mr. Knockerbicker?

HOMER [*distractedly*]: What? O yeh, sure. For our vacation.

ANGELO: You have a very old *palazzo* here, Mr. Knockerbicker. *Cinquecento*.

VIRGIL: And boy is it hideous.

MERRY [*deeply reproachful*]: Why, Virgil, how can you *say* such a thing?

ANGELO: O, no, Mr. Knockerbicker junior, you must be mistaken. This *palazzo* is very old, it is of the *rinascimento*, you understand? of the sixteenth century. So it *cannot* be hideous.

MERRY: O, don't take any account of Virgil. Have you looked out the window, Angelo? We have a real Italian yard out there, a *giardino*.

ANGELO: La signora parla italiano!

MERRY [*almost ecstatic with pleasure*]: O, no, not really, just a word or two I picked up from the hired help, but I certainly hope to learn a lot more. Yes, we have a real Italian *giardino*, and real Italian doves and real Italian chickens. I didn't learn the Italian for doves and chickens yet. But I get a big thrill just from watching those chickens and knowing every one of them is a real Italian chicken.

ANGELO [*with a glance through the window*]: You have twenty, thirty hens out there and only two cocks. Nice life for the cocks, eh?

VIRGIL: If you like responsibility.

HOMER [*belatedly understanding some at least of* ANGELO'*s remark*]: O, you mean roosters.

ANGELO: Please?

VIRGIL: Somebody sold you English English instead of American English, Angelo. In the United States we have to call them roosters, because American women have such effortlessly sexual trains of thought.

MERRY [*very rappingly*]: Virgil, will you please be quiet?

HOMER: What'd he say, Merry? I didn't get it.

MERRY: Don't let's any of us pay any attention to Virgil. He certainly has some anti-social compulsions this morning. But I'm not going to let anything spoil this wonderful place. D'you know, Angelo, living here, I can just imagine I'm back in those old days, with knights and cardinals and poison and frescoes and illuminated manuscripts. . . . O, I was just wild to get here. Last fall, I said to Mr. Knockerbicker "Homer, if it's the last thing you ever do for me, take me to Italy."

HOMER [*worrying*]: Yeh, I know, honey, but in those days they didn't have too good a concept of hygiene, and an old place like this . . .

MERRY: Homer, quit worrying. We're making out fine.

HOMER: So far honey. Knock on wood. [*Casting about anxiously.*] Where *is* some wood? Hell, this *palazzo's* all marble.

VIRGIL: There's the Coca-Cola crate.

HOMER: O, sure. [*He knocks on it.*] Thanks, Virgil.

MERRY: Now, Homer, quit fussing. What *could* happen?

HOMER [*putting an arm round her, drawing her convulsively to him and drooling a little over her hair*]: You're a brave little person, Merry. D'you know, Angelo, when we came here, they didn't even have a *shower* in this *palazzo,* only a tub.

MERRY: Relax, Homer, will you. You'll get yourself a duodenal. Just relax, and let the lovely Italian culture just seep into you.

HOMER: Maybe I'll get around to that, baby, when I got this place fixed so it's good enough for you.

MERRY: O, you take marvellous care of me, Homer. D'you know, Angelo, Homer had a shower fitted.

HOMER: Yeh, I had this shower fitted, and I installed another icebox—

MERRY: Why, yes, Angelo, Homer had a complete kitchen installed right here [*She points to the door at the right.*]—it's right through there just next door to the living room, so we don't have to have our food cooked by the hired help any more—

HOMER: When we first came, the hired help wanted to cook everything, but she was operating under pretty primitive conditions—

MERRY: O, it wasn't just the con*di*tions, Homer dear, it was the calories. I don't know, Angelo, if you ever saw a breakdown of the calorific content of olive oil, but believe you me it would horrify you. Well, the first thing Homer did, he imported a stock of low-calory cooking medium from the States, and then he fixed up this little kitchen right out there—

HOMER: Yeh, well, we have this kitchen, but there are some gadgets I wasn't yet able to find in Italy, and some we have that I imported but they're not yet operational—

ANGELO [*excitedly trying to get a word in*]: But, Mr. Knockerbicker, listen, *please.* This is why I am here.

HOMER: Why you are—I don't get it. Pardon me a moment, Angelo, I have to wipe off my lenses again. [*He does so.*]

ANGELO [*pleadingly*]: Please, Mr. Knockerbicker. I am the man who has come to fix the waste disposal unit!

HOMER [*amazed*]: No-o-o? [*Putting on his now wiped spectacles and stepping forward.*] Well, how do you like that? Hullo there again.

ANGELO: Hullo.

HOMER: Hi.

ANGELO: Ciao.

HOMER [*laughing*]: We-ell. I guess that just about takes care of it. You know, I guess I thought that as you aren't an American you wouldn't know how to fix a waste disposal unit.

ANGELO: I am the accredited Italian agent. I have here my card. [*He proffers it, then reads it aloud.*] You see. I am the accredited agent of the Atlantic Seaboard Waste Disposal Unit Corporation of New York, NY, USA.

HOMER: Well, what do you know? Isn't that swell, Merry? Now we can have that waste disposal unit operational.

ANGELO [*with self-assurance*]: You certainly can, Mr. Knockerbicker.

MERRY [*graciously social*]: Homer, would you take Angelo through there and show him where it has to be connected?

HOMER [*happily*]: I sure will. [*He ushers* ANGELO *across the room and opens the door at the right for him.*] Right through here, Angelo.

ANGELO [*pausing at the door to make a declaration*]: You are going to enjoy this waste disposal unit, Mrs. Knockerbicker. [*Reciting.*] This is the finest waste disposal unit on the market, a triumph of American technical know-how. This unit will dispose of *anything*. Say goodbye forever to malodorous, unhygienic, germ-breeding, squelchy bundles. The Atlantic Seaboard waste disposal unit takes over. Soggy, crunchy, pulpy, bony, mushy, spiny—it's all one to the Atlantic Seaboard waste disposal unit.

VIRGIL: The guy certainly is accredited.

MERRY [*on a sudden thought*]: Say, Homer, ask him if he ever fixed one before.

HOMER: You got something there, Merry. They told me this was the first they imported into Italy. Say, Angelo, did you ever fix one before?

ANGELO [*pained, and holding up his hand like a traffic policeman*]: Mr. Knockerbicker. Mrs. Knockerbicker. Please. I am the accredited agent. I fix it.

[HOMER *and* ANGELO *go through the door at the right.* MERRY, *swinging her pony tail, trips her way to the unoccupied window-seat, perches one urchin knee on it and looks out of the window.* VIRGIL *reads for a moment, then without looking up:*]

VIRGIL: You mad at me, Merry?

MERRY: Why, no, Virgil. I guess I maybe would be, if I didn't know you had problems.

VIRGIL: I got problems O.K. How'm I going to end this poem?

MERRY: Maybe it'd help you feel less mixed-up, Virgil, if you kind of explained your problem to me.

VIRGIL: I guess it's easier for composers. They just come back to the key note, and it sounds swell.

MERRY: And you want kind of a key note for your poem?

VIRGIL: It's not that simple. I need a climax—something terrible and tragic: and then a resolution: and then some kind of final chorus, to round the thing off.

MERRY: I'll keep it in mind, Virgil. Maybe I'll come up with something we can kick around together.

[HOMER *returns, much less worried than usual.*]

HOMER: He's making out fine in there. We'll soon have that unit operational. [*Going up to her and giving her a squeeze.*] And how're *you* making out, Merry? [*He places an infatuated kiss on top of her head.*] Still looking out that window?

MERRY: O, I'm as happy as I can be just so I can watch those romantic old doves and those quaint little old chickens.

HOMER [*sifting her pony tail through his fingers*]: You're just a lovely little person, Merry. You're just so satisfied with the simple things in life.

MERRY [*suddenly freezing with horror as she gazes through the window*]: Homer!

HOMER: Why, Merry! Hey, Merry! Merry, what's your problem? Merry, look at me! Virgil! She's gone quite rigid, like she was in shock. I guess I ought to pat her cheeks. Hey, Merry, Merry! [HOMER *nervously pats her cheeks.*]

MERRY: Homer, I been watching those roosters—

HOMER: Sure, Merry, I know it—

MERRY: Homer, *one of those roosters is a degenerate.*

HOMER [*agonisedly, very gently*]: My poor little Merry, my poor little Merry, why did you have to be born so sensitive? Now, listen, Merry, you quit thinking of it right now. You start right in thinking about something beautiful. You start thinking about music or lovely old paintings or beautiful literature. . . .

VIRGIL: Why don't you tell her go take a look at the waste disposal unit?

HOMER: Why, Merry, you hear what Virgil said? I think that's a swell idea. Come along now. [*He leads her across the room to the door at the right.*] If there's one thing that ought to take your mind off all the ugly, unclean things that happen in this world, it's that waste disposal unit. [*Opening the door for her.*] You go right on in there, Merry, and see how the project's making out. [HOMER *tenderly closes the door after Merry and then marches back across the room.*]

HOMER: Now what're we going to do?

VIRGIL: I don't know why, but that question always panics me. Do about what, anyway?

HOMER: That rooster, of course. I can't ask Merry to share the premises with a rooster that's a degenerate.

VIRGIL: I don't see why it's any worse than asking her to share them with a brother-in-law that's a degenerate.

HOMER [*angrily*]: Will you quit talking that way? You'd be a perfectly healthful American boy, if you'd only try.

VIRGIL: I guess that's what's unhealthful about me. I can't even try to try.

HOMER: Why not, for pity's sakes? Don't I have enough on my mind as it is?

VIRGIL: Maybe I'm afraid it would spoil my work.

HOMER: Now that's another thing. I keep trying to get round to talking with you about that. How much longer is your work going to take?

VIRGIL: I can't say. I'm kind of held up for a climax.

[HOMER *deliberates, then:*]

HOMER: You know, Virgil, I sometimes get to wondering if you wrote anything at all.

VIRGIL [*deliberates, then deciding to take up the challenge*]: O.K. I'll read it to you.

HOMER: Right now?

VIRGIL: Mm-hm.

HOMER: But you didn't finish it yet.

VIRGIL: I'll read it as far as I went. Maybe you'll come up with something for the ending.

HOMER: I don't think I have any talent.

VIRGIL: Then sit down, brother, and listen to mine.

HOMER: How can I sit, there's no place to—I guess I can stand. It won't take that long, will it?

VIRGIL: Why didn't you hire some furnishings for this *palazzo?*

HOMER: That's a very selfish request, Virgil. You're the one that sits around all day. Maybe I'll hire some furnishings when I get round to it, but the first problem is to make the basic living conditions fit for Merry.

VIRGIL: O.K. brother, you stand. But don't move around any, you could distract me.

HOMER: O.K. O.K. Quit stalling, Virgil. Shoot.

VIRGIL [*turns back to the beginning of his book, clears his throat, then breaks off for a preliminary*]: Say, Homer. I hope you know this isn't going to be poetry like you mean poetry. It's more like—did you ever read any Chinese poetry?

HOMER: Sure, I guess I read some Chinese poetry some place, some magazine or something. In English.

VIRGIL: O, my poetry's in English, too. I just wanted you to know the opening sequences are modelled on Chinese poetry.

HOMER: Virgil, do you figure you can sell this? Is there a market for it? I don't know that the Chinese market's too easy to break into. I don't know, but it could even be that poetry is scheduled.

VIRGIL: Scheduled?

HOMER: Schedule of prohibited exports. I mean, if you're thinking of *Red* China.

VIRGIL: Brother!

HOMER: O.K. O.K., I didn't say a thing, go right ahead.

VIRGIL [*announcing*]: Section One. [*Reading:*]

> The American Woman
> Is strange, terrible and beautiful,
> Like fruits from the sea.
> There is nothing she would not ask her husband to do for her.
> For this reason
> She appears to be the most independent woman in the world,
> Just as aristocrats are said to be "of independent means"
> When in fact they are supported by slave labour.

[*There is a pause.*]

HOMER: Is that all?

VIRGIL: That's all of Section One.

HOMER: Maybe I'll get to see more in it when I become better accustomed to it.

VIRGIL [*reading*]:

> Section Two.
> The American Woman has grown
> Like a cactus

In a place where there is no water.
The American Woman would rather be a lovely person
Than be herself.
The American Woman would rather be a lovely, warm, genuine, sincere person
Than simply be.

[VIRGIL *leaves a brief pause.*]

HOMER: Say, Virgil, do you think Merry's making out O.K. in there? Suppose this guy
Angelo makes a pass at her?
VIRGIL: Homer, quit worrying and concentrate. Merry can handle it.
HOMER: I doubt that she can. That guy's a Latin, he's hot-blooded—
VIRGIL: You don't seem too well acquainted with Latin mores. If he does make a pass,
he'll just pinch her fanny. That's the climactic act for Latins. Merry'll just think a
mosquito got her.
HOMER: I don't know that she—
VIRGIL: Of *course* she can handle it, Homer, she'll handle it with a flit gun. Now can
I read the third *canto?*
HOMER: Third what? Sounds like you were going horseback riding.
VIRGIL: Homer, you're not *that* illiterate. Or maybe you meant it as a gag. The third
canto is freer and more rhapsodic in style.
HOMER: O.K. O.K. I guess we'll get to hear of it if Merry has problems.
VIRGIL [*reading*]: There is only one American Woman but she has two faces: one
young, one old.
   When she is young, she is younger than you would have thought possible. When
she is old, she is older than the rocks she has persuaded her husband to buy for her.
   The young American Woman is like an ad in a magazine of a glass of milk fresh
from the icebox. She looks thirst quenching. But when you taste her, she tastes of
wood-pulp.
   The young American Woman is a wax apple. She is flawless. But she has no sap.
Except her husband.
   When you have talked with her a little while, you realise she was not begotten by
sexual intercourse. Therefore:
   When she grows old, she becomes a goddess. I love her best when she is old. For
then she commands me more.
   [*Aside*] You know, I really mean that, Homer. I'm determined to live to be a very
old man, because I want to see Merry grow old. [*Resuming:*]

I followed the American goddess
Through the beautiful shrines of Europe.
I shadowed her through the Louvre,
I nearly caught up with her in the Rue de la Paix;
I watched her buying leather goods from a tiny but very expensive basement shop
   in Florence;
I dodged between her and the sunlight in Roman colonnades;

I glimpsed her in Castile;
When I stood in the Parthenon she was there.
She loves all that is old and said to be beautiful.
She has no taste.
But she has attended many seminars on good taste.

The old American Woman
Is all locust and no wild honey.
She is dry and mottled, like peanut brittle.
If you held her and bent her, she would snap.
But you do not lay hands on a cult object.
The strands of her hair are one with the spun gold she wears at her wrists and
    neck;
Her eyes are one with the topazes she wears on her knucklebones;
The skin of her forearms is one with the alligator hide that makes her purse.
I followed the tinkle of her charms on her charm bracelet
And the tinkle of her beaten metal hair.
I followed the clacking of her heels
And the clacking of her voice,
Which is an almost perfect imitation of the human voice.
I followed. I am unnatural; I am perverse.

The American Woman is more strange and more bizarre
Than the art of the mummy-maker.
And she is more old.
Organic in form, she is not created by life,
But is slowly deposited, like a tree of crystals
Imitating a baroque pearl.
The American Woman is a wax avocado pear
From a desert under the sea

[ANGELO *bursts in from the door at the right and flings himself, across the doorway, into the posture
of the blinded Oedipus.*]

ANGELO [*sobbing and groaning*]: O no no no no no no no no no. Orrore! [*He falls silent; his
groans are quietly reiterated by a soft mechanical chug-chug from the next room. For a second everyone
is too shocked to show reaction. Then* HOMER *dashes across the room towards* ANGELO, *who
compassionately bars the way.*]

HOMER [*trying desperately to get past*]: What happened? What happened to Merry? Let
me in there, Angelo, I got to get in there and see what happened to Merry.

ANGELO: Non c'è niente da vedere.

HOMER [*distractedly over his shoulder*]: What'd he say, Virgil?

VIRGIL [*threnodically*]: He says there is nothing to see.

HOMER [*in a groan of horror*]: What?

ANGELO [*pleading distressfully*]: Mr. Knockerbicker, I *tell* her not to lean over it and peer
down it, but she wants to check I fixed it right—

HOMER [*beside himself*]: Can't you reverse the machinery or something? [*Bursting past* ANGELO.] Let me *in* there—

ANGELO [*appealing to Virgil*]: Mr. Knockerbicker junior, *you* are understanding, are you not? I *did* fix it right. If only she had believed me. Of *course* I reverse the machinery, but this is a very efficient unit. In thirty seconds, everything is—you understand, Mr. Knockerbicker junior?—*everything* . . .

[*The noise of the machinery is switched off.* HOMER *plods brokenly back into the* salone.]

HOMER: My little Merry! My little Merry! She was such a dainty little person, the last thing she would have wanted was to get mixed up with the garbage.

[*There is a moment's respectful silence.*]

Virgil, I know you will never forget that just before—why, it could even have been at the very moment—[HOMER *nearly breaks down.*] Well, anyhow, that you were just saying you wanted to live to see what a lovely lovely old lady Merry was going to grow into.

[LIA-PIA *shuffles unperturbedly into the room by the door at the left. She is followed by* MRS. VAN DEN MOST—*an older Merry and taken, of course, by the same actress.*]

LIA-PIA: Signori, ho incontrato queste signore davanti alla casa, non so cosa vuole. . . .

[LIA-PIA *shuffles out by the route she came, closing the door behind her.*]

HOMER [*horrified to reeling point*]: Mrs. van den *Most!*

MRS. VAN DEN MOST [*waggishly reproachful*]: Now, Homer. You know I asked you to call me something more intimate, such as Mom, because I think it will be so lovely for Merry to feel her family has been really integrated into her marriage.

HOMER: I didn't know—

MRS. VAN DEN MOST [*wagging a waggish finger at him*]: I know it, Homer, you didn't even know I was in Europe. Well, I figured I'd just hop over and see how you were taking care of my little girl. [HOMER *hides his face, and groans.*] I was counting on giving you a real surprise, and I must say you certainly seem to have gotten one. I wasn't even going to ring the doorbell, I was just snooping around outside, when your lovely old Italian hired help came out to feed your chickens. Those certainly are lovely chickens, Homer, I can just guess how Merry loves those chickens. And your lovely old Italian hired help brought me right along in. [*Noticing, with displeasure.*] O. Virgil's here. Hi, Virgil. I certainly hope you're beginning to get a hold on those problems of yours. [*Noticing, with pleasure.*] Why, we have company, I didn't notice.

VIRGIL: This is Signor Angelo Lumaca.

MRS. VAN DEN MOST: Why, you must be an Italian! I just love Italians, I love your *Renaissance*, I feel sure you must be a very good friend of my little girl, because she just loves your *Ren*aissance too. Now where *is* my little girl? No, don't tell me. I can guess. Merry always takes such good care of her husband, Signor Lumaca, she's a real homebody, I don't have to ask where she is. I feel positive she's right along in the kitchen. Homer just loves her homebody ways, don't you, Homer? Right from the start, that girl loved to be in the kitchen. She has such a happy temperament, she makes everyone happy. Well, I should know. Right from the start she made *me* happy. Why, d'you know, Signor Lumaca, that little girl was toilet-trained before she was one year old. It was on account of she had such a happy temperament I persuaded Mr. van den Most to let me call her Merry. Lots of folks, when they first meet her, they think she's called Mary—Maria, as you would say it, Signor Lumaca—but no, her name is really Merry, M-E-double-R-Y, because, I always tell them, she *is*. Now where *is* the kitchen? No, naughty me, I don't need to ask. I didn't pass it on my way along, so I guess it must be right through here. [*She opens the door at the right.*] I'll just go give Merry a little surprise. [*Calling:*] Merry! Merry dear! [*Popping her head back into the* salone] I didn't find Merry yet, Homer, but I saw you had a waste disposal unit installed. Now that's very thoughtful of you, Homer, I'm sure Merry appreciates that. I wouldn't have thought you could obtain one over here. Well, I guess you imported it, but I reckon it was quite a problem for you getting it operational. I wonder if you got it fixed right. I'll just go take a quick look.

[MRS. VAN DEN MOST *hurries out. At once, the machinery noise begins again.*]

ANGELO [*lunging after her*]: No! Mrs. van den Most, no! Come back! No!
HOMER [*dashing across the room*]: Stop her, Angelo! I'm coming! Stop her!

[ANGELO *and* HOMER *sprint through the door at the right. Even* VIRGIL *is sufficiently anxious to discard his book, rises from the window-seat, and stands tense while he awaits the outcome.*]

[*The noise of the W.D.U. rises to a climax, and stops.* HOMER *and* ANGELO *return to the* salone.]

ANGELO [*with an explanatory, proving-his-point gesture*]: You see, Mr. Knockerbicker—
HOMER: Virgil—
VIRGIL [*incredulously*]: No?
HOMER: } *Yes.*
ANGELO: }
HOMER [*with deep, plodding philosophy*]: The way I look at it, God proposes—
VIRGIL: And the Atlantic Seaboard waste disposal unit disposes.
HOMER [*with not altogether reluctant resignation*]: Well, everything has come to an end—
VIRGIL [*rising to exultation*]: And the Atlantic Seaboard waste disposal unit is the American male's best friend.
HOMER }
        } [*beginning a stomping dance with one another*]:
VIRGIL }

> Soggy crunchy
> Pulpy bony
> Mushy spiny

VIRGIL: Mottled shiny

HOMER: ⎤
VIRGIL: ⎦ Pulpy bony

ANGELO [*trying a last plea*]: Signori Knockerbicker, *please*—

VIRGIL [*stomping gaily*]: How're you feeling now, brother?

HOMER [*likewise*]: How'm I feeling now? [*As in a college cry*] M-E-double-R-Y.

HOMER ⎤
VIRGIL ⎦ [*in a shout in unison*]: Merry!

VIRGIL: Say goodbye forever to squelchy bundles!

ANGELO [*giving up restraint and joining the dance with a wild, free-lance fling, as he sings in a bold tenor*]: La donna è mobile! La donna è mobile!

HOMER ⎤
VIRGIL ⎬ [*stomping and chanting*]:
ANGELO ⎦

> Soggy crunchy
> Honeybunchy
> Sodden dry
> Sweetiepie
> Say goodbye
> Mushy spiny
> Dainty tiny
> Lovely happy
> Minced-up pappy
> Very merry

ANGELO [*floating his tenor above the stomp*]: La donna è mobile.

VIRGIL [*basso profondo*]: E disponibile!

[*There is a general, happy, panting collapse onto the floor.*]

VIRGIL [*happily*]: Angelo, did it take but *everything?*

ANGELO [*with happy assurance*]: Every single thing, Mr. Knockerbicker junior.

HOMER: Even the second time round?

ANGELO: Second time round was even more efficient, Mr. Knockerbicker. That machine likes something tough to bite on.

VIRGIL [*solemnly*]: Angelo, Homer, I guess we have witnessed the ultimate triumph of American technology.

Curtain

QUESTIONS

1. What class and culture is the playwright satirizing?
2. The playwright mentions that Virgil has spent ten years writing his poem. What does she mean to imply about his personality?
3. The Knockerbickers display a great deal of concern about propriety. What are some of the more absurd anxieties about doing things the "proper" way?
4. Why does the family appear so happy at the end of the play, despite the fact that Merry has disappeared down the waste disposal unit? What aspect of bourgeois life is the author commenting on?

Susan Glaspell

SUPPRESSED DESIRES
A Comedy in Two Episodes

In Collaboration with George Cram Cook

--- CHARACTERS ---

HENRIETTA BREWSTER
STEPHEN BREWSTER
MABEL

Scene—A Studio Apartment

SCENE I

*A studio apartment in an upper story, Washington Square South. Through an immense north window in the back wall appear tree tops and the upper part of the Washington Arch. Beyond it you look up Fifth Avenue. Near the window is a big table, loaded at one end with serious-looking books and austere scientific periodicals. At the other end are architect's drawings, blue prints, dividing compasses, square, ruler, etc. At the left is a door leading to the rest of the apartment; at the right the outer door. A breakfast table is set for three, but only two are seated at it—*HENRIETTA *and* STEPHEN BREWSTER. *As the curtains withdraw* STEVE *pushes back his coffee cup and sits dejected.*

HENRIETTA: It isn't the coffee, Steve dear. There's nothing the matter with the coffee. There's something the matter with *you.*

STEVE [*doggedly*]: There may be something the matter with my stomach.

HENRIETTA [*scornfully*]: Your stomach! The trouble is not with your stomach but in your subconscious mind.

STEVE: Subconscious piffle! [*Takes morning paper and tries to read.*]

HENRIETTA: Steve, you never used to be so disagreeable. You certainly have got some sort of a complex. You're all inhibited. You're no longer open to new ideas. You won't listen to a word about psychoanalysis.

STEVE: A word! I've listened to volumes!

HENRIETTA: You've ceased to be creative in architecture—your work isn't going well. You're not sleeping well—.

STEVE: How can I sleep, Henrietta, when you're always waking me up to find out what I'm dreaming?

HENRIETTA: But dreams are so important, Steve. If you'd tell yours to Dr. Russell he'd find out exactly what's wrong with you.

STEVE: There's nothing wrong with me.

HENRIETTA: You don't even talk as well as you used to.

STEVE: Talk? I can't say a thing without you looking at me in that dark fashion you have when you're on the trail of a complex.

HENRIETTA: This very irritability indicates that you're suffering from some suppressed desire.

STEVE: I'm suffering from a suppressed desire for a little peace.

HENRIETTA: Dr. Russell is doing simply wonderful things with nervous cases. Won't you go to him, Steve?

STEVE [*slamming down his newspaper*]: No, Henrietta, I won't!

HENRIETTA: But Stephen—!

STEVE: Tst! I hear Mabel coming. Let's not be at each other's throats the first day of her visit. [*He takes out cigarettes.* MABEL *comes in from door left, the side opposite* STEVE, *so that he is facing her. She is wearing a rather fussy negligee in contrast to* HENRIETTA, *who wears "radical" clothes.* MABEL *is what is called plump.*]

MABEL: Good morning.

HENRIETTA: Oh, here you are, little sister.

STEVE: Good morning, Mabel.

[MABEL *nods to him and turns, her face lighting up, to* HENRIETTA.]

HENRIETTA [*giving* MABEL *a hug as she leans against her*]: It's so good to have you here. I was going to let you sleep, thinking you'd be tired after the long trip. Sit down. There'll be fresh toast in a minute and [*rising*] will you have—

MABEL: Oh, I ought to have told you, Henrietta. Don't get anything for me. I'm not eating breakfast.

HENRIETTA [*at first in mere surprise*]: Not eating breakfast? [*She sits down, then leans toward* MABEL *who is seated now, and scrutinizes her.*]

STEVE [*half to himself*]: The psychoanalytical look!

HENRIETTA: Mabel, why are you not eating breakfast?

MABEL [*a little startled*]: Why, no particular reason. I just don't care much for breakfast,

and they say it keeps down—[*A hand on her hip—the gesture of one who is "reducing"*] that is, it's a good thing to go without it.

HENRIETTA: Don't you sleep well? Did you sleep well last night?

MABEL: Oh, yes, I slept all right. Yes, I slept fine last night, only [*laughing*] I did have the funniest dream!

STEVE: S-h! S-t!

HENRIETTA [*moving closer*]: And what did you dream, Mabel?

STEVE: Look-a-here, Mabel, I feel it's my duty to put you on. Don't tell Henrietta your dreams. If you do she'll find out that you have an underground desire to kill your father and marry your mother—

HENRIETTA: Don't be absurd, Stephen Brewster. [*Sweetly to* MABEL] What was your dream, dear?

MABEL [*laughing*]: Well, I dreamed I was a hen.

HENRIETTA: A hen?

MABEL: Yes; and I was pushing along through a crowd as fast as I could, but being a hen I couldn't walk very fast—it was like having a tight skirt, you know; and there was some sort of creature in a blue cap—you know how mixed up dreams are—and it kept shouting after me, "Step, Hen! Step, Hen!" until I got all excited and just couldn't move at all.

HENRIETTA [*resting chin in palm and peering*]: You say you became much excited?

MABEL [*laughing*]: Oh, yes; I was in a terrible state.

HENRIETTA [*leaning back, murmurs*]: This is significant.

STEVE: She dreams she's a hen. She is told to step lively. She becomes violently agitated. What can it mean?

HENRIETTA [*turning impatiently from him*]: Mabel, do you know anything about psycho-analysis?

MABEL [*feebly*]: Oh—not much. No—I— [*Brightening*] It's something about the war, isn't it?

STEVE: Not that kind of war.

MABEL [*abashed*]: I thought it might be the name of a new explosive.

STEVE: It *is*.

MABEL [*apologetically to* HENRIETTA, *who is frowning*]: You see, Henrietta, I—we do not live in touch with intellectual things, as you do. Bob being a dentist—somehow our friends—

STEVE [*softly*]: Oh, to be a dentist! [*Goes to window and stands looking out.*]

HENRIETTA: Don't you see anything more of that editorial writer—what was his name?

MABEL: Lyman Eggleston?

HENRIETTA: Yes, Eggleston. He was in touch with things. Don't you see him?

MABEL: Yes, I see him once in a while. Bob doesn't like him very well.

HENRIETTA: Your husband does not like Lyman Eggleston? [*Mysteriously*] Mabel, are you perfectly happy with your husband?

STEVE [*sharply*]: Oh, come now, Henrietta—that's going a little strong!

HENRIETTA: Are you perfectly happy with him, Mabel?

[STEVE *goes to work-table.*]

MABEL: Why—yes—I guess so. Why—of course I am!

HENRIETTA: Are you happy? Or do you only think you are? Or do you only think you
ought to be?

MABEL: Why, Henrietta, I don't know what you mean!

STEVE [*seizes stack of books and magazines and dumps them on the breakfast table*]: This is what
she means, Mabel. Psychoanalysis. My work-table groans with it. Books by Freud,
the new Messiah; books by Jung, the new St. Paul; the Psychoanalytical Review—
back numbers two-fifty per.

MABEL: But what's it all about?

STEVE: All about your sub-un-non-conscious mind and desires you know not of. They
may be doing you a great deal of harm. You may go crazy with them. Oh, yes! People
are doing it right and left. Your dreaming you're a hen— [*Shakes his head darkly.*]

HENRIETTA: Any fool can ridicule anything.

MABEL [*hastily, to avert a quarrel*]: But what do you say it is, Henrietta?

STEVE [*looking at his watch*]: Oh, if Henrietta's going to start that! [*During* HENRIETTA'*s
next speech settles himself at work-table and sharpens a lead pencil.*]

HENRIETTA: It's like this, Mabel. You want something. You think you can't have it.
You think it's wrong. So you try to think you don't want it. Your mind protects
you—avoids pain—by refusing to think the forbidden thing. But it's there just the
same. It stays there shut up in your unconscious mind, and it festers.

STEVE: Sort of an ingrowing mental toenail.

HENRIETTA: Precisely. The forbidden impulse is there full of energy which has simply
got to do something. It breaks into your consciousness in disguise, masks itself in
dreams, makes all sorts of trouble. In extreme cases it drives you insane.

MABEL [*with a gesture of horror*]: Oh!

HENRIETTA [*reassuring*]: But psychoanalysis has found out how to save us from that.
It brings into consciousness the suppressed desire that was making all the trouble.
Psychoanalysis is simply the latest scientific method of preventing and curing in-
sanity.

STEVE [*from his table*]: It is also the latest scientific method of separating families.

HENRIETTA [*mildly*]: Families that ought to be separated.

STEVE: The Dwights, for instance. You must have met them, Mabel, when you were
here before. Helen was living, apparently, in peace and happiness with good old Joe.
Well—she went to this psychoanalyzer—she was "psyched," and biff!—bang!—
home she comes with an unsuppressed desire to leave her husband. [*He starts work,
drawing lines on a drawing board with a T-square.*]

MABEL: How terrible! Yes, I remember Helen Dwight. But—but did she have such a
desire?

STEVE: First she'd known of it.

MABEL: And she *left* him?

HENRIETTA [*coolly*]: Yes, she did.

MABEL: Wasn't he good to her?

HENRIETTA: Why, yes, good enough.

MABEL: Wasn't he kind to her?

HENRIETTA: Oh, yes—kind to her.

MABEL: And she left her good, kind husband—!

HENRIETTA: Oh, Mabel! "Left her good, kind husband!" How naïve—forgive me, dear, but how bourgeois you are! She came to know herself. And she had the courage!

MABEL: I may be very naïve and—bourgeois—but I don't see the good of a new science that breaks up homes.

[STEVE *applauds.*]

STEVE: In enlightening Mabel, we mustn't neglect to mention the case of Art Holden's private secretary, Mary Snow, who has just been informed of her suppressed desire for her employer.

MABEL: Why, I think it is terrible, Henrietta! It would be better if we didn't know such things about ourselves.

HENRIETTA: No, Mabel, that is the old way.

MABEL: But—but her employer? Is he married?

STEVE [*grunts*]: Wife and four children.

MABEL: Well, then, what good does it do the girl to be told she has a desire for him? There's nothing can be done about it.

HENRIETTA: Old institutions will have to be reshaped so that something can be done in such cases. It happens, Mabel, that this suppressed desire was on the point of landing Mary Snow in the insane asylum. Are you so tight-minded that you'd rather have her in the insane asylum than break the conventions?

MABEL: But—but have people always had these awful suppressed desires?

HENRIETTA: Always.

STEVE: But they've just been discovered.

HENRIETTA: The harm they do has just been discovered. And free, sane people must face the fact that they have to be dealt with.

MABEL [*stoutly*]: I don't believe they have them in Chicago.

HENRIETTA [*business of giving* MABEL *up*]: People "have them" wherever the living Libido—the center of the soul's energy—is in conflict with petrified moral codes. That means everywhere in civilization. Psychoanalysis—

STEVE: Good God! I've got the roof in the cellar!

HENRIETTA: The roof in the cellar!

STEVE [*holding plan at arm's length*]: That's what psychoanalysis does!

HENRIETTA: That's what psychoanalysis could *un*-do. Is it any wonder I'm concerned about Steve? He dreamed the other night that the walls of his room melted away and he found himself alone in a forest. Don't you see how significant it is for an architect to have *walls* slip away from him? It symbolizes his loss of grip in his work. There's some suppressed desire—

STEVE [*hurling his ruined plan viciously to the floor*]: Suppressed hell!

HENRIETTA: You speak more truly than you know. It is through suppressions that hells are formed in us.

MABEL [*looking at* STEVE, *who is tearing his hair*]: Don't you think it would be a good thing, Henrietta, if we went somewhere else? [*They rise and begin to pick up the dishes.* MABEL *drops a plate which breaks.* HENRIETTA *draws up short and looks at her—the psychoanalytic look*] I'm sorry, Henrietta. One of the Spode plates, too. [*Surprised and resentful as* HENRIETTA *continues to peer at her*] Don't take it so to heart, Henrietta.

HENRIETTA: I can't help taking it to heart.

MABEL: I'll get you another. [*Pause. More sharply as* HENRIETTA *does not answer*] I said I'll get you another plate, Henrietta.

HENRIETTA: It's not the plate.

MABEL: For heaven's sake, what is it then?

HENRIETTA: It's the significant little false movement that made you drop it.

MABEL: Well, I suppose everyone makes a false movement once in a while.

HENRIETTA: Yes, Mabel, but these false movements all mean something.

MABEL [*about to cry*]: I don't think that's very nice! It was just because I happened to think of that Mabel Snow you were talking about—

HENRIETTA: *Mabel* Snow!

MABEL: Snow—Snow—well, what was her name, then?

HENRIETTA: Her name is Mary. You substituted *your own* name for hers.

MABEL: Well, *Mary* Snow, then; *Mary* Snow. I never heard her name but once. I don't see anything to make such a fuss about.

HENRIETTA [*gently*]: Mabel dear—mistakes like that in names—

MABEL [*desperately*]: They don't mean something, too, do they?

HENRIETTA [*gently*]: I am sorry, dear, but they do.

MABEL: But I'm always doing that!

HENRIETTA [*after a start of horror*]: My poor little sister, tell me about it.

MABEL: About what?

HENRIETTA: About your not being happy. About your longing for another sort of life.

MABEL: But I *don't.*

HENRIETTA: Ah, I understand these things, dear. You feel Bob is limiting you to a life in which you do not feel free—

MABEL: Henrietta! When did I ever say such a thing?

HENRIETTA: You said you are not in touch with things intellectual. You showed your feeling that it is Bob's profession—that has engendered a resentment which has colored your whole life with him.

MABEL: Why—Henri*etta!*

HENRIETTA: Don't be afraid of me, little sister. There's nothing can shock me or turn me from you. I am not like that. I wanted you to come for this visit because I had a feeling that you needed more from life than you were getting. No one of these things I have seen would excite my suspicion. It's the combination. You don't eat breakfast [*enumerating on her fingers*]; you make false moves; you substitute your own name for the name of another *whose love is misdirected.* You're nervous; you *look* queer; in your eyes there's a frightened look that is most unlike you. And this dream. A *hen.* Come with me this afternoon to Dr. Russell! Your whole life may be at stake, Mabel.

MABEL [*gasping*]: Henrietta, I—you—you always were the smartest in the family, and all that, but—this is terrible! I don't think we *ought* to think such things. [*Brightening*] Why, I'll tell you why I dreamed I was a hen. It was because last night, telling about that time in Chicago, you said I was as mad as a wet hen.

HENRIETTA [*superior*]: Did you dream you were a *wet* hen?

MABEL [*forced to admit it*]: No.

HENRIETTA: No. You dreamed you were a *dry* hen. And why, being a hen, were you urged to step?

MABEL: Maybe it's because when I am getting on a street car it always irritates me to have them call "Step lively."

HENRIETTA: No, Mabel, that is only a child's view of it—if you will forgive me. You see merely the elements used in the dream. You do not see into the dream; you do not see its meaning. This dream of the hen—

STEVE: Hen—hen—wet hen—dry hen—mad hen! [*Jumps up in a rage*] Let me out of this!

HENRIETTA [*hastily picking up dishes, speaks soothingly*]: Just a minute, dear, and we'll have things so you can work in quiet. Mabel and I are going to sit in my room. [*She goes out left, carrying dishes.*]

STEVE [*seizing hat and coat from an alcove near the outside door*]: I'm going to be psychoanalyzed. I'm going now! I'm going straight to that infallible doctor of hers—that priest of this new religion. If he's got honesty enough to tell Henrietta there's nothing the matter with my unconscious mind, perhaps I can be let alone about it, and then I *will* be all right. [*From the door in a low voice*] Don't tell Henrietta I'm going. It might take weeks, and I couldn't stand all the talk. [*He hurries out.*]

HENRIETTA [*returning*]: Where's Steve? Gone? [*With a hopeless gesture*] You see how impatient he is—how unlike himself! I tell you, Mabel, I'm nearly distracted about Steve.

MABEL: I think he's a little distracted, too.

HENRIETTA: Well, if he's gone—you might as well stay here. I have a committee meeting at the bookshop, and will have to leave you to yourself for an hour or two. [*As she puts her hat on, taking it from the alcove where* STEVE *found his, her eye, lighting up almost carnivorously, falls on an enormous volume on the floor beside the work-table. The book has been half hidden by the wastebasket. She picks it up and carries it around the table toward* MABEL] Here, dear, is one of the simplest statements of psychoanalysis. You just read this and then we can talk more intelligently. [MABEL *takes volume and staggers back under its weight to chair rear center,* HENRIETTA *goes to outer door, stops and asks abruptly*] How old is Lyman Eggleston?

MABEL [*promptly*]: He isn't forty yet. Why, what made you ask that, Henrietta? [*As she turns her head to look at* HENRIETTA *her hands move toward the upper corners of the book balanced on her knees.*]

HENRIETTA: Oh, nothing. Au revoir. [*She goes out.* MABEL *stares at the ceiling. The book slides to the floor. She starts; looks at the book, then at the broken plate on the table*] The plate!

The book! [*She lifts her eyes, leans forward, elbow on knee, chin on knuckles and plaintively queries*] Am I unhappy?

SCENE II

Two weeks later. The stage is as in Scene I, except that the breakfast table has been removed. During the first few minutes the dusk of a winter afternoon deepens. Out of the darkness spring rows of double street-lights almost meeting in the distance. HENRIETTA *is at the psychoanalytical end of* STEVE'S *work-table, surrounded by open books and periodicals, writing.* STEVE *enters briskly.*

STEVE: What are you doing, my dear?

HENRIETTA: My paper for the Liberal Club.

STEVE: Your paper on—?

HENRIETTA: On a subject which does not have your sympathy.

STEVE: Oh, I'm not sure I'm wholly out of sympathy with psychoanalysis, Henrietta. You worked it so hard. I couldn't even take a bath without its meaning something.

HENRIETTA [*loftily*]: I talked it because I knew you needed it.

STEVE: You haven't said much about it these last two weeks. Uh—your faith in it hasn't weakened any?

HENRIETTA: Weakened? It's grown stronger with each new thing I've come to know. And Mabel. She is with Dr. Russell now. Dr. Russell is wonderful! From what Mabel tells me I believe his analysis is going to prove that I was right. Today I discovered a remarkable confirmation of my theory in the hen-dream.

STEVE: What is your theory?

HENRIETTA: Well, you know about Lyman Eggleston. I've wondered about him. I've never seen him, but I know he's less bourgeois than Mabel's other friends—more intellectual—and [*significantly*] she doesn't see much of him because Bob doesn't like him.

STEVE: But what's the confirmation?

HENRIETTA: Today I noticed the first syllable of his name.

STEVE: Ly?

HENRIETTA: No—egg.

STEVE: Egg?

HENRIETTA [*patiently*]: Mabel dreamed she was a hen. [STEVE *laughs*] You wouldn't laugh if you knew how important names are in interpreting dreams. Freud is full of just such cases in which a whole hidden complex is revealed by a single significant syllable—like this egg.

STEVE: Doesn't the traditional relation of hen and egg suggest rather a maternal feeling?

HENRIETTA: There is something maternal in Mabel's love, of course, but that's only one element.

STEVE: Well, suppose Mabel hasn't a suppressed desire to be this gentleman's mother,

but his beloved. What's to be done about it? What about Bob? Don't you think it's going to be a little rough on him?

HENRIETTA: That can't be helped. Bob, like everyone else, must face the facts of life. If Dr. Russell should arrive independently at this same interpretation I shall not hesitate to advise Mabel to leave her present husband.

STEVE: Um—hum! [*The lights go up on Fifth Avenue.* STEVE *goes to the window and looks out*] How long is it we've lived here, Henrietta?

HENRIETTA: Why, this is the third year, Steve.

STEVE: I—we—one would miss this view if one went away, wouldn't one?

HENRIETTA: How strangely you speak! Oh, Stephen, I *wish* you'd go to Dr. Russell. Don't think my fears have abated because I've been able to restrain myself. I had to on account of Mabel. But now, dear—won't you go?

STEVE: I— [*He breaks off, turns on the light, then comes and sits beside* HENRIETTA] How long have we been married, Henrietta?

HENRIETTA: Stephen, I don't understand you! You *must* go to Dr. Russell.

STEVE: I have gone.

HENRIETTA: You—what?

STEVE [*jauntily*]: Yes, Henrietta, I've been psyched.

HENRIETTA: You went to Dr. Russell?

STEVE: The same.

HENRIETTA: And what did he say?

STEVE: He said—I—I was a little surprised by what he said, Henrietta.

HENRIETTA [*breathlessly*]: Of course—one can so seldom anticipate. But tell me—your dream, Stephen? It means—?

STEVE: It means—I was considerably surprised by what it means.

HENRIETTA: *Don't* be so exasperating!

STEVE: It means—you really want to know, Henrietta?

HENRIETTA: Stephen, you'll drive me mad!

STEVE: He said—of course he may be wrong in what he said.

HENRIETTA: He *isn't* wrong. *Tell* me!

STEVE: He said my dream of the walls receding and leaving me alone in a forest indicates a suppressed desire—

HENRIETTA: Yes—yes!

STEVE: To be freed from—

HENRIETTA: Yes—freed from—?

STEVE: Marriage.

HENRIETTA [*crumples. Stares*]: Marriage!

STEVE: He—he may be mistaken, you know.

HENRIETTA: *May* be mistaken?

STEVE: I—well, of course, I hadn't taken any stock in it myself. It was only your great confidence—

HENRIETTA: Stephen, are you telling me that Dr. Russell—Dr. A. E. Russell—told you this? [STEVE *nods*] Told you you have a suppressed desire to separate from *me?*

STEVE: That's what he said.

HENRIETTA: Did he know who you were?

STEVE: Yes.

HENRIETTA: That you were married to me?

STEVE: Yes, he knew that.

HENRIETTA: And he told you to leave me?

STEVE: It seems he must be wrong, Henrietta.

HENRIETTA [*rising*]: And I've sent him more patients—! [*Catches herself and resumes coldly*] What reason did he give for this analysis?

STEVE: He says the confining walls are a symbol of my feeling about marriage and that their fading away is a wish-fulfillment.

HENRIETTA [*gulping*]: Well, is it? Do you want our marriage to end?

STEVE: It was a great surprise to me that I did. You see I hadn't known what was in my unconscious mind.

HENRIETTA [*flaming*]: What did you tell Dr. Russell about me to make him think you weren't happy?

STEVE: I never told him a thing, Henrietta. He got it all from his confounded clever inferences. I—I tried to refute them, but he said that was only part of my self-protective lying.

HENRIETTA: And that's why you were so—happy—when you came in just now!

STEVE: Why, Henrietta, how can you say such a thing? I was *sad*. Didn't I speak sadly of—of the view? Didn't I ask how long we had been married?

HENRIETTA [*rising*]: Stephen Brewster, have you no sense of the seriousness of this? Dr. Russell doesn't know what our marriage has been. You do. You should have laughed him down! Confined—in life with me? Did you tell him that I *believe* in freedom?

STEVE: I very emphatically told him that his results were a great surprise to me.

HENRIETTA: But you accepted them.

STEVE: Oh, not at all. I merely couldn't refute his arguments. I'm not a psychologist. I came home to talk it over with you. You being a disciple of psychoanalysis—

HENRIETTA: If you are going, I wish you would go tonight!

STEVE: Oh, my dear! I—surely I couldn't do that! Think of my feelings. And my laundry hasn't come home.

HENRIETTA: I ask you to go tonight. Some women would falter at this, Steve, but I am not such a woman. I leave you free. I do not repudiate psychoanalysis; I say again that it has done great things. It has also made mistakes, of course. But since you accept this analysis— [*She sits down and pretends to begin work*] I have to finish this paper. I wish you would leave me.

STEVE [*scratches his head, goes to the inner door*]: I'm sorry, Henrietta, about my unconscious mind. [*Alone,* HENRIETTA's *face betrays her outraged state of mind—disconcerted, resentful, trying to pull herself together. She attains an air of bravely bearing an outrageous thing.—The outer door opens and* MABEL *enters in great excitement.*]

MABEL [*breathless*]: Henrietta, I'm so glad you're here. And alone? [*Looks toward the inner door*] Are you alone, Henrietta?

HENRIETTA [*with reproving dignity*]: Very much so.

MABEL [*rushing to her*]: Henrietta, he's found it!

HENRIETTA [*aloof*]: Who has found what?

MABEL: Who has found what? Dr. Russell has found my suppressed desire!

HENRIETTA: That is interesting.

MABEL: He finished with me today—he got hold of my complex—in the most amazing way! But, oh, Henrietta—it is so terrible!

HENRIETTA: Do calm yourself, Mabel. Surely there's no occasion for all this agitation.

MABEL: But there is! And when you think of the lives that are affected—the readjustments that must be made in order to bring the suppressed hell out of me and save me from the insane asylum—!

HENRIETTA: The insane asylum!

MABEL: You said that's where these complexes brought people!

HENRIETTA: What did the doctor tell you, Mabel?

MABEL: Oh, I don't know how I can tell you—it is so awful—so unbelievable.

HENRIETTA: I rather have my hand in at hearing the unbelievable.

MABEL: Henrietta, who would ever have thought it? How can it be true? But the doctor is perfectly certain that I have a suppressed desire for— [*Looks at* HENRIETTA, *is unable to continue.*]

HENRIETTA: Oh, go on, Mabel. I'm not unprepared for what you have to say.

MABEL: Not unprepared? You mean you have suspected it?

HENRIETTA: From the first. It's been my theory all along.

MABEL: But, Henrietta, I didn't know myself that I had this secret desire for Stephen.

HENRIETTA [*jumps up*]: Stephen!

MABEL: My brother-in-law! My own sister's husband!

HENRIETTA: *You* have a suppressed desire for *Stephen!*

MABEL: Oh, Henrietta, aren't these unconscious selves terrible? They seem so unlike *us!*

HENRIETTA: What insane thing are you driving at?

MABEL [*blubbering*]: Henrietta, don't you use that word to me. I don't *want* to go to the insane asylum.

HENRIETTA: What did Dr. Russell say?

MABEL: Well, you see—oh, it's the strangest thing! But you know the voice in my dream that called "Step, Hen!" Dr. Russell found out today that when I was a little girl I had a story-book in words of one syllable and I read the name Stephen wrong. I used to read it S-t-e-p, step, h-e-n, hen. [*Dramatically*] Step Hen is Stephen. [*Enter* STEPHEN, *his head bent over a time-table*] Stephen is Step Hen!

STEVE: I? Step Hen?

MABEL [*triumphantly*]: S-t-e-p, step, H-e-n, hen, Stephen!

HENRIETTA [*exploding*]: Well, what if Stephen is Step Hen? [*Scornfully*] Step Hen! Step Hen! For that ridiculous coincidence—

MABEL: Coincidence! But it's childish to look at the mere elements of a dream. You have to look *into* it—you have to see what it *means!*

HENRIETTA: On account of that trivial, meaningless play on syllables—on that flimsy basis—you are ready— [*Wails*] O-h!

STEVE: What on earth's the matter? What has happened? Suppose I *am* Step Hen? What about it? What does it mean?

MABEL [*crying*]: It means—that I—have a suppressed desire for *you!*

STEVE: For me! The deuce you have! [*Feebly*] What—er—makes you think so?

MABEL: Dr. Russell has worked it out scientifically.

HENRIETTA: Yes. Through the amazing discovery that Step Hen equals Stephen!

MABEL [*tearfully*]: Oh, that isn't all—that isn't near all. Henrietta won't give me a chance to tell it. She'd rather I'd go to the insane asylum than be unconventional.

HENRIETTA: We'll all go there if you can't control yourself. We are still waiting for some rational report.

MABEL [*drying her eyes*]: Oh, there's such a lot about names. [*With some pride*] I don't see how I ever did it. It all works in together. I dreamed I was a hen because that's the first syllable of Henrietta's name, and when I dreamed I was a hen, I was putting myself in Henrietta's place.

HENRIETTA: With Stephen?

MABEL: With Stephen.

HENRIETTA [*outraged*]: Oh! [*Turns in rage upon* STEPHEN, *who is fanning himself with the time-table*] What are you doing with that time-table?

STEVE: Why—I thought—you were so keen to have me go tonight—I thought I'd just take a run up to Canada, and join Billy—a little shooting—but—

MABEL: But there's more about the names.

HENRIETTA: Mabel, have you thought of Bob—dear old Bob—your good, kind husband?

MABEL: Oh, Henrietta, "my good, kind husband!"

HENRIETTA: Think of him, Mabel, out there alone in Chicago, working his head off, fixing people's *teeth*—for you!

MABEL: Yes, but think of the living Libido—in conflict with petrified moral codes! And think of the perfectly wonderful way the names all prove it. Dr. Russell said he's never seen anything more convincing. Just look at Stephen's last name—Brewster. I dream I'm a hen, and the name Brewster—you have to say its first letter by itself—and then the hen, that's me, she says to him: "Stephen, Be Rooster!"

[HENRIETTA *and* STEPHEN *collapse into the nearest chairs.*]

MABEL: I think it's perfectly wonderful! Why, if it wasn't for psychoanalysis you'd never find out how wonderful your own mind is!

STEVE [*begins to chuckle*]: Be Rooster! Stephen, Be Rooster!

HENRIETTA: You think it's funny, do you?

STEVE: Well, what's to be done about it? Does Mabel have to go away with me?

HENRIETTA: Do you want Mabel to go away with you?

STEVE: Well, but Mabel herself—her complex, her suppressed desire—!

HENRIETTA [*going to her*]: Mabel, are you going to insist on going away with Stephen?

MABEL: I'd rather go with Stephen than go to the insane asylum!

HENRIETTA: For heaven's sake, Mabel, drop that insane asylum! If you *did* have a suppressed desire for Stephen hidden away in you—God knows it isn't hidden now. Dr. Russell has brought it into your consciousness—with a vengeance. That's all that's necessary to break up a complex. Psychoanalysis doesn't say you have to *gratify* every suppressed desire.

STEVE [*softly*]: Unless it's for Lyman Eggleston.

HENRIETTA [*turning on him*]: Well, if it comes to that, Stephen Brewster, I'd like to know why that interpretation of mine isn't as good as this one? Step, Hen!

STEVE: But Be Rooster! [*He pauses, chuckling to himself*] Step-Hen B-rooster. And *Hen*-rietta. Pshaw, my dear, Doc Russell's got you beat a mile! [*He turns away and chuckles*] Be rooster!

MABEL: What has Lyman Eggleston got to do with it?

STEVE: According to Henrietta, you, the hen, have a suppressed desire for *Egg*leston, the egg.

MABEL: Henrietta, I think that's indecent of you! He is bald as an egg and little and fat—the idea of you thinking such a thing of me!

HENRIETTA: Well, Bob isn't little and bald and fat! Why don't you stick to your own husband? [*To* STEPHEN] What if Dr. Russell's interpretation has got mine "beat a mile"? [*Resentful look at him*] It would only mean that Mabel doesn't want Eggleston and does want you. Does that mean she has to have you?

MABEL: But you said Mabel Snow—

HENRIETTA: *Mary* Snow! You're not as much like her as you think—substituting your name for hers! The cases are entirely different. Oh, I wouldn't have *believed* this of you, Mabel. [*Beginning to cry*] I brought you here for a pleasant visit—thought you needed brightening *up*—wanted to be *nice* to you—and now you—my husband—you insist— [*In fumbling her way to her chair she brushes to the floor some sheets from the psychoanalytical table.*]

STEVE [*with solicitude*]: Careful, dear. Your paper on psychoanalysis! [*Gathers up sheets and offers them to her.*]

HENRIETTA: I don't want my paper on psychoanalysis! I'm sick of psychoanalysis!

STEVE [*eagerly*]: Do you mean that, Henrietta?

HENRIETTA: Why shouldn't I mean it? Look at all I've done for psychoanalysis—and— [*Raising a tear-stained face*] what has psychoanalysis done for me?

STEVE: Do you mean, Henrietta, that you're going to stop *talking* psychoanalysis?

HENRIETTA: Why shouldn't I stop talking it? Haven't I seen what it does to people? Mabel has gone crazy about psychoanalysis!

[*At the word "crazy" with a moan* MABEL *sinks to chair and buries her face in her hands.*]

STEVE [*solemnly*]: Do you swear never to wake me up in the night to find out what I'm dreaming?

HENRIETTA: Dream what you please—I don't care what you're dreaming.

STEVE: Will you clear off my work-table so the Journal of Morbid Psychology doesn't stare me in the face when I'm trying to plan a house?

HENRIETTA [*pushing a stack of periodicals off the table*]: I'll *burn* the Journal of Morbid Psychology!

STEVE: My dear Henrietta, if you're going to separate from psychoanalysis, there's no reason why I should separate from *you*.

[*They embrace ardently.* MABEL *lifts her head and looks at them woefully.*]

MABEL [*jumping up and going toward them*]: But what about me? What am I to do with my suppressed desire?

STEVE [*with one arm still around* HENRIETTA, *gives* MABEL *a brotherly hug*]: Mabel, you just keep right on suppressing it!

Curtain

QUESTIONS

1. Compare the tone used in describing the setting of the play with the tone of the dialogue. How does the contrast between the two set the stage for the play's humor?
2. Henrietta initiates all the conflict in Scene I. What is the source of this conflict?
3. There is a reversal of action in Scene II. How does the author create this reversal? Does the action escalate in Scene II. If so, how?
4. Does the dialogue of the play appear natural or artificial? Explain your answer.
5. What is the author satirizing in the play?

Lady Gregory

THE RISING OF THE MOON

— PERSONS —

SERGEANT
POLICEMAN X
POLICEMAN B
A RAGGED MAN

Scene: Side of a quay in a seaport town. Some posts and chains. A large barrel. Enter three policemen. Moonlight.

> [SERGEANT, *who is older than the others, crosses the stage to right and looks down steps. The others put down a pastepot and unroll a bundle of placards.*]

POLICEMAN B: I think this would be a good place to put up a notice.

> [*He points to barrel.*]

POLICEMAN X: Better ask him. [*Calls to* SERGEANT.] Will this be a good place for a placard?

[*No answer.*]

POLICEMAN B: Will we put up a notice here on the barrel?

[*No answer.*]

SERGEANT: There's a flight of steps here that leads to the water. This is a place that should be minded well. If he got down here, his friends might have a boat to meet him; they might send it in here from outside.

POLICEMAN B: Would the barrel be a good place to put a notice up?

SERGEANT: It might; you can put it there.

[*They paste the notice up.*]

SERGEANT [*reading it*]: Dark hair—dark eyes, smooth face, height five feet five—there's not much to take hold of in that—It's a pity I had no chance of seeing him before he broke out of gaol. They say he's a wonder, that it's he makes all the plans for the whole organization. There isn't another man in Ireland would have broken gaol the way he did. He must have some friends among the gaolers.

POLICEMAN B: A hundred pounds is little enough for the Government to offer for him. You may be sure any man in the force that takes him will get promotion.

SERGEANT: I'll mind this place myself. I wouldn't wonder at all if he came this way. He might come slipping along there [*points to side of quay*], and his friends might be waiting for him there [*points down steps*], and once he got away it's little chance we'd have of finding him; it's maybe under a load of kelp he'd be in a fishing boat, and not one to help a married man that wants it to the reward.

POLICEMAN X: And if we get him itself, nothing but abuse on our heads for it from the people, land maybe from our own relations.

SERGEANT: Well, we have to do our duty in the force. Haven't we the whole country depending on us to keep law and order? It's those that are down would be up and those that are up would be down, if it wasn't for us. Well, hurry on, you have plenty of other places to placard yet, and come back here then to me. You can take the lantern. Don't be too long now. It's very lonesome here with nothing but the moon.

POLICEMAN B: It's a pity we can't stop with you. The Government should have brought more police into the town, with *him* in gaol, and at assize[1] time too. Well, good luck to your watch.

[*They go out.*]

---

[1] Periodical legal proceedings.

SERGEANT [*walks up and down once or twice and looks at placard*]: A hundred pounds and promotion sure. There must be a great deal of spending in a hundred pounds. It's a pity some honest man not to be better of that.

[A RAGGED MAN *appears at left and tries to slip past.* SERGEANT *suddenly turns.*]

SERGEANT: Where are you going?

MAN: I'm a poor ballad-singer, your honor. I thought to sell some of these [*holds out bundle of ballads*] to the sailors. [*He goes on.*]

SERGEANT: Stop! Didn't I tell you to stop? You can't go on there.

MAN: Oh, very well. It's a hard thing to be poor. All the world's against the poor!

SERGEANT: Who are you?

MAN: You'd be as wise as myself if I told you, but I don't mind. I'm one Jimmy Walsh, a ballad-singer.

SERGEANT: Jimmy Walsh? I don't know that name.

MAN: Ah, sure, they know it well enough in Ennis. Were you ever in Ennis, sergeant?

SERGEANT: What brought you here?

MAN: Sure, it's to the assizes I came, thinking I might make a few shillings here or there. It's in the one train with the judges I came.

SERGEANT: Well, if you came so far, you may as well go farther, for you'll walk out of this.

MAN: I will, I will; I'll just go on where I was going. [*Goes toward steps.*]

SERGEANT: Come back from those steps; no one has leave to pass down them to-night.

MAN: I'll just sit on the top of the steps till I see will some sailor buy a ballad off me that would give me my supper. They do be late going back to the ship. It's often I saw them in Cork carried down the quay in a hand-cart.

SERGEANT: Move on, I tell you. I won't have any one lingering about the quay to-night.

MAN: Well, I'll go. It's the poor have the hard life! Maybe yourself might like one, sergeant. Here's a good sheet now. [*Turns one over.*] "Content and a pipe"—that's not much. "The Peeler and the goat"—you wouldn't like that. "Johnny Hart"—that's a lovely song.

SERGEANT: Move on.

MAN: Ah, wait till you hear it. [*Sings.*]

> There was a rich farmer's daughter lived near the town of Ross;
> She courted a Highland soldier, his name was Johnny Hart;
> Says the mother to her daughter, "I'll go distracted mad
> If you marry that Highland soldier dressed up in Highland plaid."

SERGEANT: Stop that noise.

[MAN *wraps up his ballads and shuffles towards the steps.*]

SERGEANT: Where are you going?

MAN: Sure you told me to be going, and I am going.

SERGEANT: Don't be a fool. I didn't tell you to go that way; I told you to go back to the town.

MAN: Back to the town, is it?

SERGEANT [*taking him by the shoulder and shoving him before him*]: Here, I'll show you the way. Be off with you. What are you stopping for?

MAN [*who has been keeping his eye on the notice, points to it*]: I think I know what you're waiting for, sergeant.

SERGEANT: What's that to you?

MAN: And I know well the man you're waiting for—I know him well—I'll be going. [*He shuffles on.*]

SERGEANT: You know him? Come back here. What sort is he?

MAN: Come back is it, sergeant? Do you want to have me killed?

SERGEANT: Why do you say that?

MAN: Never mind. I'm going. I wouldn't be in your shoes if the reward was ten times as much. [*Goes on off stage to left.*] Not if it was ten times as much.

SERGEANT [*rushing after him*]: Come back here, come back. [*Drags him back.*] What sort is he? Where did you see him?

MAN: I saw him in my own place, in the County Clare. I tell you you wouldn't like to be looking at him. You'd be afraid to be in the one place with him. There isn't a weapon he doesn't know the use of, and as to strength, his muscles are as hard as that board. [*Slaps barrel.*]

SERGEANT: Is he as bad as that?

MAN: He is then.

SERGEANT: Do you tell me so?

MAN: There was a poor man in our place, a sergeant from Bally-vaughan.—It was with a lump of stone he did it.

SERGEANT: I never heard of that.

MAN: And you wouldn't, sergeant. It's not everything that happens gets into the papers. And there was a policeman in plain clothes, too . . . It is in Limerick he was. . . . It was after the time of the attack on the police barrack in Kilmallock. . . . Moonlight . . . just like this . . . waterside. . . . Nothing was known for certain.

SERGEANT: Do you say so? It's a terrible county to belong to.

MAN: That's so, indeed! You might be standing there, looking out that way, thinking you saw him coming up this side of the quay [*points*], and he might be coming up this other side [*points*], and he'd be on you before you knew where you were.

SERGEANT: It's a whole troop of police they ought to put here to stop a man like that.

MAN: But if you'd like me to stop with you, I could be looking down this side. I could be sitting up here on this barrel.

SERGEANT: And you know him well, too?

MAN: I'd know him a mile off, sergeant.

SERGEANT: But you wouldn't want to share the reward?

MAN: Is it a poor man like me, that has to be going the roads and singing in fairs, to have the name on him that he took a reward? but you don't want me. I'll be safer in the town.

SERGEANT: Well, you can stop.

MAN [*getting up on barrel*]: All right, sergeant, I wonder, now, you're tired out, sergeant, walking up and down the way you are.

SERGEANT: If I'm tired I'm used to it.

MAN: You might have hard work before you to-night yet. Take it easy while you can. There's plenty of room up here on the barrel, and you see farther when you're higher up.

SERGEANT: Maybe so. [*Gets up beside him on barrel, facing right.*]

[*They sit back to back, looking different ways.*]

You made me feel a bit queer with the way you talked.

MAN: Give me a match, sergeant [*he gives it and* MAN *lights pipe*]; take a draw yourself? It'll quiet you. Wait now till I give you a light, but you needn't turn round. Don't take your eye off the quay for the life of you.

SERGEANT: Never fear, I won't. [*Lights pipe.*]

[*They both smoke.*]

Indeed it's a hard thing to be in the force, out at night and no thanks for it, for all the danger we're in. And it's little we get but abuse from the people, and no choice but to obey our orders, and never asked when a man is sent into danger, if you are a married man with a family.

MAN [*sings*]:

> As through the hills I walked to view the hills and shamrock plain,
> I stood awhile where nature smiles to view the rocks and streams,
> On a matron fair I fixed my eyes beneath a fertile vale,
> And she sang her song it was on the wrong of poor old Granuaile.

SERGEANT: Stop that; that's no song to be singing in these times.

MAN: Ah, sergeant, I was only singing to keep my heart up. It sinks when I think of him. To think of us two sitting here, and he creeping up the quay, maybe, to get to us.

SERGEANT: Are you keeping a good lookout?

MAN: I am; and for no reward too. Amn't I the fool man? But when I saw a man in trouble, I never could help trying to get him out of it. What's that? Did something hit me? [*Rubs his heart.*]

SERGEANT [*patting him on the shoulder*]: You will get your reward in heaven.

MAN: I know that, I know that, sergeant, but life is precious.

SERGEANT: Well, you can sing if it gives you more courage.

MAN [*sings*]:

> Her head was bare, her hands and feet with iron bands were bound,
> Her pensive strain and plaintive wail mingles with the evening gale,

And the song she sang with mournful air, I am old Granuaile.
Her lips so sweet that monarchs kissed . . .

SERGEANT: That's not it. . . . "Her gown she wore was stained with gore." . . . That's it—you missed that.

MAN: You're right, sergeant, so it is; I missed it. [*Repeats line.*] But to think of a man like you knowing a song like that.

SERGEANT: There's many a thing a man might know and might not have any wish for.

MAN: Now, I daresay, sergeant, in your youth, you used to be sitting up on a wall, the way you are sitting up on this barrel now, and the other lads beside you, and you singing "Granuaile"? . . .

SERGEANT: I did then.

MAN: And the "Shan Van Vocht"?[2] . . .

SERGEANT: I did then.

MAN: And the "Green on the Cape?"

SERGEANT: That was one of them.

MAN: And maybe the man you are watching for to-night used to be sitting on the wall, when he was young, and singing those same songs. . . . It's a queer world. . . .

SERGEANT: Whisht! . . . I think I see something coming. . . . It's only a dog.

MAN: And isn't it a queer world? . . . Maybe it's one of the boys you used to be singing with that time you will be arresting to-day or to-morrow, and sending into the dock. . . .

SERGEANT: That's true indeed.

MAN: And maybe one night, after you had been singing, if the other boys had told you some plan they had, some plan to free the country, you might have joined with them . . . and maybe it is you might be in trouble now.

SERGEANT: Well, who knows but I might? I had a great spirit in those days.

MAN: It's a queer world, sergeant, and it's little any mother knows when she sees her child creeping on the floor what might happen to it before it has gone through its life, or who will be who in the end.

SERGEANT: That's a queer thought now, and a true thought. Wait now till I think it out. . . . If it wasn't for the sense I have, and for my wife and family, and for me joining the force the time I did, it might be myself now would be after breaking gaol and hiding in the dark, and it might be him that's hiding in the dark and that got out of gaol would be sitting up here where I am on this barrel. . . . And it might be myself would be creeping up trying to make my escape from himself, and it might be himself would be keeping the law, and myself would be breaking it, and myself would be trying to put a bullet in his head, or to take up a lump of stone the way you said he did . . . no, that myself did. . . . Oh! [*Gasps. After a pause*] What's that? [*Grasps man's arm.*]

MAN [*jumps off barrel and listens, looking out over water*]: It's nothing, sergeant.

[2] Song of a poor old woman, personification of Ireland, foretelling the coming of the French to aid Irish rebellion; the Shan Van Vocht personification of Ireland also informs Yeats's *Cathleen Ni Houlihan*.

SERGEANT: I thought it might be a boat. I had a notion there might be friends of his coming about the quays with a boat.

MAN: Sergeant, I am thinking it was with the people you were, and not with the law you were, when you were a young man.

SERGEANT: Well, if I was foolish then, that time's gone.

MAN: Maybe, sergeant, it comes into your head sometimes, in spite of your belt and your tunic, that it might have been as well for you to have followed Granuaile.

SERGEANT: It's no business of yours what I think.

MAN: Maybe, sergeant, you'll be on the side of the country yet.

SERGEANT [gets off barrel]: Don't talk to me like that. I have my duties and I know them. [Looks round.] That was a boat; I hear the oars. [Goes to the steps and looks down.]

MAN [sings]:

> O, then, tell me, Shawn O'Farrell,
> Where the gathering is to be.
> In the old spot by the river
> Right well known to you and me!

SERGEANT: Stop that! Stop that, I tell you!

MAN [sings louder]:

> One word more, for signal token,
> Whistle up the marching tune,
> With your pike upon your shoulder,
> At the Rising of the Moon.

SERGEANT: If you don't stop that, I'll arrest you.

[A whistle from below answers, repeating the air.]

SERGEANT: That's a signal. [Stands between him and steps.] You must not pass this way. . . . Step farther back. . . . Who are you? You are no ballad-singer.

MAN: You needn't ask who I am; that placard will tell you. [Points to placard.]

SERGEANT: You are the man I am looking for.

MAN [takes off hat and wig].

[SERGEANT seizes them.]

I am. There's a hundred pounds on my head. There is a friend of mine below in a boat. He knows a safe place to bring me to.

SERGEANT [looking still at hat and wig]: It's a pity! It's a pity. You deceived me. You deceived me well.

MAN: I am a friend of Granuaile. There is a hundred pounds on my head.

SERGEANT: It's a pity, it's a pity!

MAN: Will you let me pass, or must I make you let me?

SERGEANT: I am in the force. I will not let you pass.
MAN: I thought to do it with my tongue. [*Puts hand in breast.*] What is that?

[*Voice of* POLICEMAN X *outside.*]

Here, this is where we left him.
SERGEANT: It's my comrades coming.
MAN: You won't betray me . . . the friend of Granuaile. [*Slips behind barrel.*]

[*Voice of* POLICEMAN B.]

That was the last of the placards.

POLICEMAN X [*as they come in*]: If he makes his escape it won't be unknown he'll make it.

[SERGEANT *puts hat and wig behind his back.*]

POLICEMAN B: Did any one come this way?
SERGEANT [*after a pause*]: No one.
POLICEMAN B: No one at all?
SERGEANT: No one at all.
POLICEMAN B: We had no orders to go back to the station; we can stop along with you.
SERGEANT: I don't want you. There is nothing for you to do here.
POLICEMAN B: You bade us to come back here and keep watch with you.
SERGEANT: I'd sooner be alone. Would any man come this way and you making all that talk? It is better the place to be quiet.
POLICEMAN B: Well, we'll leave you the lantern anyhow.

[*Hands it to him.*]

SERGEANT: I don't want it. Bring it with you.
POLICEMAN B: You might want it. There are clouds coming up and you have the darkness of the night before you yet. I'll leave it over here on the barrel. [*Goes to barrel.*]
SERGEANT: Bring it with you I tell you. No more talk.
POLICEMAN B: Well, I thought it might be a comfort to you. I often think when I have it in my hand and can be flashing it about into every dark corner [*doing so*] that it's the same as being beside the fire at home, and the bits of bogwood blazing up now and again. [*Flashes it about, now on the barrel, now on* SERGEANT.]
SERGEANT [*furious*]: Be off the two of you, yourselves and your lantern!

[*They go out.* MAN *comes from behind barrel. He and* SERGEANT *stands looking at one another.*]

SERGEANT: What are you waiting for?

MAN: For my hat, of course, and my wig. You wouldn't wish me to get my death of cold?

[SERGEANT *gives them.*]

MAN [*going towards steps*]: Well, good-night, comrade, and thank you. You did me a good turn to-night, and I'm obliged to you. Maybe I'll be able to do as much for you when the small rise up and the big fall down . . . when we all change places at the rising [*waves his hand and disappears*] of the Moon.

SERGEANT [*turning his back to audience and reading placard*]: A hundred pounds reward! A hundred pounds! [*turns towards audience.*] I wonder, now, am I as great a fool as I think I am?

QUESTIONS

1. In this short play, time, setting, and plot are set up very quickly. How does the author achieve this? At what point are all these basic elements in place?
2. Follow the steps by which the Man changes the Sergeant's view of capturing the fugitive and collecting the reward money. What methods does he employ, in what order, and to what effect?
3. Describe the *internal* and *external* conflicts of the Sergeant. How do they complement one another?
4. Why does the fugitive sing his ballads? What is the effect of these ballads on the Sergeant?
5. A great deal of light imagery is used in the play. Find each reference to this imagery, and explain what this imagery might represent besides a pure description of the setting and action.

David Henry Hwang

FAMILY DEVOTIONS

————————————— **CHARACTERS** —————————————

JOANNE, late thirties, Chinese American raised in the Philippines.

WILBUR, her husband, Japanese American, nisei (second generation).

JENNY, their daughter, seventeen.

AMA, Joanne's mother, born in China, emigrated to the Philippines, then to America.

POPO, Ama's younger sister.
HANNAH, Popo's daughter and Joanne's cousin, slightly older than Joanne.
ROBERT, Hannah's husband, Chinese American, first generation.
DI-GOU, Ama and Popo's younger brother, born and raised in China, still a resi-
dent of the People's Republic of China (P.R.C.).
CHESTER, Hannah and Robert's son, early twenties.

```
          AMA ————————— POPO ————————— DI-GOU
           |                |
WILBUR — m — JOANNE     HANNAH — m — ROBERT
           |                |
        JENNY            CHESTER
```

SYNOPSIS OF SCENES

ACT I. *Late afternoon, the lanai/sunroom and tennis court of a home in
Bel Air, California.*
ACT II. *Same scene, immediately following.*

ACT I

The sunroom and backyard of a home in Bel Air. Everywhere is glass—glass roof, glass walls. Upstage of the lanai/sunroom is a patio with a barbecue and a tennis court. The tennis court leads offstage. As the curtain rises, we see a single spotlight on an old Chinese face and hear Chinese music or chanting. Suddenly, the music becomes modern-day funk or rock 'n' roll, and the lights come up to reveal the set.

The face is that of DI-GOU, *an older Chinese man wearing a blue suit and carrying an old suitcase. He is peering into the sunroom from the tennis court, through the glass walls. Behind him, a stream of black smoke is coming from the barbecue.*

JOANNE: [*Offstage*] Wilbur! Wilbur!

[DI-GOU *exits off the tennis court. Enter* JOANNE, *from the house. She is a Chinese American woman, attractive, in her mid-thirties. She sees the smoke coming from the barbecue.*]

JOANNE: Aiii-ya! [*She heads for the barbecue, and on her way notices that the sunroom is a mess.*] Jenny! [*She runs out to the barbecue, opens it up. Billows of black smoke continue to pour out.*] Oh, gosh. Oh, golly. [*To offstage*] Wilbur! [*She begins pulling burnt objects out of the barbecue.*] Sheee! [*She pulls out a chicken, dumps it onto the ground.*] Wilbur! [*She pulls out another chicken, does the same.*] Wilbur, the heat was too high on the barbecue! [*She begins pulling out burnt objects and tossing them all over the tennis court.*] You should have been watching it! It could have exploded! We could all have been blown up! [*She picks up another chicken, examines it.*] You think we can have some of this? [*She pauses, tosses it onto the court.*] We'll get some more chickens. We'll put barbecue sauce on them and stick them into the microwave. [*She exits into the house holding a chicken on the end of her fork.*] Is this okay, do you think?

[WILBUR *appears on the tennis court. He is a Japanese American man, nisei, in his late thirties. His hair is permed. He wears tennis clothes.*]

WILBUR: Hon? [*He looks around.*] What's up? [*He picks a burnt chicken off the tennis court.*] Hon? [*He walks over to the barbecue.*] Who—? Why's the heat off? [*He walks around the tennis court picking up chickens.*] Jesus! [*He smears grease on his white tennis shirt, notices it.*] Aw, shit! [*He dumps all the chickens except one, which he has forgotten to pick up, back into the barbecue. He walks into the sunroom, gets some ice, and tries to dab at the stain.*] Hon? Will you come here a sec? [*He exits into the house.*]

[JENNY *appears on the tennis court. She is seventeen,* WILBUR *and* JOANNE's *daughter. She carries a large wire-mesh box.*]

JENNY: Chickie! [*Looking around*] Chickie? Chickie, where the hell did you go? You know, it's embarrassing. It's embarrassing being this old and still having to chase a chicken all over the house. [*She sees the lone burnt chicken on the court. She creeps over slowly, then picks it up.*] Blaagh! Who cooked this? See, Chickie, this is what happens—what happens when you're a bad chickie.

[CHESTER, *a young Chinese American male in his early twenties, appears on the tennis court. He tries to sneak up on* JENNY.]

JENNY: [*To chicken*] Look, if you bother Popo and Ama, I'm gonna catch shit, and you know what that means for you—chicken soccer. You'll be sorry. [CHESTER *is right behind* JENNY.] You'll be sorry if you mess with me. [*She turns around, catching* CHESTER.] Oh, good. You have to be here, too.
CHESTER: No, I don't. I've gotta pack.
JENNY: They'll expect you to be here when that Chinese guy gets here. What's name? Dar-gwo?
CHESTER: I dunno. Dah-gim?
JENNY: Doo-goo? Something.
CHESTER: Yeah. I'm not staying.
JENNY: So what else is new?
CHESTER: I don't have time.
JENNY: You luck out 'cause you don't live here. Me—there's no way I can get away. When you leaving?
CHESTER: Tomorrow.
JENNY: Tomorrow? And you're not packed?
CHESTER: Don't rub it in. Listen, you still have my green suitcase?
JENNY: Yeah. I wish *I* had an excuse not to be here. All I need is to meet another old relative. Another goon.
CHESTER: Yeah. Where's my suitcase?
JENNY: First you have to help me find Chickie.
CHESTER: Jesus!

AMA: [*Offstage*] Joanne!

CHESTER: [*To* JENNY] All right. I don't want them to know I'm here.

[CHESTER *and* JENNY *exit.* POPO *and* AMA *enter. They are* JOANNE'*s aunt and mother, respectively.*]

AMA: Joanne! Joanne! Jenny! Where is Joanne?

POPO: Probably busy.

AMA: Where is Jenny? Joanne?

POPO: Perhaps you can find, ah, Wilbur.

AMA: Joanne!

POPO: Ah, you never wish to see Wilbur.

AMA: I see him at wedding. That is enough. He was not at church again today.

POPO: Ah?

AMA: He will be bad influence when Di-gou arrive. Wilbur—holy spirit is not in him.

POPO: Not matter. He can perhaps eat in kitchen.

AMA: Outside!

POPO: This is his house.

AMA: All heart must join as one—

POPO: He may eat inside!

AMA: —only then, miracles can take place.

POPO: But in kitchen.

AMA: Wilbur—he never like family devotions.

POPO: Wilbur does not come from Christian family.

AMA: He come from Japanese family.

POPO: I mean to say, we—ah—very fortunate. Mama teach us all Christianity. Not like Wilbur family.

AMA: When Di-gou arrive, we will remind him. What Mama tells us.

POPO: Di-gou can remember himself.

AMA: No.

POPO: But we remember.

AMA: You forget—Di-gou, he lives in China.

POPO: So?

AMA: Torture, Communists. Make him work in rice fields.

POPO: I no longer think so.

AMA: In rice field, all the people wear wires in their heads—yes! Wires force them work all day and sing Communist song. Like this! [*She mimes harvesting rice and singing.*]

POPO: No such thing!

AMA: Yes! You remember Twa-Ling? Before we leave China, before Communist come, she say, "I will send you a picture. If Communists are good, I will stand—if bad, I will sit."

POPO: That does not mean anything!

AMA: In picture she sent, she was lying down!

POPO: Picture was not sent for ten years. Probably she forget.

AMA: You wait till Di-gou arrive. You will see.

POPO: See what?

AMA: Brainwash! You watch for little bit of wires in his hair.

[POPO *notices the lone burnt chicken on the tennis court.*]

POPO: What's there?

AMA: Where?

POPO: There—on cement.

AMA: Cannot see well.

POPO: There. Black.

AMA: Oh. I see.

POPO: Looks like *gao sai.*

AMA: They sometimes have problem with the dog.

POPO: Ha!

AMA: Very bad dog.

POPO: At home, dog do that?—we shoot him.

AMA: Should be punish.

POPO: Shot! [*Pause*] That no *gao sai.*

AMA: No? What then?

POPO: I don't know.

AMA: Oh, I know.

POPO: What?

AMA: That is Chickie.

POPO: No. That no Chickie.

AMA: They have a chicken—"Chickie."

[*They get up, head toward the chicken.*]

POPO: No. That one, does not move.

AMA: Maybe sick. [*They reach the chicken.*] Aiii-ya! What happen to Chickie!

POPO: [*Picking it up*] This chicken very sick! [*She laughs.*]

AMA: Wilbur.

POPO: Huh?

AMA: Wilbur—his temper is very bad.

POPO: No!

AMA: Yes. Perhaps Chickie bother him too much.

POPO: No—this is only a chicken.

AMA: "Chickie" *is* chicken.

POPO: No—this—another chicken.

AMA: How you know?

POPO: No matter now. Like this, all chicken look same. Here. Throw away. No good.

AMA: Very bad temper. Japanese man. [AMA *sees* POPO *looking for a trash can.*] Wait.

POPO: Huh?

AMA: Jenny—might want to keep it.

POPO: This?

AMA: Leave here until we know. [*She takes the chicken from* POPO.]

POPO: No, throw away. [*She takes it back.*] Stink up whole place soon.

AMA: Don't want to anger Wilbur!

POPO: You pig-head!

AMA: He do this to Chickie—think what he will do to us?

POPO: *Zin gao tza!* [Always so much trouble!]

AMA: You don't know Japanese man!

[AMA *knocks the chicken from* POPO's *hands; they circle around it like boxers sparring.*]

POPO: *Pah-di!* [Spank you!]

AMA: Remember? During war? Pictures they show us? Always—Japanese man kill Chinese!

POPO: Go away, pig-head!

AMA: In picture—Japanese always kill and laugh, kill and laugh.

POPO: If dirty, should throw away!

AMA: Sometimes—torture and laugh, too.

POPO: Wilbur not like that! Hardly even laugh!

AMA: When he kill Chickie, then he laugh!

[*They both grab the chicken;* JOANNE *enters, sees them.*]

JOANNE: Hi, Mom, Auntie. Who cleaned up the chicken?

AMA: Huh? This is not Chickie?

POPO: [*To* AMA] Tell you things, you never listen. *Gong-gong-ah!* [Idiot!]

JOANNE: When's Hannah getting here?

POPO: Hannah—she is at airport.

JOANNE: We had a little accident and I need help programming the microwave. Last time, I put a roast inside and it disintegrated. She should be here already.

AMA: Joanne, you prepare for family devotions?

JOANNE: Of course, Mom. I had the maid set up everything just like you said. [*She exits.*]

AMA: Good. Praise to God will bring Di-gou back to family. Make him rid of Communist demon.

POPO: He will speak in tongue of fire. Like he does when he is a little boy with See-goh-poh.

[WILBUR *enters the tennis court with an empty laundry basket. He heads for the barbecue.* JOANNE *follows him.*]

JOANNE: [*To* WILBUR] Hon, what are you going to do with those?

WILBUR: [*Referring to the burnt chicken*] I'm just going to give them to Grizzly. [*He piles the chickens into the basket.*]

JOANNE: All right. [*She notices that the mess in the lanai has not been touched.*] Jenny! [*To* WILBUR] But be careful not to give Grizzly any bones! [JOANNE *exits.*]

WILBUR: [*To* AMA *and* POPO] How you doin', Mom, Auntie?

AMA: [*To* POPO, *sotto voce*] Kill and laugh.

WILBUR: Joanne tells me you're pretty excited about your brother's arrival—pretty understandable, after all these years—what's his name again? Di-ger, Di-gow, something . . .

AMA: Di-gou!

WILBUR: Yeah, right. Gotta remember that. Be pretty embarrassing if I said the wrong name. Di-gou.

POPO: Di-gou is not his name.

WILBUR: What? Not his—? What is it again? Di-gow? De—?

AMA: Di-gou!

WILBUR: Di-gou.

POPO: That is not his name.

WILBUR: Oh. It's the tones in Chinese, isn't it? I'm saying the wrong tone: Di-gou? or Di-gou? Or—

POPO: Di-gou meaning is "second brother."

WILBUR: Oh, I see. It's not his name. Boy, do I feel ignorant in these situations. If only there were some way I could make sure I don't embarrass myself tonight.

AMA: Eat outside.

WILBUR: Outside?

POPO: Or in kitchen.

WILBUR: In the kitchen? That's great! You two are real jokers, you know?

AMA: No. We are not.

WILBUR: C'mon. I should bring you down to the club someday. The guys never believe it when I tell them how much I love you two.

AMA: [*To* POPO] Gao sai.

[JENNY *enters the sunroom.*]

WILBUR: Right. "*Gao sai*" to you, too. [*He starts to leave, sees* JENNY.] Wash your hands before you play with your grandmother.

JENNY: [*To* WILBUR] Okay, Dad. [*To* AMA] Do I have to, Ama?

AMA: No. Of course not.

JENNY: Can I ask you something personal?

AMA: Of course.

JENNY: Did Daddy just call you "dog shit"?

AMA: Jenny!

POPO: Yes. Very good!

JENNY: Doesn't that bother you?

POPO: [*To* AMA] Her Chinese is improving!

JENNY: We learned it in Chinese school.

AMA: Jenny, you should not use this American word.

JENNY: Sorry. It just slipped out.

AMA: You do not use such word at school, no?

JENNY: Oh, no. Of course not.

AMA: You should not use anyplace.

JENNY: Right.

POPO: Otherwise—no good man wants marry you.

JENNY: You mean, no rich man.

AMA: No—money is not important.

POPO: As long as he is good man.

[*Pause*]

AMA: Christian.

POPO: Chinese.

AMA: Good education.

POPO: Good school.

AMA: Princeton.

POPO: Harvard.

AMA: Doctor.

POPO: Surgeon.

AMA: Brain surgeon.

POPO: Surgeon general.

AMA: Otherwise—you marry anyone that you like.

JENNY: Ama, Popo—look, I'm only seventeen.

POPO: True. But you can develop the good habits now.

JENNY: I don't want to get married till I'm at least thirty or something.

POPO: Thirty! By that time we are dead!

AMA: Gone to see God!

POPO: Lie in ground, arms cross!

JENNY: Look at it this way: how can I be a good mother if I have to follow my career around?

AMA: Your career will not require this.

JENNY: Yeah, it will. What if I have to go on tour?

AMA: Dental technicians do not tour.

JENNY: Ama!

POPO: Only tour—one mouth to next mouth: "Hello. Clean your teeth?"

JENNY: Look, I'm telling you, I'm going to be a dancer.

AMA: We say—you can do both. Combine skills.

JENNY: That's ridiculous.

POPO: Be first dancing dental technician.

JENNY: I don't wanna be a dental technician!

POPO: Dancing dental technician very rare. You will be very popular.

JENNY: Why can't I be like Chester?

AMA: You cannot be like Chester.

JENNY: Why not!

POPO: You do not play violin. Chester does not dance. No hope.

JENNY: I know, but, I mean, he's a musician. Why can't I be a dancer?

AMA: Chester—his work very dangerous.

JENNY: Dangerous?

AMA: He just receive new job—play with Boston Symphony.

JENNY: Yeah. I know. He's leaving tomorrow. So? What's so bad about Boston?

AMA: Conductor—Ozawa—he is Japanese.

JENNY: Oh, no. Not this again.

AMA: Very strict. If musicians miss one note, they must kill themself!

JENNY: Don't be ridiculous. That's no reason why I can't be like Chester.

POPO: But Chester—he makes plenty money.

JENNY: Yeah. Right. Now. But he has to leave home to do it, see? I want a career, too. So what if I never get married?

AMA: Jenny! You must remember—you come from family of See-goh-poh. She was a great evangelist.

JENNY: I know about See-goh-poh. She was your aunt.

AMA: First in family to become Christian.

POPO: She make this family chosen by God.

JENNY: To do what? Clean teeth?

AMA: Jenny!

JENNY: Look, See-goh-poh never got married because of her work, right?

AMA: See-goh-poh was marry to God.

POPO: When Di-gou arrive, he will tell you his testimony. How See-goh-poh change his life.

AMA: Before, he is like you. [*To* POPO] You remember?

POPO: Yes. He is always so fussy.

JENNY: I'm not fussy.

AMA: Stubborn.

POPO: Complain this, complain that.

JENNY: I'm not complaining!

AMA: He will be very happy to meet you. Someone to complain with.

JENNY: I'm just telling you, there's no such thing as a dancing dental technician.

AMA: Good. You will be new discovery.

POPO: When Di-gou is a little boy, he never play with other children. He only read the books. Read books—and play tricks.

AMA: He is very naughty.

POPO: He tell other children there are ghosts hide inside the tree, behind the bush, in the bathroom at night.

AMA: One day, he feed snail poison to gardener.

POPO: Then, when he turns eight year old, See-goh-poh decide she will bring him on her evangelism tour. When he return, he has the tongue of fire.

JENNY: Oh, c'mon—those kind of things only happened in China.

AMA: No—they can happen here as well.

POPO: Di-gou at eight, he goes with See-goh-poh on her first evangelism tour—they travel all around Fukien—thirty day and night, preach to all villages. Five hundred people accept Christ on these thirty day, and See-goh-poh heal many sick, restore ear to deaf, put tongue in mouth of dumb, all these thing and cast out the demon. Perhaps even one dead man—dead and wither—he rise up from his sleep. Di-gou see all this while carry See-goh-poh's bag and bring her food, ah? After thirty day,

they return home. We have large banquet—perhaps twelve different dish that night—outside—underneath—ah—cloth. After we eat, See-goh-poh say, "Now is time for Family Devotions, and this time, he will lead." See-goh-poh point to Di-gou, who is still a boy, but he walk up in front of table and begin to talk and flame begin to come from his mouth, over his head. Fire. Fire, all around. His voice—so loud—praise and testify the miracle of God. Louder and louder, more and more fire, till entire sky fill with light, does not seem to be night, like middle of day, like twelve noon. When he finish talk, sun has already rise, and cloth over our head, it is all burn, gone, ashes blow away.

[JOANNE *enters, pulling* CHESTER *behind. He carries a suitcase.*]

JOANNE: Look who's here!
POPO: Chester—good you decide to come.
JOANNE: He looked lost. This house isn't that big, you know. [*Exits.*]
AMA: [*To* CHESTER] You come for reunion with Di-gou. Very good.
CHESTER: Uh—look, I really can't stay. I have to finish packing.
AMA: You must stay—see Di-gou!
CHESTER: But I'm leaving tomorrow.

[*Doorbell*]

CHESTER: Oh, no.
JOANNE: Can someone get that? ⎫
JENNY: Too late!   ⎬ [*Simultaneously*]
POPO: Di-gou!   ⎭
AMA: [*To* CHESTER] You must! This will be Di-gou!

[WILBUR *crosses with basket, now full of chicken bones.*]

WILBUR: I'll get it. Chester, good to see you made it. [*Exits.*]
JENNY: He almost didn't.
CHESTER: I'm really short on time. I gotta go. I'll see you tomorrow at the airport.
POPO: Chester! When Di-gou arrive, he must see whole family! You stay!

[CHESTER *pauses, decides to stay.*]

CHESTER: [*To* JENNY] This is ridiculous. I can't stay.
JENNY: I always have to. Just grin a lot when you meet this guy. Then everyone will be happy.
CHESTER: I don't wanna meet this guy!

[WILBUR *enters with* HANNAH *and* ROBERT, *who are* CHESTER'S *parents.* HANNAH *is* POPO'S *daughter. They are five to ten years older than* JOANNE *and* WILBUR.]

WILBUR: [*To* ROBERT] What? What do you mean?

AMA: [*Stands up on a chair; a speech*] Di-gou, thirty year have pass since we last see you—

WILBUR: [*To* AMA] Not now, Ma.

AMA: Do you still love God?

ROBERT: What do you mean, "What do you mean?" That's what I mean.

HANNAH: He wasn't there, Wilbur. [*To* AMA] Auntie! Di-gou isn't with us.

AMA: What? How can this be?

ROBERT: Those Chinese airliners—all junk stuffs—so inefficient.

AMA: Where is he?

POPO: [*To* ROBERT] You sure you look close?

ROBERT: What "look close"? We just waited for everyone to get off the plane.

AMA: Where is he?

HANNAH: [*To* AMA] We don't know, Auntie! [*To* CHESTER] Chester, are you packed?

AMA: Don't know?

CHESTER: [*To* HANNAH] No, I'm not. And I'm really in a hurry.

HANNAH: You're leaving tomorrow! Why aren't you packed?

CHESTER: I'm trying to, Mom.

[ROBERT *pulls out a newspaper clipping, shows it to* CHESTER.]

ROBERT: Look, son, I called the Chinese paper, used a little of my influence—they did a story on you—here.

CHESTER: [*Looks at clipping*] I can't read this, Dad! It's in Chinese!

ROBERT: [*Takes back clipping*] Little joke, there.

AMA: [*To anyone who will listen*] Where is he?

HANNAH: [*To* AMA] Auntie, ask Wilbur. [*To* CHESTER] Get packed!

CHESTER: All right!

WILBUR: [*Trying to explain to* AMA] Well, Mom, they said he wasn't at—

AMA: [*Ignoring* WILBUR *totally*] Where is he?!

[ROBERT *continues to study the newspaper clipping, points a section out to* CHESTER.]

ROBERT: Here—this is where it talks about my bank.

CHESTER: I'm going to pack.

HANNAH: [*To* CHESTER] Going?

CHESTER: [*To* HANNAH] You said I should—

HANNAH: [*To* CHESTER] You have to stay and see Di-gou!

[WILBUR *makes another attempt to explain the situation to* AMA.]

WILBUR: [*To* AMA] See, Mom, I guess—

AMA: [*Ignoring him again*] Where is he?

[ROBERT *continues studying his clipping, oblivious.*]

ROBERT: [*Translating, to* CHESTER] It says, "Great Chinese violinist will conduct and solo with New York Philharmonic."

CHESTER: What? It says what?

HANNAH: [*To* CHESTER] You came without being packed?

[AMA *decides to look for* DI-GOU *on her own, and starts searching the house.*]

AMA: Di-gou! Di-gou!

WILBUR: [*Following* AMA] Ma, listen. I'll explain.

HANNAH: [*To* CHESTER] How can you be so inefficient?

CHESTER: [*To* ROBERT] Dad, I just got a job playing in the violin section in Boston.

AMA: Di-gou! Di-gou!

CHESTER: [*To* ROBERT] I'm not conducting, and—

ROBERT: [*To* CHESTER] Sssh! I know. But good publicity—for the bank.

HANNAH: [*To* CHESTER] Well, I'll help you pack later. But you have to stay till Di-gou arrives. Sheesh!

CHESTER: I can't believe this!

AMA: [*Continuing her search*] Di-gou! Are you already in bathroom? [*Exits.*]

HANNAH: [*To* AMA] Auntie, he wasn't at the airport! [*To* WILBUR] Why didn't you tell her?

WILBUR: [*Following* AMA] I'm trying! I'm trying! [*Exits.*]

ROBERT: It's those Communist airlines, I'm telling you. Inefficient.

HANNAH: We asked at the desk. They didn't have a flight list.

AMA: [*Entering*] Then where is he?

WILBUR: [*Entering, in despair*] Joanne, will you come here?

ROBERT: They probably left him in Guam.

POPO: [*To* ROBERT] We give you that photograph. You remember to bring it?

ROBERT: Of course I remembered.

HANNAH: [*To* POPO] Mom, it's not Robert's fault.

POPO: [*To* HANNAH] Should leave him [*Refers to* ROBERT] in car.

HANNAH: I tried.

ROBERT: In the car?

HANNAH: He wanted to come in.

ROBERT: It's hot in the car!

AMA: [*To* ROBERT] Suffer, good for you.

POPO: [*To* HANNAH] You cannot control your husband.

ROBERT: I suffer enough.

HANNAH: He said he could help.

POPO: He is wrong again.

AMA: What to do now?

[JENNY *exits in the confusion;* JOANNE *enters.*]

JOANNE: What's wrong now?

WILBUR: They lost your uncle.

JOANNE: Who lost him?

HANNAH: We didn't lose him.

AMA: [*To* ROBERT] You ask at airport desk?

ROBERT: I'm telling you, he's in Guam.

JOANNE: [*To* HANNAH] How could you lose a whole uncle?

HANNAH: We never had him to begin with!

JOANNE: So where is he?

ROBERT: Guam, I'm telling—!

POPO: [*To* ROBERT] Guam, Guam! Shut mouth or go there yourself!

HANNAH: [*A general announcement*] We don't know where he is!

JOANNE: Should I call the police?

WILBUR: You might have looked longer at the airport.

HANNAH: That's what I said, but he [*Refers to* ROBERT] said, "Aaah, too much trouble!"

POPO: [*To* ROBERT] See? You do not care about people from other province besides Shanghai.

ROBERT: [*To* POPO] Mom, I care. It's just that—

POPO: [*To* ROBERT] Your father trade with Japanese during war.

WILBUR: Huh?

ROBERT: Mom, let's not start that—

POPO: Not like our family. We die first!

WILBUR: What's all this about?

ROBERT: Hey, let's not bring up all this other junk, right?

POPO: [*To* ROBERT] You are ashamed.

ROBERT: The airport is a big place.

WILBUR: [*To* ROBERT] Still, you should've been able to spot an old Chinese man!

ROBERT: Everyone on that plane was an old Chinese man.

AMA: True. All Communist look alike.

HANNAH: Hold it, everybody! [*Pause*] Listen, Di-gou has this address, right?

AMA: No.

HANNAH: No? [*To* POPO] Mom, you said he did.

POPO: Yes. He does.

AMA: [*To* POPO] Yes? But I did not write to him.

POPO: I did.

AMA: Now, Communist—they will know this address.

POPO: Never mind.

AMA: No safety. Bomb us.

HANNAH: Okay, he has this address, and he can speak English—after all, he went to medical school here, right? So he shouldn't have any problem.

JOANNE: What an introduction to America.

HANNAH: All we can do is wait.

ROBERT: We went up to all these old Chinese men at the airport, asked them, "Are you our Di-gou?" They all said yes. What could we do? They all looked drunk, bums.

JOANNE: Maybe they're all still wandering through the metal detectors, looking for their families, and will continue till they die.

[CHESTER *wanders onto the tennis court, observes the following section from far upstage.*]

JOANNE: I must have been only about seven the last time Di-gou visited us in the Philippines.

AMA: Less.

JOANNE: Maybe less.

WILBUR: Honey, I'm sure everyone here has a memory, too. You don't see them babbling about it, do you?

JOANNE: The last thing I remember about Di-gou, he was trying to convince you grown-ups to leave the Philippines and return to China. There was a terrible fight—one of the worst that ever took place in our complex. I guess he wanted you to join the Revolution. The fight was so loud that all our servants gathered around the windows to watch.

AMA: They did this?

POPO: Shoot them.

JOANNE: I guess this was just around 1949. Finally, Di-gou left, calling you all sorts of terrible names. On his way out, he set fire to one of our warehouses. All us kids sat around while the servants tried to put it out.

POPO: No. That was not a warehouse.

HANNAH: Yeah, Joanne—the warehouses were concrete, remember?

JOANNE: [*To* HANNAH] But don't you remember a fire?

HANNAH: Yes.

POPO: I think he burn a pile of trash.

ROBERT: [*To* WILBUR] I know how you feel. They're always yap-yap-yapping about their family stories—you'd think they were the only family in China. [*To* HANNAH] I have memories, too.

HANNAH: You don't remember anything. You have a terrible memory.

ROBERT: Look, when I was kidnapped, I didn't know—

HANNAH: Sssssh!

JOANNE: Quiet, Robert!

POPO: Like broken record—ghang, ghang, ghang.

WILBUR: [*To* ROBERT] I tell you what: you wanna take a look at my collection of tax shelters?

ROBERT: Same old stuff?

WILBUR: No. Some new ones.

[*They exit.* DI-GOU *appears on the tennis court; only* CHESTER *sees him, but* CHESTER *says nothing.* CHESTER *watches* DI-GOU *watching the women.*]

JOANNE: Anyway, he set fire to something and the flames burned long into the night. One servant was even killed in it, if I remember correctly. I think Matthew's nursemaid was trying to put it out when her dress caught fire and, like a fool, she ran screaming all over the complex. All the adults were too busy to hear her, I guess, and all the kids just sat there and watched this second fire, moving in circles and screaming. By morning, both fires were out, and our tutors came as usual. But that day, nothing functioned just right—I think the water pipes broke in Sah-Zip's room, the cars wouldn't start—something—all I remember is servants running around all day with one tool or another. And that was how Di-gou left Manila for the last time. Left Manila and returned to China—in two fires—one which moved—and a great rush of handymen.

[DI-GOU *is now sitting in their midst in the sunroom. He puts down his suitcase. They turn and see him. He sticks his thumb out, as if for hitchhiking, but it is pointed in the wrong direction.*]

DI-GOU: "Going my way?"

AMA: Di-gou!

DI-GOU: "Hey, baby, got a lift?"

POPO: You see? Our family members will always return.

JOANNE: [*To* DI-GOU] Are you—? Oh, you're—? Well, nice—How did you get here?

DI-GOU: [*Pulls a book out of his jacket*] Our diplomacy handbook. Very useful.

POPO: Welcome to America!

DI-GOU: [*Referring to the handbook*] It says, "When transportation is needed, put your thumb as if to plug a hole."

AMA: [*On chair*] Di-gou, thirty year have passed—

DI-GOU: [*Still reading*] "And say, 'Going my way?' "

AMA: Do you still believe in God?

DI-GOU: "Or, 'Hey, baby, got a lift?' "

AMA: Do you?

HANNAH: [*To* AMA] Auntie, he's explaining something.

DI-GOU: It worked! I am here!

AMA: [*Getting down off chair*] Still as stubborn as before.

DI-GOU: Hello, my sisters.

POPO: Hello, Di-gou. This is my daughter, Hannah.

HANNAH: [*To* DI-GOU] Were you at the airport? We were waiting for you.

DI-GOU: Hannah. Oh, last time, you were just a baby.

AMA: [*Introducing* JOANNE] And Joanne, remember?

JOANNE: Hello, Di-gou. How was your flight?

DI-GOU: Wonderful, wonderful.

POPO: Where is Chester? Chester! [CHESTER *enters the lanai.*] Him—this is number one grandson.

DI-GOU: Oh, you are Chester. You are the violinist, yes?

CHESTER: You're Di-gou?

DI-GOU: Your parents are so proud of you.

HANNAH: We are not. He's just a kid who needs to pack.

AMA: Where is Jenny? Jenny!

HANNAH: [*To* DI-GOU] We figured you'd be able to get here by yourself.

DI-GOU: Oh, yes. [*He sticks out his thumb.* JENNY *enters.*]

JOANNE: Jenny! Say, "Hi, Di-gou."

JENNY: Hi, Di-gou.

DI-GOU: [*To* JOANNE] This is your daughter?

JOANNE: Yes. Jenny. [*Pause*] Jenny, say, "Hi, Di-gou."
JENNY: Mom, I just did!
JOANNE: Oh. Right.
JENNY: Will you cool out?
DI-GOU: Jenny, the last time I saw your mother, she was younger than you are now.
JENNY: He's kinda cute.
JOANNE: Jenny, your granduncle is not cute.
DI-GOU: Thank you.
JENNY: [*To* JOANNE] Can I go now?
AMA: Why you always want to go?
JENNY: Sorry, Ama. Busy.
JOANNE: [*Allowing* JENNY *to leave*] All right.
DI-GOU: [*To* JENNY] What are you doing?
JENNY: Huh? Reading.
DI-GOU: Oh. Schoolwork.
JENNY: Nah. *Vogue.* [*Exits.*]
JOANNE: I've got to see about dinner. [*To* HANNAH] Can you give me a hand? I want to use my new Cuisinart.
HANNAH: All right. What do you want to make?
JOANNE: I don't know. What does a Cuisinart do?

[HANNAH *and* JOANNE *exit;* DI-GOU, AMA, POPO, *and* CHESTER *are left in the sunroom.*]

AMA: Di-gou, thirty year have pass. Do you still love God?
DI-GOU: Thirty-three.
AMA: Ah?
POPO: 1949 to 1982. Thirty-three. He is correct.
AMA: Oh. But you do still love God? Like before?
DI-GOU: You know, sisters, after you left China, I learned that I never did believe in God. [*Pause*]
AMA: What!
POPO: How can you say this?
CHESTER: Ama, Popo, don't start in on that—he just got here.
POPO: You defend him?
AMA: [*Chasing* CHESTER *out to tennis court*] You both are influence by bad people.
POPO: Spend time with bums! Communist bum, musician bum, both same.
DI-GOU: Just to hear my sisters after all these years—you may speak whatever you like.
AMA: Do you still love God?
DI-GOU: I have much love.
AMA: For God?
DI-GOU: For my sisters. [*Pause*]
POPO: You are being very difficult.
AMA: You remember when you first become Christian?
POPO: You travel with See-goh-poh on her first evangelism tour? Before we move to Philippines and you stay in China? Remember? You speak in tongues of fire.

DI-GOU: I was only eight years old. That evening is a blur to me.

AMA: Tonight—we have family devotions. You can speak again. Miracles. You still believe in miracles?

DI-GOU: It is a miracle that I am here again with you!

POPO: Why you always change subject? You remember Ah Hong? Your servant? How See-goh-poh cast out his opium demon?

DI-GOU: I don't think that happened.

AMA: Yes! Remember? After evangelism tour—she cast out his demon.

POPO: Ah Hong tell stories how he eats opium, then he can see everything so clear, like—uh—glass. He can see even through wall, he say, and can see—ah—all the way through floor. Yes! He say he can see through ground, all the way to hell. And he talk with Satan and demon who pretend to be Ah Hong's dead uncles. You should remember.

DI-GOU: I vaguely recall some such stories.

[DI-GOU *opens up his suitcase during* POPO's *following speech and takes out two small Chinese toys and a small Chinese flag. He shows them to* POPO, *but she tries to ignore them.*]

POPO: Demon pretend to be ghost, then show himself everyplace to Ah Hong—in kitchen, in well, in barn, in street of village. Always just sit there, never talk, never move, just sit. So See-goh-poh come, call on God, say only, "Demon begone."

AMA: And from then on, no more ghost, no more opium.

POPO: You—you so happy, then. You say, you will also cast out the demon.

DI-GOU: We were all just children. [*He lines the toys up on the floor.*]

AMA: But you have faith of a child.

DI-GOU: Ah Hong didn't stop eating opium, though. He just needed money. That's why two years later, he was fired.

AMA: Ah Hong never fired!

POPO: I do not think so.

DI-GOU: Yes, my tenth, eleventh birthday, he was fired.

AMA: No—remember? Ah Hong die many year later—just before you come to America for college.

DI-GOU: No, he was fired before then.

POPO: No. Before you leave, go to college, you must prepare your own suitcase. [*To* AMA] Bad memory.

AMA: Brainwash.

[ROBERT *and* WILBUR *enter;* CHESTER *exits off the tennis court.* ROBERT *and* WILBUR *surround* DI-GOU.]

ROBERT *and* WILBUR: Welcome!

WILBUR: How you doing, Di-gow?

ROBERT: [*Correcting* WILBUR] Di-gou!

WILBUR: Oh, right. "Di-gou."

ROBERT: [*To* DI-GOU] We tried to find you at the airport.

WILBUR: [*To* DI-GOU] That means "second brother."

ROBERT: So, you escaped the Communists, huh?

WILBUR: Robert and I were just—

ROBERT: Little joke, there.

WILBUR: —looking at my collection of tax shelters.

ROBERT: China's pretty different now, huh?

WILBUR: You care to take a look?

ROBERT: I guess there's never a dull moment—

WILBUR: Probably no tax shelters, either.

ROBERT: —waiting for the next cultural revolution.

WILBUR: Oh, Robert!

ROBERT: Little joke, there.

WILBUR: [*To* DI-GOU] That's how he [*Refers to* ROBERT] does business.

ROBERT: Of course, I respect China.

WILBUR: He says these totally outrageous things.

ROBERT: But your airlines—so inefficient.

WILBUR: And people remember him.

ROBERT: How long were you in Guam?

WILBUR: [*To* ROBERT] He wasn't in Guam!

ROBERT: No?

WILBUR: [*To* DI-GOU] Well, we're going to finish up the tour.

ROBERT: My shelters are all at my house.

WILBUR: Feel welcome to come along.

ROBERT: His [*Refers to* WILBUR] are kid stuff. Who wants land in Montana?

WILBUR: [*To* ROBERT] Hey—I told you. I need the loss.

[WILBUR *and* ROBERT *exit, leaving* DI-GOU *with* AMA *and* POPO. *There is a long silence.*]

DI-GOU: Who are they?

POPO: Servants.

AMA: Don't worry. They will eat outside. In America, servants do not take over their masters' house.

DI-GOU: What are you talking about?

AMA: We know. In China now, servants beat their masters.

DI-GOU: Don't be ridiculous. I have a servant. A chauffeur.

[ROBERT *reenters.*]

ROBERT: Hey, Di-gou—we didn't even introduce ourselves.

DI-GOU: Oh, my sisters explained it to me.

ROBERT: I'm Robert. Hannah's my wife. [ROBERT *puts his arm around* DI-GOU.] When we married, I had nothing. I was working in grocery stores, fired from one job after another. But she could tell—I had a good heart.

DI-GOU: It is good to see servants marrying into the moneyed ranks. We are not aware of such progress by even the lowest classes.

[*Pause*]

ROBERT: Huh?

DI-GOU: To come to this—from the absolute bottom of society.

ROBERT: Wait, wait, I mean, sure, I made progress, but "the bottom of society"? That's stretching it some, wouldn't you say?

DI-GOU: Did you meet Hannah while preparing her food?

ROBERT: Huh? No, we met at a foreign students' dance at UCLA.

DI-GOU: Oh. You attended university?

ROBERT: Look, I'm not a country kid. It's not like I was that poor. I'm from Shanghai, you know.

POPO: [*To* ROBERT] Ssssh! Neighbors will hear!

ROBERT: I'm cosmopolitan. So when I went to college, I just played around at first. That's the beauty of the free-enterprise system, Di-gou. If you wanna be a bum, it lets you be a bum. I wasted my time, went out with all those American girls.

POPO: One girl.

ROBERT: Well, one was more serious, a longer commitment . . .

POPO: Minor.

DI-GOU: What?

POPO: He go out with girl—only fifteen year old.

ROBERT: I didn't know!

POPO: [*To* ROBERT] How come you cannot ask?

ROBERT: I was just an FOB. This American girl—she talked to me—asked me out—kissed me on first date—and I thought, "Land of opportunity!" Anyway, I decided to turn my back on China.

POPO: [*To* DI-GOU] He cannot even ask girl how old.

ROBERT: This is my home. When I wanted to stop being a bum, make money, it let me. That's America!

DI-GOU: I also attended American university. Columbia Medical School.

ROBERT: Right. My wife told me.

POPO: [*To* ROBERT] But he does not date the minor!

ROBERT: [*To* POPO] How was I supposed to know? She looked fully developed!

[AMA *and* POPO *leave in disgust, leaving* ROBERT *alone with* DI-GOU.]

ROBERT: [*To* DI-GOU] Well, then, you must understand American ways.

DI-GOU: It has been some time since I was in America.

ROBERT: Well, it's improved a lot, lemme tell you. Look, I have a friend who's an immigration lawyer. If you want to stay here, he can arrange it.

DI-GOU: Oh, no. The thought never even—

ROBERT: I know, but listen. I did it. Never had any regrets. We might be able to get your family over, too.

DI-GOU: Robert, I cannot leave China.

ROBERT: Huh? Look, Di-gou, people risk their lives to come to America. If only you could talk to—to the boat people.

DI-GOU: Uh—the food here looks very nice.

ROBERT: Huh? Oh, help yourself. Go ahead.

DI-GOU: Thank you. I will wait.

ROBERT: No, go on!

DI-GOU: Thank you, but—

ROBERT: Look, in America, there's so much, we don't have to be polite at all!

DI-GOU: Please—I'm not yet hungry.

ROBERT: Us Chinese, we love to eat, right? Well, here in America, we can be pigs!

DI-GOU: I'm not hungry.

ROBERT: I don't see why you can't—? Look. [*He picks up a piece of food, a bao.*] See? [*He stuffs the whole thing into his mouth.*] Pigs!

DI-GOU: Do you mind? I told you, I'm not—

ROBERT: I know. You're not hungry. Think I'm hungry? No, sir! What do I have to do to convince you? Here. [*He drops a tray of* guo-tieh *on the ground, begins stomping them.*] This is the land of plenty!

DI-GOU: Ai! Robert!

[ROBERT *continues stomping them like roaches.*]

ROBERT: There's one next to your foot! [*He stomps it.*] Gotcha!

DI-GOU: Please! It is not right to step on food!

ROBERT: "Right"? Now, see, that's your problem in the P.R.C.—lots of justice, but you don't produce.

[WILBUR *enters, catching* ROBERT *in the act.*]

WILBUR: Robert? What are you—? What's all this?

ROBERT: [*Stops stomping*] What's the big deal? You got a cleaning woman, don't you?

[JENNY *enters.*]

JENNY: Time to eat yet? [*She sees the mess.*] Blaagh.

[HANNAH *enters.*]

HANNAH: What's all this?

JENNY: Never mind.

[JENNY *exits;* WILBUR *points to* ROBERT, *indicating to* HANNAH *that* ROBERT *is responsible for the mess.* AMA *and* POPO *also enter at this moment, and see* WILBUR's *indication.*]

DI-GOU: In China, the psychological problems of wealth are a great concern.

POPO: Ai! Who can clean up after man like this!

WILBUR: Robert, I just don't think this is proper.

AMA: Wilbur—not clean himself.

ROBERT: Quiet! You all make a big deal out of nothing!

DI-GOU: I am a doctor. I understand.

POPO: But Robert—he also has the fungus feet.

ROBERT: Shut up, everybody! Will you all just shut up? I was showing Di-gou American ways!

[WILBUR *takes* DI-GOU*'s arm.*]

WILBUR: [*To* DI-GOU] Uh—come out here. I'll show you some American ways.

[WILBUR *and* DI-GOU *go out to the tennis court.*]

ROBERT: [*To* WILBUR] What do you know about American ways? You were born here!

POPO: [*To* AMA] Exercise—good for him.

ROBERT: Only us immigrants really know American ways!

POPO: [*To* AMA, *pinching her belly*] Good for here.

HANNAH: [*To* ROBERT] Shut up, dear. You've done enough damage today.

[WILBUR *gets* DI-GOU *a racket.*]

AMA: [*To* POPO] In China, he [*Refers to* DI-GOU] receives plenty exercise. Whenever Communists, they come torture him.

WILBUR: [*On tennis court, to* DI-GOU] I'll set up the machine. [*He goes* OFF.]

ROBERT: [*In sunroom, looking at tennis court*] What's so American about tennis?

HANNAH: [*To* ROBERT] Yes, dear.

ROBERT: You all ruined it!

HANNAH: You ruined the *guo-tieh*, dear.

ROBERT: What's a few *guo-tieh* in defense of America?

DI-GOU: [*To* WILBUR] I have not played tennis since my college days at Columbia.

ROBERT: [*To* HANNAH] He [*refers to* DI-GOU] was being so cheap! Like this was a poor country!

HANNAH: He's lived in America before, dear.

ROBERT: That was years ago. When we couldn't even buy a house in a place like this.

HANNAH: We still can't.

ROBERT: What?

HANNAH: Let's face it. We still can't afford—

ROBERT: That's not what I mean, stupid! I mean, when we wouldn't be able to because we're Chinese! He doesn't know the new America. I was making a point and you all ruined it!

HANNAH: Yes, dear. Now let's go in and watch the Betamax.

ROBERT: No!

HANNAH: C'mon!

[ROBERT *and* HANNAH *exit. On the tennis court,* DI-GOU *and* WILBUR *stand next to each other, facing offstage. A machine offstage begins to shoot tennis balls at them, each ball accompanied by*

a small explosive sound. A ball goes by; DI-GOU tries to hit it, but it is too high for him. Two more balls go by, but they are also out of DI-GOU's reach. A fourth ball is shot out, which hits WILBUR.]

WILBUR: Aaaah!

[*Balls are being shot out much faster now, pummeling WILBUR and DI-GOU. AMA and POPO continue to sit in the sunroom, staring away from the tennis court, peaceful and oblivious.*]

DI-GOU: Aaah!
WILBUR: I don't—! This never happened—!
DI-GOU: Watch out!
WILBUR: I'll turn off the machine.
DI-GOU: Good luck! Persevere! Overcome! Oh! Watch—!

[*A volley of balls drives WILBUR back. AMA and POPO hear the commotion, look over to the tennis court. The balls stop shooting out.*]

ROBERT: Tennis.
AMA: A fancy machine.

[*They return to looking downstage. The balls begin again.*]

WILBUR: Oh no!
AMA: Wilbur—he is such a bad loser.
POPO: Good exercise, huh? His age—good for here. [*She pinches her belly.*]
DI-GOU: I will persevere! [DI-GOU *tries to get to the machine, is driven back.*]
WILBUR: No! Di-gow!
DI-GOU: I am overcome!
WILBUR: Joanne! [*He begins crawling like a guerrilla toward the machine and finally makes it offstage. The balls stop, presumably because WILBUR reached the machine. DI-GOU runs off the court.*]
DI-GOU: [*Breathless*] Is it time yet . . . that we may cease to have . . . such enjoyment?

[WILBUR *crosses back onto the tennis court and into the lanai.*]

WILBUR: [*To offstage*] Joanne! This machine's too fast. I don't pay good money to be attacked by my possessions! [*Exits.*]

[AMA *and* POPO *get up, exit into the house, applauding* DI-GOU *as they go, for his exercise.*]

AMA *and* POPO: [*Clapping*] Good, good, very good!

[DI-GOU *is left alone on the tennis court. He is hit by a lone tennis ball.* CHESTER *enters, with a violin case. It is obvious that he has thrown that ball.*]

CHESTER: Quite a workout, there.

DI-GOU: America is full of surprises—why do all these products function so poorly?

CHESTER: Looks like "Made in U.S." is gonna become synonymous with defective workmanship. [*Pause*] You wanna see my violin?

DI-GOU: I would love to.

CHESTER: I thought you might. Here. [*He removes the violin from its case.*] See? No "Made in U.S." label.

DI-GOU: It is beautiful.

CHESTER: Careful! The back has a lacquer which never dries—so don't touch it, or you'll leave your fingerprints in it forever.

DI-GOU: Imagine that. After I die, someone could be playing a violin with my fingerprint.

CHESTER: Funny, isn't it?

DI-GOU: You know, I used to play violin.

CHESTER: Really?

DI-GOU: Though I never had as fine an instrument as this.

CHESTER: Try it. Go ahead.

DI-GOU: No. Please. I get more pleasure looking at it than I would playing it. But I would get the most pleasure hearing you play.

CHESTER: No.

DI-GOU: Please?

CHESTER: All right. Later. How long did you play?

DI-GOU: Some years. During the Cultural Revolution, I put it down.

CHESTER: Must've been tough, huh? [CHESTER *directs* DI-GOU's *attention to the back of his violin.*] Look—the back's my favorite part.

DI-GOU: China is my home, my work. I had to stay there. [DI-GOU *looks at the back of the violin.*] Oh—the way the light reflects—look. And I can see myself in it.

CHESTER: Yeah. Nice, huh?

DI-GOU: So you will take this violin and make music around the world.

CHESTER: Around the world? Oh, you probably got a misleading press clipping. See, my dad . . .

DI-GOU: Very funny.

CHESTER: [*Smiling*] Yeah. See, I'm just playing in the Boston Symphony. I'm leaving tomorrow.

DI-GOU: I am fortunate, then, to come today, or perhaps I would never meet you.

CHESTER: You see, I wasn't even planning to come here.

DI-GOU: That would be terrible. You know, in China, my wife and I had no children—for the good of the state. [DI-GOU *moves to where he left the Chinese toys earlier in the act. He picks them up and studies them.*] All these years, I try to imagine—what does Hannah look like? What does her baby look like? Now, I finally visit and what do I find? A young man. A violinist. The baby has long since disappeared. And I learn I'll never know the answer to my question.

[*Silence*]

CHESTER: Di-gou, why did you come here?

DI-GOU: My wife has died, I'm old. I've come for my sisters.

CHESTER: Well, I hope you're not disappointed to come here and see your sisters, your family, carry on like this.

DI-GOU: They are still my sisters.

CHESTER: I'm leaving here. Like you did.

DI-GOU: But, Chester, I've found that I cannot leave the family. Today—look!—I follow them across an ocean.

CHESTER: You know, they're gonna start bringing you to church.

DI-GOU: No. My sisters and their religion are two different things.

CHESTER: No, they're not. You've been away. You've forgotten. This family breathes for God. Ever since your aunt, See-goh-poh.

DI-GOU: See-goh-poh is not the first member of this family.

CHESTER: She's the first Christian.

DI-GOU: There are faces back further than you can see. Faces long before the white missionaries arrived in China. Here. [*He holds* CHESTER's *violin so that its back is facing* CHESTER, *and uses it like a mirror.*] Look here. At your face. Study your face and you will see—the shape of your face is the shape of faces back many generations—across an ocean, in another soil. You must become one with your family before you can hope to live away from it.

CHESTER: Oh, sure, there're faces. But they don't matter here. See-goh-poh's face is the only one that has any meaning here.

DI-GOU: No. The stories written on your face are the ones you must believe.

CHESTER: Stories? I see stories, Di-gou. All around me. This house tells a story. The days of the week tell a story—Sunday is service, Wednesday and Friday are fellowship, Thursday is visitation. Even the furniture tells stories. Look around. See-goh-poh is sitting in every chair. There's nothing for me here.

DI-GOU: I am here.

CHESTER: You? All right. Here. [CHESTER *turns the back of the violin toward* DI-GOU, *again using it like a mirror.*] You look. You wanna know what I see? I see the shape of your face changing. And with it, a mind, a will, as different as the face. If you stay with them, your old self will go, and in its place will come a new man, an old man, a man who'll pray.

DI-GOU: Chester, you are in America. If you deny those who share your blood, what do you have in this country?

AMA: [*From offstage*] All right? Ready?

CHESTER: Your face is changing, Di-gou. Before you know it, you'll be praying and speaking in tongues.

AMA: [*Still offstage*] One, two, three, four!

[*The "Hallelujah Chorus" begins. The choir enters, consisting of* WILBUR, JOANNE, ROBERT, HANNAH, *and* POPO. *They are led by* AMA, *who stands at a movable podium which is being pushed into the room by* ROBERT *and* WILBUR *as they sing. (The choir heads for the center of the room, where the podium comes to rest, with* AMA *still on it, and the "Hallelujah Chorus" ends.)* ROBERT *begins singing the tenor aria "Every Valley Shall Be Exalted," from Handel's* Messiah.]

ROBERT: "Every valley, every valley . . ."

HANNAH: Quiet, Robert!

ROBERT: But I want my solo!

JOANNE: [*To* ROBERT] Ssssh! We already decided this.

ROBERT: [*Continuing to sing*] ". . . shall be exalted . . ."

JOANNE: [*Yelling offstage*] Jenny!

AMA: [*To* ROBERT] Time for Family Devotions! Set up room!

[*They begin to arrange the room like a congregation hall, with the pulpit up front.*]

ROBERT: But it's a chance to hear my beautiful voice.

JENNY: [*From offstage*] Yeah! What?

POPO: [*To* ROBERT] Hear at home, hear in car. Now set up room.

JOANNE: [*Yelling offstage*] Jenny! Devotions!

JENNY: [*From offstage*] Aw, Mom.

JOANNE: [*Yelling offstage*] Devotions!

JENNY: [*Entering*] All right.

ROBERT: [*To* HANNAH] You know what this is? This is the breakdown of family authority.

HANNAH: [*To* ROBERT] You have all the authority, dear. Now shut up.

[JENNY *goes over to* CHESTER.]

JENNY: Hey, you still here? I thought for sure you'd have split by now.

CHESTER: I will.

JENNY: You gotta take it easier. Do like me. I act all lotus blossom for them. I say, "Hi, uncle this and auntie that." It's easy.

ROBERT: Look—all this free time. [*Sings*] "Every valley . . ."

POPO: Shoot him!

[*The room is set up.*]

AMA: We begin! Family Devotions! [AMA *flips a switch. A neon cross is lit up.*]

JENNY: [*To* CHESTER] Looks like a disco.

[*Everyone is seated except* DI-GOU. *The rest of the family waits for him. He walks over and sits down.* AMA *bows down to pray. Everyone bows except* CHESTER *and* DI-GOU, *but since all other eyes are closed, no one notices their noncompliance.* AMA *begins to pray.*]

AMA: Dear Father, when we think of your great mercy to this family, we can only feel so grateful, privilege to be family chose for your work. You claim us to be yours, put your mark on our heart.

[CHESTER *gets up, picks up his violin, gets* DI-GOU's *attention.*]

AMA: Your blessing begin many year ago in China.

[CHESTER *begins playing; his music serves as underscoring to* ÁMA's *prayer.*]

AMA: When See-goh-poh, she hear your word—from missionary. Your spirit, it touch her heart, she accept you, she speak in tongue of fire.

[CHESTER *begins to move out of the room as he plays.*]

AMA: You continue, bless See-goh-poh. She become agent of God, bring light to whole family, until we are convert, we become shining light for you all through Amoy.

[CHESTER *stops playing, looks at* DI-GOU, *waves good-bye, and exits.* DI-GOU *gets up, walks to where* CHESTER *was standing before he left, and waves good-bye.*]

AMA: Let us praise your victory over Satan. Praise your power over demon. Praise miracle over our own sinful will. Praise your victory over even our very hearts. Amen.

[AMA *conducts the choir in the ending of the "Hallelujah Chorus." As they sing, she notices* DI-GOU's *chair is empty. She turns and sees him waving. They look at each other as the "Hallelujah Chorus" continues.* CURTAIN.]

ACT II

A moment later. As the curtain rises, all are in the same positions they occupied at the end of Act I. AMA *and* DI-GOU *are looking at each other. The choir ends the "Hallelujah Chorus."* DI-GOU *walks back toward his chair, and sits.* AMA *notices that* CHESTER's *seat is empty.*

AMA: Where is Chester?
HANNAH: I heard his violin.
AMA: This is family devotions.
ROBERT: The kid's got a mind of his own.
HANNAH: He probably went home to pack, Auntie. He's really in a hurry.
JENNY: Can I go look?
AMA: Why everyone want to go?
JENNY: But he forgot his suitcase. [*She points to the green suitcase, which* CHESTER *has left behind.*]
POPO: [*To* JENNY] Di-gou, he will want to hear you give testimony.

[JENNY *sits back down.*]

AMA: Now—Special Testimony. Let us tell of God's blessing! Who will have privilege? Special Testimony! Who will be first to praise? [*Silence*] He is in our presence! Open His arms to us! [*Silence*] He is not going to wait forever—you know this! He is very busy!

[ROBERT *stands up, starts to head for podium.* POPO *notices that* ROBERT *has risen, points to him.*]

POPO: No! Not him!

AMA: [*To* ROBERT] He is very bored with certain people who say same thing over and over again.

WILBUR: Why don't we sit down, Robert?

JENNY: C'mon, Uncle Robert.

HANNAH: Dear, forget it, all right?

ROBERT: But she needed someone to start. I just—

POPO: [*To* ROBERT] She did not include you.

WILBUR: Can't you see how bored they are with that, Robert?

ROBERT: Bored.

WILBUR: Everybody else has forgotten it.

ROBERT: Forgotten it? They can't.

JOANNE: We could if you'd stop talking about it.

ROBERT: But there's something new!

WILBUR: Of course. There always is.

ROBERT: There is!

JOANNE: [*To* WILBUR] Don't pay attention, dear. It just encourages him.

WILBUR: [*To* JOANNE] Honey, are you trying to advise *me* on how to be diplomatic?

JOANNE: I'm only saying, if you let Hannah—

WILBUR: You're a real stitch, you know that? You really are.

JOANNE: Hannah's good at keeping him quiet.

ROBERT: Quiet?

WILBUR: [*To* JOANNE] Look, who was voted "Mr. Congeniality" at the club last week—you or me?

ROBERT: Hannah, who are you telling to be quiet?

HANNAH: Quiet, Robert.

WILBUR: [*To* JOANNE] Afraid to answer? Huh? Who? Who was "Mr. Congeniality"? Tell me—were you "Mr. Congeniality"?

JENNY: [*To* WILBUR] I don't think she stood a chance, Dad.

WILBUR: [*To* JENNY] Who asked you, huh?

JENNY: "Mr. Congeniality," I think.

WILBUR: Don't be disrespectful.

AMA: We must begin Special Testimony! Who is first?

POPO: I talk.

JOANNE: Good.

POPO: Talk from here. [*She stands.*] Long time since we all come here like this. I remember long ago, family leave China—the boat storm, storm, storm, storm, all around, Hannah cry. I think, "Aaah, why we have to leave China, go to Philippines?" But I remember Jonah, when he did not obey God, only then seas become— ah—dangerous. And even after, after Jonah eaten by whale, God provide for him. So if God has plan for us, we live; if not [*She looks at* DI-GOU.] we die. [*She sits.*] Okay. That's all.

[*Everyone applauds.*]

AMA: Very good! Who is next?

ROBERT: I said, I'd be happy to—

HANNAH: How about Jenny?

JENNY: Me?

JOANNE: Sure, dear, c'mon.

JENNY: Oh . . . well . . .

POPO: [*To* DI-GOU] You see—she is so young, but her faith is old.

JENNY: After I do this, can I go see what's happened to Chester?

POPO: [*To* JENNY] First, serve God.

ROBERT: Let her go.

POPO: Then, you may see about Chester.

JENNY: All right. [*She walks to the podium.*]

POPO: [*To* DI-GOU] I will tell you what each sentence meaning.

DI-GOU: I can understand quite well.

POPO: No. You are not Christian. You need someone—like announcer at baseball game—except announce for God.

JENNY: [*At podium, she begins testimony.*] First, I want to say that I love you all very much. I really do.

POPO: [*To* DI-GOU] That meaning is, she love God.

JENNY: And I appreciate what you've done for me.

POPO: [*To* DI-GOU] She loves us because we show her God.

JENNY: But I guess there are certain times when even love isn't enough.

POPO: [*To* DI-GOU] She does not have enough love for you. You are not Christian.

JENNY: Sometimes, even love has its dark side.

POPO: [*To* DI-GOU] That is you.

JENNY: And when you find that side, sometimes you have to leave in order to come back in a better way.

POPO: [*To* DI-GOU] She cannot stand to be around you.

JENNY: Please. Remember what I said, and think about it later.

POPO: [*To* DI-GOU] You hear? Think!

JENNY: Thank you.

[*Everyone applauds.*]

AMA: Good, good.

JENNY: Can I go now?

ROBERT: [*To* HANNAH] What was she talking about?

AMA: [*To* JENNY] Soon, you can be best testifier—do testimony on TV.

JENNY: Can I go now?

JOANNE: All right, Jenny.

JENNY: Thanks. [*Exits.*]

ROBERT: [*To* POPO] Why don't you interpret for *me?* I didn't understand what she was talking about. Not a bit.

POPO: Good.

ROBERT: Good? Don't you want me to be a better Christian?

POPO: No. Not too good. Do not want to live in same part of Heaven as you.

ROBERT: Why not? It'll be great, Popo. We can tell stories, sing—

POPO: In Heaven, hope you live in basement.

ROBERT: Basement? C'mon, Popo, I'm a celebrity. They wouldn't give me the basement. They'll probably recognize my diplomacy ability, make me ambassador.

JOANNE: To Hell?

ROBERT: Well, if that's the place they send ambassadors.

POPO: Good. You be ambassador.

AMA: Special Testimony! Who is next?

ROBERT: [*Asking to be recognized*] Ama?

AMA: [*Ignoring him*] Who is next?

ROBERT: Not me. I think Wilbur should speak.

AMA: [*Disgusted*] Wilbur?

WILBUR: Me?

ROBERT: Yeah.

WILBUR: Well, I don't really . . .

ROBERT: Tell them, Wilbur. Tell them what kind of big stuffs happen to you. Tell them how important you are.

WILBUR: Well, I . . .

AMA: Would you . . . like to speak . . . Wilbur?

WILBUR: Well, I'd be honored, but if anyone else would rather . . .

ROBERT: We want to hear what you have to be proud of.

WILBUR: All right. [WILBUR *takes the podium;* AMA *scurries away.*] Uh—well, it's certainly nice to see this family reunion. Uh—last week, I was voted "Mr. Congeniality" at the club.

ROBERT: What papers was it in?

WILBUR: Huh?

ROBERT: Was it in the L.A. *Times?* Front page? Otis Chandler's paper?

HANNAH: [*A rebuff*] Robert!

POPO: [*To* ROBERT] Devotions is not question-and-answer for anyone except God.

ROBERT: God sometimes speaks through people, doesn't He?

POPO: He has good taste. Would not speak through you.

ROBERT: [*Undaunted, to* WILBUR] Show me one newspaper clipping. Just one!

WILBUR: Well, besides the *Valley Green Sheet* . . .

ROBERT: The *Valley Green Sheet?* Who pays for that? Junk. People line their birdcages with it.

WILBUR: Well, I suppose from a media standpoint, it's not that big a deal.

AMA: [*To* JOANNE] What means "congeniality"?

JOANNE: It means "friendly," sort of.

ROBERT: [*To* WILBUR] So why are you talking about it? Waste our time?

WILBUR: Look, Robert, it's obviously a token of their esteem.

ROBERT: Junk stuffs. Little thing. Who cares?

AMA: [*To herself*] "Mr. Friendly"?

ROBERT: It's embarrassing. What if clients say to me, "You're a bank president but

your relatives can only get into the *Valley Green Sheet?*" Makes me lose face. They think my relatives are bums.

AMA: [*To* JOANNE] He is "Mr. Friendly"?

WILBUR: Look, Robert, the business is doing real well. It's not like that's my greatest accomplishment.

AMA: [*To* JOANNE] How can he be "Mr. Friendly"? He always kill and laugh.

JOANNE: Mom!

ROBERT: [*To* WILBUR] Does your business get in the paper?

WILBUR: Computer software happens to be one of the nation's fastest-growing—

ROBERT: So what? Lucky guess. Big deal.

WILBUR: It was an educated choice, not luck!

[ROBERT *gets up, starts to head for the podium.*]

ROBERT: Anyone can make money in America. What's hard is to become . . . a celebrity.

WILBUR: You're not a celebrity!

ROBERT: Yes, I am. That's the new thing. See, I just wanted to say that—[*He nudges* WILBUR *off the podium, takes his place.*]—when I was kidnapped, I didn't know if I would live or die.

POPO: [*Turns and sees* ROBERT *at the podium*] Huh?

JOANNE: Robert, forget it!

POPO: How did he get up there?

WILBUR: [*To* JOANNE] I'm perfectly capable of handling this myself.

POPO: He sneak up there while we are bored!

WILBUR: [*To* POPO] I'm sorry you found my testimony boring.

ROBERT: [*To* WILBUR] It was. [*To the assemblage*] Now hear mine.

JOANNE: We've all heard it before.

HANNAH: [*To* ROBERT] They're tired, dear. Get down.

ROBERT: Why? They listened to Wilbur's stuff. Boring. Junk.

JOANNE: "I didn't know if I would live or die." "I didn't know if I would live or die."

ROBERT: Di-gou, he hasn't heard. Have you, Di-gou?

DI-GOU: Is this when you didn't know if you would live or die?

ROBERT: How did—? Who told him?

POPO: I cannot think of enough ways to shoot him! Rifle! Arrows!

HANNAH: [*To* ROBERT] Sit down!

ROBERT: But there's something new!

HANNAH: I think we better let him speak, or he'll never shut up.

ROBERT: She's right. I won't.

JOANNE: All right. Make it quick, Robert.

ROBERT: All right. As I was saying, I didn't know if I would live or die.

JOANNE: You lived.

ROBERT: But the resulting publicity has made me a celebrity. Every place I go, people come up to me—"Aren't you the one that got kidnapped?" When I tell them how much the ransom was, they can hardly believe it. They ask for my autograph.

Now—here's the new thing. I met these clients last week, told them my story. Now these guys are big shots and they say it would make a great movie. Yeah. No kidding. They made movies before. Not just regular movie, that's junk stuffs. We want to go where the big money is—we want to make a miniseries for TV. Like "Shogun." I told them, they should take the story, spice it up a little, you know? Add some sex scenes—we were thinking that I could have some hanky-panky with one of my kidnappers—woman, of course—just for audience sake—like Patty Hearst. I told them I should be played by Marlon Brando. And I have the greatest title: "Not a Chinaman's Chance." Isn't that a great title? "Not a Chinaman's Chance." Beautiful. I can see the beginning already: I'm walking out of my office. I stop to help a man fixing a flat tire.

HANNAH: All right, dear. That's enough.

ROBERT: Meanwhile, my secretary is having sex with my kidnapper.

HANNAH: Kidnap! Kidnap! That's all I ever hear about!

ROBERT: But, Hannah, I didn't know if I would live or die.

HANNAH: I wish you'd never even been kidnapped.

JOANNE: Well, what about Wilbur?

WILBUR: Leave me out of this.

JOANNE: Wilbur, you could be kidnapped.

WILBUR: I know, I know. It just hasn't happened yet, that's all.

HANNAH: Listen, Joanne. Count your blessings. It's not that great a thing. If they live, they never stop talking about it.

ROBERT: But the publicity!—I sign newspapers all the time!

JOANNE: I'm just saying that Robert's not the only one worth kidnapping.

HANNAH: Joanne, no one's saying that.

AMA: Yes. We all desire Wilbur to be kidnapped also.

POPO: And Robert. Again. This time, longer.

JOANNE: I mean, Wilbur has a lot of assets.

ROBERT: Wilbur, maybe next time you can get kidnapped.

WILBUR: Never mind, honey.

JOANNE: You do.

WILBUR: I can defend myself.

ROBERT: But it takes more than assets to be kidnapped. You have to be cosmopolitan.

HANNAH: Hey, wait. What kind of example are we setting for Di-gou?

ROBERT: See? That's why I'm talking about it. To show Di-gou the greatness of America. I'm just an immigrant, Di-gou, an FOB—but in America, I get kidnapped.

HANNAH: I mean, a Christian example.

DI-GOU: Oh, do not worry about me. This is all very fascinating.

JOANNE: [To ROBERT] So, you think you're cosmopolitan, huh?

ROBERT: I am. Before they let me loose, those kidnappers—they respected me.

JOANNE: They probably let you go because they couldn't stand to have you in their car.

POPO: Probably you sing to them.

ROBERT: No. They said, "We've been kidnapping a long time, but—"

JOANNE: Because we can't stand to have you in our house! [Pause]

ROBERT: [*To* JOANNE] Now what kind of example are you setting for Di-gou?

WILBUR: Joanne, just shut up, okay?

HANNAH: [*To* DI-GOU] It's not always like this.

JOANNE: [*To* WILBUR] You never let me talk! You even let him [*Refers to* ROBERT] talk, but you never let me talk!

AMA: [*To* JOANNE] He [*Refers to* WILBUR] cannot deprive you of right to speak. Look. No gun.

ROBERT: Joanne, I have to tell this because Di-gou is here.

DI-GOU: Me?

JOANNE: [*To* ROBERT] You tell it to waiters!

ROBERT: Joanne, I want him [*Refers to* DI-GOU] to understand America. The American Dream. From rags to kidnap victim.

JOANNE: [*To* ROBERT] Well, I don't like you making Di-gou think that Wilbur's a bum.

WILBUR: [*To* JOANNE] Dear, he doesn't think that.

JOANNE: [*To* DI-GOU] You see, don't you, Di-gou? This house. Wilbur bought this.

DI-GOU: It is a palace.

JOANNE: It's larger than Robert's.

HANNAH: Joanne, how can you sink to my husband's level?

ROBERT: My house would be larger, but we had to pay the ransom.

POPO: Waste of money.

JOANNE: Look, all of you always put down Wilbur. Well, look at what he's done.

WILBUR: [*To* JOANNE] Just shut up, all right?

JOANNE: [*To* WILBUR] Well, if you're not going to say it.

WILBUR: I don't need you to be my PR firm.

ROBERT: [*To anybody*] He doesn't have a PR firm. We do. Tops firm.

JOANNE: [*To* WILBUR] Let me say my mind!

WILBUR: There's nothing in your mind worth saying.

JOANNE: What?

WILBUR: Face it, honey, you're boring.

AMA: [*To* WILBUR] At least she does not torture!

WILBUR: Please! No more talking about torture, all right?

AMA: All right. I will be quiet. No need to torture me.

POPO: [*To* DI-GOU] This small family disagreement.

JOANNE: So I'm boring, huh?

WILBUR: [*To* JOANNE] Look, let's not do this here.

POPO: [*To* DI-GOU] But power of God will overcome this.

JOANNE: I'm boring—that's what you're saying?

HANNAH: Joanne! Not in front of Di-gou!

JOANNE: [*To* DI-GOU] All right. You're objective. Who do you think is more boring?

DI-GOU: Well, I can hardly—

WILBUR: Please, Joanne.

POPO: [*To* DI-GOU] Do you understand how power of God will overcome this?

JOANNE: He [*Refers to* WILBUR] spends all his time with machines, and he calls me boring!

AMA: Di-gou, see the trials of this world?

WILBUR: [*To* JOANNE] Honey, I'm sorry, all right?
JOANNE: Sure, you're sorry.
AMA: [*To* DI-GOU] Argument, fight, no-good husbands.
WILBUR: "No-good husbands"?

[ROBERT, *in disgust exits into the house.*]

AMA: [*To* DI-GOU] Turn your eyes from this. [POPO *and* AMA *turn* DI-GOU's *eyes from the fight.*]
JOANNE: [*To* WILBUR] She's [*Refers to* AMA] right, you know.
WILBUR: All right, honey, let's discuss this later.
JOANNE: Later! Oh, right.

[WILBUR *runs off into the house;* JOANNE *yells after him.*]

JOANNE: When we're with *your* family, that's when you want to talk about my denting the Ferrari.
HANNAH: Joanne! Don't be so boring!
JOANNE: [*To* HANNAH] With *our* family, it's "later."
AMA: [*To* DI-GOU] Look up to God!

[POPO *and* AMA *force* DI-GOU *to look up.*]

DI-GOU: Please! [DI-GOU *breaks away from the sisters' grip, but they knock him down.*]
POPO: Now—is time to join family in Heaven.
AMA: Time for you to return to God.
HANNAH: [*To* JOANNE] Look—they're converting Di-gou.
POPO: Return. Join us for eternity.
AMA: Pray now.

[POPO *and* AMA *try to guide* DI-GOU *to the neon cross.*]

DI-GOU: Where are we going?
AMA: He will wash you in blood of the lamb.
POPO: Like when you are a child. Now! You bow down!
HANNAH: Ask God for His forgiveness.
JOANNE: You won't regret it, Di-gou.
DI-GOU: Do you mind? [*He breaks away.*]
POPO: Why will you not accept Him?
AMA: There is no good reason.
DI-GOU: I want to take responsibility for my own life.
POPO: You cannot!
AMA: Satan is rule your life now.
DI-GOU: I am serving the people.
AMA: You are not.

POPO: You serve them, they all die, go to Hell. So what?

DI-GOU: How can you abandon China for this Western religion?

AMA: It is not.

POPO: God is God of all people.

DI-GOU: There is no God!

[*Pause*]

AMA: There is too much Communist demon in him. We must cast out demon.

POPO: Now, tie him on table.

DI-GOU: This is ridiculous. Stop this.

[*The women grab* DI-GOU, *tie him on the table.*]

POPO: We have too much love to allow demon to live.

DI-GOU: What?

POPO: [*To* JOANNE *and* HANNAH, *who are hesitating*] Now!

DI-GOU: You can't—!

POPO: Now! Or demon will escape!

AMA: We must kill demon.

POPO: Shoot him!

AMA: Kill for good.

POPO: Make demon into *jok!*[1]

DI-GOU: This is barbaric! You live with the barbarians, you become one yourself!

POPO: Di-gou, if we do not punish your body, demon will never leave.

AMA: Then you will return to China.

POPO: And you will die.

AMA: Go to Hell.

POPO: And it will be too late.

DI-GOU: I never expected Chinese children to tie down their elders. [DI-GOU *is now securely tied to the table.*]

HANNAH: All right. We're ready.

POPO: Now—you give your testimony.

DI-GOU: I'll just lie here and listen, thank you.

AMA: You tell of God's mercies to you.

JOANNE: How He let you out of China.

AMA: Where you are torture.

JOANNE: Whipped.

POPO: After thirty year, He let you out. Praise Him!

DI-GOU: I will never do such a thing!

HANNAH: If you wait too long, He'll lose patience.

POPO: Now—tell of your trip with See-goh-poh.

POPO: The trip which begin your faith.

---

[1] A Chinese rice porridge. [Author's note]

DI-GOU: I was only eight years old. I don't remember.

POPO: Tell how many were convert on her tour.

HANNAH: Tell them, Di-gou.

DI-GOU: I cannot.

JOANNE: Why? Just tell the truth.

POPO: Tell how you saw the miracle of a great evangelist, great servant of God.

HANNAH: Tell them before they lose their patience.

DI-GOU: I'm sorry. I will not speak.

POPO: Then we are sorry, Di-gou, but we must punish your body. Punish to drive out the demon and make you speak.

HANNAH: Don't make them do this, Di-gou.

AMA: If you will not speak See-goh-poh's stories in language you know, we will punish you until you speak in tongue of fire. [AMA *hits* DI-GOU *with an electrical cord, using it like a whip.*]

JOANNE: Please, Di-gou!

HANNAH: Tell them!

AMA: Our Lord was beat, nails drive through His body, for our sin. Your body must suffer until you speak the truth. [AMA *hits him.*]

HANNAH: Tell them, See-goh-poh was a great evangelist.

AMA: You were on her evangelism tour—we were not—you must remember her converts, her miracle. [*Hit*]

JOANNE: Just tell them and they'll let you go!

AMA: Think of See-goh-poh! She is sit! [*Hit*] Sit beside God. He is praising her! Praise her for her work in China.

[CHESTER *enters the tennis court; he looks into the sunroom and sees* AMA *hit* DI-GOU.]

AMA: She is watching you!

[*Hit.* CHESTER *tries to get into the sunroom, but the glass door is locked. He bangs on it, but everyone inside stands shocked at* AMA*'s ritual, and no one notices him. He exits off the tennis court, running.*]

AMA: Praying for you! Want you to tell her story! [*Hit*]

AMA: We will keep you in float. Float for one second between life and death. Float until you lose will to hold to either—hold to anything at all.

[AMA *quickly slips the cord around* DI-GOU*'s neck, begins pulling on it.* JOANNE *and* HANNAH *run to get* AMA *off of* DI-GOU. CHESTER *enters from the house, with* JENNY *close behind him. He pulls* AMA *off of* DI-GOU.]

CHESTER: Ama! Stop it!

[DI-GOU *suddenly breaks out of his bonds and rises up on the table. He grabs* CHESTER. *The barbecue bursts into flames.* DI-GOU, *holding on to* CHESTER, *begins speaking in tongues.*]

AMA: [*Looking up from the ground*] He is speaking in tongues! He has returned!

[*Everyone falls to their knees.*]

[*As* DI-GOU's *tongues continue*, CHESTER *is suddenly filled with words, and begins interpreting* DI-GOU's *babbling.*]

CHESTER: Di-gou at eight goes with See-goh-poh on her first evangelism tour. Di-gou and See-goh-poh traveling through the summer heat to a small village in Fukien. Sleeping in the straw next to See-goh-poh. Hearing a sound. A human sound. A cry in my sleep. Looking up and seeing a fire. A fire and See-goh-poh. See-goh-poh is naked. Naked and screaming. Screaming with legs spread so far apart. So far that a mouth opens up. A mouth between her legs. A mouth that is throwing up blood, spitting out blood. More and more blood. See-goh-poh's hands making a baby out of the blood. See-goh-poh hits the blood baby. Hits the baby and the baby cries. Watching the baby at See-goh-poh's breast. Hearing the sucking.

[AMA *and* POPO *spring up.*]

POPO: Such a thing never happened!
AMA: See-goh-poh never did this!
POPO: This is not tongues. This is not God. This is demon!
CHESTER: Sucking. Praying. Sucking. Squeezing. Crying.
AMA: He is possess by demon!
CHESTER: Biting. Blood. Milk.
POPO: Both have the demon!
CHESTER: Blood and milk. Blood and milk running down.
AMA: [*To the other women*] You pray.
CHESTER: Running down, further and further down.
POPO: We must cast out the demon!

[DI-GOU's *tongues slowly become English, first overlapping, then overtaking* CHESTER's *translation.* CHESTER *becomes silent and exhausted, drops to the ground.*]

CHESTER *and* DI-GOU: Down. Down and into the fire. The fire down there. The fire down there.

[DI-GOU *breaks the last of his bonds, gets off the table.*]

DI-GOU: [*To the sisters*] Your stories are dead now that you know the truth.
AMA: We have faith. We know our true family stories.
DI-GOU: You do not know your past.
AMA: Are you willing to match your stories against ours?

[DI-GOU *indicates his willingness to face* AMA, *and the two begin a ritualistic battle.* POPO *supports* AMA *by speaking in tongues.* AMA *and* DI-GOU *square off in seated positions, facing one another.*]

AMA: We will begin. How many rooms in our house in Amoy?

DI-GOU: Eighteen. How many bedrooms?

AMA: Ten. What year was it built?

DI-GOU: 1893. What year was the nineteenth room added?

AMA: 1923.

DI-GOU: On whose instructions?

AMA: See-goh-poh.

DI-GOU: What year did See-goh-poh die?

AMA: 1945. What disease?

DI-GOU: Malaria. How many teeth was she missing?

AMA: Three.

DI-GOU: What villages were on See-goh-poh's evangelism tour? [*Silence*] Do you know?

AMA: She preached to all villages in Fukien.

DI-GOU: Name one. [*Silence*] Do you know? Your stories don't know. It never happened.

AMA: It did! What year was she baptized? [*Silence*] What year was she baptized?

DI-GOU: She was never baptized.

AMA: You see? You don't remember.

DI-GOU: Never baptized.

AMA: It was 1921. Your stories do not remember.

DI-GOU: Who was converted on her evangelism tour?

AMA: Perhaps five hundred or more.

DI-GOU: Who? Name one. [*Silence*]

AMA: It is not important.

DI-GOU: You see? It never happened.

AMA: It did.

DI-GOU: You do not remember. You do not know the past. See-goh-poh never preached.

AMA: How can you say this?

DI-GOU: She traveled.

AMA: To preach.

DI-GOU: To travel.

AMA: She visited many—

DI-GOU: I was there! She was thrown out—thrown out on her evangelism tour when she tried to preach. [*Silence*]

AMA: It does not matter.

DI-GOU: You forced her to invent the stories.

AMA: We demand nothing!

DI-GOU: You expected! Expected her to convert all Amoy!

AMA: She did!

DI-GOU: Expected many miracles.

AMA: She did! She was a great—

DI-GOU: Expected her not to have a baby.

AMA: She had no husband. She had no baby. This is demon talk. Demon talk and lie.

DI-GOU: She turned away from God.

AMA: We will never believe this!

DI-GOU: On her tours she could both please you and see China.

[POPO'S *tongues become weaker; she starts to falter.*]

AMA: See-goh-poh was a great—

DI-GOU: Only on her tours could she see both China and her baby.

AMA: She was a great . . . a great evangelist . . . many . . .

DI-GOU: Where is she buried?

AMA: . . . many miracle . . .

DI-GOU: She is not buried within the walls of the church in Amoy.

AMA: . . . many miracle a great evangelist . . .

[POPO *collapses.*]

DI-GOU: In her last moment, See-goh-poh wanted to be buried in Chinese soil, not Christian soil. You don't know. You were in the Philippines. [*Pause*] I come to bring you back to China. Come, sisters. To the soil you've forsaken with ways born of memories, of stories that never happened. Come, sisters. The stories written on your face are the ones you must believe.

[AMA *rises from her chair.*]

AMA: We will never believe this! [*She collapses back into her chair, closes her eyes.*]

[*Silence*]

DI-GOU: Sisters? [*Silence*] Sisters!

[JENNY, CHESTER, JOANNE, HANNAH, *and* DI-GOU *stare at the two inert forms.*]

CHESTER: Jenny! Jenny!

[JENNY *goes to* CHESTER'S *side.*]

JOANNE: Hannah? Hannah—come here.

[HANNAH *does not move.*]

HANNAH: I see.

JOANNE: No! Come here!

HANNAH: I know, Joanne. I see.

DI-GOU: Once again. Once again my pleas are useless. But now—this is the last time. I have given all I own.

[POPO *and* AMA *have died.* DI-GOU *picks up his suitcase and the Chinese toys, heads for the door.*]

JOANNE: [*To* DI-GOU] Are you leaving?
DI-GOU: Now that my sisters have gone, I learn. No one leaves America. And I desire only to drive an American car—very fast—down an American freeway. [DI-GOU *exits.*]
JOANNE: [*Yelling after him*] This is our home, not yours! Why didn't you stay in China! This is not your family!

[JENNY *starts to break away from* CHESTER, *but he hangs on to her.* JOANNE *turns, sees the figures of* AMA *and* POPO.]

JOANNE: Wilbur! Wilbur, come here!
JENNY: [*To* CHESTER] Let go of me! Get away! [*She breaks away from* CHESTER.] I don't understand this, but whatever it is, it's ugly and it's awful and it causes people to die. It causes people to die and I don't want to have anything to do with it.

[JENNY *runs out onto the tennis court and away. On her way, she passes* ROBERT, *who has entered onto the court.* ROBERT *walks into the sunroom. Silence.*]

ROBERT: What's wrong with her? She acts like someone just died. [*Silence. He pulls up a chair next to* CHESTER.] Let's chit-chat, okay?
CHESTER: Sure, Dad.
ROBERT: So, how's Dorrie? [*Silence*] How much they paying you in Boston? [*Silence*] Got any new newspaper clippings?

[*Silence*]

[CHESTER *gets up, picks up his suitcase, walks onto the tennis court, and shuts the glass doors.*]

[AMA *and* POPO *lie in the center of the room.* JOANNE *and* HANNAH *stare at them.* ROBERT *sits, staring off into space.*]

[CHESTER *turns around, looks through the glass door onto the scene.*]

[*The* LIGHTS BEGIN TO DIM *until there is a single spotlight on* CHESTER's *face, standing where* DI-GOU *stood at the beginning of the play.*]

[*The shape of* CHESTER's *face begins to change.*]

Curtain

QUESTIONS

1. What are some of the actions and rituals in Act I that demonstrate we are in the home of a typical American family?
2. What are the major differences in values, beliefs, attitudes, and language among the three generations of the family as they are shown in Act I? How do these differences create conflict among the various characters?
3. What is the importance to Ama and Popo of See-goh-poh? Contrast their attitude about religion with Di-gou's.
4. What irony is there in Robert's dropping the tray of *guo-tieh* to demonstrate how much abundance there is in the United States? What other ironies does the author suggest through action or dialogue that reflect on the American Dream?
5. In Act I, what similarity does Chester find between himself and Di-gou? How does this similarity foreshadow what occurs in Act II?
6. What is ironic about Robert having been kidnapped? How does his kidnapping reflect the irony of American life, particularly as it applies to achieving affluence in America?
7. What is the significance of Chester's interpreting Di-gou when the latter begins to "speak in tongues"?
8. What do you believe to be the cause of the simultaneous deaths of Ama and Popo?

Estela Portillo

DAY OF THE SWALLOWS

———————— **CAST OF CHARACTERS** ————————

ALYSEA	EDUARDO
CLEMENCIA	CLARA
JOSEFA	DON MIGUEL ESQUINAS
TOMÁS	FATHER PRADO

The tierra del Lago de San Lorenzo is within memory of mountain sweet pine. There the maguey thickens with the ferocity of the sun. The desert yawns, drinking the sun in madness. The village of Lago de San Lorenzo is a stepchild of the Esquinas hacienda, both a frugal mother and a demanding father. Two hundred years before, the Esquinas family had settled in the town on a Spanish grant of fifty thousand acres. The Indians were pushed out farther into the desert. Gradually they returned, building the barrio around the hacienda, depending on it for a livilihood. The greedy vitality of the hacienda owners, the gachupins, was a wonder to the Indian. The bearded gachupins with their arrogance became the masters. *Or did they? As the barrio clustered itself around the hacienda, time and desert life, symbiotic with the Indian, conquered the conquerors.*

The Indian, with his own distinct vision of the universe, endures, unchanged, stoic, accepting of a stunted existence. The tempo of life in the village remains unbroken, woven out of myth, ritual, and the instinctive tenacity for survival. The Esquinas hacienda is the fiber upon which existence hangs. The church is the fluid hope, dissolving human suffering into enthralling and refreshing faith.

All things happen on the day of San Lorenzo. The town is invaded by swallows flying north. On this fiesta day, a good Catholic is honored by the church. He or she leads a procession to the church for a general blessing of the people and the animals of the village. But the most important ritual of the Day of San Lorenzo is the bathing of the virgins in the lake. The church bells toll eleven in the sun. The lake becomes a sacred temple where the young girls of the village bathe and wash their hair in spring water to insure a future marriage "made in heaven." No one has seen a "marriage made in heaven," but each girl secretly hugs the hope that hers will be the one. Here the young women dig their feet in the mud with lyrical intimacy, eyes burning, heart beating, the smell of pine heavy in their nostrils as they trace mountain against sky. All the women of the village have shared in this experience except one—Josefa. Yet, hers is the only house built close to the edge of the lake, some distance from the barrio.

ACT I

SCENE I

JOSEFA's *sitting room: it is an unusually beautiful room, very feminine and done in good taste. The profusion of lace everywhere gives the room a delicate, ephemeral appearance. The lace pieces are lovely: needlepoint, hairpin, limerick, the work of patience and love. Upstage left is a large bay window; from it, one can view a large tree with a bird house of unusual size and shape, an orb that can accommodate a great number of birds. The room faces south, so it is flooded with light. There is almost a melting of light into lace, a peaceful serenity. To the right is a door leading to the kitchen; there is another door leading to a bedroom. Downstage left is a door leading to the outside.*

When the curtain rises, ALYSEA *is sitting on the floor. It is before dawn, but a minute or so after the curtain rises, light begins to fill the room.* ALYSEA *is cleaning the sitting room carpet, an unusual task for this hour. Next to her is a pail. She uses a piece of cloth with quick frantic movements, rinses, and continues the rubbing of the carpet. After a while, she looks at the cloth in her hand almost in a trance, then with a growing horror. She drops it, raising herself to her knees, she stares at it, then covers her face with her hands. She sits back on the floor leaning her head against a chair, looking helpless and lost. She is sobbing quietly. After a while, she stares at the new streaming light from the window, feeling its warmth as a comfort. The sound of a milk bell interrupts the silence. When she hears it, she jumps up, looks desperately about the room, wipes the traces of tears from her eyes and goes to the window and looks out.*

ALYSEA: If I'm not at the door to pay her, she'll come right in.

[*She looks around the room one more time. She notices the long kitchen knife with traces of blood on it on a small side table next to the couch. She picks it up with the cleaning cloth gingerly, wraps the knife inside the cloth, and puts it in a drawer (side table). During this interval,* CLEMENCIA's *noisy arrival is heard.* CLEMENCIA *is an older barrio woman who has been delivering milk for many years. From the kitchen comes the sound of the door opening, the tugging of a milk can, the pouring of milk. Sighs and ejaculations about hard work are heard.* CLEMENCIA *comes into the sitting room.*]

CLEMENCIA: Ah, there you are. My centavos were not on the kitchen table. Hombre—do I have to beg for my money?

ALYSEA: I'm sorry. I just didn't get around to it.

CLEMENCIA [*staring at* ALYSEA]: You look terrible. What is the matter? Have you been up all night?

ALYSEA [*smooths hair and looks at her hands guiltily*]: We—I stayed up late. I was trying to learn a new lace pattern.

CLEMENCIA: Josefa, eh? She teaches you well, eh?

ALYSEA: Oh, yes, yes.

CLEMENCIA: And you try to please her, eh?

ALYSEA: I try.

CLEMENCIA: You do. You do. She likes you very much. She tells everybody what a fine girl you are. [*She catches* ALYSEA *looking at her hands.*] What's the matter with your hands?

ALYSEA: Hands? Oh, nothing. Nothing.

CLEMENCIA: Of course nothing! You are young. Look at mine. Rheumatism—eaten up by life. Oh, well, pain comes with age, eh?

ALYSEA: I suppose. [*She goes to the table drawer and takes out a money box. She takes out a set of keys from her apron pocket and opens it.*] Here's your money. [*Counts it out.*] Cinco—seis—siete pesos.

CLEMENCIA: Gracias. [*Peers into* ALYSEA's *face.*] You look bad. Sleep some. You can rest in this house.

ALYSEA: I will.

CLEMENCIA: You are a lucky girl. You have a good guardian angel. Aren't you glad Josefa brought you here to live with her? You are one lucky girl.

ALYSEA: She has been very kind.

CLEMENCIA: She is loved by all. A fine woman. Mañana will be her day, Ah! She will lead the procession to the church. A day to honor Josefa. She was chosen for her goodness.

ALYSEA: Tomorrow?

CLEMENCIA: You have forgotten! What is the matter with you? San Lorenzo's day. The procession to the church.

ALYSEA: Of course. How silly of me. I—I'm not myself today.

CLEMENCIA: No you're not. You need rest and some of my good milk. [*Looks around the room.*] Nice—nice. May I sit down for a minute. I started delivering two hours ago. The chill of the desert is in my bones. [*She sits without waiting for an answer.*] Isn't it different living in this beautiful house instead of that hovel you were born in—what town was that?

ALYSEA: Moteca, south of San Miguel.

CLEMENCIA: Tch, tch, tch, tch—that's a poor town. My brother's family almost died of starvation there. But you were in the city when Josefa found you, eh? Oh, that Josefa! All her life, she goes around with—that walking stick of hers—always she goes like an avenging angel. [*Looks at* ALYSEA *who is still standing.*] Sit down. Sit down. [CLEMENCIA *stands up suddenly.*] An avenging angel, that Josefa! [*Pretends to pound away with a walking stick.*] Take that! and that! She beats those devils. The man who tried to hurt you. And that old drunk buzzard, David's father, when he was beating the poor child to death. [*At the mention of* DAVID's *name,* ALYSEA *puts her hands to her temples. She is trembling.*] You *are* sick.

ALYSEA: No. I'm alright.

CLEMENCIA: She saved you. You are very lucky. You make beautiful lace like Josefa. She teaches you well. Everything she does, she does beautiful.

ALYSEA [*rises and goes to window*]: Appearances. They are very funny—aren't they? Tomorrow the church will honor Josefa. How very funny! [*She begins to laugh, but the laughter becomes a desperate sobbing.*] Oh, God!

CLEMENCIA: You must have a fever. [*Goes to* ALYSEA *and touches her forehead.*] No—but something's wrong with you. Where is Josefa?

[JOSEFA *enters. She is a tall, regal woman about thirty-five. Her bones are Indian, her coloring Aryan. She wears her hair severely back. Her movements are graceful. The cuffs and collar of her dress are of exquisite lace. She walks up to* ALYSEA *and puts her arms around her.*]

JOSEFA: Shhhhh, stop crying. [*Goes to* CLEMENCIA.] I don't often see you in my sitting room. Alysea doesn't seem to be feeling well.

CLEMENCIA: Stayed up all night, she says.

JOSEFA: Oh?

CLEMENCIA: You must make her rest.

JOSEFA: Of course.

CLEMENCIA: Well, I must be going. I'm late on my rounds. [*She sighs.*] I wish I could stay here.

JOSEFA: My home is your home.

CLEMENCIA: You are an angel.

JOSEFA: You have your money?

CLEMENCIA: Oh, yes, gracias. Now, you make her rest.

JOSEFA: I shall. Goodbye.

[JOSEFA *escorts* CLEMENCIA *to the door.* CLEMENCIA *takes one anxious look at* ALYSEA *again before she leaves.*]

CLEMENCIA: She's coming down with something.

JOSEFA: I'll take good care of her.

CLEMENCIA: Oh, you will. You will. [*Exits.*]

[JOSEFA *turns to* ALYSEA.]

JOSEFA: She's right, you know. You should rest [ALYSEA, *still in the midst of great distress, shakes her head.*] Is it wise. . . .

ALYSEA: Wise! The way you word it—wise!

JOSEFA: Very well, I'll put it another way. Must you break down now? It's such a beautiful day. We must be faithful to loveliness.

ALYSEA: How can you say that? How can you justify in that way?

JOSEFA: There are things we must do to keep our sanity, to make each moment clear. [*Pause, voice becomes lighter.*] Any sign of the swallows? Look at the tree. Oh, I love that tree.

ALYSEA: Have you gone mad? Last night. . . .

[ALYSEA *is overwhelmed with the memory; she runs out of the room.* JOSEFA *looks for a moment after her, then she touches the lace curtains.*]

JOSEFA: We pattern our lives for rare, beautiful moments—like this lace—little bits and pieces come together. My life—this lace—a crystal thing of light. She must understand. Alysea must understand—she must!

[*There is a knock at the door. She hesitates before opening. Then, she decides to do so. It is* TOMÁS, *her shiftless uncle.*]

TOMÁS: Josefa, buenos días. I thought you might be at the hacienda—ha, ha, ha. Not today?

JOSEFA: What are you doing here?

TOMÁS: The pump. . . .

JOSEFA: You fixed that already. I've told you not to come around here at this time of day.

TOMÁS: The pump, I tell you. I have to hone the cylinder. What do women know about this?

JOSEFA: I've warned you about bothering Alysea.

TOMÁS: She say that?

JOSEFA: I know you.

TOMÁS: You think bad. Woman like you always think bad of Tomás. Not good. My wife say, "Go, help Josefa. We need provisions." I come.

JOSEFA: Take whatever you need for your family.

TOMÁS: My family thanks you. Can you spare a few centavos for me?

JOSEFA: Go help yourself to beans and rice. There's apples for the children.

TOMÁS: Beans and rice—beans and rice—who can get happy on beans and rice? A few centavos? Just one bottle?

JOSEFA: Go get your provisions.

TOMÁS: No bottle for me. But you get lots of bottles for your friend, Clara.

JOSEFA: Mind your tongue.

TOMÁS: Does Don Miguel Esquinas know you buy liquor for his wife? [*Notices the pail. Peers into it.*] It's blood. Blood?

JOSEFA: Go to the kitchen and get your rice and beans. [TOMÁS *is still staring into the pail.*] Did you hear me?

TOMÁS: Rice and beans—rice and beans. Yes, yes, Doña Perfecta—Doña Perfecta—so charitable—ha, ha, ha. . . .

JOSEFA: I'm not in the mood for your sarcasm.

TOMÁS: Queen of the world. No liquor for Tomás. Lots of liquor for la Doña Esquinas. Queen of the world. Is that blood in the pail?

JOSEFA: I do not have to satisfy your curiosity.

TOMÁS: Cálmate, cálmate. [*Walks out with his eyes on the pail.*]

[JOSEFA *turns her back to him. He shrugs and leaves through the kitchen door. His grumbling is heard as he helps himself to the food.* JOSEFA *stares at the contents of the pail. She looks away and touches her temple with her fingertips. Crosses over to a rocking chair, sits, and leans back, closes her eyes and grips the arms of the chair.*]

JOSEFA: I will not fall again, that cold, blinding misery. No, no—it can't crumble—this world I put together with such care. Alysea must understand. Fires, fires winding up my soul. Last night can be forgotten. Last night can be forgiven.

[*She rises and walks to the window and stands absorbing the light; one can sense an obvious union between the light and* JOSEFA.]

JOSEFA [*softly*]: How moist your lips, my light. Through me, through me—you live. Oh, you shape my soul with such care. I am . . . air . . . and you, my spirits—the moon's cold fire, the pulsing heat of sun. [*She comes back from the intimacy and looks at the bird house.*] They will come, my swallows. They will come after the desert flight.

[*As she looks at the tree,* TOMÁS *comes through the patio outside the window. He has a sack over his shoulder.* JOSEFA *is oblivious of him until he calls out.*]

TOMÁS: Josefa, casting your spell, so early? You can't scare me, querida. I know you. I know many things. You burn inside.

[JOSEFA *stares at him unbelievingly as if his intrusion were a blasphemy. She turns away from the window.*]

TOMÁS: Hey, Josefa, why you run away? The great Doña Perfecta runs from her sweet, loving uncle. That's funny, ha, ha, ha, ha.

JOSEFA [*ominous tone*]: Go home, Tomás, go home.

[*She closes the window and walks to an unfinished damask close to the window. She sits down, unhooks the needle, and begins to work on it. Her concentration becomes a fiery intensity; this is obvious in her finger movements.* ALYSEA *comes into the room. She is now composed and refreshed. She has on a pretty dress. She sees the pail, hesitates, then forces herself to remove it, taking it into the kitchen. All this time* JOSEFA *remains absorbed in the damask.* ALYSEA *returns.* JOSEFA *looks up.*]

JOSEFA: You look so nice. For Eduardo, I suppose?

ALYSEA: He likes this dress. Did I hear someone?

JOSEFA: Tomás, sneaking around.

ALYSEA: Oh, no!

JOSEFA: Stop that! He's gone. Do you want Eduardo to see you this way? Now smile and go make some coffee. This morning I want him to have some with us before you go off on your walk.

ALYSEA: He'd like that. He's asked about you.

JOSEFA: Oh? He's a familiar face around the hacienda. Don Miguel has often said Eduardo is the most efficient foreman he has ever had. Such a handsome young man. [ALYSEA *begins to cry softly again.*] I told you to stop that. Everything's going to be alright. I promise. Last night doesn't matter.

ALYSEA: It was so horrible, so horrible. . . .

JOSEFA: Compose yourself. Last night could not be helped.

[ALYSEA *shudders in her lostness.* JOSEFA *goes to her and takes the girl's face in her hands.*]

JOSEFA: You are so dear to me, so dear. You know that. [*She strokes* ALYSEA's *hair.*] Your hair, your beautiful hair. I want so much to make you happy.

[ALYSEA *breaks away from her.*]

ALYSEA [*bitterly*]: Happy?

JOSEFA: Eduardo will be here any moment now. Go make that coffee. Suddenly I'm hungry. Bring some scones too.

ALYSEA: The lace. . . .

JOSEFA: Let that wait.

ALYSEA: It must make the morning express to the capital.

JOSEFA: Let it wait. There'll be time. Now go make that coffee.

ALYSEA: I don't think I can face Eduardo this morning.

JOSEFA: Yes, you will. And you will behave as if nothing happened. You owe me that. Do you hear? David is alright. I took him to the hospital; they took good care of him.

ALYSEA: What did you tell them?

JOSEFA: Someone had broken into the house, a criminal.

ALYSEA: We are the criminals. We did it.

JOSEFA: For the last time, control yourself. You did nothing. I did it. I did it, do you hear? You did nothing. I take full responsibility, and I hope you have enough sense not to become hysterical. Now, promise me. Promise.

ALYSEA: I—I promise.

JOSEFA: Thank you. We must be careful. Even with Eduardo.

ALYSEA: I'll get the coffee.

[ALYSEA *exits into kitchen.* JOSEFA *walks around the room at random, picks up a book, turns its pages, reads aloud.*]

JOSEFA: "El hombre toma, toma y hierre, la flor desnuda temblorosa. . . ." David? Little David? Will you forgive?

[*Crosses to workbasket, picks up piece of lace, traces pattern.*]

JOSEFA: I saw such terror in your eyes, David . . . such terror. But this piece of lace, my lace is beauty, light, all the good things. . . .

[*Exits to bedroom, clutching piece of lace.* ALYSEA *returns, crosses to window, looks out. Knock on door:* ALYSEA *opens it to* EDUARDO.]

EDUARDO: Ready?

ALYSEA: Come in.

EDUARDO: Our walk. . . .

ALYSEA: She wants to meet you.

EDUARDO: Your pagan goddess?

ALYSEA: She'll hear you.

EDUARDO: Have you told her about us?

ALYSEA: Not yet.

EDUARDO: Woman, we're leaving tonight! You haven't told her?

ALYSEA: It's hard. She's done so much for me. Brought me to this house, this room.

EDUARDO: This is her room, you said—fragile, full of light—like her.

ALYSEA: Very much so. Isn't it beautiful?

EDUARDO: Something you might see in a dream, an uncomfortable dream.

ALYSEA: Yes, yes . . . you're right! So right. I've never looked at it that way before. All that's happened. Can I blame it on a dream?

EDUARDO: Blame what? What's happened?

ALYSEA: I do want to go with you.

EDUARDO: Then, let's go—now. We can pack two horses, take the trail, find a clear field, build a cabin, plant seed, make babies. . . .

ALYSEA: Be serious. . . .

EDUARDO: I've never been more serious. There's nothing to stop us. Father Prado can marry us tonight. . . .

ALYSEA: I can't marry you.

EDUARDO: You're going to—this very night.

ALYSEA: Find a clear field, build a cabin . . . how wonderful it sounds. In pine country?

EDUARDO: Yes, in pine country.

ALYSEA: I was born in a dirty little village called Moteca. All I remember as a child was starving. When I was fourteen they came to the village. . . .

EDUARDO: Who came?

ALYSEA: Two big women dressed in satin. You can't imagine how beautiful they seemed to me who was dressed in rags. They came the city, looking for seamstresses, they said. I could sew.

EDUARDO: You went with them to the city at fourteen?

ALYSEA: Two other girls who went with me were only twelve. I can still remember the

women's body sweat, their dirty satin dresses. They took us to a house that smelled of whiskey, rotten food and cheap perfume.

EDUARDO: Your eyes—so full of pain.

ALYSEA: I want you to know how Josefa saved me.

EDUARDO: Saved you?

ALYSEA: Women with faces of cruel men told us there would be customers. We knew then we had been tricked. The twelve year olds trembled with terror, whimpering as they were led out to where men waited. I ran and tried to hide under some sordid limp dresses. But the women found me. They had a huge man who dragged me out, down some stairs, a hallway. I broke free and found my way to the street. But the man caught up with me, twisted my arm behind my back and started to shove me back into the house. The man was swearing and laughing like an animal, and the filth that came from his mouth . . . then, out of the darkness, Josefa appeared—with that walking stick of hers. She raised it over her head and beat the man, over and over again, until he lay so still, so still. She took my hand and led me away—to this place, this haven. . . .

EDUARDO: The open sky, the warm stars, the mountain top will be our haven.

ALYSEA: Oh, I want to belong to you so much. . . .

EDUARDO: And I, to you. . . . Something is the matter with you. I can feel it. What's wrong?

ALYSEA: That uncomfortable dream you sensed—no, no—much more horrible than just a dream—a nightmare, more. . . .

[JOSEFA *enters, composed, calmed.*]

JOSEFA: There you are [*to* ALYSEA]. What on earth is the matter child?

EDUARDO: Something about a nightmare.

ALYSEA: It's nothing—nothing. I'll get some coffee [*exits to kitchen*].

JOSEFA: She's been so nervous lately. Sometimes I fear I ask too much of her. I have so many orders for my lace. It's turning into a big enterprise. We've been working our fingers to the bone. . . .

EDUARDO: Ah, yes! I've heard about your beautiful lace.

JOSEFA: And where are you going for your walk?

EDUARDO: To a place where the pines blot out all the world. To a place where she believes everything I tell her.

JOSEFA: How clever of you. Are you not afraid to take walks into forbidden country?

EDUARDO: Forbidden by whom? It's beautiful country.

JOSEFA: You're not from around here, are you? The village people—all good Catholics—believe that the old pagan gods roam the area along the lake to its very source where pine country swallows up the desert.

EDUARDO: Funny—when Alysea talks about the things you do, the ways you weave your magic—I called you a pagan goddess. Now you tell me gods roam the hills—more than coincidence. But this room, your room, is too ordered to be pagan.

JOSEFA: The order of women—but have you seen my garden?

EDUARDO: Ah! that is another thing. It is wild, profuse, and all the colors of the world.

JOSEFA: You are so nice. How easily you feel what others feel. My flowers—they open to the sun and close to darkness. Then there are my night blooms, wanting from the moon, mysterious, strange, giving out the scents that excite passions. . . .

EDUARDO: You are a poet.

JOSEFA: Am I? I believe you to be a poet too. A dangerous poet, though.

[ALYSEA *comes in with coffee tray, places on coffee table.* JOSEFA *begins to serve.* ALYSEA *offers some scones to* EDUARDO.]

ALYSEA: Have one. I made them from an old recipe—Josefa's.

EDUARDO [*takes one*]: Very, very good. There is no end to your talents, Josefa.

ALYSEA: I'll leave you two for a while. I must mail this lace off with the morning express.

JOSEFA: Have some coffee with us, child.

ALYSEA: I don't feel like coffee this morning.

EDUARDO: Are you alright? You look a little pale. Have you been crying?

ALYSEA: No, no—some speck got in my eye . . . I'll be back soon. [ALYSEA *exits.*]

EDUARDO: She'll be alright, I suppose.

JOSEFA: Yes. I suspect she wants us to get to know each other.

EDUARDO: Every person in the village has given me a glowing picture of you. A saint, they call you. A giving, loving woman. . . .

JOSEFA: Stop! I am none of those things. The Josefa they talk about is a myth—like the old gods.

EDUARDO: When Alysea came in, you called me a dangerous poet. What do you mean?

JOSEFA: Gentlemen, men who feel what others feel, who have an eye for beauty can be dangerous—to women. It's so easy to fall in love with them.

EDUARDO: You flatter me.

JOSEFA: Am I not right? Don't women fall in love with you too easily?

EDUARDO: I . . . I . . . .

JOSEFA: Am I embarrassing you?

EDUARDO: I never thought you and I would be talking of such things.

JOSEFA: You forget, I am Clara's friend and her confidant.

EDUARDO: Of course. She has told you everything. I love Clara.

JOSEFA: Love or loved?

EDUARDO: Both, I suppose. It's not the first passion we felt some time ago. It's something deeper, something I cannot explain.

JOSEFA: You are dangerous. With one breath you tell me you love Clara, with the next one you'll tell me you love Alysea.

EDUARDO: You know!

JOSEFA: You come around too often, those walks of yours.

EDUARDO: What can I say?

JOSEFA: Explain it to me—this loving two women.

EDUARDO: I do not love Clara the way I love Alysea. I've asked her to be my wife.

JOSEFA: Alysea—to be your wife? Have you told her about Clara?

EDUARDO: No.

JOSEFA: How convenient.

EDUARDO: Alysea does not want to leave you. She thinks she owes you too much.

JOSEFA: It's called loyalty. Something that perhaps you owe to Clara?

[ALYSEA *returns.*]

ALYSEA: Have you two been getting along?

JOSEFA: Marvelously.

ALYSEA: Have you told him about the duendes?

JOSEFA: Really, child.

EDUARDO: Oh, you must. That's all she talks about—the mystery of your energy.

JOSEFA: It is something beyond reason.

EDUARDO: Tell me.

JOSEFA: You know the lake just beyond my property—that runs all the way to pine country.

EDUARDO: That's all I hear in the village from the young girls. Tomorrow, isn't it?—when all the girls in the village will bathe in its waters at high noon?

JOSEFA: A hopeless ritual. Poor girls! It is believed that if you bathe in the lake at high noon on San Lorenzo's day, you will find the perfect love to marry.

EDUARDO: All girls like to dream.

JOSEFA: Ah! but the reality. In this village what can they expect? Some callous Indian boy, someone who'll kiss them hotly on the lips behind some bush. Hot breath, awkward hands—and foolishly they call it love, and marry—their fate? A slavish existence. Soon they're milked dry of beauty, youth, and they call that a perfect marriage planned in Heaven.

EDUARDO: You never bathed in the lake—as a young girl—at midday—on San Lorenzo's day?

JOSEFA: Never! I was aware of the trap early in life. My desire was of a purer grain.

EDUARDO: Your desire?

JOSEFA: A pouring of self.

ALYSEA: Doesn't she say wonderful things? I don't understand them all, but they are mysterious.

JOSEFA: All alone, while the villagers were celebrating San Lorenzo's Day at night, I went to the lake. It was forbidden at night, old beliefs in roaming pagan gods. But I wanted that—the green gods of the pines, the source of the lake—and the moon— Ah! the moon.

EDUARDO: You are bewitched. . . .

ALYSEA: Tell him—tell him about the moon.

JOSEFA: One night, I went, on the saint's day. I remember the distant barrio lanterns, mixed with the laughing of happy people and the music . . . guitars. The darkness was moist, an orange moon filled the sky, and its light seemed to pour into me. I felt a green desire, a glorious longing—a suffering, a music, a stillness sung in me. I reached the lake to see it shimmer, tremble in the moonlight. I looked up and the moon was even larger than before. I felt the beginning of some strange fear. I ran and ran towards the pines. I looked around to see the moon following me. Suddenly

I was in an open field and I dared not look at the moon again. I sat down to catch my breath, and I felt the moon pouring a passionate warmth, like blood syrup, into me. I lay down on the grass, face down. So still I lay. But my senses told me I must turn around. I did, with my eyes still closed. I felt the moon take me in its arms. I opened my eyes and saw the moon—like a sea around me. No fear anymore—just a joy, open and free.

ALYSEA: She mated with the moon.

EDUARDO: My reason tells me it could not be. But looking at you, Josefa, I have to believe.

JOSEFA: The light was me. I was to bear the children of light—the moon, the burning lake, spirits—all regenerating themselves in me—shaping my soul.

[*The harsh voice of* TOMÁS *outside the window suddenly breaks the spell.*]

TOMÁS: Josefa! Mujer!

EDUARDO: Who in the Devil . . .

ALYSEA [*in a frightened voice*]: Tomás.

[JOSEFA *crosses to window.*]

JOSEFA: Stop all that shouting! What do you want?

TOMÁS: Very strange. I found David's horse.

JOSEFA: Where?

TOMÁS: Running in the pasture, wearing a broken bridle.

JOSEFA: Are you sure it's David's horse?

TOMÁS: Of course, woman.

EDUARDO: Can I be of any help?

JOSEFA: Thank you, no. He can handle it [*to* TOMÁS]. Take him back to the stable.

TOMÁS: Sí, querida.

[*At the mention of* DAVID, ALYSEA *becomes frightened, sits in utter helplessness, begins to cry.* JOSEFA *remains calm, begins to pick up cups, napkins, etc. Goes to* EDUARDO, *takes his hand, leads him to* ALYSEA.]

JOSEFA: Take her for a walk.

EDUARDO: What is wrong, my love?

[TOMÁS *comes in through kitchen door.*]

TOMÁS: That's a bad sign. Something frightened the poor horse and he broke free.

JOSEFA: Nonsense. Take him back to the hacienda.

EDUARDO [*steering* ALYSEA *towards door.*]: I'm taking you to a very special place, where we can trace the path of the swallows. Now smile. [ALYSEA *smiles half-heartedly and leans against him for safety.*]

JOSEFA: Off with you two. Now go and enjoy yourselves.

[EDUARDO *and* ALYSEA *exit.* TOMÁS *looks after them shaking his head.*]

TOMÁS: She's in bad shape—bad. I heard you had an intruder last night—ha, ha, ha. And that terrible thing that happened to that little urchin you adopted. Poor little David. Who do you suppose did that terrible thing to him? That girl—she's afraid— like you're afraid.

JOSEFA: What?

TOMÁS: This morning, why didn't you admit that was blood in the pail? David's blood, yes? No, not a word—why?

JOSEFA: Why should I tell you anything.

TOMÁS: Your smart uncle does not believe all that talk about an intruder.

JOSEFA: I don't care what you believe.

TOMÁS: Poor little boy, poor little boy—all that blood—ha, ha, ha. All those times you have saved the poor, innocent, helpless ones, you never say anything. Smart, smart. The barrio always puts the story together—in your favor—making you out an angel. You are clever.

JOSEFA: Don't be ridiculous.

TOMÁS: People have no idea how clever you really are, Doña Perfecta. You saved Alysea from the whore house, eh? You had to cripple a man for life to do it, to be sure. You wouldn't stop beating him. But nobody remembers that. You saved David from a drunken father. Now, where was it that you beat David's father? Ah, yes, as the story goes. Ah, yes, some isolated road. The drunken old man was beating the boy without mercy. Then you came, the avenging angel, and returned the favor. Oh, how conveniently you forgot to tell anyone that the old man had been left on the road until—how many days later? Of course no one cared. The old man was the villain. You are the angel.

JOSEFA: You have an evil twisted mind.

TOMÁS: Perhaps you'll get your hands on me too, eh? Ha, ha, ha.

JOSEFA: Hadn't you better see about that horse?

TOMÁS: That girl is breaking apart. You better watch out. But look at you, such pious silence. You are the dangerous one alright.

JOSEFA: All your garbage, is it leading up to some form of blackmail?

TOMÁS: After all, I'm on your side, querida. You should be—grateful. We have the same blood running through our veins, verdad?

JOSEFA: Get out of here and look after that horse.

TOMÁS: A little money.

JOSEFA: Get out.

TOMÁS: You're made of stone, mujer.

JOSEFA: You have tried my patience long enough. Stop wasting my time. Now go.

TOMÁS: You can spare a few pesos.

[JOSEFA *looks at him contemptuously, then walks out into the kitchen without another word.* TOMÁS *scratches his head and looks around the room.*]

TOMÁS: Stupid woman. I'll break her yet. I know they keep money somewhere in this room.

[*He begins to search. Comes to the table drawer, opens it. He finds the box, pries open the lock, takes the money. He suddenly sees the knife. He picks it up, stares at it, then leaves the room with it.*]

ACT II

SCENE I

Later the same morning. EDUARDO *and* ALYSEA *are back from their walk. They come into the room laughing.*

EDUARDO: No more sadness. You promised.

ALYSEA: No more sadness. Come in. Stay a while.

EDUARDO: I must get back to the hacienda. If we're leaving tonight. . . .

ALYSEA: Leaving tonight. I can hardly believe it. I feel as if I were somebody new.

EDUARDO: You are my love.

ALYSEA: Your love. . . .

EDUARDO: Is something the matter?

ALYSEA: I don't know what you mean.

EDUARDO: You—tightened up.

ALYSEA: I have a hundred things to do myself before we leave tonight. Flowers! I must cut fresh flowers. She loves them so—on the table over there.

EDUARDO: You cannot bear to leave her, can you?

ALYSEA: Oh, I want to leave—I want to leave. You don't know how much. Thank you. Thank you for saving me.

EDUARDO: Saving you? From this—this dream of a woman's world?

ALYSEA: Go now. Go do what you have to do. I must cut those flowers.

[ALYSEA *leaves him, goes to garden. He shrugs and turns to leave. The front door opens. It is* CLARA ESQUINAS. *She carries a knitting bag.*]

EDUARDO: Clara.

CLARA: I didn't. . . .

EDUARDO: Expect to find me here?

CLARA: I don't see why not. She's going with you, isn't she?

EDUARDO: Yes. We're going to be married.

CLARA: She's very lucky.

EDUARDO: I asked you to leave your husband and marry me once, remember? You never could. Clara, this is awkward.

CLARA: No reason to feel that way. Just because you've been my lover. . . .

EDUARDO: It's awkward for you too.

CLARA: Ask me again.

EDUARDO: What?

CLARA: Ask me again—to go with you—to leave my husband. Yes, yes, yes, I'll go anywhere in the world with you.

EDUARDO: It's too late, Clara. We're not good for each other.

CLARA: Why? Because I'm too old? Because I drink? Because my husband would go after us? No . . . no, he doesn't care. He only loves himself, poor man. And I am just a pitiful, ageing woman . . . How easily you forgot me after all we've been to each other. But then, you *are* so young. There are no more Springs for me!

EDUARDO: I'll always love you, Clara, for being Clara, but. . . .

CLARA: Don't worry, I won't embarrass you. See? I'm wiping away all traces of my tears.

EDUARDO: Lovely, lovely Clara. If only I had reached the core of whatever is free in you. . . .

CLARA: Free?

EDUARDO: Goodbye, Clara.

[CLARA *turns away from him. After he leaves, she opens the knitting bag, searches for a cigarette, lights it with trembling hands. Then she takes out a small flask and drinks.* ALYSEA *returns from the garden, her arms full of flowers.*]

ALYSEA: Doña Clara.

CLARA: I came for my dress. Did Josefa finish my dress?

ALYSEA: Yes. I'll get it [*goes behind a screen, comes back with a simple gown, hands it to* CLARA]. She finished it a few days ago.

CLARA: How simple, how bare.

ALYSEA: There's a reason.

CLARA: I'll try it on [*goes behind screen*]. I saw Eduardo at the door.

ALYSEA: Oh. . . .

CLARA: Has he told you about me?

ALYSEA: About you?

CLARA: Never mind. He's in love with you, isn't he?

ALYSEA: Yes.

CLARA: And you're going away with him.

ALYSEA: He told you that? He shouldn't have. I haven't told Josefa.

CLARA: I won't mention anything to her.

ALYSEA: Thank you. It must come from me. She's been so kind.

CLARA: It'll break her heart. She's so fond of you [*comes back from behind the screen*]. Well, how does it look?

ALYSEA: You look beautiful.

CLARA [*pulls* ALYSEA *to her side, both facing a mirror*]: Look at you! How young you are. How very, very young. Would you believe that all you have now, I had, once?

ALYSEA: You're very beautiful.

CLARA: The skin, the hair, the bloom of youth, the firm, firm skin. See the lines around my eyes. And this pallor. Time is so unkind.

ALYSEA: I see a lovely face.

CLARA: How kind you are. Things do not fall easily in place for me nowadays. All will fall into place for you. Make the most of it. Before you realize it, one day you'll wake up, and youth will be gone, love will be gone, all good things like that. I'm embarrassing you, aren't I. . . .

ALYSEA: I don't know what to say. You are Doña Esquinas. You have everything.

CLARA: Go with him gladly, Alysea. Hold him, keep him, love him, be young and beautiful for him.

ALYSEA: Yes, I can do that.

CLARA: Don't look at me so strangely. I'm alright. The dress! Something's missing, don't you think?

ALYSEA: Josefa made a shawl to go with it.

CLARA: A shawl!

ALYSEA: I'll go find it.

[ALYSEA *goes to bedroom.* CLARA *watches her leave, takes flask from knitting bag, drinks.*]

CLARA [*crosses to mirror*]: He did love me. Oh, Angels in Heaven, I still love him so. The feel of his arms, the smell of his skin, his lovely, lovely hands. I mustn't . . . I mustn't.

[ALYSEA *returns with shawl.*]

ALYSEA: May I?

CLARA: Of course. [ALYSEA *places the shawl over one shoulder and adjusts it to* CLARA's *waist.*]

ALYSEA: The design is Andalusian.

CLARA: The design—it's so fragile. Where on earth did she find the design to copy?

ALYSEA: It's her design.

CLARA: Her design? Of course. She's so clever. It's almost unearthly.

ALYSEA: It came to her in a dream.

CLARA: I believe it. So delicate, the filigree of angels. . . .

ALYSEA: Her duendes, she said.

CLARA: Of course—her duendes. She's so lucky. Everything she touches becomes a miracle. If I know Josefa, the design means something.

ALYSEA: Here, let me unpin it so you can hold it up to the light [*unpins shawl*].

CLARA [*holds it up to light*]: I can't seem to make it out. . . .

ALYSEA [*tracing design with finger*]: See? A transparent mountain.

CLARA: Yes, yes, I see it.

ALYSEA: The mountain of sighs.

CLARA: The mountains of Andalusia. The caves where the gypsies live, starving sometimes, dying from the cold. People so much like the earth. A dream, you say?

ALYSEA: Yes. She was overwhelmed by depression in her dream—then, all of a sudden, from the core of the mountain, a spiral of light began to grow. Fireflies!

CLARA: Fireflies! How lovely. I see the spiral, the fireflies. . . . Oh, why can't I belong to Josefa's universe? I need some wondrous sustenance to fill my soul. But the mistress of the great Esquinas Hacienda is trapped and cannot escape. There I go again, saying things you cannot understand.

[JOSEFA *enters, crosses to them.*]

JOSEFA: A dream, Clara.

CLARA: Alysea told me about it.

JOSEFA: I have some combs for your hair. Alysea, will you please get them?

[ALYSEA *exits to bedroom for combs.*]

CLARA [*places shawl back around shoulder, holds it at her waist*]: I believe this is the way you want it.

JOSEFA: You've been drinking.

CLARA: Yes, I have. Don't preach. Drink is my faithful companion.

JOSEFA: You promised me you wouldn't drink unless you felt that desperation. . . .

CLARA: I'm desperate from sunup to sundown these days.

JOSEFA: I will not let you have any more liquor. I don't see how I weakened. . . .

CLARA: You supply me with liquor because you cannot stand my misery.

JOSEFA: I don't understand your misery.

CLARA: How can you? You are the Priestess of Light. Isn't that what you told me?

JOSEFA: You must find your own light, dear Clara. I hate to see you suffer so.

CLARA: Don't bother with me. I'm hopeless.

JOSEFA: You have to commit yourself to something, something other than a man.

CLARA: That's you. Not me. To be desired by a man—what else can a woman be upon the earth?

JOSEFA: I refuse to listen to such gibberish. You cannot have him back. I'm afraid he wants Alysea.

CLARA: I'm a coward. My husband calls me a coward because I drink. He thinks I'm greedy, vain. . . .

JOSEFA: How well he describes himself. I know the unhappiness he has caused you. Don't stay with him.

CLARA: Underneath it all, he really loves me, you know. Don Miguel Esquinas with his two hundred year old pride, loves me in his cruel way, his killing way. . . . [*begins to weep softly*].

JOSEFA: Leave him.

CLARA: I can't. I can't. He wasn't like that in the beginning, you know. But I was young and fresh. Then, we discovered I could have no children, and time went on, day after day, after day . . . Time is the villain, Josefa, not men.

JOSEFA: All they do is take and destroy. Haven't you already learned that yet?

CLARA: You're wrong. A woman was made to be loved by a man. To love a man is enough for a woman. But they don't let us love them.

JOSEFA: I wish I knew how to help free you.

CLARA: Free me? [*Laughs.*]

JOSEFA: That drink is making you hysterical.

CLARA: No. No. How can you understand? What do you know of loneliness?

JOSEFA: Loneliness? The mists full of pain when we stumble and fall and loneliness stretches out tearing at your heart. Then—chaos. But you save yourself. Do you hear me, save yourself!

CLARA: Did you?

JOSEFA: Yes! When you win the struggle, something emerges from inside, something that is solely yours and, then, there is no more emptiness.

[ALYSEA *returns with combs, hands them to* JOSEFA.]

JOSEFA: Here [*places them in* CLARA's *hair*], they're perfect.
CLARA: You have transformed me.
JOSEFA: A gypsy queen. Gypsy queens are free because they know the secrets of the earth.
ALYSEA: Look! [*Points to window, runs to it.*] They're coming! The swallows are coming! The sky is full of them.

[JOSEFA *and* CLARA *join her.*]

JOSEFA: They'll come in droves now. My birdhouse will be full by tomorrow.
CLARA: At noon tomorrow, all the village girls will be at the lake, bathing in the midday sun, dreaming of the perfect marriage made in heaven.
JOSEFA: Look at the lake. It shimmers with love. See—the light on the water is singing. I can feel the music in my skin.
CLARA: I can't see what you see or feel what you feel.
ALYSEA: Only Josefa.
JOSEFA: Water—fire—breathing pines. A temple waits.

SCENE II

Early afternoon of the same day. JOSEFA *enters from the outside. She is carrying an injured swallow. She cradles it gently as she examines it.*

JOSEFA: You poor little thing. Your wing is broken.

[ALYSEA *comes through the kitchen door.*]

JOSEFA: Look, he fell from the tree. I found it in the garden, a soft piece of life, fluttering. So small, so helpless. I think it's thirsty. Get an eye-dropper. Hurry.

[ALYSEA *goes back in the kitchen.* JOSEFA *sits in her rocking chair, placing the bird gently on her lap.* ALYSEA *comes back with a cup and a dropper. She sits on the floor next to* JOSEFA *and watches her feed the bird water.*]

JOSEFA: He has life, this one.
ALYSEA: Just a baby. Let's set the wing—some twigs and thread.

[ALYSEA *leaves again.* JOSEFA *continues feeding the bird.*]

JOSEFA: You'll be alright, little one. Here you can rest in the warmth of the sun. You must have been born near here. But your mother, she must have come from the long winter, stopping in low, wet lands, cutting the cold winds. Oh, the world is harsh! harsh! But something inside her, inside you flies to the sun. Now you are safe, safe. . . .

[ALYSEA *comes back. Together they set the wing.* ALYSEA *is absorbed in what she is doing.* JOSEFA *reaches out and strokes her hair.* ALYSEA looks up and smiles, then finishes the setting of the wing.]

ALYSEA: There.
JOSEFA: Let's put it back in the birdhouse.

[*They take the bird and place it carefully in the birdhouse.*]

JOSEFA: There are so many of them now. The pines near the lake must be full of them too. [*Looks at* ALYSEA.] It's been such a beautiful year, hasn't it?
ALYSEA: No.
JOSEFA: Alysea! How can you say that? We have shared so much. [*She reaches out and strokes* ALYSEA's *hair.* ALYSEA *breaks away from her.*] What's the matter?
ALYSEA: I cannot blame you. I was a part of all that's happened.
JOSEFA: We have been so happy.
ALYSEA: I'm so miserable. I can't tell Eduardo what's between you and me.
JOSEFA: You make it sound so ugly.
ALYSEA: Isn't it?
JOSEFA: Ugly? Alysea, we share days of work; we share laughter, dreams. That is far from ugly.
ALYSEA: That's not what I'm talking about. You easily choose to forget, don't you?
JOSEFA: I suppose I do. You should try to forget.
ALYSEA: I can't! I can't! Eduardo loves me. I love him—but I feel so guilty, so unclean.
JOSEFA: I suffer the same guilt.
ALYSEA: Then why, why did you demand. . . .
JOSEFA: Demand . . . force you? Is that what you're saying?
ALYSEA: I'm sorry. We're both to blame. You've been so good to me. I can't refuse you anything.
JOSEFA: Terror and darkness overwhelms the soul—sometimes; that's why I've created a world of light, a sanctuary. Most of the time we are happy with ourselves—aren't we?
ALYSEA: Oh, yes, Josefa, of course, except . . . [*covers face with hands*] last night was one of terror and of darkness. Aren't you afraid?
JOSEFA: Afraid?
ALYSEA: Yes, afraid.
JOSEFA: I cannot afford to be afraid.
ALYSEA: Oh, my God, what we've become.
JOSEFA: We are the same, no different.

ALYSEA: The same? After what we did last night. What happened here last night was the most gross of violences. I'll show you! [*Crosses to table drawer to get the hidden knife. The drawer's empty.*] The knife! The knife! It's gone, Josefa, gone. [*Searches frantically. Stares unbelievingly.*] The money box—it's gone too. Do you suppose it was. . . .

JOSEFA: Tomás, of course—that lying, filthy thief.

ALYSEA: He'll, he'll. . . .

JOSEFA: He'll do nothing. I'll take care of him.

ALYSEA: What are we going to do—what are we going to do? He took it. He knows.

[ALYSEA *collapses in a chair; she's crying hysterically. The voice of* TOMÁS *is heard outside the window. He is singing a popular love song.* JOSEFA *goes to the window and calls out.*]

JOSEFA: Tomás, come in here. Tomás!

ALYSEA: Don't. I—I can't face him. What are we going to do?

[TOMÁS *comes through the kitchen door, still singing. He looks at* JOSEFA *and then at the terrified* ALYSEA.]

TOMÁS: Did you call me, querida? [*He strokes* JOSEFA's *arm. She breaks away.*]

JOSEFA: Keep your hands off me.

TOMÁS: Ha, ha, ha—Doña Perfecta. [*Looks at* ALYSEA.] What's the matter with you? As if I didn't know. . . .

[ALYSEA *covers her face.*]

TOMÁS: Don't cry, pretty one, Tomás is on your side. [*He flops on the sofa, spreads out his arms and looks around.*] I think I'll move in here with you two. I need a little elegance in my life. And, both of you need a man—eh? Ha, ha, ha. . . .

JOSEFA: You've been drinking.

TOMÁS: Of course I've been drinking, preciosa. You can afford it.

JOSEFA: You bought that liquor with the money you stole from this house.

TOMÁS: Yes, and I took the knife too. The knife! Doesn't that frighten you, dear niece? Look at her! What are you going to do about her?

[ALYSEA *is crying in total despair.* JOSEFA *goes to her.*]

JOSEFA: Hush, child. Go pack David's things. Remember—he needs them in the hospital. Don't cry any more. Now, go and pack.

[ALYSEA *tries to contain herself, then goes into the bedroom to pack.*]

TOMÁS: David, poor little David—ha, ha, ha.

JOSEFA: Have you ever done anything kind in your life?

TOMÁS: Why me? You are the angel of mercy.

JOSEFA: What do you intend to do?

TOMÁS: What I said—move in. And you will give me money now and then. I know about you and her. No more crumbs for me chula. I call the play.

JOSEFA: You're lying—bluffing—as usual.

TOMÁS: Am I?

[*There is a knock at the door. With great alacrity,* TOMÁS *goes to open it. It is* DON MIGUEL ESQUINAS.]

TOMÁS: Ah, Don Miguel. Come in. Come in.

[DON MIGUEL *brushes past* TOMÁS *contemptuously.* TOMÁS *bows with mock humility. He faces* JOSEFA.]

DON MIGUEL: You know what you've done?

JOSEFA: What I've done?

DON MIGUEL: Don't play the innocent with me. It's all your fault.

JOSEFA: Oh, my God, something's happened to Clara. Tell me. I must go to her. [*She starts towards the door.* DON MIGUEL *stops her.*]

DON MIGUEL: You'll never see her again.

JOSEFA: What do you mean? Where is she?

DON MIGUEL: When I hired you to be her companion, I expected you to follow my orders. I told you you must keep her away from liquor. That was your job.

JOSEFA: She is my friend.

DON MIGUEL: Your friend! You destroyed her—with all your lies and your liquor.

JOSEFA: At first, I tried—I tried to keep her from the liquor, but she suffered so. I didn't have the heart.

DON MIGUEL: How dare you take matters into your own hands! You were paid to stop her from drinking. Now she's beyond help. You know how I found her this afternoon? She was walking out into the desert—naked. Do you understand. She was irrational. I took her back to the house and she became a mad woman—throwing things—hallucinating, screaming about your spirits. She claimed they had no faces. Then she broke loose again and ran towards the lake. Not a stitch of clothing on her. I'll be the laughing stock. . . .

JOSEFA: That's all that matters to you, isn't it?

DON MIGUEL: Of course it matters to me. Do you think I deserve an alcoholic for a wife?

JOSEFA: She became that because of you.

DON MIGUEL: How dare you! You fed her the liquor! You fed her the lies!

JOSEFA: How easy it is to blame me. You just can't see, can you?

DON MIGUEL: What do you mean? She had everything. She was the wife of Don Miguel Esquinas. There was nothing she did not have.

JOSEFA: Except you.

DON MIGUEL: You stupid woman! I married her.

JOSEFA: She wanted you to love her.

DON MIGUEL: Love her? You women are insane with your disgusting sentimentality.

JOSEFA: She knew all about your women.

DON MIGUEL: That is a man's right. How dare you!

JOSEFA: She wanted a baby. How many times did she beg you for a baby?

DON MIGUEL: She couldn't have any.

JOSEFA: She begged you to let her adopt a baby.

DON MIGUEL: We settled that long ago. It was past and forgotten.

JOSEFA: It was never forgotten. She was so lonely, so lonely. She cried every night for the baby she did not have.

DON MIGUEL: Tears of a drunken woman. Adopt a baby? A baby not of the Esquinas blood? Never! An heir not of my blood? Absurd!

JOSEFA: Which of your bastards are you going to choose as your heir?

DON MIGUEL: How dare you, you, you, peasant! You'll never see her again.

JOSEFA: I'm going to her right now.

DON MIGUEL: She's gone, do you hear? Gone. A doctor and a nurse have taken her to the sanitorium. This time for good. I shall sign permanent commitment papers.

JOSEFA: You can't do that to her! You mustn't!

DON MIGUEL: I have. The matter is closed. I only came here to tell you not to show your face around the hacienda again.

[*She turns her back to him. He stands watching her for a second, then turns to leave.* TOMÁS *follows him to the door, still assuming a pose of mock humility.*]

TOMÁS: It's terrible what my niece has done. Terrible!

[DON MIGUEL *ignores him and leaves. When he is gone,* TOMÁS *turns to* JOSEFA.]

TOMÁS: Tch—tch—tch—Doña Perfecta is not perfecta, eh?

JOSEFA: She wanted so much to believe in my spirits. My poor darling . . . so lost—so lost.

TOMÁS [*grabs her arm angrily*]: Did you hear me? You are not perfect, are you? You're going to listen to me from now on.

[JOSEFA *does not move, waits for him to let go of her arm. He does. She turns away from him with contempt.*]

JOSEFA: Leave me. I do not feel well.

TOMÁS: None of your tricks, do you hear? I know about you and the girl. I put two and two together. You see, I saw the both of you, last San Lorenzo's day. I left the fiesta in town early and walked towards the lake to sober up. It was you and she—you came out of the lake and ran after her towards the pines. Kind of blurred in my mind—the drink. But I remember now.

JOSEFA: Drunken hallucinations.

TOMÁS: La reina del barrio—ha, ha, ha. You're nothing but a . . .

JOSEFA: If you have nothing else to threaten me with . . . [*She walks away from him with disdain.*]

TOMÁS: You don't fool me, reina del barrio. Look at you—pretending to be so superior. You're afraid of me.

[JOSEFA *turns abruptly and faces him haughtily. They stand in silent defiance then* TOMÁS *falters. He turns away and leaves.* JOSEFA *looks after him.* ALYSEA *comes from the bedroom wearing traveling clothes.*]

JOSEFA: He's gone. He won't do anything. I'll see to it. Do you have all the things David will need?

ALYSEA: Yes, I think so.

[JOSEFA *goes to her and strokes her cheek.*]

JOSEFA: The ride will do you good. When you come back from the hospital, we'll have supper here. We'll plan. No one, nothing can defeat us. Trust me.

ALYSEA [*breaking away from* JOSEFA]: I'm not coming back.

JOSEFA: Not coming back?

ALYSEA: Eduardo and I made plans to leave tonight. We're going to be married.

JOSEFA: Indeed. So you've made a choice. You've chosen to become a sacrifice.

ALYSEA: I do not see it that way. I love him and he loves me.

JOSEFA: How long will your precious Eduardo love you? Don Miguel was here. Clara drank herself insane. You know why? Because Eduardo left her. Promised to love her forever. He was her lover until you came along. Of course he betrayed her. What do you think he'll do to you?

ALYSEA: He loves me. I know he loves me.

JOSEFA: All your pain is still to come. Haven't I taught you anything?

ALYSEA: Oh, you taught me beautiful things, a wonder in believing—but it's all fallen apart, Josefa. David's eyes. I remember his eyes so full of terror. His eyes told me you and I were all the terror in the world.

JOSEFA: How wrong you are. The terror's out there—wherever you're going with Eduardo.

ALYSEA: The violence—the useless violence.

JOSEFA: No. One time does not erase the beauty of our days. Each day was radiant and resplendent—we created with our hearts, our hands, our minds—it was all ours. And, out of those days flowed freedom, beauty, meaning. You know that's true.

ALYSEA: Yes. It's true. That's why I can't understand. . . .

[JOSEFA *walks to the window and reaches into the birdhouse, finding the injured bird. She picks it up, fondles it, holds it against her cheek.*]

JOSEFA: Remember how he came—all broken?

ALYSEA: I came to you the same way.

JOSEFA: You came to my sanctuary, my world. The birds come here for the same reason. [*She remembers something painful, goes to the rocking chair, places the bird on her lap and strokes it gently.*]

JOSEFA: When I was seven, the swallows came as they do each year. My mother had been dead one season. The birds came one hot dry dawn and continued all day. I had walked to the edge of the desert that still hotter afternoon. Boys were catching birds, stoning them, killing them, laughing about it with a fearful joy. It was like a bad dream. The sand was a sea of dead birds. I ran towards the boys and hit them with my fists. I screamed, "Stop, stop." They laughed at me. Then for a joke, they threw me to the ground and held me down, the burning sand against my back. In spite of my terror, I opened my eyes to see a big, burly boy take a knife. In his hand he held a trembling little swallow. He cut the bird, oh, God! [JOSEFA *strokes the bird, shakes her head, closes eyes, pausing.*] I saw the bird's insides and something spilled into my face, ran into my mouth—warm—warm—salt warm. Was it tears? Was it blood? [*Stands, goes to window, caresses bird, places it in the birdhouse. The rosary bell begins to toll.* JOSEFA *looks out at sunset.*] Alysea, look! the lake is screaming with life—Oh, such colors. Stay with me. Stay with me.

ALYSEA: No. I don't belong here. The lace, the light, the garden, the peace are all yours. You were so kind and I—I could not refuse you anything. I felt in time that the Alysea with you was someone else, not me.

JOSEFA: I've never loved anyone the way I love you.

ALYSEA: No. No. never again. I was meant to love Eduardo. I know I owe you so much. But it's not the same. I can't stay here.

[ALYSEA *turns and goes into bedroom.* JOSEFA *starts to follow, then changes her mind. She sits and begins to work on the unfinished damask. She unhooks the needle and works with great concentration. After a minute or so,* ALYSEA *returns with a suitcase.* JOSEFA *does not look up, although she is aware that* ALYSEA *has come into the room.* ALYSEA *crosses behind* JOSEFA *and looks at the damask.*]

JOSEFA: What do you think?

ALYSEA: It's very beautiful.

JOSEFA: I think the design should have a name. Some nights ago I had a most vivid dream—swallows flying into tall, flowing, golden grain, and the earth was moist-sweet. And, I could hear the rustle of their wings whispering the honey language of the sun, and I, without body, was the vibration of the light in harmony with wings, with flowing grain and with—with the passionate breathing of the earth. I started working on this design—how many weeks ago. . . . Well, that doesn't matter. But look at it. It's as if my fingers knew with celestial precision the contents of that dream before I dreamt it. Look at the design.

ALYSEA [*looking intently at the design*]: I see the grain, the outline of a swallow's wing, yes. There it is.

JOSEFA: And here, the gold thread. That is I—disembodied—free—elemental. Oh, I know it!

ALYSEA: What's this up here—see? The zigzag. It looks like lightning piercing the sky. See.

JOSEFA: No. I do not see lightning. Perhaps, the traces of sweet, sweet rain.

ALYSEA: Of course, gentle Josefa, you can't see the lightning, can you? But I see it,

clearly. How strange! Beauty and terror so well intermingled. Lovely Josefa. I shall remember you and all the beauty of this place. Goodbye, sweet lady of light.

[JOSEFA *does not respond. She is absorbed with the design, tracing it meticulously with her fingers, perhaps her own way of not hearing the goodbye.* ALYSEA *picks up the suitcase, hesitates and turns to look at* JOSEFA *once more, then she goes to the door.*]

JOSEFA: Alysea.
ALYSEA: Yes?
JOSEFA: Stop by the rectory on your way to town—will you? I won't be going to rosary services tonight. Please ask Father Prado, if at all possible, to come and see me after service tonight.
ALYSEA: Of course. [ALYSEA *stands for a moment looking at* JOSEFA, *then departs.* JOSEFA *continues putting the final stitches on the damask.*]
JOSEFA: There. It's finished. My spirits have spoken.

[*She stands, rubs the back of her neck, breathes deeply. She goes to the window. It has turned dark, though the moon flows golden into the room. She looks out to the lake.*]

JOSEFA: My lover! You look like morning crystal in the water. So still, so deep. I ache for you so! Only you, you—can console me, love me, fulfill me. Only you can take me in your arms and make me whole. You beckon me so shamelessly.

ACT III

SCENE I

Late the same evening. There's a knock at the door. JOSEFA, *sitting by the light of the moon streaming through the window, rises, goes to the door. It is Father Prado.*

JOSEFA: Father, I've been waiting for you. Thank you for coming. Wait, let me turn on a light. I was sitting in the dark, thinking. [*She turns on a lamp. She leads him to the couch.*] I know I asked you to come at such a late hour.
FATHER PRADO: The hour does not matter. I'm glad to be here. Señora Escobar led the rosary since you weren't there. She always throws in some extra "Hail, Marys." Now we can talk over the plans.
JOSEFA: Plans?
FATHER PRADO: For the procession tomorrow. Isn't that why you asked me to come?
JOSEFA: I had forgotten about the procession. How terrible of me.
FATHER PRADO: You simply cannot do that, my child. You would disappoint many people. They want to honor you. They love and respect you very much.
JOSEFA: I do not deserve it.
FATHER PRADO: You? with your splendid nature, your spiritual strength. You, who have done so much for so many? You must give them a chance to repay. Give them their day.

JOSEFA: Their day.

FATHER PRADO: I shall be here early in the morning. Three rings of the church bell will summon the people to congregate by the fountain in the town square. That fountain—it was full of swallows this morning. They're here.

JOSEFA: I know. My birdhouse is full.

FATHER PRADO: Well, everything is ready. The ladies have laid out the fine embroidered altar linens you sent, made by your lovely little hands, and the surplices for the altar boys—how can I thank you? It is your way, your way. I get the feeling you are not looking forward to tomorrow.

JOSEFA: Oh Father, so many things have happened.

FATHER PRADO: Of course, of course—I understand. Terrible, terrible things.

JOSEFA: You know about Clara?

FATHER PRADO: May God help her, give her strength.

JOSEFA: Don Miguel doesn't want her back.

FATHER PRADO: He's been very patient for some years now. She's had the drinking problem for a long time.

JOSEFA: Patient! He wasn't patient; he simply ignored her—left her alone in the hacienda for months at a time. Father—sometimes, sometimes I would let her drink because I couldn't stand her anguish. It was so—so empty—like a deep, dark chasm—and she kept falling down, down, down, never coming to the bottom. She couldn't help herself. At least—at least—when she drank she pretended gaiety. It gave her some kind of strength. Nothing else seemed to help.

FATHER PRADO: Did you pray with her?

JOSEFA: Pray? No we never did.

FATHER PRADO: Then you must pray for her now.

JOSEFA: Oh Father, I'm so confused. I—I. . . . Alysea has left me. She's going to marry Eduardo. I shall never see her again.

FATHER PRADO: She's not that way. She loves you too much and is very grateful for all you did for her. She told me that before she left. She'll come back. And you should be happy for her and Eduardo.

JOSEFA: Happy?

FATHER PRADO: You look so pale. Are you feeling alright?

JOSEFA: David . . .

FATHER PRADO: I'm so sorry, my dear. I didn't want to speak of it because I thought it might upset you. A tragedy! No one but a deranged person could have done that to the poor, defenseless child.

JOSEFA: Father!

FATHER PRADO: Yes, my child. . . .

JOSEFA: I want confession now.

FATHER PRADO: Here?

JOSEFA: Please, Father.

FATHER PRADO: Of course, if that's what you want.

[*He comes to her; she falls on her knees before him.*]

FATHER PRADO: What is wrong?

JOSEFA: Forgive me, Father, for I have sinned—I have sinned—I have sinned.

FATHER PRADO: Tell me, my daughter.

JOSEFA: I'm so lost.

FATHER PRADO: All of us are, at one time or another.

JOSEFA: I am guilty of grievous sins—beyond forgiveness.

FATHER PRADO: God forgives all. His mercy is boundless.

JOSEFA: Love takes with soundless force, shapes and forms we cannot control.

FATHER PRADO: What do you mean?

JOSEFA: There was no intruder. It was I who hurt David.

FATHER PRADO: I can't believe. . . .

JOSEFA: I did it.

FATHER PRADO: Why?

JOSEFA: He saw something he was not meant to see—between Alysea and me.

FATHER PRADO: What could have been so terrible for you to hurt the child? You love David.

JOSEFA: I don't have the right to say that. What is love?

FATHER PRADO: Tell me, tell me what happened.

JOSEFA: It began a year ago.

FATHER PRADO: A year ago?

JOSEFA: Yes. Please hear me out. I don't want to excuse the things I've done. I know now that somehow I seem to hurt all the people I profess to love. Why?

FATHER PRADO: Tomorrow the people of this town are honoring you because you care for others. You are generous and kind.

JOSEFA: There's another side. The things I do for people, the miracles I create with my hands—the lace, my garden—are the deeds of Josefa, High Priestess of the Moon. Don't look at me that way—let me explain. Los duendes, my spirits, have given me certain energies, creative energies.

FATHER PRADO: You speak in riddles, my child. I know you to be most devout. Why do you talk such nonsense? You, a good Christian.

JOSEFA: I lived alone for a long time, Father—a recluse, you might say. Even when I am with people, I am still alone—because I'm different—almost as if I belong to another world. The world of the elements—sun, earth, rain, vegetation, light— mostly light. A year ago I convinced Alysea not to bathe in the lake with the barrio girls. Theirs was a hopeless dream. I told her that if there were any spirits in the lake, they belonged to the night and the moon. My energies had always been spiritual. I lived a life, a good life, thinking this was enough. I took Alysea to the lake at night, a year ago, to bathe by moonlight—to feel the spirits, to feel as one with the pines, the moon, the water. She was caught up in my magic.

FATHER PRADO: This is all news to me—as if another person were telling me all this.

JOSEFA: I kept my body mute, physical desire, for worthier things.

FATHER PRADO: You never married.

JOSEFA: No. I took care of my mother who was an invalid, until she died. I never knew my father. He deserted my mother before I was born. It was enough for me to devote my life to caring for my mother. But many times I was overwhelmed by loneliness, a lostness, until my spirits came. Then came Alysea and little David.

FATHER PRADO: You said you took Alysea to bathe in the lake at night. . . .

JOSEFA: Oh, yes . . . Forgive me. I seem to ramble so.

FATHER PRADO: Did something happen?

JOSEFA: The water had a bright warmth, as if the moon had melted into the ripples. My body became alive with a silver desire. I could not help it. There was a fire in me, lapping, wanting. I think Alysea sensed it. She left the water and started running, away from me perhaps. I became a creature I had never known before. I followed and and caught up with her. I gently held her in my arms and found her lips.

FATHER PRADO: And found her lips?

JOSEFA: Alysea became my lover that one time—a year ago. After that I felt such guilt and disgust for myself. I didn't talk about it to Alysea. I was too ashamed.

FATHER PRADO: We have all transgressed—in one way or another. The body has needs.

JOSEFA: Not my body—not my body—I told myself after it happened. It had all been some temporary madness—or have I been mad all along?

FATHER PRADO: Of course not.

JOSEFA: But, Father, it came over me again last night. That bestial desire came over me again. Against Alysea's wish I begin to caress her. Out of gratitude for what I've done for her, she refuses me nothing. David came into the room. Oh, his eyes! His eyes . . . was it only fear I saw in his eyes? His eyes were my eyes—I was looking at myself . . . Slime, smut, maggots, mire. A fury took my heart. All I could think of was—He'll tell people—he'll tell the world. I took a kitchen knife—wanting to silence him—I tried to cut his tongue. . . .

FATHER PRADO: The ways of the Devil! You were mad. I believe it.

JOSEFA: I came to my senses and saw the horror of what I was doing. I dropped the knife—but I had already wounded him. . . . I did not cut off his tongue, did I? Oh, my God. . . . I didn't—did I? The nurses—what did they say? A wound, only a wound. I remember slashing once, and then the child broke free, and I grew cold—cold with my sin—oh, the heinous Josefa. Don't you see. Look, I'll show you. [*Looks for finished damask, finds it, holds it up to him.*] See, Father? Lightning-terror. Alysea pointed it out to me, and I never knew, or would believe. I am the lightning piercing . . . I am beauty and terror intermingled. It shouldn't be—it shouldn't be . . . but it is . . . and I must separate the two. I must! I must!

FATHER: Put your trust in Christ. Follow his way. Be true to your Faith. . . .

JOSEFA: That won't work, Father. I have to separate the two.

FATHER: Your life is far from tragic. You are greatly beloved in this pueblo. I have always admired. . . . Well, that was the Josefa as seen by those who could not see.

JOSEFA: I could not see! But now I do. The Josefa of the world is empty, confined. She strikes out in terror without forethought. But the me that the spirits created! Oh, I am the light that is the fallen flame of sunset; I am my night blooms that open to the moon; I am the delicate, intricate design of my lace—belonging to something other than the world. Not the world. This body that I wear holds all my passions—yes. I am a woman of hungry passions. If I had had a husband, a lover—long before this—I would cling to the world, celebrate my body and desire. But, it was never so. My spirits took my passions, shaped them into light—That is the Josefa you admire, Father—not the one that is alien to the world.

FATHER: You are of the world. That is the reality. You are wanted in the world. Your spirit belongs to God—not to any duendes. Oh, my child, I forgive your sins. You are absolved. Kneel and pray an act of contrition. Truly repent and feel your God.

[JOSEFA *kneels and prays the act of contrition, a comforting outlet of emotion. When she finishes,* FATHER PRADO *helps her to her feet and holds her for a moment.*]

FATHER: Don't despair, my child. Don't despair. You are exhausted. Tomorrow is an important day for you. Sleep, rest. I'll take my leave now. Goodnight, my child.

[JOSEFA *accompanies him to the door. She looks around the room with fond memories, touches curtains, lace, flowers, then goes to the window.*]

JOSEFA: You are trembling, my waters, silver, deep, and the moon is waiting. I must take a stroll to the lake—I must have comfort from my spirits. Surely they know I must find the spiral of my origin. They must take me to my origin. . . .

SCENE II

Two weeks later. The birdhouse is empty now. The room is unseemly bright. CLEMENCIA *is busily dusting. Knock at the door.* CLEMENCIA *opens it.*

CLEMENCIA: Don Eduardo—Alysea—Ah, back from your honeymoon. Come in, come in. Here, I am—in Josefa's house.

EDUARDO: So you are. How do you like it here?

CLEMENCIA: It's a beautiful house. So peaceful. Such light!

ALYSEA: It's unusually bright, isn't it?

CLEMENCIA: And the garden—all in bloom. Poor Josefa. . . .

EDUARDO: Any news?

ALYSEA: We just came in from town. We heard about Josefa disappearing.

CLEMENCIA: No one knows where she is—where she went. Some believe this. Others believe that. No one knows.

EDUARDO: People in the pueblo told us they dragged the lake looking for her body. They found no trace.

ALYSEA: My poor darling Josefa.

CLEMENCIA: I know what a loss it must be to you and little David. But Father Prado has a will—she left this house to David, and I am to stay here and take care of him. Imagine me living here—no more delivering milk, getting up at the break of dawn— not that I wanted Josefa to disappear. We all love her too much. Sad—sad. The whole town sits in the evenings wondering, believing this and that—superstitions. I myself wonder if they are only superstitions.

ALYSEA: What are they saying?

CLEMENCIA: Well—some believe she went for a walk at night—into forbidden coun- try, up in the pines where the ancient gods live—and they kept her as one of their own. Others believe she was kidnapped by the intruders who hurt David.

ALYSEA: How is David?

CLEMENCIA: Coming home tonight. I'm going to cook his favorite dinner.

ALYSEA: Chicken caldo with fresh corn.

CLEMENCIA: That's what he said.

ALYSEA: Thank God—he can talk.

CLEMENCIA: A mile a minute—that child! He still does not know about Josefa. Stay for supper. He would love to see you.

EDUARDO: Thank you, but that will be impossible. We are on our way to Guadalajara. We just stopped by—or at least—Alysea wanted to see the house one last time. She says something was telling her to come.

CLEMENCIA: She wanted to say goodbye to the beautiful house where she was so happy—isn't that it, Alysea?

ALYSEA: I suppose. . . .

CLEMENCIA: You will love Guadalajara. It is paradise.

EDUARDO: Not exactly—but I do have a job waiting for me there.

CLEMENCIA: Two young people—their whole life before them—Ah! that's good. Josefa would be so happy for you. I'm sorry you had to come back to such sad news. This pueblo—I don't know what is happening.

ALYSEA: The birds are gone—that's one thing that happened. Come and look, Eduardo. The bird house is empty. Oh, no—look, not our little bird. It had a broken wing and Josefa and I mended it. It's still here—the only one. When did they leave?

CLEMENCIA: Three days ago. One of the omens. . . .

EDUARDO: What do you mean—omen?

CLEMENCIA: There have been many since Josefa disappeared. Everyone believes it's because she disappeared. You know that when the birds leave every year, they follow a straight path north. Not this time. At dawn—they took off—towards the lake and they circled the lake for hours, some coming down to rest on the reeds, to fly low on the water. The whole town went out to look. Finally, when the sun was in the West, they flew off following the path north. Very strange. Why did they do such a thing?

EDUARDO: You said "omens." Have there been others?

CLEMENCIA: Oh, yes. Two days after she disappeared, the sky up in the pine woods was filled with millions of fireflies. It looked as if the stars had come down to dance among the pines. It was so beautiful to see.

ALYSEA: A happy omen. I believe that.

CLEMENCIA: Then there was the moon. The night after she disappeared, when the moon came out—it was red, blood red—then it seemed to come down low, very low. When we looked out into the lake—the moon seemed to have turned to silver—then it seemed to fall into the lake—yes fall into the water. The world was dark for a few seconds. Then the moon appeared among the trees—yellow and bright. Those who saw it thought it was the end of the world.

ALYSEA: Josefa. . . .

CLEMENCIA: What?

ALYSEA: Oh, nothing, nothing . . . were there any other strange things that happened?

CLEMENCIA: In this very house. The first few days, everybody was looking for Josefa. When she wasn't found, Father Prado asked me to come and water her garden. You

know it's the only beautiful garden in the whole town. Well, I noticed that all the night flowers, those strange ones that give off that strong fragrance, they were all dead—all of them. The stalks brown—also the leaves. The day the moon fell into the lake, I came to dig them out to clean up a bit. Alysea, you will not believe this—neither did my eyes at the time—the flowers had come to life again. I went to the garden at night—they were opened. They were beautiful. They were dancing in the night breeze—and the fragrance was so strong, some one from the village told me they could smell it in the town. What do you think of that?

EDUARDO: Strange, indeed! But, I suppose, in one way or another, it can all be explained.

CLEMENCIA: Well, I certainly cannot explain any of it. Oh, look at the time. I must go to el mercado to get the things for David's supper. Now you stay here and enjoy the house one last time, though I hope you will come back and visit. You will, won't you?

EDUARDO: Oh, certainly we shall.

ALYSEA: I'll always come back.

CLEMENCIA: Well—I must be off. [*Exits.*]

EDUARDO: You think she's here, don't you?

ALYSEA: Oh, yes—she is!

EDUARDO: You are the most superstitious one of all.

ALYSEA: No—it's not superstition. It's more than that. Josefa believed that we humans know so little of ourselves. Creation—that that was the wonder—the mystery—the awe. No, superstitions—most of them come from fear. This has something to do with beauty, with things eternal and unexplained.

EDUARDO: You really loved her, didn't you?

ALYSEA: I still do. [*Goes to window, then looks around the room.*] Josefa, you're here. I sense you. I know you're here. . . .

EDUARDO: It must be catching. I have this strange feeling. Is it the light in this room? It is unearthly. . . .

ALYSEA: The light, the flowers, the lake, the moon, and the history of what she has become is in this. [*She picks up a piece of Josefa's lace.*] See how intricate, how fragile. Little bits and pieces coming together—a crystal thing of light—beautiful Josefa— we love you—we'll always love you.

Curtain

QUESTIONS

1. Describe the tone of the prologue. How does it prefigure the mood of the action?
2. Josefa's house seems to be shrouded in mystery. What sort of mysteries exist that are hinted at, but not explained?
3. When Josefa and Eduardo have their first dialogue in Act I, each seems to have a different concept of love. What are they?
4. Toward the end of Act I, Josefa remarks that the swallows "have a long, lonely

flight." What does she mean in light of the fact that they arrive in droves? What might the swallows symbolize?

5. Who are the magicians that Josefa refers to?

6. In Act II, Josefa tells the injured bird that they "share so much." What do they share?

7. In Act II, Alysea decides to leave the house. What might she gain by leaving? What might she lose?

8. What is the significance of the unfinished damask? Why does Josefa consider naming it "Swallow Song"?

9. In Act III, why does Josefa refer to the house as an "oasis in the desert"?

10. Josefa and Father Prado argue over the significance of the ritual. What is each one's point of view about it?

11. Why has Josefa cut off David's tongue?

12. Josefa claims she has a desire to create beauty. What sort of beauty is she referring to? What is the purpose of creating such beauty?

John A. Williams

AUGUST FORTY-FIVE
A Play in One Act

CAST

DAVID BRIGHT, Pharmacist's Mate 3rd/Class, about 20
FRANKIE, Chamorro boy, 10 or 11
DIXON, Seaman, about 20
LYONS, Cook, 3rd/Class, 30 or more
ROY, Seaman, late 20's
PERKINS, Chief Pharmacist's Mate, about 30

The action takes place during 48 hours.

SCENE I

It is the first week of August 1945, on an island in the South Pacific. It is dark; the stage is dark, and in this darkness before the curtain goes up, we hear the sound of many, many big, heavy planes. The sound builds until it is almost unbearable to hear.

Lights come up very slowly, as the sound of the planes begins to fade. We see the interior of a three-man tent, which is raised from the ground and has steps leading up into it. A table is centered.

There are footlockers at the foot of each cot. Mess kits hang on nails above the cots. The sound of the planes fades altogether now, as the lights come up full on the empty tent.

DAVID BRIGHT *enters. He is about 20, of average build and height. He wears green fatigue pants and a white T-shirt. He sits on his cot with a sigh and pulls from beneath it a bucket filled with soiled clothes and soapy water. He takes a handy stick and begins to push it up and down and around in the bucket, holding the latter between his legs so it will not topple.*

Now, in the quietness of the camp, we hear the clattering of a typewriter, perhaps two; birds; and, from time to time, voices offstage. We will hear the typewriter throughout the day scenes, except at meal times.

Everything is white, as though the sun is taking a special vengeance on the camp. We should be made to feel uncomfortable by the suggested intensity of the sun. BRIGHT *lights a cigarette and continues to pummel the clothes, although rather absently.*

We hear a Jeep, its gears being broken down from third to second to first. BRIGHT *turns and peers in the direction of the sound, which stops abruptly.* BRIGHT *strains. We hear new voices off, hearty, brisk, perfunctory.* BRIGHT *has stopped with the clothes, absorbed by what he sees. He stands to get a better view. His body seems to slump. He slides the bucket back under the cot and lays down.*

FRANKIE, *a Chamorro boy of about 10 or 11, sneaks into the tent holding a twig.* BRIGHT's *back is to him. He touches* BRIGHT *on the back with the twig.* BRIGHT *slaps at it, but* FRANKIE *has jerked the twig away. Stealthily, he pushes it back. This time* BRIGHT *slaps and hits the twig. He sits up quickly.* FRANKIE *dances away, laughing.*

BRIGHT: Cut the crap, Frankie. [FRANKIE *throws the twig at him. It misses.*] I'll kick your butt good, you little punk. [*Picks up the twig and throws it out of the tent. He lays down again.* FRANKIE *digs in his pocket, then makes throwing motions toward* BRIGHT.] I wish you would. I just wish you would.

FRANKIE [*disdainfully*]: Aw, shut up Bright. You no so hot.

BRIGHT [*snapping upright*]: Little bastard! You get away with murder around here, but not with me. Now you stop fuckin' around. [*Softer.*] Damned little gook.

FRANKIE [*edging toward the steps*]: Where's Lyons?

BRIGHT: He's a cook, isn't he?

FRANKIE: Yes—

BRIGHT: Then he'd be in the goddamn chowhall, wouldn't he? [FRANKIE *has opened his mouth to speak, but closes it. He has one foot on the steps as he studies* BRIGHT.] And don't go around calling your father by his last name.

FRANKIE: He's no my father yet. What I spoze call him?

BRIGHT: I don't give a damn *what* you call him. If *I* was him, I wouldn't adopt a smartass like you! I'd let you rot on this fuckin' rock, just where he found you!

FRANKIE: Bright, you mad for yesterday?

BRIGHT: You got *that* right! Damned right, I'm mad!

FRANKIE [*half-teasing*]: Why you fellas no like that name when white fellas call it you?

BRIGHT: It's not a nice name. It makes you fight. It makes you want to kill.

FRANKIE [*putting on a fake scowl*]: So you get mad, Bright? Very mad! [*Laughs tentatively.*]

BRIGHT: It's not funny, Frankie. You better try and understand that!

FRANKIE: And Lyons, him mad too?

BRIGHT [*sitting and pounding his feet to the floor.* FRANKIE *jumps*]: He should have kicked your little ass! You play bad games with him, Frank, and he loves you. [*Beat.*] You like the white fellas better than the black fellas, don't you, Frankie? [FRANKIE *edges back.*] In America, you'd be just like *us.* Shit, they already locked up 100,000 Jap Americans! You wouldn't be like *them.* They'd make you know that pretty quick, boy!

FRANKIE [*defensively*]: I not say I white!

BRIGHT [*snapping at him*]: You *act* like it!

FRANKIE [*now he is for real, a little boy*]: I—I not.

BRIGHT [*tense with anger*]: You think you're better than us already. So where do you and your people get off? Any white fellas offer to adopt your skinny little ass like Lyons, and take you to the States? No! Those white boys are down there all the time doin' it to your women, and your women tellin' us all the time, none for us, 'cause we got *tails!* [FRANKIE *is frightened by the anger. He sidles close to the entrance of the tent.* BRIGHT *gets up and moves close to him.*] Shit, Frankie, I'm talkin to you. They didn't wanna take your ass home, DID THEY? You don't have no right to ask a man to care for you and then you up and call him a nigger! Takin' his time, money, love . . . [*Makes a sudden move toward* FRANKIE, *who leaps out of the tent.*] A little rat, that's what you are, a little, gook *rat!*

FRANKIE [*off, in a fright-filled voice that tries to be brave*]: Bright! You nigger, Bright! Nigger! [BRIGHT *starts to rush out, stops and shakes his head.*]

DIXON [*entering as* BRIGHT *backs out of the way. He is dressed like* BRIGHT, *but wears a white sailor cap unfolded down on his head. A bag is slung over one shoulder; he holds a stick with a nail in it in the other hand*]: What's all this nigger shit, Doc? Where's Frankie runnin' to?

BRIGHT: Aw, that kid pisses me off. Shouldn't have popped my cork like *that,* though. Did I hear you cats playin' ball a while ago?

DIXON [*sitting on a cot*]: Yeh. Got fifteen points, man. Hittin from all over, like Sidat-Singh [*demonstrating*] bip! bop!

BRIGHT [*also sitting*]: Planes out again today, huh?

DIXON: Whoooeee, man. Sure wouldn't wanna be no Jap this mornin'! They got B-29s, B-24s, and I thought I saw some B-17s. They flyin' everything. They droppin' some powerful shit these days, Doc. This sumbitch spozed to be over soon. Home alive in '45!

BRIGHT: Sure you don't mean chow line till '49? Hey, them Marines still over there in the C.O.'s office?

DIXON: Yeah, Doc. You saw them cats roll in here, too? Now what's *that* all about? I hope we ain't in for another push, man. I mean that Peliliu was enough for *me.* I ain't never seen so many dead people in my life, Jim.

BRIGHT [*staring out*]: Those First Marines *loves* this 27th Special. You cats really humped that ammo into Peliliu. Lift them shells, tote them rounds.

DIXON [*proudly*]: We got a Presidential Unit Citation, too, Jim, for that shit.

BRIGHT: Sure did. Washburne didn't. Malone didn't get it. Jefferson didn't get it. Vann didn't get it—

DIXON [*interrupting*]: I *know* that, Doc. [*Beats.*] Yeah, they dead, all right. And now, down by the beach, they got shit stacked *up,* Jim! Jeeps, Recons, trucks, tires, ambulances, rations, ammo—where the sumbitches goin *this* time?

BRIGHT [*teasing*]: Aw, man, you know. Ja-*pan*.

DIXON [*scornfully*]: You fulla shit, Doc.

BRIGHT: What else they got to in*vade*, Dixon?

DIXON [*upset*]: Aw, man! You don't know what you're talkin' about.

BRIGHT [*rubbing it in*]: The other day I was over in Agaña trying to find a girl, and I came up by COMSOPAC and saw more brass than I've ever seen on this rock or any other rock. Enough gold braid to make Fort Knox look like a Salvation Army collection plate! Man, these white folks gonna kick the shit outa them Japs!

DIXON: Yeah? How come you think you know so much?

BRIGHT [*calmly*]: I feel it right in my bones, Dixon.

DIXON [*rising, troubled*]: I got to go. I don't think the cat'sll wanna hear this shit when they come in from the docks for lunch! [*Exits.*]

LYONS [*off*]: Hiya, Dixon?

DIXON [*off*]: What say, Lyons! What's for lunch?

LYONS [*off*]: Pussy!

DIXON [*off*]: Hot or cold?

LYONS [*off*]: Seen Frankie?

DIXON [*off*]: He was around not too long ago, man.

LYONS [*Enters. He's chubby, wearing soiled white pants and T-shirt and a towel around his neck*]: Hey ole buddy.

BRIGHT [*studying him*]: Lyons, I don't understand how come you don't lose some weight in that kitchen. If it's 200 degrees out here, it's got to be 300 in there—[*Breaks off at the sound of loud voices from the C.O.'s office. Both stare off until we hear the Jeep starting up and driving away. Both sit down. They are pensive.*] Seen Frankie, Doc?

BRIGHT: He was here. Went off somewhere in the boondocks.

LYONS [*removes his shoes, folds himself down on his cot sighing with pleasure*]: After that business yesterday, I wanted to see him. Explain things to him. I guess he'll be around for evening chow. Seem okay?

BRIGHT [*starts to say something, changes his mind*]: Yeah, he's okay. Any word on what the Marines wanted?

LYONS: Not yet, but if there's any scuttlebutt, we'll hear it soon enough.

BRIGHT: Fuckin' Marines. Act like they found a home with this outfit.

LYONS: Another push, you think?

BRIGHT: Yeah. Japan. That's what I told Dixon.

LYONS [*sitting up, quick*]: What? Why you say that?

BRIGHT: I was only kidding then. But, I been thinkin', Lyons. There ain't no place left to go.

LYONS [*laying down again*]: You right, Doc. Don't look good. Don't look good at all. If we do go, I guess Frankie could wait here. Maybe I should try to get him sent to my wife. What'd you do, Doc?

BRIGHT [*with infinite weariness*]: You gotta get the papers cleared before you do any-thing, Lyons. That can take a lotta time. Look how long it's takin' already. [*Beats.*] Those goddamn Marines, man. They worry me. I wish the sumbitches'd never come. They so goddamn bad. Shit. They die just like anyone else, hollerin' and screamin' for Momma and morphine. Them Japs don't read no English. They don't know the Marines is supposed to be bad.

LYONS: Remember the Japs callin' and askin' us what we were doin' there? Now them cats spoke *good* English, Doc. Made sense, too. [*Beats.*] I wish it was over. Been out here two years and ain't met more than four-five decent white men. Twenty-four months. Still a cook third class.

BRIGHT: You know they ain't about to give us too many promotions, man. Shit. I been a pecker-checker, chancre mechanic for two years, too. I ain't gonna make it to pharmacists mate deuce. I'ma develop an illness, some mysterious jungle shit.

LYONS [*alarmed*]: Don't you go fuckin' up, now, Doc. It's a sometime proposition with those white boys in the sick bay. They just lookin' to finish sick call.

BRIGHT: Don't worry, Lyons. They'd never believe me.

LYONS [*satisfied*]: Now that's more like it! [*Beats.*] Got a letter from my ole lady today. Thinks Frankie's a good-lookin' little cat. Sent her those pictures you took.

BRIGHT: You think he'll really like it back there?

LYONS: Detroit? Sure.

BRIGHT [*bitterly*]: Yeah, sure. What're a few race riots.

LYONS: Things've changed, Doc. Anyway, the word is that once you get the papers moving, it shouldn't take long.

BRIGHT: White guy said that?

LYONS: Yeah.

BRIGHT [*taking a magazine from under his pillow and opening it*]: Great.

LYONS: My wife says she's starting to buy things already. [*Laughs.*] They may be too small or too big!

BRIGHT [*monotone, skimming*]: Ain't that the truth.

LYONS: I guess I could send him on ahead. Let him get used to things back there. [*Sits up.*] Oh, I know he's got a nasty, wild mouth, Doc. All this GI shit been rubbin' off on him after he lost his folks except for that slick ole uncle. It's been hard on him.

BRIGHT: Yeah, I guess so.

LYONS [*fixing a gaze on* BRIGHT]: You don't like him much, do you Doc?

BRIGHT [*still skimming*]: I like him fine, Lyons, no shit.

LYONS: Naw you don't.

BRIGHT [*now looking up*]: He's all right, man. Honest. If you wanna adopt him, more power to you.

LYONS: He'll be all right. I can raise him right.

BRIGHT [*suddenly, as though making a decision*]: Lyons.

LYONS: Huh?

BRIGHT [*hesitates*]: What's for chow?

LYONS [*wiping his face with the towel*]: Shit on shingles.

BRIGHT [*distastefully*]: Christ!

LYONS [*mockingly*]: Chicken on Sunday!

BRIGHT [*as* LYONS *laughs*]: Aw, man. We have chicken *every* Sunday. It's a wonder we don't have a fuckin' ice cream parlor, too.

LYONS [*stretching*]: I got to get back. Trucks should be on the way. [*Sits up. Stares off and smiles.*] How do Miz Camel?

BRIGHT [*sitting up quickly*]: Say, Camel. You folks g'one be down by the stream tonight?

CAMEL [*off, sweetly*]: Hello, Lyons. Hello, Doc. You know we at the stream *every* night. Come on down.

LYONS [*giggling; falls back onto his cot*]: That faggot's somethin' else!

BRIGHT [*staring after* CAMEL]: I swear, man, that cat is startin' to look good to me, what with these goddamn crackers lockin' up *all* the pussy. They better get me off this rock, quick!

LYONS [*standing again*]: Doc, you know you done already been down there!

BRIGHT [*laying down again*]: Not yet, but the Shadow knows—I might! Dick's gettin' hard as times in '32.

LYONS [*exiting*]: See ya.

[BRIGHT *lies, hands over his eyes. Loud laughter makes him sit up again and he looks off.*]

BRIGHT [*cupping his hands around his mouth*]: You guys take your salt pills?

VOICE [*off*]: Yeah, Doc. You see those Marines?

BRIGHT: Fuck a Marine! [*As he pulls out his bucket of wash again, we hear the sound of many heavy trucks approaching camp. They stop. Off, we also hear many voices.* ROY, *a big, husky man in his late twenties, a cap pulled down over his eyes, enters and snatches his mess kit.*]

ROY: Say, Doc.

BRIGHT [*getting his kit, too*]: I'll go with you. The Marines were here this morning.

ROY: What for?

BRIGHT [*stabbing him in the chest with his finger*]: You.

Lights

SCENE II

Forty-eight hours later. We hear no planes. BRIGHT *is sitting on his cot pummeling his clothes.* DIXON *enters.*

DIXON [*sitting*]: Doc, you got it made. Mornin' sick call and evenin' sick call and sacktime in between.

BRIGHT: You got yourself a pretty good hustle, too, Dixon.

DIXON: Say, Doc, you got any of those morphine things?

BRIGHT: Syrettes?

DIXON: Yeah, that's the stuff. Gimmee a couple of those, will ya?

BRIGHT [*snorting*]: For *what?* You ain't got no battle wound.

DIXON: I got a bad toothache, Doc.

BRIGHT: So how come you didn't make sick call?

DIXON: Sell 'em to me.

BRIGHT: Get 'em from McElhenny.

DIXON: Aw, man. You know that cracker wouldn't give me anything without a lot of who-struck-john, and then pass me on to the doctor. That's a brutal sumbitch, Jim. Cats come in from the docks, their backs messed up and he give 'em a prostate massage, man. What's a finger up your ass got to do with a broke back, is what I want to know.

BRIGHT: Don't ask me. Besides some of the cats must like it—they're on sick call for the same thing every week. Anyway, man, I can't just give the shit out. The doctor keeps a check. Regulations. What're you, some kind of addick?

DIXON: Who? Me? [*Beats.*] How about some of that 190 proof alcohol you corpsmen got? You know, the shit you drink with Coke and then you can't smoke for five hours 'cause it'll blow you up?

BRIGHT: Man, can't you see I'm busy?

DIXON [*running out of hope*]: Got an extra beer?

BRIGHT [*bitingly*]: How about two atabrine tablets, two APCs, two sulfathiazole tablets, two sulfanilamide tablets, and two sulfadiazine tablets, swallowed down with a glass of potassium permanganate instead?

DIXON [*hopefully*]: Will that get me high?

BRIGHT [*disgusted*]: No, but they'll put you outa your misery. [*Both turn at the sound of trucks.*] What's that?

DIXON: A travelin' whorehouse—I hope.

BRIGHT [*tensing*]: Fuckin' Marine trucks, Dixon.

DIXON: Kiss my wrist!

BRIGHT: It's your ass they want.

DIXON: I want it, too.

CAMEL [*off, sweetly*]: Dixon! Ho, Dixon!

DIXON [*flattens on the deck*]: Lookin' for men to unload those trucks. Me, I have just gone on sick leave.

CAMEL [*off*]: Cleaning detail on the double! On the double! Dixon, Baker, Robertson, Shorter! On the double, now!

DIXON [*mimicking*]: Cleaning detail on the double now!

BRIGHT [*still looking off*]: They got some people now. Big ole sarge with a checklist.

MARINE SGT.'S VOICE [*very loud*]: 'kay you men. Five hundred helmets, and they ain't to piss in.

CAMEL [*also off*]: We know what they're for.

SGT.: Oh, you does, does you?

DIXON: He's *great* big, right?

BRIGHT: Sure is. Looks like a house with legs.

DIXON: Pot belly.

BRIGHT: Sure 'nuff. Cat looks pregnant.

DIXON: Gotta a four-five on his hip.

BRIGHT: You ain't lyin', man.

DIXON: I'ma kick that sumbitch's ass!

BRIGHT: Hummmm. When you gonna kick his ass, Dixon?

DIXON: Not right now.

SGT.:

> Five hundred pairs of fatigues.
> Five hundred pairs of flesh-outs.
> Five thousand boxes rations.
> Five hundred M-1s.

Fifty thousand rounds .30 caliber ammo.
Five hundred battle packs.
One hundred twenty crosses.
Twenty-five Stars of David—y'all got some Jews in this outfit? [*Laughs.*]

DIXON [*muttering*]: Yo momma, you cracker sumbitch. Doc, why they issue all that new shit to die in?

SGT.: Five hundred ampules, cholera vaccine. [*Voice fades.*]

DIXON: I guess you were right, Doc.

BRIGHT: I'd rather be wrong, man.

DIXON [*vehemently*]: Shit! Last time we got new stuff—shit! This ain't got nothin' to do with me, man.

BRIGHT: Eat your own shit. They'll give a Section Eight.

DIXON: Ain't my style, Doc.

BRIGHT: Blow off a toe.

DIXON [*crouching now, peering off, too*]: I need my toes for dancin'.

BRIGHT: AWOL.

DIXON: On this rock? You crazy?

BRIGHT: Then shut the fuck up! [LYONS *enters.*] Hi, man.

LYONS [*as before, sweating and wiping*]: Whaddaya say. You cats seen Frankie this mornin'?

BRIGHT: No.

DIXON: Looks to me like you don't have no time to be worryin' about no Frankie, man.

LYONS [*snapping*]: Dixon, how come you ain't down there helpin' to unload? Ain't you on the cleaning detail?

DIXON: I had to have a special conference with Doc here.

LYONS: Conference my ass!

DIXON: Another fuckin' push! Shit!

LYONS [*laying down*]: You don't have to worry about that, Dixon. They just got a new secret weapon, a gun.

BRIGHT [*turning from watching action, off*]: Another one?

LYONS: All the battlewagons been fitted with this gun and when one of them special shells lands, nothing'll grow for a thousand years.

BRIGHT: People, too, I guess, huh?

LYONS: Especially people.

DIXON: Aw, bullshit, Lyons. Last secret weapon we heard about was this phosphorous bomb. Remember one got stuck in the bomb-bay of a B-29 and that gunner had to free it? Burned that cracker from his toenails to his eyebrows.

BRIGHT: Well, they gave him some medals.

DIXON: Yeah. Let's see how they work in place of his dick. They always comin' up with some secret weapon that turns out to be as great as a box of K-rations.

BRIGHT [*disgusted*]: If they *had* somethin', they'd a used it, right? Don't make sense, they just now discoverin' somethin', right?

LYONS: I don't understand how come Frankie ain't been around in two days.

BRIGHT: Frankie was doin' all right before we got here, and he's probably doin' all right now, and will do all right when we—

LYONS: What?

BRIGHT [*a glance at* DIXON]: Nothin'. He's all right.

LYONS [*huffily*]: Oh, he's comin' home with me, all right, Doc. Don't you worry none about that!

BRIGHT: Sure, I'm hip.

DIXON [*rising now*]: They're almost done. Time to lend a hand. See you cats. [*Exits.*]

LYONS: Doc, I'm worried about Frankie.

BRIGHT: You *sure* you want to adopt that kid, Lyons?

LYONS: Yeah, I'm sure! You youngbloods don't take me serious. I want him. He wants me. He was livin' like an animal when we found him back up in the hills. He's come a long way since then.

BRIGHT: Yeah.

LYONS: It was *us* comin' damn near 15,000 miles and some of us didn't know diddley about no fuckin' Japan until Pearl Harbor. We was . . . liberators. So here's this kid. Ain't got nobody but this slick old, toothless uncle who'd rather not be bothered with him. I can't have no kids, Doc. So there's Frankie, and we hit it off right away. It made me feel good when he needed me, made me feel important. I thought a lot about the adoption, man. You can't hardly get Negro kids in adoption agencies, 'cause colored folks don't give 'em away. I hope that never changes. I can do things for the kid, Doc. I can love him. I do love him.

BRIGHT: Love's a two-way street, man. Do you really *know* this kid? What happens if those crackers start snatching Negroes again in Detroit? Back there, he ain't gonna be white and not quite black. Somethin' in between. And, maybe, just maybe, man, he'll decide that he wants to stay here. Nother thing: we go on another push you know there isn't anything for sure except bein' black. Maybe your wife wouldn't wanna be bothered if you weren't around. . . .

LYONS [*sitting up, shaking these things off*]: I'ma go to his uncle's.

BRIGHT: You haven't been listenin' to me.

LYONS: Wanna come?

BRIGHT: Naw.

LYONS [*standing, briskly*]: Gotta go. The guys'll be in for noon chow direckly. You chowin' down?

BRIGHT [*as* LYONS *exits*]: I'm not hungry. [*Lies down as if very weary and draws up his knees and closes his eyes. Lights dim. And dim again. And a third time, to denote the passage of time and late afternoon. Now we hear the trucks grinding up to the camp again, and the voices of many men. It is now about 5:30.* BRIGHT *is still asleep as* ROY, *a worried look on his face, enters carrying new equipment: fatigues, shoes, rifle, pack and helmet. He throws it all on his cot and looks at the sleeping* BRIGHT *with disgust.*]

ROY: Bright! Wake the fuck up, Doc. [*Kicks the legs of the cot.*] Doc!

BRIGHT [*bolting upright*]: What! What! Aw, shit, Roy. Don't do that, man. What time's it?

ROY [*full head of anger*]: Looka that shit! (Points to the gear.) *Look*atit! They just gave us this crap. A *push*, we're goin' on another fuckin *push*! [*Strips to his shorts and grabs a towel. Pauses in the door.*] And you layin' there sleepin'!

BRIGHT [*as* ROY *exits*]: What you want me to do, call Nimitz or Truman? [*Calling after.*] How long you guys been in?

[BRIGHT *stands and stretches. Goes to* ROY*'s cot and distastefully looks at the gear.*]

CHIEF PERKINS [*entering with a can of beer he gives to* BRIGHT. *The* CHIEF *is white, wears his cap tough-guy style, on the side of his head*]: Gettin' a little sacktime, eh, Bright?

BRIGHT: Hi, Chief. Heh, heh. Thanks for the beer. Damn! Ice cold, too.

CHIEF: Yeah, we got some ice from the kitchen. [*Sits.*] We gotta start cholera innoculations tomorrow.

BRIGHT: Where we goin' Chief?

CHIEF: Japan. Honshu. I heard it at the Fleet Hospital today.

BRIGHT: Okay, where's Honshu?

CHIEF [*drinking from his own can*]: That's where Tokyo is.

BRIGHT: Yep, that's just where it'd be all right.

CHIEF: I want you to skip sick call tonight and check out the kits against this list. [*Removes paper from his pocket and hands it over.*] Also, we need some stretcher-bearers. At least fifty. Dardano is stenciling the helmets now.

BRIGHT [*quickly*]: Tell 'im not to stencil mine. I'll take it the way it is.

CHIEF: Geneva convention. Big white circle, red cross in the middle. You know that. Make sure there're plenty of ABDs, extras, all the sulfas, morphine syrettes, and tags. The doctor will have cleared the morphine by the time you're ready.

BRIGHT: Who else is workin' on that detail, Chief?

CHIEF: Nobody. [*Stands.*] Beats the docks, don't it? [*Exits.*]

ROY [*storming in*]: What the fuck's he doin' here? [*Puts on fresh clothes from his footlocker.*]

BRIGHT: Announcing our destination—TO-KEE-YO!

ROY: Straight shit?

BRIGHT: That's what the man said. Tokyo on the island of Honshu.

ROY: Let's chow down, Doc. [*They take their mess kits and exit, meeting* LYONS, *who rushes in.*] Say, Lyons?

LYONS [*wiping off, pulling out fresh clothes*]: How you doin' man? Doc?

BRIGHT: What's the rush?

LYONS [*still dressing*]: Got a ride out to Frankie's uncle's house.

BRIGHT: Didn't you hear the news?

LYONS [*as they finish the exit*]: Why you think I'm rushin'? [*Finishes and exits.*]

DIXON [*off, but near the tent*]: Camel! Camel! Wait up. [*Beats. His voice is low, secretive.*] Goin' to chow?

CAMEL [*his voice is normal, sweet*]: No.

DIXON: What're you gonna do?

CAMEL: Why, nothing. Why do I have to *do* anything?

DIXON: Wanna go for a walk?

CAMEL: With who?

DIXON: With me, who do you think?

CAMEL [*after a pause*]: No, thank you.

DIXON [*surprised*]: Why not?

CAMEL: I don't want to.

DIXON [*incredulous*]: You sure?

CAMEL [*laughing ribbons of sweet laughter*]: Of course, I'm sure.

DIXON [*indignant, loud*]: You damned faggot, runnin' around here shakin' your skinny ass, you ain't— [CAMEL's *laughter interrupts and overrides* DIXON's *rantings. It quickly grows darker.*]

SCENE III

It is two hours later. The darkness has a silvery quality to it. The tent is empty, but all around we hear the voices of the men in the camp, singing, yelling at cards or craps, just plain talking. The PA system goes on. Perry Como sings "Dream"; Woody Herman's "Herd" blasts through "Caldonia" and "Lemon Drop"; Duke Ellington does "I'm Beginning to See the Light," and "Sentimental Lady." From time to time we hear the DJ through the following:

ROY [*entering with* BRIGHT, *who is carrying his new gear, including the stenciled helmet and M-1 carbine. He dumps it all on his cot*]: Doc, you know you ain't supposed to have no weapon.

BRIGHT [*muttering*]: Suppose my ass. [*Hefts the carbine.*] Had one of these on Peliliu. Look, Roy, I wanna be ready in case one of them jumps in my hole. I can't say to the cat, "Look here, Jim. You can't shoot me. *I'm* a pharmacist's mate, a corpsman, a medic, and I'm here on an errand of mercy."

ROY [*laughing*]: You ain't supposed to be in no hole, Doc. You *spozed* to be out there helpin' us. If we need it.

BRIGHT: An' you're gonna need it! Here come a buncha crackers walkin' through your hometown, shootin' down your kids, your ole lady, blowin' up your house— [*Beats.*] Is that how come you don't wanna be a stretcher-bearer?

ROY [*after beats*]: The war's got to be close to over. I just don't want my ass shot on a hummer, an' I mean a hummer! Look how they fucked over you with that medal you was supposed to get after Peliliu. They don't give a shit 'bout what you done, we done. I don't want to be involved in no heroics. Every man save his own ass best way he can.

BRIGHT [*patiently*]: Once you on the beach, Roy, you could get it any whichaway. Spoze that happened to you and you were layin' out there with a hole in your ass. Would you want me or stretcher-bearers to try to get to you or just leave you whinin' and cryin'? Ain't talkin' about no heroics, man; I'm talkin about obligation.

ROY [*sullenly*]: What do you think?

BRIGHT: Well, that's all there is, man. Nobody lookin' to be a hero. You think the Chief, McElhenny, Dardano, or them others gonna look after us better than we look out for our own? You gonna work with me, Roy?

ROY: Ah, shit, I guess so. We gonna have to wear those helmets?

BRIGHT [*sharing a confidence*]: Nothin' to it. Take some mud and smear it over that white circle and the red cross. Same with the arm band. Just put some goddamn mud on 'em.

ROY: Okay, man. I got the message. You goin' to the movie?

BRIGHT: I gotta get back over to the sick bay. [*There is a sudden break in the background sounds of music and voices, and we hear the DJ talking, though we cannot yet understand him, hurriedly, excitedly. A shout goes up. There are running footsteps. Voices are louder. The music resumes.*]

ROY [*as* BRIGHT *hesitates*]: What's goin' on? [*Shouts out of the entrance.*] What's goin' on?

DIXON [*flying through the entrance*]: You hear *that* shit? They dropped an atom bomb on Hiroshima.

BRIGHT [*as they huddle*]: What kinda bomb is that?

DIXON: Brighter than a hundred suns, they said. Killed every swingin' dick for miles around.

ROY [*walking around the tent, slamming his fist into his hand*]: Oh, yeah! Oh, yeah! Surrender, you bastards! Surrender!

DIXON [*excitedly*]: That's what they tole those suckers. Surrender or we'll drop another one. Oh, man, let this shit be *over*!

CAMEL [*off*]: The C.O.'s called off everything for tomorrow, work, shots . . .

DIXON [*smiling out at him*]: No shit, Camel. We *got* to celebrate! [*Sidles out of the tent.*]

[*There is another break in the music and noise. The DJ's voice, louder now, echoing through the camp, says "the bomb was released at 8:15 this morning by crews of the Pacific Strategic Air Command. President Truman has urged the Japanese government to accept his demand for unconditional surrender. We will broadcast the latest bulletins as they come in and now back to . . ." There is more music. Within the camp, the sounds of exuberance move to a higher pitch.* ROY *goes into his footlocker and brings out a bottle.*]

ROY [*breaking the seal and taking a swallow*]: Dunbar's Canadian! [*Passes it to* BRIGHT, *then gets up and starts dancing to the music.* BRIGHT *passes it back as* LYONS *comes up the steps, his face set.*] Hi, Lyons! Looks like this shit is about over! [*Passes him the bottle.*] Drink up!

[LYONS *refuses with a shake of his head.* ROY *stops dancing, looks from* LYONS *to* BRIGHT.]

LYONS: Doc?

BRIGHT: Yeah, man, what's up?

LYONS [*in a monotone*]: Step outside.

ROY: What's wrong, Lyons?

BRIGHT: You serious?

LYONS: Yeah, come *on!*

ROY [*menacingly*]: Hey!

BRIGHT [*placatingly*]: Listen, Lyons.

LYONS: You gonna fight or not?

ROY [*flexing every muscle*]: What's this all about?

BRIGHT [*standing*]: Frankie, I guess.

ROY [*restraining* BRIGHT]: So, what about Frankie?

BRIGHT: Lyons, tell him.

LYONS [*rocking on the balls of his feet*]: He's not coming home with me. This fuckin' Bright here. After what he told the kid, Frankie said he didn't want to be like *us*, didn't want to be treated the way we're treated here—

ROY [*a harsh laugh*]: Man, you're lucky.

LYONS [*without heat*]: Shut up, Roy. [BRIGHT *starts through the entrance.* LYONS *starts to follow, but* ROY *grabs his arm.*]

BRIGHT: Let him go, Roy.

ROY: No. What'd you say, Doc?

BRIGHT: I just told him the way it was for us; how it'd be for him, and that he was treating Lyons like shit.

ROY: There ain't a sumbitch in this outfit that wouldn't agree with that, Lyons. Man, the kid was rotten. He laughed at you. He was making a fool of you. You'd a got him back there—maybe—and he'd a walked away from you in a minute. Don't you dig, man? Frankie and the rest of these Chamorros, do not dig black people! The crackers got to them. Shit, they half black themselves—

LYONS [*tearing loose*]: C'mon, Doc, les go!

ROY [*thrusting himself between them as they start out*]: Oh, no! Not over that kid. Some pussy, maybe, but not Frankie. We been together for two years, man don't that count for somethin'? We've seen a whole lotta Frankies, from the Solomons all the way up here, now ain't we? *Ain't* we, Lyons? Lotas black kids down there, New Guinea, Guadalcanal . . . *Melanesians*, remember? [*Softer.*] Didn't want to adopt any of them, hey, ole buddy? That's America you wanted to take that boy to, where the school-books are poisoned. We all hoped you'd wake up, man. Doc did you a favor. He loves you more than you love yourself. *Now*, if you still wanna fight, you're gonna have to whip me first, and you know there ain't a sumbitch in this outfit that can whip me.

BRIGHT [*as* LYONS *wrenches away and throws himself down on his cot*]: Lyons? Lyons, listen, man. You just picked the wrong kid at the wrong time in the wrong war. It ain't nothin'. [*Takes the bottle from* ROY, *passes it to* LYONS. *This time he accepts, takes a deep breath and nods.*] All right man?

LYONS [*voice shaky*]: I *know* you cats are right. But it—hurts.

ROY: The whole fuckin' war hurts, Lyons. But Doc wouldn't bullshit you. None of us would. [*Takes the bottle, drinks, sighs. Peers out.*] Well, looks like this shit is just about over.

LYONS [*climbs slowly to his feet*]: Yeah, it does. I think I'll take a walk. See what's goin' on.

BRIGHT: I'll come with you.

ROY: Me, too. [*They start out with the bottle.* BRIGHT *pauses to look around the tent.*]

BRIGHT: You wrong, Roy. I think this shit's just starting.

Slow lights as they exit.

QUESTIONS

1. What mood is established in the opening description? What images in particular set this mood?

2. How would you characterize Bright? What are his attitudes, values, beliefs?
3. What are the reasons the black land-based sailors feel hostility toward the whites? What irony is there in the fact that they are participating in a war fought against Asians?
4. What does Roy mean when he tells Lyons "that's America you wanted to take that boy to, where the schoolbooks are poisoned"? In the last line of the play, Bright says, "You wrong, Roy. I think this shit's just starting." What is he referring to?

August Wilson

MA RAINEY'S BLACK BOTTOM
A Play in Two Acts

They tore the railroad down
so the Sunshine Special can't run
I'm going away baby
build me a railroad of my own
—Blind Lemon Jefferson

For my mother

CHARACTERS

Ma Rainey's Black Bottom opened on April 6, 1984, at the Yale Repertory Theater in New Haven, Connecticut, with the following cast:

> STURDYVANT   Richard M. Davidson
> IRVIN   Lou Criscuolo
> CUTLER   Joe Seneca
> TOLEDO   Robert Judd
> SLOW DRAG   Leonard Jackson
> LEVEE   Charles S. Dutton
> MA RAINEY   Theresa Merritt
> POLICEMAN   David Wayne Nelson
> DUSSIE MAE   Sharon Mitchell
> SYLVESTER   Steven R. Blye

> Director: Lloyd Richards
> Settings: Charles Henry McClennahan

Costumes: Daphne Pascucci
Lighting: Peter Maradudin
Music Director: Dwight Andrews

THE SETTING

There are two playing areas: what is called the "band room," and the recording studio. The band room is at stage left and is in the basement of the building. It is entered through a door up left. There are benches and chairs scattered about, a piano, a row of lockers, and miscellaneous paraphernalia stacked in a corner and long since forgotten. A mirror hangs on a wall with various posters.

The studio is upstairs at stage right, and resembles a recording studio of the late 1920's. The entrance is from a hall on the right wall. A small control booth is at the rear and its access is gained by means of a spiral staircase. Against one wall there is a line of chairs, and a horn through which the control room communicates with the performers. A door in the rear wall allows access to the band room.

THE PLAY

It is early March in Chicago, 1927. There is a bit of a chill in the air. Winter has broken but the wind coming off the lake does not carry the promise of spring. The people of the city are bundled and brisk in their defense against such misfortunes as the weather, and the business of the city proceeds largely undisturbed.

Chicago in 1927 is a rough city, a bruising city, a city of millionaires and derelicts, gangsters and roughhouse dandies, whores and Irish grandmothers who move through its streets fingering long black rosaries. Somewhere a man is wrestling with the taste of a woman in his cheek. Somewhere a dog is barking. Somewhere the moon has fallen through a window and broken into thirty pieces of silver.

It is one o'clock in the afternoon. Secretaries are returning from their lunch, the noon Mass at St. Anthony's is over, and the priest is mumbling over his vestments while the altar boys practice their Latin. The procession of cattle cars through the stockyards continues unabated. The busboys in Mac's Place are cleaning away the last of the corned beef and cabbage, and on the city's Southside, sleepy-eyed negroes move lazily toward their small cold-water flats and rented rooms to await the onslaught of night, which will find them crowded in the bars and juke joints both dazed and dazzling in their rapport with life. It is with these negroes that our concern lies most heavily: their values, their attitudes, and particularly their music.

It is hard to define this music. Suffice it to say that it is music that breathes and touches. That connects. *That is in itself a way of being, separate and distinct from any other. This music is called blues. Whether this music came from Alabama or Mississippi or other parts of the South doesn't matter anymore. The men and women who make this music have learned it from the narrow crooked streets of East St. Louis, or the streets of the city's Southside, and the Alabama or Mississippi roots have been strangled by the northern manners and customs of free men of definite and sincere worth, men for whom this music often lies at the forefront of their conscience and concerns. Thus they are laid open to be consumed by it; its warmth and redress, its braggadocio and roughly poignant*

comments, its vision and prayer, which would instruct and allow them to reconnect, to reassemble and gird up for the next battle in which they would be both victim and the ten thousand slain.

ACT I

The lights come up in the studio. IRVIN enters, carrying a microphone. He is a tall, fleshy man who prides himself on his knowledge of blacks and his ability to deal with them. He hooks up the microphone, blows into it, taps it, etc. He crosses over to the piano, opens it, and fingers a few keys. STURDYVANT is visible in the control booth. Preoccupied with money, he is insensitive to black performers and prefers to deal with them at arm's length. He puts on a pair of earphones.

STURDYVANT [*over speaker*]: Irv . . . let's crack that mike, huh? Let's do a check on it.

IRVIN [*crosses to mike, speaks into it*]: Testing . . . one . . . two . . . three . . .

[*There is a loud feedback. STURDYVANT fiddles with the dials.*]

Testing . . . one . . . two . . . three . . . testing. How's that, Mel?

[STURDYVANT *doesn't respond.*]

Testing . . . one . . . two . . .

STURDYVANT [*taking off earphones*]: Okay . . . that checks. We got a good reading.

[*Pause.*]

You got that list, Irv?

IRVIN: Yeah . . . yeah, I got it. Don't worry about nothing.

STURDYVANT: Listen, Irv . . . you keep her in line, okay? I'm holding you responsible for her . . . If she starts any of her . . .

IRVIN: Mel, what's with the goddamn horn? You wanna talk to me . . . okay! I can't talk to you over the goddamn horn . . . Christ!

STURDYVANT: I'm not putting up with any shenanigans. You hear, Irv?

[IRVIN *crosses over to the piano and mindlessly runs his fingers over the keys.*]

I'm just not gonna stand for it. I want you to keep her in line. Irv?

[STURDYVANT *enters from the control booth.*]

Listen, Irv . . . you're her manager . . . she's your responsibility . . .

IRVIN: Okay, okay, Mel . . . let me handle it.

STURDYVANT: She's your responsibility. I'm not putting up with any Royal Highness . . . Queen of the Blues bullshit!

IRVIN: Mother of the Blues, Mel. Mother of the Blues.

STURDYVANT: I don't care what she calls herself. I'm not putting up with it. I just want to get her in here . . . record those songs on that list . . . and get her out. Just like clockwork, huh?

IRVIN: Like clockwork, Mel. You just stay out of the way and let me handle it.

STURDYVANT: Yeah . . . yeah . . . you handled it last time. Remember? She marches in here like she owns the damn place . . . doesn't like the songs we picked out . . . says her throat is sore . . . doesn't want to do more than one take . . .

IRVIN: Okay . . . okay . . . I was here! I know all about it.

STURDYVANT: Complains about the building being cold . . . and then . . . trips over the mike wire and threatens to sue me. That's taking care of it?

IRVIN: I've got it all worked out this time. I talked with her last night. Her throat is fine . . . We went over the songs together . . . I got everything straight, Mel.

STURDYVANT: Irv, that horn player . . . the one who gave me those songs . . . is he gonna be here today? Good. I want to hear more of that sound. Times are changing. This is a tricky business now. We've got to jazz it up . . . put in something different. You know, something wild . . . with a lot of rhythm.

[*Pause.*]

You know what we put out last time, Irv? We put out garbage last time. It was garbage. I don't even know why I bother with this anymore.

IRVIN: You did all right last time, Mel. Not as good as you did before, but you did all right.

STURDYVANT: You know how many records we sold in New York? You wanna see the sheet? And you know what's in New York, Irv? Harlem. Harlem's in New York, Irv.

IRVIN: Okay, so they didn't sell in New York. But look at Memphis . . . Birmingham . . . Atlanta. Christ, you made a bundle.

STURDYVANT: It's not the money, Irv. You know I couldn't sleep last night? This business is bad for my nerves. My wife is after me to slow down and take a vacation. Two more years and I'm gonna get out . . . get into something respectable. Textiles. That's a respectable business. You know what you could do with a shipload of textiles from Ireland?

[*A buzzer is heard offstage.*]

IRVIN: Why don't you go upstairs and let me handle it, Mel?

STURDYVANT: Remember . . . you're responsible for her.

[STURDYVANT *exits to the control booth.* IRVIN *crosses to get the door.* CUTLER, SLOW DRAG, *and* TOLEDO *enter.* CUTLER *is in his mid-fifties, as are most of the others. He plays guitar and trombone and is the leader of the group, possibly because he is the most sensible. His playing is solid and almost totally unembellished. His understanding of his music is limited to the chord he is playing at the time he is playing it. He has all the qualities of a loner except the introspection.* SLOW DRAG, *the bass player, is perhaps the one most bored by life. He resembles* CUTLER, *but lacks* CUTLER'*s energy. He is deceptively intelligent, though, as his name implies, he appears to be slow. He is a rather large man with a wicked smile. Innate African rhythms underlie everything he plays, and he plays with an ease that is at times startling.* TOLEDO *is the piano player. In control of his instrument, he understands and recognizes that its limitations are an extension of himself. He is the only one in the group who can read. He is self-taught but misunderstands and misapplies his knowledge, though he is quick to penetrate to the core of a situation and his insights are thought-provoking. All of the men are dressed in a style of clothing befitting the members of a successful band of the era.*]

IRVIN: How you boys doing, Cutler? Come on in.

[*Pause.*]

Where's Ma? Is she with you?

CUTLER: I don't know, Mr. Irvin. She told us to be here at one o'clock. That's all I know.

IRVIN: Where's . . . huh . . . the horn player? Is he coming with Ma?

CUTLER: Levee's supposed to be here same as we is. I reckon he'll be here in a minute. I can't rightly say.

IRVIN: Well, come on . . . I'll show you to the band room, let you get set up and rehearsed. You boys hungry? I'll call over to the deli and get some sandwiches. Get you fed and ready to make some music. Cutler . . . here's the list of songs we're gonna record.

STURDYVANT [*over speaker*]: Irvin, what's happening? Where's Ma?

IRVIN: Everything under control, Mel. I got it under control.

STURDYVANT: Where's Ma? How come she isn't with the band?

IRVIN: She'll be here in a minute, Mel. Let me get these fellows down to the band room, huh?

[*They exit the studio. The lights go down in the studio and up in the band room.* IRVIN *opens the door and allows them to pass as they enter.*]

You boys go ahead and rehearse. I'll let you know when Ma comes.

[IRVIN *exits.* CUTLER *hands* TOLEDO *the list of songs.*]

CUTLER: What we got here, Toledo?

TOLEDO [*reading*]: We got . . . "Prove It on Me" . . . "Hear Me Talking to You" . . . "Ma Rainey's Black Bottom" . . . and "Moonshine Blues."

CUTLER: Where Mr. Irvin go? Them ain't the songs Ma told me.

SLOW DRAG: I wouldn't worry about it if I were you, Cutler. They'll get it straightened out. Ma will get it straightened out.

CUTLER: I just don't want no trouble about these songs, that's all. Ma ain't told me them songs. She told me something else.

SLOW DRAG: What she tell you?

CUTLER: This "Moonshine Blues" wasn't in it. That's one of Bessie's songs.

TOLEDO: Slow Drag's right . . . I wouldn't worry about it. Let them straighten it up.

CUTLER: Levee know what time he supposed to be here?

SLOW DRAG: Levee gone out to spend your four dollars. He left the hotel this morning talking about he was gonna go buy some shoes. Say it's the first time he ever beat you shooting craps.

CUTLER: Do he know what time he supposed to be here? That's what I wanna know. I ain't thinking about no four dollars.

SLOW DRAG: Levee sure was thinking about it. That four dollars liked to burn a hole in his pocket.

CUTLER: Well, he's supposed to be here at one o'clock. That's what time Ma said. That nigger get out in the streets with that four dollars and ain't no telling when he's liable to show. You ought to have seen him at the club last night, Toledo. Trying to talk to some gal Ma had with her.

TOLEDO: You ain't got to tell me. I know how Levee do.

[*Buzzer is heard offstage.*]

SLOW DRAG: Levee tried to talk to that gal and got his feelings hurt. She didn't want no part of him. She told Levee he'd have to turn his money green before he could talk with her.

CUTLER: She out for what she can get. Anybody could see that.

SLOW DRAG: That's why Levee run out to buy some shoes. He's looking to make an impression on that gal.

CUTLER: What the hell she gonna do with his shoes? She can't do nothing with the nigger's shoes.

[SLOW DRAG *takes out a pint bottle and drinks.*]

TOLEDO: Let me hit that, Slow Drag.

SLOW DRAG [*handing him the bottle*]: This some of that good Chicago bourbon!

[*The door opens and* LEVEE *enters, carrying a shoe box. In his early thirties,* LEVEE *is younger than the other men. His flamboyance is sometimes subtle and sneaks up on you. His temper is rakish and bright. He lacks fuel for himself and is somewhat of a buffoon. But it is an intelligent buffoonery, clearly calculated to shift control of the situation to where he can grasp it. He plays trumpet. His voice is strident and totally dependent on his manipulation of breath. He plays wrong notes frequently. He often gets his skill and talent confused with each other.*]

CUTLER: Levee . . . where Mr. Irvin go?

LEVEE: Hell, I don't know. I ain't none of his keeper.

SLOW DRAG: What you got there, Levee?

LEVEE: Look here, Cutler . . . I got me some shoes!

CUTLER: Nigger, I ain't studying you.

[LEVEE *takes the shoes out of the box and starts to put them on.*]

TOLEDO: How much you pay for something like that, Levee?

LEVEE: Eleven dollars. Four dollars of it belong to Cutler.

SLOW DRAG: Levee say if it wasn't for Cutler . . . he wouldn't have no new shoes.

CUTLER: I ain't thinking about Levee or his shoes. Come on . . . let's get ready to rehearse.

SLOW DRAG: I'm with you on that score, Cutler. I wanna get out of here. I don't want to be around here all night. When it comes time to go up there and record them songs . . . I just wanna go up there and do it. Last time it took us all day and half the night.

TOLEDO: Ain't but four songs on the list. Last time we recorded six songs.

SLOW DRAG: It felt like it was sixteen!

LEVEE [*finishes with his shoes*]: Yeah! Now I'm ready! I can play some good music now! [*He goes to put up his old shoes and looks around the room.*]
Damn! They done changed things around. Don't never leave well enough alone.

TOLEDO: Everything changing all the time. Even the air you breathing change. You got, monoxide, hydrogen . . . changing all the time. Skin changing . . . different molecules and everything.

LEVEE: Nigger, what is you talking about? I'm talking about the room. I ain't talking about no skin and air. I'm talking about something I can see! Last time the band room was upstairs. This time it's downstairs. Next time it be over there. I'm talking about what I can see. I ain't talking about no molecules or nothing.

TOLEDO: Hell, I know what you talking about. I just said everything changin'. I know what you talking about, but you don't know what I'm talking about.

LEVEE: That door! Nigger, you see that door? That's what I'm talking about. That door wasn't there before.

CUTLER: Levee, you wouldn't know your right from your left. This is where they used to keep the recording horns and things . . . and damn if that door wasn't there. How in hell else you gonna get in here? Now, if you talking about they done switched rooms, you right. But don't go telling me that damn door wasn't there!

SLOW DRAG: Damn the door and let's get set up. I wanna get out of here.

LEVEE: Toledo started all that about the door. I'm just saying that things change.

TOLEDO: What the hell you think I was saying? Things change. The air and everything. Now you gonna say you was saying it. You gonna fit two propositions on the same track . . . run them into each other, and because they crash, you gonna say it's the same train.

LEVEE: Now this nigger talking about trains! We done went from the air to the skin to the door . . . and now trains. Toledo, I'd just like to be inside your head for five minutes. Just to see how you think. You done got more shit piled up and mixed up in there than the devil got sinners. You been reading too many goddamn books.

TOLEDO: What you care about how much I read? I'm gonna ignore you 'cause you ignorant.

[LEVEE *takes off his coat and hangs it in the locker.*]

SLOW DRAG: Come on, let's rehearse the music.

LEVEE: You ain't gotta rehearse that . . . ain't nothing but old jug-band music. They need one of them jug bands for this.

SLOW DRAG: Don't make me no difference. Long as we get paid.

LEVEE: That ain't what I'm talking about, nigger. I'm talking about art!

SLOW DRAG: What's drawing got to do with it?

LEVEE: Where you get this nigger from, Cutler? He sound like one of them Alabama niggers.

CUTLER: Slow Drag's all right. It's you talking all that weird shit about art. Just play the piece, nigger. You wanna be one of them . . . what you call . . . virtuoso or something, you in the wrong place. You ain't no Buddy Bolden or King Oliver . . . you just an old trumpet player come a dime a dozen. Talking about art.

LEVEE: What is you? I don't see your name in lights.

CUTLER: I just play the piece. Whatever they want. I don't go talking about art and criticizing other people's music.

LEVEE: I ain't like you, Cutler. I got talent! Me and this horn . . . we's tight. If my daddy knowed I was gonna turn out like this, he would've named me Gabriel. I'm gonna get me a band and make me some records. I done give Mr. Sturdyvant some of my songs I wrote and he say he's gonna let me record them when I get my band together.

[*Takes some papers out of his pocket.*]

I just gotta finish the last part of this song. And Mr. Sturdyvant want me to write another part to this song.

SLOW DRAG: How you learn to write music, Levee?

LEVEE: I just picked it up . . . like you pick up anything. Miss Eula used to play the piano . . . she learned me a lot. I knows how to play *real* music . . . not this old jug-band shit. I got style!

TOLEDO: Everybody got style. Style ain't nothing but keeping the same idea from beginning to end. Everybody got it.

LEVEE: But everybody can't play like I do. Everybody can't have their own band.

CUTLER: Well, until you get your own band where you can play what you want, you just play the piece and stop complaining. I told you when you came on here, this ain't none of them hot bands. This is an accompaniment band. You play Ma's music when you here.

LEVEE: I got sense enough to know that. Hell, I can look at you all and see what kind of band it is. I can look at Toledo and see what kind of band it is.

TOLEDO: Toledo ain't said nothing to you now. Don't let Toledo get started. You can't even spell music, much less play it.

LEVEE: What you talking about? I can spell music. I got a dollar say I can spell it! Put your dollar up. Where your dollar?

[TOLEDO *waves him away.*]

Now come on. Put your dollar up. Talking about I can't spell music.

[LEVEE *peels a dollar off his roll and slams it down on the bench beside* TOLEDO.]

TOLEDO: All right, I'm gonna show you. Cutler. Slow Drag. You hear this? The nigger betting me a dollar he can spell music. I don't want no shit now!

[TOLEDO *lays a dollar down beside* LEVEE'*s.*]

All right. Go ahead. Spell it.

LEVEE: It's a bet then. Talking about I can't spell music.

TOLEDO: Go ahead, then. Spell it. Music. Spell it.

LEVEE: I can spell it, nigger! M-U-S-I-K. There!

[*He reaches for the money.*]

TOLEDO: Naw! Naw! Leave that money alone! You ain't spelled it.

LEVEE: What you mean I ain't spelled it? I said M-U-S-I-K!

TOLEDO: That ain't how you spell it! That ain't how you spell it! It's M-U-S-I-*C!* C, nigger. Not K! C! M-U-S-I-C!

LEVEE: What you mean, C? Who say it's C?

TOLEDO: Cutler. Slow Drag. Tell this fool.

[*They look at each other and then away.*]

Well, I'll be a monkey's uncle!

[TOLEDO *picks up the money and hands* LEVEE *his dollar back.*]

Here's your dollar back, Levee. I done won it, you understand. I done won the dollar. But if don't nobody know but me, how am I gonna prove it to you?

LEVEE: You just mad 'cause I spelled it.

TOLEDO: Spelled what! M-U-S-I-K don't spell nothing. I just wish there was some way I could show you the right and wrong of it. How you gonna know something if the other fellow don't know if you're right or not? Now I can't even be sure that I'm spelling it right.

LEVEE: That's what I'm talking about. You don't know it. Talking about C. You ought to give me that dollar I won from you.

TOLEDO: All right. All right. I'm gonna show you how ridiculous you sound. You know the Lord's Prayer?

LEVEE: Why? You wanna bet a dollar on that?

TOLEDO: Just answer the question. Do you know the Lord's Prayer or don't you?

LEVEE: Yeah, I know it. What of it?

TOLEDO: Cutler?

CUTLER: What you Cutlering me for? I ain't got nothing to do with it.

TOLEDO: I just want to show the man how ridiculous he is.

CUTLER: Both of you all sound like damn fools. Arguing about something silly. Yeah, I know the Lord's Prayer. My daddy was a deacon in the church. Come asking me if I know the Lord's Prayer. Yeah, I know it.

TOLEDO: Slow Drag?

SLOW DRAG: Yeah.

TOLEDO: All right. Now I'm gonna tell you a story to show just how ridiculous he sound. There was these two fellows, see. So, the one of them go up to this church and commence to taking up the church learning. The other fellow see him out on the road and he say, "I done heard you taking up the church learning," say, "Is you learning anything up there?" The other one say, "Yeah, I done take up the church learning and I's learning all kinds of things about the Bible and what it say and all. Why you be asking?" The other one say, "Well, do you know the Lord's Prayer?" And he say, "Why, sure I know the Lord's Prayer, I'm taking up learning at the church ain't I? I know the Lord's Prayer backwards and forewards." And the other fellow says, "I bet you five dollars you don't know the Lord's Prayer, 'cause I don't think you knows it. I think you be going up to the church 'cause the Widow Jenkins be going up there and you just wanna be sitting in the same room with her when she cross them big, fine, pretty legs she got." And the other one say, "Well, I'm gonna prove you wrong and I'm gonna bet you that five dollars." So he say, "Well, go on and say it then." So he commenced to saying the Lord's Prayer. He say, "Now I lay me down to sleep, I pray the Lord my soul to keep." The other one say, "Here's your five dollars. I didn't think you knew it."

[*They all laugh.*]

Now, that's just how ridiculous Levee sound. Only 'cause I knowed how to spell music, I still got my dollar.

LEVEE: That don't prove nothing. What's that supposed to prove?

[TOLEDO *takes a newspaper out of his back pocket and begins to read.*]

TOLEDO: I'm through with it.

SLOW DRAG: Is you all gonna rehearse this music or ain't you?

[CUTLER *takes out some papers and starts to roll a reefer.*]

LEVEE: How many times you done played them songs? What you gotta rehearse for?

SLOW DRAG: This a recording session. I wanna get it right the first time and get on out of here.

CUTLER: Slow Drag's right. Let's go on and rehearse and get it over with.

LEVEE: You all go and rehearse, then. I got to finish this song for Mr. Sturdyvant.

CUTLER: Come on, Levee . . . I don't want no shit now. You rehearse like everybody else. You in the band like everybody else. Mr. Sturdyvant just gonna have to wait. You got to do that on your own time. This is the band's time.

LEVEE: Well, what is you doing? You sitting there rolling a reefer talking about let's rehearse. Toledo reading a newspaper. Hell, I'm ready if you wanna rehearse. I just say there ain't no point in it. Ma ain't here. What's the point in it?

CUTLER: Nigger, why you gotta complain all the time?

TOLEDO: Levee would complain if a gal ain't laid across his bed just right.

CUTLER: That's what I know. That's why I try to tell him just play the music and forget about it. It ain't no big thing.

TOLEDO: Levee ain't got an eye for that. He wants to tie on to some abstract component and sit down on the elemental.

LEVEE: This is get-on-Levee time, huh? Levee ain't said nothing except this some old jug-band music.

TOLEDO: Under the right circumstances you'd play anything. If you know music, then you play it. Straight on or off to the side. Ain't nothing abstract about it.

LEVEE: Toledo, you sound like you got a mouth full of marbles. You the only cracker-talking nigger I know.

TOLEDO: You ought to have learned yourself to read . . . then you'd understand the basic understanding of everything.

SLOW DRAG: Both of you all gonna drive me crazy with that philosophy bullshit. Cutler, give me a reefer.

CUTLER: Ain't you got some reefer? Where's your reefer? Why you all the time asking me?

SLOW DRAG: Cutler, how long I done known you? How long we been together?

Twenty-two years. We been doing this together for twenty-two years. All up and down the back roads, the side roads, the front roads . . . We done played the juke joints, the whorehouses, the barn dances, and city sit-downs . . . I done lied for you and lied with you . . . We done laughed together, fought together, slept in the same bed together, done sucked on the same titty . . . and now you don't wanna give me no reefer.

CUTLER: You see this nigger trying to talk me out of my reefer, Toledo? Running all that about how long he done knowed me and how we done sucked on the same titty. Nigger, you *still* ain't getting none of my reefer!

TOLEDO: That's African.

SLOW DRAG: What? What you talking about? What's African?

LEVEE: I know he ain't talking about me. You don't see me running around in no jungle with no bone between my nose.

TOLEDO: Levee, you worse than ignorant. You ignorant without a premise.
[*Pauses.*]
Now, what I was saying is what Slow Drag was doing is African. That's what you call an African conceptualization. That's when you name the gods or call on the ancestors to achieve whatever your desires are.

SLOW DRAG: Nigger, I ain't no African! I ain't doing no African nothing!

TOLEDO: Naming all those things you and Cutler done together is like trying to solicit some reefer based on a bond of kinship. That's African. An ancestral retention. Only you forgot the name of the gods.

SLOW DRAG: I ain't forgot nothing. I was telling the nigger how cheap he is. Don't come talking that African nonsense to me.

TOLEDO: You just like Levee. No eye for taking an abstract and fixing it to a specific. There's so much that goes on around you and you can't even see it.

CUTLER: Wait a minute . . . wait a minute. Toledo, now when this nigger . . . when an African do all them things you say and name all the gods and whatnot . . . then what happens?

TOLEDO: Depends on if the gods is sympathetic with his cause for which he is calling them with the right names. Then his success comes with the right proportion of his naming. That's the way that go.

CUTLER: [*Taking out a reefer.*] Here, Slow Drag. Here's a reefer. You done talked yourself up on that one.

SLOW DRAG: Thank you. You ought to have done that in the first place and saved me all the aggravation.

CUTLER: What I wants to know is . . . what's the same titty we done sucked on. That's what I want to know.

SLOW DRAG: Oh, I just threw that in there to make it sound good.

[*They all laugh.*]

CUTLER: Nigger, you ain't right.

SLOW DRAG: I knows it.

CUTLER: Well, come on . . . let's get it rehearsed. Time's wasting.

[*The musicians pick up their instruments.*]

Let's do it. "Ma Rainey's Black Bottom." One . . . two . . . You know what to do.

[*They begin to play.* LEVEE *is playing something different. He stops.*]

LEVEE: Naw! Naw! We ain't doing it that way.

[TOLEDO *stops playing, then* SLOW DRAG.]

We doing my version. It say so right there on that piece of paper you got. Ask Toledo. That's what Mr. Irvin told me . . . say it's on the list he gave you.

CUTLER: Let me worry about what's on the list and what ain't on the list. How you gonna tell me what's on the list?

LEVEE: 'Cause I know what Mr. Irvin told me! Ask Toledo!

CUTLER: Let me worry about what's on the list. You just play the song I say.

LEVEE: What kind of sense it make to rehearse the wrong version of the song? That's what I wanna know. Why you wanna rehearse that version.

SLOW DRAG: You supposed to rehearse what you gonna play. That's the way they taught me. Now, *whatever* version we gonna play . . . let's go on and rehearse it.

LEVEE: That's what I'm trying to tell the man.

CUTLER: You trying to tell me what we is and ain't gonna play. And that ain't none of your business. Your business is to play what I say.

LEVEE: Oh, I see now. You done got jealous cause Mr. Irvin using my version. You done got jealous cause I proved I know something about music.

CUTLER: What the hell . . . nigger, you talk like a fool! What the hell I got to be jealous of you about? The day I get jealous of you I may as well lay down and die.

TOLEDO: Levee started all that 'cause he too lazy to rehearse.

[*To* LEVEE.]

You ought to just go on and play the song . . . What difference does it make?

LEVEE: Where's the paper? Look at the paper! Get the paper and look at it! See what it say. Gonna tell me I'm too lazy to rehearse.

CUTLER: We ain't talking about the paper. We talking about you understanding where you fit in when you around here. You just play what I say.

LEVEE: Look . . . I don't care what you play! All right? It don't matter to me. Mr. Irvin gonna straighten it up! I don't care what you play.

CUTLER: Thank you.

[*Pauses.*]

Let's play this "Hear Me Talking to You" till we find out what's happening with the "Black Bottom." Slow Drag, you sing Ma's part.

[*Pauses.*]

"Hear Me Talking to You." Let's do it. One . . . Two . . . You know what to do.

[*They play.*]

SLOW DRAG [*singing*]:

> Rambling man makes no change in me
> I'm gonna ramble back to my used-to-be
> Ah, you hear me talking to you
> I don't bite my tongue
> You wants to be my man
> You got to fetch it with you when you come.
>
> Eve and Adam in the garden taking a chance
> Adam didn't take time to get his pants
> Ah, you hear me talking to you
> I don't bite my tongue
> You wants to be my man
> You got to fetch it with you when you come.
>
> Our old cat swallowed a ball of yarn
> When the kittens were born they had sweaters on
> Ah, you hear me talking to you
> I don't bite my tongue
> You wants to be my man
> You got to fetch it with you when you come.

[IRVIN *enters. The musicians stop playing.*]

IRVIN: Any of you boys know what's keeping Ma?

CUTLER: Can't say, Mr. Irvin. She'll be along directly, I reckon. I talked to her this morning, she say she'll be here in time to rehearse.

IRVIN: Well, you boys go ahead.

[*He starts to exit.*]

CUTLER: Mr. Irvin, about these songs . . . Levee say . . .

IRVIN: Whatever's on the list, Cutler. You got that list I gave you?

CUTLER: Yessir, I got it right here.

IRVIN: Whatever's on there. Whatever that says.

CUTLER: I'm asking about this "Black Bottom" piece . . . Levee say . . .

IRVIN: Oh, it's on the list. "Ma Rainey's Black Bottom" on the list.

CUTLER: I know it's on the list. I wanna know what version. We got two versions of that song.

IRVIN: Oh. Levee's arrangement. We're using Levee's arrangement.

CUTLER: Ok. I got that straight. Now, this "Moonshine Blues" . . .

IRVIN: We'll work it out with Ma, Cutler. Just rehearse whatever's on the list and use Levee's arrangement on that "Black Bottom" piece.

[*He exits.*]

LEVEE: See, I told you! It don't mean nothing when I say it. You got to wait for Mr. Irvin to say it. Well, I told you the way it is.

CUTLER: Levee, the sooner you understand it ain't what you say, or what Mr. Irvin say . . . it's what Ma say that counts.

SLOW DRAG: Don't nobody say when it come to Ma. She's gonna do what she wants to do. Ma says what happens with her.

LEVEE: Hell, the man's the one putting out the record! He's gonna put out what he wanna put out!

SLOW DRAG: He's gonna put out what Ma want him to put out.

LEVEE: You heard what the man told you . . . "Ma Rainey's Black Bottom," Levee's arrangement. There you go! That's what he told you.

SLOW DRAG: What you gonna do, Cutler?

CUTLER: Ma ain't told me what version. Let's go on and play it Levee's way.

TOLEDO: See, now . . . I'll tell you something. As long as the colored man look to white folks to put the crown on what he say . . . as long as he looks to white folks for approval . . . then he ain't never gonna find out who he is and what he's about. He's just gonna be about what white folks want him to be about. That's one sure thing.

LEVEE: I'm just trying to show Cutler where he's wrong.

CUTLER: Cutler don't need you to show him nothing.

SLOW DRAG: [*irritated*] Come on, let's get this shit rehearsed! You all can bicker afterward!

CUTLER: Levee's confused about who the boss is. He don't know Ma's the boss.

LEVEE: Ma's the boss on the road! We at a recording session. Mr. Sturdyvant and Mr. Irvin say what's gonna be here! We's in Chicago, we ain't in Memphis! I don't know why you all wanna pick me about it, shit! I'm with Slow Drag . . . Let's go on and get it rehearsed.

CUTLER: All right. All right. I know how to solve this. "Ma Rainey's Black Bottom." Levee's version. Let's do it. Come on.

TOLEDO: How that first part go again, Levee?

LEVEE: It go like this.

[*He plays.*]

That's to get the people's attention to the song. That's when you and Slow Drag come in with the rhythm part. Me and Cutler play on the breaks.

[*Becoming animated.*]

Now we gonna dance it . . . but we ain't gonna countrify it. This ain't no barn dance. We gonna play it like . . .

CUTLER: The man ask you how the first part go. He don't wanna hear all that. Just tell him how the piece go.

TOLEDO: I got it. I got it. Let's go. I know how to do it.

CUTLER: "Ma Rainey's Black Bottom." One . . . two . . . You know what to do.

[*They begin to play.* LEVEE *stops.*]

LEVEE: You all got to keep up now. You playing in the wrong time. Ma come in over the top. She got to find her own way in.

CUTLER: Nigger, will you let us play this song? When you get your own band . . . then you tell them that nonsense. We know how to play the piece. I was playing music before you was born. Gonna tell me how to play . . . All right. Let's try it again.

SLOW DRAG: Cutler, wait till I fix this. This string started to unravel.

[*Playfully.*]

And you know I want to play Levee's music right.

LEVEE: If you was any kind of musician, you'd take care of your instrument. Keep it in tip-top order. If you was any kind of musician, I'd let you be in my band.

SLOW DRAG: Shhheeeeet!

[*He crosses to get his string and steps on* LEVEE*'s shoes.*]

LEVEE: Damn, Slow Drag! Watch them big-ass shoes you got.

SLOW DRAG: Boy, ain't nobody done nothing to you.

LEVEE: You done stepped on my shoes.

SLOW DRAG: Move them the hell out the way, then. You was in my way . . . I wasn't in your way.

[CUTLER *lights up another reefer.* SLOW DRAG *rummages around in his belongings for a string.* LEVEE *takes out a rag and begins to shine his shoes.*]

You can shine these when you get done, Levee.

CUTLER: If I had them shoes Levee got, I could buy me a whole suit of clothes.

LEVEE: What kind of difference it make what kind of shoes I got? Ain't nothing wrong with having nice shoes. I ain't said nothing about your shoes. Why you wanna talk about me and my Florsheims?

CUTLER: Any man who takes a whole week's pay and puts it on some shoes—you understand what I mean, what you walk around on the ground with—is a fool! And I don't mind telling you.

LEVEE [*irritated*]: What difference it make to you, Cutler?

SLOW DRAG: The man ain't said nothing about your shoes. Ain't nothing wrong with having nice shoes. Look at Toledo.

TOLEDO: What about Toledo?

SLOW DRAG: I said ain't nothing wrong with having nice shoes.

LEVEE: Nigger got them clodhoppers! Old brogans! He ain't nothing but a share-cropper.

TOLEDO: You can make all the fun you want. It don't mean nothing. I'm satisfied with them and that's what counts.

LEVEE: Nigger, why don't you get some decent shoes? Got nerve to put on a suit and tie with them farming boots.

CUTLER: What you just tell me? It don't make no difference about the man's shoes. That's what you told me.

LEVEE: Aw, hell, I don't care what the nigger wear. I'll be honest with you. I don't care if he went barefoot.

[SLOW DRAG *has put his string on the bass and is tuning it.*]

Play something for me, Slow Drag.

[SLOW DRAG *plays.*]

A man got to have some shoes to dance like this! You can't dance like this with them clodhoppers Toledo got.

[LEVEE *sings.*]

> Hello Central give me Doctor Jazz
> He's got just what I need I'll say he has
> When the world goes wrong and I have got the blues
> He's the man who makes me get on my dancing shoes.

TOLEDO: That's the trouble with colored folks . . . always wanna have a good time. Good times done got more niggers killed than God got ways to count. What the hell having a good time mean? That's what I wanna know.

LEVEE: Hell, nigger . . . it don't need explaining. Ain't you never had no good time before?

TOLEDO: The more niggers get killed having a good time, the more good times niggers wanna have.

[SLOW DRAG *stops playing.*]

There's more to life than having a good time. If there ain't, then this is a piss-poor life we're having . . . if that's all there is to be got out of it.

SLOW DRAG: Toledo, just 'cause you like to read them books and study and whatnot . . . that's your good time. People get other things they likes to do to have a good time. Ain't no need you picking them about it.

CUTLER: Niggers been having a good time before you was born, and they gonna keep having a good time after you gone.

TOLEDO: Yeah, but what else they gonna do? Ain't nobody talking about making the lot of the colored man better for him here in America.

LEVEE: Now you gonna be Booker T. Washington.

TOLEDO: Everybody worried about having a good time. Ain't nobody thinking about what kind of world they gonna leave their youngens. "Just give me the good time, that's all I want." It just makes me sick.

SLOW DRAG: Well, the colored man's gonna be all right. He got through slavery, and he'll get through whatever else the white man put on him. I ain't worried about that. Good times is what makes life worth living. Now, you take the white man . . . The white man don't know how to have a good time. That's why he's troubled all the time. He don't know how to have a good time. He don't know how to laugh at life.

LEVEE: That's what the problem is with Toledo . . . reading all them books and things. He done got to the point where he forgot how to laugh and have a good time. Just like the white man.

TOLEDO: I know how to have a good time as well as the next man. I said, there's got to be more to life than having a good time. I said the colored man ought to be doing more than just trying to have a good time all the time.

LEVEE: Well, what is you doing, nigger? Talking all them highfalutin ideas about making a better world for the colored man. What is you doing to make it better? You

playing the music and looking for your next piece of pussy same as we is. What is you doing? That's what I wanna know. Tell him, Cutler.

CUTLER: You all leave Cutler out of this. Cutler ain't got nothing to do with it.

TOLEDO: Levee, you just about the most ignorant nigger I know. Sometimes I wonder why I ever bother to try and talk with you.

LEVEE: Well, what is you doing? Talking that shit to me about I'm ignorant! What is you doing? You just a whole lot of mouth. A great big windbag. Thinking you smarter than everybody else. What is you doing, huh?

TOLEDO: It ain't just me, fool! It's everybody! What you think . . . I'm gonna solve the colored man's problems by myself? I said, we. You understand that? We. That's every living colored man in the world got to do his share. Got to do his part. I ain't talking about what I'm gonna do . . . or what you or Cutler or Slow Drag or anybody else. I'm talking about all of us together. What all of us is gonna do. That's what I'm talking about, nigger!

LEVEE: Well, why didn't you say that, then?

CUTLER: Toledo, I don't know why you waste your time on this fool.

TOLEDO: That's what I'm trying to figure out.

LEVEE: Now there go Cutler with his shit. Calling me a fool. You wasn't even in the conversation. Now you gonna take sides and call me a fool.

CUTLER: Hell, I was listening to the man. I got sense enough to know what he was saying. I could tell it straight back to you.

LEVEE: Well, you go on with it. But I'll tell you this . . . I ain't gonna be too many more of your fools. I'll tell you that. Now you put that in your pipe and smoke it.

CUTLER: Boy, ain't nobody studying you. Telling me what to put in my pipe. Who's you to tell me what to do?

LEVEE: All right, I ain't nobody. Don't pay me no mind. I ain't nobody.

TOLEDO: Levee, you ain't nothing but the devil.

LEVEE: There you go! That's who I am. I'm the devil. I ain't nothing but the devil.

CUTLER: I can see that. That's something you know about. You know all about the devil.

LEVEE: I ain't saying what I know. I know plenty. What you know about the devil? Telling me what I know. What you know?

SLOW DRAG: I know a man sold his soul to the devil.

LEVEE: There you go! That's the only thing I ask about the devil . . . to see him coming so I can sell him this one I got. 'Cause if there's a god up there, he done went to sleep.

SLOW DRAG: Sold his soul to the devil himself. Name of Eliza Cottor. Lived in Tuscaloosa County, Alabama. The devil came by and he done upped and sold him his soul.

CUTLER: How you know the man done sold his soul to the devil, nigger? You talking that old-woman foolishness.

SLOW DRAG: Everybody know. It wasn't no secret. He went around working for the devil and everybody knowed it. Carried him a bag . . . one of them carpetbags. Folks say he carried the devil's papers and whatnot where he put your fingerprint on the paper with blood.

LEVEE: Where he at now? That's what I want to know. He can put my whole handprint if he want to!

CUTLER: That's the damnedest thing I ever heard! Folks kill me with that talk.

TOLEDO: Oh, that's real enough, all right. Some folks go arm in arm with the devil, shoulder to shoulder, and talk to him all the time. That's real, ain't nothing wrong in believing that.

SLOW DRAG: That's what I'm saying. Eliza Cotter is one of them. All right. The man living up in an old shack on Ben Foster's place, shoeing mules and horses, making them charms and things in secret. He done hooked up with the devil, showed up one day all fancied out with just the finest clothes you ever seen on a colored man . . . dressed just like one of them crackers . . . and carrying this bag with them papers and things. All right. Had a pocketful of money, just living the life of a rich man. Ain't done no more work or nothing. Just had him a string of women he run around with and throw his money away on. Bought him a big fine house . . . Well, it wasn't all that big, but it did have one of them white picket fences around it. Used to hire a man once a week just to paint that fence. Messed around there and one of the fellows of them gals he was messing with got fixed on him wrong and Eliza killed him. And he laughed about it. Sheriff come and arrest him, and then let him go. And he went around in that town laughing about killing this fellow. Trial come up, and the judge cut him loose. He must have been in converse with the devil too . . . 'cause he cut him loose and give him a bottle of whiskey! Folks ask what done happened to make him change, and he'd tell them straight out he done sold his soul to the devil and ask them if they wanted to sell theirs 'cause he could arrange it for them. Preacher see him coming, used to cross on the other side of the road. He'd just stand there and laugh at the preacher and call him a fool to his face.

CUTLER: Well, whatever happened to this fellow? What come of him? A man who, as you say, done sold his soul to the devil is bound to come to a bad end.

TOLEDO: I don't know about that. The devil's strong. The devil ain't no pushover.

SLOW DRAG: Oh, the devil had him under his wing, all right. Took good care of him. He ain't wanted for nothing.

CUTLER: What happened to him? That's what I want to know.

SLOW DRAG: Last I heard, he headed north with that bag of his, handing out hundred-dollar bills on the spot to whoever wanted to sign on with the devil. That's what I hear tell of him.

CUTLER: That's a bunch of fool talk. I don't know how you fix your mouth to tell that story. I don't believe that.

SLOW DRAG: I ain't asking you to believe it. I'm just telling you the facts of it.

LEVEE: I sure wish I knew where he went. He wouldn't have to convince me long. Hell, I'd even help him sign people up.

CUTLER: Nigger, God's gonna strike you down with that blasphemy you talking.

LEVEE: Oh, shit! God don't mean nothing to me. Let him strike me! Here I am, standing right here. What you talking about he's gonna strike me? Here I am! Let him strike me! I ain't scared of him. Talking that stuff to me.

CUTLER: All right. You gonna be sorry. You gonna fix yourself to have bad luck. Ain't nothing gonna work for you.

[*Buzzer sounds offstage.*]

LEVEE: Bad luck? What I care about some bad luck? You talking simple. I ain't knowed nothing but bad luck all my life. Couldn't get no worse. What the hell I care about some bad luck? Hell, I eat it everyday for breakfast! You dumber than I thought you was . . . talking about bad luck.

CUTLER: All right, nigger, you'll see! Can't tell a fool nothing. You'll see!

IRVIN [IRVIN *enters the studio, checks his watch, and calls down the stairs.*]: Cutler . . . you boys' sandwiches are up here . . . Cutler?

CUTLER: Yessir, Mr. Irvin . . . be right there.

TOLEDO: I'll walk up there and get them.

[TOLEDO *exits. The lights go down in the band room and up in the studio.* IRVIN *paces back and forth in an agitated manner.* STURDYVANT *enters.*]

STURDYVANT: Irv, what's happening? Is she here yet? Was that her?

IRVIN: It's the sandwiches, Mel. I told you . . . I'll let you know when she comes, huh?

STURDYVANT: What's keeping her? Do you know what time it is? Have you looked at the clock? You told me she'd be here. You told me you'd take care of it.

IRVIN: Mel, for Chrissakes! What do you want from me? What do you want me to do?

STURDYVANT: Look what time it is, Irv. You told me she'd be here.

IRVIN: She'll be here, okay? I don't know what's keeping her. You know they're always late, Mel.

STURDYVANT: You should have went by the hotel and made sure she was on time. You should have taken care of this. That's what you told me, huh? "I'll take care of it."

IRVIN: Okay! Okay! I didn't go by the hotel! What do you want me to do? She'll be here, okay? The band's here . . . she'll be here.

STURDYVANT: Okay, Irv. I'll take your word. But if she doesn't come . . . if she doesn't come . . .

[STURDYVANT *exits to the control booth as* TOLEDO *enters.*]

TOLEDO: Mr. Irvin . . . I come up to get the sandwiches.

IRVIN: Say . . . uh . . . look . . . one o'clock, right? She said one o'clock.

TOLEDO: That's what time she told us. Say be here at one o'clock.

IRVIN: Do you know what's keeping her? Do you know why she ain't here?

TOLEDO: I can't say, Mr. Irvin. Told us one o'clock.

[*The buzzer sounds.* IRVIN *goes to the door. There is a flurry of commotion as* MA RAINEY *enters, followed closely by the* POLICEMAN, DUSSIE MAE, *and* SYLVESTER. MA RAINEY *is a short, heavy woman. She is dressed in a full-length fur coat with matching hat, an emerald-green dress, and several strands of pearls of varying lengths. Her hair is secured by a headband that matches her dress. Her manner is simple and direct, and she carries herself in a royal fashion.* DUSSIE MAE *is a young, dark-skinned woman whose greatest asset is the sensual energy which seems to flow from her. She is dressed in a fur jacket and a tight-fitting canary-yellow dress.* SYLVESTER *is an Arkansas country boy, the size of a fullback. He wears a new suit and coat, in which he is obviously uncomfortable. Most of the time, he stutters when he speaks.*]

MA RAINEY: Irvin . . . you better tell this man who I am! You better get him straight!

IRVIN: Ma, do you know what time it is? Do you have any idea? We've been waiting . . .

DUSSIE MAE [*to* SYLVESTER]: If you was watching where you was going . . .

SYLVESTER: I was watching . . . What you mean?

IRVIN [*notices* POLICEMAN]: What's going on here? Officer, what's the matter?

MA RAINEY: Tell the man who he's messing with!

POLICEMAN: Do you know this lady?

MA RAINEY: Just tell the man who I am! That's all you gotta do.

POLICEMAN: Lady, will you let me talk, huh?

MA RAINEY: Tell the man who I am!

IRVIN: Wait a minute . . . wait a minute! Let me handle it. Ma, will you let me handle it?

MA RAINEY: Tell him who he's messing with!

IRVIN: Okay! Okay! Give me a chance! Officer, this is one of our recording artists . . . Ma Rainey.

MA RAINEY: Madame Rainey! Get it straight! Madame Rainey! Talking about taking me to jail!

IRVIN: Look, Ma . . . give me a chance, okay? Here . . . sit down. I'll take care of it. Officer, what's the problem?

DUSSIE MAE [*to* SYLVESTER]: It's all your fault.

SYLVESTER: I ain't done nothing . . . Ask Ma.

POLICEMAN: Well . . . when I walked up on the incident . . .

DUSSIE MAE: Sylvester wrecked Ma's car.

SYLVESTER: I d-d-did not! The m-m-man ran into me!

POLICEMAN [*to* IRVIN.]: Look, buddy . . . if you want it in a nutshell, we got her charged with assault and battery.

MA RAINEY: Assault and what for what!

DUSSIE MAE: See . . . we was trying to get a cab . . . and so Ma . . .

MA RAINEY: Wait a minute! I'll tell you if you wanna know what happened. [*She points to* SYLVESTER.]

Now, that's Sylvester. That's my nephew. He was driving my car . . .

POLICEMAN: Lady, we don't know whose car he was driving.

MA RAINEY: That's my car!

DUSSIE MAE *and* SYLVESTER: That's Ma's car!

MA RAINEY: What you mean you don't know whose car it is? I bought and paid for that car.

POLICEMAN: That's what you say, lady . . . We still gotta check.

[*To* IRVIN.]

They hit a car on Market Street. The guy said the kid ran a stoplight.

SYLVESTER: What you mean? The man c-c-come around the corner and hit m-m-me!

POLICEMAN: While I was calling a paddy wagon to haul them to the station, they try to hop into a parked cab. The cabbie said he was waiting on a fare . . .

MA RAINEY: The man was just sitting there. Wasn't waiting for nobody. I don't know why he wanna tell that lie.

POLICEMAN: Look, lady . . . will you let me tell the story?

MA RAINEY: Go ahead and tell it then. But tell it right!

POLICEMAN: Like I say . . . she tries to get in this cab. The cabbie's waiting on a fare. She starts creating a disturbance. The cabbie gets out to try and explain the situation to her . . . and she knocks him down.

DUSSIE MAE: She ain't hit him! He just fell!

SYLVESTER: He just s-s-s-slipped!

POLICEMAN: He claims she knocked him down. We got her charged with assault and battery.

MA RAINEY: If that don't beat all to hell. I ain't touched the man! The man was trying to reach around me to keep his car door closed. I opened the door and it hit him and he fell down. I ain't touched the man!

IRVIN: Okay. Okay . . . I got it straight now, Ma. You didn't touch him. All right? Officer, can I see you for a minute?

DUSSIE MAE: Ma was just trying to open the door.

SYLVESTER: He j-j-just got in t-t-the way!

MA RAINEY: Said he wasn't gonna haul no colored folks . . . if you want to know the truth of it.

IRVIN: Okay, Ma . . . I got it straight now. Officer?

[IRVIN *pulls the* POLICEMAN *off to the side.*]

MA RAINEY [*noticing* TOLEDO]: Toledo, Cutler and everybody here?

TOLEDO: Yeah, they down in the band room. What happened to your car?

STURDYVANT [*entering*]: Irv, what's the problem? What's going on? Officer . . .

IRVIN: Mel, let me take care of it. I can handle it.

STURDYVANT: What's happening? What the hell's going on?

IRVIN: Let me handle it, Mel, huh?

[STURDYVANT *crosses over to* MA RAINEY.]

STURDYVANT: What's going on, Ma. What'd you do?

MA RAINEY: Sturdyvant, get on away from me! That's the last thing I need . . . to go through some of your shit!

IRVIN: Mel, I'll take care of it. I'll explain it all to you. Let me handle it, huh?

[STURDYVANT *reluctantly returns to the control booth.*]

POLICEMAN: Look, buddy, like I say . . . we got her charged with assault and battery . . . and the kid with threatening the cabbie.

SYLVESTER: I ain't done n-n-nothing!

MA RAINEY: You leave the boy out of it. He ain't done nothing. What's he supposed to have done?

POLICEMAN: He threatened the cabbie, lady! You just can't go around threatening people.

SYLVESTER: I ain't done nothing to him! He's the one talking about he g-g-gonna get a b-b-baseball bat on me! I just told him what I'd do with it. But I ain't done nothing 'cause he didn't get the b-b-bat!

IRVIN [*pulling the* POLICEMAN *aside*]: Officer . . . look here . . .

POLICEMAN: We was on our way down to the precinct . . . but I figured I'd do you a favor and bring her by here. I mean, if she's as important as she says she is . . .

IRVIN [*slides a bill from his pocket*]: Look, Officer . . . I'm Madame Rainey's manager . . . It's good to meet you.

[*He shakes the* POLICEMAN'*s hand and passes him the bill.*]

As soon as we're finished with the recording session, I'll personally stop by the precinct house and straighten up this misunderstanding.

POLICEMAN: Well . . . I guess that's all right. As long as someone is responsible for them.

[*He pockets the bill and winks at* IRVIN.]

No need to come down . . . I'll take care of it myself. Of course, we wouldn't want nothing like this to happen again.

IRVIN: Don't worry, Officer . . . I'll take care of everything. Thanks for your help.

[IRVIN *escorts the* POLICEMAN *to the door and returns. He crosses over to* MA RAINEY.]

Here, Ma . . . let me take your coat.

[*To* SYLVESTER.]

I don't believe I know you.

MA RAINEY: That's my nephew, Sylvester.

IRVIN: I'm very pleased to meet you. Here . . . you can give me your coat.

MA RAINEY: That there is Dussie Mae.

IRVIN: Hello . . .

[DUSSIE MAE *hands* IRVIN *her coat.*]

Listen, Ma, just sit there and relax. The boys are in the band room rehearsing. You just sit and relax a minute.

MA RAINEY: I ain't for no sitting. I ain't never heard of such. Talking about taking me to jail. Irvin, call down there and see about my car.

IRVIN: Okay, Ma . . . I'll take care of it. You just relax.

[IRVIN *exits with the coats.*]

MA RAINEY: Why you all keep it so cold in here? Sturdyvant try and pinch every penny he can. You all wanna make some records, you better put some heat on in here or give me back my coat.

IRVIN [*entering*]: We got the heat turned up, Ma. It's warming up. It'll be warm in a minute.

DUSSIE MAE [*whispering to* MA RAINEY]: Where's the bathroom?

MA RAINEY: It's in the back. Down the hall next to Sturdyvant's office. Come on, I'll

show you where it is. Irvin, call down there and see about my car. I want my car fixed today.

IRVIN: I'll take care of everything, Ma.

[*He notices* TOLEDO.]

Say . . . uh . . . uh . . .

TOLEDO: Toledo.

IRVIN: Yeah . . . Toledo. I got the sandwiches, you can take down to the rest of the boys. We'll be ready to go in a minute. Give you boys a chance to eat and then we'll be ready to go.

[IRVIN *and* TOLEDO *exit. The lights go down in the studio and come up in the band room.*]

LEVEE: Slow Drag, you ever been to New Orleans?

SLOW DRAG: What's in New Orleans that I want?

LEVEE: How you call yourself a musician and ain't never been to New Orleans.

SLOW DRAG: You ever been to Fat Back, Arkansas?

[*Pauses.*]

All right, then. Ain't never been nothing in New Orleans that I couldn't get in Fat Back.

LEVEE: That's why you backwards. You just an old country boy talking about Fat Back, Arkansas, and New Orleans in the same breath.

CUTLER: I been to New Orleans. What about it?

LEVEE: You ever been to Lula White's?

CUTLER: Lula White's? I ain't never heard of it.

LEVEE: Man, they got some gals in there just won't wait! I seen a man get killed in there once. Got drunk and grabbed one of the gals wrong . . . I don't know what the matter of it was. But he grabbed her and she stuck a knife in him all the way up to the hilt. He ain't even fell. He just stood there and choked on his own blood. I was just asking Slow Drag 'cause I was gonna take him to Lula White's when we get down to New Orleans and show him a good time. Introduce him to one of them gals I know down there.

CUTLER: Slow Drag don't need you to find him no pussy. He can take care of his own self. Fact is . . . you better watch your gal when Slow Drag's around. They don't call him Slow Drag for nothing.

[*He laughs.*]

Tell him how you got your name Slow Drag.

SLOW DRAG: I ain't thinking about Levee.

CUTLER: Slow Drag break a woman's back when he dance. They had this contest one time in this little town called Bolingbroke about a hundred miles outside of Macon. We was playing for this dance and they was giving twenty dollars to the best slow draggers. Slow Drag looked over the competition, got down off the bandstand, grabbed hold of one of them gals, and stuck to her like a fly to jelly. Like wood to glue. Man had that gal whooping and hollering so . . . everybody stopped to watch. This fellow come in . . . this gal's fellow . . . and pulled a knife a foot long on Slow Drag. 'Member that, Slow Drag?

SLOW DRAG: Boy that mama was hot! The front of her dress was wet as a dishrag!

LEVEE: So what happened? What the man do?

CUTLER: Slow Drag ain't missed a stroke. The gal, she just look at her man with that sweet dizzy look in her eye. She ain't about to stop! Folks was clearing out, ducking and hiding under tables, figuring there's gonna be a fight. Slow Drag just looked over the gal's shoulder at the man and said, "Mister, if you'd quit hollering and wait a minute . . . you'll see I'm doing you a favor. I'm helping this gal win ten dollars so she can buy you a gold watch." The man just stood there and looked at him, all the while stroking that knife. Told Slow Drag, say, "All right, then, nigger. You just better make damn sure you win." That's when folks started calling him Slow Drag. The women got to hanging around him so bad after that, them fellows in that town ran us out of there.

[TOLEDO *enters, carrying a small cardboard box with the sandwiches.*]

LEVEE: Yeah . . . well, them gals in Lula White's will put a harness on his ass.

TOLEDO: Ma's up there. Some kind of commotion with the police.

CUTLER: Police? What the police up there for?

TOLEDO: I couldn't get it straight. Something about her car. They gone now . . . she's all right. Mr. Irvin sent some sandwiches.

[LEVEE *springs across the room.*]

LEVEE: Yeah, all right. What we got here?

[*He takes two sandwiches out of the box.*]

TOLEDO: What you doing grabbing two? There ain't but five in there . . . How you figure you get two?

LEVEE: 'Cause I grabbed them first. There's enough for everybody . . . What you talking about? It ain't like I'm taking food out of nobody's mouth.

CUTLER: That's all right. He can have mine too. I don't want none.

[LEVEE *starts toward the box to get another sandwich.*]

TOLEDO: Nigger, you better get out of here. Slow Drag, you want this?

SLOW DRAG: Naw, you can have it.

TOLEDO: With Levee around, you don't have to worry about no leftovers. I can see that.

LEVEE: What's the matter with you? Ain't you eating two sandwiches? Then why you wanna talk about me? Talking about there won't be no leftovers with Levee around. Look at your own self before you look at me.

TOLEDO: That's what you is. That's what we all is. A leftover from history. You see now, I'll show you.

LEVEE: Aw, shit . . . I done got the nigger started now.

TOLEDO: Now, I'm gonna show you how this goes . . . where you just a leftover from history. Everybody come from different places in Africa, right? Come from different tribes and things. Soonawhile they began to make one big stew. You had the carrots, the peas, and potatoes and whatnot over here. And over there you had the meat, the nuts, the okra, corn . . . and then you mix it up and let it cook right through to get the flavors flowing together . . . then you got one thing. You got a stew.

Now you take and eat the stew. You take and make your history with that stew. All right. Now it's over. Your history's over and you done ate the stew. But you look around and you see some carrots over here, some potatoes over there. That stew's still there. You done made your history and it's still there. You can't eat it all. So what you got? You got some leftovers. That's what it is. You got leftovers and you can't do nothing with it. You already making you another history . . . cooking you another meal, and you don't need them leftovers no more. What to do?

See, we's the leftovers. The colored man is the leftovers. Now, what's the colored man gonna do with himself? That's what we waiting to find out. But first we gotta know we the leftovers. Now, who knows that? You find me a nigger that knows that and I'll turn any whichaway you want me to. I'll bend over for you. You ain't gonna find that. And that's what the problem is. The problem ain't with the white man. The white man knows you just a leftover. 'Cause he the one who done the eating and he know what he done ate. But we don't know that we been took and made history out of. Done went and filled the white man's belly and now he's full and tired and wants you to get out the way and let him be by himself. Now, I know what I'm talking about. And if you wanna find out, you just ask Mr. Irvin what he had for supper yesterday. And if he's an honest white man . . . which is asking for a whole heap of a lot . . . he'll tell you he done ate your black ass and if you please I'm full up with you . . . so go on and get off the plate and let me eat something else.

SLOW DRAG: What that mean? What's eating got to do with how the white man treat you? He don't treat you no different according to what he ate.

TOLEDO: I ain't said it had nothing to do with how he treat you.

CUTLER: The man's trying to tell you something, fool!

SLOW DRAG: What he trying to tell me? Ain't you here. Why you say he was trying to tell *me* something? Wasn't he trying to tell you too?

LEVEE: He was trying all right. He was trying a whole heap. I'll say that for him. But trying ain't worth a damn. I got lost right there trying to figure out who puts nuts in their stew.

SLOW DRAG: I knowed that before. My grandpappy used to put nuts in his stew. He and my grandmama both. That ain't nothing new.

TOLEDO: They put nuts in their stew all over Africa. But the stew they eat, and the stew your grandpappy made, and all the stew that you and me eat, and the stew Mr. Irvin eats . . . ain't in no way the same stew. That's the way that go. I'm through with it. That's the last you know me to ever try and explain something to you.

CUTLER [*after a pause*]: Well, time's getting along . . . Come on, let's finish rehearsing.

LEVEE [*stretching out on a bench*]: I don't feel like rehearsing. I ain't nothing but a leftover. You go and rehearse with Toledo . . . He's gonna teach you how to make a stew.

SLOW DRAG: Cutler, what you gonna do? I don't want to be around here all day.

LEVEE: I know my part. You all go on and rehearse your part. You all need some rehearsal.

CUTLER: Come on, Levee, get up off your ass and rehearse the songs.

LEVEE: I already know them songs . . . What I wanna rehearse them for?

SLOW DRAG: You in the band, ain't you? You supposed to rehearse when the band rehearse.

TOLEDO: Levee think he the king of the barnyard. He thinks he's the only rooster know how to crow.

LEVEE: All right! All right! Come on, I'm gonna show you I know them songs. Come on, let's rehearse. I bet you the first one mess be Toledo. Come on . . . I wanna see if he know how to crow.

CUTLER: "Ma Rainey's Black Bottom," Levee's version. Let's do it.

[*They begin to rehearse. The lights go down in the band room and up in the studio.* MA RAINEY *sits and takes off her shoe, rubs her feet.* DUSSIE MAE *wanders about looking at the studio.* SYLVESTER *is over by the piano.*]

MA RAINEY [*singing to herself*]:

> Oh, Lord, these dogs of mine
> They sure do worry me all the time
> The reason why I don't know
> Lord, I beg to be excused
> I can't wear me no sharp-toed shoes.
> I went for a walk
> I stopped to talk
> Oh, how my corns did bark.

DUSSIE MAE: It feels kinda spooky in here. I ain't never been in no recording studio before. Where's the band at?

MA RAINEY: They off somewhere rehearsing. I don't know where Irvin went to. All this hurry up and he goes off back there with Sturdyvant. I know he better come on 'cause Ma ain't gonna be waiting. Come here . . . let me see that dress.

[DUSSIE MAE *crosses over.* MA RAINEY *tugs at the dress around the waist, appraising the fit.*]

That dress looks nice. I'm gonna take you tomorrow and get you some more things before I take you down to Memphis. They got clothes up here you can't get in Memphis. I want you to look nice for me. If you gonna travel with the show you got to look nice.

DUSSIE MAE: I need me some more shoes. These hurt my feet.

MA RAINEY: You get you some shoes that fit your feet. Don't you be messing around with no shoes that pinch your feet. Ma know something about bad feet. Hand me my slippers out my bag over yonder.

[DUSSIE MAE *brings the slippers.*]

DUSSIE MAE: I just want to get a pair of them yellow ones. About a half-size bigger.

MA RAINEY: We'll get you whatever you need. Sylvester, too . . . I'm gonna get him some more clothes. Sylvester, tuck your clothes in. Straighten them up and look nice. Look like a gentleman.

DUSSIE MAE: Look at Sylvester with that hat on.

MA RAINEY: Sylvester, take your hat off inside. Act like your mama taught you something. I know she taught you better than that.

[SYLVESTER *bangs on the piano.*]

Come on over here and leave that piano alone.

SYLVESTER: I ain't d-d-doing nothing to the p-p-piano. I'm just l-l-looking at it.

MA RAINEY: Well. Come on over here and sit down. As soon as Mr. Irvin comes back, I'll have him take you down and introduce you to the band.

[SYLVESTER *comes over.*]

He's gonna take you down there and introduce you in a minute . . . have Cutler show you how your part go. And when you get your money, you gonna send some of it home to your mamma. Let her know you doing all right. Make her feel good to know you doing all right in the world.

[DUSSIE MAE *wanders about the studio and opens the door leading to the band room. The strains of* LEVEE'*s version of "Ma Rainey's Black Bottom" can be heard.* IRVIN *enters.*]

IRVIN: Ma, I called down to the garage and checked on your car. It's just a scratch. They'll have it ready for you this afternoon. They're gonna send it over with one of their fellows.

MA RAINEY: They better have my car fixed right too. I ain't going for that. Brand-new car . . . they better fix it like new.

IRVIN: It was just a scratch on the fender, Ma . . . They'll take care of it . . . don't worry . . . they'll have it like new.

MA RAINEY: Irvin, what is that I hear? What is that the band's rehearsing? I know they ain't rehearsing Levee's "Black Bottom." I know I ain't hearing that?

IRVIN: Ma, listen . . . that's what I wanted to talk to you about. Levee's version of that song . . . it's got a nice arrangement . . . a nice horn intro . . . It really picks it up . . .

MA RAINEY: I ain't studying Levee nothing. I know what he done to that song and I don't like to sing it that way. I'm doing it the old way. That's why I brought my nephew to do the voice intro.

IRVIN: Ma, that's what the people want now. They want something they can dance to. Times are changing. Levee's arrangement gives the people what they want. It gets them excited . . . makes them forget about their troubles.

MA RAINEY: I don't care what you say, Irvin. Levee ain't messing up my song. If he got what the people want, let him take it somewhere else. I'm singing Ma Rainey's song. I ain't singing Levee's song. Now that's all there is to it. Carry my nephew on down there and introduce him to the band. I promised my sister I'd look out for him and he's gonna do the voice intro on the song my way.

IRVIN: Ma, we just figured that . . .

MA RAINEY: Who's this "we"? What you mean "we"? I ain't studying Levee nothing. Come talking this "we" stuff. Who's "we"?

IRVIN: Me and Sturdyvant. We decided that it would . . .

MA RAINEY: You decided, huh? I'm just a bump on the log. I'm gonna go which ever way the river drift. Is that it? You and Sturdyvant decided.

IRVIN: Ma, it was just that we thought it would be better.

MA RAINEY: I ain't got good sense. I don't know nothing about music. I don't know what's a good song and what ain't. You know more about my fans than I do.

IRVIN: It's not that, Ma. It would just be easier to do. It's more what the people want.

MA RAINEY: I'm gonna tell you something, Irvin . . . and you go on up there and tell Sturdyvant. What you all say don't count with me. You understand? Ma listens to her heart. Ma listens to the voice inside her. That's what counts with Ma. Now, you carry my nephew on down there . . . tell Cutler he's gonna do the voice intro on that "Black Bottom" song and that Levee ain't messing up my song with none of his music shit. Now, if that don't set right with you and Sturdyvant . . . then I can carry my black bottom on back down South to my tour, 'cause I don't like it up here no ways.

IRVIN: Okay, Ma . . . I don't care. I just thought . . .

MA RAINEY: Damn what you thought! What you look like telling me how to sing my song? This Levee and Sturdyvant nonsense . . . I ain't going for it! Sylvester, go on down there and introduce yourself. I'm through playing with Irvin.

SYLVESTER: Which way you go? Where they at?

MA RAINEY: Here . . . I'll carry you down there myself.

DUSSIE MAE: Can I go? I wanna see the band.

MA RAINEY: You stay your behind up here. Ain't no cause in you being down there. Come on, Sylvester.

IRVIN: Okay, Ma. Have it your way. We'll be ready to go in fifteen minutes.

MA RAINEY: We'll be ready to go when Madame says we're ready. That's the way it goes around here.

[MA RAINEY and SYLVESTER exit. The lights go down in the studio and up in the band room. MA RAINEY enters with SYLVESTER.]

Cutler, this here is my nephew Sylvester. He's gonna do that voice intro on the "Black Bottom" song using the old version.

LEVEE: What you talking about? Mr. Irvin say he's using my version. What you talking about?

MA RAINEY: Levee, I ain't studying you or Mr. Irvin. Cutler, get him straightened out on how to do his part. I ain't thinking about Levee. These folks done messed with the wrong person this day. Sylvester, Cutler gonna teach you your part. You go ahead and get it straight. Don't worry about what nobody else say.

[MA RAINEY exits.]

CUTLER: Well, come on in, boy. I'm Cutler. You got Slow Drag . . . Levee . . . and that's Toledo over there. Sylvester, huh?

SYLVESTER: Sylvester Brown.

LEVEE: I done wrote a version of that song what picks it up and sets it down in the

people's lap! Now she come talking this! You don't need that old circus bullshit! I
know what I'm talking about. You gonna mess up the song Cutler and you know it.

CUTLER: I ain't gonna mess up nothing. Ma say . . .

LEVEE: I don't care what Ma say! I'm talking about what the intro gonna do to the
song. The peoples in the North ain't gonna buy all that tent-show nonsense. They
wanna hear some music!

CUTLER: Nigger, I done told you time and again . . . you just in the band. You plays
the piece . . . whatever they want! Ma says what to play! Not you! You ain't here to
be doing no creating. Your job is to play whatever Ma says!

LEVEE: I might not play nothing! I might quit!

CUTLER: Nigger, don't nobody care if you quit. Whose heart you gonna break?

TOLEDO: Levee ain't gonna quit. He got to make some money to keep him in shoe
polish.

LEVEE: I done told you all . . . you all don't know me. You don't know what I'll do.

CUTLER: I don't think nobody too much give a damn! Sylvester, here's the way your
part go. The band plays the intro . . . I'll tell you where to come in. The band plays
the intro and then you say, "All right, boys, you done seen the rest . . . Now I'm
gonna show you the best. Ma Rainey's gonna show you her black bottom." You
got that?

[SYLVESTER *nods.*]

Let me hear you say it one time.

SYLVESTER: "All right, boys, you done s-s-seen the rest n-n-now I'm gonna show you
the best. M-m-m-m-m-m-ma Rainey's gonna s-s-show you her black b-b-bottom."

LEVEE: What kind of . . . All right, Cutler! Let me see you fix that! You straighten that
out! You hear that shit, Slow Drag? How in the hell the boy gonna do the part and
he can't even talk!

SYLVESTER: W-w-w-who's you to tell me what to do, nigger! This ain't your band! Ma
tell me to d-d-do it and I'm gonna do it. You can go to hell, n-n-n-nigger!

LEVEE: B-b-b-boy, ain't nobody studying you. You go on and fix that one, Cutler. You
fix that one and I'll . . . I'll shine your shoes for you. You go on and fix that one!

TOLEDO: You say you Ma's nephew, huh?

SYLVESTER: Yeah. So w-w-what that mean?

TOLEDO: Oh, I ain't meant nothing . . . I was just asking.

SLOW DRAG: Well, come on and let's rehearse so the boy can get it right.

LEVEE: I ain't rehearsing nothing! You just wait till I get my band. I'm gonna record
that song and show you how it supposed to go!

CUTLER: We can do it without Levee. Let him sit on over there. Sylvester, you
remember your part?

SYLVESTER: I remember it pretty g-g-g-good.

CUTLER: Well, come on, let's do it, then.

[*The band begins to play.* LEVEE *sits and pouts.* STURDYVANT *enters the band room.*]

STURDYVANT: Good . . . you boys are rehearsing, I see.

LEVEE [*jumping up*]: Yessir! We rehearsing. We know them songs real good.

STURDYVANT: Good! Say, Levee, did you finish that song?

LEVEE: Yessir, Mr. Sturdyvant. I got it right here. I wrote that other part just like you say. It go like:

> You can shake it, you can break it
> You can dance at any hall
> You can slide across the floor
> You'll never have to stall
> My jelly, my roll,
> Sweet Mama, don't you let it fall.

Then I put that part in there for the people to dance, like you say, for them to forget about their troubles.

STURDYVANT: Good! Good! I'll just take this. I wanna see you about your songs as soon as I get the chance.

LEVEE: Yessir! As soon as you get the chance, Mr. Sturdyvant.

[STURDYVANT *exits.*]

CUTLER: You hear, Levee? You hear this nigger? "Yessuh, we's rehearsing, boss."

SLOW DRAG: I heard him. Seen him too. Shuffling them feet.

TOLEDO: Aw, Levee can't help it none. He's like all of us. Spooked up with the white man.

LEVEE: I'm spooked up with him, all right. You let one of them crackers fix on me wrong. I'll show you how spooked up I am with him.

TOLEDO: That's the trouble of it. You wouldn't know if he was fixed on you wrong or not. You so spooked up by him you ain't had the time to study him.

LEVEE: I studies the white man. I got him studied good. The first time one fixes on me wrong, I'm gonna let him know just how much I studied. Come telling me I'm spooked up with the white man. You let one of them mess with me, I'll show you how spooked up I am.

CUTLER: You talking out your hat. The man come in here, call you a boy, tell you to get up off your ass and rehearse, and you ain't had nothing to say to him, except "Yessir!"

LEVEE: I can say "yessir" to whoever I please. What you got to do with it? I know how to handle white folks. I been handling them for thirty-two years, and now you gonna tell me how to do it. Just 'cause I say "yessir" don't mean I'm spooked up with him. I know what I'm doing. Let me handle him my way.

CUTLER: Well, go on and handle it, then.

LEVEE: Toledo, you always messing with somebody! Always agitating somebody with that old philosophy bullshit you be talking. You stay out of my way about what I do and say. I'm my own person. Just let me alone.

TOLEDO: You right, Levee. I apologize. It ain't none of my business that you spooked up by the white man.

LEVEE: All right! See! That's the shit I'm talking about. You all back up and leave Levee alone.

SLOW DRAG: Aw, Levee, we was all just having fun. Toledo ain't said nothing about you he ain't said about me. You just taking it all wrong.

TOLEDO: I ain't meant nothing by it Levee.

[*Pauses.*]

Cutler, you ready to rehearse?

LEVEE: Levee got to be Levee! And he don't need nobody messing with him about the white man—cause you don't know nothing about me. You don't know Levee. You don't know nothing about what kind of blood I got! What kind of heart I got beating here!

[*He pounds his chest.*]

I was eight years old when I watched a gang of white mens come into my daddy's house and have to do with my mama any way they wanted.

[*Pauses.*]

We was living in Jefferson County, about eighty miles outside of Natchez. My daddy's name was Memphis . . . Memphis Lee Green . . . had him near fifty acres of good farming land. I'm talking about good land! Grow anything you want! He done gone off of shares and bought this land from Mr. Hallie's widow woman after he done passed on. Folks called him an uppity nigger 'cause he done saved and borrowed to where he could buy this land and be independent.

[*Pauses.*]

It was coming on planting time and my daddy went into Natchez to get him some seed and fertilizer. Called me, say, "Levee you the man of the house now. Take care of your mama while I'm gone." I wasn't but a little boy, eight years old.

[*Pauses.*]

My mama was frying up some chicken when them mens come in that house. Must have been eight or nine of them. She standing there frying that chicken and them mens come and took hold of her just like you take hold of a mule and make him do what you want.

[*Pauses.*]

There was my mama with a gang of white mens. She tried to fight them off, but I could see where it wasn't gonna do her any good, I didn't know what they were doing to her . . . but I figured whatever it was they may as well do to me too. My daddy had a knife that he kept around there for hunting and working and whatnot. I knew where he kept it and I went and got it.

I'm gonna show you how spooked up I was by the white man. I tried my damndest to cut one of them's throat! I hit him on the shoulder with it. He reached back and grabbed hold of that knife and whacked me across the chest with it.

[LEVEE *raises his shirt to show a long ugly scar.*]

That's what made them stop. They was scared I was gonna bleed to death. My mama wrapped a sheet around me and carried me two miles down to the Furlow place and they drove me up to Doc Albans. He was waiting on a calf to be born, and say he ain't had time to see me. They carried me up to Miss Etta, the midwife, and she fixed me up.

My daddy came back and acted like he done accepted the facts of what happened. But he got the names of them mens from mama. He found out who they was and then we announced we was moving out of that county. Said good-bye to everybody . . . all the neighbors. My daddy went and smiled in the face of one of them crackers who had been with my mama. Smiled in his face and sold him our land. We moved over with relations in Caldwell. He got us settled in and then he took off one day. I ain't never seen him since. He sneaked back, hiding up in the woods, laying to get them eight or nine men.

[*Pauses.*]

He got four of them before they got him. They tracked him down in the woods. Caught up with him and hung him and set him afire.

[*Pauses.*]

My daddy wasn't spooked up by the white man. Nosir! And that taught me how to handle them. I seen my daddy go up and grin in this cracker's face . . . smile in his face and sell him his land. All the while he's planning how he's gonna get him and what he's gonna do to him. That taught me how to handle them. So you all just back up and leave Levee alone about the white man. I can smile and say yessir to whoever I please. I got time coming to me. You all just leave Levee alone about the white man.

[*There is a long pause.* SLOW DRAG *begins playing on the bass and sings.*]

SLOW DRAG [*singing*]:

> If I had my way
> If I had my way
> If I had my way
> I would tear this old building down.

ACT II

The lights come up in the studio. The musicians are setting up their instruments. MA RAINEY *walks about shoeless, singing softly to herself.* LEVEE *stands near* DUSSIE MAE, *who hikes up her dress and crosses her leg.* CUTLER *speaks to* IRVIN *off to the side.*

CUTLER: Mr. Irvin, I don't know what you gonna do. I ain't got nothing to do with it, but the boy can't do the part. He stutters. He can't get it right. He stutters right through it every time.

IRVIN: Christ! Okay. We'll . . . Shit! We'll just do it like we planned. We'll do Levee's version. I'll handle it, Cutler. Come on, let's go. I'll think of something.

[*He exits to the control booth.*]

MA RAINEY [*calling* CUTLER *over*]: Levee's got his eyes in the wrong place. You better school him, Cutler.

CUTLER: Come on, Levee . . . let's get ready to play! Get your mind on your work!

IRVIN [*over speaker*]: Okay, boys, we're gonna do "Moonshine Blues" first. "Moonshine Blues," Ma.

MA RAINEY: I ain't doing no "Moonshine" nothing. I'm doing the "Black Bottom" first. Come on, Sylvester.

    [*To* IRVIN.]

    Where's Sylvester's mike? You need a mike for Sylvester. Irvin . . . get him a mike.

IRVIN: Uh . . . Ma, the boys say he can't do it. We'll have to do Levee's version.

MA RAINEY: What you mean he can't do it? Who say he can't do it? What boys say he can't do it?

IRVIN: The band, Ma . . . the boys in the band.

MA RAINEY: What band? The band work for me! I say what goes! Cutler, what's he talking about? Levee, this some of your shit?

IRVIN: He stutters, Ma. They say he stutters.

MA RAINEY: I don't care if he do. I promised the boy he could do the part . . . and he's gonna do it! That's all there is to it. He don't stutter all the time. Get a microphone down here for him.

IRVIN: Ma, we don't have time. We can't . . .

MA RAINEY: If you wanna make a record, you gonna find time. I ain't playing with you, Irvin. I can walk out of here and go back to my tour. I got plenty fans. I don't need to go through all of this. Just go and get the boy a microphone.

    [IRVIN *and* STURDYVANT *consult in the booth,* IRVIN *exits.*]

STURDYVANT: All right, Ma . . . we'll get him a microphone. But if he messes up . . . He's only getting one chance . . . The cost . . .

MA RAINEY: Damn the cost. You always talking about the cost. I make more money for this outfit than anybody else you got put together. If he messes up he'll just do it till he gets it right. Levee, I know you had something to do with this. You better watch yourself.

LEVEE: It was Cutler!

SYLVESTER: It was you! You the only one m-m-mad about it.

LEVEE: The boy stutter. He can't do the part. Everybody see that. I don't know why you want the boy to do the part no ways.

MA RAINEY: Well, can or can't . . . he's gonna do it! You ain't got nothing to do with it!

LEVEE: I don't care what you do! He can sing the whole goddamned song for all I care!

MA RAINEY: Well, all right. Thank you.

    [IRVIN *enters with a microphone and hooks it up. He exits to the control booth.*]

MA RAINEY: Come on, Sylvester. You just stand here and hold your hands like I told you. Just remember the words and say them . . . That's all there is to it. Don't worry about messing up. If you mess up, we'll do it again. Now, let me hear you say it. Play for him, Cutler.

CUTLER: One . . . two . . . you know what to do.

[*The band begins to play and* SYLVESTER *curls his fingers and claps his hands together in front of his chest, pulling in opposite directions as he says his lines.*]

SYLVESTER: "All right, boys, you d-d-d-done s-s-s-seen the best . . .
[LEVEE *stops playing.*]
Now I'm g-g-g-gonna show you the rest . . . Ma R-r-rainey's gonna show you her b-b-b-black b-b-b-bottom."

[*The rest of the band stops playing.*]

MA RAINEY: That's all right. That's real good. You take your time, you'll get it right.
STURDYVANT [*over speaker*]: Listen, Ma . . . now, when you come in, don't wait so long to come in. Don't take so long on the intro, huh?
MA RAINEY: Sturdyvant, don't you go trying to tell me how to sing. You just take care of that up there and let me take care of this down here. Where's my Coke?
IRVIN: Okay, Ma. We're all set up to go up here. "Ma Rainey's Black Bottom," boys.
MA RAINEY: Where's my Coke? I need a Coke. You ain't got no Coke down here? Where's my Coke?
IRVIN: What's the matter, Ma? What's . . .
MA RAINEY: Where's my Coke? I need a Coca-Cola.
IRVIN: Uh . . . Ma, look, I forgot the Coke, huh? Let's do it without it, huh? Just this one song. What say, boys?
MA RAINEY: Damn what the band say! You know I don't sing nothing without my Coca-Cola!
STURDYVANT: We don't have any, Ma. There's no Coca-Cola here. We're all set up and we'll just go ahead and . . .
MA RAINEY: You supposed to have Coca-Cola. Irvin knew that. I ain't singing nothing without my Coca-Cola!

[*She walks away from the mike, singing to herself.* STURDYVANT *enters from the control booth.*]

STURDYVANT: Now, just a minute here, Ma. You come in an hour late . . . we're way behind schedule as it is . . . the band is set up and ready to go . . . I'm burning my lights . . . I've turned up the heat . . . We're ready to make a record and what? You decide you want a Coca-Cola?
MA RAINEY: Sturdyvant, get out of my face.
[IRVIN *enters.*]
Irvin . . . I told you keep him away from me.
IRVIN: Mel, I'll handle it.
STURDYVANT: I'm tired of her nonsense, Irv. I'm not gonna put up with this!
IRVIN: Let me handle it, Mel. I know how to handle her.
[IRVIN *to* MA RAINEY.]
Look, Ma . . . I'll call down to the deli and get you a Coke. But let's get started, huh? Sylvester's standing there ready to go . . . the band's set up . . . let's do this one song, huh?

MA RAINEY: If you too cheap to buy me a Coke, I'll buy my own. Slow Drag! Sylvester, go with Slow Drag and get me a Coca-Cola.

[SLOW DRAG *comes over.*]

Slow Drag, walk down to that store on the corner and get me three bottles of Coca-Cola. Get out my face, Irvin. You all just wait until I get my Coke. It ain't gonna kill you.

IRVIN: Okay, Ma. Get your Coke, for Chrissakes! Get your coke!

[IRVIN *and* STURDYVANT *exit into the hallway followed by* SLOW DRAG *and* SYLVESTER. TOLEDO, CUTLER *and* LEVEE *head for the band room.*]

MA RAINEY: Cutler, come here a minute. I want to talk to you.

[CUTLER *crosses over somewhat reluctantly.*]

What's all this about "the boys in the band say"? I tells you what to do. I says what the matter is with the band. I say who can and can't do what.

CUTLER: We just say 'cause the boy stutter . . .

MA RAINEY: I know he stutters. Don't you think I know he stutters? This is what's gonna help him.

CUTLER: Well, how can he do the part if he stutters? You want him to stutter through it? We just thought it be easier to go on and let Levee do it like we planned.

MA RAINEY: I don't care if he stutters or not! He's doing the part and I don't wanna hear any more of this shit about what the band says. And I want you to find somebody to replace Levee when we get to Memphis. Levee ain't nothing but trouble.

CUTLER: Levee's all right. He plays good music when he puts his mind to it. He knows how to write music too.

MA RAINEY: I don't care what he know. He ain't nothing but bad news. Find somebody else. I know it was his idea about who to say who can do what.

[DUSSIE MAE *wanders over to where they are sitting.*]

Dussie Mae, go sit your behind down somewhere and quit flaunting yourself around.

DUSSIE MAE: I ain't doing nothing.

MA RAINEY: Well, just go on somewhere and stay out of the way.

CUTLER: I been meaning to ask you, Ma . . . about these songs. This "Moonshine Blues" . . . that's one of them songs Bessie Smith sang, I believes.

MA RAINEY: Bessie what? Ain't nobody thinking about Bessie. I taught Bessie. She ain't doing nothing but imitating me. What I care about Bessie? I don't care if she sell a million records. She got her people and I got mine. I don't care what nobody else do. Ma was the *first* and don't you forget it!

CUTLER: Ain't nobody said nothing about that. I just said that's the same song she sang.

MA RAINEY: I been doing this a long time. Ever since I was a little girl. I don't care what nobody else do. That's what gets me so mad with Irvin. White folks try to be put out with you all the time. Too cheap to buy me a Coca-Cola. I lets them know it, though. Ma don't stand for no shit. Wanna take my voice and trap it in them fancy boxes with all them buttons and dials . . . and then too cheap to buy me a Coca-Cola. And it don't cost but a nickle a bottle.

CUTLER: I knows what you mean about that.

MA RAINEY: They don't care nothing about me. All they want is my voice. Well, I done learned that, and they gonna treat me like I want to be treated no matter how much it hurt them. They back there now calling me all kinds of names . . . calling me everything but a child of god. But they can't do nothing else. They ain't got what they wanted yet. As soon as they get my voice down on them recording machines, then it's just like if I'd be some whore and they roll over and put their pants on. Ain't got no use for me then. I know what I'm talking about. You watch. Irvin right there with the rest of them. He don't care nothing about me either. He's been my manager for six years, always talking about sticking together, and the only time he had me in his house was to sing for some of his friends.

CUTLER: I know how they do.

MA RAINEY: If you colored and can make them some money, then you all right with them. Otherwise, you just a dog in the alley. I done made this company more money from my records than all the other recording artists they got put together. And they wanna balk about how much this session is costing them.

CUTLER: I don't see where it's costing them all what they say.

MA RAINEY: It ain't! I don't pay that kind of talk to mind.

[*The lights go down on the studio and come up on the band room.* TOLEDO *sits reading a newspaper.* LEVEE *sings and hums his song.*]

LEVEE [*singing*]:

> You can shake it, you can break it
> You can dance at any hall
> You can slide across the floor
> You'll never have to stall
> My jelly, my roll,
> Sweet Mama, don't you let it fall.

Wait till Sturdyvant hear me play that! I'm talking about some real music, Toledo! I'm talking about *real* music!

[*The door opens and* DUSSIE MAE *enters.*]

Hey, mama! Come on in.

DUSSIE MAE: Oh, hi! I just wanted to see what it looks like down here.

LEVEE: Well, come on in . . . I don't bite.

DUSSIE MAE: I didn't know you could really write music. I thought you was just jiving me at the club last night.

LEVEE: Naw, baby . . . I knows how to write music. I done give Mr. Sturdyvant some of my songs and he says he's gonna let me record them. Ask Toledo. I'm gonna have my own band! Toledo, ain't I give Mr. Sturdyvant some of my songs I wrote?

TOLEDO: Don't get Toledo mixed up in nothing.

[*He exits.*]

DUSSIE MAE: You gonna get your own band sure enough?

LEVEE: That's right! Levee Green and his Footstompers.

DUSSIE MAE: That's real nice.

LEVEE: That's what I was trying to tell you last night. A man what's gonna get his own band need to have a woman like you.

DUSSIE MAE: A woman like me wants somebody to bring it and put it in my hand. I don't need nobody wanna get something for nothing and leave me standing in my door.

LEVEE: That ain't Levee's style, sugar. I got more style than that. I knows how to treat a woman. Buy her presents and things . . . treat her like she wants to be treated.

DUSSIE MAE: That's what they all say . . . till it come time to be buying the presents.

LEVEE: When we get down to Memphis, I'm gonna show you what I'm talking about. I'm gonna take you out and show you a good time. Show you Levee knows how to treat a woman.

DUSSIE MAE: When you getting your own band?

LEVEE [*moves closer to slip his arm around her*]: Soon as Mr. Sturdyvant say. I done got my fellows already picked out. Getting me some good fellows know how to play real sweet music.

DUSSIE MAE [*moves away*]: Go on now, I don't go for all that pawing and stuff. When you get your own band, maybe we can see about this stuff you talking.

LEVEE [*moving toward her*]: I just wanna show you I know what the women like. They don't call me Sweet Lemonade for nothing.

[LEVEE *takes her in his arms and attempts to kiss her.*]

DUSSIE MAE: Stop it now. Somebody's gonna come in here.

LEVEE: Naw they ain't. Look here, sugar . . . what I wanna know is . . . can I introduce my red rooster to your brown hen?

DUSSIE MAE: You get your band, then we'll see if that rooster know how to crow.

[*He grinds up against her and feels her buttocks.*]

LEVEE: Now I know why my grandpappy sat on the back porch with his straight razor when grandma hung out the wash.

DUSSIE MAE: Nigger, you crazy!

LEVEE: I bet you sound like the midnight train from Alabama when it crosses the Maxon-Dixon line.

DUSSIE MAE: How's you get so crazy?

LEVEE: It's women like you . . . drives me that way.

[*He moves to kiss her as the lights go down in the band room and up in the studio.* MA RAINEY *sits with* CUTLER *and* TOLEDO.]

MA RAINEY: It sure done got quiet in here. I never could stand no silence. I always got to have some music going on in my head somewhere. It keeps things balanced.

Music will do that. It fills things up. The more music you got in the world, the fuller it is.

CUTLER: I can agree with that. I got to have my music too.

MA RAINEY: White folks don't understand about the blues. They hear it come out, but they don't know how it got there. They don't understand that's life's way of talking. You don't sing to feel better. You sing 'cause that's a way of understanding life.

CUTLER: That's right. You get that understanding and you done got a grip on life to where you can hold your head up and go on to see what else life got to offer.

MA RAINEY: The blues help you get out of bed in the morning. You get up knowing you ain't alone. There's something else in the world. Something's been added by that song. This be an empty world without the blues. I take that emptiness and try to fill it up with something.

TOLEDO: You fill it up with something the people can't be without, Ma. That's why they call you the Mother of the Blues. You fill up that emptiness in a way ain't nobody ever thought of doing before. And now they can't be without it.

MA RAINEY: I ain't started the blues way of singing. The blues always been here.

CUTLER: In the church sometimes you find that way of singing. They got blues in the church.

MA RAINEY: They say I started it . . . but I didn't. I just helped it out. Filled up that empty space a little bit. That's all. But if they wanna call me the Mother of the Blues, that's all right with me. It don't hurt none.

[SLOW DRAG and SYLVESTER enter with the Cokes.]

It sure took you long enough. That store ain't but on the corner.

SLOW DRAG: That one was closed. We had to find another one.

MA RAINEY: Sylvester, go and find Mr. Irvin and tell him we ready to go.

[SYLVESTER exits. The lights in the band room come up while the lights in the studio stay on. LEVEE and DUSSIE MAE are kissing. SLOW DRAG enters. They break their embrace. DUSSIE MAE straightens up her clothes.]

SLOW DRAG: Cold out. I just wanted to warm up with a little sip.

[He goes to his locker, takes out his bottle and drinks.]

Ma got her Coke, Levee. We about ready to start.

[SLOW DRAG exits. LEVEE attempts to kiss DUSSIE MAE again.]

DUSSIE MAE: No . . . Come on! I got to go. You gonna get me in trouble.

[She pulls away and exits up the stairs. LEVEE watches after her.]

LEVEE: Good God! Happy birthday to the lady with the cakes!

[The lights go down in the band room and come up in the studio. MA RAINEY drinks her Coke. LEVEE enters from the band room. The musicians take their places. SYLVESTER stands by his mike. IRVIN and STURDYVANT look on from the control booth.]

IRVIN: We're all set up here, Ma. We're all set to go. You ready down there?

MA RAINEY: Sylvester you just remember your part and say it. That's all there is to it.

[*To* IRVIN.]

Yeah, we ready.

IRVIN: Okay, boys. "Ma Rainey's Black Bottom". Take one.

CUTLER: One . . . two . . . You know what to do.

[*The band plays.*]

SYLVESTER: All right, boys, you d-d-d-done s-s-seen the rest. . . .

IRVIN: Hold it!

[*The band stops.* STURDYVANT *changes the recording disk and nods to* IRVIN.]

Okay. Take two.

CUTLER: One . . . two . . . You know what to do.

[*The band plays.*]

SYLVESTER: All right, boys, you done seen the rest . . . now I'm gonna show you the best. Ma Rainey's g-g-g-gonna s-s-show you her b-b-black bottom.

IRVIN: Hold it! Hold it!

[*The band stops.* STURDYVANT *changes the recording disk.*]

Okay. Take Three. Ma, let's do it without the intro, huh? No voice intro . . . you just come in singing.

MA RAINEY: Irvin, I done told you . . . the boy's gonna do the part. He don't stutter all the time. Just give him a chance. Sylvester, hold your hands like I told you and just relax. Just relax and concentrate.

IRVIN: All right. Take three.

CUTLER: One . . . Two . . . You know what to do.

[*The band plays.*]

SYLVESTER: All right, boys, you done seen the rest . . . now, I'm gonna show you the best. Ma Rainey's gonna show you her black bottom."

MA RAINEY [*singing*]:

> Way down south in Alabamy
> I got a friend they call dancing Sammy
> Who's crazy about all the latest dances
> Black Bottom stomping, two babies prancing
>
> The other night at a swell affair
> As soon as the boys found out that I was there
> They said, come on, Ma, let's go to the cabaret.
> When I got there, you ought to hear them say,

I want to see the dance you call the black bottom
I want to learn that dance
I want to see the dance you call your big black bottom
It'll put you in a trance.

All the boys in the neighborhood
They say your black bottom is really good
Come on and show me your black bottom
I want to learn that dance

I want to see the dance you call the black bottom
I want to learn that dance
Come on and show the dance you call your big black bottom
It puts you in a trance.

Early last morning about the break of day
Grandpa told my grandma, I heard him say,
Get up and show your old man your black bottom
I want to learn that dance

[*Instrumental break.*]

I done showed you all my black bottom
You ought to learn that dance.

IRVIN: Okay, that's good, Ma. That sounded great! Good job, boys!

MA RAINEY [*to* SYLVESTER]: See! I told you. I knew you could do it. You just have to put your mind to it. Didn't he do good, Cutler? Sound real good. I told him he could do it.

CUTLER: He sure did. He did better than I thought he was gonna do.

IRVIN [*entering to remove* SYLVESTER*'s mike*]: Okay, boys . . . Ma . . . let's do "Moonshine Blues" next, huh? "Moonshine Blues," boys.

STURDYVANT [*over speaker*]: Irv! Something's wrong down there. We don't have it right.

IRVIN: What? What's the matter Mel . . .

STURDYVANT: We don't have it right. Something happened. We don't have the goddamn song recorded!

IRVIN: What's the matter? Mel, what happened? You sure you don't have nothing?

STURDYVANT: Check that mike, huh, Irv. It's the kid's mike. Something's wrong with the mike. We've got everything all screwed up here.

IRVIN: Christ almighty! Ma, we got to do it again. We don't have it. We didn't record the song.

MA RAINEY: What you mean you didn't record it? What was you and Sturdyvant doing up there?

IRVIN [*following the mike wire*]: Here . . . Levee must have kicked the plug out.

LEVEE: I ain't done nothing! I ain't kicked nothing!

SLOW DRAG: If Levee had his mind on what he's doing . . .

MA RAINEY: Levee, if it ain't one thing, it's another. You better straighten yourself up!

LEVEE: Hell . . . it ain't my fault. I ain't done nothing!

STURDYVANT: What's the matter with that mike, Irv? What's the problem?

IRVIN: It's the cord, Mel. The cord's all chewed up. We need another cord.

MA RAINEY: This is the most disorganized . . . Irvin, I'm going home! Come on. Come on, Dussie.

[MA RAINEY *walks past* STURDYVANT *as he enters from the control booth. She exits offstage to get her coat.*]

STURDYVANT [*to* IRVIN]: Where's she going?

IRVIN: She said she's going home.

STURDYVANT: Irvin, you get her! If she walks out of here . . .

[MA RAINEY *enters carrying her and* DUSSIE MAE*'s coat.*]

MA RAINEY: Come on, Sylvester.

IRVIN [*helping her with her coat*]: Ma . . . Ma . . . listen. Fifteen minutes! All I ask is fifteen minutes!

MA RAINEY: Come on, Sylvester, get your coat.

STURDYVANT: Ma, if you walk out of this studio . . .

IRVIN: Fifteen minutes, Ma!

STURDYVANT: You'll be through . . . washed up! If you walk out on me . . .

IRVIN: Mel, for Chrissakes, shut up and let me handle it!

[*He goes after* MA RAINEY, *who has started for the door.*]

Ma, listen. These records are gonna be hits! They're gonna sell like crazy! Hell, even Sylvester will be a star. Fifteen minutes. That's all, I'm asking! Fifteen minutes.

MA RAINEY [*crosses to a chair and sits with her coat on*]: Fifteen minutes! You hear me, Irvin? Fifteen minutes . . . and then I'm gonna take my black bottom on back down to Georgia. Fifteen minutes. Then Madame Rainey is leaving!

IRVIN [*kisses her*]: All right, Ma . . . fifteen minutes. I promise.

[*To the band.*]

You boys go ahead and take a break. Fifteen minutes and we'll be ready to go.

CUTLER: Slow Drag, you got any of that bourbon left?

SLOW DRAG: Yeah, there's some down there.

CUTLER: I could use a little nip.

[CUTLER *and* SLOW DRAG *exit to the band room, followed by* LEVEE *and* TOLEDO. *The lights go down in the studio and up in the band room.*]

SLOW DRAG: Don't make me no difference if she leave or not. I was kinda hoping she would leave.

CUTLER: I'm like Mr. Irvin . . . After all this time we done put in here, it's best to go ahead and get something out of it.

TOLEDO: Ma gonna do what she wanna do, that's for sure. If I was Mr. Irvin, I'd best go on and get them cords and things hooked up right. And I wouldn't take no longer than fifteen minutes doing it.

CUTLER: If Levee had his mind on his work, we wouldn't be in this fix. We'd be up there finishing up. Now we got to go back and see if that boy get that part right. Ain't no telling if he ever get that right again in his life.

LEVEE: Hey, Levee ain't done nothing!

SLOW DRAG: Levee up there got one eye on the gal and the other on his trumpet.

CUTLER: Nigger, don't you know that's Ma's gal?

LEVEE: I don't care whose gal it is. I ain't done nothing to her. I just talk to her like I talk to anybody else.

CUTLER: Well, that being Ma's gal, and that being that boy's gal, is one and two different things. The boy is liable to kill you . . . but you' ass gonna be out there scraping the concrete looking for a job if you messing with Ma's gal.

LEVEE: How am I messing with her? I ain't done nothing to the gal. I just asked her her name. Now, if you telling me I can't do that, then Ma will just have to go to hell.

CUTLER: All I can do is warn you.

SLOW DRAG: Let him hang himself, Cutler. Let him string his neck out.

LEVEE: I ain't done nothing to the gal! You all talk like I done went and done something to her. Leave me go with my business.

CUTLER: I'm through with it. Try and talk to a fool . . .

TOLEDO: Some mens got it worse than others . . . this foolishness I'm talking about. Some mens is excited to be fools. That excitement is something else. I know about it. I done experienced it. It makes you feel good to be a fool. But it don't last long. It's over in a minute. Then you got to tend with the consequences. You got to tend with what comes after. That's when you wish you had learned something about it.

LEVEE: That's the best sense you made all day. Talking about being a fool. That's the only sensible thing you said today. Admitting you was a fool.

TOLEDO: I admits it, all right. Ain't nothing wrong with it. I done been a little bit of everything.

LEVEE: Now you're talking. You's as big a fool as they make.

TOLEDO: Gonna be a bit more things before I'm finished with it. Gonna be foolish again. But I ain't never been the same fool twice. I might be a different kind of fool, but I ain't gonna be the same fool twice. That's where we parts ways.

SLOW DRAG: Toledo, you done been a fool about a woman?

TOLEDO: Sure. Sure I have. Same as everybody.

SLOW DRAG: Hell, I ain't never seen you mess with no woman. I thought them books was your woman.

TOLEDO: Sure I messed with them. Done messed with a whole heap of them. And gonna mess with some more. But I ain't gonna be no fool about them. What you think? I done come in the world full-grown, with my head in a book? I done been young. Married. Got kids. I done been around and I done loved women to where you shake in your shoes just at the sight of them. Feel it all up and down your spine.

SLOW DRAG: I didn't know you was married.

TOLEDO: Sure. Legally. I been married legally. Got the papers and all. I done been through life. Made my marks. Followed some signs on the road. Ignored some others.

I done been all through it. I touched and been touched by it. But I ain't never been the same fool twice. That's what I can say.

LEVEE: But you been a fool. That's what counts. Talking about I'm a fool for asking the gal her name and here you is one yourself.

TOLEDO: Now, I married a woman. A good woman. To this day I can't say she wasn't a good woman. I can't say nothing bad about her. I married that woman with all the good graces and intentions of being hooked up and bound to her for the rest of my life. I was looking for her to put me in my grave. But, you see . . . it ain't all the time what you' intentions and wishes are. She went out and joined the church. All right. There ain't nothing wrong with that. A good Christian woman going to church and wanna do right by her god. There ain't nothing wrong with that. But she got up there, got to seeing them good Christian mens and wondering why I ain't like that. Soon she figure she got a heathen on her hands. She figured she couldn't live like that. The church was more important than I was. So she left. Packed up one day and moved out. To this day I ain't never said another word to her. Come home one day and my house was empty! And I sat down and figured out that I was a fool not to see that she needed something that I wasn't giving her. Else she wouldn't have been up there at the church in the first place. I ain't blaming her. I just said it wasn't gonna happen to me again. So, yeah, Toledo been a fool about a woman. That's part of making life.

CUTLER: Well, yeah, I been a fool too. Everybody done been a fool once or twice. But, you see, Toledo, what you call a fool and what I call a fool is two different things. I can't see where you was being a fool for that. You ain't done nothing foolish. You can't help what happened, and I wouldn't call you a fool for it. A fool is responsible for what happens to him. A fool cause it to happen. Like Levee . . . if he keeps messing with Ma's gal and his feet be out there scraping the ground. That's a fool.

LEVEE: Ain't nothing gonna happen to Levee. Levee ain't gonna let nothing happen to him. Now, I'm gonna say it again. I asked the gal her name. That's all I done. And if that's being a fool, then you looking at the biggest fool in the world . . . 'cause I sure as hell asked her.

SLOW DRAG: You just better not let Ma see you ask her. That's what the man's trying to tell you.

LEVEE: I don't need nobody to tell me nothing.

CUTLER: Well, Toledo, all I gots to say is that from the looks of it . . . from your story . . . I don't think life did you fair.

TOLEDO: Oh, life is fair. It's just in the taking what it gives you.

LEVEE: Life ain't shit. You can put it in a paper bag and carry it around with you. It ain't got no balls. Now, death . . . death got some style! Death will kick your ass and make you wish you never been born! That's how bad death is! But you can rule over life. Life ain't nothing.

TOLEDO: Cutler, how's your brother doing?

CUTLER: Who, Nevada? Oh, he's doing all right. Staying in St. Louis. Got a bunch of kids, last I heard.

TOLEDO: Me and him was all right with each other. Done a lot of farming together down in Plattsville.

CUTLER: Yeah, I know you all was tight. He in St. Louis now. Running an elevator, last I hear about it.

SLOW DRAG: That's better than stepping in muleshit.

TOLEDO: Oh, I don't know now. I liked farming. Get out there in the sun . . . smell that dirt. Be out there by yourself . . . nice and peaceful. Yeah, farming was all right by me. Sometimes I think I'd like to get me a little old place . . . but I done got too old to be following behind one of them balky mules now.

LEVEE: Nigger talking about life is fair. And ain't got a pot to piss in.

TOLEDO: See, now, I'm gonna tell you something. A nigger gonna be dissatisfied no matter what. Give a nigger some bread and butter . . . and he'll cry 'cause he ain't got no jelly. Give him some jelly, and he'll cry 'cause he ain't got no knife to put it on with. If there's one thing I done learned in this life, it's that you can't satisfy a nigger no matter what you do. A nigger's gonna make his own dissatisfaction.

LEVEE: Niggers got a right to be dissatisfied. Is you gonna be satisfied with a bone somebody done throwed you when you see them eating the whole hog?

TOLEDO: You lucky they let you be an entertainer. They ain't got to accept your way of entertaining. You lucky and don't even know it. You's entertaining and the rest of the people is hauling wood. That's the only kind of job for the colored man.

SLOW DRAG: Ain't nothing wrong with hauling wood. I done hauled plenty wood. My daddy used to haul wood. Ain't nothing wrong with that. That's honest work.

LEVEE: That ain't what I'm talking about. I ain't talking about hauling no wood. I'm talking about being satisfied with a bone somebody done throwed you. That's what's the matter with you all. You satisfied sitting in one place. You got to move on down the road from where you sitting . . . and all the time you got to keep an eye out for that devil who's looking to buy up souls. And hope you get lucky and find him!

CUTLER: I done told you about that blasphemy. Taking about selling your soul to the devil.

TOLEDO: We done the same thing, Cutler. There ain't no difference. We done sold Africa for the price of tomatoes. We done sold ourselves to the white man in order to be like him. Look at the way you dressed . . . . That ain't African. That's the white man. We trying to be just like him. We done sold who we are in order to become someone else. We's imitation white men.

CUTLER: What else we gonna be, living over here?

LEVEE: I'm Levee. Just me. I ain't no imitation nothing!

SLOW DRAG: You can't change who you are by how you dress. That's what I got to say.

TOLEDO: It ain't all how you dress. It's how you act, how you see the world. It's how you follow life.

LEVEE: It don't matter what you talking about. I ain't no imitation white man. And I don't want to be no white man. As soon as I get my band together and make them records like Mr. Sturdyvant done told me I can make, I'm gonna be like Ma and tell the white man just what he can do. Ma tell Mr. Irvin she gonna leave . . . and Mr. Irvin get down on his knees and beg her to stay! That's the way I'm gonna be! Make the white man respect me!

CUTLER: The white man don't care nothing about Ma. The colored folks made Ma

a star. White folks don't care nothing about who she is . . . what kind of music she make.

SLOW DRAG: That's the truth about that. You let her go down to one of them white-folks hotels and see how big she is.

CUTLER: Hell, she ain't got to do that. She can't even get a cab up here in the North. I'm gonna tell you something. Reverend Gates . . . you know Reverend Gates? . . . Slow Drag know who I'm talking about. Reverend Gates . . . now I'm gonna show you how this go where the white man don't care a thing about who you is. Reverend Gates was coming from Tallahassee to Atlanta, going to see his sister, who was sick at that time with the consumption. The train come up through Thomasville, then past Moultrie, and stopped in this little town called Sigsbee . . .

LEVEE: You can stop telling that right there! That train don't stop in Sigsbee. I know what train you talking about. That train got four stops before it reach Macon to go on to Atlanta. One in Thomasville, one in Moultrie, one in Cordele . . . and it stop in Centerville.

CUTLER: Nigger, I know what I'm talking about. You gonna tell me where the train stop?

LEVEE: Hell, yeah, if you talking about it stop in Sigsbee. I'm gonna tell you the truth.

CUTLER: I'm talking about *this* train! I don't know what train you been riding. I'm talking about *this* train!

LEVEE: Ain't but one train. Ain't but one train come out of Tallahassee heading north to Atlanta, and it don't stop at Sigsbee. Tell him, Toledo . . . that train don't stop at Sigsbee. The only train that stops at Sigsbee is the Yazoo Delta, and you have to transfer at Moultrie to get it!

CUTLER: Well, hell, maybe that what he done! I don't know. I'm just telling you the man got off the train at Sigsbee . . .

LEVEE: All right . . . you telling it. Tell it your way. Just make up anything.

SLOW DRAG: Levee, leave the man alone and let him finish.

CUTLER: I ain't paying Levee no never mind.

LEVEE: Go on and tell it your way.

CUTLER: Anyway . . . Reverend Gates got off this train in Sigsbee. The train done stopped there and he figured he'd get off and check the schedule to be sure he arrive in time for somebody to pick him up. All right. While he's there checking the schedule, it come upon him that he had to go to the bathroom. Now, they ain't had no colored rest rooms at the station. The only colored rest room is an outhouse they got sitting way back two hundred yards or so from the station. All right. He in the outhouse and the train go off and leave him there. He don't know nothing about this town. Ain't never been there before—in fact, ain't never even heard of it before.

LEVEE: I heard of it! I know just where it's at . . . and he ain't got off no train coming out of Tallahassee in Sigsbee!

CUTLER: The man standing there, trying to figure out what he's gonna do . . . where this train done left him in this strange town. It started getting dark. He see where the sun's getting low in the sky and he's trying to figure out what he's gonna do, when he noticed a couple of white fellows standing across the street from this station. Just standing there, watching him. And then two or three more come up and joined the other one. He look around, ain't seen no colored folks nowhere. He didn't know what was getting in these here fellows' minds, so he commence to walking. He ain't knowed where he was going. He just walking down the railroad tracks when he hear them call him. "Hey, nigger!" See, just like that. "Hey, nigger!" He kept on walking. They called him some more and he just keep walking. Just going down the tracks. And then he heard a gunshot where somebody done fired a gun in the air. He stopped then, you know.

TOLEDO: You don't even have to tell me no more. I know the facts of it. I done heard the same story a hundred times. It happened to me too. Same thing.

CUTLER: Naw, I'm gonna show you how the white folks don't care nothing about who or what you is. They crowded around him. These gang of mens made a circle around him. Now, he's standing there, you understand . . . got his cross around his neck like them preachers wear. Had his little Bible with him what he carry all the time. So they crowd on around him and one of them ask who he is. He told them he was Reverend Gates and that he was going to see his sister who was sick and the train left without him. And they said, "Yeah, nigger . . . but can you dance?" He looked at them and commenced to dancing. One of them reached up and tore his cross off his neck. Said he was committing a heresy by dancing with a cross and Bible. Took his Bible and tore it up and had him dancing till they got tired of watching him.

SLOW DRAG: White folks ain't never had no respect for the colored minister.

CUTLER: That's the only way he got out of there alive . . . was to dance. Ain't even had no respect for a man of God! Wanna make him into a clown. Reverend Gates sat right in my house and told me that story from his own mouth. So . . . the white folks don't care nothing about Ma Rainey. She's just another nigger who they can use to make some money.

LEVEE: What I wants to know is . . . if he's a man of God, then where the hell was God when all of this was going on? Why wasn't God looking out for him. Why didn't God strike down them crackers with some of this lightning you talk about to me?

CUTLER: Levee, you gonna burn in hell.

LEVEE: What I care about burning in hell? You talk like a fool . . . burning in hell. Why didn't God strike some of them crackers down? Tell me that! That's the question! Don't come telling me this burning-in-hell shit! He a man of God . . . why didn't God strike some of them crackers down? I'll tell you why! I'll tell you the truth! It's sitting out there as plain as day! 'Cause he a white man's God. That's why! God ain't never listened to no nigger's prayers. God take a nigger's prayers and throw them in the garbage. God don't pay niggers no mind. In fact . . . God hate niggers! Hate them with all the fury in his heart. Jesus don't love you, nigger! Jesus hate your black ass! Come talking that shit to me. Talking about burning in hell! God can kiss my ass.

[CUTLER *can stand no more. He jumps up and punches* LEVEE *in the mouth. The force of the blow knocks* LEVEE *down and* CUTLER *jumps on him.*]

CUTLER: You worthless . . . That's my God! That's my God! That's my God! You wanna blaspheme my God!

[TOLEDO *and* SLOW DRAG *grab* CUTLER *and try to pull him off* LEVEE.]

SLOW DRAG: Come on, Cutler . . . let it go! It don't mean nothing!

[CUTLER *has* LEVEE *down on the floor and pounds on him with a fury.*]

CUTLER: Wanna blaspheme my God! You worthless . . . talking about my God!

[TOLEDO *and* SLOW DRAG *succeed in pulling* CUTLER *off* LEVEE, *who is bleeding at the nose and mouth.*]

LEVEE: Naw, let him go! Let him go!
[*He pulls out a knife.*]
That's your God, huh? That's your God, huh? Is that right? Your God, huh? All right. I'm gonna give your God a chance. I'm gonna give your God a chance. I'm gonna give him a chance to save your black ass.

[LEVEE *circles* CUTLER *with the knife.* CUTLER *picks up a chair to protect himself.*]

TOLEDO: Come on, Levee . . . put the knife up!
LEVEE: Stay out of this, Toledo!
TOLEDO: That ain't no way to solve nothing.

[LEVEE *alternately swipes at* CUTLER *during the following.*]

LEVEE: I'm calling Cutler's God! I'm talking to Cutler's God! You hear me? Cutler's God! I'm calling Cutler's God. Come on and save this nigger! Strike me down before I cut his throat!
SLOW DRAG: Watch him, Cutler! Put that knife up, Levee!
LEVEE [*to* CUTLER]: I'm calling your God! I'm gonna give him a chance to save you! I'm calling your God! We gonna find out whose God he is!
CUTLER: You gonna burn in hell, nigger!
LEVEE: Cutler's God! Come on and save this nigger! Come on and save him like you did my mama! Save him like you did my mama! I heard her when she called you! I heard her when she said, "Lord, have mercy! Jesus, help me! Please, God, have mercy on me, Lord Jesus, help me!" And did you turn your back? Did you turn your back, motherfucker? Did you turn your back?
[LEVEE *becomes so caught up in his dialogue with God that he forgets about* CUTLER *and begins to stab upward in the air, trying to reach God.*]
Come on! Come on and turn your back on me! Turn your back on me! Come on! Where is you? Come on and turn your back on me! Turn your back on me, motherfucker! I'll cut your heart out! Come on, turn your back on me! Come on! What's the matter? Where is you? Come on and turn your back on me! Come on, what you scared of? Turn your back on me! Come on! Coward, motherfucker!
[LEVEE *folds his knife and stands triumphantly.*]
Your God ain't shit, Cutler.

[*The lights fade to black.*]

MA RAINEY [*singing*]:

> Ah, you hear me talking to you
> I don't bite my tongue
> You wants to be my man
> You got to fetch it with you when you come.

[*Lights come up in the studio. The last bars of the last song of the session are dying out.*]

IRVIN [*over speaker*]: Good! Wonderful! We have that, boys. Good session. That's great, Ma. We've got ourselves some winners.

TOLEDO: Well, I'm glad that's over.

MA RAINEY: Slow Drag, where you learn to play the bass at? You had it singing! I heard you! Had that bass jumping all over the place.

SLOW DRAG: I was following Toledo. Nigger got them long fingers striding all over the piano. I was trying to keep up with him.

TOLEDO: That's what you supposed to do, ain't it? Play the music. Ain't nothing abstract about it.

MA RAINEY: Cutler, you hear Slow Drag on that bass? He make it do what he want it to do! Spank it just like you spank a baby.

CUTLER: Don't be telling him that. Nigger's head get so big his hat won't fit him.

SLOW DRAG: If Cutler tune that guitar up, we would really have something!

CUTLER: You wouldn't know what a tuned-up guitar sounded like if you heard one.

TOLEDO: Cutler was talking. I heard him moaning. He was all up in it.

MA RAINEY: Levee . . . what is that you doing? Why you playing all them notes? You play ten notes for every one you supposed to play. It don't call for that.

LEVEE: You supposed to improvise on the theme. That's what I was doing.

MA RAINEY: You supposed to play the song the way I sing it. The way everybody else play it. You ain't supposed to go off by yourself and play what you want.

LEVEE: I was playing the song. I was playing it the way I felt it.

MA RAINEY: I couldn't keep up with what was going on. I'm trying to sing the song and you up there messing up my ear. That's what you was doing. Call yourself playing music.

LEVEE: Hey . . . I know what I'm doing. I know what I'm doing, all right. I know how to play music. You all back up and leave me alone about my music.

CUTLER: I done told you . . . it ain't about *your* music. It's about *Ma's* music.

MA RAINEY: That's all right, Cutler. I done told you what to do.

LEVEE: I don't care what you do. You supposed to improvise on the theme. Not play note for note the same thing over and over again.

MA RAINEY: You just better watch yourself. You hear me?

LEVEE: What I care what you or Cutler do? Come telling me to watch myself. What's that supposed to mean?

MA RAINEY: All right . . . you gonna find out what it means.

LEVEE: Go ahead and fire me. I don't care. I'm gonna get my own band anyway.

MA RAINEY: You keep messing with me.

LEVEE: Ain't nobody studying you. You ain't gonna do nothing to me. Ain't nobody gonna do nothing to Levee.

MA RAINEY: All right, nigger . . . you fired!

LEVEE: You think I care about being fired? I don't care nothing about that. You doing me a favor.

MA RAINEY: Cutler, Levee's out! He don't play in my band no more.

LEVEE: I'm fired . . . Good! Best thing that ever happened to me. I don't need this shit!

[LEVEE *exits to the band room.* IRVIN *enters from the control booth.*]

MA RAINEY: Cutler, I'll see you back at the hotel.

IRVIN: Okay, boys . . . you can pack up. I'll get your money for you.

CUTLER: That's cash money, Mr. Irvin. I don't want no check.

IRVIN: I'll see what I can do. I can't promise you nothing.

CUTLER: As long as it ain't no check. I ain't got no use for a check.

IRVIN: I'll see what I can do, Cutler.

[CUTLER, TOLEDO, *and* SLOW DRAG *exit to the band room.*]

Oh, Ma, listen . . . . I talked to Sturdyvant, and he said . . . Now, I tried to talk him out of it . . . He said the best he can do is to take twenty-five dollars of your money and give it to Sylvester.

MA RAINEY: Take what and do what? If I wanted the boy to have twenty-five dollars of my money, I'd give it to him. He supposed to get his own money. He supposed to get paid like everybody else.

IRVIN: Ma, I talked to him . . . He said . . .

MA RAINEY: Go talk to him again! Tell him if he don't pay that boy, he'll never make another record of mine again. Tell him that. You supposed to be my manager. All this talk about sticking together. Start sticking! Go on up there and get that boy his money!

IRVIN: Okay, Ma . . . I'll talk to him again. I'll see what I can do.

MA RAINEY: Ain't no see about it! You bring that boy's money back here!

[IRVIN *exits. The lights stay on in the studio and come up in the band room. The men have their instruments packed and sit waiting for* IRVIN *to come and pay them.* SLOW DRAG *has a pack of cards.*]

SLOW DRAG: Come on, Levee, let me show you a card trick.

LEVEE: I don't want to see no card trick. What you wanna show me for? Why you wanna bother me with that?

SLOW DRAG: I was just trying to be nice.

LEVEE: I don't need you to be nice to me. What I need you to be nice to me for? I ain't gonna be nice to you. I ain't even gonna let you be in my band no more.

SLOW DRAG: Toledo, let me show you a card trick.

CUTLER: I just hope Mr. Irvin don't bring no check down here. What the hell I'm gonna do with a check?

SLOW DRAG: All right now . . . pick a card. Any card . . . go on . . . take any of them. I'm gonna show you something.

TOLEDO: I agrees with you, Cutler. I don't want no check either.

CUTLER: It don't make no sense to give a nigger a check.

SLOW DRAG: Okay, now. Remember your card. Remember which one you got. Now . . . put it back in the deck. Anywhere you want. I'm gonna show you something.

[TOLEDO *puts the card in the deck.*]

You remember your card? All right. Now I'm gonna shuffle the deck. Now . . . I'm gonna show you what card you picked. Don't say nothing now. I'm gonna tell you what card you picked.

CUTLER: Slow Drag, that trick is as old as my mama.

SLOW DRAG: Naw, naw . . . wait a minute! I'm gonna show him his card . . . There it go! The six of diamonds. Ain't that your card? Ain't that it?

TOLEDO: Yeah, that's it . . . the six of diamonds.

SLOW DRAG: Told you! Told you I'd show him what it was!

[*The lights fade in the band room and come up full on the studio.* STURDYVANT *enters with* IRVIN.]

STURDYVANT: Ma, is there something wrong? Is there a problem?

MA RAINEY: Sturdyvant, I want you to pay that boy his money.

STURDYVANT: Sure, Ma. I got it right here. Two hundred for you and twenty-five for the kid, right?

[STURDYVANT *hands the money to* IRVIN, *who hands it to* MA RAINEY *and* SYLVESTER.]

Irvin misunderstood me. It was all a mistake. Irv made a mistake.

MA RAINEY: A mistake, huh?

IRVIN: Sure, Ma. I made a mistake. He's paid, right? I straightened it out.

MA RAINEY: The only mistake was when you found out I hadn't signed the release forms. That was the mistake. Come on, Sylvester.

[*She starts to exit.*]

STURDYVANT: Hey, Ma . . . come on, sign the forms, huh?

IRVIN: Ma . . . come on now.

MA RAINEY: Get your coat, Sylvester. Irvin, where's my car?

IRVIN: It's right out front, Ma. Here . . . I got the keys right here. Come on, sign the forms, huh?

MA RAINEY: Irvin, give me my car keys!

IRVIN: Sure, Ma . . . just sign the forms, huh?

[*He gives her the keys, expecting a trade-off.*]

MA RAINEY: Send them to my address and I'll get around to them.

IRVIN: Come on, Ma . . . I took care of everything, right? I straightened everything out.

MA RAINEY: Give me the pen, Irvin.

[*She signs the forms.*]

You tell Sturdyvant . . . one more mistake like that and I can make my records someplace else.

[*She turns to exit.*]

Sylvester, straighten up your clothes. Come on, Dussie Mae.

[*She exits, followed by* DUSSIE MAE *and* SYLVESTER. *The lights go down in the studio and come up on the band room.*]

CUTLER: I know what's keeping him so long. He up there writing out checks. You watch. I ain't gonna stand for it. He ain't gonna bring me no check down here. If he do, he's gonna take it right back upstairs and get some cash.

TOLEDO: Don't get yourself all worked up about it. Wait and see. Think positive.

CUTLER: I am thinking positive. He positively gonna give me some cash. Man give me a check last time . . . you remember . . . we went all over Chicago trying to get it cashed. See a nigger with a check, the first thing they think is he done stole it someplace.

LEVEE: I ain't had no trouble cashing mine.

CUTLER: I don't visit no whorehouses.

LEVEE: You don't know about my business. So don't start nothing. I'm tired of you as it is. I ain't but two seconds off your ass no way.

TOLEDO: Don't you all start nothing now.

CUTLER: What the hell I care what you tired of. I wasn't even talking to you. I was talking to this man right here.

[IRVIN *and* STURDYVANT *enter.*]

IRVIN: Okay boys. Mr. Sturdyvant has your pay.

CUTLER: As long as it's cash money, Mr. Sturdyvant. 'Cause I have too much trouble trying to cash a check.

STURDYVANT: Oh, yes . . . I'm aware of that. Mr. Irvin told me you boys prefer cash, and that's what I have for you.

[*He starts handing out the money.*]

That was a good session you boys put in . . . That's twenty-five for you. Yessir, you boys really know your business and we are going to . . . Twenty-five for you . . . We are going to get you back in here real soon . . . twenty-five . . . and have another session so you can make some more money . . . and twenty-five for you. Okay, thank you, boys. You can get your things together and Mr. Irvin will make sure you find your way out.

IRVIN: I'll be out front when you get your things together, Cutler.

[IRVIN *exits.* STURDYVANT *starts to follow.*]

LEVEE: Mr. Sturdyvant, sir. About them songs I give you? . . .

STURDYVANT: Oh, yes, . . . uh . . . Levee. About them songs you gave me. I've thought about it and I just don't think the people will buy them. They're not the type of songs we're looking for.

LEVEE: Mr. Sturdyvant, sir . . . I done got my band picked out and they's real good fellows. They knows how to play real good. I know if the peoples hear the music, they'll buy it.

STURDYVANT: Well, Levee, I'll be fair with you . . . but they're just not the right songs.

LEVEE: Mr. Sturdyvant, you got to understand about that music. That music is what the people is looking for. They's tired of jug-band music. They wants something that excites them. Something with some fire to it.

STURDYVANT: Okay, Levee. I'll tell you what I'll do. I'll give you five dollars a piece for them. Now that's the best I can do.

LEVEE: I don't want no five dollars, Mr. Sturdyvant. I wants to record them songs, like you say.

STURDYVANT: Well, Levee, like I say . . . they just aren't the kind of songs we're looking for.

LEVEE: Mr. Sturdyvant, you asked me to write them songs. Now, why didn't you tell me that before when I first give them to you? You told me you was gonna let me record them. What's the difference between then and now?

STURDYVANT: Well, look . . . I'll pay you for your trouble . . .

LEVEE: What's the difference, Mr. Sturdyvant? That's what I wanna know.

STURDYVANT: I had my fellows play your songs, and when I heard them, they just didn't sound like the kind of songs I'm looking for right now.

LEVEE: You got to hear *me* play them, Mr. Sturdyvant! You ain't heard *me* play them. That's what's gonna make them sound right.

STURDYVANT: Well, Levee, I don't doubt that really. It's just that . . . well, I don't think they'd sell like Ma's records. But I'll take them off your hands for you.

LEVEE: The people's tired of jug-band music, Mr. Sturdyvant. They wants something that's gonna excite them! They wants something with some fire! I don't know what fellows you had playing them songs . . . but if I could play them! I'd set them down in the people's lap! Now you told me I could record them songs!

STURDYVANT: Well, there's nothing I can do about that. Like I say, it's five dollars a piece. That's what I'll give you. I'm doing you a favor. Now, if you write any more, I'll help you out and take them off your hands. The price is five dollars apiece. Just like now.

[*He attempts to hand* LEVEE *the money, finally shoves it in* LEVEE's *coat pocket and is gone in a flash.* LEVEE *follows him to the door and it slams in his face. He takes the money from his pocket, balls it up and throws it on the floor. The other musicians silently gather up their belongings.* TOLEDO *walks past* LEVEE *and steps on his shoe.*]

LEVEE: Hey! Watch it . . . Shit Toledo! You stepped on my shoe!

TOLEDO: Excuse me there, Levee.

LEVEE: Look at that! Look at that! Nigger, you stepped on my shoe. What you do that for?

TOLEDO: I said I'm sorry.

LEVEE: Nigger gonna step on my goddamn shoe! You done fucked up my shoe! Look at that! Look at what you done to my shoe, nigger! I ain't stepped on your shoe! What you wanna step on my shoe for?

CUTLER: The man said he's sorry.

LEVEE: Sorry! How the hell he gonna be sorry after he gone ruint my shoe? Come talking about sorry!

[*Turns his attention back to* TOLEDO.]

Nigger, you stepped on my shoe! You know that!

[LEVEE *snatches his shoe off his foot and holds it up for* TOLEDO *to see.*]

See what you done done?

TOLEDO: What you want me to do about it? It's done now. I said excuse me.

LEVEE: Wanna go and fuck up my shoe like that. I ain't done nothing to your shoe. Look at this!

[TOLEDO *turns and continues to gather up his things.* LEVEE *spins him around by his shoulder.*]

LEVEE: Naw . . . naw . . . look what you done!

[*He shoves the shoe in* TOLEDO's *face.*]

Look at that! That's my shoe! Look at that! You did it! You did it! You fucked up my shoe! You stepped on my shoe with them raggedy-ass clodhoppers!

TOLEDO: Nigger, ain't nobody studying you and your shoe! I said excuse me. If you can't accept that, then the hell with it. What you want me to do?

[LEVEE *is in a near rage, breathing hard. He is trying to get a grip on himself, as even he senses, or perhaps only he senses, he is about to lose control. He looks around, uncertain of what to do.* TOLEDO *has gone back to packing, as have* CUTLER *and* SLOW DRAG. *They purposefully avoid looking at* LEVEE *in hopes he'll calm down if he doesn't have an audience. All the weight in the world suddenly falls on* LEVEE *and he rushes at* TOLEDO *with his knife in his hand.*]

LEVEE: Nigger, you stepped on my shoe!

[*He plunges the knife into* TOLEDO's *back up to the hilt.* TOLEDO *lets out a sound of surprise and agony.* CUTLER *and* SLOW DRAG *freeze.* TOLEDO *falls backward with* LEVEE, *his hand still on the knife, holding him up.* LEVEE *is suddenly faced with the realization of what he has done. He shoves* TOLEDO *forward and takes a step back.* TOLEDO *slumps to the floor.*]

He . . . he stepped on my shoe. He did. Honest, Cutler, he stepped on my shoe. What he do that for? Toledo, what you do that for? Cutler, help me. He stepped on my shoe, Cutler.

[*He turns his attention to* TOLEDO.]

Toledo! Toledo, get up.

[*He crosses to* TOLEDO *and tries to pick him up.*]

It's okay, Toledo. Come on . . . I'll help you. Come on, stand up now. Levee'll help you.

[TOLEDO *is limp and heavy and awkward. He slumps back to the floor.* LEVEE *gets mad at him.*] Don't look at me like that! Toledo! Nigger, don't look at me like that! I'm warning you, nigger! Close your eyes! Don't you look at me like that! [*He turns to* CUTLER.] Tell him to close his eyes. Cutler. Tell him don't look at me like that.

CUTLER: Slow Drag, get Mr. Irvin down here.

[*The sound of a trumpet is heard,* LEVEE's *trumpet, a muted trumpet struggling for the highest of possibilities and blowing pain and warning.*]

Black out

QUESTIONS

1. How does the prologue reveal the social milieu of the play and its characters?
2. What distinguishes Toledo from his two colleagues, Cutler and Slow Drag? When he says of them in Act I, "you forgot the name of the gods," what does he mean? Why does Toledo call Levee the devil? What does Toledo believe to be the chief shortcoming of African-Americans in the United States?
3. Why does Sturdyvant want to use Levee's renditions of the blues songs? Why do the other musicians resist playing them?
4. Describe the relationships among the members of the band, Ma Rainey, and the two recording producers—Sturdyvant and Irvin—in Act I.
5. In Act II, Ma Rainey describes what "White Folks" want from her. What do they want?
6. In Act II, Ma Rainey says "You sing 'cause that's a way of understanding life." What type of singing is she referring to? What does she mean by this?
7. In Act II, Toledo and Levee have an argument over "life." What does each feel about life in general? How do they differ?
8. Cutler says that whites "wanna make him [the black man] a clown." What does he mean? What special relevance does it have to the lives of Ma Rainey and the musicians?
9. Why does Levee stab Toledo?

Biographical Profiles

Chinua Achebe (b. 1930) was born in eastern Nigeria, subsequently Biafra. His first novel, *Things Fall Apart* (1958), tracing the conflicts between European and African cultures, is a masterpiece of African fiction. Additional novels, collections of short fiction, and essays have established Achebe as a foremost contemporary writer.

Anna Akhmatova (1888–1966) is considered one of the finest modern Russian poets. She was born in Odessa and raised near St. Petersburg. Her poetry, chronicling the harsh course of Soviet history, includes *White Flock* (1917), *Collected Poems* (1963), and *The Complete Poems* (1966).

Al-Tutili, one of the foremost Moorish poets living in Spain, was born, lived, and died during the Age of the Caliphs (A.D. 632–1050). Followers of Mohammed, founder of Islam, ruled there until 1492.

Paula Gunn Allen (b. 1939) was born in New Mexico, the daughter of Sioux-Laguna and Lebanese-Jewish parents. She received her Ph.D. from the University of New Mexico, and teaches at San Francisco State University. Her collected verse includes *Coyote's Daylight Trip* (1978).

Woody Allen (b. 1935) was born Allen Stewart Konigsberg in Brooklyn, New York. He attended New York University and City College of New York, but did not graduate. In 1964, he wrote his first screenplay, *What's New Pussycat?* Since then, he has become one of America's foremost film directors. Allen's literary collections include *Getting Even* (1971), *Without Feathers* (1975), and *Side Effects* (1980).

Yehuda Amichai (b. 1924) was born in Germany but emigrated to Palestine with his parents when he was a child. A poet, novelist, and short story writer, he is the author of *In This Terrible Wind* (1973) and other works.

Maya Angelou (b. 1928) was born in St. Louis, Missouri, but raised in Arkansas by her grandmother, who figures prominently in her famous autobiography, *I Know Why the Caged Bird Sings* (1969). Angelou has written other books about her experience as an African-American woman. Poet, teacher, lecturer, and civil-rights leader, Angelou was selected to read one of her poems at the 1993 inauguration of President Bill Clinton.

Aristophanes   (450?–385 B.C.), generally considered the greatest classical Greek dramatic comedian, was born toward the beginning of the Age of Pericles. Nine of his plays were written during the Peloponnesian War—the struggle between Athens and Sparta that lasted from 431 to 404 B.C. This war and the conflicts it caused form a major backdrop for Aristophanes' plays, notably *The Acharians* (425 B.C.), *Peace* (421 B.C.), and *Lysistrata* (411 B.C.). Other plays include *The Wasps* (422 B.C.), *The Birds* (414 B.C.), and *The Frogs* (405 B.C.).

Matthew Arnold   (1822–1888) was born at Laleham, England, the day before Christmas. He was educated at Winchester, Rugby, and Oxford and in 1847 was secretary to the marquis of Lansdowne. Arnold published his first collection of verse, *The Strayed Pearl and Other Poems* (1849) when he was 27. His studies and teaching led him to literary criticism; in 1852 he published *Empedocles*, a poem on Wordsworth, Byron, and Goethe. His other works include *Stanzas from the Grande Chartreuse* (1855), *Merope* (1858), *Thyrsis* (1866), and *Essays in Criticism* (1865, 1888). The obligation of a critic, he wrote, is "a disinterested endeavor to learn and propagate the best that is known and thought in the world."

Margaret Eleanor Atwood   (b. 1939) studied at the University of Toronto, in her native Canada, and at Radcliffe College, in the United States (1957–1962). She has taught at Canadian universities and is the recipient of several awards for poetry, including the E. J. Pratt, the Governor's, and the President's medals. Atwood is considered to be one of the most important contemporary writers. She is also a major novelist having written *The Handmaid's Tale* (1987) and *Cat's Eye* (1989), among other works. Among her collections of published poetry Atwood includes *Double Persephone* (1961), *The Circle Game* (1967), *The Journals of Susanna Moodie* (1970), and *Power Politics* (1971).

Wystan Hugh Auden   (1907–1973) was born in England in 1907. After college at Oxford he became a member of a group of London poets that included Stephen Spender, C. Day Lewis, Louis MacNeice, and Christopher Isherwood. This was one of the most talented collections of writers in England at that time. Auden, like many other writers of the period, saw socialism as the political system that would save the world. He fought with the Republicans during the Spanish Civil War and in 1939, after his marriage to Erika Mann, emigrated to the United States and later became a citizen. Greatly influenced by W. B. Yeats and T. S. Eliot, Auden's work was first socially concerned and then more religiously concerned. He collaborated with MacNeice on *Letters from Iceland* (1937) and with Isherwood on four plays during the decade of the 1930s. A deft employer of satire, as in "The Unknown Citizen," Auden was wedged between English and American culture. His references tend to be more English, and this is true even though he lived in Greenwich Village in New York until a few years before his death. His works include *Poems* (1930), *Look, Stranger* (1936), *Spain* (1937), *The Sea and the Mirror* (1944), *For the Time Being: A Christmas Oratorio* (1944), *Selected Poetry* (1959), and *Homage to Clio* (1960).

Kofi Awoonor   (b. 1935) was born in Ghana. He was educated in Ghana, England, and the United States. One of Africa's foremost poets, he is the author of *Rediscovery* (1964), *Ride Me, Memory* (1973), and other collections. He has also written fiction, plays, and literary and political criticism.

Isaac Babel   (1894–1939?) was born in Odessa, Russia, of Jewish background. He was a soldier during World War I and later a correspondent attached to the Red Army. Two collections of his tales are *The Story of My Dove-Cote* (1925) and *Red Cavalry* (1926). He was arrested and disappeared during the Stalinist purges of the 1930s.

Ingeborg Bachmann   (1926–1973), the 1964 Buchner Prize winner, was born in Austria and studied philosophy. She traveled widely and published poetry, plays, and prose.

Amiri Baraka   (b. 1934), poet, playwright, novelist, and essayist, was one of the moving forces behind the cultural explosion known as the Black Arts Movement during the 1960s. Born in Newark, New Jersey, as LeRoi Jones and educated at both Howard and Columbia universities, Baraka (the Muslim name he adopted in 1968) experienced the cultural training that was expected of both white and black intellectuals during the middle part of this century. This experience led Baraka to the realization that his own conception of who he was as a black man and who blacks as a people were within the larger white society was determined by the white man's visions of the world. His books include *Note* (1962), *Black Magic: Poetry 1961–1967* (1967), the play *Dutchman* (1967), and other works.

Aphra Behn   (1640–1689) was born in Kent, England. She spent part of her childhood in Surinam, Guiana, an experience that provided her with the background for her best-known novel, *Oroonoko* (1688). In 1666, when Behn was 26, she was sent on a mission as a spy in the Netherlands for Charles II, becoming known for her exploits as "the Incomparable." However, she fell out of royal favor, spent time in debtors' prison in London, and on her release turned to writing to earn a living. Behn wrote seventeen plays, twelve histories and novels, and poetry, and did translations.

Ulli Beier   (?) A distinguished linguist, Beier was a Senior Lecturer in English Literature at the University of Papua and New Guinea when he translated, edited, and compiled the traditional poetry of Nigeria's Yoruba people during the 1960s.

John Berryman   (1914–1972), born in McAlester, Oklahoma, and educated at Columbia University and Oxford, is a notable contemporary poet best known for his collections *77 Dream Songs* (1964) and *Short Poems* (1967). All of his poetry reflects psychologically intense self-reflection.

Elizabeth Bishop   (1911–1979) was born in Worcester, Massachusetts, and raised by grandparents and an aunt in Nova Scotia and Boston. She graduated from Vassar in 1934 and then traveled extensively in Europe, Mexico, and finally Brazil, where she settled more or less permanently in 1951. Bishop won the Pulitzer Prize in 1956 and the National Book Award in 1970; the bulk of her verse appears in *The Complete Poems* (1969). Her friend Marianne Moore, whom she first met in 1934, once declared that Bishop was "spectacular in being unspectacular." Bishop is natural, deliberate, commonplace, modest, yet subtly contemplative in her best verse. However, she can also be, as she remarks of one of her favorite poets, George Herbert, "almost surrealistic" in her vivid descriptions of landscapes, objects, and people.

William Blake   (1757–1827) was born in London, where during the course of his life he was a poet, an engraver, a painter, and a mystic whose views became recognizable in his work. Many of his works are based on a mythological structure created by Blake, one that bypasses or ignores organized religion of Blake's day. Blake illustrated many of his own works, which include *Poetical Sketches by W. B.* (1783), *Songs of Innocence* (1789), *Songs of Experience* (1794), and the "prophetical books"—*The Book of Thel* (1789), *The Marriage of Heaven and Hell* (1790), *The Gates of Paradise* (1793), *The Vision of the Daughters of Albion* (1793), and others.

Louise Bogan   (1897–1970) was born in Maine and attended Boston University for one year. She lived most of her life in New York City, where she supported herself by writing stories and articles and doing translations and book reviews for *The New Republic, The Nation, The New Yorker,* and other magazines. She published her first volume of poetry in 1923. Though she wrote many things simply to pay the bills, she was a perfectionist about her poetry. She reduced the contents of her final collection, *The Blue Estuaries: Poems 1923–1968,* to only 105 poems, her lifetime's work. Often her poetry depicts the situation of women and asserts the need for a separate feminine view of the world.

Arna Wendell Bontemps   (1902–1973) was born in Alexandria, Louisiana. A courtly man, he served Fisk University in Nashville as librarian and assistant to the president for much of his life. Bontemps and Langston Hughes collaborated on many collections and other works. "He sought," says Charles Nichols, "the source and shape of his creative work in his own roots—the deep South of Louisiana and Alabama. The stark, laconic, poignant stories he wrote in the early 1930's are in the realistic mode of American regionalism." The South was the place Bontemps returned to after his graduation from Pacific Union College in 1924, and two years later he won the Alexander Pushkin Poetry Prize. He became, as well an essayist, a playwright, a short story writer, a novelist, and the author of many children's books, on some of which he collaborated with Hughes, Jack Conroy, and Countee Cullen. Bontemps was one of several writers to emerge from the Harlem Renaissance (1925–1929). Perhaps his most important novel was *Black Thunder* (1936).

Jorge Luis Borges   (1899–1986) was born in Argentina. Between 1923 and 1929 he published several volumes of poetry, which were mainly nostalgic and nationalistic (*Fervor de Buenos Aires,* 1923; *Luna de enfrente,* 1925; *Cuaderno de San Martin,* 1929). He then began writing essays on literature, metaphysics, and language. When his eyesight began to fail, he turned to writing fictional narratives, and these established his reputation. Somewhat like Kafka, Borges wove together the real and the surreal to create yet another reality. Among his better-known publications are *Historia de la infamia* (1935), *Ficciones* (1945, 1956), *El Aleph* (1949), *Other Inquisitions* (1952), and *Labyrinths, Stories and Essays* (1962).

Kay Boyle   (1903–1992) left her hometown, St. Paul, Minnesota, for study in Ohio from 1917 to 1919. She was a steady and frequent contributor to the little magazines that flourished at the close of World War I. Boyle lived in Europe, mainly France, for long periods of time, and much of her fiction is set overseas. The 1936 and 1941 winner of the O. Henry Award for short fiction, Boyle also gained great prominence as a poet. The poetic touch is easily discernible in her fiction. Her first novel, *Wedding Day,* was published in 1931 and was followed five years later by *The White Horses of Vienna and Other Stories.* These brought her considerable attention and established her as a writer who touched the world with a woman's sensibilities. *The Crazy Hunter* (1940); *American Citizen,* a poem (1944); *1939* (1948); *Generation without Farewell* (1959); *The Seagull on the Step: Three Short Novels* (1958); and *Testament for my Students,* a collection of poems (1970), are among her notable works, which also include *Thirty Stories* (1946) and *Fifty Stories* (1980).

Anne Bradstreet   (1612?–1672) was the first truly dedicated poet to settle in America. Bradstreet's poems were taken to London by her brother-in-law and apparently published without her consent in a volume entitled *The Tenth Muse Lately Sprung Up in America* (1650). Around 1666, Bradstreet began to revise the poems and work on others for a second edition, which she did not live to see published in 1678.

William Stanley Braithwaite   (1878–1962), born in Boston, early on became involved with literature and writing. Between 1926 and 1929 he edited eleven collections of poetry. He was himself poet, novelist, essayist, publisher, and editor. As editor of *The Poetic Journal* and *Poetry Review,* Braithwaite published many of the contemporary imagists and Frost, Sandburg, Masters, and Lindsay—unusual for a black man and despite the racial epithets by which many of his contributors addressed him.

Gwendolyn Brooks   (b. 1917) was born in Topeka, Kansas, but was raised in Chicago's South Side. As a child, Brooks was encouraged by both of her parents to write; her mother, alluding to an earlier black American poet, predicted that she would one day be the female Paul Laurence Dunbar. Brooks attended Wilson Junior College in Chicago and published her first book of poetry, *A Street in Bronzeville,* in 1945. Her second book, *Annie Allen,* won the Pulitzer Prize in 1949, making Brooks the first black writer to win that award. Other volumes include *Bronzeville Boys and Girls* (1956); *The Bean Eaters* (1960); *In the Mecca* (1968); *Family Portraits* (1971);

an autobiography, *Report from Part One* (1972); and a novel, *Maud Martha* (1953). A major poet, Brooks has been a prodigious supporter of younger artists and an inspiration for them. She has pioneered in depicting inner-city lives and in blending classical poetics with dialect and vernacular.

Brigid Brophy (b. 1929), English fiction writer and playwright, was born in London and attended St. Hugh's College, Oxford. Her fiction and drama examine the complex sexual relationships between people, including lesbians and bisexuals.

Sterling A. Brown (1901–1989) was born in Washington, D.C. He received one of the best educations of the writers in the Harlem Renaissance, graduating from Williams College and earning an M.A. from Harvard University. Brown taught for many years at Howard University. His main contribution to scholarship has been his recording of the lyrics of blues and spirituals and his helping these forms earn standing as legitimate forms of artistic expression. His study of spirituals and the blues influenced his own poetry.

Elizabeth Barrett Browning (1806–1861), born at Durham, England, received in childhood a rich, leisurely education from her brothers' tutors. She was devoted to literature, and when she was 14 her father had published her epic poem, *The Battle of Marathon*. In 1819, she apparently suffered a spinal injury that left her a semi-invalid until her marriage to Robert Browning in 1846. Elizabeth Browning enjoyed great fame for her *Sonnets from the Portuguese* (1850) and her blank-verse novel, *Aurora Leigh* (1857).

Robert Browning (1812–1869) was born near London, of wealthy parents, and was educated at home and at the University of London. Poetry was a childhood passion, used by Browning as a therapeutic tool to rid himself of his turbulent emotions. In September 1846, he eloped to Italy with the poet Elizabeth Barrett. They were to live fairly happily together until her death fifteen years later. A fine, though often difficult, poet, he is most famous for his development, as in "My Last Duchess," of the dramatic monologue, in which he presents complex characters through their own voices.

George Gordon, Lord Byron (1788–1824), was described by a contemporary as "mad, bad, and dangerous to know." Born of aristocratic parents with titles but little wealth, Byron grew up in poverty in the Scottish city of Aberdeen. A series of coincidences left him as the sixth Lord Byron, and he completed his education at Trinity College, Cambridge. A victim of both nature (he was born with a clubfoot) and nineteenth-century medicine, he nevertheless became a fine athlete, excelling in boxing, fencing, horse racing, and swimming. Financial difficulties and personal catastrophes plagued him most of his life, which ended with his fighting and dying in faraway Greece for the thing he loved most—freedom. Byron in his lifetime enjoyed sensational popular success as the author of such romantic narratives as *Childe Harold's Pilgrimage* (1812), *The Corsair* (1814), and the unfinished *Don Juan* (1818).

Thomas Campion (1567–1620) was born in London, the son of well-to-do parents who died in his childhood. A man of many interests and talents, Campion studied at Cambridge from 1581 to 1584, but took no degree; and at Gray's Inn, but never practiced law. He obtained a medical degree, probably at Caen in 1605, and for the rest of his life practiced medicine. Poetry and music were his main preoccupations, and he was much appreciated in his own time for his productions. Campion published five collections of lute songs in his lifetime. "In these airs," he wrote, "I have chiefly aimed to couple my words and notes lovingly together." Campion was praised in modern times by T. S. Eliot as an "accomplished master of rhymed lyric."

Raymond Carver (1938–1989) grew up in a logging town in Oregon. Married and a father at 19, Carver took courses at Chico State College, in California, where he studied creative writing with writer John Gardner. Carver also studied at Humboldt State College, California, and the University of Iowa; he published six collections of short fiction, notably *What We Talk About When We Talk About Love* (1981) and *Cathedral* (1983), along with a significant body of poetry, before his death from lung cancer.

Lorna Dee Cervantes   (b. 1959) was born in San Francisco, California, of Mexican descent. She attended San Jose City College and San Francisco State University. Her first book of poems is *Emplumada* (1982).

Aimé (Fernand) Césaire   (b. 1913), long considered one of the finest modernists writing in French, was born in Martinique, West Indies. He studied at the École Normale Supérieure and the Sorbonne in Paris. Former mayor of Fort-de-France, he was also Martinique's deputy to the French National Assembly and consul general of a district in Fort-de-France. Perhaps best known for his monumental work *Notebook of a Return to the Native Land,* Césaire began his career in letters in 1946, producing voluminous works in the essay and in poetry. His volumes include *The Miracle Weapon* (*Les armes miraculeuses* 1946), *Solar Throat Slashed* (*Soleil Cou-Coupe* 1948), *Shackles* (*Ferrements* 1960), *Aimé Césaire: The Collected Poetry* (1983), and *Lost Body* (*Corps Perdu* 1949). Between 1956 and 1969, Césaire wrote four plays. He is one of the prime spokespersons of the Negritude movement, which was sparked by Langston Hughes's work during the 1920s and 1930s.

Anton Chekhov   (1860–1904), the grandson of a serf, was born in Taganrog, Russia, and studied medicine at Moscow University. He received his medical degree in 1884, the same year that his first collection of short stories was published. Chekhov wrote hundreds of stories and sketches early in his career, gaining a literary reputation and a measure of financial independence that enabled him to make writing rather than the practice of medicine his major priority. Chekhov's greatest work in both short fiction and drama came in the last years of a life drastically shortened by tuberculosis. The plays of this last period—*The Seagull* (1896), *Uncle Vanya* (1899), *The Three Sisters* (1901), and *The Cherry Orchard* (1904)—were masterpieces that established Chekhov as a great modern dramatist. Chekhov's masterpieces of short fiction are equally outstanding, a delicate mixture of comedy, pathos, and tragedy in the author's depiction of humanity.

Cho Chihun   (b. 1920) first published in *The Green Deer Anthology* of Korea with a group of poets, each of whom contributed fifteen poems. He is a Buddhist. The author of several books of poetry, he taught at Korea University.

So Chongju   (b. 1915) was born in North Cholla Province, Korea. In 1930 he was expelled from the high school he attended in Seoul for protesting Japan's colonial policies, but later studied at Chungan Buddhist College. He became a university teacher and has been publishing poetry—including seven collections—since 1938.

Kate Chopin   (1851–1904) was born in St. Louis, Missouri. At the age of 20, she married a man from New Orleans, and she lived there until her husband's premature death caused her to return to St. Louis and assume in 1887 a career in writing. Chopin gained a national reputation in the 1890s for her local-color tales about Louisiana. These stories were collected in *Bayou Folk* (1894) and *A Night in Acadie* (1897). In 1899, she published a novel, *The Awakening.* Termed by one critic an "American *Madame Bovary,*" this novel about a passionate and independent woman was severely criticized by reviewers and even banned in Chopin's native city.

Judith Ortiz Cofer   (b. 1952) was born in Puerto Rico, and emigrated to the United States four years later. She earned her M.A. in 1977, and then attended Oxford. Her works include a play, *Latin Women Pray,* and four volumes of poetry. Her work has appeared in a variety of publications since the 1970s.

Samuel Taylor Coleridge   (1772–1834) was born in the countryside (Devonshire), but was educated in London. From childhood on, his extraordinary imaginative powers made themselves known and were noted by others. He attended Cambridge University, disliked its monotony, and enlisted impulsively in the British cavalry. Though purchased out of the army by his family and returned to Cambridge, he never took his degree. This pattern of impulsiveness and incompleteness was to recur many times in the course of his life. He met William Wordsworth in 1795, and the two men exercised a stabilizing and stimulating influence on one another. Together they published *Lyrical Ballads* in 1798, one of the most revolutionary documents in English literary history. But soon the radical spirit of youth became more circumspect, and Coleridge espoused—in philosophy, politics, and religion—conservative causes. Sensitive and volatile, he is one of the most beloved poets in English. In "Kubla Khan" (1797), Coleridge uses exotic images to create a world that is both wondrous and sinister. He claimed to have composed it in a dream, as a "psychological curiosity."

Jayne Cortez   (b. 1936), an American Book Award winner in 1980, was born in Arizona and raised in California before moving to New York. Since 1969 she has published seven volumes of poetry, including *Festivals and Funerals* (1971), *Mouth on Paper* (1977), *Coagulations* (1984), and *Maintain Control* (1987).

Stephen Crane   (1871–1900), born in Newark, New Jersey, and educated at Lafayette College and Syracuse University, is a pivotal figure in American fiction, poetry, and journalism—an artist who helped to shape the modern age in literature. Although he died before the age of 29, Crane did more than any other American author to assimilate the European modes of naturalism, impressionism, and sociological realism into our national literature. His novel *Maggie: A Girl of the Streets* (1893) offended the contemporary public with its harsh portrayal of slum life and of a young woman whose life ends in prostitution and death. His short novel about the Civil War, *The Red Badge of Courage* (1895), won for Crane broader and more approving recognition and today is considered a masterpiece of war fiction.

Victor Hernandez Cruz   (b. 1949) was born in Aguas Buenas, Puerto Rico, and grew up in New York City. He has taught at San Francisco State University and at the University of California, Berkeley. Cruz's collections of verse include *Snaps* (1969), *Mainland* (1973), *Tropicalization* (1976), and *Red Beans* (1991). "My mind," comments Cruz, "is creole and can fuse many unlikely things together: outer variety, inner unity; we are an experiment in communications."

Countee Cullen   (1903–1946) grew up in Harlem, the son of a minister. He studied at New York University and Harvard. He was 23 when he published his first volume of poetry, *Color* (1926). Like McKay, Bontemps, Hughes, and others, Cullen was involved in the Harlem Renaissance. However, his principal occupation was teaching French in the New York City schools. Cullen was also an editor of various publications. In 1927 he published *Copper Sun* and *The Ballad of the Brown Girl*. *The Black Christ* followed two years later. Cullen wrote two children's books and a novel, *One Way to Heaven* (1932). A year after his death a collection of selected poems was published, *On These I Stand*.

e.e. cummings   (1894–1962) was an American poet, novelist, playwright, painter, and essayist. Cummings's first published work was his novel *The Enormous Room* (1922), which was considered a modern masterpiece. The plays *HIM* (1927) and *Santa Claus* (1946) came between the poetry. There were seven volumes between *Tulips and Chimneys* (1923) and *Poems 1923–1954* (1954). Cummings, a gifted satirist, nevertheless maintained the rhythmic cadences of natural speech.

Roque Dalton   (1935–1975), born in El Salvador, studied law and social science in his native country as well as in Chile and Mexico. During his studies abroad, Dalton became a Communist. As a result, he was exiled from and imprisoned in El Salvador several times. He was assassinated in May 1975. His works include *La Ventana en el Rostro* (Mexico, 1961), *El Mar* (Havana, 1962), and *Poemas Clandestinos* (1975).

Kamala Das   (b. 1934), poet, short-story writer, and autobiographer, was born in Malabar, India. Urging new roles for Indian women, Das has collected her poetry in *Summer in Calcutta* (1965) and *The Old Playhouse* (1973), among other works.

René Depestre   (b. 1926), born in Haiti, is a frequent contributor to *Presence Africaine* in Paris, and is considered one of the Negritude poets. Among his works are *For the Revolution, For Poetry* (1969) and *A Rainbow for the Christmas West* (1972).

Babette Deutsch   (1895–1982) was born in New York City and began publishing poetry when she was a student at Barnard College. She served as Thorstein Veblen's secretary at the New School for Social Research and married the Russian scholar Avrahm Yarmolinsky, with whom she collaborated on a number of verse translations. Deutsch wrote poetry, criticism, novels, and children's books. She is best known as a poet, a distinctive author who combines a refined intellect with emotional involvement in social and political issues. Much of her work is assembled in *Collected Poems, 1919–1962* (1963).

Emily Dickinson   (1830–1886) was born in Amherst, Massachusetts, the second child of an important local family. She attended Amherst Academy from 1840 to 1847 and spent a year at Mount Hadley Female Seminary, but ill health often forced her to interrupt her education. Aside from brief trips to Boston, Philadelphia, and Washington, Dickinson remained in Amherst all her life. She wrote poems prolifically from 1858 to 1865, but was largely uninterested in publication, arranging her poems in packets and storing them in a box—a cache that would be discovered by her sister, Lavinia, after Emily died. Only with the publication of *The Poems of Emily Dickinson* in 1955 did the bulk of her poetry—some 1,775 items—become available to readers. In much of her greatest poetry, she often deals with loneliness, loss, pain, sorrow, despair, and death. Yet Dickinson commanded many moods: she could be witty, comic, playful, irreverent. Her love lyrics are of the same order as the rest of her poetry—demanding, existing in tension with other felt emotions.

Isak Dinesen   (1985–1962) was born Karen Christentze Dinesen, near Elsinore, Denmark. In 1941 she married her cousin, Baron Boor Blixen, and went to Kenya, the source and site of her finest writing. She published her first collection of stories, *Seven Gothic Tales*, in 1934. Subsequent works include *Out of Africa* (1937), *Winter's Tales* (1942), and *Last Tales* (1957).

John Donne   (1572–1631), the first great English metaphysical poet, came from a Roman Catholic family whose ways he preferred less than those of a man about town. However, after sipping from the cup of the good life, he had a change of heart and converted to Anglicanism. He became dean of St. Paul's Cathedral in 1621. His early works were shaped by satire, irony, and eroticism and are as famous as his later poems, which, with great power and grace, express his desire for a rapprochement with God. Donne's elegies, epigrams, and devotions are an extraordinary examination of sickness and considerations of death.

Rita Dove   (b. 1952) was born in Akron, Ohio, the daughter of African-American parents who had migrated from the South. She received an M.F.A. from the writers' workshop at the University of Iowa and has been a Fulbright, Guggenheim, and National Endowment for the Humanities recipient. Her poetry collections include *The Yellow House on the Corner* (1980), *Museum* (1983), and *Thomas and Beulah* (1986).

Thomas Stearns Eliot   (1888–1965) was born in St. Louis. An outstanding student, he traveled to Europe on an academic fellowship shortly before the start of World War I. He eventually settled in London, where he quickly established himself as a radically innovative poet and an influential and often acerbic critic. He counted among his friends Virginia Woolf, James Joyce, H.D., and Ezra Pound, all important figures in the literary movement known as modernism. His first volume of poetry, *Prufrock and Other Observations,* was published in 1917, but it was his long poem *The Waste Land* (1922) that established him as the leading poet writing in English between the wars, and as the most prominent spokesman for what became known as the "lost generation." He wrote comparatively little lyric poetry after World War II, but instead concentrated on verse drama and on literary and social criticism. His poetry and plays often show a courageous intelligence in confrontation with a deep, seemingly inescapable unhappiness.

Louise Erdrich (b. 1954), of Chippewa and German-American descent, grew up in North Dakota. She now lives in New Hampshire with her husband, the writer Michael Dorris. A poet, essayist, and novelist, Erdrich is the author of *Love Medicine* (1984), *The Beet Queen* (1986), *Tracks* (1988), and with Dorris, *The Crown of Columbus* (1992).

William Faulkner (1897–1962), 1949 winner of the Nobel Prize in literature, was born in New Albany, Mississippi. His family moved to Oxford in 1902, and Faulkner attended the University of Mississippi there. He drew extensively on his family history and the people of the region he would come to make famous in his novels as Yoknapatawpha County. The interrelated problems of race and class are recurring themes in his work. These were, Malcolm Cowley said, "the tragic fable of Southern history." From his first novel, *Soldier's Pay* (1926), to *The Reivers* (1962), Faulkner's stories and novels, some of them difficult to comprehend at first reading, have been lyrical, interior, and brimming with characters and symbolism.

Lawrence Ferlinghetti (b. 1919) emerged first as a poet and publisher in the Beat scene of the 1950s in San Francisco. He founded City Lights Bookstore, which served as both focal point and publishing house for the movement. As a poet, playwright, novelist, and publisher, Ferlinghetti has been active in the struggle for control of our humanity within a society that seeks to make our behavior "normal." In his poem "Overheard Conversations," he defines his concept of poetry: "And still the whole idea of poetry being/to take control of life/out of the hand of/the terrible people." In his poetry Ferlinghetti often employs experimental and shocking language, but always strives to make it as accessible as possible.

Anne Finch (1661–1722) was born the daughter of a Southampton nobleman. By marriage she became the countess of Winchelsea. Her position, interests, and talent kept her in the thick of England's intellectual life, and she earned the respect and admiration of Pope and Swift, with whom she was known to banter in verse epistles. Her range is extensive, touching on the personal and public issues of her day, and some consider her a precursor of romanticism.

Gisele Fong is a third-generation Chinese American born in San Francisco, California. Her poetry has appeared in literary magazines and in the anthology *Making Face, Making Soul.*

Carolyn Forché (b. 1950), poet and political activist, was born in Detroit, Michigan. Her poetry, often reflecting political concerns, is collected in *Gathering the Tribes* (1976), which received the Yale Younger Poets award; and in *The Country Between Us* (1982).

Robert Frost (1875–1963) was born in San Francisco but moved at the age of 11 with his family to the New Hampshire farm country that would become identified with some of his finest poetry. He attended Dartmouth College briefly, leaving to assume a variety of jobs: bobbin boy in a Lawrence mill, shoemaker, newspaper editor, schoolteacher, farmer. Frost wrote poetry in his leisure hours; he published his first poem in 1894. He married in 1895, and after years of largely unsuccessful farming Frost sold his farm and moved his family to England in 1912, risking everything to become a poet. His first book, *A Boy's Will* (1913), was published in England, as well as his second, *North of Boston* (1914), which won critical acclaim. By the time Frost returned to America in 1915, he was a successful and celebrated, if somewhat embarrassed, poet. He won four Pulitzer prizes, for *New Hampshire* (1923), *Collected Poems* (1930), *A Further Range* (1936), and *A Witness Tree* (1942). A poet of the New England soil,

Frost spent the bulk of his mature career on farms in New Hampshire and Vermont, wintering later in his life at a palmetto patch he owned in Florida, and serving intermittently as poet-in-residence at Amherst, Harvard, Michigan, and Dartmouth.

Gabriel García Márquez   (b. 1928) was born in the small town of Aracataca, Colombia, near the Caribbean coastline. He was sent to school in Bogotá, and after his graduation in 1946 studied law. His first collection of stories was *Leaf Storm* (1965). His masterpiece is *One Hundred Years of Solitude* (1967); other novels include *The Autumn of the Patriarch* (1975) and *Love in the Time of Cholera* (1988). He received the Nobel Prize for literature in 1982.

Allen Ginsberg   (b. 1926) was born in Newark, New Jersey. He went to high school in Paterson and graduated in 1948 from Columbia University. At Columbia he published in the *Columbia Review;* there and elsewhere in New York in the late 1940s he participated in the activities of the group that came to be known as the Beat Generation. Ginsberg's travels in Europe, Asia, and South America, his advocacy of Zen Buddhism, of hallucinatory drugs, and of homosexuality, and his involvement in the civil rights campaign, war resistance, and attacks on the C.I.A. have done as much to keep him in the public eye since the appearance of *Howl and Other Poems* (1956) as has his poetry. "Kaddish," a long poem on his mother's illness and death, is perhaps his best known later work. Ginsberg defines his poetry as "Beat-Hip-Gnostic-Imagist." After some early experimentation with rhymed, metrical verse in the style of Thomas Wyatt, he began under the influence of William Carlos Williams to seek a line modeled on speech and breathing patterns. Later, the incantatory verse of Indian mantras strengthened his sense of the importance of parallelism and repetition. Influenced also by the Bible, by William Blake, and by Walt Whitman, Ginsberg strives for a prophetic poetry that embraces the sacred and profane.

Nikki Giovanni   (b. 1943) was born in Nashville, Tennessee, and was raised in Ohio. She received a B.A. in history from Fisk University in 1967 and did graduate work at the University of Pennsylvania. Giovanni was witness to the crises of the 1960s and the problems of her generation. "Blacks made the sixties," she has stated, and much of her poetry from that period deals with the need for revolutionary social change. Giovanni's more recent poetry is introspective, dealing with the basic processes of life and the struggles of the individual self. One of the most popular poets today, Giovanni has published numerous volumes of verse, including *Black Judgment* (1969), *Re-Creation* (1970), *Broadside Poem of Angela Yvonne Davis* (1970), *Gemini* (1971), *My House* (1972), *The Women and the Men* (1975), *Cotton Candy on a Rainy Day* (1978), and *Sacred Cows and Other Edibles* (1988).

Susan Glaspell   (1876–1948), American feminist, playwright, and fiction writer, was born in Davenport, Iowa, of Irish immigrant parents. She helped to found the Provincetown Players, writing the plays *Suppressed Desires* (1915), *Tribes* (1916), *Bernice* (1919), and *Alison's House* (1930), the latter which won a Pulitzer Prize.

Lady Augusta Gregory   (1852–1932), cofounder of the Abbey Theatre and a dramatist, was born in County Galway, Ireland. She wrote more than thirty plays, of which *The Workhouse Ward* (1908), *Spreading the News* (1904), and *The Rising of the Moon* (1907) are the best known.

Anthony Grooms   (b. 1955) was born in Charlottesville, Virginia, and was educated at the College of William and Mary and George Mason University. Also a fiction writer, Grooms teaches at the University of Georgia. He lives in Atlanta.

Lorraine Hansberry   (1930–1965) was born in Chicago, Illinois, into a middle-class African-American family. She moved to New York City in 1950 and began her career as a writer. Her major plays include *A Raisin in the Sun* (1953), which won the New York Drama Critics Award for best play; *The Sign in Sidney Brustein's Window* (1964); and the posthumous *Les Blancs* (1966).

Joy Harjo   (b. 1951), a Native American poet, was born in Tulsa, Oklahoma. Her collected poetry includes *The Last Song* (1975) and *She Had Some Horses* (1983).

Nathaniel Hawthorne   (1804–1869) was born in Salem, Massachusetts. Following graduation from Bowdoin College in Maine in 1825, Hawthorne returned to Salem and entered into a relatively isolated twelve-year period of writing that culminated in the publication of *Twice-Told Tales* in 1837. But it was not until 1850 that Hawthorne achieved fame with the publication of *The Scarlet Letter*. This novel, along with *The House of the Seven Gables* (1851) and his finest short fiction, centers on sin, evil, guilt, and the mysterious—almost supernatural— workings of these forces in human affairs.

Robert Hayden   (1913–1980) was born and raised in the black working-class neighborhoods of Detroit. After attending Wayne State University, he became a professor of English literature at the University of Michigan. As a poet of the black experience, Hayden employed a wide variety of styles and forms—ranging from his early use of colloquial street language to his later, more stylized work with long poems—in order to explore the complexities of his own history. Among his major poetry collections are *A Ballad of Remembrance* (1962) and *Selected Poems* (1966).

Ernest Miller Hemingway   (1899–1961) was born in Oak Park, Illinois, and he died in Ketchum, Idaho. He was for a long time a journalist; in 1954 he won the Nobel Prize in literature. Even during his career as a novelist, story writer, and playwright, Hemingway reported from various parts of the world. It is sometimes difficult to note extreme differences between his dispatches and passages in his fiction, though he believed that the two kinds of writing were distinct. Following World War I, he lived in Europe, where he knew many writers, among them Gertrude Stein, F. Scott Fitzgerald, Wallace Stevens, Morley Callaghan, and Ezra Pound. In 1923 he published *Three Stories and Ten Poems,* which was followed the next year by a collection of stories, *In Our Time. The Torrents of Spring* and *The Sun Also Rises* (1926), both novels, came next. *The Sun Also Rises* established "his reputation and set him, at the age of 26, in the limelight which he both enjoyed and resented for the rest of his life," wrote critic Philip Young.

George Herbert   (1593–1633), who was born into an illustrious and pious Anglo-Welsh family, was educated at Cambridge University. He was appointed reader in rhetoric in 1618 and was public orator from 1620 to 1627. Herbert was elected to Parliament in 1624, but in 1626 he debarred himself from civil service by taking minor religious orders; he was ordained a priest in 1630. A friend of John Donne and Francis Bacon, Herbert chose "to lose himself in an humble way," serving as a pious and charitable country parson. Aware early in 1633 that he was dying of consumption, Herbert readied a copy of his book, *The Temple*, for publication. The religious lyrics in this miscellany, which also includes hymns, prayers, and Church history, are varied in verse forms, but clear, concise, and natural in diction.

Robert Herrick   (1591–1674) was born in London of a middle-class family. He served for ten years as an apprentice goldsmith to his uncle, Sir William Herrick. Educated at St. John's College, Cambridge, and Trinity Hall, he later accepted a clerical position and lived his life as a bachelor in Devonshire (1629–1647). In terms of his poetic style, Herrick is usually classified with the Cavaliers—poets who wrote during the reign of Charles I. Other Cavaliers included Thomas Carew, Sir John Suckling, and Richard Lovelace. Early in his career, Herrick was greatly influenced by Ben Jonson. However, poems such as "To the Virgins, to Make Much of Time" and "Delight in Disorder" reveal him to be a less didactic and more playful poet than Jonson. Herrick's major collection, *Hesperides,* was published in 1648 and contained over 1,200 sacred and secular poems.

Gerard Manley Hopkins (1844–1889) was the eldest son in a middle-class, Anglican family. His childhood was apparently uneventful, but he blossomed intellectually at Oxford, where he studied with Walter Pater and was befriended by John (later Cardinal) Newman. With Newman's sponsorship and against the wishes of his family, he converted to Catholicism in 1866. Two years later he entered the Jesuit order and, in a dramatic gesture, burned the final copy of all his early poems. At this point in his life he feared that the aesthetic and the religious might not be reconcilable. Six years later, however, with the encouragement of his prefect, he wrote a long poem to honor five nuns drowned in a shipwreck and continued to write from then on. Hopkins spent his life as a teacher and as a priest, serving many different communities, some of which were poor and isolated. He made only halfhearted attempts to have his poetry published in his lifetime.

Henry Howard (1515–1547), son of the powerful duke of Norfolk, had a tumultuous youth, full of the customary pastimes of young aristocrats—vigorous games, traveling, and wenching. Along the way, he also acquired a first-rate education at the hands of private tutors. Fierce and absurdly proud, he almost had his right hand chopped off for striking a courtier; eventually, he was beheaded for suspicion of treason. With Thomas Wyatt, he helped establish the sonnet in English, and he was the first poet to publish in blank verse.

James Langston Hughes (1902–1967) was born of black American and Cherokee ancestry in Joplin, Missouri, and raised in Kansas, Illinois, and Ohio. He was elected class poet in grammar school in Lincoln, Illinois, and again in high school in Ohio. Hughes attended Columbia University briefly and then roamed the world as a seaman, traveling to Africa and Europe before returning to the United States to complete his education at Lincoln University. Hughes then moved back to New York and settled in Harlem. Best known for his poetry and for his stories of Simple, Hughes also wrote journalism, opera librettos, plays and television scripts, and was a notable anthologist of black writing. His poetry reveals a keen ear for folk vernacular, and he is a major experimenter in verse technique in his use of music rhythms. It is deceptively simple and casual, but beneath the simplicity of colloquial statement there are undercurrents of humor and irony, of social criticism, and of compassion for the gallery of figures that Hughes draws. Much of Hughes's most memorable poetry deals with the history and experience of black Americans and with the struggle against hate and oppression. Among his collections of poetry are *Weary Blues* (1926), *Fine Clothes to the Jew* (1927), *The Dream Keeper* (1932), *Shakespeare in Harlem* (1942), *Fields of Wonder* (1947), *One Way Ticket* (1949), *Montage of a Dream Deferred* (1951), and *Ask Your Mama* (1961).

David Henry Hwang (b. 1957), the son of Chinese-American immigrants, attended Stanford University, where he wrote plays as an undergraduate. Among his plays are *FOB* (1981), recipient of the Obbie Award; *Family Devotions* (1982); and *M. Butterfly* (1988), which won a Tony Award as best play.

Henrik Ibsen (1828–1906) was born in the little seaport town of Skien on the picturesque southern coast of Norway. His father was a successful merchant until 1836, when the family fortune was lost and the Ibsens had to retire to a small farm. At 15 Ibsen became an apothecary's assistant in Grimstad, where during that time he tried writing without success. In 1850, however, through the influence of Ole Bull, the famous violinist, Ibsen was appointed a "theater poet" at the Bergen Theater. Here he served his apprenticeship as reader, stage manager, playwright, and director. (His first play, *Love's Comedy*, was staged there in 1862.) Ibsen married Susannah Thoresen, who was devoted to furthering his career. A government stipend allowed them to move to Rome and later, to Dresden. Recognition came to Ibsen when *Brand* (1866) was staged, followed the next year by *Peer Gynt*. Both were written in verse. However, by the time *A Doll's House* was staged (1879), poetry had given way to prose, and

Ibsen had become a "social dramatist" and the "father of modern drama." *Ghosts* (1881) and *An Enemy of the People* (1882) were frontal assaults on marriage and convention, as were the rest of Ibsen's plays. Ibsen simplified dramatic technique, gaining greater compactness of plot; he discarded monologues and asides and episodic movement. Wrote Ibsen: "I look upon it as my appointed task to use the talents God has given me in rousing my countrymen from their lethargy and making them see the import of the great life problems."

Yussef Idriss   (b. 1927) is an Egyptian short story writer and playwright, one of the major literary figures in the Arab world. Trained as a physician, he gave up his profession in the 1970s to work as a journalist, playwright, critic, and story writer. Influenced by Gorky, Kafka, and Faulkner, Idriss combines their psychological techniques with the oral traditions of Egyptian life.

Lawson Fusao Inada   (b. 1938), born a third-generation Japanese American *(Sansei)* in Fresno, California, was once host of a radio program "Talk Story: The Written Word," in Ashland, Oregon. His work has appeared in many publications, and he is the coeditor of *AIIIEEEEE: An Anthology of Asian American Writers* (1974). He is also the author of the poetry volume *Before the War* (1972).

Shirley Jackson   (1919–1965) was born in San Francisco and educated at Syracuse University. She married the literary critic Stanley Edgar Hyman; they lived in Bennington, Vermont, where her husband taught at Bennington College. Jackson is the heiress of Poe in her talent for tales and novels of Gothic horror. What distinguishes her from Poe is her ability to modernize Gothic conventions, locating in apparently "normal" contemporary events and situations a highly convincing realm of shock, violence, and terror. Her novels include *Life Among the Savages* (1945), *Hangsman* (1951), *The Bird's Nest* (1954), *The Haunting of Hill House* (1959), and *We Have Always Lived in the Castle* (1962). Jackson's short fiction is collected in *The Lottery* (1944) and *The Magic of Shirley Jackson* (1966).

Randall Jarrell   (1914–1965) was born in Nashville, Tennessee, and received degrees in psychology and English from Vanderbilt University. During World War II, he served as an air control tower operator. Noted as much for his translations and criticism as for his poetry, Jarrell in 1956 was appointed a consultant in poetry at the Library of Congress. He also served as an editor for *The Nation, Partisan Review,* and *Yale Review.* Robert Lowell said that Jarrell was "the most heartbreaking . . . poet of his generation."

Ben Jonson   (1572–1637), dramatist, poet, and literary critic, was one of the greatest writers of the English Renaissance; among his contemporaries, he was more influential than Shakespeare or Donne. Born a few months after his clergyman father's death, into impoverished circumstances, Jonson somehow managed to attend the most noted school of the period—Westminster—and to study language and literature under the famous schoolmaster William Camden. No "mouse of the scrolls," Jonson worked as a bricklayer, a soldier (he killed an enemy in single combat), and finally as an actor and playwright. Jonson's finest comedies are *Volpone* (1606) and *The Alchemist* (1610). As a poet, Jonson preferred the "plain," or "native," style. Throughout his life, he looked to the masterpieces of antiquity for inspiration. In 1616 he published his *Works,* which showed a flawless command of all the genres of the ancient world—epigram, lyric, satire, tragedy, and comedy.

June Jordan   (b. 1936), poet, journalist, and novelist, was born in Harlem. She attended Barnard College and the University of Chicago and since 1975 has been a professor at the City University of New York. Committed to what she terms "the politics of survival and change," Jordan is a literary figure constantly giving poetry readings at schools and institutions around the nation, attempting to combat "the cult of negative realism" that she says affects the country's youth. Her poetry collections include *Some Changes* (1971), *New Days: Poems of Exile* *and Return* (1973), and *Selected Poems of June Jordan: Things That I Do in the Dark* (1977). Jordan's poems are short and structurally tight.

James Joyce (1882–1941) was born in Dublin, Ireland, a city and a country standing at the center of this literary universe. Living much of his adult life in self-imposed exile, Joyce produced a series of works in fiction, progressively more experimental in technique and vision, that established him as one of the great literary modernists of the twentieth century: *Dubliners* (1914), *A Portrait of the Artist as a Young Man* (1916), *Ulysses* (1922), and *Finnegan's Wake* (1939). Joyce was a brilliant, daring, and provocative stylist, willing to break new literary ground and to assault popular taste and conventions, notably in his treatment of human sexuality—a habit that resulted in the censorship of his masterpiece, *Ulysses*, for more than a decade.

Franz Kafka (1883–1924) was born in Prague, Czech Republic. He received a law degree from the German University in Prague in 1906 and worked subsequently in the Austrian civil service. Kafka devoted his life to writing, but at the time of his death, he directed his friend and literary executor, Max Brod, to burn all his manuscripts. Instead Brod saw Kafka's novels—*The Trial* (1925), *The Castle* (1926), and *Amerika* (1927)—and many of his short stories through production. Kafka's fiction projects a distinctive tone of the uncanny—of life and reality that tend to shift away from our ability to understand them. Typically, Kafka's protagonists embark on quests for meaning but are frustrated and ultimately alienated by the process. In many ways, Kafka's fiction captures the absurdities of modern life and the futility of seeking any lasting meaning in the twentieth century. His stories in English can be found in *The Great Wall of China* (1933), *A Franz Kafka Miscellany* (1940), *The Penal Colony* (1948), *Parables and Paradoxes* (1963), and *The Complete Stories* (1976).

Yasunari Kawabata (1899–1972), born in Osaka, became Japan's first recipient of the Nobel Prize for literature, in 1968. An orphan since infancy and a writer since high school, Kawabata was celebrated for his highly poetic short fiction and novels. His work includes *Snow Country* (1947), *Thousand Cranes* (1959), and *Palm-of-Hand Stories* (1988).

John Keats (1795–1821) was born at Finsbury, north of London, the eldest of five children. His father was killed by a fall from his horse in 1804, and when his mother remarried the same year, the children were sent to their maternal grandparents at Enfield and, later, Edmonton. In 1815, Keats went to London for medical training. He published his first poetry the following year and met many notable literary figures, including Shelley; by 1817, he had abandoned his plans for a medical career. Keats published his first collection, *Poems*, in 1817 and *Endymion* in 1818. In 1818, Keats contracted a severe sore throat during a walking tour in Scotland; he also met 18-year-old Fanny Brawne, with whom he began an affair. Keats wrote all of his major odes, including "To Autumn," in 1819; by the end of the year, his sore throat had recurred. Following hemorrhaging and an attack of blood spitting in the first half of 1820, Keats upon his doctor's advice sailed for Italy in September. *The Eve of St. Agnes and Other Poems* was published that year.

Maurice Kenny, twice nominated for the Pulitzer Prize in poetry, is the author of eighteen volumes of poetry, including *Between Two Rivers: Selected Poems, Tekonwatonti; Molly Brant, Poems of War*, and *Second Thought: A Compilation of Writings*, all published in 1992. A member of the Mohawk tribe, he is a 1984 American Book Award winner.

Jamaica Kincaid (b. 1949) was born Elaine Potter Richardson in Antigua, West Indies. Now a resident of Bennington, Vermont, she is the author of a series of fiction—*At the Bottom of the River* (1983), *Annie John* (1985), *Lucy* (1990)—exploring the impact of Caribbean culture on women's lives.

Maxine Kumin (b. 1925) was born in Philadelphia and received her B.A. and M.A. degrees from Radcliffe College. She began writing children's stories and light verse while pregnant with her third child in 1953. Since that time, she has published more than a dozen books of poetry, novels, and children's fiction. She won the Pulitzer Prize for poetry in 1973 for *Up Country* (1972). While noted for her close attention to objective details, Kumin has a talent for transforming her images into unique, sometimes grotesque statements about the processes of life.

David Herbert Lawrence   (1885–1930), the son of a coalminer and a former schoolteacher, was born in Eastwood, Nottinghamshire, England. Raised in England's industrial midlands and exposed to fierce tensions within his family life, Lawrence used these twin realities to achieve his first literary recognition with *Sons and Lovers* (1913). Thereafter, his daring, inventive, and prolific literary production; his iconoclastic personal life; and his idiosyncratic search for pure alternatives to the crassness and dehumanization of English industrial and social life made Lawrence an international literary figure. Among his significant works are *The Rainbow* (1915), *Twilight in Italy* (1916), *Women in Love* (1920), *Studies in Classic American Literature* (1923), *Lady Chatterly's Lover* (1928), *The Complete Stories* (1961), and *Complete Poems* (1964).

David Leavitt   (b. 1961) grew up in Palo Alto, California, where his father taught at Stanford University. He graduated from Yale University in 1983, and began publishing fiction in *The New Yorker, Harper's,* and elsewhere. In 1989, his first collection of stories, *Family Dancing*, was nominated for the National Book Critics Circle Award. His second collection is *A Place I've Never Been* (1990).

Doris Lessing   (b. 1919) was born in Kermanshah, Iran, and moved at an early age to a large farm in Southern Rhodesia. Escaping the loneliness and isolation of African farm life, she moved to Salisbury at the age of 18, entering quickly into artistic and political life there, joining the Communist party, and marrying the first of two husbands. (Both marriages ended in divorce.) She left Africa for London in 1949, and in 1950 she published her first novel, *The Grass Is Singing*. Her fiction since then, increasingly experimental in mode, has focused on the violence and political disorders of modern life and especially on the plight of contemporary women. Lessing's novels include *A Proper Marriage* (1954), *Retreat to Innocence* (1956), *A Ripple from the Storm* (1958), *The Golden Notebook* (1962), *Briefing for a Descent into Hell* (1971), and the tetralogy *Canopus in Argos: Archives* (1981). Her stories, many of the best drawn from her African experience, have been collected in *This Was the Old Chief's Country* (1951), *The Habit of Loving* (1957), *A Man and Two Women* (1963), *African Stories* (1963), and *Stories* (1978).

Denise Levertov   (b. 1923) was born in Ilford, Essex, England, and served as a nurse during World War II. She came to the United States in 1948 after her marriage to an American, the writer Mitchell Goodman; she has been an American citizen since 1955. Levertov acknowledges, "Marrying an American and coming to live here while still young was very stimulating to me as a writer for it necessitated the finding of new rhythms in which to write, in accordance with new rhythms of life and speech." Influenced by William Carlos Williams and Wallace Stevens, and profiting from contact with other leading contemporary poets, notably Charles Olson and Robert Duncan, Levertov seeks to capture what she terms "authentic experience" in verse. She is the author of more than a dozen volumes of poetry, including *With Eyes at the Back of Our Heads* (1960), *To Stay Alive* (1971), and *Life in the Forest* (1979). Levertov's best poetry is, in the words of Kenneth Rexroth, "clear, sparse, immediate, and vibrant."

Philip Levine   (b. 1928) was born and educated in Detroit, Michigan. After graduating from Wayne State University and working a variety of jobs, he located in Fresno, California, where he taught until retirement in 1992. He has received numerous awards, including two Pulitzers. His last of several volumes of poetry is *What Work Is* (1991).

Shirley Geok-lin Lim   was born and reared in Malacca, Malaysia. She studied at Brandeis University and has taught in the United States on both the East and West coasts since 1973.

Her first collection of poems, *Crossing the Peninsula* (1980), won the Commonwealth Poetry Prize, the first time ever won by a woman and an Asian. Two other volumes of poems have since followed.

Audre Lorde (1934–1992) was born in New York City. Self-described as "black, lesbian, mother, and cancer survivor," she published more than twelve books of poetry and non-fiction before her illness overcame her. Typical of her poetry is the collection *New York Head Shop and Museum* (1975). For many years she taught English at Hunter College of the City University of New York.

Amy Lowell (1874–1925) was born into an illustrious Boston family. As a child and young woman she often traveled to Europe, and at the age of 28, she began to write poetry. Her first volume of verse was fairly conventional, but in 1913 she met Ezra Pound and became part of the imagist movement, which she eventually dominated. She spent the last years of her life writing a biographical study of the poet John Keats. Lowell's version of imagism tempers the hard, objective, impersonal focus on a single image with a more subjective caring about the emotions of love and disappointment.

Robert Lowell (1917–1977), described by John Berryman as "a talent whose ceiling is invisible," was one of the major innovators in contemporary American poetry. Born in Boston, the great-grandnephew of James Russell Lowell, he attended Harvard University and Kenyon College. Lowell converted to Catholicism in 1940, the same year that he married the first of his three wives, novelist Jean Stafford. (His other wives, Elizabeth Hardwick and Caroline Blackwood, were also writers.) He was a conscientious objector during World War II and served a prison term for violation of the Selective Service Act. Lowell's New England heritage, his personal experience, his Catholicism, his family, and his political and historical awareness were the forces that shaped his poetry. *Lord Weary's Castle* (1946) was awarded the Pulitzer Prize in 1947; *Life Studies* (1959), the National Book Award; *Invitations* (1961), the Bollinger Translation Prize. Each of these volumes measures Lowell's progress as an experimental poet: from formal, tightly rhymed lines; to free verse; to adaptations from poets in other languages.

Mairi MacInnes was born in the north of England and educated in Yorkshire and at Oxford. She has worked as an advertising copywriter, editor, teacher, truck driver, and cook; and is married, with three children. She has lived in the United States for 25 years, as well as in Germany, Spain, and Mexico. MacInnes is author of *Admit One*, a novel; *Splinters*, verse; an anthology on censorship; a dictionary; and poems and articles.

Andrew Marvell (1621–1678), the son of an Anglican clergyman, studied at Cambridge University, served as an assistant to Milton, and was a member of Parliament from 1659 until his death. He was famous in his own time as a political satirist in both prose and poetry. However, his greatest poems express diverse attitudes, ranging from seductive Cavalier lyrics, such as "To His Coy Mistress," to deeply contemplative poems.

Bobbie Ann Mason (b. 1940) was born in Mayfield, Kentucky. Educated at the University of Kentucky and the University of Connecticut (Ph.D.), Mason has established herself as a major short story writer and novelist. She is the author of *Shiloh and Other Stories* (1962), *In Country* (1985), and *Love Life* (1990), among other works.

Annette M'Baye (b. 1927), born in Sokhone, Senegal, has worked as a teacher in Senegal and in Paris. Active for many years in radio and journalism, she is currently with Radio Senegal and serves as editor-in-chief of *Awa: Journal of the Black Woman*.

Claude McKay (1890–1948) was born in Jamaica, West Indies. Primarily a poet, McKay was a ranking figure of the Harlem Renaissance, which was one element of the entire post-World War I renaissance of American letters. After publishing two volumes of poetry in the

West Indies, McKay came to the United States in 1912. A lukewarm supporter of the new Communist society in Russia, he was disillusioned after a visit there. Two additional volumes of verse, *Spring in New Hampshire and Other Poems* (1920) and *Harlem Shadows* (1922), preceded his popular novels, *Home to Harlem* (a best-seller, 1922), *Banjo* (1929), and *Banana Bottom* (1933).

Ifeanyi Menkiti   (b. 1940), was born in Onitsha, Nigeria, and educated at Columbia University and Pomona College. He has published in the United States and abroad in a variety of publications. His novel *Affirmations* was published in 1971, and a book of poetry, *The Jubilation of Falling Bodies*, in 1978. Menkiti's subtext in his poetry is often a recapitulation of African history. He is an English professor at Wellesley College.

Josephine Miles   (1911–1985) was born in Chicago, descended from a family which came to America aboard the *Mayflower*. Miles took an undergraduate degree at UCLA and a doctorate at the University of California, Berkeley; she joined the Berkeley faculty in 1940, becoming university professor emerita in 1978. A noted scholar, especially of the metaphysical poets, Miles in her own finest verse is simple, factual, and incisive. Like William Carlos Williams, she seeks to render through the national vision the commonplace occurrences of American life. Much of her important work is collected in *Poems, 1930–1960.*

Arthur Miller   (b. 1915) was born in New York and decided that he wanted to be a writer while working in a warehouse after graduating from high school. He read *The Brothers Karamazov* during his lunch breaks, and that reading convinced him to enroll at the University of Michigan, where he began his playwriting career. He had some success at Ann Arbor and then returned to New York, where he wrote a novel, *Focus* (1945), whose subject was racism. His first major success was the play *All My Sons* (1947), which was followed two years later by the Pulitzer Prize-winning play *Death of a Salesman*. Miller continued his success with *The Crucible* (1953) and with *A View from the Bridge* (1955). From one of his short stories, the film *The Misfits* (1961) was made, starring his wife Marilyn Monroe, who also figured, it is believed, in Miller's 1964 play, *After the Fall. I Don't Need You Anymore* (1967) and *The Creation of the World and Other Businesses* (1972) are story collections. *Death of a Salesman*, wrote William Rose Benet, "exemplified Miller's contention that tragedy is possible in modern theatre and that its proper hero is the common man."

Czeslaw Milosz   (b. 1911), Polish poet, essayist, novelist, and Nobel Prize in literature recipient, was born in Lithuania. He fought against the Nazis in World War II, then came to America. He teaches at the University of California at Berkeley. His translated poetry appears in *Bells in Winter* (1978), *Collected Poems* (1988), and other volumes.

John Milton   (1608–1674) was born in London of an upper-middle-class father who was employed as a notary. He took a B.A. at Cambridge in 1629 and an M.A. in 1632. He began his literary career in earnest with the writing of *Comus* in 1634. By 1641 he was involved in the religious and political disputes that would result in the execution of King Charles I and the imposition of the Cromwell government, both of which he enthusiastically supported. His greatest work is *Paradise Lost* (1667), in which he sets out "to justify the ways of God to man." This rigorous Puritan composed the work while blind and poor.

Janice Mirikitani,   as a child was interned or "camped" by the U.S. government, though she was an American, because she was of Japanese descent. She studied at UCLA and San Francisco State University. Mirikitani has been publishing for more than twenty years. Her most recent works are *Awake in the River* (1982) and *Shedding Silence* (1987).

Marianne Moore   (1887–1972) was born in St. Louis and educated at Bryn Mawr. After teaching at a government Indian school in Pennsylvania, she moved to New York and worked at a variety of literary jobs. Her poetry won a steady stream of awards and prizes. Though Moore's life was uncomplicated and uneventful, her poetry, while at times despairing, never expresses boredom. She lived most of her life like a "church mouse," sharing apartments with her mother. They had little money, and Moore indulged herself with two pleasures. She loved zoos and filled her poetry with exotic fauna. She was also a devotee of baseball, with its "miracles of dexterity." Moore's poetry often possesses a satiric sense of the absurd.

Patricia Mora   (b. 1942) was born in El Paso, Texas, of Mexican-American ancestry. A teacher and college administrator, she has published the poetry collections *Chants* (1984) and *Borders* (1986).

Nancy Morejón   (b. 1944), one of the most distinguished poets of Cuba, was born in Havana. After studies in French language and literature at the university there, she began to write poetry that, over the years, has resulted in a prodigious amount of work. She is known throughout Latin America and elsewhere.

Bharati Mukherjee   (b. 1940) was born in Calcutta, India. She emigrated to Canada and then to the United States, where her short stories and novels have received critical acclaim. Her most recent novel, *Jasmine* (1991), is a brilliant portrayal of the absurdities of the immigrant experience.

Alice Munro   (b. 1931) grew up on a farm in Ontario, Canada. She began publishing short stories while a student at the University of Western Ontario. Her award-winning books include *Dance of the Happy Shades* (1968), *Something I've Been Meaning to Tell You* (1974), and *The Progress of Love* (1987). Her fiction of rural life are reminiscent of the stories of Flannery O'Connor and Eudora Welty.

David Mura   is a third-generation Japanese American. He is both a poet and an essayist who has published widely in *The Nation, The New Republic,* and *The American Poetry Review.* His poetry is collected in *After We Lost Our Way* (1989).

Rasipuraun Krishaswami Narayan   (b. 1906) was born in Madras, India, and today is India's most famous writer of fiction in English. He has published almost two dozen novels and short-story collections, including *Lawley Road* (1967) and *Under the Banyon Tree* (1985). Much of his fiction is set in the imaginary village of Malgusi.

Gloria Naylor   (b. 1950) was born in New York City. She worked as a missionary for Jehovah's Witnesses from 1968 to 1975, before studying at Brooklyn College and New York University. Her first novel, tracing the interconnected lives of African-American women—*The Women of Brewster Place,* 1982—won the American Book Award for best first novel. *Linden Hills* (1985) and *Mama Day* (1988) are two additional novels.

Carlos Nejar   (b. 1939) was born and lives in southern Brazil. Since his first book was published in 1960, he has received several major Brazilian literary awards and distinctions. His volumes of poetry include: *Sélesis* (1960), *Livro de Silbion* (1963), *Livro do Tempo* (1965), *O Campêador e o Vento* (1966), *Danações* (1969), *Ordenações* (1971), *Canga: Jesualdo Monte* (1971), and *Casa dos Arreios* (1974).

Pablo Neruda   (1904–1973), Chilean poet, essayist, short-story writer, and dramatist, is regarded as a major modern Latin American literary figure. He was honored with the Nobel Prize for Literature in 1971. His poetry, for which he is most famous, ranges from his early traditional verse to surrealism in the 1930s and to direct political poetry (Neruda was a Marxist) in later years. His principal works include *Residencia en la Tierra* (1937), *Selected Poems* (1970), and *New Poems* (1972).

Flannery O'Connor   (1925–1964) was born in Savannah, Georgia. She attended Georgia State College for Women, where her fondness for drawing cartoons and caricatures hinted at some of her future fiction methods. Awarded a fellowship to the Writers Workshop of the

University of Iowa, she received an M.F.A. in creative writing in 1947. Following a brief stay in New York and Connecticut, O'Connor returned to Georgia, living on her mother's farm in Milledgeville. In 1950, she learned that she had the same disease—disseminated lupus—that had killed her father; the last fourteen years of her life involved a painful battle with that illness. O'Connor wrote two novels, *Wise Blood* (1951) and *The Violent Bear It Away* (1960). Her short stories, three of which won O. Henry first prizes, are collected in *A Good Man Is Hard to Find* (1955) and *Everything That Rises Must Converge* (1965).

Simon J. Ortiz   (b. 1941) is a member of the Acoma Pueblo in New Mexico. He received his master's degree from the University of Iowa. His book *From Sand Creek* won the Pushcart Prize in 1982.

Wilfred Owen   (1893–1918), a native of Liverpool, England, and a graduate of London University, was killed on the western front just seven days before the armistice that ended World War I. He never lived to see the publication of a projected collection of verse whose subject would be, he declared in a note, "war and the pity of war." His *Collected Poems* was published in 1920 by a friend and fellow poet, Siegfried Sassoon, whom Owen had met in a military hospital. Although he won the Military Cross, Owen once asked, "am I not myself a conscientious objector with a very seared conscience?" His most powerful poems, which were written during his thirteen months of service in France, convey Owen's opposition to war and to the false idealism spawned by it.

Grace Paley   (b. 1922) was born and raised in New York City. She taught creative writing at a number of colleges before settling in at Sarah Lawrence. Of her stories Philip Roth writes that she possesses "an understanding of loneliness, lust, selfishness, and fatigue that is splendidly comic and unladylike . . . and a style whose toughness and bumpiness arise not only out of exasperation with the language, but the daring and heart of a genuine writer of prose." Paley's stories are collected in two volumes, *The Little Disturbances of Man* (1959) and *Enormous Changes at the Last Minute* (1975).

Nicanor Parra   (b. 1914), a poet and a physicist, was born in Chile, where he was influenced by the folklore of his country. Later, he came to admire the Beat poets of the 1950s. His volumes include *Poems and Antipoems* and *Emergency Poems*.

Octavio Paz   (b. 1914), Mexican poet, is concerned with the contradictions between eternal being and existence in time. He has a great lyrical gift. His masterpiece is the cyclical *Piedra de sol* (Sun Stone, 1958). His social involvement began with the Spanish Civil War. His *Laberinto de la soledad* (The Labyrinth of Solitude, 1962) examines the role of Mexico in history and the importance of its double ancestry and double heritage of civilization from the Spaniards and the Indians.

Katherine Philips   (1631–1664) was the daughter of a wealthy London businessman. She was educated in Hackney, and at the age of 16 she married a prestigious man of 54. Though her husband was a strict Puritan and a supporter of Cromwell, she herself embraced more genial and open forms of religion and government. A noted translator and accomplished poet, she was widely admired throughout England as the "English Sappho" and was the founder of a literary salon that included Cowley and Vaughan. Her collected verses appeared in a pirated version in 1664.

Luigi Pirandello   (1867–1936) was born in Girgenti, Italy, and was educated at Palermo, Rome, and the University of Bonn, in Germany. He was a professor of Italian literature at the Normal College for Women in Rome for approximately thirty years. Perhaps best known as a playwright, Pirandello did not begin writing for the stage until he was 46. Prior to that time, he gained a considerable reputation as a novelist and short story writer. His most famous play, *Six Characters in Search of an Author,* was published in 1921. His fiction works include *The Late*

Mattia Pascal (1904) and *One, None and a Hundred Thousand* (1926). Pirandello's stories, numbering in the hundreds, have been published in English under the titles *Horse in the Moon* (1932), *Better Think Twice about It* (1935), and *The Medals and Other Stories* (1939). He was the 1934 recipient of the Nobel Prize in literature.

Sylvia Plath   (1932–1963) was born in Boston, Massachusetts, and educated at Smith College and Cambridge University. At Cambridge she met and married the English poet Ted Hughes, with whom she had two children. Her style in the first and only volume of poetry that she published in her lifetime, *Colossus* (1960), is elegant and classically controlled, dominated by images and metaphors exploring the relationship between the poet and her world. Plath's later poetry, assembled notably in the posthumous volume *Ariel* (1965), reveals a preoccupation with psychic strain and death—painful warnings perhaps of her own suicide. This motif also dominates an autobiographical novel, *The Bell Jar* (1971).

Edgar Allan Poe   (1809–1849), who invented the modern detective story and contributed to the early development of both short fiction and science fiction, is a unique figure in American literary history. Born Edgar Poe in Boston, he was orphaned in 1811 by the death of his mother; subsequently he was taken in by the John Allans of Richmond, Virginia, and rechristened Edgar Allan Poe. The scandal of his drinking and gambling at the University of Virginia ultimately alienated Poe from Allan and hastened his departure from college life. After a brief education at West Point, shortened again by his debauchery and gambling, Poe in 1836 married his cousin Virginia Clemm, who was then 13. Thereafter, Poe's life became a constant struggle to support his family; he wrote stories and poems and was an editor, journalist, and reviewer. His wife died in 1847. Two years later, Poe was found unconscious in a Baltimore street; he died on December 7, 1849. Poe's influence as a poet, critic, and short-story writer has been significant. His best stories—"The Fall of the House of Usher," "William Wilson," "The Purloined Letter," and "The Cask of Amontillado," among others—did much to establish that unity of effect that Poe espoused as the hallmark of modern short fiction. Poe, of course, specialized in what he termed in *Tales of the Grotesque and Arabesque* (1940) the "terrors of the soul."

Estela Portillo   (b. 1936), was born in El Paso, Texas. She has been a teacher, college administrator, theater and television director, novelist, and practicing playwright. Her works include *Day of the Swallows* (1972) and *For Juana and Other Plays* (1983).

Ezra Loomis Pound   (1885–1972) was born in Haily, Idaho, and studied at the University of Pennsylvania and Hamilton College. He moved to Europe and became a permanent resident of Italy in 1924. His first collection of poems, *A Lume Spento* (1908), was published when he was 23. Pound was drawn to medieval and Renaissance literature, translating several works from those periods. He was a forceful critic and commentator and one of the guiding lights behind the imagist movement in England and America, which involved T. E. Hulme, Hilda Doolittle, William Carlos Williams, Amy Lowell, and others. In addition to the *Cantos* (1925, 1930, 1940, 1948, and 1956), Pound produced many poetic and prose works. He was arrested and detained after World War II for collaborating with the Italian fascists.

Alexander (Sergeyevich) Pushkin   (1799–1837), a multifaceted writer, became known as the "Father of the Russian Language" because he preferred the language of the people to the French most of the Russian nobility spoke. He was the great-grandson of an African general serving under Peter the Great. Pushkin wrote *Eugene Onegin, Boris Godunov, Mozart and Salieri*, and several other works considered classics.

Ibn Quzman,   like Al-Tutili, lived out his life sometime during the Age of the Caliphs (A.D. 632–1050). While the latter indicates a world weariness in his work, Quzman displays a sharp sense of humor.

Rahel [Blaustein] (1890–1931) emigrated to Palestine from Russia in the early 1900s. She helped to develop the *kibbutzim,* the communal agricultural settlements that flourished in modern Israel. After study in Europe, Rahel returned to Palestine and there died of tuberculosis.

Ishmael (Scott) Reed (b. 1938), poet, novelist, filmmaker, producer, playwright, and editor, is probably foremost among those collecting and publishing multiethnic writings, largely through a variety of his own publications. Reed has published nine novels and six volumes of poems, and has been nominated for the Pulitzer Prize in both poetry and fiction.

Roberto Fernandez Retamar (b. 1930) was born in Havana, Cuba. Retamar published his first collection, *Poetry Reunited,* in 1966; and while continuing to publish, was active in organizing the annual Cuban Premio Casa Awards that recognize writers in Spanish, Portuguese, English, and French.

Adrienne Rich (b. 1929) was born in Baltimore, Maryland, and received her B.A. from Radcliffe College in 1951, the same year that her first book of poems, *A Change of World,* was published. She has taught at several colleges and universities, including Swarthmore, Columbia, City College of New York, and Brandeis. Rich has received numerous awards for her poetry, among them two Guggenheim Fellowships and the National Book Award for *Diving into the Wreck* (1973). Her other volumes include *The Diamond Cutters* (1955), *Snapshots of a Daughter-in-Law* (1963), *Necessities of Life* (1966), *Poems: Selected and New, 1950–1974* (1975), *Times Power* (1988), and *Atlas of the Difficult World* (1991). A determined feminist, Rich has written: "To be a woman at this time is to know extraordinary forms of anger, joy, impatience, love, and hope."

Edward Arlington Robinson (1869–1935) was born in Head Tide and grew up in Gardiner, both barren Maine towns. He remembered his childhood as unhappy and was able to attend Harvard for only two years before the death of his father and the failure of the family business made further education impossible. He published his first volume of poetry at his own expense ($52) and soon after moved to New York to make writing his career. One of his later books of poetry came to the attention of President Theodore Roosevelt, who praised and aided Robinson. Robinson's popular reputation continued to grow during his lifetime, and today he has a firm place as a significant modern poet. Like Robert Frost, he usually writes about New England, but instead of describing a scene in nature, Robinson uses dramatic monologues to sketch New England character types: drunks, unemployed dreamers, unconventional misfits.

Theodore Roethke (1908–1963) was born in Saginaw, Michigan, and received his education at the University of Michigan and Harvard. As a boy, Roethke worked and played around his parents' greenhouses, among the most famous in America and the center of some of his finest poems. His career began with *Open House* (1941). His second volume, *The Lost Son and Other Poems,* was published in 1948, shortly after he joined the faculty at the University of Washington. *The Waking: Poems 1933–1953* won the Pulitzer Prize in 1953, and *Words for the Wind: The Collected Verse of Theodore Roethke* (1958) won the National Book Award. In 1964 he received a second National Book Award for his posthumous volume, *The Far Field.*

Christina Rossetti (1830–1894) was born in London, 12 years after her brother, Dante Gabriel Rossetti, the poet, painter, and founder of the Pre-Raphaelite group. Throughout her life, her two abiding loves were her brother, whom she idolized, and the Anglican Church, which she celebrated in many powerful, unself-conscious devotional poems. *Goblin Market* (1862), the first poem by any of the Pre-Raphaelites to become widely known, is an elaborate fantasy, full of images and events that suggest to many readers deep sexual repression.

Muriel Rukeyser (1913–1980) was born in New York City and educated at Vassar College and Columbia University. Her *Theory of Flight* won the Yale Series of Younger Poets award in 1935. The last of twelve volumes, *Collected Poems,* was published in 1978. In both her poetry and her daily life she sought to transform the world in which she lived from one filled with violence and oppression to one in which each individual could begin to understand his or her own (potential) abilities. Much of her poetry is expressly political. Rukeyser demonstrated that poetry is the ground on which the personal and political come together to change the way we think about the world.

Luis Omar Salinas   (b. 1937) was born in Robstown, Texas, and was raised and educated in California. Among his volumes are *Crazy Gypsy, Afternoon of the Unreal,* and *Darkness Under the Elms/Walking Behind the Spanish.*

Sonia Sanchez   (b. 1934) has developed one of the most complex and yet most direct voices to come out of the black cultural revolution of the late 1960s (the Black Arts Movement). After growing up in Atlanta, Georgia, and then going on to receive a B.A. from NYU in 1955, Sanchez found that she could not reconcile the difference between her childhood upbringing as a black girl in the South and her education as an intellectual in the North. Thus she began to question (and challenge) the systems that allow such distinctions and disparities to exist. A committed activist, Sonia Sanchez uses her own voice and the voice of the American black community—with its particular idioms and diction—to evoke the personal significance of a large political situation.

Bert Schierbeek   (b. 1918) was born in Glanerburg, The Netherlands and fought with the Dutch Resistance during the German Occupation (1940–1945). He was the lone survivor of his unit. He published a novel in 1945, which was followed by an autobiographical trilogy of poetry spanning the years 1950 through 1955. Several other works followed, including *Forment-era* (1989).

Léopold Sédar Senghor   (b. 1906), poet and former President of Senegal, was born at Joal-la-Portugaise, a coastal town about sixty-five miles south of Dakar. In 1928, he left the Lycée of Dakar to study in Paris, receiving a degree from the University of Paris in 1933. In the vanguard of the Negritude movement in the arts, he published his first volume of poetry, *Chants d'Ombre* in 1945 followed by *Chants pour Naett* in 1949. A noted statesman and diplomat, Senghor became President of Senegal in 1960.

Anne Sexton   (1928–1974) was born in Newton, Massachusetts. She was an indifferent student but a writer of poetry at an early age. Sexton attended Garland Junior College in Boston before eloping in the summer of 1948 with Alfred "Kayo" Sexton II. In 1953, she was hospitalized for severe depression and a suicide attempt; she subsequently began writing poetry again, on the advice of her psychiatrist. Sexton became a student of W. D. Snodgrass and Robert Lowell, and through Lowell's 1958–59 poetry seminar at Boston University she entered into a close friendship with Sylvia Plath. *To Bedlam and Part Way Back* (1960), Sexton's first poetry collection, is a confessional account of the author's confrontations with insanity and of her personal relationships with her family. In the spring of 1961, the Radcliffe Institute for Independent Study named Sexton and her friend Maxine Kumin their first scholars in poetry. Sexton's subsequent volumes, notably *All My Pretty Ones* (1962), the Pulitzer Prize-winning *Live or Die* (1966), and *Transformations* (1971), continue to trace her psychological conflicts and torments. On October 4, 1974, she had lunch with Kumin and then went home and committed suicide.

William Shakespeare   (1564–1616) was born at Stratford-on-Avon, the eldest son of a prosperous English businessman who held many civic offices and of a gentlewoman whose own family, the Ardens, were relatively wealthy landowners. By 1600, at the age of 34, he was acclaimed by many as the foremost playwright of his age, the author of fourteen plays and probably the bulk of his famous sonnets (which were not published until 1609). His early plays for the group included the histories *Richard II* (1595) and *I Henry IV* (1597); the comedies *A Midsummer Night's Dream* (1595), *The Merchant of Venice* (1596), and *Much Ado about Nothing* (1598);

and the tragedies *Romeo and Juliet* (1596) and *Julius Caesar* (1599). In the summer of 1599, the Lord Chamberlain's Men opened its own playhouse across the Thames in Southwick, naming it the Globe, with Shakespeare owning shares in both the company and the playhouse. *Julius Caesar* was the first play produced at the new playhouse. After 1600, Shakespeare devoted less time to acting and more to the writing of his greatest tragedies, *Hamlet* (1602), *Othello* (1604), *King Lear* (1606), *Macbeth* (1606), and *Antony and Cleopatra* (1606); and also to such "dark" comedies as *The Tempest* (1611), his last independently written play. Shakespeare's personal fortune also increased during this period. He had inherited Stratford property upon the death of his father in 1601, and he made other profitable transactions there in 1602 and 1605. In London, he continued to reside in rented lodgings. After 1608, following a year of personal upheaval that included the deaths of an illegitimate son and a younger brother, Shakespeare spent more time in Stratford. He died there on April 23, 1616, and was buried in the parish church.

Percy Bysshe Shelley   (1792–1822), influenced by the credos of the Enlightenment, or the Age of Reason, revolted against his conservative upbringing. At Oxford, he wrote a pamphlet in favor of atheism and was dismissed. He first married at 19, but that marriage ended in disaster. Shelley married Mary Godwin in 1816. He was a student of Greek and spent much time in Italy, where he drowned. Shelley believed that a Platonic civilization was possible, but that men needed pushing in that direction. His works, often abstract and allegorical, were lyrical and elegiac and sometimes, as with "Ozymandias," were warnings couched in irony. Among his best-known works are "Hymn to Intellectual Beauty" (1816); "Ode to the West Wind" (1819); "To a Skylark" (1819); and *Prometheus Unbound* (1819).

Sir Philip Sidney   (1554–1586) was born in Penhurst, Kent, of an aristocratic family. He attended both Oxford and Cambridge, but took no degree. He traveled to France with the English ambassador in 1572 and there witnessed the St. Bartholomew's Day Massacre, an event which turned him and his countrymen firmly toward Protestantism. Sidney became the epitome of the Elizabethan gentleman—an accomplished poet, scholar, soldier, and diplomat. Perhaps his most famous work is his *Defense of Poetry* (1595), which was published after his death from wounds received in battle. His place in English poetry has never wavered. His prose, criticism, and poetry are all considered of the highest order. Sidney's greatest achievement in poetry is the sonnet sequence *Astrophel and Stella* (1582).

Leslie Marmon Silko   (b. 1948) was born in Albuquerque, New Mexico, of mixed ancestry— Laguna Pueblo, Mexican, and white. She grew up on the Laguna Pueblo reservation, where she lives today with her husband and two children. A widely published poet, novelist, and short story writer, Silko is preoccupied in her writing with the act, process, and ritual of storytelling as a way of celebrating tradition, preserving memory, and sustaining cultural continuity. "I grew up with storytelling," she writes. "My earliest memories are of my grandmother telling me stories while she watered the morning glories in her yard. Her stories were about incidents from long ago, incidents which occurred before she was born but which she told as certainly as if she had been there."

Isaac Bashevis Singer   (1904–1991) was born in Radzymin, Poland, and came to the United States in 1935. He became a citizen in 1943. Singer was a journalist with the *Jewish Daily Forward,* writing first in Hebrew. Later, he said, "Hebrew was not a living language then," and he also wrote in Yiddish. A former rabbinical student, Singer injects elements of religion into much of his work. Since 1950 his work has been translated into English, in which language he gained great recognition, winning the 1979 Nobel Prize in literature. Of Singer, critic Thomas Lask wrote: "We are aware of a natural story teller who moves at his own pace, confident of his powers, fertile in invention, and able to hold the reader as long as he wishes. . . ." Singer published well over one hundred stories in collections that include *Gimpel* *the Fool* (1957), *The Seance* (1968), *The Spinoza of Market Street* (1961), and *The Collected Stories* (1982). His novels include *The Family Moskat* (1955) and *The Slave* (1962).

Mohan Singh (b. 1905), said to be "one of the greatest poets in the [Hindi] language," was an editor as well as a poet. Singh was strongly committed to improving life for the poor and oppressed in India.

Stevie Smith (1902–1971) was born Florence Margaret Smith in Tarkshire, England. Her nickname, "Stevie," referring to her shortness, was taken from the name of a popular jockey at the time. Until 1953, Smith worked in a London publisher's office, after which she devoted her time to writing and to broadcasts on the BBC. Known for her personal wit and charm as as well as for the wit and charm of her verse, poet and novelist Smith brought to her poetry a sense of the comic that pierced through the surface of reality. Often appearing at first irrelevant or childish because they rely on fairy tales, nursery rhymes, or childlike visions, Smith's self-illustrated poems assume a naive pose in order to probe the "agonies" of existence.

Gary Snyder (b. 1930) was born in San Francisco. In discussing Snyder's use of images culled from Buddhism, Native American folklore, experience of the wilderness, and his own social interactions, fellow poet Thom Gunn has said: "His [Snyder's] valuing of the primitive tribe and its relations to the earth is not a sentiment but a call for action. . . ." Snyder's poetry is rooted in his own widely varied experience. (Snyder has a B.A. in anthropology from Reed College; he has worked as a logger and on a Forest Service trail crew; he studied oriental languages at the University of California at Berkeley; from 1956 to 1964, he studied Buddhism in Japan; he worked on an oil tanker in the Pacific and Indian oceans before returning to Berkeley to teach.) Snyder's poems weave a fragmented web of keen observation and profound insight into a rich tapestry on which history and nature appear as two complementary pieces of the myth of humanity. This relationship underlies Snyder's poetic project because it locates poetry at the level of experience and action—at the level of change. In a 1966 *Village Voice* interview, Snyder said, "I think there's a real revolution going on somewhere below or outside the level of formal politics."

Edith Sodergran (1892–1923), a major modernist force in the literature of Sweden and Finland, was born to a wealthy Finnish-Swedish couple living in St. Petersburg, Russia. Her translated poetry, both confessional and feminist in tone, appears in *Love and Solitude* (1981) and *Complete Poems* (1984).

Cathy Song (b. 1955) was born in Hawaii and attended the University of Hawaii, Wellesley College, and Boston University. Her first collection of poetry, *Picture Bride* (1982), won the Yale Younger Poets Award. A second book of verse is *Frameless Windows, Squares of Light* (1988).

Sophocles (496?–406 B.C.) was born near Athens. His father was an arms manufacturer, and the family had status in the Athenian order of society. At 15, Sophocles was chosen to lead the paean sung by a chorus of boys in celebration of the victory over the Persians at the battle of Salamis (480 B.C.). He is believed to have been the author of about 150 plays, some of which were produced after his death. *Oedipus Rex, Electra,* and *Antigone* are his best-known works. Sophocles advanced Greek tragedy by extending dramatic action, by using three instead of two actors (later, he added a fourth), and by subordinating the chorus to the action on stage. Sophocles also improved costuming and set decorations. In his plays the action depends on motives that develop from the characters; this is true for both male and female figures.

Gary Soto (b. 1952) won the American Book Award for his reminiscence *Living Up the Street* (1985). Born of Mexican-American ancestry, Soto is a noted poet, the author of *Small Faces* (1985) and other volumes.

Wole Soyinka (b. 1934), born in Nigeria, is a noted essayist, musician, playwright, and poet. His award-winning plays have been produced throughout Africa, Europe, and America. His publications include *Five Plays* (1964) and *Ake: The Years of Childhood* (1981). He won the Nobel Prize in 1987.

Stephen Spender   (1909–1990) was born in London and educated at Oxford University. As novelist, playwright, essayist, and poet, he became one of the most outspoken and concerned literary figures of our age. For most of his life he was a professor at a variety of American and British universities, and he produced a vast body of work that attests to his concern for oppressed individuals within contemporary society. Beginning with overtly political works on the Spanish Civil War in the 1930s, Spender gradually moved toward issues of more general social concern.

Wallace Stevens   (1879–1955), a major American poet, was born in Redding, Pennsylvania. He attended Harvard University and received a degree from New York University Law School. Stevens was admitted to the New York bar in 1904, and from 1916 he was associated with Hartford Accident and Indemnity Company, becoming a vice president in 1934. Few of his associates in the insurance world knew of Stevens' private penchant for jotting down poems, but he liked the blend of business and private vocations. "It gives a man character as a poet," he once observed, "to have daily contact with a job." Stevens' first book of verse, *Harmonium*, did not appear until 1923. Later volumes, including *Ideas of Order* (1935), *The Man with the Blue Guitar* (1937), *Transport to Summer* (1947), *Collected Poems* (1954), and *Opus Posthumous* (1957), secured his reputation as a "virtuoso." A poet in and of the world, singing the American landscape more persistently than any poet since Whitman, Stevens was a bold and elegant experimenter in poetics.

May Swenson   (1913–1989) was born in Logan, Utah, and educated at Utah State University. She lived primarily in the New York metropolitan area after 1949, serving periodically as poet-in-residence at Purdue, the University of California at Riverside, and elsewhere. An award-winning poet and critic, Swenson was an experimental artist, seeking in her own words "to get through the curtain of things as they appear, to things as they are, and then into the larger, wilder space of things as they are becoming." She explored mysteries through riddles, and celebrated especially the sounds and colors of natural and urban landscapes, concentrating on the "thingness" (as the poet Chad Walsh observed) of the world. Her collections include *Another Animal* (1954), *A Cage of Spines* (1958), *To Mix with Time* (1963), *Half Sun Asleep* (1967), *New and Selected Things Taking Place* (1978), and *In Other Words* (1987).

Jonathan Swift   (1667–1745), born in Dublin, was educated in Ireland before going to England, where he became deeply involved in politics. He also became a master of satiric prose and poetry and an important political writer for the moderate Tories. Returning to Ireland, Swift was appointed dean of St. Patrick's Cathedral in 1713 and, except for brief trips, remained in Ireland for the rest of his life. His *Tale of a Tub* and *Battle of the Books* (1704); *A Modest Proposal* (1729); and most famous work, *Gulliver's Travels* (1726), all combined to create for Swift the image of a nasty misanthrope—though he was not. In fact, he joked about the label. Swift was a true political animal, unable to refrain from the battles. Sometimes he used pen names (although most people knew they were his): "Isaac Bickerstaff," "M. B. Drapier," "Cadenus," "Presto," and "Lemuel Gulliver." Swift knew—and sometimes ridiculed—many other writers, among them Addison and Steele, Pope, Parnell, Congreve, and Gay. Swift was declared insane in 1742.

John Millington Synge   (1871–1909), the son of a barrister, was born in Rathfranham, near Dublin, Ireland. His father died when Synge was 1 year old, and he was raised by an extended family consisting of his mother, grandmother, sister Annie, and various aunts. Synge entered Trinity College in 1888, his chief interests being language, history, and music. After his studies, he wandered through Europe, settling in Paris, where he met William Butler Yeats and many Irish nationalists. Synge wanted to become a critic. "Give up Paris," Yeats said. "You will never create anything by reading Racine. . . . Go to the Aran Islands. Live there as if you were one of the people themselves; express a life that has never found expression." Synge did just that, seeking creative inspiration in the peasant life of western Ireland and visiting the Aran

Islands, off the Irish coast, on an annual basis. After his return to Dublin in 1903, Synge quickly became a leader in the Irish National Theatre Company and at the Abbey Theatre, which produced his plays: *The Shadow of the Glen* (1903), *Riders to the Sea* (1904), *The Well of the Saints* (1905), *The Tinker's Wedding* (1907), and the controversial *Playboy of the Western World* (1907). An unfinished verse play, *Deidre of the Sorrows*, was written while Synge was dying of Hodgkin's disease.

Amy Tan   (b. 1952), the author of two highly acclaimed novels, *The Joy Luck Club* (1989) and *The Kitchen God's Wife* (1991), both tracing the lives of Chinese Americans, is a former business and freelance writer who was born and raised near San Francisco, California.

Sara Teasdale   (1884–1933) was born in St. Louis to wealthy, middle-aged parents. She started writing poetry in high school, and her first volume of poetry was published at her parents' expense in 1907. Over the next twenty years, she became one of the most widely read poets in America, best known for her love sonnets. She won the Pulitzer Prize for poetry in 1917 for *Love Songs*.

Hernando Téllez   (1908–1966) was born in Bogotá, Colombia, where for much of his life he was involved in the literary and journalistic life of the city. At 17 he joined the staff of the weekly *Mundo al Día*. Two years later, German Arciniegas started a magazine, *Universidad*, with Téllez's help. The formation of this publication helped to draw the intellectuals of his generation into what they called *Los Nuevos* ("the New Ones"). The group succeeded the writers and journalists of an earlier generation of Colombian—more precisely, Bogotán—fiction, nonfiction, and poetry writers. Arciniegas and Alberto Lleras Camargo, who headed *El Tiempo*, which Téllez joined in 1929, were leading figures in the New Ones. Active in national politics, Téllez in 1937 was designated the consul in Marseille, France. He returned to Colombia shortly before World War II and took up the post of subdirector of another publication, *El Liberal*. He was a senator from 1944 to 1947, and in 1959 he was appointed ambassador to UNESCO in Paris. "The prose of Téllez," wrote Richard Latcham, editor of *Stories of the Hispanic American*, "is distinguished for the qualities of spiritual contention and noble power exactly synthesized and shaded." In addition to his editorial and diplomatic activities, Téllez published *Inquietud del mundo* (*The Restless of the World;* 1943); *Bagatelas* (1944); *Diario* (1946); *Luces en el bosque* (*Lights in the Woods;* 1946); *Cenizas para el viento y otras historias* (*Ashes to the Wind and Other Stories;* 1950), *Literatura* (*Literature;* 1951); *Literatura y sociedad* (1956); and *Confesión de parte* (*In the Name of Confession;* 1966).

Dylan Thomas   (1914–1953) was born and received a grammar school education in Swansea, Wales. Deciding against attending a university, Thomas instead adopted the role of the bohemian poet, a role based in part on the style of Oscar Wilde. His first book of poems, *Eighteen Poems* (1934), won him the enthusiastic acclaim of London literati, especially that of the equally flamboyant Edith Sitwell. Like Sitwell, Thomas felt the need for poetry to act, to "narrate," and as a result his verbal virtuosity often produces images of darkly suggestive obscurity. This style was seen in contrast to the arid landscapes and alienated metaphors of the early modernists, of whom T. S. Eliot is the best example, and was claimed by some to be a turn toward a new romantic poetry. When this turn failed to materialize, however, Thomas remained a lone voice for unity amidst the modernists' roar of "fragmentation!" Emphasizing themes of unity within diversity, of wholeness encompassing contradiction, Thomas's poems create intricately woven webs of diverse images and metaphors.

Joyce Carol Thomas   (b. 1938), born in Ponca City, Oklahoma, has been a French, Spanish, and writing teacher. A Djerassi Fellow, Thomas was also an American Book Award winner in 1982. Her writings include four volumes of poetry and five novels, plus a 1981 collection of poetry, *Black Child*.

James Thurber   (1894–1961) was born in Columbus, Ohio, into a family that he claimed was "hooked on" the absurd. Some of Thurber's most humorous stories and essays retell incidents during his boyhood; it was also as a boy that an accident impaired his vision in one eye. Eventually, he would lose vision in the other and become completely blind. Before this happened, however, he studied at Ohio State University and later became a reporter and illustrator in Columbus, New York, and Paris. He was on the staff of *The New Yorker*, but left as quickly as was graciously possible. Thurber was keenly attuned to the fears and fantasies of people. "The Secret Life of Walter Mitty" was only one of many stories that explored the theme of fear and fantasy, weakness and power. Thurber's books started to come in 1929 when he wrote *Is Sex Necessary?* (with E. B. White). There followed, among others, *My Life and Hard Times* (1933), *The Middle-Aged Man on the Flying Trapeze* (1935), *The Male Animal* (a play, with Elliot Nugent, 1940), *Alarms and Diversions* (1957), and a last book of essays, *Lanterns and Lances* (1961).

Mohamud S. Togane (b. 1940), born in Somalia, came to the United States, where he studied in California, Virginia, Ohio, and then in Canada. He has been publishing since 1969. His poetry is collected in *The Bottle and the Bushman* (1989).

Melvin B. Tolson (1900–1966) was born in Moberly, Missouri. Surveying his life in an interview entitled "A Poet's Odyssey," he said: "Tennyson's protagonist says in "Ulysses," 'Much I have seen and know!' And again, 'I am a part of all that I have met. . . .'—as shoeshine boy, stevedore, soldier, janitor, packinghouse worker, cook on a railroad, waiter in a beachfront hotel, boxer, actor, football coach, director of drama, lecturer for the NAACP, organizer of sharecroppers' unions, teacher, father of Ph.D.s, poet laureate of a foreign country, painter, newspaper columnist, four-time mayor of a town, facer of mobs, I have made my way in the world since I was twelve years old." Tolson's wide experience as a black man in American culture led him to write poetry that challenged oppression wherever it occurred.

Fadwa Tuquan (b. 1917), born into a family of Arab intellectuals and poets, was raised in the historic town of Nablus, a part of territory now held by Israel. Her poetry laments the loss of the region in 1967.

Luisa Valenzuela (b. 1938), an Argentinean novelist and short story writer, was born in Buenos Aires; her mother was a well-known writer. She has lived in France and the United States. Valenzuela has published *Strange Things Happen Here* (1979), *The Lizard's Tale* (1983), and *Open Door* (1988). Her early fiction is aligned with the tradition of "magical realism," associated with Jorge Luis Borges and Gabriel García Márquez.

Gerald Vizenor (b. 1934), a Native American novelist, folklorist, and poet, was born in Minneapolis, Minnesota. He teaches at the University of California at Berkeley. His books include *Poems: Born in the Wind*, *The Heirs of Columbus*, and *Dead Voices*.

David Wagoner (b. 1926), raised in an Indiana suburb of Chicago and educated at both Penn State and Indiana Universities, brings to his present home in the Pacific Northwest—where he is currently a professor of English at the University of Washington at Seattle—a knowledge and experience of the diversity of the American people. Focusing his poetry on themes of human survival, of the violation of the natural world, and of the mythic reality of Native Americans, Wagoner expresses a deep concern for the problems and possibilities of the continued survival of the human race. A novelist as well as a prolific poet, he presents in his work a thoughtful and diverse perspective on modern American life.

Diane Wakoski (b. 1937) was born in Whittier, California, and was educated at the University of California at Berkeley. A noted poet, she is the author of numerous collections, including *Inside the Blood Factory* (1968), *Motorcycle Betrayal Poems* (1971), and *Rings of Saturn* (1986).

Alice Walker (b. 1944) was born in Eatonton, Georgia, the eighth and youngest child of African-American sharecroppers. She attended Spelman College and Sarah Lawrence College, where she began writing poetry. Her best-known novel is *The Color Purple* (1982), which won the American Book Award and the Pulitzer Prize. Her short story collections include *In Love and Trouble* (1973) and *You Can't Keep a Good Woman Down* (1981).

Margaret Walker (b. 1915), poet and novelist, was born in Birmingham, Alabama, and educated at Northwestern University and the University of Iowa. She won the Yale Award for Younger Poets in 1942 for her volume *For My People*. Walker was then teaching at Livingston College, in North Carolina, and since that time she has held several academic posts, most recently at Jackson State University, in Mississippi. In the introduction to her prizewinning novel *Jubilee* (1966), Walker observes that hers was a "talking" family, given to anecdotes, folklore, and discussions of history, politics, and race.

Chad Walsh (b. 1914), born in South Boston, Virginia, studied at the University of Virginia and the University of Michigan. He was ordained an Episcopal priest in 1949. Walsh has taught at a number of colleges in the United States and abroad, most notably in Finland. Many of his nonfiction works have been about the interaction of modern man and modern religion. Between these he has published, among other volumes of poetry, *The Unknowing* (1964), and *Garlands for Christmas* (1965). Walsh's work is marked by a humanitarian concern and a clear vision of the problems of contemporary life. Some of his works are in traditional poetic structures into which he places contemporary themes.

Eudora Welty (b. 1909) was born in Jackson, Mississippi, where she began an education that was completed at the University of Wisconsin and at Columbia University. During the Depression, she worked for the WPA as a publicist; later she became an advertising copywriter. She also wrote for radio. Welty, who has a keen eye for description, once thought about becoming a painter. Instead, she became a writer, her work first appearing in 1936; a collection of stories, *A Curtain of Green*, was published five years later. Among her novels are *Delta Wedding* (1946), *The Ponder Heart* (1954), and *The Optimist's Daughter* (1972). Though sometimes considered a Southern regionalist in the tradition of Robert Penn Warren, Faulkner, and John Crowe Ransom, Welty's main interest is in character—what the character thinks, feels, and sees; how the character adapts to the world in which she or he lives. In this sense she is closer to the Chekhovian tradition than to the American realist writers.

Phillis Wheatley (1753–1784) did not remember what part of Africa she had been taken from, nor could she recall much about her family. She arrived at the age of 7 in Boston, Massachusetts, in 1761, where John Wheatley, a minor tradesman, bought her at auction. The young girl was educated in English and Latin by her new family, and she later traveled to England with them. In 1773, her *Poems on Various Subjects, Religious and Moral* was published in England. Her fame had increased so much by 1776 that she was granted an audience by George Washington. She married John Peters in 1778; her last years were filled with poverty and illness. Wheatley's poetry is in the neoclassic tradition and typically personal in its glorification of freedom.

Walt Whitman (1819–1892) was born on Long Island, the Paumanok of his poems. He attended public schools in Brooklyn and started his career by working in rural schools, setting type, and serving as a writer for several newspapers. Whitman was editor of the influential *Brooklyn Eagle* from 1846 to 1848; he used the newspaper's editorial page to espouse abolitionism, opposition to banks and to capital punishment, and endorsement of free soil—positions that probably hastened his dismissal. Subsequently Whitman spent three months on a Louisiana paper, *The Crescent,* and the impact of the South is reflected in "I Saw in Louisiana a Live-Oak Growing" and other poems. After his return to New York, he worked as a carpenter for his father, freelanced, and then served as editor of *The Brooklyn Times* from 1857 to 1859; once again he was discharged for his outspoken editorial opinions on sex, abortion, prostitution, and slavery. During the Civil War, Whitman served as a volunteer nurse for the Army in Washington, and later was given a clerkship in the Indian Department, but was fired by the secretary of the interior, who labeled *Leaves of Grass* an "indecent book." Whitman published the first edition of *Leaves of Grass*, which contained twelve untitled poems, in 1855. At the outset of this seminal book, Whitman declared his subject: "One's-self I sing, a simple separate person/Yet utter the word Democratic, the word En Masse." Frank in its subject matter and technically experimental, *Leaves of Grass* is a mystical celebration of the body and the soul, the individual and the collective, all woven into a process of regeneration that frees humanity from the absoluteness of death. From the embryonic first edition with its magnificent centerpiece, "Song of Myself," Whitman would evolve a symbolic autobiography in later, expanded editions of *Leaves of Grass*. Stricken by paralysis, Whitman spent the last nineteen years of his life in Camden, New Jersey, generally enjoying his role as "the good gray poet."

John Alfred Williams (b. 1925) was born in Mississippi and raised in Syracuse, New York, where, after World War II, he studied at Syracuse University. He is the author of *Sissie* (1963), *The Man Who Cried I Am* (1967), *!Click Song* (1982), and other novels and short fiction. He is a professor of English and Journalism at Rutgers University.

William Carlos Williams (1883–1963), who like his friend Wallace Stevens was both a professional man and a poet, was born in Rutherford, New Jersey. He received his medical degree from the University of Pennsylvania in 1906, and from 1910 until his retirement in 1951 he was a successful pediatrician in Rutherford. Influenced by Ezra Pound when the two were at the University of Pennsylvania, and himself a major influence on such later poets as Robert Lowell and Theodore Roethke, Williams was an advocate of American images, materials, and strategies in poetry. His books include *The Collected Later Poems* (1950), *The Collected Earlier Poems* (1951), and a magnificent five-volume philosophical poem about the American experience, *Paterson* (1946–1958). Williams was a poet of particulars, seeking to lift moments of reality from the actual world and transcribe them economically in poetry. "No ideas but in things," he declared. Taking his "things" from the native surroundings of the New Jersey landscape, Williams is unrivaled in the clarity of his images depicting parts of the world.

August Wilson (b. 1945) grew up in an impoverished family in Pittsburgh. He dropped out of school, and began writing poetry and drama. Among his celebrated plays concerned with the African-American experience are *Ma Rainey's Black Bottom* (1984), *Fences* (1987), and *Joe Turner's Come and Gone* (1988).

James Wright (b. 1927) was born in Martin's Ferry, Ohio, and received his B.A. from Kenyon College. After serving in the U.S. Army during the occupation of Japan, he returned to complete a Ph.D. at the University of Washington and subsequently to take up teaching at Hunter College. Speaking of his own poetry, Wright has said, "I try and say how I love my country and how I despise the way it is treated. I try to speak of the beauty and again of the ugliness in lives of the poor and neglected." Seeing poetry as a form of social concern, Wright believes that "poetry [should] say something humanly important instead of just showing off the language." As a result, Wright's poetry often expresses a directness and engagement with the external world that is reminiscent of the lucid complexities of Robert Frost, whom Wright acknowledges as one of his models.

Richard Wright (1908–1960) was born on a cotton plantation near Natchez, Mississippi. Wright was 5 when his father, a mill worker, abandoned the family. His childhood, vividly recorded in his autobiography, *Black Boy* (1945), was characterized by persistent poverty, hardship, wanderings, and, following his mother's paralysis from strokes, intermittent stays in foster homes and orphanages. After working for a time in Memphis, Wright went to Chicago in 1927, joined the Communist party, and began to write, gaining his first recognition as a short story writer. In 1940, Wright published his first and most famous novel, *Native Son*. This novel is a brutal, naturalistic account of Bigger Thomas, a young black man victimized by his own blind impulses and by white society. Wright went into exile in France in 1947 and lived there until his death. His later work, still largely neglected, includes an account of his disenchantment with communism, "I Tried to Be a Communist," in *The God That Failed* (1950); two mildly existentialist novels, *The Outsider* (1953) and *The Long Dream* (1958); and an analysis of emerging nations in west Africa and the end of colonialism, *Black Power* (1954). Some of Wright's stories are collected in *Uncle Tom's Children* (1938) and *Eight Men* (1961). Referring to the black American experience, Wright in *12 Million Black Voices* (1941) declared, "The seasons of the plantation no longer dictate the lives of many of us."

Sir Thomas Wyatt   (1503–1542) was born in Kent and educated at Cambridge University. His life was filled with intrigues and adventures (he was even rumored to be the lover of Ann Boleyn). Before the age of 25, he had attracted the notice of Henry VIII, who used him as a deputy and an ambassador on various missions to the Continent. His Continental travels, especially his 1527 visit to Italy, bore unexpected fruit for English poetry—the sonnet. Wyatt and the hotheaded earl of Surrey, Henry Howard, introduced this verse form, which was to become one of the most important genres in the language.

Elinor Wylie   (1885–1928) was born in New Jersey and grew up in Philadelphia. She married in 1905 and later left her husband to be with Horace Wylie, whom she married soon after. Her first volume of poetry, *Nets to Catch the Wind*, was published in 1921; she published novels and poetry until her death at 43. Though she is the contemporary of T. S. Eliot and Marianne Moore, her poetry has nothing of their revolutionary "newness" of form and expression. Her best work displays a single emotion elegantly stated.

Mitsuye (May) Yamada   (b. 1923), born in Japan, came to the United States in 1926 and became a citizen in 1955. She studied at New York University, the University of Chicago, and the University of California at Irvine. She has taught at several California colleges, and has published *Camp Notes and Other Poems* (1976) and *Desert Run: Poems & Stories* (1988).

William Butler Yeats   (1865–1939), the most prolific and one of the greatest modern poets, was born in Dublin, the son of the well-known painter John Butler Yeats. His Irish Protestant family moved often between London and the Irish countryside, and Yeats grew up more Irish than Protestant, a precocious youth fascinated by poetry, philosophy, politics, folklore, and the occult. He achieved early fame as a poet and wrote extraordinary poetry his entire life. In a life full of projects and accomplishments, his work in the theater and his long study of and belief in magic deserve the most attention. In 1889 he met and fell in love with the Irish radical Maud Gonne. The passion was never reciprocated. He proposed marriage to her on several occasions and at least once made the same offer to Gonne's daughter, Iseult. He finally married another woman in 1917 and, with the help of his wife, wrote *A Vision*, which presents his systematic theory of world philosophy.

Al Young   (b. 1939), a 1982 American Book Award winner, is also a novelist of distinction, an editor, a musician, and a former disk jockey. His first volume of poetry was *Dancing* (1969), and was followed the next year by his first novel, *Snakes*. Since then, poetry collections and novels have come regularly, making Young one of the most productive of American writers.

Bernice Zamora   (b. 1938) was born Bernice Ortiz in Pueblo, Colorado. She has a Ph.D. in English and American literature from Stanford University. Her poetry, much of it celebrating the Chicana experience, is collected in *Restless Serpents* (1976).

Cyn. Zarco   (b. 1950) was born in Manila, Philippines, but now lives in California. A poet, she is the author of *Cir'cum·nav'i·ga'·tion* (1986) and other writings.

Glossary of Literary Terms

Act A major division of a play.

Affective fallacy The fallacy of wrongly evaluating a literary work by emphasizing only its emotional impact.

Allegory A narrative whose characters, symbols, and situations represent elements outside the text. For example, the character Christian in the allegory *Pilgrim's Progress* represents the Everyman who is a Christian.

Alliteration The repetition of consonant or vowel sounds at the beginning of words.

Allusion An indirect reference to some literary or historical figure or event. For example, the line in T. S. Eliot's *Love Song of J. Alfred Prufrock*, "No! I am not Prince Hamlet, nor was meant to be," is an allusion.

Ambiguity A literary device in which an author uses words with more than one meaning, deliberately leaving the reader uncertain.

Analogy A comparison of two different things on the basis of their similarity.

Anapest A metrical foot consisting of two unaccented syllables followed by an accented one (˘ ˘ ′), as in the phrase "on the ship."

Antagonist A competitor or opponent of the main character (protagonist) in a work of literature.

Antihero A protagonist in a modern literary work who has none of the noble qualities associated with a traditional hero.

Antistrophe In a Greek play, the portion of the Chorus that responds to the comments made by the first part of the Chorus, the Strophe.

Antithesis A phrase that contains words whose meanings harshly contrast with each other and are in rhetorical balance. For example, Alexander Pope's "Man proposes, God disposes" is an antithesis.

Aphorism A terse, sharp statement of a large principle or idea. Thomas Hobbes's "The life of man, solitary, poor, nasty, brutish, and short" is an aphorism.

Apostrophe   A direct, emotional address to an absent character or quality, as it if were present.

Archetype   An image or character representative of some greater, more common element that recurs constantly and variously in literature.

Aside   Lines in a play that are delivered not to another character but to the audience or to the speaker himself or herself.

Assonance   The use of similar vowel sounds in adjacent or closeby words (for example, *slide* and *mind*).

Avant garde   A term used to describe writing that is strikingly different from the dominant writing of the age—in its form, style, content, and attitude.

Ballad   A poem originally sung or singable, recounting some domestic or heroic story, usually within a four-line stanza alternating three-beat and four-beat lines.

Bathos   An unsuccessful attempt to arouse great emotion, becoming not grand but absurd or silly.

Blank verse   Unrhymed lines of iambic pentameter.

Caesura   A pause within a line of poetry, often created through punctuation.

Canto   A division of certain long poems, such as Dante's *Divine Comedy* and Byron's *Don Juan*.

Carpe diem   Latin for "seize the day," used in literature to describe poetry that examines temporary human pleasures against the backdrop of eternity—as in Marvell's "To His Coy Mistress."

Catharsis   Exhaustion and cleansing of an audience member's emotions through participation in the events of a tragedy.

Character   A person created by an author for use in a work of fiction, poetry, or drama.

Chorus   A group of singers or actors who comment on and respond to the action in a play of classical Greece; also, a refrain in a song or poem.

Classicism   A term deriving from the era of the ancient Greeks and Romans, used in English literature to describe the outlook of the eighteenth century, where writers celebrated the "classical" values of restraint, order, and stylistic elegance.

Cliché   A phrase so overused that it has lost its original punch (for example, "beating a dead horse").

Climax   A point at which the events in a play or story reach their crisis, where the maximum emotional reaction of the reader is created.

Closed poetry   Closed poetry possesses certain structural patterns, notably rhyme and rhythm, that are clearly discernible.

Coda   A closing section of some literary works, occurring after the main action has been resolved.

Colloquialism   A term used in speech but not acceptable in formal writing.

Colloquy   A debate or conversation among characters.

Comedy   A work of literature, often a play, whose first intention is to amuse and that ordinarily has a happy ending.

Comic relief   A light, amusing section of a play or story that relieves tension and often comments by its humor on the surrounding serious action.

Complication   A part of a plot in which the conflict among characters or forces is engaged.

Conceit   A metaphor extended to great lengths in a poem (for example, Donne's "The Flea").

Conflict   A struggle among opposing forces or characters in fiction, poetry, or drama.

Connotation   Implications of words or sentences, beyond their literal, or denotative, meanings.

Consonance   Repetition of consonant sounds within words.

Couplet   Two lines of verse that have unity within themselves, often because they rhyme.

Cue   In a play, words or action from one character that signal the start of another character's words or action.

Dactyl   A metrical foot containing an accented syllable followed by two unaccented syllables (′ ⌣ ⌣), as in the word "craziness."

Denotation   Literal meaning of a word or of sentences.

Denouement   The final action of a plot, in which the conflict is resolved; the outcome.

Deus ex machina   Literally, "God from a machine"—the improbable intervention of an outside force that arbitrarily resolves a conflict.

Dialogue   Conversation between two people in fiction, drama, or poetry.

Diction   The use of words; good diction is accurate and appropriate to the subject.

Dimeter   A line of poetry composed of two metrical feet.

Dionysian   A term referring to the ancient Greek values embraced by the god Dionysius and his worshipers—faith in the irrational and in the primacy of human emotions; often a descriptive term in literature.

Dramatic irony   A term used to describe the effect of words of a character in a play that have more significance than they appear to have.

Dramatic monologue   A poem spoken by a character other than the author (for example, Browning's "My Last Duchess").

Elegy   A poetic meditation on death, often occasioned by the death of a specific individual.

End-stopped lines   Lines of poetry completed with the pause of punctuation.

Enjambment   Lines of poetry whose sense and grammar continue without a pause from one line into the next.

Epic   A long poem, usually narrative, recounting the trials and victories of a great hero, a hero usually important to an entire nation or people.

Epigram   A sharp, witty saying, such as Oscar Wilde's "I can resist everything but temptation."

Epigraph   A short inscription at the start of a literary work.

Epilogue   A concluding portion of a literary work, occurring after the main action has been completed.

Epithet   A descriptive word or phrase pointing out a specific quality—as when Shakespeare is referred to as "the Bard." The word is often used to describe terms of contempt.

Epode   The third portion of the comments of the Chorus in a classical Greek play, following the strophe and the antistrophe.

Essay   Literally, "attempt"—any short piece of nonfiction prose that makes specific points and statements about a limited topic.

Euphemism   A word or phrase substituting indirect for direct statement (for example, "passed away" in place of "died").

Euphony   A use of words to pleasant musical effect.

Exposition   A portion of a narrative or dramatic work that establishes the tone, setting, and basic situation.

Fable   A short tale that presents a specific moral and whose characters are often animals.

Fantasy   A work that takes place in a world that does not exist.

Farce   A broadly comic play relying for its humor on unlikely situations and characters.

Feminine ending   An additional syllable at the end of a line that has no metrical stress.

Figurative language   Language that deliberately departs from everyday phrasing, with dramatic and imagistic effects that move the reader into a fresh mode of perception.

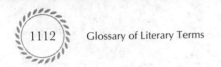

Foot   A metrical unit of a line of poetry that contains at least one stressed syllable and one or more unstressed syllables.

Foreshadowing   In a plot, an indication of something yet to happen.

Form   The structure and organization of a work of art; form expresses its content.

Free verse   Poetry that relies more on rhythm than on regular meter for its effectiveness.

Genre   A distinct kind of writing, such as mystery, gothic, farce, or black comedy.

Gothic fiction   Novels, often historical, in which weird, grotesque activity takes place; Mary Shelley's *Frankenstein* is an example of gothic fiction.

Haiku   A form of Japanese poetry now also practiced by Westerners, which in three lines of five, seven, and then five syllables presents a sharp picture and a corresponding emotion or insight.

Heptameter   A line of poetry composed of seven metrical feet.

Heroic couplet   Two lines of rhyming iambic pentameter.

Hero (or heroine)   The central character of a literary work; he or she often has great virtues and faults, and his or her trials and successes form the main action of the plot.

Hexameter   A line of poetry containing six metrical feet.

Hubris   Overbearing or insolent pride; in Greek drama, the arrogance toward the gods that leads to a character's downfall.

Humours   The four Renaissance divisions of human temperament, corresponding to the liquids of the human body—blood, yellow bile, black bile, and phlegm—which are often associated with the personalities of dramatic characters.

Hyperbole   Deliberately overstated, exaggerated figurative language, used either for comic or great emotional effect.

Iamb   A metrical foot composed of one unaccented syllable followed by one stressed syllable (⌣ ╱), as in the word "undone."

Iambic pentameter   A line containing five iambic feet, the most widely used meter in English-language poetry.

Image, imagism   A concrete expression of something perceived by the senses, using simile, metaphor, and figurative language.

Internal rhyme   Rhyme that occurs within a single line of poetry.

Irony   An effect associated with statements or situations in which something said or done is at odds with how things truly are.

Line   The fundamental element of a poem—a set of words that ends at a specific point on the page and has a unity independent of what goes before and after.

Lyric   A short, personal poem marked by strong feeling, musicality, and vivid language.

Masculine ending   The last stressed syllable in a line of poetry.

Meditative poetry   Verse with a strong and personal expression of religious feeling, especially as practiced by John Donne and others in the seventeenth century; also, a form of poetry in which the poet muses quietly and personally on a particular scene or emotion.

Metafiction   A contemporary form of fiction in which an author makes the process of writing fiction part of his or her subject.

Metaphor   An implicit comparison of an object or feeling with another unlike it, as when Eliot's "Prufrock" says, "I have measured out my life with coffee spoons."

Metaphysical poetry   Thoughtful, often religious, intellectually vigorous poetry, as practiced by John Donne and others in the seventeenth century.

Meter A rhythmic pattern in a poem created by the regular alternation of stressed and unstressed syllables.

Metonymy A figure of speech in which an object or person is not mentioned directly but suggested by an object associated with it, as when a reference to "the White House" means "the President."

Mock heroic A form of long poem in which the structures and values of the epic are used to burlesque a trivial subject (for example, Pope's "The Rape of the Lock").

Monometer A line of poetry composed of only one metrical foot.

Mood The emotional tone or outlook an author brings to a subject.

Muse Originally any one of nine Greek goddesses presiding over the arts; "the muse" usually refers to an abstract being that inspires poets to write.

Myth Ancient stories of unknown origin involving the supernatural; myths have provided cultures and writers with interpretations of the world's events.

Narrative A story that consists of an account of a sequence of events.

Naturalism Literature in which the author attempts to represent the world in a realistic and often harsh and hopeless way.

Novel A long fictional narrative that represents human events, characters, and actions.

Novella A short novel or tale.

Octameter A line of poetry composed of eight metrical feet.

Octave An eight-line stanza of poetry, often part of a sonnet.

Ode A lyric meditation, usually in elevated figurative language, upon some specific object, event, or theme.

Off rhyme A form of rhyme employing not-quite-identical sounds, such as "slip" and "slap."

Omniscient narrator A speaker or implied speaker of a work of fiction who can tell the story, shift into the minds of one or more characters, be in various places, and comment on the meaning of what is happening in the story.

Onomatopoeia An effect in which a word or phrase sounds like its sense (for example, Tennysons's "murmuring of innumerable bees").

Open poetry Related to free verse, it is not structurally restricted by rhyme or rhythm.

Ottava rima An eight-line stanza whose end-words usually rhyme in an *ababababcc* pattern; used by many English poets (for example, Byron in *Don Juan*).

Pacing Narrative or linguistic devices that keep literary works moving and interesting.

Parable A story illustrating a moral, in which every detail parallels the moral situation.

Paradox A statement that seems contradictory but actually points out a truth (for example, Wordsworth's line, "The Child is father of the Man").

Parody A literary work that deliberately makes fun of another literary work or of a social situation.

Pathetic fallacy The fallacy of attaching human feelings to nature.

Pathos The qualities in a work of art that arouse pity or sadness, especially the helpless feeling caused by undeserved bad luck.

Persona The mask through which a writer gives expression to his or her own feelings or participates in the action of a story, poem, or play.

Personification A literary strategy giving nonhuman things human characters or attitudes, as in Aesop's fables or Keats's poem "To Autumn."

Plot The sequence of events in a story, poem, or play; the events build upon each other toward a convincing conclusion.

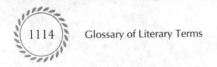

Poetry   A form of writing in which the author writes in lines, with either a metrical pattern or a free-verse rhythm.

Point of view   The angle from which a writer tells a story. Point of view can be either omniscient, limited, or through the eyes of one or more characters.

Prologue   A preface or introduction setting the scene for what is to follow.

Prose   Any form of writing that does not have the rhythmic patterns of metrical verse or free verse. Good prose is characterized by tightness, specificity, and a sense of style.

Protagonist   The leading character; the protagonist engages the main concern of readers or audience.

Proverb   A statement putting forth a great truth (for example, the Biblical proverb "Go to the ant, thou sluggard; consider his ways and be wise").

Pun   A form of word play, often serious, that relies on the double meaning of words or sounds for its effect (for example, the dying Mercutio's words to Romeo, "ask for me tomorrow and you shall find me a grave man").

Quatrain   A four-line stanza.

Realism   An approach to writing that emphasizes recording everyday experience.

Refrain   A line or group of lines repeated several times in a poem.

Resolution   The dramatic action occurring after the climax of a play, before the events themselves are played out.

Rhetoric   The study and practice of language in action—presenting ideas and opinions in the most effective way.

Rhyme   Similarity of sound between words.

Rhythm   In poetry, the regular recurrence of stressed syllables; in literature in general, the overall flow of language, having a sensory effect on the reader.

Romance   Any work of fiction that takes place in an extravagent world remote from daily life.

Romanticism   A powerful literary movement beginning in the late eighteenth century; it shook off classical forms and attitudes, embracing instead the power, promise, and political dignity of the imaginative individual.

Satire   A literary work using wit, irony, anger, and parody to criticize human foibles and social institutions.

Scansion   The act of counting out the meter of a poem.

Scene   A portion of a drama, poem, or work of fiction that occurs within one time and setting.

Science fiction   Fantasy in which scientific facts and advances fuel the plot.

Sestet   A six-line stanza of poetry, often part of a sonnet.

Setting   The background of a literary work—the time, the place, the era, the geography, and the overall culture.

Short story   A brief fictional narrative.

Simile   A comparison of two things via the word "like" or "as."

Situational irony   The contrast between what a character wants and what he or she receives, arising not through the character's fault but from other circumstances.

Soliloquy   A speech by a character who is alone on stage, talking to himself or herself or to the audience.

Sonnet   A poem of fourteen lines using some kind of metrical form and rhyme scheme and always unified with a concentrated expression of a large subject.

Sound   In literature, the combination of sensations perceived by the ear or the mind's ear.

Spondee   A metrical foot containing two stressed syllables, as in the phrase "time out."

Sprung rhythm A form of meter defined by the poet Gerard Manley Hopkins that emphasizes only the number of stresses in a line, thus making a kind of tense meter of accentual irregularity.

Stanza A portion of a poem set off by blank space before and after; more formally, a stanza may have rhyme and metrical regularity matching that of stanzas before and after.

Stereotype Widely believed and oversimplified attitudes toward a person, an issue, a style, and so on.

Stream of consciousness Writing that attempts to imitate and follow a character's thought processes.

Stress The emphasis a syllable or word naturally receives within a line of poetry, or in human speech.

Strophe In an ancient Greek play, the comments of that portion of the Chorus speaking first during a scene.

Style The property of writing that gives form, expression, and individuality to the content.

Subject The person, place, idea, situation, or thing with which some piece of literature most immediately concerns itself.

Subplot A complication within a play or piece of fiction that is not part of the main action but often complements it.

Subtext Significant communication, especially in dialogue, that gives motivation for the words being said.

Surrealism Art that values and expresses the unconscious imagination by altering what is commonly seen as reality.

Suspense Those literary qualities that leave a reader breathlessly awaiting further developments with no clear idea of what those developments will be.

Symbol Something that represents something else, the way a flag represents a country or a rose may stand for love—implying not only another physical thing but an associated meaning.

Synecdoche A kind of metaphor in which the mention of a part stands for the whole (for example, "head" refers not only to the heads of cattle but to each animal as a whole).

Synesthesia A subjective sensation or image (as of color) that is felt in terms of another sense (as of sound).

Synopsis A summary of the main points of a plot.

Syntax The arrangement of words to form sentences.

Tercet A three-line stanza, often one in which each line ends with the same rhyme.

Terza rima A series of three-line stanzas that rhyme *aba, bcb, cdc, ded,* and so on; used by Dante in the *Divine Comedy* and by Shelley, among others.

Tetrameter A line of verse composed of four metrical feet.

Theater of the absurd Avant-garde, post-World War II drama representing the hopelessness of the human condition by abandoning realistic characters, language, and plot.

Theme The main idea of a literary work created by its treatment of its immediate subject.

Tone The expression of a writer's attitudes toward a subject; the mood the author has chosen for a piece.

Tour de force A display of literary skill that is very impressive, but often empty.

Tragedy A literary work, usually a play, where the main characters participate in events that lead to their destruction.

Tragicomedy A work of literature, usually a play, that deals with potentially tragic events that are finally avoided, leading to a happy ending.

Trimeter A line of poetry containing three metrical feet.

Trochee A metrical foot consisting of an accented syllable followed by an unaccented one (′ ‿), as in the word "salty."

Understatement A passage that deliberately and ironically states or implies that something is less than it really is.

Utopia An ideal social and political state created by an author (for example, Plato, Thomas More, H. G. Wells, and Paul Goodman wrote utopias).

Verbal irony The discrepancy between things as they are stated and as they really are.

Verse A unit of poetry, usually a line or stanza; in general, any kind of literary work written in poetic lines.

Wit Originally a word that meant "intelligence," "wit" now refers to a facility for quick, deft writing that usually employs humor to make its point.

Permissions Acknowledgments

Jamaica Kincaid "Girl" from *At the Bottom of the River* by Jamaica Kincaid. Copyright © 1978, 1983 by Jamaica Kincaid. Reprinted by permission of Farrar, Straus & Giroux, Inc.

Maxine Kumin "Together" from *The Nightmare Factory* by Maxine Kumin. Reprinted by permission of Curtis Brown, Ltd. Copyright © 1970 by Maxine Kumin.

D. H. Lawrence "Piano" by D. H. Lawrence, from *The Complete Poems of D. H. Lawrence* by D. H. Lawrence, Edited by V. de Sola Pinto & F. W. Roberts. Copyright © 1964, 1971 by Angelo Ravagli and C. M. Weekley, Executors of the Estate of Frieda Lawrence Ravagli. Used by permission of Viking Penguin, a division of Penguin Books USA Inc.

David Leavitt "Gravity," from *A Place I've Never Been* by David Leavitt. Copyright © 1990 by David Leavitt. Used by permission of Viking Penguin, a division of Penguin Books USA Inc.

Doris Lessing "Flight" from *The Habit of Loving* by Doris Lessing. Copyright © 1957 by Doris Lessing. Reprinted by permission of HarperCollins Publishers, Inc., and Jonathan Clowes Ltd., London, on behalf of Doris Lessing.

Denise Levertov "Living While It May," "The Ache of Marriage," and "The Victors." From *Denise Levertov: Poems 1960–1967*. Copyright © 1964, 1966 by Denise Levertov Goodman. Reprinted by permission of New Directions Publishing Corp.

Philip Levine "Spring in the Old World." © Philip Levine, from *The Names of the Lost*, Atheneum, 1976. Reprinted by permission of the author.

Shirley Geok-lin Lim "Ah Mah." © 1995. Reprinted by permission of the author.

Shirley Geok-lin Lim "Modern Secrets" from *Modern Secrets* by Shirley Geok-lin Lim. Dangaroo Press. © Shirley Geok-lin Lim, 1989. Reprinted by permission of the author.

Audre Lorde "Oya" from *New York Head Shop and Museum* by Audre Lorde. Broadside Press, Detroit, 1975. Reprinted by permission of the publisher.

Robert Lowell "Children of Light" from *Lord Weary's Castle*, copyright 1946 and renewed 1974 by Robert Lowell, reprinted by permission of Harcourt Brace & Company.

Mairi MacInnes "VJ Day" from *Quarterly Review of Literature*, Poetry Series #3, Vol. XXII (1981). Reprinted by permission of *Quarterly Review of Literature*.

Claude McKay "America" and "Outcast." By permission of The Archives of Claude McKay, Carl Cowl, Administrator. In *Selected Poems of Claude McKay*, Harcourt Brace, 1979.

Archibald MacLeish Excerpt from "Ars Poetica," *Collected Poems 1917–1982* by Archibald MacLeish. Copyright © 1985 by the Estate of Archibald MacLeish. Reprinted by permission of Houghton Mifflin Co. All rights reserved.

Bobbie Ann Mason "Big Bertha Stories" from *Love Life* by Bobbie Ann Mason. Copyright © 1990 by Bobbie Ann Mason. Reprinted by permission of HarperCollins Publishers, Inc.

Annette M'Baye "Silhouette" from *Présence Africaine, No. 57: New Sum of Poetry from the Negro World*. Présence Africaine, Paris, 1966. Trans. Kathleen Weaver, in *The Penguin Book of Women Poets*, ed. Carol Cosman, Joan Keefe, and Kathleen Weaver. Viking Press, New York, 1979. Reprinted by permission of Présence Africaine, and Kathleen Weaver, Berkeley, CA.

Ifeanyi Menkiti "Veterans Day" from *Okike*, Vol. 1, No. 2 (December 1971). Reprinted by permission of the author.

Josephine Miles "Housewife" from *Collected Poems 1930–1983* by Josephine Miles. © 1983 by Josephine Miles. Used with permission from the University of Illinois Press.

Arthur Miller *Death of a Salesman*. Copyright 1949, renewed © 1977 by Arthur Miller. Used by permission of Viking Penguin, a division of Penguin Books USA Inc.

Czeslaw Milosz "On Prayer." © 1988 Czeslaw Milosz Royalties, Inc. From *The Collected Poems, 1931–1987* by Czeslaw Milosz, first published by The Ecco Press in 1988. Reprinted with permission.

Janice Mirikitani "Prisons of Silence" excerpted from *Shedding Silence* by Janice Mirikitani.

of California. Reprinted by permission of the University of California Press, and Miriam Lichtheim.

Luigi Pirandello "War" from *Better Think Twice About It and Other Short Stories*. Reprinted by permission of the Pirandello Estate and Toby Cole, Agent.

Sylvia Plath "Daddy" from *Ariel* by Sylvia Plath. Copyright © 1963 by Ted Hughes. Reprinted by permission of HarperCollins Publishers, Inc., and Faber and Faber Ltd.

Estela Portillo *Day of the Swallows*. Reprinted by permission of the author.

Ezra Pound "A Virginal" and "The River-Merchant's Wife: A Letter." From *Ezra Pound: Personae*. Copyright 1926 by Ezra Pound. Reprinted by permission of New Directions Publishing Corp.

Alexander Pushkin "A Sower Went Out to Sow His Seed" and "To My Old Nurse." From *Poems of Pushkin* by Alexander Pushkin, translated by Henry Jones. Copyright © 1965 by Henry Jones. Published by arrangement with Carol Publishing Group. A Citadel Press Book.

Ibn Quzman "The Radish" from *Moorish Poetry*, trans. A. J. Arberry. Cambridge, UK: Cambridge University Press, 1953. Reprinted with the permission of Cambridge University Press.

Rahel "To My Country," trans. Diane J. Mintz. From *The Penguin Book of Women Poets*, ed. Carol Cosman, Joan Keefe, and Kathleen Weaver. Viking Press, New York, 1979. Translation copyright Diane J. Mintz. Reprinted by permission of Diane J. Mintz.

Ishmael Reed "Sermonette" from *New and Collected Poems* by Ishmael Reed. Atheneum Publishers. Copyright © 1972 by Ishmael Reed. Reprinted by permission of Ellis J. Freedman, Atty., on behalf of the author.

Roberto Fernandez Retamar "A Motto from Poets: Leave Stone," trans. Tim Reynolds. From *Giant Talk: An Anthology of Third World Writings*, ed. Quincy Troupe and Rainer Schulte. Random House, New York, 1975.

Adrienne Rich "August" and Part IV of "Twenty-One Love Poems" ("I Come Home from You") are reprinted from *The Fact of a Doorframe, Poems Selected and New, 1950–1984*, by Adrienne Rich, by permission of W. W. Norton & Company, Inc. Copyright © 1984 by Adrienne Rich. Copyright © 1975, 1978 by W. W. Norton & Company, Inc. Copyright © 1981 by Adrienne Rich.

Theodore Roethke "My Papa's Waltz," copyright 1942 by Hearst Magazines, Inc. from *The Collected Poems of Theodore Roethke* by Theodore Roethke. Used by permission of Doubleday, a division of Bantam Doubleday Dell Publishing Group, Inc.

Muriel Rukeyser "Myth" from *Out of Silence*. TriQuarterly Books, Evanston, IL, 1992. © William L. Rukeyser. By permission of William L. Rukeyser.

Muriel Rukeyser "The Lost Romans" from *Collected Poems*. © Muriel Rukeyser, 1978. McGraw-Hill, New York. By permission of William L. Rukeyser.

Luis Omar Salinas "Quetzalcoatle" from *Crazy Gypsy* by Luis Omar Salinas. Fresno, California: La Raza Studies, Fresno State College. Copyright © 1970 by Luis Omar Salinas. Reprinted by permission of the author.

Sonia Sanchez "Poem at Thirty" from *Home Coming* by Sonia Sanchez. Broadside Press, Detroit, Michigan. © 1969 by Sonia Sanchez. Reprinted by permission of the author.

Bert Schierbeek "The Bicycle Repairman" from *Formentera/ The Gardens of Souza*, © Bert Schierbeek, 1984, 1986, 1989. © Translation Charles McGeehan and Guernica Editions Inc., 1989. Reprinted by permission of the publisher.

Léopold Sédar Senghor "Prayer to the Masks" from *The Collected Poetry* by Léopold Sédar Senghor, translated and with an introduction by Melvin Dixon. Copyright © 1991 by the Rector and Visitors of the University of Virginia. Reprinted by permission of the University Press of Virginia.

Index of
Literary Terms

Index of Names, Titles, and First Lines of Poems